CASES IN STRATEGIC MANAGEMENT

FIFTH EDITION
CASES IN STRATEGIC MANAGEMENT

FRED R. DAVID

FRANCIS MARION UNIVERSITY

PRENTICE HALL

Englewood Cliffs, New Jersey 07632

Acquisitions Editor: Natalie Anderson
Production Editor: Katherine Evancie
Managing Editor: Fran Russello
Interior/Cover Designer: Michaelis/Carpellis Design Associates, Inc.
Design Director: Linda Fiorditlino
Buyer: Paul Smolenski
Assistant Editor: Lisamarie Brassini
Editorial Assistant: Nancy Proycet
Cover Art: Adam Niklewicz

Printed in the United States of America

10 9 8 7 6 5 4 3 2 1

ISBN 0-02-327869-2

Prentice Hall International (UK) Limited, *London*
Prentice Hall of Australia Pty. Limited, *Sydney*
Prentice Hall Canada Inc., *Toronto*
Prentice Hall Hispanoamericana, S.A., *Mexico*
Prentice Hall of India Private Limited, *New Delhi*
Prentice Hall of Japan, Inc., *Tokyo*
Simon & Schuster Asia Pte. Ltd., *Singapore*
Editora Prentice Hall do Brasil, Ltda., *Rio de Janeiro*

Joy, Forest, Byron, and Meredith—my wife and children—
for their encouragement and love

PREFACE

The mission of Prentice Hall and I in preparing the fifth edition of *Strategic Management* was "to create the premier business policy textbook on the market, a book that is interesting and valuable to students and from which professors will enjoy teaching." To achieve this mission, Prentice Hall spared no expense. They published this edition in color and financed development of the most elaborate ancillary package available. This mission led me to include only outstanding current business policy cases and to incorporate the newest strategic management research and practice. Prentice Hall and I believe you will find this textbook to be better than any other for communicating both the excitement and value of strategic management.

A SPECIAL NOTE TO PROFESSORS

This book meets all AACSB guidelines for the business policy and strategic management course. previous editions of this text have been used at more than 400 colleges and universities. The entire research base for this text has been revised and updated since the previous edition. A net result of this activity is that every chapter is shorter in length, yet the chapters include all new examples and many new concepts. The most current concepts and practices in strategic management are presented in a style that is clear, focused, and relevant. The changes in this edition add up to the biggest revision every made on this popular text.

The first four editions achieved a reputation for excellence and differentiation in three primary areas:

1. The cases are exceptionally up-to-date and offer a good mix of large and small firms across a variety of industries.
2. The chapter material is presented in a skills-oriented, practical manner, supported by Experiential Exercises.
3. The writing style is conversational, logical, concise, interesting, and lively.

This fifth edition builds upon these traditional strengths. *All* of the cases in this edition include year-end 1992 or 1993 information. A new Experiential Exercise at the end of each chapter directs students into the business community to explore strategic management issues.

SPECIAL FEATURES IN THE TEXT

Improved Model. The comprehensive strategic-management model that appears in all chapters of this text has been improved and simplified to incorporate the latest thought and practice.

New Collection of Cases. This edition has a total of thirty-five cases. Thirteen of the cases are new and 22 of the cases are updated from the previous edition. Some of the new cases focus on large firms in trouble, such as IBM and Borden, and some focus on small businesses, such as Dave's Pit Stop Cafe and Norwood Furniture. The cases in this text are organized clearly by type of industry and size of firm. A breakdown of the cases is as follows:

- Sixteen service-oriented cases, such as Audubon Zoo—1994 and Citicorp—1994.
- Nineteen manufacturing-oriented cases, such as Boeing—1994 and Winnebago Industries—1994.
- Twenty international cases, such as Playboy Enterprises—1994 and Weyerhaeuser Corporation—1994.
- Four nonprofit cases, such as Classic Car Club of America—1994 and Walnut Creek Baptist Church—1993.
- Ten small business strategy cases, such as Circus Circus Enterprises—1994 and Splatterball—1993.

All cases have been class tested to ensure that they are interesting, challenging, and effective for illustrating strategic-management concepts. Most were written exclusively for this text and are designed to reflect current strategic-management problems and practices. This collection of cases Complements virtually any approach in teaching business policy or strategic management.

Appendix on "Using the Software." An appendix in this edition gives students all the information needed to use the *Strategy Formulator* and *Case Analyst* software materials that are available free upon adoption of this text. This new software instructional material appears in Part 6 of the text.

Hardback Edition Available. For instructors who desire a hardback text with cases, *Strategic Management* (fifth edition) contains all of the materials in this text, as well as ten chapters, 53 Experiential Exercises, and a Cohesion Case for Hershey Foods Corporation. Three themes permeate all the chapters of the hardback edition:

1. Strategic management must be a people process to be successful.
2. Global considerations affect virtually all strategic decisions.
3. Preserving the natural environment is an important strategic issue.

SPECIAL ANCILLARY MATERIALS

This text is accompanied by the most elaborate auxiliary package available with any business policy text. As described below, seven separate supplements are available free from Prentice Hall with adoption of this text.

Comprehensive Case Solutions Manual. Prepared solely by the author, the *Case Solutions Manual* provides comprehensive teacher's notes for each case. The teacher's notes feature detailed analyses, classroom discussion questions with answers, an external and internal assessment, specific recommendations, strategy-implementation material, and an epilogue for each case. Diskettes for the *Case Analyst* and *Strategy Formulator* software are provided on the back cover of the *Case Solutions Manual.*

Seventeen Color Case Video Segments. To accompany the Cohesion Case, a 21-minute color video prepared by Hershey Foods Corporation is available to adopters free of charge. Shown near the beginning of the course, the Hershey Foods video can arouse students' interest in studying the Cohesion Case and completing Experiential Exercises that apply chapter material to this case.

In addition, a collection of sixteen other color case video segments is available free of charge. The segments average 15 minutes each and were professionally prepared by firms used in cases in this text. Videos are provided to accompany the following cases: The Limited, Promus Corporation, Winnebago Industries, Playboy Enterprises, Weyerhaeuser Corporation, WTD Industries, Dell Computer, Banc One, Audubon Zoo, W.L. Gore, Borden, Nike, Pilgrim's Pride, Whirlpool, Rykä, Georgia Pacific, and McDonnell Douglas.

Updated Case Analyst *Software.* Free for all adopters of this text, *Case Analyst* is a diskette that contains income statement and balance sheet data from all cases in the text. Information on the disk is organized in Lotus 1-2-3 format. The text gives clear instructions so that IBM-compatible spreadsheet packages can be used to access the data files. Special instructions are given for the EXCEL and ENABLE spreadsheet products.

Packaged on the back cover of the *Case Solutions Manual,* the *Case Analyst* diskette is not copyright protected. Rather, professors are encouraged to make copies of the disk for students who have access to a personal computer and who want to generate pro forma financial statements for the cases being analyzed. Exceptionally fast and user-friendly, *Case Analyst* shows students the impact their recommendations will have on the firms' financial condition. Familiarity with spreadsheets is needed to use *Case Analyst* initially.

New Strategy Formulator *Software.* The *Strategy Formulator* software Prentice Hall has purchased the most widely used strategic planning software among corporations, and is making that available free for students who use this text. *Strategy Formulator* thus is a totally new software package that gives students hands-on experience using actual strategic planning software. The new *Strategy Formulator* software follows the approach presented in the chapters for formulating strategies in any type organization. Free for all adopters, this software is packaged inside the back cover of the *Case Solutions Manual.* Clear instructions for using *Strategy Formulator* are given in the text. No prior experience with computers, spreadsheets, databases, or programming is needed to use *Strategy Formulator.*

A SPECIAL NOTE TO STUDENTS

Welcome to business policy. This is a challenging and exciting course that will allow you to function as the owner or chief executive officer of different organizations. your major task in this course will be to make strategic decisions and to justify those decisions through oral and written communication. Strategic decisions determine the future direction and competitive position of an enterprise for a long time. Decisions to expand geographically or to diversify are examples of strategic decisions.

Strategic decision making occurs in all types and sizes of organizations, from General Motors to a small hardware store. Many people's lives and jobs are affected by strategic decisions, so the stakes are very high. An organization's very survival is often at stake. The overall importance of strategic decisions makes this course especially exciting and challenging. You will be called upon in business policy to demonstrate how your strategic decisions could be successfully implemented.

In this course you can look forward to making strategic decisions both as an individual and as a member of a team. No matter how hard employees work, an organization is in real trouble if strategic decisions are not made effectively. Doing the right things (effectiveness) is more important than doing things right (efficiency). For example, IBM was prosperous in the 1980s, but ineffective strategies led to annual billion dollar losses in the 1990s.

You will have the opportunity in this course to make actual strategic decisions, perhaps for the first time in your academic career. Do not hesitate to take a stand and defend specific strategies that you determine to be the best. The rationale for your strategic decisions will be more important than the actual decision, because no one knows for sure what the best strategy is for a particular organization at a given point in time. This fact accents the subjective, contingency nature of the strategic-management process. Use the concepts and tools presented in this text, coupled with your own intuition, to recommend strategies that you can defend as being most appropriate for the organizations that you study. You will also need to integrate knowledge acquired in previous business courses. for this reason, business policy is often called a capstone course; you may want to keep this book for your personal library.

This text is practitioner-oriented and applications-oriented. It presents strategic-management concepts that will enable you to formulate, implement, and evaluate strategies in all kinds of profit and nonprofit organizations. The end-of-chapter Experiential Exercises allow you to apply what you've read in each chapter to the Hershey Foods Cohesion Case and to your own university.

Be sure to use *Case Analyst* and *Strategy Formulator* because this software will save you time in performing analyses and will make your work look professional. Read and follow the guidelines provided in the appendices for using the software and for making oral presentations. Work hard in policy this term and have fun. Good luck!

ACKNOWLEDGMENTS

Many persons have contributed time, energy, ideas, and suggestions for improving this text over four editions. The strength of this text is largely attributed to the collective wisdom, work, and experiences of business policy professors, strategic-management researchers, students, and practitioners. Names of particular individuals whose published research is referenced in the fourth edition of this text are listed alphabetically in the Name Index. To all individuals involved in making this text so popular and successful, I am indebted and thankful.

Many special persons and reviewers contributed valuable material and suggestions for this edition. I would like to thank my colleagues and friends at Auburn University, Mississippi State University, East Carolina University, and Francis Marion University. These are universities where I have served on the management faculty. Professors at these schools who shaped development of this text are Bill Holley, Achilles Armenakis, and Bob Neibuhr at Auburn University; Johnny Giglioni, Dennis Ray, and Dan Cochran at Mississippi State University; Louis Eckstein, Tilton Wilcox, and Buc Keush at East Carolina University; and Tom Stanton, Jery Kinard, Don Kelley, Jim Fenton, Bob Pugh, Lucretia Zienert, and Bob Barrett at Francis Marion University.

Individuals who develop cases for the North American Case Research Association Meeting, the Midwest Society for Case Research Meeting, the Eastern Casewriters Association Meeting, the European Case Research Association meeting, and Harvard Case Services are vitally important for continued progress in the field of strategic management. From a research perspective, there is no questions that writing business policy cases represents a valuable scholarly activity among faculty. Extensive research is required to structure business policy cases in a way that exposes strategic issues, decisions, and behavior. Pedagogically, business policy cases are essential for students in learning how to apply concepts, evaluate situations, formulate strategies, and resolve implementation problems. Without a continuous stream of up-to-date business policy cases, the strategic-management course and discipline would lose much of its energy and excitement.

The following individuals wrote cases that were selected for inclusion in this text. These persons helped develop the most current compilation of cases ever assembled in a business policy text: Claire Anderson, Old Dominion University; Robert Anderson, College of Charleston; Jill Austin, Middle Tennessee State University; Stephen Barndt, Pacific Lutheran University; Henry Beam, Western Michigan University; Lynn Brumfield, Middle Tennessee State University; Carol Cumber, South Dakota State University; Jim Fenton, Francis Marion University; Caroline Fisher, Loyola University; Phil Fisher, University of South Dakota; Barbara Gottfried, Bentley College; Michelle Greene, Francis Marion University; Walter Greene, Pan American University; James Harbin, East Texas State University; Marilyn Helms, University of Tennessee at Chattanooga; Diane Hoadley, University of South Dakota, Neil Jacobs, Northern Arizona University; Mike Keeffe, Southwest Texas State University; Ted Legatski, Sam Houston State University; Dean Lewis, Sam Houston State University; Charles Manz, Arizona State University; Paula Maynes, University of Tennessee at Chattanooga; Steve McCutcheon, University of Tennessee at Chattanooga; Bill Middlebrook, Southwest Texas State University; Kent Nassen, Iowa State University; Sharon Oswald, Auburn University; Valerie J. Porciello, Bentley College; Paul Reed, Sam Houston State University; John Ross, Southwest Texas State University; Frank Shipper, Arizona State University; Charles Shrader, Iowa State University; Matthew Sonfield, Hofstra University; Randall White, Auburn University at Montgomery.

Prentice Hall employees and salespersons have worked diligently behind the scenes to make this text a leader in the business policy market. Natalie Anderson, Lisamarie Brassini, Nancy Proyect, Jo-Anne DeLuca, Tom Nixon, Bill Oldsey, Katherine Evancie, and Paul Smolenski, for example, have supported this text immensely. I appreciate the continued hard work of all Prentice Hall employees and salespersons.

I also want to thank you, the reader, for investing time and effort reading and studying this text. As we approach the twenty-first century together, this book will help you formulate, implement, and evaluate strategies for organizations with which you become associated. I hope you come to share my enthusiasm for the rich subject area of strategic management and for the systematic learning approach taken in this text.

I need to thank Mary Greene, Nichole Greene, and Angela White—my special editorial assistants at Francis Marion University—for doing an excellent job.

Finally, I want to welcome and invite your suggestions, ideas, thoughts, and comments and questions regarding any part of this text or the ancillary materials. Please call me at 803-661-1419 or write me at the School of Business, Francis Marion University, Florence, South Carolina 29501. I appreciate and need your input to continually improve this text in future editions. Drawing my attention to specific errors or deficiencies in coverage or exposition will especially be appreciated. Thank you for using this text.

F.R.D.

CONTENTS

PART 2
Cases

[a]Denotes an international organization

[b]Denotes a case updated from fourth edition of the text

[c]Denotes a new case appearing for first time in text

PART · 6

Case
Analysis

Case Introduction

HOW TO ANALYZE A BUSINESS POLICY CASE

OUTLINE	WHAT IS A BUSINESS POLICY CASE?
	GUIDELINES FOR PREPARING CASE ANALYSES
	PREPARING A CASE FOR CLASS DISCUSSION
	PREPARING A WRITTEN CASE ANALYSIS
	MAKING AN ORAL PRESENTATION
	FIFTY TIPS FOR SUCCESS IN CASE ANALYSIS

OBJECTIVES   After studying this section, you should be able to:

- ■ Describe the case method for learning strategic-management concepts.
- ■ Identify the steps in preparing a comprehensive written case analysis.
- ■ Describe how to give an effective oral case analysis presentation.
- ■ Discuss fifty tips for doing case analysis.

*T*he purpose of this section is to help you analyze business policy cases. Guidelines for preparing written and oral case analyses are given, and suggestions for preparing cases for class discussion are presented. Steps to follow in preparing case analyses are provided. Guidelines for making an oral presentation are described.

WHAT IS A BUSINESS POLICY CASE?

A *business policy case* describes an organization's external and internal condition and raises issues concerning the firm's mission, strategies, objectives, and policies. Most of the information in a business policy case is established fact, but some information may be opinions, judgments, and beliefs. Business policy cases are more comprehensive than those you may have studied in other courses. They generally include a description of related management, marketing, finance/accounting, production/operations, R&D, computer information systems, and environmental issues. A business policy case puts the reader on the scene of the action by describing a firm's situation at some point in time. Business policy cases are written to give you practice applying strategic-management concepts. The case method for studying strategic management is often called *learning by doing.*

GUIDELINES FOR PREPARING CASE ANALYSES

The Need for Practicality. There is no such thing as a complete case, and no case ever gives you all the information you need to conduct analyses and make recommendations. Likewise, in the business world, strategists never have all the information they need to make decisions: information may be unavailable, too costly to obtain, or may take too much time to obtain. So, in preparing business policy cases, do what strategists do every day—make reasonable assumptions about unknowns, state assumptions clearly, perform appropriate analyses, and make decisions. *Be practical.* For example, in performing a pro forma financial analysis, make reasonable assumptions, state them appropriately, and proceed to show what impact your recommendations are expected to have on the organization's financial position. Avoid saying, "I don't have enough information." You can always supplement the information provided in a case with research in your college library. Library research is required in case analyses.

The Need for Justification. The most important part of analyzing cases is not what strategies you recommend, but rather how you support your decisions and how you propose that they be implemented. There is no single best solution or one right answer to a case, so give ample justification for your recommendations. This is important. In the business world, strategists usually do not know if their decisions are "right" until resources have been allocated and consumed. Then it is often too late to reverse the decisions. This cold fact accents the need for careful integration of intuition and analysis in preparing business policy case analyses.

The Need for Realism. Avoid recommending a course of action beyond an organization's means. *Be realistic.* No organization can possibly pursue all the strategies that could potentially benefit the firm. Estimate how much capital will be required to implement what you recommended. Determine whether debt, stock, or a combination of debt and stock could be used to obtain the capital. Make sure your recommendations are feasible. Do not prepare a case analysis that omits all arguments and information not supportive of your recommendations. Rather, present the major advantages and disadvantages of several feasible alternatives. Try not to exaggerate, stereotype, prejudge, or overdramatize. Strive to demonstrate that your interpretation of the evidence is reasonable and objective.

The Need for Specificity. Do not make broad generalizations such as "The company should pursue a market penetration strategy." *Be specific* by telling what, why, when, how, where, and who. Failure to use specifics is the single major shortcoming of most oral and written case analyses. For example, in an internal audit, say, "The firm's current ratio fell from 2.2 in 1993 to 1.3 in 1994, and this is considered to be a major weakness," instead of, "The firm's financial condition is bad." Rather than concluding from a SPACE Matrix that a firm should be defensive, be more specific, saying, "The firm should consider closing three plants, laying off 280 employees, and divesting itself of its chemical division, for a net savings of $20.2 million in 1995." Use ratios, percentages, numbers, and dollar estimates. Businesspeople dislike generalities and vagueness.

The Need for Originality. Do not necessarily recommend the course of action that the firm plans to take or actually undertook, even if those actions resulted in improved revenues and earnings. The aim of case analysis is for you to consider all the facts and information relevant to the organization at the time, generate feasible alternative strategies, choose among those alternatives, and defend your recommendations. Put yourself back in time to the point when strategic decisions were being made by the firm's strategists. Based on information available then, what would you have done? Support your position with charts, graphs, ratios, analyses, and the like—not a revelation from the library. You can become a good strategist by thinking through situations, making management assessments, and proposing plans yourself. *Be original.* Compare and contrast what you recommend versus what the company plans to do or did.

The Need to Contribute. Strategy formulation, implementation, and evaluation decisions are commonly made by a group of individuals rather than by a single person. Therefore, your professor may divide the class into three- or four-person teams to prepare written or oral case analyses. Members of a strategic-management team, in class or in the business world, differ on their aversion to risk, their concern for short-run versus long-run benefits, their attitudes toward social responsibility, and their views concerning globalization. There are no perfect people, so there are no perfect strategists. Be open-minded to others' views. *Be a good listener and a good contributor.*

PREPARING A CASE FOR CLASS DISCUSSION

Your professor may ask you to prepare a case for class discussion. Preparing a case for class discussion means that you need to read the case before class, make notes regarding the organization's external opportunities/threats and internal strengths/weaknesses, perform appropriate analyses, and come to class prepared to offer and defend some specific recommendations.

The Case Method Versus Lecture Approach. The case method of teaching is radically different from the traditional lecture approach, in which little or no preparation is needed by students before class. The *case method* involves a classroom situation in which students do most of the talking; your professor facilitates discussion by asking questions and encouraging student interaction regarding ideas, analyses, and recommendations. Be prepared for a discussion along the lines of "What would you do, why would you do it, when would you do it, and how would you do it?" Prepare answers to the following types of questions:

1. What are the firm's most important external opportunities and threats?
2. What are the organization's major strengths and weaknesses?
3. How would you describe the organization's financial condition?
4. What are the firm's existing strategies and objectives?
5. Who are the firm's competitors and what are their strategies?
6. What objectives and strategies do you recommend for this organization? Explain your reasoning. How does what you recommend compare to what the company plans?
7. How could the organization best implement what you recommend? What implementation problems do you envision? How could the firm avoid or solve those problems?

The Cross-Examination. Do not hesitate to take a stand on the issues and to support your position with objective analyses and outside research. Strive to apply strategic-management concepts and tools in preparing your case for class discussion. Seek defensible arguments and positions. Support opinions and judgments with facts, reasons, and evidence. Crunch the numbers before class! Be willing to describe your recommendations to the class without fear of disapproval. Respect the ideas of others, but be willing to "go against the grain" of majority opinion when you can justify a better position.

Business policy case analysis gives you the opportunity to learn more about yourself, your colleagues, strategic management, and the decision-making process in organizations. The rewards of this experience will depend upon the effort you put forth, so do a good job. Discussing business policy cases in class is exciting and challenging. Expect views counter to those you present. Different students will place emphasis on different aspects of an organization's situation and submit different recommendations for scrutiny and rebuttal. Cross-examination discussions commonly arise, just as they occur in a real business organization. Avoid being a silent observer.

PREPARING A WRITTEN CASE ANALYSIS

In addition to asking you to prepare a case for class discussion, your professor may ask you to prepare a written case analysis. Preparing a written case analysis is similar to preparing a case for class discussion, except written reports are generally more structured and more detailed. There is no ironclad procedure for preparing a written case analysis because cases differ in focus; the type, size, and complexity of the organizations being analyzed also vary.

When writing a strategic-management report or case analysis, avoid jargon, vague words, redundant words, acronyms, abbreviations, sexist language, and ethnic or racial slurs, and watch your spelling. Use short sentences and paragraphs and simple words and phrases. Use quite a few subheadings. Arrange issues and ideas from the most important to the least important. Arrange recommendations from the least controversial to the most controversial. Use the active voice rather than the passive voice for all verbs; for example, say, "Our team recommends the company diversify," rather than, "It is recommended by our team to diversify." Use many examples to add specificity and clarity. Tables, figures, pie charts, bar charts, time lines, and other kinds of exhibits help communicate important points and ideas. Sometimes, a picture *is* worth a thousand words.

The Executive Summary. Your professor may ask you to focus the written case analysis on a particular aspect of the strategic-management process, such as "to identify and evaluate the organization's existing mission, objectives, and strategies," or "to propose and defend specific recommendations for the company," or "to develop an industry analysis by describing the competitors, products, selling techniques, and market conditions in a given industry." These types of written reports are sometimes called *executive summaries*. An executive summary usually ranges from three to five pages of text in length, plus exhibits.

The Comprehensive Written Analysis. Sometimes your professor may ask you to prepare a *comprehensive written analysis*. This assignment requires you to apply the entire strategic-management process to the particular organization. When preparing a comprehensive written analysis, picture yourself as a consultant who has been asked by a company to "conduct a study of our external and internal environment and make specific recommendations for our future." Prepare exhibits to support your recommendations. Highlight exhibits with some discussion in the paper. Comprehensive written analyses usually are about ten pages in length, plus exhibits.

Steps in Preparing a Comprehensive Written Analysis. In preparing a comprehensive written analysis, you could follow the steps outlined here, which follow the stages in the strategic-management process and the chapters in this text.

Step 1 Identify the firm's existing mission, objectives, and strategies.

Step 2 Develop a mission statement for the organization.

Step 3 Identify the organization's external opportunities and threats.

Step 4 Construct a Competitive Profile Matrix.

Step 5 Construct an EFE Matrix.

Step 6 Identify the organization's internal strengths and weaknesses.

Step 7 Construct an IFE Matrix.

Step 8 Prepare a TOWS Matrix, SPACE Matrix, BCG Matrix, IE Matrix, Grand Strategy Matrix, and QSPM as appropriate. Give advantages and disadvantages of alternative strategies.

Step 9 Recommend specific strategies and long-term objectives. Show how much your recommendations will cost. Itemize these costs clearly for each projected year. Compare your recommendations to actual strategies planned by the company.

Step 10 Specify how your recommendations can be implemented and what results you can expect. Prepare forecasted ratios and pro forma financial statements. Present a timetable or agenda for action.

Step 11 Recommend specific annual objectives and policies.

Step 12 Recommend procedures for strategy review and evaluation.

MAKING AN ORAL PRESENTATION

Sometimes your professor will ask you to prepare a business policy case analysis, individually or as a group, and present your analysis to the class. Oral presentations are usually graded on two parts: content and delivery. *Content* refers to the quality, quantity, correctness, and appropriateness of analyses presented, including such dimensions as logical flow through the presentation, coverage of major issues, use of specifics, avoidance of generalities, absence of mistakes, and feasibility of recommendations. *Delivery* includes such dimensions as audience attentiveness, clarity of visual aids, appropriate dress, persuasiveness of arguments, tone of voice, eye contact, and posture. Great ideas are of no value unless others can be convinced of their merit through clear communication. The guidelines presented here can help you make an effective oral presentation.

Organizing the Presentation. Begin your presentation by introducing yourself and giving a clear outline of topics to be covered. If a team is presenting, specify the sequence of speakers and the areas each person will address. At the beginning of an oral presentation, try to capture your audience's interest and attention. You could do this by displaying some products made by the company, telling an interesting short story about the company, or sharing an experience that you had related to the company, its products, or its services. You could develop or obtain a VHS video to show at the beginning of class; you could visit a local distributor of the firm's products and tape a personal interview with the business owner or manager. A light or humorous introduction can be effective at the beginning of a presentation.

Be sure the setting of your presentation is well organized, with chairs, flip charts, a transparency projector, and whatever else you plan to use. Arrive at least 15 minutes early at the classroom to organize the setting, and be sure your materials are ready to go. Make sure everyone can see your visual aids well.

Controlling Your Voice. An effective rate of speaking ranges from 100 to 125 words per minute. Practice your presentation out loud to determine if you are going too fast. Individuals commonly speak too fast when nervous. Breathe deeply before and during the presentation to help yourself slow down. Have a cup of water available; pausing to take a drink will wet your throat, give you time to collect your thoughts, control your nervousness, slow you down, and signal to the audience a change in topic.

Avoid a monotone by placing emphasis on different words or sentences. Speak loudly and clearly, but don't shout. Silence can be used effectively to break a monotone voice. Stop at the end of each sentence, rather than running sentences together with "and" or "uh."

Managing Body Language. Be sure not to fold your arms, lean on the podium, put your hands in your pockets, or put your hands behind you. Keep a straight posture, with one foot slightly in front of the other. Do not turn your back to the audience, which is not only rude but which also prevents your voice from projecting well. Avoid using too many hand gestures. On occasion, leave the podium or table and walk toward your audience, but do not walk around too much. Never block the audience's view of your visual aids.

Maintain good eye contact throughout the presentation. This is the best way to persuade your audience. There is nothing more reassuring to a speaker than to see members of the audience nod in agreement or smile. Try to look everyone in the eye at least once during your presentation, but focus more on individuals who look interested than on persons who seem bored. Use humor and smiles as appropriate throughout your presentation to stay in touch with your audience. A presentation should never be dull!

Speaking from Notes. Be sure not to read to your audience, because reading puts people to sleep. Perhaps worse than reading is memorizing. Do not try to memorize anything. Rather, practice using notes unobtrusively. Make sure your notes are written clearly so you will not flounder trying to read your own writing. Include only main ideas on your note cards. Keep note cards on a podium or table if possible so that you won't drop them or get them out of order; walking with note cards tends to be distracting.

Constructing Visual Aids. Make sure your visual aids are legible to individuals in the back of the room. Use color to highlight special items. Avoid putting complete sentences on visual aids; rather, use short phrases and then elaborate on issues orally as you make your presentation. Generally, there should be no more than four to six lines of text on each visual aid. Use clear headings and subheadings. Be careful about spelling and grammar; use a consistent style of lettering. Use masking tape or an easel for posters—do not hold posters in your hand. Transparencies and handouts are excellent aids; however, be careful not to use too many handouts or your audience may concentrate on them instead of you during the presentation.

Answering Questions. It is best to field questions at the end of your presentation, rather than during the presentation itself. Encourage questions and take your time to respond to each one. Answering questions can be persuasive because it involves you with the audience. If a team is giving the presentation, the audience should direct questions to a specific person. During the question and answer period, be polite, confident, and courteous. Avoid verbose responses. Do not get defensive with your answers, even if a hostile or confrontational question is asked. Staying calm during potentially disruptive situations such as a cross-examination reflects self-confidence, maturity, poise, and command of the particular company and its industry. Stand up throughout the question and answer period.

FIFTY TIPS FOR SUCCESS IN CASE ANALYSIS

Business policy students who have used this text over two editions offer to you the following fifty tips for success in doing case analysis:

1. View your case analysis and presentation as a product that must have some competitive factor to differentiate it favorably from the case analyses of other students.
2. Prepare your case analysis far enough in advance of the due date to allow time for reflection and practice. Do not procrastinate.
3. Develop a mind-set of "why,"continually questioning your own and others' assumptions and assertions.
4. The best ideas are lost if not communicated to the reader, so as ideas develop, think of their most appropriate presentation.
5. Maintain a positive attitude about the class, working *with* problems rather than against them.

6. Keep in tune with your professor and understand his or her values and expectations.

7. Since business policy is a capstone course, seek the help of professors in other specialty areas as needed.

8. Other students will have strengths in functional areas that will complement your weaknesses, so develop a cooperative spirit that moderates competitiveness in group work.

9. Read your case frequently as work progresses so you don't overlook details.

10. When preparing a case analysis as a group, divide into separate teams to work on the external analysis and internal analysis. Each team should write its section as if it were to go into the paper; then give each group member a copy.

11. At the end of each group session, assign each member of the group a task to be completed for the next meeting.

12. Have a good sense of humor.

13. Capitalize on the strengths of each member of the group; volunteer your services in your areas of strength.

14. Set goals for yourself and your team; budget your time to attain them.

15. Become friends with the library.

16. Foster attitudes that encourage group participation and interaction. Do not be too hasty to judge group members.

17. Be creative and innovative throughout the case analysis process.

18. Be prepared to work. There will be times when you will have to do more than your share. Accept it, and do what you have to do to move the team forward.

19. Think of your case analysis as if it were really happening; do not reduce case analysis to a mechanical process.

20. To uncover flaws in your analysis and to prepare the group for questions during an oral presentation, assign one person in the group to actively play the devil's advocate.

21. Do not schedule excessively long group meetings; two-hour sessions are about right.

22. A goal of case analysis is to improve your ability to think clearly in ambiguous and confusing situations; do not get frustrated that there is no single best answer.

23. Push your ideas hard enough to get them listened to, but then let up; listen to others and try to follow their lines of thinking; follow the flow of group discussion, recognizing when you need to get back on track; do not repeat yourself or others unless clarity or progress demands repetition.

24. Do not confuse symptoms with causes; do not develop conclusions and solutions prematurely; recognize that information may be misleading, conflicting, or wrong.

25. Work hard to develop the ability to formulate reasonable, consistent, and creative plans; put yourself in the strategist's position.

26. Develop confidence in using quantitative tools for analysis. They are not inherently difficult; it is just practice and familiarity you need.

27. Develop a case-writing style that is direct, assertive, and convincing; be concise, precise, fluent, and correct.

28. Have fun when at all possible. It is frustrating at times, but enjoy it while you can; it may be several years before you are playing CEO again.

29. Acquire a professional typist and proofreader. Do not perform either task alone.

30. Strive for excellence in writing and technical preparation of your case. Prepare nice charts, tables, diagrams, and graphs. Use color and unique pictures. No messy exhibits!

31. In group cases, do not allow personality differences to interfere. When they occur, they must be understood for what they are and put aside.
32. Do not forget that the objective is to learn; explore areas with which you are not familiar.
33. Pay attention to detail.
34. Think through alternative implications fully and realistically. The consequences of decisions are not always apparent. They often affect many different aspects of a firm's operations.
35. Get things written down (drafts) as soon as possible.
36. Read everything that other group members write, and comment on it in writing. This allows group input into all aspects of case preparation.
37. Provide answers to such fundamental questions as what, when, where, why, and how.
38. Adaptation and flexibility are keys to success; be creative and innovative.
39. Do not merely recite ratios or present figures. Rather, develop ideas and conclusions concerning the possible trends. Show the importance of these figures to the corporation.
40. Support reasoning and judgment with factual data whenever possible.
41. Neatness is a real plus; your case analysis should look professional.
42. Your analysis should be as detailed and specific as possible.
43. A picture speaks a thousand words, and a creative picture gets you an A in many classes.
44. Let someone else read and critique your paper several days before you turn it in.
45. Emphasize the "Strategy Selection" and "Strategy Implementation" sections. A common mistake is to spend too much time on the external or internal analysis parts of your paper. Always remember that the "meat" of the paper or presentation is the strategy selection and implementation sections.
46. Make special efforts to get to know your group members. This leads to more openness in the group and allows for more interchange of ideas. Put in the time and effort necessary to develop these relationships.
47. Be constructively critical of your group members' work. Do not dominate group discussions. Be a good listener and contributor.
48. Learn from past mistakes and deficiencies. Improve upon weak aspects of other case presentations.
49. Learn from the positive approaches and accomplishments of classmates.
50. Be considerate, dependable, reliable, and trustworthy.

READINGS

Fielen, John. "Clear Writing Is Not Enough." *Management Review* (April 1989): 49–53.

Holcombe, M., and J. Stein. *Presentations for Decision Makers* (Belmont, Calif.: Lifetime Learning Publications, 1983).

———. *Writing for Decision Makers* (Belmont, Calif.: Lifetime Learning Publications, 1981).

Jeffries, J., and J. Bates. *The Executive's Guide to Meetings, Conferences, and Audiovisual Presentations* (New York: McGraw-Hill, 1983).

Shurter, R., J. P. Williamson, and W. Broehl. *Business Research and Report Writing* (New York: McGraw-Hill, 1965).

Strunk, W., and E. B. White. *The Elements of Style* (New York: Macmillan, 1978).

Zall, P., and L. Franc. *Practical Writing in Business and Industry* (North Scituate, Mass.: Duxbury Press, 1978).

APPENDIX

Instructions for Using the *Strategy Formulator* and *Case Analyst* Software

*T*he *Strategy Formulator* and *Case Analyst* software that accompanies this text are user-friendly programs that run on any IBM or IBM-compatible machine with at least one floppy disk drive and 512K (or greater) memory. Step-by-step instructions for using this software are provided in this appendix. *Strategy Formulator* and *Case Analyst* will greatly reduce the time it takes you to prepare quantitative, professional exhibits to support your oral case presentations and written case assignments.

The *Strategy Formulator* program generates strategy-formation matrices that are widely used among organizations. The matrices are described in Chapters 4, 5, and 6 of the text. You will want to use *Strategy Formulator* in analyzing all business policy cases. No prior experience with computers is needed to use this software.

The *Case Analyst* program consists of a set of 33 data files that contain the income statements and balance sheets for nearly all the cases in the text. These data files are presented in Lotus 1-2-3 format (Version 2.2) and can be loaded into any spreadsheet program. *Case Analyst* enables you to generate pro forma financial statements and projected financial ratios. Pro forma analysis is described in Chapter 7 of the text. Generating pro forma financial statements is an important part of analyzing a case because you need to show what impact your recommendations will have on the firm's future.

Making a Backup Copy of the Diskettes. It is a good idea to make a working copy of both the *Strategy Formulator* and *Case Analyst* diskette. Keep the original copies in a safe place as a backup. The operating system manual that came with your computer contains instructions on how to make backup copies. If you are using a computer with a hard disk drive, follow instructions in your DOS manual for creating a subdirectory and copy the original diskette to that subdirectory.

THE *STRATEGY FORMULATOR* SOFTWARE

Strategy Formulator is an innovative program that enables managers and students to formulate strategies for organizations. This personal computer software program incorporates the most modern strategic planning techniques in a simple way. The simplicity of *Strategy Formulator* enables this software to facilitate the "process of strategic planning" by promoting communication, understanding, creativity, and forward thinking among users.

Strategy Formulator is not a spreadsheet or database program; it is a structured brainstorming tool that enhances participation in strategy formulation. The software begins with development of an organizational mission statement as described in Chapter 3. Then, the software guides the user through an internal strategic planning audit of the company, followed by an external audit of the firm as described in Chapters 4 and 5. Next, the software generates alternative strategies for the firm, using analytical tools discussed in Chapter 6.

Strategy Formulator enables students or managers to create an organizational mission statement, identify key internal strengths and weaknesses as well as key external opportunities and threats, and then generate, evaluate, and prioritize alternative strategies that the firm could pursue. Individuals can work through the software independently and then meet to discuss particular strategies.

Strategy Formulator runs on any IBM-compatible personal computer system that has a high density (HD) disk drive. It includes numerous help screens and examples and offers clear printouts. No documentation manual is needed with *Strategy Formulator*. Simply boot DOS, Type SF, and follow directions.

Strategy Formulator gives you hands-on experience using actual strategic planning software and facilitates business policy case analysis. This new software is a derivative of the CheckMATE strategic planning software that is widely used among organizations worldwide. (For additional information about CheckMATE, contact Strategic Planning Systems, P.O. Box 13065, Florence, SC 29504; Phone 803-669-6960; Fax 803-673-9460.)

The Structure and Function of Strategy Formulator. The first and second screens that appear in the *Strategy Formulator* software are given in Figures 1 and 2. Note from the first screen that the F1, F2, and F3 keys are the Save key, Load key, and Print key, respectively. Note that the second screen gives an outline or flowchart of the *Strategy Formulator* program. This second screen is a main menu that returns throughout the program; you simply highlight the particular area you wish to work on and hit Enter to begin that part of the program.

FIGURE 1

THE FIRST SCREEN
STRATEGY FORMULATOR SOFTWARE

The *Strategy Formulator* program provides a systematic approach for managers to devise strategies their organization could pursue. *Strategy Formulator* incorporates the most modern strategic planning techniques in a simple way.

The recommended approach for using *Strategy Formulator* is for managers to work through the software independently, and then meet together to discuss the results and develop a single set of joint recommendations. This approach to strategic planning facilitates communication, forward thinking, understanding, commitment, and performance. The help key (F1) is available at all times throughout the *Formulator* program to give you more information. Press the F1 key now to obtain information about the Save key (F2), Load key (F3), Print key (F4), and Escape key.

Press the return key on the highlighted topic on the menu to activate the various parts of the program.

FIGURE 2

THE SECOND SCREEN

The Structure and Function of *Strategy Formulator*
  I. Create a Mission Statement
 II. Identify Key Internal Strengths and Weaknesses
III. Identify Key External Opportunities and Threats
 IV. Generate Alternative Strategies Using:
        IE Analysis
        TOWS Analysis
        SPACE Analysis
        GRAND Analysis
  V. Refine Alternative Strategies
 VI. Select Strategies to Pursue
        Other functions:
          Load Data from Disk
          Save Data to Disk
          Print
          Quit Program

Getting Started. Insert the *Strategy Formulator* diskette into any IBM-compatible machine that has a high density (HD) disk drive and, at the prompt, type SF. (You will need to have previously loaded DOS if your system does not have that installed.)

Read the first screen. Hit the F1 key just to get familiar with the Help routine. Hit the Escape key to return to the main menu. Hit Enter to go to the second screen. Note from the second screen that you may simply highlight the "Create a Mission Statement" line and hit Enter to begin work on developing a mission statement—which is the first activity in formulating strategies. Hit Enter again when you are ready to return to the main menu. You may hit the F1 key anytime in the program for help. The Program Mechanics Help, as shown in Figure 3, will (always) appear on the screen if you hit the F1 key twice.

After completing the mission statement, highlight the next line "Identify Key Internal Strengths and Weaknesses." Hit Enter and begin development of a list of the company's key strengths and weaknesses. When you have completed this work, return to the main menu. Continue working sequentially in this manner through the program.

The Save and Load Routines. It is easy to save and load your work in the *Strategy Formulator* program. The Help Screens (F1 key) associated with the Save and Load routines are given in Figures 4 and 5.

The Print Routine. The *Strategy Formulator* software generates nine planning reports that can be printed separately or together, as indicated on a print screen as shown in Figure 6, that appears near the end of the program.

Simply highlight the reports you desire to be printed and hit Enter to begin printing your work. You could highlight the "Print All Reports" to print all of your work. If you press the F1 key, the screen shown in Figure 7 appears.

FIGURE 3

THE PROGRAM MECHANICS HELP SCREEN

- Movement between screens within a module is accomplished by pressing the UP and DOWN arrows. This is true both within the Help facility and within the main program.
- If you wish to delete to the left of the cursor, you should press the BACKSPACE key. If you wish to delete to the right of the cursor, you should press the DELETE key.
- If you wish to insert text, place the cursor where you wish to begin the insertion and press the INSERT key. When the insert mode is in operation, the cursor changes its size and the word "Insert" appears in the bottom right corner of the screen. Insert is turned off again either by pressing the INSERT key or by moving to another answer.
- You can access the HELP facility at any time by pressing the F1 key. From the Help facility, you can return to the screen you were working on by pressing the ESCAPE key.
- You can SAVE all of your work at any time by pressing the F2 key.
- You can LOAD all of your work at any time by pressing the F3 key.
- You can PRINT all or part of your work at any time by pressing the F4 key.
- You can return to the menu at any time by pressing the ESCAPE key.

FIGURE 4

THE SAVE ROUTINE HELP SCREEN

The Save routine is where the information that has been entered into the system is saved for later use.

The Drive is the disk drive where the data is saved.

The Path is the logical place on the drive where the information is saved. You should either read up on this in the DOS manual or go with the default. The default is the drive and path where the program is located.

The File Name is the name that is given to the information that is saved. This name is used later to retrieve the information. It is eight characters long.

The Directory List will give you a list of files that already exist. If you save over a file (use the same name), the contents of that file are lost. It is a good idea to save your files in two places so that there will be a backup if the primary file is lost. To do this, put a floppy disk in the drive and change the disk drive letter to the letter corresponding to the drive you are using. Usually the letter is A; sometimes it is B.

FIGURE 5

THE LOAD ROUTINE HELP SCREEN

The Load routine is where the information that has been saved on the disk is brought back into the system.

The Drive is the disk drive where the data is saved.

The Path is the logical place on the drive where the information is saved. For more information on this, you should read the DOS manual.

The File Name is the name that is given to the information that is saved. This name is used to retrieve the information. It is eight characters long.

The Directory List will give you a list of files that exist on the disk and path that are listed on the screen. The name must show up on the directory in order for the information to be read.

FIGURE 6

STRATEGY FORMULATOR PRINT REPORTS

Print ALL Reports	TOWS Analysis Report
Mission Statement Report	SPACE Analysis Report
Internal Analysis Report	GRAND Analysis Report
External Analysis Report	Alternative Strategies Report
IE Analysis Report	Selected Strategies Report

FIGURE 7

THE PRINT ROUTINE HELP SCREEN

The Print routine is accessed by hitting the F4 key or the print option on the main menu.

Within the print menu, select the report you wish by pressing the up and down arrow keys. You can print all reports or individual ones.

If there is a "printer off line" error, you should locate the on-line button on your printer and press it. This should put your printer on-line.

If there is a "printer paper out" error, you should load paper into your printer. This should correct this problem.

If you wish to bypass the program's printer error detection features for any reason, press the "D" (for disable) key. This is usually not needed, but if the user has nonstandard software or hardware, it may be necessary.

Contents of the Diskette. Income statements and balance sheets for 33 cases are provided in the Lotus 1-2-3 format (Version 2.2) on the *Case Analyst* diskette. The only two cases in the text that do not include financial statements are *W. L. Gore* and *Dave's Pit Stop Cafe*. Spreadsheets saved under Version 2.2 have a WK1 extension attached to their name. Newer versions of Lotus can read these files. Ample space is provided on the diskette for projected income statement and balance sheet information to be entered.

The 33 *Case Analyst* data files are listed below in alphabetical order.

FILE NAME	CORRESPONDING ORGANIZATION
AUDUBON WK1	*The Audubon Zoo*
BANCONE WK1	*Banc One*
BOEING WK1	*Boeing*
BORDEN WK1	*Borden*
CAMPBELL WK1	*Campbell Soup*
CCCA WK1	*Classic Car Club of America*
CIRCUS WK1	*Circus Circus Enterprises*
CITICORP WK1	*Citicorp*
DELL WK1	*Dell Computer*
DMERR WK1	*Dakota, Minnesota, & Eastern Railroad*
GEORGPAC WK1	*Georgia-Pacific*
HARLEY WK1	*Harley-Davidson*
HERSHEY WK1	*Hershey Foods*
IBM WK1	*International Business Machines*
LIMITED WK1	*The Limited*
MCDONNEL WK1	*McDonnell Douglas*
MET WK1	*The Metropolitan Museum of Art*
MHE WK1	*Material Handling Engineering*
NIKE WK1	*Nike*
NORDSTRO WK1	*Nordstrom*
NORWOOD WK1	*Norwood Furniture*
NSP WK1	*NSP Corporate Graphics*
PILGRIM WK1	*Pilgrim's Pride*
PLAYBOY WK1	*Playboy Enterprises*
PROMUS WK1	*Promus Companies*
RYKA WK1	*Rykä*
SPLATTER WK1	*Splatterball Adventure Games*
WALMART WK1	*Wal-Mart Stores*
WALNU WK1	*Walnut Creek Baptist Church*
WEYER WK1	*Weyerhaeuser*
WHIRLPOO WK1	*Whirlpool*
WINNEBAG WK1	*Winnebago Industries*
WTD WK1	*WTD Industries*

Using Case Analyst with Other Spreadsheets. Due to the historic dominance of Lotus in the spreadsheet arena, most popular spreadsheets such as Enable, Excel, and Quattro Pro can work with files created by Lotus. In most cases, the user can manipulate the Lotus file using the other spreadsheet. Once the manipulation is completed, the user has the option of saving the file in the Lotus format or in the format of the other spreadsheet. The details for working with a Lotus file will vary depending on the spreadsheet so users are advised to consult their manuals for details.

Prior Experience with Lotus. To benefit most from this diskette, you should have some prior knowledge and experience with Lotus or a comparable spreadsheet. Minimal prerequisite skills include retrieving and saving a spreadsheet, moving the cursor, using the @SUM function, and using the COPY command. For those who are not familiar with some of the other techniques used in constructing the Hershey case that follows, a brief review is provided below. This review includes details on entering data, formatting cells, editing the spreadsheet, and absolute addressing. A review of the PRINT command is presented in a later section.

Data Entry. Lotus permits users to enter numbers, labels, and formulas. To enter a number, it must begin with a digit, a plus or minus sign, or a decimal. The number should not contain commas, spaces, or a dollar sign. These symbols can be inserted by formatting commands described later. If a number is too wide for a cell, 1-2-3 may display asterisks instead of the number. If this happens, you need to increase the cell-width (/WORKSHEET COLUMN SET-WIDTH).

Labels are used mainly for row and column headings. Labels that are longer than a cell's width are continued across adjacent cells to the right, provided the cells are empty. If the first character of a label is one of those designating a number or formula, a label prefix must be used. Label prefixes determine how to display the label in the cell. The possible label prefixes are the apostrophe (') for left alignment of a label, the quotation mark (") for right alignment, and the caret (^) for centering the label. The default prefix is the apostrophe.

Formatting. The /RANGE FORMAT command can be used to format selected cells in a spreadsheet. This command yields a menu with ten options, but only three are of interest: Currency, Comma (,), and Percent. Before selecting one of the options under Format, you must select the number of decimal places to display. The number of decimals displayed does not change the internal value of the number when it is used in computations. The Currency option places a dollar sign before cell entries, commas between thousands, and negative values appear in parentheses. The , (Comma) option is the same as the Currency option except the dollar sign is suppressed. The Percent option displays the number in a percent format with a fixed number of decimal places.

Editing. Lotus provides users with a number of editing features. First, there are options under the WORKSHEET menu for inserting or deleting rows and columns and for changing the width of a column. Second, striking the F2 key permits you to edit individual cells. While in edit mode, typed characters are inserted immediately to the left of the cursor. The backspace or delete key can be used to delete characters. Third, the Erase option from the RANGE menu can be used to erase entries in a range of cells.

Absolute Addressing. Most of the cells containing assumptions for a pro forma model should be referenced using an absolute address. A cell reference is designated as absolute by preceding each coordinate by a dollar sign (e.g., an absolute address for B5 is $B$5). If a formula like (1+$A$30)*D30 were copied from the D column to the E column, the formula would appear as (1+$A$30)*E30 rather than (1+B30)*E30.

Format of the Spreadsheets on the Case Analyst *Diskette.* The financial data for each case begins in row 20 of column B. Rows 20–26 contain the name of the company and whether this portion of the spreadsheet is an income statement or balance sheet. Columns B–F are used to describe the row entries that will occupy column G and beyond. For nearly all the cases, numeric values for two consecutive years have been entered starting in column G.

Since all of the data will usually not print on one page, the user may have to insert page breaks at appropriate points. In order to accommodate wide lines, the user may have to use a compressed printing mode (i.e., 132 characters per line). To instruct your printer to print in compressed mode, the /PRINT PRINTER OPTIONS menu is used. Select the SETUP option from this menu and enter the appropriate printer code. For example, if you are using an Epson or IBM printer, the proper setup code is \015. If you are using a printer other than an IBM or Epson, you will need to consult your printer manual for the proper code. Before attempting to print in compressed mode, be sure to change the margins to the Left = 4 and Right = 136. Margins can be set by accessing the /PRINT PRINTER OPTIONS menu and selecting Margins. If you are using a printer that is capable of printing 132 characters per line in normal mode, you must access the /PRINT PRINTER OPTIONS menu and delete the code \015.

The Windows version of Lotus makes the printing process much simpler; the user can direct Lotus to fit as much information as possible on a page. In addition, the user has the option of printing in a landscape mode.

Pro Forma Statements. Pro forma (projected) financial statement analysis is an important strategic-management tool because it allows firms to examine the expected results of different strategies. A pro forma income statement and balance sheet allows managers to compute projected financial ratios under different strategy-implementation scenarios. Steps for developing pro forma financial statements are given in Chapter 8.

A Pro Forma Example Using Lotus. Financial statements from the Hershey Foods Cohesion Case on the *Case Analyst* diskette are used as an example. The steps listed below apply generally to other cases as well. A three-year (1994, 1995, and 1996) forecast will be generated from the existing data. However, realize that pro forma statements should reasonably reflect what strategies you recommend the company to pursue in the future. Thus, a constant historical growth or shrink rate may not reasonably show the effect of your strategies on the future financial condition of the firm.

Step 1 Start the Lotus 1-2-3 program. This process may vary depending on the type of computer facilities you are using. Your professor or lab instructor should provide explicit instructions for starting Lotus.

Step 2 Use the /FILE command to retrieve the case of interest. For our example, this will be the file named Hershey.

Step 3 Make sure your printer has been turned on. Use the /PRINT command to generate a paper copy of the case data. This copy of the case will be used as a worksheet.

Step 4 Determine a projected sales growth (decline) rate for Hershey. A reasonable way to determine a value for the projected sales growth (or decline) is to calculate the following ratios:

net sales for 1990/net sales for 1989 (1.12),

net sales for 1991/net sales for 1990 (1.07),

net sales for 1992/net sales for 1991 (1.11), and

net sales for 1993/net sales for 1992 (1.08).

Then use the average of these four ratios as the projected sales growth (decline) rate. This average (1.10) can be computed with Lotus or with a calculator. Now write the average in its decimal form to the left of the "Net Sales" entry on your paper copy.

Step 5 Determine the ratio of the cost-of-goods to net sales. This can be done in the same manner as the calculations for the projected sales growth (decline) rate. In particular, calculate the following ratios:

Cost of Sales 1990/net sales 1990, (.58),

Cost of Sales 1991/net sales 1991 (.58),

Cost of Sales 1992/net sales 1992 (.57), and

Cost of Sales 1993/net sales 1993 (.57).

In the Hershey case, the entries for "Cost of Sales" (row 28) are used for the cost-of-goods. Once these ratios have been determined, calculate the average, and use the decimal value of the average (.58) as the cost-of-goods-sold as a percentage-of-sales figure. On your paper copy, write the average to the left of the "Cost of Sales" entry.

Step 6 Determine percentages for other expense items from the income statement in the same manner, and enter the decimal equivalent to the left of the expense item on your paper copy.

For the next steps you will be using your computer.

Step 7 Prepare columns K, L, and M as follows. First, enter 1994, 1995, and 1996 in cells K23, L23, and M23, respectively. Second, use the Column Width option of the /WORKSHEET menu to increase the width of these columns to 12 or more. Third, to save effort, copy the data in column J to corresponding areas in columns K, L, and M. Fourth, use the /RANGE ERASE command to erase the data in this area; the data will be erased, but the format specifications for cell entries will be retained. Thus, when entries are made in these columns, they will automatically have the same format of the data in columns G–J.

Step 8 Enter your projected sales growth rate (1.10) from Step 4 in cell A25. Enter in column A your estimates for the other expenses in the appropriate row. In the Hershey example, you would enter .58 in cell A28 as the estimate for the ratio for the cost of sales to net sales.

Step 9 Use the spreadsheet to determine projected sales for the next three years. Enter the following formula in cell K25: ($A25) *J25. This represents the projected sales for 1994. Copy the formula in K25 to the range L25. .M25 to generate the projected sales for 1995 and 1996.

Step 10 Use the spreadsheet to determine the estimated "Cost of Sales" for 1994–1996. Enter the following formula in cell K28: +$A28 *J25. This represents the projected cost-of-goods-sold for 1994. For 1995 and 1996, copy the formula from cell K28 to L28 and M28. Continue this process for the remaining expenses. For entries that are totals in the J column, copy the formula stored in the total cell for column J to the corresponding cells in the projected year columns (K, L, and M).

Step 11 To create the pro forma balance sheet, calculate the projected values on your paper copy and then enter these values in the appropriate cell in column A. Use the /COPY command to copy the balance sheet data from column J to the range defined by your projected years. For example, if you are making a three-year projection, then copy column J to columns K, L, and M. After the copy is completed, replace all nonformula entries in column K by your projected values (as was done in the income statement). The value of this procedure is that the existing format specifications for column J will be copied to columns K, L, and M. Thus, the proper number of decimal places, placement of the dollar sign, and positioning of commas will be taken care of automatically. If you want to change the format, select the /RANGE FORMAT menu. Another advantage of copying column J is that all formula entries will also be copied.

Step 12 This step describes how to use the spreadsheet to calculate financial ratios of interest. The financial ratios for a case should be calculated at the bottom of the spreadsheet. Enter the name of the financial ratio as a label in column B. For long names, you may have to put the name in two rows. To calculate the ratio, enter the formula in terms of relative cell addresses in the column of the first projected year. After all ratios have been calculated for the first projected year, copy the cells containing the ratio formulas to the corresponding cells for the other projected years. The value of this procedure is that if the assumptions in column A change, the financial ratios are automatically recalculated.

A Ratio Example. A benefit of having case data on this diskette is the ease with which various financial ratios can be calculated. Recall that a listing of important financial ratios was presented in Chapter 5.

To illustrate how the ratios can be calculated, data from the Hershey case are used. It would be useful if you had a copy of the Hershey example in front of you now. An example from each ratio category is calculated for the year 1993. For each ratio, the appropriate formula in terms of cell references, the numbers used in the calculation, and the results of the calculation are displayed.

Examples of Financial Ratios for Hershey for 1993

CURRENT RATIO
- = Current assets/Current liabilities
- = +j81/j106
- = 888,996/813,845
- = 1.09

LONG-TERM-DEBT-TO-
EQUITY RATIO
- = Long-term debt/Total stockholders' equity
- = +j108/j126
- = 165,757/1,412,344
- = .12

TOTAL ASSETS
TURNOVER
- = Sales/Total assets
- = +j25/j90
- = 3,488,249/2,855,091
- = 1.22

RETURN ON TOTAL
ASSETS (ROA)
- = Net income/Total assets
- = +j47/j90
- = 193,325/2,855,091
- = .07

ANNUAL PERCENTAGE
GROWTH IN TOTAL
SALES
- = (Total sales$_{1993}$ − Total sales$_{1992}$)/Total sales $_{1992}$
- = +(j25 − i25)/i25
- = (3,488,249 − 3,219,805)/3,219,805
- = 8.34%

The user should note that not all ratios for every case can be calculated since some income statements and balance sheets do not contain the necessary information.

BANKING INDUSTRY NOTE
WRAY O. CANDILIS AND JOHN R. SHUMAN
U.S. Department of Commerce

Federally insured depository institutions held slightly more than $4.9 trillion in assets in 1993, down slightly from 1992. If the interest rates remain low and prices remain steady, however, assets in 1994 are expected to increase 1 percent to approximately $5 trillion.

Commercial banks, savings institutions, and credit unions in 1993 benefited from a widening of spreads between interest rates charged for loans and paid for deposits. Savings institutions reported a record high spread of 4.25 percent between interest earned from mortgage loans and interest paid on deposits.

Depositors in 1993 diverted funds in record volume from banks, thrifts, and credit unions to alternative investments, especially mutual funds and common stock. Commercial banks faced with higher deposit insurance and the need to improve loan quality slowed the growth of deposits and their lending activity.

Despite the slowdown in lending and runoff in deposits, commercial banks and savings institutions continued to increase profits in 1993. Banks in 1994 are expected to report profits for the third consecutive year. Savings institutions are expected to continue to decline in terms of numbers and assets, but should extend a streak of profitable quarters that dates from 1991.

Banks and savings institutions are also expected to continue their evolution into a structure featuring a regional bank-holding company that operates independent depository, commercial and consumer lending, mortgage lending and mortgage servicing, insurance, and securities units. Banks expect securities activities to become a significant growth area.

In 1987 the Federal Reserve Board allowed certain subsidiaries of banks to underwrite and deal in asset-backed securities and municipal revenue bonds. The Fed in 1989 expanded the eligible securities to corporate debt and stock. Revenues from underwriting and dealing in these securities are limited to 10 percent of the subsidiary's total revenues, yet by early 1993 bank subsidiaries accounted for 6.2 percent of the capital of all securities firms. During the 12 months ending June 30, 1993, these subsidiaries underwrote 5.5 percent of all investment-grade corporate debt. Money-center and large regional banks in 1993 also competed aggressively with traditional mutual fund sponsors by retailing mutual funds to their customers, in part as an effort to recapture some of the funds flowing from certificates of deposit to other investment vehicles. Some of these banks have limited their activity to retailing funds sponsored by traditional fund management companies. But more than 110 banks or bank-holding companies offered proprietary mutual funds, primarily to their existing client base. Bank-sponsored mutual funds in 1993 were the fastest growing segment of the mutual-fund industry, accounting for 10.6 percent of total assets, and 30 percent of new sales.

Community development banking also increased in prominence in 1993. Federal banking and savings institution regulators intensified their audits of lending to lower-income communities, and gathered public information on means to increase lending in these neighborhoods. Credit union regulators chartered four new credit unions exclusively to provide services for lower-income members, while another 140 credit unions focused services on lower-income members.

Trends and Forecasts: Commercial Banking (SIC 602) (in billions of dollars except as noted)

					PERCENT CHANGE (1990–1994)			
ITEM	1991	1992	1993[1]	1994[2]	90–91	91–92	92–93	93–94
Assets	3,545	3,653	3,689	3,763	4.3	3.1	1.0	2.0
Loans	2,288	2,281	2,327	2,420	–0.9	–0.3	2.0	4.0
Investments	706	799	878	966	16.5	13.2	10.0	10.0
Deposits	2,452	2,542	2,593	2,648	3.8	3.7	2.0	2.0
Employment(000)	1,529	1,488	1,473	1,458	–2.3	–2.7	–1.0	–1.0

[1]Estimate
[2]Forecast

Source: Board of Governors of the Federal Reserve System; U.S. Department of Labor, Bureau of Labor Statistics, Estimates and forecasts by U.S. Department of Commerce, International Trade Administration.

As economic activity maintained its steady, but modest, upward trend, businesses began once again to turn to banks for their short-term capital needs. With low interest rates and steady price levels as a backdrop, bank lending was expected to fare a little better than in the most recent past, rising 2 percent to $2,327 billion in 1993, and 4 percent to $2,420 billion in 1994. Bank lending dropped slightly both in 1991 and 1992. The growth of bank investments, on the other hand, is expected to continue to decelerate from its recent peak increase of 16.5 percent in 1991 to about 10 percent in both 1993 and 1994.

The broad variety of savings and investments instruments marketed by competing depository and nondepository financial institutions is expected to result in a relatively small 3 percent increase in commercial bank deposits in 1993 and 1994. Over the past few years, consumer bank deposits have been especially hit due to the runoff of certificates of deposit, only partly offset by the growth of passbook and money market accounts. Most of the runoff has flowed into mutual funds providing the strength being experienced in the stock and bond markets. This continuous rivalry from competitors has compelled commercial banks to enter the mutual fund business and to keep up the pressure on legislators and regulators in an effort to open up areas, such as the securities market, that previously were off-limits.

Specifically, the Federal Reserve Board has in recent years given approval to a number of banks for broader securities underwriting powers, under "Section 20" of the Glass–Steagall Act, which permits banks, through separately capitalized units, to underwrite and deal in corporate debt and equity. These activities, however, can contribute no more than 10 percent of the unit's revenues. Banks have long been able to deal in government securities.

Of the more than 30 banks that have received approval by the Board for securities underwriting privileges under Section 20, about one third are foreign banks while the rest are domestic money-center banks and big regional bank companies. It should be noted that 17 additional foreign banks have used "grandfathered" status under the International Banking Act of 1978 to deal in both commercial banking and securities underwriting activities in the United States.

Profitability of Banks. High net interest-rate margins—the spread between interest income and interest expense—and improved quality of commercial bank assets in 1992, set in a framework of a general economic upturn, resulted in lifting banks out of their 1989–1991 depressed profit picture (Table 1). These trends continued in the first half of 1993.

The average return on assets, measured by income as a percentage of average fully consolidated assets for all size categories of banks went from 0.53 percent in 1991 to 0.92 in 1992. The most progress was experienced by large banks—those with more than $5 billion in assets—and the 10 largest banks, the return on assets of the former going from 0.50 to 1.01 percent, and the latter from 0.21 to 0.65 percent.

The average return on equity, measured by net income as a percentage of average equity capital, also grew substantially for the industry as a whole, going from 7.86 percent in 1991 to 12.80 in 1992. As with the return on assets, the greatest gains were shown by large banks and the ten largest banks, the return on equity of the former increasing from 8.10 to 14.66 percent and the latter from 4.25 to 11.87 percent.

Failures and Problem Banks. The financial health of the commercial banking industry is also evident in the number of failures, which dropped from a peak of 206 in 1989 to 120 in 1992 (Figure 1). Unofficial predictions for 1993 put the number of failures at 50 to 60. The number of banks on the problem list of the Federal Deposit Insurance Corporation (FDIC) also dropped considerably, falling by nearly half from the 1987 peak.

As a consequence of bank failures and the depletion of the Bank Insurance Fund, premium rates have been steadily increasing since 1989 when banks were paying 8.3 cents for every $100 of insured deposits. Beginning in January 1993, the FDIC instituted a risk-based system with premiums ranging from 23 cents for the best-performing banks to 31 cents for the weaker ones. It was at first predicted that by the year 2002 the bank fund would reach the required level of $1.25 for every $100 of insured deposits, at which time premiums would drop to 13.5 cents per $100 of deposits and to 10 cents a year later. More recent predictions, however, based on lower bank-failure projections for the years ahead and a slowing in the growth rate of deposits, estimated that the $1.25 level for every $100 of insured deposits might be reached much

TABLE 1	Profit Rates of Commercial Banks, 1990–92		
ITEM	1990	1991	1992
Return on assets[1]	0.49	0.53	0.92
Return on equity[2]	7.57	7.86	12.80

[1]Net income as a percent of average fully consolidated assets net of loss reserves.

[2]Net income as a percent of average equity capital.

Source: Board of Governors of the Federal Reserve System.

FIGURE 1 Failed and Problem Banks

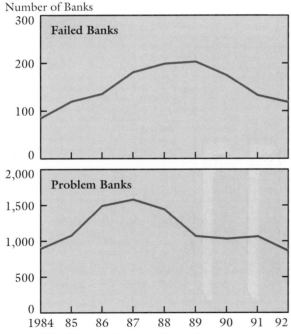

Source: Federal Deposit Insurance Corporation.

earlier than 2002, perhaps as early as 1996. Consequently, premiums are now expected to be reduced more quickly than previously predicted.

International Activities. The number of foreign bank offices in the United States rose steadily throughout the past two decades, reaching 747 by the end of 1992, and fell slightly to 720 a year later (Figure 2).

These offices include 8 branches, 224 agencies, 90 subsidiaries more than 25 percent owned by foreign banks, 17 Edge Act and Agreement Corporations, and 11 New York State Investment Companies. Nearly one-half of the offices are in New York, with most of the others in California, Illinois, and Florida. Japan, Canada, France, and the United Kingdom have the largest number of bank offices in the United States. Assets of foreign bank offices in the United States have increased significantly in recent years, rising from $198 billion in 1980 to $865 billion in 1992 or approximately one-fourth of U.S. total banking assets.

In contrast to foreign banks in the United States, U.S. banks abroad have been restructuring and consolidating their activities during the past several years. By the end of 1992, 120 Federal Reserve member banks were operating 774 branches in foreign countries and overseas areas of the United States, a decline from 916 branches at the end of 1985. Of the 120 banks, 88 were national banks operating 660 branches, and 32 were state banks operating the remaining 114 branches.

Technological Developments. Customer use of automated teller machines (ATMs) has been rising significantly over the past few years with the result that branch operating costs have been falling, according to an ATM survey conducted in 1992 by the *American Banker.* Specifically, the annual growth rate for ATMs between 1989 and 1992 has ranged between 17 and 19 percent, with the top five users of teller machines

FIGURE 2 Foreign Bank Offices in the United States

Number of Offices

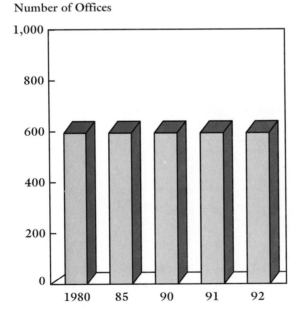

Source: Board of Governors of the Federal Reserve System.

being Bank of America with 4,500; Citibank 1,900; Wells Fargo 1,687; NationsBank 1,678; and First Interstate 1,332.

Increased ATM usage and the consequent decrease in teller transactions does not necessarily mean the demise of branches. There will always be customers who will prefer a live teller to a machine, but it will be bank officers with their sophisticated personal computers and software that will, with increased efficiency, meet new customers, handle their questions, and sell them new products.

Slower progress than the ATM growth is being shown by the debit card which can be used not only in conjunction with an ATM or the withdrawal of funds, but also in conjunction with a point-of-sale terminal for the transfer of funds from a buyer's account to a seller's account. The development of the debit card also remains quite modest in the United States, although it has had enormous success in other countries.

In the home banking field, it seems that the problems that existed in the 1980s still prevail in the 1990s. It is a relatively expensive service that requires a personal computer, a modem, and the necessary software. However, for the sophisticated customer, it offers the facility of paying bills, transferring funds, and opening new accounts. As the equipment becomes less expensive, however, and as banks offer a broader array of services, home banking could develop into a comprehensive information package that would include such nonbank activities as insurance, entertainment, travel, as well as business and sports news.

Legislative and Regulatory Issues. As a result of the passage of the Federal Deposit Insurance Corporation Improvement Act of 1991 (see *1993 U.S. Industrial Outlook*), with its mandated new disclosure rules and tougher auditing and underwriting standards, commercial bankers have been pressuring legislators and regulators to ease the regulatory burden that might have resulted from the implementation of the act. Consequently, regulators decided to rely on examiners to assure that banks are operating safely rather than to set specific managerial standards. Other examples of regulatory sensitivity to bankers' complaints include a proposal to exempt about 7,500 smaller banks from the act's proposed capital standards for banks facing unusual risk from interest rate swings, loan concentration, and other nontraditional activities; and a proposal to let large banks use their own internal systems, with examiner approval, for measuring interest-rate risk.

The principal banking bills in Congress in 1993 concerned the issues of interstate banking (to authorize nationwide branching subject to restrictions on market share of deposits), community development lending (to establish a fund to support community development by financial institutions), overhauling the Federal Reserve System (to increase accountability of the central bank), Fair Credit Reporting Act Amendments (to make it easier for consumers to obtain copies of their credit reports and correct errors), a secondary market for small business loans (to create such a market by either establishing a federal agency or reducing regulatory impediments to securitization), regulatory relief (to give well-capitalized institutions more favorable treatment, or repeal or modify some of the congressionally mandated regulations), and agency consolidation (to create a single banking oversight agency).

At the state level, legislators aimed at using state law to break down interstate banking barriers. Among the latest states to favorably consider interstate banking reform legislation are North Carolina, Alaska, and Oregon. Several Southeastern states are expected to take up similar legislation in the near future, a move that is necessary to modify the regional banking pact system these states adopted in the mid-1980s. Twenty-two states, including California and New York, require reciprocity as a condition to interstate banking, meaning they will let an out-of-state bank into their state if that bank's home state will let their banks in.

Despite strong banking industry opposition, the Financial Accounting Standards Board (FASB) adopted rules that require banks to assign market value to a broader classification of securities holdings; to value impaired or troubled loans at their current value; and thereafter to reserve against expected loss of interest on such loans. However, in a concession to the industry, FASB gave banks the option of adopting its market-value standard in the fourth quarter of 1993 instead of the first quarter of 1994, as requested by some large banks, and delaying the starting date for a new standard on valuing nonperforming loans and setting loan-loss reserves to the first quarter of 1995.

Judicial Issues. Following many years of debate over the advantages and disadvantages of the separation of commercial banking and insurance, and with billions of dollars at stake, the U.S. Supreme Court in mid-1993 ruled that 1916 law, which authorized national banks with branches in towns of less than 5,000 to sell insurance, remains in force. On demand, the U.S. Circuit Court of Appeals for the District of Columbia also decided that there is no geographic limit on where national banks affected by the Supreme Court ruling may sell insurance. In a related case, the U.S. Supreme Court declined to resolve the issue as to whether the Office of the Comptroller of the Currency may permit national banks to sell title insurance under authority of a federal law that permits national banks to exercise "all such incidental powers as shall be necessary to carry on the business of banking." In refusing to hear this appeal, the Court let stand a decision of the U.S. Court of Appeals for the Second Circuit which barred the sale of such insurance in New York, Vermont, and Connecticut. In yet another insurance case, the U.S. Circuit Court of Appeals for the Fifth Circuit ruled that annuities are insurance products, and thus subject to the so-called town of 5,000 rule. Under the ruling, a national bank could sell annuities by mail in small towns, but it would not be able to offer them from branches in larger cities.

Outlook for 1994. The turnaround in the commercial banking industry during 1992 and 1993 was much stronger than the upturn in the economy as a whole, and will probably remain so during 1994. The industry's liquidity together with its strengthened capital position will provide the means to meet the borrowing requirements of individual and corporate customers, but loan growth is expected to rise no more than 4 percent. Monetary and fiscal authorities will continue to work together to try to prevent any stalling of the economic recovery or any buildup of inflationary pressures.

CITICORP—1994

RANDY WHITE
Auburn University at
Montgomery
FRED DAVID,
Francis Marion University

Based in New York City, Citicorp (212-559-4822) is a U.S. bank-holding company and sole shareholder of Citibank, N.A. (Citi). Citi has assets exceeding $213 billion and is the largest U.S. bank. However, Citi is in trouble; its 1992 return on assets of 0.23 percent is the lowest of the top ten U.S. banks, as shown in Exhibit 1–1. In the 38 years that *Fortune* has been compiling its annual list of the largest commercial banking companies, Citi has never made as much as 1 percent on assets. In most years, it hasn't even come close. *Fortune* annually evaluates U.S. companies on eight management criteria: quality of management; financial soundness; quality of products or services; ability to attract, develop, and keep talented people; use of corporate asset; value as long-term investment; innovativeness; and, finally, community and environmental responsibility. Citi currently ranks near the bottom of *Fortune's* list, a fact that suggests the bank is poorly managed.[1]

Citi's net income declined steadily from $1.86 billion in 1988 to a loss of $457 million in 1991. Citi's net income rebounded to $722 million in 1992 and $1.9 billion in 1993.

THE BUSINESSES OF CITI

Through a network of 1,389 U.S. offices covering 32 states and the District of Columbia as well as 1,947 offices outside the United States operating in 92 countries, Citi's 81,500 employees (38,500 in the United States and 43,000 outside the United States) market financial services to individuals, businesses, governments, and financial

EXHIBIT 1-1 Top Ten U.S. Banks by Asset Size as of December 31, 1992 (*In millions of dollars except ROE and ROA*)

RANK		ASSETS	RETURN ON ASSET (%)	RETURN ON EQUITY (%)	MARKET VALUE*
1	Citicorp	213,701	.23	6.6	10,811
2	BankAmerica	180,646	.80	12.7	17,517
3	Chemical Bank	139,655	.67	12.4	10,140
4	Nations Bank	118,059	.97	15.8	13,820
5	J. P. Morgan	102,941	1.14	20.8[a]	13,006
6	Chase Manhattan	102,941	.51	11.2	5,444
7	Bankers Trust NY	72,448	.99	23.1	5,925
8	Banc One	61,417	1.31	16.3	13,403
9	Wells Fargo	52,537	.45	7.9	5,995
10	PNC Bank	51,380	1.18	15.5	7,762

*As of March 31, 1993. Market Value is the closing common stock price multiplied by the number of outstanding common shares.

[a]Year-end amounts.

Source: "Bank Scoreboard," *Business Week*, May 3, 1993, p. 150.

institutions. Citi faces intense competition from both bank and nonbank institutions and, in certain of their activities, from government agencies. Its core businesses are shown in Exhibit 1–2.

Global Consumer. The Global Consumer division provides the following broad range of consumer financial services worldwide:

1. Citiphone Banking and Citicard Banking Centers to give customers current account information to manage their money anytime and anywhere. In Japan, Citi has 21 branches and recently introduced several new services, including automatic bill payment, a direct salary payment facility, and an unsecured revolving credit line available via International Citicard which enables customers traveling in other countries to access their home bank accounts;

EXHIBIT 1-2 The Businesses of Citicorp by Net Income (Loss) as of December 31, 1993 *(In millions of dollars)*

BUSINESS FOCUS	NET INCOME (LOSS) $ MILLIONS		AVERAGE ASSETS $ BILLIONS		RETURN ON ASSETS	
	1993	1992[1]	1993	1992[1]	1993	1992[1]
Global consumer[2]						
North America, Europe and Japan	$ 665	$ 439	$ 75	$ 85	.89%	.52%
Developing economies	556	448	25	21	2.22%	2.13%
Global finance[3]						
North America, Europe and Japan	909	490	73	64	1.25%	.77%
Developing economies	761	643	36	32	2.11%	2.01%
North America commercial real estate	(621)	(1,316)	12	14	(5.18)%	(9.40)%
Cross-border refinancing portfolio	92	403	3	4	3.07%	10.08%
Corporate items[4]	(443)	(385)	4	6	(11.08)%	(6.42)%
	$ 1,919	$ 722	$ 228	$ 226	.84%	.32%
Cumulative effect of accounting change[5]	300	—	—	—	—	—
Total Citicorp	$ 2,219	$ 722	$ 228	$ 226	.97%	.32%

(1) Reclassified to conform to current year's presentation.

(2) Global Consumer results reflect after-tax restructuring charges of $143 million in 1993 and $82 million in 1992. Of these amounts, Global Consumer North America, Europe and Japan included $139 million and $74 million, respectively.

(3) Global Finance results reflect after-tax restructuring charges of $95 million in 1993 and $49 million in 1992. Of these amounts, Global Finance North America, Europe and Japan included $83 million and $31 million, respectively.

(4) Corporate Items includes the effects of asset sales, as well as business write-downs. Results for 1993 also reflect after-tax restructuring charges of $16 million, compared with $(8) million in 1992.

(5) Represents cumulative effect of adopting Statement of Financial Accounting Standards No. 109, "Accounting for Income Taxes," as of January 1, 1993.

Source: *Annual Report*, 1993.

2. A National Banking System (NBS) that enables all U.S. branches to access a customer's total banking relationship upon presentation of his/her Citicard; NBS was completed by year-end 1993;
3. Card products such as *Citigold* for affluent customers; Visa and MasterCard accounts, 29 million domestic and 8 million foreign accounts. New card brands appealing to different customer segments such as CHOICE (the price sensitive), Preferred (the upscale), Classic (security, quality, and value appeals), and affinity cards such as Citibank AAdvantage (a frequent-flier mileage reward program based on card activity). Citi's Diners Club travel and entertainment card produces more than $21 billion in worldwide sales in over 175 countries; U.S. sales have climbed to $9 billion.
4. Citibank Private Bank, the world's largest non-Swiss private bank, focuses on management services tailored to wealthy individuals, their families, and their businesses. The average level of client assets managed totaled $1 million in 1993, with locations in 31 countries.

As shown in Exhibit 1–2, Global Consumer includes two subdivisions: (1) Japan, Europe, and North America (JENA), which showed an increase in net income from $455 million in 1992 to $665 million in 1993, and (2) Developing Economies (primarily Latin America and Asia), which earned a record $556 million in 1993, up from $486 million in 1992. This increase was due primarily to solid loan demand and account growth in Argentina, Hong Kong, and Taiwan. At year-end 1993, $23.9 billion of securitized credit-card receivables were outstanding as compared to $25.6 billion in 1992.

Exhibit 1–3 reflects an increase in Global Consumer's net income from $887 million in 1992 to $1,221 million in 1993. Exhibit 1–4 describes Citi's consumer credit-loss history based on its credit-loss ratio (i.e., annual credit losses as a percent of

EXHIBIT 1-3 Global Consumer as of Years Ended December 31
(In millions of dollars)

	1993	1992	INC./ (DEC.)	%
Total revenue	$ 9,600	$ 9,285	$ 315	3
Restructuring charges	$ 233	$ 130	$ 103	79
Other operating expense	5,965	5,789	176	3
Total operating expense	$ 6,198	$ 5,919	$ 279	5
Provision for credit losses	$ 1,686	$ 2,134	$(448)	(21)
Income before taxes	$ 1,716	$ 1,232	$ 484	39
Income taxes	495	345	150	43
Net income	$ 1,221	$ 887	$ 334	38
Average assets (In billions)	$ 100	$ 106	$ (6)	(6)
Return on assets	1.22%	.84%	.38%	—

Source: *Annual Report*, 1993.

EXHIBIT 1-4 Consumer Portfolio Loss Ratios as of Years Ended December 31

	AVERAGE LOANS(1) ($ BILLIONS)	NET CREDIT LOSSES ($ MILLIONS)	1993 CREDIT LOSS RATIO	1992 CREDIT LOSS RATIO	1991 CREDIT LOSS RATIO
U.S.					
Mortgages(2)	$19.1	$ 267	1.40%	1.61%	.46%
Credit cards	8.5	440	5.18%	6.28%	5.84%
Other	16.9	331	1.96%	2.47%	2.65%
Total U.S.	$44.5	$1,038	2.33%	2.89%	2.46%
Outside the U.S.	36.9	372	1.01%	1.04%	1.05%
Total	$81.4	$1,410	1.73%	2.16%	1.97%

(1) Loan amounts are net of unearned income.
(2) Includes first and second residential mortgages.
Source: *Annual Report*, 1993.

average consumer loans). The falling credit-loss ratios are due to fewer bankruptcies and an improved housing market. Similarly, loans outside the United States also experienced lower credit loss ratios.

Exhibit 1–5 displays Citi's loss ratios for commercial loans. Regarding the U.S. portfolio, net credit losses declined to $379 million, down from $1.8 billion in 1992; the credit-loss ratio fell to 1.67 percent in 1993 from 4.54 percent in 1992, a 63 percent fall. In offices outside the United States, credit-loss ratios declined 62 percent from 1.74 percent in 1992 to 0.65 percent in 1993; net credit loss also dropped to $209 million in 1992 as compared to $511 million in 1993. Exhibit 1–6 gives the allowances for credit loss.

Global Finance. The global finance sector provides worldwide financial services to corporations, financial institutions, governments, and capital markets. Net income increased markedly from $1.13 billion in 1992 to $1.67 billion in 1993, as shown in Exhibit 1–7.

North America Commercial Real Estate. Consisting of real estate operations in the United States and Canada, the North America Commercial Real Estate division incurred a net loss of $621 million in 1993 compared to a loss of $1.3 billion in 1992, as shown in Exhibit 1–8. Increasing write-offs and write-downs affected this business, and projections indicated continuing unfavorable results. Citi is trying to restructure loans to insure repayment and recoup its losses. Citi's tactics also include continued collection efforts by a staff of 600 experienced real estate professionals in 12 offices in the United States and Canada. Exposure in this division is diversified by office, resi-

EXHIBIT 1-5 Commercial Portfolio Loss Ratios as of Years Ended December 31
(*In millions of dollars*)

	AVERAGE LOANS ($ BILLIONS)	NET CREDIT LOSSES ($ MILLIONS)	1993 CREDIT LOSS RATIO	1992 CREDIT LOSS RATIO	1991 CREDIT LOSS RATIO
In U.S. offices					
Commercial real estate loans[1]	$ 8.4	$285	3.38%	7.80%	4.06%
Other commercial loans and leases[2]	14.3	94	.66%	2.38%	2.58%
	$22.7	$379	1.67%	4.54%	3.21%
In offices outside the U.S.					
Commercial real estate loans[1]	$ 2.5	$124	4.94%	7.75%	7.18%
Other commercial loans and leases[2]	29.6	85	.29%	1.01%	1.00%
	$32.1	$209	.65%	1.74%	2.03%
			2.15%	(.89)%	26.14%
Refinancing country loans	2.8	61	.77%	1.44%	6.89%
	$34.9	$270	1.13%	2.80%	5.13%
Total	$57.6	$649			

(1) Includes mortgage and real estate loans.

(2) Includes net write-offs of real estate-related loans of $24 million, $123 million, and $51 million in U.S. offices in 1993, 1992, and 1991 respectively, with $173 million in offices outside the U.S. in 1992.

Source: *Annual Report*, 1993.

EXHIBIT 1-6 Allowance for Credit Losses as of Years Ended December 31
(*In millions of dollars or as noted*)

	LOANS ($ BILLIONS)	1993 ALLOWANCE	1992 ALLOWANCE	1991 ALLOWANCE
Global consumer ratio	$ 84.4	$1,596	$1,338	$1,137
		1.89%	1.60%	1.24%
Commercial ratio	52.1	2,545	2,221	1,650
		4.88%	4.19%	2.97%
Cross-border refinancing portfolio[1]	2.5	238	300	521
Total	$139.0	$4,379	$3,859	$3,308
Ratio		3.15%	2.76%	2.19%
Reserve for Global Consumer Sold Portfolios		$ 527	$ 544	$ 412

(1) The allowance attributable to the cross-border refinancing portfolio represented 8% of medium- and long-term loans and placements at December 31, 1993. When adjusted to add back $2.8 billion of cumulative country write-offs previously charged off, the allowance at December 31, 1993 was equivalent to 53% of similarly adjusted medium- and long-term claims, compared with 51% at year-end 1992 and 54% at year-end 1991.

Source: *Annual Report*, 1993.

EXHIBIT 1-7 Global Finance as of Years Ended December 31 (*In millions of dollars*)

	1993	1992	INC./ (DEC.)	%
Total revenue	$6,108	$5,406	$ 702	13
Restructuring charges	$ 156	$ 76	$ 80	N/M
Other operating expense	3,279	3,137	142	5
Total operating expense	$3,435	$3,213	$ 222	7
Provision for credit losses	$ 305	$ 644	$(339)	(53)
Income before taxes	$2,368	$1,549	$ 819	53
Income taxes	698	416	282	68
Net income	$1,670	$1,133	$ 537	47
Average assets (In billions)	$ 109	$ 96	$ 13	14
Return on assets	1.53%	1.18%	.35%	—

Source: *Annual Report*, 1993.

EXHIBIT 1-8 North America Commercial Real Estate as of Years Ended December 31 (*In millions of dollars*)

	1993	1992[1]	INC./ (DEC.)	%
Total revenue	$ (11)	$ (45)	$ 34	76
Operating expense	377	424	(47)	(11)
Provision for credit losses	610	1,622	(1,012)	(62)
(Loss) before taxes	$(998)	$(2,091)	$(1,093)	(52)
Income taxes	(377)	(775)	(398)	(51)
Net (loss)	$(621)	$(1,316)	$ (695)	(53)
Average assets (in billions)	$ 12	$ 14	$ (2)	(14)
Adjusted for credit-related items:				
Total revenue[2]	$ 173	$ 252	$ (79)	(31)
Operating expense[3]	150	148	2	1
Credit costs[4]	842	1,719	(877)	(51)

(1) Reclassified to conform to current year's presentation.

(2) After adding back the net cost to carry cash-basis loans and OREO.

(3) Excludes net write-downs and direct revenues and expenses related to OREO.

(4) Principally net write-offs, the net cost to carry cash-basis loans and OREO, as well as net write-downs and direct revenues and expenses related to OREO.

Source: *Annual Report*, 1993.

dential, and retail types—36 percent, 23 percent, and 20 percent, respectively. The largest geographic regions are located in the West and Mid-Atlantic—32 percent and 18 percent, respectively; total western exposure was nearly $5.0 billion, with California accounting for approximately 64 percent, whereas total mid-Atlantic exposure was $2.4 billion, with New York responsible for nearly $2 billion or 50 percent.

Cross-Border Refinancing Portfolio. As shown in Exhibit 1–9, net income fell to $92 million, a 77 percent decline. Included in the $402 million for 1992 was the collection of Brazil's past-due interest payments of $74 million for 1992 and $116 million for 1991. Medium- and long-term cross-border claims dropped markedly from $3.3 billion in 1992 to $2.9 billion in 1993, an 18 percent fall. Of the $3.3 billion, approximately $1.0 billion was placed on a cash basis. (A loan put on a cash basis indicates doubtful collection of either principal or interest.) Brazil accounted for $0.9 billion on a cash basis.

Citi anticipated that its share of remaining unpaid interest for 1991 and 1992 would be satisfied through issuance of a $220 million 12-year bond and $44 million cash payment. The $2.9 billion medium and long-term loans consisted approximately of $1.1 billion to South Africa and Venezuela, $0.4 billion to the Philippines, $0.3 billion to Uruguay, and $0.2 billion to 11 other countries. Medium- and long-term loans to 11 other countries totaled $0.2 billion. Trade and short-term obligations of $2.7 billion consisted of $0.9 billion to Argentina, $0.9 billion to Brazil, $0.1 billion to the Philippines, Uruguay, and Venezuela.

Risk Management at Citicorp. The process of risk management is central to Citicorp's continuing efforts to contain loan problems as well as improve its ability to correct present and potential deficiencies. At the core of this credit process are four groups established to coordinate and execute the bank's credit-operating process. One group is the Management Committee, whose responsibility is to allocate key corporate resources, formalize the bank's overall risk capacity, and examine individual credit decisions that could pose future problems.

A second group is the Credit Policy Committee, which insures that credit policies and standards cited in Citi's manual, *Core Credit Policies,* are adhered to. The Committee also maintains contact with both the Management Committee and the Board of Directors regarding portfolio quality, risk profile, loan problems, and credit policy issues. Depending on the severity of the problem, Citi's line managers may turn problem loans over to Institutional Recovery Management, a team organized to control and monitor difficult loan problems.

The Business Risk Review (BRR) group's responsibilities include independent and periodic reviews of both the credit process and portfolio quality so as quickly to identify problem loans. BRR members are senior line officers on rotation for approximately two to three years. BRR reports to the Audit Committee of the Board of Directors.

With regard to its North American Commercial Real Estate portfolio, Citi's strategy is to restructure existing loans through loan-collection efforts, asset sales, asset management, and appraisals. This sector includes over 600 experienced real estate personnel and staff located in 12 offices in the United States and Canada.

As a major part of the risk management process, Citi is required to adhere to capital guidelines issued by the Federal Reserve Board (FRB). For example, quali-

EXHIBIT 1-9 Cross-Border Refinancing Portfolio as of Years Ended December 31
(*In millions of dollars*)

	1993	1992[1]	INC./ (DEC.)	
Total revenue	$126	$ 196	$ (70)	(36)
Operating expense	28	29	(1)	(3)
Provision for credit losses	(1)	(254)	(253)	N/M
Income before taxes	$ 99	$ 421	$(322)	(76)
Income taxes	7	18	(11)	(61)
Net income	$ 92	$ 403	$(311)	(77)
Average assets (In billions)	$ 3	$ 4	$ (1)	(25)

(1) Reclassified to conform to current year's presentation.
N/M Not meaningful as percentage equals or exceeds 100%.
Source: *Annual Report*, 1993.

fying capital includes two parts: Tier 1 Capital is common stockholders' equity, qualifying perpetual preferred stock and minority interest in consolidated subsidiaries less goodwill and certain other deductions; Tier 2 Capital consists of perpetual preferred stock not included in Tier 1 capital and, subject to% limitations, the allowance for credit losses, qualifying senior and subordinated debt and limited-life preferred stock less certain deductions. FRB ratio guidelines are shown in Table 1–1.

Note in Table 1 that a leverage ratio of 3 percent for the highest rated banks and 4–5 percent for other banks is required. This ratio is Tier 1 capital divided by adjusted average assets. Citi's goal is to attain a 7–7.5 percent Tier 1 capital in 1994.

Strategies of the Chairman. For a number of years, as net income has declined, Chairman John Reed has felt considerable foreign pressure. Coupled with the relative improvement in net income for year-end 1992, Reed embarked on several cost-cutting measures. Table 1–2 compares Citi's facilities and staffing in 1992 with those in 1993. Note in Table 1–2 that Citi's overseas offices declined 1.6 percent, yet staffing increased 7.5 percent.

TABLE 1-1 Regulatory Ratio Guidelines as of December 31, 1993

RATIOS	REQUIRED	1993	1992	1991
Common Stockholders' Equity		4.65%	3.73%	3.39%
Tier 1 Capital	4.00%	6.62%	4.90%	3.73%
Tier 1 & Tier 2 Capital	8.00%	11.45%	9.60%	7.46%
Leverage	3.00%+	6.15%	4.74%	3.94%

Tier 1 Capital and Tier 1 & Tier 2 Capital requirements effective as of year-end 1993.

The elimination of stock dividends in 1991 was an attempt to improve its capital position. Reed himself was affected, as "almost all his net worth is tied up in Citi stock." Based on data published by *Fortune,* among the 200 top-paid CEOs in the United States Reed ranks 38th at over $4.2 million, a figure that includes salary ($1.15 million), bonus ($1.0 million), value of long-term incentives and stock grants ($1.9 million), and other items ($69,000) such as insurance, club memberships, and so on. Yet Reed ranks 138th of 200 CEOs in terms of the five-year total return to shareholders.

Reed has implemented a number of top management changes. He established a leaner management structure, reducing senior management from 95 executives in 1990 to 29 in 1992. Reed made a key decision in hiring Christopher Steffen, a 51-year-old executive who had suddenly resigned as Eastman Kodak's Chief Financial Officer after 11 weeks on the job. Before joining Kodak, Steffen had built a solid reputation as a cost-cutter and generator of profits at several companies such as Chrysler (1981–1989) and Honeywell (1989–1993). However, despite his keen intellect and financial skills, Steffen's management style was regarded as confrontational; moreover, he focused too heavily on numbers, according to some critics. It appeared that Steffen needed better skills in dealing with people.

With Steffen's hiring, Reed apparently felt that the revamping he undertook in 1991 and 1992 was crucial for implementing his desire to reengineer Citi's credit and data processes—that is, to emphasize not individual tasks but rather the delivery of the service (i.e., credit). Reed was favorably impressed after a tour of several companies—Ford Motor, Cummins Engine, and General Electric—studying their reengineering successes dealing with the work process. He reasoned that Citicorp could cut about $1 billion in costs via reengineering .

Reed felt that Steffen would be just the person to carry out the difficult but necessary cost-cutting and productivity programs. As Senior Executive Vice President, Steffen was one of Citicorp's top six officers with responsibilities covering auditing, financial controls, and productivity programs. Yet, the abrasive Steffen might be hampered by the culture of Citicorp, which had traditionally been a decentralized bank acting like a global confederation of fiefdoms. Each major division had its own legal, financial control and human-resources staff with over 100 communications networks, some of which could not converse with others.

TABLE 1-2 Offices and Staff in Domestic and Overseas Locations, Years Ended December 31, 1993, and December 31, 1992

OFFICES	1993	1992	VAR.
U.S.	1,389	1,528	33.0%
Overseas	1,947	1,979	−8.7%
Total	3,336	3,507	6.9%
STAFF			
U.S.	38,500	41,000	−18.0%
Overseas	43,000	40,000	2.6%
Total	81,500	81,000	−8.9%

Source: *Annual Report,* 1993.

Citi rebounded in 1993 with earnings of $2.2 billion and reserves standing at $4.4 billion. These reserves cover 30 percent of non-lesser developed countries' nonperforming assets. However, this level of reserves is still low by industry standards. Citi must continue improving its reserves.

Fortune in 1994 rated Citi's management very poorly. What recommendations could you offer to CEO Reed to improve Citi's effectiveness and efficiency? Citi declared no dividends in 1993 despite having a successful year. Would you recommend that Citi pay dividends for 1994? Remember that 1994 interest rates are rising slowly.

Citi does not have a mission statement, but does have a vision statement as given below. What advice would you offer CEO Reed regarding Citi's vision statement and lack of a mission statement?

Citi currently operates in 90 foreign countries. How can the firm best capitalize on being the most globally oriented commercial bank in the United States? Should other foreign countries be added to Citi's portfolio? Citi's revenue growth in developing countries in Asia and Latin America is averaging 15 percent annually compared to 1 percent growth in revenues from operations in the rest of the world. Should Citi acquire competing commercial banks to strengthen its presence in the developed world?

Prepare a three-year strategic plan for Citi. Include specific recommendations and associated costs as well as projected financial statements to show the expected impact of your suggestions.

CITICORP'S VISION

To be a global bank, unique in worldwide presence . . . dedicated to our customers . . . financially strong . . . consistent . . . committed to our staff and its development . . . delivering sustained superior performance to investors.

UNIQUE, GLOBAL
Unique in being global, operating both locally and collectively around the world in delivering financial services for the benefit of both individual and corporate customers; unique also in spirit.

CUSTOMER DEDICATION
Dedicated to serving the financial needs of our customers. Our success depends upon our importance to them. Customer needs define position, product and service offerings. We seek to build sustained relationships and recognize the importance of continuity of people. We are committed to competitive excellence, delivering customer satisfaction, and investing in the business, people and technology required to meet our customer needs.

FINANCIALLY STRONG
Our balance sheet and earnings will be a source of strength; recognized internally, by customers, investors, competitors, rating agencies, and regulators. Control, executional excellence and productivity improvements are acknowledged objectives.

CONSISTENT
Consistent and dependable: in our commitment to our people, with our customers, in the development and execution of our strategy, and in our risk profile.

STAFF AND ITS DEVELOPMENT
We seek to recruit, develop and retain the most talented people from around the world. We will reward people based on merit, teamwork, results, and shared values. We are accountable: We will take responsibility for our actions and the exercise of judgment. We treat people with trust, openness and respect, and maintain the highest ethical standards in dealing with customers, the community and each other.

DELIVERING SUSTAINED SUPERIOR PERFORMANCE TO OUR INVESTORS
Our objective is to achieve superior return on shareholders' equity. We seek the reality and reputation of being well-managed, being consistently sound in our risk-taking judgments, and being seen as one of the most respected financial institutions in the world; a unique global bank.

1. Welsh, Trish, "Best and Worst Corporate Reputations,"
Fortune, February 7, 1994, p. 8

EXHIBIT 1-10 Citicorp in Brief as of Years Ended December 31 (*In millions of dollars except per share amounts*)

	1993	1992	1991	1990	1989
Net income (loss)					
Before accounting changes	$ 1,919	$ 722	$ (914)	$ 318	$ 498
After accounting changes[1]	$ 2,219	$ 722	$ (457)	$ 458	$ 498
Net income (loss) per share[2]					
On common and common equivalent shares					
Before accounting changes	$ 3.82	$ 1.35	$ (3.22)	$ 0.57	$ 1.16
After accounting changes[1]	$ 4.50	$ 1.35	$ (1.89)	$ 0.99	$ 1.16
Assuming full dilution					
Before accounting changes	$ 3.53	$ 1.35	$ (3.22)	$ 0.57	$ 1.16
After accounting changes[1]	$ 4.11	$ 1.35	$ (1.89)	$ 0.99	$ 1.16
Return on assets and equity					
Return on total assets[3]					
Before accounting changes	.84%	.32%	(.41)%	.14%	.23%
After accounting changes[1]	.97%	.32%	(.21)%	.20%	.23%
Return on common stockholders' equity[4]					
Before accounting changes	17.7%	6.5%	(14.3)%	2.1%	4.3%
After accounting changes[1]	21.1%	6.5%	(7.9)%	3.7%	4.3%
Return on total stockholders' equity[5]					
Before accounting changes	15.3%	7.2%	(9.4)%	3.1%	4.7%
After accounting changes[1]	17.7%	7.2%	(4.5)%	4.4%	4.7%
Capital					
Tier 1 capital	$13,388	$10,262	$ 8,540	$ 7,999	$ 7,974
Tier 1 + tier 2 capital	$23,152	$20,111	$17,080	$15,998	$15,948
Tier 1 capital ratio	6.62%	4.90%	3.73%	3.26%	3.22%
Tier 1 + tier 2 capital ratio	11.45%	9.60%	7.46%	6.52%	6.44%
Common stockholders' equity as a percentage of total assets	4.65%	3.73%	3.39%	3.77%	3.57%
Total stockholders' equity as a percentage of total assets	6.44%	5.23%	4.37%	4.48%	4.37%
Common stockholders' equity per share	$ 26.04	$ 21.74	$ 21.23	$ 24.34	$ 25.36

(1) Refers to adoption of Statement of Financial Accounting Standards No. 109, "Accounting for Income Taxes," as of January 1, 1993; accounting change for venture capital subsidiaries in 1991; and accounting change for certain derivative products in 1990.

(2) Based on net income (loss) less preferred stock dividends, except where conversion is assumed.

(3) Net income (loss) as a percentage of average total assets.

(4) Earnings (loss) applicable to common stock as a percentage of average common stockholders' equity.

(5) Net income (loss) less redeemable preferred dividends as a percentage of average total stockholders' equity.

Source: *Annual Report,* 1993.

EXHIBIT 1-11 Citicorp Consolidated Statement of Operations as of Years Ended December 31 (*In millions of dollars except per share amounts*)

	CITICORP AND SUBSIDIARIES		
	1993	1992[1]	1991[1]
Interest revenue			
Interest and fees on loans	$16,408	$18,476	$20,440
Interest on deposits with banks	1,106	1,029	886
Interest on federal funds sold and securities purchased under resale agreements	2,952	1,393	637
Interest and dividends on investment securities	950	875	1,081
Interest on trading account assets	2,485	2,010	1,310
	$23,811	$23,783	$24,354
Interest expense			
Interest on deposits	$ 9,797	$10,458	$11,116
Interest on securities sold, not yet purchased	195	175	315
Interest on other borrowed money	4,155	3,414	3,438
Interest on long-term debt and subordinated capital notes	1,974	2,280	2,220
	$16,121	$16,327	$17,089
Net interest revenue	$ 7,690	$ 7,456	$ 7,265
Provision for credit losses	$ 2,600	$ 4,146	$ 3,890
Net interest revenue after provision for credit losses	$ 5,090	$ 3,310	$ 3,375
Fees, commissions, and other revenue			
Fees and commissions	$ 5,057	$ 5,084	$ 4,815
Trading account	939	326	457
Foreign exchange	995	1,005	709
Investment securities transactions	94	12	330
Other revenue	1,300	1,738	1,174
	$ 8,385	$ 8,165	$ 7,485
Other operating expense			
Salaries	$ 3,817	$ 3,683	$ 3,873
Employee benefits	1,028	965	938
Total employee expense	$ 4,845	$ 4,648	$ 4,811
Net premises and equipment expense	1,601	1,680	1,807
Restructuring charges	425	227	750
Other expense	3,744	3,502	3,729
	$10,615	$10,057	$11,097
Income (loss) before taxes and cumulative effects of accounting changes	$ 2,860	$ 1,418	$ (237)
Income taxes	941	696	677
Income (loss) before cumulative effects of accounting changes	$ 1,919	$ 722	$ (914)
Cumulative effects of accounting changes:			
Accounting for income taxes	300	–	–
Venture capital[2]	–	–	457
Net income (loss)	$ 2,219	$ 722	$ (457)

EXHIBIT 1-11 *Continued*

	1993	CITICORP AND SUBSIDIARIES 1992[1]	1991[1]
Income (loss) applicable to common stock	$ 1,900	$ 497	$ (649)
Earnings (loss) per share on common and common equivalent shares			
Income (loss) before cumulative effects of accounting changes	$ 3.82	$ 1.35	$ (3.22)
Cumulative effects of accounting changes:			
Accounting for income taxes	0.68	–	–
Venture capital[2]	–	–	1.33
Net income (loss)	$ 4.50	$ 1.35	$ (1.89)
Assuming full dilution			
Income (loss) before cumulative effects of accounting changes	$ 3.53	$ 1.35	$ (3.22)
Cumulative effects of accounting changes:			
Accounting for income taxes	0.58	–	–
Venture Capital[2]	–	–	1.33
Net income (loss)	$ 4.11	$ 1.35	$ (1.89)

(1) Reclassified to conform to current year's presentation.

(2) In addition to the cumulative effect adjustment, the venture capital accounting change had the effect of reducing the 1991 net loss by $125 million ($0.37 per share).

Source: *Annual Report,* 1993.

EXHIBIT 1-12 Citicorp Consolidated Balance Sheet As of Years Ended December 31

	CITICORP AND SUBSIDARIES	
	1993	1992
Assets		
Cash and due from banks	$ 4,836	$ 5,138
Deposits at interest with banks	6,749	6,550
Investment securities		
At cost (market value $5,666 in 1993 and $6,504 in 1992)	5,637	6,515
At lower of aggregate cost or market value		
(market value $9,088 in 1993 and $7,574 in 1992)	8,705	7,213
At fair value	1,489	1,328
Trading account assets	18,117	17,085
Federal funds sold and securities purchased		
under resale agreements	7,339	6,381
Loans, net		
Consumer	$ 84,354	$ 83,453
Commercial	54,613	56,257
Loans, net of unearned income	$138,967	$139,710
Allowance for credit losses	(4,379)	(3,859)
Total loans, net	$134,588	$135,851
Customers' acceptance liability	1,512	1,802
Premises and equipment, net	3,842	3,819
Interest and fees receivable	2,552	2,721
Other assets	21,208	19,298
Total	$216,574	$213,701
Liabilities		
Non-interest-bearing deposits in U.S. offices	$ 13,442	$ 13,572
Interest-bearing deposits in U.S. offices	38,347	44,175
Non-interest-bearing deposits in offices outside the U.S.	6,644	5,243
Interest-bearing deposits in offices outside the U.S.	86,656	81,185
Total deposits	$145,089	$144,175
Securities sold, not yet purchased	2,352	1,894
Purchased funds and other borrowings	16,777	18,120
Acceptances outstanding	1,531	1,866
Accrued taxes and other expenses	6,452	5,049
Other liabilities	12,260	11,244
Long-term debt (note 1)	15,983	16,886
Subordinated capital notes	2,150	3,250
Redeemable preferred stock	27	36
Stockholders' equity		
Preferred stock	$ 3,887	$ 3,212
Common stock ($1.00 par value)	412	392
Issued shares: 412,017,300 in 1993 and 391,888,124 in 1992		

EXHIBIT 1-12 *Continued*

	1993	CITICORP AND SUBSIDIARIES 1992
Surplus	3,898	3,598
Retained earnings	6,149	4,368
Common stock in treasury, at cost	(393)	(389)
Shares: 25,527,133 in 1993 and 25,399,438 in 1992		
Total stockholders' equity	$ 13,953	$ 11,181
Total	$216,574	$213,701

Source: *Annual Report*, 1993.

EXHIBIT 1-13 Citicorp Consolidated Statement of Cash Flows as of Years Ended December 31 (*In millions of dollars*)

	1993	CITICORP AND SUBSIDIARIES 1992	1991
Cash flows from operating activities			
Net income (loss)	$ 2,219	$ 722	$ (457)
Adjustments to reconcile net income (loss) to net cash provided by (used in) operating activities:			
Provision for credit losses	$ 2,600	$ 4,146	$ 3,890
Depreciation and amortization of premises and equipment	568	587	652
Amortization of goodwill	55	60	72
Restructuring charges	425	227	750
Business write-downs	179	–	–
Provision for deferred taxes	(612)	4	249
Cumulative effects of accounting changes	(300)	–	(457)
Venture capital activity	(161)	249	(144)
Net (gain) on sale of investment securities	(94)	(12)	(330)
Net (gain) on the sale of subsidiaries and affiliates	(77)	(417)	(168)
Changes in accruals and other, net	(1,244)	(1,648)	(1,810)
Net (increase) in trading account assets	(1,032)	(5,021)	(4,546)
Net increase (decrease) in securities sold, not yet purchased	458	162	(962)
Total adjustments	$ 765	$ (1,663)	$ (2,804)
NET CASH PROVIDED BY (USED IN) OPERATING ACTIVITIES	$ 2,984	$ (941)	$ (3,261)

EXHIBIT 1-13 *Continued*

	1993	CITICORP AND SUBSIDIARIES 1992	1991
Cash flows from investing activities			
Net (increase) decrease in deposits at interest with banks	$ (199)	$ 137	$ 854
Purchases of investment securities	(31,017)	(27,734)	(38,447)
Proceeds from sale of investment securities	7,886	5,100	8,144
Maturities of investment securities	21,599	21,604	28,882
Net (increase) in federal funds sold and securities purchased under resale agreements	(958)	(1,831)	(479)
Net (increase) in loans	(86,698)	(78,426)	(94,904)
Proceeds from sales of loans and credit card receivables	82,961	82,746	92,519
Capital expenditures on premises and equipment	(829)	(1,252)	(929)
Proceeds from sales of premises and equipment	175	342	394
Proceeds from sales of subsidiaries and affiliates	230	1,453	926
Proceeds from sales of other real estate owned (OREO)	1,740	1,052	617
NET CASH PROVIDED BY (USED IN) INVESTING ACTIVITIES	$ (5,110)	$ 3,191	$ (2,423)
Cash flows from financing activities			
Net increase (decrease) in deposits	$ 2,816	$ (2,200)	$ 4,023
Net increase (decrease) in federal funds purchased and securities sold under repurchase agreements	(1,336)	2,633	136
Proceeds from issuance of commercial paper and funds borrowed with original maturities of less than one year	335,235	360,550	424,475
Repayment of commercial paper and funds borrowed with original maturities of less than one year	(333,417)	(361,403)	(424,626)
Proceeds from issuance of long-term debt	4,682	3,460	4,783
Repayment of long-term debt and retirement of redeemable preferred stock	(6,444)	(6,365)	(4,703)
Proceeds from issuance of preferred stock	654	1,275	1,222
Redemption and repurchase of preferred stock	–	–	(650)
Proceeds from issuance of common stock	302	119	81
Dividends paid	(313)	(216)	(435)
NET CASH PROVIDED BY (USED IN) FINANCING ACTIVITIES	$ 2,179	$ (2,147)	$ 4,306
Effect of exchange rate changes on cash and due from banks	$ (355)	$ (293)	$ (392)
Net (decrease) in cash and due from banks	$ (302)	$ (190)	$ (1,770)
Cash and due from banks at beginning of year	5,138	5,328	7,098
CASH AND DUE FROM BANKS AT END OF YEAR	$ 4,836	$ 5,138	$ 5,328
Supplemental disclosure of cash flow information			
Cash paid during the year for:			
Interest	$ 14,481	$ 14,493	$ 15,379
Income taxes	$ 1,197	$ 473	$ 484
Non-cash investing activities			
Transfers from loans to OREO	$ 1,644	$ 3,761	$ 2,039

Source: *Annual Report*, 1993.

EXHIBIT 1-14 Citicorp Geographic Distribution of Revenue, Earnings (Loss), and Assets as of Years Ended December 31 *(In millions of dollars)*

	Total Revenue[1]			Income (Loss) Before Taxes and Cumulative Effects of Accounting Changes			Net Income (Loss)			Average Total Assets		
	1993	1992	1991	1993	1992	1991	1993	1992	1991	1993	1992	1991
North America[2]	$ 8,198	$ 8,309	$ 8,736	$ 247[3]	$(1,008)[3]	$(1,250)[3]	$ 556	$(379)	$(885)	$117,075	$124,795	$131,416
Caribbean, Central and South America	1,913	2,080	1,335	819	1,346	555	519	924	317	22,238	19,005	15,988
Europe, Middle East, and Africa	3,628	3,287	2,993	1,100	475	218	677	218	132	47,820	45,653	41,462
Asia/Pacific	2,336	1,945	1,686	694	605	240	467	319	(21)	41,107	36,348	33,031
Total	$16,075	$15,621	$14,750	$2,860	$ 1,418	$ (237)	$2,219[4]	$ 722	$(457)[5]	$228,240	$225,801	$221,897

(1) Includes net interest revenue and fees, commissions, and other revenue.

(2) Includes amounts attributed to United States operations (in 1993, 1992, and 1991 respectively) as follows: total revenue, $8,100 million, $8,180 million, and $8,552 million; income (loss) before taxes and cumulative effects of accounting changes, $405 million, $(722) million, and $(1,285) million; net income (loss), $659 million, $(544) million, and $(894) million; and average total assets, $111,117 million, $120,237 million, and $125,970 million.

(3) Includes approximately $22 million in 1993, $35 million in 1992, and $71 million in 1991 of tax-exempt income, reducing the federal income tax provision attributed to the United States.

(4) The 1993 results include the $300 million cumulative effect of adopting Statement of Financial Accounting Standards No. 109, "Accounting for Income Taxes."

(5) The 1991 results include the $457 million cumulative effect of the accounting change for venture capital, all of which is attributed to U.S. operations.

Source: *Annual Report*, 1993.

EXHIBIT 1-15   Citicorp Loans Outstanding as of Years Ended December 31 (In millions of dollars at year end)

CONSUMER LOANS OUTSTANDING	1993	1992
In U.S. offices		
Mortgage and real estate[1][2][3]	$22,719	$26,140
Installment, revolving credit and other		
consumer loans	22,490	21509
Lease financing	152	353
	$45,361	$48,002
In offices outside the U.S.		
Mortgage and real estate[1][4]	$13,908	$12,863
Installment, revolving credit and other		
consumer loans	25,355	23,011
Lease financing	672	746
	$39,935	$36,620
	$85,296	$84,622
Unearned income	(942)	(1,169)
Consumer loans—net	$84,354	$83,453

COMMERCIAL LOANS OUTSTANDING	1993	1992
In U.S. Offices		
Commercial and industrial[5]	$ 8,969	$10,168
Mortgage and real estate[6]	7,440	9,194
Loans to financial institutions	269	271
Lease financing	3,541	3,547
	$20,219	$23,180
In offices outside the U.S.		
Commercial and industrial[5]	$23,624	$21,332
Mortgage and real estate[6]	2,201	2,657
Loans to financial institutions	3,123	3,300
Governments and official institutions	4,807	5,055
Lease financing	800	927
	$34,555	$33,271
	$54,774	$56,451
Unearned income	(161)	(194)
Commercial loans—net	$54,613	$56,257

(1) Loans secured primarily by real estate.
(2) Includes $4.2 billion and $4.3 billion of commercial real estate loans related to community banking and private banking activities at December 31, 1993 and 1992, respectively.
(3) Includes $6.3 billion and $6.6 billion of residential mortgage loans held for sale and carried at the lower of aggregate cost or market value at December 31, 1993 and 1992, respectively.
(4) Includes approximately $1.4 billion and $1.0 billion of loans secured by commercial real estate at December 31, 1993 and 1992, respectively.
(5) Includes loans not otherwise separately categorized.
(6) Loans secured primarily by real estate.
   Source: *Annual Report*, 1993.

BANC ONE CORPORATION—1993

Headquartered in Columbus, Ohio, Banc One (614-248-5944) is a bank-holding corporation for 61 affiliate banks. The corporation uses the spelling "Banc" because Ohio and several other states forbid using the word "bank" in a bank-holding company's name. Banc One operates affiliate banks in Colorado, Illinois, Kentucky, Michigan, Texas, and Wisconsin. It also operates several additional corporations that engage in data processing, venture capital, merchant banking, trust, brokerage, equipment leasing, mortgage banking, and insurance.

Banc One ranks eighth among the top 100 U.S. banks in asset size (see Exhibit 2–1). Banc One's return on assets of 1.31 percent and its return on equity of 16.3 percent are outstanding. *Euromoney* magazine recently ranked Banc One as number six among the world's 100 best banks. There was only one other U.S. bank in the top ten—J. P. Morgan, which ranked number one.

As shown in Exhibits 2–2 and 2–3 Banc One made numerous acquisitions in 1992, expanding from its home base in Ohio into Illinois, Indiana, Michigan, Wisconsin, West Virginia, Kentucky, Texas, Arizona, Colorado, Utah. As of March 31, 1993, Banc One's assets exceeded $70 billion, with 1,277 offices in 12 states. Banc One recently entered California with its $1.2 billion acquisition of Arizona's Valley National and moved into Nebraska by acquiring FirsTier Financial, the second largest Nebraska bank, with assets of $3 billion. Banc One recently expanded into Oklahoma by acquiring the seventh-largest bank there, Central Banking Group. Overall, Banc One acquired seven bank

EXHIBIT 2-1 Top Ten U.S. Banks by Asset Size as of December 31, 1992 (in millions of dollars except ROA, ROE, and NPA)

RANK	ASSETS	ROA (%)[a]	ROE (%)[b]	NPA (%)[c]	MARKET VALUE[d]
1 Citicorp	213,701	.23	6.6	4.9	10,811
2 BankAmerica	189,646	.80	12.7	3.4	17,517
3 Chemical Bank	139,655	.67	12.4	4.4	10,140
4 Nations Bank	118,059	.97	15.8	1.7	13,820
5 J. P. Morgan	102,941	1.14	20.8[e]	0.5	13,006
6 Chase Manhattan	102,941	.51	11.2	5.3	5,444
7 Bankers Trust NY	72,448	.99	23.1	2.5	5,925
8 Banc One	61,417	1.31	16.3	1.0	13,403
9 Wells Fargo	52,537	.45	7.9	5.1	5,995
10 PNC Bank	51,380	1.18	15.5	1.6	7,762

[a]Return on Asset
[b]Return on Equity
[c]Nonperforming Asset
[d]As of March 31, 1993. Market Value is the closing common stock price multiplied by the number of outstanding common shares.
[e]Year-end amounts
Source: "Bank Scoreboard," *Business Week*, May 3, 1993, p. 150.

companies with $13.3 billion in assets and two thrifts with $700 million in assets during 1992.

Bank One celebrated its 25th anniversary in 1993 as a multibank-holding company. The corporation's net income increased from $493 million in 1990 to over $781 million in 1992, while earnings per share climbed from $2.33 to $3.28. Banc One's foreign loans of $237 million were less than .7 percent of total loans, with the United Kingdom accounting for $105 million or 44 percent of total foreign loans; Mexico had $15 million outstanding in 1992 compared to $16 million in 1991. Banc One provides technological assistance in retail banking and card processing through a joint agreement with Banco Nacional de Mexico, whose headquarters are in Mexico City.

MANAGEMENT CONTROL

Chairman John B. McCoy is the third member of the McCoy family to lead Banc One. John H. McCoy, his grandfather, served as president and guided the corporation during its early years. John G. McCoy, his father, joined the bank in 1937 and did much to build Banc One, then called City National Bank. After John H.'s death in 1958, John G. became president and CEO; upon John G.'s retirement in 1984, John B. became president and eventually chairman in 1987.

John B. had been a major driving force for Banc One's growth through implementation of the corporate culture known as the "uncommon partnership." Each affiliate bank is viewed as a partner within the corporate structure and has responsibilities to formulate its own business plan, control all personnel and lending functions, and determine all product pricing and marketing, based on local market conditions. In essence, this uncommon partnership allows local banks to set prices and decide on their own which of Banc One's family of 120 financial products to use. Banks also

EXHIBIT 2-2 Bank Affiliations Completed and Savings and Loan Assets Purchased as of December 31, 1992 (in billions of dollars)

Bank Affiliations Completed in 1992	City, State	Assets ($ billions)	Offices
TB Marine Corporation	Springfield, IL	$1.2	19
First Illinois Corporation	Evanston, IL	1.7	19
First Security Corporation	Lexington, KY	1.6	13
Bedford National Bank	Bedford, IN	.2	2
Jefferson Bancorp, Inc.	Peoria, IL	.3	5
Team Bancshares, Inc.	Dallas, TX	5.5	56
Affiliated Bankshares of Colorado, Inc.	Denver, CO	2.8	43

Savings and Loan Assets Purchased		Deposits ($ billions)	
Diamond Savings and Loan Company	Findlay, OH	$ .6	18
Savings of America	Cincinnati, OH	.1	4

Source: *Annual Report*, 1992.

develop their own marketing programs, make their own hires, and set their own salaries.

McCoy views himself as people-oriented and interested in watching them grow. However, when queried about his thoughts regarding people who made mistakes, the outspoken McCoy bluntly responded: "You learn from mistakes, not from successes, so hold up your hand and tell us. . . . But if you have a problem, and don't tell, and it's a disaster, it's your ass. . . ."

Career opportunities at Banc One abound as individuals move from the presidency of smaller affiliates up to a larger affiliate. The depth and quality of management experience CEOs exceeds 18 years. Banc One fills almost all CEO positions internally. The structure and culture of the corporation motivate both managers and employees. The fact that "80 percent of the officers and over two-thirds of all employees own stock in the company" further motivates employees and, to a large extent, reinforces the business culture. McCoy's reported annual compensation in 1992 totalled over $2.8 million—salary $907,000; bonus $980,000; other sources such as insurance and club memberships, $93,000; value of long-term incentives and stock grants, $825,000. McCoy ranked 77 of the 200 top-paid U.S. executives in 1992. Banc One's organizational chart is given in Figure 2–1.

A key to Banc One's ability to control and evaluate its decentralized operation is through a Management Information and Control System (MICS). Whenever an affiliate is brought into Banc One's structure, MICS is installed to gather and evaluate data and report the data in the same manner to each entity. Individual and comparative financial results are provided. To insure that information is timely, monthly updates and forecasts are prepared by local staff. In essence, affiliates share and compare data. The ultimate objective is "to be able to measure every aspect of our business across the company in exactly the same way for comparison purposes."

With many firms attempting to cut costs by outsourcing some of their operational activities, McCoy continues to improve and develop new technologies

EXHIBIT 2-3 Banc One Market Share[a] as of December 31, 1992 (in billions of dollars)

	ASSETS	STATE RANK
Arizona	9.8	2 nd
Colorado	2.8	3 rd
Illinois	3.9	8 th
Indiana	7.5	2 nd
Kentucky	1.7	4 th
Michigan	.6	11 th
Ohio	19.3	2 nd
Texas	18.8	3 rd
Utah	.9	4 th
West Virginia	3.0	1 st
Wisconsin	6.7	3 rd

[a]Assumes "all remaining announced affiliations are completed." (*Annual Report*, 1992, p. 5.)

Source: *Annual Report*, 1992.

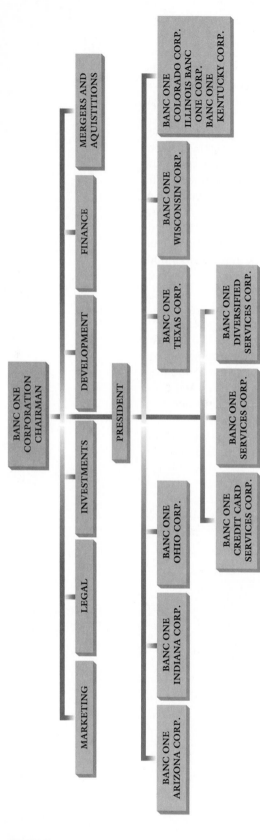

FIGURE 2-1 Banc One Corporation

within the Banc One system. For example, through a six-year alliance with Electronic Data Systems (EDS) in Dallas, Banc One began to install parts of its Strategic Banking System (SBS) in its affiliates. SBS is a state-of-the-art, total-bank-operating system keyed to the customer, thus providing to each affiliate bank a total financial picture of customer relationships. SBS integrates Banc One's product profitability and household demographic systems and gives Banc One personnel (e.g., customer service representatives, loan officers, and new account managers) immediate access to relevant information for additional sales. McCoy recently described an example of building a loyal customer base: "If Mrs. Smith walks into a branch to make a checking deposit, a message will come up on the screen that prompts our service rep to offer her a credit card with a $5,000 limit. Since she's a longtime customer, a message will appear with an offer to waive the service fee for three years." Development costs for SBS have exceeded $100 million, but EDS has incurred the greatest part of the cost and risk in developing SBS. EDS, however, retains the right to sell the system to other banks when completed.

Another joint venture was recently established with Andersen Consulting to set up a new credit and debit card-processing system called TRIUMPH. Rights to the system remain with Banc One. Banc One is the third-largest credit-card processor in the United States, providing services to some 3,000 "commercial bank, savings and loan, credit union and broker clients with 14 million cardholder accounts."

In another arrangement with three other regional banks, a new company called Electronic Payment Services (EPS) has been established "to provide automated teller machine and electronic point-of-sale systems and processing. . . ." About 13,000 ATMs could be linked to process annually 650 million point-of-sale transactions. Perhaps most telling is Banc One's commitment over the past 25 years to allocate annually 3 percent of its profits to technology research and development. Banc One is known as the technology bank. As a Kidder Peabody vice president commented, "I've never heard a bank say they were determined to spend a certain amount of their income stream on R&D and have it turn out to such advantage."

McCoy works at keeping things simple and predictable. Among his rules are to keep management in place when a bank is taken over, because those managers know the market better than anyone else; consolidate back-office functions; and never buy a bank more than one-third the size of the corporation. "That way if the deal turns out to be a bust, it won't drag down the entire bank." Banc One's mission statement and precepts are given in Figure 2–2.

RISK MANAGEMENT

Although credit decisions are made on a local basis, Banc One insures necessary remedial action for all present and potential problem loans, which are quickly identified through monthly analyses of delinquencies and nonperforming assets. Analyses have been carried out by such in-house groups as affiliate bank management, state holding company loan-review personnel, and corporate credit officers. Additionally, continuing efforts are maintained to refine credit policies dealing with appraisals, borrower's financial condition, lending outside of well-defined geographical areas, and loan concentrations to any single industry or borrower. The firm maintains that only five borrowing relationships exceed $100 million and there are only twenty other relationships which exceed $50 million. Of these only seven had more than $50 million outstanding at year end with the largest being $83 million.

FIGURE 2-2

BANC ONE CORPORATION
MISSION STATEMENT

WE BELIEVE

Enterprise and the opportunities created by individual choice are cornerstones of our "Uncommon Partnership." They produce the greatest value for the customer and the greatest stimulant to business. Those core values provide the best plan for delivering true satisfaction for every customer and the most desirable return for investors.

PRECEPTS

Based on this belief, the Board of Directors of BANC ONE CORPORATION adopted these precepts as the official guideline for the commitment and performance of our people.

One   We believe in creating an atmosphere in which our people working together:
- care about what they do
- utilize their own abilities to make the right decisions
- focus on customers and uncover innovative ways to service their changing financial needs
- promptly respond to problems and customer concerns in a professional sensitive manner.

Two   We believe in conducting our business:
- with uncompromising honesty, fairness and integrity
- to achieve superior financial performance for our shareholders
- to identify, develop, retain, and provide equal opportunity for all people who demonstrate the willingness and ability to perform and grow
- with an unflinching focus on providing a quality of services that ensures customer satisfaction.

Three We believe management should base decisions on:
- maintaining a balance between the needs of our customers, employees and shareholders
- the need to support the social, cultural, and economical programs which enhance the quality of life in our communities
- providing creative leadership to the direction and success of the financial industry
- expanding the geographic influence and customer service opportunities of the organization as enterprise and prudence permits.

We believe commitment to performance and a focus on the quality of customer service are essential to success. We believe in the everlasting process of building a great bank.

In 1992 Banc One instituted "a corporate credit development group and charged it with development of a systemwide credit training program." Thus, formal credit training for all lending employees in addition to a continuing education program for commercial credit employees was set up.

Banc One has well-defined programs to resolve and dispose of foreclosed properties through management centralization of problem assets. For example, commercial loans are placed in a nonaccrual basis after 90 days past due or if collection of the debt is doubtful. For loans put on a nonaccrual basis, all previously accrued and unpaid interest is charged against income. If recovery appears certain, interest received is included in income for future periods. Residential real estate loans are put in a nonaccrual status when 120 days past due or if deemed uncollectible. In the case of installment loans, accrued interest and the remaining principal balance are charged off at the earlier of when the loan was 120 days past due or if collection was uncertain. Average balance on installment loans is over $8,700. Credit card loans are written off when 180 days past due or collection is questionable. There are approximately 8.3 million credit card accounts, with an average balance of $581.

Banc One's expansion into 14 states with different economic, political, and regional conditions carries increased risk. Major financial institutions already exist in those states. Asked whether he felt the "empire building" should continue, McCoy responded, "If there isn't change, then I'm not going to be here, because it wouldn't be fun anymore."

Banc One's plans for 1993 include purchase of Valley National Corporation of Arizona for $11.4 billion and Key Centurion Bancshares of West Virginia for $1.6 billion. The company has an eye on Liberty National BanCorp of Kentucky for $4.7 billion and FirsTier Financial Corporation of Nebraska for $3.0 billion. Banc One strives to be the first, second, or third largest bank in each state it operates. This policy suggests further acquisitions are needed in Illinois, Utah, and Michigan, where Banc One's market share is only 2%, 6%, and 1%, respectively. Banc One also has a policy never to acquire a bank more than one-third its own combined size.

Despite the large amount of consolidation that has already taken place among financial institutions, the U.S. banking landscape remains fragmented. As of June 30, 1993, there were still 11,198 insured commercial banks and 1,825 insured thrift institutions in the country, with total domestic office deposits of $2.94 trillion. Banc One's total deposits of $59.0 billion at June 30 represented just 2.0% of total U.S. domestic deposits—and this is a banking organization that ranks fourth in the country in market share. Consolidation of the U.S. banking industry will continue and Banc One should be able to find ongoing opportunities to expand its presence.

Prepare a three-year strategic plan for Banc One. Include specific recommendations regarding whether Banc One should enter the securities business which it has avoided to date. Also, do you feel Banc One's mission statement and organizational chart are adequate? Include an acquisition plan in your recommendations for CEO McCoy.

EXHIBIT 2-4 Members of Banc One Corporation

BANC ONE OHIO CORPORATION

Ohio

Akron
Athens
Cambridge
Cincinnati
Cleveland
Columbus
Coshocton
Dayton
Dover
Fremont
Lima
Mansfield
Marietta
Marion
Portsmouth
Sidney
Steubenville
Youngstown
Bank One Ohio
  Trust Company,
  NA

Michigan

East Lansing
Fenton
Sturgis
Ypsilanti

BANC ONE DIVERSIFIED SERVICES CORPORATION

Banc One Financial Services, Inc.
Banc One Insurance Group
Banc One Investment Advisors Corporation
Banc One Leasing Corporation
Banc One Mortgage Corporation
Banc One Securities Corporation

NON-BANK AFFILIATES

Banc One Capital Corporation
Banc One Credit Card Services Company
Banc One Management and Consulting
  Corporation
Banc One Services Corporation

BANC ONE ARIZONA CORPORATION

Serving markets in:
Arizona

Utah

BANC ONE INDIANA CORPORATION

Indiana

Bloomington
Crawfordsville
Indianapolis
Lafayette
Marion
Merrillville
Rensselaer
Richmond

BANC ONE REGIONAL AFFILIATE GROUP

Colorado

BANC ONE COLORADO CORPORATION

Boulder
Colorado Springs
Denver
Greeley
Fort Collins/
  Loveland
Western Colorado

Illinois

BANC ONE ILLINOIS CORPORATION

Bloomington-
  Normal
Champaign-Urbana
Chicago
Elgin
Evanston
La Grange
Peoria
Springfield
Wilmette

Kentucky

Lexington

BANC ONE WISCONSIN CORPORATION

Wisconsin

Antigo
Appleton
Beaver Dam
Elkhorn
Fond du Lac
Green Bay
Janesville
Madison
Milwaukee
Monroe
Oshkosh
Racine
Stevens Point
West Bend
Bank One
  Wisconsin Trust
  Company, NA

BANK ONE, TEXAS, NA AND TEAM BANCSHARES, INC.

Serving markets in:
Texas

Abilene
Amarillo
Arlington
Austin
Beaumont/Orang/
  Port Arthur
Brenham
Corsicana
Dallas
Denison
Denton
Fort Worth
Fredericksburg
Greenville
Houston
Levelland
Longview
Marshall
Midland
Odessa
San Antonio
Sherman
Temple
Tyler
Waco
Wichita Falls

PENDING AFFILIATES

Key Centurion Bancshares, Inc., Charleston, West Virginia
First Community Bancorp, Inc., Rockford, Illinois
United National Bank, Denton, Texas
Parkdale Bank, Beaumont, Texas
First Financial Associates, Inc., Kenosha, Wisconsin
Colorado Western Bancorp, Inc., Montrose, Colorado

(Certain pending affiliates are subject to shareholder and regulatory approval.)

Source: Provided by Banc One Corporation (April, 1993).

EXHIBIT 2-5 Banc One Consolidated Balance Sheet as of Years Ended December 31
(in thousands of dollars except share data)

$ (THOUSANDS, EXCEPT SHARE DATA)	DECEMBER 31, 1993	1992
Assets:		
Cash and due from banks	$ 4,757,475	$ 5,186,870
Short-term investments (including Eurodollar placements and foreign negotiable certificates of deposit of $4,492 and $299,578 at December 31, 1993 and 1992)	931,959	2,267,310
Securities:		
Securities held for investment (market value approximates $16,903,201 and $16,575,168 at December 31, 1993 and 1992)	16,591,970	16,349,280
Securities held for sale (market value approximates $860,897 and $1,722,954 at December 31, 1993 and 1992)	815,941	1,658,735
Total securities	17,407,911	18,008,015
Loans and leases (net of unearned income of $676,980 and $655,983 at December 31, 1993 and 1992)	53,845,620	47,809,448
Reserve for loan and lease losses	918,153	909,896
Net loans and leases	52,927,467	46,899,552
Collection pools	22,302	420,220
Other assets:		
Bank premises and equipment, net	1,387,218	1,313,044
Interest earned not collected	624,185	598,119
Other real estate owned	193,158	288,252
Excess of cost over net assets of affiliates purchased	227,312	265,003
Other	1,439,574	1,492,734
Total other assets	3,871,447	3,957,152
Total assets	$79,918,561	$76,739,119
Liabilities:		
Deposits:		
Non-interest bearing	$13,674,976	$13,158,961
Interest bearing	47,268,205	48,595,644
Total deposits	60,943,181	61,754,605
Federal funds purchased and repurchase agreements	6,744,437	4,631,394
Other short-term borrowings	2,020,176	1,383,927
Long-term borrowings	1,701,662	1,357,462
Accrued interest payable	222,946	258,671
Other liabilities	1,252,521	1,111,474
Total liabilities	72,884,923	70,497,533

EXHIBIT 2-5 *Continued*

	DECEMBER 31,	
$ (THOUSANDS, EXCEPT SHARE DATA)	1993	1992
Commitments and contingencies (Notes 14 and 17)		
Stockholders' equity:		
Preferred stock, 35,000,000 shares authorized:		
Class B convertible, no par value, 373,076 shares issued and outstanding, at December 31, 1992		9,700
Series C convertible, no par value, 4,998,000 and 5,000,000 shares issued and outstanding, at December 31, 1993 and 1992	249,900	250,000
Common stockholders' equity:		
Common stock, no par value, $5 stated value, 600,000,000 shares authorized, 380,687,187 and 272,246,801 shares issued and outstanding, at December 31, 1993 and 1992, respectively (December 31, 1993 shares reflect the 10% stock dividend effective February 10, 1994 and the five-shares-for-four-shares stock split effective August 31, 1993)	1,903,436	1,361,234
Capital in excess of aggregate stated value of common stock	3,833,611	3,009,221
Retained earnings	1,046,691	1,611,431
Total stockholders' equity	7,033,638	6,241,586
Total liabilities and stockholders' equity	$79,918,561	$76,739,119

Source: *Annual Report,* 1993.

EXHIBIT 2-6 Banc One Consolidated Statement of Income as of Years Ended December 31 (in thousands of dollars)

$ (THOUSANDS, EXCEPT PER SHARE AMOUNTS)	1993	1992	1991
Interest income:			
Interest and fees on loans and leases	$4,759,498	$4,638,246	$4,197,706
Interest and dividends on:			
Taxable securities	812,899	994,065	874,578
Tax exempt securities	118,426	132,178	162,546
Other interest income, (including interest on Eurodollar placements and foreign negotiable certificates of deposi of $2,415, $17,161, and $22,316 in 1993, 1992, and 1991)	37,255	116,470	184,105
Interest on Collection pools	7,053	36,965	52,295
Interest on Note receivable from FDIC			18,808
Total interest income	5,735,131	5,917,924	5,490,038
Interest expense:			
Interest on deposits:			
Demand and savings deposits	599,432	737,056	884,035
Time deposits	763,713	1,121,195	1,484,089
Other borrowings	281,903	261,853	354,326
Total interest expense	1,645,048	2,120,104	2,722,450
Net interest income	4,090,083	3,797,820	2,767,588
Provision for loan and lease losses	368,507	604,131	586,239
Net interest income after provision for loan and lease losses	3,721,576	3,193,689	2,181,349
Other income:			
Income from fiduciary activities	211,796	205,120	184,506
Service charges on deposit accounts	432,296	413,494	308,937
Loan processing and service income	451,786	434,417	380,945
Securities gains	16,016	24,677	53,121
Income from management of Collection pools, net	22,777	28,226	59,301
Equity in earnings of Bank One, Texas, NA, net of income tax			57,012
Other	356,988	334,535	294,467
Total other income	1,491,659	1,440,469	1,338,289
Other expenses:			
Salaries and related costs	1,618,342	1,511,310	1,209,872
Net occupancy expense, exclusive of depreciation	151,521	174,605	124,953
Equipment expense	106,754	97,103	87,149
Taxes other than income and payroll	76,514	70,290	60,054
Depreciation and amortization	262,759	216,331	149,486
Outside services and processing	489,646	469,366	287,265
Marketing and development	148,401	119,810	94,570
Communication and transportation	224,921	196,044	160,312
Other	435,258	498,077	466,202
Total other expenses	3,514,116	3,352,936	2,639,863

EXHIBIT 2-6 *Continued*

$ (THOUSANDS, EXCEPT PER SHARE AMOUNTS)	1993	1992	1991
Income before income taxes and change in accounting principle	1,699,119	1,281,222	879,775
Income tax provision:			
Income excluding securities transactions	(572,924)	(396,244)	(197,426)
Securities transactions	(5,606)	(8,390)	(18,061)
Provision for income taxes	(578,530)	(404,634)	(215,487)
Income before cumulative effect of change in accounting principle	1,120,589	876,588	664,288
Cumulative effect of change in method of accounting for income taxes	19,391		
Net income	$1,139,980	$ 876,588	$ 664,288
Net income per common share (amounts reflect the 10% common stock dividend effective February 10, 1994 and the five-shares-for-four-shares stock split effective August 31, 1993)			
Income before cumulative effect of change in accounting principle	$ 2.93	$ 2.29	$ 1.82
Cumulative effect of change in method of accounting for income taxes	.05		
Net income per common share	$ 2.98	$ 2.29	$ 1.82
Weighted average common shares outstanding (000)	376,828	373,699	356,102

Source: *Annual Report*, 1993.

EXHIBIT 2-7 Banc One Consolidated Statements of Cash Flows as of Years Ended December 31 (in thousands of dollars)

$ (THOUSANDS)	1993	1992	1991
Cash provided by (used in) operating activities:			
Net income	$ 1,139,980	$ 876,588	$ 664,288
Adjustments:			
Provision for loan and lease losses	368,507	604,131	586,239
Depreciation and amortization	331,969	272,338	153,532
Net (increase) decrease in trading account portfolio	(14,754)	52,411	(182,222)
Net increase in warehoused mortgage loans	(428,617)	(406,340)	(221,337)
Net change in deferred loan fees and costs	(8,835)	(3,075)	6,581
Gain on sale of other assets	(21,197)	(28,845)	(79,895)
Gain on sale of loans	(1,960)	(14,536)	(25,768)
Gain on sale of investment securities	(16,016)	(24,677)	(53,121)
Net decrease in other assets	243,551	114,159	193,847
Net (decrease) increase in other liabilities	(131,480)	(13,947)	21,697
Net change in deferred income taxes	42,849	(40,366)	(11,097)
Cumulative effect of change in accounting principle	(19,391)		
Equity in earnings of Bank One, Texas, NA			(57,012)
Net cash provided by operating activities	1,484,606	1,387,841	995,732
Cash provided by (used in) investing activities:			
Purchase of securities held for sale	(350,000)		
Purchases of investment securities	(6,010,067)	(10,682,930)	(7,022,627)
Maturities of securities held for sale	476,242		
Maturities of investment securities	6,068,254	6,929,321	3,572,611
Proceeds from the sale of securities held for sale	716,764		
Proceeds from the sales of investment securities	83,525	1,369,257	3,092,568
Net increase in loans, excluding sales and purchases	(4,745,355)	(2,784,492)	(2,847,880)
Proceeds from the sales of loans	76,721	694,499	643,902
Purchases of loans and related premiums	(768,264)	(747,056)	(369,410)
Net decrease in short-term investments	1,410,165	2,430,144	336,252
Additions to bank premises and equipment	(274,836)	(268,364)	(214,452)
Disposals of bank premises and equipment	38,643	38,529	40,450
Payments received on Collection pools	398,742	885,186	718,838
Net decrease in note receivable from FDIC			321,502
Cash acquired less purchase price of final 61% interest in Bank One, Texas, NA			544,740
Net cash acquired in other acquisitions	36,148	247,327	307,082
Net decrease (increase) in mortgage servicing rights	12,283	(53,819)	(2,672)
All other investing activities, net		(8,347)	(3,520)
Net cash used in investing activities	(2,831,035)	(1,950,745)	(882,616)

EXHIBIT 2-7 *Continued*

$ (THOUSANDS)	1993	1992	1991
Cash provided by (used in) financing activities:			
Net increase in demand deposit, money market and savings accounts	588,636	4,614,205	3,099,252
Net decrease in certificates of deposits	(2,317,125)	(4,949,369)	(2,092,622)
Net increase (decrease) in short-term borrowings	2,715,250	991,844	(379,426)
Proceeds from the issuance of long-term borrowings	395,887	493,912	34,578
Repayment of long-term borrowings	(51,687)	(80,266)	(99,952)
Proceeds from issuance of stock			563,740
Cash dividends paid	(379,418)	(202,155)	(234,230)
All other financing activities, net	(34,509)	36,000	23,255
Net cash provided by financing activities	917,034	904,171	914,595
Increase (decrease) in cash and cash equivalents	(429,395)	341,267	1,027,711
Cash and cash equivalents at January 1,	5,186,870	4,845,603	3,817,892
Cash and cash equivalents at December 31,	$4,757,475	$5,186,870	$4,845,603

Source: *Annual Report,* 1993.

EXHIBIT 2-8 Banc One Loan and Lease Analysis as of Years Ended December 31 (in thousands of dollars)

	1992	1991	1990	1989	1988
Ending loan and lease balances:					
Commercial, financial, and agricultural	$12,724,081	$12,466,118	$10,136,768	$ 9,362,356	$ 9,241,961
Real estate	11,844,359	10,895,716	7,447,742	5,998,965	5,148,821
Installment, net	8,530,834	7,720,043	5,557,322	4,700,312	4,483,519
Credit card	4,813,183	4,372,938	2,386,267	1,690,260	1,878,830
Leases, net	809,976	809,872	793,167	745,229	698,191
Total loans and leases	$38,722,433	$36,264,687	$26,321,266	$22,497,122	$21,451,322
Nonperforming assets and delinquencies:					
Non-accrual loans	$ 380,474	$ 485,054	$ 440,245	$ 289,115	$ 294,776
Renegotiated loans	26,179	19,931	22,303	47,025	46,024
Other real estate owned	222,711	265,695	155,341	112,137	87,472
Total nonperforming assets	$ 629,364	$ 770,680	$ 617,889	$ 448,277	$ 428,272
Loans delinquent 90 days or more (not included in non-accrual)	$ 179,661	$ 234,594	$ 142,043	$ 92,973	$ 88,406
Loans classified as doubtful[a]	45,128	124,575	75,204	74,634	87,938
Interest foregone on nonperforming loans (after tax)[b]	$ 25,316	$ 26,913	$ 27,180	$ 20,092	$ 16,727
Reserve and loss ratios:					
Ending reserve to ending balances:					
Commercial, financial, and agricultural	1.74%	1.56%	1.45%	1.41%	1.20%
Real estate	.73	1.12	.87	.75	.80
Installment, net	1.44	1.46	1.29	1.31	1.24
Credit card	3.17	3.50	3.14	3.67	3.63
Leases, net	1.69	.98	.83	1.11	1.24
Total loans and leases	1.88	1.87	1.65	1.56	1.54
Net charge-offs to average balances:					
Commercial, financial, and agricultural	.70	1.13	1.18	.87	.74
Real estate	.38	.52	.24	.35	.66
Installment, net	1.48	1.57	1.33	1.25	1.05
Credit card	4.82	4.94	4.49	3.92	4.35
Leases, net	1.00	1.23	1.13	1.64	1.83
Total loans and leases	1.25	1.43	1.20	1.08	1.14
Recoveries to gross charge-offs	22.38	19.38	22.19	24.42	22.52
To ending loans and leases:					
Nonperforming assets	1.63	2.13	2.35	1.99	2.00
Loans delinquent 90 days or more	.46%	.65%	.54%	.41%	.41%

[a]Defined as loans with a high loss possibility after collateral liquidation based on existing facts, market conditions, and value. These loans are provided for in the reserve for loan losses, as appropriate. Any interest income recognized on these loans is immaterial.

[b]The amount of gross interest on nonperforming loans that would have been recorded during 1992 and 1991 if the loans had been current throughout the year totaled $58 million and $62 million, respectively. Of this amount, $19 million and $22 million of interest was actually recorded on nonperforming loans during 1992 and 1991, respectively. Texas is included in these amounts for the whole year of 1991 even though it was consolidated beginning October 1, 1991.

*unaudited

Source: *Annual Report*, 1992.

EXHIBIT 2-9 Banc One Loan and Lease Reserves[a] as of Year Ended December 31 (in thousands of dollars)

	COMMERCIAL, FINANCIAL AND AGRICULTURAL	REAL ESTATE	INSTALLMENT	CREDIT CARD	LEASES	UNALLOCATED	TOTAL RESERVES
Balance, December 31, 1987	$123,098	$20,162	$49,516	$62,081	$12,166	$19,500	$286,523
Reserves of entities acquired and sold, net	24,816	17,599	2,821	(543)	(48)	3,885	48,530
Provision, 1988	28,162	36,117	46,644	87,617	7,725	22,691	228,956
Gross losses	(88,217)	(34,267)	(68,628)	(96,602)	(13,818)		(301,532)
Recoveries	22,738	1,583	25,238	15,724	2,623		67,906
Net losses	(65,479)	(32,684)	(43,390)	(80,878)	(11,195)		(233,626)
Balance, December 31, 1988	110,597	41,194	55,591	68,277	8,648	46,076	330,383
Reserves of entities acquired and sold, net	6,207	10,003	1,251	8	4	266	17,739
Provision, 1989	95,614	13,516	62,464	62,645	11,196	(3,238)	242,197
Gross losses	(102,212)	(22,822)	(86,635)	(88,589)	(15,267)		(315,525)
Recoveries	22,032	2,906	28,820	19,627	3,654		77,039
Net losses	(80,180)	(19,916)	(57,815)	(68,962)	(11,613)		(238,486)
Balance, December 31, 1989	132,238	44,797	61,491	61,968	8,235	43,104	351,833
Allowance applicable to loans transferred to the Collection pool	(820)	(1,845)	(77)				(2,742)
Reserves of entities acquired and sold, net	5,556	8,476	4,843	13,926		2,897	35,698
Provision, 1990	128,341	30,195	77,434	86,085	6,683	22,047	350,785
Gross losses	(145,391)	(19,288)	(102,838)	(108,275)	(12,663)		(388,455)
Recoveries	27,451	2,625	30,608	21,220	4,291		86,195
Net losses	(117,940)	(16,663)	(72,230)	(87,055)	(8,372)		(302,260)
Balance, December 31, 1990	147,375	64,960	71,461	74,924	6,546	68,048	433,314
Allowance applicable to loans transferred to the Collection pool	(1,168)	(681)	(32)				(1,881)
Reserves of entities acquired and sold, net	51,873	36,178	30,327	32,411	900	11,231	162,920
Provision, 1991	116,433	66,894	107,632	193,992	10,212	7,566	502,729

EXHIBIT 2-9 *Continued*

	COMMERCIAL, FINANCIAL AND AGRICULTURAL	REAL ESTATE	INSTALLMENT	CREDIT CARD	LEASES	UNALLOCATED	TOTAL RESERVES
Gross losses	(146,070)	(49,977)	(138,468)	(171,818)	(14,721)		(521,054)
Recoveries	25,463	4,823	41,992	23,663	5,016		100,957
Net losses	(120,607)	(45,154)	(96,476)	(148,155)	(9,705)		(420,097)
Balance, December 31, 1991	193,906	122,197	112,912	153,172	7,953	86,845	676,985
Allowance applicable to loans transferred from the Collection pool	652	36	1				689
Reserves of entities acquired and sold, net	2,020	1,843	885	75			4,823
Provision, 1992	113,238	4,187	128,779	205,984	13,982	44,309	510,479
Gross losses	(129,428)	(50,697)	(172,906)	(233,108)	(14,189)		(600,328)
Recoveries	40,401	8,417	52,992	26,589	5,947		134,346
Net losses	(89,027)	(42,280)	(119,914)	(206,519)	(8,242)		(465,982)
Balance, December 31, 1992	$220,789	$85,983	$122,663	$152,712	$13,693	$131,154	$726,994

aunaudited

Source: *Annual Report,* 1992.

EXHIBIT 2-10 Banc One Consolidated Statement of Changes in Stockholders' Equity as of Year Ended December 31 (in thousands of dollars)

$ (THOUSANDS, EXCEPT PER SHARE AMOUNTS)	PREFERRED STOCK	COMMON STOCK		CAPITAL IN EXCESS OF AGGREGATE STATED VALUE OF COMMON STOCK	RETAINED EARNINGS	TOTAL STOCKHOLDERS' EQUITY
		SHARES	STATED VALUE			
Balance, December 31, 1990	$ 23,156	238,701,770	$1,193,508	$1,854,143	$1,443,846	$4,514,653
Net income					664,288	664,288
Cash dividends:						
Corporation:						
Common ($.76 per share)(1)					(186,968)	(186,968)
Class B Preferred ($3.00 per share)					(2,421)	(2,421)
Series C Preferred ($2.54 per share)					(12,639)	(12,639)
Pooled affiliates					(43,434)	(43,434)
Shares issued in acquisitions		1,019,632	5,098	20,702		25,800
Preferred stock offering, net of issuance costs	250,000			(5,350)		244,650
Common stock offering, net of issuance costs		7,625,000	38,125	280,965		319,090
Conversion of preferred into common	(3,742)	351,749	1,759	1,983		
Exercise of stock options, net of shares purchased		(57)	(1)	(2,792)		(2,793)
Pooled affiliate stock issuance and other		1,455,658	7,280	19,726	12,138	39,144
10% common stock dividend at fair market value		17,330,839	86,654	773,389	(860,043)	
Balance, December 31, 1991	269,414	266,484,591	1,332,423	2,942,766	1,014,767	5,559,370
Net income					876,588	876,588
Cash dividends:						
Corporation:						
Common ($.89 per share)a					(257,101)	(257,101)
Class B Preferred ($3.00 per share)					(1,486)	(1,486)
Series C Preferred ($3.50 per share)					(17,500)	(17,500)
Pooled affiliates					(25,748)	(25,748)
Shares issued in acquisitions		1,254,000	6,270	6,371	20,049	32,690
Conversion of preferred into common	(9,714)	995,789	4,979	4,735		
Exercise of stock options, net of shares purchased		569,311	2,847	(22,486)		(19,639)
Pooled affiliate stock issuance and other		2,943,110	14,715	77,835	1,862	94,412
Balance, December 31, 1992	259,700	272,246,801	1,361,234	3,009,221	1,611,431	6,241,586

EXHIBIT 2-10 *Continued*

$ (THOUSANDS, EXCEPT PER SHARE AMOUNTS)	PREFERRED STOCK	COMMON STOCK		CAPITAL IN EXCESS OF AGGREGATE STATED VALUE OF COMMON STOCK	RETAINED EARNINGS	TOTAL STOCKHOLDERS' EQUITY
		SHARES	STATED VALUE			
Net income					1,139,980	1,139,980
Cash dividends:						
Corporation:						
Common ($1.07 per share)[1]					(388,245)	(388,245)
Class B Preferred ($.75 per share)					(216)	(216)
Series C Preferred ($3.50 per share)					(17,498)	(17,498)
Pooled affiliates					(4,987)	(4,987)
Shares issued in acquisitions		4,907,702	24,539	12,269	59,409	96,217
Conversion of preferred into common	(9,800)	1,005,825	5,029	4,771		
Exercise of stock options, net of shares purchased		(575,147)	(2,876)	(44,758)		(47,634)
Pooled affiliate stock issuance and other		304,452	1,521	12,062	852	14,435
Common stock split five-for-four, effective August 31, 1993		68,189,628	340,949	(340,949)		
10% common stock dividend at fair market value		34,607,926	173,040	1,180,995	(1,354,035)	
Balance, December 31, 1993	**$249,900**	**380,687,187**	**$1,903,436**	**$3,833,611**	**$1,046,691**	**$7,033,638**

[a]Amounts reflect the effect of the 10% common stock dividends effective February 14, 1992 and February 10, 1994, and the five-shares-for-four-shares stock split effective August 31, 1993.

Source: *Annual Report*, 1993.

RETAILING INDUSTRY NOTE

JAMES WALSH
U.S. Department of Commerce

The retail trade sector (SIC 52 59) is one of the major sources of jobs in the U.S. economy, consistently accounting for about 21 percent of all nonfarm jobs in the private sector. Retail establishments are primarily engaged in selling merchandise for personal or household consumption.

Retail merchandise lines are divided into the following categories: building materials, hardware, garden supplies, and mobile home dealers (SIC 52); general merchandise stores (SIC 53); food stores (SIC 54); automobile dealers and gasoline service stations (SIC 55); apparel and accessory stores (SIC 56); home furniture, furnishings, and equipment stores (SIC 57); eating and drinking places (SIC 58); and miscellaneous retail stores (SIC 59).

In general, sales of retail establishments in SIC groups 52, 55, 57, and 59 are mostly from durable goods and sales of retail establishments in SIC groups 53, 54, 56, and 58 are mostly from nondurable goods.

Year-to-year changes in sales of retail stores concentrating on nondurable merchandise lines, such as food and clothing, tend to mirror changes in general business conditions as indicated by the gross domestic product (GDP), which is forecast to grow about 3 percent in 1994. In contrast, year-to-year changes in sales of retail stores concentrating in durable goods, such as furniture and major household appli-

Trends and Forecasts: Retail Sales (SIC 52–59) (in billions of dollars except as noted)

ITEM	1991	1992	1993[1]	1994[2]	PERCENT CHANGE (1991–1994) 91–92	92–93	93–94
All stores	1,866	1,962	2,086	2,232	5.1	6.3	7.0
Total nondurables	1,212	1,257	1,329	1,411	3.7	5.7	6.2
General merchandise	228	247	280	320	8.3	13.4	14.3
Apparel	97	105	108	112	8.2	2.9	3.7
Restaurants	197	202	207	216	2.5	2.5	4.4
Drugs	76	77	78	80	1.3	1.3	2.6
Food	377	384	387	399	1.9	0.8	3.1
Other	237	242	269	284	2.1	11.2	5.6
Total durables	654	705	757	821	7.8	7.4	8.5
Employment (millions)	19.3	19.1	19.3	NA	–1.0	1.1	NA
Average hourly earnings ($)	6.95	7.14	7.26	NA	2.7	1.7	NA

[1]Estimate.

[2]Forecast.

Source: U.S. Department of Commerce: Bureau of the Census, International Trade Administration (ITA); U.S. Department of Labor, Bureau of Labor Statistics. Estimates and forecasts by ITA.

ances, tend to exaggerate changes in business conditions by increasing more than the GDP during good years and declining more than the GDP during slowdowns. In addition to overall business conditions, retail sales reflect changes in prices, merchandise mix, and shifts to alternative channels of distribution.

This industry note focuses on the trends that influence the current and near-term demand for nondurable retail merchandise.

Industry Sales. In 1993 total retail sales reached nearly $2.1 trillion, a gain of more than 6 percent in current dollars. A major portion of the increase was due to price hikes. It is difficult to measure the precise increase in "real dollars" because of the incompatibility of retail sales data and the Consumer Price Index, which measures inflation.

Stores selling mostly nondurables accounted for nearly 64 percent of total retail sales, with 1993 revenues topping $1.3 trillion, up 5.7 percent over 1992. Sales of durable goods totaled $757 billion in current dollars, up more than 7 percent from 1992, and accounted for 36 percent of the total.

However, these year-to-year gains should be taken as only a rough approximation of the direction of change for the sales value of all consumer durables or nondurables because of the way Census Bureau data is reported. For example, Kmart reported furniture sales totaling $364 million in 1991. The Census Bureau reported all of these sales as retail sales of nondurables because Kmart's principal merchandise lines are nondurable.

Retail stores selling primarily nondurable goods, for which Census Bureau data are available, include general merchandise stores, department stores, food stores, variety stores, apparel stores, restaurants, and drug stores. Other retailers for which Census data are not available include discount stores, warehouse clubs, convenience stores, and catalog and video sales firms.

A list of the top 100 retailing firms compiled by *Chain Store Age Executive* magazine combined the sales data for the top 100 retailing firms in 1992, including data for types of retailers not collected by Census. The results indicated that discount stores accounted for 21 percent of all sales by the top retail stores selling nondurable goods, second only to supermarkets, which represented 35 percent of total sales. Warehouse clubs, a relatively recent entrant into the retail market, accounted for 6 percent of nondurable sales in 1992. (See Table 1.)

According to the *Chain Store Age Executive,* discount stores and warehouse clubs achieved their current market position mainly by underpricing department stores, variety stores, and drug stores. Supermarkets also increased their market share at the expense of drug stores, and specialty apparel stores captured markets formerly claimed by department stores. A new category of retailer—"G" stores, operated by the major gasoline companies—encroached on the market share of traditional convenience stores.

New Strategies for the 1990s. In response to increased competition from new market participants, retailers are exercising a full array of strategies, including downsizing and restructuring, changing their merchandise mix, adding services, and adapting the "quick response system" for controlling inventory management costs. Over the past decade, these strategies, singly or in combination, helped retailers faced with declining market shares and falling profit margins to prevent further erosion of their market positions and improve their overall revenues.

But these competitive strategies may not be enough for the 1990s. David Glass, president and chief executive officer of Wal-Mart, told the 1993 National Retail

TABLE 1 1992 Retail Sales of Nondurable Products (by type of store, ranked by total sales*)

ITEM	MARKET SHARE (IN PERCENT)
Supermarkets	35.0
Discount stores	21.0
Department stores	13.0
General merchandise	8.0
Specialty apparel	7.0
Warehouse clubs	6.0
Drug stores	5.0
Convenience stores	3.0
Variety stores	2.0
Total	100.0

*Based on total sales of the top 100 retailers of nondurable merchandise in 1992. Excludes revenues of catalogs and video sales channels, estimated at $2 billion.

Source: *Chain Store Age Executive,* April 1993.

Federation convention that "all concepts of doing business are changing." He pointed out that the customer of the 1990s is looking for genuine value, coupled with superior and different customer services. Others have made similar observations. P. R. Trimmer, in his book *50 Powerful Ideas You Can Use to Keep Your Customer,* called customer service "the competitive battleground for the 1990's."

The retail customer of the 1990s is significantly different from the retail customer of a decade ago, and retail strategies need to be reassessed in view of the changing demographics and new buying patterns.

The most significant demographic change is in the declining importance of households composed of married couples, dropping from 60.8 percent in 1980 to 55.3 percent in 1991. At the same time, the number of people living alone increased, influencing the consumer buying habits and forcing retailers to respond with appropriate packaging and marketing, as evidenced by the increase in "single serving" products.

Some retailers depend on groups other than households for their target markets. For instance, men between the ages of 18 and 34 are the mainstay customers of convenience stores. But the number of men in this age group is expected to decline during the 1990s, portending a difficult period for convenience stores.

Another demographic change is the projected surge in the number of teenagers and young adults in the next five years. This group will be more inclined to embrace electronic shopping channels and interactive television, sometimes referred to as "storeless" shopping.

Changing buying patterns projected for the 1990s reflect new priorities for households composed of married couples and a different life-style for single-person households.

Many married couples consisting of maturing baby boomers have changed their priorities to emphasize more leisure time. Increasingly they have rejected the day-long shopping trips of the past in favor of quick "buy and go" patterns. These changing attitudes toward shopping appear to have had an effect on the retailing scene. Sales at super regional malls—those with at least three anchor stores—dropped 7.3 percent between 1990 and 1992, after increasing 18 percent during the previous three years. During the same period, retail sales at smaller community shopping centers increased 15 percent and sales at neighborhood strip centers increased nearly 7 percent.

Consequently, superstores are being downsized to attract the 1990s consumer. In the 1980s the superstores had 220,000–260,000 square feet. In the 1990s the superstores will cover 116,000–188,000 square feet.

Retailers also have altered strategies to appeal to the increased number of people living alone. This group follows a different life-style from that of the traditional retail customer. According to Barbara Caplan, Vice President of Yankelovich, Clancy Shulman, people living alone "no longer feel that they have to do what society says, but feel that they have permission to do as they please." This group of customers tends to shun traditional buying patterns and look for unusual items and wider assortments of merchandise.

As Michael Wellman, Vice President for Marketing at Kmart, told retailers at the 1993 National Demographic and Lifestyle annual conference, "The successful retailer of the 1990's must change his operation to meet the needs of the 1990's customer." These changes will include new marketing vehicles such as "electronic retailing."

Electronic retailing, as defined by Carl Steidtmann, Director of Management Horizons, a division of Price Waterhouse, includes interactive communications via faxes, electronic data interchanges, and other interactive media. Here are some examples of electronic retailing already in place:

- An upstate New York supermarket allows its customers to electronically check out and pay for their purchases without the aid of a check-out person.
- A discount store in Maryland allows its customers to fax their orders to the store for immediate assembly and delivery to the ordering customer.
- Several "G" stores are experimenting with interactive electronic menus at the gasoline pump that list the merchandise carried in the store. The customer electronically indicates the merchandise to be purchased, pays for the gasoline and other merchandise at the pump with a credit card, and picks up the bagged selections at the store's drive-in window.

Competitive Measures. Shifts in market position during the last five years prompted retailers to adopt competitive countermeasures, including downsizing and consolidation, merchandise mix changes, more consumer services, and greater use of advanced technologies, such as quick-response systems, to control inventory costs and increase productivity.

A quick-response system usually involves a strategic alliance between a retailer and manufacturer, coupled with an Electronic Data Interchange (EDI) system, which includes sharing sales, marketing, and inventory data with vendors; bar coding on packaging to track sales and inventory; and point-of-sale scanners to track sales and implement an automated stock replenishment system. It is also essential that an EDI system be able to issue invoices and payments electronically and track consumer buyer patterns.

The most frequently cited benefits of a quick response system include increased inventory turnover and reduced inventory levels, operating costs, and frequency of out-of-stock items. A recent Garr Consulting Group survey of a cross section of retailers conducted for *Chain Store Age Executive* magazine found that 61 percent of those surveyed had entered into strategic alliances with vendors to take advantage of the benefits of a quick-response system.

The various competitive strategies undertaken by major types of retailers during the last few years are reviewed in the next section.

Department Stores. Department store sales increased from nearly $153 billion in 1988 to $183 billion in 1993, a five-year increase of nearly 20 percent, according to Census Bureau data. Despite the growth in sales volume, department stores lost market share to discount stores, warehouse clubs, and specialty apparel shops, dropping from nearly 15 percent of the market for nondurable retailers in 1988 to slightly less than 14 percent in 1993.

To adjust to the competitive pressures from other types of retailers, several department stores, including R. H. Macy and Federated Stores, filed Chapter 11 bankruptcy actions while they downsized and restructured their operations. Other department stores have changed their merchandise mix to deemphasize their durable lines and highlight their fashion apparel, gifts, and designer household items.

The Garr Consulting Group survey showed 78 percent of the department store managers interviewed reported they had entered into strategic alliances with their vendors to implement the quick-response system. In terms of sales, the top five department stores are Mays, J. C. Penny, Federated, R. H. Macy, and Dillard.

Supermarkets. Food retailers increased their sales but accounted for a smaller share of nondurable goods purchased during the 1988–1993 period. Sales rose from $326 billion in 1988 to $387 billion in 1992, a gain of nearly 19 percent, according to the Census Bureau. In terms of market share, food stores claimed more than 29 percent of the total market for nondurable retailers in 1993, down from the nearly 32 percent claimed in 1988. Supermarkets have consistently accounted for about 80 percent of all food store sales.

During the last several years, supermarkets lost sales to drugstores, discount stores, and warehouse clubs. To meet these competitive challenges, supermarkets changed their merchandise mix by dropping duplicated product lines and allocating more shelf space to fast-moving nonfood items and promotional items. Some supermarkets also have revised their marketing strategy, shifting some of their advertising dollars from weekly newspaper inserts to direct mail circulars.

According to the Garr Consulting Group survey, 46 percent of the supermarket managers surveyed said that they have entered into strategic alliances with their vendors to implement the quick-response system. In addition, a few supermarkets have expanded their consumer services, such as accepting telephone orders of groceries for home delivery.

The top five supermarkets are Kroger, American Stores, Safeway, A&P, and Winn-Dixie.

Warehouse Clubs. The number of warehouse clubs increased from 15 in 1983 to 577 in 1992, experiencing double-digit growth in sales and earnings until the early 1990s. Since then, warehouse club sales and earnings have declined.

Part of this deterioration in sales and earnings is due to competitive challenges from other types of retailers such as supermarkets. In response, warehouse clubs are downsizing and restructuring, changing their mix of merchandise, adding more services, and opening new markets. Kmart's recent sale of Pace Club to Sam's Club and Costco's merger with Price Club are examples of the new competitive strategies. Price Club and Sam's Club also entered new markets by forming joint ventures with retailers in Mexico.

The top warehouse clubs include Price Club, Sam's Club, and Waban.

Discount Stores. Sales of the big ten discount stores grew at a robust average annual rate of 11.5 percent from 1987 to 1991, according to *Chain Store Age*

Executive magazine. But discount stores' sales have begun to slow, increasing only 10.3 percent from 1990 to 1991—the latest period for which revenue figures are available. A closer look at the individual sales changes from 1990 to 1991, compared to the full 1987–1991 period, reveals a significant slowdown in the revenue of several discounters, including Hills, Ames, and Rose's. As a result, discount stores have implemented strategies to maintain their market standing, including downsizing and restructuring, changing their merchandise mix, adding services, and intensifying the use of their quick-response systems.

The Garr Consulting Group report revealed that 50 percent of the discount store managers responding to the survey said they have entered into strategic alliances with their vendors to implement their quick-response systems.

Discount stores also are changing their merchandise mix by adding groceries to their product lines. Others are adding more services, such as beauty shops and in-store opticians. A few discount stores also are expanding into new markets by forming joint ventures with retailers in Mexico.

The major discount stores include Wal-Mart, Kmart, Stop-N-Shop, Pacific Enterprises, and Ames.

Apparel Stores. Apparel and accessory stores posted sales of $108 billion in 1993, up 27 percent from the $85 billion recorded for 1988. In terms of market position, apparel and accessory stores have maintained a fairly stable 8 percent of total sales of all retailers of nondurable merchandise. Apparel and accessory stores have been effective in maintaining their market position by emphasizing fashion and value, thereby capturing consumer clothing sales previously claimed by department stores.

According to the Garr Consulting Group survey, 59 percent of the apparel store managers surveyed reported that they have entered into strategic alliances with their vendors to implement quick-response systems.

The top retail firms selling mostly apparel and accessories are Melville, The Limited, TJX Co., U.S. Shoe, and Gap.

Catalog and Video Retailers. The top six catalog retailers show an average annual increase in sales of 13.8 percent during the period 1987–1991 compared to the 5.7 percent increase registered from 1990 to 1991, the latest year for which revenue figures are available. *Chain Store Age Executive* magazine attributed the 1990–1991 slowdown to the recession, rather than competitive pressures from other direct sales channels.

Catalog retailers are maintaining their competitive edge in part by expanding into foreign markets. For example, L. L. Bean has formed four joint ventures in Japan; Lands' End is developing the British market and plans to test the market in France; and J. Crew recently hired a vice president for international development to guide their expansion into foreign markets.

Video retailers were given a boost recently by the merger of QVC and Home Shopping Network. These two video retailers claim to cover about 99 percent of the total $2.2 billion market for video sales. Some industry analysts view current video retailers as rivals for the catalog retail customer, but about half of all video retail sales —$1.1 billion—are from repeat customers. The greater competitive threat for both catalog and video retailers appears to be from general merchandise stores, such as Dillard, that are planning their own shopping channels with interactive electronic arrangements that would allow the at-home customer to make direct purchases.

The top catalog retailers are Fingerhut, Spiegel, Lands' End, and L. L. Bean. The top video retailers are QVC, Home Shopping Network, and the Fashion Channel.

Until recently, few retailers attempted to expand into foreign markets. But the easing of investment restrictions in some foreign countries, and the emerging trend of establishing affiliated firms abroad, has launched a new era in retailing.

The precise volume of exports and imports attributable to retailers is not known because merchandise trade flows are identified by type of product (e.g., manufactured, agricultural, metals, and minerals, etc.) rather than type of organization. The only export data identified by type of organization are listed in the *U.S. Direct Investment Abroad* (DIA) reports published every five years. The latest, the 1989 benchmark survey, shows the 50 U.S. retailers, with 211 foreign affiliates, exported merchandise valued at $200 million to affiliated firms in foreign markets. They included retailers of general merchandise, food, clothing, autos, garden supplies, hardware, as well as discount stores and catalog retailers. In addition, U.S. retailers reported $500 million in direct sales to foreign customers.

In 1989 major stores with at least one affiliated firm in a foreign market included Sears, J. C. Penney, Woolworth, and Carter-Hawley. The foreign affiliates of these retail parent firms were either wholly owned or majority owned by the U.S. firm. Since then, several other major U.S. retailers have established affiliated firms in foreign countries, including Toys-R-Us, Sam's Club, Kmart, Price Club, Blockbuster, and Dillard.

Most recent investments in foreign affiliates have been in Mexico because of the easing of government restrictions on joint ventures and other business activities that had previously been imposed on foreign investors. Further expansions are expected as a result of the North American Free Trade Agreement.

Foreign governments often impose restrictions on how or where foreign firms may operate or limit foreign investment to certain sectors or organizational arrangements. These constraints discourage U.S. retailers from expanding into new markets through affiliated firms in foreign countries. A major objective of the Uruguay Round of multilateral trade negotiations, as well as separate bilateral consultations, is to reduce or eliminate restrictions on investment. If the negotiations are successful, more U.S. retailers will be encouraged to expand to new foreign markets. For example, bilateral consultations with Japan have resulted in an easing of restrictions on the size of foreign retail stores, prompting Toys-R-Us and Blockbuster Video to establish affiliated firms there.

Additional U.S. investment in retail affiliates abroad may increase the demand for American exports from U.S. parent retail firms to their foreign affiliates.

Outlook for 1994. Total retail sales should reach $2.2 trillion in 1994, up 7 percent from 1993. Total revenue earned by stores concentrating in nondurable product lines will exceed $1.4 trillion, an increase of more than 6 percent over 1993, largely reflecting higher prices. These projected increases reflect the general view of business forecasters that consumer spending in 1994 will provide the underlying strength for the 3 percent growth rate in the GDP forecast for the 1993–1994 period. During 1993 consumer spending, reflecting uneasiness about the future, was projected to remain flat as consumers continued to reduce their debt burden. However, low interest rates and diminished inflationary pressures should encourage business investment and induce consumers to spend more in 1994.

THE LIMITED, INC.—1994

Based in Columbus, Ohio, the Limited (614-479-7000) continues to exploit opportunities for growth. Net sales from 1991 to 1992 increased 13 percent to almost $7 billion. New income increased in 1992 by 12.9 percent to $455 million. An additional 2.5 million square feet of selling space was added during 1992 for a total of 22.9 million square feet of selling space for all Limited stores. Stores now number 4,425. The Limited, Inc., has become the largest women's apparel specialty store and mail-order retailer in the United States.

Leslie Wexner, chairman of The Limited, believes that creativity and innovation are the essential ingredients for his company's success in the highly competitive specialty retailing industry. "I think specialty retailing is as valid, and perhaps more valid, than twenty years ago," Wexner says.

> In a world that's changing faster, the intensity of your efforts and your knowledge is obsolete faster; and it becomes increasingly difficult to be knowledgeable and/or competitive if you have a broad-based business. . . . The fashion business is a business of change, with fashion cycles on a short and long term basis always moving.

For over thirty years, Wexner's Limited stores have achieved success by "breaking the rules" in the specialty retailing industry. Instead of offering a wide variety of types of clothing, the stores offer a limited assortment of women's sportswear in large quantities and a variety of colors. The company emphasizes rapid turnover of inventory so only the newest in fashion is in the stores at all times. The Limited, Inc. has 12 retail store divisions targeted to specific groups of shoppers: The Limited, Express, Henri Bendel, Victoria's Secret Stores, Abercrombie & Fitch, Lerner New York, Lane Bryant, Structure, The Limited Too, Cacique, Bath & Body Works, and Penhaligon's.

The operations of these 12 divisions are independent so that division presidents can make needed changes very quickly. Wexner does not believe that centralized control works in the fashion industry. "Every time somebody says 'economy of scale' somebody else should jump up and say 'what about diminishing returns?'" The decentralization of operations at The Limited provides the company a distinct advantage in the turbulent retail apparel industry. Wexner believes that his company's performance suggests that The Limited has been successful in its attempt to "reinvent the large specialty store."

HISTORY

Leslie Wexner's mother and father both worked in retailing—his father for the Miller Wall specialty chain and his mother as a buyer for Lazarus. When Wexner was fourteen, his parents opened their own specialty apparel store in Columbus, Ohio. After college and one year in law school, Wexner returned to work in his parents' store until he decided what he wanted to do with his life. He planned that his work in retail would be temporary, but he says he "got hooked."

In 1963 Leslie Wexner borrowed $10,000 from an aunt and a bank to open The Limited's first store. During its first year in operation, this store achieved sales of $157,000. His strategy was to provide a "limited" assortment of quality, fashionable sportswear at medium prices. The "limited" concept worked well, and by the late

1970s Wexner began a twofold strategy of market development and product development. New stores were opened and acquired to appeal to women of different ages, different sizes, and different budget limits.

Since 1984 Wexner has tried to acquire department store chains such as Federated Department Stores, R. H. Macy, and Carter Hawley Hale (CHH). Probably the greatest disappointment in Wexner's acquisition attempts was his failed attempt to acquire CHH for $1.1 billion. At the time he submitted the offer, CHH consisted of 124 department stores, 117 specialty stores, and 841 bookstores. Some of the store names associated with CHH at the time included Thalhimers, Neiman-Marcus, Broadway, and Bergdorf Goodman. The Limited acquired about 700,000 shares of CHH stock at the time of its offer. In response to The Limited's takeover attempt, General Cinema acquired $300 million of CHH stock and CHH began buying its own stock. The Securities and Exchange Commission stepped in to stop both The Limited and CHH from unfairly attempting to control the takeover situation. These legal developments stalled Wexner's takeover attempt. After the CHH takeover attempt failed in 1986, Wexner began thinking more about internal growth than about new acquisitions. CHH recently filed for Chapter 11 bankruptcy. Wexner now says about CHH, "we wouldn't take it for free."

Throughout the 1980s Wexner acquired a variety of businesses including Lane Bryant, Victoria's Secret, Sizes Unlimited, Lerner, Henri Bendel, and Abercrombie & Fitch, each of which was in financial trouble when Wexner acquired it. He also started several store divisions during the 1980s, including Express, Structure, Limited Too, and Cacique. During the 1990s the number of acquisitions and business startups has continued to grow, but at a slower pace. The growth of The Limited, Inc. is shown in Exhibit 3–1.

OPERATIONS

Despite the industry slump during the late 1980s, The Limited, Inc., has continued to perform well. During 1992, 231 new stores were opened. Net sales increased 13 percent and net income increased by 13 percent to $455 million in 1992. The largest revenue generator for The Limited during 1992 was Express. Structure doubled its sales in 1991 and almost did it again in 1992 to approximately $348 million. Victoria's Secret Stores and Victoria's Secret Catalogue also had a successful 1992.

Wexner has been disappointed in the performance of two of The Limited's divisions since 1990. A portion of the decrease in profits for these two divisions during 1990 were explained by renovation costs. The Limited Stores were upgraded with high-tech lighting, marble floors, chrome, mirrors, and so forth, and the size of many stores was doubled. In addition, the former division president of The Limited Stores, Verna Gibson, phased out the popular Forenza private label. In its place, Gibson introduced a higher-priced line called Paul et Duffier that did not sell well. Lerner also incurred significant renovation expenses. Although some industry observers believe that Lerner's new richer-looking design, featuring piano players, overstuffed furniture, and large dressing rooms, provides a pleasant shopping environment, it did not help to increase Lerner's sales.

During 1992, The Limited flagship store continued to have merchandising problems. Estimates are that Limited sales for 1992 were $1.3 billion, a decrease of 5 percent from 1991 sales. At the beginning of the 1990s, consumers became more value-conscious and demanded higher-quality clothing than The Limited offered. Howard Gross, president of The Limited, hopes that better-quality merchandise will

EXHIBIT 3-1 Growth of The Limited, Inc.

OPERATING RESULTS (THOUSANDS EXCEPT PER SHARE AMOUNTS)

	1993	1992	% CHANGE
Net Sales	$7,245,088	$6,944,296	4%
Operating Income	$701,556	$788,698	(11%)
Net Income	$390,999	$455,497	(14%)
Net Income as a Percentage of Sales	5.4%	6.6%	
Net income Per Share	$1.08	$1.25	(14%)
Dividends Per Share	$.36	$.28	29%

YEAR-END POSITION (THOUSANDS EXCEPT FINANCIAL RATIOS)

	1993	1992	% CHANGE
Total Assets	$4,135,105	$3,846,450	8%
Working Capital	$1,513,181	$1,063,352	42%
Current Ratio	3.1	2.5	
Long-Term Debt	$650,000	$541,639	20%
Debt-to-Equity Ratio	27%	24%	
Shareholders' Equity	$2,441,293	$2,267,617	8%
Return on Average Shareholders' Equity	17%	22%	

STORES OPEN AT END OF YEAR (RANKED BY SALES)

	1993	1992
Express	673	640
Lerner New York	877	915
The Limited	746	759
Victoria's Secret Stores	570	545
Lane Bryant	817	809
Structure	394	330
The Limited Too	184	185
Bath & Body Works	194	121
Abercrombie & Fitch Co.	49	40
Henri Bendel	4	4
Cacique	108	71
Penhaligon's	7	6
Total Number of Stores	4,623	4,425
Selling Square Feet	24,426,000	22,863,000
Number Of Associates		97,500

Source: The Limited *Annual Report*, 1993.

lure its customers back to Limited stores. Lerner New York's former budget-conscience customers now spend their money at Wal-Mart, Kmart and other discount stores. In response, Lerner New York decided to move upscale and began selling moderately priced clothing. This is a risky strategy because it may take some time for potential customers to understand that Lerner provides a higher-quality product and is no longer a budget-priced store.

Business Structure. The Limited, Inc. is presently organized into 20 major operating divisions that include 12 different store types, two mail-order divisions, and six facilitating-type operations. The 20 divisions are described briefly here.

Limited Stores. This is the flagship division of the organization. Originally, merchandise in these stores was targeted to women between the ages of 16 and 25. Limited Stores has now shifted its orientation to women in the "thirtysomething" age group. These stores focus on the sale of medium-priced fashion clothing and accessories. Fifteen larger-format Limited stores called International Fashion Stores were opened in 1990, and many older stores are presently being renovated to provide additional selling space. Most of the 759 Limited stores are located in regional shopping centers or malls across the United States.

Express. The Express was recently redesigned to have a more sophisticated image instead of the neon-lit, high-tech store of the mid-1980s. Merchandise includes a unique assortment of popular-priced sportswear in the latest American and international styles. A private label brand created for Express is called Compagnie Internationale. The 640 Express stores in operation are located mostly in shopping malls.

Lerner New York. This division sells conventional women's sportswear. The Lerner stores have begun a transition from a budget-priced store to a moderately priced store. The Limited purchased the Lerner chain in 1985 for $297 million. Presently there are 915 Lerner stores in operation in malls and shopping centers across the United States.

Victoria's Secret. Victoria's Secret stores are the dominant intimate-apparel store in the world, presently selling more lingerie than industry competitors Vanity Fair and Maidenform. These stores specialize in high-quality European and American designer lingerie, with prices ranging from $5 to $2,000. In 1988 Victoria's Secret stores began selling toiletries, bath products, and fragrances. This division focuses on women aged 25 to 45, but gifts purchased by men account for a significant portion of the total sales. The stores had been decorated in a "Victorian Parlor" style, and the recently updated store design is an English-influence decor called "Bond Street." There are 545 Victoria's Secret stores in the United States.

Victoria's Secret Catalogue. This division is one the fastest-growing mail-order operations in the United States. Since its purchase by The Limited in 1982, the catalogue has steadily increased its operations. Now Victoria's Secret Catalogue is the dominant catalogue for lingerie in the world.

Lane Bryant. Lane Bryant had been in operation for 80 years; it was actually larger than The Limited, Inc., at the time it was purchased by The Limited in 1982. Lane

Bryant's market is primarily women between 30 and 50. The store specializes in the sale of medium-priced clothing, intimate apparel, and accessories for the "special-sized woman" (sizes 14 and up). Nearly all Lane Bryant stores were originally located in regional shopping centers, but Wexner has shifted Lane Bryant stores to mall locations near the other Limited stores. Because about 40 percent of American women are size 14 or larger, much growth is expected for Lane Bryant. There are presently 809 Lane Bryant stores.

Brylane. This division is the nation's largest catalogue retailer. Brylane sells women's special-sized apparel and misses sizes in their Lane Bryant Direct, Lerner Direct, and Roaman's catalogues. This division maintains a distribution center in Indianapolis, Indiana, where all orders are shipped and received.

Henri Bendel. In 1985 The Limited purchased this upscale fashion store. The store offers the best in clothing and accessories from international designers. Prices are designed for the fashion-conscious but not the budget-conscious shopper. This is the only high-priced store owned by The Limited. The first Henri Bendel store is located in New York City, and three more stores have been opened in major cities in the United States.

Abercrombie & Fitch. The Limited purchased Abercrombie & Fitch in 1988 from Oshman's Sporting Goods for $45 million in cash. The company sells traditional sportswear and outdoor sporting apparel and related gift items for younger men and women. The Limited operates 40 Abercrombie & Fitch stores.

Structure. The Limited, Inc., began testing the market for men's fashions by offering "Express for Men" in Express stores beginning in 1987. Sixty-nine Structure stores were opened in 1989, and by the end of 1992 there were 330 stores. They carry good-quality, affordable clothing in the latest styles. The store design mixes Palladian and modern architectural styles to appeal to men who "have a good sense of fine design." Structure stores generally open into Express stores so that customers can shop in both stores without having to exit to the mall area.

Limited Too. The market for girls' clothing (sizes 6–14) was tested by The Limited in the late 1980s when the Limited Too brand was offered in The Limited's flagship store. Sixty-two stores were opened during 1989, and by the end of 1992 there were 185 Limited Too Stores. Clothing sold in Limited Too stores is stylish–the newest in colors, prints, and fabrics—and moderately priced.

Bath & Body Works. In response to demand by consumers for natural personal-care products, The Limited opened six Bath & Body Works stores in 1990. These stores have a natural-market, open-air design and sell a variety of personal care products. There are now 121 Bath & Body Works stores.

Cacique. Select lingerie presented as Parisian in style is sold in 71 Cacique stores. Lingerie is made of high-quality fabrics in sophisticated designs.

Penhaligon's. The Limited purchased Penhaligon's in 1990 from Laura Ashley Holdings for approximately $11 million. The six stores, located in England, offer high-quality personal care products including perfumes, shaving accessories, soaps, and bath salts. Penhaligon products are also sold in some of the finest department stores around the world.

Mast Industries. The business of this division is to arrange for the manufacture and import of women's clothing from around the world, and to wholesale this merchandise to The Limited stores and to other companies.

Limited Distribution Services. The Limited's distribution center is located in Columbus, Ohio, with seven buildings and about 4.2 million square feet. This includes a 760,000-square-foot fulfillment center and office complex for Victoria's Secret Catalogue that was completed in 1992. The Limited also owns a mail-order center of approximately 750,000 square feet in Indianapolis, Indiana.

Limited Store Planning. This division designs store layout and develops merchandising techniques for all of The Limited's retail divisions.

Limited Real Estate. This division handles store leases for the 13 retail divisions. In 1991 the Real Estate division began a process of remodeling many stores and opening new larger-format stores (6 million square feet of selling space) for a total selling space at the end of 1991 of 20.3 million square feet. By the end of 1992, the total selling space of Limited Stores was almost 23 million square feet.

Limited Credit Services. This division handles consumer credit for both the retail and mail-order divisions. Activities of Limited Credit Services include billing, credit assessment, and credit collection. World Financial Network, Inc., a company-owned subsidiary, finances the company's private credit-card receivables.

Gryphon Development L.P.. This division, acquired by The Limited in 1992, develops and supplies fragrances for Bath & Body Works and Victoria's Secret.

COMPETITION

The retail sale of women's clothing is a very competitive business. Competitors of The Limited include nationally, regionally, and locally owned department stores, specialty stores, and mail-order catalogue businesses. Some of The Limited's major competitors are The Gap, Petrie Stores, Casual Corner, Marshall Fields, Carson Pirie Scott, Dayton-Hudson, Dillard's, May Department Stores, Charming Shoppes, Nordstrom, Sears, and J. C. Penney.

The years 1987 through 1990 were not good ones for the women's fashion industry. Many clothing retailers were purchased by debt-heavy corporations. Other retailers have gone out of business, including B. Altman, Garfinckel's, and Bonwit Teller. Leaders in the apparel retail industry have begun rethinking their strategies in hopes of improving the industry outlook for the 1990s. For example, some companies have chosen to concentrate on selling separates, whereas other companies promote collections and branded labels such as Liz Claiborne, J. G. Hook, and J. H. Collectibles. Improved customer service, including seminars and fashion shows, is a strategy adopted by many companies in the industry. Other companies have chosen to update displays, concentrate on private labels, emphasize career clothes, or to offer a mix of casual and career clothing.

According to *Stores,* The Limited, Inc. was the number one apparel chain in the United States during both 1991 and 1992. (The top ten apparel chains are shown in Exhibit 3–2.) Other specialty retailers who were in the top ten for sales volume in 1991 and 1992 include Melville Apparel, Nordstrom, TJX Cos., The Gap, Petrie Stores, Saks Fifth Avenue, U. S. Shoe, Charming Shoppes, and Kohls.

Two of The Limited's major competitors are described here.

The Gap, Inc. At the end of January 1993, The Gap had 1,307 apparel stores in operation. Several of its divisions compete directly with The Limited stores. The Gap, Inc. (885 stores), sells casual sportswear items for both men and women. GapKids (262 stores) sells children's sportswear. Banana Republic (160 stores) sells travel and outdoor sporting apparel. The Gap, Inc. also operates 22 GapKids in the United Kingdom and 24 in Canada. Financial information for The Gap, Inc., is shown in Exhibit 3–3.

EXHIBIT 3-2 Top Ten Apparel Chains (in millions of dollars)

CHAIN	1991 SALES	1992 SALES	PERCENT CHANGE
The Limited	$6,149.2	$6,944.3	12.9
Melville Apparel	3,243.2	3,486.1	7.5
Nordstrom	3,179.8	3,422.0	7.6
TJX Cos.	2,757.7	3,261.2	18.3
The Gap	2,518.9	2,960.4	17.2
Petrie Stores	1,354.5	1,438.2	6.2
Saks Fifth Avenue	1,300.0	1,350.0	3.8
U.S. Shoe Apparel	1,364.0	1,262.2	(7.5)
Charming Shoppes	1,020.7	1,178.7	15.5
Kohls	930.5	1,096.9	17.8

Source: "Top 100 Retailers," *Stores,* July 1993.

EXHIBIT 3-3 Financial Information for the Gap, Inc. (in millions of dollars except per share amount)

	1989	1990	1991	1992
Gross Revenue	1586.6	1933.8	2518.9	2960.2
Net Income	104.1	144.5	229.9	210.2
Long-Term Debt	17.5	5.0	77.5	75.0
Net Worth	338.0	465.7	677.8	887.8
Earnings Per Share	.74	1.02	1.62	1.47

Source: *Value Line.*

The Gap, Inc., is experimenting with larger-format stores that sell a complete line of merchandise including jeans, sweatsuits, shirts, sweaters, slacks, skirts, and accessories. The Gap has reduced its promotion budget because of its good location in malls and its high name recognition among young adults. During 1993 The Gap began switching 48 of its lowest performing Gap stores into discount centers called Gap Warehouse, which sell the same kinds of merchandise as do Gap stores but of lesser quality and at lower prices.

Petrie Stores Corporation. Petrie Stores sells women's clothing for teens, juniors, young misses, and larger-sized women. Some of the store names for the 1,720 Petrie chain include Petrie's, David's, Marianne, G & G, Rave, Winkelman's, Jean Nicole, Stuarts, and Plus. In 1992 the company added 36 Plus stores and 64 Combo units. The Combo units sell both large-size and junior clothing and allow the company to save in overhead costs by combining the two store types. Plans for 1993 call for 30 more Plus stores and 80 more Combo stores. Petrie Stores also owns approximately 14 percent of Toys R Us and 18 percent of Deb Shops. The majority of Petrie's apparel stores are located in shopping centers. Selected financial information for Petrie Stores is shown in Exhibit 3–4.

DEMOGRAPHIC AND SOCIETAL TRENDS

Some analysts suggest that as the baby boomers reach their late thirties, retailers and manufacturers of women's apparel have not provided for this group's needs. This large market group for women's apparel has found only youthful fashions and fads available for purchase. As a result, large numbers of customers have begun staying away from the stores entirely or purchasing fewer clothing items. Also, older shoppers (the fastest-growing demographic group) are complaining that retailers cater to younger tastes.

Many baby-boomer women, who make up about half of all U.S. working women, have little time for shopping. When they do have free time, they do not equate shopping with pleasure and prefer to relax at home. However, men are becoming much more fashion-conscious. They do more of their own shopping and make more clothing purchases on impulse than in the past.

EXHIBIT 3-4 Financial Information for Petrie Stores Corporation (in millions of dollars except per share amount)

	1989	1990	1991	1992
Gross Revenue	1257.5	1281.9	1354.5	1438.2
Net Income	32.3	13.6	16.0	14.8
Long-Term Debt	125.0	125.0	125.0	125.0
Net Worth	644.2	638.0	644.3	650.1
Earnings Per Share	.69	.29	.34	.32

Source: *Value Line.*

Currently, there is a mini baby boom, many of the new parents are older and have more disposable income than did new parents in the past. Also, the grandparents of these children are more likely to be affluent. Even though these trends would ordinarily indicate a good future for apparel retailing, there is a strong simultaneous trend away from the conspicuous consumption days of the 1980s. Retailers in the apparel industry are thus likely to struggle.

ECONOMIC CONDITIONS

The individual shopper's economic situation is not improving. The gap between rich and poor is increasing. It is estimated that by the year 2000, the number of households with annual incomes of $15,000 or less (in 1984 dollars) will increase to about 36 percent of U.S. families, or about 40 million families. The number of "downscale" shoppers is increasing. Many adults owe significant debt for cars and homes and are unable to spend much money for apparel, so they often purchase clothing at outlet malls or discount stores. Many of the women in the baby-boom group spend their disposable income on items for their children and not clothing for themselves. Occasionally, however, the downscale shopper may want to indulge himself or herself by purchasing fashion items from specialty stores.

Apparel retailers also have economic concerns. The top 30 retailers owe more than $60 billion to creditors. Several major retail chains have filed for reorganization under Chapter 11 bankruptcy. It is difficult for retail chains to predict consumer spending patterns. In 1987 spending was slow, but it improved in late 1988. However, by January 1989 spending slowed again, and 1991 was likewise a sluggish year for apparel overall. There was some consumer optimism after the presidential election in 1992, and the 1992 holiday season was a pleasant surprise for retailers. However, industry observers believe that consumers will remain cautious until they see how changes in the federal tax code and health-care reform will affect them.

If the economy continues to be weak, specialty retailers will have to take more gambles. Specialty retailers have gained a competitive advantage in the past by guessing a fashion trend early and purchasing inventory to provide that trend to customers. If a specialty retailer purchases inventory for a fashion trend but cannot turn over the inventory, the store loses profit and cannot afford to take more risks. However, if they do not gamble by trying to keep up with fashion trends, it is impossible to make a profit when the economy turns around because the merchandise will be out-of-date.

INTERNAL FACTORS FOR THE LIMITED, INC.

Marketing. Wexner believes that his company is "reinventing the specialty store business." Since the 12 Limited retail store divisions offer different price ranges and styles of clothing and related goods, Wexner has created the impact of a department store in many malls. In addition, the chain has begun an ambitious expansion. Limited executives believe that expanded-format stores are the success factor for the future. Larger stores can carry wider merchandise selections and offer better merchandise presentation. Wexner believes that "customers now want one-stop shopping and greater individuality, so they feel more secure when they see a broader assortment in one place." Many of these remodeled stores are located near each other in the malls to create the feeling of a department store for the customer. The increased size of these stores is shown in Exhibit 3–5.

EXHIBIT 3-5 Size Increases for Larger-Format Limited Stores

	GOAL-1994	1993	1992	CHANGE FROM	
				1994-1993	1993-1992
Express					
Stores	751	673	640	78	33
Selling Sq. Ft.	4,746,000	3,902,000	3,470,000	844,000	432,000
Lerner New York					
Stores	848	877	915	(29)	(38)
Selling Sq. Ft.	6,542,000	6,802,000	6,963,000	(260,000)	(161,000)
The Limited					
Stores	716	746	759	(30)	(13)
Selling Sq. Ft.	4,402,000	4,482,000	4,257,000	(80,000)	225,000
Victoria's Secret Stores					
Stores	610	570	545	40	25
Selling Sq. Ft.	2,676,000	2,346,000	2,029,000	330,000	317,000
Lane Bryant					
Stores	827	817	809	10	8
Selling Sq. Ft.	3,954,000	3,852,000	3,755,000	102,000	97,000
Structure					
Stores	499	394	330	105	64
Selling Sq. Ft.	1,942,000	1,409,000	1,076,000	533,000	333,000
The Limited Too					
Stores	234	184	185	50	(1)
Selling Sq. Ft.	747,000	566,000	567,000	181,000	(1,000)
Bath & Body Works					
Stores	319	194	121	125	73
Selling Sq. Ft.	496,000	248,000	132,000	248,000	116,000
Abercrombie & Fitch Co.					
Stores	72	49	40	23	9
Selling Sq. Ft.	581,000	405,000	332,000	176,000	73,000
Henri Bendel					
Stores	4	4	4	0	0
Selling Sq. Ft.	93,000	93,000	93,000	0	0
Cacique					
Stores	115	108	71	7	37
Selling Sq. Ft.	344,000	318,000	186,000	26,000	132,000
Penhaligon's					
Stores	7	7	6	0	1
Selling Sq. Ft.	3,000	3,000	3,000	0	0
Total Retail Divisions					
Stores	5,002	4,623	4,425	379	198
Selling Sq. Ft.	26,526,000	24,426,000	22,863,000	2,100,000	1,563,000

Source: The Limited *Annual Report*, 1993.

The Limited is experimenting with a new concept it calls "superstores." In 1991 the company opened its first mall anchor store at the Dadeland Mall in Miami, Florida. The 80,000-square-foot superstore contains six specialty stores—Limited, Limited Too, Express, Bath & Body Works, Structure, and Cacique. The entrance to The Limited also serves as a mall entrance. During the first year of the superstore operation, mall traffic at Dadeland increased and sales per square foot increased more than 20 percent for the total mall. In 1992 a 63,000-square-foot superstore opened at the mall at St. Matthews in Louisville, Kentucky.

In the past, The Limited has spent very little on advertising campaigns, relying instead on walk-in traffic in malls to sell their products. Wexner says that the company actually spends a significant amount of money on advertising because they send out hundreds of millions of catalogues per year and have nearly 4,500 storefronts where three million potential customer pass each day. Occasionally in the past the company included small advertisements in "mall shopper" magazines. In November 1989 national advertising for The Limited appeared in *Vogue, Vanity Fair,* and other women's magazines. The $10 million campaign was an attempt to increase brand recognition for the company's private labels.

The Limited's distribution center is located in Columbus, Ohio. Over 60 percent of the U.S. population is located within a 500-mile radius of Columbus, so Wexner feels this is an ideal location for a distribution center. Another advantage of the Columbus location is its nearness to New York City, the port where incoming merchandise produced in foreign countries is received by Mast Industries. All merchandise arriving in New York is shipped directly to the distribution center for allocation among The Limited's stores. A computerized distribution system aids distributors in their selections for each store's inventory. This system allows The Limited to monitor inventory levels, the merchandise mix, and the sales pattern at each store so that appropriate adjustments can be made as needed.

Production. The Limited, Inc. does not produce its own clothing, but it does have a division that contracts for the manufacture of clothing. Mast Industries specializes in contracting for production of high-quality, low-cost products. Much of the merchandise imported by Mast is marked with one of The Limited's own labels: The Limited, Compagnie Internationale, Cacique Lingerie, Structure, Victoria's Secret, and Limited Too. Leslie Wexner believes that having private label brands allows The Limited to keep merchandise inventory current and unique. Approximately 85 percent of The Limited's clothing is produced through Mast Industries.

The Limited can also maintain control over its clothing supply through Mast Industries. Mast is able to make copies of new trends in apparel and have these products on store shelves before the original design is produced for sale. Company managers try to maintain a 1,000-hour turnaround time between recognizing new style and delivering the merchandise to stores. Mast can send high-resolution, computer images of clothing designs by satellite to Far Eastern manufacturers. In addition, computer information that is collected from all individual stores is used to determine what needs to be produced in the Far East the next day. The newly produced items arrive in a few days at the Columbus distribution center and are sent to the stores.

In 1992 Mast purchased merchandise from approximately 4,800 different suppliers/factories, but no more than 4 percent of The Limited's inventory was purchased from any single manufacturer. About half of The Limited's inventory is produced outside the United States.

Finance. The Limited's income statements and balance sheets are provided in Exhibit 3–6 and Exhibit 3–7, respectively. These statements reveal increasing levels for sales, income, assets, and shareholder's equity. A consolidated statement of The Limited's shareholders' equity is given in Exhibit 3–8.

OUTLOOK

According to Leslie Wexner, "the key is our ability to change." However, while the company moves quickly to deal with immediate realities, long-range vision is never forgotten. Growth continues to be a primary objective for the future. By the mid-1990s the company plans for sales volume to be above $10 billion, with after-tax profit of about 10 percent. By the middle of the decade, Wexner expects the company's new divisions (those begun in the period 1988–1991) to account for $2 billion in sales and have more selling space than the company had in 1991. According to Kenneth Gilman, the chief financial officer:

> Some of our larger, older businesses are growing through repositioning, and others by remodeling their stores into larger-size formats. Both approaches will help the businesses achieve higher sales per square foot and sales per store. And of course the newer businesses are increasing their numbers of stores and their sales per square foot. The bottom line is that each of our businesses has a different growth profile, and each has the potential for significant and continued growth.

EXHIBIT 3-6 Income Statements for The Limited, Inc.
(in thousands of dollars per share amounts)

	1993	1992	1991
Net Sales	$7,245,088	$6,944,296	$6,149,218
Cost of Goods Sold, Occupancy and Buying Costs	(5,286,253)	(4,953,556)	(4,355,675)
Gross Income	1,958,835	1,990,740	1,793,543
General, Administrative and Store Operating Expenses	(1,259,896)	(1,202,042)	(1,080,843)
Special and Nonrecurring Items, Net	2,617	–	–
Operating Income	701,556	788,698	712,700
Interest Expense	(63,865)	(62,398)	(63,927)
Other Income, net	7,308	10,080	11,529
Gain on Issuance of United Retail Group Stock	–	9,117	–
Income Before Income Taxes	644,999	745,497	660,302
Provision for Income Taxes	254,000	290,000	257,000
Net Income	$390,999	$455,497	$403,302
Net Income Per Share	$1.08	$1.25	$1.11

Source: The Limited *Annual Report*, 1993.

Growth plans for 1993 include the following:

1. The company expects sales of $8 billion and after-tax profits of 8 percent.
2. Selling space will increase 2.5 million square feet (11 percent increase over 1992).
3. Limited Too will continue its double-digit growth from the existing base of stores.
4. 350 new stores will be opened and 290 others will be renovated.
5. Substantial gains will be made in financial performance at both Lerner New York and The Limited flagship store.

EXHIBIT 3-7 Balance Sheet for The Limited, Inc. (in thousands of dollars)

	JAN. 29, 1994	JAN. 30, 1993		
Assets				
Current Assets				
Cash and Equivalents	$ 320,558	$ 41,235		
Accounts Receivable	1,056,911	837,377		
Inventories	733,700	803,707		
Other	109,456	101,811		
Total Current Assets	2,220,625	1,784,130		
Property and Equipment, net	1,666,588	1,813,948		
Other Assets	247,892	248,372		
Total Assets	$4,135,105	$3,846,450		
Liabilities and Shareholders' Equity				
Current Liabilities				
Accounts Payable	$ 250,363	$ 309,092		
Accrued Expenses	347,892	274,220		
Certificates of Deposit	15,700	–		
Income Taxes	93,489	137,466		
Total Current Liabilities	707,444	720,778		
Long-Term Debt	650,000	541,639		
Deferred Income Taxes	275,101	274,844		
Other Long-Term Liabilities	61,267	41,572		
Shareholders' Equity				
Common Stock	189,727	189,727		
Paid-in Capital	128,906	127,776		
Retained Earnings	2,397,112	2,136,794		
	2,715,745	2,454,297		
Less: Treasury Stock, at cost	(274,452)	(186,680)		
Total Shareholders' Equity	2,441,293	2,267,617		
Total Liabilities and Shareholders' Equity	$4,135,105	$3,846,450		
Total Shareholders' Equity	1240.5	1560.1	1876.8	2267.6
Total Liabilities and Shareholder's Equity	2418.5	2872.0	3418.9	3846.4

Source: The Limited *Annual Report*, 1993.

6. The Limited will continue to build on the successes of the newer stores such as Express, Victoria's Secret, Structure, Cacique, and Panhaligon's. In addition to growth, other strategies include rebuilding and remodeling older stores, improving the merchandise mix and quality, and continuing to take advantage of company name recognition and the supplier advantages provided by Mast Industries. Wexner hopes these plans will allow The Limited to continue improving its position in the specialty retailing industry.

However, the potential for serious problems exists for Wexner. Some of these include: (1) the possibility of failure of the new, larger format stores or superstores, (2) another downturn in the women's apparel industry, (3) financial instability, especially due to expansion and remodeling debt, (4) investor disenchantment because of Wexner's risk-taking attitude, (5) a saturation of Limited stores in the U.S. malls and (6) difficulty in finding reliable foreign suppliers.

Wexner is philosophical about the ability of The Limited to compete in the women's apparel industry of the future:

> The key challenge facing us in the 90s is the same one that faces us every day: to keep taking the risk of change. Sometimes when you're trying to improve, you break something that is already fixed. Bus unless you change, and take the risk of failure, you limit your opportunities for success. That's why questioning, probing and reinventing are so important. This is how we redefined the specialty store business several times . . . and how we will continue to reinvent ourselves in the future.

EXHIBIT 3-8 Consolidated Statement of Shareholder's Equity (in thousands of dollars)

	COMMON STOCK	
	SHARES OUTSTANDING	PAR VALUE
Balance, February 2, 1991	360,598	$189,727
Net Income	–	–
Cash Dividends	–	–
Exercise of Stock Options & Other	1,188	–
Balance, February 1, 1992	361,786	189,727
Net Income	–	–
Cash Dividends	–	–
Exercise of Stock Options & Other	862	–
Warrants Issued for Acquisition	–	–
Balance, January 30 , 1993	362,648	189,727
Net Income	–	–
Cash Dividends	–	–
Purchase of Treasury Stock	(5,288)	–
Exercise of Stock Options & Other	441	–
Balance, January 29, 1994	357,801	$189,727

Source: The Limited *Annual Report*, 1993.

The following list presents some of the concerns that Wexner—and—you, might consider:

1. Is The Limited expanding too rapidly and becoming too diversified?
2. How could The Limited improve its market segmentation strategies?
3. Is the expanded format store a good idea for The Limited? What about the super-store concept?
4. Should The Limited spend more money on print and television advertising?
5. What is the likelihood of another downturn in the women's apparel industry?
6. Should The Limited attempt a takeover of a department store such as Petrie Stores or continue to grow internally?
7. How serious are the potential problems The Limited could face in the future?

NORDSTROM, INC.—1994

STEVE BARNDT
Pacific Lutheran University

Headquartered in Seattle, Washington, Nordstrom (206-628-2111) is a fashion specialty retail chain that operates 52 apparel and shoe department stores, 16 clearance clothing stores, and four youth-oriented clothing stores in Alaska, Arizona, California, Illinois, Maryland, Minnesota, New Jersey, Oregon, Utah, Virginia, and Washington. Nordstrom has attained a position of leadership and an outstanding reputation for service. Salesperson attention to the customer, selection of goods, product return policy, and amenities to make shopping an enjoyable experience are acknowledged to be extraordinary in the industry.

After many years as a regional retail chain servicing the Northwest states, expansion into California was steady through the 1980s. In 1988 the company became a national retailer with the opening of a store in Virginia. Company sales in fiscal year 1993 were $3.42 billion, whereas net earnings were $1.36 million.

HISTORY

John W. Nordstrom immigrated to the United States from Sweden in 1887 at the age of 16 and worked for a number of years as a logger, miner, and laborer. After earning $13,000 by gold mining in the Klondike, he settled in Seattle where he opened a shoe store in partnership with shoemaker Carl Wallin in 1901. In 1923 Wallin and Nordstrom opened a second store in Seattle. John Nordstrom's three sons bought his interest in the store in 1928 and Carl Wallin's in 1929, establishing the family ownership and management that has continued to the present.

In the early years under John Nordstrom, two basic philosophies were developed that have since guided business practice. The first is a customer orientation according to which the company emphasizes outstanding service, selection, quality, and value. The second is a policy of selection of managers from among employees who have experience on the sales floor. All of the Nordstrom family members who attained management positions started their careers as salesmen.

Rapid growth did not begin until after World War II. Starting with an expansion in 1950, with the opening of two new stores, growth continued so that by 1961 there were eight shoe stores and thirteen leased shoe departments in Washington, Oregon, and California. In 1963 Nordstrom diversified into women's fashion apparel with the acquisition of Best's Apparel and its stores in Seattle and Portland. Before the 1960s ended, five new Nordstrom Best stores offered clothes, shoes, and accessories had been opened.

The 1970s saw additional changes and rapid, steady growth. Management was passed to the third generation of Nordstroms in 1970, and the company went public in 1971, accompanied by a change in name to Nordstrom, Inc. Continued growth in the Northwest provided the company with 24 stores by 1978. Geographical expansion to California began in 1978 and has continued. By 1987 Nordstrom's Southern California presence was reflected in its position of first or second in market share for women's suits, women's blazers, men's tailored pants, women's dresses, women's coats, women's shoes, and men's shoes in the Los Angeles market. In early 1993, Nordstrom operated 31 stores in California including six Nordstrom Rack discount stores. The Rack line of stores was started in 1983 and by 1992 has grown to 15 in the Western states. Exhibit 4–1 shows the growth in Nordstrom, Nordstrom Rack, Place Two (youth fashion), and Last Chance (clearance) stores during the recent years ended January 31, 1993.

STRATEGIES

The Nordstrom strategy emphasizes merchandise and service tailored to appeal to the affluent and fashion-conscious shopper without losing its middle-class customers. The large Nordstrom specialty department stores cater to their target market with an unparalleled attention to the customers, guaranteed service, and a wide and deep line of merchandise. The success of this strategy has made the company one that competitors fear and attempt to follow. As has been noted, "Nordstrom is sometimes known as the 'Black Hole,' into which shoppers disappear, never to enter nearby stores."

In addition to its mainline stores, Nordstrom also operates four smaller Place Two specialty stores specializing in youth fashions, one Last Chance cut-price clearance store, and 15 Nordstrom Rack stores. The Racks serve as discount outlets offering clearance merchandise from the main stores plus some merchandise purchased directly from manufacturers. They cater to bargain shoppers who value Nordstrom quality.

EXHIBIT 4-1 Nordstrom Growth 1977–1993

YEAR ENDED JANUARY 31	COMPANY OPERATED STORES	TOTAL SQUARE FOOTAGE
1985	44	3,924,000
1986	52	4,727,000
1987	53	5,098,000
1988	56	5,527,000
1989	58	6,374,000
1990	59	6,898,000
1991	63	7,655,000
1992	68	8,590,000
1993	72	9,224,000

Source: Nordstrom *Annual Report*, 1985, 1986, 1987, 1989, and 1992.

Store architecture and merchandise differ from store to store. Each is designed to fit life-styles prevailing in the local geographic and economic environment. For example, the downtown San Francisco and Seattle stores provide their mainstay clientele, the upscale professionals, with extensive men's clothing and accessories selections. In every location merchandise selection, local tastes, and customer preferences help shape the store's interior. Approximately 70 percent of the merchandise featured is available at all Nordstrom stores, while the other 30 percent is unique to each store or region.

Product Lines. Nordstrom's specialty department stores carry focused lines of classically styled, relatively conservative merchandise. The merchandise has been described as "primarily classic and not trendy, the selection limited to styles with broad appeal." Women's fashions account for the largest share of the Nordstrom product line. However, menswear appears to be gaining in emphasis in some locations. For example, menswear comprised 18 percent of the inventory and 21 to 22 percent of total sales in the downtown San Francisco store. This is contrasted with a 16 percent share of sales from menswear company-wide. Exhibit 4–2 shows the company-wide sales breakdown by merchandise category.

Nordstrom carries both designer and private-label merchandise. In the past, private labels have been carried on 15 percent of the merchandise. Men's apparel and men's and women's shoes were the largest private-label lines where approximately 50 percent of men's clothes and 25 percent of shoes carried the Nordstrom name. Designer lines have made up the bulk of the merchandise. In its various stores Nordstrom has featured apparel lines by Claude Montana, Gianfranco Ferre, Christian Lacroix, Carolina Herrera, Carolyne Roehm, Calvin Klein, Anne Klein, Donna Karan, and Gianni Versace, among others. The Facconnable line of menswear is sold throughout the chain. Selection of lines and styles is largely based on wants indicated in direct customer feedback.

The company keeps alert to changes in both taste for and profitability of its product offerings. It has a history of change. If a new line of merchandise appears to better serve customers than an existing one, Nordstrom does not hesitate to make the switch. For example, recently the company closed out its fur salons and converted the space into departments carrying more profitable merchandise such as large-size women's apparel. The volume of its orders has allowed Nordstrom to develop a broad supplier base. No one supplier has significant bargaining power.

EXHIBIT 4-2 Merchandise Sales by Category

MERCHANDISE CATEGORY	SHARE OF 1992 SALES
Women's Apparel	39 percent
Women's Accessories	20 percent
Shoes	19 percent
Men's Apparel and Furnishings	16 percent
Children's Apparel and Accessories	4 percent
Other	2 percent

Source: Nordstrom *Annual Report,* 1992.

Merchandising. Nordstrom's merchandising is noted for its extensive inventories and dedicated, helpful sales force. However, Nordstrom also differs from rivals in several other ways. The typical store has 50 percent more salespeople on the floor than similar-sized competitors. The salesforce uses its product knowledge to show appropriate merchandise to customers, assist them in their selections, and suggest accessories. Salespeople keep track of their regular customers' fashion tastes and sizes and then call them or send notes about new merchandise in which they may have an interest. The company carries a very large inventory, providing an unusually wide selection of colors and sizes. With an inventory almost twice as large per square foot as its department store competitors, Nordstrom has a depth of inventory almost comparable to smaller specialty stores while offering a more complete line. As an indication of the inventory intensity, the San Francisco Center (downtown) store had $100 million invested in opening day inventory, including 100,000 pairs of shoes, 10,000 men's suits, and 20,000 neckties.

Nordstrom is one of the industry leaders in dividing its stores into small boutiques featuring targeted merchandise mixes. Rather than featuring a single type of merchandise, departments offer a variety of items (e.g., coats, suits, dresses, etc.) all of which are keyed to a particular lifestyle. Departments are added or changed to serve evolving customer needs. For instance, in response to growth in the number of women in higher-level management positions, women's tailored clothing departments were added. Though designer fashions are generally not given special treatment in display, the company has introduced special departments to display some of its higher-priced designer apparel.

Luxurious settings of polished wood and marble are used in place of the chrome and bright colors common in competing stores. Merchandise is arranged in departments according to life-styles. Stores feature clusters of antiques and open displays of merchandise usually arranged at right angles to each other. Mannequins are used sparingly; a piece of antique furniture is a more common display prop. Merchandise is displayed without bulky antitheft tags. In addition, there is no closed-circuit television, presenting a less intimidating atmosphere to customers. Instead, Nordstrom relies on the presence of its large sales force to discourage theft.

Nordstrom spends less than 2 percent of sales on advertising, half as much as is commonly spent. The company relies heavily on word-of-mouth to attract customers. The advertising that is used emphasizes styles and breadth of merchandise selection rather than price.

Pricing. Prices are competitive with comparable merchandise, and Nordstrom follows the same mark-up practices common to retail fashion stores. But because of the company's selectivity in providing high-quality merchandise, prices tend to be high. However, the company is committed to providing value and will not be undersold on its merchandise. If a customer finds an item carried by Nordstrom for sale at a lower price at another store, Nordstrom will match that lower price.

Consumer caution in spending during the recession that started at the end of the 1980s placed downward pressure on prices in the industry. Nordstrom responded with a shift to a greater share of value-priced merchandise. A major means of providing lower-priced, quality merchandise has been the substitution of Nordstrom-label goods for branded goods.

Customer Service. Under recent conditions of lower inflation and higher incomes, the public has raised its expectations of service. Many Americans have become tired of self-service or inattentive sales help. Two-income households and busy professionals have become hooked on convenience and are willing to pay for it. At the same time, retailers who shifted to lower levels of customer service are having difficulty in upgrading service. Understaffing in sales positions and overwork coupled with low pay and lack of a career path do not provide the conditions necessary to motivate employees to improve service.

Nordstrom has never cut service and therefore does not have to overcome structural, motivational, or cultural barriers to provide satisfying service. The company is already there—it is the undisputed leader in customer service. Nordstrom's excellent service is centered in the sales force and supported by company policy and investment in facilities and personnel. At Nordstrom a customer can expect to be in a department no longer than two minutes before a salesperson is in attendance to answer questions, explain merchandise, and make suggestions. This salesperson might lead the customer to merchandise in other departments to help the shopper find what he or she wants.

Sales clerks routinely attend customers in dressing rooms, bringing them alternate items of apparel or sizes to try on. They also routinely send thank-you notes and announcements of sales and arrival of merchandise that should be of interest to the customer. Other examples of such extraordinary out-of-the-way service by Nordstrom sales personnel include warming up customer's cars on cold days, paying parking tickets for customers who couldn't find legal parking, personal delivery of items to the customer's home, and ironing a newly bought item of apparel so the customer could wear it back to work.

Extraordinary service stems from several mutually supportive factors. First, the number of salespeople on the floor is high—50 percent higher than is common. This means the sales clerks are less rushed when waiting on customers. Second, the sales force is carefully recruited. Third, pay is higher than in comparable positions elsewhere and, in addition, is partly based on performance (volume of sales). This means that the sales clerk who satisfies customers earns more. In addition, there is a kind of peer pressure to sell more (satisfy more customers) because those who earn more are seen as role models. Last, Nordstrom has a powerful corporate culture that stresses attentiveness to the customer. This culture is well established, having been instituted under John W. Nordstrom and reinforced ever since. The company has been successful at transferring this culture to its new stores at their start-up. A key practice in establishing the Nordstrom culture in new stores is to open them under the leadership of a cadre of experienced Nordstrom managers and salespeople who provide guidance and training to the locally hired personnel. For example, when Nordstrom opens its new store in Indianapolis, about 10 percent of its employees will be moved from other Nordstrom stores.

In keeping with the feeling that the customer is king and always right, Nordstrom has a no-questions-asked merchandise return policy. The company willingly replaces or refunds the price of any item of merchandise whether new or used, with or without a sales receipt. Probably the best known of many refund tales is that of an individual who bought a pair of tires from the same store when it was under other ownership and returned them to Nordstrom for a refund. The purchase price of the pair of tires was refunded even though Nordstrom does not and never has sold tires.

Luxurious settings and furnishings make the shopper feel special. Standard extras in many of the stores include a pianist playing enjoyable music on a baby grand piano, free coat and package checking, play areas for children, extra-large dressing rooms, free gift wrap at the cash register, and tea for weary customers as they try on apparel in the dressing rooms. Newer, larger stores feature even more extras. For example, to help differentiate itself from competition the San Francisco Center store has a beauty treatment spa, four restaurants, a pub in the men's department, and valet parking.

Location. Nordstrom targets growing affluent communities for its stores. Although the majority of its stores are located in suburban shopping centers, others are located in the central business districts of large and small cities. In either type of location, Nordstrom chooses to locate close to other retailers because of the drawing power of a concentration of shopping facilities. Exhibit 4–3 shows the locations and size of Nordstrom and Nordstrom Rack stores in 1993.

As a late entrant in many regions—for example, the East, the Midwest, and Southern and Northern California—Nordstrom has had an advantage in its selection of store sites in growing high-income areas. Early entrant chains often find themselves doing business in outdated stores in older, less economically attractive areas. However, the industry is mature, with most attractive shopping districts saturated with retailers. Finding locations attractive for growth with adequate available square footage requires buying out competitors or engaging in a geographically extended search. Following its coverage of virtually all major Pacific Northwest markets in the 1970s and very early 1980s, Nordstrom channeled its growth to California. By the late 1980s Nordstrom had covered most of the attractive California markets, limiting its further growth there. This forced the company to search for expansion opportunities in several other, slower-growing geographical regions. Nordstrom currently plans to open stores in a number of selected locations spread across the East, Northeast, Southcentral, and Midwest regions, and is considering opening stores in the Southeast and Intermountain West. Such growth is opportunistic, involving new shopping-mall space in growth areas or occupancy of vacated space in older shopping centers. An example of the latter is Nordstrom's entry into the Paramus, New Jersey, market in a store vacated when May Department Stores closed its Hahne's chain. Seven distribution centers are located in regions to serve stores. These include recently opened distribution centers in Maryland and Iowa that serve the growing number of stores in surrounding states.

MANAGEMENT AND ORGANIZATION

Strategic and significant financial decisions are made at the top level in the organization, and operational decisions at the region and store level. Managers in each region, store, and department have responsibility and accountability for profit and autonomy and authority to make decisions regarding their area. This decentralized management allows managers to be entrepreneurially creative in tailoring each store's merchandise and layout to its customers. Free of decision making for regional and store operations, top management has been able to concentrate on future expansion.

The company structure can be described in terms of three levels of management responsibility—top or executive level, midlevel, and store level. The top level consists of four cochairmen of the board: brothers James F. Nordstrom, 53, and John N. Nordstrom, 55, and cousin Bruce A. Nordstrom, 59, often referred to as the "family"; plus John A. McMillan, 61, who is married to a Nordstrom. The cochairmen retain strategic management responsibility, concentrating on setting the strategic direction and making expansion location decisions. The "family" is deeply involved in providing the overall guidance to the company and exercises effective control with about 40 percent ownership. When a new store opens, one or more of the Nordstroms will be there on the selling floor. During a downturn in 1987, family

EXHIBIT 4-3 Retail Store Facilities

The following table sets forth certain information with respect to each of the stores operated by the Company. The Company also operates leased shoe departments in 11 department stores in Hawaii. In addition, the Company operates seven distribution centers and leases other space for administrative functions.

Location	Year Opened or Acquired	Present Total Store Area/Sq. Ft.	Location	Year Opened or Acquired	Present Total Store Area/Sq. Ft.
Washington Group			**Northern California Group**		
Downtown Seattle[a]	1963	245,000	Hillsdale Shopping Center	1982	149,000
Northgate Mall	1965	122,000	Broadway Plaza	1984	193,000
Tacoma Mall	1966	132,000	Stanford Shopping Center	1984	187,000
Bellevue Square	1967	184,000	The Village of Corte Madera	1985	115,000
Southcenter Mall	1968	170,000	Oakridge Mall	1985	150,000
Yakima	1972	44,000	Valley Fair	1987	165,000
Spokane	1974	121,000	280 Metro Center Rack	1987	31,000
Alderwood Mall	1979	125,000	Stonestown Galleria	1988	174,000
Pavilion Rack	1985	39,000	Downtown San Francisco	1988	350,000
Alderwood Rack	1985	25,000	Arden Fair	1989	190,000
Downtown Seattle Rack	1987	42,000	Stoneridge Mall	1990	173,000
			Marina Square Rack	1990	44,000
Oregon Group					
Lloyd Center	1963	150,000	**Alaska Group**		
Downtown Portland	1966	174,000	Anchorage	1975	97,000
Washington Square	1974	108,000			
Vancouver Mall	1977	71,000	**Utah Group**		
Salem Centre	1980	71,000	Crossroads Plaza	1980	140,000
Clackamas Town Center	1981	121,000	Fashion Place Mall	1981	110,000
Clackamas Rack	1983	28,000	Ogden City Mall	1982	76,000
Downtown Portland Rack	1986	19,000	Sugarhouse Center Rack	1991	31,000
Southern California Group			**Capital Group**		
South Coast Plaza	1978	235,000	Tysons Corner Center	1988	238,000
Brea Mall	1979	195,000	The Fashion Centre at		
Los Cerritos Center	1981	122,000	Pentagon City	1989	241,000
Fashion Valley Mall	1981	156,000	Potomac Mills Rack	1990	46,000
Glendale Galleria	1983	147,000	Montgomery Mall	1991	225,000
Santa Ana Rack	1983	21,000	City Place Rack	1992	37,000
Topanga Plaza	1984	154,000	Towson Town Center	1992	205,000
University Towne Centre	1984	130,000	Towson Rack	1992	31,000
Woodland Hills Rack	1984	48,000			
The Galleria at South Bay	1985	161,000	**Northeast Group**		
Westside Pavilion	1985	150,000	Garden State Plaza	1990	272,000
Horton Plaza	1985	151,000	Menlo Park Mall	1991	266,000
Mission Valley Rack	1985	27,000	Freehold Raceway Mall	1992	174,000
Montclair Plaza	1986	133,000	**Midwest Group**		
North County Fair	1986	156,000	Oakbrook Center	1991	249,000
MainPlace Mall	1987	169,000	Mall of America	1992	240,000
Chino Town Square Rack	1987	30,000			
Paseo Nuevo	1990	186,000	**Place Two and Clearance Stores[b]**		
The Galleria at Tyler	1991	164,000	Washington and Arizona		99,000

[a] *Excludes approximately 23,000 square feet of corporate and administrative offices.*

[b] *Includes four Place Two stores and one clearance store.*

Source: Nordstrom *Annual Report*, 1993.

members returned to the floor for stints of selling and visible leadership to help motivate meeting goals. They are visible leaders and approachable by employees and customers, but they remain reticent about themselves and the company.

While the cochairmen share strategic management, operational management is delegated to an "office of the president." In 1991 the cochairmen appointed four copresidents to manage the day-to-day operations. These four share the office by focusing on different aspects of the business. Raymond Johnson, 51, handles accessories, lingerie, children's clothes, personnel, and legal matters; Darrel Hume, 45, is in charge of store planning, finance, and men's apparel; Galen Jefferson, 43, handles women's wear and merchandise systems; and John Whitacre, 40, concentrates on shoes, restaurants, and budgeting. Each has authority to make decisions that clearly fall in their respective areas. They meet formally once a week and informally communicate with one another throughout the week as necessary. Disagreements that arise among the copresidents are usually resolved by choosing the view or course of action that best serves the customer.

The midmanagement level is comprised of the corporate treasurer; geographical group general managers for the Northern California, Southern California, Oregon, Washington and Alaska, Utah, Northeast, Midwest, and capital groups of stores; region managers responsible for smaller groups of stores in several of the geographical store groups; and various managers in charge of merchandise categories and staff support areas such as public relations, legal affairs, and sales promotion.

Operational management of the stores is the responsibility of store managers with the assistance of their staff and department managers. Stores and departments have their own buyers. Exhibit 4–4 shows the general chain of command at Nordstrom.

Throughout the company, idea generation and operational decision making are encouraged, expected, and supported at the lowest levels where the individual has the appropriate information. Managers in the sales departments routinely make decisions on what inventory to carry and whether to accept checks, set lower prices to stay competitive, and accept returned merchandise without consulting higher-level managers or staff specialists.

Units and the individuals in them are goal-driven. As one writer has put it, "the life of a Nordstrom salesperson is defined by goals. Departmental, storewide, and company goals. Qualitative and quantitative goals." Store goals are set for the year and both reflect and influence department goals. Department goals influence salesperson goals. Yearly goals are translated into monthly goals. Daily goals are more changeable and reflect pro rata accomplishment of monthly goals as well as historical performance. On a daily basis, departments aim to surpass sales of the same day last year by a set level and individual goals are adjusted accordingly. If the department is behind in reaching its monthly goal, daily goals of the department and each sales clerk are likely to be pegged higher to get back on track.

Salespeople and departments are kept aware of the level of their goal accomplishment and are provided rewards for goal achievement. Salespeople are reminded of the day's goal and may be asked during the day how they are doing. Reaching goals is praised and when longer-term goals, such as annual personal goals, are achieved, recognition is public, often in the form of an announcement or letter from a Nordstrom. Top-performing salespeople are admitted to the Pacesetters' Club. Pacesetters receive a certificate, a Pacesetter business card, a 33 percent discount on Nordstrom merchandise (rather than the standard 20 percent), and a night on the town.

The company also promotes performance and conformity to it standards of customer service through the widespread use of heroics. The exploits of employees who make

EXHIBIT 4-4   Nordstrom Management Structure

Darrel Hume
Raymond Johnson
Galen Jefferson
John Whitacre
Co-Presidents

Cynthia Paur, Ex. VP Sales Promotion	Robert Nunn, Ex. VP Shoe Division Mer. Mang.
Jack Irving, Ex. VP Men's Wear Mer. Mang.	Jammie Baugh, Ex. VP S. Calif. Gen Mang.
Gail Cottle, Ex. VP Prod Development	Blake Nordstrom, VP WA & AS Gen. Mang.
John Goesling, Ex. VP Treasurer	Cody Kondo, VP NE Gen. Mang.
Martha Wikstrom, VP Capital Gen. Mang.	James Nordstrom, VP N. Calif. Gen. Mang.
Karen Purpur Secretary	Paul Hunter, VP Rack Div. Gen. Mang.
David Lindsey, VP Store Planning	Dale Crichton, VP Cosmetics and Gift Mer. Mang.
David Mackie, VP Legal and RE	Barbara Kanaya, VP Accessories Mer. Mang.
Charles Dudley, VP Human Resources	
Joseph Demarte, VP Personnel	

unusual or extraordinary efforts to please customers or who have specially noteworthy levels of sales are communicated through the organization, formally and informally, so that they may serve as role models. This technique, along with the use of goals, serves as a powerful indicator of the kinds of behavior the company wants and rewards.

HUMAN RESOURCES

Nordstrom has about 33,000 year-long employees plus seasonal hires. The company likes to hire young people who have not learned behaviors inconsistent with the Nordstrom customer-service values and then start them in sales positions. The actual decision of whom to hire is left to the sales department managers rather than to a staff personnel department. The company's hiring practice, in conjunction with its major expansion in recent years, has left the company with a work force that is relatively young and often college educated. Even its mid- and top-level managers are young. Top managers are in their early forties to midfifties. Midlevel vice presidents range in age from low thirties to midfifties, with most less than 45 years of age.

The company follows a promote-from-within policy. Because the company is growing fast, this serves as a motivator to those who aspire to rapid advancement. Promotions to line management positions are made from among employees with sales and customer contact experience. Those who are promoted to higher-level positions are encouraged and expected to keep in contact with customers. For example, the company's buyers, who all started in sales positions, spend a large amount of their time on the sales floor to learn what customers want.

Other expectations are transmitted in various ways and will bring on corrective actions if violated. One of these is dress. Employees are expected to wear neat business attire. Further, it is understood that the attire should be acquired from Nordstrom. Personal business, including telephone calls, is not to be conducted in a customer area. Abuse of employee discount privileges, violation of criminal law, rudeness to a customer, and unacceptable personal conduct are grounds for immediate dismissal. Underperforming employees usually leave on their own as do those who are uncomfortable with constant pressure to meet goals and accommodate the customer no matter what the customer does or how he or she behaves. Those who remain are loyal to the company and accepting of its cultural values.

High pay is important in attracting, retaining, and motivating employees. Pay ranges from about $6 to $9 per hour plus commissions of 6.5 to 10 percent. Combined hourly and commission pay for first-year salespeople averages $20,000 to $22,000 per year, and after three years, about $50,000 per year. Top salespeople can earn $80,000 to $100,000 per year. With these kind of earnings, Nordstrom's sales employees' compensation is high relative to the rest of the industry.

Commission pay ties rewards directly to sales and customer service performance. The higher the sales to satisfied customers, the greater the reward. Since returned merchandise is subtracted from the sales clerk's sales and therefore decreases commission income, selling for the sake of a sale alone is discouraged. Monetary rewards and public recognition are supplemented with motivational speeches and skits, along with pep-talk meetings. The objectives of these techniques are in general to build employees' confidence in their ability to perform to higher limits, and in particular to get them worked up to capitalize on the selling opportunities associated with one of the four major annual sales.

IMAGE AND PUBLIC RELATIONS

Nordstrom is well known as a premium service retailer. Its reputation for service and selection of merchandise provides the company with a mystique. As a result, Nordstrom receives a great deal of favorable free publicity. New store openings are preceded by numerous articles in the local press that help create the perception that Nordstrom offers a superior shopping experience. Continuing favorable reports in the media reinforce that perception. For example, the press recently reported the results of a nationwide survey that ranked Nordstrom first among the top 70 U.S. retail department and discount store chains in overall customer satisfaction.

Although much publicity has been favorable, a number of unfavorable charges and accusations have surfaced in recent years. These include allegations by labor unions of wrongdoing and charges by black interest groups of discrimination. In late 1989 the United Food & Commercial Workers Union charged that Nordstrom encouraged its salespeople to work off-the-clock taking inventory, writing thank-you notes, making home deliveries, or tracking down hard-to-find garments over the phone—in other words, to do work for the company for which they were not compensated. The Washington State Department of Labor and Industries subsequently found Nordstrom in violation of state wage laws and directed the company to reimburse workers for work performed without pay. The union followed up with a class action lawsuit on behalf of 50,000 past and present Nordstrom employees in Washington, Oregon, California, Utah, Alaska, and Virginia seeking compensatory damages and penalties. Without admitting guilt, the company has agreed to pay back wages and legal fees to qualifying present and former employees. Total cost to the company has been estimated at $15 to $30 million. Earlier the company established a $15 million contingency liability reserve for retroactive wage claims.

The union also engaged in an attempt to discredit Nordstrom's image with customers. The union alleged the company requires its employees to wear garments it is promoting during work hours, then allows them to replace the merchandise back on the rack, some-times without a cleaning. Subsequently, Oregon sued Nordstrom for selling used lipstick, shoes, and other merchandise at its Oregon stores. Without admitting any wrongdoing, Nordstrom settled the suit with Oregon, paying the state $25,000. The company claims its employees are encouraged but not required to wear Nordstrom clothing. The Nordstrom clothing they wear must be purchased and employees can buy at a discount.

In an unrelated incident a sales clerk in a California Nordstrom store filed a lawsuit alleging that Nordstrom invaded her privacy through the use of a hidden video camera in a small room used by some employees as a restroom and a place in which to change clothes. Nordstrom contended that the room was not an employee lounge and the camera was there to monitor a safe containing high value merchandise.

In 1992 seven blacks filed a class action lawsuit claiming discrimination against blacks in recruitment, hiring, and promotion. Subsequently a group calling itself People Against Racism at Nordstrom (PARAN) targeted the company for a national boycott based on allegations of discrimination. Later, another six plaintiffs entered the lawsuit. However, by late 1992, 12 had withdrawn.

In spite of the charges described here, Nordstrom is generally considered to be a good community citizen. It has a record of supporting benefits for social-program fund raising in its communities. For example, in its hometown it recently provided the Seattle Housing Group with $4.7 million, more than half the cost of building a 100-unit low-income housing project.

Nordstrom started a free program called "Healthy Beginnings" to help expectant mothers avoid risks to themselves and their pregnancies. Under the program, they receive educational materials, pregnancy risk screenings, access to a toll-free hot line, and a Nordstrom gift certificate. Within the company, Nordstrom introduced a family leave program in 1991, allowing up to 12 weeks of unpaid leave to care for new-born or newly adopted children or seriously ill family members.

Nordstrom has been a leader in catering to people with disabilities. In 1992 the company was awarded an "Excellence in Access Award" for making its stores accessible to disabled customers and providing special services to them. Also in 1992 Nordstrom received an EDI (Equality/Dignity/Independence) award from the National Easter Seal Society for featuring models with disabilities in its catalogs.

Support for minorities includes a minority vendor program started in 1989 that, into 1992, had awarded $20 million in contracts to minority-owned businesses. The company committed $220,000 for advertising in West Coast African-American newspapers over ten months and contributed $10,000 to the United Negro College Fund. Within the company, 27 percent of the workforce is composed of members of minorities, as is 16 percent of its management. Further, Nordstrom claims it employs a greater percentage of African-Americans in every region where it does business than that minority's share of the population. Many special and minority interest groups support and praise Nordstrom for its efforts.

FINANCIAL POSITION

Over the ten-year period from February 1983 to January 1993, Nordstrom enjoyed continuous growth in sales. Net earnings grew each year except fiscal years 1989 and 1990. Exhibit 4–5 reveals the company's recent sales and earnings information. As shown in Exhibit 4–6, earnings per store in fiscal years 1989 to 1992 failed to continue an upward climb started in 1986.

Nordstrom is a leader in sales per square foot, a key measure of efficiency in the industry. In 1989 the department store industry averaged $173 in sales per square foot. Although Nordstrom is not directly comparable to general department stores in that it sells only apparel, shoes, and accessories that can be densely stocked, it can be compared to specialty stores. In 1988 and 1989 specialty stores averaged $248 and $243 in sales per square foot, respectively. As shown in Exhibit 4–7, Nordstrom stores averaged $398 in fiscal year 1989 and $381 in fiscal year 1992. Many of the company's new stores exceed $400 per square foot in their first year. The company's best sales record, of $600 per square foot, was reached at the South Coast Plaza store in 1987. Nordstrom stores also get off to a quicker start than is common. "On the average, it takes a Nordstrom store between one and two years before it reaches chainwide sales per square foot performance. This compares to an industry average of about three years." Note in Exhibit 4–7 that Nordstrom's per foot sales decreased in 1991, 1992 and 1993.

EXHIBIT 4-5 Consolidated Statements of Earnings (dollars in thousands except per share amount)

Year ended January 31,	1993	% OF SALES	1992	% OF SALES	1991	% OF SALES
Net sales	$3,421,979	100.0	$3,179,820	100.0	$2,893,904	100.0
Costs and expenses:						
Cost of sales and related buying and occupancy costs	2,339,107	68.3	2,169,437	68.2	2,000,250	69.1
Selling, general and administrative	902,083	26.4	831,505	26.2	747,770	25.8
Interest, net	44,810	1.3	49,106	1.5	52,228	1.8
Service charge income and other, net	(86,140)	(2.5)	(87,443)	(2.7)	(84,660)	(2.9)
Total costs and expenses	3,199,860	93.5	2,962,605	93.2	2,715,588	93.8
Earnings before income taxes	222,119	6.5	217,215	6.8	178,316	6.2
Income taxes	85,500	2.5	81,400	2.5	62,500	2.2
Net earnings	$ 136,619	4.0	$ 135,815	4.3	$ 115,816	4.0
Net earnings per share	$ 1.67		$ 1.66		$ 1.42	
Cash dividends paid per share	$ .32		$ .31		$ .30	

Source: Company reports.

EXHIBIT 4-6 Average Per-Store Performance (in thousands of dollars)

FISCAL YEAR	NUMBER OF STORES	NET SALES PER STORE	NET EARNINGS PER STORE
1983	39	19,710	1,032
1984	44	21,788	925
1985	52	25,036	963
1986	53	30,753	1,376
1987	56	34,290	1,656
1988	58	40,137	2,126
1989	59	45,273	1,948
1990	63	45,935	1,938
1991	68	46,762	1,997
1992	72	47,527	1,897

Source: Nordstrom *Annual Report,* 1987–1992.

EXHIBIT 4-7 Nordstrom Sales Per Square Foot

YEAR ENDED JANUARY 31	SALES PER SQUARE FOOT ($)	CONSUMER PRICE INDEX OF RETAIL APPAREL AND UPKEEP		SALES PER SQUARE FOOT
		Year	Index	
1981	184	1980	90.9	202
1982	200	1981	95.3	210
1983	205	1982	97.8	210
1984	243	1983	100.2	243
1985	267	1984	102.1	262
1986	293	1985	105.0	279
1987	322	1986	105.9	304
1988	349	1987	110.6	316
1989	380	1988	115.4	329
1990	398	1989	118.6	336
1991	391	1990	124.1	315
1992	388	1991	128.7	301
1993	381	1992	131.9	289

Note: Retail apparel price index is a composite including men's and boys' apparel, women's and girls' apparel, infants' and toddlers' apparel, footwear, other apparel, and apparel services.

Sources: Nordstrom *Annual Report,* 1988, 1991; U.S. Department of Commerce, *Statistical Abstract of the United States 1992;* and U.S. Labor Department, *Monthly Labor Review,* March 1993, p. 87.

Efforts to improve profitability have included both cost cutting and revenue enhancement. A continuing pressure to reduce costs was initiated in September 1990, when management directed all stores to cut expenses by 3 to 12 percent depending on store performance. The exact nature of cost reductions, whether in personnel, inventories, or advertising, was at the discretion of each store manager. The company has undertaken a systematic attack on inventory costs through information transfer. Nordstrom has instituted an improved management information system to improve its inventory ordering and vendor service. Its Vendor Information Partnership lets suppliers and Nordstrom buyers communicate and obtain updated information about inventories, status of orders, and payments. Buyers can initiate reorders through the system. The company is also evaluating a personal computer–based system that can be used to track sales demand by item by store, identify the level and location of inventories, and initiate transfer of inventory between locations.

Nordstrom spends considerably less on advertising than is common among competitors. As compared to an industry average of 4 percent of sales, Nordstrom spends less than 2 percent on advertising. Total company advertising expenditures amounted to only $58,424,000; $55,320,000; $50,412,000; $47,150,000; and $41,556,000 in fiscal years 1992, 1991, 1990, 1989, and 1988 respectively. The low level of advertising expenditures allows the company to pay more in salesperson compensation without eroding profit margins. As has been noted, Nordstrom can get by with less advertising in part by capitalizing on the mystique created by the media.

In order to boost sales in an otherwise depressed market, the company has recently increased its volume of lower-priced merchandise. This has largely been carried out by replacing nationally branded merchandise with goods produced for the company to its specifications and bearing the Nordstrom label. This has allowed selling at lower prices without major reductions in margins. Another move to boost revenues involved establishing the Nordstrom National Credit Bank in Colorado to issue and service its credit card operations. With a federally chartered national bank, Nordstrom can charge its cardholders in any state the maximum interest allowed in the state where chartered. The bank does not engage in any checking or savings and loans operations—it handles only credit card operations.

The company has used internally generated operating earnings, debt, and proceeds from the sale of common stock to finance its growth. Currently, debt is preferred over equity as a source of capital. However, Nordstrom has avoided the high level of debt that plagues many of its competitors. Incremental, store-by-store growth has been managed so that only relatively modest increases in debt have been needed to supplement operating earnings in financing growth. In fact, Exhibit 4–8 shows a decline in relative use of debt over the last five years. Capital expenditures in the near future will not require any major increase in debt. Opening new stores and modernizing present stores is expected to require the expenditure of approximately $550,000,000 through 1995. Exhibit 4–9 presents the company's recent balance sheets.

COMPANY PLANS

Growth is planned to continue at the approximate rate of three to four new large specialty department stores per year. These large stores will range in size from about 150,000 to 250,000 square feet. In addition, the Nordstrom Racks will continue their steady expansion. Distribution centers will be established to serve the stores that are in geographical areas new to Nordstrom.

EXHIBIT 4-8 Nordstrom Liquidity and Debt Ratios, Fiscal Years
1989–1993

| | YEAR ENDED JANUARY 31 | | | | |
	1993	1992	1991	1990	1989
Current Ratio	2.28	2.13	1.98	2.06	2.04
Quick Ratio	1.34	1.21	1.16	1.21	1.14
Long Term Debt/Equity	.42	.54	.59	.64	.61
Long Term Debt/Total Assets	.21	.25	.26	.27	.26
Total Debt/Total Assets	.49	.53	.57	.57	.58

Note: Total debt is calculated as total liabilities and equity less equity.

Source: Nordstrom *Annual Report*, 1991, 1992.

EXHIBIT 4-9 Consolidated Balance Sheets (Dollars in thousands)

JANUARY 31,	1993	1992
Assets		
Current assets:		
Cash and cash equivalents	$ 29,136	$ 14,651
Accounts receivable, net	603,198	608,227
Merchandise inventories	536,739	506,632
Prepaid expenses	50,771	48,128
Total current assets	1,219,844	1,177,638
Property, buildings and equipment, net	824,142	856,404
Other assets	9,184	7,833
Total assets	$2,053,170	$2,041,875
Liabilities and Shareholders' Equity		
Current liabilities:		
Notes payable	$ 38,319	$ 134,735
Accounts payable	220,176	216,432
Accrued salaries, wages and taxes	158,028	145,792
Accrued expenses	31,141	31,741
Accrued income taxes	22,216	16,402
Current portion of long-term debt	41,316	8,801
Total current liabilities	511,196	553,903
Long-term debt	440,629	502,199
Deferred income taxes	49,314	46,542
Contingent liabilities		
Shareholders' equity	1,052,031	939,231
Total liabilities and shareholders' equity	$2,053,170	$2,041,875

Source: Nordstrom *Annual Report*, 1992.

Nordstrom has no plans to expand its operations to foreign nations. At least initially, national expansion will be targeted at the Washington-to-Boston corridor, the Southeast, the Midwest, and South-central regions. When the company enters a new area it will open several stores within a very few years to make more efficient use of the required supporting distribution center and the regional staff. The company will open its new stores under the leadership of experienced employees relocated or promoted from other Nordstrom stores. As in the past, this cadre will be relied on to anchor and communicate the Nordstrom culture.

Nordstrom's pace of expansion was slowed for 1993 when two large stores originally scheduled for opening were postponed until 1994 because of construction and environmental-impact slowdowns. In 1993 only one Rack and an outlet store opened. However, plans call for opening ten new large specialty stores between 1994 and 1996 (see Exhibit 4–10). The schedule reflects an emphasis on gaining a critical mass of stores between Washington and New York City and in the upper Midwest. The Dallas store is the first in the Texas (South-central) region. Additional stores will follow. Houston, Austin, and San Antonio are being considered. The company is also actively considering or seeking store sites in Connecticut and the Atlanta, Boston, Phoenix, Detroit, Las Vegas, and Denver areas. Nordstrom particularly likes to enter areas where competitors are not very profitable and where it can woo previously neglected customer segments with its outstanding service.

The growth of off-price clothing sales at 15 percent recently compared to 6 percent for general merchandise has prompted Nordstrom to enter that market on an experimental basis. Nordstrom planned to try two different cut-price discount store concepts specifically to cater to the low-priced, branded-goods market. One of these trial stores, the Last Chance outlet store, is similar to the Rack discount stores but carries non-Nordstrom goods. The second discount-type store was to bear the Nordstrom name and open in Philadelphia in 1993. This Nordstrom Factory Direct outlet store was to offer quality Nordstrom-label merchandise.

Prepare a strategic plan for Nordstrom as it enters the mid-1990s. Include specific recommendations for growth and improved efficiency. Do you feel Nordstrom should

EXHIBIT 4-10 Planned Additions to Large Specialty Store Chain

LOCATION	YEAR
Annapolis Mall, MD	1994
Circle Centre Mall, Indianapolis, IN	1994
Old Orchard Mall, Skokie, IL	1994
Santa Anita Mall, Arcadia, CA	1994
Washington Square, Portland, OR	1994
White Plains (Westchester Co.), NY	1994
Dallas Galleria, TX	1995
Mall at Short Hills, NJ	1995
Woodfield Mall, Schaumburg, IL	1995
King of Prussia Plaza, PA	1996

Source: Nordstrom *Annual Report*, 1992.

consider offering a catalog with women's apparel, accessories, and shoes? What rate of expansion would you recommend for Nordstrom Factory Direct stores Last Chance stores, Nordstrom Rack stores, as well as the mainstream Nordstrom stores? Is the Nordstrom organizational strategy effective?

NOTES

1. This brief history of Nordstrom, Inc., draws heavily on the Nordstrom 1987 *Report*, pp. 5–12.
2. "Nordstrom's Expansion Blitz," *Chain Store Age Executive*, December 1988, pp. 49–50, 53.
3. Jan Shaw, "Executives Catch Nordstrom Fever in Opening Week," *San Francisco Business Times*, October 10, 1988, p. 10.
4. Richard W. Stevenson, "Watch Out Macy's, Here Comes Nordstrom," *New York Times Magazine*, August 27, 1989, p. 35.
5. Robert Sharoff, "Chicago Seen as Good Move for Nordstrom," *Daily News Record*, January 6, 1989, pp. 2, 11.
6. "Nordstrom's Gang of Four," *Business Week*, June 15, 1992, pp. 122–123.
7. Stevenson, "Watch Out Macy's," p. 39.

8. Melinda Wilson, "Upscale Nordstrom's May Land in Detroit," *Crain's Detroit Business*, May 23, 1989.
9. Pat Baldwin, "You Can Get Satisfaction: Nationwide Survey Ranks Nordstrom's No. 1," *Dallas Morning News*, January 9, 1993, p. 2F.
10. "Nordstrom Labor Suit is Settled," *Los Angeles Times*, January 12, 1993, pp. D1 and 2.
11. Debra Prinzing, "Nordstrom and Minorities," *Puget Sound Business Journal*, May 29, 1992, p. 12.
12. "Nordstrom Receives Easter Seal Award for Innovative Catalogs," *PR Newswire*, September 23, 1992.
13. Prinzing, "Nordstrom and Minorities," p. 12.
14. *Standard and Poor's Industry Surveys*, January 1993, p. R81.
15. "Nordstrom's Expansion Blitz," p. 50.

EXHIBIT 4-11 Consolidated Statements of Shareholders' Equity (Dollars in thousands except per share amounts)

Year ended January 31,	1993	1992	1991
Common Stock			
Authorized 250,000,000 shares; issued and outstanding 81,974,797, 81,844,227 and 81,737,910 shares			
Balance at beginning of year	$ 153,055	$150,699	$148,857
Issuance of common stock	2,384	2,356	1,842
Balance at end of year	155,439	153,055	150,699
Retained Earnings			
Balance at beginning of year	786,176	675,711	584,393
Net earnings	136,619	135,815	115,816
Cash dividends paid ($.32, $.31 and $.30 per share)	(26,203)	(25,350)	(24,498)
Balance at end of year	896,592	786,176	675,711
Total shareholders' equity	$1,052,031	$939,231	$826,410

Source: Nordstrom *Annual Report*, 1992.

EXHIBIT 4-12 Consolidated Statements of Cash Flows (Dollars in thousands)

Year ended January 31,	1993	1992	1991
Operating Activities			
Net earnings	$136,619	$135,815	$115,816
Adjustments to reconcile net earnings to net cash provided by operating activities:			
Depreciation and amortization	102,763	96,034	85,615
Change in:			
Accounts receivable, net	5,029	(32,719)	(39,234)
Merchandise inventories	(30,107)	(58,288)	(28,368)
Prepaid expenses	(2,643)	(6,263)	(20,018)
Accounts payable	3,744	12,166	8,928
Accrued salaries, wages and taxes	12,236	17,095	6,090
Accrued expenses	(600)	(2,927)	5,588
Income tax liabilities	8,586	(6,926)	13,710
Net cash provided by operating activities	235,627	153,987	148,127
Investing Activities			
Additions to property, buildings and equipment, net	(69,982)	(145,761)	(199,407)
Other, net	(1,870)	(1,393)	(1,277)
Net cash used in investing activities	(71,852)	(147,154)	(200,684)
Financing Activities			
(Decrease) increase in notes payable	(96,416)	(14,771)	46,933
Principal payments on long-term debt	(29,055)	(85,647)	(79,240)
Proceeds from issuance of common stock	2,384	2,356	1,842
Cash dividends paid	(26,203)	(25,350)	(24,498)
Proceeds from issuance of long-term debt, net	—	106,568	99,131
Net cash (used in) provided by financing activities	(149,290)	(16,844)	44,168
Net increase (decrease) in cash and cash equivalents	14,485	(10,011)	(8,389)
Cash and cash equivalents at beginning of year	14,651	24,662	33,051
Cash and cash equivalents at end of year	$ 29,136	$ 14,651	$ 24,662

Source: Nordstrom *Annual Report,* 1992.

WAL★MART STORES, INC—1994

Headquartered in Bentonville, Arkansas, Wal★Mart (501—273-4000) does not have a formal mission statement. When asked about Wal★Mart's lack of a mission, Public Relations Coordinator Kim Ellis recently replied: "We believe that our customers are most interested in other aspects of our business, and we are focused on meeting their basic consumer needs. If in fact we did have a formal mission statement, it would be something like this: 'to provide quality products at an everyday low price and with extended customer service . . . always.' "

Hawaii, Rhode Island, and Washington each received its first Wal★Mart store in 1993. Only two other states, Alaska and Vermont, do not yet have a Wal★Mart. Some towns do not want a Wal★Mart, such as Greenfield, Massachusetts, which rejected a proposed store in October 1993. The town of 18,000 was afraid a Wal★Mart outside of town would destroy downtown.

Wal★Mart has not yet entered foreign countries. With the exception of Mexico. David Glass, President and CEO of Wal★Mart, plans continued rapid expansion of the company. The major question facing Wal★Mart is where to expand and at what rate.

Wal★Mart is composed of four major divisions: Sam's Club, Wal★Mart Stores, Wal★Mart Supercenters, and McLane & Western Merchandisers. Forty-eight new Sam's Clubs were opened in fiscal year 1993 while 40 other Sam's were remodeled. Wal★Mart opened 161 new Wal★Mart stores in fiscal 1993 and remodeled another 170 stores. Wal★Mart is a company on the move.

McLane & Western, Wal★Mart's specialty distribution subsidiary, experienced record sales and earnings in 1993. McLane serves over 30,000 convenience stores and independent grocers. McLane's sales increased 16 percent to nearly $3 million in fiscal 1993. McLane recently acquired two distribution and food-processing facilities of The Southland Corporation, enhancing McLane's nationwide distribution network. McLane has entered into a service agreement with Southland that opens up a number of new supply opportunities with convenience stores across the United States. Clarksville, Arkansas, is the home of McLane's first full-line grocery distribution center. This 705,000-square-foot center opened in 1993 and serves Wal★Mart Supercenters. A second center recently open in Temple, Texas.

HISTORY

No word better describes Wal★Mart than *growth*. Wal★Mart Stores, Inc. began as a small-town variety store business in 1945, when Sam Walton opened his first Ben Franklin franchises in Newport, Arkansas. Based in rural Bentonville, Arkansas, Walton, his wife Helen, and his brother Bud operated the nation's most successful Ben Franklin franchises. "We were a small chain," said Walton of his 16-store operation. "Things were running so smoothly we even had time for our families." What more could a man want? A great deal, as it turned out.

Walton could see that the variety store was gradually dying because supermarkets and discounters were developing. Far from being secure, Walton knew that he was under siege. He decided to counterattack. He first tried to convince the top management of Ben Franklin to enter discounting. After their refusal, Walton made a quick trip around the country in search of ideas. He then began opening his own discount stores in small Arkansas towns like Bentonville and Rogers.

The company opened its first discount department store (Wal★Mart) in November 1962. The early stores has bare tile floors and pipe racks. Wal★Mart did not begin to revamp its image significantly until the mid-1970's and growth in the early years was slow. However, once the company went public in 1970, sales began to increase rapidly. If one had purchased 100 shares of the stock in 1970, they would have been worth $350,000 in 1985.

Such retailers as Target, Venture, and Kmart provided the examples that Wal★Mart sought to emulate in its growth. The old Wal★Mart store colors, dark blue and white (too harsh), were dumped in favor of a three-tone combination of light beige, soft blue, and burnt orange. Carpeting, which had long been discarded on apparel sales floors, was put back. New racks were put into use that displayed the entire garment instead of only an edge.

Wal★Mart began to expand by taking over falling chains and "Waltonizing" them. In July 1981 Walton picked up ailing Kuhn's Big-K stores—one warehouse and 92 locations—in effect acquiring cheap leases at a discount price. Wal★Mart assumed $19 million in debt and issued $7.5 million worth of preferred stock. Now Kuhn's has a new management team and $60 million in cash for a major facelift. Profits may pour in, as they did after Wal★Mart's only previous acquisition, the 1977 purchase of Mohr Value Stores. "We fixed them up and retrained the people, and now they're our best group," said Walton.

In 1987 Wal★Mart implemented two new concepts: hypermarkets, 200,000-square-foot stores that sell everything including food, and supercenters, scaled-down supermarkets. Also in 1987 Walton named David Glass as the new chief executive officer (CEO) while he remained chairman of the board.

In 1990 Wal★Mart completed the acquisition of 14 centers of McLane Company, a national distribution system in 11 states providing over 12,500 types of grocery and nongrocery products. Also in 1990 Wal★Mart sold its 14 Dot Discount Drug Stores. Sam's Clubs, in 1991, merged the twenty-eight wholesale clubs of The Whole Club, Inc., of Indianapolis, Indiana into its operations.

At the end of its 1992 fiscal year (January 31, 1993), Wal★Mart had 1,880 discount stores (including 30 supercenter stores) in 45 states and Puerto Rico, 148 Sam's Wholesale Clubs in 41 states, 3 hypermarkets, 14 McLane's distribution centers, and 13 distribution centers (see Exhibit 5–1).

OPERATIONS

Most of the 1,880 Wal★Mart stores are located in towns of 5,000 to 25,000. There are still smaller stores for communities of less than 5,000. Wal★Mart's expense structure, measured as a percentage of sales, continues to be among the lowest in the industry. Although Walton watched expenses, he rewarded sales managers handsomely. Sales figures are available to every employee at Wal★Mart. Monthly figures for each department are ranked and made available throughout the organization. Employees who do better than average get rewarded with raises, bonuses, and a pat on the back. Poor performers are only rarely fired, although demotions are possible.

All employees (called "associates") have a stake in the financial performance of the company. Store managers earn as much as $100,000 to $150,000 per year. Even part-time clerks qualify for profit sharing and stock-purchase plans. Millionaires among Wal★Mart's middle managers are not uncommon. Executives frequently solicit ideas for improving the organization from employees and often put them into use.

	WALMART	SAM'S
Alabama	74	7
Arizona	28	4
Arkansas	77	3
California	43	3
Colorado	32	3
Connecticut	1	1
Delaware	2	1
Florida	122	23
Georgia	83	9
Idaho	5	1
Illinois	97	18
Indiana	65	12
Iowa	43	3
Kansas	43	3
Kentucky	66	4
Louisiana	74	9
Maine	6	2
Maryland	7	2
Massachusettes	2	2
Michigan	22	6
Minnesota	27	7
Mississippi	57	3
Missouri	105	9
Montana	2	1
Nebraska	16	1
Nevada	5	2
New Hampshire	7	2
New Jersey	3	2
New Mexico	19	1
New York	16	3
North Carolina	74	8
North Dakota	8	2
Ohio	42	16
Oklahoma	81	6
Oregon	12	
Pennsylvania	26	5
Puerto Rico	2	
South Carolina	49	5
South Dakota	8	1
Tennessee	86	7
Texas	229	44
Utah	11	
Virginia	37	6
West Virginia	10	3
Wisconsin	47	9
Wyoming	9	
	1,880	256

Puerto Rico

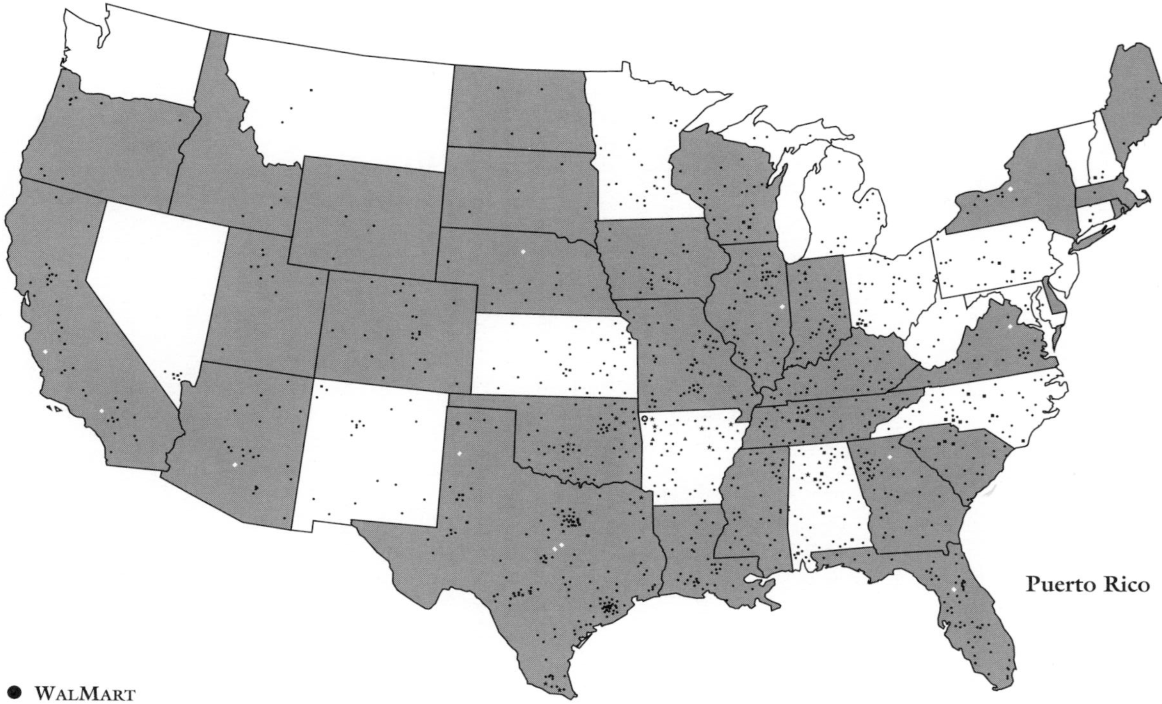

● WALMART
■ SAM'S CLUB
▲ DISTRIBUTION CENTER
★ SUPER CENTER
✪ WALMART HOME OFFICE AND THREE WALMART DISTRIBUTION CENTERS
◆ MCLANE DISTRIBUTION CENTER
✳ WESTERN MERCHANDISERS HOME OFFICE

EXHIBIT 5-1 Trade Territory Map

With Wal★Mart stock selling at 20 to 30 times earnings—an almost incredible price—Walton presided over a sizable fortune before his death in 1992. Wal★Mart stock is still 39 percent held by the Walton family. Family holdings are worth nearly $8 billion.

Continuing a Walton tradition, Wal★Mart invites over 100 analysts and institutional investors to the fieldhouse at the University of Arkansas for its annual meeting in mid-June. During the day-and-a-half session, investors meet top executives, as well as Wal★Mart district managers, buyers, and 200,000 hourly salespeople. Investors see a give-and-take meeting between buyers and district managers.

Wal★Mart unveiled in mid-1993 its first environmental demonstration store, a 121,294-square-foot facility in Lawrence, Kansas. This store is designed so that a second floor could be added if Wal★Mart vacates to allow conversion to apartments. The store is exceptionally energy efficient but costs 20 percent more than the average Wal★Mart, which costs about $2.4 million or $20 a square foot. The environmental store features on-site recycling, native plants that make up the landscaping, and solar-powered lights. Planning for this store began in 1990 when Hillary Rodham Clinton served on Wal★Mart's board of directors.

EMPLOYEE BENEFITS

Wal★Mart management takes pride in the ongoing development of its people. Training is seen as critical to outstanding performance, and new programs are implemented often in all areas of the company. The combination of grass-roots meetings, the open-door policy, videos, printed material, classroom and home study, year-end management meetings, and on-the -job training has enabled employees to prepare themselves for advancement and added responsibilities.

Wal★Mart managers stay current with new developments and needed changes. Executives spend one week per year in hourly jobs in various stores. Walton himself once traveled at least three days per week, visiting competitors' stores and attending the opening of new stores, leading the Wal★Mart cheer, "Give me a W, give me a A . . ."

Wal★Mart encourages employee stock purchases; about 8 percent of Wal★Mart stock is owned by employees. Under the Stock Purchase Plan, stock may be bought by two different methods. First, an amount is deducted from each employee's check with a maximum of $62.50 per check. An additional 15 percent of the amount deducted is contributed by Wal★Mart (up to $1,800 of annual stock purchases). Second, a lump-sum purchase is allowed in April up to $1,500 with an additional 15 percent added by the company. Wal★Mart also as of January 31, 1993 offered an associate stock ownership plan with approximately 4,000 management associates granted stock options.

Wal★Mart has a corporate profit-sharing plan with contributions of $98,327,000 as of January 31, 1991, $129,653,000 in 1992, and $166,035,000 in 1993. The purposes of the profit-sharing plan is to furnish an incentive for increased efficiency, to provide progressive recognition of service, and to encourage careers with the company by Wal★Mart associates. This is a trustee-administered plan, which means the company's contributions are made only out of net profits and are held by a trustee. The company from time to time contributes 10 percent of net profits to the trust.

Company contributions can be withdrawn only on termination. If employment with the company is terminated because of retirement, death, or permanent disability, the company contribution if fully vested, meaning the entire amount is nonforfeitable. If termination of employment occurs for any other reason, the amount that is nonforfeitable depends on the number of years of service with the company. After completion of the third year of service with the company, 20 percent of each participant's account is nonforfeitable for each subsequent year of service. After seven years of service, a participant's account is 100 percent vested.

Walton was admittedly old-fashioned in many respects. Wal★Mart store policies reflect many of his values. For example, store policies forbid employees from dating other employees without prior approval of the executive committee. Also, women are rare in management positions. Annual manager meetings include sessions for wives to speak out on the problems of living with a Wal★Mart manager. No women were in the ranks of Wal★Mart's top management. Walton also resisted placing women on the board of directors. Only 12 women have made it to the ranks of buyers (12 percent of all buyers). Wal★Mart is an EEOC/AA employer but has managed to get away with "apparent" discriminatory policies, perhaps because most Wal★Marts are located in small rural towns in the Sun Belt states.

MARKETING

The discount retailing business is seasonal to a certain extent. Generally, the highest volume of sales and net income occurs in the fourth fiscal quarter and the lowest volume occurs during the first fiscal quarter. Wal★Mart draws customers into the store by radio and television advertising, monthly circulars, and weekly newspaper adds. Television advertising is used to convey an image of everyday low prices and quality merchandise. Radio is used to a lesser degree to promote specific products that are usually in high demand. Newspaper and monthly circulars are major contributors to the program, emphasizing deeply discounted items, and are effective at luring customers into the store.

Efforts are also made to discount corporate overhead. Visitors often mistake corporate headquarters for a warehouse owing to its limited decorating and "show." Wal★Mart executives share hotel rooms when traveling to reduce expenses. The company avoids spending money on consultants and marketing experts. Instead, decisions are made based on intuitive judgments of managers and employees and on the assessment of strategies of other retail chains.

Wal★Mart advertises a "Buy American" policy in an effort to keep production at home. Consequently, Wal★Mart buyers are constantly seeking vendors in grass-roots America. For example, Wal★Mart dropped Fuji film for 3M. In addition, Wal★Mart censors products that are not conservative. The company has banned recordings and removed magazines based on lyrics and graphics, as well as stopped marketing teen rock magazines.

GROWTH IN DISTRIBUTION CENTERS

During the 1993 fiscal year, close to 77 percent of Wal★Mart's merchandise passed through one of 22 distribution warehouses, an amount greater than Kmart's or Sear's. Wal★Mart Distribution Centers are located as follows: three in Bentonville, Arkansas; two each in Searcy, Arkansas, and Laurens, South Carolina; and one each in Ft. Smith, Arkansas; Palestine, Texas; Cullman, Alabama; Mt. Pleasant, Iowa; Brookhaven, Mississippi; Douglas, Georgia; Plainview, Texas; New Braunfels, Texas; Loveland, Colorado; Seymour, Indiana; Poterville, California; Sutherland, Virginia; Greencastle, Indiana; Brooksville, Florida; and Grove City, Ohio. Wal★Mart has a total of 20,381,727 square feet of storage space. Sam's, unlike Wal★Mart stores, receive the majority of its merchandise by direct shipments from suppliers, rather than from the company's distribution centers.

Wal★Mart maintains warehouse space in Oklahoma, Arkansas, and Georgia that is utilized for seasonal merchandise. The McLane distribution centers primarily buy, sell, and distribute merchandise to the convenience store industry with an aggregate square footage of 4,213,430 square feet, including two distribution centers in San Bernardino, California, and Fredericksburg, Virginia.

Wal★Mart's distribution operations were highly automated. Terminals at each store wire merchandise requests to warehouses, which in turn either ship immediately or place a reorder. Wal★Mart computers are linked directly with over 200 vendors, making deliveries faster. Wal★Mart has one of the world's largest private satellite communication systems to control distribution. In addition, Wal★Mart has installed point-of-sale bar-code scanning in all of its stores.

Wal★Mart owns a fleet of truck-tractors that can deliver goods to any store in 38 to 48 hours from the time the order is placed. After trucks drop off merchandise, they frequently pick up merchandise from manufacturers on the way back to the distribution center. This back-haul rate averages over 60 percent and is yet another way Wal★Mart cuts costs.

MERCHANDISE

Wal★Mart stores generally have 36 departments and offer a wide variety of merchandise, including apparel for women, girls, men, boys, and infants. Each store also carries curtains, fabrics and notions, shoes, housewares, hardware, electronics, home supplies, sporting goods, toys, cameras and supplies, health and beauty aids, pharmaceuticals, and jewelry. Nationally advertised merchandise accounts for a majority of sales of the stores. Wal★Mart has begun marketing limited lines of merchandise under the brand name "Sams's American Choice." The merchandise is carefully selected to insure quality and must be made in the United States.

During the fiscal year ended January 31, 1993, sales at Wal★Mart stores by product category were as follows:

CATEGORY	PERCENTAGE OF SALES
Softgoods	28%
Hardgoods (hardware, housewares, auto supplies and small appliances)	26
Stationery and candy	11
Sporting goods and toys	10
Health and beauty aids	8
Pharmaceuticals	7
Gifts, records, and electronics	6
Shoes	2
Jewelry	2
	100%

Sales in pharmaceuticals above are a combination of owned and licensed departments. These pharmaceutical percentages includes sales of licensed departments, but Wal★Mart records as revenues only rentals received from such departments.

Sam's offers bulk displays of name-brand hardgood merchandise, some softgoods, and institutional-size grocery items. Each Sam's also carries jewelry, sporting goods, toys, tires, stationery, and books. During fiscal year 1992 Sam's began experimenting with fresh bakery, meat, and produce departments. Sam's has 131 clubs with fresh-food departments.

McLane's offers a wide variety of grocery and nongrocery products, including perishable and nonperishable items. The nongrocery products consist primarily of tobacco products, hardgood merchandise, health and beauty aids, toys, and stationery. Western Merchandisers offers a wide variety of prerecorded music, videos, and books. Both McLane and Western Merchandisers are wholesale distributors that sell their merchandise to a variety of retailers, including the Wal★Mart stores and Sam's Clubs.

OPERATIONS

Except for extended hours during certain holiday seasons, most Wal★Mart stores are open from 9:00 a.m. to 9:00 p.m. six days a week, and from 12:30 p.m. to 5:30 p.m. on Sundays, with the remainder of the stores closed on Sunday. Some Wal★Mart stores and most of the Supercenter stores are open 24 hours each day. Wal★Mart tries to meet or undersell local competition but maintains uniform prices, except where lower prices are necessary to meet local competition. Wal★Mart stores maintain a "satisfaction guaranteed" program to promote customer goodwill and acceptance.

Sam's are membership only, cash-and-carry operations. However, a financial service credit-card program (Discover Card) is available in all clubs. Qualified members include businesses and those individuals who are members of certain qualifying organizations, such as government and state employees and credit union members. Both business and individual members have an annual membership fee of $25 for the primary membership card.

Operating hours vary among Sam's, but generally are Monday through Friday from 10:00 a.m. to 8:30 p.m. Most Sam's are open on the weekend from 9:30 a.m. to 7:00 p.m. on Saturday and 12:00 noon to 6:00 p.m. on Sunday. Sam's attempts to maximize sales volume and inventory turnover while minimizing expenses.

STRATEGIES TODAY

Europe is nearly void of mass discount retailing companies, and analysts view Europe as a goldmine for Wal★Mart or Kmart. Thousands of small European retailers are worried. In Germany and France, for example, established merchants are fiercely opposing proposals to legalize late-evening and seven-day-a-week retailing, the hallmark of American discounters. In England, small retailers are trying to persuade the government to limit the spread of big discounters. Napoleon once called England "a nation of shopkeepers" and this description still applies to most of Europe. "It's like America in the 1950s" says Moulton of Lostco Wholesale Corporation in Seattle.

Wal★Mart recently entered into a joint venture interest with CIFRA, Mexico's largest retailer. The joint venture operates three Club Aurreras, four Bodegas discount stores, and one Aurrera combination store. This joint venture plans to add a large number of units during the coming years.

In fiscal 1994 Wal★Mart plans to open approximately 150 new Wal★Mart stores and 65 Sam's Clubs. The company also plans to expand or relocate approximately 100 older Wal★Mart stores and 25 Sam's Clubs, including relocation or expansion of 40 Wal★Mart Supercenters. Also planned is the construction of two new full-line distribution centers, two grocery distribution centers, a distribution center to process clothing, and a storage center.

1. What strategies would you recommend to CEO David Glass, as Wal★Mart has become the largest retailing firm in the United States?
2. Should Wal★Mart get a foothold in Europe before competitors such as Kmart seize the initiative?
3. Should Wal★Mart expand further in Mexico? expand in the United States? expand into Canada?
4. Should Wal★Mart make further acquisitions?

EXHIBIT 5-2 Ten-Year Financial Summary (dollar amounts in thousands except per share data)

WAL★MART STORES, INC. AND SUBSIDIARIES	1993	1992
OPERATING RESULTS		
Net sales	$55,483,771	$43,886,902
Net sales increase	26%	35%
Comparative store sales increase	11%	10%
Rentals from licensed departments and other income-net	500,793	402,521
Cost of sales	44,174,685	34,786,119
Operating, selling, and general and administrative expenses	8,320,842	6,684,304
Interest costs:		
Debt	142,649	113,305
Capital leases	180,049	152,558
Provision for federal and state income taxes	1,171,545	944,661
Net income	1,994,794	1,608,476
Per share of common stock[a]		
Net income	.87	.70
Dividends	.11	.09
FINANCIAL POSITION		
Current assets	$10,197,590	$ 8,575,423
Inventories at replacement cost	9,779,981	7,856,871
Less LIFO reserve	511,672	472,572
Inventories at LIFO cost	9,268,309	7,384,299
Net property, plant, equipment and capital leases	9,792,881	6,433,801
Total assets	20,565,087	15,443,389
Current liabilities	6,754,286	5,003,775
Long-term debt	3,072,835	1,722,022
Long-term obligations under capital leases	1,772,152	1,555,875
Preferred stock with mandatory redemption provisions	—	—
Shareholders' equity	8,759,180	6,989,710
FINANCIAL RATIOS		
Current ratio	1.5	1.7
Inventories/working capital	2.7	2.1
Return on assets	12.9%	14.1%
Return on shareholders'equity[b]	28.5%	30.0%
OTHER YEAR-END DATA		
Number of Wal*Mart Stores	1,880	1,720
Number of Sam's Clubs	256	208
Average Wal*Mart Store size	81,200	75,000
Number of Associates	434,000	371,000
Number of Shareholders	180,584	150,242

[a]Restated to reflect the two-for-one stock split announced January 22, 1993.

[b]On beginning of year balances.

Source:Wal*Mart *Annual Report*, 1993.

EXHIBIT 5-3 Consolidated Statements of Income (amounts in thousands except per share data)

WAL★MART STORES, INC. AND SUBSIDIARIES	FISCAL YEAR ENDED JANUARY 31		
	1993	**1992**	**1991**
REVENUES			
Net sales	$55,483,771	$43,886,902	$32,601,594
Rentals from licensed departments	36,035	28,659	22,362
Other income-net	464,758	373,862	239,452
	55,984,564	44,289,423	32,863,408
COSTS AND EXPENSES			
Cost of sales	44,174,685	34,786,119	25,499,834
Operating, selling, and general and administrative expenses	8,320,842	6,684,304	5,152,178
INTEREST COSTS			
Debt	142,649	113,305	42,716
Capital leases	180,049	152,558	125,920
	52,818,225	41,736,286	30,820,648
INCOME BEFORE INCOME TAXES			
	3,166,339	2,553,137	2,042,760
PROVISION FOR FEDERAL AND STATE INCOME TAXES			
Current	1,136,918	906,183	737,020
Deferred	34,627	38,478	14,716
	1,171,545	944,661	751,736
Net income	$ 1,994,794	$ 1,608,476	$ 1,291,024
Net Income per share	$ .87	$ .70	$ .57

Source: Wal*Mart *Annual Report*, 1993.

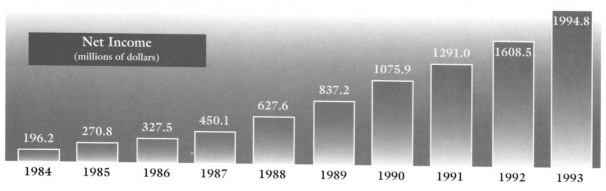

Net Income (millions of dollars)

1984	1985	1986	1987	1988	1989	1990	1991	1992	1993
196.2	270.8	327.5	450.1	627.6	837.2	1075.9	1291.0	1608.5	1994.8

EXHIBIT 5-4 Consolidated Balance Sheets (amounts in thousands)

WAL★MART STORES, INC. AND SUBSIDIARIES	JANUARY 31	
	1993	1992
ASSETS		
CURRENT ASSETS:		
Cash and cash equivalents	$12,363	$30,649
Receivables	524,555	418,867
Recoverable costs for sale/leaseback	312,016	681,387
Inventories:		
At replacement cost	9,779,981	7,856,871
Less LIFO reserve	511,672	472,572
LIFO	9,268,309	7,384,299
Prepaid expenses	80,347	60,221
Total Current Assets	10,197,590	8,575,423
PROPERTY, PLANT, AND EQUIPMENT, AT COST:		
Land	1,692,510	1,077,658
Buildings and improvements	4,641,009	2,569,095
Fixtures and equipment	3,417,230	2,683,481
Transportation equipment	111,151	86,491
	9,861,900	6,416,725
Less accumulated depreciation	1,607,623	1,338,151
Net property, plant, and equipment	8,254,277	5,078,574
Property under capital leases	1,986,104	1,724,123
Less accumulated amortization	447,500	368,896
Net property under capital leases	1,538,604	1,355,227
OTHER ASSETS AND DEFERRED CHARGES	574,616	434,165
Total Assets	$20,565,087	$15,443,389
LIABILITIES AND SHAREHOLDERS' EQUITY		
CURRENT LIABILITIES:		
Commercial paper	$ 1,588,825	$453,964
Accounts payable	3,873,331	3,453,529
Accrued liabilities	1,042,108	829,381
Accrued federal and state income taxes	190,620	226,828
Long–term debt due within one year	13,849	5,156
Obligations under capital leases due within one year	45,553	34,917
Total Current Liabilities	6,754,286	5,003,775
LONG–TERM DEBT	3,072,835	1,722,022
LONG–TERM OBLIGATIONS UNDER CAPITAL LEASES	1,772,152	1,555,875
DEFERRED INCOME TAXES	206,634	172,007

TABLE 5-4 *Continued*

WAL★MART STORES, INC. AND SUBSIDIARIES (AMOUNT IN THOUSANDS)	JANUARY 31	
	1993	1992
SHAREHOLDERS' EQUITY:		
Preferred stock ($.10 par value; 100,000 shares authorized, none issued)		
Common stock ($.10 par value; 5,500,000 shares authorized, 2,299,638 and 1,149,028 issued and outstanding in 1993 and 1992 respectively)	229,964	114,903
Capital in excess of par value	526,647	625,669
Retained earnings	8,002,569	6,249,138
Total Shareholders' Equity	8,759,180	6,989,710
Total Liabilities and Shareholders' Equity	$20,565,087	$15,443,389

Source: Wal★Mart *Annual Report*, 1993.

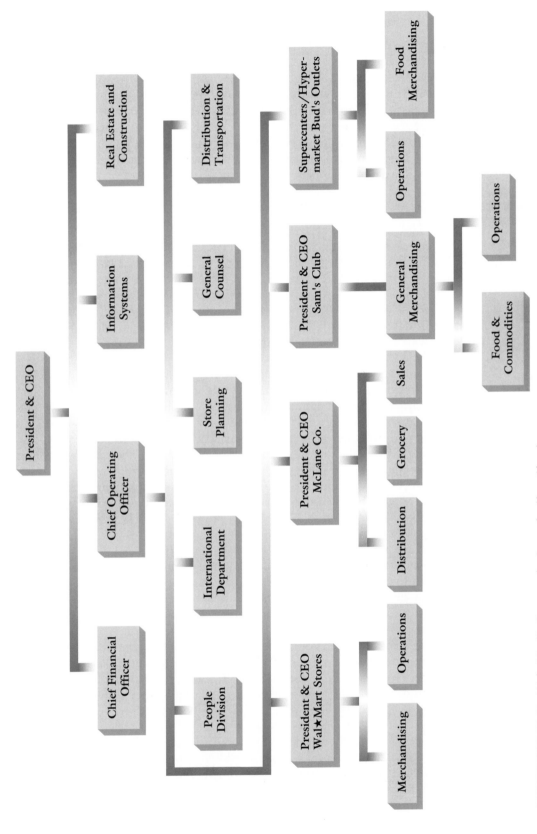

EXHIBIT 5-5 Wal★Mart's Corporate Organization Chart

NSP CORPORATE GRAPHICS—1993

NSP Corporate Graphics (205-821-0050) is based in Auburn, Alabama. In his third year as president of NSP Corporate Graphics (NSP), Michael Plumb has seen annual sales increase from $700,000 in 1982 to approximately $5.5 million in 1992. NSP's sales are on their way to a record $6 million in 1993. Product turnaround time has been cut drastically and NSP has become a leader in the screen-printing industry. Yet, numerous competitors are taking market share from NSP and are trying to put Plumb's business out of business.

NSP'S HISTORY

C. H. "Babe" McGehee and Tom Edwards became friends in the fifth grade after McGehee's family moved to the small town of Auburn, Alabama. As McGehee recalled, the early days were trying. As a "preacher's kid," he had to fight all of the boys in his class just to be accepted. After he beat up Edwards, one of the larger boys in his class, he never had further problems. Instead, the two became best friends, a friendship that was to last a lifetime. Their friendship grew in college where they pledged with the same fraternity at Auburn University. They lost touch for a while during World War II but were reunited later.

McGehee was working in construction in Mobile, Alabama, and Edwards was back in Auburn building houses with his father. Edwards convinced McGehee to join him in the construction business in Auburn. A very enterprising team, they were always in search of new opportunities. Edwards found a plant for sale that produced wooden ammunition boxes for use in the Korean conflict. The two partners bought the plant and moved it from Columbus, Missouri, to Auburn in 1952. The end of the conflict brought a significant decrease in the demand for ammunition boxes, so the partners modified the business to produce returnable wooden soft-drink containers. By 1962, the returnable glass bottle business was losing ground, and the future for a container company looked grim. When NSP's container plant was closed in 1990, it was the last remaining plant of its type in the United States.

Edwards became interested in the screen-printing business and began looking for viable prospects. Screen printing is an old form of printing on silk. Areas of silk are blocked out to make an impression on material, and ink is deposited through a screen mesh. Photographic and chemical agents are used to screen out color. Screen printing is superior to some other forms of printing because it allows heavier deposits of ink onto a surface and results in a more vibrant, longer-lasting finish.

Edwards identified Dixie Printing in nearby Opelika as their next business opportunity. Screen printing was a natural choice because the company's skill in cutting special angles for wooden soft-drink containers was readily transferred to Dixie Printing's production of plywood shapes for highway traffic signs. After cutting the plywood base, the firm applied the sign front. The partners bought Dixie Printing, convinced the former owner, Jim Crawford, to join them and move their new business to Auburn directly across the street from the container plant. The newly formed firm, National ScreenPrinters (later changed to NSP Corporate Graphics, Inc.), incorporated as a closely held corporation in 1962 with 30,000 shares of stock selling at a par value of $10 per share.

The first meeting of NSP's board of directors was held on February 2, 1962. The company had approximately sixty original stockholders then, primarily from the Auburn/Opelika area. Less than two-thirds of the stock was sold with the rest retained by the company. Within three years, NSP reached its goal of profitability. In 1985, NSP declared its first dividends at $.50 per share.

SUCCESSION OF MANAGEMENT

During the early years, McGehee spent most of his time running the container factory, while Edwards took over the operations of the screen-printing business. While Edwards was overseeing manufacturing, McGehee handled most of the personnel issues. The two occupied a single office at NSP that was equipped with two desks and a manual Royal typewriter.

Edwards was the driving leader of the new corporation. His expertise in machinery and equipment created the spirit of strong manufacturing and commitment to quality for which NSP became recognized. NSP is one of the few companies in the industry that is almost entirely automated, a tribute to the solid foundation established by Edwards. In 1979 Edwards died unexpectedly, and McGehee became president of the firm. A portrait of the two in the lobby of NSP signified Edwards's continued presence in the company.

As president, McGehee was a laissez-faire administrator who believed in the talents and capabilities of his employees and, therefore, did not interfere with their work. McGehee attributed the success of NSP to the theme of one of his favorite sayings: "No amount of planning will replace dumb luck." He admitted that during the 1970s NSP did no strategic planning.

In 1982, Michael Plumb joined NSP as sales manager, working out of his home in Atlanta, Georgia. Plumb had a degree in history from the University of Vermont. His northeastern work ethic was considered by fellow employees to be quite foreign to the NSP style, and he was often described by others as an "aggressive Yankee." Plumb's previous experience and training at 3M, Creatist, and Kux Manufacturing, along with his "slick" appearance, natural gift of gab, and knowledge of the product, made him an accomplished salesman. In 1987 his position was upgraded in title to vice president of sales.

Moving to Auburn, Plumb became a good corporate citizen, a member of Rotary, and an active member, along with his family, in the Presbyterian church. He also became a crisis center telephone volunteer. The crisis center not only taught Plumb to listen effectively (through forty hours of intense training), but also made him more aware of the problems that could be affecting his employees.

In 1989, on his seventieth birthday, McGehee stepped down as president of the corporation but remained involved as chairman of the board of directors. He envisioned another in-house candidate as his heir apparent, but in one of the few instances of disagreement with McGehee, the board of directors chose Plumb who they felt better fit the image they wanted to project as the company's chief executive. The board wanted someone with new visions, someone with a well-rounded background in the screen-printing industry. Plumb best met that need. He had experience in all three levels of screen printing: he sold to screen-printing companies, he worked for an installation company, and he sold screen printing.

In 1992, NSP was ranked in the top 15 percent (in terms of size) of all screen-printing firms in the country. Although still involved in fleet graphics, NSP has expanded its services to include all aspects of corporate graphics, signage, and design.

Michael Plumb. As CEO of NSP, Plumb's management philosophy parallels Alvin Toffler's: "Dare to image the future." Toffler suggested that managers look for "big chances," be willing to work toward specific goals, and dare to differ from conventional wisdom. Plumb believes in this philosophy without taking it to extremes. For example, when he became president of NSP, Plumb surprised employees when he did not move to the largest office but instead stayed in a smaller inner office.

Another of Plumb's personal philosophies is to "do what you do well and do it often." His special talent is sales, so he spends at least one-quarter of his time making new contacts and servicing old accounts, particularly the Federal Express account, and another quarter of his time managing sales. With competition in the industry being so fierce, Plumb spends considerable time on the road. He has his eyes set on obtaining business related to the 1996 Olympics since NSP is located only 100 miles from Atlanta. Plumb also spends time working in the plant because he feels the only way to keep current on the business is to do the job. The remainder of his time is spent in new market development and performing the normal duties of a corporate executive.

Plumb has his own philosophy of Total Quality Management which begins with employee training. He believes that a greater understanding of the total business process by all NSP employees will enhance the overall productivity and competitiveness of the firm. His plans are to train his total workforce to know and appreciate every aspect of the business.

Plumb is considered to be a challenging person, very demanding of his employees. He sets high standards for himself and expects others to have equally high goals for themselves. He is a tried-and-true person and allows no obstacles to stand in the way of his accomplishments. As a result, he seldom takes time to relax. Although he is very family-oriented and concerned about spending quality time with his family, he often finds himself thinking of business during family vacations or other outings. One of his greatest obsessions is a determination to be fair. In both his work and home life, Plumb is careful to look at all situations in terms of the fairness of the outcome.

Plumb keeps NSP's employees fully apprised of the firm's position in the industry. He takes every available moment to update the employees on NSP progress. On one occasion when the city was under a tornado alert and all employees gathered in the basement for safety, Plumb announced the previous quarter's earnings and updated all employees on new accounts. Plumb holds quarterly meetings with all employees. Seldom, if ever, is there a written, preestablished agenda. His meetings are informal and light-hearted, yet he is always in control. Still, he is quick to compliment employees for their part in any financial or productivity improvements or to answer any question pertaining to company operations. His monthly meetings with management personnel are also informal. Although ideas for new ventures surface for discussion, the direction that the company will take is usually predetermined by Plumb.

THE SCREEN-PRINTING INDUSTRY

Large-format screen printing in the United States is about a $750 million industry. In 1990, the two largest competitors—Ariston and Screen Art—merged, which placed the new company in a position of dominance. Despite the merger, the screen-printing industry is primarily comprised of many small to mid-sized firms. Very little capital is required (about $10,000) to get started in screen printing; the industry is, consequently, flooded with mom-and-pop operations. The screen-printing business is largely regionalized, with few national firms.

The fragmented market and steep competition results in characteristically low operating margins and low switching costs to the buyer of screen-printing services. This is compounded by the fact that most larger screen-printing clients use more than one vendor, which makes it difficult for any one company to solely maintain a major corporate account. Competition is so intense that an exclusive account today could be subdivided or retracted tomorrow. Survival in the industry depends on a firm's ability to diversify its business among a large number of companies.

Generally, two types of screen-printing businesses exist: (1) Firms that specialize in fleet and large graphics, and (2) silk-screen shops that concentrate on T-shirts and specialty advertising items, such as coffee cups. NSP is considered an industrial screen printer specializing in fleet graphics. However, NSP is attempting to make the switch to a niche strategy specializing in art and graphics, while still performing screen-printing functions services to existing clients.

Without reliance on the existing fleet graphics business, NSP could not survive. As a company evolving toward specialization in art and graphics, NSP has added advertising agencies to its list of customers. Plumb feels that the technical ability NSP provides can benefit advertising agencies who often contract out graphics and screen printing work.

Fleet Graphics. Fleet graphics is a successful means of corporate exposure. A 1977 study conducted by the American Trucking Association showed that an over-the-road tractor-trailer combination makes 101 visual impressions per mile during daylight hours. Assuming an average annual mileage of 100,000, this totals 10.1 million impressions. The study further measured the visual impact of local delivery vans, for a total of 16 million visual impressions per year. Nighttime use of trucks adds another 37.5 percent to the previous numbers. Statistics show that over two-thirds of motorists favor the use of fleet graphics as a means of advertising.

In response to the positive appeal of fleet graphics, much of the industry has focused on "spicing up" the distribution fleets. One company, Eastern Foods, Inc., changed its trucks and tractors for their Naturally Fresh salad dressings from brown and white with yellow stripes to an elaborately produced rolling billboard of full-color vegetables and salad dressings.

The fleet graphics business is dependent on the truck-trailer market which is considered by some to be in a state of crisis. Trailer manufacturers are cutting capacity, consolidating production into fewer manufacturing plants, and finding ways to create long-term business partnerships with motor-carrier customers. The financial demands on the industry have heightened as a result of leveraged buy-outs on the part of major trailer manufacturers. Typically, the trucking industry has been restrictive in the amount of money companies allocate toward advertising, and this has become more pronounced in recent years. Improvements to the trailer business are dependent on the U.S. economy improving.

Advertising Agencies. Advertising agencies can be classified as international, national, regional, or local. Some agencies have hundreds of employees and service scores of large clients. Saatchi & Saatchi is one of the largest firms and has billings in excess of $11 billion. With increasing frequency, large companies are taking advertising activities inhouse. Some companies are doing a combination of inhouse and agency, while others "farm out" work to independents.

All advertising agencies are not full-service companies. A full-service agency generally employs account representatives, creative people, and media buyers. The firms are generally responsible for developing the creative strategy, analyzing market data, and buying media time. Advertising agencies usually work on a 15 percent commission. Creative boutiques, on the other hand, usually are responsible for writing and creating advertisements, but do not get involved in formulating advertising strategies.

Strategic Planning. Prior to Plumb's arrival, NSP did no formal strategic planning. Planning was always "seat of the pants" or whatever seemed right at the time. For example, the decision to get into interior design graphics came with the addition of a former staff member who had previous experience in the field—no market research was conducted.

Formal planning has been on the horizon for NSP for several years. Prior to 1990, the company's one attempt at formal planning came quite by accident. At a scheduled meeting between key management personnel and a major supplier, the supplier failed to show up. Consequently, the managers found themselves at loose ends and began talking about future directions. On reflection, Plumb believes those were the best two hours they had ever spent. He believes planning is a necessary evil. In 1990, Plumb developed a mission statement and long-term objectives for NSP as presented in Exhibits 6–1 and 6–2, respectively. No strides have been made toward formalized strategic planning since 1990. Of the long-term objectives presented to the management team in 1991, only one objective, "Increase ColorFX" was added to the list and none were removed.

EXHIBIT 6-1 NSP Corporate Graphics, Inc., Mission Statement

NSP will provide our customers with high quality products and service to enhance corporate image. Long-term enduring relationships will be developed with our customers and suppliers. A consistent, caring, and conscientious posture with all our contacts will be maintained through motivated co-owners in our ESOP company. NSPeople will keep a clear focus to provide integrity and responsiveness to our customers. A reasonable profit will be reinvested equally to our shareholders and employees, knowing that NSPeople are the driving force behind our product and service.

EXHIBIT 6-2 NSP Corporate Graphics, Inc., Long-term Objectives

1. Establish market niches(s), areas of diversification
2. Strive for 100 percent UV printing, if possible
3. Establish the art department as a profit center
4. Expand the CAMGraphix (computerized graphics)
5. Expand ColorFX
6. Purchase a new die cut machine or a TA 41 machine
7. Determine the feasibility of establishing an in-house advertising agency
8. Provide a computer station for each artist
9. Perfect the accounting system to trace costs
10. Establish a positive working environment
11. Examine the employee benefits program

Source: NSP Corporate Graphics, Inc.

In 1991, Plumb decided NSP would be everything to 300 top customers. "Everything" meant doing all corporate graphics for the client—from letterhead design to interior signage to fleet graphics. There was no magic associated with the number 300, no break-even point, no market research. Plumb's only rationale for this number was to take an average of his 5.5 salespeople (including himself) and multiply that times servicing the needs of about fifty to sixty accounts each.

Today, about 30 industrial accounts are the mainstay of NSP's revenue. The company services about 200 other accounts. While his plan of 300 has not been fully realized, Plumb feels NSP will meet this goal. He has been successful in spreading revenue dependence over more than one or two firms. A few years previously, Federal Express was NSP's primary account. NSP's new focus, however, is to capitalize on the art and graphics portion of their business.

The Federal Express Account. When Plumb joined NSP, he brought the Federal Express account with him, having first called on them in 1978. After fifteen years of a close working relationship, which is uncharacteristic of the industry, Plumb still feels the need to nurture Federal Express as if the company were a new account. Federal Express comprises 18 percent of NSP's annual business, although that percentage may increase in 1993. Of the six staff artists at NSP, one is fully devoted to the Federal Express account. NSP has received Federal Express's fleet graphics business and its entire corporate identity program.

Organizational Structure. The organizational structure of NSP is depicted in Exhibit 6–3. McGehee serves as chairman of the board and Plumb is president. Jim Davis is plant manager. Davis has been with NSP about sixteen years. Betty Stallings, comptroller and business manager, has been with NSP about fourteen years.

Neil McGee, who joined NSP in 1989 as a member of the art department, serves as marketing manager. Ken Roberts also joined NSP in 1990 as sales manager. A position of multi-media director was added to the staff in August 1993 and is held by Patrick Smith.

Bobbie Griggs came to the job of personnel specialist from the production area with no previous personnel experience. In selecting someone for this position, Plumb wanted a person with intelligence and initiative, and Bobbie seemed to fit that description. She has been with the company for approximately six years.

Employee Stock Ownership Program (ESOP). Getting employees involved in the profitability of the company was an idea that McGehee and Edwards shared from the early days of operation. In early 1981, McGehee became interested in a simplified employee pension (SEP) plan and operationalized it in 1983, the same year the company's net profit first broke $100,000, and dividends of $2 per share were declared. McGehee was not completely satisfied with the SEP because he wanted employees to feel more a part of the company. He soon became convinced that an ESOP was what his company needed. If employees were given the opportunity to buy into their own company, he believed they would take a greater interest in the business and the company would benefit. In 1985 NSP became one of the first small firms in America to bring the ESOP concept to its employees.

NSP is about 30 percent employee owned. No stockholder has a controlling interest in NSP. McGehee is the largest stockholder and maintains about 12 percent of the stock. This is apparent by the slogan on each employees' name tag: "If it has to be, it is up to me." The importance of the ESOP program is even proudly displayed in all

EXHIBIT 6-3 Organizational Structure of NSP Corporate Graphics, Inc.

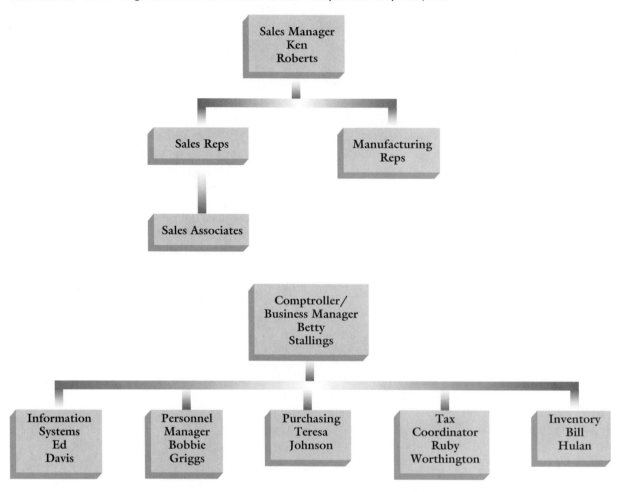

advertisements about NSP. Under terms of the plan, employees become eligible to participate after reaching age eighteen and after completing twelve consecutive months of employment. Contributions to the plan are based on a percentage of the salaries of participants, and the rate is set by the board of directors annually. Vesting in the program takes five years.

Employees annually receive a record of their ownership, and each year a distribution is made, even in years when NSP does poorly. McGehee feels the ESOP encourages quality and service because it motivates employees to work harder. As a result, craftsmanship, delivery, and installation are superior because they, as owners of the company, care about the products that are produced.

Pension Plan. The primary investment to the ESOP, according to the terms of the plan, is NSP stock. The contribution rates for 1992 and 1991 amounted to $36,940 and $54,731, respectively. During 1991, the ESOP purchased 183 shares of the Company's common stock that had been held as treasury stock. During 1989 the ESOP's purchase of 3,531 shares of the Company's common stock was financed with borrowed funds; the Company guaranteed to the lender that NSP would make contributions to the ESOP which were adequate to fund the debt service requirements of the loan.

EXHIBIT 6-3 *Continued*

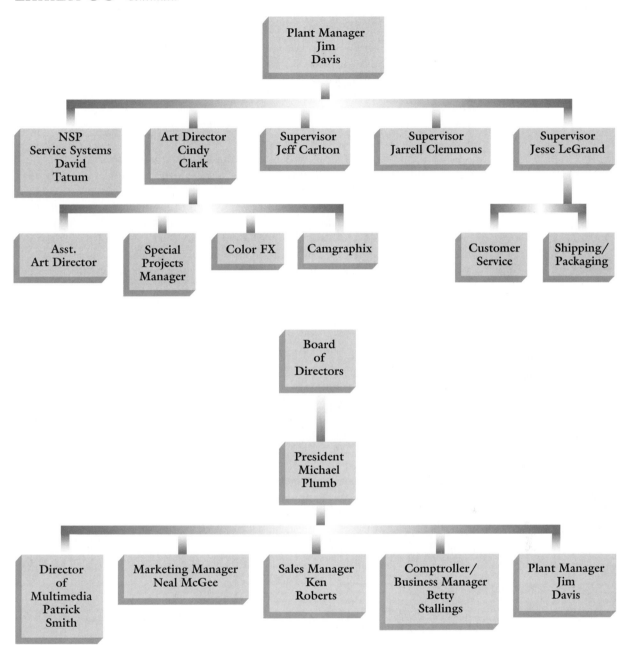

Personnel. The soul of NSP's operations is its 75 full-time employees. But no one in the company reflects the friendly, warm attitude of the NSPeople (as they fondly refer to themselves) more than Ruby Worthington. Known to employees and clients alike as "Miss Ruby," she had been receptionist and tax coordinator for fifteen years. Miss Ruby, according to Plumb, keeps the "southern warmth" in the business, something that NSP strives to retain.

Personnel activities, like most other aspects of NSP, are not formalized. Until recently, there was no employee job descriptions. Although job descriptions seem to Plumb to be another one of those necessary evils, his emphasis on formalizing the planning procedure extended to the development of descriptions for all NSP jobs to coincide with a merit system of performance evaluation. Plumb believes every employee should be able to do many jobs; cross training is the key to successful operations. This belief has been carried into the office. For example, in 1991 Bobbie Griggs continued to work half-time in the production area, and Larry Long doubled in sales. In order to achieve a completely cross-trained organization, Plumb is content to keep his operation relatively small. Job descriptions today set the standards by which employee performance is judged, something that previously was nonexistent at NSP.

Almost since its beginning, NSP operated one ten-hour shift four days per week. No one, with the exception of management and the office staff, worked on Friday. The company ran about 20 percent overtime hours. Plumb's philosophy is to pay overtime rather than hiring new employees. A team of graduate students who were analyzing NSP operations for a class project suggested that the company implement staggered shifts. Staggered shifts would allow employees to continue working four days, while at the same time covering the entire week. Staggered shifts began at NSP in November 1990. Concurrently, approximately 70 percent of the employees opted to work five eight-hour days.

Employees are on the honor system in regard to time worked. There are no time cards. The use of time cards, however, has become an issue among employees who feel that implementation of time cards are needed because too many employees are taking advantage of the honor system. Most employees do not find time cards to be an invasion of privacy, but do consider wearing uniforms problematic.

An area where Plumb has problems dealing with the honor system is in relation to sick days. Plumb is seldom sick; he has little tolerance for sickness and believes sick days are often used for extra time off. As a result, NSP's sick leave policy requires anyone who misses work due to illness on a Friday or Monday to submit a doctor's excuse.

NSP is not unionized and Plumb wants it to stay that way. Quarterly meetings are one way of allowing employees to voice concerns before problems get out of hand. Plumb noted some dissatisfaction among his staff in adjusting to his new niche strategy. Plumb feels that perhaps he is pushing his employees too hard without rewarding them for their efforts. In response, he has implemented a before-taxes profit-sharing program whereby all employees share equally in the benefits — from Michael to the people on the shop floor. Since establishment of the program, profits have been paid every quarter, averaging around $400 per person

Sales Force. Plumb is aware of the importance of a good sales force. "It used to be that if you were ethical and a nice guy you could keep a job. This is no longer the case. Today you have to be all that and good," he explained. "Today the three Ps of selling are price, product, and personality." Three sales representatives and two sales associates report to Ken Roberts. One of the sales representatives, Brad Hugall, operates out of the Auburn office, while the others operate primarily out of Georgia and Mississippi. The three manufacturer representatives extend the business into New York, Florida, and Texas. Much of their day-to-day selling is conducted by telephone.

Financial constraints are the reason for keeping the sales force small and relatively immobile. It is too costly to "go out and drum up business." Instead, Plumb elects to further develop existing accounts to provide all the corporate graphics — concentrating on exceptional art — for his accounts. This goal could be met without increasing the current size of the sales force. "If you develop a unique enough relationship with the customer, you can differentiate yourself from the masses."

NSP sales representatives operate in designated territories. The sales goal for all representatives is $1 million annually. Most are meeting that goal for 1993. Commissions are generally not affected by the profit margin on the specific sales. Compensation is based on a commission of 5 percent after a base level of $30,000 in sales is met. According to Plumb, while manufacturer representatives have added to the business, the company could not survive without full-time sales people. "It's the nature of the business—you can only count on your internal sales force," he explained.

Performance. NSP's balance sheet, statement of income and retained earnings, and statement of cash flows are displayed in Exhibits 6–4 — 6–6, respectively. In a comparison to 1990, cost of goods sold increased by 34.37 percent, operating expenses increased by 11.76 percent, and gross profits increased by a total of $660,694 in 1992. However, Comptroller Betty Stallings said 1993 will be the best year ever—"a dream year for us." "We have managed to implement controls that have finally gotten our cost of goods sold down and our profits up. We are finally headed in the right direction." Stallings added that an unexplained increase in original equipment business from existing customers like Federal Express will add to the expected increased profits in 1993. "I can't really put my finger on what we are doing right this year, but we are pleased with the results."

When Plumb took over the presidency, NSP began to take a better look at where the true costs of the business exist. NSP has implemented a "Covalent System" used for cost recovery, cost estimating, cost tracking, and cost inventory. The focus of this system is to make NSP more efficient. Maintaining good vendor relations has become as important as increasing sales. The Covalent System has also helped NSP identify product lines and markets where the company is not showing an adequate return. For example, the system indicated a poor return on its metal plate-printing operations which was then discontinued and sold. Inefficiencies in machine operations have also been identified through the Covalent System, as well as duplication of efforts. The latter became apparent in the supervision of four-color printing. Formerly, during the printing of four-color jobs an employee from the art department and the printing department would supervise the work. This unnecessary duplication increased job costs. The Covalent System allows NSP employees to know exactly where jobs are in the production process in order to keep clients more adequately informed as to a project's status. One downside of the Covalent System has been the response from employees. "I think many of our employees think we forced the system on them," Stallings said. NSP is in the process of changing the Covalent System through employee interview process.

Services Provided. NSP is a company dedicated to superior corporate art and graphics; however, the firm still does fleet graphic work. Services provided by NSP can be divided into eight categories:

1. *Truckgraphix®.* Truckagraphix® is the trademark name for NSP's larger-than-life decals for the side of company vehicles. The decals offer a more cost-effective method of identification than paint and is used by more than 85 percent of trucks on the road today. Additionally, the decals last almost four times longer than painting. NSP's capabilities span from a simple one-color mark to full-color photographic reproductions, which are light-reflective for easy visibility at night.

EXHIBIT 6-4 NSP Corporate Graphics, Inc., Schedules of Cost of Goods Sold for Years Ended December 31

	1992	1991	1990
Assets			
Current Assets			
Cash	$ 25,070	$ 102,359	$ 32,327
Trade accounts receivable (net)	1,114,853	1,072,378	981,550
Receivable from employees	4,019	1,993	—
Income tax refunds receivables	—	16,001	—
Other receivables	1,613	113	5,221
Inventories	572,532	788,288	790,665
Prepaid expenses	44,834	27,481	43,190
Total current assets	1,762,921	2,008,613	1,852,953
Property, Plant, and Equipment			
Land	10,613	10,613	10,613
Land improvements	38,197	32,212	6,031
Buildings and improvements	676,086	635,803	645,242
Furniture, fixtures, and equipment	1,535,781	1,165,500	1,112,099
Vehicles	36,858	36,858	36,492
	2,297,535	1,880,986	1,810,477
Less accumulated depreciation			
Net Property, plant, and equipment	1,057,770	881,769	764,356
	1,239,765	999,217	1,046,121
Other Assets			
Deposits	—	—	—
Total Assets	$3,002,686	$3,007,830	$2,899,134
Liabilities and Stockholders' Equity			
Current Liabilities			
Line of credit	—	291,034	268,035
Bank overdraft	—	—	—
Current portion of notes, capital			
Leases payable	100,850	41,527	62,013
Current portion ESOP note payable	—	—	—
Accounts payable	208,262	359,470	235,677
Accrued salaries and wages	37,509	41,888	32,256
Accrued interest	4,403	5,285	5,953
Accrued income tax	33,891	—	—
Deferred income tax	—	—	11,875
Payroll, sales taxes payable	14,494	17,238	66,062
Pension plan contribution payable	3,358	—	—
Total current liabilities	402,767	756,442	681,871
Long-term Liabilities			
Notes and capital leases payable net of			
current portion	289,848	37,051	59,293
ESOP note payable	195,736	223,575	307,947
Deferred income taxes	115,982	113,744	95,780
Total long-term liabilities	601,566	374,370	463,020
			(62,013)
Total Liabilities	$1,004,333	$1,130,812	$1,082,878

Source: NSP Corporate Graphics, Inc.

EXHIBIT 6-5 NSP Corporate Graphics, Inc., Balance Sheets for Years Ended December 31

	1992	1991	1990
Inventory, beginning of year	$ 788,288	$ 790,664	$ 168,740
Production department			
Purchases	2,091,337	2,042,837	1,869,483
Salaries	625,643	616,033	612,266
Scotchprint	48,146	—	—
Professional services	4,581	—	—
Application labor expenses	1,497	6,735	1,878
Depreciation	160,222	132,360	126,272
Freight	12,085	7,172	3,133
Insurance	149,088	107,450	112,428
Taxes	56,445	51,823	49,626
Supplies	99,567	95,000	91,353
Repairs and maintenance	45,564	26,460	30,819
Utilities	46,992	48,112	45,855
Contract labor	96,684	136,612	52,529
Uniforms	9,402	9,744	9,355
Rent	8,043	6,721	6,000
Refunds	—	—	140
Travel	5,557	7,604	7,176
Miscellaneous	6,906	5,034	107,997
Total costs—production	3,467,699	3,299,697	3,126,310
Art department			
Salaries	170,809	165,553	136,310
Supplies	10,465	10,194	12,440
Contract labor	47,606	26,600	20,010
Insurance	10,224	16,691	11,215
Taxes	13,682	13,429	10,900
Repairs and maintenance	8,452	2,442	3,176
Miscellaneous	3,720	1,401	5,055
Total costs—art	264,958	236,310	198,991
Application department			
Salaries	58,057	53,042	61,898
Supplies	615	988	1,899
Contract labor	2,968	5,510	361
Taxes	4,709	4,326	5,069
Travel	11,203	15,256	16,568
Repairs and maintenance	851	695	4,999
Insurance	7,293	7,223	14,681
Depreciation	3,072	3,072	3,072
Miscellaneous	239	242	7,244
Total costs—application	89,007	90,354	115,791
Goods available for sale	4,609,952	4,417,025	3,440,092
Less inventory, end of year	572,532	788,288	790,664
Costs of goods sold	$4,037,420	$3,628,737	$2,649,428

EXHIBIT 6-5 *Continued*

	1992	1991	1990
Stockholders' Equity			
Common stock—authorized 30,000 shares; $10 par value per share; issued 27,134 shares at December 31, 1989 and 22,665 shares at December 31, 1988	271,344	271,344	271,334
Additional paid in capital	602,167	602,168	575,324
Retained earnings	1,377,068	1,285,115	1,285,115
Less			
Treasury stock at cost, 3,163 shares at December 31, 1989 and 1988	(28,393)	(28,393)	(12,529)
ESOP contra account	(223,833)	(253,215)	(303,090)
Dividends paid	—	—	—
Total stockholders' equity	1,998,353	1,877,018	1,816,256
Total Liabilities and Stockholders' Equity	$3,002,686	$3,007,830	$2,899,134

Source: NSP Corporate Graphics, Inc.

EXHIBIT 6-6 NSP Corporate Graphics, Inc., Income Statement for December 31

	1992	1991	1990
Sales	$5,211,588	$4,647,779	$4,484,290
Cost of Goods Sold	4,037,420	3,628,737	2,649,428
Gross profit	1,174,168	1,019,042	1,834,862
Operating expenses			
General and administrative	388,280	335,139	304,724
Sales	544,704	522,335	518,511
	932,984	857,474	823,235
Income from operations	241,184	161,568	1,011,672
ESOP contribution	—	—	—
Other income and (expenses)	(73,046)	(97,104)	(50,797)
Net income (loss)	$ 168,138	$ 64,464	$ 960,830

Source: NSP Corporate Graphics, Inc.

Truckgraphix® is used by such customers as Eastern Foods (Naturally Fresh), Food World, and Delta Airlines (ground equipment).

2. *Creative design systems.* The company has professionally trained graphic designers who can revise and update an existing logo or create a total corporate identity program.

3. *Durabanners®.* Durabanners® is the registered name of NSP's posters and banners of the business. Made with state-of-the-art equipment, the pressure-sensitive vinyl banners are created to last up to seven years.

4. *Architectural and environmental graphics.* A new service offered by NSP, architectural and environmental graphics includes design services for both internal and external reimaging. This group includes signage, color bars, geometric shapes and symbols, and worded messages, that can be used to modernize a facility.

5. *Decor.* The decor group deals with internal signage for supermarkets, drug and soft goods retailers, hardware and auto parts stores, and convenience and department stores. This group includes such things as banners, aisle markers, shelf talkers, and displays.

6. *Corporate graphics.* A diversified venture for NSP is corporate graphics. For interested customers, NSP will design a complete graphics package for a company that includes logos and letterhead paper.

7. *Original equipment manufacturers.* NSP produces decals for installation by the manufacturer on such products as lawn mowers, ladders, boats, trailers, and snowmobiles. This market is a difficult market to break into because manufacturers rarely change this type of graphics from current suppliers.

8. *ColorFX.* A new venture for NSP is ColorFX. ColorFX is a 4-color process achieved by computerized electrostatic printing. This process allows NSP to do color processing on a small scale for customers.

9. *Service systems.* Installation is a final step to NSP's graphics. The company provides customers with either personal installation or a detailed how-to book for easy application.

Plumb believes that it is important to service NSP accounts completely. So, if a client needs something that NSP cannot provide, NSP should find someone who could. An example of this is storefront awnings. NSP had the screen-printing capabilities but did not supply awnings. Management, therefore, found a small mom-and-pop operation that could supply awnings, and the job went to NSP.

While most of NSP's graphics work is done by computer, the art department is capable of producing work far beyond computer graphics—whatever the client wants.

NEW VENTURES

For about $350 million NSP recently purchased 3M's Scotchprint machine. This new investment is "ColorFX," a take off on the *FX* and *FX2* special effects movies. ColorFX is designed to enhance NSP's art capabilities and shifts the company away from the fleet industry. At the time of the purchase, only nine companies in the U.S., six in Europe, and two in the Orient owned a Scotchprint machine. ColorFX allows NSP to do 4-color processing without color separations. With the addition of ColorFX, color processing can be done on any scale—large or small. With the change in strategy, Plumb sees the need to change attitudes. No longer will his sales force tell the customer what NSP can do, instead they will ask "what are your needs?" Thus far, the sale of ColorFX has been slower than anticipated. Customers needing ColorFX are different from fleet graphics customers, something to which the salesforce is still adjusting. Target customers for the new product are advertising agencies, outdoor advertisers, and the retail point-of-purchase market. "We are still on the learning curve," admitted Stallings. "But, we are trying to tap into the grocery business—if we can do that, we will be on our way to profitability. Right now, however, our fleet business is keeping us operating."

As might be expected, Plumb has *never* been afraid to try new ventures. He "lives on the edge" in his business—always wanting to be the first out of the starting blocks. One venture that Plumb previously entertained was the production and sales of a lighted table. Plumb commissioned two engineering professors at Auburn University to design and build a table for their use. Because the resulting table was perfectly suited for NSP's large-scale graphic work, Plumb considered producing and selling the table to competitors. "Someone is going to eventually build such a table and market it. Why shouldn't it be us?" he asked. However, members of his management staff convinced him that their time would be better served concentrating on their primary business. As a result, NSP is investigating obtaining and then selling a patent for the table.

Back-lighted signs were the last NSP venture, prior to ColorFX. Through a working agreement with the 3M Corporation, NSP has implemented a "roll 'n' ship" program that allows them to design signage on one of 3M's translucent films that can be rolled into easily transportable tubes for damage-free shipping. This program allows firms with multilocation backlighted signs to portray a consistent image.

CONCLUSION

Plumb is an aggressive entrepreneur. He spends much of his time in day-to-day operations trying to better NSP. He does not move conservatively. He is a risk taker, full of new ideas for NSP. He is convinced the only way to survive is through his niche strategy. Only two years previously, he felt the only way to survive was to diversify, to concentrate on his chosen 300 accounts and provide any service that they requested. He sees many new opportunities on the horizon including the Olympics in 1996. With NSP's close proximity to Atlanta, he feels his company is a natural to capitalize on any available business. Plumb is going to be there—and he plans to be at the forefront.

Plumb believes in NSP, and he believes in the concept of ESOP. With employees in command of the company, he feels the company can only get better. As he puts it, "We control our own destiny because we own our own destiny."

CASE
7

BETH JACK AND
MARILYN M. HELMS
The University of
Tennessee at Chattanooga

SPLATTERBALL ADVENTURE GAMES, INC.—1993

Splatterball Adventure Games, Inc., (615-842-8766), based in Chattanooga, Tennessee, conducts paintball or "simulation war" games. The company also maintains a store located in East Ridge, Tennessee, approximately five miles outside of Chattanooga. The playing field location for the game is Apison, Tennessee, approximately twenty miles from Chattanooga. The company has one principal, Mr. Doug Gray, who monitors games, conducts sales, and repairs guns. He has outside help for accounting services and hires part-time help on the field when necessary. The company has not made a profit during the past two years.

Paintball became popular on a national level in the early 1980s and includes both amateur and professional players in the sport. The development of the professional player occurred in the late 1980s. Like other sports, professional status is obtained when players earn money for playing paintball. In the case of paintball, money is earned by winning tournaments. Some of these tournaments have first place prizes as high as $30,000 for a ten member team. For a team to be designated as a professional team, three-fifths of the members must be professional players.

Paintball is played mainly in the United States. As of October 9, 1993, the periodical *Paintball News* listed 250 different paintball playing fields in 44 states in their directory. Another 14 fields in Canada and Mexico are also represented. At least 23 fields exist in California alone. It is difficult to know exactly how many fields do exist outside the United States because many are located in countries that consider the guns used in paintball illegal.

The American Paintball League (APL) was established in mid-1992 and includes more than 200 member fields. According to Mike Fugarino of APL, the sport appears to be growing steadily, but very little empirical data exists to support this hypothesis. Paintball groups are a loose coalition, with no definitive national representation beyond national periodicals. According to the September 11, 1993, issue of *Paintball News,* more than 800 people competed in the 1993 International Amateur Paintball Open in Cranberry, Pennsylvania, held in August. More than $50,000 in prize money was awarded.

Development of the sport has led to standard governing. Several different governing organizations do exist, but the most prevalent is the International Paintball Players' Associations (IPPA). This organization organizes tournaments, establishes guidelines, monitors pending legislation that may be harmful to the industry, and attempts to bring together the participants in paintball.

There are several variations in the way paintball is played depending on location of field, type of field, and field operator. Tournaments usually follow IPPA rules.

Standard equipment for all players include comfortable clothing and shoes for running through obstacles. Many people choose to wear camouflage although it is not necessary. All players must wear protective eye goggles whenever on the field. Also required are guns, carbon-dioxide tanks, and paintballs. All of the equipment, with the exception of the clothing, can be bought or rented from the field operator.

Additional equipment used by regular players includes semi-automatic guns, gun cleaners, replacement parts for guns, vests, and speedloaders. This equipment is allowed in tournament play and is used to increase the performance and ability of the players. Supplies can be ordered from vendors across the country or purchased from paintball specialty stores. Most advertise in *Paintball News,* a industry trade publication.

Games are usually played in densely wooded areas. This gives players obstacles to hide behind and adds to the difficulty of the game. The games can be played in large backyards, however there are usually not enough obstacles for effective play. Paintball is not played in parks unless prior approval is received from park managers or area officials. The paint used in the paintball is water-based and environmentally safe, but it still leaves marks on trees and other obstacles until there is enough rain to wash the paint away. Also, the plastic casing around the paintball will be left behind.

The object of paintball is to capture the opponent team's flag and return it to your own flag station. Flags remain at stations until a member of the opposing team captures it. Flag stations are simply a small area from which a flag is hung from a tree or from a pole placed in a clearing.

The area around a flag station varies from field to field. In some cases, there will be a natural barrier from which a player can defend the station. In other cases, the area is wide and open and must be defended from its perimeter. If a person who has captured the flag is shot while carrying the flag, the flag is considered "dead." It cannot simply be transferred to another teammate. That individual must return the flag to its original station to be recaptured by another team member.

There are two main differences in tournament play and casual play. In casual play, the team returning the captured flag to its own station wins the game. However, in tournament play, teams advance through round-robin brackets in a point system. Points are awarded for the number of opposing players shot, first flag pulled, and returning the flag to one's own flag station. There are point penalties for safety violations, foul or abusive language, and physical contact during a game. The maximum number of points awarded is one hundred.

Each member of a team carries a carbon-dioxide based gun that shoots the paintball. The original guns were pressed plastic with few moving parts. The carbon-dioxide came in small metal tubes that were pierced when inserted into the gun and would shoot approximately twenty to thirty rounds of paintballs. The guns now used have become more complicated with more moving parts. These guns are made of metal and often more closely resemble real guns. Manufacturers have begun to introduce new types of guns such as semi-automatics. Carbon-dioxide used in the guns can be obtained in refillable tanks and used for an entire game.

Paintballs are about the size of a large marble. They were originally made of oil-based paint enclosed in a thin plastic shell. This quickly changed because once this paint dried onto clothing, it was extremely difficult to remove. The paintballs are now water–based and come in a wide variety of colors. Most fields avoid using red so injuries are not mistaken for paint. The manufacturing process for paintballs is constantly being improved so that a more uniform ball can be made for better accuracy.

Professional teams have been reduced from fifteen member teams to either ten or five member teams. This development has occurred so that games could be played under a forty-five minute time limit. Amateur games, usually played on weekends, are not as strict about time limits and the number of members on a team. Usually the field operator will instruct individuals to form two to four teams, depending on the number of people at the field. They try not to allow more than twenty-five players on a team, if possible. Games are usually limited to one hour, although amateur games tend to end within thirty minutes. Tournament events can have an average of 20 teams participating.

The typical paintball player is male. Only three percent are women, and they tend to play primarily at the amateur level. The average professional player is between 22 and 35 years old, while the average casual player is between 18 and 30 years old. Players come from a wide variety of backgrounds, including professional managers, physicians, blue-collar workers, and students.

Tournaments are sponsored year round in the United States. For the month of October 1993, for example, 31 paintball tournaments throughout the United States were listed and 29 were listed for November 1993. More than 2,000 individuals per month participate in U.S. tournaments. The most prestigious tournament takes place every October in Nashville, Tennessee. This tournament, the International Masters

Tournament, is the biggest of its kind with a sixty-four team field and a $30,000 first prize. This tournament lasts five days and includes both five-member and ten-member team competitions. This tournament usually includes at least two British teams every year. The top eight finishers of this tournament are able to obtain sponsorship from manufacturers of paintball equipment. This tournament is also a chance for vendors to display their new products and innovations to players.

HISTORY OF SPLATTERBALL ADVENTURE GAMES, INC.

Splatterball Adventure Games, Inc. in Chattanooga, Tennessee runs local paintball games and maintains a retail store that sells paintball supplies and repairs guns. It is through this store that many games are scheduled.

The owner, Doug Gray, began his involvement with the sport of paintball in 1981 as a member of a small team based in Chattanooga. Many of the players lived in Nashville so the group decided to open a field there. Mr. Gray is still an active member of the Nashville Ridgerunners Professional Paintball Team. The field in Nashville is very successful at organizing paintball tournaments and bringing in teams from the entire Southeast region.

There is no longer a field in Chattanooga, so Mr. Gray drives two hours to Nashville almost every weekend to play the sport. Mr. Gray gets his friends and acquaintances to go to Nashville with him in order to play. During a recent trip, Mr. Gray considered opening a field of his own in Chattanooga so he could practice closer to home. Eventually, he was able to generate enough local interest in paintball to support his field in Chattanooga.

Mr. Gray leased a parcel of land approximately 20 miles southeast of Chattanooga. According to Mr. Gray, "since this was more of a hobby than business, I decided to run the operations from my home." He bought some of the plastic guns to use for rentals so he could continue to bring new players to his field.

Mr. Gray worked closely with the Nashville field in setting up his own field. His close ties enabled him to obtain many of his supplies at volume discount prices, as well as gain other advantages that would otherwise have been denied to him as an independent.

Mr. Gray's business continued to grow as paintball began to receive national attention. Businesses and groups began to schedule games for their members. As his business expanded, Mr. Gray began to carry more rental equipment and supplies for the part-time player.

Eventually the business grew so large it became difficult to manage from his home. The rental equipment took up so much room that he decided it was time to establish a center of operations. However, in order to make this feasible, Mr. Gray needed an infusion of capital for the store lease, furniture lease, and additional equipment. He estimated the total cost to be $7,500. It was at this time he took in one partner and the business incorporated with each partner owning five hundred shares of stock.

Unfortunately, the partnership was not successful. Both partners had differing ideas on how the income should be distributed. Mr. Gray wanted most of the money reinvested into the business for further growth. However, his partner decided he wanted his capital infusion paid back immediately. After one year the partnership was dissolved through Mr. Gray's purchase of his partner's five hundred shares of stock for $11,000. The original investment was $10,000, and his partner had received approximately $1,200 in capital withdrawals when the repurchase was made.

The Situation in 1993. Today, Mr. Gray is the sole stockholder of Splatterball and has decided to reevaluate what he is trying to accomplish. What is the future of Splatterball? Where is he trying to go with the business? How does he get there?

The business is quickly becoming a full-time operation. Hours of operation of the store are 11 A.M. to 3 P.M. Monday through Friday. The store is only open on weekends if no games are being played at the field. Mr. Gray would like to increase the hours of operation but is not currently in the position to do so. He has a full time job as a computer programmer, and he works from 4 P.M. to 12:15 A.M. during the week. Eventually, he would like to leave this position and have the paintball business as his primary source of income.

The store generates some walk-in business, often from people who play the game on their own property. Mr. Gray offers gun repair services and sells guns, supplies, and trade magazines. Most of Splatterball's income, however, is derived from the games. The field is available year-round but games are scheduled in advance, especially during winter months. With scheduling, necessary supplies can be ordered, and the appropriate number of field judges can be obtained. Splatterball only keeps one hundred rental guns in stock, so if extremely large groups play, Mr. Gray has to borrow guns from other fields. He has worked out an agreement with a field in Atlanta in which each field makes guns available to the other at no charge.

Since 1990, Splatterball has had its own professional and amateur teams that play regularly at the field and in national tournaments. These teams have no sponsorship, and there is no fee to become a member. Each member is responsible for all tournament entry fees and their own supplies. Mr. Gray relies heavily on his professional team members to give their support in running the store and in officiating games when they are not playing. Their compensation is in the form of discounts on supplies and gun repairs. Individuals playing the game with a group who decide that they would like to play on a regular basis are recruited as new members. These individuals will generally play with the team for six months before becoming a team member.

Currently, almost all games are scheduled on Saturdays and Sundays. Groups may schedule the field for an entire day. It is also possible for Mr. Gray to run games during the week before 2 P.M. Splatterball continues to sponsor walk-on games on weekends, enabling individuals to try paintball without having to find other players to make up two teams. In addition to the typical player, Mr. Gray has some school groups that regularly rent the field for an entire day.

Mr. Gray's business background includes several years of college courses in addition to his own trial and error experience gained since he first started Splatterball in 1981. He has taken a small business management course at a local junior college, but feels that he learned the most about management from starting the business. When asked about his management style, Mr. Gray says, "I am a doer out of necessity, but a delegator by nature. I am great at long-range planning and need to be careful not to forget the small daily details that keep me in business."

COMPETITION

Splatterball's competition is primarily from the amusement industry in general and specifically from other paintball fields. Movies, music, and sport hunting are just a few examples of the broad range of amusement competition from the leisure-time industries. Because of the great deal of physical activity involved, Mr. Gray feels he competes for the physical fitness dollar as well.

Competition between paintball fields is very friendly. The closest fields to Chattanooga are in Atlanta, Knoxville, and Nashville. A directly competing field opened in Chattanooga during 1992 but remained in business only a few months. Each of these fields are approximately a two-hour drive from Chattanooga so Gray does not compete directly with them for local players. Instead, he has worked out arrangements enabling each field to host participating regional teams in league play. This league has eight teams from Chattanooga, Nashville, Atlanta, Kentucky, and Birmingham. The teams play eight times on the first Sunday of each month from March through October at different field locations. This arrangement gives each team a chance to play at various fields on a competitive level. Although a trophy is awarded to the team accumulating the most points at the end of the tournament year, the main purpose of the league is to provide practice opportunities to prepare for major tournaments.

Most fields in this league are about the same size as the Chattanooga field, with the exception of Nashville. The Nashville field is four times the size of the Splatterball field and has an agreement with a local campground to use the campground area for major tournaments in the Spring and Fall. As it is privately held, the exact earnings of the Nashville operation is unknown but is estimated by Mr. Gray to be around $1,000,000 annually, including field operations, specialty store operations, and tournaments.

In the physical fitness area, Splatterball has been able to work in cooperation with different programs. The game has been included as an activity in an intensive six week fitness program in Chattanooga and has been used to build self-confidence as well as physical fitness. Unfortunately, the executive games segment of the paintball market has not grown as expected. There are a few small businesses that use the games for team-building exercises and require employees to participate. Their best group is the McCallie School, a local boys private preparatory high school that plays once every couple of months. Splatterball also competes with the hobby/entertainment industry in general. Often it can be heard around the field that someone played that weekend instead of hunting or buying some personal item.

COSTS

The cost of playing Splatterball depends on the experience level of the player. Novice players have lower costs, because they usually rent all their equipment. Mr. Gray charges a $22.52 flat field fee which includes a $12 gun rental, forty rounds of paint, and one small tank of carbon-dioxide. Novice players generally shoot less than more experienced players and often to not have to purchase extra paint. The typical charge is $1.08 for one tube of paint (eight rounds).

An experienced player tends to incur higher costs since most purchase their own guns which start at $150 each. Also, there is the purchase of camouflage gear and extra supplies and accessories to maintain the performance of their equipment. It is not uncommon for an experienced player to shoot thirty tubes of paint per game. Since most play a minimum of three, forty-five minute games, costs can be high.

Players that are part of a team often have higher expenses than those incurred by the experienced player. Many own several backup guns in case of gun failure. These failures are usually due to wear on parts and do not occur regularly, but if a gun fails during a tournament, the team will be short a player. Also, there are entrance fees for tournaments which can be as much as $200 per member. The July 31, 1993, issue of *Paintball News* indicated that professional tournaments are charging as much as $1,850 in entry fees and awarding up to $40,000 in prize money.

Splatterball Adventure Games, Inc. has a very "loose" accounting system. Mr. Gray has recently taken advantage of an offer of free accounting services in exchange for 100 shares of stock. Mr. Gray now owns 900 shares of the 1,500 shares with 500 shares retained by the business. Bill, the accountant, often works on weekends but does not get involved with the operation of the games.

Exhibits 7–1 and 7–2 show the current financial statements for 1991 and 1992. The largest debt is Mr. Gray's repayment of $7,500 of the original $11,000 loan used to repurchase the stock from his former partner. Other expenses, such as supplies, can usually be directly matched to sales since most supplies are received within two days of use to eliminate spoilage. Paintballs have a shelf-life of several months, but tend to become soft. Thus, the sooner they are used, the better they perform.

Mr. Gray has had an offer from two of his team members to work in the business for 150 shares of stock each. One is a computer programmer with a college degree, and the other assists in the management of his family's convenience store. These two players have helped Mr. Gray run Splatterball for four years. Neither would invest any money, but instead would reinvest their share of the profits plus provide free services. They have offered to assist in running games and working in the store to increase the hours of store operations. Both are experienced in gun repair and would be able to assist in this aspect of the business as well. Both individuals would be able to work during the hours Mr. Gray is at his full-time job. Mr. Gray has considered this offer for several years and has consulted with an attorney as to the fair value and distribution of future income either through dividends or salaries. Currently, no changes have been made and Mr. Gray continues to pay these two individuals to work in the store and assist on the field when necessary.

LEGAL ISSUES

The current legal environment is of great concern to Splatterball. Although every player signs a waiver form (See Exhibit 7–3) each time they play, these waivers have not been tested through a lawsuit. Mr. Gray has had several attorneys review his form and has always received approval.

Injuries are one of the main concerns for Mr. Gray. Two years ago a new player was hit in the eye with a paintball and lost his vision. This player had taken his goggles off even though he had been instructed not to and had signed a waiver stating he would wear the goggles at all times. In this particular instance, Splatterball was very lucky as a spectator had taken a picture of the injured player not wearing the required safety goggles. This picture prevented a negligence lawsuit. However, the potential legal problems were brought to the forefront by this incident.

The entire paintball industry has worked hard to promote safe usage practices both on and off the field. *Paintball Sports Magazine* has published several articles regarding safe usage of guns. Tournaments impose penalties against teams whenever a players is found not wearing goggles. Off the field, gun barrels are required to have plugs so if accidentally discharged, the paintball will break in the gun. Field operators monitor how hard guns are shooting the paintball. They calibrate, or chronograph, guns to ensure they do not shoot so hard as to injure a player. Even though the guns are carefully monitored, being hit by a paintball hurts. If shot from close range, the paintball leaves a bruise and occasionally a small welt. Welts, although painful, disappear within one to two days with no special attention required.

Most fields, including Splatterball, and all tournaments discourage shooting other players in the head. They have simply ruled that head shots do not count as "kills" or points. If a player is hit in the head, he or she may call a judge over to help him or her

EXHIBIT 7-1 Splatterball Adventure Games, Inc. Income Statement for the Years Ended 1991 and 1992

	1991	1992
INCOME		
Sales	$7,107.00	$11,742.00
Net Sales	7,107.00	11,742.00
COST OF GOODS SOLD		
Total Cost of Goods Sold	0.00	0.00
Gross Profit	7,107.00	11,742.00
EXPENSES		
Advertising	2,195.00	800.00
Auto Expense	15.22	
Bank Service Charges	22.50	48.00
Bank Wire Transfer Fees	18.00	
Casual Labor	175.00	300.00
Dues & Subscriptions	58.00	58.00
Entertainment	173.28	60.00
Entry Fees	278.00	180.00
Miscellaneous Expense	190.10	163.12
Office Expense	377.69	233.01
Paint & CO2 Supplies	6,280.71	8,004.73
Postage	10.24	26.68
Rent	100.00	750.00
Field Supplies	1,204.97	1,621.11
Telephone	111.88	367.48
Uniforms	128.56	
Total Expenses	11,339.15	12,612.13
Net Operating Income	(4,232.15)	(870.13)
OTHER INCOME		
Interest Income	13.00	0.00
Total Other Income	13.00	0.00
OTHER EXPENSES		
Total Other Expenses	0.00	0.00
Income Before Taxes	(4,219.15)	(870.13)

Source: Splatterball Adventure Games, Inc.

wipe off the paint. The judge will declare the player neutral until the paint is removed, and the player is put back into the game.

Whenever new players come to the field, they are given instructions before the game begins. The field operator walks over the field with new players to point out boundaries, the flag station location, and any areas players need to avoid because of potential injury.

The entire splatterball industry has worked together in regards to concerns regarding equipment. There have been attempts in several states, most notably California where there are several major fields, to ban the sale of toys that closely resemble guns.

EXHIBIT 7-2 Splatterball Adventure Games, Inc., Balance Sheet for the Years Ended 1991 and 1992

ASSETS	1991	1992
CURRENT ASSETS		
Cash	(1,777.58)	216.12
Inventory	260.99	318.00
Total Current Assets	(1,516.59)	534.12
FIXED ASSETS		
Office Equipment	189.95	149.28
Paint Guns	8,539.10	8,740.63
Field Equipment	2,592.25	2,038.44
Total Fixed Assets	11,321.30	10,928.35
OTHER ASSETS		
Total Other Assets	0.00	0.00
TOTAL ASSETS	9,804.71	11,462.47
Liabilities & Equity		
CURRENT LIABILITIES		
Accounts Payable	1,145.00	2,953.40
Notes Payable	11,363.26	7,680.42
Sales Tax Payable	515.60	698.78
Total Current Liabilities	13,023.86	11,332.60
LONG TERM LIABILITIES		
Total Long Term Liabilities	0.00	0.00
Total Liabilities	13,023.86	11,332.60
STOCKHOLDERS EQUITY		
Common Stock	1,000.00	1,000.00
Current Earnings	(4,219.15)	(870.13)
TOTAL EQUITY	(3,219.15)	129.87
TOTAL LIABILITIES AND CAPITAL	9,804.71	11,462.47

Source: Splatterball Adventure Games, Inc.

EXHIBIT 7-3 Splatterball Adventure Games, Inc., Application to Play

WAIVER OF LIABILITY AND ASSUMPTION OF RISK

1. I, the undersigned wish to play the Splatterball Adventure game. I recognize and understand that playing the game involves running certain risks. Those risks include, but are not limited to, the risk of injury relating from the impact of the paint pellets used in the Game. Injuries resulting from possible malfunction of equipment used in the Game and injuries resulting from tripping or falling over obstacles in the Game playing field. In addition, I recognize that the exertion of playing the game could result in injury or death.

2. Despite these and other risks, and fully understanding such risks, I wish to play the Game and hereby assume the risks of playing the Game. I also hereby hold harmless Splatterball Adventure Game, Inc., hereafter called the Sponsors, and John Felts (landowner) and indemnify them against any and all claims, actions, suits, procedures, costs, expenses (including attorney's fees and expenses), damages and liabilities arising out of, connected with, or resulting from my playing the Game, including without limitation, those resulting from the manufacture, selection, delivery, possession, use or operation of such equipment. I hereby release the Sponsors from any and all such liability, and I understand that this release shall be binding upon my estate, my heirs, my representatives and assigns. I hereby certify to the Sponsors that I am in good health and do not suffer from a heart condition or other ailment which could be exacerbated by the exertion involved in playing the Game.

3. I hereby promise to play the Game only in accordance with the rules of the Game as set forth by the Sponsors. In particular, I agree:

    a. to wear safety goggles at all times when I am on the playing field or at the target area, even after I have been marked with paint or the game is over and to keep the goggles snug by pulling the straps tight; I understand that serious eye injury, including loss of eyesight, could occur if the safety goggles are not on when marking pistols may be discharged anywhere near me. Should my safety goggles fog up or for any reason be such that I cannot see through them properly, I will ask someone near me, on the playing field or in the target area, to lead me out of the area I am into to one where all marking pistols are on "SAFETY". Only then will I remove my safety goggles to clean them. I understand that any "safety goggle" is subject to fogging up or getting dirty and that if I am anywhere near a marking pistol as it discharges, and my "safety goggles" are not properly on, I may get seriously and permanently injured;

    b. to avoid any physical contact of fighting with other players;

    c. to stay within the boundaries of the playing field and not to chase or run after anyone over ledges or mountainous terrain; and

    d. to keep the marking pistol I am using on "safety" (the no-shoot position) in the staging area at all times, in the target area while not shooting and on the playing field before and after each game, to aim or point the pistol at another person ONLY during an active game and never to wave or brandish the pistol about in the staging area or the target area.

    e. to avoid pointing at or shooting at the head of any player at any time.

4. For safety reasons I agree to use only equipment and/or supplies provided to me by the Sponsors while playing the game or in the target area. Written permission of the Sponsors is necessary should I elect to use other equipment or supplies. If I have chosen not to use the goggles or marking pistol available from the Sponsors, I hereby certify that the goggles or marking pistol, which I have chosen to use, are at least as safe as the Sponsor's form claims arising out of any additional risk resulting from my use of goggles or marking pistol other than those available from the Sponsors.

5. I agree to ask the Sponsor for clarification of any rule or safety procedure, for further instruction as regard anything that I don't understand about the equipment and supplies as regards anything else that may effect the safety of or playing of the Game.

6. I have read this waiver of liability and assumption of risk carefully, and understand that by signing below, I am agreeing, on behalf of myself, my estate, my heirs, representatives and assigns not to sue the Splatterball Adventure Games, Inc. or to hold them or their insurors liable for any injury including death, resulting from my playing the Game, I intend to be fully bound by this Agreement.

By virtue of my signature, I acknowledge and agree to all terms and conditions set forth on this form.

X Signature _____

Date signed _____

Is this your first visit to our field? YES ( ) NO ( )

Source: Splatterball Adventure Games, Inc.

This is due to the publicity surrounding some shootings of children because someone thought they had real guns. Because the newer guns resemble real guns, the industry is notably concerned.

Teams, field operators, and suppliers try to keep paintball games as safe as possible. Because of the nature of the sport, there are sometimes injuries, but most injuries can be avoided. These same people have also worked hard to keep the sport legal in all states through letter writing campaigns and lobbying.

THE FUTURE

Mr. Gray would eventually like to turn Splatterball into his full time job. "If I could create a larger demand in the off-season, I could depend on Splatterball as my sole source of income," he states. The addition of shareholders to ease the financial burden of expansion is another consideration of Mr. Gray's. It would enable Splatterball to run more games, especially during the week.

There is no real marketing strategy in place for Splatterball although Mr. Gray feels one is needed. He has some informational brochures available for distribution, but the main source of new business comes from word of mouth. Mr. Gray would like to implement a strategy that will not deplete too much of his personal financial resources, yet still enable him to work full time in his hobby.

Prepare a strategic plan for Mr. Gray that you feel will turn the company into a profitable business.

EXHIBIT 7-4 Slatterball Adventure Games, Inc., Marketing Brochure

SPLATTERBALL
Adventure Games, Inc.
**5725 Ringgold Road, Suite D
East Ridge, TN 37412**

One of the best ways to play Splatterball is with a group of your co-workers. Intra-corporate games are fast-becoming one of the country's most enjoyable ways to increase productivity, camaraderie and competitive drive within business groups.

Photo above shows W.U.S.Y.-US101. Southeast Tennessee's top-rated country music radio station. US101 is the current reigning champion of the Chattanooga "media league."

Please call us for more information as well as group rates and lodging information for out-of-town guests.

"Your heart is beating fast. Adrenalin races through your body, sharpening your senses to a degree you never thought possible."

EXHIBIT 7-4 *Continued*

Field Fee...$10
Equipment Rental...$15

The above rate insures you of an entire day of play. The only limitation is your own endurance and desire.

(Group rates are available. Call our information line at 499-1151 for details.)

The day rate includes:

1 Spitfire, pump action rifle.

An initial supply of paintballs(40) and a day's supply of CO_2.

Safety certified J.T. competition goggles.

(Although paint is water soluble, players are advised to wear only old clothing! Standard brush or treebark camouflage gets best results.)

5725 RINGGOLD ROAD SUITE D
EAST RIDGE, TN 37412
(615) 499-1151

The description on the opposing page can only pale in comparison to the real experience of playing Chattanooga's oldest and best known survival game.

Splatterball Adventure Games Inc. wants to introduce you to the excitement of a day in the field with friends and foes.

Paintball is one of the country's fastest growing sports...it's easy, it's exciting, it's affordable, and can be played solo or with a team. A single fee includes all the equipment, instructions, N.A.P.R.A. certified referees and even a picnic lunch depending on the size of your group.

We offer over 25 acres of various topography as a playing field, set in beautiful, woodsy hills only 20 minutes from downtown Chattanooga. Anyone in reasonable health can play...some groups may even be designed by age bracket.

"Beside you, your comrades, glancing right and left. The sound of your movement through the woods seems like thunder...your muscles taut, finger on the trigger of your weapon...the only object that will get you through the next several minutes alive. Then, a sharp retort in the creekbed ahead of you. Your breath quickens. You race for the cover of a grove of young saplings and sage brush...firing as you go. One of your buddies goes down.. In a flash, you see the enemy. Without thinking your hand swings up. By gut instinct you react. CRACK. You see the impact...and breathe easier, a smile on your lips, as the enemy stalks off the field, hand raised above his head, the sign of his own defeat in battle."

NORWOOD FURNITURE COMPANY—1993

C A S E

8

DAVID ADAMS
Marywood College

The Spring of 1993 brought a great deal of change to Norwood Furniture. In fact, so much has changed that Jess and Jan feel as though they have just gone through a time warp.* Business today is so different than what it was just a few years ago, but their original objective still is to operate a profitable family owned business selling quality furniture at above average prices to customers in and around their two store locations. Norwood Furniture's SIC code is 3970.

HISTORY

Nineteen years ago, Jess and Jan Norwood needed a recliner to replace their 20-year-old chair. Their search for a recliner proved unsuccessful. However, while at King Furniture, Jan found an antique rocker that could be used in one of their children's bedrooms. As Jess loaded the rocker into the car, Joe King, the owner, remarked, "I would like to sell this business." As they drove home, the Norwoods wondered how much Joe King really wanted for the business. They returned to the store to ask and he said, "$30,000 plus the inventory." Within months, the Norwoods purchased the business from King, who financed the capital needed by the Norwoods.

The Norwoods bought the furniture business in September 1974. Jess decided that it would be worthwhile to stay at his current job as a machinist for a year while Jan ran the business. This would provide at least one secure income. Sales kept steadily increasing and, with the increase in sales, Jess planned to enter the business full-time by June 1. However, a sudden sales decline frightened him enough that he decided to remain in his factory. Three months later, one year after the purchase, Jess had his first full-time day at the store.

By 1980, the Norwoods began to observe their business drawing customers from Wilkes-Barre (40,000) a city twenty-five miles north of Hazleton, with a population two-thirds that of Hazleton. Convinced that a market existed in Wilkes-Barre, they rented, for $400 a month, a 2,700 square feet store on Main Street.

In 1982, the Norwoods rented a store near Allentown, some sixty miles south of Hazleton. The store had space for unloading in the back area, a parking lot next door, and the rent was only $500 per month. However, according to Jess, "Business absolutely died, we couldn't believe going into such a huge community (125,000) and doing such a small amount of business." In March 1984, the Norwoods moved the store to another location on a major access route to Allentown.

In July 1986, Norwood Furniture had just completed its worst month in 4 years at its Allentown Store. Jess Norwood was reflecting on why this store, located in a city with 125,000 people, was doing less business than either of his two other stores. The location of the other stores were in cities with less than 60,000 people. Jess really felt it would be unwise, after 12 years, to change the operation drastically. Yet, he knew changes were necessary to survive. Jess and Jan finally decided to liquidate the Allentown operation and bring its manager back to the Hazleton store.

*Store locations and family member names are disguised.

In 1991, the Norwood Furniture store at Wilkes-Barre, which had been located in the downtown business district, relocated just two miles outside of Wilkes-Barre. The location is close to Nanticoke, approximately twenty miles from Scranton, and only seventy interstate miles from Binghamton, New York.

Store Locations. The store in Hazleton has about 9,800 square feet and is located on a side street, just off the main street shopping area. Parking in the downtown area is ample, with a 30 car public off-street parking area directly across the street from the store. Within the last three years, a corner store location became available, and the Norwoods purchased this space. The corner provided the missing entrance to the main street sales district and needed expansion of the sales area. This new area became the carpet display and sales area. The cut up floor design of the Hazleton store, however, makes it difficult to track customers as they move about. Generally, a sales person must stay right with the customer as they shop. For security and alerting salespeople, each entry door has an indicator bell. The Hazleton store location is illustrated in Exhibit 8–1.

The Wilkes-Barre store was originally located on the city's main business street. The extent of the furniture display areas consisted of two 20 × 60 foot areas. Walk-in customers found the store's access convenient with sufficient street and garage parking in the area. However, while at the downtown location, the Norwoods felt the impact as fellow merchants considered several alternatives to Friday night shopping which resulted in frustrated customers. Several merchants tried Thursday night, others stayed with Friday night. This factor, coupled with space constraints of their downtown store, prompted Jess, Jan, and their son John to find another store site. For several years, they had been aware of a shopping district developing just south of Wilkes-Barre. A good site was located next to a busy highway and surrounded by a

EXHIBIT 8-1 Hazleton Store Location

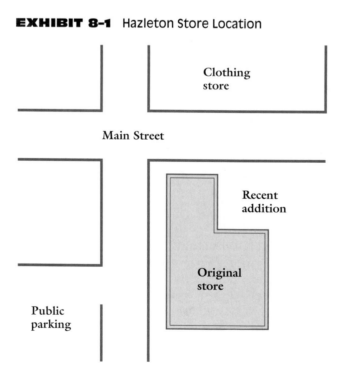

number of other businesses including Kmart, several banks, and a grocery store. The Norwoods purchased the land and obtained a bank loan.

Construction of the new Wilkes-Barre store started during the fall of 1990 and was completed in February 1991. The building has a pole construction on a concrete slab. There is track lighting throughout the store which consists of 9,000 square feet of gallery type displays of furniture and accessories. The openness of the store allows one salesperson to effectively work three customers at one time. Sales results have pleasantly surprised the Norwoods as sales have more than met their break-even level. The new Wilkes-Barre store layout is illustrated in Exhibit 8–2.

There is a two-lane highway in front of the Wilkes-Barre store. Due to development of businesses in the area, the county has begun construction of a three-lane highway less than one-half mile from the store.

COMPETITION

Surrounding the Hazleton store is a variety of stores that sell furniture. One major competitor is the Farnsworth Furniture store which features a wider price range of furniture and uses a quantity display concept.

When the Norwood's location was in the downtown business district, the major competitor was Newton's, a large general merchandise store, which sells some furniture. With the stores new location, there are no competitors within the immediate business area. Other stores in Wilkes-Barre carry only a limited number of furniture lines and have few or no waterbeds. There is only one retailer and installer of carpet within the city limits. Jan and Jess believe their operation is on the edge of becoming the number one furniture and carpet retailer in the Wilkes-Barre area.

EXHIBIT 8-2 Norwood Furniture Wilkes-Barre Store Layout

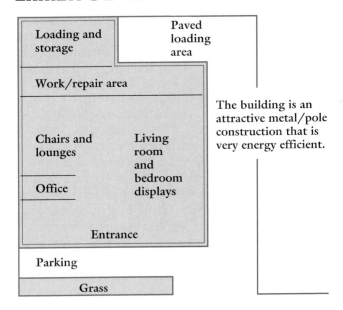

During the growth period from 1976 to 1982, the Norwoods and their two sons, John and Robert, were always the key employees. As Jess and Jan recalled, there were times when they felt the boys were too young to be doing the type of physical work needed. After spending some time away from the area, both of the sons, decided to return to the family business.

John, Jess, Jan, and one salesperson currently operate the Wilkes-Barre store seven days a week. The store hours are 9:30 A.M. to 8 P.M. Monday through Friday, 9 A.M. to 5 P.M. Saturday, and 12 P.M. to 4 P.M. Sunday. Whoever works the weekday evening shift does not have to work the weekend hours. John, however, is the principle manager of this location and spends five full days each week at the store.

Jess, Jan, Robert, and a bookkeeper are at the Hazleton store five days a week. John spends a day per week at this location, when his father or mother are at the Wilkes-Barre store. Robert moves between the two stores as need arises. By 1993, there were six people outside the family who worked at the two store locations. Although the six jobs are involved with both stores, all six employees operate out of the Hazleton store. Their responsibilities include cleaning displays, assembling furniture, delivering customer's orders, laying carpet, and performing various carpentry functions necessary for display changes. The most recent person to join the business is the new bookkeeper/accountant. The business retains a full-time (CPA) accounting firm to handle the year end audit and filing of Federal income taxes.

THE FAMILY

Jess Norwood was 37 years old when he entered the furniture sales business. He had some experience during high school working for a drugstore and feels that this experience was an excellent basis for learning the retail business. When he graduated from high school in 1957, he could not find a factory job, so he became a car salesman. Jess jokes about the empty suitcase Jan brought over one day, announcing, "If you want to live there selling cars, then here are your clothes." Soon, Jess began studying in an apprentice program for machinists. After the apprentice training program, he left to work as a machinist for a larger firm. This lasted for 10 years during which Norwood Furniture became a reality. Jess is now the full-time owner/manager for the overall operation of the two stores. He is responsible for the accounting records, including receivables and payables, purchasing, and overall functional decision making for both stores.

In 1976, Jan left being a housewife and became a manager, owner, and partner of the furniture store. Jan spent her early years working with her parents running a hotel and sporting good store. She commented that the job included "a little bit of buying, but I also spent nights in a creek catching bait for the sporting goods store." She continued this job until their first son (John) was born. Though never having had any formal business training, Jan did quite a bit of reading about operating a business and many of the ideas for their current stores originated with her. For instance, it was her idea to remodel the basement of the Hazleton store into a display area.

The oldest son, John, went to college, completed a Business Degree and to the surprise of his parents, informed them that he wanted to come back and join the furniture business. At the time, the current business did not have the income to cover his salary. However, John's interest and enthusiasm allowed a plan to be developed to expand the business's product line and eventually to enter the carpet sales market. John apprenticed as a carpet mechanic for a year before Jess decided he was ready to go out on his own. His first solo job proved the value of his training. "It was the most cut up mess you ever saw in your life," said Jess, and Jan agreed, adding "it got done and it was a good job when it was done— in fact, those customers just recently came back and bought another carpet." John is manager of the Wilkes-Barre store. His one day a week at the Hazleton store provides him the opportunity to better understand the total business operation.

Robert, the younger son, is married and has a family. Robert is manager of the Allentown location. He now works full time laying carpet, assembling furniture, and helping with sales at both the Wilkes-Barre and Hazleton stores.

Ann, their daughter, became involved in the business when she was 16 years old. She has been invaluable to her parents in providing a young woman's perspective on products and displays. Ann's interest in the area of interior decorating lead her to go to college with a major in interior design. As her father noted, "Ann's awareness of color, style, and integration of the various furniture units has added a needed dimension to our business." Ann has completed college, married, and is now working part time at the Wilkes-Barre store. In addition to helping in the store's layout and decoration, she assists customers with questions concerning interior design and during off hours does some private consulting for home decoration.

MARKETING

When the Norwoods bought the business in 1974, their main product lines were sofas and chairs. In 1981, while shopping in the Shoppingtown Mall in Albany, they noticed a store called Waterbed World. Its display was a bedroom suite called the Vintage Suite from Burlington Furniture, the same manufacturer that supplied conventional bedroom suites to the Norwoods. They contacted the Burlington salesperson and arranged to begin selling waterbeds. As Jess recalls, "when we got that waterbed suite in the store, we practically had to give it away—it didn't sell."

The first profitable load of waterbeds followed soon after when Jess and Jan took their van and 12-foot trailer to Alabama and picked up 27 waterbeds from Schwagert, Inc. Schwagert manufactured less expensive, but high quality waterbeds. Jan remembers stopping over in Atlanta, Georgia, at the Liberty Warehouse to get the mattresses. "We went in and said we had no cash, I don't even know if we have a check. Jan told them who we were, and who they could check with and we left there with, I think, about $4,000 worth of products." On the other hand, we did get a call off to John immediately, and he put a check, for the correct amount, into the mail that day. Once back to Hazleton, Jess no sooner had the headboard set down when a young man came in and said if we could deliver it tomorrow, he'd buy it. That first sale was about $400.

In the fall of 1983, a competitor in Hazleton that carried the La-Z-Boy line of recliners went bankrupt. A salesperson came into our store and announced "that he was going to place the La-Z-Boy product line in one of the three stores in the area." He then asked for an "interview." After several meetings, he asked the Norwoods if they would like to place an order. Jess and Jan agreed and purchased the minimum initial order for 25 chairs with a 150 day, 2 percent discount. These chairs sold quickly even though the Norwoods carried other well-known recliners such as Kroehler, Berkline, Futuristic, and Pontiac. The majority of their customers preferred the La-Z-Boy rocker recliner.

After the initial success, energy devoted to selling the La-Z-Boy line declined and sales declined substantially. Jess commented, "The decline was our own fault because we were so active in doing other things, we weren't paying attention to the chairs. It's hard to handle multiple stores and concentrate on everything all the time. You don't have the advertising budget for it, and you just pick on the things that are important to you and the things that are working and that are profitable. That's probably what we did, and there again, it was probably waterbeds—if you look at our books, it's probably waterbeds."

The Norwood furniture business is shifting from being a waterbed store marketing to lower end customers, to being a total furniture and furnishings store targeting middle to upper level income customers. Advertising the business now covers the entire range of media. Newspaper and radio continue to be their most effective forms with television a distant third. The Norwoods have a mobile lighted sign with removable letters in front of the Wilkes-Barre store. This lighted billboard is not the most beautiful, but it is a very effective device to attract the customer's attention.

ACCOUNTING AND FINANCE

During the first 16 years, Jess did all of the accounting, even though it was a task he did not enjoy. Jess would rather be out on the floor selling, but the $200 monthly fee an outside firm would charge, was just too much. In 1990, Jess did hire a full time bookkeeper/accountant to handle the stores' books. This person also does other jobs at the Hazelton store's location. What had appeared to be a continuous problem bothering Jess: "the yearly statements never being completed until several months after the year end closing" now seemed rectified with the addition of the new bookkeeper. The bookkeeper keeps running records of each stores operation and prepares the year-end financial tax return that summarizes each year's results for the total operation. Jess occasionally goes through the ledger to analyze how well various aspects of the business are performing. The financial statements for 1990, 1991, and 1992 are given at the end of this case (Exhibits 8–3, 8–4, and 8–5).

As 1992 was drawing to a close, Jess and Jan set two primary goals for their business. First, they want to get to a million dollar sales level; and second, they want to become the number one store in Wilkes-Barre. They feel that each goal is possible since, during the recent recession, the business has remained profitable. A concern in Jess's mind however is the, approximately, $500,000 debt load that the stores are carrying.

THE FUTURE

The Norwood store operations are running smoothly and each member of the family is participating in each store. Up-to-date records and other decision-making information has been developed by the bookkeeper. The Norwood customer base has remained stable and their policy of standing behind their products even after the manufacturer's warranty has expired is still a major selling point for people. The competition, formerly only stores selling furniture, has now become furniture stores that sell other lines of household goods such as kitchen appliances. Jess and Jan have noticed that Norwood's customers are now looking for a wide range of goods that extend beyond furniture. Jess is thinking about introducing a line of appliances to compliment the furniture and carpet business. Several customers have recently asked whether Norwoods carries kitchen appliances such as microwaves, stoves, and refrigerators.

EXHIBIT 8-3 Norwood Furniture Balance Sheet (Unaudited) December 31, 1990

	1990	1991	1992
ASSETS			
Current Assets			
Cash			
Accounts Receivable	$ 35,736	$ 31,171	$ 48,089
Inventory	14,639	22,638	30,329
	145,926	201,747	203,400
Total Current Assets	196,301	255,556	281,818
Property, Plant and Equipment:			
Land	85,000	85,000	85,000
Building	181,178	309,282	309,282
Building Improvements	78,511	69,264	69,264
Furniture and Fixtures	10,125	10,125	10,125
Delivery Equipment and Tools	49,469	49,469	80,205
Total Assets	404,283	523,140	553,876
Less: Accumulated Depreciation	95,629	107,093	124,067
Total Property, Plant and Equipment	308,654	416,047	429,809
TOTAL ASSETS	504,955	671,603	711,627
LIABILITIES AND PROPRIETOR'S CAPITAL			
Current Liabilities:			
Accounts Payable	20,249	15,858	36,905
Building Construction Cost Payable	57,380	0	0
Taxes Payable	9,338	7,022	9,429
Current Portion of Debt	8,813	316,011	62,439
Total Current Liabilities	95,780	338,891	108,773
Long-Term Liabilities:			
Note Payable—Bank Loans (Note B)	178,033	114,161	338,494
Total Long-Term Liabilities	178,033	114,161	338,494
TOTAL LIABILITIES	273,813	453,052	447,267
Owners' Equity	231,142	218,551	264,360
TOTAL LIABILITIES AND OWNERS' EQUITY	$504,955	$671,603	$711,627

Source: Norwood Furniture Company.

EXHIBIT 8-4 Norwood Furniture—Income Statement

	1990	1991	1992
SALES	$743,036	$791,629	$880,236
Less: Returns & Allowances	1,858	0	
Net Sales	741,178	791,629	880,236
Cost of Goods Sold	432,488	452,900	515,520
Gross Operating Profit	308,690	338,729	364,716
Operating Expenses			
Advertising	41,695		37,966
Car & Truck Expense	10,074		7,160
Depreciation and			
Section 179 Deduction	8,483		0
Dues and Subscriptions	0		873
Insurance	21,064		18,431
Interest—Mortgage	10,778		0
—Other	0		0
Legal and Professional Service	1,071		1,070
Office Expense	3,371		4,535
Rent or Lease:			
Machinery and Equipment	0		900
Other Business Property	10,400		0
Repairs and Maintenance	9,408		7,165
Supplies	59		1,384
Taxes and Licenses	4,046		20,606
Travel Meals & Entertainment:			
Travel	0		2,481
Meals & Entertainment	100		569
20% of (meals & entertainment) subject to limitation	20		0
Difference	80		0
Utilities	21,508		22,597
Wages	96,624		127,482
Other Expenses	13,639		4,427
Total Operating Expenses	252,420	244,137	257,646
NET OPERATING PROFIT (LOSS)	56,270	94,592	107,070
Other Expenses:			
Depreciation		11,464	16,974
Interest		37,745	29,773
Total Other Expenses		49,209	46,747
NET INCOME	56,270	45,383	60,323
Owner's Equity at Beginning of Year		231,142	218,551
Less: Owners' Withdrawals—Net		57,974	14,514
OWNERS' EQUITY AT END OF YEAR	$231,142	$218,551	$264,360

Source: Norwood Furniture Company.

EXHIBIT 8-5 Norwood Furniture 1992 Statement of Cash Flows (Unaudited)

Cash received from customers	$872,545	
Cash Paid to Suppliers	(496,126)	
Cash Paid for Expenses	(237,040)	
Cash Paid for Taxes	(18,199)	
Cash Paid for Interest	(29,773)	
Net Cash Provided by Operating Activities		$91,407
Cash Flows from Investing Activities:		
Purchase of Property, Plant & Equipment	(30,736)	
Net Cash Used by Investing Activities		(30,736)
Cash Flows from Financing Activity:		
Proceeds from issuance of Debt	273,198	
Payment of Debt	(302,437)	
Owner Withdrawals	(14,514)	
Net Cash Provided by Financing Activity		(43,753)
Net Increase (Decrease) in Cash		16,918
Cash at Beginning of Year		31,171
Cash at End of Year		48,089

Reconciliation of Net Income to Net Cash

Provided by Operating Activity

Net Income	$60,323
Add (deduct) items not using (providing) cash	16,974
(Increase) Decrease in Accts. Receivable	(7,691)
(Increase) Decrease in Inventory	(1,653)
Increase (Decrease) in Accts. Payable	21,047
Increase (Decrease) in Taxes Payable	$2,407
Net Cash Flows from Operating Activities	$91,407

Note A - Summary of Significant Accounting Policies
    Basis of Acctg.

    (Norwood) Furniture (a proprietorship) is engaged in the retail furniture business with stores in Pennsylvania. The financial statements are presented on an accrual basis of accounting. Inventory is valued using the lower of cost or market (FIFO) method.

    As a way to expand their product line, Jess is thinking about carrying used furniture. He and Jan agree that used furniture would be quite a departure from their original business objectives: "giving their customers quality at an above average margin of profit." However, just two months ago the Norwood's had a trade-in sale. Customers could trade in an old couch, sofa, or chair toward a new price of furniture. The result was a sale that far exceeded their wildest hopes and resulted in an entirely new market, people interested in buying the trade-ins. Many of the trade-ins were still excellent

EXHIBIT 8-5   *Continued*

Property, Plant and Equipment:

Depreciation of plant and equipment is provided on an accelerated depreciation method. Expenditures for maintenance and repairs are charged against operations, Renewals and betterments that materially extend the life of an asset are capitalized.

Federal Income Taxes:

The proprietorship itself is not a taxpaying entity for purposes of federal and state income taxes. Federal and state income taxes of the proprietor are computed on his total income from all sources, accordingly, no provision for income tax is made in this statement.

Note B - Long Term Debt

Note payable in equal monthly installments of $1,041 (int.=6%) collateralized by property and equipment.	$69,875	$8,527	$61,346
Mortgage payable in variable monthly installment (currently $2,517,73, including interest currently 8.875%). Amount and rate is adjusted annually in March.	242,872	12,725	230,147
Note payable in equal monthly installment of $555.10 (int.=6%).	43,599	4,158	39,441
Bank line of credit payable at Prime +1 (current int.=7%).	26,147	26,147	0
Note payable in equal monthly installments of $350 (int. at 9.25%).	10,884	3,324	7,560
Note payable in equal monthly installments of $349.61 (int. at 8.9%).	7,556	7,556	0
TOTAL	$400,933	$62,439	$338,494

Source: Norwood Furniture Company.

quality and had several years of good use left. Jess was able to set the trade-in price such that he made a good profit, and the buyer got a fair price. The trade-in sale involved delivery but did not involve guarantees, service agreements, or other contracts that linger on with the seller long after a new sale has been completed.

Jess is concerned about the closing of a clothing store located directly across the main street from their Hazleton store. Over the years, Jess has found that women coming into town for clothes shopping will often shop other stores close by.

Jess and Jan are interested in letting their sons take over the total operation. There are now grand children to enjoy, and Jess and Jan both have some health problems. Jess and Jan are unsure how to best step aside and allow their children to run the business. Develop a strategic plan for Jess and Jan to guide the Norwood Furniture Company to continued growth and profitability in the mid-to-late 1990s.

DAVE'S PIT STOP CAFE—1993*

Dave's Pit Stop Cafe (517-269-5945) is located in the center of Bad Axe, Michigan, a small town surrounded by rich agricultural land that serves as the county seat for Huron County. Huron County's two major industries are agriculture (it has long been a major producer of corn, sugar beets, and soy beans) and, during the summer months, tourism. The main road through Bad Axe is M-53, which originates in Detroit a hundred miles due south and terminates seventeen miles north of Bad Axe at the village of Port Austin on the shore of Lake Huron. M-53 makes a right angle turn to the east shortly before it enters Bad Axe, as shown in Exhibit 9–1. It turns north again at the stoplight at the center of town.

EXHIBIT 9-1 Location of Dave's Pit Stop Cafe and Selected Other Businesses, Bad Axe, MI

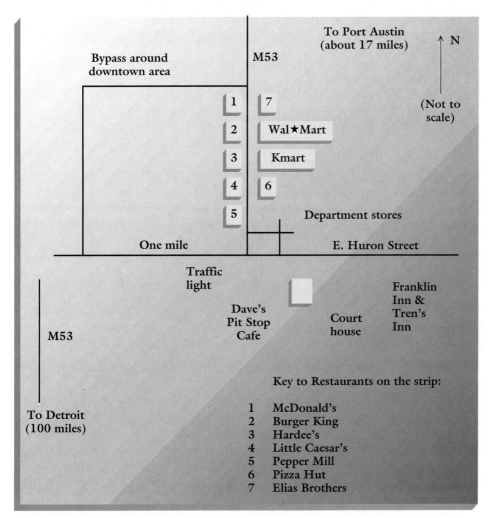

* Copyright 1993 by Henry H. Beam

EXHIBIT 9-2 Dave's Pit Stop Cafe

A block to the east, on the northwest corner, is Dave's Pit Stop Cafe. The court house and the offices of ten lawyers, several real estate and insurance agencies, and a two-person architectural firm are within a block of the cafe. According to the 1990 census, the population of Bad Axe, 3,484, has changed little for over fifty years.

In the summer of 1992, visitors to Dave's Pit Stop Cafe could not miss the rear of a 1957 Chevy sticking out of the second floor. The owner, Dave Schemansky, had wanted to do something creative to make people take a second look. Thus, he bought an original 1957 Chevrolet, tail fins and all, and had the vehicle cut in two. Then he had the rear half bolted to the exterior above the building's entrance (Exhibit 9–2). The interior walls were decorated with framed posters of automobiles and a classic pop poster of Marlon Brando on a motorcycle as he appeared in the 1954 movie, *The Wild One*. Michigan license plates dating from the 1950s were displayed on the walls, adding to the vintage automobile theme.

HOW THE PIT STOP CAME INTO BEING

"I like cars. I've always been around them and I really like them." That's what Dave Schemansky, 34, told a *Huron Daily Tribune* reporter shortly after he opened his restaurant in December, 1991. The menu, as well as the rear of the '57 Chevy mounted over the entrance, reflect this interest. All the deli sandwiches are named after automobiles of the 1950s and 1960s, such as the Cadillac Eldorado (a corned beef and swiss cheese triple decker) and the Ford Galaxie (turkey, ham, tomato, lettuce, and mayonnaise). The summer 1992 menu is shown in Exhibit 9–3. Dave's specialty is chili. Over fifteen gallons are sold daily during the winter months. In 1991, Dave won second place with his recipe at the Huron County chili cookoffs.

Dave graduated from high school in Royal Oak, a northern suburb of Detroit. His interest in cars comes naturally, since his father worked for Ford Motor Company for over forty years. Dave worked as a design technician first for General Motors, then for

EXHIBIT 9-3 The Summer 1992 Menu

"Coney Island"

1-C	Hot Dog	1.25
2-C	Coney Island Hot Dog	1.40
	Hot dog served with chili, mustard and onions	
3-C	Dave's Special	2.15
	Hot dog served with chili, mustard, onion, ground beef and cheese	
4-C	Loose Hamburger	1.75
	Served with chili, mustard and onions	
5-C	Hotdog with Saurerkraut	1.70

"Chili"

6-C	Dave's Famous Chili	1.60

"Hamburgers"

(All our burgers start with 1/3 lb. all beef served with lettuce, tomato, onion, pickle and mayo on a toasted bun.)

7-C	Hamburger	2.35
8-C	Hamburger Deluxe	3.35
	with fries and coleslaw	
9-C	Cheeseburger	2.60
10-C	Cheeseburger Deluxe	3.60
	with fries and coleslaw	
11-C	Bacon Cheeseburger	2.85
12-C	Patty Melt	2.80
	1/3 lb beef with cheese and onion grilled together on rye	
13-C	Deli Burger	4.85
	1/3 lb. hamburger, pastrami, swiss cheese, lettuce, tomato and onion, topped with Russian dressing	
14-C	Double Cheese Burger	5.00
15-C	Chili Cheese Burger	3.10

21-D	Woody	4.30
	Pastrami, swiss cheese and Russian dressing	
22-D	Biscayne	4.65
	Corned beef, swiss, cheese, cole slaw and Russian dressing	
23-D	Plymouth Sport Fury	5.95
	Hot pastrami, corned beef, swiss cheese, dipped in Russian dressing	
24-D	Rueben	4.65
	(Guaranteed to please the most discriminating) Corned beef, swiss cheese and sauerkraut on three thin slices of rye and grilled	Half 3.05
25-D	Buick Special	4.70
	Triple Decker-Roast beef, tomato, egg, lettuce and Russian dressing	Half 3.00
26-D	Dave's Limousine	6.40
	A bit of everything on large (white or rye)	

"Meat on Rye"

Corned Beef	3.95
Hot Pastrami	4.95
Roast Beef	4.05

"Just Plain Good"

Sliced Turkey	3.65
Chicken Salad	3.00
Tunafish Salad	2.75
Grilled Cheese	1.25
Egg Salad	1.50
Ham	3.25
Tuna Melt	3.75
Tuna on grilled rye bread with American cheese	

	Grilled Ham & Cheese	2.50
16-C	Mushroom Burger	4.00
	Sauted mushroom & swiss cheese	
17-C	Pitstop Burger	3.75
	Hamburger, ham & swiss cheese	
18-C	Philly Burger	3.50
	Hamburger, grilled green peppers/onions and swiss cheese	
19-C	Olive Burger	4.00
	Hamburger smothered with olives	
20-C	Garbage Burger	4.75
	Hamburger with ham, cheese, bacon, onions, mushrooms & green peppers	
21-C	Fire Pit Burger	4.75
	Hamburger, salsa sauce, refried beans, jalopena peppers and sour cream	

"Dave's Deli Delights"

(All sandwiches served with chips and a pickle)

1-D	Chevrolet Bel-Air	4.40
	Triple decker-corned beef, lettuce, tomato and Russian dressing	Half 2.85
2-D	Buick Skylark	4.65
	Triple decker-corned beef, egg, lettuce, tomato and Russian dressing	Half 3.00
3-D	Chevrolet Corvette	4.50
	Pastrami, egg coleslaw and Russian dressing	Half 2.90
4-D	Cadillac Eldorado	4.80
	Triple decker-corned beef, swiss cheese, lettuce, tomato and Russian dressing	Half 3.12
5-D	Packard	4.30
	Triple Decker-chicken salad, lettuce and tomato	Half 2.80
6-D	T-Bird	4.70
	Triple decker-turkey, bacon, lettuce, tomato and mayonnaise	Half 3.05

"Salads of the Seasons"

Tossed Salad	Sm. 1.50.........Lg.1.75
Tuna Salad Platter	4.00
Hard boiled egg, sliced tomatoes, large scoop of white meat tuna, served on a bed of crispy lettuce	
Chicken Salad Platter	4.10
Hard boiled egg, sliced tomatoes, large scoop of chicken salad, served on a bed of crispy lettuce	
Greek Salad	Sm. 3.75 Lg. 4.25
Made with selected greens, tomatoes, feta cheese, olives, onions and beets	
Julienne Salad	Sm. 3.65 Lg. 4.00
Ham, turkey, hard broiled egg, Swiss cheese and American cheese	

"Along Side"

French Fries...1.00 Chili Fries	1.50
Cheese Fries..1.30 Cole Slaw	30
Onion Chips..1.50	
Chili/Cheese Fries	1.75

"Children's Menu"

(12 Years and Under)

Hamburger	2.60
Served with fries, pop or milk	
Grilled Cheese Sandwich	2.05
Served with fries, pop or milk	
Hot Dog	2.05
Served with fries, pop or milk	

"Beverages"

Soft Drinks	Sm. 65 Lg.75
Milk (white)	Sm. 70 Lg.85
Coffee	50 ....Decaf. 50
Hot Chocolate	60

7-D	Chevrolet Impala	3.95
	Triple decker-bacon, tomato, lettuce and mayonnaise	Half 2.60
8-D	Studebaker Hawk	4.50
	Triple decker-sliced turkey, lettuce, tomato and mayonnaise	Half 2.90
9-D	Mercury	4.65
	Triple decker-ham, lettuce, tomato, swiss cheese and mayonnaise	Half 3.00
11-D	Buick Electra	4.40
	Triple decker-pastrami, coleslaw and Russian dressing	Half 2.85
12-D	Corvette Sting Ray	4.60
	Triple decker-roast beef, onion, lettuce, tomato, american cheese and mayonnaise	Half 2.95
13-D	Ford Mustang 2+2	5.95
	4 decker-corned beef, pastrami, lettuce, tomato and Russian dressing	Half 3.85
14-D	Dodge Coronet Super Bee	4.30
	Hot corned beef, swiss cheese and lettuce	
15-D	Pontiac GTO	4.25
	Hot pastrami, coleslaw, and Russian dressing	
16-D	Pontiac Firebird	4.40
	Hot corned beef, coleslaw and Russian dressing	
17-D	Plymouth Road Runner	4.50
	Turkey, coleslaw and Russian dressing	
18-D	Ford Galaxie	4.70
	Turkey, ham, tomato, lettuce, and mayonnaise	
19-D	Tucker	5.70
	Sliced turkey, pastrami, swiss cheese and Russian Dressing	
20-D	Pontiac Catalina	3.65
	Swiss cheese, lettuce, tomato and mayonnaise	

Free Delivery
with $15.00 Purchase

181 E. Huron

Bad Axe

269-2760

Ford Motor Company. However, during the difficult times in the automobile industry in the late 1980s, he was laid off, which gave him the incentive to open the restaurant. "I'd seen this building here for a long time, and I always said it had potential, if it just had atmosphere." Thus Dave leased the building, formerly used as a Dairy Queen, gutted it, and installed new plumbing, wiring, and kitchen equipment. He was assisted in the renovation by his girlfriend, Patty Bowen, who also did the bookkeeping. For seating, there were eight tables with four chairs each. All 955 square feet of space on the main level was used for the restaurant, while the 650 square feet of space on the second floor was divided between storage and a small office.

Initially, the Pit Stop opened at 6 A.M. for breakfast, but there were few customers. After a few months of operation, Dave settled on the following hours:

Monday through Wednesday	9:30 A.M. to 7:00 P.M.
Thursday and Friday	9:30 A.M. to 8:00 P.M.
Saturday	9:30 A.M. to 6:00 P.M.
Sunday	Closed

The slowest part of the day is from opening until 11:00 A.M. The busiest day is usually Friday, which is also payday for many local workers.

LARGE HELPINGS AND SERVICE

Dave takes pride in the large helpings served to customers. As he puts it, "We serve the biggest sandwiches in town—everybody gets a to-go box!" One customer who ate lunch at the cafe in June 1992, ordered the Hamburger Deluxe with french fried potatoes, coleslaw, and coffee. He was able to eat the hamburger, but, true to Dave's word, he took most of the french fries home in a to-go box. Others who eat at Dave's cafe agree that the food is good but the portions are too large for most people.

All food is prepared to order and only fresh meat is used. Dave does most of the cooking, an activity he enjoys. During busy periods, such as lunch time, two or three waitresses seat customers, take orders, and serve the food. Otherwise, there is usually only one waitress. Waitresses are paid minimum wage ($4.25 per hour in 1992).

Most people who eat at Dave's are not in a hurry. Nevertheless, there are occasional complaints about slow service or unavailability of some items on the menu. For example, at a time when the cafe was not busy, one customer waited five minutes for a waitress to bring him a menu after he was seated, and an additional fifteen minutes for the waitress to bring him his order. Another customer, who had brought his family to the cafe for lunch, was disappointed to find that Dave was out of chili, his specialty. His children ordered milk, but Dave was out of that, too, so they had soft drinks instead. Other than that, their food was fine.

COMMERCIAL DEVELOPMENT AND COMPETITION

During the 1980s, most commercial development in Bad Axe took place along a two mile section of M-53 on the northern edge of the town. Both Kmart and Wal★Mart built stores along this "strip". This strip also features two hardware stores, three medium sized supermarkets, and several gas stations with mini-marts in them. Burger King, Hardee's, and McDonald's each have a fast food franchise along this strip. Pizza is available from Little Caesar's and Pizza Hut. The Elias Brothers Big Boy restaurant at the north end and the Pepper Mill at the south end feature family style meals served by a waitress. It is a little over a mile from Dave's Pit Stop Cafe to the Pepper Mill, where the strip begins.

Dave's cafe is located in the center of town. Two small, family-owned restaurants are located nearby. Two motels, the Franklin Inn and Tren's Inn, are located less than a mile to the east of M-53. Each has a restaurant and a lounge. A large department store building in the block to the east of Dave's has been vacant for over a year. It is for sale for $125,000. For many years, it housed the Polewach store, Bad Axe's largest merchandiser prior to the arrival of Kmart. Another longtime downtown business, the D & C Variety Store, closed in December 1992. Exhibit 9–4 gives some economic data on Huron County.

FINANCIAL ASPECTS

Dave leases the building for his Pit Stop Cafe from Willet O'Dell. Willet's permanent residence had been in New Jersey, but since retiring in 1988, he and his wife spend the summer months at their cottage near Port Austin and travel most of the rest of the year. Willet has long-standing family ties to Bad Axe. The lot on which the cafe is located had belonged to Willet's grandfather at a time when it was considered the best commercial location in Bad Axe. His grandfather had operated a general merchandise store on the site until a fire destroyed it in 1920. In 1950, Willet's father leased the lot to a local businessman who built a cinder-block structure that served as a Dairy Queen during summer months. However, the lease contained no provision for the owner of the Dairy Queen building to buy the lot.

Willet inherited the lot and the lease in 1986 after the death of his mother. Tired of years of sporadic lease payments by the tenant, Willet took ownership of the Dairy Queen building in 1990 in return for forgiveness of all unpaid rent. The building and a small parking area each occupied about half the 44 foot by 100 foot lot. Additional parking (at no charge) was readily available along the streets adjacent to the restaurant.

In September 1991, a real estate consultant prepared a report for Willet which estimated the market value of the land at $27,600 and the property (land, unoccupied building, and equipment) at about $57,550. According to the tax assessment, the value of the property was $70,400. The consultant suggested a selling price for the property of $69,000. Rather than sell the property, Willet opted to lease the land and building.

Dave Schemansky was one of two individuals who expressed an interest in leasing the building for use as a restaurant. He developed a business plan which showed an estimated monthly pre-tax profit of $2,257 on estimated monthly sales of $12,500. In November 1991, Dave signed a one-year lease with monthly payments of $725. The lease contained an option, exercisable anytime during the life of the lease, for Dave to buy the lot and building for $75,000 on a land contract. (A land contract is an agreement between a buyer and a seller of real estate, with no financial institution involved. The seller holds title to the property until the final payment is made. If the buyer defaults (i.e., fails to make payments as specified in the agreement), the land contract is void and the seller keeps the property, the down payment and any payments made.) Terms were at $15,000 down payment with 9.5 percent interest on the unpaid balance for ten years. The lease also contained a clause which stated, "Tenant's failure to pay rent when due or to perform any of his obligations hereunder shall constitute a default." Once the lease had been signed, Willet spent about $7,000 to have a new roof put on the building and to have the exterior painted in bright art deco colors.

Business at the restaurant generally is brisk, with sales highest, as expected, during the summer months. Sales for August 1992 were unusually low because the city of Bad

EXHIBIT 9-4 Economic Data on Huron County

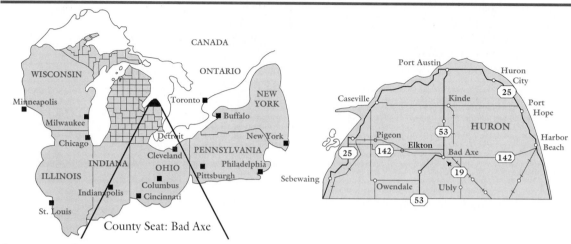

County Seat: Bad Axe

PROFILE OF HURON COUNTY, MICHIGAN
January, 1992

LOCATION SERVICES
Huron County Economic Development Corporation
250 East Huron, Room 302
Bad Axe, MI 48413

Contact: Carl Osentoski
Phone: 517/269-6431

POPULATION

1970 Census	34083
1980 Census	36459
1990 Census	34951
Median Age (as of 1990)	35.8 years

LABOR FORCE *(1990 average)*

Total Labor Force	16475
Employed	14800
Total Unemployment	1675
Unemployment Rate	10.1%
3-Year Average	9.8%

PRINCIPAL ECONOMIC BASE EMPLOYERS

Active Industries, Elkton	887	Metal stamping
Michigan Sugar, Sebewaing	380	Beet sugar
Sebewaing Industries, Sebewaing	369	Automotive stampings
NutraSweet, Harbor Beach	128	Medicinal/Botanical
U.S. Mfg., Bad Axe	120	Steering gears & boxes
Gemini Plastics	105	Plastic profile extrusions
Arjay Mfg., Bad Axe	94	Custom molding/thermoplastics
Nortec, Bad Axe	94	Custom plastic molding
Walbro Precision Plastics	94	Molded thermoplastic parts
Pigeon Mfg., Pigeon	88	Metal stamping
Thumb Tool & Engineering, Bad Axe	78	Extrusion dies
Huron Tool	70	Automotive
Hercules, Harbor Beach	69	Food seasonings
Acme Roll Forming, Sebewaing	60	Sheet metal
Derek Tool, Owendale	50	Carbide tools
Vultron, Bad Axe	50	Electronic signs
Cel-Star, Port Austin	40	Rubber products
Spartan Carbide, Bad Axe	40	Carbide tools
Port Austin Level, Port Austin	35	Levels
Lyntex Mfg., Ubly	30	Cut & sew of webbings, elastic
Total Employees:	2881	

Source: Michigan Department of Commerce, County Profiles.

Axe had the downtown streets, including the one in front of Dave's cafe, blocked off for over a week to install new sidewalks. Exhibit 9–5 gives some data on sales for the months of May 1992 through September 1992. Exhibit 9–6 shows the estimated

EXHIBIT 9-5 Data on May – September Monthly Sales

MONTH	SALES	HIGHEST DAILY SALES	DAY	LOWEST DAILY SALES	DAY	DAYS OPEN
May	$9,004.57	$649.63	Friday	$ 96.14	Monday	26
June	8,494.75	————	not available	————		
July	8,894.37	$488.58	Friday	$192.40	Tuesday	26
August	4,824.00	————	not available	————		
September (estimated)	7,500.00	————	not available	————		

Source: Dave's Pit Stop Cafe.

EXHIBIT 9-6 Expenses for the Month of July, 1992

NON-FOOD EXPENSES:

Rent	$ 725.00
Gas	65.00
Electric	310.00
Water	50.00
Phone	95.00
Waste Removal	86.00
Coke Machine	30.00
Towels	40.00
Bookkeeping	150.00
Health Insurance	287.52
Restaurant Insurance	167.00
Advertising (local radio station)	45.00
Part time help (waitresses)	1,400.00
Load repayment	685.00
Subtotal	$4,135.52
FOOD EXPENSES (ESTIMATED):	$1,600.00
Total expenses	$5,735.52

Source: Dave's Pit Stop Cafe.

expenses for operation Dave's Pit Stop Cafe for the month of July 1992. Nevertheless, Dave has struggled to make his monthly rent payments to Willet almost from the start. Failure to pay rent on time is costly, since the lease contains a clause which requires Dave to pay a penalty of five dollars per day for each day the rent is late. In June 1992, after repeated prodding from Willet, Dave paid three of the five months of back rent he owed. He also asked for a reduction in the rent to $500 a month, noting that commercial property in downtown Bad Axe rented for between 28 and 32 cents per square foot per month. Dave also claimed that he had spent $27,000, considerably more than he had anticipated, to make the improvements that resulted in his cafe.

As of August 1, 1992, Dave owed Willet $1,975 in back rent and $1,530 in late fees. He also owed about $1,400 to various contractors for work done renovating the building's interior. After some haggling about payment of the back rent, Willet and Dave agreed to modify the lease, effective August 14, 1992. The rent was reduced to $550 per month and was due on the 14th of the month rather than the 1st. Willet also waived all late payments up to August 14, 1992, and reduced future late payments from $5 to $2 per day. Dave brought his rental payments up to date as of October 14, 1992. However, he failed to make the November payment.

DAVE'S SITUATION IN DECEMBER 1992

As December 14th approached, Dave needed to make a major decision. If he did not make his December rental payment on time, he would fall two months behind in his payments. If this happened, Willet, who had grown increasingly impatient with Dave's failure to pay rent on time, would probably enforce the default provision. Dave would no longer be able to operate his Pit Stop Cafe at its present location. Willet would have to find another tenant for the building or sell it. On the other hand, if Dave wanted to exercise his option to buy the land and the building, he would need to make both the November and December rental payments by December 14th. He would then have to come up with $15,000 for the down payment by August 1993. This would be difficult, since Dave had little personal property and he had already borrowed a substantial amount from his father to start the Pit Stop Cafe.

Conduct a strategic analysis for Dave's Pit Stop Cafe. Do you feel Dave can stay in business? Should he stay in business? Prepare a strategic plan for Dave giving specific recommendations and your justifications.

CASE 10

CLAIRE ANDERSON
Old Dominion University
CAROLINE FISHER
Loyola University

AUDUBON ZOO—1994

The Audubon Zoo (504-861-2537) is located in New Orleans, Louisiana. The ancient business of making money on wild animals has become exceptionally competitive. More and more money is spent every year to build, expand, and improve zoos and aquariums in the United States, reaching over $1.2 billion in 1992. The building of mega-aquariums, known in the business as the "blue wave," cost nearly $100 million each and may feature acrylic tunnels that let you walk beneath sharks. Zoos are fighting back with multimillion-dollar exhibits with real animal sounds and exotic surroundings.

More people today go to zoos and aquariums than attend professional football, basketball, and baseball games combined; 105 million in 1992. However, the animal industry is on the defensive as never before. Animal rights groups have stepped up criticism of zoos and aquariums. The popularity of *Free Willy*, a movie about a boy and a sadly caged whale, fueled critics' attacks. Zoo attendance is increasing only slightly and governments are slashing budgets for nonprofit zoos. Zoo biologists are giving way to zoo marketers who are looking for unique ways to increase revenues, such as hosting corporate meetings, regional sales meetings, cocktail parties, weddings, and even conventions. At Zoo Atlanta, for example, 75 after-hour events brought in $200,000 in 1992, up from zero four years ago. Zoo Atlanta allows you to reserve the zoo for five hours for $6,000 and touch some of the animals. Zoo Atlanta is now taking reservations for 1996 Olympic corporate parties.

The Fort Worth Zoo caters dinner parties and business meetings. The Aquarium of the Americas in New Orleans lets you reserve an evening meeting for $4,000 for three hours, with cocktails and food costing extra. The four Sea Worlds host business after-hours events for $22 a person, park admission included, food and beverages extra.

Zoo and aquarium managers know that animal rights activists are persistent. *Free Willy* ends with a toll-free telephone number for people who want to learn more about protecting whales. "People are starting to see these places as a-*buse*-ment parks," Dan Matthews of People for the Ethical Treatment of Animals says. All zoos, aquariums, and marine theme parks are animal prisons and in the greed business, he says. Marketing campaigns strive to position zoos as protectors of species not as cagers of animals. Both zoos and aquariums are run mostly by not-for-profit foundations that constantly remind society that their income goes toward fighting animal extinction. Some zoos even change their name, such as the Bronx Zoo, which now is called the International Wildlife Conservation Park.

For-profit Sea World constantly battles an image problem, annually spending more than $1 million rescuing and rehabilitating animals. Although more than 90 percent of Anheuser-Busch's operating income comes from beer, the company's 1991 *Annual Report* is entitled "A Century of Environmental Responsibility." The *Annual Report* is devoted to the company's commitment to animal welfare.

Although activists probably will not win the release of zoo and marine animals, they could cause a whale of a problem if corporate sponsors decline. Few doubt that the industry, which goes back at least 3,000 years to China, will survive, but innovative strategies will be needed.

HISTORY

The Audubon Zoo was the focus of national concern in the early 1970s, with well-documented stories of animals kept in conditions that were variously termed an "animal ghetto," "the New Orleans antiquarium," and even "an animal concentration camp." In 1971, the Bureau of Governmental Research recommended a $5.6 million zoo improvement plan to the Audubon Park Commission and the City Council of New Orleans. The local *Times Picayune* commented on the new zoo: "It's not going to be quite like the 'Planet of the Apes' situation in which the apes caged and studied human beings but something along those broad general lines." The new zoo confines people to bridges and walkways while the animals roam amid grass, shrubs, trees, pools, and fake rocks. The gracefully curving pathways, generously lined with luxuriant plantings, give the visitor a sense of being alone in a wilderness, although crowds of visitors may be only a few yards away.

A chronology of major events in the life of the Audubon Zoo is presented in Exhibit 10–1. One of the first significant changes made was the institution of an admission charge in 1972. Admission to the zoo had been free to anyone prior to the adoption of the renovation plan. Ostensibly, the initial purpose behind instituting the admission charge was to prevent vandalism, but the need for additional income was also apparent. Despite the establishment of and increases in admission charges, admission charges have increased dramatically. Exhibit 10–4 reveals that attendance also is seasonal, with July and August being the busiest months and December and January being the slowest months.

The Audubon Park Commission launched a $5.6 million developmental program based on the Bureau of Governmental Research plan for the zoo in March

1972. A bond issue and a property tax dedicated to the zoo were put before the voters on November 7, 1972. When it passed by an overwhelming majority, serious discussions began about what should be done. The New Orleans City Planning Commission finally approved the master plan for the Audubon Park Zoo in September 1973. But the institution of the master plan was far from smooth.

Over two dozen special interests were ultimately involved in choosing whether to renovate and expand the existing facilities or move to another site. Expansion became a major community controversy. Some residents opposed the zoo expansion, fearing that "loss of green space" would affect the secluded character of the neighborhood. Others opposed the loss of what they saw as an attractive and educational facility.

Most of the opposition came from the zoo's affluent neighbors. Zoo director John Moore ascribed the criticism to "a select few people who have the money and power to make a lot of noise." He went on to say, "The real basis behind the problem is that the neighbors who live around the edge of the park have a selfish concern because they want the park as their private back yard." Legal battles over the expansion plans continued until early 1976. At that time, the Fourth Circuit Court of Appeals ruled that the expansion was legal. An out-of-court agreement with the zoo's neighbors (the Upper Audubon Association) followed shortly.

The expansion of the Audubon Zoo took it from 14 to 58 acres. The zoo was laid out in geographical sections: the Asian Domain, World of Primates, World's Grasslands, Savannah, North American Prairie, South American Pampas, and Louisiana Swamp, according to the master plan developed by the Bureau of

---

EXHIBIT 10-1 Chronology of Events for the New Zoo

1972	Voters approved a referendum to provide tax dollars to renovate and expand the Zoo. The first Zoo-To-Do was held. An admission charge was instituted.
1973	The City Planning Commission approved a master plan for the Audubon Park Zoo calling for $3.4 million for upgrading. Later phases called for an additional $2.1 million to be completed by 1978.
1974	Friends of the Zoo formed with 400 members to increase support and awareness of the Zoo.
1975	Renovations began—$25 million public and private funds—14 acres to be expanded to 58 acres.
1976	The Friends of the Zoo assumed responsibility for concessions.
1977	John Moore went to Albuquerque, Ron Forman took over as Park and Zoo director.
1980	First full time education staff assumed duties at the Zoo.
1980	Last animal removed from antiquated cage—a turning point in Zoo history.
1981	Contract signed allowing New Orleans Steamboat Company to bring passengers from downtown to the Park.
1981	Delegates from the American Association of Zoological Parks Aquariums ranked the Audubon Zoo as one of the top three zoos of its size in America.
1981	Zoo accredited.
1982	The Audubon Park Commission reorganized under Act 352, which required the Commission to contract with a non-profit organization for the daily management of the Park.
1985	The Zoo was designated as a Rescue Center for Endangered and Threatened Plants.
1986	Voters approved a $25 million bond issue for the Aquarium.
1988	The Friends of the Zoo became The Audubon Institute.
1990	The Aquarium of the Americas opened in September.
1993	Freeport-McMoran Audubon Species Survival Center opened.
1995	Audubon Center for Research on Endangered Species scheduled to open.
1995	Audubon Insectarium scheduled to open.

Source: The Audubon Institute.

Governmental Research. Additional exhibits included the Wisner Discovery Zoo, Sea Lion exhibit, and Flight Cage. See Exhibit 10–2 for a map of the new zoo.

The Audubon Zoo currently employs 625 people and has a local economic impact of $100 million annually. More than 80,000 households and 200,000 individuals are members of the Zoo. The Zoo plans to open the Freeport-McMoran Audubon

EXHIBIT 10-2   A Map of the Audubon Park Zoo

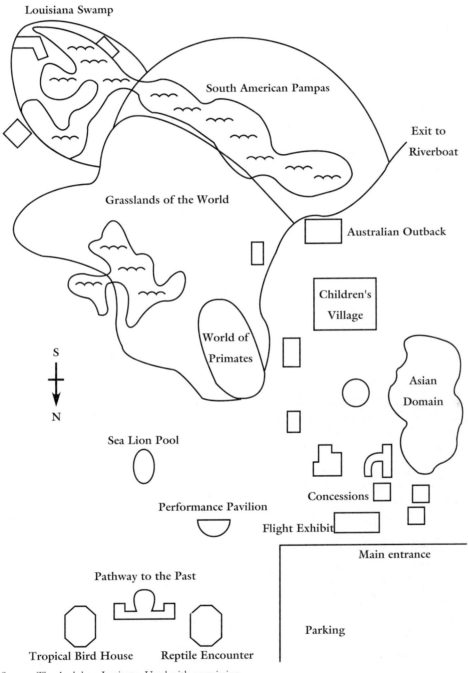

Source: The Audubon Institute. Used with permission.

Species Survival Center in 1993, the Audubon Center for Research on Endangered Species in 1995, and the Audubon Insectarium in 1995.

PURPOSE

The main outward purpose of the Audubon Zoo is entertainment. Many of the zoo's promotional efforts are aimed at creating an image of the zoo as an entertaining place to go. Obviously, such a campaign is necessary to attract visitors to the zoo. Behind the scenes, the zoo also preserves and breeds many animal species, conducts research, and educates the public. The mission statement of the Audubon Institute, which encompasses the zoo, is given in Exhibit 10–3.

OPERATIONS

Friends of the Zoo. Friends of the Zoo was formed in 1974 and incorporated in 1975 with 400 original members. The group's stated purpose is to increase support and awareness of the Audubon Zoo. Initially, Friends of the Zoo tried to raise interest and commitment to the zoo, but its activities have increased dramatically over the years to include funding, operating, and governing the zoo. Friends of the Zoo has a 24-member governing board. Yearly elections are held for six members of the board who serve four-year terms. The board oversees the policies of the zoo and sets guidelines for memberships, concessions, fund-raising, and marketing. Actual policy making and operations are controlled by the Audubon Park Commission, however, which sets zoo hours, admission prices, and so forth.

Through its volunteer programs, Friends of the Zoo staffs many of the zoo's programs. Volunteers from members of the Friends of the Zoo served as "edZOOcators," education volunteers who are specially trained to conduct interpretive education programs, and "Zoo Area Patrollers," who provide general informa-

---

EXHIBIT 10-3 Audubon Institute Mission Statement

The mission of the Audubon Institute is to cultivate awareness and appreciation of life and the earth's resources and to help conserve and enrich our natural world. The Institute's primary objectives toward this are:

Conservation: To participate in the global effort to conserve natural resources by developing and maintaining captive stocks of endangered plants, animals, and marine life, and by cooperating with related projects in the wild.

Education: To impart knowledge and understanding of the interaction of nature and man through programs, exhibits, and publications and to encourage public participation in global conservation efforts.

Research: To foster the collection and dissemination of scientific information that will enhance the conservation and educational objectives of the facilities of the Audubon Institute.

Economics: To insure long–range financial security by sound fiscal management and continued development, funding through creative means that encourage corporate, foundation, and individual support.

Leadership: To serve as a model in the civic and professional communities. To foster a spirit of cooperation, participation, and pride.

Source: The Audubon Institute.

tion about a geographic area of the zoo and help with crowd control. Other volunteers assist in the Commissary, Animal Health Care Center, and Wild Bird Rehabilitation Center or help with membership, public relations, graphics, clerical work, research, or horticulture.

In 1988, the name of the Friends of the Zoo was changed to the Audubon Institute to reflect its growing interest in activities beyond the zoo alone. It planned to promote the development of other facilities and manage these facilities once they were a reality.

Fund-Raising. The Audubon Zoo and the Audubon Institute raise funds through five major types of activities: Friends of the Zoo membership, concessions, Adopt an Animal, Zoo-to-Do, and capital fund drives. Zoo managers from around the country come to the Audubon Zoo for tips on fund-raising.

Membership. Membership in the Audubon Institute is open to anyone. Admission prices and membership fees have increased over the years, as summarized in Exhibits 10–4 and 10–5. The number of members also increased steadily, from the original 400 members in 1974 to 38,000 members in 1990, but decreased to 28,000 in 1992.

EXHIBIT 10-4 Audubon Zoo Admission Data

YEAR	SENIOR/ ADULT	CHILD
1972	$0.75	$0.25
1978	1.00	0.50
1979	1.50	0.75
1980	2.00	1.00
1981	2.50	1.25
1982	3.00	1.50
1983	3.50	1.75
1984	4.00	2.00
1985	4.50	2.00
1986	5.00	2.50
1987	5.50	2.50
1988	5.50	2.50
1989	6.00	3.00
1990	6.50	3.00
1991	7.00	3.25
1992	7.00	3.25
1993	7.50	3.50

EXHIBIT 10-4 *Continued*

ADMISSIONS FOR 1990–1993

AUDUBON ZOO

MONTH	1990	1991	1992	1993
January	38,091	18,710	27,139	35,797
February	49,881	38,296	47,411	38,878
March	125,551	99,217	104,906	87,959
April	129,408	92,776	109,825	136,157
May	126,881	89,881	119,948	132,685
June	88,600	83,655	79,607	80,636
July	95,923	81,746	77,279	90,232
August	101,309	94,022	99,724	84,118
September	57,105	51,180	39,380	51,485
October	77,948	87,642	90,131	
November	63,940	56,882	50,960	
December	26,856	32,178	30,498	
Total	981,493	826,167	876,708	737,947

AQUARIUM OF THE AMERICAS

MONTH	1990	1991	1992	1993
January		128,894	79,786	71,041
February		127,718	82,761	66,619
March		206,931	142,383	117,290
April		182,614	135,815	116,437
May		199,232	145,879	139,975
June		191,603	136,262	135,232
July		235,093	182,461	177,725
August		207,544	157,969	143,152
September	247,875	112,574	90,965	88,778
October	220,498	101,583	94,301	
November	201,021	109,766	85,670	
December	162,334	98,561	72,889	
Total	831,728	1,902,113	1,407,061	1,056,249

Source: The Audubon Institute.

Membership allows free entry to the Audubon Zoo and many other zoos around the United States. Participation in Zoobilation (annual-members-only evenings at the zoo) and the many volunteer programs described earlier are other benefits of membership.

Increasing membership required a special approach to marketing the zoo. Chip Weigand, director of marketing for the zoo, says:

> In marketing memberships, we try to encourage repeat visitations, the feeling that one can visit as often as one wants, the idea that the zoo changes from visit to visit and that there are

EXHIBIT 10-5 Audubon Zoo Membership Fees and Membership

YEAR	FAMILY MEMBERSHIP FEES	INDIVIDUAL MEMBERSHIP FEES	NUMBER OF MEMBERSHIPS
1979	$20	$10	1,000
1980	20	10	7,000
1981	20	10	11,000
1982	25	15	18,000
1983	30	15	22,000
1984	35	20	26,000
1985	40	20	27,000
1986	45	25	28,616
1987	45	25	29,318
1988	45	25	33,314
1989	49	29	35,935
1990	49	29	38,154
1991	49	30	30,171
1992	49	30	28,422

Source: The Audubon Institute.

good reasons to make one large payment or donation for a membership card, rather than paying for each visit. . . . The overwhelming factor is a good zoo that people want to visit often, so that a membership makes good economical sense.

Results of research conducted on visitors to the zoo are contained in Exhibits 10–6 and 10–7.

The zoo has a membership designed for businesses, the Audubon Zoo Curator Club, with four categories of membership: Bronze, $250; Silver, $500; Gold, $1,000; and Platinum, $2,500 and more.

Concessions. The Audubon Zoo concessions for refreshments and gifts are run by volunteer members of the Audubon Institute, and all profits go directly to the zoo. Profits from operation of the concession brought in $400,000 a year by 1980 and over $1 million in profits in 1990. In 1993, the Audubon Institute was considering leasing the concessions to a third party vendor.

Adopt an Animal. Zoo Parents pay a fee to "adopt" an animal, the fee varying with the animal chosen. Zoo Parents' names are listed on a large sign inside the zoo. They also have their own celebration, Zoo Parents Day, held at the zoo yearly.

Zoo-to-Do. Zoo-to-Do is a black-tie fund-raiser held annually with live music, food and drink, and original, high-class souvenirs such as posters or ceramic necklaces. Admission tickets, limited to 3,000 annually, are priced starting at $100 per person. A raffle is conducted in conjunction with the Zoo-to-Do, with raffle items varying from an opportunity to be zoo curator for the day to the use of a Mercedes Benz for a year. Despite the rather stiff price, the Zoo-to-Do is a popular sellout every year. Local

EXHIBIT 10-6 Respondent Characteristics of Zoo Visitors According to Visitation Frequency (in percent)

RESPONDENT CHARACTERISTIC	NUMBER OF ZOO VISITS OVER PAST TWO YEARS			
	FOUR OR MORE	TWO OR THREE	ONE OR NONE	NEVER VISITED ZOO
AGE				
Under 27	26	35	31	9
27 to 35	55	27	15	3
36 to 45	48	32	11	9
46 to 55	18	20	37	25
Over 55	27	29	30	14
MARITAL STATUS				
Married	41	28	20	11
Not Married	30	34	24	13
CHILDREN AT HOME				
Yes	46	30	15	9
No	34	28	27	12
INTERESTED IN VISITING NEW ORLEANS AQUARIUM				
Very, with Emphasis	47	26	18	9
Very, without Emphasis	45	24	23	12
Somewhat	28	37	14	11
Not Too	19	32	27	22
MEMBER OF FRIENDS OF THE ZOO				
Yes	67	24	5	4
No, but Heard of It	35	30	24	12
Never Heard of It	25	28	35	13
WOULD YOU BE INTERESTED IN JOINING FOTZ (NON-MEMBERS ONLY)				
Very/Somewhat	50	28	14	8
No/Don't Know	33	29	26	12

Source: The Audubon Institute.

restaurants and other businesses donate most of the necessary supplies, which decreases the cost of the affair. In 1985 the Zoo-to-Do raised about $500,000 in one night, more money than any other nonmedical fund-raiser in the country.

Marketing. The American Association of Zoological Parks and Aquariums report that most zoos find the majority of their visitors live within a single population center in close proximity to the park. Thus, in order to sustain attendance over the years,

EXHIBIT 10-7 Relative Importance of Seven Reasons as to Why Respondent Does Not Visit the Zoo More Often (in percent)

REASON (CLOSE ENDED)	VERY IMPORTANT WITH EMPHASIS	VERY IMPORTANT WITHOUT EMPHASIS	SOMEWHAT IMPORTANT	UNIMPORTANT
The distance of the Zoo's location from where you live	7	11	21	60
The cost of a Zoo visit	4	8	22	66
Not being all that interested in Zoo animals	2	12	18	67
The parking problem on weekends	7	11	19	62
The idea that you get tired of seeing the same exhibits over and over	5	18	28	49
It's too hot during the summer months	25	23	22	30
Just not having the idea occur to you	8	19	26	48

Source: The Audubon Institute.

zoos must attract the same visitors repeatedly. A large number of the Audubon Zoo's promotional programs and special events are aimed at just that.

Marketing goals for the Audubon Institute are to position the institute as a world leader in species preservation and resource conservation and to reinforce and maintain Audubon Zoo's position as a world-class facility. For 1991 the Audubon Institute wanted to increase attendance at the zoo by 10 percent to 1.1 million visitors. Another major objective is to raise the level of awareness of the Audubon Institute and its mission 50 percent in a three-state region.

The zoo's marketing budget is over $800,000 per year, excluding salaries. This budget includes group sales, public relations, advertising, and special events but does not include developmental fund-raising or membership. Breakdowns of the marketing budget for 1993 can be found in Exhibit 10–8.

The Audubon Zoo and the Audubon Institute conduct a multitude of very successful promotional programs. The effect is to have continual parties and celebrations going on that attract a variety of people to the zoo and raise additional revenue. Exhibit 10–9 lists the major annual promotional programs that the zoo conducts. The zoo also schedules concerts of well-known musicians, such as Irma Thomas, Pete Fountain, the Monkees, and Manhattan Transfer, and other special events throughout the year. As a result, a variety of events occur each month.

Many educational activities are held all year long: (1) a Junior Zoo Keeper program for seventh- and eighth-graders, (2) a student intern program for high school and college students, and (3) a ZOOmobile that takes live animals to such locations as special education classes, hospitals, and old-age homes.

EXHIBIT 10-8 1993 Marketing Budget

MARKETING	
Administrative	$319,200
Sales	159,700
Public Relations	99,950
Concerts/Events	166,000
Special Events	74,500
TOTAL	$819,350
Revenues from Special Events	160,000
NET BUDGET	$659,305

PUBLIC RELATIONS	
Education, Travel, and Subscriptions	5%
Printing and Duplicating	58
Professional Services	14
Delivery and Postage	3
Telephone	1
Entertainment	2
Supplies	15
Miscellaneous	2

SPECIAL EVENTS	
General and Administrative	18%
LA Swamp Fest	22
Earthfest	16
Ninja Turtle Breakfast	13
Jazz Search	9
Fiesta Latina	6
Crescent City Cats	6
Other Events	10

Source: The Audubon Institute.

Riverboat. A riverboat ride on the romantic paddle-wheeled *Cotton Blossom* takes visitors from downtown to the zoo. Originally, the trip began at a dock in the French Quarter, but it was later moved to a dock immediately adjacent to New Orleans' newest attraction, the Riverwalk, a Rouse development, on the site of the 1984 Louisiana World Exposition. Not only is the riverboat ride great fun, it also lures tourists and conventioneers from the downtown attractions of the French Quarter and the new Riverwalk to the zoo some 6 miles upstream. A further allure of the riverboat ride is a return trip to downtown on the New Orleans streetcar, one of the few remaining trolley cars in the United States. The Zoo Cruise not only draws more visitors but has generated additional revenue through landing fees paid by the New Orleans Steamboat Company, and it helps keep traffic out of uptown New Orleans.

The zoo's ability to generate operating funds has been ascribed to the dedication of the Audubon Institute, continuing increases in attendance, and creative special events and programs. A history of adequate operating funds allows the zoo to guar-

EXHIBIT 10-9 Selected Audubon Park Zoo Promotional Programs

MONTH	ACTIVITY
March	Louisiana Black Heritage Festival. A two-day celebration of Louisiana's Black history and its native contributions through food, music, and arts and crafts.
March	Earth Fest. The environment and our planet are the focus of this fun-filled and educational event. Recycling, conservation displays, and puppet shows.
April	Jazz Search. This entertainment series is aimed at finding the best new talent in the area with the winners to be featured at the New Orleans' Jazz & Heritage Festival.
April	Zoo-To-Do for Kids. At this "pint-sized" version of the Zoo-To-Do, fun and games abound for kids.
May	Zoo-To-Do. Annual black tie fund-raiser featuring over 100 of New Orleans' finest restaurants and three music stages.
May	Irma Thomas Mother's Day Concert. The annual celebration of Mother's Day with a buffet.
August	Lego Invitational. Architectural firms turn thousands upon thousands of Lego pieces into their own original creations.
September	Fiesta Latina. Experience the best the Hispanic community has to offer through music, cuisine, and arts and crafts.
October	Louisiana Swamp Festival. Cajun food, music, and crafts highlight this four-day salute to Louisiana's bayou country; features hands-on contact with live swamp animals.
October	Boo at the Zoo. This annual Halloween extravaganza features games, special entertainment, trick or treat, a haunted house, and the Zoo's Spook Train.

Source: The Audubon Institute.

antee capital donors that their gifts will be used to build and maintain top-notch exhibits. A comparison of the 1990 and 1991 statements of operating income and expense for the Audubon Institute is in Exhibit 10–10.

Fund Drives. The Audubon Zoo Development Fund was established in 1973. Corporate-industrial support of the zoo has been very strong—many corporations underwrote construction of zoo displays and facilities. A partial list of major corporate sponsors is in Exhibit 10–11. A sponsorship is considered to be for the life of the exhibit. The developmental department operates on a 12 percent overhead rate, which means that $.88 of every dollar raised goes toward the projects. By 1989 the master plan for development was 75 percent complete; the fund-raising goal was $1.5 million.

Zoo Director. L. Ron Forman, Audubon Zoo Director, is called a "zoomaster extraordinaire" and is described by the press as a "cross between Doctor Doolittle and the Wizard of Oz," as a "practical visionary," and as "serious, but with a sense of humor." A native New Orleanian, Forman quit an MBA program to join the city government as an administrative assistant and found himself doing a business analysis project on the Audubon Park. Once the city was committed to a new zoo, Forman was placed on board as an assistant to the zoo director, John Moore. In early 1977,

EXHIBIT 10-10   The Audubon Institute, Inc. Operating Income and Expenses

	1990 Zoo	1990 Aquarium	1990 Total	1991 Zoo	1991 Aquarium	1991 Total	1992 Zoo	1992 Aquarium	1992 Total
OPERATING INCOME (IN THOUSANDS)									
Admissions	3,587	3,664	7,251	2,908	8,900	11,808	2,763	7,953	10,716
Food and Gift Operations	3,496	711	4,207	2,565	2,600	5,165	2,663	2,397	5,060
Membership	1,932	2,318	4,250	1,658	1,290	2,948	1,957	646	2,603
Recreational Program	396	0	396	366	130	496	647	143	790
Visitor Services	218	0	218	198	650	848	144	315	459
Other	32	650	682	129	7	136	436	6	442
Total Income	9,660	7,343	17,003	7,824	13,577	21,401	8,610	11,460	20,070
OPERATING EXPENSES (IN THOUSANDS)									
Maintenance	1,444	1,316	2,760	1,220	2,470	3,690	1,582	2,330	3,912
Educational/Curatorial	2,526	2,783	5,311	2,117	3,500	5,617	2,197	1,808	4,005
Food and Gift Operations	2,375	483	2,858	2,010	920	2,930	1,805	1,383	3,188
Membership	840	631	1,471	528	540	1,068	612	361	973
Recreational	358	362	720	231	400	631	276	100	376
Marketing	633	593	1,226	479	1,500	1,979	492	1,569	2,061
Visitor Services	373	125	498	205	650	855	230	366	596
Administration	1,110	1,050	2,160	1,034	3,597	4,631	1,416	2,289	3,705
Construction Expenses	0	0	0	0	0	0	0	1,254	1,254
Total Expenses	9661	7,343	17,004	7,824	13,577	21,401	8,610	11,460	20,070
Net Profit	0	0	0	0	0	0	0	0	0
OPERATING INCOME									
Admissions	49%	51%	100%	25%	75%	100%	26%	74%	100%
Food and Gift Operations	83	17	100	50	50	100	53	47	100
Membership	45	55	100	56	44	100	75	25	100
Recreational Program	100	0	100	74	26	100	82	18	100
Visitor Services	100	0	100	23	77	100	31	69	100
Other	5	95	100	95	5	100	99	1	100
Total Income	57	43	100	37	63	100	43	57	100
OPERATING EXPENSES									
Maintenance	52%	48%	100%	33%	67%	100%	40%	60%	100%
Educational /Curatorial	48	52	100	38	62	100	55	45	100
Food and Gift Operations	83	17	100	69	31	100	57	43	100
Membership	57	43	100	49	51	100	63	37	100
Recreational	50	50	100	37	63	100	73	27	100
Marketing	52	48	100	24	76	100	24	76	100
Visitor Services	75	25	100	24	76	100	39	61	100
Administration	51	49	100	22	78	100	38	62	100
Construction Expenses	0	0	0	0	0	0	0	100	100
Total Expenses	57	43	100	37	63	100	43	57	100

Source: The Audubon Institute.

EXHIBIT 10-11 Audubon Zoo Major Corporate Sponsors

Amoco Foundation
American Express
Anheuser-Busch, Inc.
Arthur Anderson and Company
J. Aron Charitable Foundation, Inc.
BellSouth Corporation
BP America
Chevron USA, Inc.
Conoco, Inc.
Consolidated Natural Gas Corporation
D. H. Holmes, Ltd.
Entergy Corporation
Exxon Company, USA
Freeport-McMoran, Inc.
Host International, Inc.
Kentwood Spring Water
Louisiana Coca-Cola Bottling Company, Ltd.
Louisiana Land and Exploration Company
Martin Marietta Manned Space Systems
McDonald's Operators of New Orleans
Mobil Foundation, Inc.
National Endowment for the Arts
National Science Foundation
Ozone Spring Water
Pan American Life Insurance Company
Phillip Morris Companies, Inc.
Shell Companies Foundation, Inc.
Tenneco, Inc.
Texaco USA
USF&G Corporation
Wendy's of New Orleans, Inc.

Source: The Audubon Institute.

Moore gave up the battle between the "animal people" and the "people-people," and Forman took over as park and zoo director.

Forman was said to bring an MBA-meets-menagerie style to the zoo that was responsible for transforming it from a public burden into an almost completely self-sustaining operation. The result has not only benefitted the citizens of the city but has also added a major tourist attraction to the economically troubled city of the 1980s.

Staffing. The zoo uses two classes of employees, civil service, through the Audubon Park Commission, and noncivil service. The civil service employees include the curators and zookeepers. They fall under the jurisdiction of the city civil service system but are paid out of the budget of the Friends of the Zoo. Employees who work in public relations, advertising, concessions, fund-raising, and so on, are hired through the Friends of the Zoo and are not part of the civil service system. See Exhibit 10–12 for further data on staffing patterns.

A visitor to the new Audubon Zoo can quickly see why New Orleanians are so proud of their zoo. In a city called one of the dirtiest in the nation, the zoo is virtually spotless. This is a result of adequate staffing and the clear pride of both those who work at and those who visit the zoo. One of the first points made by volunteers guiding school groups is that anyone seeing a piece of trash on the ground must pick it up. A 1986 city poll showed that 93 percent of the citizens surveyed gave the zoo a high approval rating—an extremely high rating for any public facility.

Kudos came from groups outside the local area as well. Delegates from the American Association of Zoological Parks and Aquariums ranked the Audubon Zoo as one of the three top zoos of its size in America. In 1982 the American Association of Nurserymen gave the zoo a Special Judges Award for its use of plant materials. In 1985 the Audubon Zoo received the Phoenix Award from the Society of American Travel Writers for its achievements in conservation, preservation, and beautification.

By 1987, the zoo was virtually self-sufficient. The small amount of money received from government grants amounted to less than 10 percent of the budget. The master plan for the development of the zoo was 75 percent complete, and the reptile exhibit

EXHIBIT 10-12   Audubon Zoo Employee Structure

YEAR	NUMBER OF PAID EMPLOYEES	NUMBER OF VOLUNTEERS	ANNUAL TOTALS
1972	36	0	36
1973	49	0	49
1974	69	0	69
1975	90	0	90
1976	143	0	143
1977	193	0	193
1978	184	0	184
1979	189	0	189
1980	198	0	198
1981	245	0	245
1982	305	0	305
1983	302	56	358
1984	419	120	539
1985	454	126	580
1986	426	250	676
1987	431	300	731
1988	462	310	772
1989	300	270	570
1990	450	350	800
1991	266	325	591
1992	245	374	619
			7,937

Source: The Audubon Institute.

was scheduled for completion in the fall. The organization had expanded with a full complement of professionals and managers. (See Exhibit 10–13 for the organizational structure of the zoo.)

Although the zoo had made great progress in fifteen years, all was not quiet on the political front. In a court battle, the city won over the state on the issue of who wielded ultimate authority over Audubon Park and Zoo. Indeed, the zoo has benefitted from three friendly mayors in a row, starting with Moon Landrieu, who championed the new zoo, to Ernest "Dutch" Morial, to Sidney Barthelemy who threw his support to both the zoo and the aquarium proposal championed by Forman.

The Aquarium. In 1986, Forman and a group of supporters proposed the development of an aquarium and riverfront park to the New Orleans City Council. In November 1986, the electorate voted to fund an aquarium and a riverfront park by a 70 percent margin, one of the largest margins the city had ever given to any tax proposal. Forman hailed this as a vote of confidence from the citizens and a mandate to build a world-class aquarium that would produce new jobs, stimulate the local economy, and create an educational resource for the children of the city.

The Aquarium of the Americas opened in September 1990. The $40 million project is located adjacent to the Riverwalk, providing a logical pedestrian link for visitors between New Orleans major attractions of the Riverwalk and the Jax Brewery, a shopping center in the French Quarter. Management of the aquarium was placed under the Audubon Institute, the same organization that ran the Audubon Zoo. A feasibility study prepared by Harrison Price Company projected a probable 868,000 visitors during the first year of operation, with 75 percent of the visitors coming from outside the metropolitan area. These attendance figures were reached in only four months and six days from the grand opening. Attendance remained strong through 1992 after dropping off a little from the grand opening numbers.

Zoo director Forman has demonstrated that zoos have almost unlimited potential. A 1980 *New Orleans* magazine article cited some of Forman's ideas, ranging from a safari train to a breeding center for rare animals. The latter has an added attraction as a potential money maker since an Asiatic lion cub, for example, sells for around $10,000. This wealth of ideas was important because expanded facilities and programs are required to maintain attendance at any public attraction.

THE FUTURE

Although the zoo and aquarium enjoyed political support in 1992, New Orleans is still suffering from high unemployment and a generally depressed economy resulting from the depression in the oil industry. A few facts about New Orleans are given in Exhibit 10–14. The zoo operates in a city where many attractions compete for the leisure dollar of citizens and visitors. The Audubon Zoo must vie with the French Quarter, Dixieland jazz, the Superdome, and Mardi Gras.

The Audubon Institute has a strategic plan for the 1990s as outlined below. Evaluate the effectiveness of this plan and offer additions, changes, and deletions based on a thorough strategic analysis.

The components of the Institute's plan include:

Wilderness Park, a 300-acre preserve located on the 1,200-acre campus of the Freeport-McMoran Audubon Species Survival Center, providing a wilderness recreational area within a hardwood forest, complete with an abundance of native fauna. (Opening: Spring 1994, estimated cost $1 million)

EXHIBIT 10-13 Organizational Chart for the Audubon Park Commission

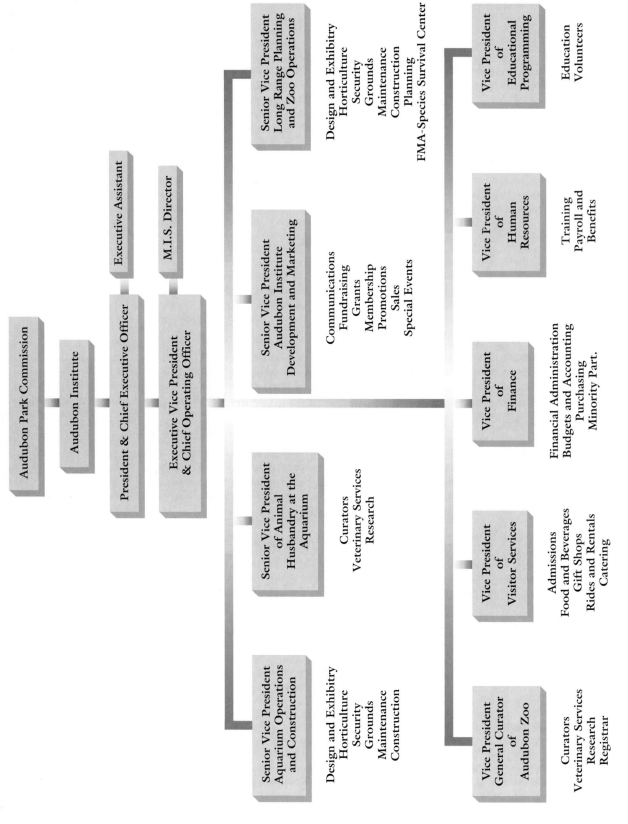

Audubon Park Commission

Audubon Institute

President & Chief Executive Officer

Executive Assistant

M.I.S. Director

Executive Vice President & Chief Operating Officer

Senior Vice President Aquarium Operations and Construction

Design and Exhibitry
Horticulture
Security
Grounds
Maintenance
Construction

Senior Vice President of Animal Husbandry at the Aquarium

Curators
Veterinary Services
Research

Senior Vice President Audubon Institute Development and Marketing

Communications
Fundraising
Grants
Membership
Promotions
Sales
Special Events

Senior Vice President Long Range Planning and Zoo Operations

Design and Exhibitry
Horticulture
Security
Grounds
Maintenance
Construction
Planning
FMA-Species Survival Center

Vice President of Educational Programming

Education
Volunteers

Vice President of Human Resources

Training
Payroll and Benefits

Vice President of Finance

Financial Administration
Budgets and Accounting
Purchasing
Minority Part.

Vice President of Visitor Services

Admissions
Food and Beverages
Gift Shops
Rides and Rentals
Catering

Vice President General Curator of Audubon Zoo

Curators
Veterinary Services
Research
Registrar

Audubon Center for Research of Endangered Species (Acres), where studies on the procreation and successful rearing of animals in captivity will take place. (opening: Fall 1995, estimated cost $15 million Federal Grant)

Insectarium and Butterfly Pavillion, a unique facility exclusively dedicated to the insect world, featuring "hands-on" exhibitry to encourage the visitor—young and old—to explore the realm of these fascinating creatures. (opening: June 1996, estimated cost $2 million)

Expansion of the Woldenberg Riverfront Park, 16 acres located downriver from the Aquarium, continuing the pattern of beautiful plantings, water features, and gracious green space already developed on the banks of the Mississippi River. (completion: June 1996, estimated cost $1 million)

Phase II of the Aquarium of the Americas, a 60,000-square-foot addition, including a 350-seat Imax theater (opening: Fall 1995) and a changing exhibits gallery. (opening: Spring 1996, estimated cost of both $10 million)

Zoo 2000, a new master plan focusing on increasing and enhancing the participatory conservation and environmental education experience of the Audubon Zoological Garden. (completion: 1997, estimated cost $17 million)

Total Estimated Cost: $46 million

EXHIBIT 10-14   A Few Facts About the New Orleans MSA

Population	1,324,400
Households	489,900
Median Age	30.8 years
Median Household EBI	$29,130
Average Temperature	70 degrees Fahrenheit
Average Annual Rainfall	63 inches
Average Elevation	5 feet below sea level
Area	363.5 square miles
	199.4 square miles of land

MAJOR ECONOMIC ACTIVITIES

   Tourism (5 million visitors per year)
   Oil and Gas Industry
   The Port of New Orleans (170 million tons of cargo/year)

TAXES

State Sales Tax	4.0%
Parish (County) Sales Tax	5.0% (Orleans)
	4.0% (Jefferson)
State Income Tax	2.1-2.6% on first $20,000
	3.0-3.5% on next $30,000
	6.0% on $51,000 & over

Parish Property Tax of 126.15 mills (Orleans) is based on 10% of appraised value over $75,000 homestead exemption.

Sources: *Sales and Marketing Management* and South Central Bell *Yellow Pages*, 1991.

THE CLASSIC CAR CLUB OF AMERICA—1994

Headquartered in Des Plaines, Illinois (708-390-0443), the Classic Car Club of America, Inc. (CCCA) was formed in 1952 by a small group of enthusiasts interested in luxury cars of the late 1920s and 1930s. A listing of certain high-priced, high-quality, and limited-production cars were designated as "Classic Cars," and the period of 1925–1942 was chosen as the limits of the "Classic Era." It was felt that cars built prior to 1925 had not yet reached technical maturity, and that after World War II the quality of most so-called luxury cars had succumbed to the economic pressures of mass production. Some pictures of Classic Cars are provided in Figure 11–1.

Over the years, the list of CCCA recognized Classics was modified and expanded, and the time period was extended to 1948 to include certain pre-World War II models that continued in production for a few years after the war. While all cars included on the list were of considerably higher price and quality than the mass-production cars of this era, there was also a wide variance in original prices and quality of these recognized Classics. For example, in 1930 a new Ford Model A (*not* a Classic) cost about $450. In comparison, two of the many CCCA-recognized Classics of that year are the Auburn Eight, which was priced as low as $1,195, and the Duesenberg Model J, which sold new in the $12,000–$14,000 range. The Auburn, although a car of middle price and quality, is considered a Classic because its styling was exceptional at the time while the Duesenberg was the highest priced and most exotic American car of the era, carrying custom-built bodies and bought by an exclusive clientele of movie stars, playboys, and other superrich personalities. Most Classics fell somewhere between these two extremes, with original prices in the $2,000–$5,000 range (a considerable amount of money at that time). Exhibit 11–1 lists those cars recognized as Classics by the CCCA in 1993.

THE COLLECTOR CAR HOBBY

The "collector car" hobby in the United States is a broad and wide-reaching activity involving a large number of Americans. Basically, a "collector car" is any automobile owned for purposes other than normal transportation. The most widely-read collector car hobby magazine, *Hemmings Motor News*, had a circulation of about 265,000 in December 1993. Another magazine, *Car Collector*, estimates that nearly one million Americans are engaged in the old car hobby. However, a figure of 350,000–500,000 would probably be a more conservative estimate of the number of Americans engaged in this hobby.

"Collector car" is a loose term, ranging from turn-of-the-century "horseless carriages" to currently-built but limited-production cars, such as Italian super-sports cars. Naturally, owners of collector cars enjoy the company of other persons with similar interests, and thus a wide variety of car clubs exist, to suit almost any particular segment of this vast hobby. The largest of these clubs, the Antique Automobile Club of America, caters to owners of virtually all cars twenty-five years old or older, and has a membership of more than 55,000.

FIGURE 11-1 Classic Cars: 1941 Packard (top left); 1934 Rolls Royce (top right); 1926 Duesenburg (bottom).

CCCA ORGANIZATION AND ACTIVITIES

When the club's 1993 fiscal year ended on October 31, 1993, the club had 5,447 members, as indicated below. (Exhibit 11–2 gives a comparison of membership figures for recent years.)

Active (regular membership—1993 dues at $30 a year)	4179
Associate (for spouses, no publications—$5 a year)	1005
Life (after ten years, one-time fee of $420)	199
Life Associate (spouse of Life— $42)	59
Honorary (famous car designers, etc.)	5
	5,447

CCCA members receive a variety of benefits from their membership including a magazine, *The Classic Car*, which is published four times a year. The magazine, which is highly respected by automotive historians, features color photos of Classics on the front and back covers, as well as forty-eight pages or more of articles and black-and-white photos of Classics. A CCCA *Bulletin* is also published eight times a year, and contains club and hobby news, technical columns, and members' and commercial ads for Classic cars, parts, and related items. A further publication is the club's *Handbook and Directory*, published annually. It contains the CCCA bylaws, judging rules, requirements for regions, etc., as well as a current listing of members and the Classic cars they own. Commercial car-related advertisements are solicited for this *Handbook and Directory*, and its cost is largely paid for by these advertisements.

The CCCA sponsors three types of national events each year. The annual meeting in January includes business meetings and a car judging meet, and is held in a different location in the United States each year. In April and July, a series of "Grand Classic" judging meets are held in ten to twelve locations around the country, with a

EXHIBIT 11-1 CCCA-recognized Classic Cars

A.C.	Farman*	N.A.G.*
Adler*	Fiat*	Nash*
Alfa Romeo	FN*	Packard*
Alvis*	Franklin*	Peerless
Amilcar*	Frazer-Nash*	Peugot*
Armstrong-Siddeley*	Hispano-Suiza*	Pierce-Arrow
Aston Martin*	Horch	Railton*
Auburn*	Hotchkiss*	Raymond Mays*
Austro-Daimler	Hudson*	Renault*
Ballot*	Humber*	Reo*
Bentley	Invicta	Revere
Benz*	Isotta-Fraschini	Riley*
Blackhawk	Itala	Roamer*
B.M.W.*	Jaguar*	Rochet Schneider*
Brewster*	Jensen*	Rohr*
Brough Superior*	Jordan*	Rolls-Royce
Bucciali*	Julian*	Ruxton
Bugatti	Kissell*	Squire
Buick*	Lagonda*	S.S. and S.S. Jaguar*
Cadillac*	Lanchester*	Stearns-Knight
Chenard-Walcker*	Lancia*	Stevens-Duryea
Chrysler*	La Salle*	Steyr*
Cord	Lincoln*	Studebaker*
Cunningham	Lincoln Continental	Stutz
Dagmar*	Locomobile*	Sunbeam*
Daimler*	Marmon*	Talbot*
Darracq*	Maserati*	Talbot-Lago*
Delage*	Maybach	Tatra*
Delahaye*	McFarlan	Triumph*
Delaunay Belleville*	Mercedes	Vauxhall*
Doble	Mercedes-Benz*	Voisin
Dorris	Mercer	Wills Ste Claire
Duesenberg	M.G.*	Willys-Knight*
du Pont	Minerva*	
Excelsior*		

* Indicates that only certain models of this make are considered Classic. Some other
  1925–1948 custom-bodied cars not listed above may be approved as Classic upon
  individual application.

Source: The CCCA.

total of 400 to 600 Classics being exhibited and judged. At CCCA judging meets,
cars are rated by a point system which takes into account the quality and authenticity
of restoration and the general condition of the car, both mechanically and cosmeti-
cally. CCCA judging meets are not publicized to the general public and access to view
the cars is restricted to club members and their guests only.

EXHIBIT 11-2   Selected CCCA Membership Data (for October 31 fiscal year end)

	1993	1992	1991	1990	1989	1988	1987	1986
Active Members	4179	4184	4156	4188	4170	4118	3935	3885
Associate Members	1005	1012	977	893	928	914	828	773
Life Members	199	195	188	185	175	170	163	160
Life Associate Members	59	60	59	56	53	50	48	45
Honorary Members	5	5	6	6	7	6	7	6
Total	5447	5456	5386	5328	5333	5258	4981	4869

Source: The CCCA.

Each year, the club sponsors several "Classic CARavans" in various parts of the United States and Canada. The "CARavan" is a tour in which members in as many as 100 Classic cars join together in a week-long planned itinerary.

The Annual Meeting, Grand Classics, and CARavans are designed to be financially self-supporting, with attending members paying fees that cover the costs of the events.

The CCCA also has members who have volunteered to be technical advisors available to assist other members. Furthermore, the club makes available for sale to members certain club-related products, such as ties and umbrellas with a Classic Car design.

The club is managed by a fifteen-member Board of Directors, with a President, Vice Presidents, Treasurer, Secretary, etc. All are club member volunteers (from all over the United States) who have shown a willingness and ability to help run the CCCA and have been elected by the total membership to three-year terms of office. They are not reimbursed for their expenses, which include attending eight Board meetings each year, most of which are held at headquarters offices which are rented in Des Plaines, Illinois (a location chosen because of its central location within the United States and its close proximity to Chicago's main airport). Another member volunteers as "Executive Administrator" and oversees the club's secretary and its daily operations. The only paid employees of the club are the full-time office secretary and the publications editor, who is a free-lance editor doing other work besides that for the CCCA. An organization chart of the CCCA is shown in Exhibit 11–3.

In addition to belonging to the national CCCA, the majority of members also pay dues and belong to a local CCCA region. In 1994 there were twenty-eight regions throughout the United States. (See Figure 11–2.) Each region sponsors a variety of local activities for members and their Classics and publishes its own magazine or newsletter. Many of the regions also derive revenues from the sale of classic car replacement parts or service items, offered to all members of the national club.

Legally separate from the CCCA and its regions, a Classic Car Club of America Museum also exists. It occupies space as part of a larger old-car museum in Hickory Corners, Michigan, and displays a variety of Classic cars that have been donated to it. The CCCA Museum, unlike the CCCA itself, is eligible to receive tax-deductible gifts of money and property (such as cars). Although the CCCA has granted the museum the right to use the "CCCA" name, the museum has a separate Board of Trustees and is run totally separate from the club.

EXHIBIT 11-3 CCCA Organizational Chart

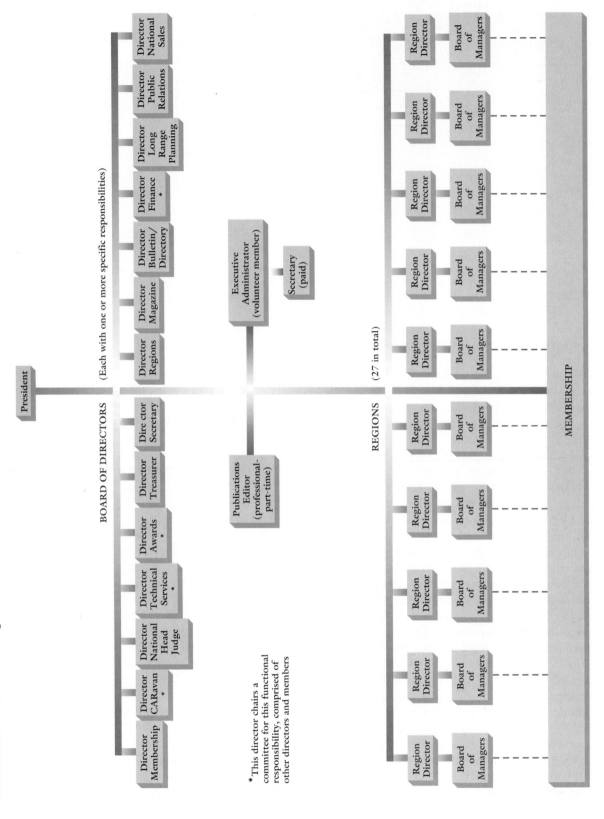

President

BOARD OF DIRECTORS

(Each with one or more specific responsibilities)

Director Membership

Director CARavan *

Director National Head Judge

Director Technical Services *

Director Awards *

Director Treasurer

Director Secretary

Director Regions

Director Magazine

Director Bulletin/ Directory

Director Finance *

Director Long Range Planning

Director Public Relations

Director National Sales

Publications Editor (professional- part-time)

Executive Administrator (volunteer member)

Secretary (paid)

* This director chairs a committee for this functional responsibility, comprised of other directors and members

REGIONS

(27 in total)

Region Director

Board of Managers

MEMBERSHIP

FIGURE 11-2   Map Showing Boundaries of Regions of Classic CAr club of America

CURRENT CONCERNS THAT FACE THE CCCA

While the officers and directors of the CCCA believe the club to be strong, both financially and in its value to its members, a variety of concerns about the future exist.

Of primary concern is the continuing effect of inflation upon the club's ability to maintain its current level of services and benefits to the membership. In particular, the cost of publications, and headquarters office administration and rent have risen considerably over the years. The board of directors has responded by both watching costs carefully and by raising annual dues several times (from $10 in the 1960s to the current $30 per year), but it recognizes that certain cost increases are unavoidable, and that raising dues too high may result in a loss of members. (Financial statements are provided in Exhibit 11–4.)

One way to overcome this problem is to increase the number of members and thus create greater revenues for the club. (The number of members who pay full dues has only increased moderately over the years. See Exhibit 11–2.) The directors know that many Classic owners do not belong to the CCCA. While CCCA members owned about 8000 Classics in 1994, no one really knows how many Classic owners are not in the club. Club efforts in recent years to increase membership have been targeted at these Classic-owning non-CCCA members. Letters have been sent to past members who failed to renew their CCCA membership (about 5–10 percent each year), region officers have contacted local non-CCCA members known to own Classics, mailings

EXHIBIT 11-4 CCCA Financial Statements (cash-flow basis)

	FY 1993	FY 1992	FY 1991	FY 1990	FY 1989	FY 1988	FY 1987	FY 1986	FY 1985	FY 1984	FY 1983
RECEIPTS											
Active Dues (dues received for current fiscal year)	$ 46,879	$ 50,168	$ 49,627	$101,009	$121,998	$ 59,067	$ 56,709	$ 58,926	$ 78,663	$ 39,999	$ 47,950
Prepaid Active Dues (dues received for next fiscal /year- See Note)	87,382	79,860	77,760	76,722	26,170	3,809	65,509	61,560	55,079	17,350	54,975
Associate Dues	1,960	2,210	1,925	3,560	4,503	2,329	2,005	2,061	3,279	931	972
Prepaid Associate Dues	3,540	3,105	2,945	2,970	1,005	130	2,275	2,165	1,851	685	1,227
Life Membership	1,260	4,320	3,990	4,830	4,333	3,066	2,730	1,799	840	2,975	7,310
Publications Sales	2,683	1,972	2,053	4,393	2,285	3,004	3,082	2,987	2,661	3,665	3,429
Bulletin Advertising	11,176	9,583	9,884	9,924	10,919	9,747	8,986	8,618	3,318	4,992	3,662
Magazine Advertising	1,815	2,526	2,100	3,850	4,510	2,400	1,975	3,329	750	1,900	3,567
Directory Advertising	10,010	11,100	14,500	9,625	14,050	9,900	8,500	0	0	0	0
Awards (member registration fees for meets, etc.)	15,975	11,328	14,509	10,860	10,3331	6,653	6,481	5,234	5,779	5,439	5,240
CARavan	32,400	26,300	27,837	30,000	26,485	27,135	11,610	12,160	51,919	25,441	11,660
National Sales Items (badges, jewelry, ties, etc.)	4,358	4,952	4,397	8,495	6,417	6,298	4,722	5,002	5,136	6,155	5,235
Interest Earned	12,531	15,889	16,707	15,179	13,881	9,983	5,543	5,466	2,588	11,772	10,416
Regional Insurance (reimbursement from regions)	2,100	4,119	2,278	3,250	270	2,530	3,210	2,280	1,845	1,780	1,110
Miscellaneous & Foreign Exchange	941	584	3,008	3,792	2,695	2,768	1,580	931	9,725	3,071	877
Total Receipts	$235,010	$228,016	$233,520	$288,459	$249,852	$148,819	$184,916	$172,518	$223,433	$126,155	$157,630
ASSETS											
Bank Balance	$25,890	$76,035	$18,626	$34,188	$8,324	$7,728	$31,438	$36,605	$18,466	$11,296	$5,356
Investments (at cost: Money market funds, CDs, etc.)	339,235	262,705	291,880	177,409	149,360	117,099	101,827	71,148	59,885	27,296	96,966
[includes life membership fund]	(66,393)	(66,600)	(62,830)	(57,034)	(51,834)	(48,021)	(44,577)	(42,962)	(37,325)	(36,845)	(37,245)

EXHIBIT 11-4 *Continued*

LIABILITIES:
None

DISBURSEMENTS

	FY 1993	FY 1992	FY 1991	FY 1990	FY 1989	FY 1988	FY 1987	FY 1986	FY 1985	FY 1984	FY 1983
Bulletin	$42,225	$25,658	$33,675	$21,510	$25,343	$23,224	$18,389	$22,651	$19,538	$20,734	$16,828
Magazine	53,219	46,277	43,788	41,019	45,724	39,031	39,091	44,697	47,972	45,788	46,598
Directory	15,447	15,985	19,150	16,225	14,776	11,085	12,925	11,647	1,784	11,739	16,181
Awards (judging, meetings, trophies, etc.)	9,805	14,386	36,474	21,588	22,619	11,662	4,094	3,386	4,038	20,378	8,888
General Administration	9,776	10,110	9,736	7,777	9,916	13,268	11,983	12,658	11,801	14,664	8,786
Office (salaries, rent, etc.)	35,483	30,996	32,239	30,030	29,049	27,186	27,190	29,431	27,750	27,326	28,573
CARavan	24,206	16,679	16,074	20,025	16,025	15,741	5,247	6,323	46,924	29,777	5,069
National Sales Items	3,340	343	2,917	3,629	7,574	2,041	6,007	2,204	2,623	2,784	1,710
Membership (recruitment)	15,641	4,802	14,181	14,289	10,053	5,836	6,341	4,872	7,246	2,950	5,670
Regional Insurance	4,447	7,284	2,279	2,788	744	2,759	6,032	2,250	2,800	1,924	1,600
Regional Relations	0	0	0	0	0	0	0	0	27	302	454
Computer Services	4,661	21,171	0	7,695	6,789	33	9,064	8,137	9,339	4,493	3,678
Miscellaneous	5,490	8,018	9,584	3,112	2,786	3,869	7,931	861	456	426	2,562
Taxes	6,952	7,404	3,122	5,515	4,002	1,523	4,709	470	1,377	6,599	0
Total Disbursements	$230,692	$209,113	$223,218	$195,201	$195,401	$157,258	$159,004	$149,587	$183,675	$189,884	$146,597
Excess Receipts over Disbursements	$4,288	$18,903	$10,302	$93,258	54,451	[8,439]	25,912	22,931	39,758	[63,729]	11,033

Source: CCCA reports.

have been made to Classic-owning persons found in directories of other old-car clubs, articles about CCCA activities as well as a few paid advertisements have been placed in various old car hobby magazines, and membership ads have been placed in single-marque car clubs (such as the Packard club) in return for allowing those clubs to place their membership ads in the CCCA's publications.

Furthermore, while some CCCA members do not own Classics, most do, for much of the pleasure of belonging to the club derives from participating in the various activities with a Classic car. Thus, while Classic enthusiasts who do not own a Classic might also be an appropriate target for CCCA new membership recruitment efforts, the primary focus has been on persons currently owning a Classic.

The club's membership recruitment efforts have only been moderately successful. While new members have offset the annual five to ten percent attrition rate, total membership has risen only slightly in recent years. Yet, unless the listing of recognized Classics is expanded, the number of Classic cars in existence is fixed, and with it, by and large, is the number of Classic owners.

There are varying opinions within the CCCA with regard to expanding the current listing of Classic cars. While there is some debate over adding further makes and models within the current 1925–1948 year limits, the main controversy concerns whether or not to add cars built after 1948.

A minority of members favor this post–1948 expansion and make several arguments. They say that some high-quality cars were built after 1948 and these should also be considered "Classic." Furthermore, they argue that the club is currently not attracting young members (only 13 percent of CCCA members are less than 45 years old), and this is because younger people are less able to afford the cost of a Classic and are also unable to "identify" with a 1925–1948 car as they can with a car of the 1950s or 1960s. Although current prices of Classics vary greatly depending on the make of car, its condition, and type of body, all prices rose significantly in the 1970s and 1980s. Also, it is true that many current CCCA members own classics because of nostalgia for cars of their youth.

On the other hand, most members of the Board of Directors, along with a clear majority of the membership, argue against the expansion of the list of Classics past 1948. The primary argument is that a Classic car is more than just a high quality luxury car. Rather, it is the product of a "Classic Era," when the truly wealthy lived a separate lifestyle from the rest of the population, and when an elite group of auto makers and custom-body craftsmen were willing and able to produce cars to meet this upper-class lifestyle. By the end of World War II, it is argued, social upheavals ended this lifestyle, and economic pressures closed down the custom-body builders and most of the independent luxury car makers, with the remaining luxury cars generally becoming simply bigger, heavier, and better-appointed versions of other cars made by multiline manufacturers. Thus, expanding beyond 1948 would alter the basic focus and philosophy of the club, and it is this narrow focus that differentiates the CCCA from other clubs and thus makes it so attractive and important to its members.

Furthermore, it is argued, while a few truly special car models were made after 1948, the quantities produced were very small, and the addition of these cars to the CCCA listing would bring in few new members to the club.

Beyond the Board's concerns about the future financial strength of the club, there is also a concern about the use of members' Classics and the nature of CCCA activities. As previously mentioned, the values of Classics has risen significantly over the years. In 1952, when the club was founded, most people viewed Classics as simply "old cars," and they could generally be bought for a few hundred to a few thousand dollars.

Today, many view Classics as major investment items, with professional dealers and auctions a significant factor in the marketplace. While some less exotic and unrestored Classic models can be found for under $15,000, most sell for $20,000 to $75,000, and the most desirable Classics, (convertible models with custom bodies, twelve- and sixteen-cylinder engines, etc.) can sell for $100,000 and more. (A very small number of especially exotic and desirable Classics have recently sold in the $500,000 to $1,500,000 range, and a 1929 Bugatti Royale reportedly sold in 1987 for over $9.8 million!) Furthermore, judging meets have become very serious events, with high scores adding significantly to a Classic's sales value. Thus, many highly desirable and/or top scoring Classics are now hardly driven at all and are transported in enclosed trailers to and from judging meets. While most Classic owners still enjoy driving their cars, and the CCCA CARavans continue to be highly popular among club members, some members yearn for the "old days" when there was less emphasis on judging and on a car's value and CCCA members would drive and park their Classics anywhere.

Still another concern of some members involves the possibility of a greater stress in future years on the conservation of gasoline in this country. If the country did focus more seriously on its high usage of gasoline, how would the public view Classic cars and the collector car hobby in general? Would the ownership and driving of cars for nontransportation purposes be considered unpatriotic or wasteful?

MEMBERSHIP SURVEY

In response to these various concerns, the CCCA board of directors established a Long-Range Planning Committee to study issues about the future of the club and to make recommendations to the Board. In 1983 and again in 1991, a membership questionnaire was sent to all members along with their membership renewal material. The response rate was excellent. Exhibit 11–5 presents the 1991 questionnaire and a tabulation of those responses which were quantifiable, along with a comparison to the 1983 survey responses.

FUTURE DIRECTION OF THE CCCA

As the club's 1994 fiscal year began, the CCCA board of directors was studying these issues. The board members knew that they could not ignore the problem of rising costs, and that their response must go beyond raising dues. While the survey clarified some of the opinions of the membership, the board did not view this survey as a ballot, with the board obligated to follow the majority preference in every question area.

Together for their regular board of directors meeting, the fifteen officers and directors of the CCCA asked themselves the following questions:

1. How should we deal with rising costs to the club?
2. What should be our policy with regard to future dues increases?
3. Should we consider the reduction of CCCA services to our membership in the future?
4. Is expansion of the listing of recognized Classics desirable?
5. What are the alternative ways to increase membership?
6. How can younger people be attracted to the CCCA?
7. Are there other possible sources of revenue to the club?
8. Were important questions not included in the previous membership surveys that should be included in a future survey?
9. Are there other long range issues or concerns that the club has not yet addressed?

1. I have been a member of the CCCA:
   1991   8% less than 2 years   19% 2-5 years   20% 5-10 years   53% more than 10 years
   (1983)   11% less than 2 years   20% 2-5 years   18% 5-10 years   51% more than 10 years

2. May age is:
   1991   0% under 25   3% 25-34   10% 35-44   24% 45-54   32% 55-64   31% 65 or over
   (1983)   1% under 25   3% 25-34   17% 35-44   30% 45-54   28% 55-64   22% 65 or over

3. My age when joining CCCA was:
   1991   7% under 25   19% 25-34   26% 35-44   26% 45-54   17% 55-64   5% 65 or over
   (1983)   not asked

4. I live in the _____ Region. (Not tabulated in this summary.)

5. I am a member of a CCCA region:
   1991   76% yes   24% no
   (1983)   69% yes   31% no
   If yes, which region: 15% Michigan, 13% So. Cal., 6.4% Pac. NW, others less than 6%.
   If not, why not? Of those responding here (54% of those who answered "no"): 30% indicated distance, 21% no time, 13% no classic or not running, 8% not invited or didn't know about it, 9% not interested, 3% lack of activities, and 16% miscellaneous of less than 2% each.

6. I have attended:

1991	(1983)	
74%	(64%)	One or more Grand Classics
27%	(19%)	One or more National CCCA CARavans
34%	(24%)	One or more Annual Meetings
65%	(52%)	One or more Regional events
13%	—	None of the above

7. I belong to how many other car clubs:

	Average	0	1	2	3	4	5	6-10	10 or more
1991	3	8%	18%	22%	19%	12%	9%	11%	2%
(1983)	3	9%	19%	23%	17%	12%	7%	11%	2%

   I am more active in some of these clubs than I am in CCCA:
   1991   42% yes   58% no
   (1983)   44% yes   56% no
   If yes, why? Of those responding here (84% of those who answered "yes"): 22% prefer a one marque club, 21% indicated distance, 16% interest in other clubs, 10% also interested in nonclassics, 10% want more activities, 8% don't own classic or not running, and 13% miscellaneous of 3% or less.

8. Compared to other clubs, the CCCA is:
   1991   32% the best   47% better than most   20% average   1% poor
   (1983)   31% the best   47% better than most   21% average   1% poor

9. Compared to other clubs, the value I receive for my CCCA dues is:
   1991   29% the best   42% better than most   28% average   1% poor
   (1983)   27% the best   40% better than most   31% average   3% poor

EXHIBIT 11-5 *Continued*

10. Overall, I rate *The Classic Car Magazine*:
1991	74% excellent	23% good	3% fair	0% poor
(1983)	74% excellent	24% good	1% fair	0% poor

11. Overall, I rate the *CCCA Bulletin*:
1991	55% excellent	39% good	6% fair	0% poor
(1993)	35% excellent	51% good	13% fair	1% poor

12. With regard to the CCA listing of recognized Classic cars:

1991	(1983)	
63%	(69%)	I basically think the current listing is good.
32%	(28%)	I think the listing should be expanded.
5%	(3%)	I think the listing should be reduced.

    Of those commenting (31%) and desiring change: 26% accept newer cars, 18% accept others in Classic era, 7% accept older cars, 11% eliminate some current Classics, 7% 1925–1948 year span, and 31% other of less than 5% each.

13. With regard to the scoring currently used at Grand Classics and Annual Meetings:

*1991	(1983)	
82%	(86%)	I basically think the current system is good.
18%	(14%)	I think the system could be improved. If so, how?

    Of those commenting (only 10%): 19% judging/scoring, 10% more points, 10% drive cars before judging, 8% recognize original cars, 11% better judges, etc., and 42% misc. of 5% or less. (*Without "don't know" so as to compare with 1983.)

14. Overall I would rate the Grand Classics as:
1991	46% excellent	32% good	3% fair	1% poor	18% don't know
(1983)	50% excellent	30% good	2% fair	1% poor	17% don't know

    or 100% basis without "dont' know"
1991	56% excellent	39% good	4% fair	1% poor	———
(1983)	61% excellent	36% good	2% fair	1% poor	———

15. Overall I would rate the Annual Meetings as:
1991	21% excellent	23% good	2% fair	0% poor	54% don't know
(1983)	15% excellent	22% good	5% fair	0% poor	59% don't know

    or 100% basis without "don't know"
1991	46% excellent	50% good	4% fair	0% poor	———
(1983)	35% excellent	53% good	12% fair	0% poor	———

16. Overall I would rate the CARavans as:
1991	32% excellent	11% good	1% fair	0% poor	56% don't know
(1983)	28% excellent	16% good	2% fair	0% poor	54% don't know

    or 100% basis without "don't know"
1991	73% excellent	25% good	2% fair	0% poor	———
(1983)	61% excellent	35% good	3% fair	1% poor	———

EXHIBIT 11-5 *Continued*

17. The CCCA has not associated itself with automobile auctions. How do you feel about this policy?
    [1991]   62% strongly agree   21% agree   4% disagree   3% strongly disagree   9% don't know
    or 100% basis without "don't know"
    [1991]   69% strongly agree   23% agree   4% disagree   3% strongly disagree
    This question was not asked in 1983.

18. I completed the previous CCCA questionnaire sent to members in 1983:
    23% yes   37% no   40% don't know
      or 100% basis without "don't know"
    38% yes   62% no

19. If there is one thing I'd recommend the CCA *not change*, it would be:
    Of those commenting (24%): 26% 1925–48 year span, 20% publications, 9% quality of cars considered
        classic, 8% CARavans, 6% happy with club, 5% Grand Classics, 4% judging\scoring, and 22% other of
        3% or less.

20. If there is one thing I'd recommend the CCCA change, it would be:
    Of those commenting (25%): 13% accept newer cars, 7% judging/scoring, 6% accept other cars in the
        classic era, 4% encourage younger people, 4% CARavans, and 66% miscellaneous 3% or less.

21. I think the CCCA could be improved by: (only 15% commenting)
    An emphasis on encouraging younger members. A desire to see newer cars accepted, and general
        "happiness" with the Club. Many miscellaneous comments too numerous to list.

22. Other comments: (only 18% responding)
    Principally a general satisfaction with the Club.
    Encourage younger people.
    Many miscellaneous comments too numerous to list.
Source: The CCCA. Used with permission.

WALNUT CREEK BAPTIST CHURCH—1993*

C A S E 12

TED W. LEGATSKI
Texas A&M University
PAUL R. REED
Sam Houston State
University
R. DEAN LEWIS
Sam Houston State
University

Reverend Dean Earl glanced out of his office window hardly noticing the workmen, barely 15 feet from his desk, putting the finishing touches on the east access road of Interstate 45. His thoughts were on his two-year effort to convince his staff and the church's board of deacons of the merits of strategic planning.

For some time, he had been concerned about the direction of Walnut Creek Baptist Church. Although so much was happening that was encouraging, there remained in his mind some lingering doubts. Was the church doing all that it could to meet the needs of the community? Was the church using its resources efficiently as well as effectively? Was the church growing at a rate that would allow it to continue its present programs and add much needed new ones? Were the church's physical facilities and grounds adequate for future growth? Was the church in control at all?

The church had an excellent professional staff with appropriate religious and theological training and a supportive board, but, as was common in many not-for-profit organizations, they lacked business administrative expertise. Reverend Earl had recognized these deficiencies and had initiated a personal investigation into strategic issues.

The pile of documents on his desk contained a Southern Baptist publication describing strategic analysis for church development, a borrowed 1992 edition of a popular strategic management textbook, plus a myriad of memos and discussion notes tracing the history of the many meetings on the subject. Last week, to his surprise, the Deacons gave him the go ahead to conduct a strategic audit of the church. The July 1994 deadline, some 12 months away, made him wonder about their degree of enthusiasm. In any event, there was nothing to say he couldn't finish earlier. Reverend Earl found his pad of lined paper in the center of the pile and began moving things around looking for his pencil. It was time to get serious, he thought!

THE EXTERNAL ENVIRONMENT

Walnut Creek Baptist Church was established in 1969 in the southern part of Montgomery County, Texas, approximately 30 miles north of downtown Houston. The church is near an exit on Interstate 45, 10 miles south of Conroe, the county seat.

The area has undergone tremendous changes since the church was started, especially since the late 1970s. The oil boom brought rapid growth to the Houston metropolitan area, including Montgomery County, which was one of the fastest-growing counties in the nation during the early 1980s. The mid-1980s brought serious recession to the area. Home prices fell by as much as 50 percent, and many residential and commercial properties fell into foreclosure. There was also a dramatic increase in small-business failures in the immediate area. By the late 1980s, many believed that the recession had hit bottom. Indeed, economic conditions, although considerably lower than before, had stabilized, and southern Montgomery County was growing once again. By December 1992 the population of southern Montgomery County was estimated at 60,000, an increase of approximately 30 percent over 1985 estimates.

*This case was prepared as a basis for class discussion. The name of the church and its pastor have been disguised. All rights reserved to the authors and the North American Case Research Association. Permission to use the case should be obtained from the authors and the North American Case Research Association.

Besides growth, a number of other basic changes had taken place. In 1969 most residents worked either in the immediate area or in Conroe. By the early-1990s, many area residents worked in downtown Houston or even farther from home. Average commuting time to downtown Houston was in excess of one hour each way; peak periods could take twice that long. It was not at all uncommon for people to leave home at 5 A.M. and not return until 7 P.M.

Another fundamental change that had occurred was a shift in basic values. Southern Montgomery County was viewed by many, especially its northern neighbors, as a "yuppie" haven. Recreational and social activities were a high priority with many residents, and the availability of these attractions was often cited by real estate salespeople. A wide variety of youth sport activities were also available. Unfortunately, there was also high alcohol and recreational drug usage in the area. Less than 25 percent of the residents were members of a local church.

While current median age data were not available at the time, local experts agreed that the area age levels were likely considerably below that of surrounding areas. The ethnic breakdown of the area population then was approximately 80 percent white, 15 percent Hispanic, and 5 percent black and other. The area is serviced by the seven Southern Baptist churches as shown in Exhibit 12–1. Selected demographics for these churches are listed in Exhibits 12–2 through 12–6.

In 1990 the Texas Department of Highways and Public Transportation had announced plans to widen Interstate 45 and its service roads. These plans would have placed the northbound service road right through the middle of the church sanctuary. There had been some speculation about whether the highway would be willing to purchase the entire 3.81-acre church property and, if so, at what price.

More recently, the highway department announced that the expansion plans had been revised. The highway department decided to shift the majority of the new right of way needed to the west side of Interstate 45 where only one building would need to be removed. Ongoing construction had moved the new service road to within three feet of the church's sign pylon and 12 feet from the church's sanctuary or main auditorium. This would soon be very disruptive to church activities, particularly Sunday services.

THE INTERNAL ENVIRONMENT

Walnut Creek Baptist Church was incorporated under the state laws of Texas and operates under a constitution and bylaws. It closely follows Southern Baptist doctrine.

Walnut Creek Baptist employs three full-time ministers in addition to Revered Earl: associate pastor/minister to adults, minister of music, and minister of youth. The Little Learners program (Mother's Day Out) also has a full-time director and one other paid staff position. In addition, there are five full-time support staff people.

Actions taken by the church are governed by a committee system. The church has established policy guidelines for thirty-one standing committees.

As with most nonprofit organizations, Walnut Creek Baptist relies heavily on volunteer workers. Workers may be true volunteers or actively recruited to perform specific roles. Training is provided when deemed necessary. A personnel policy manual for paid staff includes job descriptions and standards as well as procedures for periodic formal performance appraisals. There are formal guidelines for committees, but no similar guidelines for other volunteer positions, such as Sunday school teacher. There are no written job descriptions or procedures for performance reviews.

EXHIBIT 12-1 Southern Baptist Church Locations

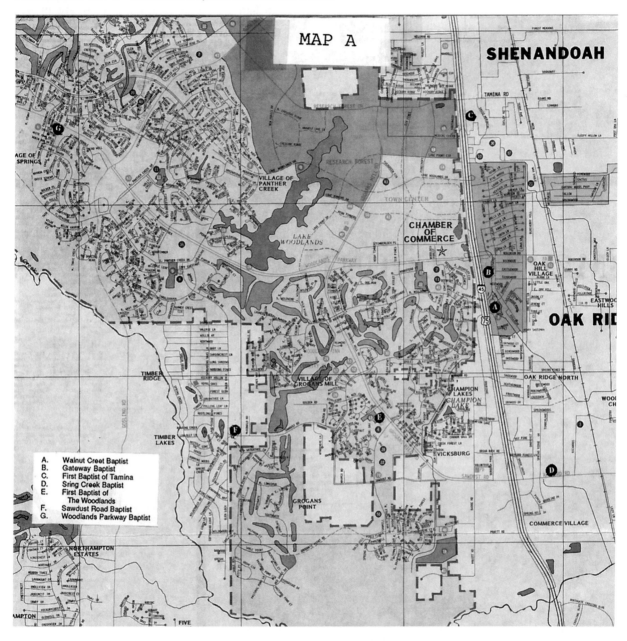

A staff member is assigned to each committee in order to coordinate its activities. The staff member assists the lay volunteers in performing the committee's duties and communicates the committee's activities to the rest of the staff during the weekly staff meetings. The chairman of each committee (normally a lay member) presents committee recommendations that require a vote of church members during congregational business meetings.

Each committee is responsible for its own long-range planning as its membership deems necessary for such planning. For example, the Little Learners Committee has been working on plans to expand the program from its present preschool status to a full elementary curriculum. Reverend Earl feels that long-range planning in the church is probably the exception rather than the rule.

The committee system includes a long-range planning committee, which historically has concerned itself exclusively with planning for new buildings and facilities. The church has no written goals that extend beyond one year and has adopted no formal long-range objectives or strategies. The church leadership does not consider this to be a problem since they believe that a clear consensus exists as to the direction that the church is and should be taking.

The pastor is responsible to the board of deacons for general policy guidance, but in actuality he receives great latitude in exercising control over church affairs. Reverend Earl's philosophy is for the church body to vote on as few matters as possible. He also believes in delegating considerable authority to the other staff members. He firmly believes that his main duties are to be engrossed in the Scriptures and to keep himself mentally, physically, and spiritually prepared to meet the needs of the church.

The church's membership is primarily middle-class, white-collar working families, with a small percentage in the higher income brackets. There are also a substantial number of single-parent families. Reverend Earl believes that these people need a stable base on which to build their lives. He believes that they are looking for relationships where they know that people care, they can find help in managing their children, and they can develop wholesome personal friendships.

Walnut Creek Baptist has sought to meet these needs by teaching and preaching basic biblical doctrine, offering programs directed toward the needs of children and youth, and presenting special seminars and other training opportunities. Extensive counseling is also available, including special programs for drug and alcohol abuse.

Reverend Earl was rather proud of Walnut Creek's marketing efforts: A 15-foot sign pylon, next to the church, supported a theater type marquee which could display messages of 10 to 12 words. The lettering was large enough to be read by travelers as they raced along I–45 at speeds well in excess of the posted 55 mph. A map showing

EXHIBIT 12-2 Southern Montgomery County Baptist Churches, Membership

		RESIDENT MEMBERSHIP		
CHURCH	YEAR ESTABLISHED	1985	1990	1992
First Baptist of Tamina	1947	146	158	158
First Baptist of the Woodlands	1978	1,003	975	1,168
Gateway Baptist	1986[a]	—	149	225
Walnut Creek Baptist	1969	2,589	2,178	2,345[b]
Sawdust Road Baptist	1979	408	510	245
Spring Creek Baptist	1967	406	150	230[b]
Woodlands Parkway Baptist	1984[c]	—	190	331

Source: Texas Baptist Annual.

[a] Gateway Baptist was formed in 1986 when approximately half the membership of Spring Creek Baptist left to form a new church.

[b] Corrected figure obtained from individual churches.

[c] Woodlands Parkway Baptist is located closest to new residential developments.

EXHIBIT 12-3 Southern Montgomery County Baptist churches, Sunday school attendance

CHURCH	1985	1990	1992
First Baptist of Tamina	27	61	90
First Baptist of the Woodlands	467	549	535
Gateway Baptist	—	65	101
Walnut Creek Baptist	1,064	950	995
Sawdust Road Baptist	149	181	151
Spring Creek Baptist	171	40	68
Woodlands Parkway Baptist	—	167	257

Source: Texas Baptist Annual.

EXHIBIT 12-4 Southern Montgomery County Baptist churches, revenues

CHURCH	1985	1990	1992
First Baptist of Tamina	$29,575	$61,438	n/a
First Baptist of the Woodlands	615,915	1,070,014	1,098,580
Gateway Baptist	—	103,780	156,210
Walnut Creek Baptist	1,370,165	1,399,769	1,386,231
Sawdust Road Baptist	115,035	148,067	164,840
Spring Creek Baptist	231,515	70,700	86,520
Woodlands Parkway Baptist	—	253,663	445,690

Source: Texas Baptist Annual.

EXHIBIT 12-5 Southern Montgomery County Baptist churches, property and debt, 1992

CHURCH	PROPERTY	DEBT
First Baptist of Tamina	n/a	n/a
First Baptist of the Woodlands	$5,000,000	$1,500,000
Gateway Baptist	30,000	0
Walnut Creek Baptist	4,127,770	615,587
Sawdust Road Baptist	450,000	88,000
Spring Creek Baptist	n/a	n/a
Woodlands Parkway Baptist	650,000	244,555

Source: Tryon Evergreen Association.

EXHIBIT 12-6 Southern Montgomery County Baptist Churches, Staff Salaries and Debt Retirement Expenditures, 1992

CHURCH	SALARIES	DEBT RETIREMENT
First Baptist of Tamina	n/a	n/a
First Baptist of the Woodlands	$287,534	$394,615
Gateway Baptist	95,887	0
Walnut Creek Baptist	341,206	236,451
Sawdust Road Baptist	64,257	41,600
Spring Creek Baptist	33,382	0
Woodlands Parkway Baptist	132,980	25,263

Source: Tryon Evergreen Association

the church's location and schedule of services had been run in the suburban edition of the yellow pages for several years. The church also locally distributed flyers three or four times a year publicizing various youth-oriented programs.

Walnut Creek Baptist is located on 3.81 acres fronting Interstate 45. No undeveloped land adjoins the property. The physical plant consists of five buildings and parking spaces for 471 cars. Three of the buildings, with a total of 18,866 square feet, are used exclusively for educational space. The Family Center contains a full-sized gymnasium, commercial kitchen, and educational space. The building has a total of 24,175 square feet, of which approximately 16,000 is available for education. The auditorium, completed in 1981, seats 1,700 people, although close to 2,000 have been accommodated with temporary seating. The building also contains the church offices and educational space. The total square footage is 51,000, with 40 percent available for educational use. Exhibit 12–7 provides a physical layout of the church property.

Southern Baptists have long held to the strategy of growing through the Sunday school. Therefore, great emphasis is usually placed in properly designing and utilizing educational space. Two rules of thumb are normally used in planning educational space. The first is to provide approximately 45 square feet of floor space per person. The second is that a church will not maintain an average Sunday school attendance in excess of 80 percent of its design capacity.

In site planning, two rules of thumb are to have two acres of land per 300 attendees and one parking space for each three people.

The church's financial affairs are directed by the treasurer and the finance/budget committee. The budget for each year is established through a process in which the various committees and ministry heads present their budget requests for the coming year. An attempt is then made to predict revenues by extrapolating figures from the previous year as adjusted by an informal assessment of current economic trends. Revenue projections are also adjusted for attendance trends.

In the last ten years, the church has never reached its revenue projection. As a result, expenditures are tightly controlled, even though funds have been authorized through the budget. A staff member authorizes all expenditures. All checks require two signatures, and the treasurer is supposed to certify that funds are available before checks are issued. There are no formal limits on the amount of an expenditure that a staff member can authorize,

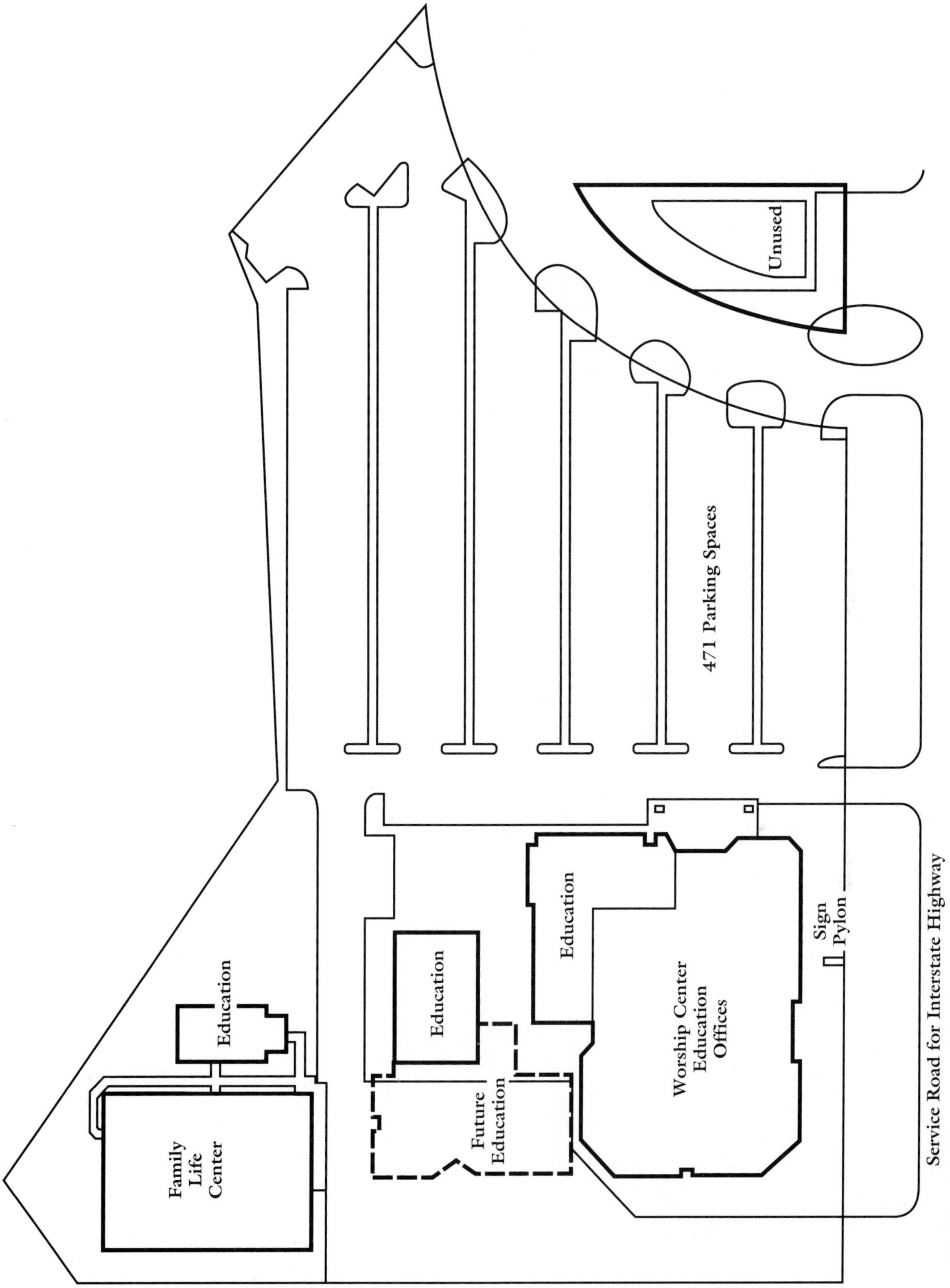

Unused

471 Parking Spaces

Family
Life
Center

Education

Education

Future
Education

Education

Worship Center
Education
Offices

Sign
Pylon

Service Road for Interstate Highway

EXHIBIT 12-7 Walnut Creek Baptist Church Site Elevation

although informal constraints are acknowledged. The church does not use a cash flow budget. An income statement and balance sheet are presented in Exhibits 12–8 and 12–9.

TOPICS FOR CONSIDERATION

Address the following questions regarding the status of Walnut Creek Baptist Church:

1. Is the church doing all that it can to meet the needs of the community?
2. Is the church using its resources efficiently and effectively?
3. Is the church growing at a rate that will allow it to continue its present programs as well as add new ones?
4. Is the church in control of its situation?
5. Are the churches current control systems appropriate?
6. Does the church have adequate physical facilities and grounds for future growth?

BIBLIOGRAPHY

Anderton, T. Lee. *Church Property/Building Guidebook. Rev.* Nashville: Convention Press, n.d.

Texas Baptist Annual, 1986. Dallas: Baptist General Convention of Texas, 1986.

Texas Baptist Annual, 1991. Dallas: Baptist General Convention of Texas, 1992.

Tryon Evergreen Baptist Association, Conroe, TX, 1992. Walnut Creek Baptist Church. *Constitution and Bylaws. Author, n.d.*

Walnut Creek Baptist Church. Policy Manual. *Author, n.d.*

EXHIBIT 12-8 Walnut Creek Baptist Church Income Statement for Years Ending December 31

	1989	1990	1991	1992
Revenues				
Tithes/offerings	$ 867,725	$ 884,328	$ 914,092	$ 922,701
Designated gifts	116,807	159,247	180,376	163,428
Restricted funds	325,165	277,900	224,766	195,667
Little Learners	51,557	69,380	95,246	100,357
Interest & bonds	12,622	8,914	7,629	4,078
Total	$1,373,876	$1,399,769	$1,422,109	$1,386,231
EXPENSES				
Missions	75,718	77,205	85,708	94,986
Activities/education	26,081	33,551	36,624	54,769
Administrative	261,724	291,335	322,880	396,189
Counseling/discipleship/evangelism	21,648	15,669	19,299	20,143
Preschool/children/youth	72,951	100,373	92,486	89,312
Wages/salaries	280,735	345,450	341,206	316,966
Debt service	452,548	387,538	234,643	291,318
Noncash Expenses	104,869	87,031	85,411	47,621
Total	$1,296,274	$1,338,152	$1,218,257	$1,311,304
Operating Income	77,602	61,617	203,852	74,927
Fees/expenses	0	0	(75)	0
Net	$ 77,602	$ 61,617	$ 203,777	$ 74,927

Source: Walnut Creek Baptist Church documents, as adjusted.

EXHIBIT 12-9   Walnut Creek Baptist Church Balance Sheet as of December 31

	1989	1990	1991	1992
ASSETS				
Current Assets				
Petty Cash	$ 55	$ 55	$ 500	$ 500
Checking	3,875	(12,047)	31,976	26,894
Savings	49,682	61,826	47,632	27,192
Restricted Savings	145,672	116,317	203,621	100,000
Bonds	1,743	0	0	1,620
Total	$ 201,027	$ 166,151	$ 283,729	$ 156,204
Fixed Assets				
Land	295,349	295,349	295,349	295,349
Improvements	2,691,165	2,703,169	2,701,660	2,691,877
Depreciation	(1,007,143)	(1,081,974)	(1,158,086)	(1,140,544)
Total	1,979,371	1,916,544	1,838,923	1,846,682
Other Assets				
Deferred Charges	56,575	53,475	54,898	13,140
Total	56,575	53,475	54,898	13,140
Total Assets	$ 2,236,973	$ 2,136,170	$ 2,177,550	$ 2,016,026
LIABILITIES				
Current Liabilities				
Accounts Payable	$ 16,845	$ 13,451	$ 0	$ 0
Bonds	48,766	54,733	187,957	863
Matured Bonds	6,003	2,867	1,124	1,124
Payroll	(69)	(95)	(56)	0
Total	71,545	70,956	189,025	1,987
Long-term Liabilities				
"B" bonds	12,250	0	0	0
1986 bonds	1,065,000	945,000	665,000	0
Bank Note Payable	0	0	0	615,587
Accrued interest	29,579	0	0	0
Total	1,106,829	945,000	665,000	615,587
Total Liabilities	1,178,374	1,015,956	854,025	617,574
GENERAL FUND				
Fund Balance	1,058,599	1,120,214	1,323,525	1,398,452
Total	$ 2,236,973	$ 2,136,170	$ 2,177,550	$ 2,016,026

Source: Walnut Creek Baptist Church documents, as adjusted.

THE METROPOLITAN MUSEUM OF ART—1994

MARILYN M. HELMS,
PAULA J. HAYNES, AND
TAMMY L. SWENSON
The University of
Tennessee at Chattanooga

Based in New York City, the Metropolitan Museum of Art, or the Met (212-535-7710), ended its 1992–93 fiscal year with an operating deficit of $1.15 million. The deficit occurred in part because of decreases in admissions income and increases in operating expenses. Although the museum suffered a decline in per-capita visitor contributions and weaker merchandise sales in 1992–93, support from endowments increased substantially. The museum also enjoyed strong gains on its investment fund, reporting a 15 percent return from the previous period.

In the 1990s, many non-profit organizations are facing decreased support from patrons, government, and corporate and private philanthropy. These issues were challenging for strategic management. In 1993, admissions income represented only 10 percent of total revenue for the year; operations depend greatly upon endowment support, both from individuals and government sources. After having cut a large portion of its support to the Metropolitan Museum of Art in 1991–92, New York City increased its operating support by $595,000 in 1992–93, thus helping to partially restore previous funding levels.

The Met depends on external sources of revenue including interest on endowments, gifts, governmental appropriations, and grants as well as internal sources of revenue from merchandising operations, auditorium rental, parking garage fees, restaurants, admissions, memberships, royalties, and fees. Operating expenses include curatorial departments, educational programs and libraries, providing public information, marketing research, stocking inventories for auxiliary operations, and administrative costs. Total expenditures are rising at a faster rate than total revenues, and management of the Museum needs to find ways to sustain financial stability.

HISTORY

The State of New York granted a charter to a group forming a corporation in the name of the Metropolitan Museum of Art on April 13, 1870. The corporation was formed for the purpose of establishing and maintaining a museum and library of art, of encouraging and developing study of fine arts and the application of arts to manufacture and practical life, of advancing the general knowledge of kindred subjects, and, to that end, of furnishing popular instruction and recreation. This mission remains unchanged through 1993 with one exception; the word "recreation" is no longer part of the mission. The museum is a nonprofit tax-exempt [501(c)(3)] organization.

CITY SUPPORT

New York City owns the museum building but collections are the property of the corporation operating the Met. The city appropriates funds to the museum for maintaining the building as well as providing utilities at no charge. In 1993, allocations totalled $14,884,799, which was 8.1 percent of the total 1993 operating revenue; these allocations represented a partial, though somewhat sluggish, recovery of city support to previous years' levels. A history of support from the City of New York is included in the Five Year Summary shown in Exhibits 13–1 to 13–4. According to Bradford Kelleher, head of the Met's merchandising and publishing activities, "people think we

EXHIBIT 13-1 The Metropolitan Museum of Art Five Year Summary

	1993	1992*	1991*	1990*	1989*†
OPERATING FUND					
Revenue and Support					
Total income from endowment including The Cloisters, less or plus endowment income stabilization reserves as noted below	$18,217,436	$15,253,879	$14,169,461	$12,815,529	$10,838,371
City of New York:					
Funds for guardianship and maintenance	7,841,471	6,853,617	9,645,657	10,193,481	9,892,601
Value of utilities provided	7,043,328	5,941,552	6,068,111	5,398,227	5,489,227
Memberships	11,588,899	11,434,836	11,723,453	10,809,726	10,557,710
Gifts and grants:					
Education, community affairs, and special exhibitions	6,941,903	6,774,915	5,784,889	5,921,025	4,419,936
General purpose contributions	18,634,992	17,885,118	15,864,740	14,126,525	11,492,125
Income for specified funds utilized	2,258,308	721,037	439,330	539,539	403,308
Admissions	8,733,207	9,115,457	8,621,001	7,304,343	10,032,361
Royalties and fees	1,260,152	1,646,293	1,814,579	1,222,951	1,438,572
Other	3,689,999	3,620,855	3,817,124	4,941,078	4,393,423
Income before auxiliary activities	86,209,695	79,247,559	77,948,345	73,272,424	68,957,634
Revenue of auxiliary activities	98,762,341	92,977,194	90,154,977	79,565,366	78,480,090
TOTAL REVENUE AND SUPPORT	184,972,036	172,224,753	168,103,322	152,837,790	147,437,724
Expenses					
Curatorial:					
Curatorial departments, conservation, cataloguing, and scholarly publications	20,477,337	21,019,361	21,470,368	19,845,456	18,219,950
Operation of The Cloisters	3,568,841	3,216,458	3,253,558	2,913,132	2,801,680
Special exhibitions	8,371,094	6,985,200	5,789,990	6,242,448	5,061,807
Education, community programs, and libraries	4,910,108	4,587,853	5,300,858	5,104,734	5,700,470
Financial, legal, and other administrative functions	6,602,448	6,175,840	6,084,069	5,542,451	5,046,463
Communications, development, and membership services	5,582,308	4,745,585	5,431,390	6,649,179	5,398,638
Operations:					
Guardianship	16,067,186	14,548,710	15,404,915	14,981,129	13,497,933
Maintenance	9,027,426	9,911,716	9,994,162	8,460,979	8,075,233
Operating services	5,982,392	5,388,269	5,359,190	4,870,045	4,572,179
Value of utilities provided by the City of New York	7,043,328	5,941,552	6,068,111	5,398,227	5,489,227
Nonexhibition capital construction and renovation	3,135,992	3,179,204	2,088,713	2,530,557	1,163,930
Expenses before auxiliary activities	90,768,460	85,699,748	86,245,324	82,538,337	75,027,510

EXHIBIT 13-1 *Continued*

OPERATING FUND	1993	1992*	1991*	1990*	1989*†
Cost of sales and expenses of auxiliary activities	95,353,942	88,809,318	83,818,862	72,894,246	68,924,676
TOTAL EXPENSES	186,122,402	174,509,066	170,064,186	155,432,583	143,952,186
Net (Decrease) Increase in Operating Fund Balance	($1,150,366)	($2,284,313)	($1,960,864)	($2,594,793)	($3,485,538)
Additional information:					
Endowment funds balance	$535,073,452	$487,930,208	$450,890,594	$425,725,761	$396,149,106
Capital Construction expenditures	$ 30,110,406	$ 33,111,821	$ 22,978,339	$ 20,434,301	$ 15,476,598
Acquisitions of art	$ 85,169,652	$ 21,242,915	$ 16,945,340	$ 18,259,644	$ 17,107,754
Income (from) to endowment income stabilization reserves	($3,398,905)	$109,932	$2,378,908	$2,123,180	$2,903,502
Full-time employees	1,673	1,607	1,627	1,659	1,568
Visitors to the Main Building and The Cloisters	4,615,588	4,667,884	4,702,078	4,558,560	4,816,388

*Fiscal years 1989–1992 have been reclassified to conform with the fiscal 1993 presentation of scholarly publications expenses.

†Fiscal 1989 amounts have not been restated to apply Financial Accounting Standard No. 93.

Source: The Metropolitan Museum of Art.

are rich because we are custodians of a treasure house, but we are not. The museum has operated at or near a deficit for 10 years."

New York City's budget problems included cuts of 36 percent in 1991–92, or a total of $3.5 million, in the city's annual support for the Met. The Met's total annual budget is $186 million. Given the cuts, William Luers, President of the Met, did not open the Museum for the 13th Annual Museum Mile Festival. It was the first time the Met did not participate in the annual three-hour event staged by the 10 museums that line the upper 5th Avenue. According to Luers, "We have always been involved in the festival but it costs between $25,000 to $30,000 to open for the one night celebration. We felt bad about not staying open, but we're cutting a lot of other things as well, including window washing, which costs $120,000 a year." As a result of the city's cuts, The Met implemented a rotating gallery closing schedule in September 1991, closing roughly half of their galleries on Tuesdays through Thursdays as a means of cutting operating costs. As of November 1993, the rotating schedule remains in effect.

COLLECTIONS AND ACTIVITIES

Located on the east side of Central Park, the Met's collections include ancient and modern art from Egypt, Greece, Rome, the Near and Far East, pre-Columbian cultures and the United States. The Cloisters, a branch museum, located in Fort Tryon Park on the far northern tip of Manhattan Island, houses the European medieval art

EXHIBIT 13-2   The Metropolitan Museum of Art Balance Sheet June 30, 1993 with Comparative Totals as of June 30, 1992

| | | | 1993 | | | 1992 |
	Operating Fund	Funds for Specified Purposes	Endowment Funds	Elimination of Interfund Receivables and Payables	Total	Total
ASSETS						
Cash	$1,552,054	$117,112			$1,669,166	$798,773
Investments, at market (Notes A, B, and I)	3,414,384	121,048,321	$537,712,825		662,175,530	593,124,807
Receivables (Notes A and C)	5,964,032	15,513,585	106,372,604		127,850,221	67,761,692
Interfund receivables, net (Note D)				(44,664,441)	($44,664,441)	—
Merchandise inventories (Notes A and E)	22,296,507				22,296,507	21,308,804
Fixed assets, at cost, net (Notes A and F)	22,034,859	12,698,535			34,733,394	26,757,614
Deferred charges, prepaid expenses and other assets	4,020,910	55,913	1,045,590		5,122,413	5,776,913
TOTAL ASSETS	$59,282,746	$149,433,466	$689,795,460	($44,664,441)	$853,847,231	$715,528,603
LIABILITIES AND FUND BALANCES						
Accounts payable	$8,810,593	$7,468,050	$102,169,384		$118,448,027	$67,093,060
Accrued expenses, primarily payroll, annual leave, and pension (Note G)	13,234,030				13,234,030	12,370,775
Interfund payables, net (Note D)	28,687,382	15,977,059		($44,664,441)	—	—
Deferred income, principally memberships, gifts, and grants	10,030,381				10,030,381	12,508,355
Notes payable (Note H)	2,672,376		7,227,624		9,900,000	25,200,000
Loan payable (Note I)			45,325,000		45,325,000	46,140,000
TOTAL LIABILITIES	63,434,762	23,445,109	154,722,008	(44,664,441)	196,937,438	163,312,190
Fund (deficit) balance (Notes J and K)	(4,152,016)	125,988,357	535,073,452		656,909,793	552,216,413
TOTAL LIABILITIES AND FUND BALANCES	$59,282,746	$149,433,466	$689,795,460	($44,664,441)	$853,847,231	$715,528,603

Source: The Metropolitan Museum of Art.

	1993	1992
REVENUE AND SUPPORT		
Return from endowment funds, including $3,398,905 allocated from and $109,932 allocated to income stabilization reserves in 1993 and 1992, respectively	$ 16,403,379	$ 13,616,046
Appropriation from the City of New York		
Funds for guardianship and maintenance	7,841,471	6,853,617
Value of utilities provided	7,043,328	5,941,552
Admissions at Main Building	8,183,991	8,572,125
Memberships	11,588,899	11,434,836
Gifts and grants:		
General purposes and education	19,054,598	18,362,940
Special exhibitions	6,522,298	6,297,094
The Cloisters:		
Return from endowment funds used in operations	1,814,057	1,637,833
Admissions and other	884,417	809,284
Royalties and fees	1,260,153	1,646,293
Other income	5,613,104	4,075,939
Revenue and support before auxiliary activities	86,209,695	79,247,559
Revenue of auxiliary activities:		
Merchandise operations	86,261,137	82,388,036
Restaurant, parking garage, auditorium, and other	12,501,204	10,589,158
TOTAL REVENUE AND SUPPORT	184,972,036	172,224,753
EXPENSES		
Curatorial:		
Curatorial departments, conservation, cataloguing and scholarly publications	20,477,337	20,829,434
Operation of The Cloisters	3,568,841	3,216,458
Special exhibitions	8,371,094	6,985,200
Education, community programs, and libraries	4,910,108	4,587,853
Membership services	2,810,876	2,510,180
Communications	449,927	189,927
Financial, legal, and other administrative functions	6,602,448	6,175,840
Development	2,321,506	2,235,405
Operations:		
Guardianship (Note A)	16,067,186	14,548,710
Maintenance (Note A)	9,027,426	9,911,716
Operating services	5,982,391	5,388,269
Value of utilities provided by the City of New York	7,043,328	5,941,552
Nonexhibition capital construction and renovation	3,135,992	3,179,204
Expenses before auxiliary activities	90,768,460	85,699,748

EXHIBIT 13-3 *Continued*

	1993	1992
Cost of sales and other expenses of auxiliary activities		
Merchandise operations	83,974,789	79,068,100
Restaurant, parking garage, auditorium, and other	11,379,153	9,741,218
TOTAL EXPENSES	186,122,402	174,509,066
EXPENSES IN EXCESS OF REVENUE AND SUPPORT	($1,150,366)	($2,284,313)

Source: The Metropolitan Museum of Art.

collection. The structure was constructed from parts of five European monasteries. Opened in 1938, the land and building were donated to the City of New York and much of the art within was donated by John D. Rockefeller, Jr. With almost 2 million square feet of space, the Met is really 21 different museums or galleries with separate curatorial departments.

The Met calls itself the largest art museum in the Western Hemisphere. They have more than two thousand employees. More than a million works of art from all over the world, ranging from the prehistoric to the contemporary, are on display. According to Kathleen Mary Arffmann, Manager of Visitor Services for the Met, when planned expansions are completed by the end of the 1990s, the Met will be the world's largest museum.

In addition to the many gallery wings, the Museum has a 250,000 volume library of art and reference materials used by graduate students in accordance with the Museum's affiliation with New York University. This Thomas J. Watson Library has a computerized online public access catalog that was initiated in November 1992. The Met has a 708 and a 246 seat auditorium; 3 classrooms; a restaurant and cafeteria; a parking garage; and a 10,000 square foot museum store. Twelve other retail stores operated by the Met exist in New York City, Connecticut, California, Ohio, New Jersey, Georgia, and Texas. The Met also has a mail order catalog with 1,500 items sent 6 times a year to almost 3 million people.

Activities at the museum include guided tours, lectures, gallery talks, concerts, formally organized educational programs for children, inter-museum loans, and permanent, temporary, and travelling exhibitions.

MANAGEMENT

The Met operates by a dual management system as shown in Exhibit 13–5. The president and director report directly to the Board of Trustees. The dual management system was started in 1978, when the board decided the Museum was too complex and large for one person to manage. Prior to the board's action in 1978, Thomas Hoving had been chief executive at the Museum since 1967. Hoving's acquisitions and expansion projects included addition of the Lehman Wing, a glass-covered garden court, in 1975; the Sackler Wing, a climate-controlled glass-roofed room housing the Temple

EXHIBIT 13-4 Statements of Changes in Fund Balances for the Years Ended June 30, 1993 and 1992

	1993			1992		
	OPERATING FUND	FUNDS FOR SPECIFIED PURPOSES	ENDOWMENT FUNDS	OPERATING FUND	FUNDS FOR SPECIFIED PURPOSES	ENDOWMENT FUNDS
FUND BALANCE BEGINNING OF YEAR ADDITIONS	($3,001,650)	$ 67,287,855	$487,930,208	($ 717,337)	$56,944,626	$450,890,594
Return from endowment funds		6,953,917			7,135,851	
Return to endowment fund income for stabilization reserves				109,932		
Investment income		2,525,740			3,104,298	
Increase in net investment appreciation		9,101,116	48,615,847		10,554,735	30,367,885
Gifts, bequests, and grants		127,952,990	24,700,641		35,911,012	8,698,786
Proceeds from sales of art		830,016			712,095	
Return from invested loan proceeds	109,932	457,407			560,395	
	109,932	147,821,186	73,316,488	109,932	57,978,386	39,066,671
DEDUCTIONS						
Expenses in excess of revenue and support	1,150,366			2,284,313		
Return from endowment fund income stabilization reserves	3,398,905					
Acquisitions of art		85,169,651			21,242,915	
Construction, renovation, and other capital expenditures		19,579,475			21,251,219	
Fellowships, reference books, and other		3,042,919			3,219,958	
Interest and other loan-related expenses		3,457,902			3,495,845	
Depreciation and amortization		645,076			562,209	
	4,549,271	111,895,023		2,284,313	49,772,146	
INTERFUND TRANSFERS						
Transfer of income stabilization reserves from (to) endowment	3,398,905	4,057,677	(7,456,582)	(109,932)	2,079,754	(1,969,822)
Other		18,716,662	(18,716,662)		57,235	(57,235)
FUND (DEFICIT) BALANCE, END OF YEAR (NOTES J AND K)	($4,152,016)	$125,988,357	$535,073,452	($3,001,650)	$67,287,855	$487,930,208

Source: The Metropolitan Museum of Art.

of Dendur, in 1978; and the American Wing in 1980. Major renovations of the Great Hall and Costume Institute were completed in 1970 and 1971.

Most of the controversy that surrounded Hoving's tenure was due to his role in institutionalizing the "blockbuster", or special event, at the Metropolitan as an answer to the financial crisis. According to Hoving, "the public is most attracted to temporary events and attendance figures were high at the large scale ticketed events." Examples of these types of events were the "Treasures of Tutankhamen" show in 1978 and 1979, during which 1.2 million tickets were sold. Other examples of large scale ticketed events include "The Great Age of Fresco," "Mexico: Splendors of Thirty Centuries," and "Harlem on My Mind." The "blockbuster" issue was a very questionable one, however. According to supporters, "the attraction of new audiences will diminish the elitist image of museums." People against such exhibitions, such as Sherman Lee, Director of the Cleveland Museum, say "the values of the marketplace, if applied carelessly, may undermine public confidence in the Museum's integrity."

As of 1993, de Montebello and William H. Luers, the president, share the responsibility of managing the Met. Philippe de Montebello, born in France and a graduate of Harvard and New York University, is primarily responsible for all curatorial functions, conservation departments, libraries, and educational activities. William H. Luers, a past United States Ambassador to Czechoslovakia, is responsible for the business side of the Metropolitan. His responsibilities include daily operations, merchandising, development, human resources, internal auditing, and all financial matters including budgeting. Even though the president is responsible for development of the Metropolitan including fund-raising, de Montebello is involved in development, as well as in acquiring donations of works of art and money. Mr. Luers stated "Philippe should be perceived as the man who gives aesthetic and artistic vision to the Museum. And I am the manager, diplomat, executive, fund-raiser and basically a communicator."

De Montebello's career in art has been pursued at the Met—initially as an associate curator and in 1977 as acting director and the following year he became director. In addition to his duties as director, he continues to write articles for art publications.

Revenues earned from additional attendees have helped support Museum's activities from 1980 to 1993. Since Lee's retirement from the Cleveland Museum, Philippe de Montebello, the current Director of the Metropolitan and Hoving's successor, has taken on responsibility of the "anti-blockbuster" cause. Mr. de Montebello's position is to "lament the cost-effective mentality that places any Museum activity that does not generate attendance or immediate income in jeopardy." For the year ended June 30, 1990, there were no large-scale exhibition events at the Metropolitan, and the total revenue from admissions decreased by 27 percent. However, during 1991 the Museum's increased admission prices and large-scale exhibition offerings increased total admission revenues. By 1993, a strategic shift was clearly taking place with the reopening of the Nineteenth Century Paintings and Sculpture Galleries in September. After spending two years and nearly $13 million on renovations, the Metropolitan Museum opened with an impressive collection of Impressionist and Post-Impressionist masterpieces. The highlight of this exhibit, Van Gogh's *Wheat Field with Cypresses,* seems to contradict earlier "anti-blockbuster" sentiments.

De Montebello feels a number of things are essential in being a top-notch director of a great museum: knowledge of your own field and, in the case of an art museum, a very broad knowledge of art and a genuine desire to communicate it. Beyond that, you have to be diplomatic, forceful, and well situated, because you have to be able to raise money. You have to be able to express yourself in order to set policy with the

EXHIBIT 13-5 The Metropolitan Museum of Art Organizational Chart

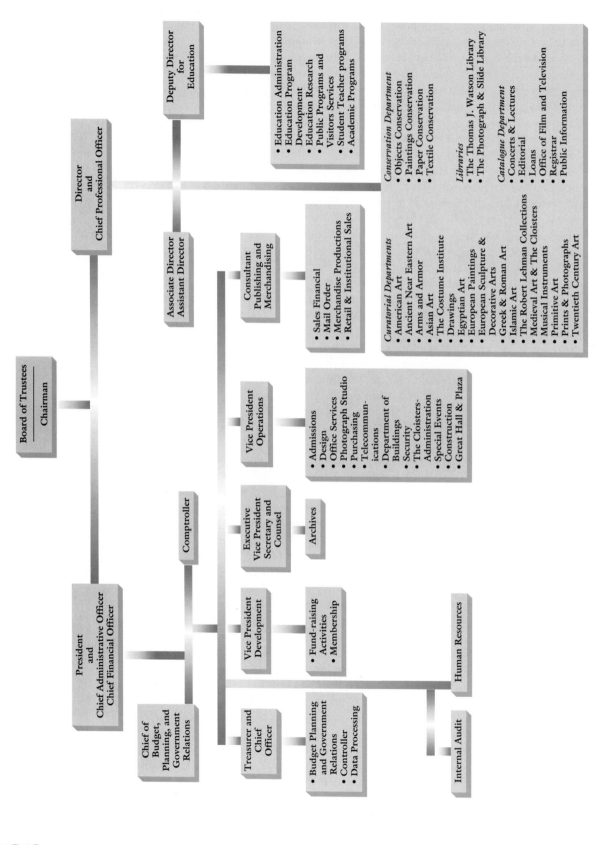

board of trustees, to work with very large staff of experts in their fields, and to arbitrate. You have to be decisive. Obviously, you must be able to be a lot of things at once.

COMPETITORS AND SPECIAL EXHIBITIONS

The Museum of Modern Art in New York, whose membership of 45,000 is off 20 percent from its 1987 peak, received a flood of new art devotees lured by a blockbuster exhibit, the Henri Matisse retrospective. According to the Museum of Modern Art (MOMA), such shows pack a box office wallop because the art is drawn from many collections. But they are getting scarcer as funding slows and insurance costs rise. To capitalize, the MOMA is boosting its direct-mail appeals and is installing a special recruitment desk in its lobby.

The MOMA saw a 15 percent increase in membership during the exhibition show's four-month run in 1991. The Philadelphia Museum of Art sent special mailings tied to their Picasso exhibition show. But such members are poor renewal candidates, warns Bonnie Coulter of the Philadelphia Museum. With fewer blockbusters in the offing, the Museum of Fine Arts in Boston focuses on upgrading membership. Washington's National Gallery of Art uses numerous special exhibitions.

When asked about the main function of a great museum, de Montebello feels the purpose is to furnish both instruction and pleasure to the general public. To do so, they collect and preserve great art, put the art on display, and conduct research. The strength of the Met is its remarkable comprehensiveness in representing the history of mankind in visual terms at a high level of quality.

According to de Montebello, all important art institutions are trying to do great things with a limited currency, which is works of art or the subjects of exhibitions. The key players are the French museums, the National Gallery in Washington, D.C., the Royal Academy in London, and the Met. Then there are other American museums that have very active programs—Los Angeles, Chicago, Boston, and Philadelphia.

FUND-RAISING AT THE MET

In 1982, the Met began a campaign to raise $150 million to offset operating deficits and enhance their endowment. Even though large gifts had been solicited for specific projects on several occasions, this campaign was the first formal, public fund-raising drive ever conducted by the Met. These funds were supposed to help the Metropolitan Museum achieve financial stability, to allow all galleries to stay open when the Museum is open, and to finance the existing educational programs, the work of curatorship, and the conservation library. The five-year drive, completed in 1987, was successful in meeting the $150 million goal; however, the Metropolitan experienced an operating deficit of $2.6 million for the 1989–90 fiscal year and a $1.9 million deficit for 1990–91. The 1992 deficit increased to $2.3 million but by 1993 had dropped back to $1.15 million, the lowest deficit in four years. The development staff implemented the following fund-raising techniques in an attempt to offset deficits. Philippe de Montebello says "there is no ministry of culture in the United States. We don't receive a check from Washington, so we have to seek ways to provide revenues."

Endowed Chairs. An effective fund-raising technique, borrowed from universities and hospitals, has been soliciting funds for existing curatorship in the form of endowed chairs. All major art dealers in New York, as well as industry leaders are approached regularly to solicit the endowments. These chairs carry the name of the donor who would add to the endowment indefinitely. The purpose of this drive is to raise the salaries of curators so the Metropolitan can be competitive within the job market by attracting the best people and retain the people they already have by increasing their existing salaries. Raises of this type would not have otherwise been possible due to the operating fund shortfalls.

Corporate Sponsorship. As governmental funding decreases, corporations have come under increasing pressure to take the lead in funding social and community programs. Based on a 1991 study performed by *American Demographics,* the largest share of corporate support goes to education (38 percent) with health and human services (34 percent) following. The study does not present a promising future for corporate sponsorship of the arts because most corporations practice "strategic philanthropy" focusing philanthropic efforts to maximize their returns. At the Metropolitan, great effort is given to matching the 30 annual special exhibits to corporations' activities to entice them to fund the exhibit, otherwise the exhibit might not be shown. One example of matching a corporation's activities to an exhibit was a gift of $500,000 from the Hunting World Group of Companies to maintain a gallery displaying American Arms.

The corporate patron program requires an annual donation of $30,000. This membership allows companies to have one party a year, at their own expense, in the Temple of Dendur, the American Wing, or the Medieval Sculpture Hall. Proceeds cover a portion of the Met's operating costs. Even though private use of public space is a controversial issue, it has proven to be a successful way to generate revenue.

Memberships. The Museum has various levels of membership and councils. The Chair's council members donate $25,000 annually and are included in governance of the Museum. Membership in this council is by invitation only. The Real Estate Council is responsible for raising money for special showings not fully financed. Each member is given 15 invitations to a special showing.

Many memberships are available to the general public. Members enjoy free admission and receive the quarterly *Bulletin* magazine and the bimonthly *Calendar.* Also they receive mail order Museum catalogues and are given 10 percent off all merchandise purchased in the Museum shop. In 1993, the Metropolitan Museum's membership was almost 100,000. Contribution levels required for all categories of membership were increased in 1991. Exhibits 13–6 and 13–7 provide a comparison of the number of members by category for 1987 through 1993.

Government Grants. For the year ended June 30, 1993, the Met received funding from local, state, and federal governments. The City of New York provided the building that houses the Museum, the utilities, and appropriated funds for maintaining the building. The State of New York provided an annual allocation from the New York State Council on the Arts for general operating and program support. Special capital funds from the Natural Heritage Trust were received to support the special exhibitions program.

Federal agencies such as the National Endowment for the Arts and the Institute of Museum Services provide support for specific projects and general operations. Funds provided from all governmental sources amounted to more than $15 million for the year

EXHIBIT 13-6 Number of Annual Members by Category

CURRENT PRICES	1993	1992	1991	1990	1989
Student ($30)	1,478	1,590	1,557	1,575	1,517
Individual ($70)	29,362	30,260	29,175	33,054	34,548
Dual ($125)*	19,268	20,187	21,261	23,299	24,485
Sustaining ($300)	7,242	6,186	6,539	7,329	7,729
Supporting					
Contributing ($600)	1,011	1,076	1,547	1,671	1,885
Donor ($900)	428	448	555	611	634
Sponsor ($2,000)	518	461	507	521	541
Patron ($4,000)	132	136	156	182	175
Upper Patron ($6,000)	26	25	51	62	51
National Association ($35)***	40,287	36,876	32,848	31,555	29,777
National Friend ($200)**	60				
Total	99,812	97,245	94,196	99,859	101,342

*Includes Life Members.

**New category for 1993.

***Nonresident Membership.

Note: Rates for all membership categories were increased an average of 21% in 1991.

Source: The Metropolitan Museum of Art.

ended June 30, 1993; only $250,000, or less than 2 percent of government funding, came from the federal government. Most government support is appropriated on an annual basis; therefore, during recessionary periods, this external funding is uncertain.

Gifts. The 1986 Tax Reform Act discouraged donations of works of art to the Metropolitan and other museums. The change in the tax law reduced the tax deduction donors could take for appreciated art objects. As a result many art objects were sold to the highest bidder at auction houses. A survey conducted by *American Demographics* found that charitable giving by corporations fell 12 percent after the 1986 Tax Reform Act became effective. In March 1991, the Metropolitan received the largest gift it had received in over 50 years, probably due to a temporary "tax window," a one year restoration of tax deductions for the full market value of art donated in 1991. Valued at $1 billion, the paintings donated by Walter Annenberg will not become the property of the Metropolitan until Mr. Annenberg's death. According to the Tax Reform Act of 1986, people who donate appreciable property, like a painting that has become more valuable, can deduct only what they paid and not the current market value if they are subject to the alternative minimum tax. This was repealed by the 1993 Tax Reform Act which reinstated the deduction for art object donations.

In 1992, a bill was passed creating a procedure to value property before a donor gives it to charity. Backers of the bill, including the Met, say their goal is to keep costly audit disputes from arising years after donors take big deductions for gifts of major artwork. The bill would allow a process for donors and the Internal Revenue Service (IRS) to agree in advance on appraisals of artwork and collectibles valued at over $50,000. While donors may inflate their charitable deduction estates, they tend to

EXHIBIT 13-7 Members of the Corporation

	1993	1992	1991	1990	1989
Honorary Fellows for Life	3	3	3	3	3
Fellows for Life	820	843	873	901	911
Fellows in Perpetuity	318	323	329	336	342
Benefactors	302	305	355	389	372
Total Corporation Members	1,443	1,474	1,560	1,629	1,628
Total Annual Members	99,812	97,245	94,196	99,859	101,342
Grand Total	101,255	98,719	95,756	101,488	102,970

Source: The Metropolitan Museum of Art.

undervalue their taxable bequests of art. The IRS has an Art Advisory Panel of outside experts to review these works of art.

Donations to 250 museums surveyed by the American Association of Museums soared 541 percent in 1991 when an eighteen-month window went into effect on June 30 for donors to get a full tax break. (In contrast, donations had fallen 50 percent from 1987 through 1990.) A 1993 provision extended the tax break indefinitely. Contributions were expected to remain strong because of this ruling, although historical data has suggested that the economy, and not the tax code, has the greatest effect on charitable giving.

According to the Business Committee for the Arts, business giving to the arts reportedly fell by 2 percent in 1992. A survey of 419 arts organization directors cited numerous challenges in soliciting corporate donations: business does not understand the benefits of art sponsorship; business is only interested in projects that draw big crowds; business wants a large return for a small contribution; business wants quantifiable results that aren't always available; and business wants more lead time than the arts organizations can provide.

ADMISSIONS

For the year ended June 30, 1993, 4.6 million people visited the Museum and the Cloisters making the Met the number one tourist attraction in New York City. Attendance decreased in 1993 due in part to the rotating gallery closings. Revenue from admissions decreased by $382,000 (4.2 percent) from the previous year. Management of the Museum has veered away from ticketing exhibitions in an effort to make special exhibitions more spontaneous and more rewarding for the frequent visitor.

HOURS OF OPERATION

Evening hours were added on Friday and Saturday nights in 1991 in place of opening on Tuesday evening in an attempt to increase attendance. Attendance on Tuesday evening averaged 2,500, while attendance on Friday and Saturday evenings ranged from 3,500 to 5,000 visitors in 1991. The trend continued through 1993. Exhibit 13–8 reveals the hours of operation and donations for admission to the Museum.

TARGET CUSTOMER

Surveys are conducted by the Metropolitan each year to determine the key demographics of their visitors. Exhibit 13–9 reveals demographics of the average visitor to the Met which is used to effectively market the Museum's services. Of the 1,357 surveyed, 48 percent were New York City residents, 39.6 percent were residents in other United States areas, and 12.4 percent were foreign visitors.

VOLUNTEERS

Approximately 800 volunteers work at the Metropolitan Museum. Three hundred of these are volunteers, who lead tours. Mostly women volunteers are now employed. As women continue to enter the work force, nonprofit organizations may have difficulty finding volunteers to work during daytime hours.

AUXILIARY OPERATIONS

A growing number of business executives serve on the board because the Museum has evolved into a big business with an investment portfolio, reproduction studio, and retail outlets. Because external funds are uncertain, greater emphasis is placed on generation of internal sources of revenue.

Museum Shops. The Met sells a wide range of goods, from expensive reproductions of statues to coffee mugs and poster art. The Met relies on such merchandise to support its operations.

Profits from merchandising has been rising faster than income from endowments, as a percent of total operating income, since 1967. Retail shops are operated within the Museum, at the Cloisters, and in twelve offsite locations. Met's sales are largely made in the museum itself, where the Met has run an expanded 10,000 square foot store since 1979. The majority of the Met's retail sales come from the onsite store. Four satellite shops are in New York: Rockefeller Center, New York Public Library, The Americana at Manhasset, and Macy's. Two are in Connecticut: Stamford Town

Center and Westfarms Mall. Two are in California: Century City Shopping Center in Los Angeles and Southcoast Plaza in Costa Mesa. One is in Ohio at Columbus City Center, and one is in New Jersey at the Mall at Shorthills. The two most recent additions include Lenox Mall in Atlanta and the Galleria in Houston. The Met does most of the original modeling and design work in manufacturing the art reproductions in its own studio, then subcontracts the actual production to small factories and artisans around the world. Final approval of reproductions for resale rests with the original's curator, who wields an absolute veto over each potential reproduction.

Because the Met is a tax-exempt nonprofit organization, it pays no taxes on profits realized from retail operations; therefore, some retailers feel the Met has an unfair advantage over businesses selling similar goods. The Museum is only required to pay sales taxes on retail items unrelated to its mission of art education, in accordance with section 511 (imposition of tax on unrelated business income of charitable organizations) of the *Internal Revenue Code*. The only regular sales activity the Met pays income tax for is rental of its membership list to other businesses. The Met is a leader in opposing changes that would increase tax burdens on nonprofit institutions.

The purpose of the unrelated business income tax is to prevent tax-exempt organizations from competing unfairly with businesses whose earnings are taxed. Unrelated business income is any income derived from any unrelated trade or business. The term is defined in section 513 of the *Internal Revenue Code* as "the case of any organization subject to the tax imposed by section 511, any trade or business the conduct of which is not substantially related (aside from the need of such organization for income or funds or the use it makes of the profits derived) to the exercise or performance by such organization of its charitable, educational, or other purpose or function constituting the basis for its exemption under section 501."

The Met's stores sell greeting cards, posters, calendars, scarves, art reproductions, postcards, sculptures, glass, and jewelry. Nearly all items offered are reproductions or adaptations from the Museum's collections. These items are not available for sale at any other retail location; they are sold only in the Museum shops or through mail order. According to Museum management, "the sale of items in the shops falls within the mission of the Museum because sale of an item makes people think about the Museum outside its walls and serves as an extension of their visit."

The Metropolitan's merchandising activities resemble those of commercial businesses in some ways but are unique in others. Differences include the requirement that all merchandise sold in the Museum must reflect the permanent (not blockbuster) collection to preclude assessment of taxes on the earnings. Therefore, the decision on the types of items to sell do not necessarily reflect customer wants. Marketing research consists of showing pictures of items in the permanent collection to randomly selected customers in the Museum shop to determine if the items should be reproduced for sale.

The Met in late 1992 installed a Fujitsu Atrium 9000 point of sale (POS) system at its largest satellite gift shop and has continued plans to begin rolling out the personal computer (PC)-based system to other stores. The system installed at the Rockefeller Center store consists of a controller terminal with 8 intelligent primary terminals and 5 satellites. The system provides full sales transaction processing, credit-check authorization, manager workstation functions, and host communications capabilities. Its interactive help function and user-friendly interface have made training sales associates easy. The Met also uses two of Fujitsu's host software packages—online host communications and host sales audit.

Groups who represent small businesses are lobbying for changes in the tax code because some commercial ventures undertaken by nonprofit institutions compete unfairly with private companies who are selling nearly the same merchandise. These groups want the tax code rewritten detailing specifically which items would be considered tax exempt.

Vagueness of the tax laws allow museums to make unfair profits from everyday items like napkins, neckties, and mugs. The museum's profit margin from shops and mail order is triple that of some department stores. The Met's inventories of gifts and merchandise is more than $22 million.

Mail Order. More than half of the Met's merchandise sales comes from a booming mail-order business operated out of a warehouse in Queens, New York. The average order of $45 is low by mail order standards but the response rate is higher than average as nine percent of those who received Christmas catalogues placed orders.

The Museum rarely advertises except to invite people to join their catalog mailing list. Six catalogs per year, containing 1,500 different items, are mailed to members and other customers. The Christmas catalog is mailed to 3 million people; the other catalogs are mailed to a smaller group. Some of the Met's merchandising policies, such as buying large quantities of an item to get it at a lower price, have led to inventory storage problems. It is not unusual for an item to remain in inventory for up to two years. The Museum manufactures molds to make copies of art in its own reproduction studio.

In 1993, the Met's mail-order operation, gift shops, and royalty agreements had sales of over $86 million and net income of about $3.5 million. Sources of merchandising revenue included 23.5 percent from sculpture, silverware, glassware, and jewelry; 21.0 percent from art books; 18.4 percent from paper goods; 16.1 percent from prints; 6.4 percent from children's products; 5.7 percent from textiles; 5.7 percent from royalties from retailers and other museums that sold products based on the Met's collection; 1.7 percent from postcards; and 1.5 percent from other products. Those not receiving a Met Christmas catalogue can order a copy of the 144-page catalogue for $1.00. Advertisements for the catalogue appear in popular magazines like *Vogue*.

The Museum leases space for offsite retail stores and for the warehouse that serves as headquarters and storage for the mail-order business. Lease costs for all rented space used for the retail operation amounted to $2,322,044 and $2,014,727 for the years ended June 30, 1993 and 1992, respectively.

Mail order competition is from other museum shops who, like the Met, have catalogues as well. For-profit catalogues like those from the Museum Company, the Nature Company, Lillian Vernon, Harriette Carter, and Walter Drake, among others, can be viewed as competitors.

The Met's catalog is also featured on the Prodigy interactive home computer information system. Prodigy customers can view and order merchandise from a variety of catalogs. Ed Sessler, Prodigy's director of merchandise marketing says Prodigy wants to become more focused and work with larger first-tier catalogers, like the Met. The Met catalog has been pleased with Prodigy. Although business started slowly, Metropolitan marketing analyst Philip Fertick says sales have increased and surpassed expectations.

Restaurants. The Museum operates a restaurant, cafeteria, and bar. The restaurant and bar are open to accommodate the evening hours on Fridays and Saturdays. In 1990, the Museum received approval from the City of New York to open a new restaurant to replace the current restaurant and cafeteria so the space could be used for additional galleries.

Other Auxiliaries. Other auxiliary operations at the Met are the parking garage and auditoriums. The parking garage, located adjacent to the Museum, is used by patrons at the rate of $8.50 for the first hour, $1.00 for each additional hour up to the fifth, $17.50 for five to ten hours, and $19.50 beyond ten hours. Included in these rates is New York City's 18.25 percent parking and sales tax.

Results of Auxiliary Operations. Net income from merchandising operations was $2,286,348 for the year ended June 30, 1993. Though total retail sales increased by 7.9 percent, mail-order sales declined by 4.5 percent, consistent with recent industry trends. The net contribution to the Museum's operations from auxiliaries totaled $3.41 million in 1993. Exhibit 13–2 gives the Met's Balance Sheet while Exhibit 13–1 provides a five year summary.

FUTURE OUTLOOK

Recession and Museum Attendance. The future financial stability of the Met is a key concern of management as 1994 begins. Fiscal instability of the City of New York could lessen future city support and declining federal funding might have an adverse affect on the Museum's operations.

According to the book *Megatrends 2000* by Naisbitt and Aburdene, researchers predict the arts will begin to replace sporting events as society's primary leisure activity. The authors cite a 1988 report by the National Endowment of the Arts which calculated that Americans spend $28 billion on sports events compared to $3.7 billion on art events. A reversal of these numbers by the year 2000 could yield substantial additional revenue for the Met. More than 500 million people visited American museums in 1991, far more than attended professional sporting events.

In 1992, charitable contributions decreased for the first time in modern history. One nationwide survey of shareholders showed that top priorities for spending money are for such things as cleaning corporate facilities and stopping environmental pollution. Contributing more money to charities ranks 8 out of 10 items. Statistics from

The Economist, show that while the French government spends approximately $30 per capita on the arts and the British $9, the United States Federal and State Governments together spend only about $2.

Museum Gift Shop Competition. Patrons want to support local culture and are spending generously on books, maps, models, posters, replicas, and other Museum shop items. In 1993, the Metropolitan ranked first of all other museum shops in sales and remained the only museum manufacturing its own line of merchandise. Second in sales was the Smithsonian Institution in Washington, D.C., with their nine Museum shops and a catalog business. As of 1993, other shops with a minimum of $1 million in annual sales included the Museum of Modern Art and Whitney Museum of American Art in New York, Boston's Museum of Fine Arts, San Francisco Museum of Modern Art, the Art Institute of Chicago, Los Angeles County Museum of Art, Philadelphia Museum of Art, and San Diego Museum of Art.

Competition for Museum shops is not solely limited to museum locations. The Museum Company, a retailer based in East Rutherford, New Jersey, operates stores in seven states and sells merchandise from the Louvre in Paris, the British Museum, and other art institutions. The Museum Company pays royalties to museums, and its 1993 revenues topped $10 million. Will Edwards, a partner in the chain of 21 Museum Company stores based in New York, objects to museums running their own retail stores in malls because they have an unfair tax advantage. The Museum Company is an entrepreneurial venture. Its first-year revenues topped $10 million. Stores are located mostly in malls. Edwards is a member of the coalition for Fair Business Practices, a group that voiced their objections to the nonprofits operating in the retail world.

Other Museum Competition. Direct competitors, or other museums, are plentiful in the New York area, including the American Museum of Natural History, the Museum of Modern Art, the Whitney Museum, and the Museum of the City of New York.

Because there are multiple demands for the free time of Museum visitors, many activities, outings, and other forms of recreation and leisure are potential substitutes. Other activities and forms of available recreation range from sporting events to theatrical presentations. The New York metropolitan area was the home of two National Basketball Association teams; three National Hockey League teams; two National Football League teams; two baseball teams; and two race tracks. Broadway, the most celebrated street in America, offers daily productions in forty theaters and numerous off-Broadway shows for both the tourist and resident of New York.

In addition, each of the five New York boroughs have many attractions from which to choose, including the Statue of Liberty, the Bronx Zoo, and the National Historic Landmark district on Staten Island. Central Park and the World Trade Center are easily accessible to all visitors via the New York City subway.

SUMMARY

Both Philippe de Montebello and William Luers are faced with having to generate additional donations externally and deciding whether to use large scale ticketed "blockbuster" exhibits. They also would like to expand the Met's retail operations and attract additional visitors to the Met in the increasingly crowded leisure markets. Developing a strategic plan for the future that would address these issues is an immediate priority for the management team to present to the Board of Trustees.

GAMING INDUSTRY NOTE

JOHN K. ROSS, III, MIKE KEEFFE, AND BILL MIDDLEBROOK
Southwest Texas State University

The gaming industry has captured a large amount of the vacation/leisure-time dollars spent in the United States. Gamblers lose over $30 billion annually on legal wagering, including wagers at racetracks and bingo parlors and in lotteries and casinos. This figure does not include dollars spent on lodging, food, transportation, and other related expenditures associated with visits to gaming facilities. Casino gambling accounts for 79 percent of all legal gambling expenditures, far surpassing second-place lotteries at 6.8 percent. The popularity of casino gambling may be credited to more frequent and somewhat higher payout as compared to lotteries and racetracks; however, as winnings are recycled, the multiplier effect restores a high return to casino operators.

Marketing research reveals that the U.S. casino player is slightly older, more affluent, and less educated than the average American. Casino players average age 49, with median household income of $39,500, and about one-half have never attended college. The average age and household income of all Americans is 47 and $27,900, respectively. More than 10 percent of all U.S households made at least one trip to a casino in 1993.

Gaming is becoming widely accepted in the United States as a form of entertainment. Nineteen states now have legalized gambling. Marketing research reveals that 55 percent of all Americans say gambling is "perfectly acceptable for anyone," 35 percent say gambling is "acceptable for others, but not for me," and 10 percent say gambling is "not acceptable for anyone." Many of the 31 states that have not yet legalized gambling have lotteries and video poker, and view gaming as a viable source of revenue that can lower the tax burden on the general population.

The state of Nevada and Atlantic City, New Jersey, dominate the gaming industry, being the established areas allowing full-fledged casino gambling. Nevada accounts for over $6 billion annually in casino revenues as compared to Atlantic City's $3.5 billion. It is believed that Nevada generates more revenue and higher profitability because of lower interest expense from old debt and lower regulatory and labor costs. Limited gaming activity (such as floating casinos, bingo, poker parlors, video gambling, lotteries, and pari-mutuel betting) is allowed in other states, but because of legal constraints in these states significant expansion beyond Nevada and Atlantic City is expected to be slow.

Besides geographical location, the primary differences in the two markets reflect the different types of consumers frequenting these markets. Whereas Las Vegas attracts overnight resort-seeking vacationers, Atlantic City's clientele are predominantly day-trippers traveling by automobile or bus. According to the Las Vegas Convention and Visitor Authority, Las Vegas is a destination market, with most visitors planning their trip more than a week in advance (81 percent), arriving by car (47 percent) or airplane (42 percent), and staying in a hotel (72 percent). Gamblers are typically return visitors (77 percent), averaging 2.2 trips per year, and like playing the slots (65 percent).

Development of new and existing markets will determine the industry's future. New theme resorts are being introduced to differentiate the market and are expected to capture most of the increase in gaming revenues. Atlantic City is expanding transportation and lodging accommodations to better enable it to attract resort and convention-related business, but it will be some time, if ever, before it can compare with Nevada.

The gaming industry is led by nine companies that account for more than 70 percent of total gaming revenues. Hilton Hotels, Promus, Caesars World, and Circus Circus are the leaders in gaming. Other revenue leaders are Bally Manufacturing, Mirage, Resorts International, Trump, Showboat, and Aztar.

MARKETPLACES

Laughlin. The city of Laughlin, Nevada, represents a market quite distinct from those of Las Vegas and Reno. Its population is 4,791 as compared to 741,459 for Las Vegas and 139,900 for Reno. Laughlin caters to the day travelers from nearby Arizona and Southern California population centers and annually attracts more than four million visitors. Ten casinos opened in Laughlin between 1986 and 1993, and some expansion of the current 9,000 hotel rooms is now under way. Such construction activities have been, at times, a disruptive factor to the tourism business because of the strain placed on the city's housing, schools, and water supplies. Laughlin has been described as the industry's fastest-growing market, with gaming revenues of about $507 million in 1993 compared to $40 million in 1985. Its future, however, depends on the extent to which it becomes a destination resort rather than a day-trip resort. Although Circus's facilities must compete with eight major casinos, they are able to maintain a 95 percent occupancy rate.

Las Vegas. Las Vegas is a more established gambling market, although growth has recently been quite explosive. More than 70 casinos operate in the Las Vegas area and collect over $5 billion annually. On the "strip," well-known casinos such as Caesar's World, Harrah's, and the Golden Nugget brought in about 80 percent of the strip's winnings and more than one-third of the statewide totals. Many cater to the upscale gambler, offering big-name entertainment, free drinks for gamblers, easy credit, and glamorous surroundings. Las Vegas draws clientele largely from Southern California and the rest of the southwestern United States. It ranks as one of the most popular convention locations in the nation and is becoming more popular for tours from Asia and Europe.

From 1989 to 1993 several new casino-hotels opened in Las Vegas, such as the Mirage, Excalibur, Luxor, Grand Slam Canyon, and O'Sheas. Additionally, MGM has begun development of the MGM Grand Hotel and Theme Park, scheduled to open in 1994. This rapid growth in Las Vegas has some observers worried; however, most expect it to be readily absorbed by the current market and increased tourism. The expected increase in family vacationers may end up exerting pressures on the more traditional gambling-only casino operations, forcing them to compete with the theme resorts.

Reno. In Reno recent growth has been much more modest, with total gambling revenues about $700 million annually. Like Las Vegas, Reno is a relatively established gaming market, with 12 major casinos catering to the upscale gambler. It draws clientele largely from Northern California and the rest of the northwestern United States.

MAJOR INDUSTRY PLAYERS

Bally Manufacturing Corporation. Bally Manufacturing Corporation is a diversified organization that operates casinos and fitness centers and produces and distributes gaming products. Bally is currently enjoying a recovery in its casino operations in both Atlantic City and Nevada. Through the first half of 1993, both the Park Place and Bally Grand saw increased revenue through winnings, with the Park Place reestablishing its position in the upper tier of Atlantic casinos. Bally has acquired 40 percent of the stock of Bally's Grand in Nevada through bankruptcy proceedings.

In addition to casinos, Bally's Scientific Games offers gaming equipment and services. They produce German wall machines and coin-operated gaming equipment; recently they were the first to sell slot machines to the former Soviet Union. Producing and selling paper-ticket lottery games is another of Bally's gaming segments, with customers in the United States as well as Costa Rica, Guatemala, and Venezuela. Finally, Bally operates 315 fitness centers and manufactures exercise bicycles, among other items, for the health club market.

Caesar's World, Inc. Caesar's World is one of the top revenue–producing casino operators in the United States. Caesar's owns and operates three casino/hotels: Caesar's Palace in Las Vegas, Caesar's Tahoe, and Caesar's Atlantic City. Altogether these properties offer 223,000 square feet of casino space and 2,600 rooms, with an average 84 percent occupancy (86 percent in Las Vegas). Caesar's probably will experience an adverse impact from the opening of the new theme park/casinos/hotels in Las Vegas and Trump's Taj Mahal in Atlantic City. Caesar's reacted to competitive pressures by renovating and adding to its properties in all three locations. In addition, it began operation of its first cruise casino called Caesar's Palace at Sea aboard a Japanese-owned luxury cruise liner. Another cruise casino is already under construction and should be operating in the near future.

Capitalizing on the Caesar's name are two other subsidiaries, Caesar's World Resorts and Caesar's World Merchandising. Caesar's World Resorts owns and operates four nongaming resorts in the Pocono Mountains of Pennsylvania. In addition, Caesar's has an agreement with a Japanese firm to manage a new noncasino resort to open in 1992 in Henderson, Nevada. Caesar's World Merchandising, Inc. markets private-label apparel, accessories, gifts, and fragrances.

Mirage Resorts (formerly Golden Nugget, Inc.). All of Mirage's gaming operations are located in Nevada. It owns and operates the Golden Nugget-Downtown, Las Vegas (which may be spun off), the Mirage on the strip in Las Vegas, and the Golden Nugget-Laughlin. The Mirage, an extremely ambitious resort venture with 3,056 hotel rooms and 95,000 square feet of casino space, became Vegas's top attraction when it opened in 1989. Constructed around a tropical theme, it offers a 20,000-gallon aquarium, a 54-foot-high volcano that erupts with pina-colada scented fumes every 15 minutes, rare white tigers in a jungle scene, tropical gardens, a multitude of restaurants, bars and shops, and an adjacent 16,000-seat outdoor sports arena. The Mirage was the first of the tourist- and family-oriented theme resorts in Las Vegas. The project cost more than $615 million and was largely financed with borrowed money.

Mirage's latest venture is Treasure Island, a pirate-theme casino/resort, which opened in October 1993. Adding 3,000 rooms to the Las Vegas market, the project cost an estimated $430 million. Its visitors will have the opportunity to watch a ship sink during a pirate battle in front of the resort and are expected to add significantly to Mirage's profit during 1994.

Hilton Hotels Corporation. The Hilton family name is well known around the world for fine hotels. Hilton owns five casino/hotels: the Las Vegas Hilton and Flamingo Hiltons in Las Vegas, two in Reno, and one in Laughlin. These casino-hotels have 12,557 guest rooms with an 85 percent average occupancy rate. Hilton gaming revenues exceed $700 million annually. Total Hilton revenues in 1993 were $1.39 billion, while profits were $103 million.

Producing slightly less revenue are the 243 other hotels and inns owned, managed, or franchised by Hilton. Although Hilton experienced a slight improvement in occupancy rate in 1993, almost all of its earnings growth occurred in the gaming operations. The company is moving rapidly into the riverboat gaming venue, with boats operating out of New Orleans and Kansas City.

Promus Companies, Inc. A relatively new company, Promus is a spin-off of Holiday Corporation (the transaction occurred in February 1990). Promus has both casino-hotel and hotel-only operations. It operates Harrah's casino/hotels in Reno, Lake Tahoe, and Laughlin; Bill's Lake Tahoe; Holiday Casino and Holiday Inn Hotel in Las Vegas; and Harrah's in Atlantic City. Promus has also ventured into the riverboat gambling market, with boats operating out of Joliet, Illinois, Vicksburg, Mississippi, and Tunica, Mississippi, and has won the rights to co-operate the only land-based casino complex in New Orleans, Louisiana. Plans call for a 120,000-square-foot casino to be completed by the end of 1994. Gaming operations contribute 80 percent to revenues and 81 percent to operating income. The Promus gaming facilities are illustrated on the U.S. map given in Figure 13–1. Note that 19 states today have legalized gambling, up from only two (New Jersey, Nevada) in 1989.

Promus's hotel segment develops real estate for the purpose of selling it while retaining franchise and management contracts. It operates over 500 hotels under the names of Embassy Suites, Hampton Inn, and Homewood Suites and is the ninth largest hotel chain in the world. Promus's 1993 revenues were a record $1.25 billion, a 12.5 percent increase over 1992, while net income rose 31.5 percent to $304 million.

MGM Grand, Inc. MGM Grand, Inc. has undergone numerous changes in recent months to prepare for the opening of its largest and potentially most profitable gamble. Although the MGM Grand Air, Inc. subsidiary has been a drain on the corporation, MGM Grand has been able to sell off its MGM Sands and Desert Inn holdings, purchase and close the Marina Hotel and Casino and the Tropicana Country Club in Las Vegas, and finance the construction of the MGM Grand Hotel and Theme Park. Situated on 115 acres directly across from the Excalibur, the MGM Grand Hotel and Theme Park has been erected at an estimated cost of over $1 billion. This complex will be the world's largest hotel, with 5,011 rooms and a 170,000-square-foot casino, and will feature a 35-acre theme park, its theme being the Wizard of Oz. Visitors will walk under a 109-foot-tall gold lion and up the yellow brick road into Emerald City, an entertainment area. Staged performances on three levels will entertain visitors riding the 50-passenger elevator.

Showboat, Inc. Showboat owns and operates one casino/hotel in Las Vegas and one in Atlantic City. The company plans to expand geographically, but debt accounting for 69 percent of Showboat's capitalization restrains growth.

Circus Circus Enterprises. Circus Circus owns and operates five casino/hotels in Nevada, two in Las Vegas and Laughlin, and one in Reno. Circus recently opened its $370 million pyramid-shaped Luxor Resort in Las Vegas to overflowing crowds. Also in 1993, Circus opened its Grand Slam Theme Park in Las Vegas. Circus's 1993 revenues grew 4 percent to $873 million, whereas its profits fell 8 percent to $110 million.

Circus Circus's plans for 1994 and 1995 include opening a huge Spanish-style casino/hotel in Reno and other casino/hotels in Sydney, Australia, and Windsor, Ontario. In addition, Circus will be opening two riverboats, one in Tunica County, Mississippi, and one in Chalmette, Louisiana.

FIGURE 13-1 Nineteen States with Legalized Gambling in the United States in 1993 (Promus casinos are highlighted)

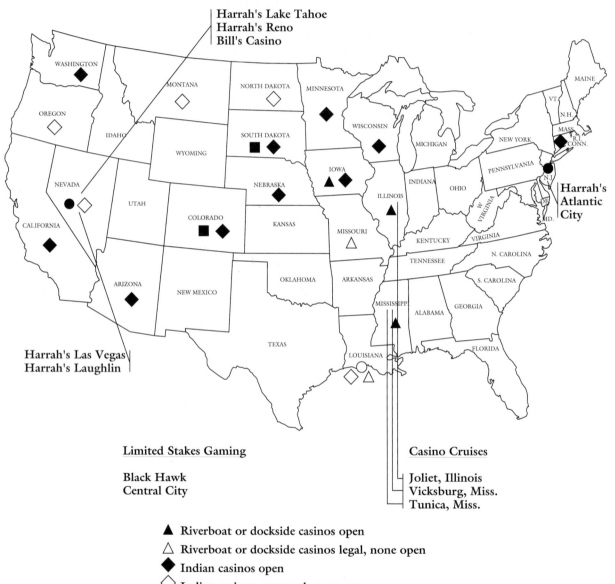

▲ Riverboat or dockside casinos open
△ Riverboat or dockside casinos legal, none open
◆ Indian casinos open
◇ Indian casinos approved, none open
● Traditional land-based casinos open
○ Traditional land-based casino approved, none open
■ Limited-stakes casinos open

PROMUS COMPANIES, INC.—1993

FRED R. DAVID
Francis Marion University

Headquartered in Memphis, Tennessee, Promus (901-762-8600) is one of the leading casino entertainment and hotel companies in the United States. Promus's hotel division operates the Embassy Suites, Hampton Inn, and Homewood Suites hotel brands. Its stock soared 150 percent in 1992, from $22 to $55 a share—18th-best on the New York Stock Exchange. About 80 percent of Promus's revenues and net income comes from gaming. Its Harrah's casino entertainment division operates seven casino properties and is expanding into riverboat and Indian gaming. Harrah's Dockside Casino in Tunica County, Mississippi, approximately 20 miles south of Memphis, is a $49 million facility featuring 32,100 square feet of casino entertainment space, with 1,460 slot machines and 54 table games. In addition to the dockside building, a 30,000-square-foot shoreside facility features a 255-seat restaurant, retail space, and a lounge. Parking for approximately 1,300 cars is adjacent to the casino. The casino maintains its own self-contained power and sewage plants. Promus is building Louisiana's first land-based casino, a 120,000-square-foot facility with 4,800 slot machines and 200 gambling tables. When completed, this casino will be the largest in the world.

CASINO ENTERTAINMENT

Gambling is on the rise in the United States, and casino entertainment is becoming more widely accepted. Nearly 30 million households in the United States have one or more gamblers, and, according to *The Harrah's Survey of U.S. Casino Gaming Entertainment,* 55 percent of the population now say they feel gambling "is perfectly acceptable for anyone" (based on research by an independent market research firm). The survey also indicates that 50 percent of the American adult population has gamed at a casino at some point in their lifetime. The survey reported a four-percentage-point increase annually in people who had visited a casino. This increase translates to an additional 4.4 million gamers and a 20 percent increase in annual trips. The survey further determined that the most rapid growth in gaming in the United States is taking place in newer jurisdictions such as riverboat and Indian reservation gaming.

Here's how the states line up on lotteries and casinos: South Dakota, Colorado, Louisiana, and New Jersey have lotteries and casinos. Nevada has casinos but no lottery. Thirty-two states—Georgia, Florida, Texas, Washington, Oregon, Montana, Idaho, California, Arizona, Nebraska, Kansas, Minnesota, Wisconsin, Iowa, Illinois, Missouri, Indiana, Kentucky, Michigan, Ohio, West Virginia, Virginia, Delaware, Maryland, Pennsylvania, New York, Rhode Island, Connecticut, Massachusetts, New Hampshire, Vermont, and Maine—and the District of Columbia have lotteries but no casinos. Some of these 32 states—Florida, Rhode Island, and New York, for example—also have other forms of parimutuel wagering, such as horse racing, greyhound racing, and jai-alai. Thirteen states—North Dakota, Wyoming, Utah, New Mexico, Oklahoma, Arkansas, Mississippi, Alabama, Tennessee, North Carolina, South Carolina, Alaska, and Hawaii—have neither lotteries nor casinos. Iowa, Illinois, Mississippi, Missouri, Louisiana, and Indiana have legalized riverboat gambling.

Harrah's operates casino hotels in all major U.S. gaming markets, including Reno, Lake Tahoe, Las Vegas, and Laughlin, Nevada; and Atlantic City, New Jersey. Harrah's casino properties comprise over 460,000 square feet of casino space, 11,000 slot machines, 500 table games, 6,000 hotel rooms or suites, approximately 80,000 square feet of convention space, 40 restaurants, three showrooms, and three cabarets. Promus's strategy is to impress upon customers that they will receive the same quality experience at any Harrah's property regardless of location. Over the last five years, Promus has invested more than $354 million in maintaining and upgrading its existing Harrah's casino hotels.

Competitors within the casino entertainment industry compete on the basis of facility features such as theme and decor, location within a market, service, and promotional activity. Harrah's competes by providing high-quality entertainment value principally through its services to guests and the interaction among employees and customers. Every Harrah's operation aims to provide comfortable and enjoyable surroundings. Harrah's targets the broad middle-market gaming customer segment and does not actively seek to attract the very high-end or the very low-end segment. Its Nevada properties account for approximately 7.5 percent of the total gaming revenue in Nevada, and Harrah's Atlantic City accounts for approximately 8.9 percent of the total gaming revenue in New Jersey.

Atlantic City. The Harrah's Atlantic City casino hotel opened in Atlantic City, New Jersey, in 1980. With approximately 61,200 square feet of casino space, it has the highest gaming revenues and operating profit of the Promus casinos. Harrah's Atlantic City is situated on 21.4 acres in the Marina area of Atlantic City and consists of dual 16-story hotel towers with 268 suites and 492 regular rooms and adjoining low-rise buildings that house the casino and a 23,000-square-foot convention center. The hotel has nine restaurants, an 850-seat showroom, a pool, a health club, a teen center with video games, child care facilities, and parking for 2,678 cars. The property also has a 107-slip marina. Occupancy at the hotel has averaged over 88 percent for the past five years. Most of the casino's customers arrive by car from within a 150-mile radius which includes Philadelphia, New York, and northern New Jersey. Harrah's Atlantic City gears its advertising and promotional campaigns to the "drive-in" market, which makes this market especially susceptible to gasoline prices and adverse weather.

Harrah's Atlantic City competes directly with 11 other casinos in Atlantic City and to a lesser degree with a casino on an Indian reservation in Ledyard, Connecticut. The casino in Ledyard opened in 1992, with slot-machine play being first offered by the Ledyard casino in early 1993. The soft regional economy continued to make it difficult for Atlantic City operators to maintain operating margins as competition for revenues increased. Note from the statistics in Table 14–1 that Promus's net income in Atlantic City has been declining.

TABLE 14–1 Promus's Net Income, Atlantic City

	1992	1991	1990	PERCENTAGE INCREASE/(DECREASE) '92 vs '91	'91 vs '90
Revenues	$312.1	$310.3	$313.9	0.6%	(1.1)%
Operating income	$ 66.2	$ 65.7	$ 74.2	0.8%	(11.5)%
Operating margin	21.2%	21.2%	23.6%	—	(2.4) pts.

Reno. Harrah's Reno, situated on approximately 3.5 acres, consists of a casino-hotel complex with a 24-story structure, a 14,500-square-foot convention center, and 64,400 square feet of casino floor space. The hotel, with seven suites and 558 rooms, has six restaurants, a 420-seat Sammy's Showroom, a pool, a health club, and an arcade. The complex can accommodate 383 cars in a valet parking garage and another 377 cars in a self-park garage. In addition to this on-site parking, Harrah's Reno also leases approximately 850 spaces nearby that are available for overflow valet parking. Occupancy at the hotel has averaged approximately 91 percent for the past five years.

Harrah's Reno caters primarily to middle- and upper-income customers. The casino's marketing programs include a club for slot-machine players that gives complimentaries based on levels of play, a showroom guest program that invites valued customers to the casino to see a show, and a limited bus program that provides subsidized transportation to the casino. The primary markets for Harrah's Reno are Northern California, the Pacific Northwest, and Canada.

Promus competes with seven major casinos in the Reno area and with five major casinos in the Lake Tahoe area. No major additions to casinos or rooms are in progress in Northern Nevada and none were anticipated for 1993 through 1995.

Lake Tahoe. Harrah's Lake Tahoe is situated on 22.9 acres near Lake Tahoe and consists of an 18-story tower and adjoining low-rise building that house a 16,500-square-foot convention center and approximately 63,200 square feet of casino space. The casino hotel, with 62 suites and 472 luxury rooms, has seven restaurants, an 800-seat South Shore Showroom, a 197-seat cabaret, a health club, a retail shop, a heated pool, and an arcade. The facility has customer parking for 791 cars in a garage and 1,161 additional spaces in an adjoining lot. Occupancy at the hotel has averaged over 81 percent for the past five years. A 400-suite Embassy Suites hotel provides an additional supply of high-quality guest rooms, conveniently located adjacent to Harrah's Lake Tahoe.

Harrah's also operates Bill's Lake Tahoe Casino, which is located on a 2.1-acre site adjacent to Harrah's Lake Tahoe casino hotel. The casino includes approximately 18,000 square feet of casino space and two casual on-premise restaurants, Bennigan's and McDonald's, operated by nonaffiliated restaurant companies. Bill's Casino appeals to those customers who enjoy a more casual atmosphere. The primary markets for the casinos are California and the Pacific Northwest. Note from the statistics given in Table 14–2 that Promus's net income has been increasing from its Reno and Lake Tahoe operations.

TABLE 14-2   Promus's Net Income, Northern Nevada Division

	1992	1991	1990	PERCENTAGE INCREASE (DECREASE) '92 vs '91	'91 vs '90
Revenues	$310.5	$304.5	$312.0	2.0%	(2.4)%
Operating income	$ 67.3	$ 56.5	$ 52.2	19.1%	8.2%
Operating margin	21.7%	18.6%	16.7%	3.1 pts.	1.9 pts.

Las Vegas. Is Las Vegas becoming Disney on the desert? The answer seems to be yes, as Vegas has become a year-round family resort. Four family attractions opened in 1993 alone: Grand Slam Canyon, Luxor, Treasure Island, and MGM Grand Adventures. All four of these theme parks are owned by competitors of Promus.

Harrah's Las Vegas is located on approximately 16.4 acres of the strip in Las Vegas and consists of a 15-floor hotel tower with 500 rooms, a 23-floor hotel tower with 491 rooms, a 32-floor hotel tower with 734 rooms, and adjacent low-rise buildings that house the 15,000-square-foot convention center and the casino. The hotel has 1,725 total rooms with 22 suites. The size and location of the property permits Promus to expand its facilities if needed.

The Harrah's Las Vegas complex has approximately 79,300 square feet of casino space, five restaurants, a 525-seat Commander's Theater, a health club, and a heated pool. There are 3,087 parking spaces available, including a substantial portion in a self-park garage. Occupancy at the hotel has averaged over 91 percent for the past five years.

Harrah's Las Vegas caters to middle-income customers. The casino has marketing programs, such as a low-priced, high-volume buffet, coupons, and merchandise give-aways, which are less expensive than the marketing programs at Promus's other casino hotels. The casino's primary markets are the Midwest, California, and Canada.

Harrah's Las Vegas is in direct competition with numerous Las Vegas strip properties. The Las Vegas market has seen a significant increase in the number of rooms and casino space during the last three years. This expansion resulted from completion of two of the largest casino hotels in the world along with major expansions by existing casinos, which added over 10,000 rooms to the market. Despite this influx of rooms and casino space, Promus's Las Vegas properties have increased revenues annually. Three major competitors are currently developing new casino facilities in Las Vegas, adding an additional 10,500 rooms to the market. Table 14–3 shows that Promus's revenues have been increasing recently in Las Vegas.

Laughlin. Harrah's Laughlin opened in August 1988 in Laughlin, Nevada. It is located on a 44.9-acre site in a natural cove on the Colorado River and features a hotel with 1,658 rooms (including 23 suites), five restaurants, and a 90-seat cabaret, all with a south-of-the-border theme. It is the only property in Laughlin with a developed beachfront on the river. Harrah's Laughlin has approximately 47,000 square feet of casino space and approximately 7,000 square feet of convention center space. The facility has customer parking for 2,789 cars and vans, including a covered parking garage, and a park for recreational vehicles. Since opening, occupancy at Harrah's

TABLE 14-3 Promus's Net Income, Southern Nevada Division

	1992	1991	1990	PERCENTAGE INCREASE/(DECREASE) '92 vs '91	'91 vs '90
Revenues	$266.3	$242.0	$239.3	10.0%	1.1%
Operating income	$ 65.8	$ 55.6	$ 57.4	18.3%	(3.1)%
Operating margin	24.7%	23.0%	24.0%	1.7 pts.	(1.0) pts.

Laughlin has averaged over 91 percent. Harrah's Laughlin caters primarily to middle-income customers and targets its advertising and promotional campaigns to the drive-in market. It is located within a four-hour drive from both the Los Angeles and Phoenix metropolitan areas, whose combined populations total approximately 15 million people.

Harrah's Laughlin completed construction in September 1992 of a $37 million expansion that included a new 701-room hotel tower and additional parking facilities, restaurant seating, and meeting space. The Laughlin gaming market has changed significantly over the past three years with the virtual doubling of available rooms and increasing casino space. Harrah's competes with nine other casinos in Laughlin. Most competitors in Laughlin are planning to expand room capacity in the next few years. The Laughlin market has been served primarily by road (car, bus, and recreational vehicle) travel from Arizona and California residents.

Riverboat Casinos. Legalization of gaming in states beyond Nevada and New Jersey created the opportunity for Harrah's to expand into new casino entertainment markets. Harrah's first riverboat in Joliet, Illinois (Harrah's Casino Cruises Joliet), opened in 1993, and other Harrah's riverboat projects are under way in Vicksburg, Mississippi, Shreveport, Louisiana, and North Kansas City, Missouri. Riverboat cruises are limited to a duration of four hours, and no gaming may be conducted while the boat is docked. Minimum and maximum wagers on games are set by the licensee and wagering may not be conducted with money or other negotiable currency. No person under the age of 21 is permitted to wager, and wagers may only be taken from a person present on a licensed riverboat. With respect to electronic gaming devices, the payout percentage may not be less than 80 percent or more than 100 percent.

Legalization of riverboat gambling in Illinois imposes a 20 percent wagering tax on adjusted receipts from gambling games. The tax imposed is to be paid by the licensed owner to the Illinois Gaming Board on the day after the day when the wagers were made. Of the proceeds of that tax, 25 percent goes to the local government where the home dock is located, a small portion to the Illinois Gaming Board for administration and enforcement expenses, and the remainder to the state education-assistance fund.

Legalization also requires that licensees pay a $2.00 admission tax for each person admitted to a gaming cruise. Of this admission tax the host municipality or county receives $1.00. The licensed owner is required to maintain public books and records clearly showing amounts received from admission fees, the total amount of gross receipts, and the total amount of adjusted gross receipts.

Joliet. Harrah's operates a riverboat gaming entertainment complex in Joliet, Illinois. The Empress is a 210-foot riverboat with 17,900 square feet of casino space, 42 table games, 569 slot machines, and a pavilion and related parking facilities on shore. A second riverboat, with 12,600 square feet of casino space, began operating in 1994 at Joliet. Revenues from the Empress in 1993 were about $75 million.

Vicksburg. Promus operates a dockside casino entertainment complex in Vicksburg, Mississippi. The project costs approximately $35.6 million and includes a 250-foot stationary riverboat with approximately 20,000 square feet of casino space, 600 slot machines, 43 table games, and a 120-room Harrah's hotel.

North Kansas City. Promus operates a riverboat casino entertainment center in North Kansas City, Missouri. Promus spent $69 million to develop the casino, which includes a 300-foot riverboat with 30,000 square feet of casino entertainment space, 1,100 slot machines, 55 table games, and related shoreside facilities.

Shreveport. Promus operates a casino entertainment complex in Shreveport, Louisiana, that features a 210-foot riverboat with 19,600 square feet of casino entertainment space, an anticipated 700 slot machines and 40 table games, and dockside facilities. Promus spent $41.3 million on this project.

For 1994, analysts expect Promus's total riverboat revenues to be about $405 million —$250 million from the two boats in Joliet, $55 million from the full-year operation of Vicksburg, and partial-year contributions from Shreveport and North Kansas City.

Indian Gaming. Promus purchased a 20 percent ownership interest in Sodak Gaming Supplies, Inc. ("Sodak") in 1992. Under terms of an agreement with International Game Technology ("IGT") expiring in 1997, Sodak is the exclusive distributor for IGT of its gaming equipment in the states of North Dakota, South Dakota, and Wyoming, and on Indian reservations within the 48 contiguous states, excluding Nevada and New Jersey. The distribution agreement may be extended beyond the current five-year term by IGT at its option.

Promus has been selected by the Ak-Chin Indian Community to negotiate an exclusive management and development agreement for a planned $18.5 million casino on the Community's land approximately 25 miles south of Phoenix, Arizona. Proceeding with the project is subject to various regulatory approvals and the resolution of uncertainties relative to gaming on Indian reservations in Arizona.

Abroad. Promus has applied for a license to operate a casino entertainment facility in Auckland, New Zealand. If the application is successful, Promus anticipates making an investment of up to $15 million in a joint venture to develop and construct the proposed casino, which would be managed by Promus.

HOTELS

Promus's hotel business consists of the Embassy Suites, Hampton Inn, and Homewood Suites brands. Each brand is targeted to a specific market segment. Although the U.S. economy appears to be recovering, it could take the hotel industry several years to absorb the current supply of rooms. But because very few new hotels are being built, demand is rising faster than supply. Hotel occupancy rates for 1993 averaged 64 percent, the highest in a decade and up from 62 percent in 1992. The average room rate edged up 2 percent to $61 in 1993 as demand grew 5.1 percent, while supply grew only 1.2 percent. Average hotel rates in key cities are as follows:

CITY	OCCUPANCY RATE	AVERAGE DAILY RATE
New York	69%	$135
Boston	72	119
Washington	65	115
San Francisco	69	111
Honolulu	81	99
Miami	84	90
Chicago	63	89
Philadelphia	62	84
San Diego	66	81

Atlanta	60	79
Los Angeles	60	76
Tampa	68	72
Houston	60	70
Dallas	63	68
Orlando	72	68
Phoenix	64	68
San Antonio–Austin	67	63
Memphis	63	62
Denver	63	61

Intense competition exists in the sale of hotel franchises and in obtaining management contracts. Promus's hotel brands are in vigorous competition with a wide range of facilities offering various types of lodging options and related services to the public. All of Promus's hotel brands outperform their respective competitive segment in terms of both revenue-per-available-room (RevPAR) and occupancy.

The more than 100 Embassy Suites hotels appeal to the traveler who has a need or desire for greater space and more focused services than are available in traditional upscale hotels. Embassy Suites hotels comprise the largest all-suite hotel system in the Unites States by number of suites and system revenues.

Hampton Inn hotels are moderately priced hotels designed to attract the business and leisure traveler desiring quality accommodations at affordable prices. Since 1984 when the brand was introduced, Hampton has grown to more than 350 hotels.

The 24 Homewood Suites hotels represent Promus's entry in the extended-stay market and target the traveler who stays five or more consecutive nights, as well as the traditional business and leisure traveler.

At the beginning of 1993, Promus's three hotel brands included 350 properties that are licensed by Promus, 66 properties that are managed by Promus, and 39 properties that are owned and operated by Promus. These properties total 68,276 rooms and suites.

Promus pursues a strategy of growth for its hotel brands by minimizing its ownership of hotel real estate and concentrating on obtaining new franchise or management contracts. As a part of this strategy, owned or leased hotels are sold and operated either by Promus under a management contract or by the purchaser under license from Promus. In recent years the declining real estate and financial markets have constrained Promus's ability to sell hotel assets, although Promus intends to continue this strategy. No major projects to construct additional company-owned hotels are currently planned.

Each of Promus's hotel brands uses a centralized business system, which includes access to reservation services and also to performance support or training, operations management, and revenue management. This network of business systems is one of the most sophisticated systems in the hotel industry. The Embassy Suites, Hampton Inn, and Homewood Suites business systems' reservation module receives reservation requests entered on terminals located at all of their respective hotels and reservation center, and major domestic airlines. The systems immediately confirm reservations or indicate accommodations available at alternate system hotels. Confirmations are transmitted automatically to the hotel for which the reservation is made. Promus's computer center in Memphis, Tennessee, houses the computers and satellite communications equipment necessary for its commercial, reservations, and property management systems.

Promus offers an unconditional money-back guarantee of service satisfaction at all three of its hotel brands. The Hampton Inn "100 Percent Satisfaction" guarantee and

Homewood Suites "Suite Assurance" guarantee have been in place since 1989; the "Embassy Suites Way" guarantee was initiated at Embassy Suites in 1991 and was expanded system-wide in the second quarter of 1992. All of Promus's hotel brands offer suites/rooms exclusively for nonsmoking guests.

To facilitate international growth, Promus has acquired a minority interest in a Hong Kong–based hotel-management and development company in order to expand Promus's hotel brands into the Asia Pacific region. Promus's participation in this venture will not require it to make substantial investments of capital. One result of the venture is a franchised Embassy Suites hotel currently under construction in Bangkok, Thailand.

Embassy Suites Hotels. Embassy Suites hotels are all-suite hotels targeted to the traveler who has a need or desire for greater space and more focused services than are available in most traditional hotels. Exhibit 14–1 sets forth information regarding all Embassy Suites hotels, including company-owned hotels, hotels operated by Embassy under management contracts or joint venture arrangements, and hotels operated by licensees. As the year 1993 began, three hotels were under construction, all of which will be licensee-operated. Embassy Suites hotels are located in 30 states and Washington, D.C. One hotel is located in Canada and another, as mentioned, is under construction in Thailand. Embassy Suites hotels generally have between 142 and 460 suites. Each guest suite has a separate living room and dining/work area, with a color television, refrigerator, and wet bar, as well as a traditional bedroom where most fea-

EXHIBIT 14-1 Embassy Suites Hotels

	LICENSED		OWNED		MANAGEMENT CONTRACTS/ JOINT VENTURES	
	NUMBER OF HOTELS	NUMBER OF SUITES	NUMBER OF HOTELS	NUMBER OF SUITES	NUMBER OF HOTELS	NUMBER OF SUITES
Fiscal Year-End 1989	40	9,470	7	1,455	51	13,032
1990 Activity:						
Additions	5	1,135	1	261	7	1,870
Conversions, net	8	2,114	—	—	(8)	(2,114)
Sales/Terminations	(11)	(2,895)	—	—	—	—
Fiscal Year-End 1990	42	9,824	8	1,716	50	12,788
1991 Activity:						
Additions	2	476	6	1,519	4	1,254
Conversions, net	2	677	1	215	(3)	(892)
Sales/Terminations	(4)	(1,171)	—	—	(7)	(1,698)
Fiscal Year-End 1991	42	9,806	15	3,450	44	11,452
1992 Activity:						
Additions	2	685	—	—	—	(3)
Conversions, net	1	221	—	—	(1)	(221)
Fiscal Year-End 1992	45	10,712	15	3,450	43	11,228

Source: Promus *Annual Report.*

ture a remote-controlled television. Most Embassy Suites hotels are built around an atrium lobby. All hotels offer a free breakfast and complimentary evening cocktails.

The following table sets forth information concerning system occupancy, average daily rate per occupied suite, and revenue per available suite for all Embassy Suites hotels:

FISCAL YEAR	OCCUPANCY RATE	AVERAGE DAILY RATE PER OCCUPIED SUITE	REVENUE PER AVAILABLE SUITE
1992	71.7%	$90.97	$65.26
1991	69.4	88.19	61.19
1990	69.8	86.73	60.56

Hampton Inn Hotels. Hampton Inn hotels are moderately priced hotels designed to attract the business and leisure traveler desiring quality accommodations at affordable prices. Exhibit 14–2 sets forth information regarding all Hampton Inn hotels, including company-owned hotels, hotels operated by Hampton Inns under management contracts or joint venture arrangements, and hotels operated by licensees. As 1993 began 26 hotels were under construction, all of which will be licensee-operated.

EXHIBIT 14-2 Hampton Inn Hotels

	LICENSED		OWNED		MANAGEMENT CONTRACTS/ JOINT VENTURES	
	NUMBER OF HOTELS	NUMBER OF ROOMS	NUMBER OF HOTELS	NUMBER OF ROOMS	NUMBER OF HOTELS	NUMBER OF ROOMS
Fiscal Year-End 1989	183	22,962	10	1,353	19	2,376
1990 Activity:						
Additions	36	4,598	3	403	—	—
Terminations	(3)	(380)	—	—	—	—
Fiscal Year-End 1990	216	27,180	13	1,756	19	2,376
1991 Activity:						
Additions	45	5,362	2	293	2	242
Terminations	(2)	(239)	—	—	—	—
Fiscal Year-End 1991	259	32,303	15	2,049	21	2,618
1992 Activity:						
Additions	32	3,216	—	(1)	2	292
Terminations	(2)	(277)	—	—	—	—
Fiscal Year-End 1992	289	35,242	15	2,048	23	2,910

Source: Promus *Annual Report.*

Hampton Inn hotels are located in 41 states in the United States and one is under construction in Canada. An average Hampton Inn hotel has from 100 to 150 rooms. The Hampton Inn hotel's standardized concept provides a guest room featuring a color television, free in-room movies, free local telephone calls, and complimentary continental breakfast. Hampton Inn hotels also offer an electronic communications alerting system and reservations system for deaf and hearing-impaired guests. Unlike full-service hotels, Hampton Inn hotels do not feature restaurants, lounges, or large public spaces. Room rates typically are below those of traditional midscale hotels.

Hampton Inns also has a modified lodging property for use in communities supporting hotels of fewer than 100 rooms. The building design for these smaller communities has the same features as a standard Hampton Inn hotel but with fewer rooms and a smaller lobby. Hampton Inn hotels compete in the segment of the lodging market that is directed primarily to business and leisure travelers desiring quality accommodations at reasonable prices. The following table sets forth information concerning system occupancy, average daily rate per occupied room, and revenue per available room for all Hampton Inn hotels:

Fiscal Year	Occupancy Rate	Average Daily Rate per Occupied Room	Revenue per Available Room
1992	71.2%	$48.91	$34.82
1991	68.6	47.22	32.39
1990	69.3	45.71	31.69

Homewood Suites Hotels. The Homewood Suites brand represents Promus's entry in the extended-stay market and is targeted for the traveler who stays five or more consecutive nights, but is a unique alternative to traditional business and leisure travelers. Exhibit 14–3 sets forth information regarding all Homewood Suites hotels, including company-owned hotels and hotels operated by licensees. As 1993 began one Homewood Suites hotel was under construction and will be licensee-operated. Homewood Suites hotels are located in 16 states and a hotel is under construction in one additional state. Homewood Suites hotels feature residential-style accommodations, including a living-room area (some with fireplaces), separate bedroom (with a king-size bed) and bath, and a fully equipped kitchen. The hotel buildings, generally two or three stories, are centered around a central community building, called the Lodge, which affords guests a high level of social interaction. Amenities include a limited complimentary breakfast and a complimentary evening social hour, a convenience store, shopping service, business center, outdoor pool, exercise center, and limited meeting facilities.

Homewood Suites recently designed a smaller, modified prototype of its standard hotel for use in suburban areas of major cities, as well as secondary cities with active industrial or commercial areas. The modified prototype reflects the signature design and amenities of a traditional Homewood Suites hotel, but with fewer suites, a smaller Lodge, and other construction modifications that will require less land.

The following table sets forth information concerning system occupancy, average daily rate per occupied suite, and revenue per available suite for all Homewood Suites hotels:

Fiscal Year	Occupancy Rate	Average Daily Rate per Occupied Suite	Revenue per Available Suite
1992	71.9%	$69.65	$50.10
1991	65.2	66.84	43.56
1990	59.3	64.49	38.34

Results of Operations. Promus's casino entertainment and hotel segments both achieved record operating results during 1992. These operating results, coupled with the lower overall cost of debt, were the primary contributors to a 75 percent increase in net income. The casino entertainment segment contributed approximately 80 percent of Promus's 1992 consolidated revenues and operating income. A summary of the performance of Promus's operating segments for three recent years is presented in Exhibit 14–4. Promus's most recent balance sheets, income statement, statements of stockholders' equity, and statement of cash flows are given in Exhibits 14–5, 14–6, 14–7, and 14–8.

CONCLUSION

Hilton Hotels, Mirage Resorts, and Circus Circus Enterprises are battling Promus for riverboat and gambling licenses and management contracts. Municipalities are becoming savvier in dealing with gaming companies by demanding more shoreline development with restaurants and hotel rooms. The net result is lower profit margins

EXHIBIT 14-3   Homewood Suites Hotels

	LICENSED		OWNED	
	Number of Hotels	Number of Rooms	Number of Hotels	Number of Rooms
Fiscal Year-End 1989	2	127	1	30
1990 Activity:				
Additions	7	724	6	790
Fiscal Year-End 1990	9	851	7	820
1991 Activity:				
Additions	5	653	1	120
Fiscal Year-End 1991	14	1,504	8	940
1992 Activity:				
Additions	2	250	—	(8)
Fiscal Year-End 1992	16	1,754	8	932

Source: Promus *Annual Report.*

for gaming companies such as Promus. Yet, opportunities abound in gaming. The state of Texas and the city of Chicago are expected to legalize riverboat gambling soon, and Promus must act quickly to get prime locations and contracts.

Promus has formed a separate division to seek new opportunities in the Indian reservation gaming market. Although Harrah's is doing well in the land-based casinos, new theme parks such as the Luxor and Treasure Island are pressuring Harrah's.

Promus's hotel operating income rose 43 percent in 1992 and hotel demand is increasing more than supply, but the hotel business is still characterized by discounting and low occupancy rates. Perhaps the greatest constraint on Promus's strategies today is the firm's debt situation. Debt at year-end 1992 exceeded $800 million, or about twice the firm's equity. A 2-to-1 debt-to-equity ratio restrains investment options. Promus may need an equity offering to finance expansion during the mid-1990s.

Should Promus expand its Hampton Inn, Embassy Suites, and/or Homewood Suites hotels? Develop a three-year strategic plan for CEO Michael Rose that will enable Promus to fulfill its Vision Statement:

> Our vision is to provide the best experience to our gaming and hotel customers by having the best people trained, empowered, and pledged to excellence, delivering the best service, quality and value to every customer, every time … guaranteed.

EXHIBIT 14-4 Operating Results by Segment

	FISCAL YEAR ENDED			PERCENTAGE INCREASE (DECREASE)	
	DECEMBER 31, 1992	JANUARY 3, 1992	DECEMBER 28, 1990	'92 vs '91	'91 vs '90
CASINO ENTERTAINMENT					
Revenues					
Casino	$711,777	$686,177	$689,789	3.7%	(0.5)%
Food and beverage	133,485	129,147	134,779	3.4%	(4.2)%
Rooms	94,092	88,749	91,653	6.0%	(3.2)%
Other	43,901	39,620	35,728	10.8%	10.9%
Less: casino promotional allowances	(92,151)	(84,750)	(84,503)	8.7%	0.3%
Total revenues	891,104	858,943	867,446	3.7%	(1.0)%
Operating expenses					
Departmental direct costs					
Casino	334,702	338,529	331,412	(1.1)%	2.1%
Food and beverage	71,551	69,702	74,225	2.7%	(6.1)%
Rooms	31,958	31,346	32,314	2.0%	(3.0)%
Other	265,683	248,571	254,006	6.9%	(2.1)%
Total operating expenses	703,894	688,148	691,957	2.3%	(0.6)%
	187,210	170,795	175,489	9.6%	(2.7)%
Property transactions	(327)	168	9	N/M	N/M
Operating income	$186,883	$170,963	$175,498	9.3%	(2.6)%
Operating income before property transactions margin	21.0%	19.9%	20.2%	1.1 pts	(0.3)pts

EXHIBIT 14-4 *Continued*

	FISCAL YEAR ENDED			PERCENTAGE INCREASE (DECREASE)	
	DECEMBER 31, 1992	JANUARY 3, 1992	DECEMBER 28, 1990	'92 vs '91	'91 vs '90
HOTEL					
Revenues					
Rooms	$124,192	$ 88,109	$ 54,415	41.0%	61.9%
Food and beverage	8,310	6,436	3,580	29.1%	79.8%
Franchise and management fees	51,719	45,320	48,881	14.1%	(7.3)%
Other	33,993	27,126	22,571	25.3%	20.2%
Total revenues	218,214	166,991	129,447	30.7%	29.0%
Operating expenses					
Departmental direct costs					
Rooms	71,191	51,256	32,121	38.9%	59.6%
Food and beverage	8,696	6,127	3,520	41.9%	74.1%
Other	89,252	75,358	79,369	18.4%	(5.1)%
Total operating expenses	169,139	132,741	115,010	27.4%	15.4%
	49,075	34,250	14,437	43.3%	137.2%
Property transactions	(5,713)	(1,354)	6,305	N/M	N/M
Operating income	$ 43,362	$ 32,896	$ 20,742	31.8%	58.6%
Operating income before property transactions margin	22.5%	20.5%	11.2%	2.0 pts	9.3pts
OTHER					
Revenues	$ 3,748	$ 5,178	$ 7,313	(27.6)%	(29.2)%
Operating expenses	2,577	6,056	10,075	(57.4)%	(39.9)%
Operating income (loss)	$ 1,171	$ (878)	$ (2,762)	N/M	68.2%

N/M = not measurable.

Source: Promus *Annual Reports.*

EXHIBIT 14-5 Consolidated Balance Sheets (in thousands, except per share amounts)

	DECEMBER 31,	
	1993	1992
ASSETS		
Current assets		
Cash and cash equivalents	$ 61,962	$ 43,756
Receivables, including notes receivable of $2,197 and $9,831,		
less allowance for doubtful accounts of $10,864 and $11,598	47,448	53,283
Deferred income taxes	21,024	15,196
Prepayments	18,063	11,697
Supplies	12,996	11,296
Other	2,065	1,919
Total current assets	163,558	137,147
Land, buildings, riverboats and equipment		
Land	245,846	243,678
Buildings, riverboats and improvements	1,143,356	1,064,363
Furniture, fixtures and equipment	435,231	375,489
	1,824,433	1,683,530
Less: accumulated depreciation	(486,231)	(435,039)
	1,338,202	1,248,491
Investments in and advances to nonconsolidated affiliates	70,050	50,985
Deferred costs and other	221,308	159,914
	$1,793,118	$1,596,537
LIABILITIES AND STOCKHOLDERS' EQUITY		
Current liabilities		
Accounts payable	$ 60,530	$ 50,669
Construction payables	26,345	—
Accrued expenses	162,969	102,716
Current portion of long-term debt	2,160	3,898
Total current liabilities	252,004	157,283
Long-term debt	839,804	877,427
Deferred credits and other	86,829	83,606
Deferred income taxes	63,460	46,623
	1,242,097	1,164,939
Minority interest	14,984	3,668
Commitments and contingencies		
Stockholders' equity		
Common stock, $1.50 par value, authorized—120,000,000 shares,		
outstanding—102,258,442 and 101,882,082 shares		
(net of 25,251 and 44,442 shares held in treasury)	153,388	152,823
Capital surplus	201,035	178,972
Retained earnings	187,203	100,857
Deferred compensation related to restricted stock	(5,589)	(4,722)
	536,037	427,930
	$1,793,118	$1,596,537

Source: Promus *Annual Report.*

EXHIBIT 14-6 Consolidated Statements of Income (in thousands, except per share amounts)

| | FISCAL YEAR ENDED | | |
	DECEMBER 31, 1993	DECEMBER 31, 1992	JANUARY 3, 1992
Revenues			
Casino	$ 812,081	$ 711,777	$ 686,177
Rooms	223,129	218,284	176,858
Food and beverage	147,616	141,795	135,583
Franchise and management fees	60,359	51,719	45,320
Other	109,390	81,642	71,924
Less: casino promotional allowances	(100,720)	(92,151)	(84,750)
Total revenues	1,251,855	1,113,066	1,031,112
Operating expenses			
Departmental direct costs			
Casino	369,335	334,702	338,529
Rooms	98,653	103,149	82,602
Food and beverage	84,733	80,247	75,829
Depreciation of buildings, riverboats and equipment	77,590	69,575	63,857
Other	318,669	287,937	266,128
Total operating expenses	948,980	875,610	826,945
	302,875	237,456	204,167
Property transactions	1,345	(6,040)	(1,186)
Operating income	304,220	231,416	202,981
Corporate expense	(27,136)	(28,450)	(26,825)
Interest expense, net of interest capitalized	(106,561)	(118,282)	(133,992)
Other (expense) income, including interest income	(714)	3,615	10,030
Income before income taxes and minority interest	169,809	88,299	52,194
Provision for income taxes	(73,262)	(36,881)	(22,183)
Minority interest	(4,754)	—	—
Income before extraordinary items	91,793	51,418	30,011
Extraordinary items, net of tax benefit (provision) of $3,415 and $(753)	(5,447)	1,074	—
Net income	$ 86,346	$ 52,492	$ 30,011
Earnings per share before extraordinary items	$ 0.89	$ 0.51	$ 0.33
Extraordinary items, net	(0.05)	0.01	—
Earnings per share	$ 0.84	$ 0.52	$ 0.33
Average common shares outstanding	102,562	101,116	90,480

Source: Promus *Annual Report.*

EXHIBIT 14-7 Consolidated Statements of Stockholders' Equity

	COMMON STOCK SHARES OUTSTANDING	AMOUNT	CAPITAL SURPLUS	RETAINED EARNINGS	DEFERRED COMPENSATION RELATED TO RESTRICTED STOCK	TOTAL
Balance - December 28, 1990	$ 79,959	$119,938	$ 77,660	$ 18,354	$(12,203)	$203,749
Net income				30,011		30,011
Public offering of common stock, net of issue costs of $6,920	21,000	31,500	94,580			126,080
Net shares issued under incentive compensation plans, less income tax provision of $1,600	409	614	(61)		5,102	5,655
Balance - January 3, 1992	101,368	152,052	172,179	48,365	(7,101)	365,495
Net income				52,492		52,492
Net shares issued under incentive compensation plans, including income tax benefit of $3,726	514	771	6,793		2,379	9,943
Balance - December 31, 1992	101,882	152,823	178,972	100,857	(4,722)	427,930
Net income				86,346		86,346
Pro-rata share of proceeds from equity investee's initial public offering, less income tax provision of $2,662			3,752			3,752
Net shares issued under incentive compensation plans, including income tax benefit of $10,467	376	565	18,311		(867)	18,009
Balance - December 31, 1993	102,258	$153,388	$201,035	$187,203	$ (5,589)	$536,037

Source: Promus *Annual Report.*

EXHIBIT 14-8 Consolidated Statements of Cash Flows

	FISCAL YEAR ENDED		
	DECEMBER 31, 1993	DECEMBER 31, 1992	JANUARY 3, 1992
Cash flows from operating activities			
Net income	$ 86,346	$ 52,492	$ 30,011
Adjustments to reconcile net income			
to cash flows from operating activities			
Extraordinary items	8,862	(1,827)	—
Depreciation and amortization	98,095	92,342	88,073
Other noncash items	27,356	25,678	21,779
Minority interest share of net income	4,754	—	—
Equity in earnings of and distributions from			
nonconsolidated affiliates	2,782	6,452	13,431
Net (gains) losses from property transactions	(1,481)	972	(5,405)
Net change in long-term accounts	2,239	(11,451)	(12,288)
Net change in working capital accounts	33,929	2,437	7,386
Tax indemnification payments to Bass	(8,459)	(13,238)	(32,186)
Cash flows provided by operating activities	254,423	153,857	110,801
Cash flows from investing activities			
Land, buildings, riverboats and equipment additions	(235,766)	(117,771)	(118,266)
Increase in construction payables	26,345	—	—
Proceeds from sales of equity investments	—	3,733	12,026
Proceeds from property transactions	25,169	3,585	6,459
Investments in and advances to nonconsolidated			
affiliates	(15,431)	(13,487)	(3,986)
Other	(27,954)	(8,334)	(13,371)
Cash flows used in investing activities	(227,637)	(132,274)	(117,138)
Cash flows from financing activities			
Debt retirements	(358,762)	(189,219)	(82,406)
Proceeds from issuance of senior subordinated			
notes, net of issue costs of $3,819 and $5,687	196,181	194,313	—
Net borrowings under Revolving Credit Facility,			
net of issue costs of $11,547	158,453	—	—
Net repayments under retired revolving credit facility	(9,000)	(16,000)	(43,000)
Minority interest contributions, net of distributions	4,548	2,908	—
Proceeds from issuance of common stock, net of issue			
costs of $6,920	—	—	126,080
Premiums paid on early extinguishment of debt	—	(4,426)	—
Cash flows (used in) provided by			
financing activities	(8,580)	(12,424)	674
Net increase (decrease) in cash and cash equivalents	18,206	9,159	(5,663)
Cash and cash equivalents, beginning of period	43,756	34,597	40,260
Cash and cash equivalents, end of period	$ 61,962	$ 43,756	$ 34,597

Source: Promus *Annual Report.*

C A S E

15

JOHN K. ROSS, III,
MIKE KEEFFE, and
BILL MIDDLEBROOK
Southwest Texas State
University

CIRCUS CIRCUS ENTERPRISES, INC.—1994

The sun bears down as you travel across the desert searching for your destination. The heat causes the air to rise in waves toward the sky as you carefully examine the horizon. At last, above the sand dunes shimmering in the heat, you see the top of the fabled pyramid. Even at this distance you can tell it is bigger than anything you imagined. The closer you get to the desert oasis where the pyramid is located, the bigger it seems in this land of dreams. Finally you stand at the base of the pyramid, at the foot of the great sphinx, anxious to explore the huge complex before you. Then the sphinx flashes its eyes at you—and you enter. Flashes its eyes? Yes, for this is Las Vegas—and you have entered the land of Circus Circus Enterprises, Inc. (702-734-0410).

Although Circus Circus Enterprises, Inc. (hereafter Circus) describes itself as a merchant and compares its stores to supermarkets and shopping malls, its products are hardly those one would find on typical store shelves. The "merchandise" of Circus is entertainment and the "stores" are huge pink-and-white-striped concrete circus tents, a 600-foot-long riverboat replica, a giant castle, and the latest addition—a great pyramid. Circus's areas of operation are the glitzy vacation and convention meccas of Las Vegas, Reno, and Laughlin, Nevada, and, if plans work out, other locations in the United States and abroad. The company's marketing of it products has been called "right out of the bargain basement," and has catered to "low rollers," although Circus now aims more at the middle-income gambler and family-oriented vacationers wanting more than a conventional gambling-oriented vacation.

Circus was purchased in 1974 for $50,000 as a small and unprofitable casino operation by partners William G. Bennett, an aggressive cost-cutter who ran furniture stores before entering the gaming industry in 1965, and William N. Pennington (see Exhibit 15–1 for Board of Directors and top managers). The partners were able to rejuvenate Circus back to profitability, went public with a stock offering in October 1983, and in the last five years had an average growth rate in earnings per share of more than 22.6 percent per year. Today, Circus is the largest casino-hotel operator in both the Las Vegas and Laughlin markets in terms of square footage of casino space and number of hotel rooms—this, despite the incredible growth in both markets. For instance although Laughlin has experienced over 100 percent growth in total hotel rooms, Circus operates nearly 30 percent of that total. Casino gaming operations provide over half of total revenue for Circus (see Exhibit 15–2), and in 1993 they reported a net income of more than $120 million and employed more than 13,600 people.

CIRCUS CIRCUS OPERATIONS

Circus defines entertainment as pure play and fun, and it goes out of the way to see that customers have plenty of opportunity for both. Each of Circus's "stores" has a distinctive personality. Circus Circus–Las Vegas is the world of the Big Top, where live circus acts perform for free every 30 minutes. Kids may cluster around video games while the adults migrate to nickel slot machines and dollar game tables. The latest addition to the original casino is the $90 million Grand Slam Canyon Adventuredome, a five-acre, glass-enclosed theme park including a four-loop roller coaster. Recent soft results at the Las Vegas property have induced management to include more rides costing an additional $5 to $8 million.

EXHIBIT 15-1 Circus Circus Enterprises, Inc.

I. DIRECTORS

Name	Age	Title
William G. Bennett	68	Chairman of the Board and CEO, Circus Circus Enterprises
William P. Pennington	70	Cofounder, Circus Circus Enterprises
Clyde T. Turner	55	President and CFO, Circus Circus Enterprises
Fred W. Smith	59	President and CEO, Donrey Media Group
James Cashman III	44	President, Cashman Equipment and Vice President, Cashman Cadillac, Inc.
Tony Coelho	na	Managing Director, Wertheim Schroder & Co., Inc.
Carl F. Dodge	77	Former Chairman, Nevada Gaming Commission, retired
Arthur M. Smith, Jr.	71	Chairman of the Board, retired, First Interstate Bank of Nevada

II. TOP MANAGEMENT

William G. Bennett	Chairman of the Board and CEO, Circus Circus Enterprises
Clyde T. Turner	President and CFO, Circus Circus Enterprises
William J. Paulos	Senior Vice President
Terry L. Caudill	Vice President, Chief Accounting Officer and Treasurer
Mike Sloan	General Counsel and Secretary

Source: *Annual Report*, 1993.

EXHIBIT 15-2 Circus Circus Enterprises, Inc. Sources of Revenue

Casinos	56.8%
Food and Beverage	15.6%
Hotel	16.9%
Other	10.6%

Source: Company reports.

Luxor, the newest Circus property, opened on October 15, 1993, when 10,000 people entered to play the 2,525 slot and video poker games and 82 table games in the 100,000-square-foot casino in the hotel atrium (reported to be the world's largest). By the end of the opening weekend 40,000 people per day were visiting the 36-story bronze pyramid that encases the hotel and entertainment facilities. Circus management is gambling that over 11 million visitors will tour the Luxor in the first year. In the Luxor you can take a cruise on one of 11 barges down an 18,000-foot River Nile past an obelisk and a sphinx, see a show in the 1,100-seat dinner theater, dine in one of the seven restaurants, exercise in the state-of-the-art health spa, or play the slots.

Circus operates nine properties in all (see Exhibit 15–3). At one end of the Vegas strip is Circus Circus–Las Vegas, a circus big-top that covers 795 hotel rooms, shopping areas, two specialty restaurants, a buffet with seating for 1,100, fast-food shops, cocktail lounges, video arcades, 110,000 square feet of casino, live circus acts, and the Grand Slam Canyon. Guests who stay in the facility's other 1,998 rooms travel by elevated monorail from the adjacent Circus Skyrise and Circus Manor, or from the nearby Circusland RV Park.

Located next to the Luxor, Excalibur is one of the first sights travelers see as they exit Interstate Highway 15. (Management was confident that the sight of a giant, colorful medieval castle would make a lasting impression on mainstream tourists and vacationing families arriving in Las Vegas.) Guests cross a drawbridge over a moat onto a cobblestone walkway where multicolored spires, turrets, and battlements loom above. The castle walls are four 28-story hotel towers containing a total of 4,032 rooms. Inside is a medieval world complete with a Fantasy Faire inhabited by strolling jugglers, fire eaters, and acrobats as well as a Royal Village complete with peasants, serfs, and ladies-in-waiting around medieval theme shops. The 100,000-square-foot casino encloses 2,600 slot machines, more than 100 game tables, a sports book, and a poker and keno area. There are 12 restaurants, capable of feeding more than 20,000 people daily, and a 900-seat amphitheater. Excalibur, which opened in June 1990, was built for $294 million, primarily financed with internally generated funds, and contributed 33 percent of the organization's revenues in the year ending January 31, 1993.

Situated between the two anchors on the Las Vegas strip are two smaller casinos operated by Circus. The Silver City Casino and Slots-A-Fun primarily depend on the foot traffic along the strip for their gambling patrons.

All of Circus's operations do well in the city of Las Vegas. However, Circus Circus 1993 operational earnings have remained relatively flat, reflecting the general economic downturn. Circus's hotel room occupancy rates in Las Vegas are typically 98 to 100 percent, due in part to low room rates ($30 to $50 at Circus Circus–Las Vegas)

EXHIBIT 15-3 Circus Circus Enterprises, Inc. Properties and Revenues by Market

	PROPERTIES	PERCENT REVENUES
Las Vegas	Circus Circus–Las Vegas	49.9
	Luxor	
	Excalibur	
	Grand Slam Canyon	
	Silver City Casino	
	Slots-A-Fun	
Laughlin	The Colorado Belle	29.6
	The Edgewater	
Reno	Circus Circus–Reno	20.5

Source: Company reports.

and popular buffets. Seating over 3,000, the restaurants at Excalibur alone are able to offer the most meals per day of any single-site commercial establishment in the world. Although Circus loses 50 cents on each meal it serves, the popular buffets generate enough cash flow each year to cover debt obligations nearly six times.

The company's other big-top facility is Circus Circus–Reno. With the addition of Skyway Tower in 1985, this big top now offers a total of 1,625 hotel rooms, 60,600 square feet of casino, a buffet that can seat 700 people, shops, video arcades, cocktail lounges, midway games, and circus acts. As a project, Circus Circus–Reno had several marginal years, but nevertheless has become one of the leaders in that market.

The Colorado Belle and the Edgewater Hotel are located in Laughlin, Nevada, a city 90 miles south of Las Vegas on the banks of the Colorado River. The Colorado Belle, opened in 1987, features a huge paddle-wheel riverboat replica, buffet, cocktail lounges, and shops. The Edgewater, acquired in 1983, has a southwestern motif, a 57,000-square-foot casino, a bowling center, a buffet, and cocktail lounges. Combined, these two properties contain 2,700 rooms and over 120,000 square feet of casino; and together, these two operations contributed 23 percent of the company's revenues in the year ended January 31, 1993.

Circus has achieved success through an aggressive growth strategy and a corporate structure designed to enhance that growth (see Exhibit 15–4). Since 1984 Circus has increased its available hotel rooms from approximately 2,500 to more than 13,000. Casino space has increased from 165,000 square feet to more than 536,000 square feet during the same period. A strong cash position, innovative ideas, and attention to cost control has allowed Circus to satisfy the bottom line during a period when competitors were typically taking on large debt obligations to finance new projects (see Exhibits 15–1, 15–2, 15–3, 15–4). Yet the market is changing.

New Ventures. Gambling of all kinds has spread across the country. No longer does the average individual need to go to Las Vegas or New Jersey. Instead, gambling can be found at the local quick market (lottery), at the bingo hall, at many Indian reservations, and along the Mississippi river. In order to maintain a competitive edge, Circus has recently announced several projects that will take it beyond the bounds of Nevada.

EXHIBIT 15-4 Circus Circus Organizational Chart

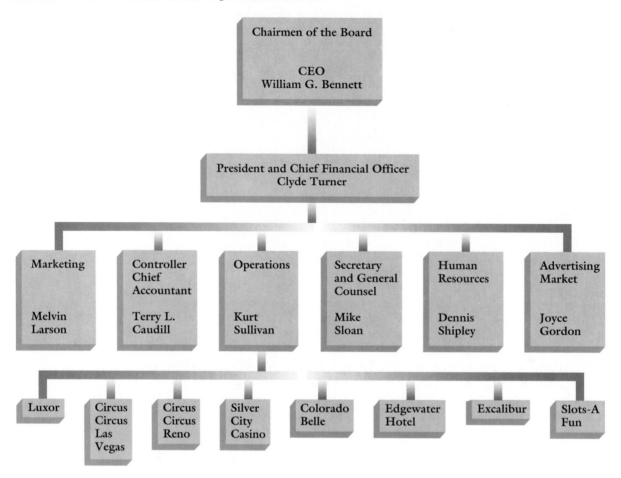

Circus has decided to join the Mississippi River gambling development by creating a riverboat casino site less than 20 miles from Memphis. Subject to licensing, Circus will own and operate one of three dockside casinos at the site. As an additional river operation, Circus is attempting to secure a riverboat license from the Indiana Gaming Commission for the town of Portage, Indiana. Located 35 miles east of Chicago, the proposed development would include a riverboat, an entertainment facility, and a small hotel. The estimated cost for this project is $80 to $100 million. Gambling is, of course, not limited to the United States and Circus is attempting to expand internationally by joining with Press Holdings Limited and Nine Network Australia to bid on a proposed casino license in Sydney, Australia. If the bid is successful, circus would own 50 percent of the casino.

Closer to home, Circus has also announced plans to bid on a casino project in Windsor, Canada. This would be a joint arrangement with Caesar's World, Inc. and Hilton Hotels to build a 75,000-square-foot casino, a 1,000-seat showroom, three dining areas, and a 300-room hotel.

Even closer to home, in May 1993 Circus formed a joint partnership with Eldorado Hotel/Casino to develop and operate Project C in downtown Reno. This will be a theme project depicting a 16th-century Spanish port on the island of Atlantis, with 1,800 rooms and 60,000 square feet of casino space at an estimated cost of $270 million.

Circus's projects are being tailored to attract mainstream tourists and family vacationers. Prices and credit limits are low, while the diversity of potential entertainment activities is substantial.

THE LEGAL ENVIRONMENT

Within the gaming industry all current operators must consider compliance with extensive gaming regulations as a primary concern. Gambling operations are subject to regulatory control by the Nevada State Gaming Control Board, the Clark County Nevada Gaming and Liquor Licensing Board, and by city governments. Gaming companies must submit detailed operating and financial reports to authorities. Nearly all financial transactions, including loans, leases, and the sale of securities, must be reported. Some financial activities are subject to approval by regulatory agencies. As Circus moves into other locations outside of Nevada, it will need to adhere to local regulations.

Although Circus can expect to exert only limited influence on regulatory matters, it took a step in 1989 to strengthen its ability to deal with regulatory concerns by electing Carl F. Dodge, a former chairman of the Nevada Gaming Commission, to its board of directors.

THE FUTURE FOR CIRCUS CIRCUS

Circus has done well by introducing theme-oriented entertainment "megastores" and can be expected to innovate more on that concept. Likewise, its focus on serving middle-income tourists by delivering family entertainment at relatively low prices (room rates range from $39) has been effective in capturing market share. Excalibur and Luxor represent a move upscale in the clientele income target, and it is not yet clear whether future projects will cater to the lower-or upper-middle-class tourists. Circus believes that customer loyalty in the gaming industry is closely tied to the merchant's ingenuity, and management believes that the philosophy that brought them this far can be expected to carry them into the future. Circus is considering ventures outside Las Vegas and Nevada as they arise. It has set aggressive performance targets for itself, including exceeding 20 percent in both the average annual growth rate in earnings per share and in return on equity, as well as sustaining its industry-leading profit margin and return on invested capital.

Circus intends to continue its growth in the Nevada markets by way of further innovation in theme-oriented entertainment, It is also expanding to other gambling locations, including Sydney, Australia, and Windsor, Ontario, with a casino and riverboats in Chalmette, Louisiana, Michigan City, Indiana, and Tunica County, Mississippi. Develop a three-year strategic plan for CEO Bennett that will fulfill Circus's mission statement, which follows.

MISSION STATEMENT

Circus, Circus is dedicated to providing a total entertainment package, including gaming, for family vacationers. Our tremendous success is based on a simple framework of innovation, expansion, and value.

Bold architecture, state-of-the-art special-effects attractions, and an emphasis on high-tech, "latest and greatest" entertainment concepts make our "megastores" the most innovative in the gaming industry. Our customers expect and receive value as well as a broad, intense entertainment experience.

We believe that our concepts of value and leading-edge entertainment will be the "heartstone" of the expansion of gaming across the country and beyond. We stand ready with both the ability and the willingness to expand into other geographic regions here and abroad.

While innovation, expansion, and value are watchwords for success, we are ultimately dependent upon people—our customers and our employees. With Circus, the customer is always king, as we constantly strive to meet rising expectations and deliver more value. Our employees, who serve those customers so well, are an integral part of our success.

Circus Circus, in partnership with our customers, is doing its share to conserve the natural environment.

EXHIBIT 15-5   Selected Financial Information

	1993	1992	1991	1990	1989	1988
Earnings Per Share*	2.05	1.84	1.39	1.30	1.29	.74
Current Ratio	.90	1.14	.88	.66	1.12	2.34
Total Liability/Total Assets	.48	.58	.77	.76	.72	.47
Operating Profit Margin	24.4%	24.9%	22.9%	28.7%	28.6%	27.6%

* Adjusted to reflect 2-for-1 stock split effective July 1991. In June 1993 the Board of Directors declared a 3-for-2 stock split.
Source: Company reports.

EXHIBIT 15-6   Eight-Year Summary

	SALES (000)	NET INCOME
FY 93	$843,025	$117,322
FY 92	806,023	103,348
FY 91	692,052	76,292
FY 90	522,376	76,064
FY 89	511,960	81,714
FY 88	458,856	55,900
FY 87	373,967	28,198
FY 86	306,993	37,375

Source: Company reports.

EXHIBIT 15-7 Circus Circus Enterprises, Inc. Annual Income (000) Fiscal Year Ended January 31

	1993	1992	1991	1990	1989	1988
Net Sales	843,025	806,023	692,052	522,376	511,960	458,856
Cost of Goods	386,971	346,663	313,269	227,942	217,891	200,005
Gross Profit	456,054	441,360	378,783	294,434	294,069	258,851
Selling, General, and Administrative Expenses	204,022	193,584	179,309	124,228	125,380	113,361
Income Before Depreciation and Amortization	252,032	247,776	199,474	170,206	168,689	145,490
Depreciation and Amortization	46,550	47,385	40,998	31,216	31,800	29,134
Nonoperating Income	820	245	(570)	1,030	1,493	4,113
Interest Expense	22,989	43,632	42,048	26,818	28,425	19,733
Income Before Tax	183,313	157,004	115,858	113,202	109,957	100,736
Provision for Income Taxes	62,330	53,656	39,566	38,138	37,478	38,809
Net Income Before Extraordinary Items	120,983	103,348	76,292	75,064	72,479	61,927
Extraordinary Items and Discontinued Operations	(-3,661)	0	0	0	9,235	(6,027)
Net Income	117,322	103,348	76,292	75,064	81,714	55,900
Outstanding Shares	58,167	56,600	54,977	62,572	57,814	75,814

Source: Company reports.

EXHIBIT 15-8 Circus Circus Enterprises Inc., Balance Sheet

ANNUAL ASSETS (000)						
FISCAL YEAR ENDED JANUARY 31,	1993	1992	1991	1990	1989	1988
Cash	43,415	34,158	18,134	19,411	20,667	14,212
Marketable Securities	0	0	0	0	0	60,097
Receivables	3,977	4,171	5,977	2,156	3,197	3,319
Inventories	16,565	15,894	16,573	9,337	15,714	10,861
Other Current Assets	14,478	13,687	13,601	10,323	8,212	8,734
Total Current Assets	78,435	695,154	717,466	41,227	47,790	97,223
Property, Plant and Equipment	851,463	695,154	717,466	612,905	455,074	413,745
Deferred Charges	9,997	9,080	9,438	9,252	0	0
Intangibles	10,563	10,927	11,290	11,654	12,328	11,198
Deposits and Other Assets	0	0	0	0	8,920	6,891
Total Assets	950,458	783,071	792,479	675,038	524,112	529,057

ANNUAL LIABILITIES (000)						
FISCAL YEAR ENDED JANUARY 31,	1993	1992	1991	1990	1989	1988
Accounts Payable	11,473	11,814	16,048	23,690	9,578	7,177
Current Long-term Debt	154	941	938	935	1,485	2,053
Accrued Expenses	47,397	45,558	43,652	35,104	29,326	30,822
Income Taxes	708	1,185	818	2,345	2,168	1,420
Total Current Liability	87,494	59,498	48,750	62,074	42,557	41,472
Deferred Charges/Increases	64,123	58,830	48,209	42,586	38,933	39,529
Long-term Debt	308,092	337,680	496,750	408,314	296,316	168,339
Noncurrent Capital Leases	0	0	0	0	0	485
Other Long-term Liability	740	867	1,221	1,340	1,394	1,174
Total Liabilities	460,449	326,196	184,843	514,314	379,200	250,999
Common Stock Net	1,599	1,590	1,571	1,912	1,907	1,903
Capital Surplus	111,516	84,026	52,302	47,376	43,273	42,035
Retained Earnings	502,257	384,935	281,587	205,295	130,370	237,290
Treasury Stock	125,353	144,355	150,617	93,859	30,638	3,170
Shareholder Equity	490,009	326,196	184,843	160,724	144,912	278,058
Total Liability and Net Worth	950,458	783,071	792,479	675,038	524,112	529,057

Source: Company reports.

EXHIBIT 15-9 Consolidated Statements of Income, Fiscal Year Ended January 31
(In thousands, except share data)

	1993	1992	1991
Revenues			
Casino	$495,012	$471,823	$414,688
Rooms	147,115	141,716	109,869
Food and beverage	135,786	129,951	112,274
Other	92,500	89,652	78,956
	870,413	833,142	715,787
Less—complimentary allowances	(27,388)	(27,119)	(23,735)
	843,025	806,023	692,052
Costs and expenses			
Casino	189,499	175,771	155,809
Rooms	68,783	64,799	52,289
Food and beverage	128,689	124,093	105,171
Other operating expenses	58,917	56,565	51,283
General and administrative	130,152	124,313	105,805
Depreciation and amortization	46,550	47,385	40,998
Preopening expense	—	—	11,177
	622,590	592,926	522,532
Operating profit before corporate expense	220,435	213,097	169,520
Corporate expense	14,953	12,706	11,044
Income from operations	205,482	200,391	158,476
Other income (expense)			
Interest, dividends and other income (loss)	820	245	(570)
Interest expense	(22,989)	(43,632)	(42,048)
	(22,169)	(43,387)	(42,618)
Income before provision for income tax	183,313	157,004	115,858
Provision for income tax	62,330	53,656	39,566
Income before extraordinary loss	120,983	103,348	76,292
Extraordinary loss on early extinguishment of debt, net of income tax benefit of $1,885	(3,661)	—	—
Net income	$117,332	$103,348	$ 76,292
Earnings per share			
Income before extraordinary loss	$ 2.11	$ 1.84	$ 1.39
Extraordinary loss on early extinguishment of debt	(0.06)	—	—
Net Income	$ 2.05	$ 1.84	$ 1.39

Source: *Annual Report*, 1993.

EXHIBIT 15-10 Consolidated Statements of Cash Flows

	YEAR ENDED JANUARY 31, INCREASE (DECREASE) IN CASH AND CASH EQUIVALENTS (IN THOUSANDS)		
	1993	1992	1991
Cash flows from operating activities:			
Net income before extraordinary loss	$120,983	$103,348	$76,292
Adjustments to reconcile net income before extraordinary loss to net cash provided by operating activities:			
Depreciation and amortization	48,182	48,870	42,395
Increase in deferred income tax	5,293	10,621	5,623
Increase (decrease) in interest payable	(4,100)	(1,668)	435
Increase (decrease) in income tax payable	(477)	367	(1,527)
(Gain) loss on sale of fixed assets	(41)	(93)	1,389
(Increase) decrease in other current assets	(1,268)	2,412	(14,335)
Increase in other current liabilities	5,598	3,415	13,678
(Increase) decrease in other noncurrent assets	(2,368)	531	(71)
Decrease in other noncurrent liabilities	(65)	(65)	(65)
Total adjustments	50,754	64,390	47,522
Net cash provided by operating activities	171,737	167,738	123,814
Cash flows from investing activities:			
Capital expenditures	(208,586)	(26,569)	(148,519)
Increase (decrease) in construction payables	27,762	(4,075)	(13,207)
Proceeds from sale of equipment and other assets	4,510	527	663
Net cash used in investing activities	(176,314)	(30,117)	(161,063)
Cash flows from financing activities:			
Net effect on cash of issuances and payments of debt with initial maturities of three months or less	69,957	(138,993)	(23,382)
Issuances of debt with original maturities in excess of three months	—	—	51,014
Principal payments of debt with original maturities in excess of three months	(100,397)	(20,320)	(39,309)
Exercise of stock options and warrants	46,491	50,806	4,585
Effect on cash of extraordinary loss	(2,155)	—	—
Purchases of treasury stock	—	(12,801)	(56,758)
Proceeds from issuance of senior subordinated notes	—	—	99,875
Other	(62)	(289)	(53)
Net cash provided by (used in) financing activities	13,834	(121,597)	35,972
Net increase (decrease) in cash and cash equivalents	9,257	16,024	(1,277)
Cash and cash equivalents at beginning of year	34,158	18,134	19,411
Cash and cash equivalents at end of year	$ 43,415	$ 34,158	$18,134
Supplemental Cash Flow Disclosures:			
Interest paid (net of amount capitalized)	$ 26,104	$ 43,727	$40,330
Income tax paid	$ 41,500	$ 30,350	$34,400

Source: *Annual Report*, 1993.

RAILROADING INDUSTRY NOTE
JOEL PALLEY

The railroad freight industry generated nearly $32 billion in operating revenues in 1993. The 12 major freight railroads accounted for almost $29 billion of that total. Amtrak, the quasi-government rail passenger corporation serving 45 states, had estimated revenues of $1.4 billion in 1993, up from $1.3 billion in 1993.

FREIGHT SERVICE

In 1993, for the seventh consecutive year, the railroad industry recorded a new high for freight traffic, which increased by nearly 2 percent as measured by revenue ton-miles (a measure than incorporates both weight and distance). Shipments (as measured by carloads) of motor vehicles and parts continued their rebound from 1991, increasing by nearly 10 percent from 1992, and metals rose by an estimated 9 percent. Intermodal traffic (trailer-on-flatcar and container-on-flatcar) grew an estimated 7 percent. Coal, the largest rail commodity, declined an estimated 3 percent because of a coal strike, reduced coal exports, and inventory reductions by electric utilities. Among other top rail commodities, chemicals increased 1 percent, while grain shipments rose 2 percent.

For the 12 months ending June 30, 1993, the freight railroad industry earned an average 7.2 percent return on its net investment base (excluding special charges). Since 1980, the year the Staggers Rail Act partially deregulated rail rates and services, the railroads have invested nearly $160 billion in track and equipment. Freight rates declined by 1.5 percent per year in real terms between 1990 and 1993, roughly the same annual rate of decline since the passage of the Staggers Act, compared to an increase of 2.9 percent per year in the five years prior to 1980.

Intermodal and Technology Issues. Railroad productivity measured by revenue ton-miles per employee continues to increase at a faster rate than that of almost any other industry, doubling between 1983 and 1992. Rail intermodal traffic has risen from 3.1 million trailers and containers in 1980 to 6.7 million in 1992. The increase is due largely to the introduction in 1984 of specialized railcars with depressed platforms that carry containers stacked two high (double-stack containers). Containers from the Far East move through West Coast ports to inland destinations under expedited schedules on such double-stack trains, carrying export and domestic traffic on the backhaul. Roughly 130 double-stack trains depart the West Coast weekly. Double-stack cars now account for approximately 40 percent of total intermodal capacity and 80 percent of containers.

Technological Innovation. The rail industry is developing an Automatic Train Control System (ATCS), which utilizes microelectronics and telecommunications to control train operations. It will be implemented in four areas—work order reporting, locomotive performance monitoring, track force equipment management, and positive train separation and control. The Department of Transportation's Federal Railroad Administration (FRA), in cooperation with the industry, will conduct a safety inquiry into this new technology and report to the Congress on the feasibility of implementing ATCS in a way that will enhance railroad's safety, efficiency, productivity, and customer service capabilities.

Safety Issues. The FRA regulates rail safety in the United States. In 1992–1993, FRA issued final rules covering bridge worker safety standards, state safety participation regulations, and the use of event recorders. FRA is continuing research for proposed rules on grade crossing warning devices, alcohol and drug testing improvements, power brakes, tank car improvements, and tank car shell thickness.

Cooperation with Mexico. Cooperative efforts between the United States and Mexico have increased the efficiency and safety of rail transportation between the two countries. Rail transportation is an important factor in supporting the increasing trade between the United States and Mexico. In anticipation of congressional approval of the North American Free Trade Agreement (NAFTA), and in response to burgeoning trade between the two countries, U.S. railroads and the Mexican National Railway (Ferrocarriles Nacionales de Mexico, or FNM) introduced innovative management and operating practices and worked together to streamline border-crossing procedures.

Under NAFTA proposals, U.S. and Canadian railroads will be able to market their own services in Mexico and use their own locomotives to carry run-through trains under agreements with FNM. Railroads and other private investors, such as shippers or steamship lines, may build and own terminals and spur lines, and finance construction of rail infrastructure. The NAFTA-member countries will also continue consultations to make their rail safety standards compatible.

Some of these concepts are being put into practice through new cooperative ventures between U.S. and Mexican railroads. The FNM has purchased Union Pacific Railroad's Transportation Control System, which provides computerized monitoring and management of yard operations, inventory, billing, scheduling, and planning functions. The system has been installed in Mexico City and is expected to be in place in Monterrey and Nuevo Laredo in 1993, with full implementation by 1994.

The Santa Fe Railway, the FNM, and Concarril, a Mexican rail car builder, have entered into an agreement to provide rail cars to Santa Fe. The Southern Pacific has invested in a Mexican company, Ferropuertos, that is building distribution centers to handle imported grain, mineral exports, and intermodal traffic moving both to and from the United States.

Some U.S. railroads that have no direct connections with the FNM in Mexico are forging new connections by utilizing the sea lanes of the Gulf of Mexico. Burlington Northern (BN) and the Mexican corporation Grupo Protexa have formed a joint transportation venture to integrate rail and barge services between interior points in Mexico and the United States. In April 1993 BN started moving trains southbound to Galveston, Texas, where the rail cars are transported on Protexa's oceangoing barges to the Mexican ports of Coatzacoalcos, Veracruz, and Altamira. From there, they are distributed by FNM to the interior of Mexico.

Eastern railroads are considering similar rail-barge links to Mexican ports from U.S. ports in the Gulf of Mexico. Such cooperative efforts will increase the competitiveness of both countries' rail industries, opening new markets for both trade and the railroads.

Rail plays a major role in moving products between the United States and Mexico. According to the USDA's 1992 report entitled *U.S.-Mexico Bilateral Trade: Estimated Modal Shares,* in 1991 the United States exported 15.8 million tons of freight by rail to Mexico, led by farm products (3.9 million tons), food and kindred products (1.9 million tons), waste or scrap materials (1.5 million tons), and primary metal products (1.5 million tons). In the same year 4.7 million tons of freight were

Trends and Forecasts: Class I Railroads (SIC 4011)

ITEM	1991	1992	1993[1]	1994[2]	PERCENT CHANGE (1991–1994)		
					91–92	92–93	93–94
Operating revenue (billion $)	27.7	28.3	28.7	29.4	2.2	1.4	2.4
Revenue ton-miles (billions)	1,036	1,064	1,080	1,110	2.7	1.5	2.8
Average employment (000)	231	222	215	208	−3.9	−3.2	−3.3

[1] Estimate.

[2] Forecast.

Source: Association of American Railroads, U.S. Department of Labor, Bureau of Labor Statistics; Railroad Retirement Board. Estimates and forecasts by the Federal Railroad Administration.

imported by rail from Mexico, including transportation equipment (1.0 million tons); miscellaneous mixed shipments of TOFC/COFC (0.8 million tons); clay, concrete, glass, and stone products (0.5 million tons); and primary metal products (0.5 million tons).

Labor Issues. Wages and other labor-related expenses are the largest component of railroad operating costs. Nationwide collective bargaining disputes over wages, work rules, and health care resulted in a one-day strike in 1991 and a two-day strike in 1992, after administrative procedures had been exhausted. Both times, Congress passed legislation ending the strike (for more information see the *1993 U.S. Industrial Outlook*, pages 40–47). All major national railroad labor contracts are in force until January 1, 1995.

Railroads are realizing greater efficiencies through reduced train crew size. The standard crew on through freight trains now consists generally of an engineer and a conductor. This standard was affirmed by the arbitration process established under the legislation which ended the 1991 dispute.

Industry Structure and Regulatory Environment. The 12 Class I freight railroad systems (defined in 1992 as systems with operating revenues of more than $250 million) and Amtrak employed an estimated 215,000 persons in 1993, down from 222,000 in 1992. In addition, in 1992 there were 33 regional railroads with 12,338 employees; 278 independently owned local railroads (not part of Class I systems) with 6,055 employees; and 192 switching and terminal railroads with 7,322 employees.

Although the pace of mergers among major railroads has slowed since the early 1980s, sales of line segments by Class I railroads to smaller operators continue. In cases where traffic volumes have declined on branch lines, Class I railroads have sold their lines to smaller, lower-cost operators. These short-line operators have improved service to local shippers while continuing to feed traffic to the major railroads.

The Staggers Act did not completely deregulate the freight railroads, but it did reduce ICC authority in areas where competition served to limit rail rates. Now more than three-quarters of freight traffic is not subject to maximum rate regulation, either because competition has kept rates at levels below the threshold for ICC authority, or because the ICC exempted the traffic altogether. The ICC has explicitly exempted traffic moving in boxcars and trailers-on-flatcars. In addition, the Commission has exempted many agricultural and manufactured commodities (including most lumber and wood products, and transportation equipment), regardless of car type, after determining that competition was sufficient to protect shippers.

During the last few years, an average of less than a dozen new rate complaints and protests have been filed per year, down sharply from an annual average of nearly 300 rate complaints or protests before the Staggers Act went into effect. (For additional background on the Staggers Rail Act, see the *1990 U.S. Industrial Outlook,* chapter 42.) Railroad-shipper contracts, legalized by the Act, have had a significant impact on the industry. Now more than 60 percent of all rail traffic moves under contract. The terms of these agreements, although filed at the ICC, are confidential; only a very general summary is released to the public. (For additional information on railroad-shipper contracts, see the *1993 U.S. Industrial Outlook,* Chapter 40, pp. 6–7).

In January 1993 the FRA released a report entitled *Small Railroad Investment Goals and Financial Options: A Report to Congress.* The study surveyed regional and shortline railroads concerning their capital needs and their interest in possible federal loan guarantees. Of 339 respondents, 76 percent filed abbreviated surveys, which were requested of those carriers not interested in, or not foreseeing a need for, a federal loan guarantee. The remaining 24 percent indicated interest in obtaining loan guarantees for track rehabilitation, financing locomotives and rolling stock, and refinancing existing loans. The study found that these carriers could not meet their goals with financing from traditional sources. Collectively, these railroads indicated that they would need to spend $1.77 billion through 1995 to maintain and upgrade their systems. They also expect to finance or fund internally $1.33 billion of these requirements, but would be unable to raise the remaining $440 million, mostly for track rehabilitation. An additional $290 million would be needed for refinancing existing loans.

Outlook for 1994. In 1994 rail traffic volume is forecast to continue the modest recovery of 1993, with revenue ton-miles increasing 3 percent. Coal traffic, the top commodity carried by the railroads, is expected to grow by 2 to 3 percent in 1994 after its 1993 decline, in line with industry and government forecasts of increased coal production. Because of the increasing importance of container and double-stack service, intermodal traffic is expected to continue to be the fastest growing area, increasing by 3 to 5 percent. Traffic in chemicals, lumber and wood products, paper, metallic ores, primary metal products, motor vehicles and parts, stone, clay, and glass, and other industrial commodities, are expected to increase as a consequence of expanding industrial production. Growth in grain traffic will depend largely on export demand, such as whether larger grain shipments are made to the former Soviet Union. Class I railroad employment is forecast to decline by approximately 3 percent to 208,000—in part with early retirements—as the railroads continue to increase their operating efficiencies.

DAKOTA, MINNESOTA & EASTERN RAILROAD—1994

PAUL REED
Sam Houston State
University
CAROL CUMBER
South Dakota State
University

The Dakota, Minnesota & Eastern (DM&E) Railroad (605-697-2400) is headquartered in Brookings, South Dakota, and operates mainly in South Dakota and Minnesota* but also has a 69-mile branch line serving Mason City, Iowa. DM&E's location in the upper Midwest is always subject to weather extremes such as floods. On July 21, 1993, Minnesota had over three million acres underwater with crop damage estimated at $1 billion. In South Dakota alone, 25 percent of all farmland was flooded and farmer losses exceeded $500 million. Corn and soybean losses would reduce DM&E revenues for the next 18 months by $1.5 to $2 million. Flood-related reduction in the construction industry had already severely hurt DM&E cement shipments. One bright spot was that wheat production was expected to be 25 percent above average in South Dakota.

Railroads of today are far different from the traditional railroads of yesterday. In essence, railroads were once responsible for hauling almost everything and everybody into and out of every city and village; in 1929 they accounted for 75 percent of all United States intercity freight ton-miles. The volume of freight handled by today's railroads is 238 percent of that of 1929, but huge market share has been lost to trucks, river carriers, and pipelines. Railroads today handle about 37 percent of all freight ton-miles and have evolved from general freight carriers to specialized freight carriers primarily handling large-volume bulk commodities, oversized or bulky loads, and general products and merchandise when combined into container- or trailer-sized lots.

The DM&E has struggled since its inception in 1986, primarily because of problems with the Chicago and North Western (C&NW) Railroad, DM&E's major customer and supplier. President John C. "Pete" McIntyre has led DM&E from start-up and is basically pleased with its progress. Revenues have continued to climb, net income has improved, and the debt-to-equity ratio has been halved. New customers have been found and many older customers increasingly have switched from truck to rail. Yet McIntyre feels DM&E will never reach its potential until it is freed from C&NW dominance and new markets are found. So on April 14, 1993, DM&E placed a request to the Interstate Commerce Commission (ICC) for relief from certain C&NW restrictions. Repair costs for the 1993 flood approximate $2 million and have put a severe strain on the DM&E budget, although federal grants may assist in the rebuilding effort.

THE DM&E'S BEGINNINGS

The Chicago and North Western (C&NW) is one of seven railroads that connect Chicago with the states of the upper Midwest. It is a conservative company with many lightly traveled lines and only marginal profits even in the best of times. The route system is directed west and northwest of Chicago, and its many rail lines crisscross northern Illinois, Iowa, Nebraska, Wisconsin, Minnesota, and South Dakota. Trackage also serves small portions of Wyoming and the Upper Peninsula of Michigan.

The mid-1970s saw many rail lines, including C&NW, suffering heavy losses or facing bankruptcy. This general malaise coupled with new legislation and more flexible regulatory agencies contributed to a massive industry restructuring. Many lines

*This case is intended for classroom discussion only, not to depict effective or ineffective handling of administrative situations. All rights reserved to the authors and the Southwest Case Research Association.

merged, were severely downsized, or disappeared with bits and pieces purchased by former competitors or entrepreneurs. C&NW was particularly active during the 1970s, purchasing and then abandoning major portions of competitors, such as Chicago GreatWestern (1,450 miles) and Minneapolis and Saint Louis (1,300 miles), plus acquiring the Minneapolis–Kansas City line of the Rock Island (600 miles). By the late 1980s, C&NW had also sold or abandoned some 4,500 miles of its own trackage, including the vast majority of its lines in Minnesota and South Dakota.

Most of the trackage of what is now the DM&E (Exhibit 16–1) had been unprofitable for C&NW for several years. In 1983 and again in 1985, C&NW petitioned to abandon the line from five miles west of Pierre to Rapid City. This action would leave South Dakota with no centrally located east-west rail transportation. C&NW's requests were met with unusually strong opposition from the State and U.S. Senator Larry Pressler, R-South Dakota. Realizing that abandonment was no longer a wise move, C&NW was faced with either continued operations or sale. All parties agreed that the former was not feasible, and therefore the C&NW initiated actions that ultimately led to the formation of the DM&E.

The C&NW contracted with a subunit of L. B. Foster, Inc., a railroad supply firm, to negotiate the sale of the line. It was obvious that the Pierre–Rapid City (PRC) section could not stand alone, so the sale package was gradually expanded eastward to Winona, Minnesota, with several north-south branch lines included. It was felt that these approximately 965 miles of railroad would generate enough traffic to adequately service the debt associated with its purchase plus provide a satisfactory return to the owner.

As discussion continued, L. B. Foster itself became interested in the proposed rail package. The company eventually developed business plans that included all operating aspects of the railroad plus pro forma financial statements, and negotiated the purchase price with C&NW. Final closing took place on September 4, 1986. The $26 million agreement was heavily leveraged with Westinghouse Credit Corporation, the primary lender, and with C&NW assuming a $4 million subordinated note. Foster provided a small portion of the equity financing along with TXL Corporation, Lombard Investments, and DM&E top management.

The buyers acquired 826 miles of track and rights to operate on an additional 139 miles. Included were 18 C&NW locomotives, averaging 35 years old, and maintenance and repair equipment. C&NW retained ownership of the tracks at DM&E's main interchanges at Winona and Mankato, Minnesota, Mason City, Iowa, and Rapid City, South Dakota. It also could exercise veto power over DM&E's rates and route proposals or any changes in existing financing. The new line also had to agree to pay substantial monetary penalties unless 89 percent of DM&E's originated traffic was loaded in C&NW freight cars.

Lack of funds coupled with the C&NW equipment agreement precluded the DM&E purchase or lease of freight cars. Additional locomotive needs were satisfied by the purchase of 22 vintage diesels from the Soo Line and Norfolk Southern railroads. Recruiting a trained workforce was a major item on the agenda. DM&E was not bound by C&NW labor union agreements and was therefore not required to have a union workforce. Beginning salaries were pegged approximately 15 percent below comparable jobs on unionized railroads but were well above the average South Dakota and Minnesota wage earners' income. A profit sharing plan offset the wage differential to some degree. Work rules were designed to permit far more flexibility than was the case with C&NW.

DM&E hiring gave initial priority to local C&NW employees because of their experience and familiarity with the lines purchased. DM&E filled approximately 60

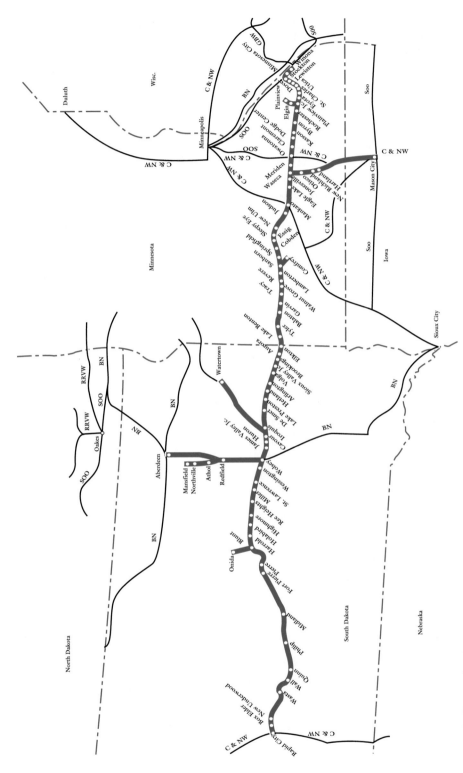

EXHIBIT 16-1 Dakota, Minnesota and Eastern Railroad

percent of its 130 positions from this source and the remaining hires came from other rail lines or had no prior railroad experience.

DM&E's early years of operation contained more than the average number of problems. Integration of new people, procedures, policies, communication channels, and the like took weeks. A concern to the newly hired president McIntyre was the purchase agreement itself. Traffic projections had been overstated and physical condition of track was far worse than estimated. Revenue projections had been based on an unrealistic level of business, and DM&E was seriously undercapitalized with no working capital available on the first day of operations. C&NW had been paid far too much for the property and by agreeing to the aforementioned C&NW restrictions, the negotiators had in effect severely limited McIntyre and his subordinates' ability to operate the road efficiently. Other problems included a serious drought that ruined crops, heavy rains that washed out miles of track, blizzards that stopped traffic, burned-out locomotive engines, and a plant explosion at the railroad's largest customer.

This almost continuous series of problems pushed DM&E to the brink of insolvency. On the positive side, misfortune seemed to bond management and workers together. By 1991 hard work had overcome many of the inherited problems, and it was apparent that the railroad had turned the corner.

ASPECTS OF DM&E

Exhibit 16–2 shows that the Winona–Rapid City main line and the track to Mason City carry the greatest freight tonnages and most traffic is eastbound. Track conditions on most of the line prevent freight train speeds in excess of 25 mph, and approximately 30 percent of the line can support only 10 mph.

DM&E serves the main line with a minimum five-day-per-week scheduled train service between Rapid City and Winona. A similar schedule handles freight between Waseca, Minnesota, and Mason City, Iowa. During peak months (June–October), two trains per seven-day week are often scheduled. Extra trains also originate at points between Pierre and Waseca to handle grain and other tonnage. Branch lines use trains on an as-needed basis. Local freights at Rochester and New Ulm, Minnesota, serve all on-line customers in Minnesota, thus relieving scheduled trains from making numerous stops.

Freight cars are sorted and blocked at the division points at Waseca and Huron, South Dakota. DM&E must turn over almost all traffic to C&NW at its four principal gateways. This forces DM&E to pay C&NW switching charges in excess of $100 per car or share revenue on all through traffic. Exhibit 16–3 gives populations of the largest cities (1990 Census) along the DM&E route and reveals ownership of the tracks.

DM&E owns and operates car and locomotive repair shops at Huron. Major repairs and overhauls are performed on locomotives. Similar services are provided on an as-needed basis to freight cars of other railroads. All active locomotives have been rebuilt or received major overhaul since start-up. The availability rate for locomotives is over 90 percent and approaches 100 percent during winter months, when many units are stored because of lower traffic requirements. During the summer–fall season, DM&E leases approximately a dozen locomotives to handle increased traffic.

Grain and grain-derived products make up 50 percent of DM&E's carloads. Grain shipments include wheat, corn, and soybeans from eastern South Dakota and the western two-thirds of Minnesota. The second major item of traffic is bentonite clay (used in foundry operations, oil drilling, iron-ore pelletizing, and cat litter), which is turned over by C&NW at Rapid City to DM&E for delivery farther east.

EXHIBIT 16-2 Dakota, Minnesota & Eastern Railroad Corporation:
1992 Freight density map (Shown in million gross tons per mile)

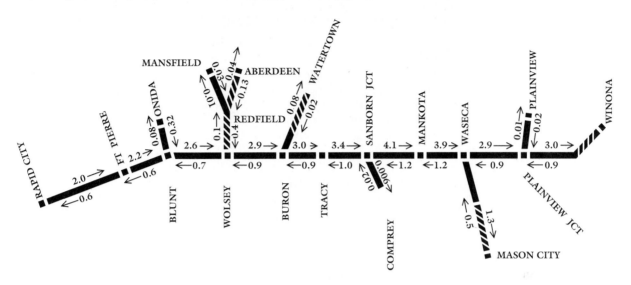

////////// Trackage rights

━━━━━━ Owned

Other major traffic sources include industrial sand, cement, wood chips, lumber, and kaolin clay (manufacturing of cement). Exhibit 16–4 shows the traffic mix since start-up.

Corporate Philosophy. In the words of Pete McIntyre, the DM&E's mission is "to provide rail users in the upper Midwest with consistent, damage-free, on time, wholesale and retail transportation service with the intent of moderate growth and profitability, recognizing its employees as valuable assets and with the aim of being customer driven." The railroad has made a long-term commitment to provide reliable freight services and not to diversify into nonrail businesses. The credo of moderate traffic growth is supported by McIntyre's emphasis on "growing the business we already have" and receiving more through traffic from connections. In 1992 DM&E had the following traffic mix: forwarded (originated and delivered on-line or to connections), 47.6 percent; overhead (received from and delivered to other railroads), 45.1 percent; and received (received from other lines for delivery to DM&E customers), 7.4 percent of total carloads. Total carloads increased from 43,000 in 1987 to over 55,000 in 1992.

DM&E strives to strengthen its position as a rail freight carrier in the upper Midwest by making its existing system more efficient. Accordingly, DM&E increased its carloadings and revenues by enlarging its market share of freight shipped by existing customers, by regaining customers who had shifted to trucks when the railroad was operated by previous owners, by serving new shippers in its territory, and by improving relations with other railroads. DM&E historically has employed a strategy

EXHIBIT 16-3   Largest Cities and Track Ownership

STATE	CITY	SIZE	TRACK OWNERSHIP
Minnesota	Winona	47,828	C&NW
	Rochester	70,745	DM&E
	Owatonna	19,386	C&NW
	Waseca	18,079	DM&E
	Mankato	31,477	C&NW
Iowa	Mason City	29,040	C&NW
South Dakota	Brookings	16,270	DM&E
	Huron	12,448	DM&E and BN
	Watertown	17,592	BN and DM&E
	Aberdeen	24,927	BN and DM&E
	Pierre	12,906	DM&E
	Rapid City	54,523	C&NW

Source: U.S. Bureau of the Census, 1990.

EXHIBIT 16-4   Historical Carloadings by Category (1987–1992)

CATEGORIES OF TRAFFIC	1987	1988	1989	1990	1991	1992
Wheat	10,888	8,919	6,664	8,949	10,532	9,883
Bentonite Clay	0	0	740	6,756	9,054	9,666
Woodchips	2,827	3,413	3,450	3,768	3,232	3,353
Corn	5,082	7,031	8,436	10,443	8,045	8,469
Cement	2,893	3,572	3,132	1,976	2,171	2,853
Industrial Sand	3,115	2,733	4,055	5,040	2,369	3,407
Lumber/Boards	165	145	109	825	656	546
Soybeans	3,090	4,061	1,902	2,915	2,766	2,973
Kaolin Clay	0	0	0	663	1,036	1,295
Soybean Oil	2,636	2,011	1,458	1,566	1,969	1,971
Wheat Flour	760	598	434	966	974	930
All Others	11,623	10,260	9,644	8,721	8,658	9,814
Total	43,079	42,743	40,024	52,588	51,462	55,160

Source: Company records.

of strengthening its existing traffic base and increasing its market share within the territory it serves rather than expanding beyond South Dakota and Minnesota. Recent activities, however, indicate that DM&E desires to acquire additional trackage owned by C&NW.

DM&E has aggressively gone after traffic from both large and small shippers. It has initiated long-term agreements with large shippers to stabilize its traffic base; given 8 to 10 percent discounts to grain shippers who make unit train shipments of 25 cars or more; and initiated pricing and service packages to provide South Dakota and Minnesota farmers' markets in Texas, the eastern United States, the Pacific coast, and the Gulf coast via the Mississippi River. DM&E continues to streamline operations and facilities through upgrading its locomotive fleet, continually improving and repairing unsatisfactory track and roadbed inherited from C&NW, adding or rescheduling train service, and opening a computerized Customer Service Center to improve rail-customer interface.

Marketing. DM&E has done considerable research and planning to identify and satisfy customer needs. Marketing vice president Lynn Anderson stresses that DM&E "must determine what our customers' expectations are: in terms of car supply, transit times, loss or damage, billing, communications, switching, car tracing, and response time. What does the customer expect from us? With this knowledge, we can expedite the action needed to provide customers with superior service." Although DM&E's innovative ideas affect shippers and receivers of all categories of traffic, the marketing of grain is of particular interest. DM&E took advantage of the Winona end of track on the Mississippi River by developing a rail-barge service that opened up new markets to shippers and receivers at prices that took advantage of cheaper barge rates. This traffic has grown from 750 carloads of grain and grain products in 1987 to nearly 9,000 in 1992. Elevators from as far west as Pierre have found this option attractive. When the Mississippi freezes in the winter DM&E has organized trains for delivery of grain to the Pacific Northwest and Texas.

Lynn Anderson's department also faces many challenges: the limited size and nature of the railroad's target markets, determined by demographics of the DM&E service area; freight car shortages, particularly during peak demand; difficulty in interchanging traffic with C&NW; prior agreements that preclude car interchange with the Soo Line at Owatonna and Winona; and the impact of weather on shippers, receivers, and DM&E itself.

Transportation Conditions. Providing safe, timely service that meets customer needs is a never-ending challenge to DM&E. Poor track, a lethargic C&NW, and intermittent locomotive shortages have too often translated into high operating costs and dissatisfied customers. A great portion of the DM&E line west of Huron is the original 72-pound (per yard) rail laid in the early 1900s. Eighty-odd years of pounding have made the track and the supporting grade increasingly unable to support 100-ton railcars moving at speeds much above 10 mph.

DM&E tracks end short of the yards at Mason City, Rapid City, and Winona, and as a result, entry, car switching, and exit are controlled by C&NW. DM&E trains are often forced to idle for several hours while waiting for C&NW yard crews to put outgoing trains together or clear tracks for incoming cars. Getting entry onto C&NW tracks through Mankato can be equally exasperating, and several-hour waits for passage of C&NW through trains or yard switching are common. These impediments are particularly irritating because DM&E pays C&NW over $2 million a year for switching services. Also, increased traffic occasionally overloads available locomotive supply, causing slow underpowered trains or tonnage being left behind for later pickup. Exhibit 16–5 shows the seasonality of DM&E traffic.

Poor track conditions have increased the average Rapid City–Winona passage from 69 to more than 80 hours and have been largely responsible for 89 derailments in

1992 at a cost of $2.2 million. Derailments through May 1993 numbered 26 at a cost of $857,000. Train crew costs have also skyrocketed, with most crews going beyond the standard eight hours and sometimes stopping their trains in place because of the federally mandated 12-hour crew maximum. Slower trains and crews "dying out" on the line require overnight motel and meal expenses or cab fares to pick up old crews and deliver fresh ones.

Crews. DM&E has 45 conductors and 43 engineers plus a management and administrative staff of 15. DM&E has been training its own conductors for the last few years and has begun a 70-day cross-training program, in conjunction with the Santa Fe railroad, where senior conductors are qualified as engineers. This dual qualification has added job stability by permitting conductors to serve as engineers during peak season and return to their former duties during slack time. Temporary conductors are used as needed.

Modern communications link train crew, home office, and customers via locomotive-mounted radio, fax machines at each railroad station, and the recently opened Customer Service Center. Crews are able to communicate instantaneously about changes in car requirements for on-line customers, schedule status, train meets, and so on and to act upon changes with dispatch.

Engineering. The DM&E engineering department maintains track, bridges, and other physical plant in a safe condition. This task includes cross-tie replacement, rail replacement, rock ballasting, surfacing (cleaning, leveling, and smoothing of track), subgrade and bridge improvements. DM&E inherited a poorly maintained railroad with 40 percent unsatisfactory cross ties, 10 defective rails per mile, and at least 50 per-

EXHIBIT 16-5   Dakota, Minnesota & Eastern Railroad (1987–1993): Carloads by Month

	1987	1988	1989	1990	1991	1992	1993
January	2,483	2,814	2,000	3.640	2,870	3.644	3,227
February	2,471	2,854	2,072	3,130	2,579	3,404	3,552
March	2,965	3,807	2,437	2,954	3,337	3,709	4,362
April	3,522	3,874	3,175	3,550	3,883	5,250	4,245
May	3,574	3,811	3,319	4,272	4,211	4,476	4,178
June	4,012	4,394	3,146	4,636	4,431	5,202	4,415
Subtotal	19,027	21,554	16,149	22,182	21,311	25,685	23,979
July	4,991	3,898	3,766	5,751	5,872	5,716	
August	4,544	3,782	4,502	6,369	5,642	5,251	
September	3,942	4,018	3,663	4,787	5,057	5,384	
October	3,919	4,310	5,118	6,329	6,149	5,778	
November	3,347	2,662	3,515	4,526	3,714	3,887	
December	3,309	2,519	3,311	2,644	3,717	3,459	
Total	43,079	42,743	40,024	52,588	51,462	55,160	

Source: Company records.

cent of the track unsafe for speeds greater than 10 mph. Added to these woes was discovery that the native clay (Pierre shale) subgrade on the PRC section was unstable during periods of heavy rains. The frequent end result is that water, clay, and ballast are squeezed to both sides of the railbed, thus causing the track to sink. Some of these soft-spot areas extend for 500 feet.

The weather is unkind to DM&E. Blizzards and cold weather block track, freeze switches, and cause rail failures. A wildfire in October 1992 raced down seven miles of track in western South Dakota, burning out or severely damaging 89 timber spans and ultimately costing DM&E $500,000. Unseasonably wet weather has played havoc on the PRC section and by late July 1993 had washed out roadbed in eastern South Dakota and at many places across Minnesota.

DM&E has spent over $34 million on track and bridge-related capital projects. More than half of this amount was from cash generated from operations, and the remainder came from federal and state loans and grants plus loans from customers. DM&E also performs normal maintenance and maintenance-support activities that are not included in capital expenditures. Exhibit 16–6 shows capital expenditures by year. Budgeted capital track expenditures for 1993 approximate $8.3 million, with $3 million spent in South Dakota and $5.3 million in Minnesota.

Through 1992, capitalized expenditures include 488,000 cross ties; 639,000 tons of rock ballast (8,520 car loads); surfacing of approximately 650 miles of track; replacement of 30 miles of rail and 1.5 miles of bridging with culvert and earthen fill; strengthening of 12 steel bridges; installation of 4,000 feet of cross-drain plastic pipe and 2,700 feet of longitudinal-drain plastic pipe; and extension of several rail sidings.

DM&E has long recognized that a targeted main-line average speed of 25 mph will never be attained until a solution to the PRC subgrade problems is found and the lightweight rail between Wolsey and Pierre, South Dakota, is replaced. DM&E estimates the "Big Fix" will cost an estimated $37 million. The project includes replacement of 104 miles of 72-pound rail, 85 miles of ditching, surfacing of the entire 170-mile PRC subdivision, with a total of 6,800 cars of ballast and installation of 35 miles of waterproof fabric between ballast and clay. Also, over 4,500 feet of perforated lateral drain pipe and 20 miles of perforated longitudinal piping will be used to remove trapped pockets of water.

The DM&E engineering department is staffed with 27 section personnel who are spread out at regular intervals along the nine sections of 850-mile owned rail. Each three-man section is responsible for maintaining a safe railroad across its section. The department's other 37 nonmanagement personnel install and maintain signals, repair bridges, inspect track, and operate a variety of equipment. This 64-man base workforce is augmented by temporary hires in the spring and summer. DM&E uses contractors for all major capital projects. This department is highly respected by the train crews.

Mechanical. The DM&E mechanical department has to maintain the locomotive fleet, repair all foreign on-line railcars, and provide service to nearly 300 newly leased covered hoppers. James Appleman's 36-member department has the equipment and expertise to perform almost any type of maintenance or repair requirement. The fact that locomotive availability remains 90 percent or higher, with units manufactured between 1952 and 1974 and averaging 39 years old, speaks for itself. The department covers 80 percent of its entire budget from foreign railcar repairs.

Human Resources. Human Resources Management (HRM) is not centrally administered. Hiring and training are done at the department level, whereas pay, benefits, performance appraisal, and administrative record-keeping are performed by the Finance and Accounting Department. DM&E recently began interviewing candidates for the newly created position of HRM director. It is assumed that HRM functions will be increasingly consolidated under this person's watch.

No function of the DM&E has higher priority than human resources, however. Pete McIntyre continually stresses the importance of all employees both as people and as the real reason for DM&E's success. Most key managers seem to embrace this attitude, though some seem to have difficulty adjusting from the confrontational leadership style too typical of the railroad industry.

DM&E schedules "employee appreciation dinners" in the summer and during the holiday season at major locations. Employees enjoy the give and take during these festivities and feel free to express their views. McIntyre and other rail officials get out on the line as often as possible but acknowledge that their hectic jobs keep them from getting needed feedback. Face-to-face communication is supplemented by a quarterly newsletter, *DM&E Enroute*, which keeps employees, customers, and supporters informed of current operations and future plans. One innovation is an open invitation for employees to phone McIntyre direct, or in his absence, leave a message. Overall,

EXHIBIT 16-6 Dakota, Minnesota & Eastern Railroad Corporation Capital Expenditures (In thousands of dollars)

	1987	1988	1989	1990	1991	1992	TOTAL
Capital Expenditures							
SD Track—West of Pierre	$2,156	$ 464	$3,099	$ 2,614	$ 955	$2,221	$11,509
SD Track—East of Pierre	2,362	713	2,768	3,429	219	1,120	10,611
Total SD Track	$4,518	$1,177	$5,867	$ 6,043	$1,174	$3,341	$22,120
MN Track	837	4,721	692	2,969	1,374	1,713	12,306
Total All Track	$5,355	$5,898	$6,559	$ 9,012	$2,548	$5,054	$34,426
Locomotive & All Other	47	1,043	1,528	1,410	1,267	1,454	6,749
Total	$5,402	$6,941	$8,087	$10,422	$3,815	$6,508	41,175
Funded by:							
SD Grant (FRA Funds)[a]	626	0	0	0	0	89	715
SD Grant (State Funds)	452	676	374	345	278	567	2,692
SD State Loan	0	0	0	0	75	0	75
SD Industry	0	296	50	0	48	76	470
SD FRA Loan	0	0	4,870	2,720	60	0	7,650
MN Grant (FRA Funds)	0	209	19	70	21	49	368
MN Grant (State Funds)	357	709	235	408	334	509	2,552
MN State Loan	0	2,898	263	967	5	0	4,133
MN Industry	0	336	129	210	0	40	715
DM&E Cash	3,967	1,817	2,147	5,702	2,994	5,178	21,805
Total	$5,402	$6,941	$8,087	$10,422	$3,815	$6,508	$41,175

[a]FRA=Federal Rail Administration.

Source: Company records.

employees have a positive attitude toward these efforts, although some feel they need more one-on-one contact. Total employment has gradually increased from 130 at start-up to 233 by April 1993. DM&E wages for its craft, clerical, and nonunion employees are shown in Exhibit 16–7. These wages are considered to be very competitive versus local rates.

DM&E remained nonunion until June 1990 when train crew, railcar repairmen, and electricians began to be represented by the United Transportation Union (UTU). One of the major complaints against DM&E was its failure to improve wages as compared to major railroads. Exhibit 16–8 shows the current DM&E and UTU wage scale agreement. Exhibit 16–9 gives a sample comparison of benefits offered by the DM&E and the Unionized National Railroad Plan.

The American Train Dispatchers Association attempted to organize DM&E dispatchers in 1989 but failed. The UTU attempted to organize DM&E engineering employees in 1991 but was rejected by a vote margin of 2 to 1. In August 1992 DM&E's car repairmen voted to decertify the UTU and form their own local union.

EXHIBIT 16-7 Craft, Clerical, and Nonunion Employees' Salary Ranges

GRADE	JOB TITLE(S)	GRADE	JOB TITLE(S)
1	Part-time or Temporary Nonexempt Employee	6	Assistant Track/B&B Foreman Machine Operator A Machine Operator B Road & Equipment Repairman
2	Administrative Assistant Accounting Clerk Operating Clerk Secretary	8	Track Inspector Track B&B Foreman Welder Signalman Mechanical Mechanic
4	Track/B&B Laborer Welder Helper Mechanical Laborer Clerk/Yard Clerk	10	Mechanical Foreman, Weekend Mechanical Foreman, Regular Mechanical Leadman

SALARY RANGES

GRADE	MINIMUM	25TH	MIDPOINT	75TH	MAXIMUM
1	5.20	5.85	6.45	7.10	7.70
2	7.15	7.75	8.40	9.00	9.65
4	9.05	9.80	10.65	11.40	12.25
6	9.55	10.35	11.20	12.00	12.90
8	10.05	10.90	11.85	12.70	13.65
10	10.80	11.70	12.70	13.60	14.60

Note: DM&E has admitted from the beginning that it could not match the train crew pay of unionized Class I railroads. Rates of pay are 15 to 25 percent below comparable wages on the C&NW. Extensive overtime on DM&E plus profit sharing and year-round employment (Class I railroads often have winter layoffs) undoubtedly narrows this gap.

Source: *DM&E Policy and Procedure Manual.*

EXHIBIT 16-8 Wage Scale Agreement, Rates of Pay

I. Regular assignments (straightaway and through freight runs). Overtime will begin at the expiration of eight (8) hours on runs of 100 miles or less.

| | PER DAY | | | | | PER MILE OVER |
	1/1/93	9/1/93	9/1/94	9/1/95	9/1/96	100 MILES
Conductor	$ 89.88	$ 93.48	$ 98.15	$102.57	$107.18	79.17¢
Engineer	$103.79	$107.94	$113.34	$118.44	$123.77	91.66¢
Brakeman	$ 83.56	$ 86.90	$ 91.25	$ 95.36	$ 99.65	74.07¢

II. Work trains and assignments that ordinarily do not leave terminal, or that operate out to points within 35 miles of the terminal.

| | PER DAY | | | | |
	1/1/93	9/1/93	9/1/94	9/1/95	9/1/96
Conductor	$100.01	$104.01	$109.21	$114.13	$119.26
Engineer	$107.67	$111.98	$117.58	$122.87	$128.40
Brakeman	$ 95.71	$ 99.54	$104.52	$109.22	$114.14

Note: DM&E uses bonus and merit pay to further reward employees. Bonuses for all nonmanagerial employees averaged $1,700 in 1990, $2,200 in 1991, and $2,700 in 1993. All but operating UTU nonmanagerial employees are eligible to receive performance appraisal–based merit pay. This incentive averaged 3 percent in 1990, 2 percent in 1991, and 3 percent in 1992. In addition, this category of employees received 3 percent across-the-board increases in 1990 and 1992.

The benefit package offered to DM&E employees equals or exceeds those provided by the major union railroads.

Source: DM&E and UTU Contract Agreement.

EXHIBIT 16-9 Sample Benefit Comparison

BENEFIT	DM&E	UNIONIZED NATIONAL RAILROAD PLAN
Life Insurance	$50,000	$10,000
Accidental D&D	$50,000	$8,000
401 (K)	Yes	Not Provided
Profit Sharing	Yes	Not Provided
Maximum Medical	$500,000	$500,000
Deductible	$100 each individual	$100 each individual
Maximum out-of-pocket	$500 individual, $1,000 family	$2,000 each person covered

Source: DM&E Benefit Brochures.

In November 1992 the International Association of Machinists failed in their attempt to organize the DM&E's mechanical employees.

Finance. DM&E has improved its financial condition since start-up. Operating revenues for 1991 were $37.9 million and traffic volume 51.4 thousand carloads, a 6.3 percent increase in revenues and a 2.2 percent decline in carloads. In 1992 operating revenue was $40.1 million with traffic volume of 55.1 thousand carloads, an increase of 5.8 and 7.2 percent respectively. During the first six months of 1993, operating revenues were $19.61 million compared to a nearly identical $19.62 million for the same period in 1992. At the same time, carloadings dropped from 25.6 thousand to 23.9 thousand, a decrease of 7.1 percent. Net income for the six-month period was 48 percent below last year. Exhibit 16–10 presents income statement data for the years 1990–1992.

Traffic volume from 1987 to 1992 increased in 7 of 12 commodity groups, with an overall increase of 22 percent. The largest increases were in bentonite clay, corn, woodchips, and kaolin clay. Major decreases in wheat and soybean oil were attributable to weather and market conditions rather than loss to other transportation modes. Increases in gross revenues were due to increased traffic and higher per car charges. (See Exhibit 16–11.)

Operating expenses rose 10.6 percent between 1990 and 1992. Increased traffic coupled with roadbed problems increased expenses in four of six categories. Decline in net income during the first six months of 1993 was attributable to increased car hire, derailment, and crew costs associated with repairing track.

Cash generated from operations is DM&E's primary source of funds for debt service, capital expenditures, and working capital. DM&E was highly leveraged at start-up and has been forced continually to ask for federal, state, and local financing to assist in roadbed maintenance. Governmental loans are at approximately 3 percent and have a delayed principle payment feature. Westinghouse Credit Corporation and C&NW loans average around 12.5 percent interest. DM&E continues to pay down its senior debt and has reduced its debt-to-equity ratio to 2.8 to 1. The ideal railroad debt-to-equity ratio is 1 to 1; 2 to 1 is considered highly leveraged in banking circles. In the May 1993 issue of *DM&E Enroute*, CFO Kurt Feaster stated that DM&E could be below 2 to 1 in two years. See Exhibit 16–12 for balance sheet information for 1990–1992.

C&NW

One of the most unusual twists in the DM&E–C&NW saga occurred in July 1992 when the C&NW unexpectedly backed out of their 1989 agreement to sell the Colony Line for $6.3 million (see Exhibit 16–13). Their excuse was that DM&E lacked financing, but McIntyre denied this charge and commented that "after months of negotiations and coming this far, we couldn't believe they would renege on their agreement." DM&E had hoped, by purchase of the Colony Line, to acquire the originating points of the 20,000 cars a year that are generated on this trackage, which would have permitted the DM&E to control subsequent routing of these cars and also increase their share of car revenues. Colony Line shippers and local and state authorities also expressed their concern about the change of events.

In August 1992 the Union Pacific Railroad (UP) requested ICC approval to acquire the majority, or even 100 percent, ownership of C&NW. Addition of

EXHIBIT 16-10 Dakota, Minnesota & Eastern Railroad Income Statements 1990–1992

	1990	1991	1992
REVENUES			
Freight	34,909	36,941	40,377
Other	660	976	577
Net Revenue	35,569	37,917	40,954
OPERATING EXPENSES			
Car Hire and Car Leases	4,927	5,332	5,723
Fuel	3,581	3,393	3,381
Accident Expense + Insurance	3,649	2,987	3,831
Transportation	5,900	6,848	7,288
Maintenance of Way (includes property tax)	3,177	3,673	3,515
Maintenance of Equipment	1,974	2,038	1,952
Total Operating Expenses	23,208	24,271	25,690
Gross Profit	12,361	13,646	15,264
GENERAL AND ADMINISTRATIVE EXPENSES			
Wages and Benefits	1,678	1,723	2,049
Professional Fees (includes audit)	830	432	599
Other	115	360	382
Other Expenses (Income)	(413)	(92)	(164)
EBITDA	10,151	11,223	12,398
Adjustments	0	0	(1,029)
ADJUSTED EBITDA	10,151	11,223	11,369
Depreciation and Amortization	2,689	2,947	3,314
EBIT	7,462	8,276	8,055
Interest—Revolver (net of interest income)	221	66	(10)
Interest—Westinghouse	2,975	2,725	2,319
Interest—CNW	697	810	991
Interest—Government Loans	235	266	249
Interest—First Bank/Tifco/etc.	117	124	148
Interest—New Debt	0	0	0
EBT	3,217	4,285	4,358
Income Tax	993	1,471	895
NET INCOME	2,224	2,814	3,463
Less Preferred Dividends—Reg.	186	186	186
Net Income Available to Common	2,038	2,628	3,277

Source: Company records.

EXHIBIT 16-11 Dakota, Minnesota & Eastern Railroad Corporation Top Eleven Commodities (1987–1992)

	GROSS FREIGHT REVENUE						REVENUE PER CARLOAD					
COMMODITY	1987	1988	1989	1990	1991	1992	1987	1988	1989	1990	1991	1992
Wheat	$ 9,687,565	$ 9,367,530	$ 7,131,587	$ 9,570,644	$11,809,116	$11,134,529	$890	$1,050	$1,070	$1,069	$1,121	$1,127
Bentonite Clay	0	0	745,517	7,913,920	9,651,590	10,806,305	—	—	1,007	1,171	1,066	1,118
Woodchips	2,781,150	3,821,725	3,755,085	4,274,558	3,544,238	3,888,649	984	1,120	1,088	1,134	1,097	1,160
Corn	1,270,934	1,830,224	2,673,626	3,803,260	2,969,148	3,278,697	250	360	317	364	369	387
Cement	2,383,082	2,931,008	2,588,389	1,602,287	1,613,215	2,219,796	824	821	826	811	743	778
Industrial Sand	509,150	510,321	746,693	971,763	462,578	684,565	164	187	184	193	195	201
Lumber/ Boards	74,893	81,599	92,333	852,319	626,959	534,014	454	563	847	1,033	956	978
Soybeans	734,869	1,261,295	726,857	1,099,612	1,042,046	1,149,938	238	311	382	377	377	387
Kaolin Clay	0	0	0	311,610	497,087	621,341	—	—	—	470	480	480
Soybean Oil	480,580	432,282	300,320	345,404	428,920	420,660	182	215	206	221	218	213
Wheat Flour	109,846	99,499	89,262	433,464	511,697	591,264	145	166	206	449	525	636
All Others	4,849,217	4,609,784	4,306,748	4,533,120	4,821,565	4,856,336	417	449	447	520	557	495
Total	$22,881,286	$24,945,267	$23,156,417	$35,711,961	$37,978,159	$40,186,094	$ 531	$ 584	$ 579	$ 679	$ 738	$ 729

Source: Company records.

the most powerful railroad in the United States to the C&NW equation, in the DM&E's opinion, would have severely restricted its already limited operational freedom. As a result, the DM&E intervened in the ICC proceedings requesting:

EXHIBIT 16-12 Dakota, Minnesota & Eastern Railroad Balance Sheets 1990–1992

	1990	1991	1992
ASSETS			
Cash	1,821	2,789	1,231
Accounts Receivable	5,061	6,937	6,555
Materials and Supplies Inventory	419	421	417
Prepaid Expenses	607	514	574
Total Current Assets	7,908	10,661	8,777
PP&E—Net	51,384	51,866	53,369
Capitalized Leases—Net	0	0	0
Deferred Finances & Other Assets	476	450	1,062
Total Assets	59,768	62,977	63,208
LIABILITIES AND STOCKHOLDERS' EQUITY			
Accounts Payable—Trade	2,963	2,400	1,834
Accounts Payable—International + Contract Allowance	1,351	1,670	1,158
Car Hire Payable	420	730	591
Notes Payable	284	283	286
Wages and Benefits Payable	1,598	1,548	1,519
Interest Payable	316	296	495
Other Accrued Liability	2,291	3,320	2,858
Total Current Liabilities	9,223	10,247	8,741
Deferred Income Tax Liability	3,050	4,427	4,784
Revolving Loan	1,616	2,000	2,000
Westinghouse Term Loans	22,071	18,959	16,105
CNW Term Loan	5,490	6,180	7,388
Government Loans—Net	10,969	10,778	10,652
First Bank	424	516	313
New Debt	0	0	0
Other Liabilities	683	876	874
Total Liabilities	53,526	53,983	50,857
Preferred Stock	1,651	1,838	2,025
Senior Preferred Stock	0	0	0
Common Stock	3,290	3,290	3,290
Retained Earnings	1,300	3,927	7,203
Treasury Stock	0	(61)	(167)
Total Stockholders' Equity	6,241	8,994	12,351
Total Liability & Stockholders' Equity	59,767	62,977	63,208

Source: Company records.

1. Enforcement of the sale of the Colony Line with trackage rights from Dakota Junction to Crawford, Nebraska, for an unrestricted connection with Burlington Northern, or trackage rights over both lines.
2. Removal of interchange restrictions at Winona, Mankato, Owatonna, and Mason City.
3. Allowing direct service to shippers at Winona and access to shippers via reciprocal switching agreement at the other three cities.
4. Modifying the car supply agreement, which requires the DM&E to use C&NW cars while at the same time not requiring the C&NW to furnish them. The DM&E could use cars from any source without C&NW penalty.

As of mid-July 1993 the entire matter remained under ICC study.

COMPETITION

DM&E's operations are subject to competition from railroads and trucks. There are several local and three major railroads that have lines in or near the DM&E service area. Aside from the C&NW, the 23,000-mile Burlington Northern (BN) trackage could prove to be a serious threat. Because of its size and resources, BN offers highly competitive rates and provides direct access to the Gulf, the Pacific Northwest, and the Midwest.

As major carriers continue selling off ancillary lines, opportunities remain for smaller railroads to pick up complementary trackage. C&NW's Minneapolis–Sioux City, Iowa, branch (277 miles), the Soo's corn lines across southern Minnesota (112

EXHIBIT 16-13 DM&E's North/South Trackage from Rapid City

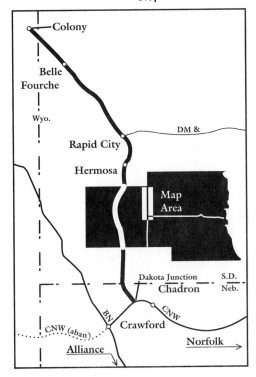

miles) and northern Iowa to the Mississippi River (253 miles), and BN's Sioux City to Aberdeen, South Dakota, route (265 miles), may fit this category for DM&E.

Trucks carry a greater share of intercity traffic than do railroads. Their innate flexibility, relatively low capital requirements, and huge network of tax-supported highways give them great advantage in smaller-volume and under-500-mile shipments. Railroads are very competitive in bulk shipments over long distances. Intermodal shipments (truck or container on rail flatcar) often offer the advantages of both modes to shippers. The DM&E faces the strongest truck competition in Minnesota.

CONCLUSION

Develop a three-year strategic plan for DM&E. Include ten major recommendations with associated costs or savings and pro forma financial statements. Prepare projected ratios to show the expected impact of your proposed strategies.

MOTORCYCLES AND MOTOR VEHICLES INDUSTRY NOTE

JOHN VANDERWOLF
Office of Consumer Goods

Constant-dollar product shipments of motorcycles and parts increased an estimated 5 percent in 1993. Imports of motorcycles were about 19 percent higher, while exports increased less than 1 percent. With domestic shipments and imports up, apparent consumption jumped 19 percent (Table 1).

The U.S. motorcycle market may have finally turned around. Since its peak in 1980 during the last oil crisis, the demand for motorcycles has slowly decreased. However, in 1992 new motorcycle registrations increased by almost 4 percent. New registrations for 1993 also are expected to be up; they were more than 5 percent higher during the first five months of the year.

The excess supply that had built up in the 1980s began to diminish in the early 1990s, as owners began looking for larger, newer motorcycles. The average age and income of motorcycle owners increased as baby boomers matured, so they began purchasing newer, bigger, more comfortable, and more expensive motorcycles. In 1980 the average age of the motorcycle owner was 24 years; in 1990 it was 31. The 26-to-35 age group generally makes more money ($34,032) than those under 25 ($14,319), according to the 1991 Consumer Expenditure Survey prepared by the Bureau of Labor Statistics. Therefore, many motorcycle owners have upgraded to a heavyweight motorcycle (an engine exceeding 750cc). The market for these motorcycles has been growing since 1987.

Table 1: Motorcycles and Parts: Domestic Shipments and Trade, 1988–94 (in millions of dollars except as noted)

ITEM	1991	1992[1]	1993[2]	1994[3]	PERCENT CHANGE (1991–1994)[4] 91–92	92–93	93–94
Product shipments	776.1	865.0	945.9		11.5	9.4	
Product shipments (1987$)	694.8	733.1	769.0	788.0	5.5	4.9	2.5
Apparent consumptions[5]	919.0	1,171.0	1,398.5		27.4	19.4	
Imports	583.9	802.7	952.6	1,025.0	37.5	18.7	7.6
Imports to apparent consumption (%)	63.5	68.5	68.1		7.9	–0.6	
Exports	441.0	496.7	500.0	525.0	12.6	0.7	5.0
Exports to shipments (%)	56.8	57.4	52.9		1.1	–7.9	

1. Estimated product shipments.

2. Estimated trade and product shipments.

3. Forecast.

4. Percent changes are calculated on more detailed data.

5. Apparent consumption = product shipments – exports + imports.

Source: U.S. Department of Commerce: Bureau of the Census; International Trade Administration (ITA). Estimates and forecasts by ITA.

The U.S. industry has benefited from this trend, as all three domestic manufacturers produce primarily large-engine class motorcycles. The two Japanese-owned manufacturing facilities in the United States produce most of their companies' heavyweight motorcycles sold in this country. However, the biggest beneficiary has been the sole U.S.-owned manufacturer, Harley-Davidson. Having saved itself from going out of business in the early 1980s, the company has rebounded to become the dominant supplier (67 percent) of heavyweight motorcycles in the U.S. market. Harley-Davidson's products have a unique style and appeal that have attracted many of the motorcycle owners in the baby boom generation.

Consumers' perceptions of motorcycle safety have been a negative force affecting demand. They often think that motorcycling is a dangerous hobby and one to avoid. However, this trend has abated to some degree. Easing consumers' safety concerns has been the decrease in accident rates of the last several years. In 1992 the rate of motorcycle accidents dropped 12 percent from 1991, to 206 accidents per 10,000 registered motorcycles. The Motorcycle Safety Foundation rider education programs have promoted the safe use of motorcycles, and the industry believes these programs have been effective.

Lessening concern about motorcycle safety and a decreasing supply of used motorcycles may explain the growth in sales of some other motorcycles, such as off-road, dual-purpose, and small-engine street motorcycles. These segments grew an estimated 10 percent in 1993.

U.S. Trade Patterns in 1992 Motorcycles, Bicycles, and Parts (SIC 3751) (in millions of dollars, percent)

EXPORTS	Value	Share	IMPORTS	Value	Share
Canada and Mexico	90	13.4	Canada and Mexico	18	1.1
European Community	306	45.5	European Community	94	6.1
Japan	81	12.0	Japan	804	52.3
East Asia NICs	28	4.2	East Asia NICs	599	39.0
South America	78	11.6	South America	3	0.2
Other	89	13.2	Other	20	1.3
World Total	671	100.0	World Total	1,537	100.0

TOP FIVE COUNTRIES	Value	Share		Value	Share
Germany	110	16.3	Japan	804	52.3
Netherlands	88	13.2	Taiwan	476	31.0
Japan	81	12.0	China	87	5.7
Canada	62	9.3	Italy	43	2.8
Argentina	54	8.1	Germany	32	2.1

Source:U.S. Department of Commerce: Bureau of the Census; International Trade Administration.

U.S. exports have become a more important factor in domestic production. The exports-to-shipments ratio reached a high of 57 percent in 1992, before dropping to 53 percent in 1993. As a result of the growth of U.S. experts, the industry's trade balance in general has improved significantly. In 1986 the trade deficit was $812 million; in 1993 it was an estimated $453 million. (The deficit reached a low of $143 million in 1991.)

Three major factors likely contributed to the 1993 slowdown in exports following 3 years of double-digit growth. First, overall economic growth in the major motorcycle markets has diminished. Second, Harley-Davidson decided to maintain 1993 production near 350 units per day, most of which is aimed to meet domestic market demand. Harley-Davidson has had difficulty meeting foreign demand for the last several years, preferring not to increase production at the expense of product quality. Therefore, many entrepreneurs stepped in and began exporting used Harleys, which is the likely reason that the exports-to-shipments ratio was so high in 1991 and 1992. However, it may be possible that the supply of used Harleys in

Trends and Forecasts: Motorcycles, Bicycles, and Parts (SIC 3751) (in millions of dollars except as noted)

ITEM	1991	1992[1]	1993[2]	1994[3]	PERCENT CHANGE (1991–1994)		
					91–92	92–93	93–94
INDUSTRY DATA							
Value of shipments[4]	1,914	2,100	2,226	—	9.7	6.0	—
Value of shipments (1987$)	1,701	1,784	1,858	1,906	4.9	4.1	2.6
Total employment (000)	10.8	11.4	12.0	—	5.6	5.3	—
Production workers (000)	8.5	9.0	9.5	—	5.9	5.6	—
Average hourly earnings ($)	11.69	11.10	11.45	—	-5.0	3.2	—
Capital expenditures	61.5	—	—	—	—	—	—
PRODUCT DATA							
Value of shipments[5]	2,112	2,300	2,449	—	8.9	6.5	—
Value of shipments (1987$)	1,877	1,954	2,044	2,087	4.1	4.6	2.1
TRADE DATA							
Value of imports	1,329	1,537	1,732	1,840	15.7	12.7	6.2
Value of exports	615	671	704	750	9.1	4.9	6.5

1. Estimate, except exports and imports.

2. Estimate.

3. Forecast.

4. Value of all products and services sold by establishments in the motorcycles, bicycles, and parts industry.

5. Value of products classified in the motorcycles, bicycles, and parts industry produced by all industries.

Source: U.S. Department of Commerce: Bureau of the Census; International Trade Administration (ITA). Estimates and forecasts by ITA.

the United States now has dried up to a degree, slowing export sales by these entrepreneurs.

The European Community (EC) is by far the largest foreign market for U.S. motorcycle exports, totaling an estimated $347 million in 1993, or 69 percent of exports. However, the market share of U.S. companies could be even greater if it were not for stringent noise emission standards in the EC—the third factor in slowing export growth. Meeting current noise regulations has forced reductions in the performance of U.S. motorcycles exported to the EC. Harley-Davidson has stated that standards proposed for 1997 cannot be met without design changes likely to be unacceptable to a majority of its customers.

U.S. manufacturers exported an estimated $93 million to Germany in 1993, down 4 percent from 1992. Germany was the largest individual country export market for U.S. motorcycles. The second-largest market was Canada at an estimated $90 million, up 24 percent from 1992. Japan was the third-largest foreign market—about $60 million, as U.S. exports there increased 10 percent.

In Japan several rules and regulations severely limit the potential export market for large U.S.-built motorcycles, including the extremely difficult operator license test for large motorcycles and the ban on carrying passengers on highways. According to the available evidence, these regulations do not contribute to safety or to other public purposes. Careful analysis of accident data demonstrates that larger motorcycles are less likely to be involved in accidents than smaller ones.

In 1993 U.S. imports of motorcycles grew an estimated 19 percent to $953 million. Japan is the largest foreign supplier of motorcycles, accounting for 86 percent of total U.S. imports. Taiwan, Germany, and Italy were the other major suppliers of motorcycles, accounting for 4 percent, 3.4 percent, and 2.6 percent of U.S. imports, respectively, in 1993.

Outlook for 1994. Constant-dollar product shipments of motorcycles and parts are forecast to increase 3 percent. Exports will be up about 5 percent and should benefit from improving economic growth in the major markets for motorcycles. Imports are expected to rise by about 8 percent in 1994. Apparent consumption will continue to grow but at a slower annual rate, estimated at 7 percent. Slower increases in personal disposable income will likely reduce the growth of personal consumption expenditures on motorcycles.

Long-term Prospects. Real domestic product shipments are expected to grow at an annual rate of 2 to 3 percent between 1993 and 1998, as both the export sector and the domestic market grow. The latter should stabilize or slightly increase. Demographic influences and safety concerns will continue to affect the domestic demand for motorcycles.

Foreign demand for motorcycles is expected to remain strong. Germany and Japan should continue to be the largest foreign markets for U.S. motorcycles. The economies of the Organization for Economic Cooperation and Development countries (major industrial nations) are expected to grow about 3 percent annually over the next four years. Growth in the U.S. share of the EC motorcycle markets will likely hinge on how effectively U.S. manufacturers are able to adapt to the new noise emission standards there.

The North American Free Trade Agreement will provide U.S. manufacturers with additional opportunities. Mexican tariffs for motorcycles, currently at 20 percent, are scheduled to be phased out over the next five years under NAFTA. Mexican tariffs for motorcycle parts, currently at 15 percent, were eliminated immediately upon implementation of the agreement. Furthermore, U.S. producers will likely benefit from increases in the Mexican standard of living, giving more consumers the chance to purchase a motorcycle.

The average age of a motorcycle owner is expected to continue to increase over the next five years, to at least 35 years. Consumers in the 35-to-54 age group generally reach their maximum earning potential. The 1992 Consumer Expenditures Survey reported that new motorcycle expenditures were the highest among these consumers.

The perception of danger associated with motorcycle riding may continue to affect sales. However, if accident rates continue to decline, any negative effects on sales should be minimized. The trend toward large touring motorcycles will contribute to lower accident rates. In general, motorcycle manufacturers should expect much better results in the next five years than they experienced in the last ten years.

HARLEY-DAVIDSON—1994

C A S E
17
FRED R. DAVID
Francis Marion University
CHARLES SHRADER
Iowa State University

Over the last decade, Harley-Davidson took itself from the brink of destruction to its current status as one of the most admired companies in the world. Headquartered in Milwaukee, Wisconsin, Harley (414-342-4680) is now winning the battle among the heavyweight motorcycle competitors—Honda, Kawasaki, Suzuki, and Yamaha. Harley has gained a 60 percent share of the heavyweight motorcycle market-share in the United States and 15 percent internationally. However, the company has an unusual—and big—problem: Because of a lack of plant capacity, Harley cannot meet demand for its motorcycles. Customers worldwide who order a new Harley must wait at least a year for delivery. Dealers are upset; they have no inventory. Consumers are upset. Harley plans to increase motorcycle production from 76,000 units in 1992 to over 100,000 units annually by 1996, but analysts contend this planned increase is still far below demand.

The Harley-Davidson corporate vision is given as follows:

> Harley-Davidson is an action-oriented, international company—a leader in its commitment to continuously improve the quality of profitable relationships with stakeholders (customers, employees, suppliers, shareholders, governments, and society). Harley-Davidson believes the key to success is to balance stakeholders' interests through the empowerment of all employers to focus on value-added activities.

HISTORY

The Harley-Davidson story began in 1903 when William Harley, aged 21 and a draftsman at a Milwaukee manufacturing firm, designed and built a motorcycle with the help of three Davidson brothers: Arthur, a pattern maker; Walter, a railroad mechanic; and William, a tool maker. At first, the brothers tinkered with ideas, motors, and old bicycle frames. Legend has it that their first carburetor was fashioned from a tin can. They were able to make a 3-horsepower, 25-cubic-inch engine and successfully road tested the first motored cycle.

Operating out of a shed in the Davidson family's backyard, the men built and sold three motorcycles. Production was expanded to eight in 1904 and in 1906 the company's first building was erected on the current site of the main offices in Milwaukee, Wisconsin. Harley-Davidson Motor Company was incorporated in 1907, and Arthur set off to recruit dealers in New England and the South. William completed a degree in engineering, specializing in internal combustion engines, and quickly applied his expertise in the company; he developed the first V-twin engine in 1909. He followed this with a major breakthrough in 1912—the first commercially successful motorcycle clutch. This made possible the use of a roller chain to power the motorcycle. The first three-speed transmission was offered in 1915.

During the early 1900s the United States experienced rapid growth in the motorcycle industry, with firms such as Excelsior, Indian, Merkel, Thor, and Yale growing and competing. Most of the early U.S. motorcycle companies turned out shoddy, unreliable products. But this was not considered to be true of Harley-Davidson and Indian cycles. Early continued success in racing and endurance made Harley a favorite among motorcyclists. The company's V-twin engines became known for power and reliability.

During World War I, Harley-Davidson supplied the military with motorcycles and became the largest motorcycle company in the world in 1918. The company built a 300,000-square-foot plant in Milwaukee in 1922. In 1949 Harley first faced international competition from British motorcycles, such as Nortons and Triumphs, which handled better and were cheaper, lighter, and just as fast, even though they had smaller engines. To counter the British threat, Harley-Davidson improved the design of their engines and increased the horsepower of their heavier cycles. The result, in 1957, was the first modern superbike: the Harley Sportster. It was also during the 1950s that Harley developed the styling that is famous to this day.

In an attempt to expand production capacity and raise capital, Harley went public in 1965 and then merged with the conglomerate AMF, Inc. (American Machine and Foundry) in 1969. Known for its leisure and industrial products, AMF expanded Harley's production capacity from 15,000 units to 40,000 units in 1974. With the expanded capacity, AMF pursued a milking strategy, favoring short-term profits rather than investment in research and development and retooling. Japanese motorcycle manufacturers, however, continued to improve, whereas Harley began to turn out heavy, noisy, vibrating, laboriously handling, poorly finished machines.

In 1975 Honda Motor Company introduced the Gold Wing, which quickly became the standard for large touring motorcycles, a segment that Harley had owned. At the time, Harley's top-of-the-line touring bike sold for almost $9,000, while the comparable Honda Gold Wing was approximately $7,000. Not only were Japanese cycles priced less than similar Harleys, but Japanese manufacturing techniques yielded operating costs that were 30 percent lower than Harley.

Motorcycle enthusiasts more than ever began to go with Japanese products because of their price and performance advantages. Even some loyal Harley owners and police department contracts were lost. The company was rapidly losing ground in both technological advances and the market. Starting in 1975 and continuing through the mid-1980s, Japanese companies penetrated the big-bore, custom motorcycle market with Harley look-alikes sporting V-twin engines. The Honda Magna and Shadow, the Suzuki Intruder, and the Yamaha Virago were representative of the Japanese imitations. The Japanese captured a significant share of the large cycle segment and controlled nearly 90 percent of the total motorcycle market.

Vaughn L. Beals, Jr., served as the Harley-Davidson manager during its six years under AMF control. Beals was uncomfortable with AMF's short-term orientation and unwillingness to confront the problems caused by imports. Consequently, in June 1981 a subgroup of Harley management, including Beals, completed a leveraged buyout of Harley-Davidson from AMF. To celebrate, Beals and the management team made a Pennsylvania-to-Wisconsin motorcycle ride, proclaiming as their slogan, "the eagle soars alone."

Beals himself was an engineer who simply loved motorcycles. He surrounded himself with a team that loved motorcycles as well. No longer was the company run by AFM's "finance guys." It was now run by a group of motorcycle riders. Under the management of Beals, Richard Teerlink, and Thomas Gelb, Harley-Davidson adopted a very efficient approach to manufacturing. Three major programs comprise the manufacturing approach: materials as needed (MAN) or just-in-time inventory, statistical operator control (SOC), and employee involvement.

Under the MAN system, Harley suppliers must comply with the company's quality requirements. Harley offers long-term contracts to suppliers who do comply and who deliver only the exact quantity needed for a given period of time. Harley also transports materials from suppliers. When the Harley transportation company makes scheduled pickups from suppliers, Harley has greater control over the shipments and is thereby able to cut costs.

Harley invests heavily in research and development. One payoff of this investment is a computer-aided design (CAD) system that allows management to make changes in the entire product line while maintaining elements of the traditional styling. Harley is recognized as an industry leader in many aspects of production, including belt-driven technology, vibration isolation, and steering geometry.

Employee involvement at Harley means the full participation of all employees in the continuous improvement process. Decisions made in quality circles are a major source of input for quality improvement. Employees participate in meetings and have a stake in the success of the company through bonus programs that share financial rewards and the Employee Stock Purchase Program. The employee involvement practices at Harley ensure high morale, low absenteeism, and few grievances.

Harley's purchasing strategy includes working with suppliers that are close to Harley's own facilities. Nearly 80 percent of the company's suppliers are located within 180 miles of Milwaukee. Proximity to suppliers means that the MAN system and just-in-time inventory practices are easier to implement. Plant productivity has continued to improve in the 1990s. For example, the York plant produced approximately 160 motorcycles a day in 1987 and 285 a day in 1990, and currently produces over 300 motorcycles a day. The concern for quality is transmitted to dealers as well. Harley mechanics at dealerships are expected to take a series of qualifying examinations dealing with 24 motorcycle repair categories. Exam questions deal with categories such as transmission, suspension, and electronics repair. Mechanics receive factory training and support, and dealers keep their customers apprised of how well the local mechanics are doing.

HARLEY DIVISIONS

Harley operates in two segments: (1) Motorcycles and Related Products and (2) Transportation Vehicles. Harley's Motorcycles and Related Products segment designs, manufactures, and sells superheavyweight (engine displacement of 851cc or above) touring and custom motorcycles and a broad range of related products. Harley is the only major American motorcycle manufacturer. The company's bike sales abroad exceeded $285 million in 1993, or 24 percent of their $1.2 billion total.

The Transportation Vehicles segment consists entirely of Holiday Rambler Corporation and its subsidiaries. Holiday Rambler is a wholly owned subsidiary that manufactures recreational vehicles, principally motorhomes and travel trailers, and specialized commercial vehicles. Holiday Rambler began manufacturing recreational vehicles in 1953 and was acquired by Harley in 1986. Holiday Rambler's recreational vehicle sales declined 12 percent in 1993 to about $65 million. Holiday Rambler's commercial vehicles (marketed under the Utilimaster brand name), which include walk-in vans and parcel delivery trucks, are built for a diverse range of specialized commercial uses.

Revenue, operating profit (loss), and identifiable assets attributable to each of Harley's segments are as follows (in thousands):

	MOTORCYCLES AND RELATED	TRANSPORTATION VEHICLES	CORPORATE
1992			
Revenue	$822,929	$282,355	$ —
Operating Income (loss)	102,300	2,137	(7,240)
Identifiable Assets	341,940	178,252	1,972
1991			
Revenue	$701,969	$237,894	$ —
Operating Income (loss)	89,551	(13,427)	(7,479)
Identifiable Assets	281,790	189,326	3,117
1990			
Revenue	$624,027	$240,573	$ —
Operating Income (loss)	90,219	825	(7,669)
Identifiable Assets	227,819	177,498	2,150

During 1992 the recreational vehicle industry reported volume increases for the first time in three years. Most of the increase was realized in the middle-to-low price segment of the market. The Recreational Vehicle division generally targets its products toward the middle-to-upper price segment of the market.

Motorcycles and Related Products. Harley's motorcycle products emphasize traditional styling, design simplicity, durability, ease of service and evolutionary change. Studies indicate that the typical Harley motorcycle owner is a male in his late thirties with a household income of approximately $53,000, who purchases a motorcycle for recreational rather than transportational purposes, and who is an experienced motorcycle rider. Approximately two-thirds of Harley's sales are to buyers with at least one year of higher education.

The superheavyweight class of motorcycles comprises four types: standard, which emphasizes simplicity and cost; performance, which emphasizes racing and speed; touring, which emphasizes comfort and amenities for long-distance travel; and custom, which emphasizes styling and individual owner customization. Touring and custom models are the only class of superheavyweight motorcycle that Harley manufactures. Harley sells 20 models of touring and custom superheavyweight motorcycles, with suggested retail prices ranging from approximately $5,000 to $16,000. The touring segment of the superheavyweight market was pioneered by Harley and includes motorcycles equipped for long-distance touring, with fairings, windshields, saddlebags, and Tour Pak. The custom segment of the market includes motorcycles featuring the distinctive styling associated with certain classic Harley-Davidson motorcycles. These motorcycles are highly customized through the use of trim and accessories. Harley's motorcycles are based on variations of five basic chassis designs and are powered by three air-cooled, twin-cylinder engines of "V" configuration that have displacement of 883 cc, 120 cc, and 1,340 cc. Harley manufactures its own engines and frames.

The top of Harley's custom product line is typically priced at approximately twice that of its competitors' custom motorcycles. The custom portion of the Harley product line represents the highest unit volumes and continues to command a price premium because of its features, styling, and high resale value. Harley's smallest displacement custom motorcycle (the 883 cc Sportster) is directly price competitive with competitors' comparable motorcycles. Surveys of retail purchasers indicate that, historically, over 80 percent of the purchasers of this Sportster model have come from competitive-brand motorcycles or are people new to the sport of motorcycling. Domestically, motorcycle sales generated 52.8 percent, 50.6 percent, and 50.7 percent of revenues in the Motorcycles and Related Products segment during 1992, 1991, and 1990 respectively.

Harley's Motorcycle Products business consists primarily of parts and accessories and rider apparel. The major product categories for motorcycle parts are replacement parts, mechanical accessories, rider accessories (MotorClothes), and specially formulated oil and other lubricants. Harley's replacement parts include original equipment parts, generally made in the United States, and a less expensive line of imported parts introduced to compete against foreign-sourced aftermarket suppliers. Harley provides a variety of services to its dealers and retail customers, including optional extended-service contracts, insurance programs, service training schools, delivery of its motorcycles, motorcycling vacations, memberships in an owners club, and customized software packages. Harley has had recent success under a program emphasizing modern store design and display techniques in the merchandising of parts and accessories by its dealers. Currently more than 370 domestic and 90 international dealerships have completed, or are in the process of, store design renovation projects. Domestic motorcycle parts and accessories sales comprised 15.3 percent, 14.9 percent, and 14.8 percent of net sales in the Motorcycles and Related Products segment in 1992, 1991, and 1990, respectively. Net sales from motorcycle parts and accessories have grown 71.2 percent over the last three years (since 1989).

Licensing. In recent years, Harley has endeavored to create an awareness of the brand among the nonriding public by licensing the trademark "Harley-Davidson" through production and sales of a broad range of consumer items, including t-shirts and other clothing, trading cards, jewelry, small leather goods, and toys. Although the majority of licensing activity occurs in the United States, Harley has expanded into international markets.

This licensing activity provides Harley with a valuable source of advertising. Licensing also has proven to be an effective means for enhancing Harley's image with consumers and provides an important tool for policing the unauthorized use of Harley's trademarks. Royalty revenues from licensing accounted for approximately 1 percent of the net sales from the Motorcycles and Related Products segment during each of the three years in the period ended December 31, 1992. Though net sales from licensing activities are small, the profitability of this business is relatively high.

Marketing and Distribution. Harley's basic channel of United States distribution for its motorcycles and related products is approximately 600 independently owned full-service dealerships. With respect to sales of new motorcycles, approximately 75 percent of the dealerships sell Harley motorcycles exclusively. All dealerships carry Harley's replacement parts and aftermarket accessories and perform servicing of Harley motorcycle products.

Harley's marketing efforts are divided among dealer promotions, customer events, magazine and direct-mail advertising, public relations, and cooperative programs with dealers. Harley also sponsors racing activities and special promotional events and participates in all major motorcycle consumer shows and rallies. In an effort to encourage Harley owners to become more actively involved in the sport of motorcycling, Harley formed a riders club in 1983. The Harley Owners Group (HOG) currently has in excess of 192,000 members worldwide and is the industry's largest company-sponsored enthusiast organization. In addition, Harley is a national sponsor of the Muscular Dystrophy Association. Harley's expenditures on domestic marketing and advertising were approximately $4.52 million, $36.1 million, and $34.7 million during 1992, 1991, and 1990, respectively.

International Sales. International sales were $240 million, $205 million, and $176 million, accounting for approximately 29 percent, 29 percent, and 28 percent of net sales of the Motorcycles and Related Products segment during 1992, 1991, and 1990, respectively. Harley believes that the international heavyweight market (engine displacements of 751cc and above) is growing and is significantly larger than the U.S. heavyweight market. Harley has wholly owned subsidiaries located in Germany, Japan, and the United Kingdom. The German subsidiary also serves Austria and France. The combined foreign subsidiaries have a network of 118 dealers, of which approximately 43 percent sell Harley motorcycles exclusively. Elsewhere, sales are managed through 17 distributors in 14 countries. These distributors service approximately 280 additional countries who primarily seek fleet sales and parts orders. Germany, Japan, Canada, and France, in descending order, represent Harley's largest export sales.

Competition. The United States and international superheavyweight/heavyweight motorcycle markets are highly competitive. Harley's competitors, Yamaha, Honda, Suzuki, and Kawasaki, have financial and marketing resources greater than Harley's as well as larger overall sales volumes and a more diversified product line. During 1992 the superheavyweight segment represented 32 percent of the total United States motorcycle market in terms of units registered. The touring and custom segments of the superheavyweight motorcycle market together accounted for 73 percent, 72 percent, and 77 percent of total superheavyweight segment retail unit sales in the United States during 1992, 1991, and 1990, respectively. Custom and touring motorcycles are generally the most expensive and most profitable vehicles in the market. Resale prices of Harley-Davidson motorcycles, as a percentage of price when new, are significantly higher than resale prices of motorcycles sold by the competitors. The primary reason for this is that production of Harley bikes is more than a year behind demand.

Harley estimates its worldwide competitive position to be as follows:

751+ cc Motorcycles Registration Data (Units in thousands)

	1992	1991	1990
North America:			
Total registrations	92.3	80.7	84.2
Harley-Davidson registrations	56.0	48.3	50.2
Harley-Davidson market share percentage	60.6%	59.9%	59.6%
Europe:			
Total registrations	128.0	104.9	96.1
Harley-Davidson registrations	12.5	10.7	8.7
Harley-Davidson market share percentage	9.7%	10.2%	9.0%
Japan/Australia:			
Total registrations	28.2	24.6	26.1
Harley-Davidson registrations	5.2	5.2	4.8
Harley-Davidson market share percentage	18.4%	21.1%	18.4%

1. Includes the United States and Canada.

2. Includes Austria, Belgium, France, Germany, Italy, Netherlands, Spain, Switzerland, and United Kingdom.

3. Data for Queensland, Northern Territory, and South Australia not available.

Employees. As of December 31, 1992, the Motorcycles and Related Products segment had approximately 4,000 employees. Production workers at the motorcycle manufacturing facilities in Wauwatosa and Tomahawk, Wisconsin, are represented principally by the Allied Industrial Workers (AIW) of the AFL-CIO, as well as the International Association of Machinist and Aerospace Workers (IAM). Production workers at the motorcycle manufacturing facility in York, Pennsylvania, are represented principally by the IAM. The collective bargaining agreements with the AIW and the Wisconsin-IAM expired March 27, 1994, and the collective bargaining agreement with the Pennsylvania-IAM expired February 2, 1994.

Transportation Vehicles.

Recreational Vehicles. The Recreational Vehicle division's motorhomes and travel trailers are designed to appeal to people interested in travel and outdoor recreational activities. These recreational vehicles are distinct from mobile homes, which are manufactured housing designed for permanent and semipermanent dwelling.

Principal types of recreational vehicles produced by the Recreational Vehicle division include Class A or "conventional" motorhomes, Class C or "mini" motorhomes, and travel trailers. Recreational vehicle classifications are based on standards established by the Recreation Vehicle Industry Association (RVIA). A motorhome is a self-powered vehicle built on a motor vehicle chassis. The interior typically includes a driver's area, kitchen, bathroom, and dining and sleeping areas. Motorhomes are self-contained, with their own lighting, heating, cooking, refrigeration, sewage-holding and water-storage facilities, so that they can be lived in without being attached to utilities. As such, they generally qualify as second homes for income-tax purposes. Although they generally are not designed to provide complete facilities for permanent or semipermanent living, motorhomes do provide comfortable living facilities for short periods of time.

Class A motorhomes are constructed of medium-duty truck chassis, which are purchased with engine and drive-train components. The living area and driver's compartment are designed, manufactured, and installed by the Recreational Vehicle Division. Class C motorhomes are built on a van or small truck chassis, which are purchased with engine and drive-train components and a finished access to the driver's compartment.

Travel trailers are nonmotorized vehicles designed to be towed by passenger automobiles, pick-up trucks, sport utility vehicles, or vans. They are otherwise similar to motorhomes in features and use. Harley produces both "conventional" and "fifth-wheel" travel trailers. Conventional travel trailers are towed by means of a bumper or frame hitch attached to the towing vehicle. Fifth-wheel trailers, designed to be towed by pick-up trucks, are constructed with a raised forward section that is attached to the bed area of the pick-up truck. This design allows a bilevel floor plan and additional living space.

Harley's premium lines of recreational vehicles are marketed under the Navigator and Imperial brand names. Models in these lines are manufactured with high-quality materials and components, including entertainment centers, solid-oak cabinetry, and brass fixtures, and may be equipped with luxury features such as microwave-convection ovens, washer/dryers, and built-in vacuum cleaner systems. These models are generally purchased by people who previously have owned recreational vehicles. The Navigator is a bus-style motorhome that carries a suggested retail price of $193,000 to $220,000. In Harley's Imperial line, suggested retail prices of motorhomes generally range between $105,000 and $125,000, and of travel trailers between $37,000 and $64,000.

Harley also produces motorhomes and travel trailers for the midrange market under the Aluma-Lite brand name. These models are produced with fewer standard features than the Imperial. Suggested retail prices for the Aluma-Lite line range between $48,000 and $95,000 for motorhomes and between $18,000 and $54,000 for travel trailers. Also in the midrange market, Harley produces the Endeavor and the Vacationer motorhome models. Suggested retail prices in these lines range between $47,000 and $76,000.

The following table presents information regarding wholesale sales of Harley's recreational vehicles during the periods indicated:

Wholesale Sales Sales, Year Ended December 31, (in thousands)

	1992	1991	1990
Premium lines	$ 71,643	$ 41,246	$ 37,561
Midrange lines	76,418	79,788	76,202
Other	—	—	2,553
Total	$148,061	$121,034	$116,316

In addition to wholesale sales of the Recreational Vehicle division's products shown above, sales by the Recreational Vehicle division also include retail sales by wholly owned Holiday World stores. The Recreational Vehicle division's sales (including retail, wholesale, and other sales) were $202.1 million, $170.6 million, and $166.5 million in 1992, 1991, and 1990, respectively. Sales of the Recreational Vehicle division accounted for 71.6 percent, 71.7 percent, and 69.2 percent of the Transportation Vehicle segment's revenues for the years ended December 31, 1992, 1991, and 1990, respectively.

Competition and Other Business Considerations. The recreational vehicle market is highly competitive among a number of manufacturers. Competition is based on price, design, quality, and service. The primary external factors affecting the recreational vehicle industry are the consumer's perception of health of the economy, interest rates, availability of retail financing, and the availability of gasoline. Harley believes that all of these items have played significant roles during the recent, three-year downcycle in the recreational vehicle industry.

Fifteen manufacturers account for approximately 87 percent of total units sold in the recreational vehicle market classifications in which the Recreational Vehicle division competes. The remaining units include products manufactured by approximately 50 additional manufacturers. Fleetwood Enterprises, Inc. accounts for approximately 37 percent and 28 percent of the Class A and travel trailer markets, respectively. Harley's share of the Class A and travel trailer markets is 5.3 percent and 2.6 percent, respectively. Harley ranks fourth in Class A market share and ninth in travel trailer market share. Coachmen and Winnebago are two other large competitors in this market.

Marketing and Distributing. The Recreational Vehicle division markets its recreational vehicle products through a network of approximately 140 dealers located throughout the continental United States, including 12 company-owned Holiday World dealers. Holiday World dealers also stock previously owned vehicles and new recreational vehicles manufactured by certain of Holiday Rambler's competitors. Holiday World dealers provide Holiday Rambler with valuable knowledge regarding consumer preferences and information regarding products of its competitors, as well as other marketing information. Holiday Rambler's sales and service agreements require dealers to maintain a service department and a supply of recreational vehicle parts, supplies, and accessories. These agreements are subject to renewal on an annual basis.

Holiday Rambler is gearing its marketing effort to be more responsive to its customers' needs. Holiday Rambler has redesigned a number of its stores, expanded its roster of dealers, and continues the development of new product offerings.

Holiday Rambler's new owner questionnaires indicate that approximately 68 percent of purchasers of Holiday Rambler's new recreational vehicles are 56 years or older, a growing segment of the U.S. population. Customer loyalty is reinforced by Holiday Rambler's sponsorship of the Holiday Ramblers Recreational Vehicle Club, Inc., a not-for-profit corporation. The club is open only to owners of Holiday Rambler's recreational vehicles and has approximately 12,500 members. The club holds 34 club-sponsored rallies and caravans each year and is provided with administrative and promotional assistance by Holiday Rambler. Holiday Rambler receives valuable feedback from its customers at these events.

COMMERCIAL VEHICLES

Through its Utilimaster Corporation subsidiary, Harley builds truck bodies for specialized commercial uses. Sales of Harley's commercial vehicles and truck bodies accounted for 24.0 percent, 23.4 percent, and 25.7 percent of the Transportation Vehicle segment's revenues in 1992, 1991, and 1990, respectively.

Utilimaster currently installs truck bodies on chassis of various sizes supplied by third parties. The truck bodies are offered in aluminum or fiberglass-reinforced plywood (FRP) construction and are available in lengths of 9 to 28 feet. Harley's products (excluding chassis) range in price from $2,300 to $34,000 although special service vehicles can sell as high as $55,000.

The principal types of commercial bodies are as follows:

Parcel Delivery Vans. Aluminum or FRP parcel delivery van bodies are installed on chopped van chassis supplied by major Detroit truck manufacturers. These parcel delivery van bodies that are manufactured by Harley range in length from 10 to 16 feet and are primarily used for local delivery of parcels, freight, and perishables.

Standard Walk-In Vans. Utilimaster manufactures its standard walk-in vans (stepvans) on a truck chassis supplied with engine and drive-train components, but without a cab. Harley fabricates the driver's compartment and body using aluminum panels. Uses for these vans include the distribution of food products and small packages.

Truck Bodies. Utilimaster's truck bodies are typically up to 28 feet in length with prepainted aluminum or FRP panels, aerodynamic front and side corners, hardwood floors, and various door configurations to accommodate end-user loading and unloading requirements. These products are used for diversified dry freight transportation. Harley installs its truck bodies on chassis supplied with a finished cab.

Mobile Rescue and Special Use Emergency Vehicles. Utilimaster builds a variety of specialty use vehicles for the fire and rescue industry. These vehicles range in length from 10 to 22 feet and usually require extensive customization to meet the needs of the local emergency agencies.

Aeromate. The Aeromate was developed for customers needing a midsize delivery vehicle that offered maneuverability, front-wheel drive, fuel efficiency, a large cargo area, and driver comfort, features not available from production vans and larger delivery vans. Its six-cylinder engine, automatic transmission, and drive train are purchased from a third party in the automotive industry and retrofitted to the Harley-built chassis. The all-aluminum truck body can hold 317 cubic feet of cargo, weighing up to one ton.

Marketing and Distribution. Utilimaster markets its commercial vehicles and bodies directly to 450 fleet accounts and to single commercial vehicles purchasers through a network of 900 automobile and truck dealers. This network is distinct from Harley's recreational-vehicle dealer network. Harley does not provide financing to these dealers or fleet accounts.

Competition. Though the Commercial Vehicle division experiences some competition from the large automotive manufacturers, which traditionally have offered a narrow selection of standardized commercial-vehicle body options for their truck chassis, its principle competition is from a small number of manufacturers with the resources to satisfy the volume requirements and specialized needs of commercial-vehicle fleet customers. These manufacturers include Grumman Corporation, Union City Body Company, Inc., and Supreme Corporation. Competition among manufacturers is based on price, quality, and responsiveness to customer requirements both in design and timing of delivery.

PROPERTIES

The following is a summary of the principle properties of the company's Motorcycles and Related Products segment:

TYPE OF FACILITY	LOCATION	SQUARE FEET	STATUS
Executive Offices, Engineering, and Warehouse	Milwaukee, WI	502,720	Owned
Manufacturing	Wauwatosa, WI	317,734	Owned
Manufacturing	Tomahawk, WI	70,327	Owned
Manufacturing	York, PA	949,380	Owned
Motorcycle Testing	Talladega, AL	11,500	Lease expiring 1996
Office and Warehouse	Morfelden-Walldorf, Germany	50,880	Lease expiring 2001
Office	Tokyo, Japan	3,090	Lease expiring 1993
Warehouse	Tokyo, Japan	6,282	Lease expiring 1993
Office	Brackley, England	2,845	Lease expiring 1995
Warehouse	Brackley, England	1,122	Lease expiring 1995

The Motorcycles and Related Products segment has three facilities that perform manufacturing operations: Wauwatosa, Wisconsin, a suburb of Milwaukee (motorcycle power train production); Tomahawk, Wisconsin (fiberglass parts production and painting); and York, Pennsylvania (motorcycle parts fabrication, painting, and assembly). Harley completed the transition to a new paint facility at its York, Pennsylvania, location during 1992.

Harley anticipates that the size of the existing facilities should be adequate to meet its current goal of being able to produce 100,000 motorcycles annually by 1996.

The principal properties of the Transportation Vehicle segment are as follows:

TYPE OF FACILITY	LOCATION	SQUARE FEET	STATUS
Executive Offices	Wakarusa, IN	51,178	Owned
Manufacturing and Warehouse	Wakarusa, IN	842,367	Owned
Factory Service Center	Wakarusa, IN	41,138	Owned
Purchasing and Quality Cont.	Wakarusa, IN	23,850	Owned
Research and Development	Wakarusa, IN	38,120	Owned
Sales Facilities	Various	8,290	Leased
Manufacturing and Offices	Nappanee, IN	169,711	Owned
Manufacturing	Mishawaka, IN	16,180	Owned
Retail Dealership Facilities	Various	201,900	Owned
Retail Dealership Facilities	Various	2,724	Leased

The Transportation Vehicles segment's units are manufactured in approximately 30 separate buildings. Additionally, the segment owns 20 buildings used for administrative, storage, and other purposes. Substantially all of the facilities are located on three sites at or near the Transportation Vehicles segment's corporate headquarters in Wakarusa, Indiana. Harley owns all of the production facilities and the underlying parcels of land. Because recreational and commercial vehicles are produced largely through a labor-intensive assembly process, the facilities do not house extensive capital equipment. The Transportation Vehicle segment's present facilities are generally adequate for their current intended use. Capacity increases may be achieved at a relatively low cost, largely by adding production employees.

FINANCIAL PERFORMANCE

Harley's financial performance improved steadily from 1988 to 1992. Harley has been able to reduce its long-term debt from $168 million in 1988 to $19 million in 1992. Harley reported worldwide net sales during 1992 of $1.1 billion. Worldwide motorcycle demand continues to outpace production, and dealers throughout the world remain on an allocation program that limits the number of motorcycles that may be ordered. Harley expects worldwide motorcycle demand to outpace production through 1996.

Harley held approximately 63 percent of the superheavyweight segment (engine displacement of 851 cc and above) of the domestic motorcycle market during 1992 and 1991. United States registrations of superheavyweight motorcycles increased by 10,637 units (14.9 percent) during 1992. Although definitive market share information does not exist for many of the smaller foreign markets, Harley estimates that it holds an average market share of approximately 13 percent in the heavyweight segment (751 cc and above) of the foreign markets in which it competes. Outside of the United States, registration data are generally not available for the superheavyweight classification.

Total international revenues in the Motorcycles and Related Products segment increased 16.6 percent to $239.5 million during 1992. Revenue from international motorcycle sales and parts and accessories sales increased 17.1 percent and 13.5 percent, respectively, during 1992, despite reported consumer concerns regarding worldwide economic conditions. Over the past three years approximately 31 percent of all motorcycle unit production has been allocated and shipped to international markets.

Worldwide, the motorcycle parts and accessories business reported a 19.5 percent revenue increase over 1991. The MotorClothes line of rider accessories increased $15.3 million (approximately 45 percent) during the same period. The MotorClothes line has begun to attract "nontraditional" customers and is increasing floor traffic at dealerships. Margins on the MotorClothes line are slightly lower than the margins generated by the other major parts and accessories lines.

The Transportation Vehicles segment reported a $44.5 million (18.7 percent) revenue increase compared to 1991. The Recreational Vehicle division provided the majority of the increase. Improvements in market conditions, as well as introductions of several new products during the year, contributed to the Recreational Vehicle division's revenue increase. The division began shipping the new "bus style" Navigator motorhome at the end of the second quarter, which generated the division's largest single source of revenue increase during 1992. Revenue also benefited from a $16.6 million increase in total sales at the division's 12 retail Holiday World stores. Approximately $9.4 million of this increase was the result of two new retail Holiday World stores, in California, which opened at the beginning of 1992.

The Motorcycles and Related Products segment reported a $48.8 million (24.4 percent) increase in gross profit compared to 1991. Motorcycle volume increases accounted for approximately one-half of the change. Improvements in the gross profit percentage were primarily the result of a shift in motorcycle mix toward higher-margin custom units. The shift in product mix accounted for approximately one-third of the segment's increase in gross profit. The Motorcycle division's focus during 1993 was on identifying and eliminating manufacturing waste and inefficiencies and improving product quality rather than expanding capacity.

The Transportation Vehicles segment reported a $13.9 million (42.8 percent) increase in gross profit compared to 1991. The gross profit percentage for the segment improved to 16.4 percent during 1992 from 13.6 percent in 1991. Gross profit in the Recreational Vehicle division showed improvement due, in part, to the introduction of the Navigator motorhome. The division also benefited from a shift in product mix within the towable lines toward higher-margin, fifth-wheel products. The gross profit percentage at the Commercial Vehicle division increased during 1992, due to higher sales volume and lower warranty costs.

THE HARLEY IMAGE

Few motorcycle companies can elicit the name recognition and brand loyalty of Harley-Davidson. Harley's appeal is based on the thrill and prestige of owning and riding the king of big bikes. Harleys are known as sturdy, powerful, macho bikes that are not for wimps and kids—true bikes for the open road.

Part of the Harley image is built on an appreciation of tradition. Harley bikes are considered to be of classic design. The teardrop gas tanks, the "soft-tail" suspensions, and the low, uneven rumble of Harley engines are believed to be the substance of fundamental motorcycling. The company has a knack for combining the old and the new. For example, Harley recently offered a bike with a "springer" front-end fork. The spring fork had not been offered on Harley motorcycles since 1949. Harley made major technological improvements in the fork but maintained the original look and offered it on a limited-edition model. The springer fork was made to appeal to someone who wanted traditional style and custom design as well as modern advancements.

A worrisome problem with the Harley image, on the other hand, is the perceived connection between Harleys and "outlaw" groups. The negative image associated with the Road Warrior films affected sales in some areas to such a degree that the company has initiated a public relations campaign. The campaign gently attacks the biker image by directing the majority of advertising at young professionals. The message is that Harley-Davidson represents fun, recreation, and reliability. The company trumpets the fact that famous professionals such as the former baseball star Reggie Jackson ride Harleys, and advertisements picturing these celebrities atop their "hogs" further help the company's image. The campaign seems to work. More doctors, lawyers, and dentists have begun to purchase Harleys.

Harley also put tighter controls on licensing its name, ensuring it is not used in obscene ways. Harley is careful not to alienate their loyal "biker" customers, however. And the company continues to promulgate—even enhance—its tough image through advertising in motorcycle magazines. For example, one ad pictures a group of rather tough-looking bikers with the caption "Would you sell an unreliable bike to these guys? We don't!" Another ad shows a junkyard filled with scrapped Japanese bikes. The caption is, "Can you find a Harley in here?"

A related image problem for Harley is that it cannot attract very many women customers. Harleys are very big and heavy. The Harley low-rider series attracts some women customers because the bikes are lower and easier to get on. Notwithstanding this partial success, some Japanese companies introduced smaller, lighter, low-riding, inexpensive Harley look-alikes in a straightforward attempt to attract women buyers. Honda's Rebel (250 cc) and Yamaha's Route 66 (V-twin, 250 cc) are two such bikes that have become fairly successful with women.

Perhaps the most objective indicator of the strength of the image came from an unlikely source—Japan itself. The Japanese have made numerous attempts to copy Milwaukee designs. For example, Suzuki's Intruder (1,400 cc) went to great lengths to hide the radiator, because Harleys were air cooled. Yamaha's Virago (1,100 cc) and Kawasaki's Vulcan (1,500 cc) were V-twin street bikes conspicuously styled in the Harley tradition. Nevertheless, some analysts feel that Japanese imitations only serve to strengthen the mystique of the original. The more the Japanese try to make look-alike bikes, the more the real thing increases in value.

HARLEY'S FUTURE

During 1992 Harley shipped 3,000 motorcycles to Japan and could have sold many more. Harley is one of only a few firms actively apologizing to its dealers for not being able to meet demand. Virtually no Harley dealers in the United States or overseas have any retail inventory of Harley bikes. Consumers must get on a one- to two-year waiting list even to purchase a new Harley. Harley must expand capacity. The major questions are where, how, and when. Harley's top management plans to reach their 100,000 annual motorcycle output goal in 1996 by boosting production at existing facilities, rather than by hiring additional employees or building any new facilities. Some analysts believe that is impossible.

Divestiture of Holiday Rambler is another strategic issue being considered by Harley's management. Potential revenues from this sale could be used to finance plant expansion. Winnebago and Coachmen likely would be interested in Holiday Rambler. Proceeds could be used to build another manufacturing facility, perhaps in Europe.

Another strategic issue concerns Harley's 49 percent–owned Eagle Credit subsidiary. Eagle is attempting to provide "one-stop" financial services to Harley dealers and customers, including a credit card, floor-plan financing, consumer loans, and insurance. Formed in January 1993, Eagle Credit has become very successful in the $700 million motorcycle loan business. The Harley credit card, introduced in 1993, has over 20,000 cards approved. Should Harley diversify further into the consumer finance market?

Develop a strategic plan for Richard Teerlink, Harley's president and chief executive officer.

EXHIBIT 17-1 Harley-Davidson, Inc. Selected Financial Data *(In thousands, except per share amounts)*

	1993	1992	1991	1990	1989
Income statement data:					
Net sales	$1,217,428	$1,105,284	$939,863	$864,600	$790,967
Cost of goods sold	880,269	808,871	706,140	635,551	596,940
Gross profit	337,159	296,413	233,723	229,049	194,027
Selling, administrative, and engineering	267,353*	199,216	165,078	145,674	127,606
Income from operations	69,806	97,197	68,645	83,375	66,421
Other income (expense):					
Interest expense, net	(831)	(4,912)	(7,312)	(9,701)	(14,322)
Lawsuit judgment	—	2,200	—	(7,200)	—
Other	(2,460)	(5,676)	(3,239)	(3,857)	910
	(3,291)	(8,388)	(10,551)	(20,758)	(13,412)
Income from continuing operations before income taxes, extraordinary items, and accounting changes	66,515	88,809	58,094	62,617	53,009
Provision for income taxes	48,072	34,636	21,122	24,309	20,399
Income from continuing operations before extraordinary items and accounting changes	18,443	54,173	36,972	38,308	32,610
Discontinued operation, net of tax	—	—	—	—	3,590
Income before extraordinary items and accounting changes	18,443	54,173	36,972	38,308	36,200
Extraordinary items, net of tax	—	(388)	—	(478)	(3,258)
Income before accounting changes	18,443	53,785	36,972	37,830	32,942
Accounting changes, net of tax	(30,328)	—	—	—	—
Net income (loss)	$ (11,885)	$ 53,785	$ 36,972	$ 37,830	$ 32,942
Weighted average common shares assuming no dilution	37,950	35,889	35,580	35,576	34,548
Per common share:					

EXHIBIT 17-1 *Continued*

	1993	1992	1991	1990	1989
Per common share:					
Income from continuing operations	$.49	$1.51	$1.04	$1.08	$.94
Discontinued operation	—	—	—	—	.10
Extraordinary items, net of tax	—	(.01)	—	(.02)	(.09)
Accounting changes, net of tax	(.80)	—	—	—	—
Net Income (loss)	$(.31)	$1.50	$1.04	$1.06	$.95
Dividends declared	$.12	—	—	—	—
Balance sheet data:					
Working capital	$142,996	$ 96,232	$ 64,212	$ 50,152	$ 51,313
Total assets	583,285	522,164	474,233	407,467	378,929
Short-term debt, including current					
maturities of long-term debt	21,369	16,965	41,089	23,859	26,932
Long-term debt, less current maturities	3,429	2,360	46,906	48,339	74,795
Total debt	24,789	19,325	87,995	72,198	101,727
Stockholders' equity	324,912	335,380	238,000	198,775	156,247

*Includes $57.0 million charge related primarily to the write-off of goodwill at the Transportation Vehicles segment (Holiday Rambler).

Source: *Annual Report*, 1993.

EXHIBIT 17-2 Motorcycle Unit Shipments and Consolidated Net Sales 1993 Compared to 1992

	1993	1992	CHANGE	% CHANGE
Motorcylce unit shipments	81,696	76,495	5,201	6.8%
Net Sales (in millions):				
Motorcycles	$ 734.3	$ 667.2	$ 67.1	10.0%
Motorcycle Parts and Accessories	199.0	155.7	43.3	27.8
Total Motorcycles and Related Products	933.3	822.9	110.4	13.4
Recreational Vehicles	192.7	202.1	(9.4)	(4.6)
Commercial Vehicles	78.9	67.9	11.0	16.2
Other	12.5	12.4	0.1	1.1
Total Transportation Vehicles	284.1	282.4	1.7	0.6
Consolidated Harley-Davidson, Inc.	$1,217.4	$1,105.3	$112.1	10.1%

Source: *Annual Report*, 1993.

EXHIBIT 17-3 Consolidated Gross Profit 1993 Compared to 1992 *(Dollars in millions)*

	1993	1992	CHANGE	PERCENT OF SALES 1993	PERCENT OF SALES 1992
Motorcycles and Related Products	$292.0	$250.0	$42.0	$31.3%	30.4%
Transportation Vehicles	45.2	46.4	(1.2)	15.9	16.4
Consolidated Harley-Davidson, Inc.	$337.2	$296.4	$40.8	27.7%	26.8%

Source: *Annual Report*, 1993.

EXHIBIT 17-4 Harley-Davidson, Inc. Consolidated Statements of Income *(In thousands, except per share amounts)*

	YEARS ENDED DECEMBER 31		
	1992	1991	1990
Net sales	$1,105,284	$939,863	$864,600
Cost of goods sold	808,871	706,140	635,551
Gross profit	296,413	233,723	229,049
Selling, administrative, and engineering	199,216	165,078	145,674
Income from operations	97,197	68,645	83,375
Interest income	956	950	1,736
Interest expense	(5,868)	(8,262)	(11,437)
Lawsuit judgment	2,200	—	(7,200)
Other-net	(5,676)	(3,239)	(3,857)
Income before provision for income taxes and extraordinary item	88,809	58,094	62,617
Provision for income taxes	34,636	21,122	24,309
Income before extraordinary item	54,173	36,972	38,308
Extraordinary item, loss on debt repurchases, net of tax	(388)	—	(478)
Net income	$ 53,785	$ 36,972	$ 37,830
Earnings per common share assuming no dilution:			
Income before extraordinary item	$1.51	$1.04	$1.08
Extraordinary item	(.01)	—	(.02)
Net income	$1.50	$1.04	$1.06
Earnings per income share assuming full dilution:			
Income before extraordinary item	$1.46	$1.04	$1.08
Extraordinary item	(.01)	—	(.02)
Net income	$1.45	$1.04	$1.06

Source: *Annual Report*, 1992.

EXHIBIT 17-5 Harley-Davidson, Inc. Consolidated Balance Sheets
(In thousands, except share amounts)

DECEMBER 31,	1993	1992
ASSETS		
Current assets:		
Cash and cash equivalents	$ 77,709	$ 44,122
Accounts receivable, net of allowance for		
doubtful accounts	86,031	93,178
Inventories	140,151	94,428
Deferred income taxes	20,296	24,120
Prepaid expenses	9,571	9,617
Total current assets	333,758	265,465
Property, plant, and equipment, net	205,768	183,787
Goodwill, net	—	56,710
Deferred income taxes	11,676	—
Other assets	32,083	16,202
	583,285	522,164
LIABILITIES AND STOCKHOLDERS' EQUITY		
Current liabilities:		
Notes payable	$ 20,580	$ 15,933
Accounts payable	56,350	58,004
Accrued expenses and other liabilities	113,043	94,264
Current maturities of long-term debt	789	1,032
Total current liabilities	190,762	169,233
Long-term liabilities	12,612	7,224
Deferred income taxes	—	10,327
Postretirement health-care benefits	54,999	—
Commitments and contingencies (Note 7)		
Stockholders' equity:		
Series A Junior Participating preferred stock,		
none issued	—	—
Common stock, 38,452,490 shares issued in		
1993 and 1992	385	385
Additional paid-in capital	137,150	131,053
Retained earnings	189,410	205,850
Cumulative foreign currency translation		
adjustment	186	757
	327,131	338,045
Less:		
Treasury stock (456,464 and 567,284 shares		
in 1993 and 1992, respectively), at cost	(1,583)	(1,028)
Unearned compensation	(636)	(1,637)
Total stockholders' equity	324,912	335,380
	$583,285	$522,164

Source: *Annual Report*, 1993.

EXHIBIT 17-6 Harley-Davidson, Inc Consolidated Statements of Cash Flows *(in thousands)*

YEARS ENDED DECEMBER 31,	1993	1992	1991
Cash flows from operating activities:			
Net income (loss)	$(11,885)	$53,785	$36,972
Adjustments to reconcile net income (loss) to net cash provided by operating activities:			
Goodwill and restructuring charges	57,024	—	—
Depreciation and amortization	33,272	29,410	22,603
Deferred income taxes	(25,922)	(993)	(2,981)
Lawsuit:			
Reversal	—	(2,200)	—
Settlement paid	—	(5,000)	—
Long-term employee benefits	57,386	1,369	1,258
Loss on disposal of long-term assets	626	1,164	1,346
Equity in net loss of joint ventures	1,427	—	—
Net changes in other current assets and current liabilities	(15,756)	10,380	(9,772)
Total adjustments	108,057	34,130	12,454
Net cash provided by operating activities	96,172	87,915	49,426
Cash flows from investing activities:			
Net capital expenditures	(55,202)	(47,229)	(47,766)
Investment in joint ventures	(10,350)	—	—
Other-net	(1,484)	(2,727)	(766)
Net cash used in investing activities	(67,036)	(49,956)	(48,532)
Cash flows from financing activities:			
Net increase (decrease) in notes payable	4,647	(23,593)	17,175
Payments on long-term debt	(1,183)	(9,420)	(1,771)
Dividends paid	(4,555)	—	—
Issuance of stock under employee stock plans	5,542	8,257	620
Net cash provided by (used in) financing activities	4,451	(24,756)	16,024
Net increase in cash and cash equivalents	33,587	13,203	16,918
Cash and cash equivalents:			
At beginning of year	44,122	30,919	14,001
At end of year	$ 77,709	$44,122	$30,919

Source: *Annual Report*, 1993.

EXHIBIT 17-7 Harley-Davidson, Inc. Consolidated Statements of Changes in Stockholders' Equity
(In thousands, except share amounts)

	Common Stock		Additional Paid-in Capital	Retained Earnings	Cumulative Foreign Currency Translation Adjustment	Treasury Stock	Unearned Compensation
	Issued Shares	Balance					
Balance December 31, 1990	18,310,000	$183	$ 87,115	$115,093	$ 995	$(771)	$(3,840)
Net income	—	—	—	36,972	—	—	—
Amortization of unearned compensation, net of cancellations	—	—	—	—	—	(218)	(1,280)
Exercise of stock options	—	—	615	—	—	5	—
Foreign currency translation adjustment	—	—	—	—	571	—	—
Balance December 31, 1991	18,310,000	183	87,730	152,065	1,566	(984)	(2,560)
Two-for-one common stock split	18,310,000	183	(183)	—	—	—	—
Net income	—	—	—	53,785	—	—	—
Amortization of unearned compensation, net of cancellations	—	—	—	—	—	(73)	923
Exercise of stock options	—	—	2,757	—	—	29	—
Tax benefit of restricted shares and stock options	—	—	5,471	—	—	—	—

EXHIBIT 17-7 *Continued*

	Common Stock		Additional Paid-In Capital	Retained Earnings	Cumulative Foreign Currency Translation Adjustment	Treasury Stock	Unearned Compensation
	Issued Shares	Balance					
Conversions of subordinated debentures	1,832,490	19	35,278	—	—	—	—
Foreign currency translation adjustment	—	—	—	—	(809)	—	—
Balance December 31, 1992	38,452,490	385	131,053	205,850	757	(1,028)	(1,637)
Net loss	—	—	—	(11,885)	—	—	—
Dividends declared	—	—	—	(4,555)	—	—	—
Amortization of unearned compensation, net of cancellations	—	—	—	—	—	—	1,001
Exercise of stock options	—	—	2,044	—	—	(566)	—
Tax benefit of restricted shares and stock options	—	—	4,053	—	—	11	—
Foreign currency translation adjustment	—	—	—	—	(571)	—	—
Balance December 31, 1993	$38,452,490	$385	$137,150	$189,410	$ 186	$(1,583)	$ (636)

Source: *Annual Report,* 1993.

EXHIBIT 17-8 Business Segments

The Company operates in two business segments: Motorcycles and Related Products and Transportation Vehicles. Information by industry segment is set forth below (in thousands):

	1993	1992	1991
Net Sales:			
Motorcycles and Related Products	$ 933,262	$ 822,929	$701,969
Transportation Vehicles	284,166	282,355	237,894
	$1,217,428	$1,105,284	$939,863
Income (loss) from operations:			
Motorcycles and Related Products	$ 136,217	$ 102,300	$ 89,551
Transportation Vehicles[a]	(59,533)	2,137	(13,427)
General corporate expenses	(6,878)	(7,240)	(7,479)
	69,806	97,197	68,645
Interest expense, net	(831)	(4,912)	(7,312)
Other:			
Motorcycles and Related Products:			
Lawsuit judgment reversal	—	2,200	—
Other	(3,249)	(3,811)	(1,355)
Transportation Vehicles	789	(1,865)	(1,884)
	(2,460)	(3,476)	(3,239)
Income before provision for income taxes, extraordinary item and accounting changes	$ 66,515	$ 88,809	$ 58,094

[a]Includes a $57.0 million charge related primarily to a write-off of goodwill in 1993.

	MOTORCYCLES AND RELATED PRODUCTS	TRANSPOR- TATION VEHICLES	CORPORATE	CONSOLIDATED
1993				
Identifiable assets	$437,813	$134,699	$10,773	$583,285
Depreciation and amortization	27,225	5,813	234	33,272
Net capital expenditures	52,324	2,766	112	55,202
1992				
Identifiable assets	$341,940	$178,252	$1,972	$522,164
Depreciation and amortization	22,630	6,639	141	29,410
Net capital expenditures	42,276	4,754	199	47,229
1991				
Identifiable assets	$281,790	$189,326	$3,117	$474,233
Depreciation and amortization	15,404	7,058	141	22,603
Net capital expenditures	43,621	2,987	1,158	47,766

There were no sales between business segments for the years ended December 31, 1993, 1992 or 1991.

(b)Foreign operations

EXHIBIT 17-8   *Continued*

Included in the consolidated financial statements are the following amounts relating to foreign affiliates:
(In thousands)

	1993	1992	1991
Assets	$ 49,109	$ 37,962	$ 31,081
Liabilities	40,769	27,716	15,882
Net sales	144,639	132,557	99,441
Net income	5,113	5,315	5,558

Export sales of domestic subsidiaries to nonaffiliated customers were $117.6 million, $106.9 million and $105.7 million in 1993, 1992 and 1991, respectively.
Source: *Annual Report*, 1993.

CASE 18

WINNEBAGO INDUSTRIES—1994

FRED R. DAVID
Francis Marion University

What has six feet of stand-up head room, kitchen, dinette, shower, toilet, and closet; sleeps four; and gets 22 miles per gallon on the highway? It's called LeSharo, a motor home made by Winnebago. Saving money is nice, but it is not the real reason people travel in a motor home. Motor homing is just plain fun. Motor homers are an adventurous lot—they like to go, see, and do. Florida residents have replaced Californians as the most active motor home campers. New Yorkers are third on the "most on the go" list. Recreational vehicle (RV) owners say that they not only save money when camping but can avoid the bother of having to stop for restaurants and bathrooms.

According to a recent study, motor home traveling is much less expensive than traveling by car or plane and staying in a motel. Motor homers stop when there is something to see and do. They often spend summers where it is cool and winters where it is warm.

The name *Winnebago* is considered synonymous with the term *motor home*. However, Winnebago—headquartered in Forest City, Iowa (515-582-3535)—today has fallen behind Fleetwood Enterprises of Riverside, California, the industry's recognized front-runner. Winnebago's fiscal year 1993 ended August 28, with a net income of $9.28 million, following four consecutive yearly losses totaling more than $62 million.

EARLY MOTOR HOMING

Motor homing has a rich history. Native Americans were the first Americans to engage in traveling with their home hundreds of years ago. They did so for both practical and recreational reasons. For them survival depended on staying close to sources of food, so as herds moved and the weather changed, Native Americans picked up their lightweight homes and traveled.

The first motor home was built in 1915 to take persons from the Atlantic Coast to San Francisco. It had wooden wheels and hard rubber tires. It was promoted as having all the comforts of an ocean cruiser. By the 1920s the house car had become a fixture in the United States and a symbol of freedom. All kinds of house cars could be seen traveling across America's dirt roads. They ranged from what looked like large moving cigars to two-story houses with porches on wheels. But these house cars featured poor weight distribution, poor insulation, and poor economy. From the 1930s to the 1950s they gave way in popularity to the trailer.

In the mid-1950s motor homes were called motorized trailers. They were overweight, underpowered, and poorly insulated, but still a vast improvement over the house cars of the 1920s. In the 1960s motor homing became much more popular, largely as a result of the innovations of Winnebago. From Forest City, Iowa, where the company was founded in 1958, Winnebago set the pace for new development of motor homes. The Winnebago name became a household word. Buyers of motor homes were asked, "When will your Winnebago be delivered?"

WINNEBAGO: 1958 TO 1992

Winnebago's phenomenal growth during the 1960s came to an end in 1970. That year was marked by a recession, and Winnebago's stock plunged nearly 60 percent before recovering. The OPEC oil embargoes of 1973 and 1974 had disastrous effects on Winnebago because gas was either unavailable or unaffordable. The company's net income averaged less than 1 percent of sales between 1973 and 1978. From a level of $229 million in 1978, Winnebago's sales dropped to $92 million in 1979.

A troubled board of directors called John Hanson, founder of the company, out of retirement in March 1979, reelecting him chairman of the board and president of Winnebago. To resolve Winnebago's problems, Hanson reduced the number of employees from 4,000 to 800 in less than nine months. He initiated the development of a propane conversion system for motor homes. This system allows users to power their vehicles with less costly propane, which eliminates worries about the supply and cost of gasoline. Hanson also pioneered the development of a lightweight, fuel-efficient motor home powered by a revolutionary heavy-duty diesel engine.

Winnebago was nearly forced into bankruptcy in 1980 when the company lost $13.5 million. But conditions improved. Employment at Winnebago increased from 800 in 1980 to 1,400 by May 1981. The company introduced a fuel-efficient, lightweight, aerodynamically designed line of motor homes. In 1982 Winnebago entered into an agreement with five manufacturers to allow use of the Winnebago name on products ranging from camping equipment to outdoor clothing. Winnebago declared its first cash dividend on common stock in October 1982: 10¢ per share. In 1983 Winnebago introduced a new family of front-wheel-drive vehicles powered by Renault diesel engines. Sales of $239 million in 1983 set a company record, and the number of Winnebago employees increased to 2,200. On August 10, 1983, Hanson was inducted into the Recreational Vehicle/Motor Home Hall of Fame in South Bend, Indiana. In 1984 Winnebago Industries won an award for the outstanding company turnaround in 1983.

In the mid-1980s, Winnebago's choice of Renault as supplier of its diesel engine for front-wheel-drive RVs came back to haunt them. The diesel engines were unreliable, and significant damage was done to Winnebago's reputation as a premier motor home manufacturer. The diesels were discontinued in 1988. However, the sad saga has not ended. In 1991 the Federal Trade Commission (FTC) decided to investigate whether Winnebago engaged in deceptive practices in selling the line of diesel-powered motor homes (1983–1986) under the names Winnebago LeSharo and Itaska

Phasar and van conversions called Centauri. Although the number of vehicles involved is small by industry standards, the problems represent one of the biggest cases of vehicle failure in terms of the percentage that failed. Apparently, the FTC is concerned about Winnebago's reluctance to deal with owners' problems effectively and take positive (reasonable) steps in resolving them.

In 1985 Winnebago's motor home sales were $395 million, up from $376 million in 1984. However, sales of other RVs and equipment, including van conversions and vans, declined to $19.3 million in 1985 from $21.2 million in 1984. Gross profits as a percentage of sales decreased in 1985 to 13.7 percent from 15.9 percent in 1984. The Winnebago Acceptance Corporation (WAC) provides financing for Winnebago dealers; its net income in 1985 was $456,000, down from $3.1 million in 1984. Overall, Winnebago's net income declined to $18 million in 1985 from $27 million in 1984.

Financial disappointments in fiscal year 1985 led to the formation of a new management team in 1986. Gerald Gilbert was elected chief executive officer and president. He had previously been president of a joint-venture company between Control Data Corporation and Honeywell, Inc. Clyde Church was elected to the newly created position of vice president of product planning and engineering. Richard Berreth was elected vice president of operations, and Bryan Hays was elected vice president of sales and marketing. Winnebago made its first appearance on the *Fortune* 500 list of the largest U.S. manufacturers in April 1986. In October Winnebago celebrated the production of its 200,000th motor home in 20 years. John Hanson (then 73) served as chairman of the board of directors.

Fiscal year 1987 was good for Winnebago, but fiscal year 1988 was bad. Net earnings declined from $19.9 million in 1987 to $2.7 million in 1988, although sales for 1988 increased to $425 million compared to $406 million in 1987. In April 1988 Winnebago signed an agreement to begin selling Winnebago products in 14 European countries. Dealerships were established in Sweden, Norway, Germany, Austria, and France. In August 1988 Winnebago signed an agreement with the Mitsubishi Corporation of Japan to sell Winnebago and Itasca motor homes in Japan. Winnebago also has an agreement with firms in Taiwan and Great Britain to begin selling its motor homes.

Fiscal 1988 was the first full year of operation of Cycle-Sat, a television advertising broadcast distribution company acquired by Winnebago. More that 500 television stations signed agreements to use the Cyclecypher system for receiving spot television commercials via satellite, and 320 stations completed installation of the equipment.

Winnebago's performance in fiscal year 1989 was disappointing. The company's share of the $2 billion U.S. motor home industry market declined to 21 percent from 22 percent the previous year, and the company lost $4.675 million.

Fiscal 1990 brought further bad news for the firm as revenues declined 25 percent, losses increased fourfold to $17.8 million, and dividends were reduced to 10¢ per share versus 40¢ in 1989.

Winnebago incurred record losses of $29.3 million in 1991, with sales declining 33 percent. This year was disastrous and brought Winnebago to its knees. Winnebago was not the lone firm in the motor home industry experiencing problems; revenues in the industry declined 10 percent to $2.98 billion, while unit sales sank 16 percent to 61,200 units. Winnebago's share of the market deteriorated to 18 percent from 20 percent.

John K. Hanson, age 80, is the active chairman of the board and CEO of Winnebago. He and his family control 47 percent of Winnebago's common stock, which hit a dismal low of $2.125 per share in 1991. Hanson is the recognized monarch of Winnebago and often acts the part. He is not the least bit hesitant in firing anyone who he believes is not performing, including CEOs. He even "coaxed" his son John to resign as deputy chairman. The youngest son, Paul, was at one time associated with the firm as a financial advisor. However, he is alleged to have lost a personal fortune of $4 million in less than a five-year period. There appears to be no family member in the wings prepared to take the ship's help from Hanson.

In 1992 Winnebago's sales increased 32 percent, but net income was a negative $10.6 million. Several new products were introduced in 1992, including the new bus-styled Vectra. The company created a new subsidiary in 1992, Winnebago Industries Europe, headquartered in Cologne, Germany, to expand operations internationally. Also in 1992 the company introduced the Winnebago Brave, Winnebago Warrior, Itasca Passage, and Itasca Sunrise. In the March–April 1992 issue of *Consumers Digest* magazine, Winnebago received the "Best Buy" ratings on several of its 1992 motor homes. Winnebago's Original Equipment Manufacturer (OEM) division, which sells component parts to outside manufacturers, increased 30 percent in 1992 to a record $17.4 million. Winnebago's Cycle-Sat subsidiary, which distributes radio and television commercials, grew in 1992 with 93 new television stations joining the Cycle-Sat network.

WINNEBAGO—1993

Winnebago rebounded in fiscal 1993 as revenues increased 30.2 percent and net income was a positive $9.7 million. The company's motor home shipments increased 22.9 percent for the year, with industry market share surpassing 19 percent. Fiscal 1993 revenues for Cycle-Sat increased 45 percent to $14.8 million as the network's client base rose 65 percent. Winnebago's OEM sales increased 12 percent in fiscal 1993 while sales of customized vans and trucks increased 25 percent. Winnebago moved its European headquarters location in fiscal 1993 to Saarbucken, Germany. European sales increased, especially in the United Kingdom. Sales in Japan were stagnant partly because of the depressed Japanese economy.

Winnebago manufactures three principal kinds of recreational vehicles: Type A motor homes, Type C motor homes, and van conversions. Type A motor homes are constructed on a chassis that already has the engine and drive components. They range in length from 22 to 37 feet and in price from $28,500 to over $103,000. An example of the Type A motor home is the luxurious Elante, which offers leather seating, central air, a double-door refrigerator, a water purification system, a four-burner range, a water heater with electronic ignition, a powered range hood with deluxe monitor panel and digital clock, a shower, and carpeting throughout. Other Type A motor homes include the Chieftain, Windcruiser, Itasca, and the new Vectra. The Winnebago Brave and Itasca Sunrise models are the company's top-selling vehicles, although the Winnebago Adventurer and Itasco Suncruiser are popular. Sales of Winnebago's Type A motor homes have increased three years in a row to a high of 6,095 vehicles in 1993.

Type C motor homes are constructed on a van chassis; the driver's compartment is accessible to the living area. Type C motor homes are compact and easy to drive. They range from 21 to 29 feet in length and have five popular floor plans. Typical options of a Type C vehicle include six feet of head room, shower, stove, sink, refrigerator, and two double beds. Winnebago's Minnie Winnie vehicle is the most popular Type C motor home in the country. The company's Itasca Sundancer, Winnebago Warrior, and Itasca Spirit also are popular. Sales of Winnebago's Type C motor homes have fallen four years in a row to a low of 1,998 vehicles in 1993.

The third type of RV manufactured by Winnebago is the van conversion. These vehicles are conventional vans manufactured by Ford, General Motors, and Chrysler that are custom tailored by Winnebago with special interiors, exteriors, windows, and vents. An example is the 19-foot Centauri, the largest van conversion available. On a recent 3,000-mile test trip, the Centauri averaged 24.11 miles per gallon. In many American households, van conversions are replacing the family car as the vehicle of choice. These vehicles can turn a long family trip from an ordeal into a pleasant adventure.

Marketing. The peak selling season for RVs has historically been spring and summer. Type A and Type C motor homes are marketed under the Winnebago and Itasca brand names and are sold through a network of 310 dealers, down from 340 in 1992, in the United States and to a limited extent in Canada and other foreign countries. Thirteen of these dealers accounted for more than 25 percent of Winnebago's motor home sales; one dealer accounted for 3.5 percent of motor home sales. Most Winnebago dealers also are dealers for automobiles and other motor home lines, but all dealers must provide complete service for RVs. Sales agreements with dealers are renewed on an annual or biannual basis.

Foreign sales by Winnebago are less that 10 percent of net sales. Foreign sales opportunities in Canada, Europe, and Japan are a priority at Winnebago. The largest international distributor is Mitsubishi Corporation, with a network of 21 authorized dealers in 46 locations throughout Japan.

Winnebago has 29 field sales and service personnel to aid its dealers. The company promotes its products through advertisements in national RV magazines, cable television, radio, newspapers, and trade shows. A substantial portion of Winnebago's sales of RVs to dealers is made on cash terms. Most dealers are financed on a "floor plan" basis under which a bank or finance company lends the dealer all of the purchase price, collateralized by a lien, or title to, the merchandise purchased. Winnebago, on request of the lending institution, will execute a repurchase agreement. These agreements provide that in the event of dealer default Winnebago will repurchase the financed merchandise.

Numerous Winnebago caravans are arranged each year to travel across the United States, Mexico, and Canada. With over 60,000 members since 1972, the Winnebago International Travelers' Club is one of the world's largest motor home associations. They organize national, state, and local Winnebago rallies, have a monthly newspaper, and offer discounts at KOA campsites nationwide.

The Winnebago Logo. Eighty percent of all Americans recognize the Winnebago name. Nine licensees currently pay royalties to Winnebago for using the company's name on products ranging from camping equipment to clothing. Presently, 2,000 retail outlets carry one or more products bearing the Winnebago logo.

Although licensing of the Winnebago name began in 1982, revenues to date have not been significant. There are now Winnebago bass and fishing boats, marine flotation devices, backpacks, sports bags, travel bags, slacks, shorts, shirts, vests, jackets, gloves, socks, hats, stoves, lanterns, grills, sleeping bags, air mattresses, tents, screenhouses, and suitcases. Winnebago's Scout 1 sleeping bag, Chieftain IV tent, Double Diamond air mattress, and other products have been advertised in many magazines.

Production Facilities. Winnebago has major production facilities in Forest City, Iowa. These facilities comprise over 1.4 million square feet and contain the company's manufacturing, maintenance, and service operations. The company also has 698,000 square feet of warehouse and executive office space in Forest City. Winnebago leases one manufacturing facility and one storage facility in Hampton, Iowa (74,000 square feet and 10,000 square feet), a manufacturing facility in Lorimor, Iowa (17,200 square feet), and a manufacturing facility in Garner, Iowa, which is subleased to Northern Iowa Electronics (NIE) (40,000 square feet). Winnebago owns a 14,400-square-foot facility in Forest City that is leased to Cycle-Sat. All corporate facilities in Forest City are located on approximately 784 acres of land owned by Winnebago. The company's European subsidiary recently purchased a 16,700-square-foot distribution and service facility in Kirkel, Germany.

Winnebago purchases its Type A and Type C chassis and engines from the Chevrolet Division of the General Motors Corporation, Ford Motor Company, Oshkosh Truck Corporation, and Toyota. General Motors is Winnebago's largest vendor for vans.

Winnebago has four 1,000-foot assembly lines for producing motor homes. Statistical process control is practiced at Winnebago and has enhanced the quality of its van products. As a motor home flows down the assembly line, quality control is carefully monitored. Units are randomly taken from the line for a thorough examination. The performance of every RV is tested before it is delivered to a dealer's lot. The company makes sure that all of its motor home components meet or exceed federal and durability standards. Some of the tests routinely performed include lamination strength, appliance performance, chip resistance, vibration, drop, salt spray, and crash tests.

Research and Development. Winnebago spent approximately $1.08 million, $1.82 million, and $1.63 million on research and development during fiscal 1993, 1992, and 1991, respectively. These activities employed 17, 34, and 28 full-time employees, respectively, during these years.

Winnebago uses computer technology to design its motor homes. The company has a state-of-the-art, computer-aided design/computer-aided manufacturing (CAD/CAM) system. This system aids in producing low-cost sheet metal parts, new paint lines for steel and aluminum parts, and modifications of assembly equipment.

Winnebago has had a 40,000-square-foot product-testing facility at Forest City since 1989. This facility houses some of the most sophisticated technology being used in the RV industry, such as a high- and low-temperature chamber for subjecting parts to extreme temperatures and high stress.

Cycle-Sat. Cycle-Sat is in the satellite courier and tape duplication business, specializing in the satellite transmission of commercials to television stations. Fiscal year 1993 was its sixth full year of operation. Cycle-Sat continues to expand its automated distribution system. Cycle-Sat has a patent for its cyclecypher and its network distribution process.

Until fiscal 1993 Cycle-Sat had been losing money annually since it began operations. Cycle-Sat has a satellite-supported duplication and distribution center in Memphis, Tennessee, and additional offices in Los Angeles, New York City, and Chicago.

WINNEBAGO'S EXTERNAL ENVIRONMENT

Winnebago's motor homes can attract a low-frills buyer desiring the most stripped-down RV, the person with expensive tastes desiring the ultimate in RV luxury, and everyone in between. RVs can be purchased or rented. Many families unable to buy a mobile home rent one to take on vacation. As the baby boomers age and approach retirement, many of them will consider selling their primary residence, purchasing and moving into a motor home, and traveling to any point they desire in North America.

The motel and hotel industries have been experiencing an oversupply of available rooms, which has resulted in extremely low room rates. Compared to the cost of owning/renting and operating an RV, the costs of staying in a motor home versus a motel are about the same if not a bit lower in favor of the motel. Motor home sales historically increase whenever travel, tourism, and vacationing gain in popularity. The converse is also true.

Lower fuel prices, interest rates, inflation rates, and a robust, fully employed economy spur motor home sales. Conversely, when the economy is stagnant or receding, and fuel prices are high along with inflation and interest rates, motor home sales suffer. In 1993, interest rates, gas prices, and inflation rates were low, so Winnebago prospered.

There are about 122,000 campsites in U.S. state parks, including 4,500 maintained by the U.S. Forest Service and 100 in the National Parks System. In addition, there are more than 15,000 private campgrounds and over 1,620 county parks. Winnebagos can access nearly all of these sites.

COMPETITORS

Twelve firms account for 80 percent of the RV industry's volume. Among the largest publicly held are Fleetwood Enterprises, Winnebago Industries, Coachmen Industries, Rexhall Industries, Mallard Coach, Kit Manufacturing, Harley-Davidson, and Skyline Corporation. Of all the competitors, Fleetwood Enterprises is first in sales, followed by Coachman and then Winnebago. The following is a list of major motor home competitors:

COMPANY	1993 REVENUES	NUMBER OF EMPLOYEES	LOCATION
Fleetwood Enterprises, Inc.	$1,589.3 M	12,000	Riverside, CA
Coachman Industries, Inc.	292.8 M	1,854	Elkhart, IN
Mark III Industries, Inc.	750.0 M	2,165	Ocala, FL
Jayco, Inc.	160.0 M	975	Middlebury, IN
Glaval Corp.	130.0 M	850	Elkhart, IN
Newmar Corp.	65.0 M	350	Nappanee, IN
Monaco Coach Corp.	65.0 M	260	Junction City, OR
Tiffin Motor Homes, Inc.	80.0 M	200	Red Bay, AL

Fleetwood. Fleetwood Enterprises is the nation's largest producer of both RVs and manufactured housing. It holds 30 percent of the RV market. The RV line includes conventional Type A motor homes, chopped-van Type C motor homes, travel trailers, fifth-wheel travel trailers, folding camping trailers, and truck campers. Motor homes represent 62 percent of Fleetwood's sales while mobile home sales comprise 38 percent of revenues.

Fleetwood stayed profitable through the recession of 1990–1991. Two factors enhance Fleetwood's RV sales performance: (1) concentration on ringing up sales even when margins must be slashed and (2) innovative marketing. Its products, even virtually identical ones, are sold under a number of names. Folding campers sell under the name Coleman (the famous brand that it acquired in 1989); motor homes sell under the names Pace Arrow, Southwind, Cambria, Limited, Flair, Jamboree, and Tioga; and travel trailers are sold as Avion, Prowler, Terry, and Wilderness brands. For Fleetwood, the payoff is more presence and enhanced sales.

Fleetwood recently acquired a Germany-based luxury-priced motorhome manufacturer named Nielsmen and Bischoff. This acquisition paves the way for expanded distribution of Fleetwood recreational vehicles in Europe. Fleetwood is adding 20 percent more production capacity to its base of 27 plants in order to meet rising demand in both its motor homes and mobile homes.

FUTURE PLANS, PROBLEMS, AND CONCERNS

Recreational vehicle demand tends to be robust in the earlier stages of an economic recovery. This phenomenon held true in 1993 in the United States and may also characterize Europe and Japan in 1994 and 1995.

Winnebago Industries, Inc. has started converting Chevrolet half-ton two-wheel-drive and four-wheel-drive pickups and Suburban sport utility vehicles featuring walnut interior wood accents and customized exteriors with fiberglass running boards, tailgate protectors, and bug screens. The pickup conversion packages will retail from $3,500 to $4,225 while the Suburban conversions will cost $5,065 to $6,500.

Winnebago Industries, Inc. plans to double its van conversion sales as part of a long-range strategy to play a major role in the market. Winnebago has previously concentrated on the motor home market. Not interested in the price wars in the entry-level van conversion segment, Winnebago is focusing instead on the mid- to high-priced models. The company's wholesale base price for a conversion is from $5,500 to $5,800. A Special Edition could range from $10,000 to $12,000. Projected van conversion sales were from 1,600 to 1,800 in FY 1993.

Fleetwood is a major manufacturer of mobile homes, including both single-wide and double-wide versions. Should Winnebago consider widening the scope of its business beyond motor homes?

Winnebago appears to suffer from management instability. Hanson has hired and fired four presidents in five years. This type of environment does not enhance the morale of management. Members of management tend to hold back innovativeness, free thinking, and the willingness to take risks for fear that such qualities could lead to their demise. Hanson is over 80 years old. Should he be encouraged to retire?

How does the opening of markets in Eastern Europe and the countries that comprise the former Soviet Union affect Winnebago? Are these the types of markets in which Winnebago should invest some of its limited capital? What emphasis should the firm place on international operation in the future? Would Mexico be a good area to target now that NAFTA is a reality?

EXHIBIT 18-1 Net Revenues by Major Product Class (Dollars in thousands)

YEAR ENDED (1)	AUGUST 28, 1993	AUGUST 29, 1992	AUGUST 31, 1991	AUGUST 25, 1990	AUGUST 26, 1989
Motor Homes	$ 326,861	$ 245,908	$ 180,878	$286,713	$389,224
	85.1%	83.4%	81.2%	86.2%	89.0%
Other Recreation Vehicle Revenues (2)	17,655	17,126	15,586	22,039	22,455
	4.6%	5.8%	7.0%	6.6%	5.1%
Other Manufactured Products Revenues (3)	20,344	18,090	13,974	11,423	10,744
	5.3%	6.1%	6.3%	3.4%	2.5%
Total Manufactured Products Revenues	364,860	281,124	210,438	320,175	422,423
	95.0%	95.3%	94.5%	96.2%	96.6%
Service Revenues (4)	19,223	13,870	12,210	12,658	15,077
	5.0%	4.7%	5.5%	3.8%	3.4%
Total Revenues	$ 384,083	$ 294,994	$ 222,648	$332,833	$437,500
	100.0%	100.0%	100.0%	100.0%	100.0%

(1) The fiscal year ended August 31, 1991 contained 53 weeks; all other fiscal years in the table contained 52 weeks.

(2) Primarily recreation vehicle–related parts and service and van conversions.

(3) Principally sales of extruded aluminum and component products for other manufacturers.

(4) Principally Cycle-Sat revenues from satellite courier and tape duplication services, NIE revenues from contract assembly of a variety of electronic products, and in years ended August 28, 1993, August 25, 1990 and August 26, 1989, WAC revenues from dealer financing.

Source: Company reports, 1993.

EXHIBIT 18-2 Unit Sales of Recreation Vehicles

YEAR ENDED a	AUGUST 28, 1993	AUGUST 29, 1992	AUGUST 31, 1991	AUGUST 25, 1990	AUGUST 26, 1989
Motor Homes					
Class A	6,095	4,161	2,814	4,613	7,367
Class C	1,998	2,425	2,647	3,820	3,401
Total	8,093	6,586	5,461	8,433	10,768
Van Conversions	1,103	876	842	1,789	1,801

aThe fiscal year ended August 31, 1991 ontained 53 weeks; all other fiscal years in the table contained 52 weeks.

Source: Company reports, 1993.

EXHIBIT 18-3 Interim Financial Information (unaudited) (Dollars in thousands except per share data)

YEAR ENDED AUGUST 28, 1993	NOVEMBER 28, 1992	QUARTER ENDED FEBRUARY 27, 1993	MAY 29, 1993	AUGUST 28, 1993
Net revenues	$83,416	$77,462	$115,915	$107,290
Operating income	939	(717)	4,562	3,503
Net income	1,117	407	4,579	3,175
Net income per share	.04	.02	.18	.13

YEAR ENDED AUGUST 29, 1992	NOVEMBER 30, 1991	QUARTER ENDED FEBRUARY 29, 1992	MAY 30, 1992	AUGUST 29, 1992
Net revenues	$60,175	$ 59,987	$ 88,883	$85,949
Operating (loss) income from continuing operations	(1,672)	(5,491)	3,142	2,933
(Loss) income from continuing operations[a]	(1,840)	(5,492)	2,830	2,733
Net (loss) income	(9,614)	(5,492)	2,220	2,317
Net (loss) income per share from continuing operations	(.07)	(.22)	.11	.11

In the fourth quarter ended August 28, 1993 the company recorded expense of $1,555,000 as a result of the Spectrum motor home recall.

[a]Before cumulative effect of change in accounting principle.

Source: Company reports, 1993.

EXHIBIT 18-4 Consolidated Balance Sheets (Dollars in thousands)

ASSETS	AUGUST 28, 1993	AUGUST 29, 1992
Current Assets		
Cash and cash equivalents	$ 11,238	$ 13,286
Marketable securities	2,309	1,215
Receivables, less allowance for doubtful accounts ($2,798 and $829, respectively)	29,239	27,515
Dealer financing receivables less allowance for doubtful accounts ($290 and $317, respectively)	6,742	102
Inventories	40,610	35,702
Prepaid expenses	3,636	3,999
Deferred income taxes	511	—
Total current assets	94,285	81,819
Property and Equipment, at cost		
Land	2,153	1,273
Buildings	38,373	38,591
Machinery and equipment	72,505	70,257
Transportation equipment	5,609	5,525
	118,640	115,646
Less accumulated depreciation	81,012	77,591
Total property and equipment, net	37,628	38,055
Long-Term Notes Receivable, less allowances ($1,362 and $1,427, respectively)	4,203	2,910
Investment in Life Insurance	11,853	8,906
Deferred Income Taxes	2,652	1,544
Other Assets	6,429	6,527
Total Assets	$157,050	$139,761

EXHIBIT 18-4 *Continued*

LIABILITIES AND STOCKHOLDERS' EQUITY	AUGUST 28, 1993	AUGUST 29, 1992
Current Liabilities		
Current maturities of long-term debt	$ 1,719	1,223
Accounts payable, trade	19,462	18,408
Accrued expenses:		
Insurance	6,445	7,143
Vacation liability	2,864	2,512
Promotional	4,636	4,405
Other	10,399	8,329
Liability on product warranties	4,091	2,375
Total current liabilities	49,616	44,395
Long-term Debt and Obligations Under Capital Lease	3,183	3,113
Deferred Compensation	18,766	16,157
Deferred Income Taxes	1,823	1,544
Minority Interest in Consolidated Subsidiary	1,969	2,474
Contingent Liabilities and Commitments Stockholder s' Equity		
Capital stock, common, par value $.50; authorized 60,000,000 shares	12,908	12,903
Additional paid-in capital	24,811	25,157
Reinvested earnings	52,245	42,967
	89,964	81,027
Less treasury stock, at cost	8,271	8,949
Total Stockholders' Equity	81,693	72,078
Total Liabilities and Stockholders' Equity	$157,050	$139,761

Source: Company reports, 1993.

EXHIBIT 18-5 Consolidated Statements of Operations (Dollars in thousands except per share data)

YEAR ENDED	AUGUST 28, 1993	AUGUST 29, 1992	AUGUST 31, 1991
Revenues			
Manufactured products	$364,860	$281,124	$210,438
Service	19,223	13,870	12,210
Total net revenues	384,083	294,994	222,648
Costs and expenses			
Cost of manufactured products	316,230	249,498	196,584
Cost of services	14,620	13,165	12,623
Selling and delivery	21,875	18,691	20,342
General and administrative	23,388	16,853	14,791
Other expense (income)	188	(952)	403
Minority interest in net loss of consolidated subsidiary	(505)	(1,173)	(766)
Total costs and expenses	375,796	296,082	243,977
Operating income (loss)	8,287	(1,088)	(21,329)
Financial expense	(96)	(585)	(340)
Income (loss) from continuing operations before income taxes	8,191	(1,673)	(21,669)
(Credit) provision for taxes	(1,087)	96	(5,398)
Income (loss) from continuing operations	9,278	(1,769)	(16,271)
Loss from discontinued operations	—	(1,026)	(13,110)
Cumulative effect of change in accounting principle (Note 1)	—	(7,774)	—
Net income (loss)	$ 9,278	$(10,569)	$(29,381)
Income (loss) per share:			
Continuing operations	$ .37	$ (.07)	$ (.65)
Discontinued operations	—	(.04)	(.53)
Cumulative effect of change in accounting principle	—	(.31)	—
Net income (loss)	$ .37	$ (.42)	$ (1.18)
Weighted average number of shares of stock (in thousands)	25,042	25,016	24,986

Source: Company reports, 1993.

EXHIBIT 18-6 Consolidated Statements of Changes in Stockholders' Equity
(Amounts in thousands)

	COMMON SHARES		PAID-IN CAPITAL	ADDITIONAL REINVESTED EARNINGS	TREASURY STOCK	
	NUMBER	AMOUNT			NUMBER	AMOUNT
Balance, August 25, 1990	25,777	$12,888	$ 26,959	$ 82,917	1,017	$11,602
Proceeds from the sale of common stock to employees	17	9	38	—	(1)	(15)
Contribution of treasury stock to employee stock bonus plan	—	—	(1,856)	—	(228)	(2,597)
Net loss	—	—	—	(29,381)	—	—
Balance, August 31, 1991	25,794	12,897	25,141	53,536	788	8,990
Proceeds from the sale of common stock to employees	12	6	16	—	(3)	(41)
Net loss	—	—	—	(10,569)	—	—
Balance, August 29, 1992	25,806	12,903	25,157	42,967	785	8,949
Proceeds from the sale of common stock to employees	9	5	(346)	—	(60)	(678)
Net income	—	—	—	9,278	—	—
Balance, August 28, 1993	25,815	$ 12,908	$ 24,811	$ 52,245	725	$ 8,271

Source: Company reports, 1993.

EXHIBIT 18-7 Consolidated Statements of Cash Flows (Dollars in thousands)

YEAR ENDED	AUGUST 28, 1993	AUGUST 29, 1992	AUGUST 31, 1991
Cash flows from operating activities:			
Net income (loss)	$ 9,278	$ (10,569)	$ (29,381)
Adjustments to reconcile net income (loss) to net cash from operating activities:			
Cumulative effect of change in accounting principle	—	7,774	—
Provision for disposal of Commercial Vehicle Division	—	416	8,118
Depreciation and amortization	7,961	8,195	11,070
Deferred income taxes	(1,340)	—	645
Loss (gain) on disposal of property, leases and other assets	630	507	(779)
Provision for doubtful receivables	1,496	916	(1,563)
Provision for lease residual reserve	—	—	733
Earned income on lease residuals	—	—	(128)
Deferred compensation and employee stock bonus plan	2,609	2,031	213
Realized and unrealized (gains) and losses on investments, net	(305)	625	(330)
Minority interest in net loss of consolidated subsidiary	(505)	(1,173)	(766)
Other	339	(68)	61
Change in assets and liabilities:			
(Increase) decrease in receivables and other assets	(1,186)	(4,853)	1,105
(Increase) decrease in inventories	(5,390)	(3,417)	17,380
Decrease in income tax refund receivables	—	6,339	3,847
Increase (decrease) in accounts payable and accrued expenses	3,227	5,063	(16,403)
Increase (decrease) in income taxes payable	1,106	—	(3,363)
Net cash provided (used) by operating activities	17,920	11,786	(9,541)
Cash flows from investing activities:			
Investments in marketable securities	(7,922)	(18,639)	(11,735)
Proceeds from sale of marketable securities	7,133	18,094	12,229
Purchases of property and equipment	(7,671)	(3,040)	(3,807)
Proceeds from sale of property and equipment	101	252	183
Investments in dealer receivables	(28,424)	—	—
Collections of dealer receivables	21,671	—	—
Investments in long-term notes receivable and other assets	(5,893)	(3,599)	(2,835)
Proceeds from long-term notes receivable and other assets	294	229	877
Proceeds from the sale of equipment under direct financing and operating leases	—	—	1,738
Net cash used by investing activities	(20,711)	(6,703)	(3,350)

EXHIBIT 18-7   *Continued*

YEAR ENDED	AUGUST 28, 1993	AUGUST 29, 1992	AUGUST 31, 1991
Cash flows from financing activities and capital transactions:			
Payments of long-term debt	**(1,528)**	(1,064)	(3,971)
Proceeds from issuance of long-term debt	**1,934**	55	1,289
Proceeds from issuance of Cycle-Sat common stock	**—**	2,500	—
Proceeds from issuance of common and treasury stock	**337**	63	62
Net cash provided (used) by financing activities and capital transactions	**743**	1,554	(2,620)
Net (decrease) increase in cash and cash equivalents	**(2,048)**	6,637	(15,511)
Cash and cash equivalents at beginning of year	**13,286**	6,649	22,160
Cash and cash equivalents at end of year	**$ 11,238**	$ 13,286	$ 6,649

Source: Company reports, 1993.

EXHIBIT 18-8 Winnebago Organizational Chart

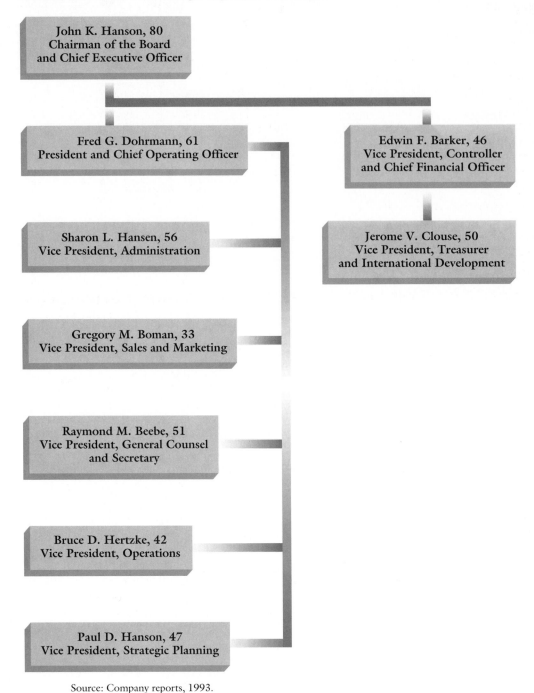

John K. Hanson, 80
Chairman of the Board
and Chief Executive Officer

Fred G. Dohrmann, 61
President and Chief Operating Officer

Edwin F. Barker, 46
Vice President, Controller
and Chief Financial Officer

Sharon L. Hansen, 56
Vice President, Administration

Jerome V. Clouse, 50
Vice President, Treasurer
and International Development

Gregory M. Boman, 33
Vice President, Sales and Marketing

Raymond M. Beebe, 51
Vice President, General Counsel
and Secretary

Bruce D. Hertzke, 42
Vice President, Operations

Paul D. Hanson, 47
Vice President, Strategic Planning

Source: Company reports, 1993.

AEROSPACE INDUSTRY NOTE

CLAYTON MOWRY
RONALD GREEN

The U.S. aerospace industry, one of America's most successful industries, is facing some difficult challenges. The three key issues confronting the aerospace sector are continuing defense cuts, increasing international competition, and a weak global economy.

Still a global leader, the U.S. aerospace industry is a critical part of the country's domestic and export economies. The aerospace industry is the nation's leading net exporter of manufactured goods, selling products worth $40 billion in 1993, and produces the largest trade surplus of any U.S. manufacturing industry (approximately $28 billion in 1993). Aerospace is also a leading technology driver, utilizing a number of the technologies identified as critical by the White House Office of Science and Technology Policy, the Department of Defense (DOD), and the Department of Commerce. The industry accounts for more than 25 percent of all the nation's research and development expenditures, making it the country's leader in R&D spending on new technologies.

INDUSTRY SALES

The aerospace industry is facing serious challenges. As a result of continued defense cuts, a weak global economy, and increased international competition, industry shipments will decline in 1994 for the third year in a row. The value of aerospace industry shipments, unadjusted for inflation, peaked in 1992 at $134 billion. Shipments in 1993 fell 11 percent, in real terms, and shipments in 1994 are expected to be 11 percent lower than 1993. Historically, at least half of the industry's revenues were derived from the military sector. Cuts in the defense budgets for aerospace products, both in the United States and in other developed countries, have reduced requirements for military aircraft, missiles, and related equipment from U.S. suppliers. Total U.S. defense spending peaked in 1985, and current budget requests indicate an annual average decline of overall spending of more than 5 percent per year through 1997. The major impact will be from procurement cuts, estimated to be down 47 percent from the peak years of the 1980s build up. Increased emphasis on dual-use technology combined with funding for defense conversion should focus future attention on research and development. Rather than canceling ongoing projects, the 1994 defense budget recommends continuing development. By contrast, the defense industry's production will continue to fall (Figure 1).

In the past, significant growth in the civil sector sustained the aerospace industry during periodic downturns in defense spending. Between 1985 and 1991, when defense aerospace shipments were declining at a rate of approximately 2 percent per year, commercial aerospace shipments increased more than 11 percent per year. This counter-cyclical characteristic of the industry has disappeared. In 1992 civil orders represented 62 percent of the industry's total order backlog—down from 65 percent in 1991. The civil sector is facing the cumulative effect of the worldwide economic downturn and a decline in global airline passenger traffic. Airline traffic reached its peak of 466 million passengers in 1990. Thereafter, a series of events began that severely damaged the economic underpinning of the industry. The Persian Gulf crisis and the worldwide recession caused the airlines'

FIGURE 1 Military Share of Aerospace Shipments and Backlog Shrinks

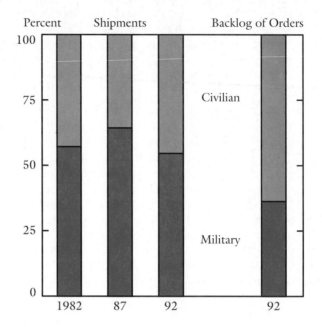

Source: U.S. Department of Commerce, Bureau of the Census, *Current Industrial Reports* #MA37D, 1983–92.

loss of $13 billion between 1990 and 1993. This weak financial performance of the airline industry has, in turn, affected aerospace equipment orders and shipments during 1992 and into 1993.

The downturn in the industry is reflected in a severe decline in employment. Between 1989 and 1993 total aerospace industry employment fell from 912,000 to 615,000 according to Bureau of Labor statistics. Total aerospace employment declined between December 1989 and June 1993 at an average rate of almost 6,000 jobs per month. Layoffs have occurred in both the commercial and military sectors. Capacity utilization for the industry, as calculated by the Federal Reserve, fell from 85 percent in mid-1990 to only 69 percent by May 1993. As long as capacity utilization remains low, prospects for reversing or stabilizing employment trends remain poor.

International Competitiveness. The U.S. aerospace industry faces increasing international challenges as well. Although the United States retains both market and technology leadership within the global aerospace industry, its position has eroded. In 1970 the United States led the global aerospace market with a share of almost 80 percent (excluding the former members of the Council for Mutual Economic Assistance, or COMECON, a group of nations led by the former Soviet Union). In 1993 U.S. aerospace shipments still led the world, but had shrunk to less than 60 percent of the worldwide market. This decline reflects the success of other countries in their efforts to foster the development and growth of their national aerospace industries, particularly Europe. Many foreign governments have ambitious plans for developing competitive aerospace industries and support the growth of these industries with subsidies for product development and production. Foreign governments have required U.S. aerospace companies to provide offsets and technology transfers and made sales con-

Trends and Forecasts: Aerospace (SIC 372, 376) (In millions of dollars except as noted)

Item	1991	1992[1]	1993[2]	1994[3]	Percent Change (1991–1994) 91–92	92–93	93–94
Industry Data							
Value of shipments[4]	131,345	133,613	120,742	101,962	1.7	–9.6	–15.6
Value of shipments (1987$)	116,911	116,287	103,510	92,313	–0.5	–11.0	–10.8
Total employment (000)	746	674	587	542	–9.7	–12.9	–7.7
Production workers (000)	362	323	279	267	–10.8	–13.6	–4.3
Average hourly earnings ($)	16.73	17.56	18.37	—	5.0	4.6	—
Capital expenditures	3,407	—	—	—	—	—	—
Product Data							
Value of shipments[5]	124,109	126,800	112,244	93,921	2.2	–11.5	–16.3
Value of shipments (1987$)	109,742	110,349	96,230	80,760	0.6	–12.8	–16.1
Trade Data							
Value of imports	12,422	12,914	11,277	10,973	4.0	–12.7	–2.7
Value of exports	42,343	43,562	39,560	33,745	2.9	–9.2	–14.7

[1] Estimate, except exports and imports.

[2] Estimate.

[3] Forecast.

[4] Value of all products and services sold by establishments in the aerospace industry.

[5] Value of products classified in the aerospace industry produced by all industries.

Source: U.S. Department of Commerce: Bureau of the Census; International Trade Administration (ITA). Estimates and forecasts by ITA.

tingent upon their own firms' supplying some of the components. In addition, some governments have encouraged consolidation and cooperation among domestic companies to reduce competition within their borders, enabling their firms to compete more effectively with established U.S. companies (Figure 2).

Europe provides the most formidable competition to the U.S. aerospace industry. According to European Community (EC) statistics, the EC aerospace industry grew almost twice as fast as the U.S. industry during the period 1978–1989. In 1990 the EC industry was nearly half the size of the U.S. industry. The emergence of the Airbus Industrie consortium, composed of the member governments of France, the United Kingdom, Germany, and Spain, is primarily responsible for the erosion of global U.S. market share. Since its inception, Airbus has received an estimated $26 billion, including interest, in direct government supports to assist in the development of its fleet of aircraft. Historically, U.S. companies have not received government assistance. European governments also support their commercial space, smaller aircraft, rotorcraft, engine, and parts industries.

Most individual EC governments have encouraged concentration in their aerospace industries, leading to diversified, national monoliths such as Deutsche Aerospace (Germany), Aerospatiale (France), Alenia (Italy), Fokker (Netherlands), and British Aerospace (U.K.). Even though Deutsche Aerospace privatized its operations in 1992 and Aerospatiale has been offered by the French government as a candidate for future privatization, the trend toward intra–EC ventures will continue

FIGURE 2 U.S. Aerospace Trade Surplus Narrows[*]

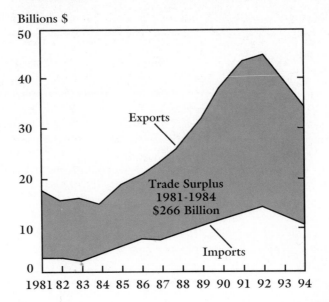

*Estimate.

Source: U.S. Department of Commerce: Bureau of the Census; International Trade Administration, Technology and Aerospace Industries Division.

to lead to even larger industry consortiums as the EC governments work to integrate their economies. An example is the recent takeover of Fokker by Deutsche Aerospace, with a possible further consolidation with Aerospatiale and Alenia's regional jet programs, the ATR-42 and the ATR-72.

In the future Japan will become a more significant competitor in several segments of the industry. Small by global standards, the Japanese aerospace industry production totaled only $8.5 billion in 1991, but the industry has grown at a rate of 9 percent a year since 1984. Targeted by the Japanese government, aerospace research and development efforts have focused on aircraft fuelage and systems components, electronics, high-speed propulsion systems, and space launch vehicles. Japan's growth in the aerospace industry stems from its partnerships and cooperative ventures with Western aerospace companies, most notably Boeing. These partnerships enabled Japanese aerospace output to grow from less than $1 billion in 1970 to more than $8.5 billion by 1991. Japan, a "program partner" in the new Boeing 777 aircraft, already possesses much of the expertise needed to produce a world-class aircraft of its own design in the future. In fact, discussions are underway for Boeing to assist its Japanese suppliers in building an 80-seat jetliner, the YSX.

China also has become a major market for U.S. aerospace products. In 1992, U.S. aerospace exports to China totaled over $2 billion. More than 40,000 U.S. aerospace jobs are estimated to have been created as a result of trade with China. It is estimated that China will need more than $40 billion in new aircraft over the next 20 years, making China one of the brighter spots in today's aerospace market. China's market remains fragile, as does its foreign relations with the United States, but the market potential is promising. China also plans to build an indigenous aerospace industry and will become both a growing subcontractor and competitor in segments of the aerospace industry, especially in lower-cost military and commuter aircraft.

The new spirit of international cooperation prevalent in the Russian aerospace industry presents both opportunities and challenges for the U.S. industry. A market that contains the world's largest airline, largest space industry, and greatest pent-up consumer demand certainly provides new long-term opportunities for U.S. aerospace companies. It is estimated that the former Soviet market will require 2,000 new aircraft for domestic service and 250 aircraft for international routes during the next 18 years. Yet it also presents the challenge of new competition. An example is the 1993 roll-out and first flight of the IL-96M, a four-engine, long-range aircraft. While the IL-96M will be powered by U.S.-built Pratt & Whitney engines and fitted with U.S. advanced avionics, it will compete with the McDonnell Douglas's MD-11 and Boeing's future 777 twin-engine aircraft. Another recent product of Russian aerospace collaboration with the West is Tupolev's TU-204, a midrange, 200-seater twin jet airliner with Rolls-Royce engines designed to compete against the Boeing 757. Prior to the dissolution of the Soviet Union, Soviet aerospace factories produced at least as many aircraft, missiles, and spacecraft as the United States. Today, most of these facilities are operating at less than 30 percent capacity. Desire for new orders for those factories, for technology, and for hard currency will force the industries of the former Soviet republics to both collaborate and compete in the international market. These factors play a key role in Russia's future participation in the Space Station. In September 1993 Vice President Gore and Russian Prime Minister Chernomyrdin agreed to the construction of a space station blending elements from the U.S. Freedom and Russian Mir projects.

Other countries also seek larger shares of the global aerospace industry, including Canada, Brazil, Indonesia, Sweden, South Korea, Israel, and Australia.

Environmental Profile. The aerospace industry has made great strides in addressing environmental problems that are aircraft related. Today, on take-off and landing, a jetliner produces less than one-quarter of the pollutants produced by a 1960s transport. Noise abatement also has been a major concern. By the year 2000, most of the commercial jet aircraft will meet stringent Stage 3 noise standards even though this will mean the retirement of many aircraft before the end of their functional lifespan. Hughes Aircraft has developed partnerships with local governments in Southern California, working to reduce the region's problem with smog. Boeing, Hughes, IBM, Autoclave Engineers Group, and five national laboratories are leading a large research and development cooperative to find more environmentally sound processing techniques for aerospace materials, including reducing the volatile organic compounds used in paints, coatings, and solvents. Environmental concerns now are considered at the earliest stages of designing an aircraft.

Pratt & Whitney, General Dynamics, Hercules, and many others have major campaigns to eliminate wastes produced in the production of aircraft parts and aircraft engines. In many cases, wastes have been reduced 60 to 90 percent. Aerospace companies have recognized that they have valuable technologies to supply to the global environmental marketplace. Several companies have formed environmental subsidiaries, such as General Dynamic's Environmental Sciences and Technologies, Lockheed's Environmental Systems & Technology Company, and Hughes' Environmental Systems, to develop and market environmental products worldwide. As traditional markets shrink, aerospace companies are expected to diversify further into the environmental technology industry.

U.S. Trade Patterns in 1992 Aerospace SIC 37A (In millions of dollars, percent)

EXPORTS	Value	Share	IMPORTS	Value	Share
Canada and Mexico	3,027	6.9	Canada and Mexico	2,309	17.9
European Community	14,782	33.9	European Community	8,911	69.0
Japan	4,442	10.2	Japan	593	4.6
East Asia NICs	9,140	21.0	East Asia NICs	258	2.0
South America	2,205	5.1	South America	168	1.3
Other	9,966	22.9	Other	674	5.2
World Total	43,562	100.0	World Total	12,914	100.0

TOP FIVE COUNTRIES

	Value	Share		Value	Share
Japan	4,442	10.2	France	4,098	31.7
France	3,714	8.5	United Kingdom	2,617	20.3
United Kingdom	3,353	7.7	Canada	2,241	17.4
Germany	2,967	6.8	Netherlands	909	7.0
China	2,112	4.8	Japan	593	4.6

See "Getting the Most Out of *Outlook '94*" for definitions of the country groupings.

Source: U.S. Department of Commerce: Bureau of the Census; International Trade Administration.

The cost of environment requirements is becoming a competitive concern. McDonnell Douglas estimates that costs related to safety, health, and environmental requirements in California alone have more than doubled since 1986. Business planning has become more difficult and time consuming in order to meet constantly changing environmental regulations. In addition to increasing production costs resulting from U.S. regulations, disparity in costs related to international environmental standards among nations could place U.S. manufacturers at a competitive disadvantage in the near future. The U.S. aerospace industry is urging negotiated international standards.

Outlook for 1994. U.S. aerospace sales should continue to decline in 1994. From January through June 1993, new aerospace orders were 24 percent lower than orders during the same period of 1992. Although the aerospace manufacturers' backlog remains quite large ($202 million), it has gradually declined since its peak in March 1991. Between the end of 1991 and the end of 1992, the backlog declined nearly 9 percent. Between January and June 1993, the backlog declined by more than 4 percent. As a result, aircraft manufacturers have been forced to reduce their production rates. For example, Boeing will cut its production of jetliners by one-third from January 1993 to mid-1994—a reduction of almost 50 percent from peak production levels of early 1992. Defense spending as a share of U.S. gross domestic product will be about 3 percent, the lowest level of the post–World War II period and half of what it was in the mid-1980s. With economic uncertainty restricting aftermarket purchases of spares, engine and parts suppliers in both military and civil segments of the industry will decline as well. Defense cutbacks have curtailed demand in the missile segment. U.S. space vehicle manufacturers will see an increase in commercial launches in 1994 due in part to long delays in launch schedules during 1993.

U.S. aerospace industry shipments will total about $102 billion in 1994. Aircraft production will continue to lead the industry with shipments of $42 billion. Shipments of engines and engine parts (SIC 3724) will fall to $17 billion, and shipments of aircraft parts (SIC 3728) will decline to $16 billion. Shipments of guided missiles and space vehicles (SIC 376) will increase 2 percent to $22 billion. Employment in that sector will decline 4 percent.

U.S. aerospace export sales, including avionics and flight simulators, are forecast to decline to about $35 billion in 1994, but will remain stronger than domestic sales (Table 1). More than 40 percent of the existing aerospace backlog is from foreign customers. Imports will also decline in 1994 to about $11 billion (Table 2). Imports will be driven primarily by increased shipments of Airbus Industrie aircraft to U.S. airlines. Aerospace companies will continue to cut back on employment as military programs are delayed or terminated.

AIRCRAFT

The large civil transport sector includes all passenger and cargo aircraft weighing more than 15,000 kilograms, typically two- and four-engine jetliners. In contrast to the booming production rates and bursting order books of the late 1980s, the large transport industry is adjusting itself to lower demand and declining orders from the airline industry, reduced production of narrow-body and wide-body aircraft, and fierce competition from Europe.

Large Transport Sector Restructuring. The future prospects for the large civil aircraft sector are mixed. Defense cuts continue to have a significant impact. U.S. military aircraft shipments, which long comprised a significant share of U.S. aircraft manufacturing, declined after reaching a record of $24 billion in 1987. Military aircraft shipments dropped to $8.4 billion in 1993 (Table 3). Boeing sells 20 percent of its products, by value, and McDonnell Douglas sells 60 percent of its products to the U.S. Government, almost all of it to the Department of Defense and the National Aeronautics and Space Administration (NASA). Exports are crucial to both companies. Boeing exports 55 percent of its aircraft and McDonnell Douglas exports approximately 25 percent of its products. Therefore, the significant reductions in DOD and foreign government military aircraft procurements, as well as the global recession, have affected the two U.S. aircraft manufacturers.

In the past, business on the commercial side has compensated for the cuts in defense. However, the 1991 conflict in the Persian Gulf, combined with the worldwide recession, stymied growth in airline traffic. Although international traffic recovered during 1992, and U.S. domestic traffic was stimulated by significant price discounting, the airline industry remained in dire financial straits. From 1990 to 1993, the U.S. airline industry lost $13 billion and is only now showing signs of partial, fitful, and inadequate recovery. After a decade of growth in the 1980s, these recent losses contributed to large-scale layoffs by airlines, aircraft manufacturers, and suppliers. Although deregulation fostered increased price competition among airlines, the economic downturn and slowdown in traffic reduced or even eliminated profit margins in the short term for many carriers, with some companies declaring bankruptcy. Braniff, Eastern, and Pan Am went out of business. Numerous smaller airlines

TABLE 1 U.S. Total Exports of Aerospace Vehicles and Equipment, 1992–1994 (Values in millions of dollars)

Items	1992[1] Units	1992[1] Value	1993[2] Units	1993[2] Value	1994[3] Units	1994[3] Value
Aerospace vehicles and equipment, total	—	45,030	—	40,118	—	34,777
Civilian aircraft	2,086	24,337	1,808	21,077	1,735	15,489
Under 4,536 kg. unladen weight, new	586	297	500	187	510	191
4,536–15,000 kg. unladen weight, new	60	295	48	254	50	260
Over 15,000 kg. unladen weight, new	387	22,379	275	19,500	195	13,900
Rotocraft, new	212	118	190	106	180	100
Nonpowered aircraft, new	—	7	—	12	—	13
Used or rebuilt	841	1,241	795	1,018	800	1,025
Military aircraft	428	2,083	500	1,311	500	1,384
New	331	1,909	370	1,250	380	1,284
Used	97	174	130	61	120	100
Aircraft engines and parts	—	6,699	—	6,361	—	6,394
Piston engines and parts	—	315	—	291	—	294
Complete engines, new and used	7,278	104	7,170	108	7,200	109
Engine parts	—	211	—	183	—	185
Turbine engines and parts[4]	—	6,384	—	6,070	—	6,100
Complete engines, new and used	18,540	2,484	27,150	2,580	26,000	2,600
Engine parts	—	3,900	—	3,490	—	3,500
Propellers, rotors, and parts	—	289	—	296	—	300
Landing gear and parts	—	362	—	310	—	320
Aircraft parts and accessories, n.e.c.	—	8,496	—	8,321	—	8,400
Avionics	—	795	—	663	—	700
Flight simulators	—	205	—	200	—	210
Guided missiles and parts	—	1,428	—	1,200	—	1,210
Space vehicles and parts	—	336	—	379	—	370

[1]Revised.

[2]Estimate.

[3]Forecast.

[4]Category changed to include reaction engines, other than turbojets—except missile and rocket—and their parts.

Source: U.S. Department of Commerce: International Trade Administration (ITA), Bureau of the Census. Estimates and forecasts by ITA.

such as Air Florida, People Express, and Ozark have merged or disappeared; others, such as TWA, Northwest, and Continental, are close to emerging or have recently emerged from Chapter 11 bankruptcy.

To help address these problems, President Clinton created the National commission to Ensure a Strong Competitive Airline Industry on April 7, 1993. The Commission's mandate was to investigate, study, and make policy recommendations about the financial health and future competitiveness of the U.S. airline and aerospace industries. The report summarizing the Commission's findings was released on August 19, 1993. Key recommendations contained in this report include: 1) cre-

TABLE 2 U.S. Total Imports of Aerospace Vehicles and Equipment, 1992–1994 (Values in millions of dollars)

ITEMS	1992[1] UNITS	1992[1] VALUE	1993[2] UNITS	1993[2] VALUE	1994[3] UNITS	1994[3] VALUE
Aerospace vehicles and equipment, total	—	14,473	—	13,154	—	11,463
Civilian Aircraft	620	3,866	664	3,442	649	3,474
Under 4,536 kg. unladen weight, new	118	104	122	60	125	62
4,536–15,000 kg. unladen weight, new	126	1,272	130	1,154	132	1,170
Over 15,000 kg. unladen weight, new	64	2,007	52	1,775	50	1,800
Rotocraft, new	148	179	140	192	142	195
Nonpowered aircraft, new	—	3	—	1	—	2
Used or rebuilt	164	301	220	260	200	245
Military aircraft	77	55	70	16	65	16
New (quantity of powered aircraft only)	26	50	32	14	30	13
Used	51	5	38	2	35	3
Aircraft engines and parts	—	6,124	—	5,344	—	4,116
Piston engines and parts	—	100	—	94	—	96
Complete engines, new and used	2,987	43	2,400	41	2,500	42
Engine parts	—	57	—	53	—	54
Turbine engines and parts[4]	—	6,204	—	5,250	—	4,020
Complete engines, new and used	2,849	3,017	2,480	2,630	2,158	2,020
Engine parts	—	3,007	—	2,620	—	2,000
Propellers, rotors, and parts	—	26	—	22	—	23
Landing gear and parts	—	78	—	61	—	53
Aircraft parts and accessories, n.e.c.	—	3,284	—	3,347	—	2,920
Avionics	—	511	—	478	—	435
Flight simulators	—	205	—	75	—	80
Guided missiles and parts	—	108	—	103	—	96
Space vehicles and parts	—	216	—	266	—	250

[1]Revised.

[2]Estimate.

[3]Forecast.

[4]Category changed to include reaction engines, other than turbojets—except missile and rocket—and their parts.

Source: U.S. Department of Commerce: International Trade Administration (ITA), Bureau of the Census. Estimates and forecasts by ITA.

ation of an independent Federal corporate entity within the Department of Transportation (DOT) to manage air traffic control and related functions; 2) establishment of a financial advisory committee to review the financial condition of individual airlines; 3) negotiation of multilateral agreements for passenger and cargo services, replacing the current system of bilateral agreements; 4) permitting foreign

TABLE 3   Shipments of Complete U.S. Aircraft, 1990–1994 (Values in millions of dollars)

	AIRCRAFT TOTAL		CIVIL TOTAL		LARGE TRANSPORTS		GENERAL AVIATION[1]		ROTOCRAFT		MILITARY TOTAL	
YEAR	UNITS	VALUE	UNITS	VALUE	UNITS	VALUE	UNITS	VALUE	UNITS	VALUE	UNITS	VALUE
1990	3,486	39,206	2,268	24,476	521	22,215	1,144	2,007	603	254	1,218	14,730
1991	2,934	40,776	2,181	29,035	589	26,856	1,021	1,968	571	211	753	11,741
1992[1]	2,465	41,828	1,833	32,246	610	30,268	899	1,836	324	142	632	9,582
1993[2]	2,079	36,483	1,429	28,097	429	26,310	710	1,660	290	127	650	8,386
1994[3]	1,851	28,475	1,311	20,555	306	18,715	730	1,720	275	120	540	7,920

1. Revised.
2. Estimate.
3. Forecast.

Source: U.S. Department of Commerce; International Trade Administration (ITA); general aviation (through first half 1993), General Aviation Manufacturers Association; rotorcraft (through first half 1993); Aerospace Industries Association. Estimates and forecasts by ITA.

investors to hold up to 49 percent voting equity in U.S. airlines; 5) increasing Export-Import Bank funding levels for large and small aircraft; and 6) enactment of a statute of repose for general aviation aircraft that would limit the liability of manufacturers of these aircraft to 15 years from the date of manufacture. The Commission made over 60 specific recommendations, but its omissions were equally significant. The Commission did *not* recommend major revisions to the present deregulated structure or suggest increased U.S. government supports or loan guarantees for the purchase or retrofitting of aircraft to meet Stage 3 aircraft noise standards. The Commission reasoned that although the U.S. International Airline Transport Association projected U.S. airline losses of $2 billion in 1993, airline over-expansion and aircraft over-capacity need to be addressed through market forces.

In addition to U.S. airline losses, international airlines are facing the difficulties of both a sluggish world economy and the competitive challenges derived from increased deregulation and international competition. This combination of events has led to restructuring policies by airlines, a slowdown in aircraft orders, and order deferrals. As a result, aircraft manufacturers have had to cut production rates of most models and are often confronted with unsold or "white tail" aircraft produced without a firm customer. These disruptions have undercut manufacturers' efforts to adjust to the defense cuts by transferring employees from defense to commercial product lines. At this time, both segments of the industry remain in a recession. Even significant international customers, such as the leasing company Guinness Peat Aviation Group of Ireland, have been forced to restructure in order to avoid bankruptcy and are canceling or rescheduling orders.

Strong competition from the European-based Airbus Industrie is further exacerbating the effects of lower demand. While U.S. aircraft manufacturers maintain 65 percent of the current world backlog of firm orders for large aircraft (Boeing with 56 percent and McDonnell Douglas with 9 percent), Airbus has established a firm control of the number two position with 34 percent and other European manufacturers with 1 per-

Trends and Forecasts: Aircraft (SIC 3721) (In millions of dollars except as noted)

Item	1991	1992[1]	1993[2]	1994[3]	Percent Change (1991–1994)		
					91–92	92–93	93–94
Industry Data							
Value of shipments[4]	58,090	58,900	53,000	41,500	1.4	−10.0	−21.7
Value of shipments (1987$)	48,449	47,045	41,309	36,630	−2.9	−12.2	−11.3
Total employment (000)	258	241	219	200	−6.6	−9.1	−8.7
Production workers (000)	125	114	102	95.0	−8.8	−10.5	−6.9
Average hourly earnings ($)	17.82	18.78	19.63	20.45	5.4	4.5	4.2
Capital expenditures	1,046	—	—	—	—	—	—
Product Data							
Value of shipments[5]	52,514	53,870	47,000	36,425	2.6	−12.8	−22.5
Value of shipments (1987$)	43,798	43,027	36,633	27,765	−1.8	−14.9	−24.2
Trade Data							
Value of imports	3,438	3,921	3,458	3,490	14.0	−11.8	0.9
Value of exports	24,173	26,419	23,414	16,900	9.3	−11.4	−27.8

[1] Estimate, except exports and imports.

[2] Estimate.

[3] Forecast.

[4] Value of all products and services sold by establishments in the aircraft industry.

[5] Value of products classified in the aircraft industry produced by all industries.

Source: U.S. Department of Commerce: Bureau of the Census; International Trade Administration (ITA). Estimates and forecasts by ITA.

cent. Helping to increase the pressure on the U.S. companies, Airbus introduced several new aircraft models over the last few years: the A340 in October 1991, the A330 in October 1992, and the A321 in May 1993. Airbus launched a 130-seat derivative of the A320—the A319—in 1993. Boeing and McDonnell Douglas have introduced their own new aircraft models: Boeing will deliver its first 777 aircraft, a twin-engine long-range jet, in May 1995, and has announced its intention to upgrade the line of 737 aircraft; McDonnell Douglas will deliver its first MD-90, a narrow-body, low-noise-level aircraft, in October 1994. During 1993 Boeing and McDonnell Douglas exported 275 large transport aircraft valued at $19.5 billion, and were the most significant contributors to the trade performance of the U.S. aerospace industry. The value of large civil transport exports are expected to fall 29 percent in 1994; imports will rise 1 percent.

All of these factors have affected the two U.S. producers. Both McDonnell Douglas and Boeing have announced reduced production rates for their aircraft and have had to resort to layoffs. Boeing announced planned layoffs of 28,000 workers for 1993 and the first half of 1994. By June 1993 McDonnell Douglas had trimmed its workforce by almost 59,000 or 44 percent below the peak levels of June 1990.

Foreign Markets. To help stem the tide of this declining demand and overcapacity, U.S. manufacturers are looking to Asia to provide future growth markets and partnerships for increasing their competitiveness. McDonnell Douglas has increased its ties with the People's Republic of China (PRC). In 1992 McDonnell Douglas successfully concluded a contract with the PRC to produce 40 narrow-body aircraft as part of their "trunkliner" program—35 were previously coproduced with the PRC. Boeing has made their three major Japanese suppliers "program partners" on the 777, and is also expanding its relationships with smaller Asian countries like Taiwan. This region of the world is attracting U.S. aircraft manufacturers with access to inexpensive capital, high-quality manufacturing, and lower production costs.

Over the long term, this segment of the aerospace industry should see increased growth. Demand in world commercial markets, particularly the expanding economies of Asia and the Pacific Rim, is expected to show increases over the next 10 to 15 years. In fact, the larger share of the commercial transport market is now overseas. The U.S. share, as a percentage of the world market, will shrink. Airline traffic, especially international traffic, is expected to show strong growth throughout the rest of the decade and the industry expects to deliver more than 14,000 aircraft over the next 20 years. Many new commercial sales are expected to come from the replacement of older, less fuel-efficient aircraft that will not meet airlines' requirements or federal and international noise and emissions standards.

Wide-body, longe-range aircraft, those targeted for the fast-growing international markets in Asia, will experience the most growth. Industry forecasts predict annual deliveries of about 225 long-range aircraft in 2011, compared with only 129 per year in 1992. In this product segment, the U.S.-made aircraft, the Boeing 747 and the Douglas MD-11, are competing against the A340, which is Airbus's first entrant into the long-range market.

The U.S. industry will continue to confront fierce competition from Airbus Industrie. However, there are indications that the U.S. and EC aerospace industries may be able to cooperate in the future. One example is the joint feasibility study being conducted by Boeing and the four major European aircraft manufacturers (Aerospatiale, Deutsche Aerospace, British Aerospace, and CASA) to determine the potential market for a Very Large Commercial Transport (VLCT) that would carry more than 600 passengers over long-range routes. A second example is the bilateral and multilateral negotiations to reduce the level of government supports provided to the aerospace industry. On July 17, 1992, the U.S. government and the European Commission signed a bilateral agreement that restricts government supports provided to the large civil aircraft sector. Specifically, the agreement prohibits all production supports and sets limits of 33 percent on the level of permissible government funding for new aircraft programs (down from 70 to 90 percent of existing Airbus aircraft). This agreement is viewed by the U.S. government and the domestic aerospace industry as a critical step in leveling the competitive playing field for U.S. large transport manufacturers who have suffered significantly from the competition of government-supported Airbus. Multilateral negotiations, which are focusing on broadening the product and country coverage of the bilateral agreement, began in July 1992 and continued through 1993. As part of these negotiations, the United States is seeking to strengthen the disciplines in the bilateral agreement by further reducing the level of government support allowed on new aircraft programs and adopting a stronger dispute settlement mechanism. The U.S. Government and the European Commission are also holding consultations to monitor and enforce each party's adherence to the 1992 bilateral agreement.

Aircraft Engine Manufacturing. The aircraft engine (SIC 3724) and aircraft parts (3728) industries face the same challenges confronting the U.S. large aircraft manufacturers. In 1993 U.S. manufacturers of aircraft engines, engine parts, and aircraft parts shipped an estimated $41 billion of products and employed 236,400 workers. This is down from shipments of $47.4 billion and employment of 276,000 in 1992. Shipments for this sector are expected to fall 18 percent in 1994 to $33.4 billion.

The recent deferrals and cancellations of aircraft orders by the airlines have directly affected the engine orders associated with those aircraft. The worldwide backlog of orders for civil turbofan engines stood at 5,800 at the beginning of 1992, but declining production rates at Boeing an McDonnell Douglas will stretch that backlog out several years. Therefore, the engine companies have been forced to restructure while they continue to invest heavily in the development of new products and technologies to take advantage of the recovery when it finally comes. All three major engine companies—General Electric (GE) and United Technologies' Pratt & Whitney (P&W) division in the United States, and Rolls Royce in the United Kingdom—are in the midst of costly programs to develop new engines to power the next generation of wide-body aircraft. GE is investing in the GE90, Rolls Royce is working on the Trent and P&W on the PW4000.

Aerospace suppliers of aircraft structures, systems, and components also face the same problems and are undergoing unprecedented consolidation, with many companies destined to exit the industry ranks for good. Boeing and McDonnell Douglas

Trends and Forecasts: Aircraft Engines and Engine Parts (SIC 3724) (In millions of dollars except as noted)

ITEM	1991	1992[1]	1993[2]	1994[3]	PERCENT CHANGE (1991–1994)		
					91–92	92–93	93–94
Industry Data							
Value of shipments[4]	22,746	24,075	21,000	17,250	5.8	−12.8	−17.9
Value of shipments (1987$)	19,211	19,621	16,680	13,350	2.1	−15.0	−20.0
Total employment (000)	122	109	95.4	90.0	−10.7	−12.5	−5.7
Production workers (000)	67.3	59.5	50.5	47.5	−11.6	−15.1	−5.9
Average hourly earnings ($)	15.56	15.80	16.20	16.35	1.5	2.5	0.9
Capital expenditures	771	—	—	—	—	—	—
Product Data							
Value of shipments[5]	21,315	22,561	19,450	15,752	5.8	−13.8	−19.0
Value of shipments (1987$)	18,002	18,387	15,450	12,190	2.1	−16.0	−21.1
Trade Data							
Value of imports	4,990	5,752	5,403	5,350	15.3	−6.1	−1.0
Value of exports	6,994	6,642	6,528	6,600	−5.0	−1.7	1.1

[1] Estimate, except exports and imports.

[2] Estimate.

[3] Forecast.

[4] Value of all products and services sold by establishments in the aircraft engines and engine parts industry.

[5] Value of products classified in the aircraft engines and engine parts industry produced by all industries.

Source: U.S. Department of Commerce: Bureau of the Census; International Trade Administration (ITA). Estimates and forecasts by ITA.

have concentrated their purchases on a smaller number of high-quality suppliers. In 1992 the number of aerospace/defense suppliers dwindled to about 30,000 companies, down from 120,000 in the mid-1980s. More than 60 percent of the value of each U.S. aircraft is produced by subcontractors. Fuselage, wing, and empennage structures, hydraulic, electrical, pneumatic, and environmental systems, avionics, composite structures, and assorted other parts are manufactured by thousands of other U.S. and foreign suppliers to the prime aircraft manufacturers.

These consolidations translate into job losses. All three of the big aircraft engine manufacturers have announced workforce reductions. P&W is cutting its peak 1991 workforce of 44,000 down to 30,000, while GE is reducing its payroll from 36,000 to 30,000. Rolls Royce is shrinking its workforce by 10 percent. Similar reductions are expected from the large suppliers of aircraft systems, such as Raytheon, GM-Hughes, Martin Marietta, Allied Signal, and TRW. Employment in the U.S. aircraft engines and engine parts (SIC 3724) and aircraft parts (SIC 3728) sectors fell 16 percent between 1990 and 1992. Long-term prospects are for continued declines on the military side and stabilizing employment on the commercial side.

In spite of the reduced demand, the U.S. engine segment is maintaining its global market position in the face of difficult economic conditions and foreign competition. Profit margins for new engines have been squeezed by the present perilous state of airline finances. In addition, since airlines fly less and require fewer spare engines in a recession, the engine manufacturers' lucrative spare parts business has been adversely affected.

Aircraft parts suppliers face the additional challenge of further globalization of large transport aircraft. Boeing and McDonnell Douglas gradually have increased the foreign content of their aircraft. For example, the percentage of foreign products (excluding the engines) installed on the Boeing 727, launched in 1959, was approximately 2 percent. Foreign products (excluding the engines) installed on the 767, launched in 1978, represent closer to 15 percent, and on the 777, launched in 1990, it may be almost 30 percent. For McDonnell Douglas, foreign products (excluding the engines) range from 15 to 20 percent of the aircraft value on the MD-11 and MD80/90, up significantly from the content on the older DC-9 and DC-10.

Military Aircraft Sector. U.S. military aircraft manufacturers shipped only $8.4 billion in complete aircraft in 1993 and are downsizing to adapt to the worldwide decline in defense spending for aircraft. U.S. manufacturers expect to ship only 540 aircraft or $7.9 billion in sales in 1994, less than half the number shipped in 1987. Historically, the U.S. government accounted for 80 percent of military aircraft sales. DOD's Foreign Military Sales program and direct exports of military aircraft have accounted for the remaining 20 percent. The reduced threat from the former Soviet Union has made defense spending a significant target for budget cuts. Although the United States has become the world's largest arms exporter with the collapse of the Soviet Union, the international market for aircraft has decreased as well. The latest Pentagon budget request indicated a cumulative real decline in DOD budget authority of more than 40 percent since 1985. The 1994 budget request also projects a 7 percent reduction in procurement funds. While procurement of aircraft has declined significantly, research, development, testing, and evaluation funding has remained stable, providing some haven for U.S. providers of advanced military aircraft technologies.

The budget cuts have hit all military aircraft: fixed-wing and helicopter, combat and transport, as well as production and development programs, resulting in cancellations and delays. DOD canceled the Navy A-12 attack fighter in 1991 after sched-

Trends and Forecasts: Aircraft Parts and Equipment, NEC (SIC 3728) (In millions of dollars except as noted)

ITEM	1991	1992[1]	1993[2]	1994[3]	PERCENT CHANGE (1991–1994)		
					91–92	92–93	93–94
Industry Data							
Value of shipments[4]	21,544	23,286	20,030	16,220	8.1	–14.0	–19.0
Value of shipments (1987$)	18,865	19,735	16,580	12,555	4.6	–16.0	–24.3
Total employment (000)	187	167	141	125	–10.7	–15.6	–11.3
Production workers (000)	108	96.3	79.8	78.3	–10.8	–17.1	–1.9
Average hourly earnings ($)	15.05	16.00	16.80	17.47	6.3	5.0	4.0
Capital expenditures	1,006	—	—	—	—	—	—
Product Data							
Value of shipments[5]	25,288	26,766	23,020	18,645	5.8	–14.0	–19.0
Value of shipments (1987$)	22,144	22,683	19,060	15,120	2.4	–16.0	–20.7
Trade Data							
Value of imports	3,888	3,132	2,325	2,030	–19.4	–25.8	–12.7
Value of exports	9,953	9,050	8,703	9,020	–9.1	–3.8	3.6

[1] Estimate, except exports and imports.

[2] Estimate.

[3] Forecast.

[4] Value of all products and services sold by establishments in the aircraft parts and equipment, NEC industry.

[5] Value of products classified in the aircraft parts and equipment, NEC industry produced by all industries.

Source: U.S. Department of Commerce: Bureau of the Census; International Trade Administration (ITA). Estimates and forecasts by ITA.

ule delays, cost overruns, and technical problems. Programs such as the Army's RAH-66 light helicopter and the Air Force's F-22 fighter, B-2 strategic bomber, and C-17 transport have been funded at levels lower than originally planned. Total C-17 procurement may be cut or procurement schedules stretched out. Although the C-17 program has suffered from cost overruns and technical problems in the past, 1993 was a turning point for the program. The C-17 survived heavy Congressional scrutiny and a successful resolution of the technical problems is expected.

Lost jobs are the ultimate price of defense cuts. Defense firms have cut hundreds of thousands of jobs over the past 5 years, and military aircraft companies are no exception. During 1992 alone, the prime military aircraft manufacturers, McDonnell Douglas, General Dynamics, Northrop, Lockheed, Rockwell, and Grumman, cut more than 29,000 jobs. These same companies have announced plans to cut another 20,000 jobs during 1993–1994. In the first half of 1993, aerospace employment declined at a 15 percent rate with commercial employment declining faster than military. Unlike past business cycles, the commercial sector is not able to absorb job losses in the military aircraft sector. As the restructuring winds down, the rate of job loss is expected to slow to between 5 and 10 percent in 1994. Increases in employment may not occur until the second half of this decade.

Exports provide little buffer from domestic spending cuts. Global defense spending is on the decline everywhere. U.S. manufacturers are finding it more difficult to compete in the European defense market as Europe's own military aircraft industry has been consolidated in an attempt to hold on to a larger share of declining local markets and to maintain a viable European defense industrial base.

Overcapacity resulting from years of Cold War production is intensifying competition worldwide. In 1990 U.S. manufacturers produced only about one-third of the world's military aircraft. Russia, the Ukraine, and other newly independent states produced thousands of military aircraft. Now operating at production rates less than one-third of capacity, these facilities in the former Soviet Union are scrambling for international sales. Both new and used MIG aircraft are being offered in aircraft competitions around the world. Other major competitors, such as France and the United Kingdom, are struggling to find international customers for their aircraft. China, Brazil, Italy, Taiwan, and Sweden are developing or producing fighters for international sales. Sales that are being made are often at break-even prices and require substantial concessions such as offsets and technology transfer. Most of the 1994 U.S. military exports will be helicopters as the need for sophisticated, front-line fighters decreases. The recent arms build-up in the Persian Gulf region is coming to an end, and the latest reduction in tensions between Israel and its neighbors will continue to reduce the need for new front-line fighters.

MISSILES AND SPACE LAUNCH VEHICLES

Shipments of U.S. missile systems, space launch vehicles, and related equipment are forecast to increase at a real rate of nearly 3 percent in 1994. Defense cutbacks and continued decline in the aerospace industry have curtailed demand in the missile segment, which is forecast to increase by only 2 percent. The space launch industry will increase commercial launches in 1994 due in part to long delays in launch schedules during 1993.

Missile Systems. In the wake of the cold war, Pentagon officials are shifting priorities away from nuclear weaponry and toward missile systems that will provide enhanced strategic conventional capability. New weapons programs in missiles and space will focus on U.S. ability to deter or win regional, non-nuclear conflicts. The president's budget request for fiscal year (FY) 1994 includes procurement of 24 Trident II nuclear missiles at a cost of more than $1.1 billion.

Improvements to the U.S. missile and space arsenal will highlight capabilities for precision strikes on command and control centers and knocking down enemy tactical ballistic missiles. Smarter and more lethal systems that increase standoff attack capabilities, such as the Tri-Service Stand-Off Attack Missile (TSSAM), will also take priority. Requested FY94 funding for initial procurement of the TSSAM was $195 million, while research and test outlays for the program are $433 million.

The Army and Navy are seeking to develop deep-strike missile systems to engage enemy targets quickly and improve reaction times. The Army Tactical Missile System (ATACMS) is a ground-based, deep-strike system that would coincide with Air Force attack capabilities. The Pentagon requested $144 million in the FY94 budget to procure 255 ATACMs. The Navy relies on its Tomahawk cruise missile for precision strikes against targets deep in enemy territory. The Navy plans to procure 216 Tomahawks in FY94 at a cost of $248 million.

On the defensive side of missile procurement, high priority will be given to the ground-based Anti-Tactical Ballistic Missiles (ATBM) and theater missile defensive systems over space-based interceptors. The FY94 budget request for the Strategic Defense Initiative Organization (SDIO) remained at the same $3.8 billion funding level of 1993. Funding for Theater High-Altitude Area Defense Missile (THAAD) and the Patriot/ERNT programs will receive priority under the new plan, while the Brilliant Pebbles program will be scaled back from $219 million in FY93 to $73 million in FY94, mainly for research and development.

Overall, 1994 DOD missile outlays are expected to increase by 2 percent, followed by cuts of 2 percent and 3 percent in 1995 and 1996, respectively.

The export market will become increasingly competitive in 1994 as European and Russian manufacturers compete with U.S. companies for shrinking defense spending overseas. Sales of U.S. missile systems (SIC 3761) through Foreign Military Sales programs reached an estimated $338 million in 1993, down significantly from $599 million in 1992. Air-to-air missiles represent the majority of this market. The United States has led this market in the past as foreign buyers looked to equip American-made fighters with U.S. missiles. The French MICA and Russian built AS-12 air-to-air missiles now pose a challenge to U.S. AIM-120 AMRAAM as well as the popular

Trends and Forecasts: Guided Missiles and Space Vehicles (SIC 3761) (In millions of dollars except as noted)

Item	1991	1992[1]	1993[2]	1994[3]	PERCENT CHANGE (1991–1994) 91–92	92–93	93–94
Industry Data							
Value of shipments[4]	23,399	22,089	21,625	22,035	−5.6	−2.1	1.9
Value of shipments (1987$)	24,787	23,599	22,956	24,081	−4.8	−2.7	4.9
Total employment (000)	136	119	97.1	93.0	−12.5	−18.4	−4.2
Production workers (000)	45.0	37.6	31.5	31.2	−16.4	−16.2	−1.0
Average hourly earnings ($)	19.07	20.05	20.85	21.50	5.1	4.0	3.1
Capital expenditures	450	—	—	—	—	—	—
Product Data							
Value of shipments[5]	16,075	15,400	14,846	15,306	−4.2	−3.6	3.1
Value of shipments (1987$)	17,028	16,452	15,760	16,728	−3.4	−4.2	6.1
Trade Data							
Value of imports	1.8	4.1	12.6	6.3	127.8	207.3	−50.0
Value of exports	318	599	338	523	88.4	−43.6	54.7

[1] Estimate, except exports and imports.

[2] Estimate.

[3] Forecast.

[4] Value of all products and services sold by establishments in the guided missiles and space vehicles industry.

[5] Value of products classified in the guided missiles and space vehicles industry produced by all industries.

Source: U.S. Department of Commerce: Bureau of the Census; International Trade Administration (ITA). Estimates and forecasts by ITA.

Sidewinder and Sparrow missiles. Unfortunately for U.S. suppliers, Israel has decided not to purchase the AIM-120 Advanced Medium Range Air-to-Air Missile (AMRAAM) in 1994, fearing similar escalating purchases by Saudi Arabia and other Arab states. Israel will rely on upgrades to the existing AIM-7 Sparrow and AIM-9 Sidewinder missiles.

Several European missile manufacturers are expected to merge in 1994–1995 to compete with larger and already consolidated U.S. companies. Shrinking defense budgets in Europe are expected to result in the consolidation of missile manufactures to benefit from joint R&D and economies of scale in production for European, U.S., and export market sales. Paris-based Matra-Hachette and the U.K.'s British Aerospace are contemplating the first move. British Aerospace was selected in 1992 to build the European Advanced Short Range Air-to-Air Missile (ASRAAM).

Space Launch Vehicles. The international market for commercial launch services for medium and large geosynchronous communications satellites declined from 14 launches in 1992 to 9 launches in 1993 because of delays in launch schedules. Geosynchronous, also known as geostationary, refers to satellites that travel at the same speed as the earth's rotation so the satellite appears to remain in the same place. The market is forecast to double in 1994 with 18 commercial launches scheduled. The actual number may be less if launch service companies are again unable to meet their aggressive schedules.

After five years of competing for commercial launch services, U.S. providers General Dynamics and McDonnell Douglas are holding on to a 36 percent share of the international market. The French/European consortium, Arianespace, had seven launches on its manifest for 1993 and plans ten launches in 1994. Arianespace controlled 62 percent of the large geosynchronous (GEO) commercial market in 1993. Arianespace currently has a launch backlog of 39 satellites worth approximately $3 billion. China's Long March Industry Corporation launched two commercial payloads in 1993 and has two launches on its manifest in 1994.

Commercial launch manifests for 1994 are crowded due to several launch failures in 1993. The failures caused long delays in international launch schedules as investigators determined causes and rockets lay idle awaiting green lights or modifications. Although expected launch rates may double in 1994, U.S. commercial launch providers still face another year of flat demand for satellite launch services. The demand for commercial launches of medium and large communications satellites leveled off at about 10 to 14 per year and is projected to remain that way for the next five years. The initial surge in demand for Expendable Launch Vehicles (ELVs) caused by the 1986 Challenger disaster, and aided by the U.S. government policy shift to dedicated launch vehicles, has subsided. Commercial launch service providers have since caught up with the backlog of commercial and military launches. Launch capacity will continue to exceed demand over the next five years as more international players enter the already crowded market for commercial launch services.

The U.S. Department of Transportation (DOT) licensed four large vehicle launches for geosynchronous communications satellites in 1993 and one launch for a Strategic Defense Initiative Organization (SDIO) experimental satellite. The communications satellite launches include two UHF satellites, the NATO IVB satellite, and the Telestar 401 satellite. Four of the five GEO launches were set for December 1993.

The government remains the largest consumer of U.S. space launch services, albeit a declining one. DOD, NASA, and the National Oceanic and Atmospheric Administration (NOAA) have had a joint requirement for about a dozen expendable launch vehicles per year, two or three of which are procured commercially, plus another three to four small orbital or suborbital launches. However, the declining strategic military threat and concomitant decline in defense spending has resulted in a downward revision in DOD's launch plans. Previously, the U.S. government used refurbished strategic missiles to meet some of its medium- and large-capacity launch requirements. A DOD directive now prohibits this practice because it unfairly competed with private U.S. launch services.

The United States lofted 14 expendable launch vehicles (ELVs) and eight Space Shuttle missions from Cape Canaveral, Florida, and four ELVs from Vandenberg Air Force Base in California in 1992. The French company Arianespace launched seven Ariane-4 boosters from Kourou in French Guiana. Russia conducted 33 launches from Plesetsk and 21 from the Baikanour Cosmodrome in Kazakhstan. The People's Republic of China conducted two launches out of Jiquan in addition to two flights of the Long March ELV from Xichang. Japan and India each launched one rocket.

U.S. commercial launch service providers will face increasingly fierce foreign competition in 1994. The European Space Agency is testing its next generation of the Ariane booster, the Ariane V, which will be able to put three medium-size satellites or several small satellites into orbit with a single launch at a reduced cost. In

Trends and Forecasts: Space Propulsion Units and Parts (SIC 3764) (In millions of dollars except as noted)

					PERCENT CHANGE (1991–1994)		
ITEM	1991	1992[1]	1993[2]	1994[3]	91–92	92–93	93–94
Industry Data							
Value of shipments[4]	3,658	3,453	3,336	3,234	−5.6	−3.4	−3.1
Value of shipments (1987$)	3,867	4,125	3,925	3,717	6.7	−4.8	−5.3
Total employment (000)	27.7	25.6	23.1	22.8	−7.6	−9.8	−1.3
Production workers (000)	9.5	8.3	8.1	7.9	−12.6	−2.4	−2.5
Average hourly earnings ($)	19.05	—	—	—	—	—	—
Capital expenditures	102	—	—	—	—	—	—
Product Data							
Value of shipments[5]	4,530	4,299	4,188	4,092	−5.1	−2.6	−2.3
Value of shipments (1987$)	4,789	5,136	4,927	4,703	7.2	−4.1	−4.5
Trade Data							
Value of imports	0.5	0.4	0.4	0.2	−20.0	0.0	−50.0
Value of exports	6.7	12.6	0.7	9.1	88.1	−94.4	530.0

[1] Estimate, except exports and imports.

[2] Estimate.

[3] Forecast.

[4] Value of all products and services sold by establishments in the space propulsion units and parts industry.

[5] Value of products classified in the space propulsion units and parts industry produced by all industries.

Source: U.S. Department of Commerce: Bureau of the Census; International Trade Administration (ITA). Estimates and forecasts by ITA.

January 1993 the U.S. Government approved Lockheed Corporation's request to enter into a joint venture with Russia's Khrunichev Enterprise, maker of the Proton launch vehicle. The new company, called Lockheed Khrunichev Energiya or LKE, will provide marketing and integration support for the Russian-made Proton. Negotiations to allow the launch of Western communications satellites on the Proton were completed in 1993 allowing Russia eight GEO launches through the year 2000. Launch prices for Russian ELVs are required to meet a 7.5 percent threshold below the lowest Western bid for a given contract. Proton launches to low earth orbit (LEO) will be considered on a case-by-case basis. Russia has already received U.S. permission to launch a satellite for the international consortium INMARSAT. The Proton is currently the most powerful commercial ELV in the world, with the ability to loft several small communications satellites to low earth orbit or two large satellites to geosychronous orbit. The PRC, originally expected to capture a limited share of the market, has had difficulties winning launch contracts. China's 1989 Memorandum of Agreement (MOA) with the United States allowing the Chinese to launch nine satellites over six years expires at the end of 1994. Negotiations are expected to resume in 1994 to renegotiate a follow-up agreement to the 1989 MOA.

Trends and Forecasts: Space Vehicle Equipment, NEC (SIC 3769) (In millions of dollars except as noted)

ITEM	1991	1992[1]	1993[2]	1994[3]	PERCENT CHANGE (1991–1994)		
					91–92	92–93	93–94
Industry Data							
Value of shipments[4]	1,907	1,810	1,751	1,723	−5.1	−3.3	−1.6
Value of shipments (1987$)	1,731	2,162	2,060	1,980	24.9	−4.7	−3.9
Total employment (000)	14.2	12.9	11.8	11.6	−9.2	−8.5	−1.7
Production workers (000)	7.7	7.6	7.4	7.1	−1.3	−2.6	−4.1
Average hourly earnings ($)	18.36	—	—	—	—	—	—
Capital expenditures	31.4	—	—	—	—	—	—
Product Data							
Value of shipments[5]	4,387	3,904	3,740	3,701	−11.0	−4.2	−1.0
Value of shipments (1987$)	3,981	4,664	4,400	4,254	17.2	−5.7	−3.3
Trade Data							
Value of imports	103	104	78.2	96.4	1.0	−24.8	23.3
Value of exports	899	839	577	693	−6.7	−31.2	20.1

[1] Estimate, except exports and imports.

[2] Estimate.

[3] Forecast.

[4] Value of all products and services sold by establishments in the space vehicle equipment, NEC industry.

[5] Value of products classified in the space vehicle equipment, NEC industry produced by all industries.

Source: U.S. Department of Commerce: Bureau of the Census; International Trade Administration (ITA). Estimates and forecasts by ITA.

The trend towards larger vehicles, with dramatically increased lift capabilities such as the Proton and Ariane V launch vehicles, is expected to curtail the number of commercial launches in coming years. The ability to launch multiple satellites on a single rocket could reduce demand for launch vehicles even in a growing market for satellite-based telecommunications, remote sensing, and direct broadcast services. Currently, the ability to "multiple-manifest" commercial launches for different customers remains largely unproven. Delivery lead times and changing launch schedules cause problems for customers and launch service providers. The ability to efficiently schedule and launch two GEO telecommunications satellites for different customers could prove to be a determining factor in lowering the cost per pound to orbit.

Developing the next Pc-265 c-265generation U.S. launch vehicle remains a low funding priority in FY94. The president's budget proposal scales back funding for the Spacelifter program, delaying yet again the development of a new rocket to replace the nation's current stable of ELVs. The National Aerospace Plane (NASP) program was also the victim of tighter budgets. In FY94 the United States will reduce funding for research and development in space transportation technologies. Lack of support for developing a new vehicle was reflected in the Senate Armed Services Committee suggestion that DOD investigate the possibility of launching payloads on non-U.S. launch vehicles. The House version of the budget retained the requested $53.9 million for spacelifter and added $36.74 million to the NASP program.

Strides toward developing a new single-stage-to-orbit (SSTO) technology highlighted industry R&D efforts last year and work continues in 1994. On August 18, 1993, the McDonnell Douglas Delta Clipper Experimental (DC-X) SSTO vehicle made a successful hover test, rising 150 feet in the air, moving laterally 350 feet, and landing. The DC-X will test the SSTO concept to demonstrate the viability of leapfrogging ahead of foreign competition in the international launch services industry. The House Armed Services Committee requested $75 million in additional funding in FY94 to continue the DC-X program and build a larger version of the experimental vehicle. The House committee also recommended that the SSTO program be shifted from the Ballistic Missile Defense Organization (BMDO) to the Advanced Research Projects Agency (ARPA).

NASA announced initial funding in both FY93 and FY94 for a four-phase study on developing new launch vehicles to meet expected demand in nonmilitary launch markets. The work will be conducted by a consortium of five aerospace companies including Boeing, Martin Marietta, Lockheed, General Dynamics, and Rockwell International.

Although funding for the next generation of launch vehicles has not increased, the Department of Defense announced a winner in the hotly contested Medium Launch Vehicle–3 competition (MLV-3). In April of 1993 the McDonnell Douglas Delta II ELV was awarded the contract to launch replacement satellites for the NAVSTAR Global Positioning System (GPS). Under the new contract, the Air Force has options for 36 launches valued at over $1 billion. The contract calls for McDonnell Douglas to "launch on demand" within 40 days of an Air Force notice.

In 1994 the new and growing segment of the space transportation industry continues to be the small- and medium-launch vehicle industry. Small launch vehicles serve the market for lightweight payloads (from a few hundred to 2,000 pounds) launched to low earth orbit or suborbital microgravity applications. These payloads consist primarily of suborbital scientific microgravity experiments as well as small telecommunications satellites, commonly known as microsats or lightsats. Medium vehicles serve the small communications and remote sensing markets with lift capabilities from 3,000 to 6,000 pounds to low earth orbit.

Lockheed Corporation announced it will enter the market for launch vehicles capable of placing payloads into low earth orbit (LEO) with a family of rockets to debut in 1995. The French company, Aerospatiale, is also considering the small vehicle market using Russian propulsion units to develop new lightweight vehicles capable of carrying single or multiple LEO payloads. These new vehicles would compete with Orbital Sciences Taurus ELV on the low end of lift capacity at approximately 3,200 pounds to LEO. McDonnell Douglas has also proposed a new launcher called the Delta-Lite, which would compete in the high-end of the market at 5,000 pounds to LEO. EER's Conestoga rocket was scheduled to carry NASA's COMET reentry vehicle in the summer of 1993, but funding problems caused a delay and the launch date is undetermined.

In the long term, the U.S. launch industry is working to focus efforts on lowering the cost per pound to orbit for commercial payloads. Three options—upgrading the existing fleet of vehicles, developing a new vehicle with off-the-shelf technology, and investing in new leap-frog technology—are at the center of the debate. Over the past three years, Congress has watched the National Launch System (NLS), Spacelifter, and a host of new single-stage-to-orbit and two-stage-to-orbit vehicles claim the next generation mantel. Projected costs for a completely new launch system are $8 to $10 billion over ten years. Marshaling these billions of dollars under increasingly tighter budgets will continue to be the major challenge facing U.S. launch service companies and policy makers over the next several years.

CASE
19

FRED R. DAVID
Francis Marion University

MCDONNELL DOUGLAS CORPORATION—1994

Our shared vision is to become the preeminent team of customer-focused people, creating the highest quality aerospace products and services which contribute to world peace, understanding and achievement. (John McDonnell, CEO, McDonnell Douglas Annual Report, 1992.)

Headquartered in St. Louis, Missouri, McDonnell Douglas Corporation (MDC) 314-232-0232 is the nation's largest defense contractor, the world's largest builder of military aircraft, the world's third largest commercial aircraft maker, and the third largest NASA contractor. However, MDC's earnings fell from $423 million in 1991 to $161 million in 1992. Company debt increased 19 percent to $2.8 billion. MDC's stock price fell from $73 to $48 per share during 1992.

MDC's 1992 earnings were substantially below 1991's as a result of three factors. First, there were $383 million of pretax charges in the C-17 program as a result of exceeding a fixed-price ceiling on development and initial production. Second, operating earnings of MDC's commercial aircraft business fell by $182 million. Third, the new accounting rule for retiree health benefits reduced 1992 earnings by $133 million.

MDC closed three fabrications plants in the United States during 1992 in order to raise average plant utilization to more than 75 percent by 1994, when in-house fabrication work will be consolidated at remaining plants. MDC reduced employment by 32 percent during 1990–1992, while industry employment fell 24 percent in the same period. Demand for both commercial aircraft and military aircraft is declining, so MDC may be in serious trouble. The company needs a clear strategic plan for the mid-1990s.

Operating earnings for MDC's military aircraft segment were $19 million in 1992, $404 million in 1991, and negative $48 million in 1990. Excluding the C-17, MDC's ten biggest government aerospace programs as a group (F/A-18, F-15, AV-8B, T-45 trainer aircraft, AH-64 Apache helicopter, Tomahawk and Harpoon missiles, Advanced Cruise Missile, Delta Launch vehicle, and Space Station) had 1992 earnings equal to nearly 10 percent of revenues. That is a fair return by industry standards and is up from 9 percent in 1991 and 8 percent in 1990. Seven of the ten projects had improved margins in 1992.

MDC is the prime contractor for three major military aircraft programs that are likely to remain in production into the next decade; although total U.S. government purchases of aerospace products—the F/A-18 Hornet, the C-17 Globemaster III, and the T-45 Goshawk—are declining, MDC expects positive earnings from the C-17 program in 1993 with delivery of the final aircraft in the development program. Flight and ground testing of the new military transport will continue into 1994.

With a larger wing, a lengthened fuselage, and higher thrust engines, the F/A-18 E/F will have the range and payload capabilities to perform the bulk of the U.S. Navy's strike and fighter missions well into the next century. The next-generation Hornet is central to the U.S. Navy's new "From the Sea" war-fighting doctrine, which shifts its focus from open-ocean warfare to regional and coastal operations. The advanced Hornet will have up to 40 percent more range than earlier versions, combined with greater weapons-carrying capacity, improved survivability, and capacity for future growth. The first flight of the F/A-18 E/F is scheduled for late 1995.

MDC's most important achievement in 1992 was the award of a $3.7 billion contract from the U.S. Navy to begin development of a major upgrade of the Hornet, called F/A-18 E/F. Coupled with continuing purchases by the Navy of F/A-18 C/D models, this development program firmly establishes the Hornet as the cornerstone of U.S. naval aviation well into the next century. MDC expects to remain the nation's largest defense contractor in 1993, measured by prime Department of Defense contract awards. However, Lockheed and Martin Marietta, which have enlarged their defense businesses through major acquisitions, are challenging MDC for the number one position in total sales to the government.

Internationally, the Hornet program now has been selected as the front-line fighter of six countries outside the United States: Finland, Switzerland, Kuwait, Canada, Australia, and Spain. Deliveries to the Finnish air force will begin in 1995 and continue through 2000. In Switzerland selection of the F/A-18 over the F-16 and several European-made fighters was reaffirmed by the Swiss Federal Council in 1991 and approved by the Swiss parliament in 1992. However, the Swiss order is subject to a positive outcome on a national referendum in 1993. The Israeli air force is evaluating several advanced combat aircraft, including the F/A-18. By year-end 1992, 1,150 Hornets had been delivered to the U.S. Navy and Marine Corps and to other nations.

MDC won a $3 billion order for the F/A-18 Hornet from Finland in the most fiercely contested international fighter plane competition in 1992. MDC also won a $5 billion order for 72 F-15 Eagles from Saudi Arabia and a $400 million order for 13 AV-8B Harrier II Plus aircraft from Italy. The Saudi Arabian F-15 sale was a great example of teamwork at a grassroots level. Thousands of people at MDC and its suppliers joined together in rallying U.S. congressional and presidential support for the sale. The sale extends F-15 production into 1998, preserving 7,000 jobs at MDC.

The C-17 Globemaster III is a central element in the U.S. Air Force's post–cold war strategy of "global reach, global power." The giant aircraft will provide large cargo airlift capability from U.S. bases to austere airfields anywhere in the world. Air Force plans call for production and delivery of 120 Globemaster IIIs for that mission. During 1992 MDC delivered four initial production C-17s to the Air Force for the flight test program. In the first half of 1993, MDC delivered the fifth and sixth production aircraft, which were the last aircraft covered in the development and initial production contract.

MDC expects the C-17 to be profitable in 1993. However, with 75 percent of flight testing still to go, additional problems may be identified during testing. MDC is under firm contract for 10 production C-17s, and Congress has approved funding for ten more aircraft. Production of an additional eight aircraft was authorized in the 1993 defense bill.

The sale of 72 F-15 Eagles to Saudi Arabia extends production of the F-15 into 1998. Additionally, the Saudi order will permit MDC to compete with the F-15 for other international orders in coming years. Saudi F-15 deliveries are expected to begin in 1995.

MDC is supporting U.S. Navy and Marine Corps efforts, which could lead to remanufacturing of existing AV-8B Harrier day attack aircraft to the Harrier II Plus radar/night attack configuration—providing an aircraft with greatly improved capabilities and a new service life at approximately two-thirds the cost of a new Harrier II Plus.

The first production aircraft deliveries of the T-45A Goshawk to the U.S. Naval Air Station in Kingsville, Texas, began in early 1992. By midyear, Kingsville formed the first T-45 training squadron. Current Navy plans call for 268 aircraft to be delivered through the year 2003. The program suffered a setback recently, however, when its first test aircraft veered from the runway and sustained major damage after landing at Edwards Air Force Base, California. Test flights resumed after the cause of the accident was established. Nine St. Louis–assembled T-45s were delivered to the Navy in 1992.

The majority of the U.S. Army's procurement of AH-64 Apache helicopters are expected to be delivered by late 1993. However, orders from the United Arab Emirates, Greece, and other countries have extended Apache deliveries into mid-1995 and hold open the door for additional foreign military sales. Projected international orders would sustain the production line into 1996, when the U.S. Army plans to begin a modernization program to remanufacture its Apache fleet into a new and more capable AH-64 C/D configuration. The first two AH-64D Longbow prototypes flew for the first time in 1992, each ahead of contract schedule. The MD Explorer, the first all-new commercial helicopter in the 1990s, featuring the NOTAR system, celebrated its first year of service in October. To date, more than 30 MD 520Ns have been delivered worldwide. In 1992 MDC delivered 57 MD 500 Series helicopters.

COMMERCIAL AIRCRAFT

MDC's commercial aircraft business continued to make a profit in 1992, operating in a cyclical market that has gone from boom to bust as a result of three consecutive years of heavy losses by U.S. and world airlines. As a result of weak market conditions, MDC delivered only 84 MD-80 twin jets in 1992, compared with 138 in 1991. Even so, the program generated sufficient earnings to more than offset a small losss in the new MD-11 trijet line. There will be a further decrease in twin jet deliveries in 1993. The ability of airlines to pay for MD-80 and MD-11 deliveries scheduled in 1993 is a major concern. Projections of positive cash flow for the MD-11 and the commercial transport business as a whole in 1993 are based on scheduled deliveries and payment of aircraft as ordered. MDC is working closely with some airline customers to help financial arrangements to complete deliveries on time.

In 1992 the world's airlines and leasing companies placed firm orders for fewer than 325 new jetliners, net of cancellations. By contrast, airlines and leasing companies placed net firm orders for more than 1,600 aircraft in 1989. With the large number of orders received from 1987 to 1990, MDC faced the challenge of increasing production rapidly to satisfy customer requirements for new aircraft with near-term delivery schedules. In adjusting to fewer new orders and the cancellation of a number of existing orders since then, MDC has faced the radically different challenge of reducing cost structures and scaling back production while continuing to make on-time deliveries of quality products and continuing to work on new models or new-generation aircraft.

Development and production milestones were met in preparing the MD-90—an advanced derivative of the MD-80—for its rollout and first flight in 1993 and entry into its flight test and certification program. The MD-90 will be the quietest and most environmentally clean aircraft in the 150-seat aircraft class when it enters airline service in 1994. The MD-11 jetliner reached a key milestone in 1993. The unit cost of a newly delivered MD-11 fell below the sales price on a consistent basis for the first time. Although the MD-11 did not achieve improved earnings in 1993, it generated positive cash flow. The MD-11 trijet was the biggest single consumer of cash of all MDC programs in 1992.

MDC delivered 42 MD-11 trijets in 1992—11 more than in 1991, the first full year of production. At year end, 76 MD-11s were in service, with 14 operators, carrying more than one-half million passengers and traveling more than 10 million miles each month. As of December 31, 1992, the MD-11 program status included 97 firm orders, 127 options and reserves, and 76 deliveries, for a total of 300 aircraft. On the same date, the MD80/90 program included 186 firm orders, 227 options and reserves, and 1,047 deliveries, for a total of 1,460 aircraft. MDC is scheduled to deliver more than 30 trijets and more than 40 twin jets in 1993. However, the ability of some airlines to pay for deliveries scheduled in 1993 is a major concern. Increased MD-11 trijet deliveries in 1992 offset reduced MD-80 twin jet deliveries. MDC delivered 84 MD-80 twin jets in 1992, as compared with 138 in 1991 and 139 in 1990. The decreased MD-80 deliveries in 1992 reflect the overall softness in the commercial aircraft market. MDC delivered 42 MD-11 trijets in 1992, compared with 31 in 1991 and 3 in 1990.

MDC was almost even with Airbus Industrie in total seats delivered in 1992—each with about 19 percent of the industry total. MDC was also close to matching Airbus in new firm orders, net of cancellations, with 11 percent of the industry total for 1992 compared with 13 percent for Airbus. Swissair, Delta, Altitalia, Martinair, and International Lease Finance Corporation all placed firm orders for MD-11s in 1992. SAS, a Scandinavian airline, became the first airline in Europe to order the MD-90. In a modification of an existing order, SAS added six MD-90s while reducing their MD-80 orders by seven.

In MDC's biggest commercial win in 1992, MDC and the People's Republic of China reached agreement on a major aircraft purchase and coproduction program. In a competition with the Boeing 737, MDC twin jets were selected by the PRC for its Trunkliner program. Final assembly of 40 twin jets (a combination of MD-80s and MD-90s) will be performed in China. The agreement with China calls for discussions by 1995 that could lead to orders for up to 130 additional MD-90s.

Operating revenues in the commercial aircraft segment decreased 2 percent after increasing 72 percent in 1991. The commercial aircraft segment reported operating earnings of $109 million in 1992 and $291 million in 1991, and operating losses of

$83 million in 1990. Factors contributing to lower 1992 earnings for the segment were reduced margins on the MD-11 trijet and higher research and development expenditures. Research and development costs, which were lower in 1992 for the MD-11 trijet, increased on the MD-90. In addition, research and development costs were incurred in 1992 on the MD-12, a proposed four-engine jumbo airliner.

Despite higher deliveries and revenues, the MD-11 program incurred operating losses in 1992 after recording a small operating profit in 1991. Contributing to the 1991 operating profit was the retention of $40 million of advance payments made by commercial airline customers that defaulted in their contracts in 1991. Because costs on the MD-11 program did not decline as rapidly as planned, MDC has raised its cost estimate for the total program.

MISSILES, SPACE, AND ELECTRONIC SYSTEMS

The missiles, space, and electronic systems division had record earnings in 1992. Revenues increased by 6 percent, mostly as a result of increased work on Space Station Freedom, the largest single program in this division. Revenues had decreased by 6 percent in 1991. Space Station Freedom will provide participants with new opportunities for research in life sciences, materials and earth sciences, and astrophysics.

Operating earnings of the missiles, space, and electronic systems segment were $197 million in 1992 as compared to $168 million in 1991 and $167 million in 1990. Increased 1992 operating earnings reflect improved margins on the Harpoon, Tomahawk, ACM, and Delta programs, partially offset by a decrease in earnings on electronic systems programs.

MDC is responsible for the largest part of the Space Station Freedom program: building the initial segments that are first launched into space. In 1992 MDC and NASA took several important steps toward making Space Station Freedom ready for first element launch in 1996. In preparation for the integration and testing of elements that will be sent into space, MDC has substantially completed construction of a 178,000-square-foot office tower and a high bay assembly and test building at the space station's Clear Lake Development Facility in Houston, Texas.

An important milestone was reached when 21 detailed design reviews of space station elements and systems were completed in preparation for a critical design review in 1993. Space Station Freedom accounted for about 40 percent of 1992 revenues in MDC's space systems business. The decision to "restructure" the program, announced by President Clinton's administration in 1993, raises uncertainties as to the configuration and schedule of the program, including the portion of the program for which MDC is responsible.

During 1992 MDC's Delta launch program continued to enhance its record as the world's most reliable launch system. There were 11 Delta launches in 1992, bringing the total number of successful consecutive launches to 39. The Delta program has strongly improved earnings, partly as a result of reduced manufacturing costs at the Delta assembly plant in Pueblo, Colorado, and improved cycle time for launch processing at the Cape Canaveral Air Force Station in Florida.

MDC is working on a contract won in 1991 for a single-stage rocket technology (SSRT) experiment for the Strategic Defense Initiative Organization to demonstrate technology readiness for a single stage-to-orbit reusable launch vehicle. Integration, assembly, and test activities are already under way, and test firings and demonstration flights were completed in 1993.

MDC's missiles business led the way for its segment in improved financial performance in 1992. The Tomahawk and Harpoon/SLAM missile programs had an outstanding year in terms of winning new business, driving down costs, and improving profitability. The Tomahawk meets the need for weapon systems that enable the United States to project power quickly—and convincingly. In the eight years since MDC entered the program as a dual-source producer, the inflation-adjusted price of the Tomahawk missile has dropped by more than two-thirds, and overall program savings for the U.S. government have been estimated at $3.5 billion.

MDC has won the majority production share in the last two annual dual-source competitions to build Navy Tomahawks. MDC is currently working under a $179 million contract to build 114 Tomahawks, which represented 65 percent of the Navy's 1992 procurement. In January 1993 MDC received a $201.6 million contract to build another 120 Tomahawks and to remanufacture an additional 120 missiles in inventory into upgraded Block III Tomahawks. That contract represents 60 percent of total Tomahawk procurement for 1993.

Overseas customers ordered 122 Harpoon anti-ship missiles in 1992, which was ten fewer than in 1991. Over 40 percent of the 5,919 Harpoons produced since the program began 21 years ago have been delivered to a total of 20 overseas customers. U.S. orders for the basic Harpoon missile stopped in 1989.

MDC's electronic systems business lost money in 1992 as a result of $38 million in loss provisions in the laser crosslink program. The laser crosslink is an advanced product that enables satellites to communicate directly with one another in orbit, reducing dependency on ground stations. Under a fixed-price development contract, MDC has incurred losses totaling $119 million in this program since its inception in 1980. TRW, the program's prime contractor, expects MDC to deliver five additional units in 1993 and 1994.

Most of the other parts of MDC's electronic systems business continued to operate profitably in 1992. Work performed in complex software, microprocessors, and lasers contributes to many MDC products. MDC is a leader in the military command, control, communications, and intelligence (C^3I) field. For 1993 Congress approved 36 Mast Mounted Sights, an electro-optical system that enables helicopter pilots and ships' crews to detect and designate targets for attack helicopters, by day or night or in inclement weather.

OTHER MCDONNELL DOUGLAS OPERATIONS

McDonnell Douglas Finance Corporation (MDFC). MDFC reduced its total assets by 22 percent to $2 billion as it disposed of a number of businesses in 1992 and continued to sharpen its focus on core markets of aircraft and commercial equipment leasing. During the year MDFC reduced its exposure in noncore lending and leasing operations by more than one-half. The disposition of several of the finance company's operations and portfolios was the principal factor in causing a substantial reduction in MDC's 1992 revenues for businesses grouped under "financial services and other."

MDFC's aircraft financing and commercial equipment leasing were solidly profitable. The aircraft financing operation provided $255 million in financing for MDC commercial aircraft customers. Aircraft transactions completed in 1992 varied in type from bridge notes on an MD-88 aircraft for Aerolineas Argentinas, to predelivery notes on eight MD-82s for USAir, and to lease financing of a new MD-83 for Reno Air, a recently formed carrier. MDFC also helped arrange the financing of two MD-11 aircraft for Varig and another three for China Eastern. At year end the aircraft-leasing operation portfolio totaled $1 billion, with MDC-built aircraft accounting for 76 percent of the value. The commercial equipment leasing operation wrote $51 million in new leases in 1992 and ended the year with a portfolio worth $557 million. Included in its business is the lease of corporate aircraft and other large equipment items.

McDonnell Douglas Realty Company (MDRC). MDRC manages a 4.6-million-square-foot portfolio valued in excess of $500 million. In 1992 the company provided increased consulting services to MDC by negotiating rental reductions, auditing existing lease arrangements, and consolidating lease facilities to utilize space more efficiently. MDRC's revenue and the total asset value of its portfolio increased approximately 7 percent in 1992, and its commercial portfolio continued to perform above average, with less than 12 percent vacancy rates. MDRC in 1992 continued to work on the development of two new MDC facilities near Houston, Texas, that will serve the space station program.

McDonnell Douglas Travel Company (MDTC). In a poor year for the travel industry MDTC generated $152 million in business travel sales, almost matching 1991 business volume. MDTC was established in 1986 and is a travel agency serving MDC and all its divisions, as well as external customers.

McDonnell Douglas Technical Services Company (MDTSC). MDTSC was established in 1989 to provide MDC and other employers with a pool of experienced and skilled workers (including retirees) to fill specific needs on short notice. MDTSC's business increased by 60 percent in 1992 as its five branch offices placed professionals in over 2,000 contract assignments within MDC and at commercial clients. MDTSC has further increased its capabilities by developing a resource pool instantly accessible from its online computer database of more than 50,000 potential employees.

CONCLUSION

The sale of McDonnell Douglas Information Systems International (MDISI) in the first quarter of 1993 completed a four-year program to divest all MDC businesses in the information systems field. In total, including MDISI, divestitures in the information systems field resulted in pretax gains of about $375 million on proceeds of more than $900 million.

MDC's long-term strategy is to obtain partners around the world interested in sharing in the risks and rewards of the commercial aircraft business. MDC was not able to bring an international alliance together in 1992. MDC also plans to divest of its laser systems business and portions or all of McDonnell Douglas Helicopter Company.

MDC must reverse recent declines in earnings. Should the company diversify into nonaircraft-related businesses? Should MDC acquire an ailing U.S. airline? Should MDC seek a merger with Boeing in an attempt to compete more effectively with Airbus? Prepare a strategic plan for CEO McDonnell that will best assure prosperity for MDC in the mid- to late 1990s.

EXHIBIT 19-1 Selected Financial Data

	REVENUES			EARNINGS			FIRM BACKLOG (UNAUDITED)[†]		
MILLIONS OF DOLLARS	1993	1992	1991	1993	1992	1991	1993	1992	1991
Military aircraft	$ 6,852	$ 7,238	$ 7,795	$ 83	$ 8	$ 394	$ 7,997	$ 7,619	$ 9,540
Commercial aircraft	4,760	6,595	6,752	40	102	283	9,172	13,364	17,913
Missiles, space and									
electronic systems	2,575	3,169	2,979	338	191	163	2,210	3,069	2,995
Financial services and other	287	352	519	31	20	26			
Operating									
revenues/earnings	14,474	17,354	18,045	492	321	866			
Non-operating income/net	13	11	16	(5)	(4)	(13)			
Discontinued operations				37	57	66			
General corporate expenses				(9)	(12)	(6)			
Postretirement benefit									
curtailment				70	1,090				
Interest expense				(89)	(309)	(232)			
Income taxes				(100)	(388)	(258)			
Cumulative effect of									
accounting change					(1,536)				
	$14,487	$17,365	$18,061	$ 396	$ (781)	$ 423	$19,379	$24,052	$30,448

	ASSETS[†]			PROPERTY, PLANT AND EQUIPMENT ACQUIRED			DEPRECIATION AND AMORTIZATION		
MILLIONS OF DOLLARS	1993	1992	1991	1993	1992	1991	1993	1992	1991
Military aircraft	$ 3,715	$ 3,960	$ 4,328	$23	$ 70	$ 49	$149	$191	$212
Commercial aircraft	4,561	5,850	5,529	1	29	51	70	89	79
Missiles, space and									
electronic systems	1,330	1,524	1,741	38	116	70	48	102	102
Financial services and other	2,340	2,222	2,793		2		49	71	102
Continuing operations	11,946	13,556	14,391	62	217	170	316	453	495
Corporate	80	133	133	2		1	7	12	4
Discontinued operations		92	77						
	$12,026	$13,781	$14,601	$64	$217	$171	$323	$465	$499

[†]Amounts as of December 31.

Source: McDonnell Douglas *Annual Report*, 1993.

EXHIBIT 19-2   Consolidated Statement of Operations

YEARS ENDED DECEMBER 31 (MILLIONS OF DOLLARS, EXCEPT SHARE DATA)	1993	1992	1991
Revenues	$14,487	$17,365	$18,061
Costs and expenses:			
Cost of Products, services and rentals	12,822	15,567	15,561
General and administrative expenses	720	825	1,003
Research and development	341	509	429
Postretirement benefit curtailment	(70)	(1,090)	
Interest expense:			
Aerospace segments	89	309	232
Financial services and other segment	126	159	221
Total Costs and Expenses	14,028	16,279	17,446
Earnings from Continuing Operations Before Income Taxes and Cumulative Effect of Accounting Change	459	1,086	615
Income taxes	100	388	258
Earnings from Continuing Operations Before Cumulative Effect of Accounting Change	359	698	357
Discontinued operations:			
Earnings from operations, net of income taxes		20	(8)
Gain on disposals, net of income taxes	37	37	74
	37	57	66
Earnings Before Cumulative Effect of Accounting Change	396	755	423
Cumulative effect of initial application of new accounting standard for postretirement benefits		(1,536)	
Net Earnings (Loss)	$ 396	$ (781)	$ 423
Earnings (Loss) Per Share:			
Continuing operations	$ 9.17	$ 17.97	$ 9.32
Discontinued operations:			
Earnings from operations		.50	(.22)
Gain on disposals	.93	.96	1.93
Cumulative effect of accounting change		(39.53)	
	$ 10.10	$ (20.10)	$ 11.03
Dividends Declared Per Share	$ 1.40	$ 1.40	$ 1.40

Source: McDonnell Douglas *Annual Report,* 1993.

EXHIBIT 19-3 Consolidated Balance Sheet

DECEMBER 31 (MILLIONS OF DOLLARS AND SHARES)	1993	1992
Assets		
Cash and cash equivalents	$86	$82
Accounts receivable	555	604
Finance receivables and property on lease	2,357	2,262
Contracts in process and inventories	5,774	7,230
Property, plant and equipment	1,750	1,991
Other assets	1,504	1,612
Total Assets	$12,026	$13,781
Liabilities and Shareholders' Equity		
Liabilities:		
Accounts payable and accrued expenses	$2,190	$3,018
Accrued retiree benefits	$1,388	1,544
Income taxes	574	572
Advances and billings in excess of related costs	1,251	1,384
Notes payable and long-term debt:		
Aerospace segments	1,625	2,767
Financial services and other segment	1,513	1,474
	8,541	10,759
Minority Interest	72	
Shareholders' Equity:		
Preferred Stock—none issued		
Common Stock—issued and outstanding:		
1993, 39.3 shares; 1992, 39.2 shares	39	39
Additional capital	335	327
Retained earnings	3,043	2,702
Translation of foreign currency statements	(4)	(10)
Unearned ESOP compensation		(36)
	3,413	3,022
Total Liabilities and Shareholders' Equity	$12,026	$13,781

Source: McDonnell Douglas *Annual Report*, 1993.

EXHIBIT 19-4 Consolidated Statement of Shareholders' Equity

Years Ended December 31 (Millions of dollars)	1993	1992	1991
Common Stock			
Beginning balance	$ 39	$ 38	$ 38
Shares issued to employee savings plans		1	
	39	39	38
Additional Capital			
Beginning balance	327	287	283
Employee stock awards and options	6	2	4
Shares issued to employee savings plans	2	38	
	335	327	287
Retained Earnings			
Beginning balance	2,702	3,538	3,168
Net earnings (loss)	396	(781)	423
Cash dividends declared	(55)	(55)	(53)
	3,043	2,702	3,538
Translation of Foreign Currency Statements	(4)	(10)	14
Unearned ESOP Compensation			
Beginning balance	(36)		
Prepayment of future employee benefits		(50)	
Shares allocated to employees	36	14	
		(36)	
Shareholders' Equity	$3,413	$3,022	$3,877

Source: McDonnell Douglas *Annual Report*, 1993.

EXHIBIT 19-5 Consolidated Statement of Cash Flows

YEARS ENDED DECEMBER 31 (MILLIONS OF DOLLARS)	1993	1992	1991
Operating Activities			
Earnings from continuing operations			
before cumulative effect of accounting change	$ 359	$ 698	$ 357
Adjustments to reconcile earnings from continuing operations			
before cumulative effect of accounting change			
to net cash provided (used) by operating activities:			
Depreciation of property, plant and equipment	258	353	370
Depreciation of rental equipment	50	58	89
Amortization of intangible and other assets	15	54	40
Gain on sale of assets	(44)		
Pension income	(138)	(107)	(55)
Postretirement benefit curtailment	(70)	(1,090)	
Non-cash retiree health care costs	20	133	
Change in operating assets and liabilities:			
Accounts receivable	40	97	2
Finance receivables and property on lease	(521)	(316)	111
Contracts in process and inventories	1,445	43	(1,098)
Accounts payable and accrued expenses	(822)	(22)	612
Income taxes	(5)	217	240
Advances and billings in excess of related costs	(112)	(703)	38
Discontinued operations		(2)	(26)
Net Cash Provided (Used) by Operating Activities	475	(587)	680
Investing Activities			
Property, plant and equipment acquired	(64)	(217)	(171)
Proceeds from sale of property, plant and equipment		173	
Finance receivables and property on lease	414	529	706
Proceeds from sale of discontinued businesses	181	70	200
Proceeds from sale of assets	32		
Other, including discontinued operations	11	(51)	(2)
Net Cash Provided by Investing Activities	574	504	733
Financing Activities			
Net change in borrowings (maturities 90 days or less)	(830)	574	(1,087)
Debt having maturities more than 90 days:			
New borrowings	681	1,461	487
Repayments	(954)	(2,009)	(743)
Minority interest	72		
Payments from (to) ESOP—net	36	(36)	
Proceeds of stock options exercised	5		
Dividends paid	(55)	(54)	(67)
Net Cash Used by Financing Activities	(1,045)	(64)	(1,410)
Increase (Decrease) in Cash and Cash Equivalents	4	(147)	3
Cash and cash equivalents at beginning of year	82	229	226
Cash and cash equivalents at end of year	$ 86	$ 82	$ 229

Source: McDonnell Douglas *Annual Report*, 1993.

The Boeing Company (206-655-2121), headquartered in Seattle, Washington, is the largest aerospace firm in the United States, as measured by total sales, and the world's leading manufacturer of commercial aircraft. For the past three years, Boeing has also had the distinction of being the nation's largest exporter. Jetliners currently in production include the 737, 747, 757, and 767—with the new 777 model scheduled for delivery in 1995. Boeing manufactures helicopter, military aircraft, electronic systems, and missiles.

The year 1992 was difficult for most airline carriers, which are Boeing's primary customer. While world passenger traffic recovered from the decline in 1991, stiff competition among carriers drove down fares and depressed yields. As a result, many airlines recorded substantial losses. The market for new aircraft was correspondingly down in 1992, with Boeing announcing new orders valued at $17.8 billion, compared with $20.6 billion the year before.

Because of lower demand and the growing number of requests by airlines to defer orders, Boeing cut production rates on Boeing 737, 747, 757, and 767 jetliners. By mid-1994, Boeing will be producing 21 jetliners per month, compared with 32.5 at year-end 1992. Development of the new Boeing 777 wide-body aircraft is on schedule, however, with the first delivery scheduled in 1995.

In defense and space Boeing recorded an operating profit of $204 million on sales of $5.4 billion in 1992. The tight federal budget climate, the change of administration, falling defense expenditures, and the end of the cold war raise many questions over the prospects for the defense business. Boeing is therefore in a precarious position, facing falling demand for both its commercial aircraft and defense products. The company needs a clear strategic plan for the future.

COMMERCIAL AIRCRAFT

Airline demand for new aircraft has declined, so Boeing has reduced production rates on the 737, 747, 757, and 767 models. In 1993 production of the 757 decreased to five per month, production of 737s fell to ten per month, and 767 monthly production decreased to three. In the second quarter of 1994, 747 production will be cut from five to three aircraft per month.

Boeing has about a 60 percent share of the world market for commercial jets, with announced orders valued at $17.8 billion. Approximately 80 percent of Boeing's airline orders are from non-U.S. carriers. Boeing's recent aircraft deliveries are as follows:

MODEL	1992	1991	1990
737	218	215	174
747	61	64	70*
757	99	80	77
767	63	62	60
Total commercial	441	421	381
707 military derivatives	5	14	4
Total jet transports	446	435	385
Commuter aircraft**	6	59	64

*Includes two Air Force One units.
**The de Havilland commuter aircraft division was sold in March 1992.

Development of Boeing's new 777 twinjet is proceeding on schedule. More than 80 percent of the engineering requirements have been released to manufacturing; major assembly has begun; flight testing of the first 777 will start in June 1994; and the first delivery is scheduled for May 1995. Sized to fit the market segment between the company's 767 and 747 aircraft, the 777 will carry 375–400 passengers in a two-class configuration and will be the widest, most spacious airplane in its class. The 777 represents a major step forward in customer-oriented design, offering many improvements in interior flexibility, passenger comfort, and flight-deck design.

In developing the 777, Boeing worked more closely with its airline customers than ever before. Customers were invited to play an integral part in the design process to ensure that every feature of the new aircraft was configured to meet their needs. Since the 777 program was launched in October 1990, Boeing has received 118 orders from 11 customers, with options for 95 more.

The smallest member of the Boeing jetliner family is the 737 series. The Boeing 737 is the world's best selling commercial aircraft, with more than 3,000 planes ordered since the first 737 flew in 1967. Customers now have three 737 models to choose from, with seating configurations ranging from 100 to 172 seats. Boeing received 114 orders for 737s in 1992.

The Boeing 757 and 767 are medium-capacity, fuel-efficient twinjets that meet FAA requirements for extended-range operations. The 757 can carry 186 passengers in mixed-class seating as far as 4,600 nautical miles. The 767 is larger, carrying about 260 passengers in mixed class, with a range on some versions in excess of 6,000 nautical miles. Boeing announced 38 orders for 757s and 21 orders for 767s in 1992.

The United Parcel Service has become a major customer for the 767 freighter, with an order for 30 aircraft and an option for 30 more. The order is the largest ever received by Boeing for an all-cargo airplane. Design engineering for the new freighter has begun, with certification and delivery scheduled in October 1995. The 767 freighter will be capable of carrying 56 tons of payload as far as 3,000 nautical miles, or 45 tons as far as 4,000 nautical miles.

The flagship of the Boeing airplane family, the 747-400, can carry 400 passengers more than 7,000 nautical miles, and offers airline customers the lowest seat-mile costs of any aircraft in the world. In 1992 Boeing received 28 new orders for the 747-400.

A new freighter version of the 747-400 was delivered in late 1993. The 747-400F gives Boeing's airline customers the capability of carrying 20 tons more payload on the routes they can fly compared to 747-200 freighters, or carrying the same payload 800 nautical miles farther.

For several years Boeing has been researching the market and optimum configuration for an aircraft even larger than the current 747-400. Boeing has signed an agreement with four European aerospace companies to study the feasibility of developing a new 550-800 seat jetliner. Participating in the one-year study are Germany's Deutsche Aerospace, France's Aerospatiale, British Aerospace, and CASA of Spain. The companies bring four different perspectives to the study, as well as considerable engineering and production resources.

Boeing believes that the cost, resource requirements, and risk associated with a large new airplane are so great that no single company could undertake the program alone. Moreover, preliminary research indicates that the market for such an airplane would be limited and could sustain only one product of the size being studied.

Boeing has also joined forces with a number of other companies to study the prospects for the next-generation supersonic transport, known as the High Speed Civil Transport (HSCT). Many technical barriers remain to producing an HSCT that would be environmentally acceptable and offer operating efficiencies that would keep ticket prices reasonably competitive with subsonic fares.

The European Airbus consortium remains Boeing's most formidable competitor in the commercial aircraft industry. Although the United States and the European community reached an agreement in 1992 that limits direct subsidies to 33 percent of development costs for new models, Airbus still receives hundreds of millions of dollars in government aid to launch new products. Boeing supports the current agreement as a step forward, but continues to urge U.S. trade representatives to negotiate an end to all direct subsidies.

In the highly competitive market for commercial aircraft, Boeing's reputation for customer service is an effective marketing tool. In mid-1993 the company opened a new spare parts distribution center adjacent to the Seattle-Tacoma airport. The 720,000-square-foot facility consolidated three existing spares operations and provided capacity to meet requirements into the next century. Boeing receives nearly 3,000 orders for spare parts each day. Another important part of customer service is training for pilots, mechanics, and maintenance people. Boeing trains about 2,100 pilots and 4,600 mechanics annually for airline customers around the world. Construction of a new $100 million customer services training center began in 1993.

A number of new Boeing manufacturing facilities recently started operations. A 937,000-square-foot skin and spar mill near Tacoma, Washington, produces parts. The plant houses 14 milling machines with beds over 100 feet long, including several 270-foot mills that are the largest machines of their type in the world. These mills allow for two 105-foot wing skins to be machined at once. Upper and lower wing-skin panels and stringers for the 777 and all wide-body models are produced at the plant, which is designed to significantly reduce flowtime on parts. In-process time is expected to fall from an 80-day average to ten days or less.

Boeing's new 518,000-square-foot Integrated Aircraft Systems Laboratory allows for the integrated testing of new airplane systems before they are installed in the airplane. One of the first important goals of the new facility is thorough testing of the 777 systems to ensure the new aircraft will be service-ready from the day it is first delivered.

Construction of the expanded factory and office facilities in Everett, Washington, where the new 777 is produced, has been completed. By mid-1993 about 6,500 employees of the 777 Division had relocated to the new facilities. In March 1992 Boeing completed the sale of Boeing of Canada de Havilland Commuter Aircraft Division to Bombardier, Inc. and the province of Ontario for $50 million.

In Wichita, Kansas, at Boeing's new 1,000,000-square-foot manufacturing plant, improvements to chemical milling and processing minimize the effects on air quality and ground water. The facility has the largest chemical milling recycling system in the world, recovering aluminum and other chemicals for commercial use. Environmental considerations have played a big part in the design and development of the 777. In the 777's interior cabin, water-based inks—rather than traditional solvent-based inks—are being used to silk-screen the wall coverings with colors and patterns. The environmental benefit is the elimination of certain solvents that are considered smog formers.

Other environmental innovations in the 777 program include remotely controlled paint booths that capture and prevent emissions; filtered vacuum units for removing dust during the drilling and grinding of composite materials; and the elimination or reduction of numerous toxic chemicals used in manufacturing aircraft parts.

Defense and space segment revenues were $5.4 billion for 1992, down from the $5.8 billion level for the prior two years. The company's defense and space business is broadly diversified, and no single program accounted for more than 16 percent of total 1990–1992 defense and space business revenues.

The defense and space segment, after incurring substantial operating losses in 1989 and 1990 aggregating nearly $900 million, regained profitability by the fourth quarter of 1991 through organizational consolidation and restructuring, termination of certain fixed-price development contracts, and better technical, cost, and schedule performance. This improved performance trend continued in 1992, resulting in an operating profit of $204 million for 1992 compared to an operating loss of $102 million for the year 1991.

The company has discontinued the separation of its defense and space operations for industry-segment reporting to better reflect the integrated nature of the market and internal operations of the previously segregated military transportation products and related systems segment and the missiles and space segment. The organizational consolidation of the company's various defense and space divisions into the Defense & Space Group reflects the singular nature of this business segment within the company. Because of common market and product and process characteristics, continued segmentation under the previous classifications would not be meaningful.

The principal defense and space programs, based on 1992 revenues, included B-2 bomber subcontract work, Space Station Freedom work packages, CH-47 helicopter, F-22 Advanced Tactical Fighter, E-3 AWACS, KC-135 tanker update modifications, V-22 Osprey tiltrotor transport, RAH-66 Comanche helicopter, E-6 submarine communications aircraft, Avenger air defense system, A-6 re-wing, B-1B bomber avionics, Inertial Upper Stage rocket booster, and Minuteman and Peacekeeper support. U.S. government classified projects also continue to contribute to defense and space segment revenues. Based on current programs and schedules, Boeing projects total 1993 sales to be in the $26 billion range.

Early in 1992 Boeing delivered the final E-3 Airborne Warning and Control System (AWACS) aircraft built for the French and United Kingdom air forces. The AWACS system is now being offered on the military derivative 767 airplane, and the company is actively pursuing foreign sales. The Japanese government has announced that it intends to place an initial order for two 767 AWACS in 1993. The U.S. government is expected to support sales to other overseas customers as well. The Defense & Space Group is continuing its modernization of the existing U.S. and NATO AWACS fleet.

The U.S. Navy, citing its changing role in the post–cold war environment, issued a termination for the P-3 Update IV program, under which Boeing was developing an advanced avionics system for the submarine-hunting fleet of aircraft. Despite the P-3 cancellation, Boeing is optimistic about opportunities for this product in the international marketplace.

The V-22 Osprey helicopter program entered the engineering and manufacturing development (EMD) phase in 1992, during which four new V-22s were built and two existing aircraft modified to the production-representative configuration. EMD is valued at $2 billion, which is shared by the Osprey's codevelopers, Boeing and Bell Helicopter Textron. Boeing delivered 40 remanufactured CH-47D Chinook helicopters, 35 to the U.S. Army, and 5 to the Spanish army in 1992. The company also delivered two new CH-47Ds to an Asian customer.

In December 1992 the U.S. Army and a Boeing/Sikorsky team finalized the restructuring of demonstration-validation phases of the new RAH-66 Comanche armed-reconnaissance helicopter. This prototyping and flight-test phase is valued at nearly $2 billion through 1997. Boeing has a contract to replace components in all U.S. Navy and Marine Corps H-46 helicopters. Kit production is valued at about $350 million.

In 1992 Congress voted to cap B-2 bomber production at 20 aircraft. Boeing produces the outboard wing and aft center sections of the bomber, as well as the fuel system and critical elements of the mission-management systems. Boeing completed delivery of major B-2 components in 1993 and continued to support the B-2 program through flight testing and the operational phase for several years.

The first prototype hardware for NASA's Space Station Freedom was produced in 1992 and tested at the Marshall Space Flight Center in Huntsville, Alabama. Boeing is NASA's prime contractor for the station's living and laboratory modules.

Production of the original order for 325 Avenger air defense missile fire units for the U.S. Army was completed in 1992, with the assembly line continuing work on a $436 million order for 679 more Avenger units. Boeing is continuing tests to integrate missiles other than the U.S.-built Stinger on the Avenger units as part of an aggressive foreign sales effort in 1993.

The Inertial Upper Stage (IUS) space booster celebrated its tenth anniversary by deploying a Defense Support Program surveillance satellite in 1992 and a NASA Tracking and Data Relay Satellite in 1993. Boeing has delivered 23 IUS vehicles, the most reliable upper-stage booster rocket in the U.S. inventory, and has a long-lead contract to build three more for the U.S. Air Force.

BOEING COMPUTER SERVICES

Boeing Computer Services supplies the company's need for advanced computing and telecommunications. The division also develops and manages large, complex information systems for the Department of Defense, NASA, and other federal government agencies. In 1992 one of the division's major responsibilities was to provide computer-aided design, computer-aided manufacturing, and systems integration for the 777 program. One of the major goals of the 777 program is to achieve 100 percent digital product definition, digital preassembly, and digital data exchange. In support of this goal, Computer Services electronically interconnected all Boeing facilities involved in the 777 program as well as key suppliers and partners worldwide, thereby improving the cost-efficiency of 777 development and production.

Recent development and delivery of enhanced solid-model viewing of 777 design data enhances the ability of engineers to detect and correct design errors prior to the manufacturing process. Implementing the principles of Continuous Quality Improvement as a management tool has improved efficiency of operations and reduced the cost of information systems. This division has consolidated and streamlined its organization to provide better support to all internal and external customers.

OTHER BOEING CONCERNS

Labor Contracts. Three-year labor agreements were reached in the fourth quarter of 1992 with the International Association of Machinists and Aerospace Workers and the United Auto Workers, representing approximately 50,000 employees and 98 percent of all hourly employees. Labor contract negotiations with the Seattle Professional

Engineering Employees Association (SPEEA), representing approximately 28,000 engineering and technical employees, reached an impasse in December after union members rejected the company's offer. Boeing implemented certain provisions of its final contract proposals to SPEEA prior to year end. In February 1993 SPEEA members voted to accept the company's offer.

Backlog. Total firm backlog of unfilled orders at December 31, 1992, was $87.9 billion, compared with $97.9 billion at the end of 1991. Of the total December 31 backlog, $82.6 billion or 94 percent was for commercial customers (including foreign governments) and $5.3 billion or 6 percent was for the U.S. government. Comparable figures at the end of 1991 were $92.8 billion or 95 percent commercial, and $5.1 billion or 5 percent U.S. government.

In evaluating the company's firm backlog for commercial customers, certain risk factors should be considered. Approximately 55 percent of the firm backlog for commercial jet airplanes is scheduled to be delivered after 1994, including all 777 aircraft. Deliveries of 777s begin in 1995. A continuation of the weak economic environment in many areas of the world could result in additional customer requests to negotiate the rescheduling or possible cancellation of firm orders.

CONCLUSION

As indicated in Exhibits 20–1 to 20–5, Boeing's net income fell 60 percent in 1992 while long-term debt increased 35 percent. Revenues dropped 16 percent in 1993. Further U.S. defense cuts are expected and more of Boeing's airline customers are facing demise. In the face of these odds, prepare a strategic plan for CEO John Fery. Keep in mind Boeing's current mission statement (from its *Annual Report*): "To be the number one aerospace company in the world and among the premier industrial concerns in terms of quality, profitability, and growth."

EXHIBIT 20-1 Boeing Company Corporate Headquarters, August 1, 1993

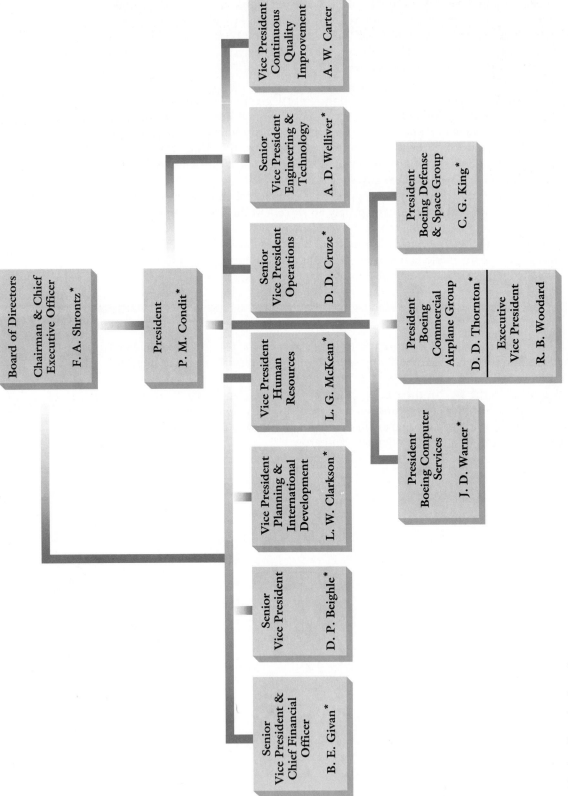

Board of Directors

Chairman & Chief Executive Officer

F. A. Shrontz *

President

P. M. Condit *

Senior Vice President & Chief Financial Officer

B. E. Givan *

Senior Vice President

D. P. Beighle *

Vice President Planning & International Development

L. W. Clarkson *

Vice President Human Resources

L. G. McKean *

Senior Vice President Operations

D. D. Cruze *

Senior Vice President Engineering & Technology

A. D. Welliver *

Vice President Continuous Quality Improvement

A. W. Carter

President Boeing Computer Services

J. D. Warner *

President Boeing Commercial Airplane Group

D. D. Thornton *

Executive Vice President

R. B. Woodard

President Boeing Defense & Space Group

C. G. King *

*Member, Executive Council.

Source: Company report.

EXHIBIT 20-2 Consolidated Statements of Net Earnings (Dollars in millions except per share data)

YEAR ENDED DECEMBER 31	1993	1992	1991
Sales and other operating revenues	$25,438	$30,184	$29,314
Costs and expenses	23,747	28,144	27,360
Earnings from operations	1,691	2,040	1,954
Other income, principally interest	169	230	263
Interest and debt expense	(39)	(14)	(13)
Earnings before federal taxes on income and cumulative effect on change in accounting	1,821	2,256	2,204
Federal taxes on income	577	702	637
Earnings before cumulative effect of change in accounting	1,244	1,554	1,567
Cumulative effect to January 1, 1992, of change in accounting for postretirement benefits other than pensions		(1,002)	
Net earnings	$ 1,244	$ 552	$ 1,567
Earnings per share:			
Before cumulative effect of change in accounting	$ 3.66	$ 4.57	$ 4.56
Cumulative effect to January 1, 1992, of change in accounting for postretirement benefits other than pensions		(2.95)	
	$ 3.66	$ 1.62	$ 4.56
Cash dividends per share	$ 1.00	$ 1.00	$ 1.00

Source: *Annual Report*, 1993.

EXHIBIT 20-3 Consolidated Statements of Financial Position (Dollars in millions except per share data)

DECEMBER 31,	1993	1992
ASSETS		
Cash and cash equivalents	$ 2,342	$ 2,711
Short-term investments	766	903
Accounts receivable	1,615	1,428
Current portion of customer financing	218	229
Deferred income taxes	800	115
Inventories	10,485	11,073
Less advances and progress billings	(7,051)	(8,372)
Total current assets	9,175	8,087
Customer financing	2,959	2,066
Property, plants and equipment, at cost	13,232	12,293
Less accumulated depreciation	(6,144)	(5,569)
Deferred income taxes	63	212
Other assets	1,165	1,058
	$20,450	$18,147
LIABILITIES AND SHAREHOLDERS' EQUITY		
Accounts payable and other liabilities	$ 5,854	$ 5,248
Advances in excess of related costs	226	639
Income taxes payable	434	232
Current portion of long-term debt	17	21
Total current liabilities	6,531	6,140
Accrued retiree health care	2,148	2,004
Long-term debt	2,613	1,772
Contingent stock repurchase commitment	175	175
Shareholder's equity:		
Common shares, par value $5.00—		
600,000,000 shares authorized;		
349,256,792 shares issued	1,746	1,746
Additional paid-in capital	413	418
Retained earnings	7,180	6,276
Less treasury shares, at cost—		
1993—9,118,995; 1992—9,836,313	(356)	(384)
Total shareholders' equity	8,983	8,056
	$20,450	$18,147

Source: *Annual Report*, 1993.

EXHIBIT 20-4 Consolidated Statements of Cash Flows (Dollars in millions)

YEAR ENDED DECEMBER 31,	1993	1992	1991
CASH FLOWS—OPERATING ACTIVITIES:			
Net earnings	$1,244	$552	$1,567
Adjustments to reconcile net earnings to net cash provided by operating activities:			
Effect of cumulative change in accounting for postretirement benefits other than pensions		1,002	
Depreciation and amortization—			
Plant and equipment	953	870	768
Leased aircraft, other	72	91	58
Deferred income taxes	(536)	(26)	95
Gain/undistributed earnings—affiliates	(1)	(13)	1
Changes in operating assets and liabilities—			
Accounts receivable	(187)	635	(41)
Inventories, net of advances and progress billings	(733)	(138)	458
Accounts payable and other liabilities	606	229	(140)
Advances in excess of related costs	(413)	(28)	(416)
Federal taxes on income	202	206	(453)
Change in prepaid pension expense	(134)	(202)	(403)
Change in accrued retiree health care	144	184	40
Net cash provided by operating activities	1,217	3,362	1,534
CASH FLOWS—INVESTING ACTIVITIES:			
Short-term investments	137	(388)	623
Customer financing additions	(1,560)	(1,156)	(223)
Customer financing reductions	626	16	123
Plant and equipment, net additions	(1,317)	(2,160)	(1,850)
Proceeds from sale of affiliate		50	
Other	8	(19)	(3)
Net cash used by investing activities	(2,106)	3,657)	(1,330)
CASH FLOWS—FINANCING ACTIVITIES:			
Debt financing	837	482	993
Shareholders' equity—			
Cash dividends paid	(340)	(340)	(343)
Treasury shares acquired		(109)	(127)
Stock options exercised, other	23	35	23
Net cash provided by financing activities	520	68	546
Net increase (decrease) in cash and cash equivalents	(369)	(277)	750
Cash and cash equivalents at beginning of year	2,711	2,938	2,188
Cash and cash equivalents at end of year	$2,342	$2,711	$2,938

Source: *Annual Report,* 1993.

EXHIBIT 20-5 Foreign sales by geographic area consisted of the following:

The Company operates in two principal industries: Commercial Aircraft, and Defense and Space. Commercial Aircraft operations principally involve development, production, and marketing of commercial jet transports and providing related support services, principally to the commercial airline industry. Defense and Space operations involve research, development, production, modification, and support of military aircraft and related systems, space systems, and missile systems. No single product line in the Defense and Space segment represented more than 10 percent of consolidated revenues, operating profits, or identifiable assets.

YEAR ENDED DECEMBER 31,	1993	1992	1991
Asia	$ 8,870	$ 7,108	$ 5,458
Europe	4,698	7,165	8,745
Oceania	635	1,911	1,659
Africa	264	430	558
Western Hemisphere	149	872	1,436
	$14,616	$17,486	$17,856

Defense sales were approximately 6 percent, 3 percent, and 5 percent of total sales in Europe for 1993, 1992, and 1991, respectively. Defense sales were approximately 2 percent, 5 percent, and 5 percent of total sales in Asia for 1993, 1992, and 1991, respectively. Exclusive of these amounts, Defense and Space sales were principally to the U.S. government.

Corporate income consists principally of interest income from corporate investments. Corporate expense consists of noncapitalized interest on debt and other general corporate expenses. Corporate assets consist principally of cash, cash equivalents, short-term investments, and deferred income taxes.

YEAR ENDED DECEMBER 31,	1993	1992	1991
REVENUES			
Commercial Aircraft	$20,568	$24,133	$22,970
Defense and Space	4,407	5,429	5,846
Other industries	463	622	498
Operating revenues	25,438	30,184	29,314
Corporate income	169	230	263
Total revenues	$25,607	$30,414	$29,577
OPERATING PROFIT			
Commercial Aircraft	$ 1,646	$ 1,990	$ 2,246
Defense and Space	219	204	(102)
Other industries	16	27	(2)
Operating profit	1,881	2,221	2,142
Corporate income	169	230	263
Corporate expense	(229)	(195)	(201)
Earnings before taxes	$ 1,821	$ 2,256	$ 2,204

EXHIBIT 20-5 *Continued*

IDENTIFIABLE ASSETS AT DECEMBER 31

Commercial Aircraft	$12,686	$10,178	$ 7,806
Defense and Space	3,525	3,687	4,262
Other industries	202	264	196
	16,413	14,129	12,264
Corporate	4,037	4,018	3,660
Consolidated assets	$20,450	$18,147	$15,924

DEPRECIATION

Commercial Aircraft	$710	$ 598	$ 484
Defense and Space	230	241	269
Other industries	67	73	51
Total depreciation	$ 1,007	$ 912	$ 804

CAPITAL EXPENDITURES, NET

Commercial Aircraft	$ 1,120	$ 1,890	$ 1,445
Defense and Space	164	212	317
Other industries	33	58	88
Total capital expenditures, net	$ 1,317	$ 2,160	$ 1,850

Source: *Annual Report*, 1993.

FOREST PRODUCTS INDUSTRY NOTE

KATHLEEN RICE, GARY STANLEY, AND BARBARA WISE

I. WOOD PRODUCTS

Fifteen manufacturing sectors make up SIC 24 (Lumber and Wood Products). Most of the lumber and wood products industry is concentrated in the Pacific Northwest and the Southeast. Secondary concentrations are found across the Midwest, Northeast, and in Appalachia. Establishments classified in SIC 24 engage in the cutting and subsequent processing of timber into other products.

The construction sector is the main end-use market for most of the industry's products. Other end-use markets include furniture, cabinets and fixtures, wood chips, and pallets and skids. The furniture and cabinets sectors of the construction industry are particularly important to producers of nonstructural panel products (particleboard, medium-density fiberboard, hardboard, and plywood). Other value-added products consist of hardwood and softwood plywood, millwork, and reconstituted panel products. More than 80 percent of the softwood lumber, 65 percent of structural panels (softwood plywood and oriented strand board [OSB]), and the majority of all millwork are used in construction-related activities.

Residential construction grew about 4 percent in 1993, with more than 1 million new-single family units added. This level of single-family housing construction will probably be maintained over the next several years.

Construction activity in Florida, Louisiana, and Hawaii picked up in 1993 in large part to rebuild following Hurricane Andrew, which hit southern Florida and Louisiana in September 1992, and Hurricane Iniki, which struck Hawaii less than two weeks later, causing more than $1 billion of damage on the island of Kauai. Only about 60 percent of the required rebuilding of residential and business property has occurred during 1993. The extreme flooding in the Midwest along the Mississippi, Missouri, and Illinois rivers during the summer of 1993 has also created a demand for new housing and farmland structures. This demand for reconstruction coupled with the shortage of domestic timber will increase the level of imports of softwoods from Canada.

Lumber and wood products shipments increased less than 1 percent (in constant dollars) in 1993, to an estimated $78.1 billion. Production remained flat or declined in most product sectors, with the value-added sectors, such as millwork and paneling, registering minor gains.

Since 1988 sales by the U.S. Forest Service (USFS) and the Bureau of Land Management (BLM) of timber from the Pacific Northwest declined by almost 80 percent (from about 26 million cubic meters in 1988 to about 7 million cubic meters in 1992). According to industry sources, more than 125 lumber and panel products mills in the Pacific Northwest have closed in the past three years partly as a result of the inadequate log supplies from federal and state lands.

Environmental Profile. Since the U.S. Fish and Wildlife Service (FWS) listed the northern spotted owl as a threatened species in June 1990, about 7 million acres of previously available federal and state timberlands can no longer be harvested. In response, President Clinton proposed a Forest Plan in July 1993 aimed at providing a "sustainable economy and a sustainable environment in the Pacific Northwest." The program is not expected to be implemented before late 1994. Industry estimates put the lands removed from harvest at about 25 percent of the total in the Pacific Northwest, and at about 11 percent of the national total.

Timber harvesting has been severely restricted or curtailed completely within the approximately 2 million hectares of the Pacific Northwest that have been designated as the habitat of the endangered owl. The USFS and BLM have been enjoined by federal courts from allowing any further timber sales—regardless of their location—until management plans are adopted and cleared by the FWS.

Preservationists will continue efforts to curtail or restrict logging on national forest lands not only in the Pacific Northwest but in other timberlands, including the Southeast and Midwest. The Endangered Species Act will be reevaluated by Congress in 1994.

International Competitiveness. Despite slow to moderate growth in many foreign markets, exports of wood products rose in 1993 to $7.1 billion, an increase of more than 15 percent over 1992. Almost all of the increase was the result of higher prices. The volume of exports was essentially flat. The relatively weak U.S. dollar and intense marketing efforts by the industry were major factors in the rise in exports.

Japan, Canada, and Mexico were again the major markets for U.S. exports, accounting for about two-thirds of shipments. Other significant markets were South Korea, Germany, and the United Kingdom. Softwood logs and softwood lumber remained by far the largest export commodities.

U.S. imports of solid wood products also increased in 1993, to about $7.7 billion. The major supplier of solid wood products is Canada, with softwood lumber the main commodity. Increases in softwood lumber imports, which were needed to make up for tight domestic supplies, accounted for most of the import increase of more than

U.S. Trade Patterns in 1992: Wood, Excluding Buildings SIC 241-244,249 (In millions of dollars, percent)

EXPORTS			IMPORTS		
	Value	Share		Value	Share
Canada and Mexico	1,553	23.0	Canada and Mexico	4,815	71.5
European Community	1,271	18.9	European Community	272	4.0
Japan	2,710	40.2	Japan	9	0.1
East Asia NICs	698	10.4	East Asia NICs	1,153	17.1
South America	23	0.3	South America	267	4.0
Other	483	7.2	Other	223	3.3
World Total	6.737	100.0	World Total	6,739	100.0

TOP FIVE COUNTRIES					
	Value	Share		Value	Share
Japan	2,710	40.2	Canada	4,520	67.1
Canada	1,040	15.4	Indonesia	404	6.0
Mexico	513	7.6	Mexico	295	4.4
South Korea	319	4.7	Taiwan	239	3.5
Germany	302	4.5	China	238	3.5

Source: U.S. Department of Commerce: Bureau of the Census; International Trade Administration.

14 percent from the year-earlier level. Other principal suppliers to the U.S. market were Indonesia, Taiwan, Mexico, China, Brazil, and Malaysia.

Outlook for 1994. Shipments of solid wood products should increase in 1994, as the U.S. economy and the economies of most trading partners improve. Solid, if not spectacular, growth in U.S. residential construction and household furniture should bring about an increase of more than 1 percent in domestic wood products shipments.

Imports and exports will increase modestly in 1994; both are expected to increase by about 2 percent, thus remaining about equal. Tight supply conditions in the U.S. market will lead to another increase in softwood lumber imports from Canada.

LOGGING

Commercial forest land, capable of growing 20 cubic feet per acre each year, covers about 195 million hectares, or one-fifth of the U.S. land base; a high proportion (70 percent) is privately owned. The U.S. Forest Service (USFS) estimates that commercial timberlands in the United States contain more than 23 billion cubic meters of timber. Currently, net annual growth exceeds removals (harvests) by more than 30 percent. More than 1 million hectares of U.S. forest land are replanted or seeded each year.

Trends and Forecasts: Logging (SIC 2411) (In millions of dollars except as noted)

					Percent Change (1991–1994)		
Item	1991	1992[1]	1993[2]	1994[3]	91–92	92–93	93–94
Industry Data							
Value of shipments[4]	11,434	13,149	16,516	—	15.0	25.6	—
Value of shipments (1987$)	8,912	9,534	9,438	9,627	7.0	-1.0	2.0
Total employment (000)	78.1	—	—	—	—	—	—
Production workers (000)	65.4	—	—	—	—	—	—
Average hourly earnings ($)	9.80	—	—	—	—	—	—
Capital expenditures	293	—	—	—	—	—	—
Product Data							
Value of shipments[5]	10,728	12,337	15,612	—	15.0	26.5	—
Value of shipments (1987$)	8,362	9,011	8,921	9,099	7.8	-1.0	2.0
Trade Data							
Value of imports	199	219	252	284	10.1	15.1	12.6
Value of export	2,715	2,749	3,374	3,711	1.3	22.7	10.0

[1] Estimate, except exports and imports.

[2] Estimate.

[3] Forecast.

[4] Value of all products and services sold by establishments in the logging industry.

[5] Value of products classified in the logging industry produced by all industries.

Source: U.S. Department of Commerce: Bureau of the Census; International Trade Administration (ITA). Estimates and forecasts by ITA.

Notwithstanding the large domestic resource base, tight log supplies prevailed in 1993 throughout the Pacific Northwest. The volume of USFS and Bureau of Land Management (BLM) timber sales continued to decline in 1992 and 1993. Harvesting in the Pacific Northwest has fallen by more than 75 percent since 1989 (about 7 million cubic meters in 1992, compared with more than 26 million cubic meters in 1989). This is a result of forest management constraints imposed after the northern spotted owl was listed as a threatened species under the Endangered Species Act. Environmental litigation also was a factor.

The logging industry harvested an estimated 465 million cubic meters of sawlogs, veneer logs, pulpwood, and related wood products in 1993, valued at $15.6 billion. Softwood logs, followed by pulpwood and hardwood logs, were the industry's leading commodities, accounting for more than three-fourths of total shipments.

Softwood log production was estimated at 178 million cubic meters in 1993, down about 1 percent from 1992. Lower harvests in the Pacific Northwest accounted for the decline. Harvest levels in the South increased, but not enough to offset the decline in the Pacific Northwest. Hardwood log production in 1993 is estimated at 44 million cubic meters. Stumpage prices for both softwood and hardwood logs were sharply higher in 1993, a factor of regional availability of timber and the market for wood building products.

The volume of uncut federal timber under contract in the Pacific Northwest fell to a historical low in 1992–1993. Again, President Clinton's announced Forest Plan will have an unknown impact on the industry.

International Competitiveness. Exports of sawlogs, veneer logs, pulpwood, and related wood products were valued at $2.7 billion in 1992 and were expected to reach almost $3.4 billion in 1993, an increase of about 23 percent. The volume of exports declined slightly, however.

Japan, South Korea, and China were the leading export markets for softwood logs in 1993, accounting for more than 95 percent of total sales overseas. The volume of log exports to South Korea and China were significantly lower in 1993 because of restrictions on the export of U.S. logs from the Pacific Northwest and increased competition from New Zealand.

The value of hardwood log exports was expected to increase by less than 2 percent in 1993, while the volume of shipments declined by an estimated 3 percent. U.S. hardwood log exports were about 1.1 million cubic meters and were valued at $302 million. Canada and Japan were the industry's leading export markets, accounting for almost 48 percent of total export sales, with each market accounting for about one-fourth of the total. Other foreign markets included Germany, Italy, and Taiwan.

Outlook for 1994. Shipments of sawlogs, veneer logs, pulpwood, and related wood products are expected to increase by about 2 percent in 1994. This forecast is dependent upon lifting of court injunctions that have halted sales from the Pacific Northwest, higher demand in the nations to which the United States exports, and congressional review of how the Fish and Wildlife Service selects threatened and endangered species.

LUMBER

Industry shipments declined by 1 percent (in constant dollars) in 1993, to an estimated $25 billion. Prices continued to increase during 1992 and 1993, with softwood lumber reaching an all-time high of almost $500 per thousand board feet in March 1993. Prices have since leveled off to an average of about $340 per thousand board feet.

The sawmills and planing mills industry (SIC 2421) primarily produces lumber, which accounts for about 70 percent of the industry's total value of shipments. Softwood lumber accounts for about three-quarters of total lumber production, and hardwood lumber makes up the rest. The remaining 30 percent consists of wood chips, softwood flooring, furniture stock, and other general sawmill products, including untreated railway ties.

Since 1990 softwood lumber production in the Pacific Northwest has steadily declined, from 9.8 billion board feet in 1989 to less than 7.5 billion board feet in 1993. Softwood lumber production also declined in the Inland Region (Rocky Mountain States), from 11.3 billion board feet in 1989 to about 9 billion board feet in 1993. Southern yellow pine lumber production increased from 12.5 billion feet to more than 14 billion board feet in 1993.

Residential construction—particularly single-family homes—is the principal softwood lumber market. In 1993 single-family housing starts increased about 4 percent. Higher housing starts combined with the slight decline in lumber production resulted in higher lumber prices. The additional demand was met by higher softwood lumber imports, primarily from Canada.

Trends and Forecasts: Sawmills and Planing Mills, General (SIC 2421) (In millions of dollars except as noted)

ITEM	1991	1992[1]	1993[2]	1994[3]	PERCENT CHANGE (1991–1994)		
					91–92	92–93	93–94
Industry Data							
Value of shipments[4]	17,485	20,111	24,929	—	15.0	24.0	—
Value of shipments (1987$)	16,341	16,900	16,731	17,066	3.4	-1.0	2.0
Total employment (000)	130	126	122	—	-3.1	-3.2	—
Production workers (000)	116	113	109	—	-2.6	-3.5	—
Average hourly earnings ($)	9.33	—	—	—	—	—	—
Capital expenditures	464	—	—	—	—	—	—
Product Data							
Value of shipments[5]	17,515	20,043	24,846	—	14.4	24.0	—
Value of shipments (1987$)	16,369	16,843	16,675	17,008	2.9	-1.0	2.0
Trade Data							
Value of imports	2,638	3,472	4,956	5,501	31.6	42.7	11.0
Value of exports	2,203	2,322	2,573	2,702	5.4	10.8	5.0

[1] Estimate, except exports and imports.

[2] Estimate.

[3] Forecast.

[4] Value of all products and services sold by establishments in the sawmills and planing mills, general industry.

[5] Value of products classified in the sawmills and planing mills, general industry produced by all industries.

Source: U.S. Department of Commerce: Bureau of the Census; International Trade Administration (ITA). Estimates and forecasts by ITA.

Repair and remodeling of residential and nonresidential structures is another major market for the sawmills and planing industry. In 1993 home improvement spending rose 5 percent in constant dollars, from $51.3 billion to $53.9 billion. This further helped to inflate the price of lumber.

Employment in the industry has declined steadily since 1988 and was down another 3 percent in 1993, from 126,000 the previous year to 122,000. The decline occurred mostly in the Pacific Northwest where, over the past six years, more than 125 sawmills have closed or curtailed operations because of the shortage of timber.

The court-imposed restrictions on logging in the Pacific Northwest have spurred the lumber industry to conduct research into new processes and alternative materials. Recyclable products and greater sawmill efficiency, including energy-saving techniques, continue to be important industry goals.

International Competitiveness. The value of the U.S. lumber industry's exports has increased by almost 27 percent from 1989 to 1993, rising from a little more than $2 billion to almost $2.6 billion. In 1993 alone exports increased by 11 percent. The value of exports of softwood lumber (the major product of this industry) was up more than 7 percent, while actual volume was down about 2 percent in 1993. All softwood lumber exports for 1992 were valued at more than $1.3 billion, the same as in 1991, while the volume of exports was down by more than 14 percent.

Japan is the largest foreign market for softwood lumber, importing more than 36 percent of the total value of U.S. exports. Mexico, with 15 percent, follows, and Canada is third, importing about 11 percent.

Hardwood lumber exports exceeded $974 million in 1993, a 13 percent increase over the previous year. Major export markets for U.S. hardwood lumber are Canada, Japan, Italy, Taiwan, the United Kingdom, and Germany. Exports to Canada were about $200 million in 1992, an increase of more than 16 percent over 1991. Exports to Japan were about $133 million in 1992; exports in 1993 are expected to increase by more than 10 percent.

In 1993 additional softwood lumber imports from Canada helped to offset declines in domestic shipments. Canada provides about 98 percent of all softwood lumber imports and accounts for about 32 percent of domestic consumption. The value of imports from Canada increased 32 percent in 1992, to $3.2 billion, and are expected to increase in 1993 by about 42 percent, increasing Canada's share of domestic consumption substantially.

Outlook for 1994. Industry shipments are expected to increase in 1994 by about 2 percent (in constant dollars). Prices leveled off in 1993 to an average of about $340 per thousand board feet. Continued price volatility can be expected in 1994.

The 4- and 5-percent increases in single-family housing starts and repair and remodeling predicted for 1994 are major incentives for the industry to increase production and remain competitive with foreign lumber imports.

MILLWORK

Aided by an increase in housing starts and by a continuing high level of expenditures for residential repair, remodeling, and home improvement (RRHI) projects, the millwork industry experienced increased demand for its primary commodities in recent years.

New residential construction continues to be the leading end-use market for millwork products, accounting for about 55 percent of demand. The RRHI end-user segment is becoming increasingly important to the millwork industry. The reason is that despite reduced mortgage interest rates, the slow U.S. economy continues to dissuade many consumers from purchasing new houses or moving up to larger ones.

The millwork industry manufactures a wide range of fabricated millwork products. These include wood millwork commodities with metal, vinyl, and other plastic overlays. Doors are the industry's sales leader, accounting for about 30 percent of total shipments. Next come wooden windows (including aluminum, metal, and vinyl clad) and sashes (26 percent), standard and prefinished moldings (12 percent), and wooden frames for doors and windows (more than 3 percent).

The remaining 28 percent of the industry's annual sales are made up of various millwork products, including wooden blinds, shutters, screens, shades, folding and stationary stairwork, porch columns and rails, trellises, carvings, ornaments, and similar products.

International Competitiveness. The U.S. millwork industry continued to run a trade deficit in both 1991 and 1992. Aided by a weak dollar and strong foreign demand (especially from Canada and Mexico), exports reached $207 million in 1991 compared to $143 million in imports the previous year. In 1992 the pattern was

Trends and Forecasts: Millwork (SIC 2431) (In millions of dollars except as noted)

ITEM	1991	1992[1]	1993[2]	1994[3]	PERCENT CHANGE (1991–1994) 91–92	92–93	93–94
Industry Data							
Value of shipments[4]	8,969	9,837	10,789	—	9.7	9.7	—
Value of shipments (1987$)	7,868	8,065	8,226	8,473	2.5	2.0	3.0
Total employment (000)	84.9	86.6	86.0	—	2.0	-0.7	—
Production workers (000)	66.7	68.8	67.9	—	3.1	-1.3	—
Average hourly earnings ($)	9.96	10.26	10.47	—	3.0	2.0	—
Capital expenditures	141	—	—	—	—	—	—
Product Data							
Value of shipments[5]	8,464	9,283	10,181	—	9.7	9.7	—
Value of shipments (1987$)	7,424	7,610	7,762	7,995	2.5	2.0	3.0
Trade Data							
Value of imports	225	306	350	395	36.0	25.8	—
Value of exports	207	272	325	320	31.4	-4.4	—

[1] Estimate, except exports and imports.

[2] Estimate.

[3] Forecast.

[4] Value of all products and services sold by establishments in the millwork industry.

[5] Value of products classified in the millwork industry produced by all industries.

Source: U.S. Department of Commerce: Bureau of the Census; International Trade Administration (ITA). Estimates and forecasts by ITA.

repeated: exports rose strongly but were unable to catch up with the volume of imports. As of May 1993 exports were trailing imports by $24 million.

The major customers for U.S. exports over the last four years have been Canada (55 percent), Mexico (more than 17 percent), Japan (7 percent), and the United Kingdom (6 percent).

Mexico is by far the leading exporter to the United States, accounting for almost 49 percent of U.S. imports of millwork. Canada is a distant second with only 14 percent of the dollar volume. Thailand is in third place with 9 percent.

Outlook for 1994. The U.S. millwork industry should experience higher sales in 1994 with the expected increase in residential construction and RRHI activity. Millwork product shipments are forecast to increase by more than 3 percent in constant dollars.

HARDWOOD VENEER AND PLYWOOD

Shipments of hardwood veneer and plywood increased about 3 percent in 1993 (in constant dollars) to $2 billion. Both domestic and overseas markets were generally stronger, reflecting the modest U.S. recovery and growth in some foreign markets. The market for hardwood plywood, especially paneling, which is used extensively in mobile-home construction, experienced a surge in demand following Hurricane Andrew in September 1992.

Establishments classified in the hardwood veneer and plywood industry (SIC 2435) produce hardwood plywood, hardwood veneer (face and technical veneers), hardwood-type products (such as laminated veneer lumber), and prefinished hardwood plywood paneling. These products are used in a wide range of applications, including residential and nonresidential construction, repair and remodeling, manufactured housing, furniture, and cabinets and fixtures.

Hardwood plywood shipments accounted for an estimated 45 percent of total product shipments in 1993, followed by hardwood veneer (25 percent), hardwood plywood-type products (20 percent), and prefinished hardwood plywood paneling (10 percent). Prefinished hardwood plywood paneling's share of total product shipments has declined steadily over the past decade, largely because of changing consumer tastes. Prefinished hardwood plywood paneling was long the product of choice, but in the 1980s gypsum board became the top choice.

Production of stock hardwood plywood (4 by 6 to 10 feet) increased for the ninth year in a row in 1993, to an estimated 78 million square meters, compared with 42 million square meters in 1985. Stock hardwood plywood comes in a wide range of thicknesses (the most common is 3/4 inch, or 19.05 mm). Production is fairly evenly divided between the East and West. While output was rising in both regions in 1992, tight raw material supplies in the West resulted in a much smaller gain in that region.

Stock hardwood plywood production makes up almost 50 percent of total hardwood plywood production. The hardwood plywood industry also produces three other types of panels—architectural or decorative panels, made-to-size panels, and cut-to-size panels. There are no production estimates available, but indications are that output rose to accommodate key end-use sectors (construction, furniture, and cabinet and fixtures).

Hardwood plywood producers use both veneer and other types of core material in the manufacturing process. Other types of core include not only lumber, but also reconstituted panel products, such as particleboard, medium density fiberboard

(MDF), and oriented strand board (OSB). About three-fourths of the industry's production is manufactured with veneer cores. On a percentage basis, the use of MDF lumber cores has increased substantially over the past decade; however, it still accounts for less than 15 percent of total hardwood plywood production. More than a dozen species of wood are used as face veneers in the production of hardwood plywood, but birch-faced (much of it imported from Canada) and oak-faced (primarily red oak) hardwood plywood account for more than three-fourths of the total. Use of these two species has increased over the past decade because of increased use of light-colored woods for furniture.

International Competitiveness. U.S. hardwood veneer and plywood exports increased to a record $303 million in 1993, marking the sixth consecutive annual increase. The largest overseas markets were Germany, Canada, Mexico, and Japan. Hardwood veneer exports amounted to 76 percent of the industry's exports, with Germany and Canada the leading foreign markets (accounting for 30 percent and 14 percent, respectively). Japan took 7 percent, followed by the United Kingdom (5 percent), and Spain and Belgium (between 4 and 5 percent each). Hardwood plywood exports increased nearly 47 percent in 1993, to an estimated $72.5 million.

Trends and Forecasts: Hardwood Veneer and Plywood (SIC 2435) (In millions of dollars except as noted)

ITEM	1991	1992[1]	1993[2]	1994[3]	PERCENT CHANGE (1991–1994) 91–92	92–93	93–94
Industry Data							
Value of shipments[4]	1,897	1,997	2,092	—	5.3	4.8	—
Value of shipments (1987$)	1,727	1,934	1,998	2,048	12.0	3.3	2.5
Total employment (000)	17.3	17.4	17.9	—	0.6	2.9	—
Production workers (000)	14.8	14.8	15.3	—	0.0	3.4	—
Average hourly earnings ($)	8.03	8.28	8.53	—	3.1	3.0	—
Capital expenditures	45.5	—	—	—	—	—	—
Product Data							
Value of shipments[5]	1,743	1,837	1,917	—	5.4	4.4	—
Value of shipments (1987$)	1,587	1,778	1,831	1,877	12.0	3.0	2.5
Trade Data							
Value of imports	588	729	758	792	24.0	4.0	4.5
Value of exports	248	278	303	333	12.1	9.0	9.9

[1] Estimate, except exports and imports.

[2] Estimate.

[3] Forecast.

[4] Value of all products and services sold by establishments in the hardwood veneer and plywood industry.

[5] Value of products classified in the hardwood veneer and plywood industry produced by all industries.

Source: U.S. Department of Commerce: Bureau of the Census; International Trade Administration (ITA). Estimates and forecasts by ITA.

The largest markets were Canada (41 percent), Mexico (23 percent), and Japan (11 percent).

Hardwood veneer and plywood imports increased by 4 percent in 1993, to an estimated $758 million. Most of this increase came as temperate hardwood plywood and veneer from Canada, as well as new sources such as Russia and Paraguay. Indonesia is the largest supplier of tropical and temperate hardwood plywood to the United States, supplying more than 40 percent of total imports. Indonesia purchases U.S. veneer-grade hardwood logs, which are processed into veneer and then overlaid on lauan plywood cores for export to the United States. Imports of tropical hardwood plywood and veneer fell about 11 percent in 1993, in part because of increased concerns over the effects of logging in tropical forests.

Outlook for 1994. Moderate growth in the furniture and construction sectors should lead to higher production levels in 1994. All sectors of the industry should experience some increase, even producers of prefinished hardwood plywood paneling, whose production dropped substantially over the past decade.

Exports are projected to increase for the seventh straight year because of increased worldwide demand for temperate veneer and hardwood plywood. Exports to Japan, which increased about 27 percent in 1993, are expected to rise again. Japan, one of the world's largest consumers of tropical wood products, is increasingly coming under fire because of growing concern even within the country itself about tropical deforestation. Imports are forecast to increase 4 to 5 percent to meet rising demand in the residential construction and furniture industries.

SOFTWOOD PLYWOOD AND VENEER

Shipments for the softwood plywood and veneer industry declined slightly in 1993. However, prices were significantly higher so that the value of industry shipments increased to an estimated $5.7 billion. Softwood plywood production decreased to 17 million cubic meters, compared with 17.1 billion cubic meters in 1992. Higher prices resulted in large part from higher raw material costs and increased demand in traditional end-use markets, such as housing and repair and remodeling.

There were 117 softwood plywood mills operating in 1993, down from 121 in 1992. Mills closed were located in Oregon and Washington. Mills in the Pacific Northwest, many of which are heavily dependent on timber from federal lands, now account for less than one-fourth of softwood plywood production, down from nearly 40 percent in 1985. At the same time, plywood mills in the South have increased production. Southern plywood mills now account for about 65 percent of softwood plywood production.

Residential construction is the biggest end-use market for softwood plywood and veneer, accounting for nearly one-third of demand. In addition to single-family housing, repair and remodeling, industrial applications and nonresidential construction are important markets. New housing starts were up 4 percent in 1993, and the value of home improvement projects increased 5 percent during the same period. The market for private nonresidential building construction fell in 1993 because of overbuilding in earlier years.

Although these factors suggest strong demand for plywood products, supply difficulties in the Pacific Northwest and increased incursions by substitute products such as oriented strand board (OSB) in traditional markets have dampened growth of plywood shipments. OSB, a structural panel, has been gaining popularity in the construction industry since the mid-1980s. It is estimated that OSB now makes up about 30 percent of structural panel shipments in the United States.

In addition, increased acceptance of laminated veneer lumber in the construction industry has created an additional end-use market for softwood veneer, which formerly was sold exclusively to the plywood industry. Separate shipment data are not available for softwood veneer, but many plywood mills have reported increased competition for veneer supplies from laminated veneer lumber mills, with resulting increases in prices.

International Competitiveness. Exports of softwood plywood and veneer continued to grow in 1993, to an estimated $340 million. EC countries (particularly the United Kingdom, Netherlands, Germany, and Belgium) constituted the major export market. Exports to EC countries remained steady or declined slightly. Exports to Mexico and Japan increased substantially.

Resolution of issues relating to performance standards for softwood plywood in construction applications allowed implementation in 1993 of previously agree tariff reductions on softwood plywood under the U.S.-Canada Free Trade Agreement. Under the agreement, plywood tariffs were reduced by 50 percent effective January 1, 1993, to be followed by a staged reduction to zero over the next five years. Exports

Trends and Forecasts: Softwood Veneer and Plywood (SIC 2436) (In millions of dollars except as noted)

ITEM	1991	1992[1]	1993[2]	1994[3]	PERCENT CHANGE (1991–1994)		
					91–92	92–93	93–94
Industry Data							
Value of shipments[4]	4,592	5,380	5,653	—	17.2	5.1	—
Value of shipments (1987$)	4,320	4,475	4,457	4,524	3.6	-0.4	1.5
Total employment (000)	31.7	31.2	30.8	—	-1.6	-1.3	—
Production workers (000)	28.6	28.3	28.0	—	-1.0	-1.1	—
Average hourly earnings ($)	10.78	10.89	10.99	—	1.0	0.9	—
Capital expenditures	86.7	—	—	—	—	—	—
Product Data							
Value of shipments[5]	3,972	4,654	4,892	—	17.2	5.1	—
Value of shipments (1987$)	3,737	3,872	3,857	3,914	3.6	-0.4	1.5
Trade Data							
Value of imports	35.5	59.0	74.4	93.7	66.2	26.1	25.9
Value of exports	275	336	340	357	22.2	1.2	5.0

[1] Estimate, except exports and imports.

[2] Estimate.

[3] Forecast.

[4] Value of all products and services sold by establishments in the softwood veneer and plywood industry.

[5] Value of products classified in the softwood veneer and plywood industry produced by all industries.

Source: U.S. Department of Commerce: Bureau of the Census; International Trade Administration (ITA).

to Canada rebounded in 1993 and constituted nearly 15 percent of all plywood exported.

Outlook for 1994. The availability of timber in the Western United States will continue to be the biggest concern for the softwood plywood industry in 1994. In addition, engineered wood products such as OSB will continue to make inroads into construction, plywood's largest end-use market.

In constant dollars, shipments of softwood plywood and veneer are projected to increase 1 to 2 percent in 1994, driven by an expected 4 percent increase in housing starts, a 5 percent increase in the home repair and remodeling sector, and improved exports. Demand should also increase marginally as homes in the Midwest are repaired and rebuilt following the summer floods of 1993.

Exports should continue to grow, as the economies in the U.K., Canada, and Mexico (each a major export market) are expected to experience modest growth in 1994. At the same time, imports should grow substantially as tight domestic supplies make this market attractive to overseas producers.

Under the North American Free Trade Agreement (NAFTA), the construction market in Mexico should offer opportunities for plywood exporters. Mexican tariffs on veneer will drop to zero immediately, and tariffs on plywood products will be phased out over a ten-year period. Currently, consumption of softwood plywood greatly exceeds production in Mexico. Because of inadequate reforestation programs in the past, this situation is likely to offer opportunities for plywood exporters for some time to come.

II. PAPER PRODUCTS

The United States paper and allied products industry is recognized worldwide as a high-quality, high-volume, low-cost producer that benefits from a large consumer base, a modern technical infrastructure, adequate raw materials, and a highly skilled labor force. The industry ranks eighth among U.S. manufacturing industries in the value of its shipments, and third among the nondurables sectors in sales. It ranks second in capital expenditures, according to the most recent Bureau of the Census data. Although the paper industry is one of the largest U.S. consumers of energy, ranking third behind metals and chemicals, it also has the highest rate of self-generated energy, totaling over 56 percent in 1992–1993.

The primary-products sector encompasses pulp, paper, and paperboard manufacturing (SIC 261, 262, and 263). These capital-intensive industries obtain cellulose fibers from timberlands, or from purchased virgin and recycled fibers. They produce commodity grades of wood pulp, printing and writing papers, sanitary tissue, industrial-type papers, containerboard, and boxboard. According to a reliable industry survey, this sector operated 544 paper and paperboard mills and 207 pulp mills in 1992, with total employment of 196,700.

The more labor-intensive converting sector, with 68 percent of the industry's employees, consists of 14 fairly distinct industries that use primary products, such as paper and paperboard, in the manufacture of coated papers, bags, boxes, and envelopes. Some companies in this sector are integrated with primary manufacturers, especially in the production of sanitary tissue products, corrugating shipping containers, folding cartons, flexible packaging, and envelopes. Other converters purchase paper, paperboard, and plastic film from the primary sector, and transform those materials into finished products. Most converters are fully independent operations,

Trends and Forecasts: Paper and Allied Products (SIC 26) (In millions of dollars except as noted)

ITEM	1991	1992[1]	1993[2]	1994[3]	PERCENT CHANGE (1991–1994) 91–92	92–93	93–94
Industry Data							
Value of shipments[4]	128,824	131,282	130,000	135,797	1.9	-1.0	4.5
Value of shipments (1987$)	113,395	114,529	115,146	118,600	1.0	0.5	3.0
Total employment (000)	621	622	620	623	0.2	-0.3	0.5
Production workers (000)	477	478	477	479	0.2	-0.2	0.4
Average hourly earnings ($)	13.34	13.71	13.92	—	2.8	1.5	—
Capital expenditures	9,009	—	—	—	—	—	—
Product Data							
Value of shipments[5]	124,658	127,102	125,891	131,505	2.0	-1.0	4.5
Value of shipments (1987$)	109,811	110,909	111,507	114,852	1.0	0.5	3.0
Trade Data							
Value of imports	10,473	10,424	11,361	11,823	-0.5	9.0	4.1
Value of exports	9,332	10,122	9,827	10,416	8.5	-2.9	6.0

[1] Estimate, except exports and imports.

[2] Estimate.

[3] Forecast.

[4] Value of all products and services sold by establishments in the paper and allied products industry.

[5] Value of products classified in the paper and allied products industry produced by all industries.

Source: U.S. Department of Commerce: Bureau of the Census; International Trade Administration (ITA).Estimates and Forecast by ITA.

but those linked with primary-product producers account for the lion's share of industry sales.

INDUSTRY PERFORMANCE

Aggregate shipments of the U.S. paper and allied products industry were estimated at $130 billion in current dollars in 1993, down less than 1 percent from 1992. The small decline was directly attributable to continued depressed prices that affected some leading grades of pulp, paper, and board, and to deep regional discounting, which significantly lowered the actual unit prices of many delivered products. Nevertheless, volume of shipments was up for many primary products, including some principal grades of paper and paperboard, in both domestic and foreign markets. Several segments of the converting sector also achieved moderate growth, including production of corrugated box, sanitary paper products, and some printing and writing paper.

The pulp, paper, and paperboard sectors (SIC 261, 262, 263) accounted for about 40 percent of the value of the industry's total shipments in 1993.The sector made significant real growth in output and in sales of some printing and writing papers and of boxboard, but shipments of market pulp and containerboard declined.

The larger, more labor-intensive converting sector, which accounted for the remaining 60 percent of paper industry shipments, also achieved significant real growth in certain sectors in 1993, particularly corrugated and folding-carton shipping containers and boxes, sanitary paper products, and envelopes. This sector is concentrated largely in populous metropolitan areas—especially in the Northeast, the Southeast, the Great Lakes region, and California—where end-user markets are accessible and transportation costs can be minimized.

Poised for Growth. By controlling operating rates and improving sales and distribution methods, manufacturers have drawn down inventories of paper and paperboard to near-normal levels, in contrast to the levels during previous business downturns. For the first time in recent years, improvements and rebuilds of existing machinery and equipment were reported to have exceeded the installation of new machines—a significant savings to the industry at a time of reduced profitability. Additions to plant capacity in 1993 were only about 2 percent more than those made in 1992, keeping operating rates high—92 percent for primary paper production and 95 percent for paperboard manufacture—without leading to price reductions for most grades. As a result, the industry was in a relatively strong economic position through 1993 amid growing indications of increased business activity, and should be able to maintain it well into 1994 at least.

In the three years through 1994, a survey in mid-1993 found, U.S. companies planned to spend a total of $13.4 billion on mill improvements, 4 percent less than indicated in the survey a year earlier, following declines of 8 percent in 1992 and 11 percent in 1991. The latest survey suggested that the trend would turn positive as the global economy improved.

With the industry's expansion winding down from the record pace of 1987–1990, environmental improvements have replaced capacity additions as the driving force behind capital spending plans. Environmental programs account for nearly 15 percent of total spending plans, up from 14 percent in 1992. Stricter state environmental standards have prompted projects to add secondary treatment plants, control odorous emissions, and reduce the use of elemental chlorine.

Earnings and Jobs Decline. Earnings declined more sharply than sales through the first half of 1993. A few companies' profits improved slightly in the second quarter, but the industry experienced a 23 percent drop from the second quarter of 1992 and 15 percent from the first quarter of 1993, when surging prices of its wood products buoyed the industry's earnings from sales of those products. Cash flow was held down by depressed prices, especially for containerboard, market wood pulp, and certain printing and writing paper grades.

Employment in the paper industry was about 620,000 in 1993, down slightly from 1992 and 2 percent below the record of 630,000 in 1989. Principal causes of the declines were mergers, acquisitions, consolidations, and the phasing out of older, less-efficient machinery and operations.

Strikes dropped off dramatically, from 19 in 1983 to only one in 1992–1993. The United Paper Workers International Union, which represents a large majority of employees, has agreed to contracts as long as five and six years. Wage increases averaged less than 3 percent in 1993, than in 1992. U.S. companies also have been able to cut labor costs by eliminating Sunday premium pay and redesigning work practices and job descriptions.

Perhaps the most serious friction between labor and management is over health care. As in other industries, rapidly escalating insurance costs threaten the viability of many companies. With health-insurance premiums estimated to equal almost half of operating profits, negotiations will center on the extent of employee health coverage and the dollar amount of medical cost-sharing.

Corporate restructuring continued, especially among large companies, both in the United States and abroad. Although mergers and takeovers declined in 1993 because of the uncertain economy and poor cash flows, some major acquisitions were followed by divestitures, consolidations, and closings of less-profitable operations.

International Competitiveness. After narrowing for four straight years, to $302 million in 1992, the U.S. paper industry's trade deficit quadrupled in 1993 to $1.5 billion. When one factors in trade of recovered paper (not included in SIC data), where U.S. exports of $560 million far exceeded imports of $26 million, the 1993 trade deficit falls to $1 billion.

Although U.S. export tonnage was essentially unchanged from the 1992 level, the value of exports decreased about 3 percent in 1993, following a 9 percent rise in 1992, further reflecting softness in prices for U.S. paper and allied products. Because of poor economic conditions in Asia and Europe, the U.S. industry was unable to take advantage of the dollar's lowest international value in years. Exports of kraft linerboard, the industry's single largest export, were hit especially hard by a decline in foreign demand. Despite low prices and the dollar's low value, exports of this commodity, used in the construction of corrugated shipping containers, fell 8 percent in value in 1993, primarily as a result of lower sales to the European Community and Japan. Other regions that reduced purchases of U.S. paper and allied products included Scandinavia, the Caribbean, Taiwan, South Korea, and China. A few countries substantially increased purchases from the U.S., however: Mexico, up 11 percent; Canada, up 8 percent; and Thailand, up 18 percent.

Canada remained the largest market with 21 percent of the total, followed by the EC with 19 percent, Mexico with 15 percent, and Japan with 12 percent.

The continued growth of U.S. exports of paper and allied products to Canada in 1993, despite Canada's economic difficulties, was due largely to the U.S.-Canada Free Trade Agreement. By eliminating all paper-industry tariffs between the nations on January 1, 1993, it made U.S. paper and allied products very competitive in Canada, especially converted paper and paperboard packaging.

With the North American Free Trade Agreement (NAFTA), U.S. paper exports to Mexico will accelerate as well. U.S. exports to Mexico increased 70 percent over the past five years, to $1.4 billion in 1993 from $841 million in 1988. NAFTA phases out market barriers to the majority of primary pulp, paper, and paperboard grades over a five-year period. It eliminates corrugated-box tariffs and nontariff barriers over seven years, and tariffs on most converted products over ten years.

In the General Agreement on Tariffs and Trade (GATT), the paper industry continues to press U.S. and foreign government and industry officials to eliminate all barriers to the import and export of paper and allied products.

The U.S. and Japanese governments met several times during 1993 to assess the effectiveness and status of the Paper Agreement they had signed in April 1992. Its primary objective was to open Japan's $60 billion paper market to foreign suppliers. The agreement requires the Japanese government to encourage Japanese paper distributors, converters, printers, and corporate users to increase imports, develop long-term relationships with foreign suppliers, establish nondiscriminatory purchasing practices, and adopt specific purchasing guidelines that are applicable to both domestic and foreign suppliers. Under the agreement the Japanese government must focus its efforts on important local users of paper products, including 164 major companies that are participants in the Ministry of International Trade and Industry's import expansion program.

Exports and Imports Increase. Exports have played an increasingly important role in the U.S. paper industry, accounting for nearly 8 percent of U.S. paper goods shipments in 1993, or about $9.8 billion. Exports' share of total shipments has increased since 1990, when they constituted less than 7 percent all shipments.

Imports of paper and allied products surged 9 percent in 1993 and accounted for almost 9 percent of the total U.S. consumption of those products, or $11.4 billion. The principal supplier to the United States in 1993 was Canada, with 78 percent of all U.S. imports. Other principal suppliers included Finland, Germany, Japan, the United Kingdom, and Brazil.

The jump in imports was led by Canadian newsprint, up 17 percent; printing and writing paper, up 12 percent; and wood pulp, up 12 percent. The increase in imports of Canadian newsprint in 1993 reversed a five-year decline. Canadian newsprint, which until the early 1980s supplied about 60 percent of total annual U.S. consumption, has become significantly less competitive with U.S. virgin and recycled newsprint in recent years, because of higher production costs, U.S. requirements for high-quality recycled newsprint, and major additions to U.S. production capacity. Canadian-supplied newsprint now accounts for slightly more than 48 percent of U.S. newsprint consumption, compared with about 52 percent in 1991.

U.S. Trade Patterns in 1992 Paper and Allied Products SIC 26 (in millions of dollars, percent)

EXPORTS	Value	Share	IMPORTS	Value	Share
Canada and Mexico	3,119	30.8	Canada and Mexico	8,016	76.9
European Community	2,436	24.1	European Community	841	8.1
Japan	1,189	11.7	Japan	222	2.1
East Asia NICs	1,534	15.2	East Asia NICs	376	3.6
South America	466	4.6	South America	270	2.6
Other	1,377	13.6	Other	698	6.7
World Total	10,122	100.0	World Total	10,424	100.0

TOP FIVE COUNTRIES	Value	Share		Value	Share
Canada	1,836	18.1	Canada	7,870	75.5
Mexico	1,283	12.7	Finland	381	3.7
Japan	1,189	11.7	Germany	243	2.3
Germany	493	4.9	Brazil	238	2.3
South Korea	486	4.8	Japan	222	2.1

Source: U.S. Department of Commerce: Bureau of the Census; International Trade Administration.

Environmental Profile. In 1993 the domestic industry attained a wastepaper recovery rate of 41 to 42 percent, surpassing its 1995 goal of 40 percent. Recycled paper constituted nearly 31 percent of fiber used at domestic paper and paperboard mills in 1993, up from 29 percent in 1992. Almost half of the recovered paper and paperboard consisted of old corrugated scrap and recovered boxes and containers; old newsprint was the second-largest recovery component. About one-third of the primary paper and board mills in operation during 1993 used wastepaper as their principal fiber component, and at another 50 percent, waste materials constituted up to half of the fiber mix. Most mill additions in 1993 were planned to use recycled fibers as a significant portion of their papermaking materials.

The U.S. government tightened its requirements in 1993 for recycled fiber content in the large quantity of printing and writing papers it purchases. About 95 percent of the bulk paper bought by the Government Printing Office in 1993 reportedly consisted of recycled fibers. The Environmental Protection Agency (EPA) began in 1993 to revise its 1988 minimum-content guidelines for paper products the government buys. These guidelines specify minimum secondary fiber and post-consumer content. In addition to national efforts, many states and local jurisdictions continued to press in 1993 for tougher recycling and packaging legislation. EPA continued to revise water-effluent and air-emission limitations and standards for the industry under the Clean Water Act and the Clean Air Act.

The guidelines, due out early in 1994 for promulgation in the second half of 1995, are expected to address dioxins and other substances, with potential implications for bleached pulp mills. Amendments to the Clean Air Act, signed into law at the end of 1990, provide extensive changes to existing regulations regarding sources of ozone, carbon monoxide, and particulate matter, which could have a profound effect on pulp and paper mills in regions where ambient air quality does not meet health-based national standards. Paper companies will be required to demonstrate, on a case-by-case basis, that they are in compliance with all existing air standards, or that the benefits of a mill significantly outweigh the costs of complying with antipollution regulations.

Because the European Community is the U.S. paper industry's largest regional export market, the EC's recent draft legislation on packaging and packaging waste, precipitated by the restrictive actions of Germany and other member countries, is of growing concern in the United States and other paper-trading countries. The objectives are to reduce the amount of packaging waste produced, require the recovery of packaging waste, and minimize the volume of such waste that goes into final disposal. With ten years, 90 percent of packaging waste would have to be recovered and 60 percent recycled. Other proposals include an EC packaging tax to ensure collection of waste and to fund recycling projects. Strict provisions are included to ensure that member states do not use these levies as barriers to trade. Nevertheless, an EC packaging tax, and the imposition of packaging-waste-recovery requirements on manufacturers, retailers, and distributors, could add to the costs of U.S. paper exports and reduce general product competitiveness.

Outlook for 1994. Supported by stronger domestic demand for packaging and industrial-type paper grades and by strengthening export markets, real growth of 3 percent is expected in shipments of paper and allied products in 1994. Successful conclusion of the NAFTA and GATT agreements could bring a substantial rise in U.S. exports.

U.S. exports should increase at least 6 percent in 1994, and the gain could be significantly higher if trade barriers are lowered in Japan, Mexico, and the EC. Imports will continue to expand in 1994, especially newsprint, pulp, and printing and writing paper from Canada. Shipments of paper and allied products to the EC should expand because of the U.S. paper industry's largely successful efforts to meet the new EC guidelines and product standards.

The U.S. industry already has a significant presence in Western Europe, and will attempt further to strengthen its EC market share through joint ventures or acquisitions of local papermaking operations, especially in the more lucrative sectors of printing and writing papers and of sanitary tissue manufacture.

PULP MILLS

Commodities in this sector (SIC 2611) include a number of chemical and mechanical paper-grade pulps and special alpha and dissolving pulps, which are sold on the open market rather than used in integrated manufacture. The various grades of pulp can be made from softwoods, hardwoods, or other fibrous raw material sources that include recovered secondary fiber, rags, or agricultural products including cotton linters, kenaf, bagasse, or straw. Shipments by this industry, both export and domestic, constitute 12 to 16 percent of total U.S. production and do not include domestic transfer shipments to affiliated paper and board mills.

Following a record-breaking 1992, U.S. market pulp shipments declined more than 2 percent in 1993 to less than 9 million metric tons (t). Causes included depressed foreign sales in key markets, sluggish domestic demand, falling prices, continued global overcapacity, and significant increases in consumption of recovered paper in the United States and abroad. The one bright spot for the domestic industry was an increase of nearly 10 percent in the volume of domestic shipments, reversing a downward slide since 1988. Exports represented two-thirds of the volume of all U.S. shipments in 1993, slightly smaller than the 70 percent market share that exports held in 1992.

Industry Developments. The domestic market pulp industry's dominant product is paper-grade pulp, accounting for nearly 95 percent of total domestic sales, or 8 million t, in 1993. Bleached softwood kraft pulp constituted 58 percent of production, but bleached hardwood kraft pulp continued to increase its fiber market share to 38 percent. Higher domestic production of coated and uncoated free sheet papers, which contain at least 90 percent bleached chemical wood pulp by fiber weight, increased the demand for U.S. virgin papermaking fibers from domestic paper and board manufacturers. In 1993 the remaining sales in SIC 2611 consisted primarily of bleached and unbleached sulfite pulp (nearly 3 percent) and unbleached kraft pulp (2 percent).

The consumer market for global pulp is going through a transition, driven largely by changes in Europe. The European Community, representing more than 40 percent of total pulp demand, obtains 20 percent of its pulp from the United States and 11 percent from Japan. Tremendous interest and investment brought about by environmental and public pressures (especially in Europe), have been directed in the past several years to the development and production of totally chlorine-free (TCF) market pulps, made without the use of chlorine compounds in the bleaching process. Chlorine (primarily elemental chlorine gas) had been identified as the main cause of toxic dioxin compounds in pulp-mill effluents.

Chemical paper-grade market pulp, used primarily in the manufacture of printing and writing papers, is produced in about 37 countries. About 63 percent, or 22.8 million t, of world output came from the NORSCAN countries (United States, Canada, Sweden, Finland, and Norway) in 1993. In recent years, the market share of NORSCAN producers has come under increased pressure from low-cost, state-of-the-art pulp mills in Latin America, Western Europe, and Africa. These countries not only enjoy abundant, fast-growing solid wood resources (especially eucalyptus and tropical pine species), but also have lower costs for labor, environmental protection, and basic operations.

Prices Continue to Decline. Prices for market pulp continued a four-year decline in 1993 as a result of excess global supply and inventories, increased use of secondary fiber, and soft world demand for virgin papermaking fibers. From the 1990 record price of $840 per metric ton for northern bleached softwood kraft, which is the global benchmark pulp grade, prices fell to $440 per metric ton in 1993, their lowest level since the price collapse of 1985. Other pulp grades, including southern bleached softwood kraft, experienced similar price declines.

Extensive downtime and production curtailments at pulp mills, designed to remove excess pulp from the consumer market, sharply reduced the U.S. market pulp sector's operating rates for 1993. In June 1993 the market pulp sector operated at 85 percent of capacity, down from 93 percent in the same period in 1992. One of the few positive trends for U.S. market pulp producers in 1993 was inventory reduction. From 882,000 t (a 41-day supply) at the end of 1992, producers' inventory levels declined to 769,000 (a 32-day supply) by mid-1993.

Trends and Forecasts: Pulp Mills (SIC 2611) (In millions of dollars except as noted)

| ITEM | 1991 | 1992[1] | 1993[2] | 1994[3] | PERCENT CHANGE (1991–1994) | | |
					91–92	92–93	93–94
Industry Data							
Value of shipments[4]	5,329	5,612	5,200	5,619	5.3	-7.3	8.1
Value of shipments (1987$)	4,898	5,265	5,133	5,251	7.5	-2.5	2.3
Total employment (000)	16.8	16.5	16.7	16.9	-1.8	1.2	1.2
Production workers (000)	12.8	12.7	12.9	13.0	-0.8	1.6	0.8
Average hourly earnings ($)	18.36	18.73	19.15	—	2.0	2.2	—
Capital expenditures	991	—	—	—	—	—	—
Product Data							
Value of shipments[5]	5,741	6,047	5,603	6,054	5.3	-7.3	8.0
Value of shipments (1987$)	5,277	5,673	5,531	5,658	7.5	-2.5	2.3
Trade Data							
Value of imports	2,142	2,104	2,073	2,114	-1.8	-1.5	2.0
Value of exports	2,920	3,236	2,709	2,844	10.8	-16.3	5.0

[1] Estimate, except exports and imports.

[2] Estimate.

[3] Forecast.

[4] Value of all products and services sold by establishments in the pulp mills industry.

[5] Value of products classified in the pulp mills industry produced by all industries.

Source: U.S. Department of Commerce: Bureau of the Census; International Trade Administration (ITA). Estimates and forecasts by ITA.

Recovered-paper consumption by U.S. paper and board mills continued to increase in 1993, causing a decrease in demand for virgin papermaking fibers. In 1993 U.S. paper and board mills consumed approximately 81 million t. Of that total, 57 million t (or 70 percent) was virgin wood pulp and 24 million t (or 30 percent) was recovered paper and paperboard. The quantity of wood pulp consumed in 1993 was unchanged from the previous year while the quantity of recovered paper and board consumed was up more than 8 percent.

Continued capacity increases by North American market pulp producers, combined with essentially flat world demand, contributed to sluggish market conditions in 1993. U.S. market pulp capacity surged nearly 4 percent and Canadian capacity rose 3 percent in 1993. These start-ups, along with the completion of other projects in Western Europe and Asia, added more than 1.5 million t of market pulp capacity during 1992–1993.

International Competitiveness. The United States trades large quantities of pulp annually, and has enjoyed a positive trade balance in this commodity grouping since 1987. A surge in imports of Canadian wood pulp, however, sharply narrowed the trade surplus in 1993. The principal grade of market pulp traded by the United States is bleached and semi-bleached kraft pulp, accounting for nearly 80 percent of pulp exports and 86 percent of imports in 1993.

In 1993 the volume of U.S. exports of pulp decreased about 8 percent to 5.6 million t. Because prices fell as well, the value of exports plunged more than 16 percent. U.S. exporters shipped pulp to 74 countries in 1993, but the major importers were Japan with 18 percent of total U.S. exports; South Korea, 12 percent; Mexico, 10 percent; and Italy, 7 percent.

Although U.S. pulp imports increased nearly 10 percent in 1993, to 5.5 million t, and accounted for almost 10 percent of total U.S. wood pulp consumption, declining prices caused the value of pulp imports to drop nearly 2 percent. The only significant suppliers of pulp imports were Canada, 86 percent, and Brazil, 10 percent of U.S. imports.

Outlook for 1994. A turnaround in the world economy should result in higher sales of U.S. market pulp in 1994. Domestic and foreign market shipments should increase 2 percent to nearly 9 million t. Higher demand by European and Asian producers of printing and writing paper should contribute to the expansion.

The volume of U.S. exports of pulp should increase more than 8 percent to 6 million t, widening their market share to nearly 70 percent of all U.S. market pulp shipments. U.S. imports are also expected to increase in 1994, as Canadian pulp exports to the large U.S. market increase by 6 percent. As the world's largest paper and board manufacturer, the United States will continue to be the target of many countries pulp export efforts. U.S. pulp producers will need to monitor their own capacity utilization rates, consumer and producer inventory levels around the world, and relationships with worldwide paper and board production to prevent further significant increases in surplus pulp in the market.

PAPER AND PAPERBOARD MILLS

U.S. primary paper and paperboard (SIC 262, 263) production rose more than 2 percent to 76 million metric tons (t) in 1993, primarily because of increased domestic demand for printing-and-writing-paper grades. The value of sales declined slightly, however, to just over $46 billion, because of lower prices for most grades of paper and paperboard, resulting in operating losses for most U.S. paper and board companies. The price declines were due to a continuing oversupply around the world.

Operating rates remained about as high in 1993 as in 1992, with paper mills operating around 92 percent and paperboard mills operating at 95 percent. Despite a record-low U.S. dollar, export volumes of paper and board showed only marginal growth, reflecting decreased demand in principal export markets, including Europe and most of Asia. Domestic sales of primary paper were boosted by higher demand from leading users of printing and writing papers, especially from advertisers, printers, magazine and catalog publishers, and business forms and office and personal stationery. The domestic paperboard sector, in contrast, experienced a year of inventory drawdowns, reduced prices, sluggish domestic demand, and lower foreign demand for U.S. casemaking materials, resulting in minimal growth in 1993 shipments.

In 1993 the paperboard sector produced 38.6 million t of containerboard, boxboard, and related products, and the paper sector generated 37.8 million t of output. In 1993 shipments of paper commodities, which have a higher per unit value than paperboard, were valued at $30.8 billion, down nearly 4 percent from 1992, and paperboard shipments were valued at $15.2 billion, down more than 10 percent.

Domestic Paper Mills. The industry (SIC 262) produces four principal commodities: Printing and writing paper, newsprint, tissue, and packaging and industrial papers. The largest sector, printing and writing paper, accounted for 22 million t, or nearly 58 percent of all production by the paper industry in 1993. Shipments by domestic paper mills rose 3 percent in 1993, driven by higher demand from the value-added, high-end advertising, commercial printing and publishing end-user segments. The growth in shipments of printing and writing paper was paced by higher sales of uncoated free sheet, coated groundwood, and coated free sheet.

Uncoated free sheet is the single largest paper grade produced by the domestic industry, accounting for 52 percent of total printing and writing paper shipments and 30 percent of all paper commodities. Shipments of this grade increased nearly 4 percent in 1993. The higher demand allowed the industry to sustain several price increases during the year. Operating rates remained in the 90–93 percent range, but additional capacity added during the year makes a similar performance unlikely in 1994.

Shipments of uncoated groundwood increased more than 7 percent in 1993, to more than 4 million t. This grade represents more than 18 percent of domestic shipments of printing and writing paper. Increases in magazine startups and in advertising strengthened demand for coated groundwood papers, which represent more than two-thirds of the total magazine paper used in 1993.

After several years of strong growth, shipments of newsprint increased only 1 percent in 1993, to 6 million t, accounting for nearly 17 percent of total U.S. paper shipments. Despite a 1 percent increase in U.S. newspaper publishers' consumption of newsprint, overall sales were somewhat disappointing because newsprint exports declined more than 10 percent. Demand for newsprint was sluggish and capacity additions were minimal, so that operating rates for the industry were in the 95–97 percent range and prices were stable.

Paperboard Mills. After several years of strong growth, U.S. production of paperboard (SIC 263) increased less than 2 percent in 1993. Exports, a strong market for several years, declined moderately in 1993, reflecting the world economic slowdown, especially in Europe and much of Asia.

Trends and Forecasts: Paper and Paperboard Mills (SIC 262, 263) (In millions of dollars except as noted)

| ITEM | 1991 | 1992[1] | 1993[2] | 1994[3] | PERCENT CHANGE (1991–1994) | | |
					91–92	92–93	93–94
Industry Data							
Value of shipments[4]	48,357	47,830	47,156	48,692	-1.1	-1.4	3.3
Value of shipments (1987$)	43,135	43,324	43,582	44,672	0.4	0.6	2.5
Total employment (000)	181	180	180	182	-0.6	0.0	1.1
Production workers (000)	138	137	137	138	-0.7	0.0	0.7
Average hourly earnings ($)	17.55	17.99	18.10	—	2.5	0.6	—
Capital expenditures	5,790	—	—	—	—	—	—
Product Data							
Value of shipments[5]	47,148	46,679	46,024	47,523	-1.0	-1.4	3.3
Value of shipments (1987$)	42,072	42,282	42,536	43,599	0.5	0.6	2.5
Trade Data							
Value of imports	6,949	6,774	7,316	7,535	-2.5	8.0	3.0
Value of exports	4,135	4,349	4,393	4,613	5.2	1.0	5.0

[1] Estimate, except exports and imports.

[2] Estimate.

[3] Forecast.

[4] Value of all products and services sold by establishments in the paper and paperboard mills industry.

[5] Value of products classified in the paper and paperboard mills industry produced by all industries.

Source: U.S. Department of Commerce: Bureau of the Census, International Trade Administration (ITA). Estimates and forecasts by ITA.

U.S. production of paperboard is essentially split into two product lines: containerboard and boxboard. Containerboard sales, representing 69 percent of all paperboard production in 1993, totaled 26.7 million t, an increase of only 1 percent. Boxboard production came to 11.9 million t.

Production of containerboard for domestic use, representing 61 percent of all U.S. production, increased less than 2 percent in 1993 to 24 million t.

Containerboard primarily consists of linerboard and corrugating medium, which are the base components used to manufacture corrugated shipping containers and other corrugated products. Domestic linerboard production in 1993 totaled 16.4 million t, about 61 percent of total containerboard output and about 42 percent of all U.S. paperboard production. Unbleached kraft linerboard accounts for more than 92 percent of U.S. linerboard production, but white-surface, high-performance, and recycled linerboard grades have shown the strongest growth in recent years. In 1993 U.S. production of recycled linerboard more than doubled, to more than 1 million t. Total domestic production of corrugating medium gained less than 1 percent, however, to 7 million t. This product represents 30 percent of U.S. containerboard production and just under 19 percent of U.S. paperboard production.

Domestic boxboard production, continuing its recent strong performance, increased more than 4 percent in 1993, driven by higher domestic demand for packaging end-uses (which increased nearly 4 percent) and nonpackaging boxboard grades (up more than 6 percent). The latter includes fiber cans, tubes, and drums; construction-related gypsum wallboard; and panelboard used in automobile production. Boxboard for domestic packaging uses saw its strongest performance in several years, spurred in part by slightly higher consumer spending on nondurable goods.

International Competitiveness. U.S. exports of primary paper and board were essentially unchanged in 1993 as paper-related exports rose slightly and paperboard products fell a bit. Despite a lower-valued U.S. dollar and lower unit values on most paper and board grades, total paper and board exports increased only 1 percent to nearly 7 million t.

Exports of the various printing and writing paper grades increased 11 percent in 1993 to more than 1 million t, following a 24 percent surge in 1992. Two printing- and writing-paper commodities, uncoated free sheet and coated groundwood, were responsible for most of the increase, with export increases of 14 percent (to 465,300 t) 23 percent (to 191,000 t) respectively. Principal U.S. export markets for uncoated free sheet in 1993 were Canada, 54 percent, and Mexico, 14 percent. For coated groundwood, the leading U.S. export markets were Canada, 35 percent; Mexico, 19 percent; Japan, 18 percent; and the Netherlands, 13 percent.

The economic downturns in Europe and Asia in 1993 were characterized by a reduction in those U.S. export markets' shipments of nondurable goods, a principal end-use for corrugated boxes. Overall, U.S. paperboard exports declined nearly 3 percent to 4 million t. Exports of unbleached kraft linerboard, accounting for 60 percent of all paperboard exports, fell 8 percent to less than 3 million t as foreign demand for U.S. containerboard fell. One paperboard grade whose exports did expand vigorously was recycled paperboard. Foreign demand for this folding carton board expanded 16 percent in 1993 to 256,820 t.

U.S. paper and board imports surged more than 15 percent to 12 million t in 1993, driven by a moderate turnaround in the U.S. economy. The largest import gains were in newsprint, up more than 18 percent to 7 million t, almost all from Canada. Because most prices remained flat or fell slightly, the value of newsprint imports increased only 8 percent to $7.3 billion. The wide range of paper grades, including newsprint and printing and writing paper, accounted for 11 million t, or about 92 percent of total U.S. imports of paper and board.

U.S. imports of printing and writing paper, which made up 26 percent of total imports, increased nearly 14 percent to 3.1 million t in 1993. This growth was attributable to large increases in U.S. imports of coated groundwood (more than 24 percent) and uncoated free sheet printing and writing papers (17 percent). U.S. printing- and writing-paper imports come primarily from Canada, Scandinavia, and the European Community.

U.S. imports of the paperboard grades, although still relatively small, increased 10 percent in 1993, to 907,000 t. The United States imported significantly larger quantities of kraft containerboard and virgin and recycled boxboard, primarily because of strong demand by U.S. corrugated box plants and folding carton plants. The leading supplier of paperboard to the United States was Canada, accounting for 90 percent of total imports.

Outlook for 1994. U.S. paper and paperboard shipments will increase more than 3 percent in value in 1994 as domestic demand remains strong and U.S. producers enjoy higher sales overseas. Exports of paper and board should increase 5 percent, and imports, buoyed by a stronger U.S. economy, should increase at least 3 percent.

The U.S. industry will continue to direct most of its additional output overseas, especially to printers, publishers, and boxmakers in Asia, Latin America, and the EC. But the domestic market will continue to claim about 90 percent of domestic output.

Domestic paper and board producers are expected to add 1.5 million t of capacity in 1994, adding to the overcapacity that prevailed in 1993, especially in printing and writing paper. If the global economy improves enough in 1994, the additional output could be easily absorbed by foreign converters and packagers. If not, operating rates in domestic paper and board mils will probably be flat or slightly lower, and pressure on domestic producers to schedule extended periods of mill downtime will increase.

WEYERHAEUSER COMPANY—1994

C A S E
21

MICHELLE R. GREENE
AND FRED R. DAVID
Francis Marion University

Headquartered in Tacoma, Washington, Weyerhaeuser's (206-924-2058) sales and net income increased 7.4 percent and 55.7 percent in 1993.

Weyerhaeuser's vision statement is to be "the best forest products company in the world." Their strategies for realizing this vision are: "making total quality the Weyerhaeuser way of doing business. Relentless pursuit of full customer satisfaction. Empowering Weyerhaeuser people. Leading the industry in forest management and manufacturing excellence. Producing superior returns for our shareholders."

THE PAST

The name Weyerhaeuser originally became identified with forest products in 1858 when a young German immigrant named Frederick Weyerhaeuser acquired a lumberyard and sawmill in western Illinois. The success of his first venture led Weyerhaeuser to purchase timberland in Wisconsin and Minnesota. Weyerhaeuser wanted to control other forests but soon realized he needed financial assistance to realize his goal. He began to seek partners in his timber business. Weyerhaeuser and his associates soon became a major force in the American timber and lumber industries.

In 1900 Weyerhaeuser organized a group of midwestern investors to buy forest land in the Pacific Northwest. The venture became one of the largest private land transactions in American history. Weyerhaeuser and 15 partners purchased 900,000 acres of timberland from the Northern Pacific Railway for $6 per acre. Then 65 years old, Weyerhaeuser could scarcely have dreamed that his enterprise would become a giant in American industry. The investors' group named the company for Weyerhaeuser and opened its first office in Tacoma. The company was incorporated in 1900 as the Weyerhaeuser Timber Company.

In addition to acquiring a sawmill, buying timber, and selling wood products, the new company kept harvested lands for reforestation. Weyerhaeuser was always determined to plant and care for more trees than his company harvested each year. The company's high-yield forestry today is a scientific forest-management program designed to produce more timber than is cut while protecting fish and wildlife. The program includes planting seedlings within a year after harvest, fertilizing heavily, and rehabilitating brushlands.

THE PRESENT

Weyerhaeuser Company earnings increased soundly in 1993 to $579 million on $8.3 billion in sales, up from $372 million and $7.7 billion in 1992. Weyerhaeuser in 1993 sold its baby diaper business—a successful but noncore operation—for $44 million and also divested its tax-deferred annuities and mutual fund business (GNA Corporation) for $36 million. This sale is the largest divestiture ever made by Weyerhaeuser. GNA also was a profitable investment for Weyerhaeuser over its nine years of ownership.

Weyerhaeuser recently completed the purchase from Procter & Gamble Company of two pulp mills, three sawmills, timberlands in Georgia, and a forest-management license in Alberta. Weyerhaeuser has strengthened its engineered fiber products business with another acquisition, an oriented strand board mill at Slave Lake, Alberta. The formerly idle mill provided needed additional capacity and flexibility to meet the growing demand for Weyerhaeuser's oriented strand products.

Weyerhaeuser is modernizing its pulp and paper complexes in Plymouth, North Carolina ($500 million); Longview, Washington ($400 million); and Kamloops, British Columbia ($80 million). The projects are part of one of the largest modernization programs in company history. Installation of state-of-the-art systems at all three facilities will allow for the elimination of elemental chlorine from the pulp-manufacturing process, improve product quality to meet ever-increasing customer demands, reduce energy and chemical costs, and significantly enhance air and water quality. Another benefit will be the use of additional recycled paper for increased production at Plymouth. Scheduled completion of the projects is late 1994 to mid-1995.

Weyerhaeuser recently celebrated the 25th anniversary of its high-yield forestry strategy that brought the company to leadership in forestry management. In the international arena, Weyerhaeuser celebrated the 20th anniversary of its business relationship with the People's Republic of China. Weyerhaeuser was the first U.S. forest products company to ship an industrial product to China through contacts made at the 1972 Guangzhou Trade Fair. Weyerhaeuser, now the leading U.S. exporter of forest products, provides China with corrugating medium, linerboard, logs, lumber, paper and pulp. In 1993 Weyerhaeuser celebrated the 30th anniversary of establishing a Weyerhaeuser office in Tokyo.

Weyerhaeuser and Svenska Cellulosa of Sweden have entered into an agreement that will enable the corrugated packaging business of both of the companies to better satisfy the increasing requirements of international customers. One of Weyerhaeuser's greatest achievements was earning registration from the International Organization for Standardization (ISO) for quality of both products and processes at four of the company's pulp and paper facilities.

THE COMPANY STRUCTURE

Weyerhaeuser has 37,000 employees, of which 34,200 are employed in its timber-based businesses. Approximately 17,000 employees are covered by collective bargaining agreements. Approximately 2,800 of the company's employees are involved in the activities of its real estate and financial services subsidiaries. In 1993 the company's sales to customers outside the United States totaled $2.2 billion, which included $1.8 billion of exports from the United States and Canada. The company's other two large subsidiaries are timberlands/wood products and pulp/paper/packaging.

Timberlands/Wood Products. Weyerhaeuser's wood products businesses produce and sell softwood lumber, plywood, and veneer; composite panels; oriented strand board; hardboard; hardwood lumber and plywood; doors; treated products; logs; chips; and timber. These products are sold primarily through the company's own sales organizations. Building materials are sold to wholesalers, retailers, and industrial users.

Weyerhaeuser owns approximately 5.5 million acres of commercial forest land in the United States, of which 50 percent is located in the South and 50 percent in the Pacific Northwest. The company also has long-term license agreements in Canada covering approximately 17.8 million acres, of which 14 million acres are considered to be productive forest land. Weyerhaeuser's combined total timber inventory on U.S. and Canadian lands is approximately 245 million cunits (a cunit is 100 cubic feet of solid wood) of which approximately 75 percent is softwood species. The company is engaged in extensive planting, suppression of nonmerchantable species, precommercial and commercial thinning and fertilization, all of which increase the yield from its fee timberland acreage.

Timberlands and Wood Products reported strong 1993 earnings—the highest since 1980—with plywood, engineered fiber products, and building materials distribution businesses posting record profits for the year. Timber supply restrictions in the public forests of the Pacific Northwest have reduced West Coast raw material availability and caused significant price increases, while reductions in international timber supply translated into stronger business results in Japan and China. Plans to protect the northern spotted owl led to reduced harvest on company-owned lands.

Weyerhaeuser has had a serious challenge with the new forest practice rules in Washington. The new rules are some of the most comprehensive in the United States and address such issues as size and timing of harvest acres, wetlands and streamside management zones, use of chemicals and critical habitat reserves. Weyerhaeuser participates actively in the regulatory process and supports its goals.

Annual production levels for Weyerhaueser's different lumber products are given in Exhibit 21–1. Note that demand for all lumber products increased. Southern lumber prices attained record levels in several product lines because the Western harvest

EXHIBIT 21-1 Weyerhaeuser Annual Production Levels for Wood Products (Millions of dollars)

NET SALES	1993	1992	1991	1990	1989
Raw materials					
(logs, chips and timber)	$1,021	$ 872	$ 843	$ 834	$ 893
Softwood lumber	1,669	1,097	938	1,016	1,229
Softwood plywood and veneer	567	498	412	411	490
Oriented strand board, composite					
and other panels	623	495	383	381	424
Hardwood lumber	154	127	118	117	119
Hardwood plywood and doors	141	116	117	135	236
Treated products	84	67	65	80	95
Miscellaneous products	209	145	72	99	180
	$4,468	$3,417	$2,948	$3,073	$3,666

Source: Weyerhaeuser *Annual Report,* 1993.

reduction resulted in more pressure on the South to make up the shortfall. Production for the year was hampered by an unusually wet spring, which slowed log supplies to the mills and mill startups. The southern lumber business has expanded its product mix by adding the Barnesville, Georgia, mill, which was part of an acquisition from Procter & Gamble. Weyerhaeuser today has 56 manufacturing facilities within its Timberlands and Wood Products division, as shown in Exhibit 21–2. Note in Exhibit 21–3 that Weyerhaeuser is operating at over 90 percent capacity in all categories except hardwood lumber.

Pulp, Paper, and Packaging. Weyerhaeuser's pulp, paper, and packaging revenues decreased in 1993, as shown in Exhibit 21–4. There were declines in all categories except pulp and chemicals. Note that the 1993 composite sales figures show a 12.9 percent decrease. For the year market pulp demand showed a modest improvement. Domestic newsprint prices continue to deteriorate with very slow growth in the domestic market and negative growth in the Japanese market. Substantial overcapacity in printing and writing papers has resulted in continued low industry-operating

EXHIBIT 21-2 Weyerhaeuser Principal Manufacturing Facilities—Timberlands and Wood Products.

Softwood lumber, plywood and veneer	35
Composite panels	6
Oriented strand board	5
Hardboard	1
Hardwood lumber	8
Hardwood doors	1

Source: Weyerhaeuser *Annual Report*, 1993.

EXHIBIT 21-3 Weyerhaeuser Timberlands and Wood Products—Annual Production (Millions)

	CAPACITY	1993	1992	1991	1990	1989
Logs—cubic feet	—	673	749	782	817	839
Softwood lumber—board feet	3,215	3,135	2,782	2,687	2,719	2,759
Softwood plywood and veneer— square feet (3/8")	1,246	1,188	1,125	966	1,076	1,069
Composite panels—square feet (3/4")	609	564	540	493	505	587
Oriented strand board—square feet (3/8")	1,440	1,443	1,234	1,208	1,156	1,121
Hardboard—square feet (7/16")	130	120	118	90	119	131
Hardwood lumber—board feet	255	221	210	196	202	212
Hardwood doors (thousands)	561	522	469	448	556	833

Source: Weyerhaeuser *Annual Report*, 1993.

rates and price reductions of 40 percent on high-volume grades. Note in Exhibit 21–5 that Weyerhaueser is operating at nearly 100 percent capacity in all its pulp, paper, and packaging categories, except MSF packaging. Recycled paper usage continues to be an important part of the raw material for the company's products. More than 23 percent of the raw material for the company's pulp and papermaking operations is recycled fiber, up from 15 percent in 1989.

Weyerhaeuser recently strengthened its pulp and paper businesses by acquiring a softwood kraft papergrade mill in Grande Prairie, Alberta, and a fluff pulp mill in Oglethorpe, Georgia, both from Procter & Gamble Company. The two newly acquired pulp mills increased market pulp capacity by 40 percent and further strengthened Weyerhaeuser's world leadership in fluff and softwood papergrade.

In containerboard packaging, the $105 million modernization of the No. 1 paper

EXHIBIT 21-4 Weyerhaeuser Pulp, Paper, and Packaging Sales (Millions of dollars)

NET SALES	1993	1992	1991	1990	1989
Pulp	$ 823	$ 711	$ 803	$ 865	$ 917
Newsprint	322	326	288	293	321
Paper	648	673	655	751	733
Paperboard and containerboard	255	321	361	366	373
Container and packaging products	1,302	1,323	1,175	1,183	1,261
Recycling	77	93	90	88	85
Chemicals	32	31	34	28	31
Personal care products	—	514	450	338	347
Miscellaneous products	120	117	147	140	147
	$3,579	$4,109	$4,003	$4,052	$4,215

Source: Weyerhaeuser *Annual Report*, 1993.

EXHIBIT 21-5 Weyerhaeuser Pulp, Paper, and Packaging—Annual Production (Thousands)

	CAPACITY	1993	1992	1991	1990	1989
Pulp—air-dry metric tons	2,130	2,096	1,506	1,527	1,386	1,275
Newsprint—metric tons	675	618	588	461	459	486
Paper—tons	1,015	1,007	971	889	900	919
Paperboard—tons	220	217	229	238	217	221
Containerboard—tons	2,360	2,269	2,240	2,224	2,171	2,168
Packaging—MSF	36,800	32,795	31,040	27,583	26,146	25,764
Recycling—tons	—	1,847	1,692	1,415	1,204	1,163
Personal care products—standard cases	—	—	16,743	14,902	11,471	12,019

Source: Weyerhaeuser *Annual Report*, 1993.

machine at Valliant, Oklahoma, has been completed and producing high-performance linerboard. Weyerhaeuser is converting the linerboard machine at Plymouth, North Carolina, to produce a 100 percent recycled product. The company expects corrugated packaging demand to rise with improvement in general economic conditions and export containerboard shipments to grow with the later pickup in the European economies and economic recovery in the Far East.

The newsprint business in 1993 was unable to increase its domestic and export market shares during a difficult period of oversupply in the marketplace. Slow growth in the domestic market and negative growth in the Japanese market hampered sales of the large incremental volumes associated with the start-up of North Pacific Paper Corporation's (NORPAC) new newsprint machine. The business has achieved full operation of the expanded facility and successfully developed and introduced two new product grades into the Japanese market. Overall, Weyerhaeuser operated 84 pulp, paper, and packaging manufacturing plants in 1993, as shown in Exhibit 21–6.

Real Estate and Financial Services. Through its financial services subsidiary, Weyerhaeuser is involved in a broad range of financial services. The principal operating groups of Weyerhaeuser Financial Services (WFS) are Weyerhaeuser Mortgage Company and Mortgage Securities Corporation. Weyerhaeuser Mortgage Company has offices in 12 states, with a serving portfolio of $8.4 billion covering more than 112,000 loans throughout the country. Earnings for 1993 were $76.4 million, up 13 percent from 1992. However, as shown in Exhibit 21–7, total revenues of WFS fell 51.8 percent in 1993. Mortgages are resold in the secondary market through mortgage-backed securities to financial institutions and investors.

Weyerhaeuser Real Estate Company (WRECO) earned $18.3 million in 1993, up 42 percent from 1992. The 1993 low interest rates and improving consumer confidence resulted in revenues increasing to $829 million as housing starts increased in all regions of the nation except California and the Pacific Northwest. WRECO's total revenues for 1993 are given in Exhibit 21–8. Note that all categories increased.

Foreign Operations and Export Sales. Weyerhaeuser exports logs to China and Korea; pulp, containerboard, lumber, and plywood to Europe; and pulp, newsprint, paperboard, containerboard, logs, lumber, and wood chips to Japan. Exhibit 21-9

EXHIBIT 21-6 Weyerhaeuser Pulp, Paper, and Packaging—Principal Manufacturing Facilities

Pulp	8
Newsprint	1
Paper	5
Paperboard	1
Containerboard	5
Packaging	36
Recycling	21
Chemicals	7

Source: Weyerhaeuser *Annual Report*, 1993.

gives the company's recent export sales to Japan versus other foreign countries. Note that the company's total export sales declined 3 percent in 1993, but exports to Japan increased 4 percent.

Finance. Weyerhaeuser's consolidated financial information is given in Exhibits 21–10 through 21–13. A list of Weyerhaeuser's top managers appears in Exhibit 21–14.

Weyerhaeuser is facing fierce competition among lenders for loan-origination volume, spurred by continuing lower mortgage interest rates and continued refinance activity. Strategic expansion of the current origination system of 40 retail branches and seven wholesale branches is planned for the coming year. Continued focus is on responding to customer needs, improving processes, and enhancing efficiency and quality throughout the business.

THE WEYERHAEUSER FUTURE

Because of environmental concerns and new regulations in the Pacific Northwest, Weyerhaeuser perhaps should acquire timberlands elsewhere in the United States and the world. The majority of its current timber is located in the Pacific Northwest. Should Weyerhaeuser purchase timber in South America, Asia, or the northeastern United States?

Weyerhaeuser's sales to customers outside the United States fell 3.7 percent in 1993. With passage of the North American Free Trade Act on November 17, 1993, trade barriers between the United States and Mexico have been lifted. The Latin American region in general is an area where Weyerhaeuser could prosper. Should Weyerhaeuser focus on producing and marketing its products in Mexico? Prepare a strategic plan for CEO John W. Creighton, Jr., that will guide Weyerhaeuser to continued prosperity in the remaining years of this decade.

EXHIBIT 21-7 Net Sales and Revenues—WFS (Millions of dollars)

	1993	1992	1991	1990	1989
Interest	$110	$144	$209	$278	$383
Investment income	116	452	454	369	314
Loan origination and servicing fees	127	103	98	89	92
Premiums	14	21	19	23	21
Other revenues	34	112	82	49	41
	$401	$832	$862	$808	$851

Source: Weyerhaeuser *Annual Report*, 1993.

EXHIBIT 21-8 Net Sales and Revenues—WRECO (Millions of dollars)

	1993	1992	1991	1990	1989
Single-family units	$615	$569	$591	$644	$718
Multi-family units	30	4	16	15	12
Residential lots	43	39	25	35	44
Commercial lots	41	6	17	10	27
Commercial buildings	3	5	30	23	66
Acreage	27	20	16	31	55
Other	70	47	49	53	53
	$829	$690	$744	$811	$975

Source: Weyerhaeuser *Annual Report*,1993.

EXHIBIT 21-9 Weyerhaeuser's Export Sales

	1993	1992	1991
Export sales:			
Customers in Japan	$ 952,000	$ 912,000	$ 887,000
Customers outside Japan	493,000	589,000	663,000
Total export sales	$1,445,000	$1,501,000	$1,550,000
Total net sales and revenues	$9,545,000	$9,266,000	$8,773,000

Source: Weyerhaeuser *Annual Report*, 1993.

EXHIBIT 21-10 Weyerhaeuser Operations by Division

Business Segments	Sales to and Revenue from Unaffiliated Customers	Intersegment Sales and Revenue	Total Sales and Revenue	Approximate Contribution to Earnings	Depreciation, Amortization and Fee Stumpage	Capital Expenditures	Assets
1993:							
Timberlands and wood products	$4,467,751	$ 352,314	$4,820,065	$ 891,431	$161,903	$ 240,760	$ 2,582,832
Pulp and paper products	3,579,042	6,189	3,585,231	60,854	263,961	652,092	5,731,965
Real estate	828,713	—	828,713	18,326	9,123	15,007	1,863,615
Financial services	401,711	—	401,711	76,437	33,976	4,737	1,892,180
Corporate and other	269,181	28,409	297,590	(46,961)	17,968	54,885	1,274,185
	9,546,398	386,912	9,933,310	1,000,087	486,931	967,481	13,344,777
Eliminations	(1,606)	(386,912)	(388,518)	—			(706,324)
Interest expense				(292,459)			—
Less: capitalized interest				100,825			—
Income before income taxes and extraordinary item				808,453			—
Income taxes				(281,168)			—
Extraordinary item				52,052			—
	$9,544,792	—	$9,544,792	$ 579,337	$486,931	$ 967,481	$12,638,453
1992:							
Timberlands and wood products	$3,416,832	$ 340,368	$3,757,200	$ 515,394	$149,504	$ 246,096	$ 2,374,152
Pulp and paper products	4,109,080	28,822	4,137,902	251,091	254,956	931,913	5,614,490
Real estate	690,342	—	690,342	12,897	7,310	7,869	1,693,741
Financial services	832,389	—	832,389	67,633	48,685	2,646	8,148,285
Corporate and other	220,032	29,907	249,939	(106,863)	42,291	16,990	1,201,418
	9,268,675	399,097	9,667,772	740,152	502,746	1,205,514	19,032,086

EXHIBIT 21-10 *Continued*

Business Segments	Sales to and Revenue from Unaffiliated Customers	Intersegment Sales and Revenue	Total Sales and Revenue	Approximate Contribution to Earnings	Depreciation, Amortization and Fee Stumpage	Capital Expenditures	Assets
Eliminations	(2,206)	(399,097)	(401,303)	—	—	—	(873,683)
Interest expense	—	—	—	(262,209)	—	—	—
Less: capitalized interest	—	—	—	85,406	—	—	—
Income before income taxes	—	—	—	563,349	—	—	—
Income taxes	—	—	—	(191,300)	—	—	—
	$9,266,469	—	$9,266,469	$ 372,049	$502,746	$1,205,514	$18,158,403
1991:							
Timberlands and wood products	$2,948,358	$ 366,988	$3,315,346	$ 155,386	$157,506	$ 161,589	$ 2,223,886
Pulp and paper products	4,002,738	19,685	4,022,423	108,287	245,533	472,412	4,928,239
Real estate	744,366	—	744,366	(175,331)	8,197	7,485	1,500,250
Financial services	862,403	—	862,403	60,409	46,843	3,518	7,956,631
Corporate and other	215,501	29,062	244,563	(148,212)	43,243	18,367	1,186,906
	8,773,366	415,735	9,189,101	539	501,322	663,371	17,795,912
Eliminations	(753)	(415,735)	(416,488)	—	—	—	(810,038)
Interest expense	—	—	—	(265,240)	—	—	—
Less: capitalized interest	—	—	—	86,853	—	—	—
Income (loss) before income taxes and effect of accounting changes	—	—	—	(177,848)	—	—	—
Income taxes	—	—	—	76,900	—	—	—
Effect of accounting changes	—	—	—	(61,000)	—	—	—
	$8,772,613	—	$8,772,613	$(161,948)	$501,322	$ 663,371	$16,985,874

Interest expense of $95,309, $151,519 and $219,441 before the elimination of intercompany interest of $0, $3,403 and $6,455 in 1993, 1992, and 1991, respectively, is included in the determination of "approximate contribution to earnings" for financial services.

Certain reclassifications have been made to conform prior years' data to the current format.

Source: Weyerhaeuser *Annual Report*, 1993.

EXHIBIT 21-11 Weyerhaeuser Consolidated Statement of Earnings For the Three Years in the Period Ended December 26, 1993 (Dollar amounts in thousands except per share figures)

	1993	1992	1991
Net sales and revenues:			
Weyerhaeuser:	$8,314,368	$7,743,738	$7,165,844
Real estate and financial services	1,230,424	1,522,731	1,606,769
Net sales and revenues	9,544,792	9,266,469	8,772,613
Costs and expenses:			
Weyerhaeuser:			
Costs of products sold	6,251,612	5,919,199	5,581,388
Depreciation, amortization and fee stumpage	443,832	446,751	446,282
Selling, general and administrative expenses	592,586	591,845	572,605
Research and development expenses	44,456	42,981	56,257
Taxes other than payroll and income taxes	136,897	121,793	120,283
Restructuring and other charges	—	—	290,000
	7,469,383	7,122,569	7,066,815
Real estate and financial services:			
Costs and operating expenses	835,400	979,478	1,026,546
Depreciation and amortization	43,099	55,995	55,040
Selling, general and administrative expenses	206,174	252,337	232,055
Taxes other than payroll and income taxes	9,191	11,700	9,838
Restructuring and other charges	—	—	155,000
	1,093,864	1,299,510	1,478,479
Total costs and expenses	8,563,247	8,422,079	8,545,294
Operating income	981,545	844,390	227,319
Interest expense and other:			
Weyerhaeuser:			
Interest expense incurred	214,813	189,648	197,337
Less interest capitalized	23,179	12,845	18,950
Other income (expense), net	60,339	35,050	9,977
Real estate and financial services:			
Interest expense incurred	172,955	220,677	280,889
Less interest capitalized	77,646	72,561	67,903
Other income (expense), net	53,512	8,828	(23,771)
Earnings (loss) before income taxes, extraordinary item and effect of accounting changes	808,453	563,349	(177,848)
Income taxes before extraordinary item and effect of accounting changes	281,168	191,300	(76,900)
Earnings (loss) before extraordinary item and effect of accounting changes	527,285	372,049	(100,948)
Extraordinary item, net of applicable taxes of $33,732	52,052	—	—
Effect of accounting changes	—	—	(61,000)
Net earnings (loss)	$579,337	$372,049	$(161,948)
Per common share:			
Earnings (loss) before extraordinary item and effect of accounting changes	$2.58	$1.83	$(.50)
Extraordinary item	.25	—	—
Effect of accounting changes	—	—	(.30)
Net earnings (loss)	$2.83	$1.83	$(.80)
Dividends paid	$1.20	$1.20	$1.20

Source: Weyerhaeuser *Annual Report*, 1993.

EXHIBIT 21-12 Weyerhaeuser Consolidated Balance Sheet (Dollar amounts in thousands)

	DECEMBER 26, 1993	DECEMBER 27, 1992
Assets		
Weyerhaeuser		
Current assets:		
Cash and short-term investments, including		
restricted deposits of $14,351 and $23,706	$ 73,257	$ 40,985
Receivables, less allowances of $9,798 and $9,614	782,507	769,910
Inventories	762,471	723,904
Prepaid expenses	280,511	168,079
Total current assets	1,898,746	1,702,878
Property and equipment	5,606,072	5,612,220
Construction in progress	666,177	322,376
Timber and timberlands at cost, less fee stumpage		
charged to disposals	604,773	591,610
Other assets and deferred charges	191,946	208,948
Total assets	8,967,714	8,438,032
Real estate and financial services		
Cash and short-term investments, including restricted		
deposits of $34,042 and $38,432	86,598	483,340
Receivables, less discounts and allowances of $6,589		
and $5,868	135,347	172,897
Mortgage and construction notes and mortgage loans		
receivable	830,569	857,963
Investments	60,355	5,232,428
Mortgage-backed certificates and restricted		
deposits	349,757	614,252
Real estate being processed for development, less reserves of		
$29,783 and $76,920	738,597	617,087
Land being processed for development, less reserves of		
$19,132 and $28,053	699,611	711,129
Deferred acquisition costs	39,751	295,314
Other assets	730,154	735,961
Total assets	3,670,739	9,720,371
	$12,638,453	$18,158,403

Source: Weyerhaeuser *Annual Report,* 1993.

EXHIBIT 21-12 *Continued*

	DECEMBER 26, 1993	DECEMBER 27, 1992
Liabilities and shareholders' interest		
Weyerhaeuser		
Current liabilities:		
Notes payable	$ 4,624	$ 14,684
Current maturities of senior long-term debt	14,522	113,607
Accounts payable	492,040	386,561
Accrued liabilities	565,002	623,163
Total current liabilities	1,076,188	1,138,015
Senior long-term debt	2,997,890	2,658,867
Convertible subordinated debentures	—	193,035
Limited recourse income debenture	—	187,963
Deferred income taxes	904,332	760,876
Deferred pension and other liabilities	535,162	511,839
Minority interest in subsidiaries	109,314	93,476
Commitments		
Total liabilities	5,622,886	5,544,071
Real estate and financial services		
Notes and commercial paper	289,038	280,351
Future annuity and contract reserves	—	5,529,700
Collateralized mortgage obligation bonds	307,416	543,157
Long-term debt	1,997,146	2,195,715
Other liabilities	455,871	419,420
Commitments		
Total liabilities	3,049,471	8,968,343
Shareholders' interest		
Common shares: authorized 400,000,000 shares, issued 206,072,890 shares, $1.25 par value	257,591	257,591
Other capital	411,096	404,250
Cumulative translation adjustment	(73,363)	(36,481)
Retained earnings	3,391,217	3,057,702
Treasury common shares, at cost: 983,952 and 1,795,595	(20,445)	(37,073)
Total shareholders' interest	3,966,096	3,645,989
	$12,638,453	$18,158,403

Source: Weyerhaeuser *Annual Report*, 1993.

EXHIBIT 21-13 Weyerhaeuser Consolidated Statement of Cash Flows (*Dollar amounts in thousands*)

For the Three Years in the Period Ended December 26, 1993	Consolidated			Weyerhaeuser Company			Real Estate and Financial Services		
	1993	1992	1991	1993	1992	1991	1993	1992	1991
Cash flows provided by operations:									
Net earnings (loss)	$ 579,337	$ 372,049	$ (161,948)	$ 511,594	$ 332,043	$ (89,185)	$ 67,743	$ 40,006	$ (72,763)
Non-cash charges to income:									
Depreciation, amortization and fee stumpage	486,931	502,746	501,322	443,832	446,751	446,282	43,099	55,995	55,040
Deferred income taxes, net	93,033	125,300	(43,000)	107,591	97,192	(6,530)	(14,558)	28,108	(36,470)
Contributions to employee investment plans	2,462	31,577	25,420	2,462	31,577	25,420	—	—	—
Extraordinary item, including current tax benefit	(90,419)	—	—	(90,419)	—	—	—	—	—
Deferred income taxes on extraordinary item	38,367	—	—	38,367	—	—	—	—	—
Effect of accounting charge	—	—	198,000	—	—	187,000	—	—	11,000
Effect of accounting changes — deferred taxes	—	—	(137,000)	—	—	(122,505)	—	—	(14,495)
Restructuring and other charges	—	—	445,000	—	—	290,000	—	—	155,000
Changes in working capital:									
Receivables	(93,196)	(191,078)	20,060	(55,155)	(120,186)	5,606	(38,041)	(70,892)	14,454
Inventories, prepaid expenses, real estate and land	(246,356)	(174,519)	3,183	(164,475)	(31,551)	(30,341)	(81,881)	(142,968)	33,524
Mortgages held for sale	22,758	164,686	168,875	22,758	—	—	22,758	164,686	168,875
Other liabilities	177,629	289,041	372,262	61,971	(78,407)	66,676	115,658	367,448	305,586
(Gain) loss on disposition of assets	(16,352)	9,868	7,776	(2,741)	9,509	8,476	(13,611)	359	(700)
Gain on sales of businesses	(111,750)	(2,742)	—	(70,199)	—	—	(41,551)	(2,742)	—
Other	18,826	(17,222)	(67,451)	34,325	7,789	27,514	(15,499)	(25,011)	(94,965)
Net cash provided by operations	861,270	1,109,706	1,332,499	817,153	694,717	808,413	44,117	414,989	524,086
Cash flows from investing in the business:									
Property and equipment	(926,899)	(574,715)	(647,887)	(907,155)	(564,200)	(636,884)	(19,744)	(10,515)	(11,003)
Timber and timberlands	(40,582)	(41,436)	(15,484)	(40,582)	(41,436)	(15,484)	—	—	—
Mortgage and investment securities acquired	(776,424)	(4,556,619)	(1,765,701)	—	—	—	(776,424)	(4,556,619)	(1,765,701)

EXHIBIT 21-13 *Continued*

Acquisition of businesses	—	—	—	(589,363)	(589,363)	—	—	(589,363)
Proceeds from sale of:								
Property and equipment	3,556	3,328	26,756	47,703	52,034	26,954	51,259	53,710
Businesses	—	—	411,684	22,668	—	204,100	22,668	615,784
Mortgage and investment securities	1,280,131	4,276,056	509,982	—	—	—	1,280,131	509,982
Other	(43,767)	(77,157)	(19,718)	(6,460)	58,942	(5,675)	(50,227)	(25,393)
Net cash flows from investing in the business	(536,784)	(364,907)	132,536	(588,457)	(1,084,023)	(722,358)	(1,125,241)	(589,822)
Cash flows from financing activities: Sale of debentures, notes and CMO bonds	213,247	664,665	360,007	633,755	117,451	930,882	847,002	1,290,889
Sale of industrial revenue bonds	—	—	—	40,900	151,840	135,400	40,900	135,400
Savings deposits, net	(142,465)	(618,467)	—	—	—	—	(142,465)	(618,467)
Notes and commercial paper borrowings, net	140,769	(82,378)	(140,102)	(585,773)	503,813	(519,837)	(445,004)	(659,939)
Sales of receivables	—	—	—	64,417	—	64,417	64,417	—
Proceeds from issuance of investment contracts	566,469	430,566	60,943	—	—	—	566,469	60,943
Cash dividends on common shares	—	—	—	—	(243,965)	(245,822)	(241,814)	(245,822)
Intercompany cash dividends on common shares	(23,000)	(22,300)	(435,000)	—	22,300	435,000	—	—
Payments on debentures, notes, bank credit agreements, income debenture, capital leases and CMO bonds	(423,900)	(469,942)	(419,243)	(78,654)	(222,783)	(823,851)	(502,554)	(1,243,094)
Exercise of stock options	—	—	—	4,438	27,060	20,571	4,438	20,571
Other	2,678	—	—	(675)	(10,231)	5,134	2,003	5,134
Net cash flows from financing activities	333,798	(97,856)	(573,395)	(140,406)	345,485	(62,523)	193,392	(635,918)
Net increase (decrease) in cash and short-term investments	321,100	(47,774)	(396,742)	79,550	(43,821)	2,272	400,650	(364,470)
Cash and short-term investments at beginning of year	210,014	531,114	483,340	5,256	84,806	40,985	215,270	524,325
Cash and short-term investments at end of year	$531,114	$483,340	$86,598	$84,806	$40,985	$73,257	$615,920	$159,855
Cash paid (received) during the year for:								
Interest, net of amount capitalized	$215,997	$150,202	$102,432	$160,157	$181,630	$203,618	$376,154	$306,050
Income taxes	47,194	$(7,762)	$(3,234)	$26,056	$(10,138)	$161,236	$73,250	$158,002

Source: Weyerhaeuser *Annual Report*, 1993.

EXHIBIT 21-14 Top Managers at Weyerhaeuser

DIRECTORS

William H. Clapp
John W. Creighton, Jr.
W. John Driscoll
Don C. Frisbee
Philip M. Hawley
E. Bronson Ingram
John I. Kieckhefer
William D. Ruckelshaus
Richard H. Sinkfield
George H. Weyerhaeuser

SENIOR OFFICERS

John W. Creighton, Jr.
President and
Chief Executive Officer

Charles W. Bingham
Executive Vice President,
Timberlands, Raw Materials
and External Affairs

William R. Corbin
Executive Vice President,
Wood Products

Steven R. Hill
Senior Vice President,
Human Resources

Norman E. Johnson
Senior Vice President,
Technology

William C. Stivers
Senior Vice President and
Chief Financial Officer

CORPORATION

John S. Coates
Vice President and
Managing Director,
Pension Fund Investments

David R. Edwards
Vice President and Treasurer

Clifford R. Hall
Vice President,
Information Technology

Mack L. Hogans
Vice President,
Government Affairs

Robert C. Lane
Vice President and
General Counsel

John S. Larsen
Vice President,
Office of the Environment

Richard K. Long
Vice President,
Corporate Communications

Sandy D. McDade
Secretary

Susan M. Mersereau
Vice President, Quality,
Corporate Region Services
and Aviation

Larry W. Pollock
Vice President and
Director of Taxes

Darien E. Roseen
Vice President,
Strategic Planning

Edward L. Soule
Vice President,
Corporate R&D

Kenneth J. Stancato
Vice President and
Controller

Marvin E. Waters
Vice President,
Labor Relations

TIMBERLANDS

Conor W. Boyd
Vice President, Washington

J. Carl Jessup
Vice President, South

Scott R. Marshall
Vice President, Policy,
Finance and Strategic Planning

Rex McCullough
Vice President,
Forestry Research

John P. McMahon
Vice President, Timberlands,
External and Regulatory Affairs

Edward P. Rogel
Vice President,
Human Resources

John H. Wilkinson
Vice President, Oregon

WOOD PRODUCTS

Arnold B. Curtis
Vice President,
Hardwood Business Group

Lynn E. Endicott
Vice President;
Purchasing and Transportation

Thomas M. Luthy
Vice President,
Engineered Fiber Products

John N. Purcell
Vice President,
Western Lumber

John D. Selig
Vice President,
Southern Lumber

Steven J. Sery
Vice President,
Canadian Lumber

David T. Still
Vice President, Building
Materials Distribution

D.J. Young
Vice President, Plywood

PULP, PAPER AND PACKAGING

Peter G. Belluschi
Vice President, Newsprint and
Bleached Paperboard

Michael J. Cordry
Vice President, Quality

R.L. Erickson
Vice President,
Manufacturing and
Technology

Carl W. Geist, Jr.
Vice President,
Pulp and Recycling

Ronald J. Glick
Vice President,
Counterboard Packaging

George D. Henson
Vice President, Recycling

Richard E. Lodmill
Vice President, Chemicals

Robert F. Meyer
Vice President, Fine Paper

WEYERHAEUSER REAL ESTATE COMPANY

C. Stephen Lewis
President and Chief Executive
Officer

WEYERHAEUSER FAR EAST

William E. Franklin
President

WEYERHAEUSER FINANACIAL SERVICE, INC.

Donald E. Lange
President and Chief Executive
Officer, Weyerhaeuser
Mortgage Company

WESTWOOD SHIPPING LINES

Arnfinn Giske
President and Chief Executive
Officer

WEYERHAEUSER CANADA LTD.

George H. Weyerhaeuser, Jr.
President and Chief Executive
Officer

U.S. NATIONAL AFFAIRS OFFICE

Frederick S. Brown
Vice President, Federal
Relations

WTD INDUSTRIES—1994

For the fiscal year ending April 30, 1993, WTD Industries, Inc. (503–246–3440), reported net income of $23.11 million compared to $2.99 million for fiscal 1992. Emerging from Chapter 11 bankruptcy in November 1992, WTD may be over the worst of its failed strategies in the early 1990s. Headquartered in Portland, Oregon, WTD operates twelve lumber mills in the Pacific Northwest.

MICHELLE R. GREENE
and Fred R. David
Francis Marion University
STEVE BARNDT
Pacific Lutheran University

HISTORY

WTD Industries was founded by Bruce L. Engel, a Portland, Oregon, lawyer, educated at Reed College and the University of Chicago School of Law. In 1981 Engel became involved in an effort to save a client's financially troubled sawmill business in Glide, Oregon. Ultimately, Engel and a partner acquired the bankrupt mill in exchange for assuming $2 million in debts. His original idea was to make changes necessary to achieve profitability, operate it until industry conditions improved, and then sell the mill. Subsequently, success with the first sawmill and other opportunities for bargain acquisitions in a depressed industry caused Engel to shift to objectives of growth and profitable operation of wood-products-converting facilities. A second mill at Silverton, Oregon, was acquired in 1982. In 1983 sawmills located at Philomath, Oregon, were acquired, and the business was incorporated as WTD Industries. Through it all, Engel has not revealed what the letters WTD stand for, even to managers and employees of the company.

In 1984 WTD added another softwood sawmill operation, this one near Corvallis, Oregon, and its first hardwood sawmill at Philomath, Oregon. The next year WTD started operations in Washington with newly acquired softwood and hardwood mills at Sedro Woolley, Olympia, and South Bend. Three more mills were added in 1986—Valley and Aberdeen in Washington and Tillamook in Oregon. Late in 1986 WTD went public with 1,850,000 shares of common stock. Net proceeds in excess of $15 million fueled a major expansion in 1987.

Thirteen companies were acquired in 1987—seven in Oregon, five in Washington, and one in Montana. In addition to WTD's first geographic expansion outside of the Pacific Northwest, 1987 also marked the company's growth into nonsawmill production operations. Five of the 1987 acquisitions were plants producing veneer, and one was a plywood plant. Although it is contrary to company strategy to invest in timberlands, WTD purchased 17,000 acres in 1987 near the Philomath mills. By mid-1991, most of the timber in this land had been harvested.

Growth in 1988 was modest by comparison to 1987 with only three acquisitions—sawmills in Washington and Oregon and a plywood plant in New York. Seven softwood lumber sawmills located at Alturas, California; Custer, South Dakota; West Burke, Vermont; Judith Gap, Montana; and Portland, Cottage Grove, and Central Point, Oregon, were acquired in 1989 and 1990. In addition, the conversion of a hardwood mill at Tillamook, Oregon, to a higher-capacity softwood mill was completed in 1990. Partially offsetting acquisitions, four lumber or veneer mills were sold or otherwise liquidated in the period 1989–1991.

The cutback in home building in 1990 with its consequent reduction in demand for lumber resulted in lumber prices that were 15 percent lower than average. At the same time, log costs increased 7 percent because of export log demand and cutbacks in the harvest of timber from public lands. Even with reductions in operating costs by way of curtailing of operations in selected locations and a reduction of overhead, WTD's poor financial performance precluded its meeting all the covenants associated with debt agreements. WTD had $221 million in assets and $460 million in sales in 1990, but experienced a severe downturn in 1991 as sales declined to $244 million and assets dropped to $106 million. When its bank line of credit was declared in default, WTD and each of its subsidiaries filed for Chapter 11 bankruptcy on January 30, 1991, and emerged from bankruptcy on November 22, 1992.

Net sales for fiscal 1993 increased 15.4 percent to $246 million while net income increased 694 percent to $23 million. WTD's long-term debt, however, is a staggering $64 million, up from $519 thousand in 1992.

WTD'S OPERATIONS

WTD produces and sells a variety of wood products, including softwood lumber, hardwood lumber, softwood veneer, and wood chips. Softwood lumber, consisting of studs and other dimension lumber in a wide range of widths, lengths, and thicknesses, is the major product, accounting for 72 percent of sales. The predominant species that are converted into softwood lumber are Douglas fir, hemlock, white fir, lodgepole pine, ponderosa pine, spruce, and larch. Although softwood lumber, along with all other products, is branded with the name of WTD's marketing organization and its logo, these products are basically commodities competing against similar, substitute products.

The second-highest source of sales, accounting for 13 percent of the total, is chips, a residual product made from the parts of logs not suitable for conversion into lumber or veneer. Chips are used to make pulp for later conversion into paper products. Less important products include veneer, hardwood lumber, and plywood. Veneer, a thin layer of wood peeled from logs, is used in the lay-up of plywood. Hardwood lumber is produced in sizes appropriate for cabinet and furniture manufacturers. The major species is alder, although some maple is also cut. Plywood plants use veneers to produce sheathing, underlayment, and sanded and marine plywood in standard sizes. The company's plywood and veneer plants were closed during 1991.

With the minor exception of a few specialty or highly finished products such as special cuts of wood for furniture, WTD is a producer of undifferentiated products. The company aims to produce and move these commodity-like products in volume, relying on high per-worker output. Labor productivity improvements in the company's existing mills are responsible for boosting aggregate lumber production by about 50 percent.

On a quarter-to-quarter basis, WTD's financial results have varied widely and will continue to vary as a result of seasonal fluctuations and market factors affecting the demand for logs, lumber, and other wood products. The industry is subject to fluctuations in sales and earnings as a result of such factors as industry production in relation to product demand and variations in interest rates and housing starts. Currency fluctuations affect the forest products industry when exchange rates spur log exports and drive up domestic log prices.

The industry is also affected by weather conditions and changing timber management policies. Fire danger and excessively dry or wet conditions temporarily reduce logging activity and may increase open-market log prices. Timber management policies of various governmental agencies change from time to time, periodically causing actual or feared shortages in some areas. These policies change because of environmental concerns, public-agency budget issues, and a variety of other reasons. Therefore, past results for any given year or quarter are not necessarily indicative of future results.

It is the company's practice to curtail production at facilities from time to time because of adverse weather or other conditions that impair log flow, imbalances between log costs and product prices, or other factors that cause the cost of operation to exceed the cost of shutdown. Management may also permanently close facilities when their future profit-making ability under expected operating conditions is not deemed promising. Management believes its labor practices and compensation systems, as well as relatively low capital cost in relation to production capacity, give it the flexibility to curtail operations and resume production as conditions warrant.

Raw materials comprise the majority of the cost of products sold by the company. Historically, a strong correlation has existed between log costs and lumber prices. However, endangered-species litigation, increased log export demand, and erratic demand for lumber and plywood altered this relationship in recent years. Since that time the relationship between lumber prices and log costs has generally been more favorable, allowing for improved results. There can be no assurance that a favorable relationship between log costs and lumber prices will exist in the future.

Over the last two years, harvests of federal timber have declined markedly because of preservationist litigation and court rulings associated with the northern spotted owl. Although WTD relies primarily on open-market logs to source its mills, log costs have risen substantially as a result of reduced raw material availability. There can be no assurance that the company will be able to obtain sufficient raw materials at prices that allow production to remain at or exceed current levels.

WTD has sold eighteen mills and is today focusing on twelve "core mills" located in Washington, Oregon, and Vermont, as illustrated in Figure 22–1.

FINANCES

Gross profit for fiscal 1993 was 8.0 percent of sales, compared to 8.6 percent for fiscal 1992. While prices increased about 15 percent and log costs increased about 13 percent in 1993 over 1992, the costs of manufacturing lumber (excluding log cost) rose 9 percent. This cost increase was primarily the result of a 4 percent decrease in production. Selling, general, and administration expenses for 1993 were 5.1 percent of sales compared to 5.6 percent of sales in 1992.

Working capital decreased by $6.9 million for fiscal 1993, to $39.2 million. This was the result of working capital provided by operations and the sale of idle facilities, offset by capital spending, the costs of holding and disposing of idle facilities, and principal payments and reclassifications made in connection with the company's reorganization plan. Substantially all of the company's assets are pledged as security for its various debt instruments.

INVENTORY STRATEGY

Inventories of logs influence profitability in two ways. The first is that assured and continuous availability is necessary for an efficient conversion process and the satisfaction of customer's order delivery requirements. The second is that logs are a costly resource and can represent a substantial tie-up of working capital as well as a major factor in determining profit margin. Although lumber prices tend slightly to lead log

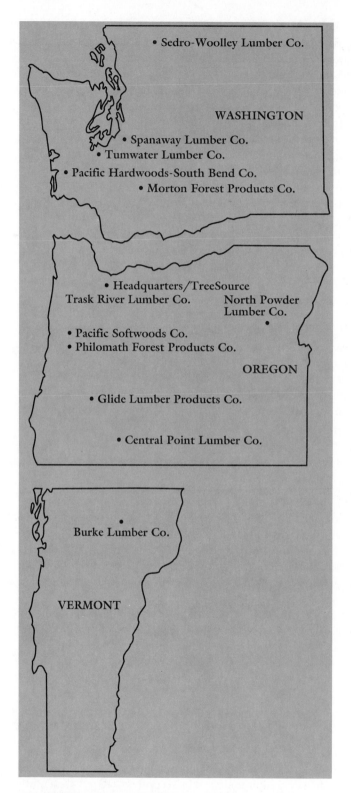

FIGURE 22-1 WTD Plant Locations

prices, moving in the same direction and maintaining a more or less constant relationship over the long term, short-term variations can and do occur. For example, increased foreign demand for logs, activities by environmental interest groups to restrict sales of government timber, and weather conditions unfavorable for logging have all decreased log supply and raised prices independent of domestic demand for lumber. With the cost of purchased logs at delivery accounting for two-thirds of finished product costs at WTD, such a shortage-induced rise in log prices without a rise in lumber prices can turn a profitable operation into an unprofitable one.

From 1987 to 1990 shortages of logs at reasonable prices led to the closing of 46 Northwest sawmills that were less well managed or positioned. Since then the imbalance has intensified because of the continued high demand for high-quality export logs and severe cutbacks in government sales of timber harvest contracts associated with protecting the spotted owl.

Traditional industry response among its larger competitors to lessen risks associated with uncertain availability and the potential of high open-market log prices has been to line up inventories of standing timber sufficient for two years or more of production and stockpile substantial inventories of logs at the mills. These firms typically secure control over timberlands either through ownership or harvest rights. The timber-owning competitors are in a position either (1) to buy on the open market or through harvest contracts when log prices are low and to harvest owned timber (presumably on the books at a lower, historical cost) when log prices are high or (2) to give priority to filling their needs from owned timber on a continuing basis. In either strategy there is a potential to sustain higher operating margins.

Competitors who lack their own timberlands usually contract with timberland owners or the government for the right to harvest timber over a number of years. Such contracts are subject to competitive bidding, and bid prices reflect the near-term profit potential of lumber-manufacturing operations and availability of timber. Companies that own timber contracts can be expected to do well during periods of rising lumber prices and poorly when lumber prices fall. In fact, WTD owes its start to the fact that in the late 1970s many sawmill owners committed themselves to high-priced timber contracts prior to an industry downturn. When lumber prices fell, they found themselves faced with bankruptcy.

WTD purposely avoids owning large inventories of logs, preferring to buy in the open market at prices that closely follow lumber market prices. WTD's strategy has always been to buy logs and convert them into lumber within a matter of weeks, before the profit margin can be eroded. The ability to follow this strategy provided consistent, although modest, profits. WTD today owns a small amount of fee timberlands in the vicinity of various mills. The following table shows the percentages of logs supplied by open-market purchases, timber contracts and fee timberlands, and total log footage required:

YEAR ENDED APRIL 30,	OPEN MARKET	TIMBER CONTRACTS	FEE TIMBER	LOG REQUIREMENTS
1988	73%	20%	7%	616,000 MBF
1989	70	21	9	680,000
1990	69	25	6	766,000
1991	75	19	6	408,000
1992	88	8	4	338,000
1993	90	6	4	306,000

MBF = thousand board feet.

In support of its inventory strategy, WTD aims to maintain log inventories equal to approximately three weeks' operating requirements. Larger inventories are carried only when it is necessary to collect selected materials for specialty orders, when weather or seasonal factors prevent regular deliveries, or when open-market buying is not possible, necessitating the purchasing of timber-cutting contracts. The latter are sold primarily by government agencies and ordinarily require the cutting and removal of public timber within three years. WTD attempts to harvest timber under these contracts within one year, preferably within three to four months to minimize the risk of a reduced margin from falling lumber prices. In keeping with WTD's acceptance of variable costs in place of fixed costs, all forest operations are contracted to logging companies. This includes road building, cutting, and delivery to the mills.

Reliance on a supply of reasonably priced logs has left the company vulnerable to imbalances between log supply and demand. Problems first arose in late 1987 when two softwood sawmills, both of which normally rely on timber-harvesting contracts with government agencies, were faced with a shortage of logs and unprofitably high prices created by foreign demand and forest fires. The company was forced to shut the two mills down temporarily until a supply of acceptably priced logs could be assured. In calendar years 1988 and 1989, several mills were temporarily closed from time to time because of log shortages. Unprofitable operations caused by shortage-induced high costs of raw materials became more widespread in 1990 and resulted in the closure of 21 lumber and plywood mills in 1990 and 1991. In the first half of 1991, log costs and lumber prices came back into a more normal relationship but not before the cost-revenue imbalance had precipitated WTD's bankruptcy. The following table gives WTD's inventory of logs, lumber, veneer, and supplies for 1993:

| | APRIL 30, | |
	1993	1992
Logs	$ 7,569	$10,913
Lumber and veneer	9,515	8,958
Supplies	1,238	1,457
	$18,322	$21,328

Growing government recognition that the Northwest is experiencing a timber shortage had spurred governmental action. At one time, pressure from organized environmentalist special interest groups seeking to protect the habitat of the spotted owl had virtually stopped the sale of old-growth timber from federal lands in the West. In response to the spotted owl's endangered species status and environmentalist and forestry pleas, the government reached a compromise that has reopened the sale of federal timber but at drastically reduced levels. The extent to which logging on federal, state, and private lands will be restricted to preserve the spotted owl at the expense of jobs has become a hotly contested political issue on the West Coast. Further compromises are possible. For example, the federal government is considering use of its authority to place temporary bans on the export of logs from state land in order to increase the supply of logs to domestic sawmills.

Major competitors such as Weyerhaeuser have invested in new technologies, some using computers and lasers, to increase the yield of higher-value products. Other technologies are commonly being incorporated to reduce labor content and increase capacity. However, WTD has focused on employee productivity incentives rather then investing in expensive automated machinery to increase production. Although the company purposely avoids investing in costly automated plants and machinery, it does invest in projects offering major savings or immediate production improvements that have paybacks of three years or less. For the most part this has meant modest capital expenditures, approximating annual depreciation costs, to replace and upgrade worn and inefficient equipment. As an example of the difference in WTD's approach to investment in technology, WTD invested $1 million to replace old parts at its Glide, Oregon, mill, while International Paper invested $90 million in a computer-driven mill process at its competing mill in Gardiner, Oregon.

All marketing, sales, and distribution of WTD's products are the responsibility of Treesource, Inc. (503–246–8600), a wholly owned subsidiary in Portland, Oregon. Through this centralized sales and marketing unit, WTD gains economies of scale not available to independent mills. Treesource is able to coordinate production at various mills to satisfy customer orders, arrange lowest-cost transportation, and fill orders for an assortment of products beyond the capability of any single mill. In addition, centralized credit management offers economies in credit checking, monitoring, and collecting. Since each salesperson is responsible for the marketing and sales for one or two of the company's mills, fewer salespeople are needed than if each mill were responsible for its own sales.

Treesource has targeted the construction, industrial, and remodel-and-replace (do-it-yourself) segments. Of these, the construction segment is the most active. Most sales are to distributors and wholesalers, industrial users, and retailers. Products sold to distributors and wholesalers, the largest customer segment, include softwood lumber for the residential construction, commercial construction, and remodel-and-replace segments plus hardwood boards for the construction and remodel-and-replace segments. Major customers include such large distributors as Georgia-Pacific, Weyerhaeuser, and Dixieline. The second-largest channel, sales to retailers including chain merchandisers, provides softwood and hardwood lumber for the remodel-and-replace user. Sales to industrial buyers, the third-largest segment, includes hardwood for furniture and cabinet manufacturers. Direct sales of intermediate materials, including veneer plus products that are immediately usable by the customer (e.g., railroad ties), are a minor market. The majority of WTD's sales are to buyers in the United States. Exports, primarily to Canada but also to Europe, Australia, and the Far East, are expanding. WTD's 1993 target market mix is

1. Stocking distributors 53%
2. Office wholesale 30%
3. Retail 9%
4. Remanufacturers 5%
5. Other 3%

Most sales are arranged through telephone contact between salesperson and buyer. The company offers competitive delivered prices, a variety of products, availability of products, and reliability as competitive advantages. WTD also offers a 1 percent discount if an account is paid within ten days, providing an effective incentive for prompt payment. In addition, WTD attempts to create a name familiarity by identifying all product lots with the Treesource trademark and name of the producing mill after they are packaged or strapped. WTD's ten largest customers in 1993 are

Georgia-Pacific Corporation

San Diego Wholesale

Weyerhaeuser Company

North Pacific Lumber Co.

Furman Lumber, Inc.

BMC West Corporation

Reliable Wholesale Lumber, Inc.

Timber Products Sales Co.

Mid-Pac Lumber Co.

Boise Cascade Corporation

Transportation is the third-highest cost component of a delivered product, exceeded only by logs and labor. Treesource arranges for the transportation of products from all WTD mills and as a result is able to secure volume discounts that help WTD to lower costs and be price competitive. Shipments of products are normally made direct from the mill to the buyer's destination via rail, truck, or barge.

Activities that benefit or apply to more than one mill are performed at a centralized location in order to gain advantages of functional specialization and scale. Sales, market development, engineering, finance, and legal services are the key activities that are centralized. Log-buying specialists are located at the individual mills because of their need to be familiar with and responsive to local conditions, suppliers, and mill needs. However, a vice president position is responsible for developing and overseeing log procurement strategies. With most support functions performed elsewhere by others, local mill managers can concentrate on operations. In May 1993 WTD employed approximately 1,100 employees, down from over 2,600 a few years earlier.

ENVIRONMENTAL REGULATION

WTD is subject to federal, state, and local waste, disposal, and pollution control regulations, including air, water, and noise pollution; these regulations have required, and are expected to continue to require, additional operating and capital expenditures. During 1992 WTD incurred expenditures of approximately $250,000 for waste disposal and pollution control.

During fiscal 1993 WTD spent approximately $400,000 for cleanup of discontinued facilities, although actual costs may exceed this amount depending on the possible presence of pollutants discovered in the cleanup process. With respect to ongoing facilities, WTD incurred expenses in fiscal 1993 in complying with various state and federal environmental programs, such as developing Spill Prevention Control Countermeasure plans, applying for stormwater discharge permits under the National Pollutant Discharge Elimination System, and complying with federal underground storage tank regulations.

WTD is also formulating plans to manage log-yard waste (bark and other debris) at each operating facility. WTD spend approximately $650,000 for fiscal 1993 with respect to these matters and other routine environmental compliance.

WTD is in need of a clear strategic plan to remain profitable. Prepare a strategic plan for CEO Bruce Engel. Should WTD acquire timberlands outside of the Pacific Northwest? Should WTD focus on softwood rather than on hardwood processing? Is it time for WTD to put itself for sale on the market? How much is the company worth?

EXHIBIT 22-1 WTD Industries, Inc. and Subsidiaries Consolidated Statements of Operations (In thousands, except per share data)

YEAR ENDED APRIL 30,	1993	1992	1991
Net sales	$246,887	$213,896	$ 243,931
Cost of sales	227,040	195,386	250,468
Gross profit (loss)	19,847	18,510	(6,537)
Selling, general and administrative expenses	12,615	12,047	20,957
Reorganization charges	563	3,272	58,000
Operating income (loss)	6,669	3,191	(85,494)
Other income (expense)			
Interest expense	(2,864)	(235)	(10,197)
Miscellaneous	151	36	589
	(2,713)	(199)	(9,608)
Income (loss) before income taxes	3,956	2,992	(95,102)
Provision for income taxes (benefit)	1,543	1,167	(9,950)
Income (loss) before extraordinary items	2,413	1,825	(85,152)
Extraordinary items			
Gain on debt restructure, net of tax provision of $7,700	12,102	—	—
Tax benefit to NOL carryforward	9,243	1,167	—
	21,345	1,167	—
Net income (loss)	23,758	2,992	(85,152)
Accumulated preferred dividends	647	—	—
Net income (loss) applicable to common shareholders	$ 23,111	$ 2,992	$ (85,152)
Net income (loss) per common share—primary			
income (loss) before extraordinary items	$ 0.29	$ 0.73	$ (34.17)
Extraordinary items	3.46	0.47	—
	$ 3.75	$ 1.20	$ (34.17)
Net income (loss) per common share—fully diluted			
income (loss) before extraordinary items	$ 0.28	$ 0.73	$ (34.17)
Extraordinary items	3.43	0.47	—
	$ 3.71	$ 1.20	$ (34.17)

Source: WTD *Annual Report*, 1993.

EXHIBIT 22-2 Consolidated Balance Sheets (In thousands)

APRIL 30,	1993	1992
Assets		
Current assets		
Cash and cash equivalents	$ 2,124	$ 4,738
Accounts receivable, net	19,583	14,788
Inventories	18,322	21,328
Restricted cash	—	7,606
Prepaid expenses	2,399	2,416
Timber, timberlands and timber-related assets	18,998	17,530
Total current assets	61,426	68,406
Notes and accounts receivable	161	224
Timber and timberlands	847	716
Property, plant and equipment, at cost		
Land	2,572	2,732
Buildings and improvements	9,953	9,008
Machinery and equipment	59,553	56,473
	72,078	68,213
Less accumulated depreciation	37,839	32,211
	34,239	36,002
Construction in progress	493	1,538
	34,732	37,540
Idle assets	974	4,979
Less costs of disposal	574	2,077
	400	2,902
Other assets	2,473	3,773
	$100,039	$113,561

Source: *Annual Report*, 1993.

EXHIBIT 22-3 Consolidated Balance Sheets (In thousands, except share information)

APRIL 30,	1993	1992
Liabilities and stockholders' equity (deficit)		
Current liabilities		
Accounts payable	$ 7,390	$ 8,524
Accrued expenses	8,549	7,546
Reserve for disputed and unallowed prepetition claims	1,204	—
Timber contracts payable	2,695	4,750
Current maturities of long-term debt	2,333	1,424
Total current liabilities	22,171	22,244
Long-term debt, less current maturities	64,184	519
Liabilities subject to compromise	—	134,351
Commitments and contingencies		
Stockholders' equity (deficit)		
Preferred stock, no par value; 10,000,000 shares authorized:		
Series A	20,581	—
Series B	5,756	—
Common stock, no par value	23,123	15,205
Additional paid-in capital	15	15
Retained earnings (deficit)	(35,791)	(58,773)
	13,684	(43,553)
	$100,039	$113,561

Source: *Annual Report*, 1993.

EXHIBIT 22-4 WTD Industries, Inc. and Subsidiaries Consolidated Statements of Cash Flows (In thousands)

YEAR ENDED APRIL 30,	1993	1992	1991
Cash provided by (used for) operating activities:			
Net income (loss)	$23,758	$ 2,992	$(85,152)
Adjustments to reconcile net income (loss) to cash provided by (used for) operations:			
Depreciation, depletion and amortization	13,124	8,178	11,968
Deferred income tax	—	—	(3,187)
Gain on sale of marketable securities	—	—	(239)
Reorganization charges	563	898	58,000
Gain on debt restructure, before income tax provision	(19,802)	—	—
Accounts receivable	(4,795)	(5,404)	17,291
Inventories	2,974	(8,963)	24,667
Prepaid expenses	208	1,285	(2,212)
Income tax refund receivable	—	6,317	—
Timber, timberlands and timber-related assets, current	(7,975)	(3,472)	—
Accruals and payables	(6,449)	6,409	(9,651)
Income taxes payable	—	—	(301)
Cash provided by operating activities	1,606	8,240	11,184
Cash provided by (used for) investing activities:			
Notes and accounts receivable	63	10	70
Net reductions of (additions to) timber and timberlands	(155)	(1,137)	3,944
Acquisition of property, plant and equipment	(5,319)	(3,410)	(2,781)
Proceeds from sale of securities	—	8	1,431
Cost of holding idle facilities	(996)	(2,860)	(979)
Proceeds from sale of idle facilities	4,819	5,324	—
Other investing activities	207	552	2,398
Cash provided by (used for) investing activities	(1,381)	(1,513)	4,083
Cash provided by (used for) financing activities:			
Notes and acceptances payable	—	—	(8,414)
Proceeds from long-term borrowings	—	142	95
Principal payments on long-term debt	(9,646)	(369)	(2,497)
Other assets	(33)	(696)	161
Restricted cash	7,606	(5,453)	(2,153)
Dividends paid on preferred stock	(776)	—	—
Issuance of common stock	10	—	—
Cash used for financing activities	(2,839)	(6,376)	(12,808)
Increase (decrease) in cash and cash equivalents	(2,614)	351	2,459
Cash balance at beginning of year	4,738	4,387	1,928
Cash balance at end of year	$ 2,124	$ 4,738	$ 4,387
Cash paid (refunded) during the year for:			
Interest	$ 2,628	$ 87	$ 11,590
Income taxes	$ —	$(6,317)	$ (6,612)

Source: *Annual Report*, 1993.

EXHIBIT 22-5 Consolidated Statement of Changes in Stockholders' Equity (deficit) (in thousands)

	Series A Preferred Stock		Series B Preferred Stock		Common Stock		Paid-in Capital	Retained Earnings (Loss)	Stockholders' Equity (Deficit)
	Shares	Amount	Shares	Amount	Shares	Amount			
Balance at April 30, 1990	—	—	—	—	6,229	$15,205	$15	$23,387	$ 38,607
Net loss	—	—	—	—	—	—	—	(85,152)	(85,152)
Balance at April 30, 1991	—	—	—	—	6,229	15,205	15	(61,765)	(46,545)
Net income	—	—	—	—	—	—	—	2,992	2,992
Balance at April 30, 1992	—	—	—	—	6,229	15,205	15	(58,773)	(43,553)
Four-for-ten reverse split	—	—	—	—	(3,737)	—	—	—	—
Shares issued pursuant to reorganization plan	269	$20,581	197	$10,730	1,869	2,934	—	—	34,245
Shares converted	—	—	(91)	(4,974)	3,176	4,974	—	—	—
Stock options exercised	—	—	—	—	11	10	—	—	10
Dividends paid	—	—	—	—	—	—	—	(776)	(776)
Net income	—	—	—	—	—	—	—	23,758	23,758
Balance at April 30, 1993	269	$20,581	106	$5,756	7,548	$23,123	$15	$(35,791)	$ 13,684

Source: *Annual Report*, 1993.

GEORGIA-PACIFIC CORPORATION—1994

In 1993 Georgia-Pacific (404-521-4000) headed in a new direction. The company's chief executive officer and chairman of the board, T. Marshall Hahn, Jr., who had been the company's leader for ten years, retired as CEO on May 3. Later in the year he also retired as chairman of the board, but continued to serve on the board of directors. Hahn was replaced by A. D. Correll, who previously was the company's president and chief operating officer. Georgia-Pacific's sales increased 4 percent in 1993 to $12.3 billion, but net income declined to negative $18 million.

HISTORY

Although his grandfather had advised against entering the timber business, in 1927 Owen R. Cheatham bought a wholesale lumber and timber yard in Augusta, Georgia. Cheatham had only half the money needed to buy the company, so he went to the man for which his old prep school had been named, J. Hunt Hargrave. Hargrave agreed to loan Cheatham a quarter of the sum needed if the president of the Planters Bank, J. Hurt Whitehead, would match it. His new company, the Georgia Hardwood Lumber Company, was incorporated in Georgia on September 26.

The Great Depression of 1929 ruined many businesses, but Cheatham was innovative. He went to Europe and discovered the Depression was ending more quickly there than in the United States. A building boom was under way in Europe and lumber was needed. His company could buy lumber at depressed prices in the United States, ship it abroad, and sell it for increased prices in Europe.

The export business to Europe enabled Cheatham to expand his company in the United States. After World War II, five mills were in operation in Georgia, Alabama, Arkansas, Mississippi, and South Carolina. The company also had an office in New York and was opening one in Portland, Oregon.

The reason for opening an office in Portland was a new product called plywood. At the time, people believed plywood could only be made successfully from Douglas fir, which grew in the Pacific Northwest. Cheatham, who was a pioneer in the plywood business when most competitors thought plywood could not be made profitably, found that plywood would bring three times the return of lumber. Upon this knowledge, the company acquired Bellingham Plywood Corporation, a large plywood plant in Bellingham, Washington, and acquired the Washington Veneer Company in 1948. Three other plywood manufacturing operations were also purchased in Olympia, Washington; Springfield, Oregon; and Savannah, Georgia.

On April 2, 1951, the company name was changed to Georgia-Pacific Plywood Company. The concept of dynamic conservation was introduced that year with the purchase of a new sawmill and related timberlands in Toledo, Oregon. Dynamic conservation was based on the fact that timber is the only natural resource that continually replaces itself. The primary element of dynamic conservation was scientific forestry, which made trees grow faster and stronger, and produced new and better seed stock from the healthiest trees in the forest. Because of the rate of cutting by former owners of the sawmill, there was only enough timber in the area to last another nine years. Georgia-Pacific wanted to modernize the plant and close the sawmill. Enough adjacent timberland was acquired so that all the reserves were put on the dynamic conservation schedule. Georgia-Pacific invested more than $60 million in building a new plywood mill, paper mill, and pulp mill. By 1960, the year Toledo was supposed to disappear, employment was up 50 percent, payrolls were up 100 percent, purchases of services and supplies from local merchants were up 65 percent, and the population of Toledo was up 33 percent.

By 1966 Georgia-Pacific had completed construction of its fourth and fifth pine plywood plants in Louisville, Mississippi, and Emporia, Virginia. Georgia-Pacific entered into Latin America for the first time with the purchase of Companhia Amazones in 1965 at the price of $2.145 million. That acquisition brought in more than 600,000 acres of timber and timberland, along with a veneer plant, in Brazil near the mouth of the Amazon. Georgia-Pacific enhanced its position in the chemicals business in 1966 by acquiring National Polychemicals, Inc. in Conway, North Carolina, and Lufkin, Texas. These facilities operated production of phenol and urea formaldehyde resin.

GEORGIA-PACIFIC TODAY

Georgia-Pacific does not maintain a central research laboratory for the development of new wood and paper products. Instead, research and development activities take place at the individual plants and other decentralized laboratories. Georgia-Pacific feels that employees are best acquainted with the potential of new products at decentralized laboratories.

Forestry research, aimed at improving seedling growth rate and quality, is conducted extensively throughout the United States and Canada. The research usually takes place where Georgia-Pacific owns and operates fee timberland. Forest research employees are continually seeking to improve reforestation methods and timber management techniques. The company's containerboard and packaging division opened a new research facility in Atlanta, Georgia, in 1992.

Georgia-Pacific employs approximately 52,000 people, most of whom are members of unions; the company considers its relationship with its employees to be good. Seventy-seven union contracts were renewed in 1993, including five at large paper facilities. Georgia-Pacific has 253 manufacturing facilities in the United States, one recycled-paper mill in Canada, and two wood-moulding manufacturing facilities in Mexico. The company has two major operating divisions: the Building Products Divisions and the Pulp and Paper Division.

Building Products Division. Georgia-Pacific is the leading manufacturer and distributor of building products in the United States. The company produces plywood, oriented strand board and other wood panels, lumber, gypsum wallboard, chemicals, and other products. Georgia-Pacific is the leading wholesaler of building products in the United States, with 139 distribution centers located in 46 states. The centers serve traditional lumberyards, consumer-oriented home centers, makers of mobile homes, and other manufacturers. Eleven centers are millwork and specialty centers that primarily sell wood mouldings, doors, and windows. In order to offer a broader line of products and to supplement Georgia-Pacific's product lines, the distribution centers also purchase products from other manufacturers. In 1992 these purchases were approximately $2.1 billion, which was up from $1.7 billion in 1991. Outside purchases comprise almost half of all materials sold at the centers. Purchased products include wood panels, lumber and roofing, doors, insulation, vinyl siding, and adhesives, as well as product lines that they do not manufacture, such as nails and other metal products.

The building products division had net sales of $6.112 billion in 1992, a 13.1 percent increase from 1991. Sales of this division accounted for 52 percent of Georgia-Pacific's total sales in 1992. Georgia-Pacific exports consisted of $141 million in 1992. Georgia-Pacific ships building products to 60 countries and has building products sales offices in Europe and Mexico. Although Georgia-Pacific's largest export markets are in the Caribbean and Europe, Mexico has been the company's fastest-growing market since 1990.

The building products division's business is affected by the number of housing starts, the level of home repairs, remodeling, additions, commercial building activity, the availability and cost of mortgage funds, and changes in the industry's capacity. In 1992 the economy was sluggish but lower mortgage interest rates helped to support an increase in housing construction. Prices for structural panels and lumber rose to record high levels in 1992 as logging restrictions on government lands resulted in more mill closures in the West and a tightening supply and demand balance.

Wood Panels. Georgia-Pacific is the industry's largest producer of structural wood panels and accounts for about 20 percent of domestic structural panel capacity. There are 43 wood panel plants located primarily in the southern United States that produce 9.7 billion square feet of panels per year. In 1992 Georgia-Pacific's wood panel division had total sales of $2.543 billion, a 21.3 percent increase in sales from 1991. The wood panel division accounts for 22 percent of the company's total sales.

Georgia-Pacific operates 24 plywood and oriented strand board plants. Specialty applications of plywood account for 60 percent of its plywood production. These specialty applications include decorative siding, sanded plywood, and concrete form. Many other wood panel applications are produced at 19 mills, primarily for industrial and construction applications. Items such as hardboard, particleboard, panelboard, softboard, and fiberboard are made from logs, sawdust, shavings, and chips. These types of wood panels are used in the production of furniture, housing, shelving, fixtures, toys, automotive parts, and siding panels. A breakdown of Georgia-Pacific's annual production in the wood panel division follows:

	NUMBER OF FACILITIES	ANNUAL CAPACITY
Soft plywood (3/8")	18	5,019
Hardwood plywood (sm)	2	495
Hardboard (1/8")	8	1,395
Particleboard (3/4")	8	1,148
Oriented strand board (3/8")	4	952
Panelboard (1/8")	1	379
Softboard (1/2")	1	250
Fiberboard (3/4")	1	100
	43	9,738

Georgia-Pacific operates four oriented strand board plants. Oriented strand board (OSB) is a nonveneered sheathing grade product made from strands of wood that are arranged in perpendicular layers and bonded into a panel by a resin. Like the uses of plywood, OSB is used for roof decking, sidewall sheathing, and floor underlayment. Georgia-Pacific's newest OSB plant is located in Mt. Hope, West Virginia, and has an annual capacity of 325 million square feet.

Lumber. Georgia-Pacific is the second-largest producer of lumber in the United States, accounting for about 5 percent of domestic lumber production. Approximately 2.6 billion board feet of lumber is produced annually. Georgia-Pacific had total lumber sales of $2.055 billion in 1992, an increase of 13 percent from 1991. Lumber sales for 1992 accounted for 17 percent of the company's total sales. The company operates 43 lumber mills located primarily in the South. Several types of wood are produced by these mills including southern pine, a variety of Appalachian and southern hardwoods, cypress, redwood, cedar, spruce, western pine, Douglas fir, and pressure-treated southern pine. Georgia-Pacific recently purchased a softwood lumber mill in Philomath, Oregon, to process Douglas fir and western hemlock logs from company-owned timberlands. The 43 mills account for 2.739 billion board feet of production.

Gypsum. Georgia-Pacific is the third largest producer of gypsum products in the United States. The company operates ten gypsum board plants with an annual capacity of 3.1 billion square feet of gypsum board. The company owns gypsum reserves of about 125 recoverable tons. Some of its gypsum products are wallboard, fire-door cores, plaster, and joint compound, all primarily used in residential and commercial construction. In 1992 the company's gypsum product sales totaled $216 million, a decrease of 2.7 percent from 1991. These sales figures have been declining since 1986. Sales from the gypsum products account for only 2 percent of Georgia-Pacific's total sales. Although the company's sales of gypsum products went down in 1992, the production of gypsum had a 45 percent increase from 1991, which had a production level of 1.955 billion square feet. Georgia-Pacific conducts gypsum research at its gypsum research and development center in Decatur, Georgia.

Chemicals. Georgia-Pacific is one of the forest industry's leading suppliers of resins, adhesives, and paper chemicals. The company operates 16 plants with a production of 2.962 billion pounds of thermosetting resins. The chemicals division accounted for $240 million of sales in 1992, a 7.6 percent increase from 1991, and overall accounts for 2 percent of total sales. More than 2 billion pounds of thermosetting resins are shipped annually to Georgia-Pacific mills and outside customers. Georgia-Pacific recently purchased a phenolic resins coatings business that produces highly specialized resins used in marine varnishes, metal cans and tanks, food containers, and other products. The company conducts chemical research in its Tacoma, Washington, facility.

Timber and Timberlands. Georgia-Pacific owns more than 6 million acres of timber and timberlands in the United States and Canada. The lumber is primarily near the company's lumber mills. Georgia-Pacific controlled 927,000 acres of timberland in 1992, which was a slight increase from 1991. Timberlands owned in fee consisted of 5.722 million acres in 1992, a decrease of 4.1 percent from 1991. Geographically, 70 percent of Georgia-Pacific's timber is located in the South, 20 percent is located in the East, and 10 percent is in the West. Georgia-Pacific's timber includes southern pines and hardwoods; Douglas fir, hemlock, and other species from the Pacific Northwest; redwood, Douglas fir, true firs, and western pines in Northern California; and numerous species of hardwoods and softwoods in Maine, West Virginia, and Wisconsin, and New Brunswick, Canada.

Georgia-Pacific owns the underlying mineral rights on the majority of its fee lands in the United States. Mining of metallurgical coal and production of oil and gas generates royalty income for Georgia-Pacific that is not material in amount. The company does not expect to realize any material income from these operations in the foreseeable future.

Pulp and Paper Division. Georgia-Pacific pulp and paper division produces a variety of items including containerboard and packaging, communication papers, market pulp, tissue, and envelopes. The company operates 103 facilities in the United States and one in Canada. Annual capacity of pulp, paper, and paperboard includes 8.6 million tons, which accounts for 8 percent of the total annual capacity in the United States. The pulp and paper division had total sales of $5.711 billion in 1992, a 6.2 percent decrease from 1991. This decrease in sales changed the balance between the building products division and the pulp and paper division. The pulp and paper division had operated as the leading sales contributor for Georgia-Pacific for the past two years.

The pulp and paper division's products are affected primarily by changes in industry capacity. The level of economic growth in the United States, currency exchange rates, and foreign market conditions also influence pulp and paper demand. In 1992 sluggish demand in the United States and export markets and excess capacity and inventories in the industry combined to keep prices and profits depressed in the pulp and paper division.

Containerboard and Packaging. Georgia-Pacific produces containerboard, corrugated containers and packaging, bleached board, and kraft paper. The company operates four containerboard mills and 37 corrugated packaging plants. With an annual capacity of 3.9 million tons of containerboard and packaging, Georgia-Pacific is the nation's second-largest producer of containerboard, accounting for about 12 percent of the United States capacity. The containerboard and packaging division had $2.001 billion of sales in 1992, a .3 percent decrease from 1991. These sales accounted for 17 percent of Georgia-Pacific's total sales in 1992.

After the containerboard is processed, about 50 percent of the production is transferred to a corrugated packaging plant. The remainder is sold to independent converters. In addition to making corrugated packaging with the containerboard, Georgia-Pacific's corrugated packaging plants manufacture double- and triple-wall containers and packaging, bulk bins, water-resistant packaging, and high-finish and preprinted packaging for point-of-sale displays. Georgia-Pacific exports about 15 percent of its containerboard, primarily to Central America, Western Europe, and the Far East.

Georgia-Pacific produces about 364,000 tons of bleached paperboard annually. The bleached paperboard is used primarily in frozen food containers, food service items, and other products. The company in its two plants annually produces 350,000 tons of kraft paper, which is used in the production of grocery bags and multiwall bags.

Communication Papers. Georgia-Pacific is the largest producer of uncoated free-sheet paper in the United States. Eight paper mills are in production with an annual capacity of 2.2 million tons, accounting for approximately 16 percent of annual capacity in the United States. Such communication paper items include office reprographics and commercial printing, business forms, stationery, tablets, envelopes, and checks. In 1992 Georgia-Pacific produced 2.223 billion tons of communication papers, an 11 percent increase from 1991.

A 1992 study of buying criteria and brand familiarities of merchants, printers, and other end-users convinced Georgia-Pacific to consolidate its communication papers product lines. To heighten its brand recognition, Georgia-Pacific is now marketing its business and printing paper products under the brand name of Georgia-Pacific Papers. Text and specialty papers are marketed under the name Nekoosa, which is operated by the company's Hopper Paper Division.

Market Pulp. Georgia-Pacific is the world's second-largest producer of market pulp. The company's seven pulp mills produce approximately 1.9 million tons of pulp annually. In 1992 Georgia-Pacific produced 1.891 million tons of market pulp, a 3.3 percent increase from 1991 production. This production level accounted for approximately 20 percent of the domestic capacity. The company produces southern softwood, southern hardwood, and northern hardwood pulps for use in the manufacture of many paper grades. The company is also a major supplier of fluff pulp and other specialty pulps.

Georgia-Pacific recently converted its Brunswick, Georgia, pulp mill to fluff pulp, which now represents 550,000 tons of company output per year. Fluff pulp is used primarily in disposable diapers and other sanitary items. These types of products are currently experiencing growing demand, particularly in developing countries.

Because of the increasing use of recycled fiber in the United States, the company is expected to have limited growth in domestic demand. However, increased paper consumption in export markets is expected to boost total market pulp demand. Georgia-Pacific exports approximately 65 percent of its market pulp, employing its direct sales force at offices in France, Germany, Italy, Japan, Switzerland, Taiwan, and the United Kingdom.

Tissue. Georgia-Pacific is the fifth-largest producer of tissue in the United States. The company operates five tissue mills with an annual capacity of over 500,000 tons of tissue. In 1992 these mills produced 578,000 tons of tissue, a 10.9 percent increase from 1991's production level of 521,000 tons. Georgia-Pacific's 1992 sales of tissue was $682 million, an increase of 2.7 percent from 1991.

The company operates six converting facilities that produce consumer and commercial tissue products such as paper towels, napkins, and bath tissue. Most of Georgia-Pacific's consumer tissue products are sold under the brand names Angel Soft, Sparkle, Coronet, MD, and Delta. The commercial tissue products are produced for industrial, food-service, office, hotel, motel, and hospital markets.

Paper Distribution and Tissue. Georgia-Pacific operates 80 distribution centers in 31 states under the name Butler Paper Company. Customers include commercial printers, in-plant printers, copy centers, and major corporations. Butler sells printing, writing, and industrial papers obtained from many manufacturers, including their own mills. The company's envelope production is handled by the Mail-Well Envelope Division, which operates 17 plants. In 1992 Mail-Well produced 15 billion envelopes, a 15.4 percent increase from 1991 production levels. The envelope division, along with the paper distribution division, had total sales of $1.208 billion in 1992, a 1 percent decrease from 1991. These sales figures have continually decreased since its beginning in 1990, prompting Georgia-Pacific in March 1993 to announce plans to sell the Butler Paper Company to Alco Standard Corporation.

Georgia Pacific and the Natural Environment. Georgia-Pacific is committed to responsible forest practices and conservation methods. The company supports regulations that benefit the environment, human health, and safety based on sound science and prudent economic analysis. Georgia-Pacific is dedicated to operating all of its facilities in compliance with applicable environmental laws, regulations, and permits. Through an environmental audit program, the company monitors compliance with this policy.

With the hiring of Lee M. Thomas as senior vice-president of environmental and government affairs in March 1993, Georgia-Pacific aims to insure compliance with environmental laws and regulations. Thomas, a former administrator of the United States Environmental Protection Agency, will also be chairman of the company's Environmental Policy Committee, which will have direct access to Georgia-Pacific's board of directors and will regularly provide the board with environmental reports.

Georgia-Pacific is always trying to protect the environment as evidenced on April 18, 1993, when the company signed an agreement with Interior Secretary Bruce Babbitt to protect the endangered red-cockaded woodpecker. The woodpecker is primarily located in the southern United States.

GEORGIA-PACIFIC'S FUTURE

At the April 2, 1993 timber summit in Seattle, Washington, Georgia-Pacific and other major forest products companies agreed with President Bill Clinton to provide more environmental protection of the Pacific Northwest. Since the Pacific Northwest is a controversial timber-cutting area of the country, should Georgia-Pacific focus on other areas of the country? Should the company seek expanded operations in foreign markets? Economies of scale are becoming more and more important in being a successful forest products company. Should Georgia-Pacific acquire a major competitor, supplier, or distributor?

The production of paper from recycled materials is becoming increasingly important, driven by user needs and environmental concerns. Georgia-Pacific leads in the recycling effort with over 100 products on the market. However, other companies are catching up to and exceeding Georgia-Pacific in the recycling effort. Should Georgia-Pacific invest more time and money in producing recycled materials?

Prepare a strategic plan for CEO Correll that could enable Georgia-Pacific to return to profitability. Note that, as shown in the attached exhibits, the company's net income was negative in 1991, 1992, and 1993, while company debt further increased. The trend in earnings must be reversed for Georgia-Pacific to remain competitive in the forest products industry.

EXHIBIT 23-1 Statements of Income—Georgia-Pacific Corporation and Subsidiaries (Millions, except per share amounts)

| | YEAR ENDED DECEMBER 31 | | |
	1993	1992	1991
Net sales	$12,330	$11,847	$11,524
Costs and expenses			
Cost of sales	9,814	9,397	9,164
Selling, general and administrative	1,190	1,170	1,137
Depreciation and depletion	764	789	724
Interest	513	565	584
Other (income) loss	26	—	(344)
Total costs and expenses	12,307	11,921	11,265
Income (loss) before income taxes, extraordinary item and accounting changes	23	(74)	259
Provision (benefit) for income taxes	41	(14)	293
(Loss) before extraordinary item and accounting changes	(18)	(60)	(34)
Extraordinary item—loss from early retirement of debt, net of taxes	(16)	(9)	(45)
Cumulative effect of accounting changes, net of taxes	—	(55)	(63)
Net (loss)	$ (34)	$ (124)	$ (142)
Per share			
(Loss) before extraordinary item and accounting changes	$ (.21)	$ (.69)	$ (.40)
Extraordinary item—loss from early retirement of debt, net of taxes	(.18)	(.10)	(.52)
Cumulative effect of accounting changes, net of taxes	—	(.64)	(.73)
Net (loss)	$ (.39)	$ (1.43)	$ (1.65)
Average number of shares outstanding	87.7	86.4	85.8

Source: Georgia-Pacific *Annual Report*, 1993.

EXHIBIT 23-2 Statements of Cash Flows—Georgia-Pacific Corporation and Subsidiaries (*Millions*)

| | YEAR ENDED DECEMBER 31 | | |
	1993	1992	1991
Cash provided by (used for) operations			
Net (loss)	$ (34)	$ (124)	$ (142)
Adjustments to reconcile net (loss) to cash provided by operations:			
Depreciation	711	747	673
Depletion	53	42	51
Deferred tax benefit	(125)	(133)	(25)
Amortization of goodwill	59	59	60
Stock compensation programs	53	42	67
Gain on sales of assets	(32)	(33)	(38)
Amortization of debt issue costs, discounts and premiums	7	6	35
Other (income) loss	26	—	(344)
Extraordinary item, net of taxes	—	—	45
Cumulative effect of accounting changes, net of taxes	—	55	63
(Increase) decrease in receivables	(174)	(87)	92
(Increase) decrease in inventories	(93)	61	(43)
Change in other working capital	40	193	45
Increase (decrease) in taxes payable	(158)	13	(2)
Change in other assets and other long-term liabilities	56	27	43
Cash provided by operations	389	868	580
Cash provided by (used for) investment activities			
Capital expenditures			
Property, plant and equipment	(421)	(347)	(490)
Timber and timberlands	(46)	(37)	(38)
Total capital expenditures	(467)	(384)	(528)
Proceeds from sales of assets	260	55	1,251
Other	5	(4)	23
Cash provided by (used for) investment activities	(202)	(333)	746
Cash provided by (used for) financing activities			
Repayments of long-term debt	(576)	(566)	(2,055)
Additions to long-term debt	511	754	610
Fees paid to issue debt	(5)	(7)	(4)
Increase (decrease) in bank overdrafts	52	(50)	27
Increase (decrease) in commercial paper and other short-term notes	(41)	(519)	226
Cash dividends paid	(142)	(140)	(140)
Cash (used for) financing activities	(201)	(528)	(1,336)
Increase (decrease) in cash	(14)	7	(10)
Balance at beginning of year	55	48	58
Balance at end of year	$ 41	$ 55	$ 48

Source: Georgia-Pacific *Annual Report*, 1993.

EXHIBIT 23-3 Balance Sheets—Georgia-Pacific Corporation and Subsidiaries (*Millions, except shares and per share amounts*)

	DECEMBER 31	
	1993	1992
Assets		
Current assets		
Cash	$ 41	$ 55
Receivables, less allowances of $32 and $35	377	331
Inventories		
Raw materials	367	321
Finished goods	786	792
Supplies	262	282
LIFO reserve	(213)	(203)
Total inventories	1,202	1,192
Other current assets	26	29
Total current assets	1,646	1,607
Timber and timberlands, net	1,381	1,402
Property, plant and equipment		
Land and improvements	237	247
Buildings	1,074	1,101
Machinery and equipment	9,550	9,420
Construction in progress	125	64
Total property, plant and equipment, at cost	10,986	10,832
Accumulated depreciation	(5,538)	(5,001)
Property, plant and equipment, net	5,448	5,831
Goodwill	1,832	1,891
Other assets	238	181
Total assets	$10,545	$10,912

EXHIBIT 23-3 *Continued*

	DECEMBER 31	
	1993	1992
Liabilities and shareholders' equity		
Current liabilities		
Bank overdrafts, net	$ 173	$ 121
Commercial paper and other short-term notes	650	691
Current portion of long-term debt	57	257
Taxes payable	35	193
Accounts payable	582	563
Accrued compensation	184	179
Accrued interest	114	132
Other current liabilities	269	316
Total current liabilities	2,064	2,452
Long-term debt, excluding current portion	4,157	4,019
Other long-term liabilities	827	731
Deferred income taxes	1,095	1,202
Commitments and contingencies		
Shareholders' equity		
Common stock, par value $.80; authorized 150,000,000 shares; 90,269,000 and 88, 111,000 shares issued	71	70
Additional paid-in capital	1,202	1,094
Retained earnings	1,217	1,393
Long-term incentive plan deferred compensation	(56)	(39)
Other	(32)	(10)
Total shareholders' capacity	2,404	2,508
Total liabilities and shareholders' equity	$10,545	$10,912

Source: Georgia-Pacific *Annual Report,* 1993.

EXHIBIT 23-4 Statements of Shareholders' Equity—Georgia-Pacific Corporation and Subsidiaries (*Millions, except shares*)

Common Stock Shares Issued		Total	Common Stock	Additional Paid-In Capital	Retained Earnings	Long-term Incentive Plan Deferred Compensation	Other
86,704,000	Balance at December 31, 1990	$2,975	$69	$ 995	$1,939	$(30)	$ 2
	Net loss	(142)	–	–	(142)	–	–
	Cash dividends declared—$1.60 per common share	(140)	–	–	(140)	–	–
	Common stock issued:						
145,000	Stock option plan	8	–	8	–	–	–
580,000	Employee stock purchase plans	20	1	19	–	–	–
	Long-term incentive plan	25	–	23	–	2	–
(8,000)	Other	(10)	–	–	–	–	(10)
87,421,000	Balance at December 31, 1991	2,736	70	1,045	1,657	(28)	(8)
	Net loss	(124)	–	–	(124)	–	–
	Cash dividends declared—$1.60 per common share	(140)	–	–	(140)	–	–
	Common stock issued:						
186,000	Stock option plan	12	–	12	–	–	–
112,000	Employee stock purchase plan	4	–	4	–	–	–
392,000	Long-term incentive plan	22	–	33	–	(11)	–
	Other	(2)	–	–	–	–	(2)

EXHIBIT 23-4 *Continued*

Common Stock Shares Issued		Total	Common Stock	Additional Paid-In Capital	Retained Earnings	Long-term Incentive Plan Deferred Compensation	Other
88,111,000	Balance at December 31, 1992	2,508	70	1,094	1,393	(39)	(10)
	Net loss	(34)	–	–	(34)	–	–
	Cash dividends declared—$1.60 per common share	(142)	–	–	(142)	–	–
	Common stock issued:						
107,000	Stock option plans	7	–	7	–	–	–
1,575,000	Employee stock purchase plans	55	1	54	–	–	–
476,000	Long-term incentive plan	26	–	43	–	(17)	–
	Other	(18)	–	4	–	–	(22)
90,269,000	Balance at December 31, 1993	$2,402	$71	$1,202	$1,217	$(56)	$(32)

Source: Georgia-Pacific *Annual Report*, 1993.

EXHIBIT 23-5 Georgia-Pacific Corporation and Subsidiaries (Millions)

(MILLIONS)	YEAR ENDED DECEMBER 31					
	1993		1992		1991	
Net sales						
Building products	$ 7,067	58%	$ 6,112	52%	$ 5,405	47%
Pulp and paper	5,231	42	5,711	48	6,089	53
Other operations	32	–	24	–	30	–
Total net sales	$12,330	100%	$11,847	100%	$11,524	100%
Net (loss)						
Building products	$973	126%	$ 691	100%	$344	32%
Pulp and paper	(187)	(24)	(8)	(1)	362	34
Other operations	10	1	9	1	17	2
Other income (loss)ª	(26)	(3)	–	–	344	32
Total operating profits	770	100%	692	100%	1,067	100%
General corporate	(205)		(166)		(165)	
Interest expense	(513)		(565)		(584)	
Cost of accounts receivable sale program	(29)		(35)		(59)	
(Provision) benefit for income taxes	(41)		14		(293)	
(Loss) before extraordinary item and accounting changes	(18)	(9)	(60)	(34)		
Extraordinary item-loss from early retirement of debt, net of taxes	(16)		(45)			
Cumulative effect of accounting changes, net of taxes	–		(55)		(63)	
Net (loss)	$ (34)		$ (124)		$ (142)	

EXHIBIT 23-5 Continued

(MILLIONS)	YEAR ENDED DECEMBER 31					
	1993		1992		1991	
Depreciation, depletion and goodwill amortization						
Building products	$ 215	26%	$ 206	24%	$ 232	30%
Pulp and paper	595	72	626	74	537	68
Other and general corporate	13	2	16	2	15	2
Total depreciation and goodwill amortization	$ 823	100%	$ 848	100%	$ 784	100%
Capital expenditures[b]						
Building products	$ 146	31%	$ 111	29%	$43	8%
Pulp and paper	261	56	217	56	436	83
Timber and timberlands	46	10	37	10	38	7
Other and general corporate	14	3	19	5	11	2
Total capital expenditures	$ 467	100%	$ 384	100%	$ 528	100%
Assets						
Building products	$ 1,726	16%	$ 1,634	15%	$ 1,681	16%
Pulp and paper	6,909	66	7,414	68	7,208	68
Timber and timberlands	1,380	13	1,402	13	1,377	13
Other and general corporate	530	5	462	4	363	3
Total assets	$10,545	100%	$10,912	100%	$10,629	100%

[a] Other income represents the results of various asset divestitures. If theses amounts had been included in segment operating profits, pulp and paper operating profits would have been $(213) million in 1993 and $546 million in 1991 and building products operating profits would have been $504 million in 1991.

[b] The capital expenditure amounts reported above represent additions, at cost, to property, plant and equipment and timber and timberlands.

Source: Georgia-Pacific *Annual Report*, 1993.

EXHIBIT 23-6 Selected Financial Data Financial Position, End of Year (*Dollar amounts, except per share, are in millions*)

	1993	1992	1991
Financial position, end of year			
Current assets	$ 1,646	$ 1,607	$ 1,562
Timber and timberlands, net	1,381	1,402	1,377
Property, plant and equipment, net	5,448	5,831	5,567
Net assets of discontinued operations	–	–	–
Goodwill	1,832	1,891	1,949
Other assets	238	181	174
Total assets	10,545	10,912	10,629
Current liabilities	2,064	2,452	2,722
Long-term debt	4,157	4,019	3,743
Other long-term liabilities	827	731	633
Deferred income taxes	1,095	1,202	795
Redeemable preferred stock	–	–	–
Shareholders' equity	$ 2,402	$ 2,508	$ 2,736
Working capital	$ (418)	$ (845)	$ (1,160)
Other statistical data			
Capital expenditures (including acquisitions)	$ 467	$ 384	$ 528
Capital expenditures (excluding acquisitions)	467	384	528
Per common share			
Market price: High	75.00	72.00	60.25
Low	55.00	48.25	36.25
Year-end	68.75	62.38	53.63
Book value	26.60	28.47	31.30
Total debt to capital	57.0%	57.0%	60.1%
Current ratio	.8	.7	.6

Source: Georgia-Pacific *Annual Report*, 1993.

EXHIBIT 23-7 Sales and Operating Profits by Industry Segment—Georgia-Pacific Corporation and Subsidiaries (*Millions*)

	1993		1992		1991		1990***	
Net sales								
Building products								
Wood panels	$ 2,913	24%	$ 2,543	22%	$ 2,097	18%	$ 2,296	18%
Lumber	2,672	22	2,055	17	1,819	16	1,966	16
Chemicals	267	2	240	2	223	2	247	2
Gypsum products	236	2	216	2	222	2	270	2
Roofing	180	1	185	2	183	2	192	2
Other	799	7	873	7	861	7	952	7
	7,067	58	6,112	52	5,405	47	5,923	47
Pulp and paper								
Containerboard and packaging	1,902	15	2,001	17	2,008	17	2,440	19
Communication papers	1,195	10	1,070	9	1,134	10	1,360	11
Tissue	713	6	682	6	664	6	719	6
Market pulp	622	5	681	6	645	6	779	6
Paper distribution and envelopes	748	6	1,208	10	1,218	10	1,027	8
Other	51	–	69	–	420	4	377	3
	5,231	42	5,711	48	6,089	53	6,702	53
Other operations	32	–	24	–	30	–	40	–
Continuing operations	$12,330	100%	$11,847	100%	$11,524	100%	$12,665	100%
Operating results*								
Building products	$ 973	126%	$ 691	100%	$ 344	32%	$ 423	29%
Pulp and paper	(187)	(24)	(8)	(1)	362	34	979	67
Other operations	10	1	9	1	17	2	17	1
Other income (expense)**	(26)	(3)	–	–	344	32	48	3
Continuing operations	$ 770	100%	$ 692	100%	$ 1,067	100%	$ 1,467	100%

*Operating results are before income taxes, interest, cost of accounts receivable sale program, general corporate expenses, unusual items, extraordinary items and accounting changes.

**Other income (expense) includes a net $26 million pretax loss in 1993, a net $344 million pretax gain in 1991 and a net $48 million pretax gain in 1990 resulting from asset divestitures and pretax restructuring charges of $135 million in 1983. If these amounts had been included in segment operating profits, pulp and paper operating profits would have been $(213) million in 1993, $546 million in 1991, $939 million in 1990 and $13 million in 1983; building products operating profits would have been $504 million in 1991, $511 million in 1990 and $277 million in 1983; and other operations operating profits would have been $13 million in 1983.

***Sales and operating profits of Great Northern Nekoosa Corporation and its subsidiaries have been included beginning on March 9, 1990.

Source: Georgia-Pacific *Annual Report*, 1993.

EXHIBIT 23-8 Operating Statistics—Georgia-Pacific Corporation and Subsidiaries

	AS OF DECEMBER 31, 1993	
	NUMBER OF FACILITIES	ANNUAL CAPACITY
Pulp and paper		
Paper (t.tons)		
Containerboard and packaging		
Linerboard and medium	4	2,941
Other paperboard	5	664
Kraft paper	2	342
Communication papers	8	2,223
Tissue	5	573
Groundwood papers	–	–
Market pulp (t.tons)	6	1,880
Total paper and market pulp	30	8,623
Converting		
Corrugated packaging (m.sq.ft.)	37	27,963
Tissue (t.tons)	6	610
Envelopes (billion envelopes)	17	15
Other	12	
Total paper, market pulp and converting	102	
Distribution centers	0**	
Building products		
Wood panels		
Softwood plywood (3/8") (m.sq.ft.)	17	5,019
Hardwood plywood (sm) (m.sq.ft.)	2	600
Hardboard (1/8") (m.sq.ft.)	8	1,395
Particleboard (3/4") (m.sq.ft.)	8	1,210
Oriented strand board (3/8") (m.sq.ft.)	4	952
Panelboard (1/8") (m.sq.ft.)	1	379
Softboard (1/2") (m.sq.ft.)	1	250
Medium-density fiberboard (3/4") (m.sq.ft.)	1	100
Lumber (m.bd.ft.)	40	2,732
Moulding (m.bd.ft.)	2	21
Gypsum board (m.sq.ft.)	10	3,063
Roofing-shingles (t.squares)	5	9,484
Formaldehyde (m.lbs.)	13	1,891
Thermosetting resins (m.lbs.)	16	3,014
Other	19	
Total building products	147	
Distribution centers	137	
Other operations	2	
Resources (as of December 31)		
North American timberlands (t.acres)		
Owned		
Controlled		

The Corporation has 248 manufacturing facilities in the United States, one recycled-paper mill in Canada, and 2 wood moulding manufacturing facilities in Mexico.

  *The production of Great Northern Nekoosa facilities has been included beginning on March 9, 1990.

  **Butler Paper assets were sold in July, 1993.

  ***Excludes 540,000 fee acres and 98,000 controlled acres of timberland sold in January 1991.

Source: Georgia–Pacific *Annual Report,* 1993

EXHIBIT 23-8 *Continued*

PRODUCTION

1993	1992	1991	1990*	1989	1988	1987	1986	1985	1984	1983
3,030	2,889	2,936	3,139	1,419	1,297	1,318	1,146	976	740	452
567	526	522	544	555	458	393	368	368	374	377
343	377	358	354	350	356	348	394	452	529	541
2,119	2,002	1,994	1,780	1,161	970	868	731	552	574	518
594	576	556	553	519	511	490	496	476	486	487
–	–	603	531	–	–	–	–	–	–	–
1,940	1,829	1,793	1,667	1,194	870	718	611	587	629	601
8,593	8,199	8,762	8,568	5,198	4,462	4,135	3,746	3,411	3,332	2,976
29,998	25,411	24,010	31,356	16,640	16,577	15,750	14,572	13,703	11,880	8,427
543	521	491	497	467	462	446	437	432	422	422
13	13	13	12	–	–	–	–	–	–	–
5,462	5,133	4,968	5,395	5,341	5,545	5,050	4,706	4,414	4,443	4,430
477	458	424	437	420	456	357	335	311	343	442
1,388	1,330	1,202	1,203	1,203	1,198	1,159	349	368	361	346
1,089	977	932	984	1,062	1,004	695	425	410	381	400
1,045	1,011	851	969	873	793	652	525	173	96	51
366	365	332	344	318	330	295	248	290	311	299
247	234	237	252	242	238	231	241	239	243	241
98	92	79	88	74	62	59	75	76	69	77
2,580	2,568	2,570	2,674	2,426	2,324	1,956	1,784	1,684	1,650	1,603
21	23	22	36	29	30	30	8	–	–	–
2,409	2,112	1,955	2,309	2,403	2,406	2,620	2,473	2,495	2,412	2,242
7,274	7,447	7,775	7,674	8,106	7,155	6,976	7,361	7,789	7,539	5,973
1,809	1,614	1,540	1,547	1,454	1,394	1,309	1,233	1,188	1,169	1,081
2,761	2,571	2,377	2,470	2,372	2,362	2,136	1,805	1,650	1,527	1,451
5,821	5,942	5,969	8,203***	5,430	5,480	4,910	4,700	4,760	4,920	4,630
681	707	922	1,047***	670	1,010	670	530	480	480	530

sm = surface measure basis
t = thousands
m = millions
Source: Georgia–Pacific *Annual Report*, 1993.

EXHIBIT 23-9 Georgia–Pacific Corporation Officers

A.D. Correll
Chairman and Chief Executive Officer

James C. Van Meter[1]
Vice Chairman and Chief Financial Officer

W.E. Babin
Executive Vice President-Pulp and Paper

Davis K. Mortensen
Executive Vice President-Building Products

Donald L. Glass
Senior Vice President-Building Products
Manufacturing and Sales

James F. Kelley
Senior Vice President-Law and General
Counsel

Maurice W. Kring
Senior Vice President-Containerboard and
Packaging

George A. MacConnell
Senior Vice President-Distribution and
Millwork

John F. McGovern[2]
Senior Vice President-Finance

David W. Reynolds
Senior Vice President-Human Resources and
Administration

Lee M. Thomas
Senior Vice President-Environmental,
Government Affairs and Communications

[1] Resigned February 28, 1994

[2] Named Chief Financial Officer February 28, 1994

James E. Bostic, Jr.
Group Vice President-Communication Papers

Gerard R. Brandt
Group Vice President-Packaged Products

Willie L. Duke
Group Vice President-Softwood Lumber

Duncan B. Facey
Group Vice President-Distribution Division

Clint M. Kennedy
Group Vice President-Pulp and Bleached Board

John F. Rasor
Group Vice President-Forest Resources

J. Wayne Amy
Vice-President-Metal Products

Joseph J. Armetta
Vice-President-Distribution Division Midwest
Region

Jerry P. Collier
Vice President-Millwork

Rebecca M. Crockford
Vice President-Compensation and Benefits

David S. Dimling
Vice President-Sales and Marketing
Communication Papers

David R. Fleiner
Vice-President-Structural Panels

EXHIBIT 23-9 *Continued*

William C. Howard
Vice President-Environmental Engineering and
Technical Support

Stephen K. Jackson
Vice President-Distribution Division Northeast
Region

Jerry L. Kincaid
Vice President-Manufacturing Communication
Papers

William A. Mamrack
Vice President-Taxes

John E. Masaschi
Vice President-Industrial Wood Products
Division

Charles H. McElrea
Vice President-Pulp and Paper Logistics and
Purchasing

Robert J. Millikan
Vice President-Engineering and Technology
Pulp and Paper

Dewey L. Mobley
Vice President-Western Wood Products
Manufacturing Division

William B. Nagle, Jr.
Vice President-Lumber Distribution

Source: Georgia-Pacific *Annual Report*, 1993.

Kelly E. Powell, Jr.
Vice President-Distribution Division Western
Region

William D. Rose
Vice President-Specialty Manufacturing and
Sales

Robert A. Starling
Vice President-Distribution Division Southern
Region

James R. Taylor
Vice President-Chemical Division

James E. Terrell
Vice President and Controller

Douglas A. Thom
Vice President-Packaging

Michael A. Vidan
Vice President-Gypsum and Roofing Division

Carl Wilson
Vice President-Information Resources

James T. Wright
Vice President-Human Resources

Kenneth F. Khoury
Secretary

Danny W. Huff
Treasurer

SHOES AND APPAREL INDUSTRY NOTE

JOANNE TUCKER
AND JAMES BYRON

The nonrubber footwear industry (SIC 314) produces all types of footwear except rubber protective and rubber-soled fabric-upper (the traditional "sneakers") footwear, both of which are classified in SIC 3021 (Table 1). Nonrubber footwear is constructed with leather, vinyl, plastic, or textile uppers or combinations of these materials for both genders and all ages. In 1993, industry shipments increased about 4 percent to an estimated $3.9 billion, from $3.8 billion in 1992. In constant dollars, the increase was more than 1 percent. Unit shipments increased less than 1 percent to 172 million pairs in 1993, from 171 million pairs in 1992. By quantity, the rate of change varied among the industry's four major sectors: house slippers (SIC 3142) were down 5 percent; men's footwear, except athletic (SIC 3143) increased 1 percent; and women's footwear, except athletic (SIC 3144) and footwear, except rubber, NEC(SIC 3149) were up between 3 and 4 percent each.

Production Up. In 1993, production of nonrubber footwear increased almost 1 percent to more than 165 million pairs, from more than 164 million pairs in 1992. This marked the first annual increase since 1988 and only the fourth since 1968, when production peaked at about 642.4 million pairs. Over the subsequent 25-year period, U.S. production has declined at a compound annual rate of about 5 percent. In 1993, production, by quantity, was up for three sectors and down only for slippers.

House Slippers. Shipments of house slippers declined about 5 percent to more than 45 million pairs in 1993. Their product value dropped to an estimated $268 million. Slippers accounted for 26 percent of the quantity but only 7.5 percent of the value of total nonrubber footwear product shipments, primarily because most slippers are produced from lower-cost vinyls and textiles. The ratio of imports to apparent consumption for slippers was about 28 percent by quantity, the lowest of the four sectors.

Men's Footwear, Except Athletic. Men's nonathletic footwear includes dress and casual shoes, work shoes, and boots. Shipments of men's footwear increased about 1 percent, to 43.3 million pairs in 1993 from 42.8 million pairs in 1992. Value increased about 3 percent in 1993 to an estimated $1.84 billion. Men's footwear accounted for 25 percent by quantity and 51 percent by value of nonrubber footwear shipments in 1993. More than 90 percent of men's footwear was made with leather uppers. By quantity, imports as a percentage of total consumption of men's footwear were an estimated 76 percent in 1993.

Women's Footwear, Except Athletic. Shipments of women's footwear increased more than 3 percent to 58 million pairs in 1993. Value increased about 6 percent to an estimated $1.3 billion. Women's footwear accounted for 34 percent by quantity and 35 percent by value. Import penetration for women's footwear was an estimated 90 percent.

Footwear, Except Rubber, NEC. Shipments of footwear for youths and boys, misses, children, infants and babies, and athletic and other miscellaneous types of

TABLE 1   Trends and Forecasts: Footwear, except Rubber (SIC 314) (*In Millions of Dollars except as noted*) 1991-1994

ITEM	1991	1992[1]	1993[2]	1994[3]	PERCENT CHANGE 91–92	92–93	93–94
INDUSTRY DATA							
Value of shipments[4]	3,775	3,778	3,918	4,134	0.1	3.7	5.5
3142 House slippers	277	295	290	293	6.5	−1.7	1.0
3143 Men's footwear	2,064	2,093	2,158	2,287	1.4	3.1	6.0
3144 Women's footwear	1,154	1,158	1,228	1,302	0.3	6.0	6.0
3149 Footwear NEC	280	232	242	252	−17.1	4.3	4.1
Value of shipments (1987$)	3,199	3,126	3,174	3,236	−2.3	1.5	2.0
3142 House slippers	251	274	261	256	9.2	−4.7	−1.9
3143 Men's footwear	1,686	1,665	1,685	1,719	−1.2	1.2	2.0
3144 Women's footwear	1,028	997	1,032	1,063	−3.0	3.5	3.0
3149 Footwear NEC	233	190	196	198	−18.5	3.2	1.0
Total employment (000)	53.1	50.3	48.2	48.2	−5.3	−4.2	0.0
Production workers (000)	46.0	43.2	41.0	41.4	−6.1	−5.1	1.0
Average hourly earnings ($)	6.83	7.17	7.53	7.83	5.0	5.0	4.0
Capital expenditures	31.5	—	—	—	—	—	—
3142 House slippers	2.4	—	—	—	—	—	—
3143 Men's footwear	18.1	—	—	—	—	—	—
144 Women's footwear	9.1	—	—	—	—	—	—
3149 Footwear NEC	1.9	—	—	—	—	—	—
PRODUCT DATA							
Value of shipments[5]	3,495	3,491	3,622	3,822	-0.1	3.8	5.5
3142 House slippers	256	273	268	271	6.6	−1.8	1.1
3143 Men's footwear	1,763	1,788	1,843	1,954	1.4	3.1	6.0
3144 Women's footwear	1,186	1,190	1,261	1,337	0.3	6.0	6.0
3149 Footwear NEC	289	240	250	260	−17.0	4.2	4.0
Value of shipments (1987$)	2,971	2,896	2,943	3,001	−2.5	1.6	2.0
3142 House slippers	232	253	241	236	9.1	−4.7	−2.1
3143 Men's footwear	1,441	1,422	1,439	1,468	−1.3	1.2	2.0
3144 Women's footwear	1,057	1,025	1,060	1,092	−3.0	3.4	3.0
3149 Footwear NEC	241	196	203	205	−18.7	3.6	1.0
TRADE DATA							
Value of imports	8,315	8,590	9,385	10,042	3.3	9.3	7.0
Value of exports	306	342	329	368	11.8	−3.8	11.9

1. Estimate, except exports and imports.
2. Estimate.
3. Forecast.
4. Value of all products and services sold by establishments in the footwear, except rubber industry.
5. Value of products classified in the footwear, except rubber industry produced by all industries.

Source: U.S. Department of Commerce: Bureau of the Census; International Trade Administration (ITA). Estimates and forecasts by ITA.

footwear increased about 3 percent to an estimated 25 million pairs in 1993. Value increased about 4 percent to $250 million. Shipments of footwear in this group accounted for 15 percent by quantity and 7 percent by value. Production of misses' and athletic footwear increased in 1993, but children's and infants' and babies' footwear declined.

Consumption of athletic footwear, including imports and domestic production of rubber-fabric "sneakers," reached a high of about 565 million pairs in 1992 but declined about 1 percent in 1993. Athletic footwear represented about 38 percent of combined nonrubber and rubber-fabric footwear consumption of about 1.5 billion pairs in 1993. Imports of juvenile footwear were up about 7 percent in the first half of 1993 from the same period in 1992, but imports of athletic nonrubber footwear declined.

Footwear Consumption Up. Apparent consumption of nonrubber footwear increased about 2 percent in 1993 to an estimated 1.1 billion pairs. Per capita consumption also increased for the third consecutive year by about 1 percent, to 4.43 pairs. Driven by demand for imported nonrubber athletic footwear, per capita consumption increased sharply during the early 1980s, peaking at 4.8 pairs in 1986. Per capita consumption declined to 4.3 pairs in 1990 and has increased only slightly since then. Per capita consumption of combined nonrubber and rubber/canvas footwear was 5.65 pairs in 1993, down from 1992 because of a drop in "sneaker" consumption of about 6 percent.

Personal consumption expenditures (PCE) on both rubber and nonrubber footwear were up only 0.4 percent in 1993 to an estimated $32.4 billion. However, PCE on footwear in constant (1987) dollars were down almost 2 percent. Inventories at all levels of distribution increased during the year, as both sales and prices at the retail level weakened.

Retailers' outdoor business was good throughout 1993. Lightweight hikers, waterproof boots, outdoor crosstrainers, and sport sandals were in demand and consumption of these types is expected to grow in 1994. Styles shifted away from the athletic look to an outdoor look but incorporated the same comfort technology, such as padded linings, collars, and insoles that made athletic shoes so popular. Water-resistant leather uppers, including suedes, predominated, especially in boots.

Factory Prices, Profits Up. The average factory price for nonrubber footwear increased about 2 percent to an estimated $21.16 per pair in 1993. This was the smallest annual increase in three years and reflected the intense pressure on prices from imported footwear. The producer price index (PPI) for nonrubber footwear was up almost 2 percent for January–June 1993, compared with the same period in 1992.

According to an analysis of publicly held footwear companies, six producers that manufactured athletic footwear overseas earned the most profits in 1992. The entire group of 31 companies saw total sales increase 7 percent and profits rise 22 percent over 1991. Six athletic footwear companies accounted for 60 percent of the group's sales and 80 percent of its profits. Nike was among the top five performers in seven financial ratios and Reebok was similarly ranked in four ratios. But with slower growth in athletic footwear, composite performances for the group were not as solid as they have been. The financial performance of individual companies, particularly among the small and medium-sized manufacturers, was much improved in 1992 over 1991. Median return on sales for the group grew from nearly 3 percent in 1991 to more than 4 percent in 1992, and median return on equity rose from more than 7 percent to slightly more than 11 percent over the same period.

An article in *Footwear News* (July 1993) indicated that consumers' footwear buying habits had shifted to form, function, and comfort and away from brands. Many were seeking lower-priced goods in strip shopping centers and outlet stores instead of in shopping malls. The same article found that, as a group, 18 publicly held U.S. footwear resource companies (companies that either produce domestically or source abroad) reported a 4.8 percent increase in sales in 1992 over 1991, but a 19.5 percent decline in profits. However, 94 percent of the group's total profits came from the two largest athletic footwear producers. Four companies, including the third largest athletic producer, recorded losses in 1992. The new profit-to-sales ratio for the group was 4.1 percent in 1992, down from 5.4 percent in 1991. In 1992, the profit-to-equity ratio was 14.1 percent, down from 18.7 percent in 1991. For a group of five footwear retailers, the same survey showed that sales increased 7.8 percent in 1992 over 1991, and profits were up 9 percent.

Plants, Employment Down. The *Census of Manufacturers for 1987* lists 379 companies operating 471 establishments in the nonrubber footwear industry. In 1966, about 990 plants were in operation. Based on published reports of plant closings, these declines have continued since 1987. Ten closings were recorded in 1992. Many of the plants recently closed were owned by the largest manufacturing and retailing companies, which chose to source more footwear from lower-cost producers overseas. In 1993, total employment declined about 4 percent to an estimated 48,200. Production employment declined also by about 5 percent.

About 47.5 percent of nonrubber footwear produced in 1992 had leather uppers, down from 51 percent in 1991. About 15 percent had leather outsoles. Leather upper use was highest in men's footwear (95 percent) and women's footwear (65 percent). Juvenile types averaged about 31 percent and athletics 75 percent.

New Technology. The industry considers new technology essential to increase productivity and lower costs. Increased use of computers has already integrated design, management, manufacturing, and marketing functions, emphasizing such nonprice factors as quality and quick delivery in competition with imports. Emphasis has been placed on linking computer-aided design (CAD) and computer-aided manufacturing (CAM) systems and software. As a result, tooling can be produced from CAD data and linked to auto-stitchers, milling, and turning machines. There has been a resurgence of interest in three-dimensional CAD, which produces more accurate shoe patterns and reduces the number of prototypes required.

Computers also enable manufacturers to combine several operations or machines under fewer operators, reducing handling time and improving quality. Computerized robots have also been developed for handling and transferring operations within and between these production modules. Much of this new technology has been developed and used in Europe and, depending on the availability of capital, can be readily transferred to Far Eastern producers. However, the labor-saving benefits of such technology would not be as great for producers with low unit labor costs. The net effect of such technology would be to reduce the costs of U.S. production relative to Far Eastern production, although the latter will continue to maintain a competitive advantage for most footwear.

Nonrubber footwear imports rose almost 3 percent in 1993 to an estimated 1 billion pairs, from 974 million pairs in 1992. The customs value increased more than 9 percent to $9.4 billion. The unit value of nonrubber footwear imports in 1993 was about $9.39, up from 1992, but still almost 60 percent below the unit value of domestic production (Table 2).

Imports increased from 175 million pairs in 1968 to 405 million pairs in 1979, when they stabilized during a four-year period of Orderly Marketing Agreements (OMAs) with South Korea and Taiwan. Following expiration of these OMAs in June 1981, imports increased by more than 100 million pairs a year until 1986, reaching 941 million pairs. Following a decline to less than 900 million pairs in 1989, nonrubber footwear imports rose to the record level of 1 billion pairs in 1993. Over the 25-year period since 1968, imports have increased at a compound annual rate of about 7 percent.

During the first six months of 1993, the five largest suppliers, by quantity, of nonrubber footwear to the United States were China (56 percent), Brazil (12 percent), Indonesia (8 percent), Taiwan (almost 6 percent), and the Republic of Korea (4 percent). These five countries accounted for nearly 85 percent of all U.S. nonrubber footwear imports for the six-month period. Although the United States imported nonrubber footwear from more than 90 countries during this period, only four other countries—Italy, Thailand, Spain, and Hong Kong—captured more than 1 percent of U.S. nonrubber footwear imports.

TABLE 2 U.S. Trade Patterns in 1992 Footwear, Except Rubber SIC 314 (*In millions of dollars, percent*)

EXPORTS	VALUE	SHARE	IMPORTS	VALUE	SHARE
Canada and Mexico	65	19.1	Canada and Mexico	145	1.7
European Community	115	33.5	European Community	1,292	15.0
Japan	39	11.3	Japan	3	0.0
East Asia NICs	15	4.3	East Asia NICs	5,715	66.5
South America	21	6.2	South America	1,166	13.6
Other	87	25.6	Other	269	3.1
World Total	342	100.0		8,590	100.0

TOP FIVE COUNTRIES	VALUE	SHARE		VALUE	SHARE
Canada	46	13.4	China	2,970	34.6
Japan	39	11.3	Brazil	1,099	12.8
United Kingdom	25	7.2	South Korea	1,074	12.5
France	24	7.1	Italy	772	9.0
Italy	23	6.8	Taiwan	696	8.1

Source: U.S. Department of Commerce: Bureau of the Census; International Trade Administration.

U.S. imports of nonrubber footwear were up nearly 10 percent for the first six months in 1993 compared with the same period in 1992. Imports from China rose 28 percent and were expected to increase by 140 million pairs in 1993 to almost 650 million pairs. More production continued to shift to China from Taiwan and Korea, formerly the two major exporters, because of lower costs. A large measure of technological and financial support for mainland China's rapidly expanding footwear operations comes from Taiwanese manufacturers. Indonesia, up 23 percent, and Brazil, up 16 percent, both recorded substantial export growth to the United States during the period January–June 1993 compared with the same period in 1992. Korea's exports to the United States dropped 45 percent and Taiwan's declined 37 percent.

China accounted for more than 35 percent of U.S. imports of nonrubber footwear with leather uppers during January–June, 1993. In addition, Brazil (23 percent), Indonesia (9 percent), Korea (8 percent), and Italy (6 percent) ranked in the top five suppliers, accounting for more than 80 percent of the total. China and Brazil were the largest suppliers of men's leather footwear. Brazil, China, and Italy were the largest suppliers of women's leather footwear, and China and Brazil were the largest suppliers of juvenile footwear. China (40 percent) and Indonesia (25 percent) were the largest suppliers of leather athletic footwear. China was the largest supplier to the United States in all 19 major gender or material subcategories of nonrubber footwear imports except women's leather footwear, where it ranked second behind Brazil.

U.S. leather footwear imports accounted for 53 percent of all nonrubber footwear imports during January–June 1993, unchanged from the same period in 1992. The import share of footwear with vinyl or plastic uppers for January–June 1993 was 44 percent, and of items with textile uppers 3 percent. The import share with leather uppers has dropped from a high of 59 percent in 1990 due to the substitution of cheaper vinyl, plastic, and other materials for more expensive leather. For January–June 1993, leather's share was highest for athletic and men's nonrubber footwear imports and lowest for juvenile and slipper types.

U.S. manufacturers export ever larger quantities of cut footwear parts to developing countries, where they are assembled and re-exported to the United States as finished or partly finished footwear. Under the U.S. Harmonized Tariff Schedule (Heading No. 9802), duties are assessed only on the value-added content. Moreover, U.S. duties on partially finished but unlasted nonrubber footwear are less than 5 percent, compared with 8.5 percent or more for completed leather footwear. Frequently, final manufacturing operations that require less labor, such as bottoming, finishing, and packing are performed in the United States. For January–June 1993, such partially completed leather footwear imports totaled more than 13 million pairs, up about 12 percent over the same period in 1992. The largest suppliers were the Dominican Republic, Mexico, Thailand, India, and China.

Exports Down. U.S. exports of nonrubber footwear declined about 4 percent in 1993 to more than 20 million pairs. Value declined more than 1 percent to an estimated $337 million. The average unit price was about $16.44, up from $15.98 in 1992. U.S. producers compete effectively in high-cost developed country markets, including all of the European Community countries. European demand was steady for U.S. branded men's moccasins, boat shoes, hiking boots, Western boots, and work boots.

The United States exported 10 million parts of nonrubber footwear valued at $156 million during the first half of 1993. Mexico took more than 16 percent of the total, by quantity, followed by Canada (9 percent), Russia (8 percent), Poland (8 percent), Japan (7 percent), France (5 percent), and the United Kingdom (4 percent).

U.S. exports of nonrubber footwear to Mexico were made up largely of low-priced juvenile types with vinyl uppers. For the first half of 1993, U.S. footwear exports to Russia were up 20 percent over the same period in 1992 by quantity, and included mostly men's and women's leather footwear.

U.S. exports of nonrubber footwear to Japan were unchanged in the first half of 1993 compared with 1992. About 24 percent of these exports were men's leather types, and 43 percent were athletic types. The latter are exempt from Japan's stringent global tariff-rate quotas on leather nonathletic footwear. These quotas and required licensing procedures restrict Japan's leather footwear imports and discourage U.S. manufacturers from developing the Japanese market. Japan's quota of about 7 million pairs annually in 1993 represents only a small fraction of its leather footwear market, which is estimated to exceed 180 million pairs a year.

Trade Legislation. Several attempts by Congress to pass footwear import quota legislation since 1985 failed to survive presidential vetoes, and it is very unlikely that further attempts will be made. Legislation extending the Caribbean Basin Initiative (CBI) passed in late 1990, and continues to exempt footwear and leather products, among others, from duty-free status. Footwear is statutorily exempt from duty-free treatment accorded beneficiary developing countries under the Generalized System of Preferences (GSP) program.

Most U.S. producers were concerned about increased imports from Mexico following the removal of duties on footwear under the North American Free Trade Agreement (NAFTA). NAFTA provides for a 15-year staged reduction of U.S. duties on rubber footwear, including rubber-fabric types. These U.S. duties range from 37 to 67 percent. Most nonrubber footwear, including leather types which are dutiable at 8.5 to 12 percent, would receive a shorter phaseout period of 10 years. NAFTA rules of origin for footwear would require that non-North American parts undergo a tariff shift at the tariff heading level and that footwear meet a regional content requirement of 55 percent. These strict rules are intended to ensure that third countries could not use Mexico as an export platform or transhipment site to gain duty-free access to the U.S. market. U.S. footwear imports from other Central and South American countries could also increase significantly if accorded duty-free status under Administration-proposed trade initiatives with these countries.

OUTLOOK FOR 1994

Shipments of nonrubber footwear are expected to increase about 1 percent in 1994, to 174 million pairs. Shipments will increase in three sectors: men's footwear by 2 percent to 44 million pairs; women's footwear by 3 percent to 60 million pairs; and footwear, except rubber NEC, by 1 percent to 25.5 million pairs. Shipments of slippers will decline about 2 percent to 45 million pairs. Imports, by quantity, are expected to increase 1 percent and exports by 7 percent. Consequently, apparent consumption will increase only 1 percent and per capita consumption will remain unchanged. Import penetration will remain unchanged from 1993 at 87 percent of apparent consumption.

II. APPAREL

The apparel products industry (SIC 23), also known as the sewn products industry, consists primarily of firms that produce wearing apparel, both cut and sewn and knit to shape, for all population groups. Apparel accounted for 74 percent of total SIC 23 shipments in 1992.

The apparel products industry increased its shipments by 2 percent in 1993, about the same growth as in the previous year. Shipments were nearly 1 percent higher, following a small decline in 1992, because price increases for apparel products decelerated. The shipment gains have occurred in response to sharp increases in consumer spending for clothing, although imports also have benefited from higher spending (Table 3). Some of the increased production, however, reflected inventory buildup in late 1992 and early 1993, similar to what occurred in the overall economy. This inventory rise probably will hold down production to some extent until stocks are worked down.

Total employment in the apparel products industry was about 939,000 workers in 1993. Employment has been declining since 1977, and this is reflected in all product lines, particularly outerwear. In 1992, the number of production workers increased slightly, although total employment registered a small decline, reflecting cost-saving cuts in management positions. Production workers constituted 84 percent of the work force in 1993, compared with 68 percent for all U.S. manufacturing. The aver-

TABLE 3 Trends and forecasts: Apparel and Other Textile Products (SIC 23) *(In millions of dollars except as noted)* 1991-1993

				PERCENT CHANGE	
ITEM	1991	1992[1]	1993[2]	91-92	92-93
INDUSTRY DATA					
Value of shipments[3]	65,345	66,652	68,052	2.0	2.1
Value of shipments (1987$)	59,021	58,790	59,391	−0.4	1.0
Total employment (000)	960	959	939	−0.1	−2.1
Production workers (000)	815	816	799	0.1	−2.1
Average hourly earnings ($)	6.73	6.91	7.06	2.7	2.2
PRODUCT DATA					
Value of shipments[4]	62,649	64,115	65,461	2.3	2.1
Value of shipments (1987$)	56,634	56,552	57,130	−0.1	1.0
TRADE DATA					
Value of imports	27,230	32,462	35,449	19.2	9.2
Value of exports	3,708	4,625	5,556	24.7	20.1

1. Estimate, except exports and imports.
2. Estimate.
3. Value of all products and services sold by establishments in the apparel and other textile products industry.
4. Value of products classified in the apparel and other textile products industry produced by all industries.

Source: U.S. Department of Commerce: Bureau of the Census; International Trade Administration (ITA). Estimates and forecasts by ITA.

age number of hours worked weekly by production workers grew to 37.2 in 1992, the highest level in at least 20 years. This growth indicates not only the industry's increased activity, but also its hesitancy in hiring permanent workers until the economy is in a solid recovery. Average hours may increase marginally in 1993.

Despite improvements in technology, manufacturing processes in this industry are still quite labor-intensive. Wages and profit margins are low relative to other manufacturing industries. In 1993, the hourly earnings of production workers averaged $7.10, 2 percent above 1992. Employees making men's coats and suits averaged the highest hourly wages, while children's wear workers earned the least. Earnings of apparel and fabricated textile product workers were about 40 percent below the average for all U.S. manufacturing employees and about 35 percent below workers in nondurable goods industries in 1993.

Apparel. Inflationary pressures in the apparel industry continued to ease in 1993, with the rate of price increases slowing for the third year in a row. A slowdown in inflation in the overall economy, little pressure from raw materials costs, and continuing declines in employment due to productivity gains all contributed to keep inflation in check.

Personal consumption expenditures on clothing expanded sharply at the end of 1992 and the beginning of 1993, following declines the two prior years, but then tapered off somewhat around mid-year. Despite the second-half slowdown, constant-dollar personal consumption expenditures for clothing expanded at a faster rate than total consumption expenditures and at a much faster pace than other nondurable spending. (Usually, toward the beginning of an economic recovery, nondurable spending lags behind purchases of durable goods, such as autos and appliances, that had been postponed during the recession.)

Retail sales of apparel and accessory stores in mid-1993 were running about 5 percent higher than in 1992. This was slightly less than the previous year's increase but well ahead of the 1991 pace. Retail inventories increased in 1992 and, at mid-year 1993, were about 9 percent above mid-year 1992. Weather disasters may have contributed to the inventory buildup in 1993. The ratio of inventories to sales in 1993 rose for the first time in 6 years.

Because labor is such a significant cost component in apparel manufacturing, producers in low-wage developing countries enjoy a significant cost advantage over U.S. producers, creating intense competition and downward pressure on profits. In addition, consumers persisted in searching for value, buying more sale merchandise in department stores and shifting some purchasing to discount and factory outlet stores. Apparel manufacturers continued to shift sourcing out of the country, most recently to the Caribbean, Central America, or South America. Major companies produced an estimated 70 percent of their sales in U.S. plants in 1993.

Structurally, the domestic industry is made up of a few large companies and many small and medium-size firms. According to one study, in 1993, the larger apparel firms appear to have become more diversified, accounting for 75 percent of apparel sales and all of the growth in volume. The divergence between the performance of the larger firms and many of the smaller companies widened, as profits of the latter group declined in 1992. As a result, the larger companies had most of the funds needed for reinvestment in the industry.

Men's and Boys' Apparel. Shipments of men's and boys' clothing, which outperformed the apparel industry in 1992, slowed somewhat in 1993, although boys' wear was still strong. Production of suits and coats continued the uptrend begun in 1992, following years of decline, helped by a move toward European styling, industry consolidation, and the general absence of inflation in this sector. Production of men's and boys' shorts, sweatshirts, knit sport shirts, and jeans also showed significant increases. Dress shirts, ties, and slacks recorded only slight gains. Dress shirt purchases were mainly for replenishment. Underwear shipments grew only slightly in value as a result of overproduction and price competition. Shipments of both men's and boys' sweaters continued to decline. In terms of sales, brand-name apparel recorded an above-average performance, but consumers generally looked for value.

Employment in men's and boys' outerwear fell in 1993, following the first increase in several years in 1992. Employment in the underwear segment, however, continued to expand. Hourly earnings grew faster than the industry average. Sharply expanding exports in both outwear and underwear accounted for a large portion of the growth in shipments.

Women's, Girl's, and Children's Apparel. Women's outerwear shipments outperformed the industry average in 1992 and 1993, partially because of a strong showing in exports. European women recently began buying more U.S. clothing, and now markets are opening up for high-status designer apparel in the Far East, including China. Employment in the women's outerwear sector continued to decline sharply, and earnings increases were below average, largely because of the heavy impact of imports on the women's apparel industry. Women's and children's underwear showed little change in shipments between 1992 and 1993.

Retail sales of women's apparel slowed somewhat in 1993, following a reasonable performance in 1992. The lackluster economic picture, coupled with a lack of significant fashion change, had a negative impact on sales. Designer apparel has been particularly hard hit as consumers turned more toward value in apparel purchases and discount pricing. Women's activewear, jeans, and skirts are the brightest spots in this segment of the apparel industry. Sweaters sales have been slow.

Girls' wear sales showed considerable strength in the beginning of 1993, following a good year in 1992. As with boys' wear, demographic trends have had a major impact on this segment of the market. More children have been born in recent years to older, better educated, and more affluent parents who tend to spend more money on them. Imports of girls' wear had little growth in 1993, but exports continued to make gains. Employment in girls' and children's wear manufacturers continued to decline steeply, while average hourly earnings increased modestly.

Environmental Issues. Apparel companies and their suppliers are embracing the "green" movement. Companies address environmental issues for a number of reasons, including concern for the earth, winning over those consumers who buy only environment-friendly products, or simply taking advantage of a popular movement. Among the rising trends in the industry are the use of organic cotton that is grown without pesticides; new low-impact dyeing methods and vegetable-based, nontoxic dyes; the use of cotton grown in natural shades of tan, brown, and green that needs no dyeing; and the use of respun fibers made from waste trimmings of textile mills or from old clothing that has been cleaned, shredded, and spun into new yarn.

INTERNATIONAL COMPETITIVENESS

The trade deficit in apparel products has been growing in recent years (Figure 1). It increased from $28 billion in 1992 to an estimated $30 billion in 1993, despite a 20 percent gain in exports and import growth of 9 percent, half the rate in 1992. The increase in the value of imports overwhelmed the export advance because imports continue to be substantially larger than exports in value terms.

Although the sewn products industry (SIC 23) is historically not export-oriented, manufacturers have increasingly turned their attention to overseas markets in recent years, rather than depend solely on the slow-growing U.S. market. Exports accounted for about 9 percent of product shipments in 1993, up from 4 percent in 1989. The depreciation in the exchange rate value of the dollar and the growing demand abroad for quality apparel and fabricated textile products contributed to the surge in exports the past several years. In 1993, exports, which were affected by depressed economic conditions in all the major apparel markets abroad, grew at the slowest rate in more than 4 years, but still managed a 20 percent gain. Some of the export growth consisted of shipments of garment parts for assembly abroad and subsequent reimport, but exports of finished apparel for sale in foreign markets increased sharply as well. Apparel components that are shipped to other countries for assembly and eventual return to the U.S. market under the HTSUS 9802 (previously 807) program receive preferential duty treatment. (The importer pays duty only on the value added abroad under this program.)

U.S. manufacturers have taken advantage of their reputation for high quality, U.S. Government-sponsored foreign trade fairs and export seminars, and long-term export strategies to expand their shipments abroad. Occasionally, modifications in design and fit are necessary to sell in foreign markets, but many customers are looking for the American look and ease of care and wearing. In addition to direct exports, greater numbers of U.S. retailers and catalog houses have established sales outlets in other countries to sell U.S. apparel products. Men's outerwear and home furnishings remain the largest export categories. Men's and boys trousers are the most important products exported to Japan, Canada, and the European Community (EC), followed

FIGURE 1 U.S. Trade Deficit Grows in Apparel and Fabricated Textile Products

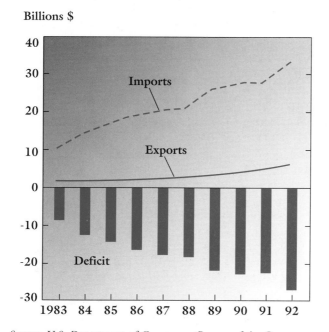

Source: U.S. Department of Commerce, Bureau of the Census.

by men's and boys' knit shirts. Menswear and women's outwear exports recorded particularly steep increases in 1993. Children's wear and women's and children's underwear continue to make strong export gains.

Japan, the EC countries, and Canada are the largest customers for U.S. apparel, with steep gains in shipments the past few years. Sales of completed garments to Mexico also grew sharply. After the United States and Canada implemented a free trade agreement in 1989, the U.S. share of the Canadian apparel market grew sharply. During the same period, however, the U.S. share of the Mexican market dropped following liberalization of Mexican import barriers (Figure 2). If the recently negotiated North American Free Trade Agreement (NAFTA) is implemented, U.S. exports are expected to regain some of their lost share in the Mexican market. Under the agreement, virtually all trade restrictions would be eliminated within 10 years, some much sooner. The expected benefit to the Mexican economy resulting from implementation of the agreement should boost demand for U.S. exports there.

Although small in value, exports of U.S. clothing have been growing rapidly to Eastern Europe and China, where demand is increasing for upscale goods, status symbols, and Western looks. U.S. manufacturers that are able to take advantage of opportunities in these countries should experience a surge in their exports. Exports of cut apparel parts to the Caribbean Basin countries have advanced sharply in recent years, particularly to the Dominican Republic and Costa Rica, which are the leading participants in HTSUS 9802 garment assembly operations.

The largest suppliers of imports of apparel products to the U.S. market in 1993 were China, Hong Kong, South Korea, and Taiwan, but only China increased its shipments of sewn products to the United States. These four countries accounted for nearly half of U.S. imports of all apparel and fabricated textile products. In 1993, the largest import increases, in addition to those from China, were from countries with

FIGURE 2 United States Share of Canadian and Mexican Apparel Imports

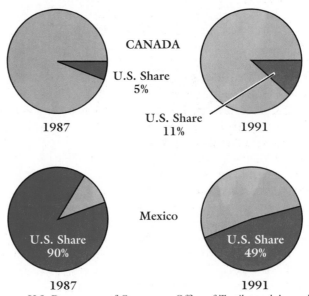

Source: U.S. Department of Commerce, Office of Textiles and Apparel.

large HTSUS 9802 operations, namely Mexico, the Dominican Republic, and the Philippines. Arrivals of HTSUS 9802 goods now account for 15 percent of all apparel imports, up from 9 percent as recently as 1990. Apparel imports in 1993 grew at less than half the 19 percent rate in 1992 (Tables 4 and 5).

LONG-TERM PROSPECTS

Factors contributing to a favorable long-term outlook for the industry include the growing recovery in economic activity and consumer spending, and continuing growth in exports and investment. Environmental and health issues and the need for further technological advancement and quality improvement are among the challenges facing the industry.

The continuing recovery of the economy should lead to a pickup in consumer confidence. The decline in consumer debt is expected to level off, while new housing starts should gain momentum. These factors should lead to increases in consumer spending on apparel and fabricated textile products. Favorable demographic and technological trends also should help boost shipments.

During the next several years, the U.S. apparel marketplace will become even more competitive, with more overseas producers vying with U.S. manufacturers for shares of the market. More U.S. companies also are shifting assembly operations to other countries to lower their production costs. U.S. producers can use new technology to strengthen the industry's productivity, quality, flexibility,

TABLE 4 U.S. Trade Patterns in 1992 Apparel and Other Textile Products SIC 23 (*In millions of dollars, percent*)

	EXPORTS			IMPORTS	
	VALUE	SHARE		VALUE	SHARE
Canada and Mexico	1,427	30.9	Canada and Mexico	2,436	7.5
European Community	493	10.6	European Community	1,600	4.9
Japan	521	11.3	Japan	210	0.6
East Asia NICs	103	2.2	East Asia NICs	17,942	55.3
South America	198	4.3	South America	656	2.0
Other	1,883	40.7	Other	9,619	29.6
World Total	4,625	100.0	World Total	32,462	100.0

	TOP FIVE COUNTRIES				
	VALUE	SHARE		VALUE	SHARE
Mexico	943	20.4	China	5,447	16.8
Dominican Republic	570	12.3	Hong Kong	4,336	13.4
Japan	521	11.3	South Korea	2,728	8.4
Canada	484	10.5	Taiwan	2,539	7.8
Costa Rica	277	6.0	Mexico	1,945	6.0

Source: U.S. Department of Commerce: Bureau of the Census; International Trade Administration.

TABLE 5 U.S. Trade Patterns in 1992 Apparel SIC 231, 232, 233, 234, 235, 236, 237, 238 (*In millions of dollars, percent*)

	EXPORTS			IMPORTS	
	VALUE	SHARE		VALUE	SHARE
Canada and Mexico	909	24.4	Canada and Mexico	1,529	5.1
European Community	415	11.1	European Community	1,418	4.8
Japan	490	13.2	Japan	101	0.3
East Asia NICs	56	1.5	East Asia NICs	16,870	56.7
South America	153	4.1	South America	612	2.1
Other	1,701	45.7	Other	9,235	31.0
World Total	3,723	100.0	World Total	29,765	100.0

TOP FIVE COUNTRIES					
	VALUE	SHARE		VALUE	SHARE
Mexico	662	17.8	China	4,823	16.2
Dominican Republic	556	14.9	Hong Kong	4,301	14.4
Japan	490	13.2	South Korea	2,619	8.8
Costa Rica	275	7.4	Taiwan	2,302	7.7
Canada	247	6.6	Dominican Republican	1,233	4.1

Source: U.S. Department of Commerce: Bureau of the Census; International Trade Administration.

and response time, thereby becoming stronger competitors in the international area.

Exports will continue to provide a significant share of the growth in shipments of apparel products, even though U.S. firms will still encounter stiff challenges from foreign competitors. When major industrialized economies expand more rapidly, the favorably valued U.S. dollar should help companies increase sales abroad of quality U.S. goods. U.S. manufacturers should continue to take advantage of export opportunities in countries such as Japan, Canada, and Mexico, where trade barriers have been reduced. A successful conclusion to the NAFTA agreement should lead to increased opportunities south of the border, and may serve as a model for similar agreements with other Latin American countries. The increased economic integration of the European market is expected to benefit U.S. exporters by eliminating national barriers to trade. In addition, the economic and political reforms in Eastern Europe and the newly independent states of the former Soviet Union may create additional opportunities for U.S. exports and investment in the apparel sector.

W. L. GORE & ASSOCIATES, INC.—1994

FRANK SHIPPER
Salisbury State University
CHARLES MANZ
Arizona State University

On July 26, 1976, Jack Dougherty, a newly minted MBA from the College of William and Mary was bursting with resolve and dressed in a dark blue suit. This was his first day of work at W. L. Gore & Associates. He presented himself to Bill Gore, shook hands firmly, looked him in the eye, and said he was ready for anything. What happened next was one thing for which Jack was not ready. Gore replied, "That's fine, Jack, fine. Why don't you look around and find something you'd like to do." Three frustrating weeks later he found that something, a machine that laminates the company's patented GORE-TEX membrane to fabric. By 1982, Jack had become responsible for all advertising and marketing in the fabrics group. This story is part of the folklore that is heard over and over about Gore, a well-known company based in Newark, Delaware.

In 1994, the orientation process for new employees at Gore (302-738-4880) is slightly more structured. New Associates (employees) take a journey through the business as they settle into their positions, regardless of the specific position for which they are hired. (In this case, the word Associate is used and capitalized because in W. L. Gore & Associates' literature the word is always used instead of employees and is capitalized. In fact, the case writers were told that Gore "never had 'employees'— always 'Associates.' ") A new sales Associate in the Fabric Division may spend six weeks rotating through different areas before beginning to concentrate on sales and marketing. Among other things the new hire may learn is how GORE-TEX fabric is made, what it can and cannot do; how Gore handles customer complaints; and how it makes investment decisions.

Anita McBride related her first on-the-job experience at W. L. Gore & Associates in a similar way. She had previously worked for a structured organization. When she came to Phoenix, her sponsor said, "Well, here's your office—it's a wonderful office— and Here's your desk," and walked away. Anita thought, "Now what do I do."

> She continues: you know? I was waiting for a memo or something, or job description. Finally, after another month, I was so frustrated, I felt, "What have I gotten myself into?" And so I went to my sponsor and said "What the heck do you want from me? I need something from you." And he said, "If you don't know what you're supposed to do, examine your commitment and opportunities."

W. L. Gore is a loosely structured, privately-held company, with worldwide sales of about $950 million. Sales are derived from four divisions: 1) Gore-Tex Consumer and Technical Fabrics, 2) Electronic Products, 3) Medical Products, and 4) Industrial Products.

HISTORY

W. L. Gore & Associates is a company that evolved from the late Wilbert L. Gore's experiences personally, organizationally, and technically. He was born in Meridian, Idaho, near Boise in 1912. By age six, he had become an avid hiker in the Wasatch Mountain Range in Utah. In those mountains, at a church camp, he met Genevieve, his future wife. She is called Vieve by everyone. In 1935, they got married and became partners. He would make breakfast and she would make lunch. The partnership lasted a lifetime.

Wilbert, called Bill by everyone, received a bachelor of science degree in chemical engineering in 1933 and a masters of science in Physical Chemistry in 1935 from the University of Utah. He began his professional career at American Smelting and Refining in 1936. He moved to Remington Arms Company in 1941. He moved once again to E. I. DuPont de Nemours in 1945. He held positions as research supervisor and head of operations research. While at DuPont, he worked on a team to develop applications for polytetrafluoroethylene, frequently referred to as PTFE in the scientific community and known as "Teflon" by DuPont's consumers (it is known by consumers under other names from other companies). On this team, Bill felt a sense of excited commitment, personal fulfillment, and self-direction. He followed the development of computers and transistors and felt that PTFE had the ideal insulating characteristics for use with such equipment.

Bill tried a number of ways to make a PTFE-coated ribbon cable without success. A breakthrough came in his home basement laboratory. He was explaining the problem to his son, Bob. Bob saw some PTFE sealant tape made by 3M and asked his father, "Why don't you try this tape?" His father then explained to his son that everyone knows you cannot bond PTFE to itself. Bob went on to bed.

Bill Gore remained in his basement lab and proceeded to try what everyone knew would not work. At about 4 A.M., he woke up his son waving a small piece of cable around saying excitedly, "It works, it works." The following night, father and son returned to the basement lab to make ribbon cable coated with PTFE.

For the next four months, Bill Gore tried to persuade DuPont to make a new product—PTFE coated ribbon cable. After talking to a number of key decision-makers, it became clear that DuPont wanted to remain a supplier of raw materials and not a fabricator.

Bill began to discuss with his wife, Vieve, the possibility of starting their own insulated wire and cable business. On January 1, 1958, their wedding anniversary, they founded W. L. Gore & Associates, Inc. The basement of their home served as their first facility. After finishing dinner on their anniversary, Vieve turned to her husband of 23 years and said, "Well, let's clear up the dishes, go downstairs, and get to work." They viewed this as another partnership.

Bill Gore was 45 years old with five children to support when he left DuPont. He left behind a career of 17 years, and a good and secure salary. To finance the first two years of the business, the Gores mortgaged their house and took $4,000 from savings. All of their friends told them not to do it.

The first few years were rough. In lieu of salary, some of their employees accepted room and board in the Gore home. At one point, 11 Associates were living and working under one roof. The order, which was almost lost, that put the company on a profitable footing came from the City of Denver's water department. One afternoon, Vieve answered a phone call while sifting PTFE powder. The caller indicated that he was interested in the ribbon cable, but wanted to ask some technical questions. Bill was out running some errands. The caller asked for the product manager. Vieve explained that he was out at the moment. Next he asked for the sales manager and finally, the president. Vieve explained that they were also out. The caller became outraged and hollered, "What kind of company is this anyway?" With a little diplomacy, the Gores were able eventually to secure an order for $100,000. This order put the company over the hump and it began to take off.

W. L. Gore & Associates has continued to grow and develop new products primarily derived from PTFE, including their best known product, GORE-TEX fabric. GORE-TEX is a registered trademark of W. L. Gore & Associates. In 1986, Bill Gore died while backpacking in the Wind River Mountains of Wyoming. Until the time of his death, he had functioned as chairman. His son, Bob, assumed the presidency, a position he continues to occupy. Vieve remains as the only other officer, secretary-treasurer.

THE OPERATING COMPANY

W. L. Gore & Associates is a company without titles, hierarchy, or any of the conventional structures associated with enterprises of its size. The titles of president and secretary-treasurer are used only because they are required by the laws of incorporation. In addition, Gore's corporate mission is simply stated as "make money and have fun." When questioned about the absence of formal policies and a code of ethics typical of other corporations, an Associate states, "The company belief is that its four basic operating principles cover ethical practices required of people in business, and Gore will not tolerate illegal practices." Gore's management style has been referred to as un-management. The organization has been guided by Bill's experiences on teams at DuPont and has evolved through his study of how people view their full potential.

In 1965, W. L. Gore & Associates was a thriving and growing company with a facility on Paper Mill Road in Newark, Delaware, and about 200 Associates. One warm Monday morning in the summer, Bill Gore was taking his usual walk through the plant. All of a sudden, he realized that he did not know everyone in the plant. The team had become too big. As a result, the company instituted a policy that no facility will have over 150–200 Associates. Gore's expansion policy is "Get big by staying small." The purpose of maintaining small plants is to accentuate a close-knit and interpersonal atmosphere.

Today, W. L. Gore & Associates consists of 44 plants worldwide with over 5,860 Associates. In some cases, the plants are clustered together on the same site as in Flagstaff, Arizona, where four plants are located on the same site. Twenty-seven Gore plants are in the United States and 17 are overseas. Gore's overseas plants, located in Scotland, Germany, France, and Japan manufacture electronics, medical, industrial, and fabric products.

Gore electronic products are found in unconventional places where conventional products will not do. In space shuttles, for example, Gore microwave assemblies withstand the heat of ignition and the cold of space. In addition, Gore's signal transmission products are found in the world's fastest companies. Gore cables are underground, in oil drilling operations, and undersea, on submarines that require superior microwave signal equipment and no-fail cables that can survive high pressure. The Gore Electronic Products Division has a history of anticipating future customer needs with innovative products. Gore electronic products are well known in industries such as oil exploration and robotics for their ability to last under adverse conditions.

In the medical arena, GORE-TEX expanded PTFE is considered an ideal replacement for human tissue in many situations. In patients suffering from cardiovascular disease, the diseased portion of arteries is often replaced by tubes of expanded PTFE that are strong, biocompatible, and able to carry blood at arterial pressures. Gore has a dominant share in this market. Other Gore medical products include patches for soft tissue repairs such as aneurysms and hernias. GORE-TEX sutures allow for tissue attachment and offer the surgeon silklike handling coupled with extreme strength. In 1985, W. L. Gore & Associates, Inc., won Britain's Prince Philip Award for Polymers in the Service of Mankind. The award recognized especially the life-saving achievements of the Gore medical products team.

The industrial products division produces a number of products including sealants, filter bags, cartridges, clothes, and coatings. These products tend to have specialized and critical applications. Gore's reputation for quality appears to influence the industrial purchasers of these products.

The Gore Fabrics Division supplies laminates to licensed manufacturers of ski wear; running suits; footwear; gloves; hunting, fishing, golfing, and cycling garments; and foul-weather gear. Firefighters and U.S. Navy pilots wear GORE-TEX fabric gear as do some Olympic athletes. The U.S. Army has adopted a total garment system built around a GORE-TEX fabric component.

GORE-TEX membrane for fabric application has 9 billion pores randomly dotting each square inch and is feather light. Each pore is 700 times larger than a water vapor molecule, yet thousands of times smaller than a water droplet. Wind and water cannot penetrate the pores, but perspiration can escape. As a result, fabrics bonded with GORE-TEX membrane are waterproof, windproof, and breathable. The laminated fabrics bring protection from the elements to a variety of products—from survival gear to high-fashion rain wear. Recently, other manufacturers, including 3M, have brought out products to compete with GORE-TEX fabrics. Gore, however, continues to have a commanding share of this market.

Bill Gore knew that products alone do not make a company. He wanted to avoid smothering the company in thick layers of formal "management." He felt that they stifled individual creativity. As the company grew, he devised an innovative way to assist new Associates to get started and to guide their progress. This was seen as particularly important when it came to compensation. W. L. Gore & Associates has developed what they call their "sponsor" program to meet these needs. When people apply to Gore, they are initially screened by personnel specialists as in most companies. For those who meet the basic criteria, there are interviews with other Associates. Before anyone is hired, an Associate must agree to be their sponsor. The sponsor is to take a personal interest in the new Associate's contributions, problems, and goals. The sponsor is both a coach and an advocate. The sponsor guides the new associate's progress, helping and encouraging, dealing with weaknesses and concentrating on strengths. Sponsoring is not a short-term commitment. All Associates have sponsors and many have more than one. When individuals are hired initially, they will have a sponsor in their immediate work area. If they move to another area, they will have a sponsor in that work area.

Because the sponsoring program looks beyond conventional views of what makes a good Associate, some anomalies occur in the hiring practices. Bill Gore has proudly told the story of "a very young man" of 84 who walked in, applied, and spent five very good years with the company. The individual had 30 years of experience in the industry before joining Gore. His other Associates had no problems accepting him, but the personnel computer did. It insisted that his age was 48. The individual success stories at Gore come from diverse backgrounds.

An internal memo by Bill Gore described three kinds of sponsorship expected and how they might work as follows:

1. The sponsor who helps a new Associate *get started* on his job. Also, the sponsor who helps a present Associate get started on a new job (starting sponsor).

2. The sponsor who sees to it that the Associate being sponsored *gets credit* and recognition for contributions and accomplishments (advocate sponsor).

3. The sponsor who sees to it that the Associate being sponsored is *fairly paid* for contributions to the success of the enterprise (compensation sponsor).

A single sponsor can perform any one or all three kinds of sponsorship. A sponsor is a friend and an Associate. All the supportive aspects of the friendship are also present. Typically, two Associates advocate for each other.

In addition to the sponsor program, Gore Associates are asked to follow four guiding principles:

1. Try to be fair.
2. Use your freedom to grow.
3. Make your own commitments, and keep them.
4. Consult with other Associates prior to any action that may adversely affect the reputation or financial stability of the company.

The four principles are often referred to as fairness, freedom, commitment and waterline. The waterline terminology is drawn from an analogy to ships. If someone pokes a hole in a boat above the waterline, the boat will be in relatively little real danger. If someone, however, pokes a hole below the waterline, the boat is in immediate danger of sinking.

The operating principles were put to a test in 1978. By this time the word about the qualities of GORE-TEX fabric were being spread throughout the recreational and outdoor markets. Production and shipment had begun in volume. At first a few complaints were heard. Next, some of the clothing started coming back. Finally, much of the clothing was being returned. The trouble was that the GORE-TEX fabric was leaking. Waterproof was one of the two major properties responsible for GORE-TEX fabric's success. The company's reputation and credibility were on the line.

Peter W. Gilson who led Gore's fabric division says, "It was an incredible crisis for us at that point. We were really starting to attract attention; we were taking off—and then this." Peter and a number of his Associates in the next few months made a number of those below the waterline decisions.

First, the researchers determined that oils in human sweat were responsible for clogging the pores in the GORE-TEX fabric and altering the surface tension of the membrane. Thus, water could pass through. They also discovered that a good washing could restore the waterproof property. At first this solution known as the "Ivory Snow Solution" was accepted.

A single letter from "Butch," a mountain guide in the Sierras, changed the company's position. Butch wrote how he had been leading a group and, "My parka leaked and my life was in danger." As Gilson says, "That scared the hell out of us. Clearly our solution was no solution at all to someone on a mountain top." All of the products were recalled. As Gilson says, "We bought back, at our own expense, a fortune in pipeline material. Anything that was in the stores, at the manufacturers, or anywhere else in the pipeline."

In the meantime, Bob Gore and other Associates set out to develop a permanent fix. One month later, a second-generation GORE-TEX fabric had been developed. Gilson, furthermore, told dealers that if at any time a customer returned a leaky parka, they should replace it and bill the company. The replacement program alone cost Gore roughly $4 million.

ORGANIZATIONAL STRUCTURE

Bill Gore refers to the structure as a lattice organization, as portrayed in Exhibit 24–1. The characteristics of this structure are:

1. Direct lines of communication—person to person—with no intermediary
2. No fixed or assigned authority
3. Sponsors, not bosses

EXHIBIT 24-1 W. L. Gore's Lattice Structure

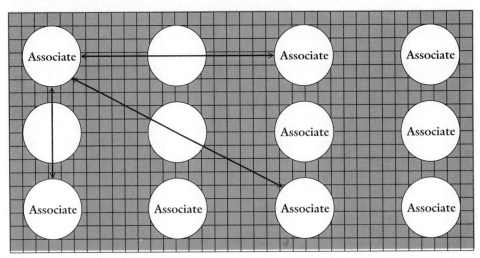

Source: W. L. Gore Associates.

4. Natural leadership defined by followership
5. Objectives set by those who must "make them happen"
6. Tasks and functions organized through commitments.

The structure within the lattice is described by the people at Gore as complex and evolves from interpersonal interactions, self-commitment to group-known responsibilities, natural leadership, and group-imposed discipline.

Bill Gore once explained this structure by saying, "Every successful organization has an underground lattice. It's where the news spreads like lightning, where people can go around the organization to get things done." Another description of what is occurring within the lattice structure is constant cross-area teams—the equivalent of quality circles going on all the time. When a puzzled interviewer told Bill that he was having trouble understanding how planning and accountability worked, Bill replied with a grin, "So am I. You ask me how it works—every which way."

One thing that might strike an outsider in the meetings and the other places in the Gore organization is the informality and amount of humor. Meetings tend to be only as long as necessary. Words such as "responsibilities" and "commitments," are, however, commonly heard. This in an organization that seems to take what it does very seriously, but its members do not take themselves too seriously.

Gore, for a company of its size, may have the shortest organizational pyramid. The pyramid consists of Bob Gore, son of co-founders Bill and Vieve Gore, as president and CEO and Vieve, Bill Gore's widow, as secretary-treasurer. All the other members of the Gore organization are referred to as Associates. Words such as "employees," "subordinates," and "managers" are taboo in the Gore culture.

Gore does not have managers, it has leaders. Bill Gore described in an internal memo the kinds of leadership and the role of leadership as follows:

1. The Associate who is recognized by a team as having a special knowledge, or experience (for example, this could be a chemist, computer expert, machine operator, salesman, engineer, lawyer). This kind of leader gives the team *guidance in a special area*.
2. The Associate the team looks to for coordination of individual activities in order to

achieve the agreed upon objectives of the team. The role of this leader is to persuade team members to *make the commitments* necessary for success (commitment seeker).

3. The Associate who proposes necessary objectives and activities and seeks agreement and team *consensus on objectives*. This leader is perceived by the team members as having a good grasp of how the objectives of the team fit in with the broad objective of the enterprise. This kind of leader is often also the "commitment seeking" leader in 2. above.

4. The leader who evaluates relative contribution of team members (in consultation with other sponsors), and reports these contribution evaluations to a compensation committee. This leader may also participate in the compensation committee on a relative contribution and pay and *reports changes in compensation* to individual Associates. This leader is then also a compensation sponsor.

5. The leader who coordinates the research, manufacturing, and marketing of one product type within a business, interacting with team leaders and individual Associates who have commitments regarding the product type. These leaders are usually called *product specialists*. They are respected for their knowledge and dedication to their product.

6. *Plant leaders* who help coordinate activities of people within a plant.

7. *Business leaders* who help coordinate activities of people in a business.

8. *Functional leaders* who help coordinate activities of people in a "functional" area.

9. *Corporate leaders* who help coordinate activities of people in different businesses and functions and who try to promote communication and cooperation among all Associates.

10. *Intrapreneuring Associates* who *organize new teams* for new businesses, new products, new processes, new devices, new marketing efforts, new or better methods of all kinds. These leaders invite other Associates to "sign up" for their project.

It is clear that leadership is widespread in our lattice organization and is continually changing and evolving. The fact that leaders are frequently *also* sponsors should not confuse the different activities and responsibilities.

Leaders are not authoritarians, managers of people, or supervisors who tell us what to do or forbid us doing things; nor are they "parents" to whom we transfer our own self-responsibility. However, they do often advise us of the consequences of actions we have done or propose to do. Our actions result in contributions, or lack of contributions, to the success of our enterprise. Our pay depends on the magnitude of our contributions. This is the basic discipline of our lattice organization.

Many other aspects of the company are arranged along egalitarian lines. The parking lot does not have reserved parking spaces except for customers and the handicapped. There is only one area in each plant in which to eat. The lunchroom in each new plant is designed to be a focal point for Associate interaction. As Dave McCarter of Phoenix explains, "The design is no accident. A lunchroom in Flagstaff has a fireplace in the middle. We want people to like being here." The locations of the plants are also no accident. Sites are selected based on transportation access, a nearby university, beautiful surroundings, and climate appeal. Land cost is never a primary consideration. McCarter justifies the selection by stating, "Expanding is not costly in the long-run. The loss of money occurs by stymieing people into a box."

Not all people function well under such a system, especially initially. For those accustomed to a more structured work environment, there are adjustment problems. As Bill Gore said, "All our lives, most of us have been told what to do, and some people don't know how to respond when asked to do something—and have the very real option of saying no—on their job. It's the new Associate's responsibility to find out what he or she can do for the good of the operation." The vast majority of the new Associates, after some initial floundering, adapt quickly.

For those who require more structured working conditions and cannot adapt, Gore's flexible work place is not for them. According to Bill, for those few, "It's an unhappy situation, both for the Associate and the sponsor. If there is no contribution, there is no paycheck."

As Anita McBride, an Associate in Arizona, says, "It's not for everybody. People ask me do we have turnover, and yes we do have turnover. What you're seeing looks like utopia, but it also looks extreme. If you finally figure the system, it can be real exciting. If you can't handle it, you gotta go. Probably by your own choice, because you're going to be so frustrated."

In rare cases, an Associate "is trying to be unfair," in Bill's own words. In one case, the problem was chronic absenteeism and in the other, the individual was caught stealing. "When that happens, all hell breaks loose," said Bill Gore. "We can get damned authoritarian when we have to."

In the early years, Gore & Associates has faced a number of unionization drives. The company neither tries to dissuade an Associate from attending an organizational meeting nor retaliate when flyers are passed out. Each attempt has been unsuccessful. None of the plants has been organized to date. Bill believed that no need existed for third-party representation under the lattice structure. He asked the question, "Why would Associates join a union when they own the company? It seems rather absurd." Overall, Associates appear to have responded positively to the Gore system of un-management and un-structure. Bill estimated the year before he died, 1985, that "The profit per Associate is double" that of DuPont.

The lattice structure is not without its critics. As Bill Gore stated, "I'm told from time to time that a lattice organization can't meet a crisis well because it takes too long to reach a consensus when there are no bosses. But this isn't true. Actually, a lattice, by its very nature works particularly well in a crises. A lot of useless effort is avoided because there is no rigid management hierarchy to conquer before you can attack a problem."

The lattice has been put to the test on a number of occasions. For example, in 1975, Dr. Charles Campbell, the University of Pittsburgh's senior resident, reported that a GORE-TEX arterial graft had developed an aneurysm. An aneurysm is a bubblelike protrusion that is life-threatening. If it continues to expand, it will explode. Obviously, this kind of problem has to be solved quickly and permanently.

Within only a few days of Dr. Campbell's first report, he flew to Newark to present his findings to Bill and Bob Gore and a few other Associates. The meeting lasted two hours. Dan Hubis, a former policeman, who had joined Gore to develop new production methods, had an idea before the meeting was over. He returned to his work area to try some different production techniques. After only three hours, a potentially damaging problem to both patients and the company was resolved. Furthermore, Hubis's redesigned graft has gone on to win widespread acceptance in the medical community. Today there are more than 3 million implants worldwide.

Other critics have been outsiders who had problems with the idea of no titles. Sarah Clifton, an Associate at the Flagstaff facility, was being pressed by some outsiders as to what her title was. She made one up and had it printed on some business cards—SUPREME COMMANDER. When Bill Gore learned what she did, he loved it and recounted the story to others.

Another critic, Eric Reynolds, founder of Marmot Mountain Works, Ltd., of Grand Junction, Colorado, and a major Gore customer, said "I think the lattice has its problems with the day-to-day nitty-gritty of getting things done on time and out the door. I don't think Bill realizes how the lattice system affects customers. I mean after you've established a relationship with someone about product quality, you can call up one day and suddenly find that someone new to you is handling your problem. It's frustrating to find a lack of continuity." He goes on to say, "But I have to admit that I've personally seen at Gore remarkable examples of people coming out of nowhere and excelling."

Bill Gore was asked a number of times if the lattice structure could be used by other companies. His answer was, "No. For example, established companies would find it very difficult to use the lattice. Too many hierarchies would be destroyed. When you remove titles and positions and allow people to follow who they want, it may very well be someone other than the person who has been in charge. The lattice works for us, but it's always evolving. You have to expect problems." He maintained that the lattice system works best when put in place in start-up companies by dynamic entrepreneurs.

RESEARCH AND DEVELOPMENT

Research and development, (R & D), like everything else at Gore, is unstructured. R & D takes place in teams in every business throughout the company. The company holds hundreds of patents, although most inventions are held as proprietary or trade secrets. Innovations come from Associates throughout the organization—managment, sales, R & D teams, and so forth. Bill Gore believed that all people had it within themselves to be creative.

The best way to understand how research and development works is to see how innovation has previously occurred at Gore. In 1969, the wire and cable division was facing increased competition. Bill Gore began to look for a way to straighten out the PTFE molecules. As he said, "I figured out that if we ever unfold those molecules, get them to stretch out straight, we'd have a tremendous new kind of material." He thought that if PTFE could be stretched, air could be introduced into its molecular structure. The result would be greater volume per pound of raw material without affecting performance. Thus, fabricating costs would be reduced and the profit margins would be increased. Going about this search in a scientific manner with his son, Bob, the Gores heated rods of PTFE to various temperatures and then slowly stretched them. Regardless of the temperature or how carefully they were stretched, the rods broke.

Working alone late one night in 1969 after countless failures, Bob, in frustration, yanked at one of the rods violently. To his surprise, it did not break. He tried it again and again with the same results.

The next morning Bob demonstrated his breakthrough to his father, but not without some drama. As Bill Gore recalled, "Bob wanted to surprise me, so he took a rod and stretched it slowly. Naturally, it broke. Then he pretended to get mad. He grabbed another rod and said, 'Oh the hell with this,' and gave it a pull. It didn't break—he'd done it." The new arrangement of molecules changed not only the wire and cable division, but led to the development of GORE-TEX fabric and what is now the largest division at Gore, plus a host of other products for medical, industrial, and electronic applications.

Initial field-testing of GORE-TEX fabric was conducted by Bill and Vieve in the summer of 1970. Vieve made a hand-sewn tent out of patches of GORE-TEX fabric. They took it on their annual camping trip to the Wind River Mountains in Wyoming. The very first night in the wilderness, they encountered a hail storm. The hail tore holes in the top of the tent, but the bottom filled up like a bathtub from the rain. As

Bill Gore stated, "At least we knew from all the water that the tent was waterproof. We just needed to make it stronger, so it could withstand hail."

The second largest division began on the ski slopes of Colorado. Bill was skiing with his friend Dr. Ben Eiseman of the Denver General Hospital. As Bill Gore told the story, "We were just to start a run when I absentmindedly pulled a small tubular section of GORE-TEX out of my pocket and looked at it. 'What is that stuff?' 'Got no idea.' I said. 'Well give it to me,' he said, 'and I'll try it in a vascular graft on a pig.' Two weeks later, he called me up. Ben was pretty excited. 'Bill,' he said 'I put it in a pig and it works. What do I do now?' I told him to get together with Pete Cooper in our Flagstaff plant and let them figure it out." Now hundreds of thousands of people throughout the world walk around with GORE-TEX vascular grafts.

Every Associate is encouraged to think, experiment, and follow a potentially profitable idea to its conclusion. For example, at a plant in Newark, Delaware, a machine that wraps thousands of feet of wire a day was designed by Fred L. Eldreth, an Associate with a third-grade education. The design was done over a weekend. Many other Associates have contributed their ideas through both product and process breakthroughs.

Without a research and development department, innovations and creativity work very well at Gore & Associates. The year before he died, Bill Gore claimed that "The creativity, the number of patent applications and innovative products is triple" that of DuPont.

ASSOCIATE DEVELOPMENT

As Ron Hill, an Associate in Newark, said, Gore "will work with Associates who want to advance themselves." Associates are offered many in-house training opportunities. They do tend to be technical and engineering focused because of the type of organization Gore is, but the company also offers in-house programs in leadership development. In addition, the company has cooperative programs with Associates to obtain training through universities and other outside providers. Gore will pick up most of the costs for the Associates. The emphasis in Associate development as in many parts of Gore is that the Associate must take the initiative.

PRODUCTS

Associates in four divisions organize themselves around opportunities in electronics, medical, industrial, and fabrics, as stated earlier. The Electronic Products Division produces cable assemblies and advanced materials for various demanding applications in aerospace, defense, computers, and telecommunications. Gore electronic and industrial application products have earned a reputation for unequaled reliability. Most of the wire and cable is used where conventional cables cannot operate. For example, Gore wire and cable assemblies were used in the space shuttle *Columbia* because they would stand the heat of ignition and the cold of space. Gore wire was used in the moon vehicle shuttle that scooped up samples of moon rocks and Gore's microwave coaxial assemblies have opened new horizons in microwave technology. Back on earth, the electronic wire products help make the world's fastest computers possible because electrical signals can travel through them at up to 93 percent of the speed of light. Because of the physical properties of the GORE-TEX material used in their construction, the electronic products are used extensively in defense systems, electronic switching for telephone systems, scientific and industrial instrumentation, microwave communications, and industrial robotics. Reliability is a watchword for all Gore products.

In medical products, reliability is literally a matter of life and death. GORE-TEX expanded PTFE is an ideal material used to repair the damage caused by cardiovascular disease. When human arteries are seriously damaged or plugged with deposits that interrupt the flow of blood, the diseased portions can often be replaced with GORE-TEX grafts. GORE-TEX vascular grafts and patches are not rejected by the body because the patient's own tissues grow into the graft's open porous spaces. GORE-TEX vascular grafts come in many sizes to restore circulation in nearly all areas of the body. They have saved limbs from amputation and saved lives. Some of the tiniest grafts relieve pulmonary problems in newborns. GORE-TEX expanded PTFE is also used to help people with kidney disease. Associates have developed a variety of surgical reinforcing membranes, known as GORE-TEX cardiovascular patches. Another medical product developed by Gore is a nonshredding dental floss.

Through the waterproof, breathable GORE-TEX fabrics division, Gore technology has traveled to the roof of the world on the backs of renowned mountaineers. GORE-TEX fabric is waterproof and windproof, yet breathable. Those features have qualified GORE-TEX fabric as essential gear for mountaineers and adventurers facing extremely harsh environments. The PTFE membrane blocks wind and water, but allows sweat to escape. That makes GORE-TEX fabric ideal for anyone who works or plays hard. Backpackers have discovered that a single lightweight GORE-TEX fabric shell will replace a poplin jacket and a rain suit, and dramatically out perform both. Skiers, sailors, runners, golfers, bicyclists, hunters, fishermen, and other outdoor enthusiasts have also become big customers of garments made of GORE-TEX fabric. General sportswear, as well as women's fashion footwear and handwear of GORE-TEX fabric, are as functional as they are beautiful. Boots and gloves, both for work and recreation, are waterproof and breathable thanks to GORE-TEX liners. GORE-TEX garments are even becoming standard items issued to many military personnel. Wetsuits, parkas, pants, headgear, gloves, and boots, keep the troops warm and dry in foul weather missions. Other demanding jobs also require the protection of GORE-TEX fabric because of its unique combination of chemical and physical properties.

The GORE-TEX fibers products, like the fabrics, end up in some pretty tough places. The outer protective layer of the NASA's spacesuit is woven from GORE-TEX fibers. They are impervious to sunlight, chemicals, heat, and cold. They are strong and uniquely resistant to abrasion.

Industrial filtration products, such as GORE-TEX filter bags, reduce air pollution and recover valuable solids from gases and liquids more completely than alternatives; they also do it more economically. They could make coal-burning plants virtually smoke free, contributing to a cleaner environment.

The Industrial Products Division also produces joint sealant, a flexible cord of porous PTFE that can be applied as a gasket to the harshest industrial applications, sealing them to prevent leakage of corrosive chemicals, even at extreme temperature and pressure. Steam valves packed with GORE-TEX valve stem packing are guaranteed for the life of the valve when used properly.

GORE-TEX microfiltration products are used in medical devices, pharmaceutical manufacturing, and chemical processing. These membranes remove bacteria and other microorganisms from air or liquids, making them sterile and bacteria free.

Compensation at W. L. Gore & Associates takes three forms—salary, profit-sharing, and an Associates' Stock Ownership Program (ASOP). Gore's ASOP is similar legally to an ESOP (Employee Stock Ownership Plan). Gore simply does not use the word "employee" in any of its documentation. Entry-level salary is in the middle for comparable jobs. According to Sally Gore, daughter-in-law of the founder, "We do not feel we need to be the highest paid. We never try to steal people away from other companies with salary. We want them to come here because of the opportunities for growth and the unique work environment." Associates' salaries are reviewed at least once a year and more commonly twice a year. The reviews are conducted by a compensation team for most workers in the facility in which they work. Their pay is proportional to their contributions to Gore's success. Positions do not have designated pay levels. Associates are ranked in relation to each other within similar job areas. The sponsors for all Associates act as their advocate during this review process. Prior to meeting with the compensation committee, the sponsor checks with customers or whoever uses the results of the person's work to find out what contribution has been made. In addition, the evaluation team will consider the Associate's leadership ability, willingness to help others to develop to their fullest.

Besides salaries, W. L. Gore & Associates has profit-sharing and ASOP plans for all Associates. Profit sharing typically occurs twice a year, but is dependent on profitability. The amount is also dependent on time in service and annual rate of pay. In addition, the firm buys company stock equivalent to 15 percent of the Associates' annual income and places it in an (ASOP) retirement fund. Thus, an Associate becomes a stockholder after being at Gore for one year. Bill wanted every Associate to feel that they themselves are the owners.

The principle of commitment is seen as a two-way street. W. L. Gore & Associates tries to avoid layoffs. The company uses a system of transfers as attrition within a plant or cluster of plants when faced with downsizing.

MARKETING STRATEGY

Gore's marketing strategy is based on making the determination that it can offer the best valued products to a marketplace, that people in that marketplace appreciate what it manufactures, and that Gore can become a leader in that area of expertise. The operating procedures used to implement the strategy follow the same principles as other functions at Gore.

First, the marketing of a product revolves around a leader who is referred to as a "product champion." According to Dave McCarter, "You marry your technology with the interests of your champions as you've got to have champions for all these things no matter what. And that's the key element within our company. Without a product champion you can't do much anyway, so it is individually driven. If you get a person interested in a particular market or a particular product for the marketplace, then there is no stopping them."

Second, a product champion is responsible for marketing the product through commitments with sales representatives. Again, according to Dave McCarter, "We have no quota system. Our marketing and our sales people make their own commitments as to what their forecasts are. There is no person sitting around telling them that that is not high enough, you have to increase it by 10 percent, or whatever somebody feels is necessary. You are expected to meet your commitment, which is your forecast, but nobody is going to tell you to change it. . . . There is no order of command, no chain involved. These are groups of independent people who come together to make unified commitments to do something and sometimes when they can't make those agreements . . . you may pass up a market place, but that's OK because there's much more advantage when the team decides to do something. . . ."

Third, the sales representatives are on salary. They are not on commission. They participate in the profit-sharing and ASOP plans in which all other Associates participate.

In the implementation of its marketing strategy, Gore relies on cooperative and word-of-mouth advertising. Cooperative advertising is especially used to promote GORE-TEX fabric products. Those products are sold through a number of clothing manufacturers and distributors, including Apparel Technologies, Lands End, Austin Reed, Timberland, Woolrich, North Face, Grandoe, and Michelle Jaffe. Gore engages in cooperative advertising because the Associates believe positive experiences with any one product will carry over to purchases of other and more GORE-TEX fabric products. Apparently, this strategy is paying off. Richard Zuckerwar, President of The Grandoe Corporation, said about his company's introduction of GORE-TEX gloves, "Sports activists have had the benefit of GORE-TEX gloves to protect their hands from the elements. . . . With this handsome collection of gloves . . . you can have warm, dry hands without sacrificing style."

The power of informal marketing techniques extends beyond consumer products. According to Dave McCarter, "In the technical end of the business, company reputation probably is most important. You have to have a good reputation with your company." He went on to say that without a good reputation, a company's products would not be considered seriously by many industrial customers. In other words, the sale is often made before the representative calls. Using its marketing strategies, Gore has been very successful in securing a market leadership position in a number of areas ranging from waterproof outdoor clothing to vascular grafts.

FINANCIAL INFORMATION

Gore is a closely held private corporation. Financial information is as closely guarded as proprietary information of products and processes.

According to Shanti Mehta, an Associate, Gore's return on assets and sales rank it among the top 10 percent of the Fortune 500 companies. According to another source, W. L. Gore & Associates is working just fine by any financial measure. It has had 33 straight years of profitability and positive return on equity. The compounded growth rate for revenues at W. L. Gore & Associates from 1969 to 1989 was over 18 percent discounted for inflation. In 1969, total sales were about $6 million and in 1989, $600 million. As illustrated in Exhibit 24–2, Gore's total sales for 1992 climbed to over $740 million. This growth has been financed without any debt.

CONCLUSION

Gore was founded on the principles of self-management, empowerment, and smallness. The principle that leaders are defined only by the presence of followers is observed whenever possible. Gore's culture allows leaders who have not been successful to be reabsorbed into the team with relatively little pain.

EXHIBIT 24-2 Growth of Gore's Sales vs. Growth of Gross Domestic Product

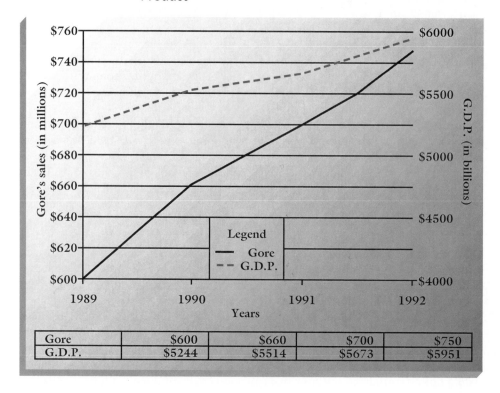

	1989	1990	1991	1992
Gore	$600	$660	$700	$750
G.D.P.	$5244	$5514	$5673	$5951

Gore is unique in many ways. To what extent could their uniqueness work effectively in other organizations? Which elements of Gore's uniqueness do you feel should be adopted by other companies?

BIBLIOGRAPHY

Aburdene, Patricia, and John Nasbitt. *Re-inventing the Corporation*. New York: Warner Books, 1985.

Angrist, S. W. "Classless Capitalist." *Forbes,* May 9, 1983, pp. 123–4.

Franlesca, L. "Dry and Cool." *Forbes,* August 27, 1984, p. 126.

Hoerr, J. "A company where everybody is the boss." *Business Week,* April 15, 1985, p. 98.

Levering, Robert. *The 100 Best Companies to Work for in America,* Chapter on W. L. Gore & Associates, Inc. Reading, MA: Addison-Wesley, 1984.

McKendrick, Joseph. "The Employees as Entrepreneur. " *Management World,* January 1985, pp. 12–13.

Milne, M. J. "The Gorey Details." *Management Review,* March 1985, pp. 16–17.

Posner, B. G. "The first day on the job." *Inc.,* June 1986, pp. 73–75.

Price, Kathy. "Firm Thrives Without Boss." *AZ Republic,* February 2, 1986.

Rhodes, Lucien. "The Un-manager." *Inc.,* August 1982, p. 34.

Simmons, J. "People Managing Themselves: Un-management at W. L. Gore Inc." *The Journal for Quality and Participation,* December 1987, pp. 14–19.

"The Future Workplace." *Management Review,* July 1986, p.22–23.

Trachtenberg, J. A. "Give Them Stormy Weather." *Forbes,* March 24, 1986, Vol. 137, No. 6, pp.172–174.

Ward, Alex. "An All-Weather Idea." *The New York Times Magazine,* November 10, 1985, Sec. 6.

Weber, Joseph. "No Bosses. And Even 'Leaders' Can't Give Orders." *Business Week,* December 10, 1990, pp. 196–197.

"Wilbert L. Gore." *Industry Week,* October 17, 1983, pp. 48–49.

NIKE INC.—1994

The athletic shoe industry has grown dramatically in the last several years, but experts predict that athletic shoe sales will increase only slightly in the next few years. Consumer trend watchers believe that the youth market now demands brands such as Tiva sandals and Doc Marten's work boots instead of branded athletic shoes. In addition, there is some evidence that consumers are purchasing casual shoes and moderately priced athletic shoes instead of branded athletic shoes. As a result, competition in an already competitive industry will become more intense. Headquartered in Beaverton, Oregon, Nike's (503-641-6453) CEO Philip Knight says media experts have tried to explain the athletic shoe industry in oversimplified terms:

> Although to some it may appear to be a simple industry, success within it is complicated by the huge human factor. The industry defies automation. It is not a single product model, nor a single manager, nor one ad, nor a single celebrity, not even a single innovation that is the key to Nike. It is the people and their unique and creative way of working together, that has brought our shareholders earnings increases of over $140 million during the last two years.

For the fiscal year 1993, revenues at Nike increased by 15 percent to $3.9 billion, and net income increased by 11 percent to $365 million. Philip Knight hopes to maintain his company's competitive advantage through the 1990s by marketing athletic shoes, clothing, and accessories around the world and by making a few acquisitions that will strengthen the company's core businesses. If Nike is to live up to its namesake "the goddess of victory," Knight and his team of workers will have to stay ahead of competitors in the marathon race for dominance in the athletic shoe industry.

HISTORY

Philip Knight, a dedicated long-distance runner, developed a plan to make low-cost running shoes in Japan and to sell them in the United States as part of his work toward an MBA degree at Stanford University. After graduation, Knight teamed up with Bill Bowerman, his former track coach at the University of Oregon to make his plan a reality. Since Bowerman's hobby was making handcrafted lightweight running shoes, his expertise was very valuable to entrepreneur Knight. In 1964, Bowerman and Knight each contributed $500 and started Blue Ribbon Sports. Knight negotiated with a Japanese athletic shoe manufacturer, Onitsuka Tiger Company, to manufacture the shoes that Bowerman had designed. Blue Ribbon Sports shoes gained a cult following among serious runners because Knight distributed the shoes, called Tigers, at track meets.

In 1971, Blue Ribbon Sports received a trademark on its Swoosh logo, and they introduced the brand name Nike that same year. Blue Ribbon Sports parted ways with Onitsuka Tiger in 1972 and contracted with other Asian manufacturers to produce the company's shoes. Blue Ribbon Sports officially changed its name to Nike in 1978. During the late 1970s and early 1980s, Nike researchers used their technological expertise to develop several types of athletic shoes that revolutionized the industry. The company became more and more successful every year with profits increasing steadily during this time.

In 1984, after five years of 44 percent annual growth, Nike missed the emerging market for aerobic shoes. The company had concentrated its efforts on an unsuccessful line of casual shoes. Reebok took the lead in the athletic shoe industry when it began selling large numbers of its fashion-oriented aerobic shoes to women.

Nike stock prices decreased by 60 percent in 1984 and between 1983 and 1985 profits declined by 80 percent. Some analysts suggested that the decreases in stock prices and profits were the fault of managers who became complacent after the firm's early success. During the early 1980s, Philip Knight focused his attention on international operations and left daily decision making to other managers. Other top managers switched from job to job and this led to poor coordination between the design, marketing, and production efforts of the company. An excess inventory of 22 million pairs of shoes in 1985 forced Nike to cut prices to reduce the inventory. This excess in inventory also caused Nike to release some of its manufacturing capability in the Far East. Much of this capacity was picked up by Reebok. After Nike lost the top spot in the industry, it had to lay off 350 employees in 1986.

Knight took several steps to try to reestablish Nike's dominance in the industry. He created small management teams to focus on narrow markets. He also put a stop to the job changing of top executives. New advertising campaigns were developed that stressed the technology of the shoes. Focus groups were used to determine customers' athletic shoe needs. The company also began to add touches of fashion, including color, to its many new products. All of these changes helped Nike regain a slight leadership position in the industry in 1988.

In 1988, Nike purchased New Hampshire-based Cole-Haan for $64 million. The subsidiary has several brand names including Country, Sporting, Classic, Bragano, and Cole-Haan. A new footwear category, Tensile Air was introduced in 1990. The Tensile Air is a dress shoe with the Nike air-cushioning system. Nike's casual footwear business grew 16 percent the following year, lead by Cole-Haan. Nike also acquired the Cole-Haan Accessories Company in 1990, a distributor of premium quality belts, braces, and small leather goods.

PRESENT CONDITIONS

Nike sells athletic shoes, accessories, and clothing for men, women, and children. The company's products are sold to approximately 15,000 retail accounts in the United States including department stores, footwear stores, and sporting goods stores. Nike also sells its products through independent distributors, licensees, and subsidiaries in 80 countries around the world. Nike passed the $1 billion sales mark in Europe in 1993 and had sales of $178 million in the Asia/Pacific Region in 1993. Distribution rights for Australia and New Zealand were acquired by Nike in 1992. Nike is also moving aggressively into Latin American countries. Domestic and international revenues for Nike are shown in Exhibit 25–1.

Nike has diversified its operations in several different ways in recent years. In 1990, Nike opened a retail store called NikeTown in Portland, Oregon. A second NikeTown was opened in 1992 in Chicago. Nike does not plan to become a major retail force, but believes that these stores help educate consumers about the breadth of Nike products. In addition, Nike began experimenting with the store-in-a-store concept when it opened its first Nike Concept Shop in Macy's Union Square in San Francisco in 1992. Nike acquired Tetra Plastics, the manufacturer of the plastic film in Nike's air sole shoes, in 1991 for $37.5 million. In 1993, Nike purchased a cap making company called Sports Specialties.

	1992	PERCENT CHANGE	1991	PERCENT CHANGE	1990	PERCENT CHANGE
Domestic footwear	$1,747,600	4	$1,676,400	22	$1,368,900	29
Domestic apparel	361,400	11	325,700	22	266,100	28
Other brands	161,900	16	139,400	16	120,500	26
Total United States	2,270,900	6	2,141,500	22	1,755,500	29
International footwear	867,500	33	651,700	76	369,400	32
International apparel	266,800	27	210,400	91	110,300	58
Total International	1,134,300	32	862,100	80	479,700	38
Total Nike	$3,405,200	13	$3,003,600	34	$2,235,200	31

Year Ended May 31

Source: Nike, Inc., Form 10–k, 1993.

COMPETITION

The athletic shoe industry has grown from $2 billion to almost $10 billion at whole-sale from 1985 to 1993. Nike, Reebok, Keds, and L.A. Gear are the top four sellers of athletic shoes in the United States. (See Exhibit 25–2.)

Some of the other two dozen competitors in the industry include Adidas, Puma, New Balance, K-Swiss, Kangaroo, Converse, and British Knights. The most intense competition has been among three of the industry leaders: Nike, L.A. Gear, and Reebok. The secret to success for these three competitors is that they contract for the manufacture of shoes to low-wage factories in Far East countries. This strategy allows each company to concentrate on marketing, image, and research and development.

Reebok International, Ltd. Reebok designs and develops athletic shoes and clothing worldwide. Reebok sells 175 models of shoes in 450 different color combinations for aerobics, tennis, fitness, running, basketball, cycling, volleyball, and walking. The company also owns Avia, a line of high performance athletic shoes. The company has diversified its offerings recently to include more types of casual shoes, sports clothing, and other types of athletic shoes. Some examples of these new products include Reebok Outdoor shoes, City Trails (women's hiking-style shoes), F-16 (men's leather casual shoes), BlackTop basketball shoes, and the Shaquille O'Neal shoe. In 1992, Reebok discontinued its Rockport, Boston Whaler, and Ellesse brands.

In the early 1980s, Reebok sold aerobic shoes primarily to women, but by the mid-1980s large numbers of men were buying Reebok shoes. Men now account for 45 percent of Reebok sales. The company's shoes are designed to make a fashion statement and are marketed to build on this image. Reebok CEO Paul Fireman believes that "Reebok is basically about freedom of expression." During 1992 Reebok opened three retail stores called Reebok Station with locations in Boston, Santa Monica, and New York City. Reebok has been successful in selling its

EXHIBIT 25-2 U.S. Branded Athletic Footwear Industry—Market Share

	1991	1992	1993(E)	1994(E)
Nike	29%	30%	32%	32%
Reebok	23	24	24	25
Keds	6	6	6	5
L.A. Gear	9	5	5	6
ASICS	3	4	5	6
Converse	3	4	4	5
Fila	1	3	3	3
Adidas	3	3	3	3
Avia	2	2	2	2
K-Swiss	2	2	2	2
Others (a)	19	17	14	11
Total U.S. Revenue (millions)	$5,789	$6,048	$6,050	$6,100
Percent change	4.8%	4.5%	0.0%	0.8%

(E) Estimate.

(a) Category includes over 15 companies with the largest single share equaling 1.9% in 1991 and 1.7% in 1992.

Source: Sporting Goods Intelligence (12/92); Kidder, Peabody & Co. Inc. estimates.

products to international markets. In 1992, foreign operations were 34 percent of total sales and 38 percent of net income. Selected financial information for Reebok is shown in Exhibit 25–3.

L.A. Gear, Inc. L.A. Gear markets athletic shoes, leisure shoes, casual clothing, and accessories (sport bags, hats, watches). The company was formed in 1983 and went public in 1986. The company's products are marketed on fashion, but they are manufactured to look like they offer technology. In just five years of operation, the company became the number three seller of athletic shoes in the United States. (Presently, L.A. Gear is the number four seller of athletic shoes in the United States.) Selected financial information for L.A. Gear is included in Exhibit 25–4.

International Competition. Competition is increasing in Europe. Adidas, a German company, is the number one seller of athletic shoes in Europe. Nike and Reebok are second and third, respectively. Nike had a 21 percent share and Reebok a 16 percent share of the international market in 1992. Analysts believe that doing well in the European market is crucial to the continued success of companies in the athletic shoe industry. Nike sales in the European, Asian, and Latin American markets increased 24 percent to about $1.4 billion in 1992 (36 percent of Nike's worldwide revenue). Reebok's total international revenues were about $1 billion. Both Nike and Reebok hope to continue increasing their revenues in the international retail market. Adidas and Puma, the two top European-owned competitors, will be fighting to maintain their share of the competitive market for athletic shoes.

EXHIBIT 25-3 Reebok selected financial information (In millions of dollars except per-share amounts)

	1989	1990	1991	1992	1993
Gross Revenues	1,822.1	2,159.2	2,734.5	3,943.5	2,915.2
Net Income	175.0	176.6	234.7	249.4	224.4
Long-term Debt	111.3	105.8	170.4	116.0	111.0
Return on Equity (%)	20.7	17.7	28.5	30.0	26.7
Net Profit Margin (%)	9.6	8.1	8.6	8.4	7.6
Earnings Per Share	1.53	1.54	2.37	2.69	2.55

Note: Reebok International (617-341-5000) is based in Stoughton, Massachusetts.

EXHIBIT 25-4 L.A. Gear selected financial information (In millions of dollars except per-share amounts)

	1990	1991	1992	1993
Gross Revenues	819.6	619.2	430.2	410.1
Net Income	25.6	(46.6)	(56.6)	(30.9)
Long-term Debt	0.0	0.0	0.0	0.0
Return on Equity (%)	12.4	(35.3)	(64.7)	(45.4)
Net Profit Margin (%)	3.1	(7.5)	(13.1)	(7.5)
Earnings Per Share	1.28	(2.40)	(2.67)	(1.34)

Note: L.A. Gear (310-822-1995) is based in Los Angeles, California.

CHANGES IN THE ATHLETIC SHOE INDUSTRY

The athletic shoe industry has changed tremendously since "sneakers" were invented. In 1873, the "sneaker" was developed from India rubber and canvas material. Dunlop became the dominant seller of sneakers in 1938. Keds and PF Fliers dominated the children's market in the 1960s. Adult standard brands such as Adidas and Converse were well accepted by sports enthusiasts for years. When Nike entered the market in the late 1960s, the industry changed forever. In addition to new competition, life-styles began to change and companies began to contract manufacturing rather than invest in plant and equipment to manufacture their own products.

Changes in Life-style. The primary buyers of athletic shoes are between the ages of fifteen and thirty-four. Since the late 1970s, these buyers have become much more brand conscious. In addition, athletic shoes have replaced other casual shoes as the primary street shoe for many consumers. Less than 10 percent of the people who wear athletic shoes buy them for the sport for which they were intended. Some trend watchers believe that athletic shoe companies will have some difficulty selling their products to the youth market in the next few years because of the youth demand shift to work boots and sandals.

Large numbers of baby boomers are interested in staying fit and healthy and have changed their diet and increased their physical activity. However, only one adult in five (aged 25–55) exercises as much as twice a week. In the 1980s, people became obsessed with fitness, and by 1991 sales in the fitness equipment industry exceeded $30 billion. Presently only 10 percent of the U.S. adult population gets the surgeon general's recommended amount of exercise (twenty minutes of vigorous exercise, three times per week).

The number of people aged forty-five and older is expected to increase by 18 million during the 1990s. The years forty-five to fifty-four are generally the peak earning and spending years for adults. As the baby boomers move into this age group, they will demand more attention from consumer goods companies.

Contract Manufacturing. Many athletic shoe companies contract with manufacturing companies in the Far East to produce their shoes. Some of the countries that manufacture shoes for Nike, L.A. Gear, and Reebok include South Korea, Taiwan, China, Thailand, Malaysia, and Indonesia. The athletic shoe companies develop design specifications and new technology for the shoes in the United States and then send these to the factory to be produced.

Even with recent changes in exchange rates in these countries and tariffs of 8.5 percent to 37.5 percent, it is still very cost effective to have shoes made overseas. A shoe that costs approximately $14 to make will be sold wholesale for $25 to $30.

The primary advantage of foreign contract manufacturing is that no capital investment is required and the athletic shoe companies can operate with very little long-term debt. There are also several disadvantages to contract manufacturing. Some countries, such as Korea, that have produced large numbers of athletic shoes in the past are developing the expertise and contacts to begin producing more sophisticated electronics products and do not have the available capacity to continue producing athletic shoes. Some additional disadvantages of overseas production include labor unrest, political unrest, delays caused by shipping, and unreliability of quota systems (embargos).

NIKE INTERNAL FACTORS

Four primary internal factors for Nike include: superior research and development efforts for the company's products, marketing expertise, social responsibility, and financial returns.

Nike Research and Development. Nike spent approximately $20 million on product research, development, and evaluation in 1992. This surprisingly low figure allows Nike to keep on the cutting edge in technology because R and D in the athletic shoe industry is largely design innovation and does not require a large investment in equipment.

In 1980, the company formed the Nike Sport Research Laboratory (NSRL), which uses video cameras and traction testing devices to research several types of concerns including children's foot morphology, "turf toe," and apparel aerodynamics. In addition, NSRL evaluates ideas that have been developed by the Advanced Product Engineering (APE) group. APE is involved in long-term product development. Shoes are created for five years in the future. This group developed cross-training shoes, the Nike Footbridge stability device, inflatable fit systems, and the Nike 180 air-cushioning system. Researchers make shoe molds in the model shop and evaluate the shoe tension and adhesion in the testing lab.

Nike continues to rely on superior technological developments to differentiate its products from competitors. The company presently sells approximately 300 models of athletic shoes in 900 styles for 24 different sports including basketball, tennis, cross-training, baseball, hiking, cycling, cheerleading, and windsurfing. Exhibit 25–5 indicates the major developments of Nike technology from 1964 to present.

Marketing. Since Nike does not actually produce shoes, the main focus of the company is creating and marketing the products. Nike positions its products as high-performance shoes designed with high-technology features. The general target market for Nike athletic shoes is males and females between eighteen and thirty-four years old.

Nike advertises its products in a variety of ways and targets its ads to specific groups or types of people. In 1992 Nike targeted women in its advertising for the first time since 1988. The "Instant Karma" ad campaign for women cost Nike approximately $12 million. Nike began a $20 million advertising campaign in Europe in 1993. The com-

EXHIBIT 25-5 Nike, Inc., Technological Developments

DATE	DEVELOPMENT	PURPOSE
1964	Lightweight shoe	Reduces weight for better performance
1975	"Waffle" sole shoe	High traction, lightweight
1979	Nike Air Sole	Air-cushioning system lessens the impact of the heel on pavement to prevent injuries
1987	Visible Air line (10 shoe models)	Gas-cushioning system prevents injury (window allows consumer to see the air bag)
	Cross-training shoe	Suitable for several different types of sports including running, baseball, and aerobics
1989	Air Pressure	Provides a tighter fit (pump shoe with a separate device to pump up the shoe)
1990	Air 180	Provides air-cushioning in heel and front of the shoe; heel cushion is 50 percent larger than previous models (consumer has a 180-degree view of the heel air bag)
	Built-in pump shoe	Provides a tighter fit, with the convenience of a built-in pump
1991	Huarache Fit Technology	Combination of neoprene and lycra spandex provides runners with a form-fitting, supportive, and lightweight shoe
1993	Air Max Cushioning technology	Provides 30 percent more cushioning

pany continues to spend advertising dollars on TV ads during professional and college sports events, prime time programs, and late night programs. Prime time ads are intended to reach a broad range of adults and late-night TV advertising is geared toward younger adults. Print media such as *Sports Illustrated, People, Runner's World, Glamour, Self, Tennis, Money, Bicycling,* and *Weight Watchers* are also very important in advertising Nike products. Nike has been successful in its attempts to build loyalty by licensing Nike gear to college sports teams. Some of the universities that made agreements to wear Nike gear during 1993 and 1994 include the University of Miami, Pennsylvania State University, University of Southern California, Florida State University, Duke University, University of Michigan, and University of Nevada-Las Vegas.

Some of the celebrity spokespersons for Nike include Michael Jordan, Andre Agassi, and Bo Jackson. Michael Jordan's Nike contract, to market the Air Jordan basketball shoe, is the most lucrative endorsement contract in sports. Agassi receives $2 million per year to endorse Nike athletic shoes and apparel, including the Challenge Court tennis shoe. Jackson is featured in Nike's cross-training advertisements. Several popular advertising campaigns are listed in Exhibit 25–6.

Nike opened a new 630,000 square foot apparel distribution center in Memphis in 1992 that is called Nike Next Day. Footwear is distributed from centers in Greenland, New Hampshire; Beaverton, Oregon; Wilsonville, Oregon; Yarmouth, Maine; and Memphis, Tennessee. The company operates a "Futures" ordering program that allows retailers to order up to six months in advance with a guarantee to receive their orders within a certain time period and at a certain price. However, retailers can receive apparel orders the next day if they place their orders by 7 PM the day before.

EXHIBIT 25-6 Nike, Inc., Advertisements

THEME	VISUAL IMAGE
"Hangtime"	Air Jordan basketball shoe is promoted featuring Michael Jordan and Spike Lee.
"Bo Knows"	The range of Nike shoes (20 different sport categories) is illustrated.
"Just Do It"	People from many walks of life are shown exercising in Nike shoes.
"Multiple Bo's"	Bo Jackson meets Sonny Bono and fourteen other Bo Jacksons who represent different sports.
"Announcers"	TV sports announcers discuss Nike shoe performance and breadth of product line. (Super Bowl XXIV)
"Rock and Roll Tennis"	Andre Agassi shows his tennis skills in rock-video format.
"Instant Karma"	Print campaign targets women.
"I am not a role model"	Charles Barkley says sports stars are not role models, but parents should be role models.
"Aerospace Jordan"	Cartoon character Bugs Bunny, Looney Tunes bad guy Marvin Martin, and Michael Jordan travel to Mars. (Super Bowl XXVII)
"Running," "Go Slow," "Aerobics"	A series of three TV ads for women stressing comfort and developing a sense of self.

Social Responsibility. Nike has received some criticism in the past few years regarding the contracting of the manufacturing of its shoes. Some consumers are concerned about the exploitive practices of managers in some Asian countries. A reporter for the *Portland Oregonian* stated that 6,700 Indonesian employees work in a plant where the temperature is 100 degrees and paint and glue smells are suffocating. To emphasize their concerns about companies that manufacture products overseas, the Made in America Foundation urged consumers to send their "old, dirty, smelly, worn-out Nikes" to Philip Knight, the Nike CEO. Operation PUSH (a Chicago civil rights organization) organized a boycott of Nike in 1990 in an attempt to force the company to increase its hiring of minorities.

Nike has developed several programs that show the company's concern about social responsibility issues. For example, Nike and the Boys and Girls Clubs of America began a program called the Kids Movement in 1993 to promote fitness among young people. Nike also provides funds for the Children's Television Workshop program *Ghostwriter,* a show that promotes literacy. The "Just Do It" corporate giving program provides funding for programs for young people who live in the inner-city. In addition to these programs, Nike demonstrates its concern for the environment by using recycled materials in the soles of its Air Escape outdoor shoe and plans to expand the technology to its entire shoe line.

Finance/Accounting. Nike, Inc., income statements and balance sheets for 1991 to 1993 are provided in Exhibits 25–7 and 25–8, respectively. These statements reveal increases for sales, income, assets, and shareholders' equity. Consolidated statements

EXHIBIT 25-7 NIKE, Inc., Consolidated Statement of Income *(In thousands, except per-share data)*

	YEAR ENDED MAY 31,		
	1993	1992	1991
Revenues	$3,930,984	$3,405,211	$3,003,610
Costs and expenses:			
Cost of sales	2,386,993	2,089,089	1,850,530
Selling and administrative	922,261	761,498	664,061
Interest	25,739	30,665	27,316
Other expense (income)	1,475	2,141	(43)
	3,336,468	2,883,393	2,541,864
Income before income taxes	594,516	521,818	461,746
Income taxes	229,500	192,600	174,700
Net income	$ 365,016	$ 329,218	$ 287,046
Net income per common share	$ 4.74	$ 4.30	$ 3.77
Average number of common and common equivalent shares	77,063	76,602	76,067

Source: Nike, Inc., *Annual Report,* 1993.

EXHIBIT 25-8 NIKE, Inc., Consolidated Balance Sheet *(In thousands of dollars)*

	YEAR ENDED MAY 31,		
	1993	1992	1991
ASSETS			
Current Assets:			
Cash and equivalents	$ 291,284	$ 260,050	$ 119,804
Accounts receivable, less allowance for doubtful accounts of $19,447, $20,046 and $14,288	667,547	596,018	521,588
Inventories	592,986	471,202	586,594
Deferred income taxes	26,378	27,511	25,536
Prepaid expenses	42,452	32,977	26,738
Total current assets	1,620,647	1,387,758	1,280,260
Property, plant and equipment	571,032	497,795	397,601
Less accumulated depreciation	193,037	151,758	105,138
	377,995	346,037	292,463
Goodwill	157,894	110,363	114,710
Other assets	30,927	28,703	20,997
	$2,187,463	$1,872,861	$1,708,430
LIABILITIES AND SHAREHOLDERS' EQUITY			
Current Liabilities:			
Current portion of long-term debt	$ 52,985	$ 3,652	$ 580
Notes payable	108,165	105,696	300,364
Accounts payable	135,701	134,729	165,912
Accrued liabilities	138,563	134,089	102,088
Income taxes payable	17,150	42,422	45,792
Total current liabilities	452,564	420,588	614,736
Long-term debt	15,033	69,476	29,992
Non-current deferred income taxes	29,965	27,074	30,613
Other non-current liabilities	43,575	23,728	
Commitments and contingencies	—	—	—
Redeemable Preferred Stock	300	300	300
Shareholders' equity:			
Common Stock at stated value:			
Class A convertible—26,691, 26,919 and 27,438 shares outstanding	159	161	164
Class B—49,161, 48,591 and 47,858 shares outstanding	2,720	2,716	2,712
Capital in excess of stated value	108,451	93,799	84,681
Foreign currency translation adjustment	(7,790)	686	(4,428)
Retained earnings	1,542,486	1,234,333	949,660
	1,646,026	1,331,695	1,032,789
	$2,187,463	$1,872,861	$1,708,430

Source: Nike, Inc. *Annual Report,* 1992, 1993.

of Nike shareholders' equity and cash flow are shown in Exhibits 25–9 and 25–10 respectively; Exhibit 25–11 presents revenue data for 1991 to 1993.

FUTURE OUTLOOK

Even with limited growth and intense competition in the U.S. athletic shoe market, Nike is expected to perform well in the future. With its innovative marketing and advertising, it should remain a force in the industry. However, there is concern in the industry that consumers will become less brand loyal and begin purchasing moderately priced athletic shoes at discount stores instead of the higher priced Nike products. According to Philip Knight,

> Brands are powerful when they communicate underlying value. In our industry, and probably in other consumer products, consumers will not trade down if there is value and quality in the high end.

There is a tremendous opportunity in the international market for Nike. "In the United States, there are four people for every pair of Nikes; France has 11, Japan 50, and China 11,821. That's a lot of Air Jordans waiting to be sold."[1] The greatest potential growth area for Nike is in the overseas market. It seems that Nike truly lives by the credo they created—"Just Do It."

Consider the following questions regarding Nike's future:

1. Should Nike narrow its product line in athletic shoes?
2. What types of acquisitions would you suggest to Philip Knight for Nike?
3. Should Nike begin producing some of its own products?
4. How should Nike market its shoes internationally? Where?
5. What changes in product and advertising should the company pursue to appeal to the aging baby boomers?
6. How can Nike maintain a competitive advantage over L.A. Gear, Reebok, and Keds?

NOTES

1. Yang, Dori Jones, "Nike's New Trends," *Business Week*, p. 38.

BIBLIOGRAPHY

Arthur, Charles. "Fashions's Fancy Footwork." *Business*, July, 1990, pp. 86–88.

Benoit, Ellen. "Lost Youth." *Financial World*, September 20, 1988, pp. 28–31.

Clay, Bobby. "It is the Shoes." *Black Enterprise*, March 1993, pp. 82–86.

Gill, Penny. "Stores Let Shoes Shine." *Stores*, August 1992, p. 48.

Gould, Les. "How Nike Guarantees Next-Day Delivery to All Its Customers." *Modern Materials Management*, September 1992, pp. 53–55.

Lippert, Barbara. "Defining Women." *Adweek*, March 1, 1993, p. 28.

Lippert, Barbara. "Speed Freaks." *Adweek*, February, 1, 1993, p. 22.

"Nike." *Business and Society Review*, Winter 1993, p. 77.

Ostroff, Jeff. "Targeting the Prime-Life." *American Demographics*, January 1991, pp. 30–52.

Schnorbus, Paula. "Running On Air." *Marketing & Media Decisions*, March 1988, pp. 55–58.

"Where Nike and Reebok Have Plenty of Running Room." *Business Week*, March 11, 1991, pp. 56–60.

Yang, Dori Jones. "Nike's New Trends." *Business Week*, October 4, 1993, p. 38.

EXHIBIT 25-9 NIKE, Inc., Consolidated Statement of Shareholders' Equity *(In thousands of dollars)*

	Common Stock				Capital In Excess Of Stated Value	Foreign Currency Translation Adjustment	Retained Earnings	Total
	Class A		Class B					
	Shares	Amount	Shares	Amount				
Balance at May 31, 1990	14,051	$168	23,435	$2,706	$78,582	$ 1,035	$701,728	$784,219
Stock options exercised			276	2	6,099			6,101
Conversion to Class B Common Stock	(393)	(4)	393	4				—
Two-for-one Stock Split October 5, 1990	13,780	—	23,754	—				—
Translation of statements of foreign operations						(5,463)		(5,463)
Net income							287,046	287,046
Dividends on Redeemable Preferred Stock							(30)	(30)
Dividends on Common Stock							(39,084)	(39,084)
Balance at May 31, 1991	27,438	164	47,858	2,712	84,681	(4,428)	949,660	1,032,789
Stock options exercised			214	1	9,118			9,119
Conversion to Class B Common Stock	(519)	(3)	519	3				—

EXHIBIT 25-9 *Continued*

	Common Stock				Capital In Excess Of Stated Value	Foreign Currency Translation Adjustment	Retained Earnings	Total
	Class A		Class B					
	Shares	Amount	Shares	Amount				
Translation of statements of foreign operations						5,114		5,114
Net income							329,218	329,218
Dividends on Redeemable Preferred Stock							(30)	(30)
Dividends on Common Stock							(44,515)	(44,515)
Balance at May 31, 1992	26,919	161	48,591	2,716	93,799	686	1,234,333	1,331,695
Stock options exercised			342	2	14,652			14,654
Conversion to Class B Common Stock	(228)	(2)	228	2				—
Translation of statements of foreign operations						(8,476)		(8,476)
Net income							365,016	365,016
Dividends on Redeemable Preferred Stock							(30)	(30)
Dividends on Common Stock							(56,833)	(56,833)
Balance at May 31, 1993	26,691	$159	49,161	$2,720	$108,451	$ (7,790)	$1,542,486	$1,646,026

Source: Nike, Inc., *Annual Report*, 1993.

EXHIBIT 25-10 NIKE, Inc., Consolidated Statement of Cash Flows *(In thousands of dollars)*

Year Ended May 31,	1993	1992	1991
Cash provided (used) by operations:			
Net income	$365,016	$329,218	$287,046
Income charges (credits) not affecting cash:			
Depreciation	60,393	47,665	34,473
Deferred income taxes and purchased tax benefits	4,310	8,222	(2,668)
Other non-current liabilities	19,847	9,992	4,769
Other, including amortization	12,951	9,355	5,626
Changes in certain working capital components:			
(Increase) decrease in inventory	(97,471)	115,392	(274,966)
Increase in accounts receivable	(62,538)	(74,430)	(119,958)
Increase in other current assets	(5,133)	(6,239)	(6,261)
(Decrease) increase in accounts payable,			
accrued liabilities and income taxes payable	(32,083)	(3,337)	83,061
Cash provided by operations	265,292	435,838	11,122
Cash provided (used) by investing activities:			
Additions to property; plant and equipment	(97,041)	(106,492)	(164,843)
Disposals of property, plant and equipment	5,006	4,065	1,730
Acquisition of subsidiaries:			
Goodwill	(52,003)	—	(31,482)
Net assets acquired	(25,858)	—	(6,081)
Additions to other non-current assets	(3,036)	(7,494)	(10,511)
Cash used by investing activities	(172,932)	(109,921)	(211,187)
Cash provided (used) by financing activities:			
Additions to long-term debt	1,536	45,901	5,149
Reductions in long-term debt including current portion	(5,817)	(3,467)	(9,974)
(Decrease) increase in notes payable	(2,017)	(194,668)	269,262
Proceeds from exercise of options	7,055	4,159	3,211
Dividends—common and preferred	(53,017)	(43,760)	(36,070)
Cash (used) provided by financing activities	(52,260)	(191,835)	231,578
Effect of exchange rate changes on cash	(8,866)	6,164	(2,158)
Net increase in cash and equivalents	31,234	140,246	29,355
Cash and equivalents, beginning of year	260,050	119,804	90,449
Cash and equivalents, end of year	$291,284	$260,050	$119,804
Supplemental disclosure of cash flow information:			
Cash paid during the year for:			
Interest (net of amount capitalized)	$ 20,800	$29,200	$ 27,200
Income taxes	235,200	184,100	159,900

Source: Nike, Inc., *Annual Report,* 1993.

EXHIBIT 25-11 Nike, Inc., Revenue and Assets by Geographic Areas *(In thousands of dollars)*

YEAR ENDED MAY 31,	1993	1992	1991
Revenues from unrelated entities:			
United States	$2,528,848	$2,270,880	$2,141,461
Europe	1,085,683	919,763	664,747
Other international	316,453	214,568	197,402
	$3,930,984	$3,405,211	$3,003,610
Inter-geographic revenues:			
United States	$ 3,583	$ 7,265	$ 9,111
Europe	—	—	—
Other international	9,350	9,076	11,892
	$ 12,933	$ 16,341	$ 21,003
Total revenues:			
United States	$2,532,431	$2,278,145	$2,150,572
Europe	1,085,683	919,763	664,747
Other international	325,803	223,644	209,294
Less inter-geographic revenues	(12,933)	(16,341)	(21,003)
	$3,930,984	$3,405,211	$3,003,610
Operating income:			
United States	$ 401,096	$ 356,589	$ 325,257
Europe	177,716	173,175	134,069
Other international	65,236	51,602	51,745
Less corporate, interest and other income			
(expense) and eliminations	(49,532)	(59,548)	(49,325)
	$ 594,516	$521,818	$ 461,746
Assets:			
United States	$1,347,507	$1,095,180	$1,156,091
Europe	429,660	453,794	370,104
Other international	128,080	79,862	94,212
Total identifiable assets	1,905,247	1,628,836	1,620,407
Corporate cash and eliminations	282,216	244,025	88,023
Total assets	$2,187,463	$1,872,861	$1,708,430

Source: Nike, Inc., *Annual Report*, 1993.

VALERIE PORIELLO,
ALLAN HOFFMAN,
BARBARA GOTTFRIED
Bentley College

"Rykä has a great story to tell. We are the only athletic footwear company that is exclusively for women, by women, and now supporting women."—Sheri Poe

It was the day after Christmas 1990 when Sheri Poe, president and chief executive officer of Rykä Inc. (617-762-9900), knew she was on the verge of the marketing break she'd been waiting for. Poe had sent several free pairs of Rykä athletic shoes to Oprah Winfrey. Now Poe was going to be featured as a successful female entrepreneur on Winfrey's popular talk-show, with a television viewing audience numbering in the tens of millions—almost entirely women. Rykä's new line of Ultra-Lite aerobic shoes had just begun to penetrate the retail market. Poe could not have planned for a better advertising spot than Winfrey tossing pairs of Rykä shoes into the studio audience exclaiming, "Can you believe how light these are?"

After the "Oprah" broadcast, the Ultra-Lite line became an overnight success. Lady Footlocker immediately put the Ultra-Lite shoe line in 200 stores, up from the 50 that had been carrying Rykä's regular line of athletic shoes. Retailers were swamped by consumer requests for Rykä products, and the sharp upturn in consumer demand quickly exhausted their inventories. It took Poe over three months to catch up with the orders. Many industry analysts believe that the shot in the arm provided by the Ultra-Lite sales literally saved the company.

Based in Norwood, Massachusetts, Rykä Inc. designs, develops, and markets athletic footwear for women, including aerobic, aerobic/step, cross-training, walk-run, and walking shoes. The company's products are sold all over the world in sporting goods, athletic footwear specialty, and department stores. As a new entrant in the highly competitive athletic footwear industry, the fledgling Rykä Corporation had no choice but to rely on low-budget "guerrilla marketing" tactics such as the "Oprah" show appearance. Since that time, however, Rykä has turned to more traditional marketing techniques such as radio and glossy magazine advertising. Rykä print ads appear regularly in *City Sports, Shape, American Fitness, Elle,* and *IDEA Today;* magazines that particularly target women aged 21-35, who care not just about how they look, but are serious about physical fitness.

Rykä today is a company in financial trouble. Net profits have been negative for the last several years. Perhaps a new mission is needed. Rykä's current mission statement is given below:

Rykä shoes are made for top performance. You'll find that Rykä shoes will help you look good and feel great, no matter how demanding your fitness program.

Rykä shoes are designed, engineered, and manufactured by women for women. Because a woman's needs in a comfortable, attractive, high-performance athletic shoe are different from a man's.

As you lace up for your first workout in your new Rykä shoes, you'll feel the difference. With every pair of Rykä shoes goes the positive energy of women who believe in other women.

Step forward with confidence, and be your best.

Rykä was organized in 1987, when it commenced operations. The company was cofounded by Martin P. Birrittella and his wife, Sheri Poe. Prior to founding Rykä, Birrittella had worked at Matrix International Industries as a vice president of sales and marketing from 1980 to 1986. At Matrix, he was responsible for developing and marketing footwear and health and fitness products, and has two patents pending for shoe designs that have been assigned to Matrix. From 1982 to 1985, Sheri Poe was national sales manager for Matrix. She then moved to TMC Group, a $15-million giftware maker based in New Hampshire, where she was national accounts manager from May 1986 to June 1987.

Sheri Poe is one of only two women CEOs in the state of Massachusetts. Poe admits being an exercise fanatic who really knew nothing about making athletic shoes when she cofounded Rykä. In 1986, Poe had injured her back in an aerobics class and was convinced that the injury had been caused by her shoes, which had never fit properly. After an exhaustive search for footwear that would not stress her body, Poe realized that many other women were probably having the same trouble as she was finding a shoe that really fit and decided to start her own women's athletic footwear company. She believed that rather than adapting men's athletic shoes for women, Rykä should design athletic shoes especially suited for women's feet and bodies. Rykä introduced its first two styles of athletic shoes in 1987 and began shipping the shoes a year later.

Poe had considerable difficulty obtaining venture capital to start a women's athletic shoe company. Potential investors questioned her ability to compete with industry leaders such as Nike and Reebok, given that she had no money and no retail experience—then turned down her requests for loans. Ironically, some of those same venture capitalists now call Poe to ask how they can get in on her $8 million business.

Since she couldn't get anything out of the venture capitalists, Poe leveraged her own house, then turned to family and friends to help finance the company. She also continued to search for more open-minded commercial investors and eventually discovered a Denver investment banker who was willing to do an initial public offering. Poe got a $250,000 bridge loan before the initial public offering—which happened to be about the time the stock market crashed in October 1987. Nevertheless, Rykä went public on April 15, 1988, and despite the unstable market, four million shares in the company were sold at one dollar each in less than a week. The Denver firm completed a second offering before failing. Poe then turned to Paulson Capital Corporation in Oregon for a third offering in 1990.

Sheri Poe believes that by having a woman president Rykä inspires other women to buy the company's products. As she points out, "we're the only company that can tell women that the person running the company is a woman who works out every day." Even Nike doesn't have a woman making all of its product decisions. Poe's image and profile is the most critical component in Rykä's marketing strategy. Rather than using professional models, Rykä's print advertisements feature Poe working out; and in the company's recent venture into television advertising spots, Poe is the company spokesperson. The caption on a recent ad for Rykä's 900-series aerobic shoes reads, "Our president knows that if you huff and puff, jump up and down, and throw your weight around you eventually get what you want," cleverly referring to Poe's own determination to succeed, and including her audience as coconspirators who know how hard it is for a woman to make it in the business world because they have "been there" themselves.

As part of Rykä's unique marketing strategy, Poe appears on regional television and radio shows throughout the country and has been interviewed by numerous magazines and newspapers. Feature articles on Poe and Rykä have appeared in *Entrepreneurial Woman*, *Executive Female*, and *Working Woman*. Poe has successfully worked the woman angle: she particularly appeals to today's working women because although she has become something of a celebrity, she considers herself a down-to-earth woman who also happens to be a successful executive, and a (divorced, and now remarried) mother. A *Boston Business Journal* article describes her as a CEO whose title "does not cramp [her] style. . . she eschews power suits for miniskirts and jeans, drives herself to work, and lets calls from her kids interrupt her meetings."

THE ATHLETIC FOOTWEAR INDUSTRY

The $11 billion athletic footwear industry is highly competitive. Three major firms control the market: Nike, Reebok, and L.A. Gear. Second string competitors include Adidas, Avia, Asics, and Converse. All of these companies have greater financial strength and more resources than Rykä. While Rykä's sales were $12.1 million in 1992, Nike's were $3.4 billion, Reebok's $3.0 billion, and L.A. Gear's $430 million.

Annual growth in the athletic footwear market has shrunk to approximately 4 percent and it is considered a mature market. Despite the subdued growth characteristics of the overall industry, however, a number of its submarkets are expanding via high specialization, technological innovation, and image and fashion appeal.

Product Specialization. The athletic footwear industry is divided into various submarkets by specialization. Product use categories include: basketball, tennis, running, aerobic, cross-training, walking, etc. Rykä competes only in the latter three markets: aerobic, walking, and cross-training shoes.

Aerobic Segment. The aerobic segment of the athletic shoe industry accounts for approximately $500 million in annual sales. Reebok pioneered the segment and continues to be the industry leader. The market is made up primarily of women and has grown rapidly in recent years. Rykä's number one market is aerobics; 80 percent of Rykä's sales are from the Ultra-Lite and step aerobic lines.

Walking Segment. The second major market Rykä competes in is the walking segment. This high-growth market is now the fourth largest product category in the athletic shoe industry. More than 70 million people walk for exercise and spend $2 billion annually on footwear. Reebok leads this market and is concentrating its marketing efforts on young women. Nevertheless, while the male and younger female walking markets have experienced some growth, the walking segment is primarily focused on women 45–55 years old. Ten percent of Rykä's sales are derived from its Series 500 walking shoe and the company expects the walking shoe segment to be its greatest growth category.

Cross-Training Segment. Rykä also competes in the cross-training segment of the athletic shoe market. Cross-training shoes are popular because they can be used for a variety of activities. Nike created this segment and maintains the lead in market share. Overall sales for the segment are currently at $1.2 billion, and growth is strong. Rykä earns 10 percent of its revenues from its cross-training shoes.

Technological Innovation. Reebok and Nike are fast moving toward the goal of identifying themselves as the most technologically advanced producers of performance shoes. Rykä understands that it must keep up with research and development to survive. Rykä has introduced its nitrogen footwear system, Nitrogen/ES—the "ES" stands for Energy Spheres. The system was developed over a two-year period by a design team with over 35 patents in shoe design and state-of-the-art composite plastics. The idea is that the ES ambient air compression spheres contain nitrogen microballoons that provide significantly more energy return than the systems of any of Rykä's major competitors. Consumer response to the Nitrogen/ES shoe was overwhelming, so Rykä has discontinued sales of a number of models that did not include this special feature.

Two patents were filed for the Nitrogen/ES System. One has been granted; the other is pending. Although patents are intended to provide legal protection, the cost of defending patents can be quite high. With the vast resources available to Rykä's competition, it would be easy for Reebok or Nike to adopt Rykä's technology at little or no risk of an infringement suit. Rykä's limited financial resources would disable them from enforcing their rights in an infringement action.

Fashion. Rykä has focused on performance rather than fashion because Poe believes that fashion-athletic footwear is susceptible to trends and the economy, but performance shoes will not be affected because women always need to protect their bodies. Nevertheless, a large segment of athletic footwear consumers purchase products based on looks rather than function. In fact, the fashion market is a mainstay of Rykä's major competitors, especially Reebok, the originators of the fashion aerobic shoe market; 80 to 90 percent of fashion aerobic shoe buyers do not participate in the sport.

Although Rykä shoes are as technologically advanced as Reebok, Nike or L.A. Gear's, they are often overlooked by fashion-conscious consumers unfamiliar with the Rykä name. Despite the fact that Rykä's sales have grown even during these recessionary times, retailers haven't always carried Rykä shoes because they prefer to stock only those brands which are easily recognizable. The lack of a nationally recognized name is a serious concern for any company; thus for Rykä, as for its competitors, expensive, leading edge advertising campaigns have played an essential part in its marketing initiatives.

A ROCKY START

Given the saturation of the athletic footwear market, athletic shoe companies need more than a good product to stay alive; they need powerful marketing and advertising. Rykä concentrates much of its energies on marketing. As a new manufacturer in an already crowded industry, Poe understands the possibility of being marketed right out of business by big competitors with deep pockets like Nike and Reebok. Rykä's approach is to offer similar products, but focus on the most cost-effective ways to reach a target market, thus carving out a niche that the industry giants have overlooked.

To protect a niche, it is critical to stay one step ahead of the competition. Unfortunately for Rykä, Poe had to learn this lesson the hard way. When the company was first founded, it tried unsuccessfully to challenge the brand name manufacturers in all product categories, including running, tennis, aerobics, walking, and cross-training shoes. However, given its limited capital and the huge advertising budgets of Reebok, Nike, and L.A. Gear, Rykä could not compete in all of these different markets at once. Instead, Rykä cut back and chose to focus on aerobic shoes, and, secondarily, on their walking shoe line. Thus, in addition to limiting product line breadth, Rykä has designed its marketing approach to attract a specific set of customers rather than a broad audience. Poe does not believe that Rykä has to be a giant to succeed. Rather, she contends that Rykä needs to maximize its ability to perform in a particular niche within a large industry.

A NEW DIRECTION

In the already-crowded athletic footwear industry, the various competitors are continually jockeying for a better market position and competitive edge. Currently, women are, and will probably continue to be, the fastest growing segment of the athletic footwear market. Women's athletic footwear accounts for 55 percent of Reebok's sales, 60 percent of Avia's, 45 percent of L.A. Gear's, and 17 percent of Nike's $2.2 billion in domestic sales. In recent years, Reebok and Nike have fought for the number one spot in the women's market, and Reebok initially prevailed; but in each of the past two years, Nike has posted a 30% growth in the market. This unparalleled growth in the women's athletic footwear market is the most important trend in the sporting goods industry today, and it is on this niche that Rykä is staking its future.

An important part of the Rykä mission stems from the fact that their shoes are specifically made for women. While the big name shoe companies were merely making smaller sizes of men's shoes made on men's lasts, Rykä developed a fitness shoe built specifically for women with a patented design for better shock absorption and durability. Rykä had a first mover advantage in this segment and had a sustained competitive advantage in that none of the other companies in the athletic shoe industry can boast having a business strategy focused on women. All other contenders have other lines or are concentrated in other niches. Ultimately, however, it is the Ultra-Lite midsole, Rykä's most significant and successful product advancement, that keeps Rykä up with its competition in its market. The Rykä Ultra-Lite aerobics shoe weighs 7.7 ounces or roughly 30 percent of the weight of a regular aerobic shoe. Within two months of its introduction in December 1990, the company had sold all of its Ultra-Lites at a unit price of $70 a pair (retail). It took three months before additional shoe orders could be filled. Some investment firms were concerned that Rykä might not be able to capitalize on the success of its new line given its difficulty keeping retailers supplied with sufficient quantities. Eventually, Rykä did lose some ground to Nike and Reebok—both of which quickly jumped into the lightweight aerobic shoe market. Despite the competition, however, Rykä's Ultra Lite lines are a success, accounting for close to 90 percent of its total sales today.

After establishing a solid foundation in the aerobics category, Rykä again turned its attention to product differentiation. Its current product line includes the Series 900 Aerobic/Step shoes, the Series 700 Aerobic shoes, the Series 800/Cross-Training shoes, and the Series 500 Walking shoes. To make sure its shoes were not perceived as "too specialized," Rykä designed the Aerobic Step 50/50 and a lightweight version of it, the Step-Lite 50/50, each of which can be worn for both high-impact and step aerobics.

Rykä also designed a dual purpose walk/run shoe, the 570, for women who complement their walking routine with running, but don't want to own shoes for every activity. Rykä is now considering entering the medical footwear market because an increasing number of podiatrists and chiropractors are recommending Rykä walking shoes to their patients.

THE RYKÄ ROSE FOUNDATION

The Rykä ROSE (Regaining One's Self Esteem) Foundation is a not-for-profit organization created by Sheri Poe to help women who have been the victims of violent crimes. The foundation was launched in 1992, and Poe herself personally pledged $250,000. Poe founded the ROSE Foundation because she was raped at age 19. The trauma resulting from the rape led to further suffering from bulimia. She sees herself as a survivor who needed to do something to help fellow victims, "For me, having a company that just made a product was not enough. I wanted to do something more."

Rykä has made a commitment to donate 7 percent of its pretax profits to the foundation and to sponsor special fund-raising events to help strengthen community prevention and treatment programs for women who are the victims of violent crimes. Rykä includes information on the foundation in brochures that are packaged with each box of shoes in the hope that its social conscience may favorably influence some consumers. But for Poe, it is more than a marketing ploy. She considers Rykä's financial commitment to the ROSE Foundation a natural extension of the company's commitment to women.

The foundation has created alliances with health clubs, nonprofit organizations, and corporations, in an effort to reach women directly with educational materials and programs. In addition, the ROSE Foundation funds a $25,000 grants program to encourage organizations to develop creative solutions to the widespread problem of violence against women. One of the foundation's beneficiaries, the National Victim Center, received an award of $10,000 to set up a toll-free (800) telephone number for victims and their families through which they can obtain immediate information, referrals, and other types of assistance.

Poe hopes that the foundation will act as a catalyst for coalition-building to help stop violence against women. But she also envisions the foundation as a means of involving retailers in marketing socially-responsible programs directly to women. Lady Foot Locker has taken advantage of this opportunity and became the first retailer to join forces with the ROSE Foundation. In October 1993, Lady Foot Locker conducted a two-week promotional campaign in their 550 United States stores in conjunction with the ROSE Foundation. The retailer distributed free education brochures and held a special sweepstakes contest to raise awareness about the issue of violence against women. Customer response was overwhelmingly positive, and Lady Foot Locker is considering a future partnership with the ROSE Foundation. Foot Locker, Champs and Athletic X-press have also expressed interest in the foundation.

MVP Sports, a New England retailer, has also participated in Rykä's activities to help stop violence against women. The company, which operates eight stores in the New England area, sponsored a two-week information-based campaign featuring Sheri Poe that included radio, TV, and newspaper advertisements. In addition, Doug Barron, president of MVP Sports, was so impressed with the concept and progressive thinking of the Rykä ROSE Foundation that he decided his company would donate $2 to the foundation for each pair of Rykä athletic shoes sold during the 1992 holiday season. Poe sees MVP Sports' support as an important first step toward actively involving retailers in Rykä's efforts to help prevent violence against women and is reaching out to other retailers who, she hopes, will follow suit.

Poe considers Rykä and its foundation unique. As she sees it, the company has a great story to tell. It is the only athletic footwear company that is exclusively for women, by women, and now supporting women—"the first athletic shoe with a 'soul.'" And Poe is banking on her hunch that the foundation will appeal to Rykä customers who appreciate the idea that their buying power is helping women less fortunate than they are.

Nevertheless, Poe's choice to make Rykä a socially responsible company right from the beginning, rather than waiting until the company is fully established, has had consequences for its financial status. Some industry analysts have suggested that Rykä would be better off funneling any extra cash back into the company until it is completely solvent, and its product lines and their name recognition are automatic. But others argue that the reputation Rykä has garnered as an ethical company, as concerned about social issues as about the "bottom line," effectively appeals to kindhearted women consumers. For them, the ROSE Foundation is worth in "good press" whatever it has cost the company in terms of actual investment dollars, because the company has effectively carved out a niche that speaks on many different levels to women's ethical and consumer concerns.

MARKETING

Rykä's promotional strategy is aimed at creating both brand awareness and sales at the retail level. By garnering the support of professional sports organizations early on, Rykä acquired instant name recognition in a variety of key audiences. Rykä entered into a six-figure, eight-year licensing agreement with the U.S. Ski Team which permitted Rykä to market its products as the official training shoes of the Team. In addition, the American Aerobics Association International boosted Rykä's brand name recognition when it replaced Avia with Rykä as the association's preferred aerobics shoes. *Shape* magazine labeled Rykä number one in its aerobic shoe category.

Rykä has also begun sponsoring both aerobics teams and aerobics competitions. In 1992, twenty-five countries competed in the World Aerobic championships in Las Vegas, Nevada. The Canadian Team was sponsored by Rykä Athletic Footwear. Rykä was the premier sponsor and the official shoe of the Canadian National Aerobic championship held in Vancouver, BC. To ensure the success of the event and build awareness for the sport of competitive aerobics, Rykä successfully promoted the nationals through retailers, athletic clubs, and individuals. Given that virtually every previous aerobics competition worldwide had been sponsored by Reebok, Canada's selection of Rykä as their official sponsor marked a significant milestone for Rykä, as well as marking Rykä's international recognition as a core brand in the women's athletic market.

The Rykä Training Body. Early on, Sheri Poe determined that the most effective way to reach Rykä's female aerobic niche would be through marketing to aerobics instructors and targeted Rykä's advertising accordingly. In fact, Rykä spends almost as much as industry leaders on print advertisements in aerobics instructors' magazines and very little on print advertising elsewhere. On the other hand, unlike its big competitors, Rykä does not use celebrity endorsements to sell its products, because the company markets on the theory that women will care more about what feels good on their feet than about what any particular celebrity has to say.

Beyond advertising in aerobics magazines, Rykä has successfully used direct mail marketing techniques to target aerobics instructors. The Rykä Training Body is comprised of more than 40,000 women employed as fitness instructors and personal trainers throughout the country. They receive product information four to six times per year, as well as discounts on shoes. Rykä also has a group of its instructors tied to specific local retailers. The instructors direct their students to those retailers, who then offer discounts to the students. Finally, Rykä-affiliated instructors offer demonstrations to educate consumers about what to look for in an aerobics shoe.

In addition to increasing sales, the relationship between Rykä and the aerobics profession has led to significant product design innovations. Aerobic instructors' suggestions, based on their own experience, as well as on feedback from students in their classes, has led to improvements such as more effective cushioning and better arch support in the shoes. Poe considers these teachers as the link to Rykä's customers. In fact, as a direct result of instructor feedback, Rykä was the first manufacturer to respond to the new step-aerobics trend by developing and marketing lightweight shoes specifically designed to support up and down step motions.

Salespeople. Rykä's marketing efforts are also aimed at the people who sell Rykä products. In Rykä's early days, Poe and her advertising manager, Laurie Ruddy, personally visited retail stores to meet salespeople and "sell" them on Rykä products. Now, the vice president of sales and marketing maintains contact with retailers using incentive programs, giveaways, and small monetary bonuses to keep salespeople excited. The company also provides premiums, such as fanny packs or water bottles for customers.

Advertising Budget. Given the highly competitive nature of the athletic footwear industry, effective advertising is crucial in distinguishing among brands and creating brand preference. Back in 1989, Rykä was particularly capital-intensive, given that it was trying to penetrate the athletic shoe market. Its $3.5 million loss that year is largely attributable to advertising spending of approximately $2.5 million, but that amount was nothing compared to Nike, Reebok, and L.A. Gear who, combined, spent more than $100 million on advertising during the same period. At that time, Rykä advertised only in trade publications, so recognition among consumers was lagging.

More recently, Rykä ads have appeared in *Shape, City Sports, American Fitness, ELLE,* and *Idea Today* magazines. Rykä's brand recognition has grown dramatically, even though Rykä's advertising and marketing budget is only about 9 percent of sales. Poe attributes Rykä's marketing success to its direct marketing techniques, especially its targeting of certified aerobic instructors to wear Rykä shoes.

In October 1992, after three successive quarters of record sales and little profitability, Poe announced that Rykä was going to expand its direct marketing to consumers, even if it required increased spending to penetrate the marketplace beyond aerobics instructors. But Rykä is still in another league compared to industry giants when it comes to budgets. Rykä's total advertising budget is approximately $1.5 million, while Nike spent about $20 million recently on a 1991 pan-European campaign to launch a single product, and Reebok is currently spending $28 million on its "I Believe . . ." ad campaign which specifically targets women.

OPERATIONS

As is common in the athletic-footwear industry, Rykä shoes are made by independent manufacturers in Europe and the Far East, including south Korea and Taiwan, according to Rykä product specifications. Rykä's first three years were rough, in large part because of the poor quality of the products provided by its manufacturer in

Taiwan. Now, however, the shoes are made in Korea with strict quality-control measures in effect. The company relies on a Far Eastern buying agent, under Rykä's direction, for the selection of suppliers, inspection of goods prior to shipment, and shipment of finished goods.

Rykä's management believes that this sourcing of footwear products minimizes company investment in fixed assets as well as reducing cost and risk. Given the extent of the underutilized factory manufacturing capacity in countries outside of South Korea and Taiwan, Rykä's management believes that alternative sources of product manufacturing are readily available, should the company have need of them. Because of the volatility of international and economic relations in today's global marketplace, and in order to protect itself from complete dependence on one supplier, Rykä has resolved to keep itself free of any long-term contract with manufacturers beyond the terms of purchase orders issued. Orders are placed on a volume basis through its agent and Rykä receives finished products within 120 days of an order. If necessary, Rykä may pay a premium to reduce the time required to deliver finished goods from the factory to meet customer demand.

The principal raw materials in Rykä shoes are leather, rubber, ethylvinyl acetate, polyurethane, cambrelle, and pigskin, all of which are readily available both in the United States and abroad. Nevertheless, even though Rykä could locate new sources of raw materials within a relatively short period of time if it needed to for its overseas manufacturers, its business could be devastated by any interruption in operations, whereas Reebok and Nike have large stockpiles of inventory and would be less affected by any difficulties with suppliers.

Distribution. Rykä products are sold in sporting-goods stores, athletic-footwear stores, selected high-end department stores, and sport-specialty retailers including Foot Locker, Lady Foot Locker, Athlete's Foot Store, Foot Action, US Athletics, Oshman's, and Nordstroms. Rykä's major distribution relationship is with the 476 Lady Foot Locker stores in the United States and 250 Lady Foot Locker stores in Canada. Today, 400 Lady Foot Locker stores display permanent Rykä signage, identifying Rykä as a brand especially promoted by Lady Foot Locker. Both Sheri Poe and Amy Schecter, vice president of retail marketing for Lady Foot Locker, agree that Rykä shoes have seen solid sales in Lady Foot Locker stores, and the Lady Foot Locker's display of permanent Rykä signage expresses the confidence Lady Foot Locker has in Rykä's future success.

FOOTACTION USA, a division of the Melville Corporation and the second largest specialty footwear retailer in the country, recently began selling Rykä athletic shoes on a trial basis in 40 stores. The trial was so successful, FOOTACTION agreed to purchase five styles of Rykä shoes for its stores, and today 150 FOOTACTION stores carry Rykä products nationally.

Rykä has received orders from three large retail sporting goods chains, adding well over 200 store outlets to its distribution network. The twelfth largest sporting goods retailer in the country, MC Sporting Goods, based in Grand Rapids, Michigan, now carries five styles of Rykä athletic shoes in each of its 73 stores. In addition, Rykä has received orders from the Tampa, Florida-based Sports and Recreation, which will sell four styles of Rykä athletic shoes in all of its 23 sporting goods stores. Charlie Burks, head footwear buyer for Sports and Recreation, based his decision to stock Rykä shoes on his sense that the chain's customers are looking for new, exciting styles of athletic shoes at affordable prices, and that Rykä delivers on performance, fashion, and value. Rykä shoes are also carried in more than 135 Athletic Express stores.

In the competitive athletic footwear industry, distributors and retailers have considerable clout. Lady Foot Locker and Foot Locker retailers accounted for 13 percent of Rykä's net sales several years ago, but today, no single customer or group under common control accounts for more than 10 percent of its total revenue.

Human Resources. When Rykä was in its early stages, Poe set out to gain credibility through human resources. The company offered industry-standard salaries, stock options, and the opportunity for significant input into the day-to-day operations of the company. In addition, Poe attracted four top executives from Reebok for positions in sales, advertising, and public relations. This high-powered team performed so effectively that sales doubled between Rykä's first and second years. But, total executive compensation was too much for the young company. Poe realized that a change in strategy was necessary, and three of the four Reebok veterans have since left.

Rykä now employs 22 people at its Norwood headquarters, as well as 35 sales representatives across the country. Rykä's small size gives it a certain flexibility, enabling the company to concentrate on continual streamlining and improvement, so that new ideas and adjustments can be implemented and in the stores within 120 days.

Rykä recently appointed Roy S. Kelvin as vice president and chief financial officer to reinforce its commitment to the financial community. Poe sees Kelvin, a former New York investment banker, as instrumental to helping the company grow, but there is also a sense in which Poe's appointment of Kelvin is her acknowledgment of the fact that she's competing for funds in an "old-boy's" network, so it is extremely valuable to have an "old-boy" to help build up her list of contacts. Kelvin's main priorities are helping to secure domestic financing, reduce operating expenses, and improve profit margins.

FINANCIALS

Rykä originally financed its operations principally through public stock offerings, warrant exercises, and other private sales of its common stock, netting an aggregate of approximately $7.2 million. In July, 1990 Rykä completed its public stock offering, which raised net proceeds of $3.5 million, allowing the company to market its products aggressively. Rykä has sold shares to private investors who control 65 percent of the shares.

Rykä's product costs are higher than those of the industry leaders for several reasons. First, because Rykä is significantly smaller than the industry leaders, it cannot take advantage of volume production discounts. Second, the company has opted to pay somewhat higher prices for its products than would be charged by alternate suppliers in order to achieve and maintain higher quality. Finally, higher production costs have resulted from Rykä's inventory financing arrangement with its Korean Trading company, which includes financing costs, commissions, and fees as part of cost of sales.

Rykä has taken on some formidable competition in the form of Nike and Reebok. For Rykä to prosper, Sheri Poe must successfully carve out a niche in the women's athletic shoe market before they run out of money. Time is becoming increasingly scarce. As indicated on Rykä's financial statements (Exhibits 26–1 through 26–6), the company lost nearly $500,000 in 1991 and $300,000 in 1992. Sales are increasing, but profits are nonexistent. Prepare a strategic plan that will enable CEO Poe to guide Rykä to prosperity in the mid-to-late 1990s.

EXHIBIT 26-1 Rykä Inc. and Subsidiary Consolidated Balance Sheets—Assets

| | DECEMBER 31, | |
	1993	1992
Assets		
Current assets		
Cash and cash equivalents	$ 83,753	$1,029,161
Accounts receivable, net of allowance for doubtful		
accounts of $665,605 in 1993 and $446,034 in 1992	2,789,728	2,958,629
Inventory	3,280,648	3,260,617
Prepaid advertising	0	723,460
Prepaid expenses and other current assets	160,916	240,511
Total current assets	6,315,045	8,212,378
Security deposits and other assets	28,253	21,485
Equipment, furniture and fixtures, net	87,514	85,366
Total assets	$6,430,812	$8,319,229

Source: Rykä Inc. *Annual Report,* 1993.

EXHIBIT 26-2 Rykä Inc. and Subsidiary Consolidated Balance Sheets—Liabilities and Stockholders' Equity

| | DECEMBER 31, | |
	1993	1992
Liabilities and stockholders' equity		
Current liabilities		
Accounts payable (including $1,028,150 in 1993		
payable to factories)	$ 1,324,603	$ 497,179
Payable to Lender	2,627,493	3,100,000
Payable to Factor	500,000	0
Accrued expenses	525,724	145,000
Notes payable to stockholder	125,000	375,000
Current portion of capital lease obligations	10,405	17,795
Total current liabilities	5,113,225	4,134,974
Obligations under capital leases, less		
current portion	7,473	17,878

EXHIBIT 26-2 *Continued*

| | DECEMBER 31, | |
	1993	1992
Commitments and contingencies		
Stockholders' equity		
Preferred Stock, $0.01 par value, 1,000,000 shares authorized; none issued or outstanding		
Common Stock, $0.01 par value, 30,000,000 shares authorized; 23,721,356 and 23,101,948 shares issued and outstanding at December 31, 1993 and 1992, respectively	237,213	231,019
Additional paid-in capital	14,780,493	14,214,459
Accumulated deficit	(13,707,592)	(10,279,101)
Total stockholders' equity	1,310,114	4,166,377
Total liabilities and stockholders' equity	$ 6,430,812	$ 8,319,229

Source: Rykä Inc. *Annual Report*, 1993.

EXHIBIT 26-3 Rykä Inc. and Subsidiary Consolidated Statements of Operations

| | YEAR ENDED DECEMBER 31, | | |
	1993	1992	1991
Net sales	$ 14,350,282	$12,193,643	$7,977,925
Cost of goods sold	11,199,119	8,867,375	5,231,346
Gross profit	3,151,163	3,326,268	2,746,579
Operating expenses:			
General and administrative	1,645,553	1,042,211	1,098,925
Provision for losses on doubtful accounts	631,835	197,034	189,000
Sales and marketing	2,085,077	1,526,299	1,098,080
Advertising costs	1,162,825	196,319	298,689
Research and development	361,780	148,958	155,576
Total operating expenses	5,887,070	3,110,821	2,840,270
Operating income (loss)	(2,735,907)	215,447	(93,691)
Other (income) expense:			
Interest expense	699,231	516,455	418,469
Interest income	(6,647)	(4,195)	(12,648)
Total other expense	692,584	512,260	405,821
Net loss	$ (3,428,491)	$ (296,813)	$ (499,512)
Net loss per share	$ (0.15)	$ (0.01)	$ (0.03)
Weighted average shares outstanding	23,573,316	19,847,283	18,110,923

Source: Rykä Inc. *Annual Report*, 1993.

EXHIBIT 26-4 Rykä Inc. and Subsidiary Consolidated Statements of Stockholders' Equity

	COMMON STOCK		ADDTIONAL PAID-IN	ACCUMULATED	
	SHARES	AMOUNT	CAPITAL	DEFICIT	TOTAL
Balance at January 1, 1990	13,242,500	$132,425	$7,109,898	$(5,394,264)	$1,848,059
Issuance of shares for cash in July 1990, in connection with public offering	4,700,000	47,000	4,653,000		4,700,000
Registration costs related to public offering			(1,182,834)		(1,182,834)
Exercise of stock options	62,642	626	21,925		22,551
Net loss				(4,088,512)	(4,088,512)
Balance at December 31, 1990	18,005,142	180,051	10,601,989	(9,482,776)	1,299,264
Issuance of shares for services	30,000	300	9,600		9,900
Exercise of stock options	101,000	1,010	24,240		25,250
Net loss				(499,512)	(499,512)
Balance at December 31, 1991	18,136,142	181,361	10,635,829	(9,982,288)	834,902
Issuance of shares for cash in September 1992, in connection with warrant call	4,021,046	40,210	3,980,836		4,021,046
Redemption of unexercised warrants in September 1992			(169,739)		(169,739)
Registration costs related to warrant call			(644,046)		(644,046)
Exercise of stock options	944,760	9,448	411,579		421,027
Net loss				(296,813)	(296,813)
Balance at December 31, 1992	23,101,948	$231,019	$14,214,459	$(10,279,101)	$4,166,377

Source: Rykä Inc. *Annual Report*, 1992.

EXHIBIT 26-5 Rykä Inc. and Subsidiary Consolidated Statements of Cash Flows

	YEAR ENDED DECEMBER 31,		
	1993	1992	1991
Cash flows from operating activities			
Net loss	$(3,428,491)	$(296,813)	$ (499,512)
Adjustments to reconcile net loss to cash used for operating activities:			
Depreciation and amortization	51,142	62,711	52,034
Provision for losses on doubtful accounts	631,835	197,034	189,000
Advertising credits	614,217		
Issuance of Common Stock for services	31,050		9,900
Changes in operating assets and liabilities:			
Accounts receivable	(462,934)	(1,395,354)	(1,152,403)
Inventory	(20,031)	(1,016,458)	(1,293,102)
Prepaid advertising	109,243	(604,099)	
Prepaid expenses other current assets	79,595	(163,115)	39,043
Accounts payable and accrued expenses	1,208,148	(52,684)	(31,437)
Net cash used for operating activities	(1,186,226)	(3,268,778)	(2,686,477)
Cash flows from investing activities			
Purchase of equipment, furniture and fixtures, net of capital leases	(53,290)	(33,398)	(6,227)
(Increase) decrease in security deposits and other assets	(6,768)	(5,398)	91,310
Net cash provided by (used for) investing activities	(60,058)	(38,796)	85,083

EXHIBIT 26-5 *Continued*

	YEAR ENDED DECEMBER 31,		
	1993	1992	1991
Cash flows from financing activities			
Payable to Lender, net	(472,507)	200,000	2,300,000
Advances from Factor, net	500,000		
Proceeds from notes payable to stockholder	125,000	375,000	
Repayment of notes payable to stockholder	(375,000)		
Repayments of capital lease obligations (32,591)	(17,795)	(32,583)	
Proceeds from exercise of stock options and warrants (net of redemptions)	541,178	4,272,334	25,250
Payment for registration costs		(644,046)	
Net cash provided by financing activities	300,876	4,170,705	2,292,659
Net increase (decrease) in cash and cash equivalents (308,735)	(945,408)	863,131	
Cash and cash equivalents, beginning of year	1,029,161	166,030	474,765
Cash and cash equivalents, end of year	$83,753	$1,029,161	$166,030
Supplemental disclosures of cash flow information:			
Cash paid during the year for interest	$370,945	$548,455	$318,469
Cash paid during the year for income taxes	—	—	—
Supplemental disclosure of noncash activity:			
Footwear sold in exchange for prepaid advertising	—	$494,856	—
Equipment, furniture and fixtures capitalized under capital leases	—	—	$14,698

Source: Rykä Inc. *Annual Report,* 1993.

EXHIBIT 26-6 Rykä Inc. Percentage of Net Sales by Category for the Years Ended December 31, 1993, 1992, and 1991

CATEGORY	1993	1992	1991
Aerobic	65%	80%	80%
Cross-Training	19	5	10
Walking and Walk/Run; Hikers	16	15	10

Source: Rykä Inc. *Annual Report,* 1993.

EXHIBIT 26-7 Rykä Inc., 1993 representatives

Territory #1 (WA, OR, MT, ID, AK)
*Peggy Finnigan 714-252-0240
same (fax)

Territory #2 (Northern California)
*Pat Miller 707-746-5784
707-746-5785 (fax)
P.O. Box 215 and/or 342 East 2nd St.
Benicia, CA 94510

Territory #3 (TX, LA, MS, AR, OK)
*Richard Hart 717-792-5774
717-792-5196 (fax)

Territory #4 (Southern California)
(AZ, NV, CO, WY, UT, NM)
*Peggy Finnigan 714-252-0240
same (fax)
86 Almador
Irvine, CA 92714

Jeanne Northrop 303-296-0980
303-431-1865
451 E 58th Avenue #3367
Denver, CO 80216

Mindy Jaffe (HI) 808-922-4222
same (fax)
Cellular 808-285-2855
234 Ohua Avenue #118
Honolulu, HI 96815

Territory #5 (FL, Puerto Rico)
*Pat Best (West Coast)
813-864-4624
Sunshine Sports
3000 34th Street South
St. Petersburg, FL 33715

*Al Maduro (East Coast, Puerto Rico)
305-382-3877
305-387-9446 (fax)
Sunshine Sports
11785 S.W. 134th Ct.
Miami, FL 33186

Representatives:
Dave Jenkins 407-779-1737
133 North East 1st Street
Satellite Beach, FL 32927

Territory #6 (OH, MI, IN, KY)
*Dave Phillips 513-459-0121
same (fax)
3478 Cutter Lane
Maineville, OH 45039

Frank Karr 502-425-6502
502-429-6668 (fax)
9013 Cardiff Road
Louisville, KY 40242

Chris Karr 317-257-2260
317-257-4066 (fax)
6242 N Rural Street
Indianapolis, IN 46220

Territory #7 (ME, NH, VT, MA, RI, CT)
*Bob Morgan 617-383-6346
617-383-1955 (fax)
698 Jerusalem Road
Cohasset, MA 02025

Tom O'Brien 617-471-2472
617-471-2855
189 Everett Street No. 5
Quincy, MA 02169

Territory #8 (NJ, NY, PA, MD, DE, VA)
*Richard Hart 717-792-5774
717-792-5196 (fax)
111 Weldon Drive
York, PA 17404

(MD, VA)
Keith Jones 301-663-8605
same (fax)
5967 Grove Hill Road
Frederick, MD 21702

Hank Mason 315-652-7416
315-652-1570 (fax)
115 Glenwood Drive
Liverpool, NY 13090

Mike Elison 215-874-4418
same (fax)
422 Camelot Drive
Brookhaven, PA 19015

EXHIBIT 26-7 *Continued*

Territory #9 NYC, NJ
  *Thad Budzinski 609-588-9698
  609-588-0019 (fax)
  38 Willow Court
  Mercerville, NJ 08619

Territory #10 (KS, MO, IA, NE, ND,
SD, WI, MN, IL)
  *Gene Wayenberg 314-997-4696
  314-997-6963 (fax)
  Great Athletic Wear
  1702 Robin Knoll Lane
  . St. Louis, MO 63146

  Representatives:
  ((Northern) IL, (Southern) WI)
  Rich Neuffer 815-337-0131
  9804 Autum Lane
  Woodstock, IL 60098

  (MN, SD, ND, WI)
  Dennis Fitzpatrick 612-641-1417
  612-646-5876 (fax)
  2095 Shelby Avenue
  St. Paul, MN 55104

(KS, MO)
  Denny Hobson 913-648-0111
  916-648-0669 (fax)
  Hobson & Associates
  7208 West 80th
  Suite 206
  Overland Park, KS 66204

Territory #11 (NC, SC)
  *Mark Diehl 704-365-9482
  704-366-1139 (fax)
  5012 Crooked Oak Lane
  Charlotte, NC 28226

Territory #14 (GA, TN, AL)
  *Lissy Cowdery 404-257-0775
  same (fax)
  470 River Valley Road
  Atlanta, GA 30328

Canadian Distributor
  Myke & Christine Penfold
  416-738-5291
  416-738-4818 (fax)
  333 Confederation Parkway
  Concord, Ontario, Canada L4K 4S1

*Head representative
Source: Rykä Inc. *Annual Report,* 1993.

COMPUTERS INDUSTRY NOTE
TIM MILES
JONATHAN STREETER
HEIDI HOFFMANN

Industry shipments of equipment by the U.S. computer industry will be more than $66 billion in 1994, an increase of 6 percent following 8 percent growth in 1993. Imports will rise faster than exports, resulting in a higher computer trade deficit of about $17 billion in 1994. U.S. manufacturers will continue to restructure their operations and reduce employment, while they face significant challenges in the complex "infotainment" market during the next 5 years.

The computer-equipment sector encompasses electronic computers (SIC 3571), storage devices (SIC 3572), computer terminals (SIC 3575), and computer peripheral equipment, NEC (SIC 3577). Electronic computers include digital computers of all sizes, as well as computer kits assembled by the purchaser. Computer storage devices are such equipment as magnetic and optical disk drives and tape storage units. The category of computer terminals covers teleprinters. Computer peripherals are printers, plotters, graphics displays, and other input/output equipment. Parts and

TABLE 1   Trends and Forecasts: Computers and Peripherals (SIC 3571, 3572, 3575, 3577) (in millions of dollars except as noted)

ITEM	1991	1992[1]	1993[2]	1994[3]	PERCENT CHANGE (1991–1994) 91–92	92–93	93–94
Industry Data							
Value of shipments[4]	54,703	58,000	62,500	66,200	6.0	7.8	5.9
Total employment (000)	227	215	200	190	−5.3	−7.0	−5.0
Production workers (000)	76.2	72.5	69.1	66.4	−4.9	−4.7	−3.9
Average hourly earnings ($)	12.52	12.72	12.81	—	1.6	0.7	—
Capital expenditures	1,813	—	—	—	—	—	—
Product Data							
Value of shipments[5]	49,144	52,100	56,300	59,700	6.0	8.1	6.0
Trade Data							
Value of imports	26,424	32,137	40,170	46,196	21.6	25.5	14.5
Value of exports	25,182	26,304	27,066	29,231	4.5	3.1	7.8

[1]Estimate, except exports and imports.

[2]Estimate.

[3]Forecast.

[4]Value of all products and services sold by establishments in the computers and peripherals industry.

[5]Value of products classified in the computers and peripherals industry produced by all industries.

Note: Census reclassified some parts for electronic computers (3571) to component industries (367) for 1988-1990.

Source: U.S. Department of Commerce: Bureau of the Census, International Trade Administration (ITA). Estimates and forecasts by ITA.

components for computers and peripherals are included, as appropriate, in each of these industries. However, since 1988, the U.S. Bureau of the Census has reclassified some parts, such as printed circuit boards and integrated microcircuits, originally reported in electronic computers, in their respective component industries.

In 1993, the U.S. computer industry experienced its second straight year of recovery from the 1990–91 recession, led by an increase in domestic computer demand of 20 percent to an estimated $69.4 billion (Figure 1). During the first half of 1993, shipments rose at a much higher rate than they did in the same period in 1992; new orders showed their strongest annual growth in 9 years; and inventories were at a relatively low level. Despite some uncertainty about the economy, U.S. business purchases of computer systems and peripherals increased substantially, reflecting the efforts of many corporations to reduce costs and boost productivity through the use of this equipment. These purchases helped the industry offset a decline in Federal computer hardware spending and slower growth in exports.

Product shipments of U.S.-based manufacturers were up an estimated 8 percent (in current dollars) in 1993, to $56.3 billion. Computer systems grew faster than peripheral equipment deliveries and represented more than 50 percent of total shipments (Figure 2). The mix of systems shipments was toward cheaper and increasingly more powerful workstations and personal computers, as users continued to shift many of their applications from mainframes and minicomputers to these smaller platforms. Peripheral shipments were largely storage devices and input/output equipment such as printers.

Computer manufacturers were concerned about the effect that mid-1993 shortages of dynamic random access memory (DRAM) chips, flash memory devices, and flat panel display screens would have on the production and pricing of their systems. Regarding DRAM supply, companies reported lead times for 1- and 4-megabit chip

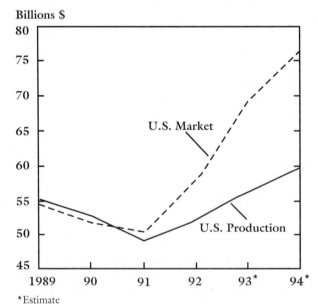

FIGURE 1 Computers: U.S. Market Grows Faster Than U.S. Production

Billions $

*Estimate
Source: U.S. Department of Commerce: Bureau of the Census; International Trade Administration, Office of Computers and Business Equipment.

deliveries of up to 14 weeks and significant price increases for these devices. Many of the smaller U.S. computer systems firms were in a vulnerable position compared with the larger vendors, which were insulated to some extent by long-term contracts with DRAM suppliers. Debate arose within the industry over whether the explosion of a Japanese epoxy resin plant in July 1993 would further exacerbate the imbalance between DRAM supply and demand by late 1993. Some industry observers speculated in August that personal computer prices might rise as much as $150 per system by year end.

Faced with financial losses stemming from declining demand for some products and fierce price competition across a broad spectrum of computer equipment, several U.S. computer manufacturers continued to restructure their domestic and foreign operations and reduce the number of positions during 1993. Total industry employment in the United States fell 7 percent to 200,000 workers (Figure 3). The bulk of the 15,000 jobs lost came from administrative, technical, sales, and support personnel. Layoffs were greater among systems firms than peripheral equipment suppliers. IBM and Digital Equipment Corporation (DEC) announced cutbacks totaling about 70,000 employees worldwide. Many smaller U.S. firms and some subsidiaries of foreign companies in the United States also trimmed their work forces. U.S. production worker employment was once again adversely affected by plant closings. The number of factory workers declined nearly 5 percent to 69,100, but remained a little more than one-third of the industry's labor force.

The U.S. computer equipment industry has used automation as a competitive tool to raise productivity, lower costs, and bring products to market quickly. A 1992 sur-

FIGURE 2 Composition of U.S. Computer Production, 1993*

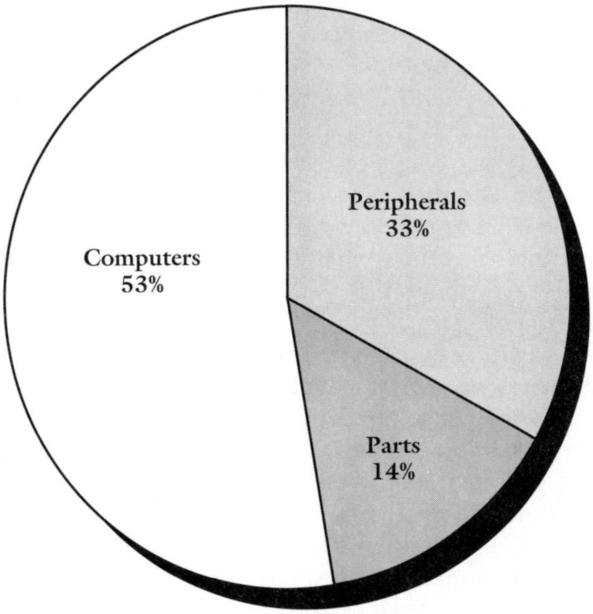

Peripherals
33%

Computers
53%

Parts
14%

Total = $56.3 Billion

*Estimate

Source: U.S. Department of Commerce: Bureau of Census; International Trade Administration, Office of Computers and Business Equipment.

FIGURE 3 Declining Employment in the U.S. Computer Industry, 1987–94

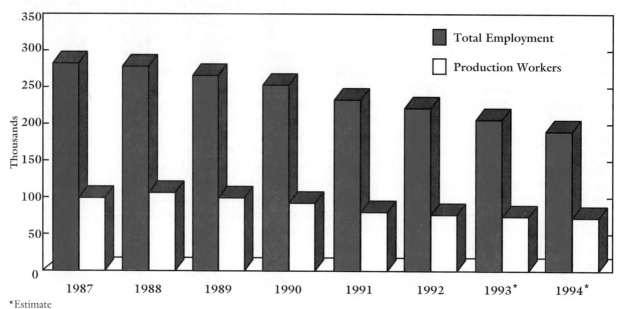

*Estimate
Source: U.S. Department of Commerce: Bureau of Census; International Trade Administration, Office of Computers and Business Equipment.

vey by the Automation Forum showed that the industry's investment in automation reached $2.1 billion in 1991, a 23 percent increase over the 1989 level. Most of this investment was in production automation software (28 percent of the total) and computer-aided product design and engineering hardware and software (25 percent). The industry was the fifth-largest spender on automation in the United States, but actually led all other U.S. industries in investment per production worker at $20,220. In terms of the demand for computers to automate design, engineering, and manufacturing, U.S. industries spent $11.6 billion on computer equipment during 1991. Among the major users were the automotive, aircraft and aerospace, and electronics industries.

Research and development (R&D) has always been critical to this industry's ability to maintain its technological leadership. Data compiled by *Business Week* in its annual R&D Scoreboard survey shows that a combined sample of 87 U.S. computer firms raised their R&D spending by 4 percent, to $14.2 billion, in 1992 (Table 2). This growth was low relative to the 7 percent average increase for all U.S. industries. However, the computer equipment industry surpassed all other U.S. electronics industries and industrial sectors in absolute spending and only lagged behind health care in the percentage of sales devoted to R&D. Three U.S. computer firms—IBM, DEC, and Hewlett-Packard—ranked among the top 10 R&D spenders in the United States.

Legislation was introduced in Congress in mid-1993 to upgrade the 3-year old High Performance Computing and Communications Initiative (HPCCI), which focuses on developing a national high-speed communications network, primarily for the use of scientists and academic researchers. The High Performance Computing and High Speed Networking Applications Act of 1993 (H.R. 1757), if passed, will allocate $1 billion over 5 years to develop applications that allow broader use of this network in health care, public education, and manufacturing. It also will boost Federal funding of research on supercomputers, advanced networking technologies,

TABLE 2   U.S. R&D spending, 1992 (In billions of dollars, percent)

INDUSTRY	R&D SPENDING	PERCENT OF SALES
Computer equipment	14.2	8.3
Automotive	12.3	4.0
Health care	11.8	9.7
Electrical and electronics	8.0	6.0
Chemicals	5.6	4.3
Aerospace	4.6	4.4
Telecommunications	3.7	3.1

Source: *Business Week*, Aug. 9, 1993.

and software. The European Commission is considering a proposal for a similar 5-year, large-scale, $4.5 billion project on high-performance computing and networking research.

INTERNATIONAL COMPETITIVENESS

The top 100 computer companies worldwide account for a majority share of the international market for information equipment and services. Their sales expanded at a healthy rate of almost 10 percent, to $318 billion in 1992, according to *Datamation* magazine's annual survey of these companies. The U.S. suppliers' share of this group's total remained steady at 61 percent, while the Japanese share fell two percentage points to 25 percent. Major factors behind this share loss may have been the downturn in Japanese computer demand during 1992 and increased competition from U.S. firms in Japan, particularly in the personal computer segment of that market.

Many of the leading U.S. computer equipment suppliers have continued to move aggressively into software and computer services as price competition in hardware has intensified and their profits have dwindled. In 1991 (the latest year available for purposes of comparison), U.S. computer systems and peripheral sales were only slightly more than half of their total revenues (Table 3). European companies were even more involved in computer software and services. In contrast, their competitors in Japan and other Asian nations still derived most of their revenues from computer equipment.

The U.S. computer industry appeared to have ceded its position as the world's leading computer-equipment producer to European Community (EC) manufacturers by 1992 (Figure 4). However, because EC statistics include business machines, such as typewriters and electronic cash registers, the EC industry's computer production is overstated somewhat. Digital Equipment, Hewlett-Packard, IBM, and other U.S. firms also contribute substantially to this industry's output through their European subsidiaries. The production of the Japanese computer industry has risen at a rapid pace, 13 percent annually since 1982, and may surpass that of U.S.-based suppliers by the middle of this decade. Like their U.S. counterparts, both EC and Japanese computer-equipment manufacturers have suffered from recession in their domestic and key overseas markets during the early 1990s. They have reacted in much the same way to losses by restructuring their operations and by instituting hiring freezes or signifi-

TABLE 3 Revenues of Information Equipment and Services Firms, 1991

| | PERCENT | | TOTAL REVENUES |
ITEM	HARDWARE	SOFTWARE	(IN BILLION DOLLARS)
United States	54	46	174
Europe	42	58	29
Japan	69	31	78
Other Asia	93	7	3

Source: *Datamation.*

FIGURE 4 U.S., EC, and Japanese Computer Production, 1982–92 (In billions of dollars)

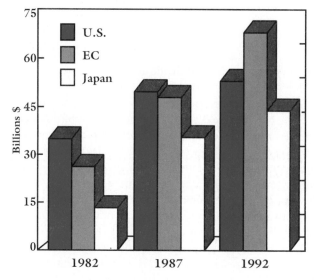

Note: European Community (EC) production includes a relatively small amount of business equipment.

Source: U.S. Department of Commerce, Bureau of the Census; JEIDA; EC Commission.

cantly cutting back their work forces. The European computer industry reduced employment, for example, by nearly 21,000 workers during 1992–93.

Although it has remained the top exporter of computers, the U.S. industry has lost considerable ground to the Japanese since 1982 (Figure 5). Japanese computer exports have risen 21 percent annually over the past 10 years, nearly twice the rate of the United States and the EC. Peripherals have accounted for almost half of the value of these exports, followed by parts (more than a 30 percent share). Computer systems have played only a minimal role. The Japanese also have increased the amount of computer

FIGURE 5 U.S., EC, and Japanese Computer Exports, 1982–92 (In billions of dollars)

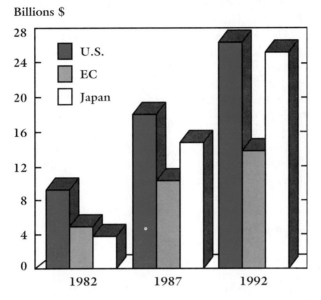

Note: European Community (EC) exports include a relatively small amount of business equipment.

Source: U.S. Department of Commerce, Bureau of the Census; JEIDA; EC Commission.

TABLE 4 U.S. Computer Trade by Product, 1993* (in millions of dollars except as noted)

PRODUCT	EXPORTS	PERCENT CHANGE 1992–93	IMPORTS	PERCENT CHANGE 1992–1993	TRADE BALANCE
Computer systems	8,390	−2.3	6,427	33.1	1,963
Peripherals	6,767	8.3	20,888	21.6	−14,121
Parts	11,909	3.8	12,854	27.4	−945
Total	27,066	2.9	40,170	25.3	−13,104

*Estimate by ITA.

Note Detail may not sum to total due to rounding.

Source: U.S. Department of Commerce: International Trade Administration (ITA).

production that is exported from 28 percent to more than 50 percent during this period and have a computer trade surplus that currently exceeds $15 billion. In contrast, the EC industry has traditionally exported no more than 20 percent of its production outside the region, concentrating its efforts within the 12 EC member countries. The EC's trade deficit has more than quadrupled in 10 years to more than $20 billion. Imports from non-EC countries have accounted for one-third of European computer consumption, with the United States and Japan as the leading suppliers.

Higher U.S. Trade Deficit. The U.S. computer trade deficit was expected to more than double to an estimated $13 billion in 1993, if trends in U.S. exports and imports through the first 5 months of the year continue (Table 4). Most of this deficit will result from a substantial imbalance in peripherals trade. Japan alone may account for two-thirds of the deficit. Roughly 58 percent of U.S. computer demand will be served by imports.

Computer exports rose only 3 percent to $27 billion during 1993, hurt by weak demand in key overseas markets. The growth was led by peripherals and parts, which together represented nearly 70 percent of export value. Systems exports were down slightly. Exports to Canada and Latin America were up 11 percent and 24 percent, respectively, but were offset by relatively flat shipments to Asia and Europe. Europe has traditionally been the largest regional market, receiving about half of U.S. computer equipment exports (Tables 5 and 6). Canada has emerged as the leading single country market.

Spurred on by a strong upturn in U.S. demand, U.S. computer imports increased 26 percent over their 1992 level, to $40 billion. Asia supplied the bulk of this import value, mainly from Japan, Singapore, Taiwan, and South Korea. Japanese firms were major sources of U.S. imports of peripherals and parts. However, other Asian manufacturers and U.S. subsidiary operations in this region have become significant providers to the U.S. market of personal computers, disk drives, printers, monitors, and components such as motherboards and power supplies.

Cumulative foreign direct investment in the U.S. computer industry fell nearly 18 percent, to $2.4 billion, in 1992, reflecting the sluggish economies of many of the major investing nations. Reduced EC investment was largely responsible for this

TABLE 5 U.S. Trade Patterns in 1992 Computers and Peripherals SIC 3571, 3572, 3575, 3577 (in millions of dollars, percent)

EXPORTS			IMPORTS		
	Value	Share		Value	Share
Canada and Mexico	4,673	17.8	Canada and Mexico	3,168	9.9
European Community	10,410	39.6	European Community	2,673	8.3
Japan	3,308	12.6	Japan	11,226	34.9
East Asia NICs	3,226	12.3	East Asia NICs	14,298	44.5
South America	1,389	5.3	South America	114	0.4
Other	3,297	12.5	Other	658	2.0
World Total	26,304	100.0	World Total	32,137	100.0

TOP FIVE COUNTRIES					
	Value	Share		Value	Share
Canada	3,603	13.7	Japan	11,226	34.9
Japan	3,308	12.6	Singapore	5,488	17.1
United Kingdom	2,811	10.7	Taiwan	4,418	13.7
Germany	2,606	9.9	Canada	2,218	6.9
Netherlands	1,679	6.4	South Korea	1,394	4.3

Source: U.S. Department of Commerce: Bureau of the Census; International Trade Administration.

TABLE 6   U.S. trade patterns, 1993* computers and peripherals SIC 3571, 3572, 3575, 3577 (in millions of dollars, percent)

EXPORTS			IMPORTS		
	Value	Share		Value	Share
Canada	3,789	14.0	Canada	5,222	13.0
Latin America	2,977	11.0	Latin America	803	2.0
Europe	11,909	44.0	Europe	6,026	15.0
Asia/Pacific	8,120	30.0	Asia/Pacific	28,119	70.0
Africa	271	1.0	Africa	—	—
World Total	27,066	100.0	World Total	40,170	100.0

TOP FIVE COUNTRIES					
	Value	Share		Value	Share
Canada	3,789	14.0	Japan	11,649	29.0
United Kingdom	3,248	12.0	Singapore	7,632	19.0
Japan	2,977	11.0	Canada	5,222	13.0
Germany	2,707	10.0	Taiwan	4,419	11.0
Netherlands	2,165	8.0	United Kingdom	3,615	9.0

*Estimate by ITA based on January to May 1993 data.

Source: U.S. Department of Commerce: Bureau of the Census; International Trade Administration.

FIGURE 6   Foreign Direct Investment in the U.S. Computer Industry, 1992 (in millions of dollars)

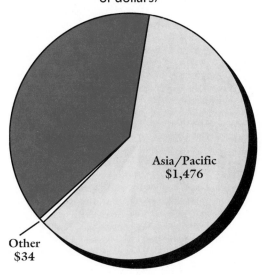

Asia/Pacific
$1,476

Other
$34

Total = $2.4 Billion

Source: Department of Commerce, Bureau of Economic Analysis.

decline. Japan continued to be the principal investor nation, accounting for 60 percent of the total (Figure 6).

The overseas investment of U.S. computer firms dropped by 11 percent to $20.4 billion, as spending was cut back appreciably in Europe and, to a lesser extent, in Canada (Figure 7). However, their investment buildup in Asia continued with Singapore as the major beneficiary. Spending by U.S. suppliers to expand their personal computer and peripheral equipment manufacturing operations in Singapore rose 70 percent to $1.3 billion. Although investment data are unavailable, trade journal sources indicate that China was an important area of joint-venture activity for U.S. PC and workstation suppliers during 1992.

A debate over the relative contributions of U.S. multinational firms and the affiliates of foreign companies to the U.S. economy has raged in academic circles for several years. The issue has assumed importance more recently in the new Administration's efforts to shape its own distinctive trade policy. At the computer- and business-equipment level, data compiled by the U.S. Department of Commerce's Bureau of Economic Analysis reveal that the U.S. parents of these multinationals have played a much more critical and positive role in the U.S.-based computer industry and the economy than U.S. affiliates of foreign firms. U.S. parent firms' total assets, sales of goods and services, employment, new plant and equipment expenditures, U.S. income tax payments, and R&D spending and intensity were many times greater in 1991 than their foreign counterparts. The parents' U.S. value-added content and employee compensation were also substantially higher. More significantly, these parents have consistently recorded trade surpluses since 1987, while the U.S. affiliates of foreign computer companies have experienced a growing deficit ($2 billion by 1991) and have become a major contributor to the worsening U.S. trade position. The import dependence of the parent firms has been much lower.

FIGURE 7 Overseas Investment of the U.S. Computer Industry, 1992 (in billions of dollars)

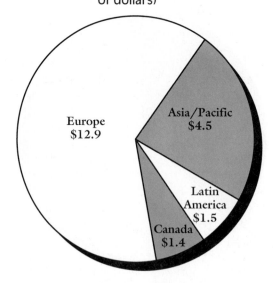

Total = $20.4 Billion

Source: U.S. Department of Commerce, Bureau of Economic Analysis.

The Computer Systems Policy Project (CSPP), a coalition of chief executive officers from 13 major U.S. computer firms, released a study in mid-1993 that provided additional perspectives on this issue. The CSPP companies had combined worldwide revenues totaling more than $123 billion in 1991, devoted 12 percent of their revenues to R&D, employed more than 400,000 Americans directly, and created 2 million more jobs indirectly in such fields as software design, computer programming, and services. Roughly 80 percent of their R&D jobs and 60 percent of their production workers remain in the United States. Spending to educate, train, and retrain their work forces and customers amounted to $2.3 billion during 1991. These and other firms in the U.S. computer industry also have supplied users with the world's most technologically advanced products. The real price performance (improvement in performance in relation to real prices) of these products has increased 25 percent annually over the past 40 years.

ENVIRONMENTAL PROFILE

SEMATECH and the Microelectronics and Computer Technology Corp. (MCC), along with the Department of Energy (DOE) and the Environmental Protection Agency (EPA), released in early 1993 a study entitled *A Workstation Life Cycle Environmental Study*, which urged U.S. electronics companies and those in other industries to become more environmentally conscious. One of the study's recommendations called for U.S. firms to improve their competitiveness by implementing programs to recycle products more efficiently and reduce pollution substantially. Its R&D-related recommendations included proposals supporting joint industry/government research efforts on environmental technology, and asked Federal laboratories to redirect their relevant resources toward conducting R&D in this area. Congress has been considering environmental legislation addressing several of the issues raised in the study.

Computer-equipment use accounts for 5 percent of the U.S. commercial-energy consumption and may reach 10 percent by the year 2000, according to EPA estimates. Personal computers, for example, consume between 150 and 240 watts when turned on and are the biggest energy consumers among the computer and business equipment used in the U.S. Government (Figure 8). In an effort to reduce this power consumption, the President issued an Executive Order in April 1993 directing Federal agencies to purchase only computer equipment that meets the criteria of the EPA's Energy Star program beginning in October 1993. The criteria require each part of a computer system—central processing unit, monitor, and printer—to enter a standby mode when it is not in use and to consume no more than 30 watts of power.

About 70 computer manufacturers had agreed to develop energy-efficient products by mid-1993. Many of them also made a commitment to convert their existing product lines to conform to the Energy Star criteria. Estimates of the program's cost savings vary. The U.S. government expects that Energy Star will slash at least $40 million from its annual electricity bill. The EPA believes "green" personal computers (PCs) could reduce the average U.S. user's electricity bill by $80 per year. On a national scale, EPA also predicts that the use of these PCs could cut electricity consumption by 25 billion kilowatt hours annually by the year 2000, thereby eliminating the need for 10 coal-fired power plants and reducing carbon-dioxide emissions by nearly 20 million tons.

During 1991, the U.S. computer industry raised its spending to control air and water pollution by 27 percent, to more than $14 million, through changes in production processes and end-of-line techniques. It also incurred $59 million in pollution abatement operating costs, including payments to government for public sewerage services and solid waste management.

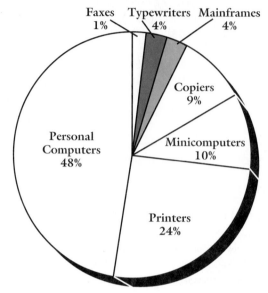

FIGURE 8 Share of U.S. Government Power Consumption in Computers and Business Equipment, 1992

Faxes 1%
Typewriters 4%
Mainframes 4%
Copiers 9%
Personal Computers 48%
Minicomputers 10%
Printers 24%

Source: General Services Administration.

Recycling has assumed greater importance as an issue within the industry. Carnegie Mellon University has estimated that approximately 15 million used computers could end up in U.S. landfills by 2005 at a cost to the taxpayer that could approach $1 billion. Several U.S. computer firms have started to recycle processor boards and power supplies along with other reusable components such as batteries and printer toner cartridges. They also are reprocessing parts to recover sheetsteel, plastics, and precious metals.

OUTLOOK FOR 1994

Product shipments by the U.S. computer-equipment industry should rise by 6 percent in current dollars to nearly $60 billion, assuming slower growth in the U.S. market and an expected resurgence in exports. The U.S. market should expand at only half its 1993 rate as domestic business spending on computer systems and peripherals begins to subside after 2 years of substantial growth. Intense price competition, particularly in low-end systems and peripherals, may continue, and exports should benefit from a long-awaited recovery in overseas demand, if key foreign economies emerge from recession and the dollar remains relatively stable. Imports should moderate in response to lower U.S. demand, but will still increase faster than exports. As a result, the U.S. computer trade deficit should increase to about $17 billion in 1994. Imports may total 60 percent of the U.S. market.

SUPERCOMPUTERS

Supercomputer systems are distinguished from other computers by their high processing speeds and their ability to handle numerically intensive problems which are too large for conventional computers. Many of the features which have historically distinguished supercomputers from other types of computer hardware have become more widespread in the computer industry, with the advent of high-speed networking, increasingly advanced mainframes, and powerful workstation clusters. One remaining distinction, however, is that supercomputers are an "enabling" technology. This means that the definition of supercomputers has more to do with applications (software) than hardware. Although advancements in hardware technology and networking have led vendors of mainframes and workstations to call their products "supercomputers," true supercomputers are those systems which are capable of processing the most advanced scientific and commercial applications such as weather forecasting.

Supercomputers now are divided into two main categories: those with one or more high-powered processors and those with many low-powered processors. The former are often referred to as "traditional" or "vector" supercomputers because they were designed to process scientific vector calculations. These systems are physically large, often require liquid cooling systems, and are expensive to acquire and operate. Computers in the latter category are often referred to as scalable parallel systems because the number of processors for an individual model can scale from a few to very many, while using the same software and operating system. These computers are smaller and less expensive than traditional systems, are air-cooled, and account for the vast majority of shipments of supercomputer "nodes" (processing units). The ability to process data using more than one processor (parallel processing) is a characteristic common to both classes of supercomputers.

Initially, scalable systems were considerably less expensive than vector supercomputers, but price distinctions between the two have rapidly begun to disappear. Traditional supercomputers are now available in less expensive, less powerful air-cooled versions. Scalable systems can be configured to have so many processing units that they can become physically larger than many mainframe systems. Supercomputers in both classes now range in price from $350,000 to $35 million. Vector supercomputers continue to account for the majority of manufacturers' annual revenues.

INTERNATIONAL COMPETITIVENESS

The export market has been an area of incremental growth for U.S. supercomputer manufacturers, allowing them to remain competitive in an increasingly saturated domestic market. Most supercomputer vendors ship more than 50 percent of their units overseas, although higher-end, higher-revenue systems tend to find their largest market in the United States. Europe is the single largest export market for U.S. firms, with Germany, France, and the United Kingdom accounting for most sales. The European Community's keen interest in supercomputing has resulted in demand for systems rather than the creation of domestic competition. European users in government, industry, and academia also have contributed significantly to the software base in the high-performance computing arena.

The hardware efforts of European suppliers have been restricted to the scalable parallel field, and their sales of these systems tend to be greatest in their home markets. The increasing competitiveness of European high-performance technology, and the firms' movement away from specialty processors, such as transputers, means that U.S. vendors now begin to see some signs of local competition in Europe.

Overall, European supercomputer sales fell slightly, to less than $500 million in 1993. The majority of revenues came from vector sales, although most units shipped were scalable systems. Despite increased Japanese competition at the high end, U.S. supercomputers accounted for upwards of 80 percent of all such installations in Europe, and about 85 percent of all public-sector, research-facility, and university sites. U.S. vendors also have the lion's share of the European market for scalable systems, despite competition from Parsytec in Germany, Telmat in France, and Meiko in the United Kingdom.

Japan. The Japanese supercomputer market is the second-largest individual market after the United States, but is marked by a more difficult sales environment for U.S. firms. Japanese government efforts to foster a domestic industry are partially to blame, but Japanese industry's inclination to purchase from domestic sources also makes it unusually difficult for foreign firms to enter that market. The private sector accounts for close to 70 percent of all supercomputer sales in Japan; U.S. supercomputers account for only about 25 percent of that market. Japanese computer users have traditionally looked to single-vendor solutions for their hardware needs, which favors such vertically integrated giants as NEC, Fujitsu, and Hitachi.

OUTLOOK FOR 1994

The global market for all types of supercomputers is expected to remain stable, at nearly $1.7 billion. There should be a reduction in sales of traditional supercomputers, by nearly 5 percent, to about $800 million, as manufacturers of those systems move into the scalable market. There is little likelihood that any new firms will enter the field because of rising prices of scalable, parallel computers, and distributed computing.

Lower system prices for newly introduced low-end vector supercomputers have reduced dollar-value sales of traditional supercomputers. However, the market should grow marginally in unit sales.

The outlook for parallel systems also is relatively weak, compared with their rapid growth from 1988 to 1992. Overall, scalable systems will account for approximately 30 percent of worldwide supercomputer revenues in 1994. The industry may well have hit at least a temporary plateau, as researchers and scientists around the world determine how they will switch from traditional supercomputers to new platforms.

MAINFRAMES

Mainframe computers, once the workhorses of the business computing world, are being challenged by a rising tide of new, competitive technologies. On the one hand, the strong demand for cheaper, less powerful systems, which are inexpensive to operate and can be placed directly under the control of individual users, has resulted in the rapid rise of personal computers and workstations. Supercomputers have become the dominant systems at the opposite end of the user spectrum, since mainframes generally have not been capable of providing the advanced scientific operations that many researchers and scientists need.

Mainframe firms have responded by making computers more available to individuals via networks and more capable of advanced scientific uses through the attachment of vector processors. At the same time, companies have continued to make rapid advances in disk-storage capacity and processing performance. Today, mainframe computers range in price from approximately $3 million for low-end systems to as high as $30 million for systems with supercomputer-like capabilities. Nevertheless, a major displacement of mainframe computers by other products has already taken place, and the future market for such large systems will reflect a significant, although diminished, position in the computing world.

The performance of mainframes is generally rated by their ability to process millions of instructions per second (MIPS). Low-end, single-processor mainframes now have processing speeds of about 50 MIPS, while the fastest multiple-processor systems are capable of more than 350 MIPS. As logic and memory-chip technology advances, however, through the use of high-density packaging and very large scale integration (VLSI), the performance parameters defining the mainframe computer will continue to rise. At the same time, the cost per unit of increased performance will fall further. Although the cost per MIPS performance in 1983 was approximately $200,000, by 1993 it had dropped to less than $50,000 and is predicted to decline again in 1994 to less than $40,000. The cost of disk storage also has fallen to about $10 per million bytes (megabytes), while capacity has dramatically risen, so that high-end storage units can store up to 90 billion bytes (gigabytes) of information.

The value of U.S.-based mainframe shipments, which stagnated in 1992 at about $12.4 billion, dropped by more than 8 percent (in current dollars) to about $11.3 billion in 1993, because of substantial price competition and lower-than-expected sales due to downsizing. Unit shipments, which dropped sharply in 1992, fell again in 1993, but only by 4 percent. General concerns about the state of the economy convinced some large-scale users to hold off on new equipment upgrades, despite the advent of new-generation systems with attractive performance characteristics and pricing. Substantial price reductions in 1993 by such industry leaders as IBM and Amdahl, as well as the Japanese firms Fujitsu and Hitachi, also lowered revenues. Nevertheless, the worst of the decline in demand for mainframes may have taken place by mid-1993, as caution by core customers has been increasingly balanced by their need to maintain essential computing capabilities.

Mainframe installations in the United States declined from about 27,000 in 1989 to about 24,000 in 1993. Enhanced performance of large-scale systems has spurred the consolidation of mainframe sites into smaller, centralized units.

INTERNATIONAL COMPETITIVENESS

Japanese firms in the late 1980s severely eroded U.S. dominance in the mainframe industry, and have continued to make inroads into the world's $25 billion market through both corporate acquisition and increased sales. By 1993, Japanese manufacturers accounted for 30 percent of world revenues in an essentially stagnant mainframe market, reducing the U.S. share to 63 percent and that of European-made systems to 7 percent. A weak European market and recession in Japan also have been obstacles for U.S. firms, which are traditionally export-oriented. An interesting side effect of the worldwide slowdown was IBM's shift of some mainframe production work from Japan back to the United States in 1993, due to the markedly increased value of the Japanese yen against the U.S. dollar. As European currencies, and especially the French franc, lost value against the dollar, however, U.S. firms were faced with the prospect of increasing prices in an already depressed and competitive European market.

OUTLOOK FOR 1994

Mainframe manufacturers in the United States will be faced with continuing stagnation and severe price competition, with revenues expected to fall another 3 percent to almost $11 billion. Unit shipments, however, are expected to stabilize to some degree. Domestic sales will continue to be the strongest market for mainframe makers, while the Japanese and European economies begin their struggle toward recovery. Unfortunately, the large layoffs resulting from reduced business and wholesale restructuring over the past two years at several firms will likely be repeated in 1994, as the effects of downsizing and competitive pricing continue. On the other hand, deeply reduced prices for increasingly sophisticated mainframe systems should convince reluctant consumers to begin investing in new computing equipment, despite the continued difficult economic environment.

MIDRANGE

The midrange segment of the computer industry consists of those systems which serve multiple numbers of networked users, either locally or remotely. Computers falling into this segment of the market are generally less expensive and less powerful than mainframes, and are distinguished from high-end workstations in that they serve from two to several hundred users. Prices of midrange systems have ranged between $20,000 and $1million. This category of computers is diverse and complex, consisting of everything from manufacturing-oriented systems, where factory workers enter and receive production data, to processors handling networked, department store, sales terminals that capture sales data and make inventory calculations. The diversity of products and customers in the midrange market makes it difficult to pinpoint technology trends and specific economic factors that characterize the segment as a whole. Nevertheless, the wide use of midrange computers as business tools makes them subject to the same economic factors that broadly affect the manufacturing, retail, and service sectors.

The midrange computer market showed continued signs of weakness in 1993, with total revenues falling about 3 percent (in current dollars) to $25.2 billion. Cumulative discounting in 1992 and 1993 by industry leaders facing eroded market shares has forced unit values to historically low levels. Other major factors driving prices down include the weak world economy, increased competitiveness as vendors move to open systems, and technological changes that enable reductions in manufacturing costs. Despite lower overall industry revenues in 1993, unit shipments increased by almost 2 percent.

INTERNATIONAL COMPETITIVENESS

U.S. midrange vendors are leading suppliers in most foreign countries, other than Japan, reaping fully 50 percent of their revenues outside of the United States. In most major foreign markets, U.S. firms are represented by wholly-owned subsidiaries, whereas in other regions they employ distributors and agents. The strongest U.S. export markets are Canada and Europe, where the United States has at least a 50-percent share. Although U.S. firms are well positioned there, economic difficulties in those markets have had a major dampening effect on midrange revenues in recent years. Nevertheless, while the European recession appeared to deepen in 1993, overall computer exports to Canada increased slightly.

In Japan, the large domestic firms have more than two-thirds of the midrange market and enjoy a significant advantage in terms of brand loyalty and exposure to potential users. U.S. firms which do well selling in heterogeneous computing environments have had difficulty in convincing the Japanese to give up their one-brand (mainframe-to-PC) operating environment. Even though U.S. midrange computers offer more advanced systems software and applications, Japanese users are reluctant to switch to open systems if the cost of converting proprietary software becomes prohibitive.

In the developing world, U.S. firms maintain a competitive advantage in terms of technology, but may lose out in pricing competition with the less costly products of Asian competitors. Promising markets in South America, such as Argentina and Chile, are still relatively small, but are the focus of some attention as markets stagnate elsewhere.

OUTLOOK FOR 1994

Advances in component technology and software, especially in the open-systems area, will spur activity in the midrange market, although little growth is expected in 1994. There will be continued confusion as the distinction between various types and capabilities of midrange systems blurs, and the marketing efforts of suppliers crossover, with mainframes at the high end and workstations at the low end. A moderate recovery in the U.S. economy will probably not make up for the slack demand in Canada and the European Community. Sales in the Japanese market also may be affected by businesses' cautious approach to investment there. Increased competitive pressures will again depress the value of sales, although low to moderate unit growth is expected. The long, steep decline in midrange unit prices, however, may slow significantly as manufacturers assess the extent to which they can make further cuts in costs, without affecting their ability to meet demand. Large-scale layoffs, which made headlines in 1992 and 1993, have brought midrange producers to higher levels of productivity. Thus, even in a relatively flat market, their refocus on core businesses should allow them to operate in 1994 without additional losses in revenues or employment.

WORKSTATIONS

Workstations are single and multiuser computers that make use of high-speed microprocessors to provide technical and business users with superior performance. On the low end, they compete with high-end personal computers, a distinction that has been blurred by the introduction of more powerful, mainstream microprocessors, such as Intel's Pentium. On the high end, they compete with mini-supercomputers in raw performance, and with midrange computers as network servers. Workstations have been sold to the scientific and engineering community since their introduction in the early 1980s, but have more recently become popular in the mainstream business markets, where they are used for electronic publishing, business graphics, financial services, mapping, and office automation.

The most significant feature of workstations is their high-performance, 32-bit reduced instruction set computing (RISC) microprocessors. U.S. shipments of RISC workstations are growing rapidly (Figure 9). Based upon the RISC philosophy of keeping the number of primary instructions for the system's operation small, designers have been steadily increasing workstation performance. More than 90 percent of RISC systems run some version of the UNIX operating system, which provides strong software development, communications, multitasking, and network support capabilities. Although UNIX is ostensibly an "open" system, most vendors have offered a proprietary version to tie customers to their specific hardware platform. Even though UNIX has enabled workstation companies to push the performance of their hardware, software developers have been hesitant to provide applications software for some versions. This situation contrasts sharply with the enormous number of applications that have been written for the DOS- and Windows-based personal computers (PCs).

Workstation unit shipments in the United States grew more than 6 percent, to 227,772 systems, in 1993, according to Dataquest, Inc. The U.S. industry is highly concentrated with five companies holding more than 85 percent of the market. The traditional computer vendor's workstation product lines have provided welcome profits, as demand has declined for mainframe and midrange systems and the substantial support they required. Various industry experts agree that workstation vendors have established strong management, technology, and marketing skills, and will realize above-average profitability and continued market-share gain in the technical-computing sector. The number of vendors in the industry has remained fairly constant, with the exception of the withdrawal of NeXT from the hardware workstation market. That company will maintain a presence in the software market with its NeXTStep operating system.

FIGURE 9 U.S. RISC Workstations Shipments

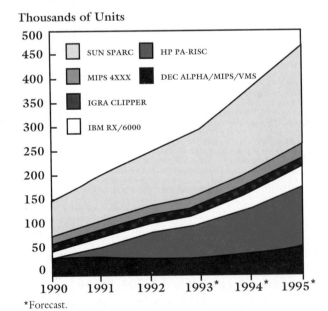

Thousands of Units

*Forecast.

Note: RISC = reduced instruction set computing.

Source: InfoCorp.

Workstation companies are aggressive in their releases of new products and existing product enhancements. Product upgrades are announced on the average of every 6 to 9 months; major product announcements come every 18 to 24 months, thereby deterring new market entrants. Clone vendors, a powerful force in the PC market, have had relatively little success in winning workstation market share, probably due to this sector's relatively strong emphasis upon performance rather than price, where the clone vendors have a marketing advantage. Average system prices are falling as workstations move into more commercial applications. In the server market, workstations are dramatically less expensive than other server options, such as midrange and mainframe computers.

INTERNATIONAL COMPETITIVENESS

The European workstation market consumed 180,117 units in 1993, according to Dataquest. Datapro International estimates that workstation unit shipments there will increase at a compound annual growth rate of about 21 percent through 1995. Demand for workstations used as servers in commercial applications will grow faster than those used in technical and graphical applications. Prices vary widely across Europe, although the differences are diminishing. The general industrial sector accounted for nearly two-thirds of European workstation shipments, mainly to technical and scientific users. The financial sector and other nontechnical users accounted for the rest.

The European workstation market is controlled by the same five U.S. companies that dominate the U.S. market. These companies sell primarily through direct sales forces and value-added resellers in Europe. Since workstations are a relatively new market segment, these companies are likely to further develop dealer and distributor networks over the next few years. Some of the major vendors have standard European pricing, while others allow their resellers to determine the price of the system and service. Local taxes, such as the value-added tax in the United Kingdom, also influence the price of the product. U.S. workstation vendors have entered into several OEM (original equipment manufacturer) relationships with European computer companies, none of which have become significant competitors to U.S. vendors in their home market.

Japanese workstation vendors, on the other hand, have been successful at turning technology licensing agreements with U.S. workstation vendors into products for their home market. Several Japanese vendors have licensed the right to manufacture the RISC processors designed by U.S. workstation vendors. The majority of systems sold in Japan are based on these microprocessors. Japanese vendors have developed systems for both the high- and low-end workstation markets.

OUTLOOK FOR 1994

Workstation shipments are expected to continue their strong growth, led by systems shipped to former mainframe and midrange users. More users are expected to downsize from large, proprietary systems to smaller, open environments, primarily based on UNIX workstations and servers. Workstations will continue to be the system of choice for scientific and technical users.

As workstation vendors focus their attention on selling to the mainstream business markets, their greatest challenge will lie in weaning DOS/Windows-based PC users away from their familiar operating systems environments by showing the advantages of the high-performance UNIX-based RISC systems. If the new technology promised by DOS/Windows software vendors stumbles in the marketplace, UNIX workstations will look more attractive to business users for their high-end needs and create a new market for workstation vendors. Some RISC vendors are already adjusting their strategy and pricing to capitalize on this potentially large market.

Competition within the workstation market will continue to be driven by lower prices, higher volumes, and better technology. The dominant workstation vendors will each continue on aggressive growth paths, announcing upgrades at least once in 1994, and introducing new, complementary product lines that will provide advanced multiprocessing and multitasking capabilities. Current users will have an impressive upgrade path as vendors begin to introduce 64-bit architectures.

The U.S. market will remain the largest single-country market, with more than 250,000 units shipped in 1994, a 10 percent increase. Japan and Europe will consume nearly 200,000 units each. By the end of 1994, the world's installed base of workstations should total more than 4 million units.

PERSONAL COMPUTERS

Personal computers (PCs) are general application computers based on microprocessor chips with a resident operating system and local programming capability. They are mainly oriented toward single users, but an increasing number are in multiuser settings or employed as network and file servers. There is a growing array of types and sizes grouped into two broad categories—stationary and portables. Stationary systems include desktop and deskside or "tower" configurations. Portables, comprising about 20 percent of the U.S. market, are divided into transportables, A/C and battery-powered laptops, notebooks, sub-notebooks, handheld, and pen-based models. Typical units with a monitor sell for $1,000 to $2,000, although prices range from below $500 for used or older computers to more than $25,000 for the most sophisticated, fully configured systems.

Although performance distinctions are blurring, PCs are differentiated from more powerful workstations, historically used in engineering and scientific applications, by slower microprocessors, less graphics capabilities, and lower display resolutions. Workstations generally run on a UNIX operating system, rather than PC operating systems, such as DOS, OS/2, and Macintosh OS.

The industry expansion of the 1980s, fed by a proliferation of suppliers, has slowed considerably, allowing the major suppliers to stabilize their positions and to retain or regain market share. The share of the top 10 vendors has remained between 50 and 60 percent over the last several years, but could increase due to escalating company acquisitions. The top three PC suppliers (IBM, Apple, and Compaq) continued to dominate the industry, although their market share has dropped from more than 50 percent in 1987 to approximately 30 percent in 1993.

Shipments of personal computers (desktops, desksides, and portables) to the U.S. market in 1993 were 13.2 million units, up 15 percent, according to IDC. (This marks a return to the double-digit growth rates enjoyed by the industry during most of the 1980s, after the bearish markets of 1990 and 1991.) The 1993 estimates include computers manufactured and assembled in the United States by domestic firms and foreign subsidiaries, and imported systems produced offshore by either U.S. or foreign-owned companies.

The value of the U.S. market in 1993 increased slightly to approximately $25 billion according to industry sources. Since 1991, market value has been growing slower than unit shipments and exhibited negative growth in 1991 due to significant price reductions. This is yet another sign of a maturing market with relative product saturation in the largest buying segments—government and business. The U.S.-installed base of PCs exceeded 70 million units compared to half that many in Europe. With heavy discounting of all computer models, sales at the high-end have not offset volume sales of less expensive machines as in past years. The 1993 PC market was most heavily affected by severe price erosion, accelerated product cycles, the increasing popularity of portables and workstations, and the success of new distribution channels.

Although abating somewhat, price wars continued to dominate the PC landscape in 1993. Pushed by intense competition among a plethora of PC suppliers, greater use of commodity-based mass marketing channels, and increased focus on the more price-sensitive buyers in homes, schools, and small businesses, vendors continued to slash list prices, cut dealer margins, and introduce low-cost lines aimed at the consumer and home markets. Intense price discounting began in 1991 and accelerated the following year as the industry set records for price reductions. Reductions in street prices, which declined on average by one-third in 1992, were not as steep in 1993. For example, street prices for some 80486-based PCs declined less than 5 percent during the first half of 1993. At some point, profit margins will be cut to the bone, and additional decreases will depend upon reduced component or manufacturing costs. Industry analysts expect price competition to moderate further in 1994.

Shortened, product-life cycles accompanied rapid price reductions. Estimated PC product-life has decreased from 5 years in 1981 to 6 months today, with R&D and market introduction phases shrinking accordingly. Component suppliers have contributed to this phenomenon. In the face of competition from other chip manufacturers, Intel expanded and stepped up product introductions in 1993, while continuing its efforts to move customers to 80486-based PCs with reductions of i486 microprocessor prices. The combination of falling prices and decreasing product cycles put severe pressure on PC suppliers' bottom lines in 1993.

The expansion of the microcomputer industry continued with the introduction of a growing variety of pen-based and hand-held computers at one end and multi-processor and multiuser systems at the other. Although still in the majority and benefiting from price cuts and the rebirth of the home market, traditional desktop PCs faced stiff competition from the portable and workstation ranks. Because desktop shipments are projected to decline from 80 percent of total PC sales to 65 percent by 1997, vendors are looking for help from the high-growth ends of the product spectrum.

The improved availability of PCs in consumer outlets at attractive prices increased sales to the more volatile, but less penetrated, small business sector, totaling more than 4 million firms with less than 100 employees. According to Link Resources, over 67 percent of these firms had PCs in 1993. Demand for PCs among businesses with less than 10 employees is forecast to grow 20 percent in 1993 to over 1.7 million units.

More than 31 million U.S. households owned PCs in 1993; the installed base was over 38 million. The value of shipments in 1993 exceeded $6 billion, while unit sales grew 5 percent to more than 5 million. Market growth was mostly driven by price cuts of 30 to 40 percent and the introduction of new low-cost PCs targeted at the home buyer. However, more than half of the sales went to satisfy pent up demand for more powerful PCs needed to run new graphical operating environments, such as Windows. Because major brands were sold through mass merchandizing channels, consumers received greater exposure to computers. Buyers also spent an average of $1,750 for their PCs than the previous year, using money saved from price reductions on systems to purchase more performance or additional software and peripherals. With improved system performance, users positioned themselves to accommodate the more power- and storage-hungry software of the future.

INTERNATIONAL COMPETITIVENESS

Foreign markets have become increasingly important to U.S. suppliers as they seek to expand sales. Some producers now sell as much PC equipment overseas as they do domestically. According to IDC estimates, the world market for personal computers totaled $68 billion in 1993, an 8 percent increase in current dollars. Unit shipments grew 14 percent to more than 33 million, with an active installed base of 157 million PCs. The largest national markets were the United States (39 percent of global shipments) and Japan (7 percent), followed by the major Western European countries. By region, the Western Hemisphere represented about 40 percent of the world market; Europe, 33 percent; and Asia, most of the rest. The U.S. share of the world market will continue to decline in the future as computer use expands abroad. While markets in the more developed countries mature, dramatic growth will occur in much of the rest of the world as industrial and government infrastructures are modernized. The potential of these developing markets holds great promise for U.S. companies.

Western Europe. In common with the U.S. market, PC sales in Western Europe have dropped from the steady double-digit growth of the 1980s. Following a 12 percent increase in 1992, IDC estimated that the Western European PC market grew 7 percent in 1993 to 10.5 million units, reflecting slow economic growth in the region. Steep price declines caused market value to remain unchanged at $21 billion. Although market sophistication has lagged behind the United States, Europe is catching up. Representing less than 1 percent of the market in 1993, shipments of PCs with Intel 80xx and 80286 processors have been declining since 1989. As in the United States, PCs with 80486 processors dominated sales with more than 60 percent of the market, while the market share for 80386SX and DX chips dropped precipitously to 21 percent from 53 percent in 1992, according to Dataquest. Sales of PCs with the more powerful RISC and Pentium processors are forecast to reach 2 million units by 1995.

According to Dataquest, the four largest PC markets in Europe last year were Germany (2.4 million units), the United Kingdom (2.3 million), France (1.5 million), and Italy (1 million). Commodore was the leading supplier in Europe, with about 12 percent of unit shipments, followed by IBM, Apple, Compaq, and Olivetti. The future growth of PC sales in Europe is linked to the development of broader distribution networks in each country and to the attractiveness of aftersales service and support packages provided by dealers. The home market also is becoming an important segment.

Japan. Personal computers are not yet as widely used in Japan as in Western Europe or the United States. The PC-installed base at the end of 1993 is estimated to be approximately 14 million units, according to IDC. This is about one-fifth the size of the U.S.-installed base. Factors that have contributed to this limited use include skepticism about the benefits of personal computers among Japanese businessmen, limited office and desk space, and the relatively higher prices for PC hardware and software in Japan compared with the United States.

In 1992, the Japanese PC industry was marked by sluggish export sales, reduced domestic production, and slowing domestic demand. Unit sales to the domestic market were down 6 percent, the first annual decline. But the 1993 market is expected to recover because of escalating hardware and software price wars, the release of the Japanese version of Windows 3.1, growing support for open systems and the DOS-V operating system, and the Japanese government's promotion of PCs in schools. Dataquest has forecast that the 1993 Japanese PC market totaled 2.3 million units and $4.6 billion, up 7 percent and 6 percent, respectively, from 1992. Almost 40 percent of unit shipments were laptop and notebook computers. In 1992, about 25 percent of PCs sold were based on Intel 80486 microprocessors; 80386-based computers accounted for 60 percent; and XT and AT computers fell to 7 percent. Macintosh units made up the rest.

Business users accounted for 60 percent of shipments, where the principal business applications were Japanese-language word processing and spreadsheets. However, Japanese business users have been moving toward networking and more powerful PC platforms with larger storage capacity and more robust operating systems and complex applications. The home and education sectors represent more than 30 percent of sales. Led by demand for high-end PCs and notebook computers, the market is projected to grow at a 9 percent average annual rate through the mid-1990's.

OUTLOOK FOR 1994

The U.S. PC market will experience favorable growth rates in 1994, although less than in 1993. According to Dataquest, the PC market should grow 13 percent, to 16.3 million units, with revenue increasing slightly to $27.6 billion. While unit sales should improve, market competition will continue to put intense pressure on revenue and profit margins. Prices for mainstream 80486 computers should continue to fall during the first half of 1994, especially if Intel further reduces the price of the 486 chip in conjunction with shipments of the new Pentium chip. Prices should begin to stabilize, however, as buyers and vendors evaluate the features and impact of the new PC platforms coming into the market. Marketing requirements will shift as the market matures further. A growing portion of sales will go to the replacement market characterized by more sophisticated buyers, who require more technology-intensive solutions. However, interest from first-time buyers also will increase, stimulated by declining prices and the availability of more useful, easier-to-use software packages.

The next generation of personal computers were introduced in 1993, and will become more widely available in 1994. These systems are characterized by 32-bit multitasking operating systems, 64-bit bus architectures, more powerful RISC-featured microprocessors, multimedia capabilities, more networking and work group computing, instant communications, and mobile computing. IDC predicts that worldwide sales of Pentium-based systems will exceed 700,000 in 1994, while shipments of the Windows NT operating system will approach 1.2 million. During this upcoming technology-intensive phase, PCs will be propelled into application areas once reserved for mainframes and minicomputers.

Sales to national, state, and local governments are a small but growing segment of the market. According to Federal Sources Inc., the Federal Government's spending on computers, communications equipment, and related services will grow 2 percent in the fiscal year that began October 1993. A 4 percent drop at the Department of Defense will be more than offset by a 7 percent increase for the civilian agencies. Future demand will be stimulated by improvements in the procurement process, more emphasis on enhancing Federal employee productivity through technology, and the ongoing modernization of government programs.

Multimedia products will have a greater impact on the PC market in 1994, as the installed base of multimedia-capable and ready PCs expands and the number of multimedia titles proliferates. Multimedia is a broadly defined cornucopia of technologies designed to combine full-motion video, animation, still pictures, voice, music, graphics, and text into a fully integrated and interactive system. These new integrated capabilities bring computers a step closer to realizing their enormous potential. Potential uses include training, education, publishing, entertainment, voice and video mail, teleconferencing, public information, and document-imaging and archival systems. Although estimates vary widely depending upon one's definition, some industry sources foresee a $13 billion market by 1995.

Multimedia is still an evolving set of technologies and products. Many issues concerning technical standards remain, such as those involving video-data compression, graphics and auto file formats, interface and storage specifications, and communications protocols. There is also a question of where the market will take off first, in the home or the office. This is an arena where U.S. computer manufacturers, communication service providers, consumer electronics conglomerates, and entertainment moguls will compete and collaborate to determine the future of the personal computer.

Another growth area is overseas, where PC sales in many countries will grow faster than in the United States. Unit-shipment growth in 1994 is projected to be 16 percent worldwide, including 13 percent each in Western Europe and Japan, according to Dataquest. Factory revenue for PC shipments outside the United States should exceed $45 billion. As a result, U.S. firms will place more emphasis on investing abroad and developing and adapting products for foreign markets.

PORTABLE COMPUTERS

Today's portable computers are divided into three fairly distinct types—laptops, notebooks, and handhelds—that vary broadly by their method of entering, storing, displaying, and processing data. Laptops have been relegated to applications which demand very powerful hardware, such as computer-aided design (CAD) and video presentations. Notebooks serve the more traditional general-purpose user who wants to do a large amount of wordprocessing and manipulate sizable spreadsheets. The handheld systems have less powerful versions of these capabilities combined with more intuitive functions, such as phone lists and messaging.

With the advent of the handheld class of computer, designers are taking advantage of new technologies to bring more functions out of the office and into these personal devices. Most of the functions designed for handheld devices attempt to electronically mimic the functions of some types of office equipment or supplies, such as writing instruments, paper forms, fax machines, or telephones. The next step to computers becoming truly "personal" is to design a handheld system that can bridge the gap between consumer and office electronics, so that the same device will be used in the living room, in the car, or on the beach.

The portable market is experiencing strong overall growth, even as the form factor (shape and size) changes and component technology advances. According to Dataquest, 6.9 million portable computers were shipped worldwide in 1993, with handheld computers comprising less than 10 percent of the total (Figure 10). However, by 1996, handhelds will make up nearly 40 percent of the market.

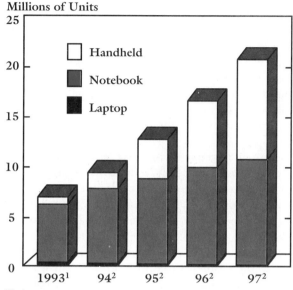

FIGURE 10 Worldwide Portable Computer Shipments Will Grow Rapidly

Millions of Units

[1]Estimate.

[2]Forecast.

Source: Dataquest, Inc.

In the United States, 50 percent of portable computers are sold through dealer channels, since most notebooks are purchased in large quantities by large corporate users. Product cycles have been reduced to an average of 18 months.

INTERNATIONAL COMPETITIVENESS

Several U.S., European, and Japanese companies are jointly developing products for the handheld area. In most cases, these companies have joined to penetrate more successfully the consumer electronics market with advanced computer-based products. Because breaking into the volume-driven consumer marketplace has proven to be a highly risky venture in the past, companies have formed strategic partnerships to spread the costs and the risk over more than one company. Through these partnerships, vendors also have ensured a supply of strategic components and in some cases gained valuable knowledge of marketing and manufacturing for the consumer market. As in the PC market, the profit margins probably will be established at the thinnest possible point to gain market share. Thus, potential vendors cannot base their market entry on a profit-making scenario, but rather on the potential to sell the follow-on peripherals, services, and software. For many vendors, tie ups are necessary to survive the nonprofitable stage of system development.

Japan's portable computer market is becoming increasingly competitive. The market has been dominated by one proprietary architecture, with a limited amount of useful applications software. The recent introduction of less expensive portables, based on a U.S. standard and its associated massive software library, has greatly invigorated that market. Portables already make up close to half of Japanese PC shipments, compared with around 20 percent of the U.S. PC market. As foreign vendors move into the Japanese market, more portables are being sold directly by the vendor than through traditional dealer distribution channels.

The European market also is experiencing steady growth in spite of its troubled economic picture. During 1993, European portable computer sales grew to 1.9 million units. The European market is very competitive, with many of the leading players holding roughly the same market shares as they do in the United States.

The most remarkable characteristic of the East Asian portable computer industry is the huge number of portable computer manufacturers. Despite an ongoing prediction that third-tier vendors will be driven out of business in price wars, nearly 200 vendors fill the advertising pages of such periodicals as *Asian Computer Sources.*

Domestic imports of portable computers are classified under Harmonized Systems Tariff Schedule number 8471.20.0090. Based on 6 months of data, the United States was expected to import nearly 1.9 million units in 1993, an increase of 58 percent. Imports from Japan will comprise 44 percent of total imports. The rest of Asia will account for another 42 percent. Canada, although increasing by an astronomical 485 percent in 1993, had only 13 percent of the total. In general, portable computer imports are increasing in average value, except for those from Hong Kong. The average value of portables from Japan was the highest—nearly $2,000 per unit—probably due to the high-end systems with color active-matrix displays.

OUTLOOK FOR 1994

The worldwide market for portable computers will be almost 9 million units, with handheld systems growing faster—as much as 100 percent—than notebooks and laptops. Handheld computers will benefit from improved communications and handwriting recognition capability, although they will continue to lack enough software applications to appeal to the general public.

Several different Pentium-based portable systems will be introduced by early 1994, but their market acceptance will be slowed until prices are reduced and other advanced component technology for this high-performance microprocessor (such as the battery) is incorporated. Component shortages will continue to play a role in notebook and laptop products, especially the high end. The supply of active-matrix LCD's, for example, will be tight until several fabrication facilities in Japan are ramped up to full production.

DELL COMPUTER CORPORATION—1994

BILL J. MIDDLEBROOK,
MICHAEL J. KEEFFE
AND JOHN K. ROSS III
Southwest Texas
State University

Headquartered in Austin, Texas, Dell Computer Corporation (512-338-4400) is a company with skyrocketing sales and new income. Sales and profits for 1993 increased 126 percent and 99 percent, respectively.

Customer satisfaction and customer service are two of the most repeated catch phrases in major corporations. CEO Michael Dell does not want service and satisfaction simply to be repeated by his corporate employees and support staffs; he requires them to practice what he preaches. Dell's commitment to customer satisfaction and service—known at Dell as Direct Relationship Marketing—can be shown through the policies of the corporation. First, there is an unconditional 30-day money-back guarantee for all of Dell's computer systems and a "no questions asked" return policy.

Second, Dell's toll-free technical support organization is available from 7 A.M. to 7 P.M., coast to coast (including Mexico). These technicians solve 95 percent of customer problems in less than six minutes. Additionally, a TechFax system is available twenty-four hours a day, seven days a week. Customers can request technical information through a fax catalogue, and problem-solving instructions are returned by fax. A third-party network of on-site service representatives can be dispatched when problems are not solved over the phone. If necessary, unresolved problems are expedited to the design engineers to ensure complete customer satisfaction. Dell users can also access an on-line technical support group via CompuServe. Finally, Michael Dell openly invites customers to write or call him with comments about the quality of Dell's products and the level of support received from service and support personnel.

This emphasis on quality and service has won accolades from customers and industry analysts. Dell has consistently been recognized as the best in customer support and satisfaction, ahead of all other computer manufacturers. J.D. Power and Associates, known for their automobile rankings, again this year rate Dell number one in customer satisfaction in its third annual end-user survey for the computer industry. Dell's mission statement follows:

> It is the mission of Dell Computer to provide individuals, small businesses, government agencies, educational institutions and large corporations with an affordable alternative within the global PC market.
>
> Dell Computer pledges to provide the highest quality and most technologically advanced personal computers at the lowest possible price and to back those computers with the highest level of customer service.
>
> Dell Computer will continually look for new value added services to provide to its current and future customers.
>
> Dell Computer believes its commitment to service sets itself apart from its competition and helps to give customers in the global PC market a true alternative when making a computer purchase.
>
> Dell Computer strongly believes it must coexist with the environment and will continually work to promote its preservation.
>
> Dell Computer realizes the importance, and its obligation, to its employees and shareholders and will continue to operate in their best interest.

The most publicized story of a company start-up in the computer industry is that of Steven Jobs and Stephen Wozniak designing and marketing Apple computers. These young entrepreneurs took a concept from a garage manufacturing arena and evolved Apple into a multimillion-dollar organization. The story of Michael Dell and the development of the Dell Computer Corporation rivals that of Jobs and Wozniak.

In 1983 Dell, then a freshman pre-med student at the University of Texas, decided to earn additional money by selling disk-drive kits and random access memory (RAM) chips at computer user meetings in Austin, Texas. Within a few months he had sufficient funds to acquire excess personal computers (PCs) at reasonable prices from IBM dealers having difficulties meeting their sales quotas. He modified these machines and began selling them through contacts in the local area and was reported to be grossing approximately $80,000 per month by April 1984. In May 1984, Dell formed the Dell Computer Corporation to sell PC's Limited brand computers and conducted operations out of his dormitory room. After dropping out of school (against his parents' wishes), he began attending computer trade fairs where he sold IBM PC-compatible computers, one of the first custom "clones" on the market.

The results of Dell's endeavors were immediate. During the first year of business, sales were approximately $6 million and grew to $257 million within the next four years. In 1988 the brand name was changed to Dell and sales continued to grow such that by 1990 the organization had sold $546 million in PC compatibles and peripheral equipment and $2.1 billion in fiscal 1993.

In 1987, Dell established its first international subsidiary in the United Kingdom to enter the growing European computer market. European countries had a lower PC saturation rate than the United States, and there were no large PC manufacturers in Europe. From 1988 to 1991, the organization developed wholly owned subsidiaries in Canada, France, Italy, Sweden, Germany, Finland, and the Netherlands and is in the process of launching other subsidiaries in Europe. An Irish manufacturing facility opened in 1991 to provide systems for the European market. In addition, a support center located in Amsterdam provides technical support throughout Europe. By February of 1993, European sales totaled $240 million and constituted 30 percent of total sales. Currently, 40 percent of sales are derived from international subsidiaries after only five years of operations.

In January 1993, Dell made a bold move by entering the Japanese market. Dell computer KK of Japan employs a staff of forty workers to provide a full range of sales, service, and technical assistance. Telephone sales are supplemented with an outside sales force and through two major retailers in Tokyo. As the first computer company to attempt telemarketing in Japan, Dell was met with skepticism by some industry observers. Initial reports indicate that the Japanese are very enthusiastic about the marketing approach and are responding in greater numbers than originally forecasted. Although successful, Dell is expected to have less than 1 percent of the Japanese market in 1993.

Dell Computer Corporation today has approximately 4,200 employees worldwide. Mr. Dell has surrounded himself with people having expertise in computer engineering and marketing; he serves as both chief executive officer (CEO) and chairman of the board of directors. The company currently operates on the principles espoused by Dell during its inception: customer service and a personal relationship with Dell system users.

The short history of the PC industry is one of booms and slumps. The stellar performance of the industry during the early to mid-1980s was followed by a consolidation of existing companies and a slowdown in sales during the 1986–1987 period. Industry sales increased through 1990, and projections show that corporate capital-equipment spending should grow at a 7 to 8 percent annual rate into the early 1990s. Some analysts contend that the growth rate of the PC industry is uncertain as the growth rate of the economy slows. For example, Volpe & Covington, a San Francisco-based PC investment consulting firm, believes that a 15 percent long-term growth in revenues for high-end PCs and a 12 percent compound growth rate for the industry is a reasonable assumption. Other analysts contend that PC sales will grow at only 5 to 7 percent in the 1990s, less than half as fast as sales grew in the late 1980s. In 1992, computer and peripheral sales totaled over $142 billion. This amount grew to $155 billion in 1993 and is projected to exceed $167 billion in 1994.

PC Industry Strategies. Two macroindustry strategies for competing in the PC industry can be combined with two macrosegments of the PC market to assess competitors and competitive approaches. First, PC manufacturers can approach the market as either innovators or imitators. IBM is the accepted innovation leader as both computer manufacturers and customers watch IBM's product development and base production and purchase decisions on current IBM products. Other computer manufacturers approach the market as innovators by developing hardware and software to satisfy specific market segments.

Some firms approach the market building clone PCs. These firms (sometimes called value-added remarketers) use the base MS-DOS technology of innovators and attempt to improve on the system configuration and/or differentiate their product on some basis such as marketing channel used, service and support, product reliability, and/or price. Essentially, value-added remarketers buy components and software from various vendors to configure systems sold under their own brand labels. The success of the imitative approaches is evidenced by the performance of companies such as Compaq, Prime Computer, Inc., CompuAdd, and Dell. Many clone firms believe that to be successful in the PC industry they must be concerned with market pressures to reduce price. They constantly monitor costs and search for ways to reduce those costs.

PC Markets. Macrosegments in the PC industry are usually defined as business, home, government, or education users. Business users want high performance, reliability, and value in a system for their computing needs. State-of-the-art technology, the ability to network and communicate with other systems, customer service and support, and cost are primary purchase determinants for the business user. One of the fastest-growing segments in the business market is the portables market, which is expected to grow at an annualized rate of 20 percent for the next few years.

Home market demand was initially created by innovators, early adopters, and the early majority groups of the adoption or diffusion of innovation cycle. Most home users are price conscious, planning to spend less than $1,200 for a system, and they value ease of operation and service as well as support from the manufacturer. This market should not be as lucrative as it was in the early to mid-1980s, but replacement sales (sales to previous PC owners) and sales to those still intending to buy a home PC should make this market moderately attractive. (For a list of competitors by market share, see Exhibits 27–1, 27–2 and 27–3.)

EXHIBIT 27-1 Worldwide Microsystems Shipped (in millions)

COMPANY	1989	1993*
IBM	2.7	4.4
Apple	1.5	3.2
COMPAQ	0.7	2.5
Sharp	1.4	1.9
NEC	1.1	1.7
Dell	0.1	1.4
Commodore	1.5	1.3
Packard Bell	0.3	0.9
Toshiba	0.4	0.8
AST	0.2	0.8
All others	13.5	22.2

*Projected
Source: infoCorp.

EXHIBIT 27-2 United States Microsystems Units Shipped (in millions)

COMPANY	1989	1993*
IBM	1.5	1.8
Apple	1.1	1.7
COMPAQ	0.4	1.1
Dell	0.1	0.9
Packard Bell	0.2	0.8
Gateway 2000	**	0.6
Hewlett-Packard	0.1	0.4
AST	0.2	0.4
Tandy	0.6	0.4
Commodore	0.4	0.3
All others	5.0	7.2

*Projected
**<100,000
Source: infoCorp.

Government and education users comprise the remaining macrosegments of the PC market. Both of these segments represent large, important segments yet typically yield lower margins than either the business or home markets. Typical purchase decisions are based on a bidding system, with the contract going to the lowest qualified bidder. The education market was considered important for its proposed ability to generate long-term brand loyalty among early users (students). Apple was one of the

EXHIBIT 27-3 Market share, 1992–1993* (percent)

COMPANY	MARKET SHARE 1993 *	MARKET SHARE 1992
IBM	13.9	11.7
Apple	13.5	13.0
COMPAQ	9.5	5.7
AST	6.2	2.7
Dell	5.7	3.8
Top 5	48.8	36.9

*Projected

Source: International Data Corp. *Wall Street Journal,* Thurs., Oct. 21, 1993, page B1.

earliest entrants into this market. It is questionable, however, if the long-term benefits of brand loyalty by early users is actually realized.

This segment, like the business segment, is interested in integrated systems designed to perform to buyers' specific needs. Increased competition for this market has led to increased downward pressures on prices.

Competitors. Major competitors of Dell include most traditional PC manufacturers such as IBM, Compaq, Zenith, and Tandy. These firms rely on selling through a professional sales force or through retail outlets. Competitors of Dell using a direct marketing and/or retailing approach (primarily value-added remarketers) include CompuAdd, which offers a full line of machines; Northgate, which offers machines similar to Dell at savings of up to $2,000 over Dell equipment; and Everex, which offers machines similar to Dell but claim that they are faster than Dell PCs. CompuAdd is located in Austin, Texas; Northgate in Plymouth, Minnesota; and Everex in Freemont, California. None of these firms have the service and satisfaction reputation of Dell.

Changes in the industry will be driven by several factors as the market matures. First, the Gartner Group, a market research firm, estimates that the number of customers replacing their outdated systems are expected to outnumber first-time purchasers by 1995.

Second, an investment report on the PC distribution industry shows that PC saturation rates are relatively low. Only about 33 percent of white-collar workers use PCs on the job, and only 17 percent of all domestic households have a PC. This becomes more important when one considers that the largest growth opportunities are in small to medium-sized accounts (businesses with fewer than 500 employees) that employ more than 70 percent of white-collar workers.

Third, the ratio of price to performance for equivalent functions continues to improve approximately 20 to 25 percent per year, which makes the purchase of state-of-the art machines more attractive to many segments. And fourth, competition should intensify. Value-added remarketers more than doubled during the 1988–1989 period, with the number of firms increasing from 350 to more than 1,000. Coupled with increased demand by business users, improved software and networking capabil-

EXHIBIT 27-4 Dell Computer Corporation, Selected Annual Financial Ratios

	01/31/93	02/02/92	02/03/91
Quick ratio	0.95	1.39	0.90
Current ratio	1.73	2.23	1.67
Sales/cash	21.13	5.75	14.91
Receivables turnover	5.38	5.39	6.09
Receivables days sales	66.86	66.73	59.12
Inventories turnover	6.64	7.03	6.17
Net sales/working capital	5.61	3.15	5.74
Net sales/current assets	2.36	1.74	2.31
Net sales/total assets	2.17	1.59	2.07
Total liab/total assets	0.60	0.51	0.58
Times interest earned	NA	NA	NA
Net income/net sales	0.05	0.06	0.05
Net income/total assets	0.11	0.09	0.10

ities, and increased competition through differentiation and focus-oriented marketing strategies, industry analysts forecast additional changes in both market approaches used by major competitors and further segmentation of the market. The 1990s should be a period of change for the industry, rivaling changes that occurred during the 1980s.

DELL COMPUTER OPERATIONS

Dell's success can be attributed to its commitment to customer service and satisfaction and the marketing of state-of-the-art systems to business users through direct marketing strategies.

Product Line. Dell offers an extensive and competitive product line ranging from inexpensive first-time-user computers to those with the latest technological developments. This strategy has resulted in a continuing evaluation and modification of Dell's product line with new products constantly being offered and other products being discontinued. Currently Dell is working with Microsoft to deliver factory installed Windows NT in high end workstations and networks as the software becomes available. Dell also plans to sell IBM's competing OS/2 operating system preinstalled. The ever changing demands of computer technology and the market have made product forecasting and planning difficult and risky.

Manufacturing. Dell's computers for the domestic market are manufactured in facilities in Austin, Texas. The purchase of a 126,000 square-foot manufacturing facility in 1989 doubled Dell's manufacturing capability. The 135,000-square-foot facility in Limerick, Ireland, is expected to satisfy the growing international demand for Dell Systems.

EXHIBIT 27-5 Dell Computer Corporation Officers

OFFICERS

NAME	AGE	TITLE
Dell, Michael S.	28	Chairman of the Board, CEO
Kocher, Joel J.	36	President, Worldwide Marketing, Sales and Service
Henry, G. Glenn	50	Senior Vice President
Flaig, L. Scott	48	Senior Vice President
Meredith, Thomas J.	42	Chief Financial Officer, Treasurer
Thomas, Thomas L.	43	Chief Information Officer
Ferrales, Savino R.	42	Vice President
Salwen, Richard E.	47	Vice President, Legal Counsel
Medica, John	34	Vice President, Portable Products Group

The manufacturing strategy utilized at Dell is one of building each computer system to the buyer's specifications. Buyers can add options to customize their system for their own needs. The order is then assembled and shipped with peripherals and upgrades requested by the customer. Manufacturing at Dell actually consists of the assembly and testing of vendor-procured parts, assemblies, and subassemblies. The assembly line is not automated at present, and Dell has not indicated plans to automate. In addition, Dell utilizes a total quality approach where enthusiastic workers compete in product-quality competitions for bonuses and recognition.

Marketing. One factor leading to Dell's success is the organization's marketing style. Dell approaches the market from a service and customer satisfaction standpoint combined with lower prices than comparable brands. Sales leads are generated through several sources, the primary source being advertising in PC and business publications. An outside sales force located in major markets addresses the needs of large corporate customers.

Dell's sales force is channelized according to the market it serves: small/medium business and home users, corporate buyers, and government/education/medical. Each of these sales channels is supported by its own marketing, customer service, and technical support organization. This organizational structure ensures high accountability for the satisfaction of each customer, as well as feedback from daily direct contact with the customer. PC makers dealing through the retail channel do not have this advantage and are not able to respond as quickly to market and service demands as the direct channel. Additional face-to-face exposure occurs at industry shows.

Dell's entire product line is sold by telephone sales representatives who answer more than 8,000 incoming calls on a busy day. In addition to answering customer-initiated calls, the Austin-based sales force responds to sales leads and supports the efforts of its team members in the field.

Sales orders are downloaded to the manufacturing facility several times each day, and all systems are custom-configured according to the customer's specifications. Trucks load at Dell's manufacturing facility throughout the day, and overnight services are utilized for expedited orders. Lead times on systems vary from three to seven days.

Internationally, Dell is similar in marketing approach and culture to its domestic operation. Dell's wholly owned subsidiaries give it access to over 70 percent of the available worldwide market for PCs.

Dell sells to major buyers through a small (twenty-five-person) sales force located in major metropolitan areas throughout the United States and services those accounts with management teams consisting of sales, customer service, and technical support representatives. Dell believes that the small- to medium-sized business represents the greatest growth potential for PC-based systems.

Dell has also arranged to sell its systems through integrators like Electronic Data Systems (EDS) and Anderson Consulting, which will increase its sales potential. This move from traditional channels was prompted by the fact that the mail-order market is only 16 percent of a $35 to $40 billion market, less than one-fifth the size of sales of computer stores. Dell currently has 25 percent of the mail-order market.

RETAIL

Dell has contracted with CompUSA, Inc., a Dallas-based chain of twenty superstores, to sell Dell products. CompUSA is a computer version of Toys "Я" Us, with approximately 21,000 square feet of retail space per store, a service center with a fast service pickup for corporate clients, and over 5,000 items at discount prices. CompUSA is adding new stores in major metropolitan areas and sells Dell systems for the same prices as Dell's direct sales.

Dell has added Staples Office Supply Superstores to its mass merchandising channel. Staples markets to a less sophisticated computer user than does CompUSA. Although Dell systems are sold through this superstore channel, Dell maintains its same level of customer support to these buyers. Users who purchase Dell systems through CompUSA and Staples are entered into Dell's customer data base as if they had ordered directly through Dell.

Dell's mass merchandising move may provide a serendipitous opportunity for the company even though computer retailing is seen by some industry analysts as poised for a shakeout. Dataquest, Inc., believes that traditional retailers will see their share of PC sales shrink through 1994. Analysts state that marketers will have to move toward the ends of the retail spectrum by either concentrating on high-volume, low-price selling or specializing in market niches or other customized services that mass marketers neglect in order to be successful. Smaller operations that emphasize service along with price are already showing the greatest gains. Superstores may be one retail format that not only survives the shakeout but prospers. Dell sells its Precision Line of Computers through Sam's Clubs, a division of Wal★Mart Stores Incorporated, and also through Price Club, another mass merchandising chain.

Research and Development. During the last few years, Dell's revenue growth has allowed the organization to devote considerable resources to building a first-class technological capability. Research and development spending for fiscal 1992 was $31.3 million, up 26 percent from 1991.

Finance. Financial summaries of Dell are presented in Exhibits 27–6 through 27–11. The organization does not pay dividends to investors, relying instead on appreciation of stock price. It has experienced good sales and profit growth. Dell is currently searching for ways to reduce costs without sacrificing customer service and technological performance of its systems.

ISSUES AND CONCERNS

The most pressing concern of investors regarding Dell operations is Michael Dell. Dell has been very successful in building his organization with an entrepreneurial style of management. On a scale of one to ten, Dell rates himself ten as a competitor, innovator, goal setter, entrepreneur, and exporter. He rates himself lowest in the areas of production and finance. Although Mr. Dell was recently cited as Entrepreneur of the Year by *Inc.* magazine, his critics wonder if he is capable of making the transition of moving the corporation from a Stage 1 entrepreneurial mode to a Stage 2 professional management company.

Another concern is Dell's current move to include retail sales in addition to its traditional strength of telemarketing. This move is designed to broaden Dell's appeal to small businesses and the home PC user, but retailers historically have not shown loyalty to any particular brand of machine and may stock several different brands in their stores. Additionally, Dell's emphasis on telemarketing is a double-edged sword.

EXHIBIT 27-6 Dell Computer Corporation, Consolidated Statement of Income (In thousands of dollars, except per share data)

	FISCAL YEAR		
	1993	1992	1991
Net sales	$2,013,924	$889,939	$546,235
Cost of sales	1,564,472	607,768	364,183
Gross profit	449,452	282,171	182,052
Operating expenses:			
Marketing and sales	220,907	142,932	88,662
General and administrative	47,075	39,223	26,354
Research, development and engineering	42,358	33,140	22,444
Total operating expenses	310,340	215,295	137,460
Operating income	139,112	66,876	44,592
Financing and other income (expense)	4,180	6,539	(1,020)
Income before income taxes	143,292	73,415	43,572
Provision for income taxes	41,650	22,504	16,340
Net income	$ 101,642	$ 50,911	$ 27,232
Earnings per share	$ 2.59	$ 1.40	$ .91
Weighted average shares outstanding	39,235	36,274	30,064

Source: Dell Computer Corporation, *Annual Report,* 1993.

Telemarketing does reduce the need for a field sales force and eliminates channel markups, but Dell is considered by some to be little more than a dim, dusty warehouse that sells cheap, undistinguished PCs.

Lastly, the question also arises whether Dell can continue to grow as quickly as it would like and still have the same emphasis on service, performance, and satisfaction. There is intense competition as the industry matures and growth slows. Dell is still one of the infants in an industry populated by giants, and it must be wary of financial and technological colossuses potentially entering its market niche.

EXHIBIT 27-7 Dell Computer Corporation, Consolidated Statement of Financial Position (In thousands of dollars, except per share data)

	JANUARY 31, 1993	FEBRUARY 2, 1992
Assets		
Current assets:		
Cash and cash equivalents	$ 14,948	$ 55,460
Short-term investments	80,367	99,392
Accounts receivable, net	374,013	164,960
Inventories	303,220	126,554
Other current assets	80,239	65,814
Total current assets	852,787	512,180
Property and equipment, net	70,462	44,661
Other assets	3,756	2,722
	$927,005	$559,563
Liabilities and stockholders' equity		
Current liabilities:		
Accounts payable	$295,133	$ 97,389
Accrued liabilities	171,473	114,816
Income taxes	27,233	17,329
Total current liabilities	493,839	229,534
Long-term debt	48,373	41,450
Other liabilities	15,593	14,399
Commitments and contingencies		
Stockholders' equity:		
Preferred stock: $.01 par value; shares authorized: 5,000,000; none outstanding	—	—
Common stock: $.01 par value; shares authorized: 100,000,000; shares issued and outstanding: 36,857,948 and 35,801,620, respectively	369	358
Additional paid-in capital	177,978	165,745
Retained earnings	208,544	106,902
Cumulative translation adjustment	(17,691)	1,175
Total stockholders' equity	369,200	274,180
	$927,005	$559,563

Source: Dell Computer Corporation, *Annual Report,* 1993.

EXHIBIT 27-8 Dell Computer Corporation, Selected Consolidated Financial Data (In thousands of dollars, except per share and operating data)

	FISCAL YEAR ENDED				
	JAN 31, 1993	FEB 2, 1992	FEB 3, 1991	FEB 2, 1990	JAN 27, 1989
Income statement data:					
Net Sales:					
Domestic	$1,283,899	$566,392	$ 358,877	$300,257	$ 218,204
International	730,025	323,547	187,358	88,301	39,606
Consolidated net sales	$2,013,924	$889,939	$ 546,235	$388,558	$ 257,810
Gross Profit	$ 449,452	$282,171	$ 182,052	$109,586	$ 80,512
Operating income	$ 139,112	$ 66,876	$ 44,592	$ 11,414	$ 21,550
Net income	$ 101,642	$ 50,911	$ 27,232	$ 5,114	$ 14,428
Earnings per share	$ 2.59	$ 1.40	$ .91	$ .18	$ .53
Shares used in per share calculation	39,235	36,274	30,064	28,843	27,019
Balance sheet data:					
Working capital	$ 358,948	$282,646	$ 95,163	$ 57,970	$ 63,126
Total assets	$ 927,005	$559,563	$ 264,222	$171,774	$ 167,032
Long-term obligations	$ 50,621	$ 43,740	$ 4,207	$ 6,041	$ 5,472
Stockholders' equity	$ 369,200	$274,180	$ 112,005	$ 79,761	$ 75,257
Operating data:					
Current ratio	1.7	2.2	1.7	1.7	1.7
Inventories/working capital	.8	.4	.9	1.2	1.6
Debt to equity ratio	.15	.15	.00	.08	.36
Return on average assets	14 %	12 %	12 %	3 %	13 %
Return on average equity	32 %	26 %	28 %	7 %	34 %
Effective tax rate	29.1%	30.7%	37.5%	38.2%	31.8%

Source: Dell Computer Corporation, *Annual Report*, 1993.

EXHIBIT 27-9 Dell Computer Corporation Financial Condition and Results of Operations

| | PERCENTAGE OF NET SALES FISCAL YEAR ENDED | | |
	JANUARY 31, 1993	FEBRUARY 2, 1992	FEBRUARY 3, 1991
Net sales:			
Domestic	63.8%	63.6%	65.7%
International	36.2	36.4	34.3
Consolidated net sales	100.0	100.0	100.0
Cost of sales	77.7	68.3	66.7
Gross profit	22.3	31.7	33.3
Operating expenses:			
Marketing and sales	11.0	16.1	16.2
General and administrative	2.3	4.4	4.8
Research, development and engineering	2.1	3.7	4.1
Total operating expenses	15.4	24.2	25.1
Operating income	6.9	7.5	8.2
Net financing and other income (expense)	.2	.7	.2
Income before income taxes	7.1	8.2	8.0
Provision for income taxes	2.1	2.5	3.0
Net Income	5.0%	5.7%	5.0%

Source: Dell Computer Corporation, *Annual Report*, 1993.

EXHIBIT 27-10 Dell Computer Corporation Consolidated Statement of Cash Flows (In thousands of dollars)

| | FISCAL YEAR | | |
	1993	1992	1991
Cash flow from operating activities:			
Net income	$ 101,642	$ 50,911	$ 27,232
Charges to income not requiring cash outlays:			
Depreciation and amortization	19,597	13,832	8,955
Other	149	5,841	3,660
Changes in:			
Operating working capital	(162,521)	(70,962)	4,036
Non-current assets and liabilities	2,111	871	6,946
	(140,664)	(50,418)	(23,597)
Net cash (used in) provided by operating activities	(39,022)	493	50,829
Cash flow from investing activities:			
Net sales (purchases) of short-term investments	19,025	(99,392)	—
Capital expenditures	(47,251)	(32,630)	(9,485)
Net cash used in investing activities	(28,226)	(132,022)	(9,485)
Cash flow from financing activities:			
Net proceeds from short-term borrowings	8,500	—	—

EXHIBIT 27-10 *Continued*

	FISCAL YEAR		
	1993	1992	1991
Borrowings from long-term debt	7,270	41,450	—
Repayments of borrowings	(711)	(2,577)	(8,791)
Net proceeds from issuance of common stock	—	105,659	—
Issuance of common stock under employee plans	12,244	6,112	2,595
Net cash provided by (used in) financing activities	27,303	150,644	(6,196)
Effect of translation exchage rate changes on cash	(567)	(282)	1,479
Net (decrease) increase in cash	(40,512)	18,833	36,627
Cash at beginning of period	55,460	36,627	—
Cash at end of period	$ 14,948	$ 55,460	$ 36,627

Source: Dell Computer Corporation, *Annual Report*, 1993.

EXHIBIT 27-11 Dell Computer Corporation Consolidated Statement of Stockholders' Equity (In thousands of dollars, except share data)

STOCKHOLDERS' EQUITY					
	COMMON STOCK	PAID-IN CAPITAL	RETAINED EARNINGS	TRANSLATION ADJUSTMENT	TOTAL
Balances at February 2, 1990	$282	$ 51,455	$ 28,759	$ (735)	$ 79,761
Net income	—	—	27,232	—	27,232
Issuance of stock under employee plans	8	2,587	—	—	2,595
Foreign currency translation adjustment	—	—	—	2,417	2,417
Balances at February 3, 1991	290	54,042	55,991	1,682	112,005
Net Income	—	—	50,911	—	50,911
Issuance of 5,762,250 shares of common stock, net	58	105,601	—	—	105,659
Issuance of stock under employee plans	10	6,102	—	—	6,112
Foreign currency translation adjustment	—	—	—	(507)	(507)
Balances at February 2, 1992	358	165,745	106,902	1,175	274,180
Net income	—	—	101,642	—	101,642
Issuance of stock under employee plans	11	12,233	—	—	12,244
Foreign currency translation adjustment	—	—	—	(18,866)	(18,866)
Balances at January 31, 1993	$369	$177,978	$208,544	$(17,691)	$369,200

Source: Dell Computer Corporation, *Annual Report*, 1993.

EXHIBIT 27-12 Dell Computer Corporation Offices

CORPORATE
HEADQUARTERS
  Dell Computer Corporation
  9505 Arboretum Boulevard
  Austin, Texas 78759-7299
  Tel: (512) 338-4400, (800) 289-3355
  Fax: (512) 338-8700

INTERNATIONAL OFFICES
AUSTRALIA:
  Dell Computer Pty Ltd
  Unit 13, 25 Frenchs Forest Rd.
  Frenchs Forest NSW 2086
  Australia
  Tel: (61) 2-930-3355
  Fax: (61) 2-930-3311

AUSTRIA:
  Dell Computer GES.m.b.H
  Inkustraße 1-7, Haus H/7
  3400 Klosterneuburg
  Tel: (43) 2243-34100
  Fax:(43)2243-34102

BELGIUM & LUXEMBOURG:
  N.V. Dell Computer S.A.
  Doornveld 1, Bus 15
  1731 Asse-Zellik
  Belgium
  Tel: (32) 2-466-91-99
  Fax: (32) 2-466-47-89

CANADA:
  Dell Computer Corporation
  121 Granton Drive, Unit 12
  Richmond Hill, Ontario
  Canada L4B3N4
  Tel: (416) 764-4200
  Fax: (416) 764-4209

CZECH REPUBLIC:
  Dell Computer s.r.o.
  Osadni 12a 17000 Prague 7
  Czech Republic
  Tel: (42) 2-879250
  Fax: (42) 2-808237

EUROPEAN MARKETING AND OPERATIONS:
  European Marketing & Operations
  Dell Computer Corporation
  Western Road
  Bracknell, Berkshire
  U.K. RG12 1RW
  Tel: (44) 344-860-456
  Fax: (44) 344-714-697

EUROPEAN SUPPORT CENTRE:
  European Support Centre
  p.a. Dell Computer BV
  Zekeringstraat 45B
  1014 BP, Amsterdam
  The Netherlands
  Tel: (31) 20-684-9291
  Fax: (31) 20-682-3596

FINLAND:
  Dell Computer OY
  Vattuniemenranta 2
  00210 Helsinki
  Finland
  Tel: (358) 0-692-3122
  Fax: (358) 0-692-2847

FRANCE (MONTPELLIER):
  Dell Computer S.A.
  BP 9646
  34054 Montpellier Cedex 1
  France
  Tel: (33) 6706-6000
  Fax: (33) 6706-6001

FRANCE:
  Dell Computer
  2, Parc Club Ariane BP-285
  78053 St. Quentin en Yvelines Cedex
  France
  Tel: (33)-1-30 60 69 00
  Fax:(33)-1-30 60 69 01

GERMANY:
  Dell Computer GmbH
  Monzastr. 4
  6070 Langen
  Germany
  Tel: (49) 6103-701-0
  Fax:(49) 6103-701-701

EXHIBIT 27-12 *Continued*

IRELAND:
Dell Products (Europe) B.V.
Raheen Industrial Estate
Raheen, Limerick
Republic of Ireland
Tel: (353) 61-304091
Fax: (353) 61-304090

IRELAND(Bray):
Dell Computer Corporation
Boghall Road
Bray
Co. Wicklow
Tel: (353) 1 2860500
Fax: (353) 1 2862020

ITALY:
Dell Computer SPA
Via Enrico Fermi, 20
20090 Assago Milano
Italy
Tel: (39) 2-457941
Fax: (39) 2-45794001

JAPAN:
Dell Computer Corporation
Gotanda Nagase Bldg.
2-8-3, Higashi Gotanda
Shinagawa-Ku, Tokyo 141
Japan
Tel: (81-3) 5420-5901
Fax: (81-3) 5420-7366

MEXICO:
Dell Computer de Mexico, S.A. de C.V.
Blvd. M. de Cervantes Saavedra 61
Colonia Granda
11520 Mexico, D.F.
Tel: (525) 228-7800
Fax: (525) 228-7840

NETHERLANDS:
Dell Computer BV
Zekeringstraat 45 B
1014 BP Amsterdam
The Netherlands
Tel: (31) 20-6812666
Fax: (31) 20-6812751

NORWAY:
Dell Computer AS
Drammensveien 302-304
N-1324 Lysaker
Norway
Tel: (47) 67 12 57 11
Fax: (47) 67 12 55 03

POLAND:
Dell Computer Poland
Stawki Str. 2, XIV Floor
00-193 Warsaw
Poland
Tel: (482) 635-7641
Fax: (482) 635-7162

SOUTHEAST ASIA:
PROCUREMENT OFFICE:
Dell Computer Corporation
Southeast Asia Procurement Office
No. 8, Lane 6 Hang ChouS. Road, Sec. 1
Taipei, Taiwan
Republic of China
Tel: (886) 2-391-2100
Fax: (886) 2-391-3354

SPAIN:
Dell España S.A.
Barajas Park
San Severo s/n
28042 Madrid
Spain
Tel: (34) 1-329-10-80
Fax: (34) 1-329-26-10

SWEDEN:
Dell Computer AB
Kanalvägen 8, Box 709
194 27 Upplands Våsby
Sweden
Tel: (46) 08-590 713 50
Fax: (46) 08-590 737 89

SWITZERLAND:
Dell Computer SA
220 route de Ferney
Ch-1218 Grand-Saconnex-Geneva
Tel: (41) 22-788-40-00
Fax: (41) 22-788-38-66

EXHIBIT 27-12 *Continued*

UNITED KINGDOM:

Dell Computer Corporation Ltd.

Milbanke House, Western Road

Bracknell, Berkshire

RG12 1RW

United Kingdom

Tel: (44) 344 720000

Fax: (44) 344 860187

Source: Dell Computer Corporation, *Annual Report*, 1993.

CASE 28

FRED R. DAVID
Francis Marion
University

IBM CORPORATION—1994

The year 1993 was the worst in IBM's history. Net losses were $8.1 billion on revenues of $62.7 billion. Big Blue was a company in Big Trouble. IBM reduced its workforce by 45,000 in 1993 to a total of 256,000. By the end of 1994 and with divestiture of the Federal Systems Company, the IBM workforce should drop to 215,000. Brown Brothers Harriman & Company, an investment brokerage firm, has concluded that "Technological changes in the computer business will preclude IBM from ever returning to its former greatness."

Headquartered in Armonk, New York, IBM's (914-765-1900) CEO Louis Gerstner, Jr., was recently criticized when he made the following comment in a speech:

> The last thing IBM needs right now is a vision. I could spend a lot of time focusing this company on a mission statement, and would love it. But there would be debate instead of action, when the most important thing we have to do is implement better and sooner. I want to stay away from abstractions and deal with the marketplace. Our mission is to be the most successful information technology company in the world. O.K., you want a vision statement? Fine, you got it, now let's go back to work.

IBM does not have a mission statement. Yet CEO Gersner says "Setting strategies is our single highest priority after making IBM profitable. We are hard at work—day and night—developing tough-minded strategies for every one of our businesses." IBM was granted 1,087 U.S. patents in 1993, more than any other company in the world.

OPERATIONS

IBM continues aggressively to restructure its worldwide business operations to reduce costs and regain a competitive posture. As indicated in Exhibit 28–1, more than 90 percent of IBM's revenues are derived from computer hardware, computer software, computer services, and computer maintenance. Revenues from computer services rose 32.1 percent in 1993, but revenues from the other three categories declined as shown. It is interesting that more than 50 percent of IBM's revenues came from non-hardware sources in 1993.

EXHIBIT 28-1 IBM Selected Income and Expense Items

PERCENTAGE OF TOTAL REVENUE				PERCENTAGE CHANGES*	
1991	1992	1993	INCOME AND EXPENSE ITEMS	1993-92	1992-91
			REVENUE:		
57.3%	52.3%	48.8%	Hardware sales	(9.4)%	(9.0)%
16.2	17.2	17.5	Software	(1.4)	5.8
8.6	11.4	15.5	Services	32.1	31.7
11.4	11.8	11.6	Maintenance	(4.4)	3.0
6.5	7.3	6.6	Rentals and financing	(10.9)	11.9
100.0	100.0	100.0	Total revenue	(2.8)	(0.4)
49.5	54.4	61.5	Total cost	10.0	9.3
50.5	45.6	38.5	Gross profit	(18.0)	(9.9)
			EXPENSES:		
33.0	30.3	29.2	Selling, general and administrative	(6.4)	(8.7)
10.3	10.1	8.9	Research, development, and engineering	(14.8)	(1.8)
5.8	18.0	14.3	Restructuring charges	—	—
49.1	58.4	52.4	Total operating expenses	—	—
0.9	0.9	1.8	Other Income, principally interest	94.2	(4.8)
2.2	2.1	2.0	Interest expense	(6.4)	(4.4)
			NET EARNINGS:		
3.5	2.2	0.0	Before restructuring charges and accounting changes	—	—
(4.4)	(7.7)	(12.9)	Net loss	—	—

*Percentage changes displayed as (-) are not meaningful.
Source: IBM *Annual Report*, 1993.

HARDWARE SALES (DOLLARS IN MILLIONS)	1993	1992	1991
Total revenue	$30,591	$33,755	$37,093
Total cost	20,696	19,698	18,571
Gross profit	$ 9,895	$14,057	$18,522
Gross profit margin	32.3%	41.6%	49.9%

Hardware and Software. As indicated above, worldwide gross profit dollars from hardware sales decreased 29.6 percent in 1993, primarily due to a 27.6 percent decrease in processors such as the System 390 processor and the Application/System/400. IBM produces and markets both high-end and midrange processors as well as workstations.

IBM's personal computer systems revenue increased 23.3 percent in 1993 due partly to strong growth in RISC System/6000. IBM shipped about 4.3 million personal computers in 1992 compared to 3.3 million units the prior year. In 1993, other hardware sales revenue increased 68.1 percent, primarily due to higher original equipment manufacturer (OEM) growth.

IBM's 1993 gross profit dollars in software decreased 7.5 percent while revenues declined to $10.9 million (see below).

Services and Maintenance. IBM's services revenue, excluding maintenance, grew 32.1 percent in 1993 while services gross profit dollars increased 10.1 percent. Federal Systems Company, a part of IBM's services operations, was sold in the first quarter of 1994. As indicated in the table on the opposite page, IBM's maintenance revenue decreased 4.4 percent in 1993. A summary of IBM's revenues by classes of similar products or services is given in Exhibit 28–2.

SOFTWARE *(DOLLARS IN MILLIONS)*	1993	1992	1991
Total revenue	$10,953	$11,103	$10,498
Total cost	4,310	3,924	3,865
Gross profit	$ 6,643	$ 7,179	$ 6,633
Gross profit margin	60.7%	64.7%	63.2%

EXHIBIT 28-2 IBM Revenue by Classes of Similar Products or Services *(Dollars in millions)*

	CONSOLIDATED			U.S. ONLY		
	1993	1992[+]	1991[+]	1993	1992[+]	1991[+]
Information technology:						
Processors*	$10,071	$13,916	$14,954	$ 3,179	$ 4,818	$ 4,717
Personal systems*	9,728	7,887	8,505	4,417	3,033	3,210
Other workstations*	2,006	2,671	3,216	689	874	1,040
Storage*	5,122	6,259	7,184	2,101	2,554	2,825
Other peripherals*	2,262	3,026	3,294	971	1,244	1,424
Software	10,953	11,103	10,498	3,898	3,883	3,760
Maintenance	7,295	7,635	7,414	2,726	2,809	2,884
Services	9,711	7,352	5,582	5,100	3,546	2,697
Financing and other	5,568	4,674	4,119	2,622	1,872	1,870
Total	$62,716	$64,523	$64,766	$25,703	$24,633	$24,427

[+]Reclassified to conform with 1993 presentation.

*Hardware only, includes applicable rental revenue, excludes functions not embedded, software, and maintenance.

Source: IBM *Annual Report*, 1993.

Services (Dollars in Millions)	1993	1992	1991
Services	$ 7,648	$ 5,530	$ 4,144
Federal Systems Company	2,063	1,822	1,438
Services revenue excluding maintenance	$ 9,711	$ 7,352	$ 5,582
Cost	8,279	6,051	4,531
Gross profit	$ 1,432	$ 1,301	$ 1,051
Gross profit margin	14.7%	17.7%	18.8%
Maintenance revenue	$ 7,295	$ 7,635	$ 7,414
Cost	3,545	3,430	3,379
Gross profit	$ 3,750	$ 4,205	$ 4,035
Gross profit margin	51.4%	55.1%	54.4%
Total services revenue	$17,006	$14,987	$12,996
Cost	11,824	9,481	7,910
Gross profit	$ 5,182	$ 5,506	$ 5,086
Gross profit margin	30.5%	36.7%	39.1%

Services revenue, excluding maintenance, continued to show overall strong growth, increasing 32.1 percent in 1993 over 1992, following an increase of 31.7 percent in 1992 over 1991.

GLOBAL FACTORS

Exhibit 28–3 reveals that IBM markets its products and services globally. Revenue in the United States was $25.7 billion, up 4.3 percent, while 1993 revenue from non-U.S. operations generated revenue of $37.0 billion, a 7.2 percent decrease from 1992. Note that IBM's Asia Pacific operations increased to over $10 billion in 1993 but the company's Europe/Middle East/Africa revenues declined 12.8 percent to $21.8 billion. In the Europe/Middle East/Africa area, European operations account for about 95 percent of IBM's revenue.

MANAGEMENT AND FINANCE

Members of IBM's top management team are listed in Exhibit 28–4. The company's 1993 financial statements are provided in Exhibits 28–5 through 28–8. Note that the company's long-term debt increased 18.6 percent, partly to cover expenses since net profits were negative $8.1 billion.

PARTNERS

The rush of new technology, the expense of staying on the leading edge, the demands of customers, and worldwide competition have required IBM and other high-tech companies to form a wide range of alliances and partnerships. The costs of developing the 256-million-bit memory chip (in a three-way pact with Siemens and Toshiba) may, for example, reach a billion dollars. With these stakes, sharing costs, risk, and knowledge is essential.

EXHIBIT 28-3 IBM Geographic Areas (*Dollars in millions*)

	1993*	1992*	1991*
United States			
Revenue—Customers	$ 25,703	$ 24,633	$ 24,427
Interarea transfers	7,297	7,524	7,668
Total	$ 33,000	$ 32,157	$ 32,095
Net loss	(5,566)	(5,545)	(2,443)
Assets at December 31	38,333	42,109	43,417
Europe/Middle East/Africa			
Revenue—Customers	$ 21,779	$ 24,971	$ 26,114
Interarea transfers	1,071	1,154	838
Total	$ 22,850	$ 26,125	$ 26,952
Net (loss) earnings	(1,695)	(1,728)	1,256
Assets at December 31	24,566	26,770	30,725
Asia Pacific			
Revenue—Customers	$ 10,020	$ 9,672	$ 9,275
Interarea transfers	1,452	1,875	1,680
Total	$ 11,472	$ 11,547	$ 10,955
Net (loss) earnings	(443)	126	469
Assets at December 31	12,778	12,837	13,241
Americas			
Revenue—Customers	$ 5,214	$ 5,247	$ 4,950
Interarea transfers	3,458	3,452	3,932
Total	$ 8,672	$ 8,699	$ 8,882
Net (loss) earnings	(251)	157	204
Assets at December 31	7,359	6,990	7,121
Eliminations			
Revenue	$(13,278)	$(14,005)	$(14,118)
Net (loss) earnings	(32)	125	(84)
Assets	(1,923)	(2,001)	(2,031)
Consolidated			
Revenue	$ 62,716	$ 64,523	$ 64,766
Net loss	(7,987)	(6,865)	(598)
Assets at December 31	81,113	86,705	92,473

*Net (loss) earnings before effect of changes in accounting for postemployment benefits (1993), income taxes (1992), and nonpension postretirement benefits (1991).

In a decade, IBM has moved from a do-it-yourself, inwardly directed company to an enterprise that reaches out for new ideas and approaches that mesh with its own talents and strengths. The quest to satisfy customers has blurred traditional competi-

EXHIBIT 28-4 IBM's Board of Directors

Harold Brown
Counselor
Center for Strategic and
International
Studies and General Partner
Warburg, Pincus & Company

James E. Burke
Retired Chairman of the Board
Johnson & Johnson

Thomas F. Frist, Jr.*
Chairman, Columbia/
HCA Healthcare Corporation

Fritz Gerber
Chairman and Chief Executive
Officer
Roche Holding Ltd. and
Executive Chairman
Zurich Insurance Company

Louis V. Gerstner, Jr.
Chairman of the Board and
Chief Executive Officer
IBM

Judith Richards Hope*
Senior Partner
Paul, Hastings, Janofsky & Walker

Nannerl O. Keohane
President
Duke University

Charles F. Knight
Chairman of the Board and
Chief Executive Officer
Emerson Electric Co.

Thomas S. Murphy
Chairman and Chief Executive
Officer
Capital Cities/ABC, Inc.

John R. Opel*
Retired Chairman of the Board
IBM

Paul J. Rizzo
Vice Chairman of the Board
IBM

John B. Slaughter
President
Occidental College

Lodewijk C. van Wachem
Chairman of the Supervisory Board
Royal Dutch Petroleum Company

Edgar S. Woolard, Jr.
Chairman and Chief Executive
Officer
E.I. du Pont de Nemours and
Company

*Directors who will be retiring effective
April 25, 1994.

IBM'S MANAGEMENT — MEMBERS OF WORLDWIDE MANAGEMENT COUNCIL

Louis V. Gerstner, Jr.
Chairman of the Board and
Chief Executive Officer

Paul J. Rizzo
Vice Chairman of the Board

James A. Cannavino
IBM Senior Vice President
Strategy and Development

Gerald M. Czarnecki
IBM Senior Vice President
Human Resources and
Administration

Donato A. Evangelista
IBM Senior Vice President and
General Counsel

Ellen M. Hancock
IBM Senior Vice President and
Group Executive

Steven A. Mills
General Manager
IBM Software Solutions Division

Robert J. LaBant
IBM Senior Vice President and
Group Executive

Robert M. Howe
IBM Vice President and General
Manager
IBM Consulting Group and
Business Transformation Services

Dennie M. Welsh
IBM Vice President and
General Manager, Services

Ned C. Lautenbach
IBM Senior Vice President and
Group Executive and Chairman
IBM World Trade Corporation

Hans-Olaf Henkel
IBM Vice President, Chairman of
the Board and Chief Executive
Officer
IBM World Trade Europe/EMEA

Lucio Stanca
President, IBM SEMEA

Nick Temple
President, IBM United
Kingdom

Robeli J. Libero
IBM Vice President, President and
General Manager
IBM Latin America

Robert M. Stephenson
IBM Vice President, President and
Representative Director
IBM Asia Pacific

Kakutaroh Kitashiro
President and Chief Executive
Officer, IBM Japan

G. Richard Thoman
IBM Senior Vice President and
Group Executive

Robert J. Corrigan
IBM Vice President and President
IBM Personal Computer Company

Nobuo Mii
IBM Vice President and President
IBM Power Personal Systems
Division

James T. Vanderslice
IBM Vice President and President
IBM Printing Systems Company

John M. Thompson
IBM Senior Vice President and
Group Executive

Nicholas M. Donofrio
IBM Senior Vice President and
General Manager
IBM Large Scale Computing
Division

William J. Filip
IBM Vice President and General
Manager
IBM RISC System/6000 Division

Leland R. Reiswig, Jr.
President
IBM Personal Software
Products Division

David M. Thomas
IBM Vice President and General
Manager
IBM AS/400 Division

Patrick A. Toole
IBM Senior Vice President and
Group Executive

Michael J. Attardo
IBM Senior Vice President and
General Manager
IBM Microelectronics Division

Lutz F. Hahne
IBM Vice President and General
Manager
IBM Application Solutions
Division

Ed Zschau
IBM Vice President and General
Manager
IBM Storage Systems Division

Jerome B. York
IBM Senior Vice President and Chief
Financial Officer

James J. Forese
IBM Vice President and President
IBM Credit Corporation

Lawrence A. Zimmerman
IBM Vice President and
Controller

Frederick W. Zuckerman
IBM Vice President and Treasurer

David B. Kalis
IBM Vice President
Communications

Abby F. Kohnstamm
IBM Vice President
Corporate Marketing

James C. McGroddy
IBM Vice President
Science and Technology, and
Director of Research

tive boundaries. Today, IBM has more than 20,000 business partnerships worldwide and more than 500 equity alliances with agents, dealers, distributors, software firms, services companies, and manufacturers.

Apple Computer is IBM's partner in Taligent to develop object-oriented software, and in Kaleida to create multimedia standards. Hewlett-Packard and IBM are jointly developing and manufacturing high-speed fiber-optic communications components. Wang and Mitsubishi sell IBM systems under their logos, and Digital Equipment is a partner in offering business recovery services. Alliances not only divide high development and production costs, but also reduce critical time-to-market, pool scarce human skills, provide access to new markets and distribution channels, fill product gaps, and—most of all—help IBM get to the customer first, with the best.

COMPETITORS

IBM is larger than all other U.S. computer manufacturers combined. The top ten computer manufacturers in the United States are listed in Exhibit 28–9 along with their 1993 sales, profits, and R&D expenditures.

CONCLUSION

IBM must reverse trends that otherwise will lead to bankruptcy. In the face of mounting criticism, IBM's chief strategist, Bernard Puckett, resigned in November 1993 and was replaced by James Cannavino. CEO Gerstner is being criticized for

EXHIBIT 28-5 Consolidated Statement of Operations *(Dollars in millions except per share amounts)*

FOR THE YEAR ENDED DECEMBER 31:	1993	1992	1991
Revenue:			
Hardware sales	$30,591	$33,755	$37,093
Software	10,953	11,103	10,498
Services	9,711	7,352	5,582
Maintenance	7,295	7,635	7,414
Rentals and financing	4,166	4,678	4,179
Total Revenue	62,716	64,523	64,766
Cost:			
Hardware sales	20,696	19,698	18,571
Software	4,310	3,924	3,865
Services	8,279	6,051	4,531
Maintenance	3,545	3,430	3,379
Rentals and financing	1,738	1,966	1,727
Total Cost	38,568	35,069	32,073
Gross profit	24,148	29,454	32,693
Operating Expenses:			
Selling, general, and administrative	18,282	19,526	21,375
Research, development, and engineering	5,558	6,522	6,644
Restructuring charges	8,945	11,645	3,735
Total Operating Expenses	32,785	37,693	31,754
Operating (Loss) Income	(8,637)	(8,239)	939
Other income, principally interest	1,113	573	602
Interest expense	1,273	1,360	1,423
(Loss) earnings before income taxes	(8,797)	(9,026)	118
(Benefit) provision for income taxes	(810)	(2,161)	716
Net loss before changes in accounting principles	(7,987)	(6,865)	(598)
Effect of changes in accounting principles	(114)	1,900	(2,263)
Net Loss	(8,101)	(4,965)	(2,861)
Preferred stock dividends	47	—	—
Net loss applicable to common shareholders	$ (8,148)	$ (4,965)	$ (2,861)
Per Share of Common Stock Amounts:			
Before changes in accounting principles	$ (14.02)	$ (12.03)	$ (1.05)
Effect of changes in accounting principles	(.20)	3.33	(3.96)
Net loss applicable to common shareholders	$ (14.22)	$ (8.70)	$ (5.01)

Average Number of Common Shares Outstanding:
1993—573,239,240; 1992—570,896,489; 1991—572,003,382

EXHIBIT 28-6 Consolidated Statement of Financial Poslition *(Dollars in millions)*

AT DECEMBER 31:	1993	1992
Assets		
Current Assets:		
Cash	$ 873	$ 1,090
Cash equivalents	4,988	3,356
Marketable securities, at cost, which approximates market	1,272	1,203
Notes and accounts receivable—trade, net of allowances	11,676	12,829
Sales-type leases receivable	6,428	7,405
Other accounts receivable	1,308	1,370
Inventories	7,565	8,385
Prepaid expenses and other current assets	5,092	4,054
Total Current Assets	39,202	39,692
Plant, Rental Machines, and Other Property	47,504	52,786
Less: Accumulated depreciation	29,983	31,191
Plant, Rental Machines, and Other Property—Net	17,521	21,595
Investments and Other Assets:		
Software, less accumulated amortization (1993, $10,143; 1992, $8,531)	3,703	4,119
Investments and sundry assets	20,687	21,299
Total Investments and Other Assets	24,390	25,418
Total Assets	$81,113	$86,705
Liabilities and Stockholders' Equity		
Current Liabilities:		
Taxes	$ 1,589	$979
Short-term debt	12,097	16,467
Accounts payable	3,400	3,147
Compensation and benefits	2,053	3,476
Deferred income	3,575	3,316
Other accrued expenses and liabilities	10,436	9,352
Total Current Liabilities	33,150	36,737
Long-term debt	15,245	12,853
Other liabilities	11,177	7,461
Deferred income taxes	1,803	2,030
Total Liabilities	61,375	59,081
Stockholders' Equity:		
Preferred stock, par value $.01 per share—shares authorized: 150,000,000		
Shares Issued: 1993—11,250,000; 1992—None	1,091	—
Common stock, par value $1.25 per share—shares authorized: 750,000,000		
Shares Issued: 1993—581,388,475; 1992—571,791,950	6,980	6,563
Retained earnings	10,009	19,124
Translation adjustments	1,658	1,962
Treasury stock, at cost (shares: 1993—2,679; 1992—356,222)	—	(25)
Total Stockholders' Equity	19,738	27,624
Total Liabilities and Stockholders' Equity	$81,113	$86,705

EXHIBIT 28-7 Consolidated Statement of Cash Flows *(Dollars in millions)*

FOR THE YEAR ENDED DECEMBER 31:	1993	1992	1991
Cash Flow from Operating Activities:			
Net loss	$(8,101)	$ (4,965)	$(2,861)
Adjustments to reconcile net loss to cash provided from operating activities:			
Effect of changes in accounting principles	114	(1,900)	2,263
Effect of restructuring charges	5,230	8,312	2,793
Depreciation	4,710	4,793	4,772
Amortization of software	1,951	1,466	1,564
Loss (gain) on disposition of investment assets	151	54	(94)
Other changes that provided (used) cash:			
Receivables	1,185	1,052	(886)
Inventories	583	704	(36)
Other assets	(10)	(3,396)	5
Accounts payable	359	(311)	384
Other liabilities	2,155	465	(1,179)
Net cash provided from operating activities	8,327	6,274	6,725
Cash Flow from Investing Activities:			
Payments for plant, rental machines, and other property	(3,154)	(4,751)	(6,497)
Proceeds from disposition of plant, rental machines, and other property	793	633	645
Investment in software	(1,507)	(1,752)	(2,014)
Purchases of marketable securities and other investments	(2,721)	(3,284)	(4,848)
Proceeds from marketable securities and other investments	2,387	3,276	5,028
Net cash used in investing activities	(4,202)	(5,878)	(7,686)
Cash Flow from Financing Activities:			
Proceeds from new debt	11,794	10,045	5,776
Payments to settle debt	(8,741)	(10,735)	(4,184)
Short-term borrowings less than 90 days—net	(5,247)	4,199	2,676
Proceeds from preferred stock	1,091	—	—
Common stock transactions—net	122	(90)	67
Payments to purchase and retire common stock	—	—	(196)
Cash dividends paid	(933)	(2,765)	(2,771)
Net cash (used in) provided from financing activities	(1,914)	654	1,368
Effect of exchange rate changes on cash and cash equivalents	(796)	(549)	(315)
Net change in cash and cash equivalents	1,415	501	92
Cash and cash equivalents at January 1	4,446	3,945	3,853
Cash and cash equivalents at December 31	$ 5,861	$ 4,446	$ 3,945
Supplemental Data:			
Cash paid during the year for:			
Income taxes	$ 452	$ 1,297	$ 2,292
Interest	$ 2,410	$ 3,132	$ 2,617

EXHIBIT 28-8 Statement of Stockholders' Equity *(Dollars in millions)*

1991	PREFERRED STOCK	COMMON STOCK	RETAINED EARNINGS	TRANSLATION ADJUSTMENTS	TREASURY STOCK	TOTAL
Stockholders' Equity, January 1, 1991	$—	$6,357	$32,912	$3,309	$(25)	$42,553
Net loss			(2,861)			(2,861)
Cash dividends declared—common stock			(2,771)			(2,771)
Common stock issued under employee plans (1,857,904 shares)		172				172
Purchases (7,306,058 shares) and sales (7,201,997 shares) of treasury stock under employee plans—net			(125)		(6)	(131)
Common stock purchased and retired (2,127,400 shares)		(24)	(172)			(196)
Tax reductions—employee plans		26				26
Translation adjustments				(113)		(113)
Stockholders' Equity, December 31, 1991	—	6,531	26,983	3,196	(31)	36,679
1992						
Net loss			(4,965)			(4,965)
Cash dividends declared—common stock			(2,765)			(2,765)
Common stock issued under employee plans (442,581 shares)		26				26
Purchases (8,097,681 shares) and sales (8,073,124 shares) of treasury stock under employee plans—net			(129)		6	(123)
Tax reductions—semployee plans		6				6
Translation adjustments				(1,234)		(1,234)

EXHIBIT 28-8 *Continued*

1991	PREFERRED STOCK	COMMON STOCK	RETAINED EARNINGS	TRANSLATION ADJUSTMENTS	TREASURY STOCK	TOTAL
Stockholders' Equity, December 31, 1992	—	6,563	19,124	1,962	(25)	27,624
1993						
Net loss			(8,101)			(8,101)
Cash dividends declared—common stock			(905)			(905)
Cash dividends declared—preferred stock			(47)			(47)
Preferred stock issued (11,250,000 shares)	1,091					1,091
Common stock issued under employee plans (3,765,854 shares)		159				159
Common stock issued to U.S. pension plan fund (5,828,970 shares)		258				258
Purchases (6,099,023 shares) and sales (6,452,566 shares) of treasury stock under employee plans—net			(62)		25	(37)
Translation adjustments				(304)		(304)
Stockholders' Equity, December 31, 1993	$1,091	$6,980	$10,009	$1,658	$—	$19,738

EXHIBIT 28-9 Top Ten U.S. Computer Manufacturers 1992 Sales, Profits, and R&D Expenditures (In Millions of Dollars)

COMPANY	SALES	PROFITS	R&D EXPENDITURES
IBM	$62,716	$–7,987	$5,083
Hewlett-Packard	20,317	1,177	1,620
Digital-Equipment	13,636	–92	1,753
Apple Computer	8,445	–34	602
Compaq Computer	7,191	462	173
Sun Microsystems	4,493	188	381
Dell Computer	2,750	–10	372
Quantum	2,002	–510	315
Tandem Computers	2,022	–22	313
Conner Peripherals	2,151	–445	

focusing on cost cutting rather than formulating an overarching vision and strategy for IBM.

The vision thing keeps coming up, too. Jack Cooper, chief information officer of Seagram Company, a big IBM customer, recently remarked, "I give CEO Gerstner another two to six months to work out a strategy. After that, I think its absolutely critical that he have a vision." In a recent Forrester Research Inc., survey of 50 of the 1,000 largest U.S. companies, 42 percent said they plan to cut back on IBM purchases, 26 percent said they are watching IBM closely and may reduce purchases later, and only 2 percent plan to increase their business with IBM.

While IBM and CEO Gerstner are struggling with direction and strategy, the company's competitors are working overtime to muscle IBM out of the market. CEO Platt of Hewlett-Packard says, "We get up every morning and think about killing them." This is a "dog-eat-dog business."

Prepare a strategic plan to guide the IBM Corporation successfully to the year 2000. Include a clear mission statement, a comprehensive internal and external audit, as well as specific recommendations and projected financial statements.

MAGAZINE PUBLISHING INDUSTRY NOTE
ROSE MARIE BRATLAND

The U.S. printing and publishing industry, with approximately 60,000 firms and between 1 million and 2 million employees, remains shadowed by the aftereffects of the 1990–91 recession. With two-thirds of the industry's shipments tied to advertising, a buoyant economy is required to end the gradual erosion of the print media's share of total U.S. advertising expenditures. Rising levels of business and consumer confidence should expand advertising budgets in 1994 and increase the number of advertising pages in the nation's newspapers and magazines.

Printers and publishers serve the nation's communication needs, supplying an array of printed products ranging from almanacs to yearbooks. The industry's cost pressures have led to product specialization in an effort to achieve economies of scale. The 1990–91 recession had a severe impact on industry investment, with estimated 1992–93 capital expenditures 10 to 15 percent below the 1990 peak of $5.8 billion. Capital investment programs focus on increasing plant efficiencies, and have resulted in lowering the ratio of production workers to total employment to 53 percent in 1993 from 65 percent in 1973.

Demand for printed products is determined by a number of factors, including general economic activity, disposable personal income, advertising expenditures, business formations and transactions, and appropriations for schools, libraries, and institutions. The United States is the world's largest market for printed products and a favorable set of demographic factors over the period 1993–98 should reinforce this preeminent position. The U.S. population should reach 270 million in 1998, an increase of more than 12 million over 1993. The number of U.S. households should expand to 101 million in 1998, a gain of almost 5 million from 1993. School enrollments—elementary, secondary, and college—should expand by close to 5 million, to 68 million in 1998, from 63 million in 1993.

Growing competition from the electronic media and a squeeze on leisure time are forcing U.S. printers and publishers to reappraise their traditional markets. Printed products originally issued as books, directories, newsletters, and reference materials increasingly appear in the form of audio books, laser disks, compact disks, software, facsimile, and on-line information. To date, these electronic products supplement rather than supplant demand for printed products, but inroads by these electronic media should become more evident by the close of the decade. Gains by the electronic media are well perceived by leading U.S. printers, several of whom have established facilities to produce electronic materials such as compact disks for their publishing customers.

ENVIRONMENTAL PROFILE

Meeting environmental challenges is affecting the cost structures of both printers and publishers. Printers' concerns with toxins, carcinogens, and volatile organic compounds (VOCs) have led to increased use of alcohol-free fountain solutions, water-based inks, and solvent-less developers and finishers. More use of recycled paper and greater care in the disposal of materials now classified as hazardous result in higher printing production costs. Publishers' environmental issues center on the nation's dwindling space for landfills. Greater use of recycled paper throughout the printed product spectrum, coupled with growing legislative efforts to separate more printed products for recycling purposes from the stream of consumer waste, add to publishers' costs.

Since the United States is the world's largest market for printed products, most U.S. printers and publishers have at best a peripheral interest in international trade. Yet the United States is the second largest exporter of printed products (exceeded only by Germany), with 1993 shipments of slightly more than $4 billion. Major markets for U.S. printed product exports are Canada, the United Kingdom, Japan, and Mexico, with combined purchases accounting for two-thirds of the total. Approximately 60 percent of U.S. printed product exports consist of books and periodicals, but a wide variety of other items, including greeting cards, catalogs, labels, posters, decals, playing cards, calendars, and other trade advertising materials contribute to export markets totaling $1.6 billion in 1993 (Table 1).

Imports of printed products reached $2.2 billion in 1993, with combined shipments from Canada, the United Kingdom, Hong Kong, and Germany representing approximately 54 percent of the total. Shipments of books constituted 46 percent of all U.S. printed product imports in 1993, with some U.S. publishers contracting with Pacific Rim or Mediterranean suppliers who offer attractive pricing.

The next five years should provide significant opportunities for those U.S. printers and publishers seeking an international presence. Successful conclusion of the North American Free Trade Agreement (NAFTA) and the Uruguay Round of the General Agreement on Tariffs and Trade (GATT) will reduce or eliminate trade barriers to

TABLE 1 U.S. Trade Patterns in 1992 Printing and Publishing (SIC 27) (*In millions of dollars, percent*)

	EXPORTS			IMPORTS	
	Value	Share		Value	Share
Canada and Mexico	1,940	50.6	Canada and Mexico	473	22.6
European Community	794	20.7	European Community	695	33.2
Japan	295	7.7	Japan	173	8.3
East Asia NICs	203	5.3	East Asia NICs	633	30.2
South America	94	2.4	South America	32	1.5
Other	507	13.2	Other	87	4.1
World Total	3,833	100.0	World Total	2,093	100.0

	TOP FIVE COUNTRIES				
	Value	Share		Value	Share
Canada	1,721	44.9	Canada	396	18.9
United Kingdom	408	10.6	United Kingdom	302	14.4
Japan	295	7.7	Hong Kong	251	12.0
Mexico	219	5.7	Japan	173	8.3
Australia	187	4.9	Singapore	120	5.7

Source: U.S. Department of Commerce: Bureau of the Census; International Trade Administration.

exports of U.S. printed products and strengthen protection of international copyrights. By addressing the information requirements of global markets—and assisted by the dominance of English as the world's language of commerce and the professions—the U.S. printing and publishing industry should dominate in providing information services to an increasingly international clientele.

PERIODICALS

Periodical advertising continued to recover in 1993, but at a slower-than-expected pace. After experiencing an upswing in 1992, the industry expected to see strong growth throughout 1993. Nagging uncertainty about the nation's economic recovery kept advertisers from substantially increasing their advertising budgets for magazines. Circulation was expected to be flat for the year or down slightly. Magazine industry receipts totaled $22.8 billion, up slightly more than 1 percent in constant dollars from 1992 (Table 2).

TABLE 2   Trends and Forecasts: Periodicals (SIC 2721) (*In millions of dollars except as noted*)

					PERCENT CHANGE (1991–1994)		
ITEM	1991	1992[1]	1993[2]	1994[3]	91–92	92–93	93–94
INDUSTRY DATA							
Value of shipments[4]	20,345	21,667	22,772	24,366	6.5	5.1	7.0
Value of shipments (1987$)	15,735	16,018	16,194	16,517	1.8	1.1	2.0
Total employment (000)	111	108	109	111	-2.7	0.9	1.8
Production workers (000)	20.7	19.5	19.3	19.7	-5.8	-1.0	2.1
Average hourly earnings ($)	13.21	13.64	14.05	14.47	3.3	3.0	3.0
Capital expenditures	223	—	—	—	—	—	—
PRODUCT DATA							
Value of shipments[5]	19,424	20,473	21,517	23,023	5.4	5.1	7.0
Value of shipments (1987$)	15,022	15,292	15,460	15,769	1.8	1.1	2.0
TRADE DATA							
Value of imports	121	136	163	179	12.4	19.9	9.8
Value of exports	705	731	768	829	3.7	5.1	7.9

[1]Estimate, except exports and imports.
[2]Estimate.
[3]Forecast.
[4]Value of all products and services sold by establishments in the periodicals industry.
[5]Value of products classified in the periodicals industry produced by all industries.

Source: U.S. Department of Commerce: Bureau of the Census; International Trade Administration (ITA). Estimates and forecasts by ITA.

Advertising in consumer periodicals during the first half of 1993 recorded its strongest first-half gains in revenue and advertising pages since 1989. However, after a sharp gain in advertising pages during the first quarter, advertising pages were flat for consumer magazines during the second quarter. Advertising gains for the business press were also more impressive early in the year but slowed during the second quarter. Advertisers were cautious in their advertising spending because of lower-than-expected consumer purchasing and their own uneasiness about the health of the economy.

Competition from television, special advertising promotions, and direct mail became more intense as publishers vied for shrinking advertising dollars. Magazines continued to fight their image as a secondary advertising medium by offering advertisers targeted markets for their products through a growing number of special-interest publications and ancillary products.

Industry cost-cutting measures implemented during the recession were expected to boost profit gains during 1993. Over the year, publishers focused on the effectiveness of magazine advertising, the profitability of circulation, and on the growing importance of pleasing their readers. In addition, publishers directed their attention to recycling issues and state and Federal tax proposals affecting magazines.

Advertising Recovery Slows. After experiencing their strongest first quarter in eight years, consumer magazines' advertising growth halted in the second quarter. Publishers Information Bureau reported that for the first quarter, advertising pages rose about 6 percent and advertising receipts climbed about 12 percent from the first quarter 1992 level. During the first seven months of 1993, advertising pages were up nearly 2 percent from the same period in 1992, and advertising revenues increased about 6 percent, reflecting the slowdown in growth during the second quarter and advertising page and revenue declines in July. In many instances, large advertisers reconsidered their advertising commitments to magazines and canceled or cut back their scheduled advertising on short notice as business growth slowed. Publishers resorted to advertising rate discounting and special offers to attract advertisers. For the year, advertising pages grew 1 to 2 percent, and advertising receipts rose 5 to 6 percent. Consumer magazine groups recording the most growth in advertising revenues in 1992 included woman/fashion/service, outdoor and sports, national business titles, and computer magazines. In 1993, advertising recovery for magazines was spotty; some magazines in special-interest segments did well while others in the same group recorded declines.

Most of the top 10 consumer magazine advertising categories recorded revenue gains during the first half of 1993. Categories showing the largest increases were drugs/remedies, direct-response companies, business/consumer services, and toiletries/cosmetics. Computer/office equipment/stationery and cigarettes/tobacco experienced substantial declines.

Business and professional magazines as a group saw no growth in advertising pages in 1992, and very little overall growth in pages was likely in 1993. *International Business Communication's 1994 Business Press Outlook* projected an 8 to 9 percent gain in advertising revenues in 1993, based on the 250 business publications tracked. American Business Press, the major trade association for business publishers, expected advertising revenues to rise about 4 percent in 1993. Advertising recovery for business publications groups was mixed, with some sectors performing very well, and others doing poorly. Groups that did well included computers, electronics, telecommunications, and long-term health care. Those performing poorly included aviation and aerospace, advertising and marketing, and construction-related publications.

From 1982 to 1992, advertising's share of total magazine receipts have declined slightly for both consumer magazines and the business press. In 1982, advertising accounted for 55 percent of total consumer magazine receipts. By 1992 it had fallen to 51 percent. Over the same decade, advertising receipts for business and professional publications dropped from 63 percent of total receipts to 60 percent. A growing number of business and professional magazines have gone from controlled circulation (sent free to industry executives and professionals) to paid circulation as advertising revenues have become more difficult to obtain. As their advertising receipts have become more unpredictable, consumer magazines have looked more to increasing circulation revenues.

Circulation Declines. Economic uncertainty, weak consumer confidence, and modest gains in real disposable personal income took their toll on consumer magazine circulation in 1992 and 1993. Although a record number of new magazines were started in 1992, magazine suspensions increased in a number of magazine groups in 1992 and 1993.

Audit Bureau of Circulation (ABC) data for 1992 reported that for the 570 consumer magazines tracked, total circulation fell for a second consecutive year. Annual combined circulation per issue for single-copy and subscription circulation each declined by about 1 million. Single-copy circulation totaled about 71 million per issue, while subscriptions numbered about 292 million per issue for consumer magazines. This was the first time since 1976 that subscription circulation fell for these ABC-audited magazines, although in 1991 subscription circulation was virtually unchanged from the previous year.

Newsstand magazines accounted for 20 percent of total consumer magazine circulation in 1991, but for 31 percent of total magazine circulation revenues; subscription represented 80 percent of circulation and 69 percent of circulation receipts.

Over the past decade, publishers have charged higher cover prices for newsstand editions of their publications than for subscriptions and have also increased rates on newsstand prices more rapidly. However, higher magazine cover prices in recent years have led to declining newsstand sales as consumers became more cautious in their purchasing. In the past few years, publishers have resisted increasing magazine cover prices but have attempted to make subscription sales more profitable. According to ABC data on the 50 leading magazines' cost to readers, the average single-copy price of a magazine rose from $2.65 in 1990 to $2.67 in 1992, an increase of less than 1 percent. By comparison, the average subscription price rose 2 percent, going from $27.11 in 1990 to $27.77 in 1992. During the 1987–90 period the average yearly single-copy price climbed 20 percent, as the average yearly subscription price increased 11 percent.

Changing Industry Profile. The *Gale Directory of Publications* listed 11,143 U.S. periodicals (consumer, farm, and business) for 1992, 96 fewer than in 1991. The *Consumer & Farm Magazines* publication of Standard Rate and Data Service reported a total of 2,318 consumer and farm publications in 1992, 42 more than in 1991. According to Samir Husni's *Guide to New Consumer Magazines*, a record 679 new magazine titles were launched in 1992, an increase of 126 over 1991. The largest number of startups were erotica and life-style/service magazines, but health, food, and children's publications also recorded strong gains. Many of the new magazines were special issues and one-time publications. *Esquire* launched two special issues in 1992, *Esquire Gentleman* and *Esquire Sportsman*. In early 1993, *Scientific American* published *Scientific American Medicine*, a one-time newsstand publication.

Magazines targeted to the baby boomers or their children, the so-called baby boomlets, were successful launches even during the recent recession. Hot magazine groups in the last five years have been children and teen magazines, which have doubled in number. New titles include *The Simpsons*, *Disney Adventures*, and *American Girl*. Spinoffs from established magazines have been popular, with such titles as *Discover for Kids*, *Money for Kids*, and *Field & Stream Jr.* Personal finance titles for the boomers have also done well. New launches, *Smart Money* and *Worth*, were aimed at this group.

A number of magazines targeted age or demographic sectors of the population by publishing a number of special editions. Several parenting magazines, including *Child* and *American Baby*, offered editions tailored to the age of a reader's child. Other recent publications targeted to a niche market include *Emerge*, a newsweekly for Black Americans, *The Senior Golfer*, targeted at aging baby boomers, and *Skiing for Women*.

Several prominent consumer and trade publications ceased to publish in 1993 as cautious advertisers, declining readership, and saturated magazine sectors made the survival of some magazines increasingly difficult. Conde Nast Publications' folding of *HG (House & Garden)*, a 92-year old home magazine, sent shock waves through the magazine industry. Univision publications suspended *Mas*, a general interest, Spanish-language lifestyle magazine with controlled circulation of 630,000. Among business journals, the 120-year old *Home Improvement Center* folded, as did *Magazine Week*, the only weekly trade title serving the magazine industry. Ziff-Davis, a computer publishing giant, closed both *Corporate Computing* and *PC Sources*.

Acquisition activity in 1993 focused on Conde Nast Publications' $170 million purchase of Knapp Communications Corp., publisher of *Bon Appetit* and *Architectural Digest*, giving Conde Nast a dominant position in the home decor and epicurean markets. This followed an announcement late in 1992 that Time Inc. would form a joint venture with American Express Publishing to manage several of AmEx's magazines, including *Travel & Leisure* and *Food & Wine*. Rather than acquiring properties, publishers focused on redesigning their publications, creating spinoff magazines and other products, including fax and videotext editions.

Employment and Production Costs. After a three-year period of downsizing to improve efficiency and cut costs, many magazine publishing companies began hiring in 1993. Publishers sought employees who could perform a number of jobs because of lean hiring budgets. Total employment rose about 1 percent to an estimated 109,000. The number of production workers was about 19,300, slightly less than in 1992.

Overall production and distribution costs rose moderately in 1993. Magazine publishers expected some publication grades of paper to rise as much as 9 percent during 1993, but anticipated no increases in ink prices. No postal rate increases took effect, but Congress passed legislation that would phase in higher postal rates for nonprofit magazines over a five-year period.

ENVIRONMENTAL PROFILE

Recycling has become an important issue. A few publishers have switched to coated recycled paper for their magazines, while others are gradually converting. Still others have no plans to use paper with recycled content. Many publishers are aware that the magazine industry must initiate a voluntary recycling program to keep Congress from enacting mandatory recycling requirements for the industry. Some major publishers are still reluctant to consider using recycled paper because of its higher cost, lower quality, and limited availability. Publishers are beginning to realize that they need to demand more recycled paper before paper producers will begin producing more and better quality recycled paper.

Although the Environmental Protection Agency (EPA) has not proposed any mandatory requirements for printing and writing papers, the agency revised its guidelines for Government procurement of recycled paper in 1993. This was of concern to publishers since any guidelines the EPA sets are likely to become the industry's standards.

According to one industry estimate, U.S. output of recycled printing and writing paper is 6 percent of total production, about the same level as 15 years ago. *Folio Magazine* reports that about 80 percent, or about 6 million tons, of high-grade printing and writing paper is disposed of in landfills annually.

INTERNATIONAL COMPETITIVENESS

Export growth slowed for U.S. magazines in 1993. Exports totaled an estimated $768 million, a gain of about 5 percent from 1992. Between 1989 and 1992, U.S. periodical exports grew at an average annual rate of 18 percent. The principal markets for U.S. magazines in 1992 were Canada (74 percent), the United Kingdom (7 percent), and Mexico (5 percent). While U.S. exports to Canada rose at an average yearly rate of 16 percent between 1989 and 1992, they dropped 1 percent in 1992 from their 1991 level (Table 3). U.S. exports to Mexico, France, the United Kingdom, the Netherlands, and Bermuda recorded strong growth between 1989 and 1992. Most of these markets showed average annual growth rates of more than 25 percent during

TABLE 3   U.S. Trade Patterns in 1992 Periodicals (SIC 2721) (*In millions of dollars, percent*)

EXPORTS			IMPORTS		
	Value	Share		Value	Share
Canada and Mexico	573	78.3	Canada and Mexico	83	61.1
European Community	95	13.0	European Community	36	26.6
Japan	8	1.1	Japan	8	6.2
East Asia NICs	9	1.3	East Asia NICs	4	3.0
South America	11	1.6	South America	3	1.9
Other	35	4.8	Other	2	1.3
World Total	731	100.0	World Total	136	100.0

TOP FIVE COUNTRIES					
	Value	Share		Value	Share
Canada	538	73.6	Canada	78	57.6
United Kingdom	52	7.1	United Kingdom	20	14.8
Mexico	35	4.7	Japan	8	6.2
Netherlands	22	3.1	Spain	5	3.7
France	13	1.8	Mexico	5	3.5

Source: U.S. Department of Commerce: Bureau of the Census; International Trade Administration.

this period. Over the past few years, softness in the economies of many industrialized countries curtailed discretionary consumer purchases of items such as magazines. International distributors expect magazine sales to show substantial growth as global economic activity improves.

Some magazine publishers have found that with their revenues declining at home, they must seek readers abroad. More of them are exploring international markets not only in Europe but in Latin America, the Middle East, Africa, and Asia. Recently, Rodale Press, publisher of *Runner's World*, and General Media International, publisher of *Longevity*, launched South African editions of their publications through joint ventures. *Ms.* magazine began distributing in the United Kingdom, Australia, and New Zealand. *National Geographic* and *Time* are exploring the feasibility of launching Japanese-language editions of their magazines. Hearst Corporation has joined with Televisa S.A. of Mexico to have more of its titles translated into Spanish-language editions for the Latin American market. Currently, Spanish-language editions of Hearst's *Cosmopolitan*, *Harper's Bazaar*, *Popular Mechanics*, and *Good Housekeeping* are distributed in Latin America. A Canadian edition of *Sports Illustrated*, launched in 1993, encountered protests from Canadian magazine publishers. Under new Canadian government regulations, U.S. companies will have to obtain government approval for future Canadian editions of their magazines. For nearly 30 years, the Canadian government has imposed a number of restrictions on foreign magazines doing business in Canada.

U.S. publishers have been more cautious in approaching the Eastern European market, although a growing number of European publishers have sought business and investment opportunities in this area. These foreign publishers believe the market offers fast growth potential. The printing and publishing sector in Eastern Europe is in need of technical assistance for its publishing, printing, and distribution operations. Those foreign companies providing assistance are most likely to gain a strong foothold. *Reader's Digest* is planning to launch a Czech edition, and recently *Playboy* started a Polish edition.

Opportunities for U.S. magazine publishers in the world market continue to grow. Many U.S. publications are special-interest titles which are not available in other countries. The United States is the only country worldwide with a sufficiently large, affluent, and educated population to support a large number of special-interest titles. These titles appeal to a small segment of a country's population, and in most countries the population statistics do not support narrowly focused magazines. In addition, since English is widely read and spoken abroad, the language barrier does not greatly impede American magazine sales overseas. Ron Scott, a magazine industry consultant, notes in *Folio Magazine* that for many smaller U.S. special-interest magazines, international newsstand distribution offers an opportunity to sell a sizable number of copies and establish a presence in the international market.

U.S. imports of magazines climbed an estimated 20 percent in 1993, to about $163 million. Major suppliers in 1992 were Canada (58 percent), the United Kingdom (15 percent), and Japan (6 percent).

OUTLOOK FOR 1994

Publishers expect 1994 to be a better year for magazine advertising and circulation as economic activity picks up. Projected growth in Gross Domestic Product (GDP) and corporate profits should encourage companies to increase their advertising budgets. If advertisers and consumers are more confident about the economy in 1994, U.S. magazine industry receipts could rise 2 to 3 percent in constant dollars. Advertising pages will likely increase modestly for consumer and business and professional publications, in the range of 2 to 4 percent, while circulation for both magazine groups will probably be flat or up less than 1 percent.

Even though real disposable personal income is expected to grow at a slightly slower rate than in 1993, increasing consumer confidence could produce more stability in magazine circulation than has existed over the past few years. With so many new titles, the shakeout of weaker titles could continue in 1994, especially in the absence of strong advertising growth.

Major costs, such as for printing, paper, and ink, should increase an average of 2 to 3 percent in 1994, unless demand rises sharply. No postal rate increases are expected before early 1995.

PLAYBOY ENTERPRISES, INC.—1994

More copies of *Playboy* magazine are sold each month than either *Newsweek* or *Cosmopolitan*. The approach to doing business at Playboy Enterprises, Inc. (PEI)(312-751-8000), is characterized by Christie Hefner, chairman and chief executive officer, as "a commitment to think globally and act locally." That statement represents the essence of PEI's business strategy toward the year 2000. Emphasis is being placed on global expansion to take advantage of Playboy's name recognition and the demise of communism worldwide. The Playboy name and logo is the world's second-best known symbol, after Coca-Cola's logo. PEI is headquartered in Chicago, Illinois.

PEI's net income has declined four years in a row, to $365,000 in 1993. The number of U.S. households subscribing monthly to the Playboy Service on television is declining. PEI's newsstand sales declined 13 percent in 1993 and advertising revenues also declined. PEI's magazine circulation revenues declined 2 percent in 1993. U.S. and Canadian newsstand sales of *Playboy* magazine fell 19 percent in 1993. A strategic plan is needed to reverse these recent declines in Playboy's business.

PEI was organized in 1953 to publish *Playboy* magazine. Christie Hefner succeeded her father, Hugh Hefner, as chairman of the board and CEO in 1988. Hugh Hefner still owns 71 percent of PEI's stock. PEI's three divisions are publishing, entertainment, and product marketing.

PUBLISHING

Playboy is the number one selling men's magazine in the world and remains the driving force behind all of the company's businesses. The publishing division reported a 13 percent increase in earnings to $14.4 million on a 7 percent rise in revenues to $162.8 million in 1993. In 1993, PEI launched its 16th international edition of the magazine in Poland, introduced a new line of trading cards, and began developing a CD-ROM product jointly with IBM.

Playboy magazine reported earnings growth of 15 percent in 1993, but magazine revenues fell 1 percent to $101.2 million. The magazine benefitted from lower paper and printing expenses, higher subscription prices, and the rollout of a $4.95 newsstand cover price nationwide. The magazine also announced a 5 percent increase in advertising rates, effective with the January 1994 issue. *Playboy* maintained its 3.4 million circulation rate base for the seventh straight year in fiscal 1993 and experienced a 2 percent increase in advertising pages. *Playboy's* circulation continued to exceed those of major magazines *GQ*, *Esquire*, and *Rolling Stone* combined. The magazine is read by 12 million readers each month and *Playboy's* female audience has grown to over 2.1 million, as given in Exhibit 29–1, the circulation ranking of various consumer magazines done annually by the Audit Bureau of Circulations (ABC).

Subscription sales, which provide 44 percent of *Playboy* magazine revenues, rose 5 percent in fiscal 1993, but the increase did not offset the decline in newsstand sales. Subscription revenues were impacted favorably by a higher average subscription price, and elimination of long-term, discounted subscription rates. Sales from *Playboy's* subscriber file of 2.7 million names also continued to generate high margin income.

PEI publishes the U.S. edition of *Playboy* magazine in 15 advertising editions: eight regional, two state, four metro and one upper-income zip-coded edition. All contain the same editorial material but provide targeting opportunities for advertisers. Net advertising revenues of the U.S. edition of *Playboy* magazine for the years ended June 30, 1993, 1992, and 1991 were $30.4 million, $30.4 million, and $32.7 million, respectively.

PEI has consolidated the printing of *Playboy* magazine and newsstand specials at Quad/Graphics, Inc., located in Wisconsin. Paper is the principal raw material used in the production of *Playboy* magazine and the company uses a variety of types of high-quality coated paper that is purchased from a number of suppliers. Lower negotiated paper prices contribute materially to reduction in manufacturing costs. Paper costs as a percentage of *Playboy* magazine revenues have declined from 22.5 percent in fiscal 1991 to 17.7 percent for the fiscal year ended June 30, 1993.

Consolidation of the convenience store industry and increased competition for display space in traditional retail stores contributed to the decline in newsstand sales in

EXHIBIT 29-1 Circulation Ranking of Various Consumer Magazines

SELECTED U.S. CONSUMER PUBLICATIONS	CIRCULATION (1)	RANKING (2)
Reader's Digest	16.3	1
TV Guide	14.6	2
National Geographic	9.6	3
Time	4.3	9
Sports Illustrated	3.6	10
People	3.5	11
Playboy	3.4	12
Newsweek	3.3	14
Cosmopolitan	2.7	18
Penthouse	1.2	41
Rolling Stone	1.2	45
Business Week	0.9	72
GQ	0.7	98
Esquire	0.7	106

Source: Audit Bureau of Circulations.

fiscal 1993. In an effort to increase sales during the coming year, PEI plans to capitalize on excitement generated by the company's 40th anniversary celebration. PEI is taking an aggressive approach to expand distribution to nontraditional channels such as music, video, and liquor stores, which register high male traffic.

Playboy magazine continues to focus on securing new advertisers from underdeveloped categories, such as fashion, fragrance, automotive, travel, and home electronics, in order to broaden its advertising mix and reduce dependency upon any one advertising category. *Playboy's* advertising sales account for 30 percent of the magazine's revenues. Advertising by category for fiscal 1993 is given in Exhibit 29–2.

The PEI marketing department sponsors a number of annual events with *Playboy* advertisers, such as the Winter Ski Fest and a three-on-three basketball tournament in Daytona Beach. PEI also offers advertisers opportunities to tie in to the Playboy Jazz Festival in Los Angeles through advertising in the Jazz Festival program and corporate sponsorship of certain program elements. Sony was the official consumer electronics sponsor of the 1993 Playboy Jazz Festival.

Playboy magazine's editorial vitality, diversity, and cultural connection are evident in the fiction, articles, investigative reporting, interviews, celebrity profiles, and entertainment and service features that are monthly staples of the publication. Regular columns on politics, books, movies, music, style, men, women, and relationships reflect contemporary social and cultural issues and further the magazine's ongoing dialogue with its readers.

PEI has successfully developed newsstand specials, calendars, international editions, and trading cards, which utilize material from *Playboy's* editorial, art, and photography libraries and capitalize on its loyal customer base.

Playboy-related businesses contributed operating income of $8.4 million in fiscal 1993, but these earnings were down modestly from 1992 due to lower average copy sales for newsstand specials and a smaller 900-number operation (see Exhibits 29–3, 29–4, and 29–5). Royalties from international publishing remained even with last year, although a new trading card deal generated new revenue and operating income.

In fiscal 1993, PEI produced 16 newsstand specials and a *Playmate* calendar. The company also entered into an agreement with Sarah Lazin Books to develop books

---

EXHIBIT 29-2 *Playboy* Advertising for Fiscal 1993

ADVERTISING CATEGORY	PERCENTAGE OF AD PAGES
Retail/Direct Mail	25
Beer/Wine/Liquor	21
Tobacco	18
Apparel/Footwear/Accessories	10
Toiletries/Cosmetics	8
Automotive	4
Home Electronics	4
Other	10
	100

Source: *Playboy Annual Report,* 1993.

EXHIBIT 29-3 Playboy Publishing Group Revenues and Operating Incomes
(In millions of dollars)

	REVENUES YEARS ENDED JUNE 30,			OPERATING INCOME YEARS ENDED JUNE 30,		
	1993	1992	1991	1993	1992	1991
Playboy Magazine	$101.2	$102.2	$100.3	$7.9	$7.0	$6.1
Playboy-Related Businesses	22.0	21.7	22.3	8.4	9.1	10.3
Subtotal	123.2	123.9	122.6	16.3	16.1	16.4
Catalogs	39.4	28.1	18.1	4.9	2.5	0.7
Administrative Expenses, New						
Magazine Development and Other	0.2	0.3	—	(6.8)	(5.8)	(4.8)
Total	$162.8	$152.3	$140.7	$14.4	$12.8	$12.3

EXHIBIT 29-4 *Playboy* Magazine's Average Net Paid Circulation Per Issue

	AVERAGE NET PAID CIRCULATION PER ISSUE (*IN MILLIONS*)		APPROXIMATE PERCENT OF CIRCULATION FROM	
FISCAL YEAR	FIRST SIX MONTHS	SECOND SIX MONTHS	SINGLE COPY SALES	SUBSCRIPTIONS
1993	3.4	3.4	21	79
1992	3.5	3.4	22	78
1991	3.5	3.5	23	77

Source: Audit Bureau of Circulations (ABC).

EXHIBIT 29-5 *Playboy* Magazine U.S. Edition Subscription and Worldwide Newsstand
Circulation Figures (In thousands, except per copy prices)

	YEARS ENDED JUNE 30,		
	1993	1992	1991
Subscription Revenues	$44,900	$42,600	$40,300
Average Monthly Subscribers	2,816	2,801	2,707
Newstand Revenues	$23,500	$27,100	$25,500
Average Monthly Newsstand Copies	652	781	787
Average Newsstand Cover Price	$ 5.04	$ 4.72	$ 4.39

Source: *Playboy* Form 10K, 1993, p. 5.

around editorial themes from *Playboy* magazine. This deal resulted in the publication of *The Playboy Interviews* in fiscal 1993 and the development of *Playboy Stories*, an anthology of some of the magazine's finest fiction.

Playboy's editorial vision and philosophy are exported globally through international editions published in Argentina, Australia, Brazil, Czech Republic, Germany, Greece, Hong Kong, Hungary, Italy, Japan, Mexico, the Netherlands, Spain, Taiwan, and Turkey. Up to 70 percent of the material in each edition is locally produced, with the remaining text and pictorials originating from the U.S. *Playboy* and other editions. PEI reviews and approves the content of the foreign editions so that they retain the distinctive style, look, and flavor of the U.S. edition, while meeting the needs of their respective markets. The terms of the license agreements for *Playboy* magazine's foreign editions vary, but in general are for a term of at least five years and carry a guaranteed minimum royalty as well as a formula for computing earned royalties in excess of the minimum. Royalty computations are generally based on both circulation and advertising revenues. In fiscal 1993, the three largest-selling editions—Germany, Japan and Brazil—accounted for 48 percent of the total licensing revenues from foreign editions.

Playboy entered into its first overseas publishing joint venture in fiscal 1993, with Autraco Holding Company, to produce a Polish edition. The deal is a departure from the licensing strategy that the company has employed since 1972, when the first foreign edition of *Playboy* was launched, and reflects the company's intent to invest in more global ventures and to become more involved in managing the Playboy brand abroad. PEI plans to launch a South African edition in November 1993 through a license agreement with Times Media Limited, a diversified media company based in Johannesburg.

PEI owns a 20 percent interest in the *duPont Registry*, a monthly magazine and shoppers' guide targeted to collectors of classic, luxury, and exotic cars. In fiscal 1993, this magazine broadened its retail distribution base and reported advertising and circulation increases.

PEI's catalog earnings for fiscal 1993 nearly doubled to $4.9 million, while revenues increased 40 percent to $39.4 million. Catalog operations are the fastest growing segment within the publishing group. The *Playboy* catalog offers Playboy fashions and accessories, home videos, gifts, calendars, art products, back issues of the magazine, and newsstand specials. In fiscal 1993, the catalog expanded its lingerie section to feature the "Romantics by Playboy" line. The growth was largely due to higher sales volume and response rates for *Critics' Choice Video*, which was partially attributable to the acquisitions of assets to two competing catalogs, *Blackhawk Films* and *Postings*, and the merging of their mailing lists with that of *Critics' Choice Video*.

Critics' Choice Video is one of the largest circulation catalogs of prerecorded videocassettes serving the sell-through market, the fastest-growing segment of the video industry. The catalog features more than 2,000 titles, including major theatrical releases and special-interest videos. The company acquired 80 percent of Critics' Choice Video, Inc., in fiscal 1989 and purchased the remaining 20 percent in fiscal 1994 for $3.0 million.

Moving closer to its goal of becoming the catalog leader in home entertainment software, PEI will test a music catalog, *Collectors' Choice Music*, in fiscal 1994. The 100-page catalog will be mailed to 500,000 music customers. It will feature more than 1,300 titles in CD and cassette formats from a wide assortment of music categories—classical, pop, rock, rhythm and blues, jazz, and country. It also will offer an extensive library of hard-to-find recordings.

PEI signed two major agreements in fiscal 1993 to produce new media brand extensions of Playboy products. In conjunction with IBM's Multimedia Publishing Studio, the company will publish *The Playboy Interview 1962–1992*, a CD containing nearly all of the interviews published since the feature's inception in 1962, the subjects' photographs, and a comprehensive index that will allow researchers to quickly access interviews by them. The CD will retail for about $39.95 and will be available through computer retail outlets and via direct mail.

Playboy's entertainment and publishing groups are working together to develop interactive entertainment software through an agreement with Philips Interactive Media of America. Among the releases that PEI will develop and market in fiscal 1994 is *40 Years of Playboy*, a multimedia review of *Playboy's* editorial highlights and an interactive forum through which users can access Playmate photos and create music videos utilizing their favorite pictures.

ENTERTAINMENT

The entertainment division's strategy is to build a library of Playboy programming that can be packaged in multiple formats for worldwide distribution. Today, Playboy programming is available via broadcast, cable and pay television, and direct-to-home technology. It also is offered on video and laserdisc formats and soon will be available on CI-I. To strengthen brand identification of Playboy programming around the world, PEI consolidated all of its television services and programming under the name "Playboy TV" in fiscal 1993 and developed a logo to market the services.

The entertainment division made substantial progress in fiscal 1993. Revenues were up 31 percent to $42.6 million as a result of growth from domestic pay television, international television, and worldwide home video. Earnings declined however to $1.8 million from $3.7 million in fiscal 1992 (see Exhibit 29–6).

Playboy signed important international broadcast license agreements in fiscal 1993 that expanded the audience of Playboy TV to 64 territories and home video to 35 countries. Three new multiyear agreements will result in tiers of Playboy programming being offered on overseas networks for the first time. These deals will enable Playboy to have an ongoing branded presence in international markets and are expected to generate higher and more consistent revenues than selling programs on a show-by-show basis.

The access growth rate of Playboy's domestic pay-per-view service continues to outpace the industry growth rate of homes equipped with addressable cable technology. Access to Playboy TV increased 25 percent, from 7.3 million homes at the start of fiscal 1993 to 9.1 million at the end. Industry analyst Paul Kagan Associates, Inc., estimates that there are now 18 million U.S. addressable homes. Tele-Communications, Inc. (TCI), the largest multiple system operator in the country, entered into its first long-term agreement with PEI in February 1993 to carry the Playboy TV network. As TCI continues to outfit its ten million basic cable homes with pay-per-view technology, the number of Playboy addressable homes should rise commensurately.

PEI's library of 500 hours of programming is available to all of the entertainment division's distribution channels and to launch new media and distribution pipelines. Exclusive programming is a hallmark of Playboy TV and sets the domestic service apart from all other pay offerings. Approximately 60 percent of the network's program lineup is originally produced. The company expects to invest approximately $19 million in new programming in fiscal 1994.

EXHIBIT 29-6 *Playboy* Entertainment Group Revenues and Operating Income (In millions of dollars)

	YEARS ENDED JUNE 30,		
	1993	1992	1991
REVENUES			
Domestic Pay Television:			
Pay-Per-View	$ 8.0	$ 6.0	$ 3.8
Monthly Subscription	8.6	9.8	11.4
Home Satellite Dish and Other	4.7	2.7	2.6
Total Domestic Pay Television	21.3	18.5	17.8
Domestic Home Video	10.1	7.0	2.7
International Television and Home Video	9.8	5.4	3.5
Other	1.4	1.6	1.0
Total Revenues	$42.6	$32.5	$25.0
OPERATING INCOME			
Profit Contribution Before Programming Expense	$15.4	$12.7	$10.4
Programming Expense	(13.6)	(9.0)	(7.5)
Total Operating Income	$ 1.8	$ 3.7	$ 2.9

Source: *Playboy* Form 10K, 1993, p. 9.

Fiscal 1993's programming investment funded approximately 89 hours of new programming, including *Playboy's Love & Sex Test*, *Playboy's Secret Confessions and Fantasies*, and the dramatic, sexy soap opera *Eden*. *Eden*, which was created by the producers of *Falcon Crest*, attracted the interest of USA Network, which licensed and began airing an edited version of the program on its basic cable service in June 1993. *Eden* is the first Playboy TV series to gain national exposure on another network, and the program received good ratings in its late-night time slot. Exhibit 29–7 categorizes the Playboy programs.

Playboy magazine's editorial forum provides both unique programming concepts and cross-promotional opportunities. Some of the magazine's celebrity pictorials and editorial features, such as the "Movies" column and the "Playboy Advisor," have been translated into segments on Playboy TV. Other features provide greater syndication and sponsorship potential. In fiscal 1993, the entertainment group produced the *Reebok Preseason College Football Special* around *Playboy's Pigskin Preview*, and the *1993 Playboy All-American team*. The show aired in September 1993 in 92 television markets nationwide.

Playboy's pay television business reported a 15 percent rise in fiscal 1993 revenues to $21.3 million. However, earnings were down slightly due to increased investments in sales, marketing, and distribution resources, including a new transponder on the Hughes Communications Galaxy V satellite. The new transponder is accessed by more cable operators than was Playboy's previous satellite and provides multichannel possibilities through compression.

EXHIBIT 29-7 Playboy Entertainment Group Company-Produced Series Information

TITLE OF SERIES	FISCAL YEAR FIRST SOLD	LENGTH OF EPISODES (MINUTES)	GENRE
Playboy Late Night			
Series I	1990	60	magazine-format
Series II	1991	30	magazine-format
Series III	1992	30	magazine-format
Inside Out	1991	30	anthology
Eden	1993	30	dramatic series
Playboy's Secret Confessions and Fantasies	1993	30	hosted series
Playboy's Love & Sex Test	1992	30	game show

Source: *Playboy* Form 10K, 1993, p. 9.

Pay-per-view sales growth has slowed due to the uncertainty surrounding the 1992 Cable Act, which affects rates and requires cable systems to obtain permission from broadcasters to retransmit their signals and reserve up to one third of their channels for relaying the signals of local broadcasters. Even though pay television services are not subject to the new regulations, the access growth rate for Playboy TV did not rise as fast as anticipated during the second half of fiscal 1993.

At June 30, 1993, the cable systems where Playboy Television was offered included approximately 16.8 million cable households. Of these households, 12.1 million could purchase Playboy Television on a monthly basis, 2.5 million could purchase only on a pay-per-view basis, and 6.6 million could purchase the programming both ways. CEO Hefner believes that the company's potential pay-per-view audience has grown at a faster rate than the pay-for-view market because Playboy Television has been able to add MSOs by offering a consistent level of "buy rates" (percentage of homes actually purchasing the service) compared to other pay-per-view services, a pricing structure that is profitable to the cable affiliate and a commitment to high quality original programming. Projections by Paul Kagan Associates, Inc., in February 1993 call for 15 percent average annual increases in addressable households through 1995. PEI expects its pay-per-view access to continue to expand at a faster rate than the industry in the near term as additional MSOs make Playboy Television available to their cable affiliates.

The number of monthly subscribers has declined as PEI's marketing focus has shifted to systems that have pay-per-view technology. As of June 30, 1993, Playboy Television had approximately 232,000 monthly subscribing households, down from 281,000 at June 30, 1991. PEI has used its pay-per-view service to gain access to additional MSOs and cable affiliates, some of which were unwilling to carry Playboy Television on a monthly subscription basis, giving the cable affiliates and PEI an opportunity to increase overall revenues. CEO Hefner believes the availability of a monthly subscription option for Playboy Television in addressable systems would benefit the company. (Subscription and pay-per-view figures are compared in Exhibit 29–8.)

In the long run, PEI expects to benefit from the new cable rulings. Cable operators will be encouraged to look for new revenue sources that are not regulated. The recent signing of TCI and Cox Cable Communications to carry the Playboy service is reflective of operators' confidence in the future of Playboy TV and pay-per-view.

EXHIBIT 29-8 Cable Households in Relation to Playboy Television

| | CABLE HOUSEHOLDS | | | PLAYBOY TELEVISION | |
	TOTAL CABLE HOUSEHOLDS	ADDRESSABLE CABLE HOUSEHOLDS	HOMES	PAY-PER-VIEW BUYS	MONTHLY SUBSCRIBERS
June 30, 1991	52,550	15,100	4,700	2,118	314
June 30, 1992	54,300	16,750	7,300	3,136	281
June 30, 1993	56,050	18,150	9,100	4,393	232
Compound Annual Growth Rate (1991-1993)	3.3%	9.6%	39.1%	44.0%	(14.0)%

Source: *Playboy* Form 10K, 1993, p. 10.

PEI provides Playboy Television vial encrypted signal, on both a pay-per-view and subscription basis, to home satellite dish viewers. As of June 30, 1993, Playboy Television was available on a pay-per-view basis to approximately 130,000 such viewers, and there were also approximately 67,000 subscription customers. At June 30, 1992, Playboy Television was available to 65,000 home satellite dish viewers on a pay-per-view basis and had approximately 41,000 subscribers. PEI receives an established fee per subscriber, which depends in part on the sales volume of the distributor. In January 1992, PEI began expanding its satellite distribution through agreements with additional distributors to supplement its former exclusive distribution agreement. In December 1992, new encryption technology was introduced by the industry in the home satellite dish market so that former "pirates" are no longer able to receive programming without subscribing to pay television services. CEO Hefner expects this development to continue to have a positive impact on the level of PEI revenues derived from this market.

In fiscal 1994, the entertainment group will explore changes to the pricing, promotion, and advertising mix and plans to test shorter program blocks and 24-hour transmission to boost revenue per home. The Playboy network is predominantly available ten hours a night on a per night and per month basis. The number of monthly subscribers continued to decline in fiscal 1993 primarily from nonaddressable systems. These older systems now represent approximately 10 percent of PEI's total monthly subscriber base. Revenues from monthly subscriptions are expected to increase as more cable systems begin offering Playboy programming on both a pay-per-view and monthly basis.

Playboy's home video business reported a 45 percent increase in revenues in 1993. This business issued 25 new titles, achieved unit volume growth, released the bulk of its titles on laserdisc, and continued its successful video distribution relationship with Uni Distribution Corp. Core releases, such as the *Playmate of the Year* video and *Video Playmate Calendar*, continue to do well. Eleven of the top 100 videos on *Billboard's* 1992 sales charts were Playboy titles. The company extended its product line with the introduction of a *Celebrity Video Centerfold*. The first release featured Jessica Hahn and was a chartbuster, jumping to number two on *Billboard's* top 40 chart list in its third week of release.

The entertainment division plans to produce fewer titles in fiscal 1994 in order to capitalize on its strong backlist of more than 75 titles. New releases will include a *Celebrity Video Centerfold* featuring Diane Parkinson and a video on *Playboy's* 40th anniversary Playmate.

The Playboy-Sharper Image tapes for couples continue to be sold in The Sharper Image's stores and catalogs and through retail distribution. The "For Couples Only" line remains extremely popular with both men and women. The company plans to expand its marketing efforts to women to further increase sales and expand the dual audience for the product.

Playboy moved into the home shopping arena in 1993 by producing and airing its first infomercial, *Secrets of Making Love*, on broadcast and cable television. Starring Morgan Brittany, the infomercial promoted two Playboy videos, an audiotape of music for lovers, and a massage kit. The ongoing successful sales of this program have led to the production of a second infomercial, which promises a new relationship series to be released in fiscal 1994.

The international television and home video operations reported an 80 percent increase in revenues to $9.8 million in fiscal 1993. Playboy's fiscal 1993 agreement with HBO Olé, the first and largest multinational pay television network reaching all of Latin America and the Caribbean, significantly broadened the global reach of Playboy programming. Under terms of the deal, programs such as *Playboy Late Night* and *Eden* will begin airing in a consistent Playboy timeslot.

In fiscal 1993, PEI increased its international television market to 64 countries, from 17, largely as a result of entering into its first multiyear, exclusive agreement to supply blocks of Playboy-branded programming ("programming tier") for exhibition throughout Latin America. While continuing to sell individual series, the company has expanded its existing foreign network relationships by entering into a programming tier agreement with overseas pay television distributors. These agreements enable PEI to have an ongoing branded presence in international markets and are expected to generate higher and more consistent revenues than selling programs on a show-by-show basis. Through separate distribution agreements, PEI also distributes its U.S. home video products to countries in Latin America, Europe, Australia, and Asia. These products are based on the videos produced for the U.S. market, with dubbing or subtitling into the local language where necessary.

At the close of fiscal 1993, the entertainment division formed a strategic alliance with Taurus Programming Services, which plans to launch a pay television service on Spanish cable systems during the latter part of calendar 1993. The agreement calls for the nightly broadcast of a two-hour block of Playboy programming on this new service and grants Playboy advertising time to promote Playboy products, such as home videos and the Spanish edition of *Playboy*.

PEI will pursue other such relationships to further its tier strategy. In fiscal 1994, PEI plans to introduce two new series, *Playboy's Hot Rocks* and *Erotic Fantasies*, to the overseas market. Home video growth from new agreements with distributors in Chile, Columbia, Croatia, Slovenia, and Venezuela will supplement international television sales.

PRODUCT MARKETING

Playboy and the rabbit head design are among the most recognized trademarks in the world. The company leverages the power of its brand recognition, design expertise, art collection, and loyal customer base to develop and market apparel, accessories, and other products to consumers in more than 50 countries.

The Playboy and Playmate product lines consist primarily of men's and women's clothing, accessories, watches, jewelry, fragrances, small leather goods, stationery, and home fashions. These products are marketed in North America, Europe, Asia, Australia, and South America, primarily through mass merchants and other retail outlets, by licensees under exclusive license agreements that authorize the manufacture, sale, and distribution of products in a designated territory. Royalties are based on a fixed or variable percentage of the licensee's total new sales, in some cases against guaranteed minimum. In fiscal 1993, approximately 62 percent of the royalties earned from licensing the company's trademarks was derived from licensees in the Far East, 24 percent from licensees in the United States, and the remainder from Europe, Australia, Canada, and other territories.

The product marketing group reported earnings of $1.0 million on a 7 percent increase in revenues to $9.5 million in fiscal 1993. Revenues grew primarily from expansion in the art products business and significant product marketing growth in Asia. Royalties from international product marketing, which provided nearly half of the division's fiscal 1993 revenues, rose 10 percent. However, earnings declined modestly. Additionally, PEI sustained a loss in its events business, which led to the restructuring of that operation at year-end to significantly reduce future expenses.

Popularity of the Playboy name stems from its association with fun, sexiness, and quality. Aspirational, adventurous, and romantic are a few of the many characteristics that define the Playboy customer. Overseas, the Playboy logo benefits from its strong identification with Western freedoms, American lifestyle, and a desire for "the good life."

The product marketing division worked toward unifying the Playboy brand image around the world in fiscal 1993. The group held its first international product licensing conference, which brought licensees together to meet other executives who manage international Playboy businesses and to exchange ideas about Playboy products. PEI also began developing plans to cross-market products through advertising, public relations, and promotions and through clustering multiple products around themes. An advertising campaign developed around two cluster concepts is expected to be launched in Western Europe in fall 1994.

The major accomplishments of the international product marketing program in fiscal 1993 were continued expansion in China; the development of a relationship with the MBf Group, a multinational Malaysian-based conglomerate, to manufacture and market Playboy condoms; and the restructuring of the licensing program in Japan.

Licensee Chaifa Investment, Ltd. increased the number of Playboy boutiques operating within department stores in China from 34 to 65; opened its first freestanding Playboy shop in Shanghai; and built a factory in Shantou to manufacture Playboy products, provide for direct distribution of merchandise throughout the country, and reduce the cost of Playboy products compared to imports. Chaifa plans to open additional freestanding stores and boutiques during fiscal 1994, bringing the total number of Playboy shops in China to approximately 100.

In Japan, Playboy reorganized its manufacturing and distribution network and established direct relationships with a number of former sublicensees to produce Playboy goods. This increases the company's royalties and allows for greater marketing control.

PEI intends to sign licensees for several new product categories in the European market, including lingerie, swimwear, sunglasses, and bath products. Additionally,

Playboy is moving to a position of active brand management from passive licensing by becoming more directly involved in the development of advertising, merchandising strategies, and store concepts.

Since *Playboy* magazine's founding, the company has provided reliable, factual information on human sexuality and outlined the responsibilities that go along with sexual freedom. With the escalating global health threats posed by AIDS and unprotected sex, the company decided to develop a line of Playboy condoms and use its knowledge and influence on sex-related issues to deliver an important message about safe sex. Playboy condoms were launched late in calendar 1993 under a licensing agreement with the MB*f* Group. A multibillion-dollar financial services and consumer products conglomerate based in Kuala Lumpur, Malaysia. The product line will be introduced initially in Taiwan, with subsequent launches in the Asian region. A portion of the proceeds generated from condom sales will be donated to a newly formed foundation that will distribute grants to locally based organizations supporting sex education and AIDS prevention efforts.

Playboy's decision to upgrade the image of its domestic consumer products to match Playboy magazine standards resulted in the termination and expiration of nearly all product licensing agreements in the United States over the past two years. The loss in royalties from Playboy's former licensees caused a drop in domestic revenues and a related decline in fiscal 1993 operating performance.

The product marketing division has developed several new products, including a line of lingerie marketed under the name "Romantics by Playboy." Playboy also signed designer Becky Bisoulis, known for her elaborate bridal wear and lace fashions, to create a signature collection of Playboy lingerie for the fall 1994 season. PEI is now looking to secure appropriate direct and retail distribution for the product lines.

Special Editions, Ltd. (SEL), which markets original art, limited-edition prints, posters, and art products, reported higher revenues as a result of strong sales from art watches and ties, and a significantly smaller operating loss in fiscal 1993 compared to the prior year. SEL's second watch collection, which featured designs by Keith Haring, Karl Wirsum, and Bas Van Reek, sold exceptionally well, as did the subsidiary's first collection of Keith Haring silk ties.

A collection of art watches utilizing designs by architect Stanley Tigerman and California painter Wayne Thiebaud and a new Keith Haring art tie collection are being developed for sale in fiscal 1994. SEL also plans to release, through an exclusive deal with the Pablo Picasso estate, an art watch featuring the painter's 1924 pen and ink drawing *The Guitar*.

The original art and limited-edition print segment of the business improved in fiscal 1993, due in large part to sales generated by the program SEL developed around emerging artist Charles Dwyer, Jr. SEL also successfully produced and marketed several new limited-edition prints and posters of works by Patrick Nagel and Salvador Dali.

PEI entered the stationery and museum notecard market during 1993. The company produced two series of notecards featuring works by *Playboy* contributing artist LeRoy Neiman—The Equestrian Collection and The Impressionist Collection. Additional works by *Playboy* artists are being considered for new notecard sets planned for introduction in fiscal 1994.

In October 1987, PEI bought the Sarah Coventry brand in order to expand sales by leveraging its brand management expertise. This subsidiary continues to be a solid performer, although fiscal 1993 revenues and earnings growth were inhibited by financial difficulties experienced by its primary jewelry licensee. During 1993, PEI negotiated a more favorable licensing contract with New Dimensions Accessories, Ltd., formerly R. N. Koch, and signed a deal for the distribution of the jewelry line through home parties.

PUBLIC AFFAIRS

PEI established the Playboy Foundation in 1965 to provide financial support for organizations dedicated to protect civil rights and civil liberties, promote First Amendment rights and freedom of expression, and support research and education on human sexuality and reproductive rights. In fiscal 1993, the Foundation awarded nearly $290,000 in grants and in-kind contributions to organizations working in these areas. The magazine provided more than one-half million dollars in free advertising space to nonprofit groups working on AIDS research and services, the First Amendment, and natural environment issues. A basic tenet of *The Playboy Philosophy* is that the First Amendment is the keystone to all other rights. Playboy established the Hugh M. Hefner First Amendment Awards in 1979 to honor individuals who have championed freedom of expression.

Another important component of PEI's philosophy is that the company has a responsibility to give back to its communities—"doing well by doing good." In 1985, the Foundation established the Neighborhood Relations Boards, composed of nonexecutive employees who award grants to small- and medium-sized organizations that serve traditionally disadvantaged people. In fiscal 1993, the Neighborhood Relations Boards awarded grants to 34 groups in Chicago, New York, and Los Angeles.

Playboy actively encourages its employees to get involved in their communities. The Foundation's Matching Gift program matches employee contributions to nonprofit organizations dollar for dollar (up to $350 per employee per year), and the Time Match program provides $2 for each hour that an employee volunteers for a nonprofit group. In fiscal 1993, 21 percent of Playboy's employees participated in the Matching Gift and Time Match programs, resulting in contributions to 121 nonprofit organizations across the country.

FUTURE PLANS

PEI wants to capitalize on trends in Europe and Asia toward democracy and freedom. Which new countries worldwide should be targeted by PEI for entry? Which of PEI's three divisions should receive the greatest emphasis and resources in the early 1990s? Should the company focus more on publishing, licensing, television, telephone, videos, or artwork? How can PEI improve its corporate image among critics who contend that their business is obscene and unethical?

Should PEI make a major acquisition in the near future to begin publishing other magazines, such as *Cosmopolitan*, *Woman's Day*, or *Ladies' Home Journal*, *Gentleman's Quarterly*, or *Esquire*? Which of these magazines could feasibly be acquired? What should be PEI's offering price? There are rumors that PEI itself could be the target of an acquisition soon. How much is the company worth today?

PEI incurred a $4.5 million operating loss in its first quarter of fiscal 1994 and reduced its workforce 10 percent, about 60 jobs. Circulation of *Playboy* magazine slid to 3.4 million in early 1994, down 50 percent from its record 6.8 million copies sold in 1972. The magazine's average reader is a 33-year old male with household income of $33,700; half of its readers are married. Should PEI target other customers? Should PEI enter the gaming business? The company was denied a casino license in New Jersey in 1982 but the gaming industry is a growing business today.[1] What are your recommendations to Christie Hefner to reverse the company's declining profitability and to grow internationally? Ms. Hefner plans to launch the company's 17th foreign edition soon in South Africa. Develop a comprehensive strategic plan for PEI. The company's current mission statement is given as follows:

> PEI is a preeminent international media and entertainment company with a worldwide recognized brand and many windows of opportunity to expand the Playboy franchise and develop other related entertainment franchises globally by leveraging Playboy's strengths of publishing, brand management, and marketing.

NOTES

[1]Carey, Susan. "Playboy Looks Overseas as U.S. Climate Grows Hostile." *Wall Street Journal,* 29 Sept. 1993, p. B4.

EXHIBIT 29-9 Playboy Enterprises, Inc., Consolidated Statements of Operations for the Years Ended June 30 (*In thousands, except per share amounts*)

	1993	1992	1991
Net revenues	$214,875	$193,749	$174,042
Costs and expenses			
Cost of sales	(180,700)	(162,149)	(144,196)
Selling and administrative expenses	(33,149)	(29,116)	(27,556)
Total costs and expenses	(213,849)	(191,265)	(171,752)
Operating income	1,026	2,484	2,290
Nonoperating income (expense)			
Investment income	274	2,086	3,522
Interest expense	(405)	(258)	(298)
Critic's Choice Video minority interest	(860)	(118)	—
Other, net	444	392	376
Total nonoperating income (expense)	(547)	2,102	3,600
Income from continuing operations before income taxes and extraordinary item	479	4,586	5,890
Income tax expense	(114)	(2,764)	(3,479)
Income from continuing operations before extraordinary item	365	1,822	2,411
Discontinued operations			
Loss on disposal	—	—	(120)
Income before extraordinary item	365	1,822	2,291
Extraordinary item—tax benefit resulting from utilization of loss carryforwards	—	1,688	2,219
Net income	$365	$3,510	$4,510
Weighted average number of common shares outstanding	18,871	18,521	18,563
Income (loss) per common share			
Income (loss) before extraordinary item			
From continuing operations	$.02	$.10	$.13
From discontinued operations	—	—	(.01)
Total	.02	.10	.12
Extraordinary item applicable to continuing operations	—	.09	.12
Net income	$.02	$.19	$.24

Source: Playboy Enterprises, Inc., *Annual Report*, 1993.

EXHIBIT 29-10 Playboy Enterprises, Inc., Selected Financial and Operating Data for the Years Ended June 30 (*In thousands*)

	1993	1992	1991
Net Revenues			
Publishing			
Playboy magazine			
Subscription	$ 44,919	$ 42,635	$ 40,314
Newsstand	23,470	27,051	25,518
Advertising	30,406	30,667	32,683
Other	2,386	1,818	1,780
Total *Playboy* magazine	101,181	102,171	100,295
Playboy-related	22,008	21,737	22,283
Catalogs	39,411	28,054	18,135
Other	163	385	—
Total Publishing	162,763	152,347	140,713
Entertainment			
Domestic pay television			
Pay-per-view	8,006	6,031	3,835
Monthly subscription	8,575	9,832	11,400
Home satellite dish and other	4,732	2,591	2,538
Total domestic pay television	21,313	18,454	17,773
Domestic home video	10,133	7,009	2,668
International television and home video	9,822	5,447	3,454
Other	1,329	1,629	1,075
Total Entertainment	42,597	32,539	24,970
Product Marketing	9,515	8,863	8,359
Total Net Revenues	$214,875	$193,749	$174,042
Operating Income			
Publishing			
Playboy magazine	$ 7,947	$ 6,991	$6,122
Playboy-related	8,426	9,097	10,272
Catalogs	4,888	2,472	684
Administrative expenses, new magazine			
development and other	(6,909)	(5,809)	(4,790)
Total Publishing	14,352	12,751	12,288
Entertainment			
Before programming expense	15,364	12,645	10,451
Programming expense	(13,553)	(8,972)	(7,535)
Total Entertainment	1,811	3,673	2,916
Product Marketing	1,015	2,676	3,487
Corporate Administration and Promotion	(16,152)	(16,616)	(16,401)
Total Operating Income	$ 1,026	$ 2,484	$ 2,290

Source: Playboy Enterprises, Inc., *Annual Report*, 1993.

EXHIBIT 29-11 Playboy Enterprises, Inc., Consolidated Balance Sheets as of June 30
(*In thousands, except share data*)

	1993	1992
Assets		
Cash and cash equivalents	$ 1,903	$ 8,773
Short-term investments	50	10,447
Receivables, net of allowances for doubtful accounts of $2,343 and $1,903	22,772	14,824
Inventories	21,666	18,021
Programming costs	31,659	16,197
Deferred subscription acquisition costs	7,608	8,481
Other current assets	7,916	7,509
Total current assets	93,574	84,252
Property and equipment		
Land	292	343
Buildings and improvements	8,032	8,921
Furniture and equipment	19,727	20,206
Leasehold improvements	8,026	6,388
Total property and equipment	36,077	35,858
Accumulated depreciation	(18,490)	(19,530)
Property and equipment, net	17,587	16,328
Programming costs—noncurrent	1,096	7,601
Trademarks	9,449	8,514
Other noncurrent assets	6,061	4,516
Total assets	$127,767	$121,211
Liabilities		
Current financing obligations	$ 322	$ 318
Accounts payable	14,967	14,197
Accrued salaries, wages and employee benefits	4,138	3,677
Net liabilities of and reserves for losses on disposals of discontinued businesses	369	1,128
Income taxes payable	845	358
Accrued retail display allowance	2,417	2,994
Deferred revenues	36,318	39,254
Other liabilities and accrued expenses	5,257	6,416
Total current liabilities	64,633	68,342
Long-term financing obligations	1,347	1,669
Other noncurrent liabilities	6,406	7,944
Total liabilities	72,386	77,955
Commitments and contingencies		
Shareholders' Equity		
Common stock, $.01 par value		
Class A—7,500,000 shares authorized; 5,042,381 issued	50	50
Class B—30,000,000 shares authorized; 16,477,143 and 15,127,143 issued	165	151
Capital in excess of par value	36,344	24,655
Retained earnings	27,401	27,036
Less cost of 341,327 Class A common shares and 1,285,643 and 1,296,667 Class B common shares in treasury	(8,579)	(8,636)
Total shareholders' equity	55,381	43,256
Total liabilities and shareholders' equity	$127,767	$121,211

Source: Playboy Enterprises, Inc., *Annual Report*, 1993.

EXHIBIT 29-12 Officers of Playboy Enterprises, Inc.

CORPORATE OFFICERS

Hugh M. Hefner
   Founder, Chairman Emeritus and Editor-in-Chief
Christie Hefner
   Chairman and Chief Executive Officer
David I. Chemerow
   Executive Vice President, Finance and Operations,
   and Chief Financial Officer
Anthony J. Lynn
   Executive Vice President and President,
   Entertainment Group
Michael S. Perlis
   Executive Vice President and President, Publishing
   Group
Richard S. Rosenzweig
   Executive Vice President
Howard Shapiro
   Executive Vice President, Law and Administration,
   and General Counsel
Robert B. Beleson
   Senior Vice President and Chief Marketing Officer
Rebecca S. Maskey
   Senior Vice President, Finance, and Treasurer
Martha O. Lindeman
   Vice President, Corporate Communications and
   Public Affairs
Michael R. Nott
   Vice President and Corporate Controller
John A. Ullrick
   Vice President, Management Information Systems
Robert D. Campbell
   Assistant Treasurer
Irma Villarreal
   Corporate Counsel and Secretary

GROUP OFFICERS

Publishing Group
Michael S. Perlis
   President and Publisher, *Playboy*
Arthur Kretchmer
   Senior Vice President, Editorial Director and
   Associate Publisher, *Playboy*
Irwin Kornfeld
   Senior Vice President, Advertising and Marketing,
   and Associate Publisher, *Playboy*

Barbara L. Gutman
   Senior Vice President, Circulation and Ancillary
   Businesses
Robert F. O'Donnell
   Senior Vice President and General Manager,
   New York
James P. Radtke
   Senior Vice President and General Manager,
   Chicago
Haresh Shah
   Senior Vice President, International Publishing
Gary Cole
   Vice President, Photography, *Playboy*
Marilyn Grabowski
   Vice President, West Coast Photography, *Playboy*
Maria D. Mandis
   Vice President, Production
Patricia Papangelis
   Vice President and Executive Editor, Newsstand
   Specials
Tom Staebler
   Vice President and Executive Art Director, *Playboy*,
   and President, Special Editions, Ltd.
Herbert M. Laney
   President, Catalogs

Entertainment Group
Anthony J. Lynn
   President
Richard V. Sowa
   Executive Vice President, Chief Operating Officer
   and President, Distribution
Richard P. Rosetti
   President, Production
Richard Bencivengo
   Senior Vice President, Programming and
   Production, Pay Television
Myron DuBow
   Senior Vice President, Business and Legal Affairs
Michael K. Fleming
   Senior Vice President and General Manager, Pay
   Television
Mary E. Herne
   Senior Vice President, International Distribution
   and Development

EXHIBIT 29-12 *Continued*

Jeffrey M. Jenest
   Senior Vice President and General Manager, Home Video
Sol Weisel
   Senior Vice President, Production Operations
Stephen M. Astor
   Vice President, Marketing
Marshal Backlar
   Vice President, Production
Suzanne Barron
   Vice President, International Home Video
Michael Hassan
   Vice President, Special Markets, Pay Television
Jeffrey R. Lai
   Vice President, Business and Legal Affairs
Barry A. Leshtz
   Vice President, Sales and Marketing, Home Video
Lawrence L. Logan
   Vice President and Creative Director
Brian W. Quirk

Vice President, National Sales and Affiliate Relations, Pay Television
Deborah R. Redleaf
   Vice President, Finance

Product Marketing
Robert B. Beleson
   Chief Marketing Officer
Cindy Rakowitz
   Vice President, Public Relations
Lisa L. Weaver
   Vice President, International Licensing

Playboy Foundation
Cleo F. Wilson
   Executive Director
Burton Joseph
   Chairman, Board of Directors

Source: Playboy Enterprises, Inc., *Annual Report*, 1993.

APPLIANCES INDUSTRY NOTE

ARIEH ULLMANN AND JOHN HARRIS

STATE UNIVERSITY OF NEW YORK AT BINGHAMPTON

Product shipments of appliances increased 3 percent in 1993, to a record $17.7 billion. While housing starts increased only about 4 percent during the year, consumer confidence fell from 77 in January, as measured by the Conference Board, to 59 in August (1985=100), a level more typical of a recession year than a recovery year.

The appliance industry is dominated by five major corporations that produce complete lines of basic, major household appliances: Whirlpool, General Electric, White Consolidated Industries, Maytag, and Raytheon, in that order. State-of-the-art major appliances of high quality are offered at low prices because of intense competition among well-capitalized companies, high volume production, heavy capital investment, and a market open to foreign producers. Imports constitute more than 50 percent of the domestic market in several categories of small appliances, because of the high labor content of these appliances.

The major U.S. producers are now moving to become global manufacturers. Most have plants in Western Europe, and some have begun to expand into Central and Eastern Europe and China (Table 1).

Energy Efficiency Standards. The National Appliance Energy Conservation Act of 1987 set national efficiency standards for several categories of major household appliances, including refrigerators and freezers, water heaters, dishwashers, clothes washers and dryers, and kitchen ranges and ovens. The statute directs the Department of Energy (DOE) to tighten the standards in future years, taking into consideration life-cycle costs (initial cost plus operating cost). DOE has since revised energy conservation standards for refrigerators, dishwashers, clothes washers, and clothes dryers. The standards for refrigerators became effective in 1993, and the others are scheduled to take effect in May 1994. The 1994 standards can be met through several changes including more efficient motors, horizontal-axis clothes washers, auxiliary water heaters, lower water temperatures in the rinse cycle, reduced water usage per cycle, and better insulation and automatic heat sensor-controlled shutoffs for clothes dryers.

DOE has proposed new energy efficiency standards for water heaters, room air conditioners, direct heating equipment, televisions, kitchen ranges and ovens, pool heaters, mobile home furnaces, and fluorescent lamp ballasts. The proposed standards are expected to be published early in 1994. After a comment period, the final standards are likely to be published late in 1994 becoming effective before 1998.

ENVIRONMENTAL PROFILE

Energy efficiency and chlorofluorocarbons (CFCs) remain major issues for the appliance industry. For more than 50 years, CFCs have been used as coolants in refrigerators and freezers, as well as in the production of foam insulation. However, because CFCs allegedly damage the earth's protective layer of atmospheric ozone, the United States has pledged to halt CFC production by 1996 under the Montreal Protocol of 1987. In addition, DuPont, a major U.S. producer, has stated that it will end CFC production by the end of 1994. This accelerated phaseout places more pressure on manufacturers to finish testing substitutes, solve problems in material compatibility and toxicity, and meet energy-efficiency requirements. Most manufacturers are

TABLE 1   Trends and Forecasts: Household Appliances (SIC 363) (*In millions of dollars except as noted*)

Item	1991	1992[1]	1993[2]	1994[3]	Percent Change (1991–1994) 91–92	92–93	93–94
INDUSTRY DATA							
Value of shipments[4]	17,692	18,900	19,540	—	6.8	3.4	—
3631 Household cooking equip	2,891	3,064	3,198	—	6.0	4.4	—
3632 Household refrigerators	3,721	3,989	3,972	—	7.2	-0.4	—
3633 Household laundry equip	3,206	3,372	3,352	—	5.2	-0.6	—
3634 Elect housewares & fans	3,112	3,490	3,700	—	12.1	6.0	—
3635 Household vacuums	1,805	1,912	2,048	—	5.9	7.1	—
3639 Home appliances nec	2,958	3,073	3,270	—	3.9	6.4	—
Value of shipments (1987$)	16,826	17,998	18,551	19,210	7.0	3.1	3.6
Household cooking equip	2,914	3,094	3,172	3,270	6.2	2.5	3.1
3632 Household refrigerators	3,688	3,939	3,890	4,060	6.8	-1.2	4.4
3633 Household laundry equip	3,059	3,261	3,394	3,530	6.6	4.1	4.0
3634 Elect housewares & fans	2,892	3,220	3,380	3,460	11.3	5.0	2.4
3635 Household vacuums	1,615	1,720	1,815	1,870	6.5	5.5	3.0
3639 Home appliances nec	2,658	2,764	2,900	3,020	4.0	4.9	4.1
Total employment (000)	104	104	106	107	0.0	1.9	0.9
Production workers (000)	83.8	84.2	85.7	86.5	0.5	1.8	0.9
Average hourly earnings ($)	11.20	11.34	11.29	—	1.2	-0.4	—
Capital expenditures	496	—	—	—	—	—	—
PRODUCT DATA							
Value of shipments[5]	16,089	17,186	17,730	—	6.8	3.2	—
3631 Household cooking equip	2,942	3,118	3,255	—	6.0	4.4	—
3632 Household refrigerators	3,621	3,881	3,865	—	7.2	-0.4	—
3633 Household laundry equip	2,860	3,008	3,114	—	5.2	3.5	—
3634 Elect housewares & fans	2,608	2,926	2,956	—	12.2	1.0	—
3635 Household vacuums	1,834	1,943	2,081	—	5.9	7.1	—
3639 Home appliances nec	2,224	2,310	2,459	—	3.9	6.5	—
Value of shipments (1987$)	15,348	16,417	16,905	17,500	7.0	3.0	3.5
3631 Household cooking equip	2,966	3,150	3,230	3,330	6.2	2.5	3.1
3632 Household refrigerators	3,589	3,832	3,785	3,950	6.8	-1.2	4.4
3633 Household laundry equip	2,729	2,909	3,030	3,150	6.6	4.2	4.0
3634 Elect housewares & fans	2,424	2,700	2,835	2,900	11.4	5.0	2.3
3635 Household vacuums	1,642	1,749	1,845	1,900	6.5	5.5	3.0
3639 Home appliances nec	1,998	2,077	2,180	2,270	4.0	5.0	4.1
TRADE DATA							
Value of imports	3,258	3,830	4,100	4,400	17.6	7.0	7.3
Value of exports	2,139	2,365	2,510	2,700	10.6	6.1	7.6

[1]Estimate, except exports and imports.
[2]Estimate.
[3]Forecast.
[4]Value of all products and services sold by establishments in the household appliances industry.
[5]Value of products classified in the household appliances industry produced by all industries.

Source: U.S. Department of Commerce: Bureau of the Census; International Trade Administration (ITA). Estimates and forecasts by ITA.

expected to use hydrofluorocarbon-134a (HFC-134a) as the refrigerant and hydrochlorofluorocarbon-141b (HCFC-141b) as the foaming agent. The use of HCFC-141b is likely to be only a temporary substitute, since U.S. production is expected to be phased out by Jan. 1, 2003.

Some appliance manufacturers in Europe are already offering CFC-free refrigerators and freezers, most using the mentioned substitutes. Early 1993 models were priced about 7 percent higher than those with CFCs, however.

A U.S. manufacturer may soon use high-insulation vacuum panels in place of foam insulation. The latest versions of these panels reportedly have insulation values up to R-65-80 per inch, far higher than the R-8 achieved with foam produced with CFC-11 or the R-7.5 with HCFC-141b. If the use of these vacuum panels proves to be technologically feasible and cost-competitive, it could result in a substantial increase in a refrigerator's interior space while substantially contributing to energy efficiency. The panels might also be used in other appliances, such as water heaters.

INTERNATIONAL COMPETITIVENESS

Appliance imports and exports increased at nearly the same rate in 1993, imports about 7 percent to $4.1 billion and exports 6 percent to $2.5 billion. The leading suppliers of appliances to the United States were Mexico, China, Japan, South Korea, and Taiwan, in that order (Table 2).

TABLE 2 U.S. Trade Patterns in 1992 Household Appliances (SIC 363)
(*In millions of dollars, percent*)

	EXPORTS		IMPORTS		
	Value	Share		Value	Share
Canada and Mexico	1,135	48.0	Canada and Mexico	909	23.7
European Community	323	13.7	European Community	482	12.6
Japan	77	3.3	Japan	464	12.1
East Asia NICs	207	8.7	East Asia NICs	1,725	45.0
South America	177	7.5	South America	40	1.0
Other	445	18.8	Other	210	5.5
World Total	2,365	100.0	World Total	3,830	100.0
		TOP FIVE COUNTRIES			
	Value	Share		Value	Share
Canada	732	30.9	Mexico	738	19.3
Mexico	403	17.1	China	726	19.0
Taiwan	89	3.8	Japan	464	12.1
Germany	84	3.6	South Korea	304	7.9
Japan	77	3.3	Taiwan	299	7.8

Source: U.S. Department of Commerce: Bureau of the Census; International Trade Administration.

Mexico is expected to increase its lead regardless of the fate of the North American Free Trade Agreement, because of the growing integration of its appliance industry with that of the United States. Some U.S. appliance manufacturers have established joint ventures with Mexican companies to produce stoves, refrigerators, and laundry equipment in Mexico. These plants are expected to increase production in future years to supply markets in both countries as well as others. Asian countries with lower labor costs will remain the major suppliers of small appliances, for which transportation costs are less of a factor.

The leading markets for U.S. appliances are Canada, Mexico, Japan, Germany, and Saudi Arabia, in that order. Exports to Canada have more than doubled in the past four years as tariffs declined under the U.S.-Canada Free Trade Agreement, under which all Canadian tariffs on U.S. appliances will be eliminated by 1998. Likewise, U.S. appliance exports to Mexico have nearly doubled in the past four years because of major tariff reductions by Mexico and increasing shipments of parts to U.S.-affiliated appliance factories in Mexico.

U.S. export competitiveness depends to a large extent on the value of the dollar with respect to the currencies of its trading partners and competitors. The overall, real trade-weighted value of the dollar has been stable since 1988, after falling 30 percent from its peak in 1985. Even in 1993, the overall, trade-weighted value of the dollar changed only slightly, with strength in European markets offsetting weakness in Japan. During the five years of stability since 1988, U.S. trade in appliances has had time to readjust to the damage caused when an overvalued dollar in the mid-1980s encouraged imports and discouraged exports. The ratio of household appliance imports to exports is currently 1.6. While this is a substantial improvement over the ratio of 2.6 in 1987, it is substantially worse than the ratio of 1.0 which existed in the mid-to-late 1970s. It is unlikely that trade patterns will continue to shift all the way back. Since the mid-1970s, duty-free treatment of imports under the Generalized System of Preferences has resulted in the developing countries becoming major suppliers of many of the small electric household appliances sold domestically.

MANUFACTURING AND DISTRIBUTION

Home appliances are generally classified as laundry (washers and dryers), refrigeration (refrigerators and freezers), cooking (ranges and ovens), and other appliances (dishwashers, disposals, and trash compactors). Many appliance manufacturers also make floor care goods such as floor polishers and vacuum cleaners.

Manufacturing operations consist mainly of preparation of a metal frame to which the appropriate components are attached in automated assembly lines and by manual assembly. Manufacturing costs comprise about 65 to 75 percent of total operating cost with labor representing less than 10 percent of total cost. Optimal-sized assembly plants have an annual capacity of about 500,000 units for most appliances except microwave ovens. Unlike other industries such as textiles, variable costs play an important role in the cost structure; changes in raw material and component costs are also significant. Component production is fairly scale sensitive. Doubling compressor output for refrigerators, for instance, reduces unit costs by 10–15 percent. There are also some scale economies in assembly, but introduction of robotics tends to reduce those while also improving quality, performance, consistency, and flexibility.

Distribution of major appliances occurs through contract sales to home builders or local builder suppliers. Traditionally, these customers were very cost conscious and prefer less expensive appliance brands. Retail sales represent a second distribution channel through which national chain stores and mass merchandisers, like Sears, as well as department, furniture, discount, and appliance stores act as intermediaries. In recent years, independent appliance stores which in the past sold about a third of all white goods are more and more being replaced by national chains such as Sears' Brand Central and mega-appliance dealers such as Circuit City. Consolidation of appliance distributors has led to the current situation in which about 45 percent of the total appliance volume is being sold through 10 powerful mega-retailers, led by Sears with a market share of about 29 percent. A third, less visible channel is the commercial market such as laundromats, hospitals, hotels, and other institutions.

Consolidation. Before World War II, appliance manufacturers produced many varieties of one product. In the mid-1940s, there were over 250 firms manufacturing appliances in the United States, including all the major U.S. automobile firms except for Chrysler. The industry experienced a period of mergers in the 1950s and 1960s while sales grew approximately 50 percent due to increased reliability, advances in technology, and a decline in prices. With the 1970s came high inflation and interest rates, but unit sales still continued to climb.

The last merger wave occurred in 1986 when Electrolux purchased White Consolidated, Whirlpool acquired KitchenAid, and Magic Chef was bought by Maytag. Maytag's acquisition of Jenn-Air and Magic Chef increased its overall revenues by giving brand name appliances to Maytag at various price points. Likewise, Whirlpool's acquisition of KitchenAid and Roper, respectively, broadened Whirlpool's presence at the high-end and low-end of the market. The number of domestic appliance manufacturers today varies by type of product, with seven for home laundry appliances, fifteen for home refrigeration and room air conditioning equipment, and five for dishwashers.

Broad Product Scope. In the 1980s, the market continued to grow primarily thanks to the acceptance by the American people of the microwave oven. Microwave oven unit sales tripled from 1980 to 1989, while washers and dryers increased in sales 34 and 52 percent, respectively. Appliance manufacturers realized that they must offer a complete line of appliances even if they did not manufacture all of them themselves which was one reason for the merger activity and practice of inter-firm sourcing. For example, Whirlpool made trash compactors for Frigidaire (Electrolux/White Consolidated), In-Sink-Erator (Emerson Electric), and Sears. General Electric manufactured microwave ovens for Caloric (Raytheon), Jenn-Air, and Magic Chef (Maytag).

Today, five major competitors control 98 percent of the core appliance market (cooking equipment, dishwashers, dryers, refrigerators, and washers) each of which offers a broad range of product categories and brands targeted to different customer segments. With 33.8 percent domestic market share, Whirlpool is ahead of GE (28.2 percent), a reversal of GE's leadership position two years earlier. Electrolux (15.9 percent), Maytag (14.2 percent), and Raytheon (5.6 percent) follow. Whirlpool holds market share leadership positions in several appliance categories.

Market Saturation. Competition in the United States is fierce. Industry demand depends on the state of the economy, disposable income levels, interest rates, housing starts, and the consumers' ability to defer purchases. Saturation levels remain high and steady; over 70 percent of households have washers and over 65 percent dryers. The market for refrigerators is saturated. Sales of electric ranges have slowed as microwave oven sales have accelerated. With many homes having more than one gas or electric range, the market has become saturated. Yet, even microwave sales, which jumped from 3.5 million units in 1980 to more than 10 million units by 1989, have started leveling out.

Factors of Competition. All rivals work hard at keeping costs down. Over four years, Electrolux spent over $500 million to upgrade old plants and build new ones for its acquisition, White Consolidated Industries. General Electric automated its Louisville, Kentucky, plant which, over ten years, halved the work force and raised output by 30 percent. Had appliance manufacturers been making automobiles, the price of a Cheverolet Caprice would have risen from $7,209 in 1980 to $9,500 in 1990 and not $17,370.

Toward the end of the 1980s, it became even more important to lower costs, monitor margins, and achieve economies of scale. The Big Four were renovating and enlarging existing facilities. Maytag built new facilities in the south to take advantage of lower cost, nonunion labor. Others built twin-plants on the Mexican border to profit from cheap labor. A third trend was towards focus factories where each plant produced one product category only, covering all price points.

Also, all competitors started to push into the high-end segment of the market which was more stable and profitable. Once the domain of Maytag, it became increasingly crowded with the appearance of GE's Monogram line, Whirlpool's acquisition of KitchenAid, and White's Euroflair models. This trend had its roots in the 1980s which brought an increase in new home construction, home expansions, and remodelings. It was estimated that each new home would purchase four to six new appliances. More upscale models were being used as compared to a previous tendency for builders to economize by buying the cheapest national brand appliances.

Quality, too, became an important feature in the competitive game as symbolized by Maytag's lonely repairman. The number of service calls dropped across the board in the wake of rising consumer expectations. Defects rates dropped from 20 per 100 appliances made in 1980 to 10 twelve years later. Relationships with suppliers changed as companies used fewer of them than in years past. Contracts were set up over longer terms to improve quality and keep costs low with just-in-time deliveries.

A recent development is demand by powerful distributors for fast delivery. Distributors seek to curtail inventory costs, their biggest expense.

> We would like to carry even more brands, but we have to find a way to move product more quickly. Sharing information with manufacturers is critical. Logistics is more than distribution; they cover disposal of major appliances, next-day delivery guaranteed in a three-hour period, and emergency repairs. But we have to work with manufacturers to get the costs down,

declared Bernard Brennan, CEO of Montgomery Ward, at a recent meeting of the Association of Home Appliance Manufacturers. As a consequence, General Electric created its Premier Plus Program which guarantees three-day delivery. Also, sales departments are reorganized so one sales representative covers all of a manufacturer's brands of a given product category. Customer information services via 800-telephone lines are now common.

Innovation. Two developments, government regulation and advances in computer software, combined with intense competition have accelerated product innovation. New energy standards to be enforced under the 1987 National Appliance

Energy Conservation Act limit energy consumption of new appliances with the objective to reduce energy usage in appliances by 25 percent every five years. At the same time, the possible ban on ozone-depleting chlorofluorocarbons (CFCs) in refrigerators by 1995 has forced the industry to redesign its refrigerators. Pressures have also been exerted to change washer and dishwasher designs to reduce water consumption.

In 1989, the Super Efficient Refrigerator Program, Inc. (SERP) was organized by the Natural Resources Defense Council, a few utilities, and the Environmental Protection Agency. The SERP organizers created a $30 million price contest financed by 24 utilities to develop a refrigerator prototype free of CFCs and which was at least 25 percent more energy efficient than the 1993 federal standards. Whirlpool won the entire $30 million and has to manufacture and sell over 250,000 refrigerators between January 1994 and July 1997.

Advances in computer technology is the second development accelerating innovation. New programs called fuzzy logic or neural networks, which mimic the human brain's ability to detect patterns, are being introduced in many industries including white goods. In Asia, elevators, washers, and refrigerators using fuzzy logic to recognize usage patterns are already widespread. In late 1992, AEG Hausgeräte AG, a subsidiary of Daimler Benz's AEG unit, introduced a washer using fuzzy logic to automatically control water consumption depending on the size of the load and to sense how much dirt remained in clothes. United Technology is working on a line of air conditioners that automatically adjust room temperature based on the number of people in a room and their preference for comfort, humidity, and air flow.

Outlook. For the future, demand conditions in the United States continue to look unattractive with growth rates forecast around 1 to 2 percent from a level which is 15 percent below 1988 industry shipments. At the prevailing saturation levels, demand is mostly restricted to replacement purchases (79 percent) with the remainder going to new housing and new household formation.

The one positive element in this otherwise bleak outlook is a demographic trend in that the aging baby boomers are demanding more stylish appliances with new features. The late 1980s saw new technologies in cooking surfaces: ceramic-glass units, solid elements, and modular grill configurations. Other new customer-oriented features include the self-cleaning oven, automatic ice cube makers, self-defrosting refrigerators, pilotless gas ranges, and appliances that can be preset. Manufacturers' own brands normally are first accessorized, followed by the national retailers they outfit. Sears and Montgomery Ward usually copy the previous year's most successful products. However, the industry is so competitive that no one manufacturer can keep an innovation to itself for more than a year without a patent. Finally, consumers have become more concerned with the way appliances look. Sleek European styling is fashionable with smooth lines, rounded corners, and a built-in look with electronic controls. Another trend is the white-on-white look which suggests superior cleanability and makes a kitchen look larger.

GLOBALIZATION

The white goods industry is as American as baseball and apple pie. In 1992, 98 percent of the dishwashers, washing machines, dryers, refrigerators, freezers, and ranges sold in America were made in America. Exports represent around 5 percent of shipments. Manufacturing plants of the industry leaders are located in places such as Newton, Iowa (Maytag); Benton Harbor, Michigan (Whirlpool); and Columbus,

Ohio (White Consolidated Industries). Combined, these companies practically own the market for each major appliance with one exception—microwave ovens. These represent the lion's share of imports which make up about 17 percent of total appliance sales.

The acquisition of White Consolidated Industries by AB Electrolux of Sweden in 1986 marked a major change in the industry. Until then, foreign competition was largely restricted to imports of microwave ovens, a segment which was controlled by Far Eastern competitors from Korea (Goldstar, Samsung) and Japan (Sharp, Matsushita). Aware of the fate of other industries, many expected that it was only a matter of time before these companies would expand from their beachhead in microwave ovens and compact appliances into other segments. Indeed, the general manager of the overseas office of Matsushita, the market leader in Japan's white goods industry, stated:

> Foreign makers are right to expect that Matsushita and other Japanese companies will enter the U.S. and European markets soon enough. The traditional makers won't be number 1 and number 2 forever.

Europe's Promise. Of prime attractiveness to U.S. manufacturers is Europe. As a continent, Western Europe represents 27 percent of the global market and, if Eastern Europe and the Middle East and Africa are included, 43 percent; Asia's share is 27 percent; North America follows with 24 percent and Latin America with 6 percent. Western Europe is rapidly moving towards a unified market of some 320 million consumers which is not nearly as saturated as Canada and the United States. Appliance demand is expected to grow at 5 percent annually. Political changes in Eastern Europe have integrated these countries into the world trade system and thus added to Europe's long-term attractiveness.

The European white goods industry has experienced a consolidation similar to that in the United States. In the late 1980s, six companies—Electrolux Zanussi, Philips Bauknecht, Bosch-Siemens, Merloni-Indesit, Thompson, and AEG—controlled 70 percent of the market (excluding microwave ovens and room air conditioners). Until the mid-1980s most companies were either producing and selling in only one national market or exporting to a limited extent to many European markets from one country. Observed Whirlpool CEO Whitwam: "What strikes me most is how similar the U.S. and European industries are." Research by Whirlpool indicates that washers were basically alike in working components around the globe.

However, the European market is very segmented and consumer preferences differ greatly from country to country with regard to almost every type of appliance. For example: The French prefer to cook their foods at high temperatures, splattering grease on oven walls. Thus, oven ranges manufactured for France have self-cleaning ability. However, this feature is not a requirement in Germany where lower cooking temperatures are the norm. In contrast to Americans who prefer to stuff as many clothes into the washer as possible, Europeans overwhelmingly prefer smaller built-in models. Northern Europeans like large refrigerators because they prefer to shop only once a week. In contrast, consumers in the south of Europe prefer small ones, because they visit the open-air markets daily. Northerners like their freezers at the bottom of the refrigerators, southerners on top. Also, the continental European "engineering" mentality dislikes the U.S. and British one-touch button models, but prefers the build-in concept which was developed in the U.S. where it failed to attract buyers. In France, 80 percent of washing machines are top-loaders, while elsewhere in Western Europe, 90 percent are front-loaders. Also, European washers frequently contain heating elements, and the typical European homemaker prefers to wash towels at 95 degrees centigrade. Gas ranges are common throughout Europe, except for Germany where 90 percent are electric.

Given these differences, some observers are skeptical about the possibility of establishing pan-European models which would yield a sustainable competitive advantage through manufacturing, procurement, and marketing efficiencies. They claim that the European market is actually many smaller individual markets made up of the respective countries. Furthermore, many of these national markets feature strong competitors.

AB Electrolux is a force practically in all of Europe with an overall 25 percent market share. Over 20 years, the $14-billion multinational firm from Sweden has undertaken more than 200 acquisitions in 40 countries which span five businesses: household appliances, forestry and garden products, industrial products, metal and mining, and commercial services. Its expertise in managing acquisitions and integrating newly acquired units into the organization is unequalled. For instance, in 1983, Electrolux took over the money losing Italian white goods manufacturer with 30,000 employees, 50 factories, and a dozen foreign sales companies. Within four years, the Swedes turned this company which in 1983 lost Lit. 120 billion into an efficient organization netting Lit. 60 billion. The acquisitions of Zanussi of Italy, Tricity in Britain, and three Spanish companies in anticipation of the changes in Western Europe marked the beginning of a new era in this mature industry. Industrial design centers and research centers are being established in Stockholm, Sweden, Venice, Italy, and Columbus, Ohio, to share product and operation ideas and to accelerate product development among the many brands. Instead of combining production, marketing, and sales on a market-by-market basis, a search for synergies began, first to establish pan-European brands for a unified Europe, and then to explore cross-Atlantic opportunities. The newly formed Electrolux Components Group is charged with taking advantage of the available integration opportunities, primarily by coordinating and developing strategic components worldwide. However, in 1993 Electrolux' pan-European strategy ran into trouble. The recession, combined with Europe's market fragmentation, reduced profits far below the targeted 5 percent margin. In contrast to North America, the varying consumer preferences compelled Electrolux to offer 120 basic designs with 1,500 variants in Europe.

In Germany, Bauknecht (Philips) as well as Siemens-Bosch and AEG-Telefunken are dominant; in Britain General Electric Corporation's Hotpoint leads; and in France, Thomson-Brandt are forces to be reckoned with. Merloni from Italy pursues a different approach by flooding Europe with machines produced in Italy with lower cost labor. In 1987, Merloni gobbled up Indesit, an Italian producer in financial troubles, in order to enlarge its manufacturing base and take advantage of Indesit's marketing position in many European countries. However, in the late 1980s, no brand had more than 5 percent of the overall market, even though the top ten producers generated 80 percent of the volume.

General Electric is another important rival. In 1989, GE entered into an appliance joint venture with Britain's General Electric Corporation (GEC), which has a strong presence in the low price segment of the European market, especially the UK, and thus complements GE's high-end European products.

In the same year, Maytag also entered the European market. It had acquired the Hoover Division through the purchase of Chicago Pacific. Hoover, best known for its vacuum cleaners, in the UK also produced washers, dryers, and dishwashers in a highly integrated process in aging facilities. Hoover is also present in Australia and, through a trading company, services other parts of the world. By acquiring Hoover, Maytag assumed a significant debt load and experienced a negative reaction from the stock market. However, the company's official strategy entails continued globalization via expansion in Europe and the Pacific Rim.

AEG is cooperating with Electrolux in washer and dishwasher production and development; Bosch-Siemens has an alliance with Maytag; the European Economic Interest Group combined several manufacturers with France's Thompson-Brandt as the leader. In spite of this trend toward consolidation, Whirlpool competes among nearly 100 European manufacturers of home appliances.

Asia. Asia, the world's second largest home appliance market, is expected to experience rapid economic growth in the near future primarily thanks to the booming economies of the Pacific Rim countries. Home appliance shipments are expected to grow at least 6 percent per annum through the 1990s—more than in Europe or North America. The market is dominated by some 50 widely diversified Asian manufacturers, primarily from Japan, Korea, and Taiwan, with no clear leader emerging yet. The biggest promise lies in the huge markets of the world's most populous states—China and India.

Latin America. Another market promising attractive growth for appliances is Latin America, once these countries follow Chile's example and emerge from decades of political instability, economic mismanagement, and hyperinflation. The North American Free Trade Agreement (NAFTA) has lowered tariffs and stimulated trade. Appliance shipments to Latin America and Mexico should expand at a faster pace than in North America and Europe.

OUTLOOK FOR 1994

Product shipments of appliances are expected to increase nearly 4 percent in real terms in 1994. Private housing starts are expected to increase 4 percent in 1994, the same rate estimated for 1993. Real improvement is expected in consumer confidence, which in 1993 actually dipped close to the levels last seen during the serious 1981–82 recession. Some argue that these low confidence levels were not a true reflection of the economy, but partly reflected consumer concerns about the federal tax increases, health care reform, and NAFTA, all of which were debated during 1993 and are expected to be settled by early 1994 at the latest.

WHIRLPOOL CORPORATION—1994

ARIEH A. ULLMANN
State University of
New York at Binghamton

Headquartered in Benton Harbor, Michigan, Whirlpool Corporation (616-923-5000) is one of the world's leading manufacturers and marketers of major home appliances. The company's plants are located in twelve countries and its products are distributed in over 120 countries under major brand names. Whirlpool's net earnings for 1993 were $51 million, down 75 percent from 1992. CEO David Whitwam needs a clear strategic plan for the rest of the 1990s decade. Whirlpool's vision statement is:

> Whirlpool, in its chosen lines of business, will grow with new opportunities and be the leader in an ever-changing global market. We will be driven by our commitment to continuous quality improvement and to exceeding all of our customers' expectations. We will gain competitive advantage through this, and by building on our existing strengths and developing new competencies. We will be market-driven, efficient and profitable. Our success will make Whirlpool a company that worldwide customers, employees and other stakeholders can depend on.

HISTORY

Located two hours by car from Chicago, Whirlpool was founded in St. Joseph, Michigan, in 1911. At the time, the company was producing motor-driven wringer-washers under the name Upton Machine, with the hopes of selling them in large quantities to large distributors. In 1916, the first order was sold to Sears, Roebuck and Co. This enduring relationship with its oldest and largest customer continues today with Sears representing 19 percent of Whirlpool's sales. In 1929, Upton merged with Nineteen Hundred Corp., of Binghamton, New York, and plants operated in both locations until Binghamton was closed in 1939. In 1948, the Whirlpool brand automatic washer was introduced. This established the dual distribution system—one product line for Sears, the other for Nineteen Hundred. The Nineteen Hundred Corp. was renamed Whirlpool in 1950 with the addition of automatic dryers to the company's product line.

In 1955, Whirlpool merged with Seeger Refrigerator Co., of St. Paul, Minnesota, and the Estate range and air conditioning divisions of R.C.A. The company, now named Whirlpool-Seeger Corporation, established the RCA Whirlpool brand name which was used until 1967. In 1957, the name was changed back to Whirlpool Corporation. In the same year, the Appliance Credit Corporation was established as a wholly owned finance subsidiary whose name later was changed to Whirlpool Financial Corporation. Also in 1957, Whirlpool, for the first time, entered the foreign market through the purchase of equity interest in Multibras S.A. of Sao Paulo, Brazil, later renamed Brastemp S.A.

In 1967, Whirlpool was the first competitor in the industry to take advantage of AT&T's new 800-line service and created the Cool-Line Telephone Service which provided customers a toll-free number to call for answers to questions and help with service.

Over the years, Whirlpool consistently upgraded its manufacturing capacity by constructing new plants and closing old ones. In 1968, it completed the Elisha Gray II Research and Engineering Center in Benton Harbor thereby establishing a solid R&D basis. In 1986, the KitchenAid division of Hobart Corporation was purchased from Dart & Kraft which marked Whirlpool's entry into the upscale segment of the appliance market. In the same year, Whirlpool sold its central heating and cooling business to Inter-City Gas Corp. of Canada.

Whirlpool diversified in 1985 with the acquisition of Mastercraft Industries Corp., a Denver-based manufacturer of kitchen cabinets. A year later, a second cabinet maker, St. Charles Manufacturing Co., was acquired through the newly formed Whirlpool Kitchens, Inc. In March 1989, Whirlpool Kitchens was sold due to lack of fit. Whirlpool Kitchens had been losing money and had discontinued operations in 1988.

In 1988, Whirlpool's North American operations were reorganized into four brand-oriented business units: Whirlpool Appliance Group, KitchenAid Appliance Group, Kenmore Appliance Group, Inglis Limited. This structure was supposed to allow the company to capitalize on the success of its brands while at the same time reap scale effects through an integrated manufacturing network. KitchenAid served the upscale market based on its reputation for quality blenders and dishwashers, the Whirlpool brand served the mid-price segment, and the Roper brand name, which Whirlpool acquired in 1988 and which was part of the Whirlpool Group, focused on the lower segment and provided Whirlpool with gas range production capability. Thus, within the North American Appliance Group (NAAG) a clear market segmentation existed which ensured complete coverage and minimal overlap. NAAG's scope had been further extended with the acquisition of Emerson Electric's dishwasher and trash compactor business.

In 1992, as a result of a year-long strategic reassessment of the entire company, a new organizational structure was designed for NAAG. Effective January 1, 1993, the new organizational units focus on process management, brand management, customer management, product and service creation, manufacturing, and logistics. The new structure is intended to provide better support for a customer-oriented strategy. The sales and distribution organizations are responsible for brand and customer management for the retail and contract sales business. Marketing focuses on product and service creation and on enhancing brand awareness and loyalty. Logistics is responsible for managing availability and inventory through the warehouses, plants, and vendors. A separate unit, the Kenmore organization, is charged with supporting Sears, Whirlpool's largest single customer.

In June 1993, Whirlpool was named winner in the $30 million Super Efficient Refrigerator Program (SERP), a success which CEO Whitwam attributed to the multidisciplinary team which had been assembled from all over the world: "Each member of the Whirlpool team is an expert in his or her field," Whitwam said. "Their combined efforts and unrelenting focus on bringing a SERP refrigerator to market has resulted in the development of a superior product in a remarkably short time." The first SERP model will be a 22 cubic foot side-by-side refrigerator/freezer to be introduced in 1994. The SERP models eliminate CFCs completely by using a different refrigerant and blowing agent to expand foam insulation between the walls of the refrigerator liner and cabinet. Energy efficiency gains are achieved through better insulation, a high-efficiency compressor, and an improved condenser fan motor in conjunction with a microchip controlled adaptive defrost control which incorporates fuzzy logic. Jeff Fettig, vice president, group marketing and sales for NAAG adds: "I can say that these changes allow us to surpass SERP's very tough requirement that the refrigerators be at least 25 percent more efficient than 1993 federal energy standards." Whirlpool had entered the SERP contest because it was consistent with the company's strategy to exceed customer expectations. Again Fettig: "The SERP program allows us to accelerate the development process and bring these products to the market sooner. Future products will be designed with these consumer expectations [regarding environmental friendliness] in mind, giving people even more reason to ask for a Whirlpool-built product next time they are in the market for a major home appliance."

Since 1988, NAAG had increased its regional market share by nearly a third. The North American business remained Whirlpool's core group: "NAAG has been the source of much of the cash flow required to fund the company's expansion into new markets, and accounts for nearly 60 percent of corporate revenues." Major home appliances constitute a $19 billion basic consumer durable industry in the United States. Exhibit 30–1 traces historical shipment patterns in the main appliance categories. Clearly apparent are the industry's comparatively slow average growth and moderate cyclicality. Refrigerators are the largest product line, followed by washers, dryers, and dishwashers.

Market share data for the years 1988 and 1992 are presented on Exhibit 30–2 and demonstrate the concentrated nature of the industry, Whirlpool's particular predominance in laundry products, and the gradual increases in the company's market shares. The share slippage in refrigeration between 1988 and 1992 partly reflects considerable restructuring in that area, and has probably now reversed.

WHIRLPOOL'S CEO

Among Whirlpool's top management, David R. Whitwam is known as a champion of Whirlpool's globalization. Born in Madison (Wisconsin), Whitwam graduated with honors from the University of Wisconsin with a B.S. in economics. After eight years in the United States Army and the Wisconsin National Guard, he joined Whirlpool as a marketing management trainee in July 1968. One year later, he was named territory sales manager at the South California sales division. From there job descriptions did not change, only the locations. Whitwam spent time in New York and then in Southern California.

A soft-spoken man with midwestern charm, Whitwam was never one to gloat, but his success in California was immense. His forward thinking and innovative spirit sparked Ed Herrelko, vice president of marketing and sales for Caloric, to exalt, "He's a legend out there."

Whitwam moved to corporate headquarters in Benton Harbor in 1977 when he was named merchandising manager for Range Products. From that post came a promotion to director of builder marketing, and then vice president, Whirlpool Sales, in 1983. In 1985, he was elected to the company's board of directors. On December 1, 1987, he assumed his current position as president, CEO and chairman of the board of Whirlpool Corporation. Since then, he has transformed a domestically oriented $4 billion company into a $7 billion global force.

WHIRLPOOL INTERNATIONAL B.V.

Among those most strongly convinced of the promise of the European market was David Whitwam: "The only people who say you can't have a pan-European brand are the people who don't have one themselves." Whitwam elaborates on the company's rationale for globalization:

> The U.S. appliance market has limited growth opportunities, a high concentration of domestic competitors and increasing foreign competition. Further, the U.S. represents only about 25% of the worldwide potential for major appliance sales.

EXHIBIT 30-1 Shipments of Major Home Appliances in the United States (thousand units)

YEAR	DISH-WASHER	DISPOSER	DRYERS	ELECTRIC RANGES	MICROWAVES	REFRIG-ERATORS	ROOM AIR CONDITIONERS	WASHERS	OTHER	TOTAL
1985	3,575	4,105	3,914	3,551	10,883	6,081	3,022	5,279	3,610	44,020
1986	3,918	4,269	4,245	3,741	12,444	6,510	2,816	5,765	3,877	47,585
1987	4,032	4,439	4,637	3,841	12,610	6,972	3,798	5,998	4,325	50,652
1988	3,907	4,233	4,601	3,708	10,988	7,227	4,637	6,190	4,542	50,033
1989	3,668	4,363	4,574	3,529	10,598	7,099	5,091	6,252	4,287	49,461
1990	3,637	4,137	4,320	3,444	8,126	7,101	4,150	6,192	4,516	45,623
1991	3,571	4,002	4,313	3,309	7,012	7,273	2,834	6,197	4,596	43,107
1992	3,820	4,195	4,717	3,574	7,588	7,761	2,910	6,515	5,091	46,171
1993E	4,033	4,366	4,980	3,716	7,697	7,875	3,075	6,728	5,174	47,644
1994E	4,070	4,501	5,098	3,822	7,812	8,076	3,124	6,931	5,230	48,664

Source: Merrill Lynch Forecast.

Most importantly, our vision can no longer be limited to our domestic borders because national borders no longer define market boundaries. The marketplace for products and services is more global than ever before and growing more so every day.

Consumers in major industrialized countries are living increasingly similar lifestyles and have increasingly similar expectations of what consumer products must do for them. As purchasing patterns become more alike, we think that companies that operate on a broad global scale can leverage their strengths better than those which only serve an individual national market. Very likely, appliance manufacturing will always have to be done regionally. Yet the ability to leverage many of the strengths of a company on an international basis is possible only if that company operates globally.

In 1988, Whitwam and Whirlpool made their boldest move so far towards global dominance in the white goods industry. They announced a joint venture with N.V. Philips, the second largest appliance manufacturer in Europe behind Electrolux. The

EXHIBIT 30-2   U.S. Market Shares for Major Appliances

	WHIRLPOOL	GENERAL ELECTRIC	FRIGIDAIRE	MAYTAG	RAYTHEON
Compactors					
92	70%	14%			
88	67	14			
Dishwashers					
92	31	40	20%	8%	
88	19	40	7	7	
Dryers (electric)					
92	52	18	12	15	3%
88	52	16	11	12	3
Dryers (gas)					
92	53	14	10	17	4
88	52	16	11	12	3
Ranges (electric)					
92	30	30	17	17	7
88	13	30	10	10	7
Ranges (gas)					
92		19	25	27	22
88			7	24	15
Refrigerators					
92	25	35	17	13	8
88	28	35	21	10	5
Washers					
92	52	16	11	17	4
88	50	17	10	16	4
Overall 1992	34	28	16	14	6
Overall 1988	31	26	18	15	6

Note: Frigidaire is owned by AB Electrolux.
Source: Appliance Manufacturer Magazine.

deal for a 53 percent interest in Philips' worldwide Major Domestic Appliance Division was consummated in 1989, for $361 million in cash; the new company was called Whirlpool International B.V. (WIBV).

In 1991, Whirlpool exercised its option to purchase from Philips the remaining interest in WIBV. With this move, Whirlpool became the world's largest appliance manufacturer, overtaking archrival AB Electrolux. (Exhibit 30–3 compares Whirlpool market share in the United States and Europe with its competitors.)

Philips' decentralized organization was phased out and WIBV split into two customer-focused business units—one for the Bauknecht brand, and the other for the dual-branded Philips/Whirlpool products and Ignis and Laden products. Brands were thus positioned to fit the niches and conditions in Europe, an approach employed earlier in the United States where each brand was given a particular segment. Bauknecht—Philips' most profitable brand—was aimed at the high end of the market, Philips/Whirlpool at the middle, and Ignis was designed for the lower end. Sales and marketing were kept completely separate for the Bauknecht and Whirlpool appliance groups, yet nonmarketing support from each of the 14 countries was combined. The manufacturing organization was also completely revamped. However, several plants located strategically were maintained—in contrast to Maytag. This turned out to be a significant advantage in a Europe with fragmented consumer tastes. Explained Lisa Mendheim of Maytag, referring to the company's Hoover operations: "We're very limited in adapting washers and dryers made in Wales to European standards." Logistics, distribution, after-sales service, and information were tied together with assembly under one person. Distribution was reconfigured towards a pan-European approach and 10 out of 28 finished goods warehouses were closed.

A global outlook was instilled in the management team. Instead of having primarily Dutch managers, the top seven-member team comprised five nationalities. Managers were rotated between Europe and the United States to foster global thinking. This move paid off recently when the VIP Crisp microwave oven, developed by a

EXHIBIT 30-3 Core Appliance Market Share of Major Competitors in the United States and Europe in 1991 vs. 1989

PERCENT OF MARKET SHARE			PERCENT OF MARKET SHARE		
UNITED STATES	1991	1989	EUROPE	1991	1989
Whirlpool	33.9	32.7	Electrolux	19	20.5
General Electric	28.2	25.5	Bosch-Siemens	13	11.0
Electrolux	15.9	18.4	Whirlpool	10	11.5
Maytag	14.2	14.8	Miele	7	na
Raytheon	5.6	na	Thompson	6	na
Other	2.2	8.6	AEG	5	na
			Merloni		10.0
			Maytag		2.0
			Other	40	40.0

Source: Bray (1993); *Appliance,* September 1992.

new "advanced global technology unit" in Norrköping, Sweden, was introduced and quickly became Europe's best-selling model. The VIP Crisp has a heated base plate which allows Italians to bake crisp pizza crusts and the British to fry eggs. Now the company is starting to import the VIP Crisp to the United States.

WIBV also made a series of moves to establish itself in the emerging markets of central and eastern Europe, which represents about 11 percent of the world appliance market and promises attractive growth opportunities over the long term. Bauknecht was first in setting up a distribution system in East Germany after the opening of the border. WIBV has developed distribution networks in the entire region and established a wholly owned sales subsidiary in Hungary, Whirlpool Hungarian Trading, Ltd. In May 1992, a 43.8 percent minority investment in Whirlpool/Tatramat a.s., a joint venture in Slovakia, was acquired which in October started manufacturing and selling automatic washers and marketing products assembled at other WIBV locations. In 1993, sales subsidiaries were opened in Poland and the Czech Republic adding to WIBV's position in eastern Europe. By the end of 1992, WIBV with headquarters in Eindhoven, Holland, employed 14,000 people and maintained manufacturing facilities in six countries.

WIBV has started redesigning its products in order to increase manufacturing efficiency, improve product quality and customer satisfaction. WIBV, now called Whirlpool Europe B.V. (WEBV), has been restructured. WEBV replaced the Bauknecht and Philips/Whirlpool Appliance Groups with centralized sales and marketing functions which support all of Whirlpool's European brands. National sales subsidiaries have been consolidated into three sales regions in order to take account of the growing European cross-border trade. The marketing function includes separate, brand-oriented components to strengthen brand identity while at the same time ensuring coordination internally. Manufacturing and technology activities are organized around product groups and development centers with Germany focusing on laundry and dishwashing products and Italy focusing on refrigeration and cooking. Key support functions (consumer services, information technology, logistics, planning) are maintained as separate, centrally managed entities. Explained WEBV president Hank Bowman: "The idea is to put systems support in place so we can deliver products more accurately and in a more timely manner." A central account-management function services transnational buying groups. WEBV now has responsibility for the Middle East and Africa which formerly were housed in Whirlpool Overseas Corporation (WOC) and which accounted for $100 million in sales, mainly in the form of kits, in an attempt to boost local content and thus preempt the emergence of the domestic-content rules. WEBV supports WOC by supplying products, components, and technology sold by WOC in its geographic domain. In June 1993, WEBV sold its refrigerator plant in Barcelona (Spain) to an Italian appliance maker in order to make better use of its remaining facilities.

By mid-1993, WEBV had established itself as the third largest appliance manufacturer in Europe behind Electrolux and Bosch-Siemens and anticipated that by achieving increased efficiencies coupled with volume growth it would raise operating margins to the North American level. Exhibit 30–4 illustrates Whirlpool's globalization milestones and Exhibit 30–5 details western European appliance shipments. Excluding microwaves and room air conditioners, aggregate western European volumes are 5 to 10 percent higher than in the United States. Shipments accelerated upward between the mid- and late-80s, and have since flattened. The largest distinct submarket within Europe is Germany (including the Benelux countries and Switzerland), followed by the United Kingdom and France. About one-third of European production takes place in Italy.

EXHIBIT 30-4 1990 Milestones of Whirlpool's Globalization

1990	A program is launched to market appliances in Europe under the dual brands Philips and Whirlpool.
	Formation of a joint-venture company with Matsushita Electric Industrial Co. of Japan to produce vacuum cleaners for the North American market.
	Creation of Whirlpool Overseas Corporation as a wholly owned subsidiary to conduct industrial and marketing activities outside North America and Western Europe.
	Inglis Limited becomes a wholly owned subsidiary.
1991	Whirlpool acquires remaining interest in WIBV from Philips Electronics N.V.
	Creation of two new global business units: Whirlpool Compressor Operations and Whirlpool Microwave Cooking Business.
1992	Creation of Whirlpool Tatramat in the Slovak Republic. Whirlpool Tatramat a.s. will manufacture clothes washers for Slovakia and neighboring countries and import other WIBV major appliances for sale.
	Begins gradual phaseout of dual-branded advertising to sole Whirlpool brand by removing the Philips name in Europe.
	Whirlpool assumes control of SAGAD S.A. of Argentina from Philips.
	Reorganization of Whirlpool Europe. The name is changed from WIBV to WEBV.
	Didier Pineau-Valencienne, chairman and CEO of Groupe Schneider S.A., France, becomes a Whirlpool director, the first non-American on the board.
1993	Reorganization of NAAG. Start of the implementation of a new Asian strategy.
	Sales subsidiaries are opened in Poland and the Czech Republic.
	In May, Whirlpool announces joint venture with Teco Electric & Machinery Co., Ltd., of Taiwan to market and distribute home appliances in Taiwan.

EXHIBIT 30-5 Western European Appliance Shipments (thousand units)

	1988	1989	1990	1991	1992
Refrigerators	11,350	11,845	12,450	12,670	12,750
Freezers	4,205	4,255	4,590	4,680	4,605
Washers	10,140	10,220	10,730	10,800	10,845
Dishwashers	3,335	3,615	3,820	3,925	4,040
Tumble Dryers	2,625	2,400	2,325	2,490	2,475
Cookers	4,840	4,685	4,800	4,615	4,430
Built-in Ovens	3,390	3,405	3,500	3,590	3,765
Total Core	39,885	40,425	42,215	42,770	42,910
Microwave Ovens	7,845	7,615	6,590	7,400	7,300
Total Market	47,730	48,040	48,805	50,170	50,210
Percent Change	11.5%	0.6%	1.6%	2.8%	0.1%

Source: Industry data.

Another initiative which encountered widespread skepticism in the industry was development of a compact washer dubbed the "world washer," which went into production in new manufacturing facilities in Brazil in 1990, and in Mexico and India in 1991. Lightweight, with substantially fewer parts than its U.S. counterpart, it had good test scores and received favorable evaluations based on such features as stainless steel and porcelain baskets. According to Samuel J. Pearson, director international engineering, its performance was equal to or better than anything on the world market while competitive on price with the most popular models in these markets.

Although many of the circumstances surrounding the decision to start world washer production in India, Brazil, and Mexico differed, all three countries saw a clear opportunity. Whirlpool estimated that about 10 to 15 percent of India's 840 million people could afford clothes washers while only about 250,000 lower quality machines were sold annually. Further, a weakened U.S. dollar provided the right "window" that Whirlpool and its partners needed to get the new design into production before competitors could capitalize on the same opportunities. The goal of the world washer effort was to develop a complete product, process, and facility-design package versatile enough to satisfy conditions and market requirements in various countries but with low initial investment requirements. At the same time, the world washer established a beachhead especially against the Far Eastern rivals.

The development was preceded by extensive market research and intensive analysis of almost every washer model marketed in Japan, Korea, Europe, New Zealand, and the United States. Originally, it was planned to replicate the project design in each of the three countries. It eventually proved necessary to develop three slightly different variations. "Each of the affiliates presented different expertise, both in the washer business and in working with various materials," said Lawrence J. Kremer, senior vice president, Global Technology and Operations. "Our Mexican affiliate, Vitromatic, has porcelain and glassmaking capabilities. Porcelain baskets made sense for them. Stainless steel became the preferred material for the others."

Costs also varied widely, further affecting both product and process decisions. "In India, for example, material costs may run as much as 200 to 800 percent higher than elsewhere, while labor and overhead costs are comparatively minimal," added Kremer. Another consideration were the garments to be washed in each country. "Saris—those beautiful, 18-foot lengths of cotton or silk with which Indian women drape themselves—posed a special challenge," recalled Pearson.

The plants also varied subtly from each other, although the goals were identical—minimizing facility investment, avoiding big finish systems and welding stations requiring extensive machinery for material cleanup, and protecting the environment. Brastemp, Whirlpool's Brazilian partner, put its new plant in Rio Claro, 100 kilometers northwest of Sao Paulo. Made of precast concrete, it was designed as a creative convection cooling system to address the high humidity. In India, the new facility was built in Pondicherry, just 12 degrees north of the equator. Although the plant looked similar to that in Brazil—except for the overhead fans—the method of construction was different. Concrete was hand mixed on location, then carried in wicker baskets to forms constructed right next to the building site. The Indian construction crew cast the concrete, allowed it to cure, and, then, using five or six men, raised each three-ton slab into place using chain, block, and tackle. Finally, two plants made up the facility in Monterrey. Internacional de Lavadores housed the flexible assembly lines as well as stamping and a few machine operations. Viplasticos, the adjacent facility, had injection moulding and extrusion processes.

Pearson underscored the fact that the project resulted not only in new plants and a new product, but in team members from very different cultural backgrounds who have gained experience in how to manage a project differently, employing a small team with the authority to do many things. "Our foreign colleagues have become partners in every sense of the word," Pearson said. "When we make the final hand-off to Gopal Srinivasan in India, to Francisco Fiorotto in Brazil, and to Luis Hernandez in Mexico, we will be placing the ventures in the hands of good people, good colleagues, good friends."

WHIRLPOOL OVERSEAS CORPORATION

Whirlpool Overseas Corporation (WOC) is a wholly owned subsidiary that conducts marketing and industrial activities outside North America and Europe. It includes U.S. Export Sales, the Overseas Business Group acquired from Philips in the WIBV transaction, and three wholly owned sales companies in Hong Kong, Thailand, and Australia. Industrial activities encompass technology sale and transfer, kit and component sales, joint venture manufacturing, and project management for affiliates. WOC oversees the activities in Brazil and the joint venture in India.

One of the key responsibilities of WOC is to feed new technologies from Whirlpool's bases in North America and Europe to its other units. A second responsibility is to ensure optimal brand positioning in each country and to analyze specific appliance design for their suitability to various markets. Conditions could vary greatly from country to country requiring design modifications. For instance, the company sold so-called giant ovens in Africa and the Middle East. These ovens were 39" and 42" wide compared to the standard 30" in the United States and were large enough to roast a sheep or goat.

WOC has strengthened its position in South America by taking over control of SAGAD, Philip's white goods operation in Argentina. A joint venture was recently created with Whirlpool's affiliates to distribute Whirlpool's and the affiliates' products to independent distributors. As a result of these moves, Whirlpool and its affiliates are the leading marketers and manufacturers of major home appliances in the region.

WOC's activities are based on the belief that global leadership requires a strong presence in all major markets. Given the company's major presence in North America, Europe, and its 30-year history in South America, Asia represented the last, and what many believed, biggest challenge and opportunity. "In the United States, households are equipped with between seven and nine major appliance products. In Asia, which already accounts for 40 percent of the world market, it's more like four appliances per home," remarked Roger E. Merriam, vice president sales and marketing, WOC. With growing income levels, significant market growth could be expected.

WOC was recently reorganized as a regional structure concentrating on Latin America and Asia. WOC Asia with headquarters in Tokyo was further subdivided into three sub-regions: Asia Pacific (South East Asia, India, Australia), Greater China (Hong Kong, Peoples Republic of China, Taiwan), Japan. This regional structure allows Whirlpool to expand from its infancy position in this region of a market share of 1 percent against the strong local manufacturers. Some of Whirlpool's products are being met with good customer acceptance. For instance, a top-load automatic washer sold in Hong Kong has about one third of the market. Whirlpool moved very quickly in Asia, creating a headquarters in Tokyo and establishing sales subsidiaries and regional offices. Whirlpool realized that a viable position implied more than selling imports from NAAG and WEBV and having kits assembled by licensees. This belief was also reinforced by the fact that consumer preferences in Asia were different from those in the United States and Europe. For instance, Japanese usually wash with cold water. But in order to get their clothes clean, Japanese machines have soak cycles which can range from 30 minutes to several hours. In May 1993, Whirlpool announced a joint venture with Teco Electric & Machinery Co., Ltd., to market and distribute home appliances in Taiwan. Teco is Whirlpool's largest international distributor of Whirlpool products.

To show its commitment to people, Whirlpool has introduced PartnerShare, a stock option plan for its 22,000 U.S. employees, hoping to encourage employee ownership and dedication to building shareholder value. A gain-sharing program at the Benton Harbor components division slashed rework by 31 percent and total scrap cost by 62 percent and its parts-per-million rejection rate by 99 percent over the last 3 years. The program provides each of the plant's 265 employees with an extra $2,700 of pay annually.

The growth objective had resulted in many acquisitions and joint ventures in recent years as well as the aggressive expansion of Whirlpool brands into new territories. The world washer and the SERP win are testimony of the company's growth and innovation orientation.

By 1994, Whirlpool's global direction and assembly of its geographic position were largely complete. However, by its own admission, Whirlpool is not a truly global home-appliance company yet, but has made significant progress towards becoming the leader in the global home-appliance industry.

> But being a real global home-appliance company means more than just trading in countries around the world. It means identifying and respecting genuine national or regional differences in what customers demand from products and services—and simultaneously recognizing and responding to similarities across markets.

CONCLUSION

Prepare a strategic plan for CEO Whitwam who is concerned about Whirlpool's $51 million loss for 1993. Conduct an internal and external strategic analysis and formulate specific strategies that can best assure prosperity for Whirlpool in the latter 1990s. (Exhibits 30–6 through 30–15 provide Whirlpool management and financial information.)

EXHIBIT 30-6 Whirlpool Product Shipments, Revenues, and Operating Earnings

Principal Locations	Principal Products
Affiliates	Automatic dryers
Great Teco Whirlpool Limited	Automatic washers
Taipei,Taiwan	Cooking products
TVS Whirlpool Limited	Dishwashers
Madras, India	Microwave ovens
Manufacturing Facility	Refrigerators
Pondicherry, India	Room air conditioners
Sales Subsidiaries	Major Brand Names
Bangkok, Thailand	Bauknecht
Hong Kong	Ignis
Kuala Lumpur, Malaysia	KitchenAid
Melbourne, Australia	Roper
Singapore	Whirlpool

EXHIBIT 30-7 Revenues by Business Unit

	1993	1992	BETTER/(WORSE) $	BETTER/(WORSE) %
North American Appliance Business	$4,559	$4,162	$ 397	10%
European Appliance Business	2,225	2,463	(238)	(10)
Other	584	472	112	24
Total Appliance Business	$7,368	$7,097	$ 271	4%

Operating Profit by Business Unit

	1993	1992	BETTER/(WORSE) $	BETTER/(WORSE) %
North American Appliance Business	$459	$417	$42	10%
European Appliance Business	123	113	10	9
Other	(78)	(83)	5	6
Total Appliance Business	$504	$447	$57	13%

Other includes Latin America, Whirlpool Asia, European compressor operations, Corporate Center costs and intercompany eliminations.

Source: Whirlpool *Annual Report,* 1993.

EXHIBIT 30-8 Revenue Information (Millions of dollars)

	PERCENT	1993	1992	1991
Major Home Appliances				
Home Laundry Appliances	32.9%	$2,481	$2,489	$2,300
Home Refrigeration and				
Room Air Conditioning				
Equipment	34.4	2,588	2,525	2,329
Other Home Appliances	30.5	2,299	2,083	1,921
	97.8	7,368	7,097	6,550
Financial Services	2.2	165	204	207
	100.0%	$7,533	$7,301	$6,757

Source: Whirlpool *Annual Report*, 1993.

EXHIBIT 30-9 Whirlpool 1993 Consolidated Balance Sheets December 31 (Millions of dollars)

December 31,	Whirlpool Corporation (Consolidated)		Supplemental Consolidating Data			
			Whirlpool with WFC on an Equity Basis		Whirlpool Financial Corporation (WFC)	
	1993	1992	1993	1992	1993	1992
Assets						
Current Assets						
Cash and equivalents	$ 88	$ 66	$ 81	$ 52	$ 7	$ 14
Trade receivables, less allowances of $36 in 1993 and $35 in 1992	866	851	866	851	—	—
Financing receivables and leases, less allowances	814	980	—	—	814	980
Inventories	760	650	760	650	—	—
Prepaid expenses and other	102	119	95	98	7	20
Deferred income taxes	78	74	78	74	—	—
Total Current Assets	2,708	2,740	1,880	1,725	828	1,014
Other Assets						
Investment in affiliated companies	320	282	320	282	—	—
Investment in WFC	—	—	239	293	—	—
Financing receivables and leases, less allowances	793	912	—	—	793	912
Intangibles, net	725	795	725	795	—	—
Deferred income taxes	127	—	127	—	—	—
Other	55	64	55	59	—	5
	2,020	2,053	1,466	1,429	793	917
Property, Plant and Equipment						
Land	69	73	69	73	—	—
Buildings	586	588	586	588	—	—
Machinery and equipment	2,181	2,052	2,157	2,031	24	21
Accumulated depreciation	(1,517)	(1,388)	(1,504)	(1,377)	(13)	(11)
	1,319	1,325	1,308	1,315	11	10
Total Assets	$6,047	$6,118	$4,654	$4,469	$1,632	$1,941

EXHIBIT 30-9 *Continued*

	WHIRLPOOL CORPORATION (CONSOLIDATED)		SUPPLEMENTAL CONSOLIDATING DATA			
			WHIRLPOOL WITH WFC ON AN EQUITY BASIS		WHIRLPOOL FINANCIAL CORPORATION (WFC)	
DECEMBER 31,	1993	1992	1993	1992	1993	1992
Liabilities and Stockholders' Equity						
Current Liabilities						
Notes payable	$992	$1,425	$ 160	$ 322	$ 832	$1,050
Accounts payable	742	688	689	646	53	41
Employee compensation	177	164	172	157	5	7
Accrued expenses	587	495	581	477	6	18
Income taxes	97	87	93	79	4	8
Current maturities of long-term debt	168	28	83	14	85	67
Total Current Liabilities	2,763	2,887	1,778	1,695	985	1,191
Other Liabilities						
Deferred income taxes	167	213	67	109	100	104
Accrued pensions and expenses	219	203	219	203	—	—
Postretirement obligation	318	—	318	—	—	—
Long-term debt	840	1,215	607	862	233	378
	1,544	1,631	1,211	1,174	333	482
Minority Interests	92	—	17	—	75	—
Stockholders' Equity						
Capital stock	79	76	79	76	8	8
Paid-in capital	152	47	152	47	26	26
Retained earnings	1,686	1,721	1,686	1,721	208	236
Unearned restricted stock	(9)	(18)	(9)	(18)	—	—
Cumulative translation adjustments	(77)	(49)	(77)	(49)	(3)	(2)
Treasury stock—at cost	(183)	(177)	(183)	(177)	—	—
	1,648	1,600	1,648	1,600	239	268
Total Liabilities and Stockholders' Equity	$6,047	$6,118	$4,654	$4,469	$1,632	$1,941

Source: Whirlpool *Annual Report*, 1993.

EXHIBIT 30-10 Whirlpool 1993 Consolidated Statements of Earnings (millions of dollars except share data)

	Whirlpool Corporation (Consolidated)			Supplemental Consolidating Data					
				Whirlpool with WFC on an Equity Basis			Whirlpool Financial Corporation (WFC)		
Year Ended December 31,	1993	1992	1991	1993	1992	1991	1993	1992	1991
Revenues									
Net sales	$7,368	$7,097	$6,550	$7,368	$7,097	$6,550	$ —	$ —	$ —
Financial services	165	204	207	—	—	—	193	235	233
	7,533	7,301	6,757	7,368	7,097	6,550	193	235	233
Expenses									
Cost of products sold	5,503	5,365	4,967	5,503	5,365	4,967	—	—	—
Selling and administrative	1,433	1,323	1,257	1,305	1,242	1,181	155	113	102
Financial services interest	59	82	91	—	—	—	72	95	101
Intangible amortization	25	27	27	25	27	27	—	—	—
Restructuring costs	31	25	22	31	16	22	—	9	—
	7,051	6,822	6,364	6,864	6,650	6,197	227	217	203
Operating Profit (Loss)	482	479	393	504	447	353	(34)	18	30

EXHIBIT 30-10 *Continued*

SUPPLEMENTAL CONSOLIDATING DATA

YEAR ENDED DECEMBER 31,	WHIRLPOOL CORPORATION (CONSOLIDATED)			WHIRLPOOL WITH WFC ON AN EQUITY BASIS			WHIRLPOOL FINANCIAL CORPORATION (WFC)		
	1993	1992	1991	1993	1992	1991	1993	1992	1991
Other Income (Expense)									
Interest and sundry	6	38	49	19	21	33	(9)	20	18
Interest expense	(113)	(145)	(138)	(105)	(134)	(130)	—	—	—
Earnings (Loss) Before Income Taxes, Other Items and Accounting Change	375	372	304	418	334	256	(43)	38	48
Income taxes	148	154	130	167	142	113	(19)	12	17
Earnings (Loss) Before Equity Earnings, Minority Interests and Accounting Change	227	218	174	251	192	143	(24)	26	31
Equity in WFC	—	—	—	(28)	26	31	—	—	—
Equity in affiliated companies	16	(13)	1	16	(13)	1	—	—	—
Minority interests	(12)	—	(5)	(10)	—	(5)	(2)	—	—
Net Earnings (Loss) Before Cumulative Effect of Accounting Change	231	205	170	229	205	170	(26)	26	31
Cumulative effect of accounting change for postretirement benefits	(180)	—	—	(178)	—	—	(2)	—	—
Net Earnings (Loss)	$51	$205	$170	$51	$205	$170	$(28)	$26	$31
Per share of common stock:									
Primary earnings before accounting change	$3.19	$2.90	$2.45						
Primary earnings	$0.67	$2.90	$2.45						
Fully diluted earnings before accounting change	$3.11	$2.79	$2.40						
Fully diluted earnings	$0.67	$2.79	$2.40						
Cash dividends	$1.19	$1.10	$1.10						
Average number of common shares outstanding (millions)	72.3	70.6	69.5						

Net earnings (loss) before cumulative effect of accounting change	$231	$205	$170	$229	$205	$170	$(26)	$26	$31
Depreciation	241	275	233	239	271	228	2	3	3
Deferred income taxes	(31)	9	3	(27)	2	(7)	(4)	7	10
Equity in net losses (earnings) of affiliated companies, including dividends received	(14)	16	(1)	(14)	16	(1)	—	—	—
Equity in net loss (earnings) of WFC	8	—	—	28	(26)	(31)	—	—	—
Loss on business disposition	—	—	—	8	—	—	—	—	—
Provision for doubtful accounts	75	55	55	8	15	25	67	40	30
Amortization of goodwill	28	27	27	28	27	27	—	—	—
Minority interests	10	—	5	10	—	5	—	2	—
Other	43	15	(19)	23	(4)	(19)	20	—	—
Changes in assets and liabilities, net of effects of business acquisitions and dispositions:									
Trade receivables	(76)	(83)	58	(75)	(83)	58	—	—	—
Inventories	(145)	(7)	109	(145)	(7)	109	12	(25)	—
Accounts payable	101	5	162	89	29	139	—	—	19
Other-net	158	61	15	165	37	27	—	16	(5)
Cash Provided by Operating Activities	$629	$578	$817	$566	$482	$730	$71	$69	$88

Source: Whirlpool *Annual Report*, 1993.

EXHIBIT 30-12 Whirlpool 1993 Business Segment Information (Millions of dollars)

GEOGRAPHIC SEGMENTS—MAJOR HOME APPLIANCES

	NORTH AMERICA	EUROPE	OTHER AND (ELIMINATIONS)	MAJOR HOME APPLIANCES
Net Sales				
1993	$4,547	$2,410	$ 411	$7,368
1992	$4,266	$2,645	$ 186	$7,097
1991	$4,016	$2,479	$ 55	$6,550
Operating profit				
1993	$ 341	$ 129	$ 34	$ 504
1992	$ 327	$ 101	$ 19	$ 447
1991	$ 274	$ 82	$ (3)	$ 353
Identifiable assets				
1993	$1,742	$1,758	$1,154	$4,654
1992	$1,570	$1,917	$ 982	$4,469
1991	$1,529	$2,284	$ 759	$4,572
Depreciation expense				
1993	$ 137	$ 101	$ 1	$ 239
1992	$ 138	$ 132	$ 1	$ 271
1991	$ 124	$ 104	$ —	$ 228
Net capital expenditures				
1993	$ 188	$ 116	$ 3	$ 307
1992	$ 170	$ 111	$ 3	$ 284
1991	$ 179	$ 104	$ —	$ 283

INDUSTRY SEGMENTS	MAJOR HOME APPLIANCES	FINANCIAL SERVICES	OTHER AND (ELIMINATIONS)	CONSOLIDATED
Revenues				
1993	$7,368	$193	$(28)	$7,533
1992	$7,097	$235	$(31)	$7,301
1991	$6,550	$233	$(26)	$6,757
Operating profit (loss)				
1993	$ 504	$(34)	$ 12	$ 482
1992	$ 447	$ 18	$ 14	$ 479
1991	$ 353	$ 30	$ 10	$ 393

The financial services business segment operates primarily in North America.

EXHIBIT 30-13 Whirlpool 1993 Stockholder Information

	1993	1992	1991	1990
Key Ratios				
Operating profit margin	6.4%	6.6%	5.8%	5.3%
Pre-tax margin[3]	5.0%	5.1%	4.5%	3.3%
Net margin [4]	3.1%	2.8%	2.5%	1.1%
Return on average stockholders' equity	14.2%	13.1%	11.6%	5.1%
Return on average total assets[5]	4.0%	3.3%	2.9%	1.4%
Current assets to current liabilities	1.0	0.9	1.0	1.1
Total debt-appliance business as a percent of invested capital[6]	31.6%	41.7%	46.1%	37.6%
Price earnings ratio	20.8	15.4	15.9	22.6
Fixed charge coverage[7]	3.2	2.6	2.3	1.8
Other Data				
Number of common shares outstanding (in thousands):				
Average	72,272	70,558	69,528	69,443
Year-end	73,068	70,027	69,640	69,465
Number of shareholders (year-end)	11,438	11,724	12,032	12,542
Number of employees (year-end)	39,590	38,520	37,886	36,157
Total return to shareholders (five year annualized)[8]	25.8%	17.0%	6.7%	2.8%

(1)Accounting changes: 1993—Accounting for postretirement benefits other than pensions, 1987—Accounting for income taxes and 1986—Accounting for pensions.

(2)The Company's kitchen cabinet business was discontinued in 1988.

(3)Earnings from continuing operations before income taxes and other items, as a percent of revenue.

(4)Earnings from continuing operations before accounting change, as a percent of revenue.

(5)Earnings from continuing operations before accounting change plus minority interest divided by average total assets.

(6)Cash, debt, minority interests and stockholders' equity.

(7)Ratio of earnings from continuing operations (before income taxes, accounting change and interest expense) to interest expense.

(8)Stock appreciation plus reinvested dividends.

Source: Whirlpool *Annual Report,* 1993.

EXHIBIT 30-14 Whirlpool Senior Management

SENIOR MANAGEMENT

Executive Officers

David R. Whitwam
  Chariman of the Board
  and Chief Executive Officer

William D. Marohn
  President and Chief Operating Officer

Executive Vice Presidents
H.W. (Hank) Bowman
  Whirlpool Europe B.V.

Robert Frey
  President, Whirlpool Asia Appliance Group

Ralph F. Hake
  North American Appliance Group

Ronald L. Kerber
  Chief Technology Officer

Senior Officers

Vice Presidents
Bradley J. Bell
  Treasurer

Bruce K. Berger
  Corporate Affairs

E.R. (Ed) Dunn
  Human Resources
  and Assistant Secretary

Jeff M. Fettig
  Group Sales and Marketing, NAAG

Robert D. Hall
  Global Procurement Operations

Stephen F. Holmes
  Group Manufacturing and
  Technology, NAAG

Halvar Johansson
  Group Manufacturing and
  Technology, WEBV

Source: Whirlpool *Annual Report,* 1993.

James E. LeBlanc
  Chairman of the Board, President
  and Chief Executive Officer,
  Whirlpool Financial Corporation

Charles D. (Chuck) Miller
  Marketing, NAAG

Robert G. Thompson
  Controller

William D. Marohn
  President and Chief Operating Officer

Michael J. Callahan
  Chief Financial Officer

Ralph F. Hake
  North American Appliance Group

James R. Samartini
  Chief Administrative Officer

Bruce K. Berger
  Corporate Affairs

Jeff M. Fettig
  Group Sales and Marketing, NAAG

Edward J.F. Herrelko
  Sales and Distribution, NAAG

Daniel F. Hopp
  General Counsel and Secretary

Kenneth W. Kaminski
  Sears Group, NAAG

Ivan Menezes
  Group Marketing, WEBV

P. Daniel Miller
  President, Whirlpool do Brasil

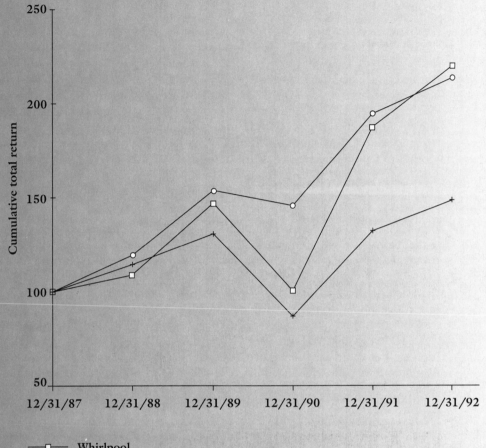

EXHIBIT 30-15 Five-Year Cumulative Return: Whirlpool, S & P Index and S & P Household Furniture and Appliance Group

- ☐ Whirlpool
- ○ S & P 500
- + S & P Household Furniture Appliance

*Cumulative total return is measured by dividing (i) the sum of (A) the cumulative amount of the dividends for the measurement period, assuming dividend reinvestment, and (B) the difference between share price at the end and the beginning of the measurement period; by (ii) the share price at the beginning of the measurement period.

Source: Whirlpool Corporation, 1992 Proxy Statement.

MATERIAL HANDLING ENGINEERING (SINGAPORE) LTD.—1993

Headquartered in Singapore, Material Handling Engineering (MHE) (phone 65-861-0670, fax 65-861-3271) has subsidiaries throughout the Asian region and a customer base that includes hundreds of companies worldwide. With revenue (called turnover in Singapore) at nearly S$21.5 million (one Singapore dollar is worth approximately U.S. $0.60), MHE is the largest material-handling company in Singapore. Peter Boo, founder and CEO of the company, has a goal of MHE becoming a S$100 million company by the end of this decade. In the short-term, he also has to make sure the 26 percent decrease in 1992 turnover does not repeat itself. Nor does Boo want to incur another year of losing $492,000 as annual net income.

HISTORY

When Peter Boo completed high school, he became a draftsman for a local material-handling (conveyors, automated carts, etc.) company. Boo continued his education by taking technical courses at Singapore Polytechnic and satisfied his compulsory military duty requirement by serving evenings and some weekends. Working in various phases of the company's business gave Boo the experience needed to start his own material-handling company.

With two employees and a small factory having only 32 square meters of usable space, Boo founded MHE in 1975 "to engage in the design, fabrication, and installation of conveyor-based integrated automation systems." Since banks in Singapore were reluctant to lend money to start-ups, Boo used his own funds to purchase and equip his factory.

Boo considered several names for his company, finally settling on Material Handling Engineering because it was descriptive, and the logo he created (see Exhibit 31–1) looked like a conveyor belt. Early customers were companies who knew Boo from his previous company affiliation or those referred by his friends. Those clients generated S$120,000 in turnover for MHE in its first year of operation.

Boo knew the only way his company could grow would be to satisfy its customers who would then refer other customers to MHE. The following mission statement has helped Material Handling Engineering become the leader in its field in Singapore and the Asian region:

> To be a world leader in automated materials handling systems and automation related businesses. To accomplish our mission, we believe in: total and continuous quality service to customers, enhancing the quality of working life for employees, support to suppliers for mutual growth, being good corporate citizens, and providing adequate return on shareholders' investments.

THE COMPANY

Ownership and Organization. MHE has authorized share capital of S$10 million (50 million shares at S$0.20) and has issued 27.5 million shares, most controlled by Peter Boo and his wife Lee Bee Lian. Other investors who own more than 300,000 shares each include the following:

EXHIBIT 31-1 MHE Ltd. Company Logo

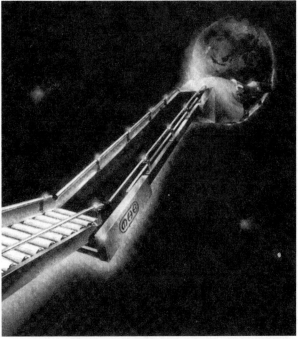

Source: Material Handling Engineering, Ltd.

HSBC (Singapore) Nominees Pte. Ltd.	7,052,000 shares	
Southeast Asia Venture Investment Co.	1,529,039	"
United Overseas Bank Nominees Ltd.	800,000	"
Venture Investment (Singapore) II Ltd.	396,727	"
Malaysian Ventures Bhad	395,727	"

Eight other non-family investors own more than 100,000 shares.

MHE is listed on SESDAQ (Stock Exchange of Singapore Dealing and Automated Quotation) which is similar to NASDAQ (National Association of Securities Dealers' Automated Quotations System). Shareholders of the company have approved a share option scheme to enable certain senior executives of the company to subscribe for shares in the capital of the company. Under that plan, options to subscribe up to an aggregate of 51,000 ordinary shares of S$1.00 each and 510,000 ordinary shares of S$0.20 each in the capital of the company are offered to executives.

Peter Boo is chairman and chief executive officer of the company, while his wife is the director of purchasing. Serving on the board of directors with them is Derrick Lee Meow Chan, Eric Cheong Yuen Chee, and Robert Iau Kuo Kwong. Since the Boo family controls most of the stock, the board is primarily advisory; however, Boo contends that he does take board members' suggestions seriously. Other departments of MHE are headed by capable executives who also may own part of the company.

Company Structure. MHE is the original company founded by Peter Boo; however, growth needs have been met by acquiring or starting subsidiary companies in Singapore and other parts of the world. MHE and its subsidiaries are referred to as the Group which is composed of ten companies wholly or partially owned by MHE (see Exhibit 31–2). Each subsidiary specializes in different products or services.

Products. MHE manufactures and distributes products to satisfy a wide range of customer needs and has been licensed by several foreign companies to be the exclusive distributor of their products. MHE's products are described below.

Conveyors and Components. Conveyor systems, customized to meet specific customer needs, have always been MHE's bread-and-butter products. The company specializes in turnkey projects designed and manufactured to meet the material handling needs of diverse customers in countries around the world.

Free-flow Chain System. This flexible conveyor system allows operators full freedom in carrying out their tasks at their own pace while the conveyor is running. This is an improvement over the conventional belt system where products move along continuously.

PCB Insertion Conveyors. These provide efficient assembly of components onto printed circuit boards and allow easy adjustments of conveyor widths to suit different boards.

Minibelt Portable Conveyors. This slim-lined range of belt conveyors are designed for light duty automation applications. These portable belt conveyors are among MHE's fastest-selling products.

Factory Automation. MHE has a factory automation unit to deal with products aimed at enhancing the intelligence and productivity of mechanical systems. Robots, palletizers, vision and identification systems, knowledge-based systems produced by MHE and its subsidiaries can be integrated into conveyors presently manufactured by the Group.

Security Systems. Through its subsidiary Premier Security Technology Pte. Ltd., MHE produces security products such as monitoring systems, safes, bank vaults, and prison doors.

Complementary Products. Products that MHE is licensed to manufacture or sell for other companies include the following:

BUSHMAN automatic revolving storage systems

KAWAHARA lift tables

ICAL vibratory equipment

GORING KERR industrial metal detectors

DINGS magnetic devices

FLOVEYOR aeromechanical conveyors

LOGAN baggage-handling systems

MECOM mail distribution systems

EXHIBIT 31-2 Material Handling Engineering Ltd. Group Structure and Current Activities

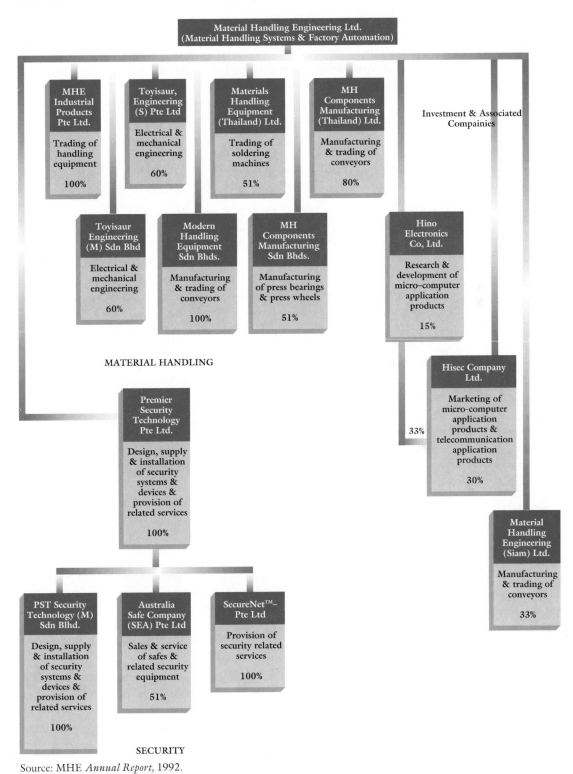

MATERIAL HANDLING

SECURITY

Source: MHE *Annual Report*, 1992.

RITE HITE dock leveler

KOKI ministar II

CONVERT autowarehouse system

TECHNO PAK high-speed conveyor system

Total System Solutions. Material Handling Engineering's extensive product line and the experience of its people enable it to provide customers with all the services needed for a turnkey project. Mr. Boo explains the steps in a typical project:

Consultancy. "Our years of practical experience in varied turnkey projects has sharpened our skills tremendously in multifarious industries be it bottling, electronics, engineering, mining, or others. MHE's professional team of engineers, through in-depth discussions and extensive consultations, analyzes and identifies the customer's requirements and budget with quality and international standards as main priorities."

Design. "No two customers are alike. With our team of trained designers, together with the computer-aided design systems, we can translate engineering concepts into effective working plans for fabrication. Safety, durability, and competitive operating costs form the basis of the whole system."

Fabrication. "Our new plant houses the fabrication facilities and the manpower necessary to turn our plans into reality. Our highly skilled technical personnel closely follow the blueprints of every design to faithfully reproduce the desired product. Quality assurance is ensured at every stage of the process through careful inspection and testing."

Installation and Commissioning. "Prompt and smooth installation of the total system is ensured through our highly trained and experienced technicians who at no time compromise the quality and reliability of the system. Proper training of the customer's staff is also provided before the final hand-over."

Back-up Service. "A project is not considered complete without an efficient and prompt back-up service to attend to the customer's every need at all times. Our quality service is why many satisfied customers come back to us time and again with repeat orders, sometimes even for their plants outside Singapore."

Turnkey Projects. MHE's ability to do large turnkey projects has enabled it to design, manufacture, and install:

- a coal preparation plant and ship loading conveyor system in Indonesia;
- assembly line systems for computer, television, and other electronics manufacturing plants in Singapore, Malaysia, Indonesia, and India;
- drum-filling handling systems for oil companies in Singapore;
- can- and bottle-handling systems for major beverage bottlers in Singapore and Malaysia;
- an assembly plant for washing machines;
- a mail- and parcel-sorting system;
- airport baggage-handling systems in Singapore and Thailand; and
- a complete loading and unloading facility for a regional refrigerated warehouse.

While the majority of these projects has been in Singapore, MHE does have an expanding client list in other countries (see Exhibit 31–3). For example, in 1991 MHE won contracts for S$10 million worth of work to be done for several companies in Turkey.

EXHIBIT 31-3 MHE's Global Customers

Source: MHE *Annual Report,* 1992.

Facilities. Material Handling Engineering is located at 107 Gul Circle. The building is in one of Singapore's industrial parks and has 6,300 square meters of usable space on 13,400 square meters of land. New factory and equipment worth S$3.8 million is large enough to meet MHE's production needs for the foreseeable future. While MHE owns the building, it only leases the land. The Singapore government owns most of the land in the country and only leases it to residential and commercial builders. MHE has a thirty-year lease on the land.

The new building is large enough to allow most fabricated conveyor systems to be set up and tested before being shipped to customers. There is also ample space to store raw materials and supplies, and there is adequate office space for all MHE's employees. Mr. Boo proudly describes some of the attributes of the new facilities:

■ *Computerization.* "We have invested in computerization of our administration, engineering design, accounting, and inventory systems. With the new computer-aided design (CAD) system, we can now produce two- and three-dimensional layout drawings for presentation to customers. In addition, from the database created, the bill of materials (BOM) can be generated on-line from the drawings. This BOM can be further extended to office automation applications for purchasing, material requirements planning and control, and project management, to ensure delivery promises are kept and material costs controlled. With office automation, administrative work and coordination will be enhanced through the use of local area networks (LAN)."

■ *Autowarehouse.* "We have an automated storage and retrieval system and an automated carousel system which improve operational efficiency. These systems are also used for demonstrations to our customers as we are marketing such systems to meet their storage needs."

■ *Fabrication and assembly.* "We have 1,080 square meters (72m long by 15m wide) of space for fabrication work, as well as a similar amount of space for assembly work. Within the assembly area, we can now preassemble a complete line for customers to inspect before delivery. We are now geared to undertake big turnkey projects in the developed countries as well as the Second and Third World countries."

■ *Spray booth and oven.* "We have our own spray booth and oven, allowing us to do painting that we could not do before. This helps to shorten the through-put time and improve the quality of surface finish."

Markets and Competition. The world automation market is estimated to be about U.S. $38 billion with material transport systems representing about 10 percent of the entire market. Peter Boo wants MHE to capture as much of the market as possible. However, it is difficult to identify a focused target market for MHE since so many different manufacturing and service companies need material handling systems. Companies with assembly lines, packages to be sorted, baggage to be moved, and so forth are potential customers who need to be courted. Mr. Boo believes that "any company with something to move, sort, or handle is a prospective customer."

MHE has no direct competition in Singapore. The few local companies that offer similar products are too small to compete with MHE for large, turnkey projects. The competition is from international companies with the capability to do large projects. MHE competes with other companies when it solicits projects in other countries, and it competes with those same companies for large projects in Singapore.

Many of the major companies in Singapore are large multinationals that often give their material-handling projects to companies from their home countries. For example, Western Electric (Singapore) recently opened a new plant with a state-of-the-art

S$5 million conveyor system that was installed by a U.S. material-handling company. To be as competitive as possible, MHE enters into joint ventures and partnerships with other companies to bid on large projects.

Personnel Relations. MHE's employees are constantly being trained and updated. While most companies pay lip service to the importance of their employees, MHE really means it. There is a severe shortage of workers in Singapore (unemployment is about 2 percent), so there is fierce competition for capable people willing to work. There is no minimum wage in Singapore, but competition for workers keeps average wages high. MHE attracts workers with good working conditions, above average wages, and an aggressive recruiting program. MHE is usually able to fill its manpower needs, but sometimes must hire inexperienced, untrained workers.

Training is something that is very important to MHE. Mr. Boo says, "We have formulated and implemented a three-year training program for employees. To date, more than one-third of our staff has received training. We are setting aside 5 percent of our profits each year for human resource development. Our goal is to have 100 percent of our staff trained." A training room was built in the new facilities where daily training is conducted. Managers, who are trainers, coaches, and counselors, benefit from external programs and in turn teach their subordinates.

MHE has lower than average turnover because the company tries to satisfy employees' needs. The company offers competitive wages and an attractive benefits package. Most workers are members of the Metal Industries Workers' Union which maintains good relations with management. Workers occasionally demand higher wages, but Mr. Boo says, "They can't justify their demands, so we pay them what we think they should get." In addition to above-average pay, workers receive annual bonuses which can amount to as much as three months' pay. In addition, Mr. Boo is working on a profit-sharing plan that will offer more incentive to workers to increase their productivity.

Production. A new building with state-of-the-art manufacturing equipment assures efficient production of MHE material-handling products. Since most projects are unique, MHE manufactures primarily customized products designed by its own technicians. Much of the routine production is done by subcontractors who work at MHE's facilities until a particular project is completed. "We are only interested in value-added production," says Mr. Boo who claims that his previous experience allows him to walk through the facility and identify manufacturing mistakes. He says, "I am a hands-on manager, unlike many people who have management experience but no manufacturing know-how."

Marketing. The company does only minimal formal advertising. There is an advertisement in the yellow pages, and the company has several brochures which are given to prospective customers. Mr. Boo claims that most of MHE's new customers are referred by previous customers, making him a firm believer in the value of word-of-mouth advertising. Mr. Boo and his managers use their networks to secure new projects and to publicize awards the company receives. For example, MHE recently received the National Productivity Award from the National Productivity Council, and Mr. Boo was named Entrepreneur of the Year at an International Entrepreneurship Conference. This kind of free advertising enhances MHE's image and attracts new customers.

Expansion and Diversification. It would be virtually impossible for any company to enjoy meaningful growth if it restricted its operations to Singapore. Mr. Boo knew that when he started his company so, from the beginning, MHE has had a global orientation. At first, MHE bid on turnkey projects in other countries, then as it grew, it began acquiring or building subsidiary companies in other countries (see Exhibit 31–2).

These companies, along with Material Handling Engineering, form the Group, which supplies products and services to each other and to unaffiliated customers. MHE currently generates about 75 percent of the Group's turnover; however, this percentage will decline as subsidiaries grow and others are acquired.

Most of MHE's subsidiaries are in the material-handling business; however, MHE recently incorporated a wholly owned subsidiary, Premier Security Technology (PST), as part of its plan to go into communication electronics. PST agreed to acquire the assets, business, and operations of the security division of Premier Cooperative Society for S$201,716.

The acquisition of PST was soon followed by the establishment of SecureNet (S) Pte. Ltd., a wholly owned subsidiary company providing security services and specialized central alarm monitoring services to PST. PST Security Technology Sdn Bhd was established to tap the vast Malaysian market. Security services were expanded when Australia Safe Company (SEA) Pte. Ltd. was acquired in 1992. ASC deals with safes, bank vaults and prison doors under the established brand name of Australia Safe.

MHE and its subsidiaries now do business in all Asian countries. Approximately 50 percent of 1992 turnover was generated by exports (see Exhibit 31–4) with Japan being the major non-Asian export market. With additional acquisitions and expansion of foreign subsidiaries, Mr. Boo expects more of MHE's turnover to be generated by exports in the future.

FINANCE

From 1975 to 1985, MHE experienced steady but modest growth, achieving turnover of S$3.7 million by the end of 1985. The late 1980s and 1990 saw turnover increase to S$16.8 million (see Exhibit 31–5). The best year in the Group's history was 1991 when turnover increased by more than 70 percent to S$29.2 million. This growth spurt, attributable to acquisition and expansion, was short-lived, however, as turnover for 1992 decreased to S$21.5 million.

Experiencing a nearly S$8 million reduction in turnover from 1991 to 1992 was quite discouraging, but Mr. Boo is confident that the company will prosper as economic conditions improve. He gives the following explanation for the reduction in MHE's turnover:

> The 1992 financial year was a challenging and eventful year for the Group. The effects of recession in most of the industrialized world were felt in Singapore, and slower growth was registered by the economy. The prevailing mood of caution and restraint resulted in a reduced level of capital investment in Singapore and the region. It was under such adverse economic conditions that the Group's turnover decreased by 26 percent to S$21.5 million. This decrease of some S$8 million was due primarily to the absence of sales to Turkey, a reflection of the economic uncertainties in that region. . . .
>
> With completion of a good foundation and the proper definition of future goals and directions for our security business; and the reinforcement of our lead in the material handling industry, I believe we now have prepared the ground for our next stage of growth. Our

EXHIBIT 31-4   MHE's Turnover by Local and Export Markets

Local (50.3%)

Export (49.7%)

Analysis of Export Market

USA (7.7%)

Others (1.2%)

Europe (2.0%)

Japan (16.8%)

Middle East (5.2%)

Asean
(excluding
Singapore)
(67.1%)

Source: Material Handling Engineering Limited, *Annual Report,* 1992.

efforts at growth may, however, be somewhat thwarted by the continuing uncertainties over recovery in the global economic environment.

Financial statements for 1992 (see Exhibits 31–6 through 31–8) show that the S$1.4 million profit (before taxes) in 1991 was replaced with a loss of nearly one-half million dollars in 1992. The company continues to be fiscally prudent. Debt is manageable, and MHE can issue an additional 25 million shares if it has major capital requirements.

FUTURE PLANS

Peter Boo's goal is to control a diversified company with annual turnover of S$100 million by the end of this decade. Material-handling products and security systems have enabled MHE to grow to a S$21.5 million company, but additional acquisitions may be necessary to get the company to its S$100 million goal.

EXHIBIT 31-5 MHE's Five-year Financial Summary

	1992 $'000	1991 $'000	1990 $'000	1989 $'000	1988 $'000
Turnover	21,484	29,171	16,801	16,181	12,897
Net (Loss)/Profit before Tax	(492)	1,428	503	1,790	1,929
Net (Loss)/Profit after Tax & Extraordinary Item Attributable to Shareholders	(599)	1,357	709	1,890	1,383
Shareholders' Fund	13,069	13,979	9,690	9,375	2,473
Total Assets	24,019	24,183	22,226	14,889	8,846
Total Liabilities	10,395	9,510	11,772	5,514	5,073
(Loss)/Earnings per Share (cents) (Note 1)	(2.20)	5.00	2.00	9.00	28.11
Net Tangible Assets per Share ($) (Note 1)	0.48	0.53	0.40	0.44	0.39
Net Dividends	275	385	275	375	82
Gross Rate of Dividend (%) (Note 2)	5.00	7.00	5.00	7.50	10.00

(1). The (loss)/earnings per share and net tangible assets per share are calculated based on the number of shares in issue during the year, or, where there is a movement in the number of shares issued, calculations are based on the weighted average of the number of shares in issue during the year.

	No. of Shares in Issue During the Year	
1988	6,100,000	
1989	20,929,830	(Weighted average)
1990	25,000,000	
1991	27,291,667	(Weighted average)
1992	27,500,000	

(2). The dividend proposed for the year 1992 and dividends paid for the years 1991, 1990 and 1989 are tax exempt. Dividend paid for the year 1988 is non tax exempt.

Source: MHE *Annual Report*, 1992.

One area that has fascinated Mr. Boo for several years is biotechnology. He has not formulated specific plans, but Mr. Boo wants to participate in this rapidly expanding field before it becomes too crowded. His intention is to have MHE assist in food production using relatively new techniques like hydroponics and genetic engineering.

Diversification will not detract from MHE's primary field of material handling. Singapore's manpower shortage leaves the government with two alternatives—import people or encourage automation. The first alternative is not particularly appealing to the government. Officially, the government encourages the immigration of people with professional and technical skills but discourages the immigration of less skilled workers. As for the second alternative, encouraging automation, the government is more proactive. The government of Singapore has established a S$65 million fund to encourage companies to automate their businesses to the fullest extent. Material Handling Engineering Ltd. expects to profit handsomely from that fund.

EXHIBIT 31-6 MHE's Profit and Loss Accounts for the year ended June 30,1992

	THE GROUP		THE COMPANY	
	1992 $	1991 $	1992 $	1991 $
Turnover	21,484,120	29,171,344	15,728,639	26,460,520
Operating (Loss)/Profit	(455,648)	1,466,542	419,803	1,508,117
Share of Losses of Associated Companies	(36,082)	(39,030)	—	—
(Loss)/Profit Before Taxation	(491,730)	1,427,512	419,803	1,508,117
Taxation	(245,097)	(219,131)	(152,000)	(164,000)
(Loss)/Profit after Taxation	(736,827)	1,208,381	267,803	1,344,117
Minority Interests	137,554	149,100	—	—
(Loss)/Profit Attributable to the Shareholders	(599,273)	1,357,481	267,803	1,344,117
Retained Profits at Beginning of Year	3,067,263	2,298,167	3,548,708	2,589,591
	2,467,990	3,655,648	3,816,511	3,933,708
Exchange Differences Arising on Consolidation	(36,205)	(203,385)	—	—
Profits Available for Appropriation	2,431,785	3,452,263	3,816,511	3,933,708
Dividends	(275,000)	(385,000)	(275,000)	(385,000)
Retained Profits at End of Year	2,156,785	3,067,263	3,541,511	3,548,708
(Loss)/Earnings Per Ordinary Share (Cents)	(2) cts	5 cts		

Source: MHE *Annual Report*, 1992.

EXHIBIT 31-7 MHE's Consolidated Statement of Changes in Financial Position for the year ended June 30, 1992

	1992 $	1991 $
Source of Funds		
From operations:		
(Loss)/profit before taxation	(491,730)	1,427,512
Adjustments for non-cash items:		
Depreciation	1,011,122	746,399
Amortisation of deferred development expenditure	83,704	82,044
Amortisation of goodwill	80,378	6,400
Amortisation of preliminary expenses	28,556	25,404
Development cost written off	1,868	11,328
Fixed assets written off	6,061	—
Other adjustments:		
Exchange differences arising on consolidation	(89,020)	11,049
Profit from sale of fixed assets	(31,830)	(11,709)
Share of losses of associated companies	36,082	39,030
	635,191	2,337,457

EXHIBIT 31-7 *Continued*

	1992	1991
	$	$
From other sources:		
Proceeds from sale of fixed assets	**115,153**	87,577
Net proceeds from issue of shares	—	3,520,100
Term loans	**500,000**	—
Staff loan repaid	**47,837**	—
Proceeds from shares issued to minority shareholders	—	78,784
	1,298,181	6,023,918
Application of Funds		
Purchase of intangibles	**410,877**	118,007
Purchase of fixed assets	**1,793,401**	1,811,334
Purchase of investments	**502,593**	—
Repayment of term loans	**321,701**	575,395
Tax paid	**82,646**	67,554
Dividends paid	**385,000**	275,000
Staff loans	—	30,712
	3,496,218	2,878,002
Net (Decrease)/Increase in Working Capital	**(2,198,037)**	3,145,916
Represented by:		
(Decrease)/Increase in inventories	**(588,246)**	1,303,672
(Decrease) in debtors	**(388,934)**	(948,087)
Decrease/(Increase) in creditors	**684,015**	(1,748,288)
	(293,165)	(1,392,703)
Movements in net liquid funds:		
(Decrease)/Increase in fixed deposits	**(876,375)**	233,301
Increase in bank and cash balances	**309,452**	608,989
(Increase)/Decrease in bank overdrafts	**(1,337,949)**	3,696,329
	(2,198,037)	3,145,916

The effects of the acquisition of subsidiaries have been reflected in the separate assets and liabilities of the Group. The effects are analysed as follows:

	$
Net assets acquired:	
Goodwill	319,889
Fixed assets	68,450
Inventories	504,860
Debtors	675,280
Bank and cash balances	753,306
Creditors	(1,423,203)
	898,582
Discharged by cash	898,582

Source: MHE *Annual Report*, 1992.

EXHIBIT 31-8 MHE's Balance Sheets June 30, 1992

	THE GROUP		THE COMPANY	
	1992 $	1991 $	1992 $	1991 $
Non-Current Assets				
Fixed assets	9,627,563	8,882,917	5,415,545	5,338,197
Subsidiary companies	—	—	4,302,948	3,392,848
Associated companies	73,336	109,418	146,437	146,437
Intangibles	545,253	327,818	—	—
Staff loans	11,027	58,864	11,027	58,864
Investments	594,193	219,000	594,193	219,000
Current Assets				
Inventories	3,868,683	4,456,929	2,309,949	3,709,892
Trade debtors	7,198,680	7,274,541	4,138,512	6,645,689
Due by subsidiaries	—	—	2,854,847	569,237
Due by an associated company	9,934	12,186	9,934	2,914
Short term investment	127,400	—	127,400	—
Other debtors, deposits and prepayments	494,532	805,354	213,171	309,104
Fixed deposits with financial institutions	210,149	1,086,524	210,149	450,000
Bank and cash balances	1,258,649	949,197	235,512	885,323
	13,168,027	14,584,731	10,099,474	12,572,159
Less				
Current Liabilities				
Trade creditors	3,465,143	4,391,127	1,645,829	3,943,529
Hire purchase and leasing creditors	389,438	322,153	137,918	138,335
Due to subsidiaries	—	—	—	153,265
Other creditors and accrued liabilities	2,124,039	1,877,623	1,173,340	1,239,144
Term loans	1,047,555	504,806	780,000	280,000
Bank overdrafts	1,561,581	223,632	1,237,065	64,634
Taxation	101,456	51,376	50,451	33,421
Proposed dividend	275,000	385,000	275,000	385,000
	8,964,212	7,755,717	5,299,603	6,237,328
Net Current Assets	4,203,815	6,829,014	4,799,871	6,334,831
Non-Current Assets				
Term loans	867,819	1,232,269	420,000	700,000
Hire purchase and leasing creditors	234,615	306,347	72,491	113,450
Deferred taxation	328,370	216,000	324,000	216,000
	(1,430,804)	(1,754,616)	(816,491)	(1,029,450)
	13,624,383	14,672,415	14,453,530	14,460,727
Share Capital and Reserves				
Share capital	5,500,000	5,500,000	5,500,000	5,500,000
Share premium	5,412,019	5,412,019	5,412,019	5,412,019
Retained profits	2,156,785	3,067,263	3,541,511	3,548,708
Interests of the Share-holders of the Company	13,068,804	13,979,282	14,453,530	14,460,727
Minority Interests	555,579	693,133	—	—
	13,624,383	14,672,415	14,453,530	14,460,727

Source: MHE *Annual Report*, 1992.

FOOD INDUSTRY NOTE
WILLIAM JANIS, CORNELIUS KENNEY, AND ELENA VASQUEZ

The processed food and beverage industry sector (SIC 20) is the nation's largest manufacturing sector. In 1993, the value of food and beverage industry shipments reached an estimated $404 billion, up more than 2 percent over 1992. Exports rose almost 3 percent, while exports of higher value-added processed foods and beverages rose almost 12 percent, a turbulent international economy notwithstanding. Adjusted for inflation, processed food and beverage sector industry shipments rose slightly more than 1 percent in 1993; between 1988 and 1992, real sectoral shipment value rose about 1 percent annually (Table 1).

Industry expectations for 1994 are clouded by concerns about the pace of domestic and international economic recovery, a possible softening in export demand, and increasingly acrimonious food processor-food retailer relationships. Adjusted for inflation, total food and beverage industry shipments are likely to rise about 1 percent in 1994. A rebounding U.S. economy and a pickup in export demand would contribute to accelerated industry growth.

TABLE 1   Trends and Forecasts: Food and Kindred Products (SIC 20) *(In millions of dollars except as noted)* 1991–1994

					PERCENT CHANGE		
ITEM	1991	1992[1]	1993[2]	1994[3]	91–92	92–93	93–94
Industry Data							
Value of shipments[4]	387,601	394,039	404,342	415,406	1.7	2.6	2.7
Value of shipments (1987$)	344,351	347,649	352,013	355,533	1.0	1.3	1.0
Total employment (000)	1,475	1,475	1,461	1,458	0.0	-0.9	-0.2
Production workers (000)	1,070	1,068	1,068	1,066	-0.2	0.0	-0.2
Average hourly earnings ($)	10.10	10.36	10.58	—	—	2.6	2.1
Capital expenditures	9,362	—	—	—	—	—	—
Product Data							
Value of shipments[5]	363,943	369,988	379,661	390,051	1.7	2.6	2.7
Value of shipments (1987$)	323,763	326,835	330,977	334,341	0.9	1.3	1.0
Trade Data							
Value of imports	19,779	20,869	20,785	21,087	5.5	-0.4	1.5
Value of exports	19,918	22,504	23,101	24,307	13.0	2.7	5.2

[1] Estimate, except exports and imports.
[2] Estimate.
[3] Forecast.
[4] Value of all products and services sold by establishments in the food and kindred products industry.
[5] Value of products classified in the food and kindred products industry produced by all industries.

Source: U.S. Department of Commerce: Bureau of the Census; International Trade Administration (ITA). Estimates and forecasts by ITA.

In 1993, aggregate food and beverage industry shipments value increased between 2 and 3 percent (nominal), or slightly more than 1 percent in real terms, as a number of factors dampened growth. Consumers continued to express concern about the overall economy by reducing their spending and, in some cases, by changing buying habits and purchase preferences.

For the first half of 1993, personal consumption expenditures (PCE) for food and beverages consumed at home and away from home rose at an annual rate of more than 2 percent over 1992. Interestingly, expenditures outside the home increased more than in-home food purchases. Many consumers, however, responded to unsettled economic times not only by spending less overall, but also by increasing their purchases of less costly, private-label foods and beverages. In addition, increasing numbers of shoppers have begun trading at "warehouse club" outlets, which stock extra large items at attractive prices.

Most industry analysts consider the U.S. food and beverage processing sector mature and developed. Population growth, economic conditions, and foreign trade patterns affect growth. In 1993, the U.S. population grew by less than 1 percent, consumers were concerned about their economic well-being, and foreign customers struggled with recession.

In addition, an increasing number of food and beverage processors adopted a wholesale pricing strategy centered around lower prices without discounts, merchandise deals, or other purchase incentives. This pricing approach results in smaller gross sales but does not necessarily affect net sales and may even increase them because it reduces promotional costs.

The economic troubles affecting most of the world in 1993 had a dampening effect on U.S. processed food and beverage exports. Total processed food and beverage export value rose only modestly, while exports of lower value-added products, such as meat, poultry, seafood, most dairy products, and grain-based intermediate products declined moderately. Foreign demand for U.S.-produced higher value-added products, such as processed fruits and vegetables, alcoholic beverages, ready-to-eat meals, bakery items, and candy products increased significantly in 1993.

Value-Added. The industry sector is divided here into two groups—higher value-added industries and lower value-added industries—for further analysis. (The Census Bureau derives value added by subtracting the cost of materials, supplies, containers, fuel, electricity, and contract work from the value of industry shipments.) The higher value-added industries manufacture retail-ready, packaged, consumer brand-name products of which at least 40 percent of the industry shipment value is added through sophisticated manufacturing.

Industry analysts attribute the increased foreign demand for higher value-added U.S. products, such as roasted nuts, frozen fruits and vegetables, ice cream, jellies, and canned fruits and vegetables to several factors. A rapidly growing middle class in developing and emerging countries accounted for some of the increased demand. Also, Russia, Ukraine, and other countries of the former Soviet Union had a great appetite for higher value-added foods and beverages, especially alcoholic beverages. Observers believe that some of these shipments moved through brokers and traders in several member states of the European Community.

Mirroring the strength of higher value-added food and beverages abroad, the value of industry shipments of the higher value-added group substantially out-performed lower value-added industries in 1993 (Tables 2 and 3). The value of industry shipments of the higher value-added group increased an estimated 3 percent and

TABLE 2 Trends and Forecasts: Higher Value-Added Foods and Beverages (*In millions of dollars except as noted*) 1991–1994

					PERCENT CHANGE		
ITEM	1991	1992[1]	1993[2]	1994[3]	91–92	92–93	93–94
Industry Data							
Value of shipments[4]	192,654	197,770	203,883	210,218	2.7	3.1	3.1
Value of shipments (1987$)	169,621	174,487	179,024	184,037	2.9	2.6	2.8
Total employment (000)	814	816	813	812	0.2	−0.4	−0.1
Production workers (000)	557	549	549	548	−1.4	0.0	−0.2
Average hourly earnings ($)	11.27	11.60	11.87	—	2.9	2.3	–
Capital expenditures	5,969	—	—	—	—	—	—
Product Data							
Value of shipments[5]	182,570	183,105	188,920	195,154	0.3	3.2	3.3
Value of shipments (1987$)	161,032	165,495	169,798	174,553	2.8	2.6	2.8
Trade Data							
Value of imports	8,719	9,724	9,395	9,535	11.5	−3.4	1.5
Value of exports	5,725	6,660	7,462	8,458	16.3	12.0	13.3

[1]Estimate, except exports and imports.

[2]Estimate.

[3]Forecast.

[4]Value of all products and services sold by establishments in the higher value-added foods and beverages industry.

[5]Value of products classified in the higher value-added foods and beverages industry produced by all industries.

Note: This aggregation includes those industries defined as higher value-added in the text.

Source: U.S. Department of Commerce: Bureau of the Census; International Trade Administration (ITA). Estimates and forecasts by ITA.

accounted for 50 percent of total value; in contrast, the value of the lower value-added group's industry shipments rose about 2 percent.

Adjusted for inflation, the value of shipments of the higher value-added industry group rose more than 2 percent in 1993. The relatively large increase in real shipments value compared with nominal value change (3 percent) reflects processors' price restraints, new efficiencies, and a changing product mix. The lower value-added industry group did not fare as well; adjusted for inflation, group value of shipments contracted fractionally due to declines in the meat and poultry and the fats and oils industries of 1 percent and 3 percent, respectively.

INTERNATIONAL COMPETITIVENESS

Recognizing that domestic markets are expanding slowly, many U.S. food and beverage processors emphasized export sales in 1993. A weaker U.S. dollar and economic concerns abroad have contributed to record export sales in 1993. As U.S. firms become more skillful in cultivating overseas customers and the international economy improves, exports are likely to increase substantially.

TABLE 3 Trends and Forecasts: Lower Value-Added Foods and Feeds (*In millions of dollars except as noted*) 1991–1994

					PERCENT CHANGE		
ITEM	1991	1992[1]	1993[2]	1994[3]	91–92	92–93	93–94
Industry Data							
Value of shipments[4]	194,947	196,269	200,459	205,188	0.7	2.1	2.4
Value of shipments (1987$)	174,730	173,162	172,989	171,496	–0.9	–0.1	–0.9
Total employment (000)	662	659	648	646	–0.5	–1.7	–0.3
Production workers (000)	513	519	519	518	1.2	0.0	–0.2
Average hourly earnings ($)	8.86	9.07	9.26	—	2.4	2.1	—
Capital expenditures	3,393	—	—	—	—	—	—
Product Data							
Value of shipments[5]	181,373	186,883	190,741	194,897	3.0	2.1	2.2
Value of shipments (1987$)	162,731	161,340	161,179	159,788	–0.9	–0.1	–0.9
Trade Data							
Value of imports	11,060	11,145	11,390	11,552	0.8	2.2	1.4
Value of exports	14,193	15,844	15,639	15,849	11.6	–1.3	1.3

[1] Estimate, except exports and imports.

[2] Estimate.

[3] Forecast.

[4] Value of all products and services sold by establishments in the lower value-added foods and feeds industry.

[5] Value of products classified in the lower value-added foods and feeds industry produced by all industries.

Note: This aggregation includes those industries defined as lower value added in the text.

Source: U.S. Department of Commerce: Bureau of the Census; International Trade Administration (ITA). Estimates and forecasts by ITA.

U.S. exports of processed foods and beverages reached an estimated $22.5 billion in 1993, an increase of about 3 percent over 1992. Despite this marginal gain, U.S. processed food and beverage exports continued to outpace imports, a pattern first established in 1991. U.S. imports of processed foods and beverages edged down an estimated 1 percent in 1993 to $20.8 billion, reversing an increase of more than 5 percent in 1992.

Foreign demand for lower value-added intermediate processed foods and beverages declined slightly in 1993. However, exports of higher value-added products were expected to rise a substantial 12 percent. Because of weakening foreign demand for lower value-added products, which represent the majority of U.S. food and beverage exports, total export value rose almost 3 percent.

Exports of higher value-added processed foods and beverages, including bakery products, breakfast cereal, and chewing gum reached about $7.5 billion in 1993, up nearly 12 percent from 1992. Between 1989 and 1993, exports of these products expanded more than 16 percent annually. Increases in foreign demand boosted the

TABLE 4 U.S. Trade Patterns in 1992 Food and Kindred Products (SIC 20) (*In millions of dollars, percent*)

EXPORTS	VALUE	SHARE	IMPORTS	VALUE	SHARE
Canada and Mexico	5,189	23.1	Canada and Mexico	4,694	22.5
European Community	3,659	16.3	European Community	5,187	24.9
Japan	6,077	27.0	Japan	333	1.6
East Asia NICs	2,585	11.5	East Asia NICs	3,146	15.1
South America	682	3.0	South America	2,320	11.1
Other	4,313	19.2	Other	5,190	24.9
World Total	22,504	100.0	World Total	20,869	100.0

TOP FIVE COUNTRIES

	VALUE	SHARE		VALUE	SHARE
Japan	6,077	27.0	Canada	3,667	17.6
Canada	3,244	14.4	Thailand	1,324	6.3
Mexico	1,946	8.6	France	1,083	5.2
South Korea	1,226	5.4	Australia	1,081	5.2
Netherlands	792	3.5	Mexico	1,026	4.9

Source: U.S. Department of Commerce: Bureau of the Census; International Trade Administration.

share of higher value-added food and beverage exports relative to total exports from more than 23 percent in 1989 to more than 32 percent in 1993.

In 1993, exports from five industries among the higher value-added group of industries accounted for 47 percent of the total. Processed nuts led the list with a share of more than 10 percent with exports of $776 million, unchanged from 1992. U.S. manufacturers of processed nuts have strong technical and marketing expertise.

With $729 million in 1993 exports, frozen fruits, fruit juices, and vegetables were second among the top five product categories at nearly 10 percent of the total. Exports of these goods rose almost 5 percent from 1992. U.S. companies operate efficient, large-scale plants to reduce their costs of production. In turn, these enterprises can offer attractive products and prices to foreign purchasers. Major buyers overseas also have developed distribution networks to handle these highly perishable products.

In 1993, U.S. exports of miscellaneous processed foods, including herbal teas, spices, vinegar, and yeast, rose nearly 33 percent to $719 million, or more than 9 percent of total U.S. exports of higher value-added processed foods and beverages. Herbal teas represented about 59 percent of this category.

With a 9-percent share of total U.S. exports of higher value-added processed foods and beverages, 1993 exports of canned fruits, juices, and vegetables reached $675 million, up 3 percent. These shelf-stable products went primarily to Canada ($248 million), Japan ($82 million), Taiwan ($31 million), Hong Kong ($31 million), and Mexico ($28 million).

In 1993, dry, condensed, and evaporated dairy products valued at $605 million accounted for 8 percent of total exports of higher value-added processed food and beverages. Exports increased 22 percent. The leading U.S. customers were Mexico ($159 million), India ($53 million), Canada ($50 million), Japan ($41 million), and Taiwan ($25 million). The United States spent $59 million on export subsidies for powdered milk in 1993, compared with $1.8 billion by the European Community for all of its dairy export subsidies.

Despite recessionary economic conditions in many countries and reduced discretionary income, foreign consumers still purchased more U.S. higher value-added foods and beverages because prices of U.S. foods and beverages compared favorably with prices of similar products.

U.S. food and beverage companies continued to place more emphasis on promoting and exporting their products. Firms devoted more resources to exporting because domestic U.S. demand for processed food and beverages is growing less rapidly than during the 1980s. When the economies of major U.S. customers recover, the industry expects its current promotion and export efforts to lead to increased sales abroad.

Exports of higher value-added foods and beverages to five countries—Canada, Japan, Mexico, Germany, and the United Kingdom—represented an estimated $4.3 billion, or about 57 percent of the 1993 export total. These products often involve sophisticated manufacturing processes. Canada, benefitting from the U.S.-Canada Free Trade Agreement (CFTA), purchased $1.9 billion worth of U.S. higher value-added food and beverages, up 10 percent from 1992. By reducing Canadian tariffs, the CFTA has generated additional U.S. exports to Canada. Japan purchased $1 billion in U.S. higher value-added food and beverages in 1993, down from $1.1 billion in 1992, due in part to a worsening of Japan's recession.

Mexico has emerged as a significant market for U.S. higher value-added foods and beverages. In 1993, U.S. enterprises sent an estimated $634 million worth of higher value-added food and beverages to Mexico, up 36 percent from 1992 (Table 5). This reflects the continuing easing of Mexican trade restrictions during the past several years.

Exports from U.S. processed food and beverage industries selling lower value-added foods and feed, such as meat, butter, cheese, flour, animal feed, fats, and oils, dipped about 1 percent in 1993 to $15.6 billion. Between 1989 and 1993, exports of these items expanded more than 4 percent yearly. The share of lower value-added food and feed relative to total exports dropped from about 76 percent in 1989 to about 68 percent in 1993.

Three factors influenced the performance of U.S. exports of lower value-added processed foods and feed. First, the European Community (EC), a major competitor, spent $4.8 billion in 1993 to subsidize dairy products, eggs, poultry, and refined sugar, an increase of 22 percent over 1992 (Table 6). By contrast, U.S. export subsidies for lower value-added foods came to about $198 million. Most U.S. export subsidies go to raw commodities, such as wheat.

Second, the food and beverage processing industries of some major U.S. customers, such as the EC, Japan, and South Korea, continued to incorporate new technological and marketing techniques, reformulate products, and modernize plants. Distribution and sales channels have become more efficient. Facing sluggish domestic demand in 1993, foreign food and beverage enterprises sought ways to trim costs and prices, thus displacing some U.S. exports of lower value-added processed food and feed.

Finally, exchange rates played a role in slowing U.S. exports of lower value-added processed food and feed in 1993. Many food and beverage companies in countries

TABLE 5 U.S. Trade Patterns in 1992 Higher Value-Added Foods and Beverages (SIC 2023, 2024, 203, 2043, 2045, 2047, 205, 2064, 2066, 2067, 2068, 2082, 2084, 2085, 2086, 2095, 2096) (*In millions of dollars, percent*)

EXPORTS	VALUE	SHARE	IMPORTS	VALUE	SHARE
Canada and Mexico	2,173	32.6	Canada and Mexico	2,152	22.1
European Community	1,283	19.3	European Community	4,006	41.2
Japan	1,098	16.5	Japan	161	1.7
East Asia NICs	690	10.4	East Asia NICs	983	10.1
South America	187	2.8	South America	1,046	10.8
Other	1,229	18.5	Other	1,376	14.2
World Total	6,660	100.0	World Total	9,724	100.0

TOP FIVE COUNTRIES

	VALUE	SHARE		VALUE	SHARE
Canada	1,708	25.6	Canada	1,429	14.7
Japan	1,098	16.5	France	995	10.2
Mexico	466	7.0	Mexico	723	7.4
Germany	306	4.6	United Kingdom	622	6.4
United Kingdom	302	4.5	Brazil	592	6.1

Source: U.S. Department of Commerce: Bureau of the Census; International Trade Administration.

with weakening currencies vis-à-vis the U.S. dollar sought to reduce costs by turning to alternative foreign suppliers and reformulated their products.

Japan, Canada, Mexico, South Korea, and the Netherlands, the top five importers of U.S. lower value-added processed foods and feed, accounted for more than 55 percent of total 1993 exports in this category.

In 1993, total imports of processed food and beverages dipped less than 1 percent to $20.8 billion after a rise of more than 5 percent in 1992. The share of higher value-added products was more than 45 percent in 1993, down from more than 46 percent in 1992. Lower value-added goods represented the rest, about 55 percent of all 1993 imports. From 1989 to 1993, imports of higher value-added foods and beverages rose more than 2 percent annually, while those of lower value-added processed food and feed increased about 2 percent yearly.

Imports of higher value-added foods and beverages from five countries—Canada, France, Mexico, the United Kingdom, and the Netherlands—accounted for an estimated $4.5 billion, or 48 percent of the 1993 total. Imports of lower value-added food and feed from five countries—Canada, Thailand, Australia, New Zealand, and Ecuador—represented an estimated $5.3 billion, or 47 percent of the 1993 total.

TABLE 6   U.S. Trade Patterns in 1992 Lower Value-Added Foods and Feeds (SIC 201, 2021, 2022, 2026, 2041, 2044, 2046, 2048, 2061, 2062, 2063, 207, 2083, 2087, 2091, 2092, 2097) (*In millions of dollars, percent*)

EXPORTS	VALUE	SHARE	IMPORTS	VALUE	SHARE
Canada and Mexico	3,016	19.0	Canada and Mexico	2,542	22.8
European Community	2,376	15.0	European Community	1,181	10.6
Japan	4,979	31.4	Japan	172	1.5
East Asia NICs	1,895	12.0	East Asia NICs	2,163	19.4
South America	495	3.1	South America	1,274	11.4
Other	3,084	19.5	Other	3,814	34.2
World Total	15,844	100.0	World Total	11,145	100.0

TOP FIVE COUNTRIES

	VALUE	SHARE		VALUE	SHARE
Japan	4,979	31.4	Canada	2,238	20.1
Canada	1,536	9.7	Australia	1,012	9.1
Mexico	1,480	9.3	Thailand	1,003	9.0
South Korea	1,065	6.7	New Zealand	738	6.6
Netherlands	615	3.9	China	435	3.9

Source: U.S. Department of Commerce: Bureau of the Census; International Trade Administration.

PERSONAL CONSUMPTION EXPENDITURES

U.S. consumer spending for food and beverages appeared to rebound somewhat in 1993, a welcome respite after a lackluster performance in 1991 and 1992. Personal consumption expenditures (PCE) for all food and beverages increased more than 3 percent to $647 billion. Spending for food and drink away-from-home rose 4 percent, while at-home food and beverage purchases gained almost 3 percent.

Adjusted for inflation, PCE for all food and beverages increased 1 to 2 percent in 1993. Away-from-home spending climbed between 2 and 3 percent, as at-home PCE expanded a more modest 1 percent. The estimated 1993 results proved encouraging. Between 1989 and 1992, total food and beverage purchases (in constant dollars) increased only 0.2 percent annually. During the same four-year period, real expenditures for food and beverages consumed at home edged up only 0.1 percent. In contrast, purchases away from home rose almost 1 percent yearly from 1989 to 1992, equalling the real gain in total PCE (Table 7).

Changing consumer demographics, a slowing growth of population, shifting buying habits, and concerns about the economy affected both the amount and types of outlays for food and beverages. The U.S. population is expanding by less than 1 percent annually, and immigrants constitute about one-fourth of this increase. The population is continuing to age as the size of U.S. households shrinks.

Economic concerns not only caused spending restraint but also prompted greater purchases of less costly private-label products and greater patronage of warehouse-club type operations. More women working outside the home and a higher number of single-person households caused a redistribution of the food and beverage dollar away from at-home outlays and toward away-from-home outlays.

Spending for food and drink is declining as a share of all PCE. In 1993, the portion of PCE devoted to food and beverages accounted for an estimated 15 percent of the total, compared with more than 18 percent in 1982. Between 1982 and 1993, the share of away-from-home food and drink purchases decreased minimally from 5.2 percent to 4.9 percent. In contrast, consumer spending for food and beverages at home dropped considerably more, from 13 percent in 1982 to nearly 10 percent in 1993.

More women in the work force, more single-person and single-parent families, and more travel combined to increase the away-from-home market as a share of total consumer spending for food and beverages. During 1982–93, the away-from-home market expanded from 28.2 percent of all food and beverage purchases to 32.6 percent; the at-home market declined by a commensurate amount.

During the 1980s, consumers became more concerned about health, fitness, and substance abuse. These concerns continued to prevail into the 1990s and affected spending for alcoholic beverages. In 1993, the estimated PCE for alcoholic beverages inched up just 0.3 percent and accounted for 11.7 percent of all food and beverage spending, down from 13.3 percent in 1982.

Adjusted for inflation, expenditures for alcoholic beverages declined 0.5 percent annually between 1982 and 1992. Alcoholic beverage spending is likely to continue its decline now that only 50 percent of business meals is tax deductible. Potentially

TABLE 7	Personal Consumption Expenditures for Food, Nonalcoholic and Alcoholic Beverages, 1989–92 (*In millions of dollars*)			
ITEM	1989	1990	1991	1992
All food and beverages	565,146	601,351	617,138	630,379
Food and beverages at home	373,675	398,444	407,354	415,281
Food and nonalcoholic beverages	330,129	351,829	359,442	365,625
Alcoholic beverages	43,546	46,615	47,912	49,656
Food and beverages away from home	180,590	191,364	198,503	203,493
Food and nonalcoholic beverages	156,911	165,885	171,889	177,889
Alcoholic beverages	23,679	25,479	26,614	25,603
Other food and nonalcoholic beverages	10,881	11,543	11,281	11,606
Furnished to employees[1]	10,325	10,976	10,769	11,116
Consumed on farms	556	567	512	490

[1] Includes military personnel.

Source: U.S. Department of Commerce, Bureau of Economic Analysis.

higher excise taxes on alcoholic beverages to help pay for health-care reform could further reduce consumption.

Population Changes. Population growth, demographic shifts, and household composition affect food and beverage consumption and spending. Total U.S. population increased slowly throughout the 1980s, and modest growth is continuing in the 1990s. Between 1980 and 1990, total population expanded just 0.95 percent annually and grew 1.1 percent from 1991–92. The Census Bureau estimates that total population is likely to increase about 0.9 percent yearly during the remainder of the 1990s.

An expanding immigrant population (mainly from South America and Asia) will have a notable effect on the industry, which must produce foods and beverages that meet the taste standards of different cultures.

Demographic shifts have also affected demand for food and beverages. The U.S. population is aging. From 1980 to 1990, the median age rose from 30 to 33 years. The fastest-growing age group is the 35-and-over set, with the greatest expansion in the 45–54 age group, which is forecast to increase nearly 45 percent during the remainder of the 1990s.

The 35–44 age group is expected to grow almost 16 percent by 2000, as the 65-and-over group increases by almost 11 percent, reaching an estimated 34.9 million people by 2000. The growing number of older consumers suggests that significant gains in consumer expenditures for foods and beverages will hinge on meeting the needs and preferences of older shoppers.

The changing composition of U.S. households also influences consumer expenditure patterns. In addition to becoming older, the average U.S. household is getting smaller. In 1992, the average household numbered 2.62 persons, a 14-percent decline since 1972.

Between 1985 and 1992, the number of U.S. households reached 95.7 million, increasing more than 10 percent; however, single-person households totaled 24 million, up 16 percent since 1985. In addition, one-parent family households also increased 19 percent since 1985. The trend toward smaller households with increasing numbers of single-person and one-parent households is expected to continue.

The combination of an aging population characterized by decreasing household size and greater numbers of single-person and one-parent households suggests that total spending for food and beverages is likely to increase slowly. More single-person and one-parent households indicate expansion of the away-from-home (food service) market at the expense of the retail grocery industry. Food and beverage processors will be pressed to provide products tailored to older and single-person households to minimize the natural appeal of away-from-home eateries. Because domestic market growth will be limited, manufacturers will likely compete very aggressively for market share and intensify export efforts to fatten sales and profits.

Consumers' Expenditure Survey. In 1991, the typical U.S. household spent $4,568 for food and beverages, including alcohol, at-home and away-from-home, according to the Bureau of Labor Statistics' Consumer Expenditure Survey. The typical household committed 58 percent of total food and beverage spending to food and nonalcoholic beverages for at-home use, 35 percent to away-from-home use, and 7 percent to alcoholic beverages purchased at home and away from home.

The typical U.S. household devoted almost 15 percent of after-tax income to the purchase of food and beverages in 1991. Two-person households spent the least, 13.7

percent, of after-tax income on food and drink, followed by three-person and four-person households, which committed 14.1 percent and 14.8 percent, respectively. The smallest and largest consumer units, one-person and five-or-more persons, spent more after-tax income than average for food and drink, 15.6 percent and 17.9 percent, respectively.

Households of five or more persons chose to spend more after-tax income (11.9 percent) for food and nonalcoholic beverages at-home; four-person households spent 9 percent, while two-person households spent the least for at-home foods, 7.7 percent of after-tax income.

One- and two-person households committed 6.2 percent and 5.9 percent, respectively, after taxes for away-from-home meals and drinks. Three- and four-person households spent the least of after-tax income, 5.1 percent, away from home, while five-or-more-person households spent 5.4 percent.

In addition to allocating more money for restaurant meals, one-person households also spent the most after-tax income on purchases of alcoholic beverages, 1.9 percent, followed by two-person households at 1.1 percent. Three-, four-, and five-person households each spent 0.7 percent on beer, wine, and distilled spirits.

Food and beverage purchase patterns changed somewhat between 1987 and 1991. Consumers elected to dedicate less of their at-home food and beverage budget to meat, poultry, seafood/fish, eggs, fruits and vegetables, and dairy products. Some of the spending shifts, especially in the case of meats, eggs, and some dairy products, reflect shoppers' concerns about health and nutrition.

Shoppers spent more of their 1991 food budget for cereal and bakery products and the so-called "other foods" category, which includes products such as most of the higher value-added prepared foods, nonalcoholic beverages, table spreads, and confectionery products. In 1991, consumers spent 46 percent on "other foods" and cereal and bakery products, compared with less than 42 percent in 1987.

Between 1987 and 1991, the Consumer Price Index (CPI) for red meat rose about 21 percent, compared with increases of 17 percent and 14 percent for poultry and fish/seafood, respectively. Per capita consumption of red meat declined almost 5 percent during this period while poultry per capita consumption increased more than 14 percent.

Prices also influenced shoppers' purchases of fruits and vegetables. During the 1987–92 period, the CPI for fresh fruits and vegetables rose 47 percent and 27 percent, respectively; prices of processed fruits and vegetables also increased, but more modestly, 19 percent and 20 percent, respectively. Per capita consumption of fresh fruit declined almost 8 percent as preserved fruit consumption fell by almost 10 percent.

NEW FOOD AND BEVERAGE LABELING

By May 1994, all U.S. sellers of processed food and beverages must conform to detailed regulations for labeling of nutritional information for their products. The rules, authorized by the Nutrition Labeling and Education Act (NLEA) of 1990, also cover serving sizes, health messages, and descriptive terms such as "light" and "low fat." The new regulations are enforced by the U.S. Food and Drug Administration.

To meet the requirements of the NLEA, most U.S. food and beverage companies have designed new labels to accommodate both NLEA information and commercial messages. Certain processors have completed the changes before the deadline. In turn, these manufacturers have used the new labeling as a selling point to differentiate their products in a crowded marketplace.

The new, more informative labeling regulations may prove especially difficult for many foreign food and beverage processors, particularly companies unaccustomed to such extensive product analysis and disclosure. Some industry analysts view the new requirements as a barrier to trade that could be challenged in the General Agreement on Tariffs and Trade (GATT). Supporters of the rules state that all enterprises, both domestic and foreign, must comply. These observers argue that the NLEA will provide vital consumer information to improve the health of U.S. consumers and that GATT would dismiss any complaint.

In August 1993, the U.S. Department of Agriculture (USDA), which regulates U.S. meat and poultry, issued recommendations on the thawing, handling, cooking, and post-preparation refrigeration of raw meat and poultry. New labels, for both retail consumers, and food service companies, will summarize these suggestions. Simultaneously, USDA will increase the number of meat inspectors, more closely monitor production plants, and accelerate efforts to develop rapid microbiological tests to detect food-borne pathogens. The American Meat Institute estimates that new regulation would cost the entire meat and poultry sector $135 million annually. Several highly publicized deaths from tainted meat contributed to greater public concern about food safety.

FOOD RETAILING

Notwithstanding consumers' overall concerns about the economy, food store and eating/drinking place sales strengthened somewhat in the first six months of 1993. Liquor sales declined, however, by more than 3 percent. Retail sales of all eating and drinking places rose 5 percent during the first six months of 1993, compared with a rise of more than 2 percent in 1992, when restaurant sales rose 3 percent and drinking place sales slumped almost 8 percent. During the first half of 1993, operators of eating and drinking places exercised considerable pricing restraint, which appears to have stimulated sales. For the period, the CPI for away-from-home food sales rose slightly more than 1 percent, compared with an average annual increase of close to 4 percent between 1987 and 1992.

Food store sales also increased by slightly more than 2 percent during the first six months of 1993, compared with a rise of slightly less than 2 percent for all of 1992. The CPI for food-at-home actually declined, about 1 percent for the first half of 1993, compared with an average annual CPI increase of 4 percent. The improved food store sales picture reflects pricing, a growing demand for private-label goods, and the increasing importance of nontraditional food sales outlets.

In 1992, nontraditional grocery sales outlets—hypermarkets, wholesale clubs, so-called deep discounters, and food mass merchandisers—accounted for 7 percent of all commodity volume (ACV) and about 1 percent of competing units, according to Willard Bishop Consulting, Ltd. By 1997, the company estimates, nontraditional outlets will represent more than 11 percent of ACV and 1.5 percent of competitive units.

Owners of food retailing outlets, especially supermarkets, believe that the nontraditional outlets are costing them sales, at least in part because processors and manufacturers sell competitive name-brand items to the warehouse clubs and similar retailers at lower prices. Because the nontraditional food outlets usually buy products in multipacks or larger sizes than traditional outlets, the cost per product unit is less than for goods packaged in conventional sizes. Savings from shopping at nontraditional outlets can be meaningful if shoppers are able to store larger sizes and quantities and are willing to spend extra travel time in exchange for convenience.

Traditional grocery sellers see the threat to their future and hold processors and wholesalers partially responsible. Conventional retailers may seek ways to penalize processors, who remain unhappy with retailers about expensive slotting allowances and penalties for the substandard sales performance of new products. One way retailers are attempting to cope with weak sales and new competition is by upgrading and expanding their private-label products.

In 1992, private-label food and beverages accounted for a reported 19.4 percent of all retail food and beverages sold. The popularity of less costly private-label items usually increases during periods of economic slowdown or uncertainty.

The quality and packaging of private-label food and beverages has been improving for some time. Modern manufacturing technologies, quality control, and improved packaging are ubiquitous throughout the processed food and beverages industry sector. Private-label products are gaining market shares in segments where they earlier had little appeal, including beer, breakfast cereal, and soft drinks. Many consumers perceive little quality difference between nationally branded items and private-label substitutes. The willingness of large numbers of consumers to pay a premium for nationally branded foods and beverages is in question.

Nevertheless, significant forces restrain the further growth of the market for private-label food and beverages. As the share of private-label processed foods and beverages increases, product development and innovation may slow considerably. Advertising, now funded by manufacturers, will likely decrease and the costs of growing the business will fall almost exclusively on retailers. Manufacturers of private-label foods and beverages can finance research and development for new products only by persuading supermarket customers to pay slightly more for the new items, an outcome probably unacceptable to weary and wary consumers.

OUTLOOK FOR 1994

Food and beverage processors and retail food store operators approach 1994 with some concern. While inflation is expected to remain under control, processors and retailers are concerned about the pace of domestic and international economic recovery and the expected growth of nontraditional retail food outlets. Processors of name-brand products will strive to stem the flow of less costly generic goods while retailers will attempt to offset the effects of new, nontraditional competition. Adjusted for inflation, the value of shipments of the food and beverage sector is forecast to rise about 1 percent in 1994 (Table 8).

Processors are also concerned about the passage of NAFTA and the fate of the Uruguay Round of trade talks. Successful conclusion of both trade pacts will mean new export opportunities in future years. However, some processors fear a backlash, which would adversely affect 1994 U.S. export sales in the event of a less-than-successful conclusion of the two sets of trade negotiations. U.S. processors are further concerned about the rate of economic recovery worldwide. For 1994, the value of processed food and beverage exports is forecast to rise about 6 percent to more than $24 billion.

NAFTA would provide at least three significant advantages to the U.S. processed food and beverage industry sector. First, the agreement would begin a series of gradual mutual tariff reductions between the United States and Mexico over a 15-year period. Second, Mexico would abolish all of its import licenses. Lastly, NAFTA would require mutual recognition of distinctive products. For example, Canada and Mexico would both recognize the uniqueness of bourbon and Tennessee whiskey, a condition

TABLE 8 Estimates and Forecasts for the Processed Food and Beverage Sector, 1992–94
(*In millions of dollars*)

			PERCENT CHANGE	
SIC	DESCRIPTION	1992[1]	1993[1]	1994[2]
201	Processed meat, poultry, and hides	88,856	90,112	91,368
202	Dairy products	51,099	52,274	53,686
203	Preserved fruits and vegetables	47,132	48,907	50,681
204	Grain mill products	48,697	50,591	52,485
205	Bakery products	27,043	27,449	28,025
206	Sugar and confectionery products	22,305	22,982	23,660
207	Fats and oils	18,980	19,260	19,896
208	Beverages	56,037	57,807	59,577
209	Miscellaneous foods	33,890	34,959	36,028
20	Total	394,039	404,341	415,406

[1] Preliminary estimate.
[2] Forecast.

Source: U.S. Department of Commerce, Bureau of Census and International Trade Administration (ITA). Estimates and forecasts by ITA.

predicated upon the elimination of Mexican tariffs on these alcoholic beverages. Only bourbon and Tennessee whiskey distilled in the United States according to U.S. laws and regulations would be sold in Canada or Mexico. In return, the United States would provide similar treatment to Canadian whiskey and Mexican tequila and mezcal.

After many difficulties and delays, the Uruguay Round of multilateral trade negotiations gained new momentum in 1993. Nevertheless, processed food and agricultural issues remain a major hurdle to agreement among the 111 member countries of the General Agreement on Tariffs and Trade (GATT).

The European Community (EC) and, in particular, France, have strong doubts about restricting their food and agricultural export subsidies and reducing barriers to imports from the United States and other countries. Imported processed foods and beverages face a common external tariff throughout the EC. The EC also assesses variable levies on the specific ingredients of imported processed food and beverages to raise prices of these products to levels prevailing in the EC.

A successful conclusion to the Uruguay Round would translate into considerable new export opportunities for U.S. manufacturers of processed foods and beverages. Most of the industry would benefit from a successful GATT agreement by allowing food and beverage manufacturers to invest more easily in GATT-member countries. The proposed investment rules would offer more clarity about the level of business risk for food and beverage companies. For example, a GATT agreement probably would not permit countries to seize assets without compensation, demand export requirements, or set domestic content regulations.

Since 1985, the share of private-label food and beverages sold in the United States has risen consistently, to more than 19 percent of total grocery food and beverage sales in 1992. Perhaps sales of private-label food and beverages will exceed 25 percent of the total in 1994. Many consumers will still search for the best combination of price and value. Industry analysts are debating, on the other hand, whether large numbers of consumers will return to nationally branded goods once the economy improves significantly.

Despite growing sales of private-label food and beverages, important factors may limit further expansion of the market. Many consumers think nationally branded foods and beverages offer greater consistency of quality than private-label substitutes. Major manufacturers of foods and beverages support their products through advertising, marketing, and promotion expenditures to maintain brand loyalty. Private-label goods do not have these advantages.

As the share of private-label processed foods and beverages increases, product development and innovation may slow considerably. Supermarket chains with their own factories do not have incentives to spend money on new product development and innovation for private-label goods because they cannot recover these expenditures over limited production cycles. Manufacturers of private-label foods and beverages could only finance research and development for new products by persuading their supermarket customers to pay a bit more for new products.

<hr>

CAMPBELL SOUP COMPANY—1994

Based in Camden, New Jersey, Campbell Soup Company (609-342-4800) saw its earnings fall from $490 million in 1992 to only $8 million in 1993. Campbell's earnings in Europe fell from $44.7 million in 1992 to negative $170.4 million in 1993. Campbell's financial objectives for fiscal 1994 are to achieve earnings per share growth of 12 to 15 percent, maintain return on equity of at least 24 percent, and maintain cash return on assets of at least 24 percent. To reach these objectives, Campbell Soup Company needs a clear strategic plan for the years 1994–2000. A mission statement recently proposed for Campbell follows.

MISSION STATEMENT FOR CAMPBELL SOUP COMPANY

Campbell Soup Company aims to offer nutritional food products to people all over the world. Our worldwide growth strategy focuses on what we do best—soup and biscuits. We are working aggressively to capture tomorrow's opportunities today.

Campbell Soup Company brand power is our pride, our inheritance, our future. With a powerhouse of trademarks that proclaims innovation, quality and consumer trust, Campbell will leverage brand strengths to deliver profitable, sustainable volume.

Campbell will concentrate on using methods and technologies while relying on the skills and experience of our people to build and expand low-cost business systems. This will ensure gains in productivity, quality and service to our manufacturing processes and marketing base.

We will continue to evaluate our business portfolio to ensure that our time, talent and money are applied to areas providing maximum return on investment. The intent is to deliver consistent financial results which keep us in the top quartile versus the best companies in the food industry. We are committed to strengthen our organization, create competitive advantage and achieve our vision, "Campbell Brands Preferred Around the World".

Throughout the 1970s and 1980s, Campbell Soup Company was largely run by the founder's son, John Dorrance, Jr. Dorrance died in early 1989 and disagreement spread throughout the Dorrance family, which owns 58 percent of Campbell's stock. Campbell's chief executive officer at the time, Gordon McGovern, resigned soon after Dorrance's death. Then in 1990, Campbell elected a new CEO, David Johnson, who previously was CEO of Gerber Products Company. After less than two months on the job, Johnson replaced Campbell's U.S. division with a North American division. This decision was based on Johnson's belief that there would soon be a North American free-trade agreement (FTA) to link the United States, Canada, and Mexico. The U.S.-Canada FTA had just been signed by both nations. Johnson continues to serve as Campbell's president and CEO today.

Campbell's philosophy is to "market locally, manufacture regionally, and resource globally—with common technology, knowledge, and supplies." Campbell currently has three major divisions: Campbell North and South America, Campbell Biscuit and Bakery, and Campbell Europe/Asia. In addition, the company has 26 subsidiaries. Each top executive has total responsibility for his or her division, from marketing and developing new products to manufacturing and logistics. These top executives are thus accountable for profits and revenues in their division. The officers as of 1992 are listed in Exhibit 32–1.

Campbell's 70 top executives are required to own at least three times their annual salary in Campbell stock. Members of Campbell's board of directors must purchase/own at least 1,000 shares of Campbell's stock. These two requirements assure that the company's top management team is totally committed to seeing the firm prosper.

Real disposable income for U.S. citizens has dropped in recent years and food as a percentage of total personal consumption expenditures also has decreased. Weak economies worldwide have limited sales of Campbell's premium-priced products such as ready-to-serve soups and Pepperidge Farm cookies. The U.S. population is not growing much, so the fight for food volume growth in the U.S. market is intense. Opportunities to increase revenues are greater abroad than in the United States. In addition to higher population growth and food consumption abroad, some international markets continue to be dominated by small, regional food processors that are sometimes inefficient producers and/or marketers.

Europe is beginning to follow the U.S. trend of seeking convenience in cooking and packaging. This trend allows food companies to offer more "value-added" products such as soups; chicken that already has been cut into pieces, boned, and skinned; marinated meats; ready-to-serve microwavable meals; single-serve portions; and cereals containing fruit and nuts.

Barriers to entry in the food industry are nearly insurmountable since this is a volume-driven business. Economies of scale for production, marketing, and distribution efficiencies are very important. For example, in cereals, the largest players—Kellogg, General Mills, and Philip Morris—are gaining market share at the expense of the three smaller cereal manufacturers—Ralston, Quaker, and Nabisco. There is a consolidation

EXHIBIT 32-1 Campbell Soup Company Officers as of October 1992

David W. Johnson
 President and Chief
 Executive Officer

Herbert M. Baum
 Executive Vice President.
 President, Campbell North
 and South America Division

John M. Coleman
 Senior Vice President—Law and
 Public Affairs and Corporate
 Secretary

James R. Kirk
 Senior Vice President—Research
 & Development and Quality
 Assurance.
 President, Campbell Research
 and Development

Richard A. Shea
 Senior Vice President.
 President, Campbell Biscuit and
 Bakery Division. President,
 Pepperidge Farm, Incorporated

Frank E. Weise, III
 Senior Vice President—Finance
 and Chief Financial Officer

Anthony J. Adams
 Vice President.
 Vice President—Marketing
 Research, Campbell North
 and South America Division

David L. Albright
 Vice President.
 President, Confectionery Group

Stephen R. Armstrong
 Vice President—Human
 Resources

James J. Baldwin
 Vice President—Taxes

Robert F. Bernstock
 Vice President.
 President and CEO,
 Campbell Soup Company Ltd
 (Canada)

Francis A. DuVernois
 Vice President.
 Vice President—Operations,
 Campbell North and South
 America Division

Brenda E. Edgerton
 Vice President—Treasurer

Leo J. Greaney
 Vice President—Controller

Ralph A. Harris
 Vice President—Corporate
 Development

Kathleen MacDonnell
 Vice President.
 Sector Vice President—Prepared
 Foods, Campbell North and
 South America Division

Charles V. McCarthy
 Vice President.
 President, Campbell Sales

Raymond A. Meillier
 Vice President.
 Vice President—Finance,
 Campbell North and South
 America Division

Edward S. Moerk
 Vice President.
 President, Campbell Europe
 Biscuits

Gary S. Moss
 Vice President.
 Vice President—Marketing
 Services, Campbell North and
 South America Division

George P. Nulty
 Vice President.
 Vice President—Purchasing,
 Campbell North and South
 America Division

Carlos Oliva Funes
 Vice President.
 President, Swift-Armour
 Sociedad Anonima
 Argentina

John L. Patten
 Vice President.
 President, Campbell Food
 Service, Campbell North
 and South America Division

Alfred Poe
 Vice President.
 Sector Vice President—
 Condiments & Sauces,
 Campbell North and South
 America Division.
 President, Vlasic Foods, Inc.

J. Neil Stalter
 Vice President—Corporate
 Communications

Robert Subin
 Vice President.
 President, Campbell
 Europe/Asia Division

F. Marty Thrasher
 Vice President.
 Sector Vice President—Soup,
 Campbell North and South
 America Division

Harry Walleasa
 Vice President—Management
 Information Systems

Source: Campbell Soup Company, 1993 *Annual Report.*

of food companies around the world, especially in Europe. As companies develop brand names that sell well around the world, they reap greater marketing efficiencies and profits.

There is a real fight among U.S. food companies for supermarket shelf space and freezer space. Firms that win space have a better chance of capturing the customer's attention and dollars. Price wars are a threat for food companies like Campbell. The areas most sensitive to price wars are frozen dinners and shelf-stable items. Regarding frozen foods, freezer space is particularly limited in supermarkets due to the extra cost of building and maintaining freezers. Thus when ConAgra recently started getting lots of freezer space for its Healthy Choice frozen dinners, price wars broke out. Campbell's Swanson brand frozen dinners compete directly with ConAgra's Healthy Choice.

CEO Johnson is considering a number of acquisitions to increase Campbell's economies of scale and distribution outlets; he is especially interested in European firms. Increases in the value of the dollar versus foreign currencies make it tougher for foreign companies to acquire U.S. firms but make it less expensive for U.S. companies to acquire foreign firms. However, a strengthening U.S. dollar hurts earnings of U.S. food companies with strong international operations.

CAMPBELL BRAND POWER

The year 1993 at Campbell could be described as one of extensive "brainstorming." This is Campbell's term for product development. The company aggressively extended many products using creativity and innovation. New products such as Pepperidge Farm gravy "borrowed" trademarks from other Campbell products. Godiva chocolate, known for luxury and indulgence, "lent" its name to a popular new line of coffees and a liqueur. Prego spaghetti sauce extended its savory benefits to a new pizza sauce line, with first-year results exceeding expectations. These brand-extension successes added more than $30 million to sales.

The volume of Campbell's Home Cookin ready-to-serve soups surged 14 percent in 1993, supported by a new campaign, *It doesn't get any better than Campbell's best.* The line features a redesigned label and two new varieties—New England Clam Chowder and Chicken Vegetable. In the competitive "healthy soup" category, Campbell's Healthy Request 98-percent-fat-free, ready-to-serve varieties captured a leadership position. Campbell's multiuse line added Campbell's Golden Corn and Italian Tomato and relaunched Cream of Asparagus to expand the business. Campbell's Double Noodle dry soup variety debuted in 1993, increasing dry soup volume 11 percent. Campbell introduced Campbell's Cream of Chicken & Broccoli, Chunky Old Fashioned Potato, and Swanson Vegetable Broth in 1993. The company launched a new advertising campaign headlined, *Campbell's Never Underestimate the Power of Soup* in 1993.

Campbell's biscuit and bakery business features many well-known brands. Pepperidge Farm's launch of Goldfish cookies in 1993 offers a novelty Goldfish pack for kids. The company's Distinctive cookie line inspired recent introductions of Double Chocolate and Hazelnut Milano varieties. Frozen garlic bread and rolls were introduced in 1993. Delacre, the pan-European brand, holds number-one market share in cookie assortments, and Arnott's, the Pacific Rim brand, ranks as the world's seventh largest biscuit—or cookie and cracker—brand.

Strong volume performance was posted in 1993 by Swanson frozen dinners, led by Hungry Man entrees and Fun Feast children's meals. In the grocery arena, Franco-

American launched Spaghetti-Os pasta varieties using the kids' cartoon character, Garfield. V8 vegetable juices reached a new audience with the launch of V8 Picante, a mild-flavored salsa drink, in 1993. Meal enhancement introductions included Marie's line of Luscious Low-Fat salad dressings and Vlasic Pickles To Go single-serve pickles.

Campbell increased marketing spending 12 percent in 1993. Helping to build Campbell brands are programs such as *Prego . . . Serving Your Community*, which supports charities with spaghetti dinner fund raisers. "Hearty School Lunch" teamed *Campbell Food Service* with the American Heart Association to offer menus, recipes, and nutrition information to schools nationwide. Celebrating the 20th anniversary of the *Labels for Education* program, Campbell produced an acclaimed television special, *"Portrait of a Teacher,"* hosted by actress Phylicia Rashad in 1993.

GLOBAL MARKETING

Campbell's worldwide growth strategy focuses on what the company does best: soup and biscuits. Campbell is relentlessly pursuing its vision, *Campbell Brands Preferred Around the World*. Currently, 95 percent of Campbell soups are sold in markets with just 5 percent of the world's population. In the United Kingdom, Campbell's condensed varieties are now the fastest-growing soups. Volume climbed a remarkable 18 percent during 1993.

In Mexico, Campbell's new Crema de Chile Poblana condensed soup variety has become a top seller. In Canada, Campbell's "Chunky" soups scored record volume and earnings in 1993. Progress in the Australian market continues with introductions of two new condensed varieties, Mushroom and Bacon and Italian Tomato. Strong growth in Campbell's Hong Kong business has led to expansion of Swanson broths into Taiwan, while markets in Indonesia, Singapore, Malaysia, and Thailand also are growing. Campbell is currently conducting taste tests in Argentina and Poland.

Campbell introduced condensed soups and broths to China in 1993. China's 1.2 billion people each consume almost six servings of soup per week. Campbell is exploring the possibility of manufacturing soup in China to generate additional savings and establish a base for long-term profitability throughout Asia.

Since acquiring a majority ownership in Arnott's Limited in Australia, Campbell's Biscuit and Bakery group derives more than half of its sales and operating earnings from outside North America. Pepperidge Farm, which mainly targets consumers in the Americas, recently expanded into Canada and Mexico. During 1993, fresh bakery items, along with cookies and crackers, were also introduced to Canadians.

In Europe, Campbell's new line of Delacre premium homemade-style cookies, Biscuits Maison de Delacre, is very popular. With simultaneous introductions in France, Belgium, Holland, and Germany, this was the industry's first-ever pan-European launch—in overall coordination of product, advertising, public relations, promotion, and packaging.

Campbell's Golden V8 vegetable juice, rich in beta carotene and made from golden tomatoes, was launched in Japan in 1993. The growing popularity of Mexican salsa in the United States led to the introduction of V8 Picante, a vegetable juice mixture of tomatoes, chilies, jalapeño peppers and lime, to American consumers. In addition, V8 vegetable juice entries to Mexico and China, along with a new uniform formula for V8 in Europe, are contributing to Campbell's revenues. Exhibit 32–2 lists Campbell Soup Company principal subsidiaries, affiliates, and operations around the world.

SUBSIDIARIES AND AFFILIATES

United States
 Campbell Finance Corp.
 Campbell Investment Company
 Campbell Sales Company
 Campbell's Fresh, Inc.
 Casera Foods, Inc.
 Godiva Chocolatier, Inc.
 Herider Farms, Inc.
 Joseph Campbell Company
 Mrs. Paul's Kitchens, Inc.
 Pepperidge Farm,
  Incorporated
 Royal American Foods
  Corporation
 Sanwa Foods, Inc.
 Vlasic Foods, Inc.

Other Countries
 Swift-Armour Sociedad
  Anonima Argentina
  (Argentina)
 Campbell's Australasia Pty.
  Limited (Australia)
 N.V. Biscuits Delacre S.A.
  (Belgium)
 N.V. Campbell Food &
  Confectionery
  Coordination Center
  Continental Europe, S.A.
  (Belgium)
 N.V. Godiva Belgium S.A.
  (Belgium)
 Campbell Soup Company
  Ltd (Canada)
 Campbell Foods P.L.C.
  (England)
 Campbell's U.K. Limited
  (England)
 Societe Francaise des
  Biscuits Delacre S.A.
  (France)
 Campbell Soup Asia
  Limited (Hong Kong)
 Campbell Japan
  Incorporated (Japan)

Campbell's de Mexico,
 S.A. de CV (Mexico)
Compania Envasadora
 Loreto, S.A. (Spain)

OPERATIONS

Campbell North and South America Division

Atlanta, Georgia (ramen noodles)
Barceloneta, Puerto Rico
 (canned foods)
Blandon, Pennsylvania
 (mushrooms)
Bonduel, Wisconsin (pickles)
Brampton, Ontario
 (distributor refrigerated foods)
Bridgeport, Michigan (pickles)
Chatham, Ontario (canned foods,
 ingredients, juices)
Chestertown, Maryland
 (ingredients)
City of Industry, California
 (pickles, ramen noodles)
Dixon, California (ingredients)
Douglas, Georgia (canned
 foods, ingredients)
Dudley, Georgia (mushrooms)
Fayetteville, Arkansas
 (frozen foods, ingredients)
Fennville, Michigan (mushrooms)
Guasave, Mexico (ingredients)
Hillsboro, Texas (mushrooms)
Howe, Indiana (mushrooms)
Imlay City, Michigan (pickles)
Jackson, Ohio (mushrooms)
Listowel, Ontario (frozen foods,
 distributor ingredients)
Marshall, Michigan (canned
 foods, refrigerated foods)
Maxton, North Carolina
 (canned foods)
Mexico City, Mexico
 (distributor food products)
Miami, Florida (frozen foods)
Millsboro, Delaware (pickles)
Milwaukee, Wisconsin
 (ingredients)

Modesto, California (frozen
 foods)
Montevideo, Uruguay
 (distributor food products)
Napoleon, Ohio (canned foods)
Omaha, Nebraska (frozen foods)
Paris, Texas (canned foods)
Pescadero, California
 (mushrooms)
Philadelphia, Pennsylvania
 (frozen foods)
Rosario, Argentina (meat prod-
 ucts, canned foods, frozen foods)
Sacramento, California
 (canned foods)
St. Marys, Ontario (ingredients)
Salisbury, Maryland
 (frozen foods)
Seville, Spain (olives)
Sidney, Ohio (dry foods)
South Plainfield, New Jersey
 (ingredients)
Stockton, California
 (ingredients)
Tecumseh, Nebraska
 (ingredients)
Thornton, Illinois
 (refrigerated salad dressings)
Toronto, Ontario (canned foods)
Villagran, Mexico (canned foods,
 frozen vegetables)
Visalia, California (olives)
Wauseon, Ohio (ingredients)
West Chicago, Illinois
 (mushrooms)
Worthington, Minnesota
 (canned foods, ingredients)

Campbell Biscuit and Bakery Division

Aiken, South Carolina (bakery)
Burbank, California (bakery)
Clinton, Connecticut
 (mail order)
Denver, Pennsylvania
 (biscuit, bakery)

EXHIBIT 32-2 *Continued*

Downers Grove, Illinois *(bakery)*
Downingtown, Pennsylvania
  (frozen foods)
Ede, The Netherlands *(biscuit)*
Lambermont, Belgium *(biscuit)*
Lakeland, Florida
  (biscuit, bakery)
Nieppe, France *(biscuit)*
Norwalk, Connecticut *(bakery)*
Pleyben, France *(biscuit)*
Richmond, Utah
  (biscuit, frozen foods)
Salt Lake City, Utah
  (food service products)
Tholen, The Netherlands
  (biscuit)
Willard, Ohio *(biscuit)*

Campbell Europe/Asia Division
EUROPE
Belgium
  Brussels *(confectionery)*
  Lier *(confectionery)*
  Manage *(confectionery)*
  Puurs *(food products)*

England
  Braintree *(frozen foods)*
  King's Lynn *(canned foods)*
  Peterlee *(frozen foods)*
  Salford *(frozen foods)*
  York *(refrigerated foods)*
France
  Thiviers *(canned foods)*
  Bondues *(confectionery)*
Germany
  Cuxhaven *(refrigerated salads)*
  Hamburg *(refrigerated salads)*
  Frankfurt am Main *(canned foods)*
  Maisach *(distributor food products)*
  Ratingen *(distributor of imported foods specialties)*
Ireland
  Middleton *(frozen and refrigerated foods)*
Italy
  Stradella *(canned foods)*
  Treviso *(canned foods)*

Scotland
  Glasgow *(frozen foods)*
The Netherlands
  Breda *(confectionery)*
  Raamsdonkveer *(confectionery)*
  Zoetermeer *(trading of imported food specialties)*
  Zundert *(frozen foods)*

ASIA
Australia
  Melbourne *(juices)*
  Mernda *(mushrooms)*
  Shepparton *(canned foods)*
Hong Kong
  Hong Kong
    (distributor food products)
Japan
  Tokyo *(distributor food products)*
New Zealand
  Auckland
    (distributor food products)

UNITED STATES
  Reading, Pennsylvania
    (confectionery)

Source: Campbell Soup Company, 1993 *Annual Report.*

INFORMATION SYSTEMS

Campbell concentrates on using methods, technologies and brain power in the most efficient manner possible to eliminate non-value-added steps while improving overall processes. Campbell has upgraded its record-keeping databases to a universal system that tracks every step of the manufacturing process. This marks the transition to a worldwide Campbell Integrated Manufacturing Information System (CIMIS) and looms as the biggest and most promising computer system undertaking in company history. At Campbell's U.S. plants alone, savings from CIMIS are estimated at $22 million annually.

As one of the first companies to adopt Efficient Consumer Response (ECR), Campbell brings value to the grocery shopper while taking costs out of the total supply chain. Driven by every-day-low-procurement pricing, reengineered promotion programs offer incentives without adding cost. In addition, Category Management and Continuous Product Replenishment programs improve overall efficiencies by maximizing return on retail space and reducing inventories, respectively. Total ECR program benefits translate to about a $30-million earnings improvement by 1996.

Campbell's world-class manufacturing and product development technologies rank among the most innovative in the industry. At the new Technology Center in Camden, the best technical and manufacturing concepts are perfected before production begins at plant locations. Along with developing and applying many new technologies—such as fat-sparing and sodium-sparing techniques—the Center is streamlining costs, improving productivity, and providing competitive advantage. During fiscal 1993, savings from new technologies totaled about $25 million.

CAMPBELL NORTH AND SOUTH AMERICA

Operating earnings for Campbell North and South America were $635 million in 1993, compared to $790 million in 1992. Net sales were $4.6 billion in 1993, an increase of 2 percent over 1992. Soup volume was up 2.5 percent despite the one less week, with strong performances by Home Cookin and Healthy Request ready-to-serve soups. In the competitive frozen food business, Swanson kids' meals and Great Start breakfast sandwiches did well. The newly introduced Pepperidge Farm gravies delivered strong volume growth as did Food Service frozen products, Vlasic pickles, and Argentina operations.

The Campbell North and South America Division was formed in January 1992, to take advantage of the emerging "common market" linking Canada, the United States, Mexico, and Argentina. The western hemisphere's eventual emergence as a powerful trading bloc will provide a critical advantage toward competing with trading blocs of the Pacific Rim countries and the European Common Market. Locations in North and South America are identified in the map in Exhibit 32–3.

Major business sectors comprising Campbell North and South America include soup, prepared foods, pork and beans, V8, condiments, and sauces. Soup has made the Campbell name synonymous with quality and convenience has grown. From the days when an ad featuring the famous Campbell Kid proudly boasted "21 kinds of soup . . . 10 cents a can" the familiar red and white labeled condensed soups have since led the way for the more recent introductions of dry, microwavable, and ramen noodle soups. In October 1991, Campbell Soup Company further strengthened its position in the fast growing ramen noodle market when it acquired Sanwa Foods Inc., the third largest marketer of ramen noodle products in the United States.

Americans purchase more than 2.5 billion cans of Campbell's soups annually, and on average have nine cans on their pantry shelf at any time during the year. Campbell Soup brands include Home Cookin, Chunky, and Healthy Request. Integral parts of the soup business are Swanson's canned chicken, beef, and vegetable broths.

Campbell's share of the total prepared soup market is 56 percent, with total wet soup share at 81.8 percent. Campbell's ready-to-serve soups account for almost 10 percent of Campbell's total wet soup share. Other components of the total prepared soup market include dehydrated and ramen noodle soups in several types of packaging including pouches, single-serve cups, and block forms.

Swift-Armour A.S.A., headquartered in Buenos Aires, with production facilities in Rosario, began operation in Argentina in 1907 and has remained a leading producer of beef products. Acquired in 1980 by Campbell Soup Company, the Swift-Armour brand is well known for its beef and other products. Since 1990, Argentina has experienced an economic boom that has benefitted long-suffering Argentines. Consumers now have more disposable income, and as a result Swift-Armour's domestic sales are up strongly. Market share for all Swift-Armour canned meat products has increased from 50 to 62 percent. The present plant at Rosario operates at 100 percent capacity but a new plant is scheduled to open in early 1993 to replace the current facility. Swift-Armour's domestic product lines include canned meats, marmalades, edible fats, ketchup, canned vegetables, and canned fruits under the Swift label, and pastas and edible oils under the La Patrona brand.

In 1992, Swift-Armour began an aggressive marketing campaign to introduce Campbell product lines into Argentina after market tests showed an excellent predisposition for the products among consumers. Argentines prefer cream soups such as Campbell's mushroom, celery, chicken asparagus, and the split pea and bean soup varieties. Campbell's Teddy Bear soup offers appeal for the children's market. V8 juice is an entirely new category to the Argentine market and its introduction offers great growth potential for this popular beverage.

Swift-Armour is the largest beef exporter in Argentina and exports canned meat to some 50 countries. Frozen meat is exported to the United States, Italy, and Japan, and most of the beef which is processed into Campbell's soups in the United States comes from Swift-Armour. In addition, the agribusiness division manages 570,000 acres with over 100,000 head of cattle.

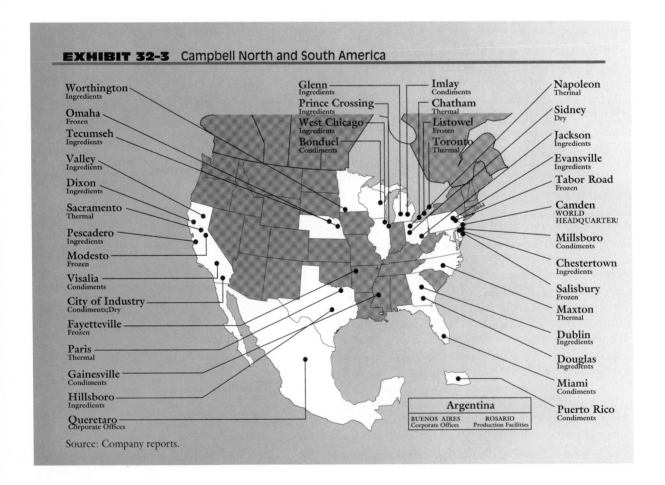

EXHIBIT 32-3 Campbell North and South America

Source: Company reports.

The Biscuit and Bakery Division reported operating earnings of $101 million in 1993. Net sales increased 23 percent to $999 million. These increases stem mainly from attaining 58 percent ownership of Arnotts in fiscal 1993, which contributed $170 million in sales. Previously, Campbell owned 33 percent and accounted for its investment on the equity method. Arnotts has strong earnings growth in the year.

Pepperidge Farm volume increased slightly for the year with sales trends improving significantly in the fourth quarter led by the introduction of Goldfish cookies and frozen garlic bread and rolls. Earnings of Delacre in Europe were down because of a sluggish European economy, the costs of starting up new production lines, and the introduction of the new Biscuits Maison, patterned after Pepperidge Farm's American Collection and Old Fashioned cookies.

In September 1990, Campbell Soup Company consolidated its U.S. and international biscuit and bakery operations into one organization to facilitate the strategic exchange of information between the businesses and, in turn, to grow the company's worldwide brands and products. The new organization comprises Pepperidge Farm, Incorporated; Biscuits Delacre; and Arnotts Biscuits Limited. Campbell Biscuit and Bakery locations are indicated on the map in Exhibit 32–4.

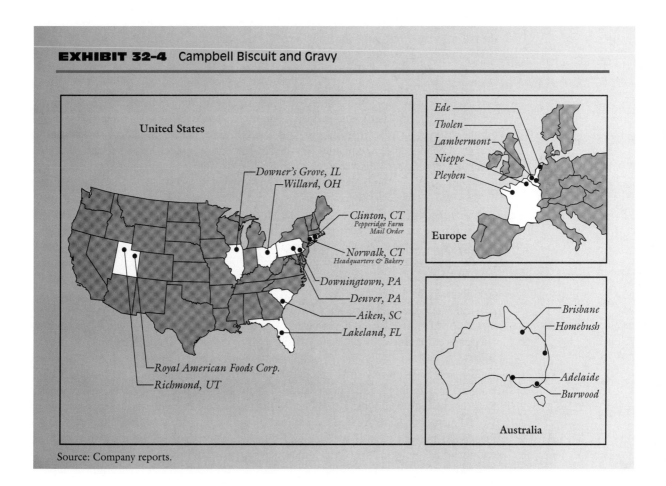

EXHIBIT 32-4 Campbell Biscuit and Gravy

Source: Company reports.

The brands offer a wide variety of fresh baked goods including breads, rolls, croutons, stuffing, cookies, and crackers; snack items including Arnotts' macadamia nuts; and frozen foods including pastries, cakes, pizzas, danish, single-serve desserts, and muffins. The products are offered through traditional marketing outlets as well as, in the case of Pepperidge Farm, through food service, thrift stores, and mail order distribution.

In 1991, Pepperidge Farm completed its $181 million bakery and biscuit plant in Denver, Pennsylvania—the most technologically advanced bakery in the world. The breakthrough technology employed in this new facility provides impetus to drive profitable volume growth through new products.

CAMPBELL EUROPE/ASIA

Campbell Europe/Asia reported an operating loss of $91 million after special charges of $144 million. Before these charges, operating earnings increased 23 percent over 1992 to $53 million, due primarily to significant improvements in the United Kingdom and Germany. Sales increased 2 percent to $1.02 billion in 1993 from $1.0 billion in 1992. Both sales and earnings benefitted from the acquisition of Fray Bentos, the leading premium canned-meat brand in the United Kingdom, and from the company's acquisition of the remaining 50 percent ownership of the Spring Valley juice business in Australia. Campbell Europe locations are shown on the map in Exhibit 32–5.

Campbell's international presence can be found in Great Britain, Europe, and Asia under Betis, Pleyben, Exeter, Unger, Freshbake, Groko, Logro, Beeck, Kattus, Probare, Lacroix, Granny's, Lamy-Lutti, Devos-Lemmens, Imperial, Kwatta, Tubble Gum, Laforest Perigord, Chantenac and many other food and confectionery brands, including world famous Godiva chocolates.

Campbell Frozen Food has four plants located in Glasgow, Salford, Braintree, and Peterlee in Scotland and England servicing the retail and food service markets. The main products are savory pastries and pies, sausages, quiche, sausage rolls, shepherd's pie, ready meals, meat products such as burgers, and snacks and small cake confectionery products. Brand names include Campbell's, Freshbake, and private label for supermarket stock.

Groko (Zundert, Netherlands) was formed in 1957, following the merger of two Dutch food companies. Acquired by Campbell Soup Company in 1979, Groko processes and distributes frozen, prepared vegetable and potato products exclusively to major supermarket chains with distribution contracted through independent frozen food distributors.

Campbell Asia is based in Hong Kong and oversees trading in Hong Kong, Singapore, Malaysia, Taiwan, and Korea. Sales agents and exporters handle sales to the Philippines, Guam, Indonesia, and the Pacific Islands. Campbell brands include Campbell's condensed soups, Chunky Ready-to-Serve, Swanson Broth, Swanson Condensed, Campbell's Beans, V8 and Tomato Juices, Franco-American pasta and gravies, Prego, and Spring Valley juices.

Campbell Australia is headquarted in Melbourne, Australia, with a plant at Shepparton to serve the Pacific Basin island countries including New Zealand, Indonesia, and the Philippines. In addition to Campbell's red and white label soups, the division markets Chunky and Chunky-for-One brand soups, V8 Juice and Spring Valley fruit juices, Campbell's spaghetti sauce, tomato paste, Heat 'n' Serve canned meals, Real Stocks (liquid cooking stock), and Oriental Sauces. Baco luxury flavored milk and Iso-Tonic sports drink are brands featured in the Australasia market. Campbell's commands 26 percent of this market, and another enterprise, Melbourne Mushrooms, command 31 percent of the bulk and prepackaged fresh mushroom market.

Campbell Japan is responsible for the sales of Campbell products throughout Japan. There are three sales offices located in Tokyo, Okinawa, and Osaka. Products sold

EXHIBIT 32-5 Campbell Europe

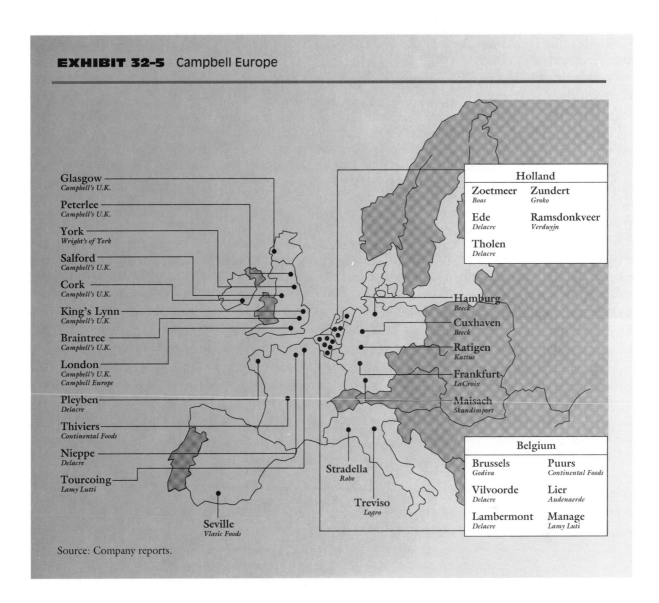

Source: Company reports.

include condensed and ready-to-serve soup, premium chocolate, red juices, and biscuits under the Campbell's Godiva Chocolates, V8, Pepperidge Farm, and Delacre brands.

NEW STRATEGIES

Campbell has consolidated its frozen food operations, closed its facilities in Salisbury, Maryland and Philadelphia, Pennsylvania, and shifted certain operations to the Omaha, Nebraska, plant. Campbell plans to divest a number of businesses over several years and to make further acquisitions. Campbell in 1993 acquired the majority interest in Arnotts Limited in Australia. Arnotts was Australia's leading biscuit manufacturer. By virtue of this acquisition, Campbell's Biscuit and Bakery division ranks as the fourth largest biscuit maker in the world. During 1993, Campbell established a biscuit headquarters in Hong Kong, where consumer trials of cookies and crackers have begun. Other test markets include Singapore, Taiwan, and Korea.

Campbell recently acquired Fray Benthos, the United Kingdom's leading brand of premium canned meats. This leverages the company's heat-processing technology used to produce canned soup, as well as its meat-processing expertise. Identify and evaluate some other foreign food companies that Campbell could potentially acquire; make some specific recommendations to CEO Johnson in this regard. Should Johnson alter Campbell's organizational structure? Would a product type structure (e.g., a soup division, a frozen foods division, a cookies division) be more effective than the geographic/product combination type structure? Develop several alternative organizational charts for Johnson and specify the advantages and disadvantages of each design for the company.

Let's say CEO Johnson asks you to go to your college library and gather information necessary to develop a five-year strategic plan for Campbell Soup Company. Include a mission statement for Campbell Soup Company. Include five-year pro forma financial statements to show the impact of your recommendations and an EPS/EBIT analysis to determine whether Campbell should use debt or stock to raise additional capital. (Exhibits 32–6 through 32–11 provide 1993 statements from

EXHIBIT 32-6 Campbell Soup Company Consolidated Statements of Earnings (*Millions of dollars except per share amounts*)

	1993 (52 WEEKS)	1992 (53 WEEKS)	1991 (52 WEEKS)
NET SALES	$6,586.2	$6,263.2	$6,204.1
Cost and expenses			
Cost of products sold	4,027.8	3,963.1	4,095.5
Marketing and selling expenses	1,208.3	1,050.0	956.2
Administrative expenses	306.7	282.3	306.7
Research and development expenses	68.8	59.7	56.3
Interest expense	82.8	101.9	116.2
Interest income	(9.0)	(15.3)	(26.0)
Other expense	28.0	22.2	31.8
Divestiture and restructuring charges	353.0	—	—
Total costs and expenses	6,066.4	5,463.9	5,536.7
Earnings before taxes	519.8	799.3	667.4
Taxes on earnings	262.6	308.8	265.9
Earnings before cumulative effect of accounting changes	257.2	490.5	401.5
Cumulative effect of accounting changes	249.0	—	—
NET EARNINGS	$ 8.2	$ 490.5	$ 401.5
PER SHARE			
Earnings before cumulative effect of accounting changes	$ 1.02	$ 1.95	$ 1.58
Cumulative effect of accounting changes	.99	—	—
NET EARNINGS	$ .03	$ 1.95	$ 1.58
Weighted average shares outstanding	251.9	251.7	254.0

Source: Campbell Soup Company, 1993 *Annual Report*.

Campbell's *Annual Report*.) CEO Johnson must reverse the negative financial trends mentioned at the beginning of this case. Do all you can to help Campbell achieve the specific objectives outlined earlier.

EXHIBIT 32-7 Campbell Soup Company Consolidated Balance Sheets (*Millions of dollars*)

	AUGUST 1, 1993	AUGUST 2, 1992
CURRENT ASSETS		
Cash and cash equivalents	$ 62.6	$ 112.1
Other temporary investments, at cost which approximates market	6.9	5.6
Accounts receivable	646.3	577.1
Inventories	804.2	717.9
Prepaid expenses	166.2	88.9
Total current assets	1,686.2	1,501.6
PLANT ASSETS, NET OF DEPRECIATION	2,264.4	1,965.8
INTANGIBLE ASSETS, NET OF AMORTIZATION	596.0	441.8
OTHER ASSETS	350.9	444.6
Total assets	$4,897.5	$4,353.8
CURRENT LIABILITIES		
Notes payable	$669.4	$ 293.7
Payable to suppliers and others	510.0	497.8
Accrued liabilities	498.9	363.9
Dividend payable	63.5	49.2
Accrued income taxes	108.7	95.1
Total current liabilities	1,850.5	1,299.7
LONG-TERM DEBT	461.9	693.3
NONPENSION POSTRETIREMENT BENEFITS	369.7	—
OTHER LIABILITIES	511.4	333.2
Total liabilities	3,193.5	2,326.2
SHAREOWNERS' EQUITY		
Preferred stock; authorized 40.0 shares; none issued	—	—
Capital stock, $.075 par value; authorized 280.0 shares; issued 271.2 shares	20.3	20.3
Capital surplus	149.1	116.2
Earnings retained in the business	2,002.0	2,224.5
Capital stock in treasury, 19.5 shares in 1993 and 20.1 shares in 1992, at cost	(428.6)	(401.9)
Cumulative translation adjustments	(38.8)	68.5
Total shareowners' equity	1,704.0	2,027.6
Total liabilities and shareowners' equity	$4,897.5	$4,353.8

Source: Campbell Soup Company, 1993 *Annual Report*.

EXHIBIT 32-8 Campbell Soup Company Consolidated Statements of Cash Flows (*Millions of dollars*)

	1993	1992	1991
CASH FLOWS FROM OPERATING ACTIVITIES			
Net earnings	$8.2	$490.5	$401.5
To reconcile net earnings to net cash provided by operating activities:			
Divestitures and restructuring provisions	353.0	—	—
Cumulative effect of accounting changes	249.0	—	—
Depreciation and amortization	242.2	216.2	208.6
Deferred taxes	(48.0)	34.4	35.5
Other, net	41.2	25.1	63.2
Net change in accounts receivable	(73.4)	(16.6)	17.1
Net change in inventories	(90.2)	7.1	48.7
Net change in other current assets and liabilities	(29.6)	(12.4)	30.6
Net cash provided by operating activities	652.4	744.3	805.2
CASH FLOWS FROM INVESTING ACTIVITIES:			
Purchases of plant assets	(366.3)	(336.5)	(361.1)
Sales of plant assets	37.7	25.5	43.2
Businesses acquired	(261.9)	(30.8)	(180.1)
Sales of businesses	9.5	2.6	67.4
Net change in other assets	(19.0)	(55.0)	(57.8)
Net change in other temporary investments	(1.3)	7.2	9.7
Net cash used in investing activities	(601.3)	(387.0)	(478.7)
CASH FLOWS FROM FINANCING ACTIVITIES:			
Long-term borrowings	1.6	5.8	402.8
Repayments of long-term borrowings	(222.7)	(221.6)	(129.9)
Net change in borrowings with less than three month maturities	389.4	80.5	(137.9)
Other short-term borrowings	55.7	77.1	117.3
Repayments of other short-term borrowings	(98.0)	(74.4)	(206.4)
Dividends paid	(216.4)	(166.4)	(137.5)
Treasury stock purchases	(42.3)	(149.6)	(175.6)
Treasury stock issued	35.5	19.2	47.7
Other, net	—	(.1)	(.1)
Net cash used in financing activities	(97.2)	(429.5)	(219.6)
Effect of exchange rate changes on cash	(3.4)	5.4	(8.7)
NET CHANGE IN CASH AND CASH EQUIVALENTS	(49.5)	(66.8)	98.2
Cash and cash equivalents at beginning of year	112.1	178.9	80.7
CASH AND CASH EQUIVALENTS AT END OF YEAR	$62.6	$112.1	$178.9

Source: Campbell Soup Company, 1993 *Annual Report.*

	PREFERRED STOCK	CAPITAL STOCK	CAPITAL SURPLUS	EARNINGS RETAINED IN THE BUSINESS	CAPITAL STOCK IN TREASURY	CUMULATIVE TRANSLATION ADJUSTMENTS	TOTAL SHAREOWNERS' EQUITY
Balance at July 29, 1990	—	$20.3	$61.9	$1,653.3	$(107.2)	$63.5	$1,691.8
Net earnings				401.5			401.5
Cash dividends ($.56 per share)				(142.2)			(142.2)
Treasury stock purchased					(175.6)		(175.6)
Treasury stock issued under Management incentive and Stock option plans			45.4		12.4		57.8
Translation adjustments						(29.9)	(29.9)
Sale of foreign operations						(10.0)	(10.0)
Balance at July 28, 1991	—	20.3	107.3	1,912.6	(270.4)	23.6	1,793.4
Net earnings				490.5			490.5
Cash dividends ($.71 per share)				(178.6)			(178.6)
Treasury stock purchased					(149.6)		(149.6)
Treasury stock issued under Management incentive and Stock option plans			8.9		18.1		27.0
Translation adjustments						44.9	44.9
Balance at August 2, 1992	—	20.3	116.2	2,224.5	(401.9)	68.5	2,027.6
Net earnings				8.2			8.2
Cash dividends ($.915 per share)				(230.7)			(230.7)
Treasury stock purchased					(42.3)		(42.3)
Treasury stock issued under Management incentive and Stock option plans			32.9		15.6		48.5
Translation adjustments						(107.3)	(107.3)
Balance at August 1, 1993	—	$20.3	$149.1	$2,002.0	$(428.6)	$(38.8)	$1,704.0

Source: Campbell Soup Company, 1993 *Annual Report.*

EXHIBIT 32-10 Campbell Soup Company Changes in Number of Shares (*Thousands of shares*)

	ISSUED	OUTSTANDING	IN TREASURY
Balance at July 29, 1990	271,245.4	258,538.0	12,707.4
Treasury stock purchased		(6,790.8)	6,790.8
Treasury stock issued under Management incentive and Stock option plans		2,260.4	(2,260.4)
Balance at July 28, 1991	271,245.4	254,007.6	17,237.8
Treasury stock purchased		(3,986.1)	3,986.1
Treasury stock issued under Management incentive and Stock option plans		1,146.7	(1,146.7)
Balance at August 2, 1992	271,245.4	251,168.2	20,077.2
Treasury stock purchased		(1,104.5)	1,104.5
Treasury stock issued under Management incentive and Stock option plans		1,642.5	(1,642.5)
Balance at August 1, 1993	271,245.4	251,706.2	19,539.2

Source: Campbell Soup Company, 1993 *Annual Report*.

EXHIBIT 32-11 Campbell Soup Company Notes to Consolidated Financial Statements (*Millions of dollars*)

	1993	1992	1991
Net sales			
United States	$4,743.6	$4,649.2	$4,495.6
Europe	1,050.2	1,042.6	1,149.1
Other countries	916.7	652.4	656.0
Adjustments and eliminations	(124.3)	(81.0)	(96.6)
Consolidated	$6,586.2	$6,263.2	$6,204.1
Earnings (loss) before taxes			
United States	$ 716.6	$ 809.6	$ 694.8
Europe	(170.4)	44.7	48.8
Other countries	99.4	69.6	55.0
	645.6	923.9	798.6
Unallocated corporate expenses	(52.0)	(38.0)	(41.0)
Interest, net	(73.8)	(86.6)	(90.2)
Consolidated	$ 519.8	$ 799.3	$ 667.4
Identifiable assets			
United States	$2,286.6	$2,802.4	$2,693.4
Europe	668.7	831.0	711.3
Other countries	1,542.2	720.4	744.3
Consolidated	$4,897.5	$4,353.8	$4,149.0

Source: Campbell Soup Company, 1993 *Annual Report*.

BORDEN—1994

Headquartered in Columbus, Ohio, Borden's (614-225-4000) net income for 1993 was a negative $630.7 million, down 73 percent from 1992. A. S. D'Amato, chairman and chief executive officer of Borden, provided his view of Borden in the company's 1992 *Annual Report:*

> My view of Borden operating results—and those since the fourth quarter of 1990 when we last reported improved earnings—can be expressed in two words: totally unacceptable. In my opinion, the reasons for Borden's lack of performance in recent years are fundamental and recurring. They require drastic remedy. The retailers who make up Borden's primary customer base have changed both in composition and operation. Borden's marketing has not. Today's retailers demand a highly-focused, integrated "one-company" approach. Yet, until recently, Borden operated eight sales and seven separate distribution organizations within the Company. In one instance, we had as many as 28 people representing various Borden brands calling on a single nationwide retailer.

Mr. D'Amato resigned in 1993. The new Borden President and Chief Executive Officer is Ervin R. Shames. The new Borden Chairman is Frank J. Tasco. Borden has three major operating divisions: North American Foods, International Foods, and Packaging and Industrial Products. Exhibit 33–1 presents a 1993 summary of the divisions' brands, strengths, and strategies. Exhibit 33–2 lists Borden's principal products by brand.

NORTH AMERICAN FOODS

The North American Foods division of Borden includes North American pasta and sauce, niche grocery products, and U.S. dairy operations. In 1993, these businesses incurred a loss in operating income of $2.3 million, on a sales decline of 12.1 percent to $2.67 billion.

Borden is the leader in a wide range of small-to-medium-sized grocery products that are among the best-known brands in the U.S. food industry—Cracker Jack candied popcorn, Eagle Brand sweetened condensed milk, ReaLemon lemon juice, Wyler's bouillon, and Snow's clam products to name just a few. Together, these products provide Borden with a major presence in North American supermarkets. Borden also is the U.S. foodservice industry's leading supplier of individual-serving products and a major supplier of bulk-size items. Overseas, Borden has a growing European grocery products business, including a joint interest in Spain's number one soup and bouillon producer.

Pasta and Sauce. Borden is the world's largest pasta company. Its flagship Creamette brand is America's best-selling pasta. Borden's Catelli brand leads in Canada; Adria is number one in Brazil; and the Albadoro and Monder brands in Italy are regional favorites. Borden accounts for nearly one-third of North American retail branded dry pasta dollar sales. Borden also is the only major North American pasta company with a full line of pasta sauces, led by Classico—the best-selling U.S. and Canadian premium pasta sauce.

Borden's U.S. and Canadian pasta and sauce sales declined in 1993. However, sales of Classico were up 12 percent in 1993. Classico sales were supported by television advertising and direct mail marketing in key markets. The program will be extended to additional markets in 1994. Classico results also benefitted from the introduction of a seventh flavor, di Sorrento with onion and garlic, and full-year sales of Classico di Parma four cheese sauce and Classico di Salerno with sweet peppers and onions.

EXHIBIT 33-1 Borden at a Glance

NORTH AMERICAN FOODS 1993 SALES: $2,672 MILLION

MAJOR BRANDS AND BUSINESSES	STRENGTHS	STRATEGIES
Pasta and Sauce		
• Creamette pasta sold across the United States	• North American pasta leader participating in all market segments—dry branded, private label, foodservice, ingredient	• Recover, expand volume through improved customer service
• Catelli pasta and sauce in Canada	• Creamette and Catelli—both number one nationally	• Improve efficiency, costs through better supply chain management
• Regional U.S. and Canadian pasta brands including Prince, R•F, Anthony's, Gioia and Ronco	• Leading regional brands	• Strengthen brands with added marketing support, emphasizing quality
• Classico premium pasta sauce	• Only major pasta maker with a full line of sauces	
• Aunt Millie's pasta sauce	• Pasta quality edge	
	• Classico—best-selling premium sauce in United States and Canada	• Leverage overall advantages in scale, capacity, cost, brand reach
	• Low-cost production base	• Develop new products
	• Unmatched capacity, distribution	
Dairy		
• Borden, Meadow Gold, Viva and Lite Line milk, ice cream, frozen desserts, cultured products	• Strong consumer brand recognition	• Recover lost volume through improved pricing and trade promotion policies
• Borden process cheese and Lite Line diet cheese products	• Dairy leader in many regional markets	• Reduce costs through improved distribution, better plant utilization, lower overhead
	• Number one in sliced diet cheese domestically	
	• Elsie the Cow—one of the most recognized food trademarks	• Develop new products. Further upgrade ice cream quality
Niche Grocery		
• Market basket of familiar food brands, including:	• Number one or strong number two positions in small to medium size grocery categories	• Increase advertising and other marketing support behind key products
–Cracker Jack popcorn and peanuts,	• Significant presence overall in U.S. supermarkets	• Reposition products for new appeal, uses
–Eagle Brand sweetened condensed milk,	• Track record of good profits and returns	• Improve quality and value
–ReaLemon juice,	• Opportunities for growth	• Develop new products that offer added value to consumers
–Wyler's bouillon and		
–Cremora non-dairy creamer		

EXHIBIT 33-1 *Continued*

INTERNATIONAL FOODS 1993 SALES: $930 MILLION

MAJOR BRANDS AND BUSINESSES	STRENGTHS	STRATEGIES

European Bakery

- Nur Hier, Nuschelberg, Stefansback, Lecker Backer, Kamps, and bakeries in Germany; Prima Pek in Hungary
- Weber, Jaus and Golden Toast packaged baked goods and breads sold in supermarkets and other retail outlets across Germany

- Unmatched German retail network
- Among the leaders in industrial/commercial baked goods
- Largest hamburger bun supplier in Germany

- Expand German retail bakery network through internal growth, acquisitions, as well as German hamburger bun business through new plant
- Expand further into Central Europe
- Lower costs of industrial operation
- Develop new products

International Dairy

- KLIM milk powder
- Dairy and cheese business in Latin America

- World's second-leading milk powder: Borden's most global brand
- Well established in growing Pacific Rim and Latin American markets

- Expand recently launched varieties—KLIM Lite Line low fat and KLIM Super Kid and Growing Up specially fortified milk powders
- Use joint venture plant in China to support growth in other areas of the Far East as well

European Grocery and Pasta

- Joint interest in Spain's Gallina Blanca dry soup and bouillon business
- Niche grocery products including ReaLemon juice across Europe and Cocio bottled chocolate drinks in Scandinavia
- Monder dry-filled pasta and Albadoro regional pasta in Italy

- Market leadership in Spain in dry soup and bouillon; expanding positions in other nations
- Strong positions in most niche markets
- Leading European brand of dry-filled pasta

- Build soup and bouillon exports to Africa, Latin America and Asia
- Add bouillon business in China via joint venture plant
- Expand niche grocery brands to other European countries
- Export Italian pasta beyond Europe to Asia and North America

PACKAGING AND INDUSTRIAL PRODUCTS
1993 SALES: $1,904 MILLION

Adhesives and Resins

- High performance adhesives and industrial resins for home building, construction, foundry and industrial applications

- World leader in forest products adhesives; presence in most global markets
- Major supplier of foundry and industrial resins

- Expand leadership position globally
- Selectively expand to meet customer needs
- Maintain technical leadership with value-added products

EXHIBIT 33-1 *Continued*

PACKAGING AND INDUSTRIAL PRODUCTS 1993 SALES (CONT.)

MAJOR BRANDS AND BUSINESSES	STRENGTHS	STRATEGIES
Decorative Products • The best-known consumer and commercial wallcovering brands including Wall-Tex, Sunworthy, Borden Home, Borges, and Crown	• World leader in wallcovering • Largest share of market in North America and United Kingdom • Strong position across all retail channels of trade	• Grow volume with new products such as coordinated home furnishings and licensed products (e.g. Disney) • Expand distribution with in-store merchandising via mass marketers and home centers • Continue cost reductions
Consumer Adhesives • Elmer's adhesives and home improvement products • Krazy Glue instant glues	• Top-selling consumer adhesives and instant glues with strong consumer brand recognition	• Grow sales volume for Elmer's and Krazy Glue adhesives with new products, increased consumer advertising
Plastic Film and Packaging • Resinite and Sealwrap vinyl foodwraps; Proponite food packaging; and Loadmaster, Resinex and Resinite palletwrap films	• U.S. leader in vinyl foodwraps • Good position in European and Far Eastern flexible packaging	• Improve profitability with cost reductions and operating efficiencies

Source: Borden *Annual Report,* 1993.

Albadoro S.p.A., one of Borden's two Italian pasta companies, posted higher sales and income in 1992, and increased plant capacity by 20 percent in 1993 to help meet the growing worldwide demand for high quality Italian pasta. Monder Aliment, S.p.A. in Italy, a leading marketer and exporter of dry filled pastas, added several new products in 1993 and achieved a record share of Italian sales.

Gallina Blanca, Borden's joint venture Spanish food company and a world leader in dry soups and bouillon, remained number one in Spain by offering several new varieties, including low sodium and children's soups. Gallina Blanca achieved record sales of Jumbo bouillon in key African markets and began bouillon production in China during 1993 through a joint venture.

Catelli Healthy Harvest pasta and sauces were introduced in 1993 in Canada. The line features whole wheat and other pastas with added fiber and protein, and pasta sauces that are low in fat and sodium.

Borden recently began operations at its St. Louis pasta hyperplant—North America's largest and one of the world's most advanced pasta plants. New pasta lines are being added at hyperplants in Phoenix, Arizona; Lowell, Massachusetts; and Warren, Michigan; and an expansion of a Montreal, Quebec, pasta and sauce hyper-

EXHIBIT 33-2 Principal Borden Products by Brand

NORTH AMERICAN FOODS

PASTA AND SAUCE	NICHE GROCERY	DAIRY

PASTA AND SAUCE

Classico pasta sauce
Creamette
Silver Award
Albadoro

Regional:
Anthony's (Southern California, Arizona and Nevada)
Aunt Millie's spaghetti sauce (Northeast)
Bravo (western New York)
Dutch Maid (Northeast and North Central)
Gioia (western New York)
Globe A-1 (California)
Goodman's (Northeast and Miami)
Luxury (Gulf Coast)
Merlino's (Pacific Northwest)
Mrs. Grass (Chicago)
New Mill (Midwest)
Prince pasta and sauce (Northeast and North Central)
R•F (Midwest, Southwest and Colorado)
Red Cross (Midwest and Tennessee)
Ronco pasta and sauce (Southeast and Mid-South)
Vimco (Pennsylvania and Ohio)
Winsom (Midwest)

Canada:
Catelli pasta and sauce, Catelli Healthy Harvest pasta and sauce, Creamette, Lancia pasta and sauce, Romi, Splendor, Gattuso pasta and pasta/pizza sauce, Golden Wheat and Bravo sauce

Puerto Rico:
Criada pasta sauce

NICHE GROCERY

Bennett's sauces
Borden egg nog
Borden, Serv, Americana, Chatsworth and Pitch 'R' Pak individual portion control and bulk foodservice products
Campfire marshmallows
Cary's maple syrup
Coco Lopez cream of coconut and fruit drink mixes
Cracker Jack caramel and butter-toffee coated popcorn and peanuts
Cremora and Cremora Lite non-dairy creamer
Eagle Brand sweetened condensed milk
Kava acid neutralized instant coffee
MacDonald's maple syrup
Maple Orchards maple syrup
MBT broth
Meadow Gold sweetened condensed milk
Mrs. Grass soup and dip mixes
None Such mincemeat
ReaLemon lemon juice from concentrate and 100% pure refrigerated lemon juice
ReaLime lime juice from concentrate
Soup Starter, Stew Starter and Minestrone Starter dry soup mixes
Steero bouillon and broth products
Wyler's bouillon and broth products

Regional:
Borden, Gregg's and Re-Mi foodservice mayonnaise, salad dressings and soup bases (Midwest, Southeast and Southwest)

DAIRY

Borden whole, lowfat, reduced lactose, skim and chocolate milks and buttermilk, cottage cheese, sour cream, whipping cream and other creams, egg nog, orange juice and fruit drinks; Hi-Protein lowfat milk; Light sugar-free chocolate lowfat milk and nonfat yogurt; Lite Line protein-fortified skim milk, cottage cheese, sour cream and yogurt; Fat Free sour cream; and Thirstee Smash fruit drinks

Borden ice cream and frozen novelty bars, sandwiches and pops, frozen yogurt and yogurt pops; Eagle Brand ice cream; Fat Free frozen desserts; Lady Borden ice cream; Light ice milk; and Frostick, Mississippi Mud and Juice Stix frozen novelties

Borden process cheese products—regular, light and fat free, Lite Line cheese products and CheezTwo process cheese substitute

Fisher cheese substitute products, Sandwich-Mate slices and Ched-O-Mate, Pizza-Mate, Salad-Mate and Taco-Mate shredded products

Meadow Gold whole, lowfat, skim and chocolate milks and buttermilk, cottage cheese, sour cream, whipping cream and other creams, egg nog, orange juice and fruit drinks; Viva lowfat milks, protein-fortified skim milk, cottage cheese, sour cream and yogurt, sugar-free chocolate lowfat milk, nonfat yogurt and

EXHIBIT 33-2 *Continued*

NORTH AMERICAN FOODS		
PASTA AND SAUCE	**NICHE GROCERY**	**DAIRY**
	Country Store instant mashed potatoes (Midwest and Southwest)	cottage cheese; and Mountain High yogurt
	Dime Brand sweetened condensed milk (Southwest)	**Regional:** KLIM whole milk powder (New York)
	Laura Scudder's natural peanut butter (Mountain, Western and Texas)	**Puerto Rico:** Nevada and Carnaval ice
	Magnolia Brand sweetened condensed milk (New York and Miami)	
	Sippin Pak aseptic fruit drinks (Southeast and Southwest)	
	Star Brand sweetened condensed milk (New York)	
	Canada: Eagle Brand sweetened condensed milk, Cracker Jack caramel and butter-toffee coated popcorn, ReaLemon lemon juice from concentrate, and Milk Mate milk flavorings	
	Puerto Rico: Borden cheeses Coco Lopez cream of coconut and cream fruit drink mixes La Famosa juices and nectars	

Source: Borden *Annual Report,* 1993.

plant was completed. Borden recently closed two small pasta plants at Winnipeg, Manitoba, and Harahan, Louisiana.

To rectify Borden's problems in Pasta and Sauce, a new President and all new sales managers were hired in 1993. A new pasta marketing campaign was launched with television and radio advertising expenditures for Borden pasta brands reaching $8 million annually in 1994, up from $3 million in 1993.

Niche Grocery. Sales and net income of Borden's Niche Grocery operations declined in 1993 although several brands did well, such as Borden's Eagle Brand sweetened condensed milk, Cracker Jack candied popcorn, and Wyler's and Steero

Bouillon. Income was down in ReaLemon juice, Cremora and Cremora Lite non-dairy creamers, Mrs. Grass dry soups, Borden egg nog, Cracker Jack butter toffee, Cremora and Cremora Lite, and Borden's Snow's and Doxsee clam products.

Borden's cheese income was down in 1993 despite the national rollout of the Singleskeeper recyclable/recloseable package for Borden single-wrap cheese slices being completed. Outstanding consumer response to the Singleskeeper package helped Borden maintain its number two position in branded cheese. Borden Fat Free cheese slices in American, Sharp Cheddar and Swiss flavors are popular.

DAIRY

The Borden Dairy incurred a 1993 operating loss of about $25 million, while sales declined to about $1.1 billion. Dairy marketing was reorganized along product lines to provide tighter direction to the fluid milk business and to coordinate the marketing of higher margin ice cream, frozen desserts, and cultured products. A new president of Borden Dairy was hired in September 1993 and a number of new products were introduced, including Cracker Jack ice cream, Borden and Meadow Gold fat-free sour cream, Borden fat-free cheese slices, and Moooore Milk Singles.

The company's Borden, Meadow Gold, Viva, and Lite-Line brands are market leaders in fluid milk, ice cream and other frozen desserts, and cultured products, ranging from regular to lowfat to nonfat. Borden's fluid milk and cultured products businesses are concentrated in the South and West, while ice cream and frozen desserts are distributed across most of the nation. Borden also has dairy operations in Japan and Central America.

Sales of Borden's Lite-Line and Viva protein fortified skim milk have been increasing. A new regional distribution center in Houston, Texas, enables Borden to improve customer service. Sales of the company's Lady Borden premium ice cream have been expanded to the Midwest and Southeast. Increased advertising support and several new flavors have helped to boost Lady Borden ice cream sales. Borden recently launched its Fat Free frozen novelties in three flavors in key Midwest markets. Further expansion is planned for 1994.

Borden and Meadow Gold frozen yogurt and desserts are doing especially well in the Northeast and the Mid-Atlantic region. A major effort to revitalize Borden dairy brands is planned for 1993. The program includes national advertising and public relations campaigns. Packaging for all Borden dairy products has been redesigned to prominently feature an updated Elsie the Cow and a new, bolder Borden trademark. New dairy television commercials featuring an animated Elsie the Cow are appearing.

INTERNATIONAL FOODS

The International Foods division of Borden includes European bakery products, international milk powder, Latin American dairy, and European grocery and pasta products. This division's 1993 sales and net income declined 2.3 percent and 29.9 percent, respectively, to $930 million and $67.3 million. Borden is moving selectively elsewhere overseas—building on existing strengths and longstanding brand franchises, such as KLIM skim milk powder. KLIM International Milk Powder is the world's number-two-selling brand of milk powder. The KLIM brand was instrumental in getting Borden started overseas in the 1920s and is now Borden's most global brand. Sold in over 85 countries, KLIM is among the world's most popular brands of milk powder. Borden is building on KLIM brand strengths through line extensions that take advantage of improved living standards and increased consumer sophistication in many of its markets and by adding to the list of countries where KLIM milk powder is sold.

The first KLIM line extension was KLIM Lite-Line lowfat milk powder launched in 1991. KLIM Lite-Line initially was sold in the Far East, where it quickly became the best-selling brand of lowfat milk powder and is now expanding into the Middle East and Central America.

KLIM Super Kid, a specially fortified whole milk powder for children from the ages of three to seven, followed in 1992 and has done well in its Far Eastern introductory markets. Borden is expanding its presence in China. The company has acquired a joint interest in a Chinese milk powder plant and is doubling its size to produce KLIM brand milk powder.

Borden's KLIM milk powder posted even sales and net income in 1993 compared to 1992. KLIM Lite-Line lowfat milk powder was successful in several Far Eastern markets and in the Middle East and Central America. In its Far Eastern markets, KLIM Lite-Line is the best-selling brand of lowfat milk powder. KLIM Super Kid specially fortified whole milk powder for children three to seven was successful in Taiwan, Hong Kong, Singapore, and Malaysia.

Borden is trying to revitalize Lady Borden ice cream in Japan with more contemporary packaging, new flavors, a new convenience store line, consumer promotions, and increased advertising support. A reformulated Lady Borden Classic premium ice cream has regained much of the distribution in Japan that it had lost after the end of a local licensing agreement in 1991. Borden's Lady Borden Home Made ice cream is being repositioned for maximum appeal to youthful Japanese consumers of superpremium ice cream. A state-of-the art process cheese plant was completed at Nagano, Japan, in June. The plant produces Borden brand sliced cheese in the Singleskeeper package, cheese snacks, shredded natural cheese, and cheese powder for distribution across Japan.

EUROPEAN BAKERY PRODUCTS

Borden is Germany's largest producer and retailer of bakery products, primarily sweet snacks and specialty breads. Borden bought the 17-store Klems bakery in Wuppertal, near Dusseldorf, and the Zo-store Heede chain near Kassel in 1993. In total, Borden operates over 400 retail bakery outlets across Germany.

In Europe, Borden is focusing on promising growth opportunities in sweet snacks. The Company exited from the highly competitive salty snacks category in 1992 with the sale of its U.K. and Spanish units. Sales in Borden's European sweet snacks business have doubled since 1987 and are expected to grow to $600 million annually by 1996. Borden is already a leader in German sweet snacks and is rapidly expanding its presence elsewhere in Central Europe.

The flagship Wilhein Weber GmbH sweet snacks unit is one of Germany's largest commercial bakers, selling packaged products under the Weber, Jaus, and Golden Toast brand names through supermarkets and other retail outlets across the country. Weber manages six German regional bakery chains nationwide and has a joint interest in retail bakeries in Hungary. Borden's European Bakery Products had high sales and net income in 1993.

A sixth retail German bakery chain was acquired in October 1992. Kamps GmbH operates a chain of 23 retail outlets serving the Dusseldorf area. Kamps is being expanded into the nearby cities of Cologne, Duisburg, Essen, and Dortmund. Borden's sales are increasing.

In eastern Germany with the addition of delivery routes for packaged baked goods and growth of the Lecker Backer and Nur Hier retail chains, more outlets are planned for 1994.

Borden's joint venture in Hungary operates five retail stores in Budapest.

PACKAGING AND INDUSTRIAL PRODUCTS/DOMESTIC AND INTERNATIONAL

Borden's packaging and industrial products division has primary responsibility for non-food consumer products, films, resin, adhesives, and includes pasta in Brazil. Sales were up 1.3 percent in 1993 to $1.90 billion, but operating income declined 15.0 percent to $167.7 million. The division's results benefitted from sales and income gains in forest products adhesives and industrial resins, Latin American operations, worldwide wallcoverings, and consumer adhesives. These gains were offset primarily by declines in North American plastic films and packaging. Exhibits 33–3 and 33–4 present products and financials for three years for this division in context with the combined foods divisions.

Consumer Adhesives. Sales and income of Borden's consumer adhesives held steady in 1993 after posting slight gains in 1992. School Glue Gel was added to the Elmer's line of consumer adhesives complementing its popular Glue-All and original School Glue. Results in Krazy Glue instant glues and Accent craft paints declined. Borden's Latin America resin and plastic film sales and income improved. A resin plant in Cubatao, Brazil closed, 1993 as did a Borden pasta plant in Porte Alegre, Brazil. In pasta, Adria remains Brazil's best-selling national brand.

Borden's forest products adhesives, industrial resins, and specialty adhesives were recently consolidated into a single worldwide operation. Borden developed several new forest products adhesives, including low-formaldehyde-emitting resins, and faster-curing and moisture-tolerant phenolic resins. New resin technology also was developed for electronics, advanced composite materials, and high-speed lithography. Borden completed a 50 percent increase in phenolic resin capacity at Louisville, Kentucky, as well as forest products adhesives expansions at Edmonton, Alberta; Springfield, Oregon; and Sheboygan, Wisconsin.

Further expansions are planned at Peterlee in the United Kingdom and at Sarawak in Malaysia. Recent acquisitions in the United Kingdom complemented Borden's position as the leading European supplier of advanced foundry resins and included new technology for an advanced binder system. Borden's forest products adhesives operations in Australia, Malaysia, and the Philippines also posted higher sales and income. Sales and income in Far Eastern films and plastic packaging were up slightly, with expanded film sales throughout the Pacific Rim.

Borden is the world leader in forest products adhesives (used in making plywood, particle board, and other wood products) and pioneered industrial adhesives more than 60 years ago. The company ranks number one in U.S. vinyl food wrap films and is a leader in many of its European and Far Eastern plastic packaging businesses. Borden also has strong positions in foundry and other industrial resins, high-technological coatings, printing inks, and specialty adhesives.

EXHIBIT 33-3

BORDEN INTERNATIONAL FOODS, AND PACKAGING AND INDUSTRIAL PRODUCTS

Pasta and Sauce
Brazil—Adria, Italianissimo, OA, Paty, Raineri, Soltinho and Romanini
Italy—Albadoro and Monder
Panama—Imperial Roma and Napoli

European Bakery
Germany—Weber, Jaus, Kamps, Klems, Klemme, Nur Hier, Nuschelberg, Stefansback, Wriedeler, Lecker Backer, Heede and Golden Toast baked goods and specialty breads
Hungary—Prima Pek baked goods and specialty breads

Niche Grocery
Belgium—ReaLemon lemon juice from concentrate, Hemo chocolate drink, Lemaitre chocolate truffles and Vrancaert truffles
Colombia—Cremora non-dairy creamer
Denmark—Cocio and Congo bottled chocolate milk, Chocola chocolate drink and Chocolet lowfat chocolate milk
Spain—Gallina Blanca dry soup mixes, Hoy Menu side dishes and Avecrem bouillon (exported to Middle East and Africa as Jumbo dry soup mixes and bouillon), Salsas ala Carta instant sauce and Sopas Hechas aseptic soups
Sweden and Norway—Cocio chocolate milk

Dairy
Worlwide export—KLIM whole, KLIM Line lowfat, KLIM Superkid and KLIM Growing Up milk powders
Bahamas and Costa Rica—Milk, ice cream and other dairy products, KLIM whole milk powder
Colombia—KLIM, El Rodeo, Rosemary and Chicolac, whole and active skim milk powders and Borden cheeses
Panama—KLIM whole milk powder and Borden ice cream, frozen yogurt, cheeses, juices and nectars

Non-Food Consumer
Decorative Products—Birge, Borden Home Wallcoverings, Borderlines, Borges, Crown, Fashion House, Foremost, Guard, James Seeman Studios, Mitchell Designs, Satinesque, ShandKydd, Storeys, Sun-Tex, Sunwall 54, Sunwall 27, Sunworthy, Trillium and Wall-Tex wallcoverings
Elmer's household, carpenter's and specialty glues, cements, building adhesives, caulking compounds and sealants, Weather-Tite wood glues and fillers, Fill'N Finish wood filler, GluColors decorative glues, Slide-All lubricant, Squeez N Caulk caulks, Stix-All adhesive and Wonder Bond adhesive
Krazy Glue instant glues and Aron Alpha industrial adhesives
Accent, Country Colors and Hobby Craft artist/craft brush-on paints

International:
Argentina—Cascola, Cascamite and Casco 1002PVA glues, Cascotac contact cement, Rolofreeze, Rolopac, Rolopaper and Rolumino household wraps and Prontoflame fire starter
Brazil—Adezite sealant putty and specialty vinyl tapes, Cascola, Cascolar, Cascofix, Cascamite, Cascorez, Cascophen and Cola Madeira glues, Cascolor color school glue, Cascor vinyl and acrylic paints, Cascolax floor coatings, Durepoxi epoxy putty, Flexite silicone sealant, Rolopac film and Krazy Glue instant glues
Canada—Sunworthy wallcoverings, Elmer's household, carpenter's and specialty glues and other products and Krazy Glue instant glues
Columbia—EGA glues and adhesives, Rally car care products, Al Greco paints and coatings, Chinola shoe and leather care products, Efro, Alpino and Relussiente floor waxes and cleaners, Durepoxi epoxy putty and Chris air freshener
Ecuador—Elmer's, Blancola, Cascotack, EGA, Parcola and Economicola glues and adhesives, Turbo Rally car care products, Rolopac, Rolopaper, Rolominio and Rolofreeze household wraps. Polo-Shoe leather care products. Poliflex, American Wax and Poligloss household waxes, Clean-All floor cleaners and Durepoxi and Rally epoxy putties

EXHIBIT 33-3 *Continued*

BORDEN INTERNATIONAL FOODS, AND PACKAGING AND INDUSTRIAL PRODUCTS

France—Heller plastic model kits
Germany—Borges wallcoverings
Philippines—Elmer's glues and
adhesives
United Kingdom—Crown and
Storeys wallcoverings,
Humbrol paints and adhesives
and Airfix model kits
Uruguay—Cascola and Cascolax
glues, Cascola contact cement
and Rolopac household wrap

Films and Adhesives
ALpHASET, Betaset and other
foundry resins and refractory
coatings
Astromel, Astrolube, Acat and
other melamine resins and
saturating products
Broadcast banner fabric
Casco, Cascophen, Cascoset and
other forest products
adhesives

Cascamid, Cascolok, Cascote
and other wet strength paper
resins
CILC N KOTE and
Hydrosperse printing inks
LUV and other industrial
coatings and resins
Loadmaster, Resinex and
Resinite palletwrap
films
Ovenex food trays
Proponite and OPPtimum
packaging films
Resinite and Sealwrap foodwrap
films

International:
Film Products—Belgium, France,
Italy, Netherlands, Spain and
United Kingdom; Canada;
Argentina, Brazil, Colombia,
Ecuador and Uruguay;
Australia, Japan, New Zealand
and Taiwan

Forest products adhesives—
France, Spain and United
Kingdom; Canada; Argentina,
Brazil, Colombia, Ecuador
and Uruguay; Australia,
Malaysia and Philippines
Foundry resins—France, Spain
and United Kingdom;
Argentina, Brazil and
Colombia; Australia, Japan,
Malaysia and Philippines
Rigid plastic packaging—France,
Italy, Netherlands and United
Kingdom
Specialty adhesives—France and
United Kingdom; Argentina,
Brazil, Colombia, Ecuador
and Uruguay; Australia,
Malaysia and Philippines

Source: Borden *Annual Report,* 1993.

Worldwide Decorative Products. Borden is the world's largest wallcovering company. Sales held even and net income was slightly higher in 1993. Its Wall-Tex, Sunworthy, Borden Home, Borges, and Crown brands are the best-known wallcoverings in North America and the United Kingdom and hold a strong position in Germany. Borden's business also includes laminated decorative overlays used for interiors and furniture manufacture. Its Elmer's and Krazy Glue brands are favorites among consumers in household adhesives, home improvement products, and instant glue.

Borden wallcoverings improved despite an industrywide slowdown in residential and commercial wallcoverings sales. Particularly strong gains were posted in Borden commercial wallcoverings. A Guard line of environmentally friendly commercial wallcoverings was recently introduced, supported by trade advertising. Borden increased its offerings in the highly profitable coordinated home wallcoverings/bedding ensemble segment of the home fashions market. A new line of licensed Disney character wallcoverings, borders, and wall murals was introduced in 1993, as were Borderlines and Paintable Impressions.

EXHIBIT 33-4 Borden Three-Year Comparison of Division Sales and Operating Income
(*Dollars in millions*)

YEAR ENDED DECEMBER 31,	1993		1992		1991	
Division Sales						
North American Foods	$2,671.5	48%	$3,039.0	52%	$3,085.9	52%
International Foods	930.4	17	951.9	16	967.0	16
Packaging and Industrial Products	1,904.4	35	1,880.8	32	1,871.2	32
Total	$5,506.3	100%	$5,871.7	100%	$5,924.1	100%
Division Operating Income (Loss)						
North American Foods	$(24.4)	(12)%	$49.8	21%	$337.3	55%
International Foods	51.0	26	41.8	18	90.5	15
Packaging and Industrial Products	167.7	86	142.4	61	186.9	30
Total	194.3	100%	234.0	100%	614.7	100%
Discontinued operations, net of tax	(555.8)		(85.9)		15.0	
Other income and expense not allocable to divisions and income taxes	(269.2)		(512.5)		(334.8)	
Net income (loss)	$(630.7)		$(364.4)		$294.9	

Source: Borden *Annual Report,* 1993.

Plastic Film and Packaging. Results in Borden's North American Plastic Film and Packaging operations were hurt in 1993 by higher raw material costs and strong price competition in all major products. Income in European plastic films and packaging were down due to a sluggish European economy. Dollar sales of Resinite and Sealwrap vinyl foodwrap films were up in 1993 due to higher product pricing and increased demand industrywide. Sales of Loadmaster palletwrap film outperformed industry growth by nearly two to one.

Borden has become the exclusive North American marketer of advanced oriented polypropylene (OPP) films from Moplefan, S.p.A., a leader in European high-technology films. Marketed under the OPPticoat and OPPtiwrap trademarks, the new films are used principally in food packaging and complement Borden's existing line of Proponite OPP films. LUV high technology coatings posted weak sales and income in 1993, benefitting from a growing demand in the United States, Canada, and Europe for Borden's patented fiber-optic coatings.

MANAGEMENT

Borden is a good corporate citizen in protecting the environment and has adopted the Borden Principles of Environmental Responsibility and the Borden Principles of Social Responsibility. Reinforcing these principles are companywide policies and programs regarding fair employment practices, minority purchasing, charitable contributions, environmental protection, and product packaging.

Borden has Equal Employment Opportunity (EEO) programs in place at every U.S. location, with the goal of full representation of qualified minorities and women among the Borden workforce. The result is a diverse domestic workforce in which minorities represent 24 percent of the total, well above the 18-percent national average.

Borden established a pioneering minority purchasing program more than 20 years ago, and it has continued a leadership role by making certain that minority suppliers have opportunities to win business from Borden. In 1993, Borden purchased goods and services totaling $78 million from minority suppliers and made tax payments totaling $51 million through minority-owned banks.

Borden's tradition of caring about people who are less fortunate and in need dates back to Gail Borden. His great concern for people—in particular children who needed a source of pure milk—led him to invent condensed milk and then to found The Borden Company more than 135 years ago. That legacy continues today through the Borden Foundation, which serves as the company's principal conduit for charitable contributions. Among the Foundation's most important efforts is its five-year-old Ten Cities Program with the National Urban League, which allocates special grants to League chapters to enhance the lives of children in their communities. Programs have been conducted so far in 17 Urban League chapters.

Borden devotes considerable resources to meet its environmental responsibilities. It has companywide programs to reduce waste, minimize pollution, and protect the environment. Several Borden plants were recognized in 1993 for outstanding efforts. For example, the state of California recently paid tribute to Borden's forest products adhesives plant at Fremont for cutting its water use in half over a five-year period, even as it expanded production. Other forest products adhesives plants have dramatically reduced waste and have achieved zero discharge of hazardous liquid waste.

Borden's Dallas, Texas, dairy was honored for its perfect wastewater compliance record. Borden's wallcoverings plant in Columbus, Ohio recycles over 4 million pounds of scrap vinyl and corrugated cardboard annually.

Recognizing the growing concern over solid waste, Borden has established a corporatewide product packaging policy. Borden pledges to use packaging that meets environmental concerns while maintaining product quality and safety. Borden has reduced the thickness of packaging materials, used lighter weight materials, and eliminated unnecessary packaging. These include lighter weight containers for Cremora and Cremora Lite nondairy creamers, ReaLemon juice, Eagle Brand sweetened condensed milk, and thinner plastic films for individually wrapped cheese slices and packaged pastas.

Borden uses 100 percent recycled fiberboard for nearly all of its domestic pasta boxes and an increasing amount of recycled content glass, steel, and aluminum in its packaging. New containers are marked with industry symbols to remind and encourage consumers to recycle. Corrugated cartons and shippers used by Borden are made from recycled materials, while shipping boxes from Borden Snacks are reused on average between five and six times. Currently under evaluation is the use of 100-percent recycled polyethylene terephthlate (PET) resin for the Borden Singleskeeper cheese container.

MARKETING

Borden traditionally has gone to market as a group of separate and distinct businesses—without coordinating its efforts to common customers. At a time when many major food retailers are moving rapidly to centralized buying, Borden has had eight separate sales organizations, seven distribution operations, and five distinct information systems in North America alone.

The leading national retail chains want to deal with Borden as one company rather than as a set of separate businesses. This requires Borden to take an integrated approach to sales, marketing, and distribution, and pull together all of its efforts as one company. Borden initiated this new strategy in 1992 when a large retail customer asked to coordinate through one Borden person rather than deal with 28 people as it had in the past. A companywide team was formed to serve this huge national retailer as a single strategic supplier. The result was a substantial increase in overall sales of Borden products, including significant new business. Exhibits 33–5 and 33–6 provide the figures in consolidated statements of income and balance sheets.

Borden will benefit from taking a one-company approach in advertising and promotion, distribution, purchasing, and information management. In advertising and promotion, Borden is consolidating its spending in fewer agencies and firms, and negotiating new arrangements in the way it buys and produces media advertising and sales promotion materials. Until recently, Borden worked with 19 separate advertising agencies and more than 100 sales promotion firms in North America alone. As a bigger client to fewer firms, Borden will receive superior creative work and better marketing support.

In distribution, Borden is moving to integrate its seven separate operations into a single system. The company is consolidating such functions as customer service, accounts receivable, and invoicing. Borden has begun to consolidate warehouse delivery systems for all dry grocery products, including pasta and foodservice, and to establish a one-company management of systems, backhaul, transportation, and warehousing for all Borden operations.

Information management is a crucial element in Borden's one-company approach to sales and marketing. Borden will replace information systems unique to each business with an integrated Borden system. The new system will meet the growing demand for comprehensive sales information on all Borden products and yet provide flexibility to meet the special needs of each business.

Borden is rebuilding the equity in its three biggest, most underutilized assets: the Borden name, the Borden slogan, and Elsie the Cow. Recent research shows that the Borden name has outstanding recognition nationwide. Virtually all consumers sampled nationally recognize the name. The Borden slogan—"If it's Borden–it's got to be good"—continues to represent quality and trust to millions of American consumers. More than seven of every 10 people in a national sample were aware of the slogan. And, despite years of underuse, Borden's 56-year-old Elsie the Cow trademark is still recognized by more than one of every two American adults.

In the past, Borden's approach to its businesses provided little reason to capitalize on the Borden name, slogan, and Elsie. As a result, Borden missed enormous opportunities to reach younger consumers with these still powerful marketing tools. Major new initiatives are underway to put all three back to work behind groups of products. New television advertising will carry the Borden slogan and display a family of Borden products. The Borden name also is being extended beyond dairy, starting with a new Borden snacks line.

Elsie herself has had a makeover, giving her a softer, more contemporary look. She is the focus of an umbrella marketing campaign that began in March 1993 for a full range of Borden dairy products—milk, cheese, ice cream, cultured products, and Eagle Brand sweetened condensed milk. The campaign includes a mix of new advertising, packaging, and public relations, highlighted by Elsie's first national television appearances since the 1970s. The television commercials feature an animated Elsie, husband Elmer, and kids Beauregard ("Beau") and Beulah ("Bea"). They focus on the quality of Borden dairy products and link each product to fresh, wholesome Borden milk.

EXHIBIT 33-5 Borden Business Segments (*In millions*)

YEAR ENDED DECEMBER 31,		1993[a]	1992[b]	1991[c]
Net Sales	Foods	$3,673.8	$4,055.5	$4,119.5
	Non-food consumer and industrial	1,832.5	1,816.2	1,804.6
	Total	$5,506.3	$5,871.7	$5,924.1
Operating Profit	Foods	$ 22.7	$ 92.4	$ 428.8
	Non-food consumer and industrial	171.6	141.6	185.9
	Total segments	194.3	234.0	614.7
	General corporate expense, net	(153.3)	(141.9)	(16.5)
	Interest expense	(125.1)	(116.6)	(167.0)
	Pretax (loss) income from continuing operations	$ (84.1)	$ (24.5)	$ 431.2
Identifiable Assets	Foods	$2,085.6	$3,496.9	$3,689.5
	Non-food consumer and industrial	1,114.3	1,395.4	1,438.1
	Total segments	3,199.9	4,892.3	5,127.6
	Discontinued operations	222.2		
	Corporate assets	449.6	353.7	333.7
	Total	$3,871.7	$5,246.0	$5,461.3
Depreciation and Amortization	Foods	$ 163.7	$ 165.7	$ 157.2
	Non-food consumer and industrial	48.7	49.8	46.2
Capital Expenditures	Foods	$ 102.3	$ 202.9	$ 303.4
	Non-food consumer and industrial	59.1	74.6	66.0
Geographic Net sales Information	United States	$3,620.9	$3,928.7	$3,903.2
	Europe	914.8	979.2	1,083.2
	Other	970.6	963.8	937.7
	Total	$5,506.3	$5,871.7	$5,924.1
Operating profit	United States	$ 82.7	$ 155.1	$ 421.4
	Europe	73.7	54.4	92.1
	Other	37.9	24.5	101.2
	Total	$ 194.3	$ 234.0	$614.7
Identifiable assets	United States	$2,408.0	$3,534.4	$3,602.6
	Europe	695.2	858.0	1,027.4
	Other	546.3	853.6	831.3
	Discontinued Operations	222.2		
	Total	$3,871.7	$5,246.0	$5,461.3

[a]The $38.4 restructuring and other charges to segment operating profit in 1993 is allocated as follows: $38.4 for the foods segment; and $22.1 for U.S. operations, and $16.3 for other foreign operations. The remainder of the restructuring charge not allocable to operating profit: $76.5 is included in general corporate expense.

[b]The $270.7 restructuring charge to segment operating profit in 1992 is allocated as follows: $215.7 for the foods segment and $55.0 for the non-food consumer and industrial segment; and $165.9 for U.S. operations, $38.1 for European operations and $66.7 for other foreign operations. The remainder of the restructuring charge not allocable to operating profit: $27.1 is included in general corporate expense and $79.4 is related to discontinued operations.

[c]The $61.2 restructuring charge to segment operating profit in 1991 is allocated as follows: $48.7 for the foods segment and $12.5 for the non-food consumer and industrial segment; and $34.5 for U.S. operations, $7.4 for European operations and $19.3 for other foreign operations. The remainder of the restructuring charge not allocable to operating profit: $6.0 is included in general corporate expense and $4.4 is related to discontinued operations.

Source: Borden *Annual Report*, 1993.

EXHIBIT 33-6 Borden Consolidated Statements of Income (*In millions except per share data*)

YEAR ENDED DECEMBER 31,		1993	1992	1991
Revenue	Net sales	$5,506.3	$5,871.7	$5,924.1
Costs and Expenses	Cost of goods sold	4,078.6	4,301.9	4,268.5
	Marketing, general and administrative expenses	1,223.7	1,163.6	1,023.9
	Restructuring charges	114.9	297.8	67.2
	Interest expense	125.1	116.6	167.0
	Equity in income of affiliates	(16.0)	(19.4)	(24.0)
	Minority interest	40.7	39.7	2.8
	Other (income) and expense, net	23.4	(4.0)	(12.5)
	Income taxes	(27.2)	14.2	151.3
		5,563.2	5,910.4	5,644.2
Earnings	(Loss) income from continuing operations	(56.9)	(38.7)	279.9
	Discontinued operations:			
	(Loss) income from operations	(65.8)	(85.9)	15.0
	Loss on disposal	(490.0)		
	(Loss) income before extraordinary item and cumulative effect of accounting changes	(612.7)	(124.6)	294.9
	Extraordinary loss on early retirement of debt		(10.8)	
	Cumulative effect of change in accounting for:			
	Postemploymet benefits	(18.0)		
	Postretirement benefits other than pensions		(189.0)	
	Income taxes		(40.0)	
	Net (loss) income	$ (630.7)	$ (364.4)	$ 294.9
Share Data	(Loss) income from continuing operations	$ (.40)	$ (.27)	$ 1.90
	Discontinued operations:			
	(Loss) income from operations	(.47)	(.60)	.10
	Loss on disposal	(3.47)		
	(Loss) income before extraordinary item and cumulative effect of accounting changes	(4.34)	(.87)	2.00
	Extraordinary loss on early retirement of debt		(.07)	
	Cumulative effect of change in accounting for:			
	Postemployment benefits	(.13)		
	Postretirement benefits other than pensions		(1.32)	
	Income taxes		(.28)	
	Net (loss) income per common share	$ (4.47)	$ (2.54)	$ 2.00
	Cash dividends paid per common share	$ 0.90	$ 1.185	$ 1.12
	Average number of common shares outstanding during the period	141.0	143.4	147.6

Source: Borden *Annual Report*, 1993.

Borden also will present its dairy products in more contemporary packaging with a unified Borden look. The packaging prominently features Elsie, makes dramatic use of color, and provides a clean, modern, and appetizing look that ties the entire line together. To complement the new advertising and packaging, Borden is gearing up a full-scale national public relations campaign. It will help to re-establish Borden as a flagship brand and to turn a new, younger generation of consumers into loyal Borden customers.

THE BORDEN FUTURE

In Borden's 1993 *Annual Report,* Ervin R. Shames reveals his 1994 plans for Borden as follows:

- We plan to divest 20 percent of Borden's 1993 revenue base, including North American snacks, seafood, jams and jellies, and several other businesses.
- We plan to strengthen dairy and packaging and industrial products and pasta.
- We plan to enlarge our marketing budget, and reduce our costs by $85 million.

EXHIBIT 33-7 Borden Consolidated Balance Sheets (*In millions except share and per share data*)

DECEMBER 31,	1993	1992
ASSETS		
Current Assets		
Cash and equivalents	$ 100.3	$ 186.0
Accounts receivable (less allowance for doubtful accounts of $8.9 and $10.3, respectively)	334.7	889.6
Inventories:		
Finished and in process goods	319.4	400.9
Raw materials and supplies	171.0	240.2
Other current assets	142.6	210.8
Net assets of discontinued operations	222.2	
	1,290.2	1,927.5
Investments and Other Assets		
Investments in and advances to affiliated companies	91.3	96.1
Deferred income taxes	225.4	
Other assets	126.6	255.8
	443.3	351.9
Property and Equipment		
Land	105.5	125.6
Buildings	609.6	815.5
Machinery and equipment	1,949.3	2,389.5
	2,664.4	3,330.6
Less accumulated depreciation	(1,327.7)	(1,542.5)
	1,336.7	1,788.1
Intangibles		
Intangibles resulting from business acquisitions (net of accumulated amortization of $189.8 and $222.9, respectively)	801.5	1,178.5
	$3,871.7	$5,246.0
LIABILITIES AND SHAREHOLDERS' EQUITY		
Current Liabilities		
Debt payable within one year	$410.6	$706.6
Accounts and drafts payable	433.3	589.7
Restructuring reserve	145.9	139.4
Income taxes	56.5	55.1
Other current liabilities	325.2	317.0
	1,371.5	1,807.8
Other		
Long-term debt	1,240.8	1,329.9
Deferred income taxes	47.1	66.8
Non-pension postemployment benefit obligations	353.8	317.7
Other long-term liabilities	103.8	79.3
Minority interest	508.8	518.2
	2,254.3	2,311.9
Shareholders' Equity		
Common stock—$0.625 par value		
Authorized 480,000,000 shares		
Issued 194,983,374 shares	121.9	121.9
Paid-in capital	88.1	83.0
Accumulated translation adjustment	(171.1)	(128.3)
Minimum pension liability	(95.5)	(3.2)
Retained earnings	835.1	1,592.5
	778.5	1,665.9

EXHIBIT 33-7 *Continued*

DECEMBER 31,	1993	1992
Less common stock in treasury (at cost)—53,625,339 shares and 54,342,642 shares, respectively	(532.6)	(539.6)
	245.9	1,126.3
	$3,871.7	$5,246.0

EXHIBIT 33-8 Borden Officers

Frank J. Tasco
  Chairman
Ervin R. Shames
  President and Chief Executive
  Officer

Corporate Executive Vice President
Joseph M. Saggese
  President, Packaging and
  Industrial Products Division
  Domestic and International

Corporate Senior Vice President
Allan L. Miller
  Chief Administrative Officer

Corporate Vice Presidents
Judy Barker
  Social Responsibility
  President, The Borden
  Foundation
W. Bailey Barton
  Health, Safety and Environment
Karen L. Johnson
  Consumer Affairs
Randy D. Kautto
  Human Resources
David A. Kelly
  Treasurer
Philip J. Keuper

Pulic Affairs
George P. Morris
  Chief Strategic Officer
  Vice President, Finance
  North American and
  International Foods
Francis J. Proto
  General Auditor
Eugene N. Skiest
  Science and Technology
Charles N. Timperman
  Corporate Development
George J. Waydo

Operating Executives
North American Foods:
Robert W. Allen
  Senior Group Vice President-
  President, Dairy Products
Peter C. Cline
  Group Vice President,
  North American Snacks
John F. Dix
  Group Vice President,
  Niche Grocery Products
  Vice President, Shared Sales
Craig G. Hammond
  Vice President, Operations

Ronald C. Kesselman
  Group Vice President,
  Foodservice and Seafood
  Products
  Vice President,
  Sales and Marketing Services
Russell S. Mentzer
  Vice President-President,
  North American Pasta Products

International Foods:
Dan O'Riordan
  Senior Group Vice President-
  President,
  International Foods
Ole Norgaard
  Group Vice President,
  Dairy International

**Packaging and Industrial
Products Division
Domestic and International**
Sumner S. Feinstein
  Group Vice President,
  Worldwide Decorative Products
Jerold J. Golner
  Group Vice President,
  North American Plastic
  Operations
Robert G. Jenkins
  Group Vice President,
  Worldwide Resins

EXHIBIT 33-8 *Continued*

Corporate Staff Departments	Steven C. Dove	Richard W. Pennell
Paul J. Josenhans	Assistant Treasurer	Assistant General Controller
Secretary and Associate	Terrence W. Gasper	Nancy G. Brown
General Counsel	Assistant Treasurer	Assistant General Counsel
Ellen German Berndt	George W. Sanborn	Lawrence L. Dieker
Assistant Secretary	Assistant Treasurer	Assistant General Counsel
H. Cort Doughty, Jr.	Thomas V. Barr	James A. King, Jr.
Assistant Secretary	Assistant General Controller	Assistant General Counsel
Richard H. Byrd	Edmund M. Konopka	Ronald P. Moran
Assistant Treasurer	Assistant General Controller	Assistant General Counsel

Source: Borden *Annual Report*, 1993.

EXHIBIT 33-9 Borden Consolidated Statements of Cash Flows (*In millions except per share data*)

	YEAR ENDING DECEMBER 31,	1993	1992	1991
Cash Flows From Operating Activities	Net (loss) income	$(630.7)	$(364.4)	$294.9
	Adjustments to reconcile net income to net cash from operating activities:			
	Depreciation and amortization	224.0	227.6	216.9
	Loss on disposal of discontinued operations	637.4		
	Change in accounting estimates	94.1		
	Restructuring	52.5		
	Non-pension postemployment benefit obligation	36.1	316.5 317.7	(65.0)
	Net changes in assets and liabilities:			
	Trade receivables	47.8	(30.3)	19.9
	Inventories	21.2	1.0	7.6
	Trade payables	(0.5)	(4.4)	(15.1)
	Current and deferred taxes	(242.4)	(175.3)	63.4
	Other assets	(34.2)	(9.6)	(99.0)
	Other, net	(132.9)	14.1	(74.8)
	Discontinued operations	79.9		
		152.3	292.9	348.8
Cash Flows From Investing Activities	Capital expenditures	(177.0)	(286.2)	(376.0)
	Divestiture of businesses	53.4	123.0	94.1
	Purchase of businesses	(9.5)	(20.1)	(29.5)
		(133.1)	(183.3)	(311.4)

EXHIBIT 33-9 *Continued*

	Year Ending December 31,	1993	1992	1991
Cash Flows From	(Decrease) increase in short-term debt	(536.2)	255.5	(310.4)
Financing Activities	Reduction in long-term debt	(128.7)	(266.1)	(244.2)
	Minority interest			500.0
	Long-term debt financing	274.6	45.2	223.1
	Sale of receivables	400.0		
	Dividends paid	(126.7)	(170.4)	(165.0)
	Issuance of stock under stock options and benefits and awards plans	12.1	3.9	7.2
	Acquisition of treasury stock			(1.6)
		(104.9)	(131.9)	9.1
	(Decrease) increase in cash and equivalents	(85.7)	(22.3)	46.5
	Cash and equivalents at beginning of year	186.0	208.3	161.8
	Cash and equivalents at end of year	$100.3	$186.0	$208.3
Supplemental				
Disclosures of	Interest paid	$133.3	$130.4	$177.5
Cash Flow Information	Taxes paid	20.5	67.1	102.6

Source: Borden *Annual Report*, 1993.

PILGRIM'S PRIDE—1994

JAMES L. HARBIN
East Texas State
University—Texarkana

CASE
34

"Sell it or smell it" is the unbending maxim that everyone in the chicken business faces. Because a chicken cannot be stopped from laying or growing, all producers, both literally and figuratively, live or die by the laws of supply and demand.

Headquartered in Pittsburg, Texas, Pilgrim's Pride (903-855-1000) is one of fifty survivors out of approximately 4,000-plus firms in existence a few decades ago. Lonnie "Bo" Pilgrim, one of seven children raised during the Great Depression, has taken his concern from a small-farm supply store forty years ago, to one producing over $888 million in 1993 sales. Currently, Pilgrim's is the fifth largest producer of poultry products and the 22nd largest egg producer in the United States. They produce more that 1.1 billion pounds of dressed poultry and 41 million dozen table eggs, annually, and employ more that 10,000 employees. Net income for 1993 was a record $21 million, up from a $29 million loss in 1992.

This remarkable growth has taken place in a commodity industry about which, every year for the past fifty years, economists have been predicting doom and gloom. Citing industry sales as an indicator, experts have also deduced that the chicken industry has finally matured. The big question facing Pilgrim's today is: can it continue to grow through (1) additional marketing techniques; (2) further cost curtailment; (3) increased integration; and (4) improved genetics and growing techniques; while at the same time facing competitors who are larger and just as savvy.

LONNIE A. "BO" PILGRIM'S BACKGROUND AND PHILOSOPHY

Bo Pilgrim's story is the classic one of deprivation to determination and then to success. Born in Northwest Texas in 1928, he was a middle child of seven. Bo's father died when he was nine; and he left home at twelve to live with his grandmother.

His entrepreneurial spirit has early roots. One of his first goals in life was "to be able to buy a soda when I wanted it. My father would on occasion give me money for a cold drink, but only after I had finished some work he wanted done for it," says Bo. He learned early that he could buy his own soft drinks by buying them from his father's general merchandise store and selling them at a profit to the local factory workers. He later peddled newspapers, raised chickens and hogs, hauled gravel, picked peas and cotton, and sacked groceries—all before he turned eighteen.

Bo is a tireless worker at age sixty-five. Getting up with the chickens would aptly describe Mr. Pilgrim. "Bo" still works 12-hour days, taking time out for a daily exercise regimen of treadmill work and swimming (he had a heart attack about 10 years ago). "People retire too early," says Pilgrim, "they should retire when they don't enjoy working anymore. I won't retire!"

He likens business to "a game, even a war." Commenting on how he spends his time, "I spend one third of my working days dealing with the government, one third with lawyers, and the remaining one third of my time is spent constructively."

"Today we don't appreciate how much we have and how easy it is to get things. I'm definitely hooked on the free enterprise system," comments Bo. "In fact, when I visited with President Reagan a few years ago, I reminded him that the chicken and egg industry had never had any kind of subsidy. I also shared my belief that the government should not be in the business of protecting the inefficient."

Mr. Pilgrim recently expressed his thoughts on entrepreneurship:

It is more than just shooting from the hip. A company has four resources: people, dollars, time, and facilities. Our company's objective is to gain optimum use of these four through planning, building pride, and rewarding your employees.

Educated in a three-room school without electricity, Bo still believes in "old-fashioned Christian values" and the idea that "there is more to life than just making a dollar." He has had three children with his wife of thirty-six years; and for the past thirty-plus years has taught a Sunday school class. When asked about his secret of success, Bo responded:

Take your abilities, season them with experience on the job and combine that with drive and motivation and you will be successful. The way to make a difference in your life is to make that *mind-boggling* decision not to be average.

THE COMPANY

Pilgrim's History. Pilgrim's Pride is engaged in the production, processing, and marketing of fresh chicken and further processed and prepared chicken products. Pilgrim's produces approximately 27 million pounds of chicken per week, establishing it as the fifth largest producer in the United States. Pilgrim's offers a broad range of nearly 250 chicken products across the fresh, frozen-prepared, and individually quick frozen categories. Additionally, they can develop and produce new products to meet specific customer needs.

The company offers a line of processed and prepared chicken products, which includes breast fillets, nuggets, tenders, patties, and deli foods. These products, which undergo one or more further processing steps (including deboning, cutting, forming, battering, breading, and cooking), are packaged in quantities. These are then sold to supermarkets and to food service distributors like Sysco and Kraft General Foods (which resell them to restaurants, hospitals, and the like), fast-food chains, and whole-sale discount clubs.

In large part, because commodity chicken downcycles had almost bankrupted Pilgrim's twice over the years, the company has increasingly emphasized value-added and branded products, including its chill pack and further processed and prepared food lines. In the late 1980's Pilgrim's spent $25 million on a prepared chicken plant. These products generate higher prices per pound, exhibit lower price volatility, and result in higher and more consistent profit margins than non-value-added products such as whole ice-pack chicken.

In order to crack the food service business with processed and prepared chicken, Pilgrim's had to price their products below Tyson Foods, Inc. (their chief competi-tor), at a loss to Pilgrim's Pride. The company also had to spend approximately $6 to $8 million a year on advertising, promotion, and supermarket slotting allowances to entice this business.

Pilgrim's Pride lost about $50 million over three years trying to enter the prepared chicken market. In fiscal 1988 the company lost a net $8 million on $506 million in sales. Disgruntled investors dumped the stock, which had just had an initial public offering in January of 1987. The value of Bo Pilgrim's stake shrank by 76 percent, to $61 million.

Pilgrim's finally turned the corner with a strategic retreat from the supermarkets and a major advance into the food service market. Retail products now account for a mere 2 percent of Pilgrim's prepared chicken sales. But in food service they have posi-tioned their company as an alternative to Tyson, aimed at those customers leery of being too dependent on one supplier. "A lot of buyers gave us information to help us duplicate the products they were buying from Tyson," Pilgrim says. With customers such as Kraft General Foods, Wendy's, and Kentucky Fried Chicken, the company now has been able to raise its prices to be in line with Tyson.

Pilgrim's Mission. A large group of Pilgrim's employees representing all areas of the company recently met to brainstorm their direction, vision, and mission. The group was fearful that rather than developing a mission, they might end up with a "mission statement." The difference according to Monty Henderson, president/CEO, is "that a Mission Statement becomes very wordy and usually winds up as a long para-graph or two that no one can remember . . . even the authors, and usually winds up in a file somewhere. A Mission by contrast is known by everyone, practiced daily by everyone, and becomes a way of life."

After lots of discussion about their business, their customers, and their competi-tion, they came to a consensus that their vision is "To achieve and maintain leadership in each product and service that we provide." To achieve this vision of product and service leadership, the group felt that their mission must be: "Our Job Is Customer Satisfaction . . . Every Day."

Pilgrim's Marketing. Pilgrim's has a consumer-oriented market strategy. The company's marketing activities and expenditure levels have increased annually as new products and geographic markets have developed. As a result of its marketing activi-ties, the company has achieved significant consumer awareness for the Pilgrim's Pride brand name in southwestern and western metropolitan markets. The company believes that this brand awareness is beneficial to the introduction and acceptance of new products, such as its further processed and prepared food lines.

The company utilizes television, radio, and newspaper advertising, point-of-sale and coupon promotions, and other marketing techniques to develop consumer awareness and brand loyalty for its products. Bo Pilgrim is the featured spokesman in the company's television and radio commercials, and his likeness in a pilgrim's hat appears on all the company's branded products. Advertising slogans have included "Better from the egg to the leg"; "It's a mind-boggling thing"; "The honest chicken from real pilgrim's"; and "Real chickens from real pilgrim's."

The company maintains an active program to identify consumer preferences primarily by testing new product ideas, packaging designs, and methods through taste panels and focus groups located in key geographic markets. This program led to the identification and introduction of new products such as the company's whole boneless chicken, leaner chicken, and the entire further processed and prepared foods line.

Pilgrim's has nineteen regional distribution centers. There are eight in Texas, three in Arkansas, two in Arizona, one in Oklahoma, and five in Mexico.

Pilgrim's Competition. Pilgrim's competes with other integrated chicken companies and to a lesser extent with local and regional poultry companies that are not fully integrated. Pilgrim's has been competing for retail grocery sales of chill-pack products since 1982 and fast-food product sales of whole and precut chickens since 1965. It currently supplies Church's, Kentucky Fried Chicken, Wendy's, Grandy's, and Chili's.

The primary competitive factors in the chicken industry include price, product line, and customer service. Although its products are competitively priced and generally supported with in-store promotions and discount programs, the company believes that product quality, brand awareness, and customer service are the primary methods through which it competes. Pilgrim's produces and markets further processed and prepared chicken products. Currently, Pilgrim's believes that it has only one competitor (Tyson) with a more complete line of value-added products.

The top five chicken producers today, measured by production volume, control more than half the market. They are Tyson Foods, Inc., Springdale, Arkansas; ConAgra, Inc., Omaha, Nebraska; Gold Kist, Inc., Atlanta, Georgia; Perdue Farms, Inc., Salisbury, Maryland; and Pilgrim's.

The egg industry is more fragmented than the chicken industry with approximately sixty producers accounting for approximately 56 percent of total sales. Pilgrim's competes with many larger and smaller egg producers, primarily on the basis of product quality, reliability, price, and service.

Tyson, the number one poultry processor, solidified its position in 1989 with the purchase of Holly Farms Corporation for $1.3 billion dollars. Since then Tyson has acquired Louis Kemp Seafood and Arctic Alaska Fisheries. "They don't want to just sit on chicken as their core business," says Mark Plummer, an analyst for Stephens, Inc., "if you look at Tyson's strategy they clearly want to be in fish, pork, turkey, and beef; they want to become an international food company." The following is taken from Tyson's 1992 annual report:

> Our marketing strategy for success is simple-segment, concentrate, dominate. We identify a promising market segment, concentrate our resources in it and ultimately gain for Tyson Foods a dominate share of that segment. Our customers include all of the nation's top 50

food service distributors, 88 of the top 100 restaurant chains, 100 of the top retail super-market chains and every major wholesale club.

Pilgrim's Finances. After enjoying their best year to date in 1986, earning approximately $19 million on $375 million in sales, Pilgrim's arranged for a public offering of seven million shares. This represented nearly 20 percent of existing stock with Lonnie Pilgrim retaining nearly 80 percent. The initial stock offer sold in the $12 range during January of 1987. After the large drop in the Dow during October of 1987, the stock sold in the $3–4 range. It was one of the hardest hit stocks of that period.

In March of 1988 it was announced by the *Wall Street Journal* that Bo Pilgrim was selling his 80 percent stake in Pilgrim's Pride to Tyson Foods for $9 a share, or about $162 million. Most industry analysts weren't surprised that the boss was bailing out. Pilgrim's Pride at that time had one of the most highly leveraged balance sheets of the major poultry producers and wasn't weathering the latest downturn in the chicken industry well. Approximately a week later, the deal fell through and Tyson went on to buy Holly Farms.

Although net sales have increased every year to a high of $887 million in 1993, Pilgrim's finished the previous year with the largest loss in the history of the company.

THE BROILER INDUSTRY

The domestic integrated broiler industry encompasses the breeding, growing, processing, and marketing of chicken products. The production of poultry is one of the largest agricultural industries in the United States. Prior to World War II, the broiler industry was highly fragmented with numerous small, independent breeders, growers, and processors. The industry has experienced consolidation during the last forty-five years resulting in a relatively small number of larger, more integrated companies. Integration of the industry has led to lower profit margins at each independent production stage and enhanced the need for coordination between production stages.

The broiler industry is characterized by intense price competition, resulting in an emphasis on improving genetic, nutritional, and processing technologies in an effort to minimize production costs. These factors, coupled with the feed conversion advantages of chickens, have enabled the industry to enjoy consistently lower production costs per pound than other competing meats. As an example of the adoption of improved methods and technology, certain industry participants have moved toward product packaging at the plant level, including deep-chill processing as an alternative to ice-packing whole chicken and shipping in bulk form. Deep-chill processing rapidly lowers the temperature of chickens to slightly above freezing, thus extending freshness and shelf life.

MARKET OUTLOOK FOR 1994

Industry-wide broiler production appears to be under control moving into 1994. Supply flock data indicate production increases of 5 to 6 percent in early 1994. This modest increase in the level of production should allow for positive net returns to industry players considering per capita consumption is expected to continue to rise. Consumption could get an additional boost from increasing disposable income and the growing popularity of new chicken-based product introductions. For example, early indications are that products such as KFC's Rotisserie Gold are very successful. Typically, new products such as this will generate "copy cat" products, fueling additional demand.

On the expense side of the equation the wild card is grain costs. As a result of this year's flooding in the Midwest, corn and soybean meal have increased more than 30 and 15 percent, respectively. Should U.S. grain exports (particularly to Russia) continue to strengthen, grain supplies could become even tighter. Longer term, higher grain prices can actually be positive for chicken producers as the meat conversion ratio is less than 2 to 1 (2 pounds of feed to produce 1 pound of meat) for broilers versus 8 to 1 for beef. Under such a large divergence poultry clearly has the cost advantage, particularly as feed ingredient costs increase.

In any event, the majority of poultry production consists of value-added product, resulting in earnings and margins that are much more stable than a typical fresh (commodity) broiler producer. As the amount of further processing increases, grain cost as a percentage of the total cost of production is substantially reduced compared to that of fresh product, resulting in greater stability. For example, Tyson's feed ingredient cost as a percentage total is approximately 30 to 35 percent, compared to 60 to 65 percent for most fresh producers.

Broiler exports in 1994 are expected to remain strong. The USDA estimates 1.9 billion pounds of U.S. broiler meat will be exported. Top 1993 markets include Hong Kong, Japan, Mexico, and Poland. Producers are also experiencing increased business from private enterprise in the former Soviet Union. Export markets provide an important outlet for dark meat product, which is less desirable in the United States. In addition, exports reduce domestic broiler meat supplies, helping to support prices.

Industry Profitability. Industry profitability is primarily a function of consumption of chicken and competing meats and the cost of feed grains. Historically, the broiler industry operated on a fairly predictable cycle of about three years, a year of good profits, followed by a year of expanded output and declining profits, followed by a year of losses and production cuts.

The chicken companies have spent much of their energy trying to escape the commodity cycle through marketing. Frank Perdue, with his classic commercials, was the first to demonstrate that a company could charge a premium for a brand-name bird. Today, the biggest producers all play the brand-loyalty game. This leaves the chicken producers in an odd situation; they are commodities concerns trying to behave like consumer-products companies. Prudential-Bache's John McMillin says, "In the 1990's the chicken industry will be better capitalized, more competitive and less profitable."

Industry profitability can be significantly influenced by feed costs, which are influenced by a number of factors unrelated to the broiler industry, including government legislation that provides discretion to the federal government to set price and income supports for grain. Historically, feed costs have averaged approximately 50 percent of total production costs of non-value-added products and have fluctuated substantially with the price of corn, milo, and soybean meal. Assuming that finished product prices and other factors remain constant, very small movements in feed costs may result in large changes in industry profits from non-value-added chicken products. By comparison, feed costs typically average approximately 25 percent of total production costs of further processed and prepared chicken products such as nuggets, fillets, and deli products, and as a result, increased emphasis on sales of such products by chicken producers reduces the sensitivity of earnings to feed cost movements.

Although feed costs may vary dramatically, the cost of producing chicken is not as severely affected by changing feed ingredient prices as are the production costs of beef and pork. Chickens require approximately two pounds of dry feed to produce one pound of live meat, compared to cattle and hogs, which require approximately eight to four pounds, respectively, of feed.

Across the southeastern United States, where 85 percent of the country's chickens are processed, the poultry industry is brooding about a barrage of bad publicity. Chicken processing plants are said to be dirty; rotten meat is reaching the market; salmonella-tainted chickens are poisoning people; and the chicken growers who contract with the processors are being ripped off. Even Ross Perot has publicly lambasted Bill Clinton's record by saying that the Arkansas poultry business is "not an industry of tomorrow."

Leaders of the South's largest agribusiness concede that they have a problem. In September of 1993, a coalition of the Arkansas Poultry Federation, Hudson Foods, Pilgrim's, and Tyson Foods ran full-page ads in several Arkansas newspapers to counter this image problem. Its main caption was "Here in Arkansas, it wasn't a Goose that laid the Golden Egg. It was a Chicken." It further stated such things as: "one out of twelve working Arkansans is employed by the poultry industry; it's a three-billion-dollar-plus industry in Arkansas; salaries and benefits average more than $25,000 each employee; and the poultry industry is the largest taxpayer in Arkansas."

The industry's biggest worry may be microscopic in physical size. Chickens in battery farms (and those in farmyards) often live in their own dung, which encourages the growth of bacteria such as salmonella and campylobacter. These contaminate the meat during processing. About six million Americans are made ill by such bacteria every year, and 1,300 die. Scientists at the Centers for Disease Control say chickens may be the cause in up to half of those cases.

The industry's high-tech, fast-paced production lines—which process some 200,000 birds a day at a single plant—heighten fecal contamination. Bacteria often spread among birds as they speed along conveyors from hot collective baths through wet mechanical feather-pickers to tanks of cold water. Partly to hold down the price of poultry, the industry has not tried to produce cleaner chickens, relying instead on consumers to cook the meat thoroughly.

Injury and illness rates for poultry workers are double the rates of manufacturing generally, according to the Labor Department. And new technology is often used to reduce stress for chickens—to make their meat more tender—rather than for workers. "The industry has one foot in the 21st century when it comes to chickens, but they left one foot back in the 19th century when it comes to people," says Bob Hall, research director of the Institute of Southern Studies, a labor-funded advocacy group in Durham, North Carolina.

Conditions on the production line can be tough. Repetitive motion from such tasks as pulling out chicken guts can cause disabling injuries. Employees frequently spend shifts in either a freezing cooler or 95°F heat. Conditions can be so crowded that blood from a chicken one worker handles can sometimes splash onto a co-worker. The line speed—up to 90 chickens a minute—is double the rate a decade ago.

In the past twenty years the number of major U.S. processors has shrunk from more than 100 to about 30. This consolidation has resulted in a highly centralized and vertically integrated industry in which a half-dozen major players control over 43 percent of American production. As a result, the country has been carved up into regional buying monopolies where each region's dominant processor can dictate terms to the growers.

The processors provide growers with chicks and feed, then slaughter and market the birds. The growers provide chicken houses, the utilities, and labor. Further, the growers receive only short-term contracts from the processors with no formal assurances of long-term business relationships.

A recent report from the Texas Commissioner of Agriculture concluded that while "the grower makes a substantial capital investment and takes most of the risk, he or she is not sharing in the success of the industry." In some cases growers have received as little as $579 in annual income per 20,000-bird-capacity broiler house.

The processors defend their practices. Industry spokesmen point out that growers are guaranteed a price for adult chickens, typically about 3.5 to 4 cents a pound. Thus, the processors contend, growers are sheltered from much of the risk of the volatile chicken market. Bill Roenigk, spokesman for the National Broiler Council, a processor trade group, says studies have shown that broiler farmers' average return on investment is 5 percent, or higher than that in many other agriculture operations.

CHANGING TASTES

Chicken has experienced greater growth in per-capita consumption than most other major meat categories over the last twenty years. From 1965 to 1985, the United States per capita consumption of chicken increased 74 percent while the consumption of beef increased 7 percent. Exhibit 34–3 illustrates per capita consumption of chicken relative to turkey, fish, beef and pork.

The major factors influencing this growth are consumer awareness of the health and nutritional characteristics of chicken, the price advantage of chicken relative to red meat, and the development of more convenient further processed and prepared chicken products. The principal health and nutritional characteristics include lower levels of fat, cholesterol, and calories per pound for chicken relative to red meat. When compared with other meats, chicken has a significant price advantage, which has increased over time.

Recent growth in the consumption of chicken has been enhanced by new product forms and packaging, which increase convenience and product versatility. These products typically undergo one or more further processing steps, including deboning, forming, battering, breading, and cooking. Production of these further processed products is the fastest-growing segment of the broiler industry. The market share of the further processed product group has increased.

In 1987 the United States became a nation of bird eaters. According to the Department of Agriculture, per capita consumption of poultry rose to 78.2 pounds. At the same time, per capita consumption of beef fell to 75.7 pounds. That marked the end of more than three decades of dominance by beef (before that, pork was king).

Notwithstanding an occasional salmonella scare, birds are perceived as more healthful than beef. A 100-gram piece of chicken contains 3.7 grams of saturated fat, compared with 20.7 grams of saturated fat in a piece of T-bone steak weighing the same amount, according to the Agriculture Department.

Chicken is also cheap. Chickens are selling for less than they did in 1923, when Mrs. Wilmer Steele of Ocean View, Delaware, sold what chicken historians say was the nation's first flock of commercial broilers (she got 62 cents a pound).

And perhaps most significantly, chicken companies have lately increased profit margins by producing scores of what the industry calls value-added items: chicken parts that have been boned or skinned or marinated or otherwise processed for the convenience of consumers. Just as anyone can cook a steak, anyone can now cook a shrink-wrapped chicken breast.

The poultry sector isn't solely chicken; it also includes turkey, duck, goose, and quail. But the poultry industry in America is chicken-driven; and, in fact, consumption of chicken alone bypassed beef around 1990 (although beef backers say pounds-per-capita figures aren't strictly fair, because chicken at retail has more bones in it than beef does). Recently chicken nuggets accounted for about 10 percent of total U.S. broiler output. McNuggets showed chicken companies what could happen if they went beyond selling what are called, in the trade, "feathers-off, guts-out birds."

Since McNuggets hit the market nationally in 1982, chicken producers have been swamping supermarkets with value-added products—teriyaki tidbits, breaded wings, whole cooked birds with salt and spices injected into their flesh—and consumers have responded. "Demand has expanded for poultry since 1983 in a way that I've never seen demand for any meat take off since World War II." says Patrick Luby, vice president and corporate economist at Oscar Mayer Foods Corporation in Madison, Wisconsin.

Value-added chicken should, of course, properly be called value-subtracted. It is the whole bird, not its processed parts, that offers consumers the greatest value—and that value is considerable when compared with beef and pork.

Why is chicken, pound for pound, cheaper than the competition? The answer has to do with the fact that a chicken is highly efficient at converting feed to flesh. To produce a pound of flesh, a chicken consumes less than two pounds of feed compared with between six and eight for a cow and three for a pig.

Also, a chicken doesn't live long. The shorter a creature's life cycle, the quicker its generations can be manipulated genetically. Chicken breeders have steadily developed birds that grow bigger on less feed in less time. They may be approaching the limits of practicality on this score; modern chickens have "put on so much weight that they have some real problems mating," says Walter Becker, professor emeritus of genetics and cell biology at Washington State University.

Furthermore, chickens don't graze. Raising cattle requires an investment in land; raising chickens doesn't. Chickens used to need to run around in the sun; otherwise, they would develop a vitamin D deficiency and rickets. But in the 1920s, poultry producers solved the vitamin D problem by adding cod-liver oil to chicken feed. Since then they have been able to raise thousands of chickens in confinement, allowing about 0.7 square foot per bird.

EXHIBIT 34-1 Location of Pilgrim's facilities

EXHIBIT 34-2 Top Chicken Companies, 1993

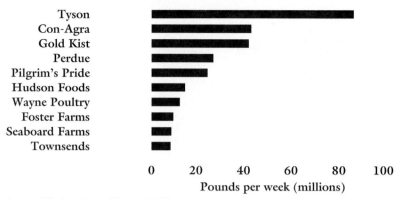

Pounds per week (millions)

Source: Pilgrim *Annual Report*, 1993.

EXHIBIT 34-3 Per Capita Consumption—*Pounds per Year*

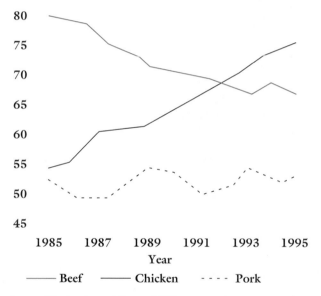

——— Beef   ——— Chicken   - - - - Pork

Source: Pilgrim *Annual Report*, 1993.

Exhibit 34-4 Selected Financial Data—Pilgrim's Pride Corporation and Subsidiaries
(In thousands, except per share data)

| | YEARS ENDED | | | | |
	1993[a]	1992[b]	1991	1990	1989
Operating Results Summary					
Net sales	$887,843	$817,361[c]	$786,651	$720,555	$661,077
Gross margin	110,213	34,646	75,567	74,190	83,356
Operating income (loss)	56,102	(13,475)	31,039	33,379	47,014
Income (loss) before income taxes and					
extraordinary charge	32,838	(33,712)	12,235	20,463	31,027
Income tax expense (benefit)	10,543	(4,048)	(59)	4,826	10,745
Income (loss) before extraordinary charge	22,295	(29,664)	12,294	15,637	20,282
Extraordinary charge—early repayment of					
debt, net of tax	(1,286)	—	—	—	—
Net income (loss)	21,009	(29,664)	12,294	15,637	20,282
Income (loss) per common share:					
Income (loss) before					
extraordinary charge	$ .81	$ (1.24)	$ .54	$ .69	$ .90
Extraordinary charge—early repayment					
of debt	(.05)	—	—	—	—
Net income (loss)	.76	(1.24)	.54	.69	.90
Cash dividends per common share	.03	.06	.06	.06	.06
Balance Sheet Summary					
Working capital	$ 72,688	$ 11,227	$ 44,882	$ 54,161	$ 60,313
Total assets	422,846	434,566	428,090	379,694	291,102
Short-term debt	25,643	86,424	44,756	30,351	9,528
Long-term debt, less current portion	159,554	131,534	175,776	154,277	109,412
Total stockholders' equity	132,293	112,112	112,353	101,414	87,132
Key Indicators—As a Percent of Sales					
Gross margin	12.4%	4.2%	9.6%	10.3%	12.6%
Selling general and administrative expenses	6.1%	5.9%	5.7%	5.7%	5.5%
Operating income (loss)	6.3%	(1.6)%	3.9%	4.6%	7.1%
Net interest expense	2.9%	2.8%	2.5%	2.3%	2.7%
Net income (loss)	2.4%	(3.6)%	1.6%	2.2%	3.1%

(a) 1993 had 53 weeks.

(b) During 1992, the Company changed the fiscal year-end of its Mexican subsidiaries from August to September to coincide with that of its domestic operations. 1992 operating results include the operations of the Mexican subsidiaries for the twelve months ended September 26, 1992. Operating results for the Mexican subsidiaries during the month of September, 1991 have been reflected as a direct addition to stockholders' equity.

(c) Excluded from net sales in 1992 is approximately $2.2 million of business interruption insurance proceeds resulting from a fire at the Company's prepared foods plant in Mt. Pleasant, Texas.

Source: Pilgrim's *Annual Report*, 1993.

EXHIBIT 34-5 Consolidated Statements of Income (Loss)—Pilgrim's Pride Corporation and Subsidiaries

		YEARS ENDED	
	OCTOBER 2, 1993 (53 WEEKS)	SEPTEMBER 26, 1992 (52 WEEKS)	SEPTEMBER 28, 1991 (52 WEEKS)
Net sales	$887,843,000	$817,361,000	$786,651,000
Business interruption insurance	–	2,225,000	–
	887,843,000	819,586,000	786,651,000
Costs and expenses:			
Cost of sales	777,630,000	784,940,000	711,084,000
Selling, general and administrative	54,111,000	48,121,000	44,528,000
	831,741,000	833,061,000	755,612,000
Operating Income (loss)	56,102,000	(13,475,000)	31,039,000
Other expenses (income):			
Interest expense, net	25,719,000	22,502,000	19,777,000
Miscellaneous	(2,455,000)	(2,265,000)	(973,000)
Total other expenses, net	23,264,000	20,237,000	18,804,000
Income (loss) before income taxes and extraordinary charge	32,838,000	(33,712,000)	12,235,000
Income tax expense (benefit)	10,543,000	(4,048,000)	(59,000)
Net income (loss) before extraordinary charge	22,295,000	(29,664,000)	12,294,000
Extraordinary charge-early repayment of debt, net of tax	(1,286,000)	–	–
Net Income (loss)	$ 21,009,000	$ (29,664,000)	$ 12,294,000
Net income (loss) per common share before extraordinary charge	$ .81	$ (1.24)	$ .54
Extraordinary charge per common share	(.05)	–	–
Net income (loss) per common share	$ .76	$ (1.24)	$ .54

Source: Pilgrim *Annual Report*, 1993.

EXHIBIT 34-6 Consolidated Balance Sheets—Pilgrim's Pride Corporation and Subsidiaries

	OCTOBER 2, 1993	SEPTEMBER 26, 1992
Assets		
Current Assets		
Cash and cash equivalents	$ 4,526,000	$ 11,550,000
Trade accounts and other receivables, less allowance for		
doubtful accounts	59,608,000	52,383,000
Inventories	91,794,000	89,428,000
Prepaid expenses	1,260,000	7,179,000
Other current assets	9,843,000	9,979,000
TOTAL CURRENT ASSETS	167,031,000	170,519,000
Other Assets	13,114,000	10,031,000
Property, Plant and Equipment		
Land	14,824,000	15,063,000
Buildings, machinery and equipment	317,657,000	315,392,000
Autos and trucks	25,877,000	24,622,000
Construction-in-progress	7,863,000	2,939,000
	366,221,000	358,016,000
Less accumulated depreciation and amortization	123,520,000	104,000,000
	242,701,000	254,016,000
	$422,846,000	$434,566,000
Liabilities and Stockholders' Equity		
Current Liabilities		
Notes payable to banks	$ 12,000,000	$ 64,979,000
Accounts payable	38,330,000	48,798,000
Accrued expenses	30,370,000	24,070,000
Current portion of long-term debt	13,643,000	21,445,000
TOTAL CURRENT LIABILITIES	94,343,000	159,292,000
Long-Term Debt, less current portion	159,554,000	131,534,000
Deferred Income Taxes	36,656,000	31,628,000
Stockholders' Equity		
Preferred stock, $.01 par value, authorized 5,000,000		
shares; none issued	–	–
Common stock, $.01 par value, authorized 45,000,000		
shares; 27,589,250 issued and outstanding in		
1993 and 1992	276,000	276,000
Additional paid-in capital	79,763,000	79,763,000
Retained earnings	52,254,000	32,073,000
Total Stockholders' Equity	132,293,000	112,112,000
Commitments and Contingencies	–	–
	$422,846,000	$434,566,000

Source: Pilgrim *Annual Report*, 1993.

EXHIBIT 34-7 Consolidated Statements of Stockholders' Equity—Pilgrim's Pride Corporation and Subsidiaries

FOR THE THREE YEARS ENDING OCTOBER 2, 1993	NUMBER OF SHARES	COMMON STOCK	ADDITIONAL PAID-IN CAPITAL	RETAINED EARNINGS	TOTAL
Balance at September 29, 1990	22,589,250	$226,000	$49,890,000	$51,298,000	$101,414,000
Net income for year				12,294,000	12,294,000
Cash dividends declared ($0.06 per share)				(1,355,000)	(1,355,000)
Balance at September 28, 1991	22,589,250	226,000	49,890,000	62,237,000	112,353,000
Net income for the month ended September 28, 1991, excluded below due to the change in fiscal year-end of Mexican subsidiaries				931,000	931,000
Net loss for year				(29,664,000)	(29,664,000)
Common stock issued	5,000,000	50,000	29,873,000	–	29,923,000
Cash dividends declared ($0.06 per share)				(1,431,000)	(1,431,000)
Balance at September 26, 1992	27,589,250	276,000	79,763,000	32,073,000	112,112,000
Net income for year				21,009,000	21,009,000
Cash dividends declared ($0.03 per share)				(828,000)	(828,000)
Balance at October 2, 1993	27,589,250	$ 276,000	$79,763,000	$52,254,000	$132,293,000

Source: Pilgrim *Annual Report*, 1993.

EXHIBIT 34-8 Consolidated Statements of Cash Flows—Pilgrim's Pride Corporation and Subsidiaries

	YEARS ENDED		
	OCTOBER 2, 1993 (53 WEEKS)	SEPTEMBER 26, 1992 (52 WEEKS)	SEPTEMBER 28, 1991 (52 WEEKS)
Cash flows from operating activities:			
Net income (loss)	$ 21,009,000	$(29,664,000)	$ 12,294,000
Adjustments to reconcile net income (loss) to cash provided by (used in) operating activities:			
Depreciation and amortization	26,034,000	24,090,000	19,860,000
(Gain) loss on property disposals	(2,187,000)	(620,000)	173,000
Provision for doubtful accounts	2,124,000	1,045,000	882,000
Deferred income taxes	5,028,000	(5,382,000)	(2,436,000)
Extraordinary charge	1,904,000	–	–
Net income for the month ended September 28, 1991, excluded above due to the change in fiscal year of Mexican subsidiaries	–	931,000	–
Changes in operating assets and liabilities:			
Accounts and other receivables	(6,555,000)	(9,720,000)	(1,033,000)
Inventories	(2,366,000)	7,807,000	(16,974,000)
Prepaid expenses	4,175,000	(4,416,000)	3,207,000
Accounts payable and accrued expenses	(4,168,000)	14,598,000	3,989,000
Other	(28,000)	(242,000)	(99,000)
Net cash flows provided by (used in) operating activities	44,970,000	(1,573,000)	19,863,000
Investing activities:			
Acquisitions of property, plant and equipment	(15,201,000)	(18,043,000)	(60,518,000)
Proceeds from property disposal	2,977,000	3,766,000	148,000
Other assets	713,000	(536,000)	1,056,000
Net cash used in investing activities	(11,511,000)	(14,813,000)	(59,314,000)

EXHIBIT 34-8 *Continued*

	OCTOBER 2, 1993 (53 WEEKS)	YEARS ENDED SEPTEMBER 26, 1992 (52 WEEKS)	SEPTEMBER 28, 1991 (52 WEEKS)
Financing activities:			
Proceeds from notes payable to banks	28,419,000	163,629,000	210,500,000
Repayments on notes payable to banks	(81,398,000)	(156,150,000)	(197,850,000)
Proceeds from long-term debt	126,468,000	—	31,600,000
Payments on long-term debt	(106,302,000)	(11,502,000)	(8,346,000)
Cost of refinancing debt	(5,510,000)		
Extraordinary charge, cash items	(1,188,000)	—	—
Proceeds from leasing transaction	—	565,000	—
Net proceeds from sale of stock	—	29,923,000	—
Cash dividends paid	(828,000)	(1,355,000)	(1,355,000)
Cash provided by (used in) financing activities	(40,339,000)	25,110,000	34,549,000
Effect of exchange rate changes on cash and cash equivalents	(144,000)	(49,000)	99,000
Increase (decrease) in cash and cash equivalents	(7,024,000)	8,675,000	(4,803,000)
Cash and cash equivalents at beginning of year	11,550,000	2,875,000	7,678,000
Cash and cash equivalents at end of year	$ 4,526,000	$ 11,550,000	$ 2,875,000
Supplemental disclosure information:			
Cash paid during the year for:			
Interest (net of amount capitalized)	$ 23,015,000	$ 22,507,000	$ 20,983,000
Income taxes	$ 3,688,000	$ 1,455,000	$ 2,273,000

Source: Pilgrim *Annual Report*, 1993.

EXHIBIT 34-9 Pilgrim Operations

	YEARS ENDED		
	OCTOBER 2, 1993 (53 WEEKS)	SEPTEMBER 26, 1992 (52 WEEKS)	SEPTEMBER 28, 1991 (52 WEEKS)
Sales to unaffiliated customers:			
United States	$699,089,000	$656,741,000	$645,081,000
Mexico	188,754,000	160,620,000	141,570,000
Consolidated Sales	$887,843,000	$817,361,000	$786,651,000
Operating profit (loss):			
United States	$46,471,000	$ (1,565,000)	$ 19,693,000
Mexico	9,631,000	(11,910,000)	11,346,000
	$ 56,102,000	$ (13,475,000)	$ 31,039,000
Identifiable assets:			
United States	$288,761,000	$297,369,000	$297,473,000
Mexico	134,085,000	137,197,000	130,617,000
	$422,846,000	$434,566,000	$428,090,000

Source: Pilgrim *Annual Report*, 1993.

EXHIBIT 34-10 Pilgrim Corporate Officers

Lonnie A. "Bo" Pilgrim[1]
Chief Executive Officer
Lindy M. "Buddy" Pilgrim[1]
President of U.S. Operations and Sales
and Marketing
Monty K. Henderson[1]
President and Chief Operating Officer
Clifford E. Butler[1]
Chief Financial Officer, Secretary and
Treasurer
David Van Hoose
President
Mexican Operations
Richard A. Cogdill[1]
Senior Vice President
Corporate Controller
O.B. Goolsby, Jr.
Senior Vice President
Prepared Foods

Robert L. Hendrix
Senior Vice President
Netex Complex
Mike Martin
Senior Vice President
Complex Manager
DeQueen and Nashville, AR Complex
James J. Miner, Ph.D.
Senior Vice President
Farm Production
Robert N. Palm
Senior Vice President
Complex Manager
Lufkin and Nacogdoches, TX
Complex

[1] Member of the Executive Committee
Source: Pilgrim *Annual Report*, 1993.

HERSHEY FOODS CORPORATION—1994

Do you know which of the following candies are made by Hershey Foods: Mr. Goodbar, Reese's, Kit Kat, Big Block, Whatchamacallit, Allsorts, Rolo, Krackel, BarNone, Mounds, Almond Joy, 5th Avenue, Snickers, and Baby Ruth? The answer is all of them except Snickers, made by M&M Mars, and Baby Ruth, by Nestlé. Mars and Nestlé are Hershey's two major competitors. Snickers is the best-selling candy bar in the world.

In Hershey, Pennsylvania, you can walk down Chocolate Avenue, stroll sidewalks lit with lights in the shape of Hershey Kisses, visit the Hershey Zoo, and see the Chocolate Kiss Tower in Hershey Park. Hershey is the home of Hershey Foods Corporation, which produces more than 33 million Hershey Kisses every day. Since the turn of this century, Hershey Foods has grown from a one-product, one-plant operation to a $2 billion company with many U.S. and international plants providing an array of quality chocolate and confectionery products and services. According to Hershey, chocolate is low in cholesterol, caffeine, and sodium, as shown in Exhibit 1.

Hershey entered 1994 as the largest candy maker in the United States, with a 21.5 percent share of a $10 billion retail market. M&M Mars is second, with a 20 percent market share. Hershey also is the largest pasta manufacturer in the United States, having recently surpassed Borden. Hershey manufactures and sells pasta under a variety of names, including American Beauty, San Giorgio, Skinner, Perfection, Light 'n Fluffy, P&R, and Delmonico.

All but 11 percent of Hershey's sales and 2 percent of profits are generated in domestic markets. How long can Hershey survive as an almost exclusively domestic producer of candy and pasta, while its competitors gain economies of scale and experience in world markets?

HISTORY

Milton Hershey's love for candy making began with a childhood apprenticeship under candy maker Joe Royer of Lancaster, Pennsylvania. Hershey was eager to own a candy-making business. After numerous attempts and even bankruptcy, he finally gained success in the caramel business. Upon seeing the first chocolate-making equipment at the Chicago Exhibition in 1893, Hershey envisioned endless opportunities for the chocolate industry. He founded the Hershey Chocolate Company in 1893.

By 1901, the chocolate industry in America was growing rapidly. Hershey's sales reached $662,000 that year, creating the need for a new factory. Milton Hershey moved his company to Derry Church, Pennsylvania, which was renamed Hershey in 1906. The new Hershey factory provided a means of mass-producing a single chocolate product. In 1909, the Milton Hershey School for Orphans was founded. Mr. and Mrs. Hershey could not have children, so for years the Hershey Chocolate Company operated mainly to provide funds for the orphanage. Hershey's sales reached $5 million in 1911.

In 1918, the entire Hershey business was donated to the Milton Hershey School for Orphans. In 1927, the Hershey Chocolate Company was incorporated under the laws of the state of Delaware and listed on the New York Stock Exchange. That same year, 20 percent of Hershey's stock was sold to the public. Between 1930 and 1960, Hershey went through tremendous growth; the name "Hershey" became a household word. Milton Hershey died in 1945.

In 1963, Hershey acquired the H. B. Reese Candy Company, maker of Reese's Peanut Butter Cups, Reese's Pieces, and Reese's Peanut Butter Chips. Later acquisitions included San Giorgio Macaroni and Delmonico Foods, both pasta manufacturers, in 1966, and the Cory Corporation, a provider of coffee services to U.S. and

---

EXHIBIT 1   Chocolate Myths: Some Questions and Answers as Provided by Hershey

IS CHOCOLATE HIGH IN SATURATED FAT, THE FAT THAT RAISES BLOOD CHOLESTEROL LEVELS?

Milk chocolate is actually low in cholesterol. A 1.55-ounce *Hershey's* milk chocolate bar contains only 10 milligrams of cholesterol, all of which comes from the milk used in the milk chocolate. (An 8-ounce glass of whole milk has approximately 36 milligrams of cholesterol.)

Cocoa is cholesterol-free and, because it is low in fat (14 percent by weight), it is the only chocolate baking ingredient included in fat-restricted diets by the American Heart Association.

WHAT IS VANILLIN AND WHY DOES HERSHEY USE IT IN ITS MILK CHOCOLATE?

Vanillin is a vanilla-like flavoring used in some of our products. It is more readily available, less expensive and more consistent in quality than vanilla. It has been used by virtually all chocolate manufacturers for many years.

IS CHOCOLATE HIGH IN CAFFEINE?

Related to the hyperactivity issue is the belief that chocolate contains

large amounts of caffeine. The reality is, however, that a 1.55-ounce *Hershey's* milk chocolate bar contains only 10 milligrams of caffeine. How does this compare to other foods? A 5-ounce cup of regular automatic drip coffee contains 137 milligrams, a 12-ounce can of a regular cola beverage contains approximately 30–46 milligrams, and a 5-ounce cup of instant decaffeinated coffee contains approximately 3 milligrams of caffeine.

DOES CHOCOLATE CONTAIN HIGH LEVELS OF CHOLESTEROL?

It was once believed that all dietary saturated fats increased blood cholesterol levels. Not anymore. Recent studies have shown that stearic acid, one of the primary saturated fats found in chocolate, behaves differently from other saturated fats. In fact, stearic acid has no effect on, or may actually lower, blood cholesterol levels.

DOES CHOCOLATE PROMOTE TOOTH DECAY?

Tooth decay is a food-related disease. Sugars, as a group, play a role in tooth decay as do most foods. Tooth decay occurs for a variety of reasons, such as genetic makeup, lack of good oral hygiene, food

lingering in the mouth, consistency of the food and the frequency of consumption. A fact not commonly known, however, is that chocolate promotes less tooth decay than do crackers, raisins, or granola bars. Chocolate actually appears to modify the cavity-causing potential of its sugar. It contains a component that blocks the production of plaque, the first stage of tooth decay. In addition, the cocoa butter in chocolate melts quickly and helps to clear the mouth, thereby reducing the potential to cause cavities.

IS CHOCOLATE HIGH IN SODIUM?

A 1.55-ounce *Hershey's* milk chocolate bar contains only 40 milligrams of sodium; a *Special Dark* chocolate bar contains 5 milligrams; a *Mr. Goodbar* chocolate bar contains 20 milligrams. In fact, by Food and Drug Administration standards, many of *Hershey's* products qualify as "low sodium." Much higher amounts of sodium are found in other common foods. For example, an ounce of cheddar cheese has 198 milligrams, and a slice of whole wheat bread has 132 milligrams.

Source: Hershey Foods Corporation

Canadian businesses, in 1967. In 1968, Hershey Chocolate Corporation changed its name to Hershey Foods Corporation. Between 1976 and 1984, William Dearden served as Hershey's chief executive officer. An orphan who grew up in the Milton Hershey School for Orphans, Dearden diversified the company to reduce its dependence on fluctuating cocoa and sugar prices.

In 1977, Hershey acquired Y&S Candy Corporation, a manufacturer of licorice-type products, such as Y&S Twizzlers, Nibs, and Bassett's Allsorts. In 1978, Hershey purchased Procino-Rossi, a pasta company, and in 1979 it acquired Skinner Macaroni Company and Friendly Ice Cream Corporation. Richard Zimmerman replaced William Dearden as chief executive officer of Hershey in 1984. That year, Zimmerman divested the company of Hershey's Cory Foods division and acquired A. B. Marabou of Sweden. He purchased Franklin Restaurants in 1985. In 1986, Hershey acquired the Dietrich Corporation, maker of Luden's Throat Drops, Luden's Mellomints, Queen Anne chocolate-covered cherries, and 5th Avenue candy bars. On April 28, 1986, Dearden retired from Hershey's board of directors after a liftetime association and 29-year career with the corporation.

Hershey acquired the Canadian confectionery and snack nut operations of Nabisco Brands Ltd. in June 1987. These businesses include bar and bagged candy items such as Oh Henry!, Eat-More, Cherry Blossom, Glosettes, Lowney, Life Savers, Breath Savers, Planter nuts, Beaver nuts, Chipits chocolate chips, Moirs boxed chocolates, Care*Free gum, and Bubble Yum gum. Hershey's debt as a percentage of total capitalization increased to 29 percent by year-end 1987, but the company achieved record sales, earnings, and dividends that year.

In 1988, Hershey acquired Peter Paul/Cadbury's U.S. candy operations, which included plant facilities in Hazleton and York, Pennsylvania, and Naugatuck, Connecticut. This agreement allowed Hershey to manufacture and market the following new products in the United States: Mounds, Almond Joy, York Peppermint Pattie, Cadbury Dairy Milk, Cadbury Fruit & Nut, Cadbury Caramello, and Cadbury Creme Eggs. Hershey received rights to market the Peter Paul products worldwide. This acquisition cost Hershey $285 million, plus assumption of $30 million of Cadbury's debt. The York facility was closed on January 20, 1989, and its operations moved to Hershey's Reading, Pennsylvania, plant.

Hershey Foods revised its mission statement in 1989 to read as below:

Hershey Foods Corporation's mission is to become a major diversified food company and a leading company in every aspect of our business as:

The number one confectionery company in North America, moving toward worldwide confectionery market share leadership.

A respected and valued supplier of high-quality, branded consumer food products in North America and selected international markets.

During 1989, Hershey's Sherbrooke Canadian plant was closed, and other Canadian manufacturing facilities were combined into Hershey's existing facility at Smith Falls, Ontario. Also during 1989, Hershey introduced five new baking items, and the Symphony chocolate bar moved into national distribution. Hershey test-marketed the first microwave pasta, called Perfection. A newly formed venture group introduced a line of chocolate bar flavored puddings to selected East Coast markets in late 1989.

In 1990, Hershey acquired Ronzoni Foods Corporation from Kraft General Foods Corporation for $80 million. The purchase included the dry pasta, pasta sauces, and cheese businesses of Ronzoni Foods. The acquired businesses had sales of approximately $85 million and strengthened Hershey's position as the number two branded pasta supplier in the United States.

In 1991, Hershey acquired Gubor Schokoladen, a German manufacturer and marketer of high-quality assorted pralines and seasonal chocolates. Gubor has two manufacturing plants in Germany and provided Hershey with increased European presence. Also in 1991, Hershey established an employee stock ownership plan (ESOP), which was funded by a 7.75 percent loan of $47.9 million from the company. In October 1991, Hershey purchased Nacional de Dulces (NDD) and renamed this company Hershey Mexico. Hershey Mexico has its main offices and manufacturing plant in Guadalajara, Mexico. It produces, imports, and markets chocolate products for the Mexican market under the Hershey brand name.

In April 1992, Hershey divested of Petybon S. A., its pasta and biscuit manufacturer in Brazil. Also in 1992, Hershey divested its stake in Freia Marabou, a Norwegian confectioner, for $220 million in cash. Company plans for 1993 include spending $200 million of this cash to repurchase its own common stock. Hershey's revenues and net income increased 11 percent in 1992, while long-term debt fell to $174 million, the lowest level in a decade.

Hershey Foods Corporation today is comprised of five divisions: Hershey Chocolate U.S.A., Hershey Canada, Inc., Hershey International, Ltd., Hershey Refrigerated Products, and Hershey Pasta Group. For the corporation as a whole, strategic objectives are to achieve a return on net assets of 12 percent without acquisitions and 10 percent with a major acquisition. Growth in earnings per share is targeted to be double-digit, and an "A" debt rating is to be maintained. Hershey's current organizational chart is provided in Exhibit 2.

Hershey Foods' mission statement today is given as follows:

Hershey Foods Corporation's mission is to be a focused food company and a leader in every aspect of our business as:

The number one confectionery company and number one branded pasta company in North America, and moving toward worldwide confectionery market share leadership.

A respected and valued supplier of other high quality, branded consumer food products in North America and selected international markets.

HERSHEY CHOCOLATE U.S.A.

Hershey has chocolate and confectionery manufacturing operations in Hershey, Pennsylvania; Oakdale, California; Stuarts Draft, Virginia; Reading, Pennsylvania; Hazleton, Pennsylvania; Lancaster, Pennsylvania; and Naugatuck, Connecticut. Hershey Chocolate U.S.A. produces an extensive line of products, including bar candies, bagged candies, syrup, baking ingredients, chocolate drink mixes, granola bars, dessert toppings, and dessert puddings. These products are produced in numerous packaged forms, marketed under more than 40 brand names, and sold in over one million retail outlets in the United States.

Hershey Chocolate U.S.A. achieved record sales and earnings in 1992, as indicated in Exhibit 3. Several new products were introduced during the year, including

EXHIBIT 2   Hershey's Organizational Chart

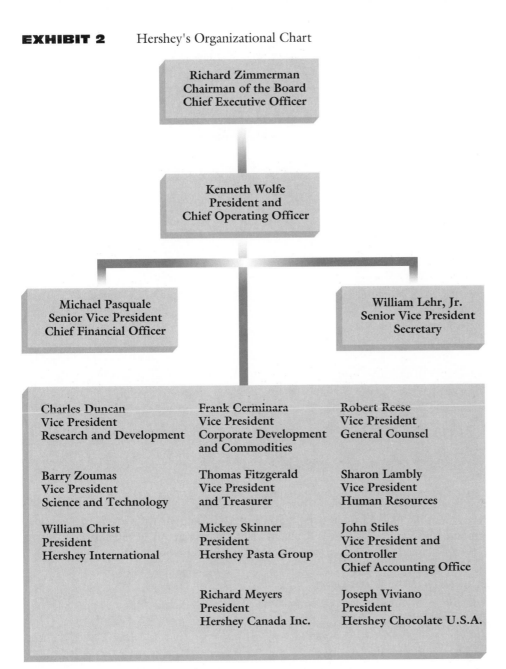

Source: Adapted from information in Hershey's 1992 *Annual Report*.

Amazin' Fruit gummy bears fruit candy. Hershey worked closely with McDonald's Corporation and the Nickelodeon cable television network to initially provide Amazin' Fruit. Y&S Twizzlers and Nibs candies are Hershey's other major non-chocolate candies. Hershey also is the leader in licorice-type candies. Another new product introduction by the Hershey Chocolate division is the Cookies 'n' Mint chocolate bar. Established candy brands that contributed significantly to growth

EXHIBIT 3 Hershey's Sales and Income by Product Area (in millions of dollars; 1993 and 1994 figures are estimated)

	1992	PERCENTAGE CHANGE	1993	PERCENTAGE CHANGE	1994	PERCENTAGE CHANGE
NET REVENUES						
Hershey Chocolate USA	$2,420.8	11	$2,650.0	9	$2,850.0	8
Pasta Operations	366.0	8	395.0	8	440.0	11
Canadian Operations	233.0	1	250.0	7	280.0	12
International Operations	200.0	33	285.0	43	375.0	32
Total Revenues	$3,219.8	11	$3,580.0	11	$3,945.0	10
OPERATING PROFITS						
Hershey Chocolate USA	$412.2	6	$449.0	9	$481.0	7
Operating Profit Margin	17.0%		16.9%		16.9%	
Pasta Operations	$ 36.8	12	$ 39.5	7	$ 44.6	13
Operating Profit Margin	10.1%		10.0%		10.1%	
Canadian Operations	$ 14.8	0	$ 15.5	5	$ 17.2	11
Operating Profit Margin	6.4%		6.2%		6.1%	
International Operations	$9.0	0	$ 14.1	57	$ 20.2	43
Operating Profit Margin	4.5%		4.9%		5.4%	
Total Operating Margin	$472.8	6	$518.1	10	$563.0	9
Operating Profit Margin	14.7%		14.5%		14.3%	

Source: *Hershey Internal Report.*

included Hershey's Miniatures chocolate bars, Reese's Peanut Butter Cups, York Peppermint Patties, Kit Kat bars, Y&S Twizzlers candy, Mr. Goodbar, Mounds, Almond Joy, Symphony, and Whatchamacallit candy bar. All of Hershey Chocolate U.S.A.'s confectionery and grocery products are listed below:

CONFECTIONERY PRODUCTS

Amazin' Fruit Gummy Bears Candy
BarNone Candy Bar
Cadbury's Dairy Milk Chocolate Bar
Cadbury's Krisp Chocolate Bar
Cadbury's Roast Almond Chocolate Bar
5th Avenue Candy Bar
Hershey's Cookies 'n' Mint Chocolate Bar
Hershey's Golden Collection Almond
Hershey's Kisses Chocolates
Hershey's Milk Chocolate Bar
Hugs
Krackel Chocolate Bar
Mr. Goodbar Chocolate Bar
Nibs Candy

Almond Joy Candy Bar
Cadbury's Creme Eggs Candy
Cadbury's Fruit & Nut Chocolate Bar
Cadbury's Mini Eggs Candy
Caramello Candy Bar
Helps Cough Suppressant Tablets
Hershey's Golden Collection Solitaires
Hershey's Kisses with Almonds Chocolates
Hershey's Milk Chocolate Bar with Almonds
Hershey's Miniatures Chocolate Bars
Kit Kat Wafer Bar
Luden's Throat Drops
Mounds Candy Bar
Reese's Crunchy Peanut Butter Cup

Reese's Peanut Butter Cups
Reese's Pieces Candy
Skor Toffee Bar
Super Twizzlers Candy
Symphony Chocolate Bar with Almonds and Toffee Chips
Whatchamacallit Candy Bar

Reese's Peanut Butter Chips
Rolo Caramels in Milk Chocolate
Special Dark Chocolate Bar
Symphony Chocolate Bar
Twizzlers Candy
Y&S Candy
York Peppermint Pattie

GROCERY PRODUCTS

Hershey's Baking Chocolate
Hershey's Chocolate Drink
Hershey's Chocolate Milk Mix
Hershey's Cocoa
Hershey's Mint Chips
Hershey's Premium Chocolate Chunks
Hershey's Syrup
Hershey's Vanilla Chunks
Reese's Peanut Butter

Hershey's Chocolate Chips
Hershey's Chocolate Milk
Hershey's Chocolate Shoppe Toppings
Hershey's Fudge Toppings
Hershey's Premium Baking Bars
Hershey's Sweetened Coconut Flakes
Hershey's Vanilla Chips
Mini Chips Semi-Sweet Chocolate

Hershey faces seasonal demand for its products. Confectionery sales are generally lowest during the second quarter of the year and highest during the third and fourth quarters, due largely to the holiday seasons. For example, in 1992, Hershey generated only 19 percent of annual sales during the second quarter. In contrast, 30 percent of annual sales were generated during the fourth quarter. For the third quarter of 1993, Hershey's confection volume was up 14 percent, due partly to strong demand for Hugs and Cookies 'n' Mint. Analysts estimate sales of $100 million of Hugs and $400 million of Kisses.

Conventional wisdom in the candy industry is that a person rarely selects the same candy bar twice in a row; consequently, product variety is crucial to success. In addition, marketing issues relative to health, nutrition, and weight consciousness are important. Hershey's marketing strategy for its products is based on consistently superior product quality, mass distribution, and best possible consumer value in terms of price and weight. The firm utilizes a variety of advertising and promotional programs to implement its strategy. The media Hershey uses most for advertising are network television, followed by syndicated television, spot (local) television, magazines, and network and spot radio. Hershey's advertising expenses increased 21 percent in 1992 to $536 million. A comparison of candy advertising expenditures for Hershey versus Mars is given in Exhibit 4.

For the year ended August 31, 1993, Hershey's confectionery market share rose 1.4 percent, to 33.8 percent. The quality of share improvement is reinforced by M&M Mars' 12-month market share drop of 2.8 percent, to 26.5 percent. The market share gap between the two companies is an unprecedented 7.3 share points (the gap rarely reaches 6 percent). At the end of the second quarter 1993, the share gap was 6.5 points.

Hershey Chocolate U.S.A. recently completed construction of a 160,000-square-foot chocolate-processing facility in Hershey, Pennsylvania. The facility operates with a team concept among employees and managers to foster a sense of ownership. Adjoining this new facility is another new 180,000-square-foot chocolate plant. Building these new facilities has been in response to the U.S. confectionery market's growing 4 percent annually in sales volume. The nonchocolate segment, which accounts for about one-third of the overall sweets market, is growing at 6.5 percent

EXHIBIT 4   First-Quarter 1993 Advertising Expenditures for Candy by Hershey Foods Corporation and Mars Inc. (in millions of dollars)

	1992	1993	PERCENTAGE CHANGE
HERSHEY FOODS CORP.			
Hershey's Bar None candy bar	—	4.8	—
Reese's peanut butter cups	3.5	4.2	20.0%
Hershey's Chocolate Kisses	2.6	3.9	50.0%
York Peppermint Patties	—	3.7	—
Kit Kat candy bar	4.0	3.6	(10.0%)
Amazin' Fruit candies	0.1	3.4	—
Hershey's candy bars	3.4	3.2	(5.9%)
Hershey Symphony bar	3.4	3.1	(8.8%)
Cadbury Creme Eggs	2.1	2.6	23.8%
Fifth Avenue candy bar	1.3	2.5	92.3%
Mr. Goodbar candy	1.3	1.5	15.4%
Peter Paul Mounds and Almond Joy	2.5	1.2	(52.0%)
Reese's Pieces candy	1.3	0.9	(30.8%)
Cadbury Caramello candy	1.6	0.9	(43.8%)
Hershey's candies	—	0.6	—
Twizzlers	—	0.3	—
Others	1.8	0.3	(83.3%)
Total	28.9	40.5	40.1%
MARS INC.			
M&M candies	8.8	5.6	(36.4%)
Snickers candy bar	7.9	4.0	(49.4%)
Dove candy bar	0.2	3.9	1,850%
Snickers Peanut Butter candy bar	—	2.6	—
Twix candy bar	1.5	2.1	40.0%
Milky Way Dark candy	—	1.7	—
Milky Way candy	0.6	1.5	83.3%
Skittles candy	1.0	1.1	10.0%
Milky Way II candy	—	0.4	—
3 Musketeers candy bar	0.5	0.2	(60.0%)
Starburst candies	—	0.1	—
Bounty coconut candy bar	—	0.1	—
Others	7.6	0.1	(98.7%)
Total	28.1	23.4	(16.7%)

Source: Company Data.

annually, while the chocolate segment is growing at 2.5 percent. Hershey has only 4 percent of the nonchocolate confectionery market, while the leader is RJR Nabisco, with 18 percent. RJR's Life Savers and Gummy Life Savers compete with Hershey's Amazin' Fruit Gummy Bears.

Hershey Canada has manufacturing facilities in Smith Falls, Ontario, Montreal, Quebec, and Dartmouth, Nova Scotia. Hershey Canada has attained market share leadership in practically every phase of the Canadian confectionery market, despite a 9 percent decline in the Canadian dollar exchange rate in 1992. Some Hershey Canada candy products that sell especially well are the Oh Henry! and Lowney brand names, hard candy sold under the brand names Life Savers and Breath Savers, nuts under the Planters name, gum under the Care*Free and Bubble Yum brands, and the Skor toffee bar.

Canadian tax on confectionery sales was reduced from 13.5 percent to 7 percent in 1991. This tax reduction action continues to benefit Hershey Canada sales. The Canadian division of Hershey markets the following products:

CONFECTIONERY PRODUCTS

Almondillos Chocolates
Bridge Mixture Candy
Eat-More Candy
Goodies Candy
Hershey Chocolate-Covered Almonds
Hershey Milk Chocolate Bar
Life Savers Candy
Moirs Chocolates
Oh Henry! Chocolate Bar
Planters Nuts
Skor Toffee Candy Bar
Special Dark Chocolate Bar

Breath Savers Mints
Cherry Blossom Candy
Glosette Candy
Hershey Almond Bar
Hershey Kisses Milk Chocolates
Hershey Raisins and Almonds Bar
Lowney Candy
Nibs Candy
Ovation Chocolate Covered Sticks
Reese's Peanut Butter Cups Candy
Special Crisp Candy Bar
Twizzlers candy
Y&S Candy

GROCERY PRODUCTS

Brown Cow Chocolate Syrup
Chipits Chocolate Chips
Hershey's Chocolate Chips
Hershey's Instant Chocolate Syrup
Strawberry Cow Strawberry Syrup

Chipits Baking Chocolate
Chipits Cocoa
Hershey's Cocoa
Hershey's Syrup
Top Scotch Butterscotch Syrup

Hershey's Canadian operation generates $250 million in annual sales, about 7 percent of the company total. The Canadian confectionery market is estimated at approximately $1 billion wholesale, with chocolate bars accounting for about 56 percent. Hershey is number three in chocolate bars and number one in boxed chocolates, a fast-growing segment that accounts for 16 percent of the market. Hershey's first-quarter 1993 Canadian sales rose 7 percent, but this increase was negated by a drop in the value of the Canadian dollar. Third-quarter 1993 Canadian sales increased another 7 percent, the result of a 17 percent volume increase and a 10 percent price decline due again to a weakening Canadian dollar. This quarter also was the first time in history when a Hershey candy product became the best seller in Canada. The product was Oh Henry!

Hershey's export sales have been increasing in recent years, benefiting immensely from a weak U.S. dollar in most foreign countries. Much of the results were due to higher sales of Hershey Kisses chocolates, Hershey's milk chocolate bar with almonds and Almond Joy bars in Mexico and higher sales of Hershey Kisses in the Philippines, South Korea, and Singapore. A new market for Hershey products was established in New Zealand in 1992. Exhibit 5 provides export information for confectionery products.

Hershey's recent sales and earnings in Mexico and Germany, however, have been lower than expected. Hershey International's licensing revenues have been growing recently, especially the Snow Brand Milk Products venture in Japan and the Maeil Dairy

EXHIBIT 5 International Trade in Confectionery Products, 1989–91 (in thousands of dollars)

	EXPORTS		
COUNTRY	1989	1990	1991
Canada	43,363	102,003	118,655
Mexico	40,346	42,039	54,917
Japan	34,446	33,151	26,130
South Korea	12,342	14,477	10,046
Philippines	6,056	6,212	9,415
Hong Kong	6,006	6,135	7,113
Taiwan	8,289	7,555	6,260
Australia	2,245	3,829	4,438
Saudi Arabia	2,181	2,029	3,751
Venezuela	417	1,159	2,359
All others	21,886	23,025	27,791
Total	177,577	241,614	270,875

	IMPORTS		
	1989	1990	1991
Canada	29,334	52,022	80,608
Germany	36,507	40,356	59,986
United Kingdom	17,893	22,080	30,797
Italy	12,081	12,239	18,220
Netherlands	30,885	34,640	15,933
Brazil	17,322	17,951	15,198
Mexico	10,586	10,704	13,425
Switzerland	8,239	14,056	13,195
Spain	10,075	10,630	10,811
France	6,083	5,891	8,291
All others	66,924	68,986	74,001
Total	245,929	289,555	340,465

Source: U.S. Department of Commerce, Bureau of the Census.

Industry venture in South Korea. In 1992, Hershey divested itself of its Petybon pasta operations in Brazil and acquired 100 percent ownership of the Hershey Japan operations.

Hershey's international division contributes about $200 million to annual sales, or 6 percent of the total. The division focuses heavily on the German and Mexican markets, both of which have been weak. Together, sales in Mexico and Germany were off 5 percent (down 3 percent in price, down 2 percent in volume) in the first quarter of 1993. However, exports to both countries increased, and the overall international operating income rose 15 percent on better cost controls. Total exports now amount to about $60 million and are increasing rapidly. Hershey recently consolidated its Japanese operation, which added $15–20 million in sales. Elsewhere, Hershey has licensing agreements in Korea and New Zealand. Analysts foresee annual sales growth of 10 to 15 percent in foreign markets, with profits growing at a double-digit clip. However, at current growth rates, the international business will remain a small part of Hershey's business. Analysts believe Hershey should expand geographically, perhaps through a major acquisition.

For the first quarter of 1993, Hershey's international sales declined another 5 percent, and volume fell 2 percent. Lack of presence anywhere in the world except Mexico, Germany, and Japan severely hurts Hershey.

HERSHEY REFRIGERATED PRODUCTS

The Refrigerated Products division of Hershey recently introduced Hershey's Free chocolate bar flavor puddings. This product is cholesterol-free, contains no artificial sweeteners, and has only 100 calories per serving. Introduction of this new product, though, hurt Hershey's regular puddings, which experienced a decline in volume for the first time ever.

HERSHEY PASTA GROUP

What is pasta? Pasta is paste or dough made from semolina milled from durum wheat, a class of hard wheat grown in the United States, primarily in North Dakota. It is formed into shapes such as spaghetti and macaroni, then dried, boxed, and readied for sale. Hershey's pasta sales have been growing 5 percent annually compared to an industry growth rate of 2.5 percent. Hershey's Ronzoni, San Giorgio, and American Beauty brands overtook Borden's Creamette brand in 1993, with 27.7 percent share to Borden's 27.6 percent. Two other major competitors in the U.S. pasta market, Quaker Oats and CPC, continue to lose market share to Hershey and Borden.

Hershey first expanded its business from cocoa-based confectionery products into pasta with the acquisition in 1966 of San Giorgio Macaroni, Inc., of Lebanon, Pennsylvania. Later that year Hershey acquired a Louisville, Kentucky, firm known as Delmonico Foods, Inc. Subsequently, Hershey acquired additional pasta product companies in a variety of regions, including Procino-Rossi Corp., Auburn, New York, in 1978; Skinner Macaroni Company, Omaha, Nebraska (1979); American Beauty Brand (purchased from Pillsbury Company) (1984); G&R Pasta Company, Inc., Philadelphia, Pennsylvania (1986); Ronzoni Foods Corporation (from Kraft General Foods) (1990); and American Italian Pasta Company, Excelsior Springs, Missouri (1990). With these regional acquisitions Hershey's Pasta Group is able to manufacture and distribute pasta throughout the United States under the following brand names: San Giorgio, Skinner, Delmonico, P&R, Light 'n Fluffy, American Beauty, Perfection, Pastamania, and Ronzoni.

Products of the Hershey Pasta Group are divided into four general categories: long goods, short cuts, egg products and specialties. A brief listing of the major items in each category follows:

LONG GOODS

Capellini
Linguine
Perciatelli/Long Macaroni
Spaghettini
Angel Hair

Fettucine
Margherite
Spaghetti
Vermicelli

SHORT CUTS

Alphabets
Dumplings
Elbows
Orzo
Fideo Cortado
Occhi Dilupo
Rings/Spaghetti Rings
Mafalda
Shells
Macarrones
Mezzani rigati

Ditalini/Salad Macaroni
Ancini Pepe
Fusilli
Ridged Mostaccioli
Radiatore
Rigatoni
Rotelle Curly-Macaroni/Twirls
Rotini/Twists
Ziti
Tubetti
Mezzani

EGG PRODUCTS

Egg Fettucini
Egg Pastina
Pot Pie Bows
Spinach Noodles

Kluski
Noodles Fine, Medium, Extra-wide
Pot Pie Squares

SPECIALTIES

Long Fusilli
Lasagne
Healthy Ribbons

Jumbo Shells
Manicotti
Cannelloni

The popularity of pasta has increased over the last ten years. Per capita consumption of pasta has grown from 12.8 pounds in 1980 to almost 20 pounds today. Hershey recently expanded pasta production capacity in its Winchester, Virginia, plant. This is a state-of-the-art facility that provides Hershey with much-needed capacity. Foreign manufacturers of pasta, especially companies in Italy and Turkey, are now marketing pasta in the United States at accelerating rates.

HERSHEY'S OPERATIONS

Social Responsibility. Hershey Foods Corporation is committed to the values of its founder, Milton S. Hershey—the highest standard of quality, honesty, fairness, integrity, and respect. The firm makes annual contributions of cash, products, and services to a variety of national and local charitable organizations. The corporation operates the Milton Hershey School for socially disadvantaged children and is the sole sponsor of the Hershey National Track and Field Youth Program. Hershey also makes contributions to the Children's Miracle Network, a national program benefiting children's hospitals across the United States.

Research and Development. Hershey engages in research and development activities to develop new products, improve the quality of existing products, and improve and modernize production processes. The company's recent research and development expenditures are listed below (in millions of dollars):

Year	Research and Development
1984	$9.9
1985	11.2
1986	12.5
1987	12.9
1988	15.7
1989	16.1
1990	19.2
1991	22.8
1992	24.2

Hershey recently completed a test market of its reduced calorie and fat candy bar. Test results suggest that consumers desire the real thing—calories, fat and all—when they indulge in a candy bar. This finding is consistent with a general trend in the U.S. away from fitness, exercise, and nutrition toward a more sedentary life-style.

Finance. Hershey's 1992 financial statements are given in Exhibits 6 through 9. Note that both revenues and net income increased 11 percent in 1992, while long-term debt declined 38 percent. Hershey's total number of full-time employees declined to 13,700 in 1992. For 1993, revenues of Hershey Chocolate, Pasta, Canadian, and International operations are expected to increase 9, 8, 7, and 43 percent, respectively.

Advertising and Promotion. M&M Mars in the early 1990s seemed lethargic in terms of advertising, promotion, and new product introductions. Hershey has tried to capitalize on this by spending more on advertising and promotion, which increased 21 percent in 1992 alone. Hershey's recent expenditures on advertising and promotion are given below (in millions of dollars):

Year	Advertising	Promotion
1987	$ 97	$171
1988	99	230
1989	121	256
1990	146	315
1991	117	325
1992	137	398

GLOBAL ISSUES

The chocolate/cocoa products industry is SIC 2066 while candy/confectionery is SIC 2064. Demand for chocolate increased nearly 4 percent in both 1991 and 1992, following a sharp decline in 1990 when price increases reduced consumption. The confectionery industry introduced nearly 400 new candy products in 1991 and 1992.

U.S. exports of candy increased 32 percent in 1992 to $359 million, while imports increased 24 percent to $420 million. Canada and Mexico represent about 64 percent

EXHIBIT 6   Hershey Food Corporation, Consolidated Statements of Income
(in thousands of dollars except per share amounts)

FOR THE YEARS ENDED DECEMBER 31,	1992	1991	1990
Net Sales	$3,219,805	$2,899,165	$2,715,609
Costs and Expenses:			
Cost of sales	1,833,388	1,694,404	1,588,360
Selling, marketing and administrative	958,189	814,459	776,668
Total costs and expenses	2,791,577	2,508,863	2,365,028
Gain on Business Restructuring, Net	—	—	35,540
Income before Interest and Income Taxes	428,228	390,302	386,121
Interest expense, net	27,240	26,845	24,603
Income before Income Taxes	400,988	363,457	361,518
Provision for income taxes	158,390	143,929	145,636
Net Income	$ 242,598	$ 219,528	$ 215,882
Net Income per Share	$ 2.69	$ 2.43	$ 2.39
Cash Dividends Paid per Share:			
Common Stock—Regular	$ 1.030	$ .940	$ .840
Common Stock—Special	—	—	.150
Class B Common Stock—Regular	.935	.850	.755
Class B Common Stock—Special	—	—	.135

Source: *Annual Report*, 1992.

of total export value, while Canada and Germany represent 41 percent of the import value. Mexico's candy tariffs currently are 20 percent compared to the U.S. tariff of 7 percent. Note that none of the high-candy-consumption countries of Western Europe are major markets for U.S.-made candy.

The main distribution channels for chocolate are grocery, drug, and department stores as well as vending machine operators. Almost all of these distributors are local, regional, or national; only a few are multinational. While chocolate producers have not yet developed globally uniform marketing programs, the situation is changing. European unification extended grocery and department store channels of distribution. For example, Safeway, a U.S. grocery chain, now operates stores in

Hershey Foods Corporation, Consolidated Balance Sheets
(in thousands of dollars)

DECEMBER 31,	1992	1991
ASSETS		
Current Assets:		
Cash and cash equivalents	$ 24,114	$ 71,124
Accounts receivable—trade	173,646	159,805
Inventories	457,179	436,917
Prepaid expenses and other	105,966	76,633
Investment interest	179,076	—
Total current assets	939,981	744,479
Property, Plant, and Equipment, Net	1,295,989	1,145,666
Intangibles Resulting from Business Acquisitions	399,768	421,694
Other Assets	37,171	29,983
LIABILITIES AND STOCKHOLDERS' EQUITY	$2,672,909	$2,341,822
Current Liabilities:		
Accounts payable	$ 127,175	$ 137,890
Accrued liabilities	240,816	226,267
Accrued income taxes	5,682	22,000
Short-term debt	259,045	57,620
Current portion of long-term debt	104,224	26,955
Total current liabilities	736,942	470,732
Long-term Debt	174,273	282,933
Other Long-term Liabilities	92,950	80,907
Deferred Income Taxes	203,465	171,999
Total liabilities	$1,207,630	$1,006,571
Stockholders' Equity		
Preferred Stock, outstanding shares: none in 1992 and 1991	—	—
Common Stock, outstanding shares:		
74,929,057 in 1992 and 74,921,282 in 1991	74,929	74,921
Class B Common Stock, outstanding shares:		
15,257,279 in 1992 and 15,265,054 in 1991	15,257	15,265
Additional paid-in capital	52,129	52,509
Cumulative foreign currency translation adjustments	2,484	26,424
Unearned ESOP compensation	(44,708)	(47,902)
Retained earnings	1,365,188	1,214,034
Total stockholders' equity	1,465,279	1,335,251
	$2,672,909	$2,341,822

Source: Annual Report, 1992

EXHIBIT 8   Hershey Foods Corporation, Consolidated Statements of Cash Flows

FOR THE YEARS ENDED DECEMBER 31,	1992	1991
Cash Flows Provided from (Used by) Operating Activities		
Net income	$ 242,598	$ 219,528
Adjustments to reconcile net income to net cash provided from operations:		
Depreciation and amortization	97,087	85,413
Deferred income taxes	21,404	20,654
Gain on business restructuring, net	—	—
Changes in assets and liabilities, net of effects from business acquisitions:		
Accounts receivable—trade	(13,841)	(6,404)
Inventories	(20,262)	(43,949)
Accounts payable	(10,715)	4,070
Other assets and liabilities	(20,707)	94,270
Other, net	649	(26,242)
Net Cash Provided from Operating Activities	296,213	347,340
Cash Flows Provided from (Used by) Investing Activities		
Capital additions	(249,795)	(226,071)
Business acquisitions	—	(44,108)
Sale of equity interest	—	—
Purchase of investment interest	(179,076)	—
Other, net	6,581	(1,510)
Net Cash (Used by) Investing Activities	(422,290)	(271,689)
Cash Flows Provided from (Used by) Financing Activities		
Net increase in short-term debt	201,425	56,489
Long-term borrowings	1,259	23,620
Repayment of long-term debt	(32,173)	(27,861)
Repayment of assumed debt	—	—
Loan to ESOP	—	(47,902)
Proceeds from sale of Common Stock to ESOP	—	47,902
Cash dividends paid	(91,444)	(83,401)
Net Cash Provided from (Used by) Financing Activities	79,067	(31,153)
Increase (Decrease) in Cash and Cash Equivalents	(47,010)	44,498
Cash and Cash Equivalents as of January 1	71,124	26,626
Cash and Cash Equivalents as of December 31	$ 24,114	$ 71,124
Interest Paid	$ 29,515	$ 24,468
Income Taxes Paid	$ 151,490	$ 119,038

Source: Annual Report, 1992

EXHIBIT 9 Hershey Foods Corporation, Net Sales, Income and Income Taxes, and Assets by Geographic Segments (in thousands of dollars)

DECEMBER 31,	1992	1991	1990
Net sales:			
Domestic	$2,871,438	$2,566,448	$2,508,542
International	348,367	332,717	207,067
Total	$3,219,805	$2,899,165	$2,715,609
Income before interest and income taxes:			
Domestic	$ 419,317	$ 381,549	$ 344,303
International	8,911	8,753	6,278
Gain on Business Restructuring, Net	---	---	35,540
Total	$ 428,228	$ 390,302	$ 386,121
Identifiable assets as of December 31:			
Domestic	$2,353,230	$2,003,425	$1,820,434
International	319,679	338,397	258,394
Total	$2,672,909	$2,341,822	$2,078,828

Source: Annual Report, 1992

Canada, Britain, Germany, and Saudi Arabia. As global channels of distribution become more available for chocolate manufacturers, global marketing uniformity will become more prevalent in the industry. Global cultural convergence is accelerating the need for more global marketing uniformity in the confectionery industry. Despite the global success of the movie E.T., about an extraterrestrial being who happens to be fond of Hershey's Reese's Pieces, Hershey did not promote this product globally.

The confectionery industry is characterized by high manufacturing economies of scale. Hershey's U.S. factory, for example, occupies more than two million square feet, is highly automated, and contains a great deal of heavy equipment, vats, and containers. It is the largest chocolate plant in the world. High manufacturing costs in any industry encourage global market expansion, globally standardized products, and globally centralized production.

The confectionery industry is also characterized by high transportation costs for moving milk and sugar, the primary raw materials. This fact motivates companies such as Hershey to locate near their supply sources. Since milk can be obtained in large volumes in many countries, chocolate producers have many options in locating plants. This is true also because producing chocolate is not labor-intensive, and it does not require highly skilled labor.

Product development costs in the confectionery industry are relatively low, since the process largely involves mixing different combinations of the same ingredients. Whenever product development costs are low in an industry, firms are spurred to globalize existing brands rather than develop new ones.

Industry analysts expect the candy industry to continue to grow. Consumption of chocolate, according to industry analysts, is closely related to national income, although the Far East is an exception to this rule. Candy consumption varies in the major markets of the developed nations. Americans consume about 22 pounds of candy annually per person, and Europeans consume about 27 pounds of candy per person.

Chocolate accounts for about 54 percent of all candy consumed. Northern Europeans consume almost twice as much chocolate per capita as Americans. Among European countries, Switzerland, Norway, and the United Kingdom consume the most chocolate, while Finland, Yugoslavia, and Italy consume the least. The Japanese consume very little chocolate—about 1.4 kilos per capita. Throughout Asia and southern Europe, there is a preference for types of sweets other than chocolate, partly because of a high incidence of lactose intolerance (difficulty in digesting dairy products).

Many consumers worldwide are becoming more and more weight-conscious and health-oriented. Numerous organizations and individuals discourage candy consumption and promote the need for exercise and nutrition. The teenage customer base that historically has consumed so much chocolate is shrinking in the United States and most other countries. This clientele is being replaced by older, wealthier consumers, who prefer more sophisticated chocolates. In countries where birth rates and numbers of youth are still growing, disposable income tends to be low, posing a barrier to entry. The confectionery industry overall is thus undergoing transition.

Cocoa beans are the most important raw material used in the production of Hershey's products. This commodity is imported from West Africa, South America, and Far Eastern equatorial regions. West Africa accounts for approximately 60 percent of the world's crop. Cocoa beans exhibit wide fluctuations in price, flavor, and quality, due to (a) weather and other conditions affecting crop size; (b) consuming countries' demand requirements; (c) producing countries' sales policies; (d) speculative influences; and (e) international economics and currency movements. Cocoa bean prices are determined by a provisional International Cocoa Agreement formed by certain producing and consuming countries. The average price of cocoa beans for 1993 had fallen to 9 cents per pound, down from 53 cents per pound in 1991. To minimize the effects of cocoa bean price fluctuations, Hershey purchases large inventories of cocoa beans and cocoa products. Hershey also purchases and sells cocoa future contracts. Hershey maintains West African and Brazilian crop-forecasting operations and continually monitors economic and political factors affecting market conditions.

Hershey's second most important raw material is sugar. Sugar is subject to price supports under domestic farm legislation. Due to import quotas and duties, sugar prices paid by U.S. users are substantially higher than prices on the world market. The average wholesale list price for refined sugar has remained stable at 30 cents per pound over recent years.

Other raw materials that Hershey Corporation purchases in substantial quantities include semolina milled from durum wheat, milk, peanuts, almonds, and coconut. The prices of milk and peanuts are affected by federal marketing orders and subsidy programs of the U.S. Department of Agriculture. Raising and lowering price supports on milk and peanuts greatly affect the cost of Hershey's raw materials. Market prices of peanuts and almonds are generally determined in the latter months of each year, following harvest time.

Tariffs imposed by different countries can greatly impede or promote globalization within an industry, especially in the country where the product is manufactured. For example, U.S. tariffs on chocolate are very low, ranging from 35 cents per pound for mass-produced chocolate to about $2.50 per pound for some premium brands. Even a ten-cent difference in price among competing brands, however, makes a big difference to consumers.

Nationalistic tariffs as they impact candy are falling but still are high enough to be a concern. Japan, Korea, and Taiwan, for example, have reduced their tariffs on imported chocolate from 20 percent to 10 percent. Europe is retaining its 12 percent tariff on chocolate imports from outside Europe. The United States has a 5 percent tariff on solid chocolate products and a 7 percent tariff on all other chocolate confectionery products. Technology standards across countries are similar to tariffs in that they vary and can impact global strategy plans. Japan, for example, prohibits the sale of chocolates that contain the additives BHT and TBHQ, which are approved by the U.S. Food and Drug Administration.

COMPETITORS

The $10 billion U.S. confectionery industry is composed of six major competitors, who control nearly 70 percent of the market: Hershey, Mars, Jacobs Suchard of Switzerland, Nestlé of Switzerland, RJR Nabisco, and Leaf Inc. The remaining 30 percent is divided among many local and regional candy manufacturers.

Based in Switzerland, Nestlé clearly has an edge internationally, being the world leader in many food categories including candy, with 98 percent of its revenues coming from international sales. Hershey's other competitors also do much of their business in foreign markets. For example, Jacobs Suchard obtains 95 percent from international sales, Cadbury-Schweppes, 50 percent, and Mars, 50 percent, while Hershey is the least with 10 percent. Hershey's two major candy competitors are Mars and Nestlé.

Nestlé's chocolate business generally totals $4.5 billion wholesale, Jacobs Suchard, $1.8 billion, Mars, $4.5 billion, Cadbury, $2 billion, and Hershey, $4.5 billion. In total, all firms in the chocolate business sell $20 billion wholesale annually, and revenues are growing at 10 percent worldwide each year.

Mars. Hershey overtook Mars in 1988 as the leading candy manufacturer in the United States, but Mars has a stronger presence in Europe, Asia, Mexico, and Japan. Mars gained 12 percent of the market in Mexico after only one year of entering that market. Analysts estimate Mars' worldwide sales and profits to be just over $7 billion and $1 billion respectively. Mars was recently successful in introducing its Bounty chocolate, originally a European candy, into the United States without prior test marketing. Mars, unlike Hershey, uses uniform marketing globally. For example, the company's M&M candies slogan, "It melts in your mouth, not in your hands," is used worldwide. In contrast, Hershey's successful BarNone candy is named Temptation in Canada.

Based in Hackettstown, New Jersey, Mars is controlled by the Mars family through two brothers, John and Forrest, Jr. A marketing executive at Mars recently said, "Being no. 2 doesn't sit well with the brothers, and that's the biggest motivator." Mars was the first candy company to persuade merchants to put candy displays near cash registers in 1979. Mars is one of the world's largest private, closely held companies. It is a secretive company, unwilling to divulge financial information and corporate strategies. Recently, Mars has not been performing well, and there are reports of high turnover in its executive and sales ranks.

Unlike Hershey, Mars has historically relied upon extensive marketing and advertising expenditures to gain market share, rather than on product innovation. Mars has been repackaging, restyling, and reformulating its leading brands, including Snickers, M&Ms, Milky Way, and 3 Musketeers, but that strategy is now being supplemented with extensive product development. New Mars products include Bounty, Balisto, and PB Max. It also successfully developed and marketed frozen Snickers ice cream bars. The product was so successful that it dislodged Eskimo Pie and Original Klondike from the number one ice cream snack slot without any assistance from promotional advertising. Mars has world-class production facilities in Hackettstown, New Jersey; from that plant it ships products worldwide. In addition, it has manufacturing plants in Mexico and in several European locations.

Mars entered Russia in 1992 and today virtually owns the chocolate market there. Kentave, one of the three Mars distributors in Moscow, sells $5 million of Mars candy monthly. Kentave estimates Mars's total monthly sales in Russia to be about $20 million.

Nestlé. Nestlé, according to many analysts, is the number one food company in the world, with sizable exposure in Europe, the Far East, and South America. Nestlé sells products in over 360 countries on all five continents, many in the Third World. It is the world's largest instant coffee manufacturer, with Nescafé the dominant product. Nestlé also produces and markets chocolate and malt drinks and is the world's largest producer of milk powder and condensed milk. Its coffee creamer product, Carnation Coffeemate, holds a sizable portion of that market.

Nestlé's chocolate and confectionery products carry some popular brand names, including Callier, Crunch, and Yes. With the acquisition of Rowntree, additional notable brands were added to the product line, including Kit Kat, Smarties, After Eight, and Quality Street. The Perugina division produces Baci. Through the RJR Nabisco acquisition, Nestlé acquired Curtiss Brand, a U.S. confectionery producer with such products as Baby Ruth and Butterfinger. Nestlé manufactures chocolate in 23 countries, notably Switzerland and Latin America. Each factory is highly automated, employing an average of 250 people.

Another major product concentration for Nestlé is frozen foods and other refrigerated products. Findus in Europe and Stouffer in the United States, with well-known brands such as Lean Cuisine, represent the bulk of the group's frozen food sales. Nestlé also manufactures a fast-developing range of fresh pasta and sauces in Europe and the United States under the name Contadina. Through the Carnation division, it also manufactures and sells pet foods, including Friskies, Gourmet, and Fancy Feast.

Other Nestlé businesses include the Stouffer hotel chain in the United States and Mexico. Nestlé also has some presence in pharmaceuticals and cosmetics, including a majority interest in Alcon, a manufacturer of eye-care products in the United States, and a 28 percent interest in L'Oreal, the world's largest cosmetics manufacturer.

Nestlé's financial performance, due to its international emphasis, can be dramatically affected by currency value fluctuations. Because of downward fluctuations in foreign currencies against the Swiss franc, Nestlé recorded a conservative 8 percent reduction in profits in 1990. The decline in profits was also influenced by the recession in the United States and worldwide, the Persian Gulf War, and the deterioration of the Brazilian economy. Since 25 percent of Nestlé's revenues and profits come from coffee, any adverse economic occurrences in South America, particularly Brazil, affect the company. Nestlé plans to continue to play to its strength, international markets outside the United States, to combat Hershey.

Hershey's global market share in the chocolate confectionery industry is only 10 percent, lowest among its competitors. A major strategic issue facing Hershey today is where, when, and how to best expand geographically. Perhaps Hershey should expand into Russia, since Mars is doing so well there already. China is another large untapped market.

More and more firms are becoming environmentally proactive in their manufacturing and service delivery processes. Environmentally responsible firms market themselves and their products as being "green-sensitive." Concern for the natural environment is an issue Hershey should address before competitors seize the initiative. Developing environmentally safe products and packages, reducing industrial waste, recycling, and establishing an environmental audit process are strategies that could benefit Hershey.

Some analysts contend that Hershey's organizational chart reflects an outdated structure. Some corporate positions could be consolidated; Hershey divisions perhaps should be based on product rather than on geographic area. Alternatives to the organization's present structure may be needed to effectively expand manufacturing and marketing operations globally.

Hershey's recent divestiture of Freia Marabou, a Norwegian confectioner, for $220 million adds more working capital for a major acquisition. Analysis is needed to identify and value specific acquisition candidates. In developing an overall strategic plan, what specific recommendations would you present to CEO Richard Zimmerman? What relative emphasis should Hershey place on chocolate versus pasta in 1994 through 1996? Should Hershey diversify more into nonchocolate candies since that segment is growing most rapidly? Should a new manufacturing plant be built in Asia or Europe? Design global marketing strategy that could enable Hershey to boost exports of both chocolate and pasta. Should Hershey increase its long-term debt or issue stock to raise the capital needed to implement your recommended strategies? Develop pro forma financial statements to fully assess and evaluate the impact of your proposed strategies.